DO YOU WANT TO BE PA
OF A LIFETIME?
TOURS TO DUBAI – APRIL 2023
SRI LANKA – JULY 2023

Website: Gillespiesports.com.au/+61 8 8293 3400
coaching@gillespiesports.com.au

UNDER 13 SQUAD TEAM PHOTO OF TOUR TO DUBAI, 2022

Back Row - Graham Sedunary, Levi Singh, Warwick Raymond, Paul Tregloan (All Coaches)
Front Row Jett Thomas, Max Tresidder, Riley Tissen, Rayan Bihari, Jude Thomas, Euen Beavan
Middle Row Nate McCleary, Lincoln Allen, James Murphy, Brad Wilson, Puffin Biswas, Harvey
Stephens.

WELCOME

Welcome to the Edition XI of the Australian Cricket Digest. It's great to get the first XI done and dusted and I hope the content has improved each year for you the reader, who parts with their hard-earned dollars. How many more editions there will be is anyone's guess!

It has been a fascinating period of cricket with Australia comfortably winning the Ashes, before going on to do well in both Pakistan and Sri Lanka, where in the past we have struggled. Our women have been sensational once again, winning multi-format series against India and England, then claiming the 50-over World Cup in New Zealand before winning Gold at the Commonwealth games.

It has also been a sad twelve months as we have lost some of the greats of the game. Ashley Mallett and Alan Davidson went in late 2021, but then came some real shocks in 2022. Rod Marsh went first, then came the unbelievable news that Shane Warne had died in Thailand, while on holiday. Then not long after when we least expected it, Andrew Symonds died in a vehicle accident in North Queensland. For many, on the back of Marsh and Warne's passing, the loss of Symonds was just a bit too much bad news to take.

Thanks to Cricket's best historian and writer David Frith for contributing once again, this time with a piece on former Australian spin bowler and journalist Bill O'Reilly. Given we have a piece on "Tiger" it only be appropriate to have Andrew Faulkner write about Bill's great mate Clarrie Grimmett. Last year Andrew wrote a fine piece on Bradman at Kensington, this year he gives some insights on Grimmett and the historic club. Andrew also reckons his history book on Kensington Cricket Club will finally be out in 2023, for his sake and a lot of other keen readers, I hope it is too!

Bharat Sundaresan continues his association with the Digest as he writes about the tour of Sri Lanka, which was not just about the cricket but meant so much to the locals who came out in massive numbers to watch, despite the major financial crisis in the country.

Many thanks to the many scorers around the country who do a great job. In particular I would like to thank Ian Wright and Robyn Sanday from Cricket NSW, as well as Jim Hamilton from Cricket Victoria.

The Digest wouldn't have lasted this long without some great financial support. Can I again thank Peter Chisholm (Morgan's Financial Limited), Paul Tregloan (Gillespie Sports), Chris Kouteris (Kouteris Financial Services) and last but not least Gerard Abood, one of Australia's best Umpires who runs ACL Lawyers in Sydney.

Thanks again to Barry Nicholls for his book reviews once again. His updated *Establishment Boys* is out, so do yourself a favour and get a copy for Christmas, as it has a stack of great yarns.

Ken Piesse (cricketbooks.com.au) has helped again with some advertising, while Roger Page (rpcricketbooks@iprimus.com.au) continues to distribute copies far and wide, so I urge you to get in touch with either of them first, if you're after any cricket books old or new. Thanks to Michael Bollen at Wakefield Press who has published and distributed the Digest in recent years.

Thanks to Adelaide freelance photographer Peter Argent for his photos including the cover shot of Usman Khawaja. The efforts of Graphic Print Group are appreciated once again, especially to Greg Lindsay who has helped with the Digest for all 11 years. Also cheers to Murray Hobbs who has been involved with recent editions.

Also, a special thanks to my chief proof-reader Paul Scott, who has found a few typos and made some sound suggestions. He is a bit too pro New South Wales cricket sometimes, but I won't hold that against him.

All feedback, good or bad is welcomed at Lawrie.colliver@gmail.com.

Here's to a great season in 2022-23,

Lawrie Colliver, Editor Australian Cricket Digest

CONTENTS
Volume XI

Editor's Notes	4
Features	
Player of the year – Usman Khawaja	6
Five great characters of Australian cricket celebrated by Lawrie Colliver	8
A view from the ground - Sri Lanka v Australia, 2022 by Bharat Sundaresan	10
Bill O'Reilly – A tribute by David Frith	12
The Allan Border Statue	13
The Fox and Kensington by Andrew Faulkner	14
Book Reviews by Barry Nicholls	16
Australia in International Cricket 2021-22	
The Ashes, 2021-22	21
ICC World Twenty20, 2021	41
Australia Twenty20 series v Sri Lanka, 2022	47
Australia in Pakistan, 2022	53
Australia in Sri Lanka, 2022	68
Australia A in Sri Lanka, 2022	83
The Australian Domestic Summer	
Sheffield Shield – Western Australia breaks a long drought	86
First-Class Averages 2021-22	129
Marsh Cup – WA grabs another one-day title	132
KFC Big Bash League – Scorchers win it for the fourth time	157
Australians in Overseas Twenty20	212
Toyota Futures League	213
Interstate Under 19 carnival	214
District/Grade Cricket Review	215
Women's Cricket	**232**
India in Australia 2021-22	233
England in Australia, 2021-22	239
ICC Women's World Cup, 2022	245
Australia in Ireland, 2022	252
Commonwealth games in Birmingham, 2022	254
Records Section	257
Scorchers take out the WBBL title	261
Tasmania wins their first WNCL title	304
Premier League Cricket	311
Under 19's National Carnival	313
Men's Records Section	**314**
Obituaries	318
Players Register 2022-23	
Men's State squads/WNCL squads	321
BBL/WBBL squads	330
Australian Cricket Hall of fame	338
Umpires and Match Referees panel for 2022-23	339
Cricket Australia Contracted player details	340
Australia v Zimbabwe, 2022	341
Future tours, 2022-23 Fixtures	343

Twelve months of strong performances

The Australian Men's and Women's teams gave their supporters plenty to cheer about in 2021/22. The Women's team had series wins over India and England, won the 50-over World Cup and took out Commonwealth Games Gold Medal. The wins and trophies continue to mount up for Australia's best female sporting team. Against the odds the Men started 2021/22 winning their first ICC World T20 in the UAE, then took out the Ashes and won the Test series in Pakistan. All very strong performances.

Pat Cummins – Australia's new Test skipper

With Tim Paine quitting on the eve of the Ashes, Cummins jumped into the hot seat and has taken to the Test captaincy very well, leading with calmness and common-sense. The Sri Lanka series was drawn, but his team achieved a much better result than the previous tour in 2016, where Australia was flogged 3-0. The one major negative he had to handle was the sacking of Coach Justin Langer. With the majority of public opinion on the side of Langer, Cummins was careful what he said in the media and in the end handled matters very well.

Tim Paine and Justin Langer depart the scene

Heading into this summer's Ashes, Tim Paine resigned the Australian Test captaincy after a private matter that became public. Given the nature of what is supposed to have happened and the fact it came into the public sphere four years later, it's hard to feel sorry for Paine. To give him his due, as Captain he did a fine job picking up the pieces of Australia's credibility when he took over the captaincy and guided it through to some turbulent times.

Justin Langer's situation was different, in that the team he was coaching had just won the World Twenty20 and Ashes and had regained a lot of the goodwill from the Public after the Ball tampering episode in South Africa in 2018. It became clear that his intense methods had become too much for some more experienced players and despite assurances that he would change his style, the players won the battle and Langer was out the door. But once again, one must give Langer plenty of credit for what he has done and achieved in the four years he was coach.

Champions pass, their performances and personalities won't be forgotten

It's been a shocking twelve months in terms of Australian players passing away. Alan Davidson, Ashely Mallett, Rod Marsh, Shane Warne and Andrew Symonds, all gone in a short space of time. When the Boxing Day Test against South Africa begins later in the year, it will be weird to see the Shane Warne Stand at the MCG, but to not have him doing commentary on the game. For those who love the BBL, it will be strange that Andrew Symonds won't be around to give his thoughts on the game. Rod Marsh was a folk hero to many of my generation brought up watching cricket in the late 1970s and early 1980s.

Western Australian Cricket gets a treble

Western Australia won the Sheffield Shield ending a long drought of 23 years without that title. It was the icing on the cake having won the Marsh Cup, with the Scorchers taking out the BBL. Congratulations to coach Adam Voges, WA skipper Shaun Marsh and Scorchers skipper Ashton Turner. There is certainly an abundance of talent in the west and throw in the fact they only could play one BBL match at home, makes that achievement all the more remarkable.

Chris Lynn gets his No Objection Certificate, will play in BBL and in Overseas T20

Cricket Australia made the right move in late August to allow Chris Lynn to sign with the Strikers and also play in the UAE T20 that runs towards the end of the BBL. They've avoided a possible legal case over restraint of trade and fans get to see him play in a possible 10 games, when it was quite likely at one point, he wouldn't be playing at all. Lynn can't be blamed for wanting to chase the extra dollars at this point of his career, particularly when he has battled shoulder problems which could end his career. The change of scenery will do him good, as perhaps the short boundaries square of the wicket at Adelaide Oval will also.

Keep the game moving please!

There are many unnecessary delays in cricket, let's make this the summer of "Keep the game moving". We need to stop drinks when there is under 10 minutes before an official break. Glove changes, slow reviews, continued questioning of the shape of the ball and captains taking a week to change the field. Many BBL games take too long, **I propose a countdown clock of 45 seconds between overs** to speed things up. If the fielding team aren't ready, an extra player comes into the inner circle for that over. Should speed it up!

BBL massive year

It shapes up as a very big year for the BBL. Barring any major disruptions it will be a full 14-match home and away season, with teams getting seven games at home. Prior to the Pandemic, Crowds had started to slip, largely because of the over saturation of the product. The overseas player draft created plenty of interest and in the end clubs largely wanted players who were available for the whole tournament. Faf du Plessis at 38 years of age was a poor choice as a CA marketing ploy, and was always unlikely to get picked up.

The season ahead – there's plenty on!

By the time many of you read this, Australia will have already played six One-day Internationals and will be getting ready for a two match T20 series with West Indies. Then comes a T20 Series with England, the World T20, ODI's versus England, two-Tests against the West Indies and then three Tests against South Africa. Chuck in the BBL, Marsh Cup and Sheffield Shield, there is something for everyone.

Stockbroking | Wealth Management | Corporate Advice

Invest in your future with Morgans

Morgans is Australia's largest national full-service stockbroking and wealth management network with offices in all states and territories.

For 40-years our experienced advisers have been committed to helping Australians to nurture, grow and protect their wealth.

Our services

- Stockbroking
- Wealth Management
- Financial Planning
- Superannuation Advice
- Portfolio Administration

- Retirement Planning
- Self-Managed Super Funds
- Fixed Interest and Cash Management
- Corporate Advice

Your financial future is our focus.

Get in touch

Creating wealth for our clients since 1982

Morgans Financial Limited ABN 49 010 669 726 AFSL 235410 | A participant of ASX Group.

PLAYER OF THE YEAR – USMAN KHAWAJA

Usman Khawaja started the 2021-22 season unsure if he would play for Australia again, by the end of his commitments in Galle in July 2022, he was one of the mainstays of the top six. From the moment he peeled off twin centuries in the Fourth Ashes Test at the SCG in early January, he hardly put a foot wrong to become a mainstay in the Australian Test team.

In a quiet start, he didn't pass 20 for Queensland in his first three digs but had some luck late on the day two against South Australia in a Shield game at Adelaide Oval. Khawaja appeared to glove a bouncer from Nathan McAndrew to be caught but the umpire said "Not out" and he went on to bat all of day three, to make 174. He then made 119 versus Tasmania on Townsville and then got 70 out of a total of 129 on a Gabba "greentop" against a strong Western Australian attack.

Queensland returned to South Australia to play at Rolton Oval, Khawaja made just four and when South Australia was all out for a paltry 102, Khawaja as skipper rightly enforced the follow-on, rather than being selfish and going in for another hit. His decision paid off as Queensland won, but Travis Head made a fine hundred on a tricky pitch and days later got the nod for the First Test side with Khawaja the one to miss out.

After the Third Test Head contracted COVID and was ruled out of the fourth at the SCG, which meant Khawaja was back in. He took his chance and played magnificently to score two hundreds in the match, making it impossible for him to be dropped. The reverse sweep was a key scoring stroke in his two innings. With Head back for the final Test, opener Marcus Harris was left out and Khawaja went up the order to open. He failed in both digs on a difficult pitch in Hobart but was still selected for the much awaited Test tour of Pakistan, the place of his birth.

Khawaja retained his spot as opener for the First Test in Rawalpindi, but a lost toss meant he had to field for two days before getting the pads on. Khawaja batted with assurance to make 97, sharing an opening stand of 156 with David Warner in a match that ended in a boring draw, where just 14 wickets fell. In the second Test in Karachi, Australia had the luck with the toss and batted, Khawaja setting his stall to make 160 in over nine hours as Australia's made 9-556 declared. The left-hander largely played the spinners off the back foot, trusting himself to get bat on ball should the odd ball keep low. Australia pressed hard to win that Test, coming up three wickets short when it ended in a draw.

Heading into the decider, Australia batted first and Khawaja was there at the forefront making a fine 91 in over five hours in a total of 391. Khawaja made an excellent unbeaten 104 in the second innings, with Pakistan set 351 to win in the final innings. Thanks to some fine spin bowling by Nathan Lyon who took five wickets, Australia won by 115 runs with Khawaja named Man of the series for his 496 runs at an incredible 165.33.

After a few months off, Khawaja headed to Sri Lanka for a two-Test series. On a pitch that spun from ball one, Khawaja used every bit of his technique to make 71, continuing to play the spinners late and with soft hands as he had in Pakistan. He also employed the reverse sweep again to great effect, giving the spinners a touch up as Australia recorded a ten-wicket win.

In the second Test, Khawaja was bowled by a beauty by Rajitha for five in the first innings and made only 29 in the second, as Australia crumbled to lose nine wickets in the final session of the fourth day, to lose by an innings. To summarise, in an incredible six months his Test average has ballooned from 40.66 to 47.19, which now puts his record right up there with many fine Australian batsmen. He turns 36 during the summer, it will be interesting to see if he can continue to produce at Test level.

Photo: Peter Argent

USMAN KHAWAJA IN FIRST CLASS CRICKET, 2021-22

Format	M	Inns	NO	Runs	Best	Average	100/50
Sheffield Shield	6	10	1	529	174	58.78	2/3
Ashes	2	4	1	255	137	85.00	2/-
Tests in Pakistan	3	5	2	496	160	165.33	2/2
Tests in Sri Lanka	2	4	1	137	71	45.67	-/1
Total	**13**	**23**	**5**	**1417**	**174**	**78.72**	**6/6**

Moran Cricket Collectibles

Dealing in:

- Books & periodicals
- Wisdens
- Cigarette & trade cards
- Postcards & badges
- Ceramics
- Autographed items
- Assorted cricketana

Catalogues Issued

MCC
PO Box 226
Gunnedah NSW 2380

Phone: (02) 6742 7022
Email: tony@morancricket.com
Website: morancricket.com

SHANE WARNE, ANDREW SYMONDS, ROD MARSH, ALAN DAVIDSON AND ASHLEY MALLETT

It is hard to believe that in the past twelve months, five significant figures in Australian cricket have passed away. Some old and sadly some not so. Alan Davidson had a long life and was firmly involved right up until passing away aged 92. Both Rod Marsh and Ashley Mallett were in their seventies, they both had a good crack at life, but in the case of Shane Warne and Andrew Symonds, it was such a shock as there seemed to be a lot more to come.

When I started producing this Digest it occurred to me after a few editions that it needed to be not just about Stats and numbers, but also about characters and stories. Never have I felt more strongly about this now after the passing of five great Australian Cricketing Characters this year.

One could easily reel off their greatest moments in order, a stack of statistics and later in the article I will mention some of these. But this journal is also about what they were also like as people, said by those who were lucky enough to know them.

I'll start with Shane Warne. For many he will be remembered for his great talent as a leg-spinner, a match winner and as a bowler who could provide an unforgettable moment. The unveiling of the "flipper" to bowl Richie Richardson at the MCG in 1992, the "Gatting ball" in 1993, the flipper to dismiss Alec Stewart in the First Ashes Test at the Gabba in 1994, the hat-trick in the next Test at the MCG, caught by David Boon. The ball to dismiss South Africa's Hansie Cronje in the 1999 World Cup at Edgbaston. His 700th Test wicket in front of a massive crowd at the MCG.

For his entertaining off-field life which while it didn't always set a good example for the youth at the time, had everybody talking. Then for his commentary and media work, as he always had an opinion and wasn't frightened to give it. Then for finding a way to get into the same room as actress Elizabeth (as Shane called her, not Liz) Hurley at the Races and eventually becoming engaged to her. Despite all his fame as a Cricketer, I think that was when Warney really went Worldwide.

For his generosity of time and fund raising. Travelling to Sri Lanka in 2004 to help after the awful tsunami. Selling his Australian cap for $1 million to raise money after the bushfires in 2019/20. His kindness and fostering of team spirit with his TV work cricket production colleagues, putting on a BBQ at his house in St Kilda on Boxing Day for a number of years and paying for it all. It was always a giggle when he kept reminding his Fox colleagues about the cost over the following days.

As fans we have much to be grateful to Andrew Symonds for. His great skill in making 143 against Pakistan in Johannesburg in the opening game of the 2003 World Cup hours after Shane Warne had been sent home. For scoring a century when Australia needed it in the 2006/07 Ashes and sharing a partnership with his great mate Matthew Hayden in the centre of the MCG. For his brilliant catching and ability to run out batsmen at will. Also, for being himself. Lover of the outdoors, fishing, drinking spiced Rum, his young family, tackling and bumping spectators who were stupid enough to run out on the field when he was out there. As a broadcaster after a nervous and quiet start, Symonds was starting to really evolve into a good analyst. He was starting to take the role a lot more seriously. But his analysis was very good, "Keep the game simple" he used to say.

He too had his foibles, on occasion getting a bit too drunk and staying out too late, which resulted in him getting in trouble with team management. But he was the typical Aussie character. If you were like me and in his company often in the past few seasons, you were often having a laugh within minutes of being around him.

As a kid growing up watching Rod Marsh, you loved him for just flying the flag. Former Australia keeping great Wally Grout apparently said that when England batting great Ken Barrington walked out to bat you felt he had a Union Jack trailing behind him. One got that sense with Marsh. He had a rocky start, dropping several chances in his first Test in 1970 against England, but knuckled down and by 1972 had established himself and became a fixture in the Australian team for what was over a decade. He was first Australian keeper to make a hundred in a Test match (1972/73) and he kept to some of Australia's fastest bowling ever in 1974/75 and 1975/76 home series and apparently said when keeping to Jeff Thomson for the first time, "Geet that hurts but I bloody love it".

His efforts in the 1977 Centenary Test playing with a photo of the first Australian Test wicket-keeper Jack Blackham in his pocket, will be long remembered. Keeping superbly and making a century in the second innings. One of the early things I learned about Marsh was his sportsmanship in calling Derek Randall back on 161 in the second innings when he knew an "edge" hadn't carried to him. My Dad, the man who fostered my interest in the game, said that's what you're meant to do. The fact was that apparently the ball didn't take the edge either, so Marsh could have been congratulated on two counts for calling Randall back. He was a key figure in World Series Cricket, then finished his playing career in style, playing his final Test with great mates Dennis Lillee and Greg Chappell.

His influence on a new generation of players coming through the Cricket Academy was profound. Later he saw the bigger picture and went to start up the England Cricket Academy, later becoming an England selector as well. He helped them turn around their game and now the Ashes is one of the biggest events in the game, which for years Australia won every series.

He was a caring and terrific father to his sons, Daniel, Paul and Jamie. He took them all to Augusta, Georgia for a once in a lifetime trip to the US Masters Golf. In 2019, he and his great mate Dennis Lillee were kind enough to grace Adelaide their presence to raise money for the Variety club. It was a memorable day, the stories flowed along with the food, beer and wine. I managed to have a quick word to Rod and told him he must have done a good job of raising his lads, because Jamie had kindly sent me a *Masters* program in the mail when he could have easily forgotten, amongst all the excitement of being on that special family trip. Former Australian cricketer and Fox Cricket commentator Adam Gilchrist summed it up best when he said that "Rod Marsh was one of the greatest wicketkeepers of all time and was also "one of the great blokes". Gilchrist believes the former wicketkeeper's true legacy lies as "a man who loved his mates and a cold beer as much as the game itself". "Greg Chappell said he 'played with plenty who would die for the baggy green, but Marsh stood apart because he'd kill for it too'.

Alan Davidson was one of Australia's greatest all-rounders, a hard-hitting batsman and a fine left-arm pace bowler who could dangerously swing the ball in late to the right handers. Old footage wasn't around much in the early days of my cricket education, but I do remember with excitement as a teenager when the ABC put on late at night a show of highlights and interviews of the 1960 Tied Test. How "Davo" excelled in that match and again at Old Trafford in 1961, when he smashed off-spinner David Allen all around the park, for his mate skipper Richie Benaud to bowl England out on the last day to retain the Ashes. I was lucky to be able to read "Fifteen Paces", as it was one of the first cricket books in my library.

Finally, to Ashley Mallett, one of the few great off-spinners Australia has produced, and then as a journalist and writer of many fine cricket books. He did well in his Test debut at the Oval in 1968 taking five wickets, but after that got less chances as captain Bill Lawry and the Australian selectors preferred mystery spinner John Gleeson to him. Things changed somewhat when Ian Chappell took over the Captaincy in 1971, Mallett got more opportunities and was a key figure in the Oval Test win of 1972, taking five wickets in a match which saw Australia level the series 2-2. In the 1974/75 Ashes it was all about Lillee and Jeff Thomson, but Mallett contributed greatly as he took some astonishing gully catches and finished with 17 wickets at 19.94 as Australia cleaned up 4-1.

His efforts as a journalist and as a prolific book writer in later years filled bookcases around the country. He wrote some brilliant books on former teammates, from skipper Ian Chappell to Doug Walters and Jeff Thomson, which gave a great first-hand insight to the personalities they were. Then later on came *Thwack – The glorious sound of summer*, a wonderful compendium of short stories and his final major book, a biography on Neil Harvey.

There was one last small booklet he wrote that came out after his death about his old skipper at South Australia, Les Favell. It's only 12 pages and has some lovely stories. Meeting Don Bradman, becoming friends with the great man Dr Donald Beard, playing in the great South Australian teams of the period. Then a final poignant few words on the last page of the book. "*He (Favell) was so good to me when I first moved to Adelaide. Les was like a father to me and his incredible confidence as a batsman and leader helped me build belief in my own game. In another life and in another place Les Favell could well have been a cavalier swordsman. Indeed, a swordsman of the musketeer brigade, a man who extolled the creed 'all for one and one for all' on the field of battle*". I think that creed in Mallett's words also applies to all five in the way they played and lived their lives. They were great to us also the fans, so thanks and Rest In Peace.

TOURING SRI LANKA IN 2022 *by Bharat Sundaresan*

THERE ARE three scenes from Australia's 2022 tour of Sri Lanka that will remain etched forever in the memories of those of us who were there. There was the sea of yellow at the R Premadasa Stadium in Colombo where thousands of Sri Lankans sang in praise of Aaron Finch & Co for having helped lift their spirits at a time of such despair. There was the sea of sorrow all around the country as thousands of Sri Lankans lined up in endless queues for fuel and other bare essentials. And there was the sea of heroes all around the Galle International Cricket Stadium as thousands of Sri Lankans marched towards what they believed was a new, bright future.

These remarkable scenes also summed up this most dramatic of tours, which was as much about the cricket as it was about being witness to the victory of people power in a country riddled with the worst economic crisis in its history. And it's very important to put into context very early on. That the Australian players didn't just spend a month-and-a-half playing some high-quality cricket, they also played a role in helping a beleaguered country somewhat get back to its feet.

For, when the T20I series began in earnest in the first week of June, everyday life in Sri Lanka was in the mire. The cricket brought them solace. They filled up stadiums in Kandy and Colombo and roared out their gratitude to the Australian team. But there was no respite in sight. The fuel crisis worsened. The economy fell further into strife. Their voices for change fell on deaf ears. The rallies and protests against the incumbent government and leaders waged on endlessly even as power cuts and shortage in medical supplies brought the rest of the country to a standstill.

Like some of the fans at the Premadasa put it, "for the few hours we are the cricket, we forget all the negativity in our real lives. This is our real escape."

And for good measure, both teams gave them enough reasons at the cricket for it to feel like the ultimate 'escape'.

Though Australia started off very strongly in the T20Is, the Sri Lankans pulled things back wonderfully in the final encounter, with captain Dasun Shanaka producing one of the moments of the tour with a fantastic finisher's knock. With the captain smashing a breath-taking half-century, the hosts chased down 59 off the last three overs to pull off a great escape on the field. For the T20I world champions, it was about consolidating their growing prowess in a format that hasn't always been their strength and building towards their title defence in a few months' time at home. Josh Hazlewood's burgeoning reputation as a T20 bowler was the highlight for the visitors.

That set the tone for Sri Lanka to claim the ODI series despite once again losing the opening game to a Glenn Maxwell special. We saw the rise of young guns Pathum Nissanka and Charith Asalanka, as they put the Aussies to the sword in consecutive matches, setting up wins for their team. Recording their highest ever ODI run-chase against Australia in the third match was one of the best nights in Sri Lankan cricket history. The dramatic turnaround orchestrated by their spinners while David Warner & Co were coasting to victory in the fourth ODI was even better. The fifth ODI was all about the Sri Lankans showing their gratitude to the Aussies, coming decked in yellow and screaming, "thank you Australia" at the end of the night despite their team having been trounced in the dead rubber. While there were some positives for the Australians, there were more question marks about some of their tactics and techniques on the really slow pitches of the subcontinent, that they might encounter next year at the ODI World Cup in India.

Warner spoke a lot about how the turning pitches during the ODIs would play to their advantage come the two Tests in Galle. And they certainly did in the first Test as Australia took revenge for their humbling at the same venue six years earlier. On a surface that was custom-designed to suit the home team, it was Sri Lanka who slipped and stuttered and fell in a heap as Nathan Lyon and Mitchell Swepson ran amok. After failing to make the most of winning the toss and batting first, Dimuth Karunaratne's team batted with no direction in the first innings, before showing no determination in the second. In between the two collapses though, Cameron Green announced himself as a nearly finished-product with bat in hand, producing his best Test innings to do in very alien conditions. So good was his footwork and conviction at the crease that he if anything ended up laying a blueprint for the rest of his senior colleagues to follow.

Having been rolled over in less than 23 overs in their second innings, not many gave Sri Lanka any hope of turning their misfortune around come the second Test. The six-day gap that had resulted from the early finish did allow the groundstaff in Galle to roll some more grass into the surface and leave it more sustainable for a Test match. And it was Australia's turn to not bat the opposition out of the game after Steve Smith and Marnus Labuschagne regained their century-scoring touch, with classy knocks. It was Smith's first ton in 18 months and was another masterclass on batting in the subcontinent. It also made up for his disappointing run-out in the first Test.

The door had been left ajar for Sri Lanka to get back in. And they stormed back in, courtesy one of the most dominating innings played by a Sri Lankan in Tests, as Dinesh Chandimal took apart the Aussie bowling to record his maiden double ton. That his knock came at a time thousands of locals continued protesting and marching towards Galle Fort only summed up the tour and its significance in a nutshell. And around the time, the Sri Lankan public reclaimed their fort, their team had regained their self-pride on the field. They had also dragged the Aussies through the dust, having kept them on the field for 181 overs. A deflated and fatigued Aussie batting line-up were perfect prey for 30-year-old debutant Prabath Jayasuriya to hunt down on the wearing pitch. And he did just that, adding six wickets to the six he'd snared in the first innings to finish with the fourth best match figures on debut in Test history. There was no mystery about him though, just pure, classical left-arm spin, with exceptional use of drift to boot.

It brought a slightly premature end to Australia's hopes of building up for that tour to India next year with back-to-back series wins in the subcontinent. But the 1-1 series result fairly represented how evenly fought the Tests were overall. Australia might have had to share the Warne-Muralitharan Trophy eventually, but they left the Sri Lankan shores as ultimate winners, having brought hope for and having won over the people of a country in much need of it.

GK Money

If it's your first home or if it's time to renovate, refinance or invest, we're here to help make it happen.

1300 859 643

gkmoney.com.au

BILL O'REILLY - *by David Frith*

"Tiger" seemed rather cool. I'd slipped into the press-box seat next to his at Adelaide Oval, but he wasn't his usual genial self. It was some time before the source of the problem revealed itself. "I see England's been up to its old tricks again," groaned Bill O'Reilly, who for some years had been one of my father figures. He could only have been referring to the recent Falklands war. And he was.

I needed to find an adequate retort quickly. So I said: "What would Australia do, Bill, if a foreign power landed on Lord Howe Island and claimed it as their own? Would it just stand by?"

There was a long pause, during which I think he saw the point. Crisis over. A cherished friendship had been retrieved.

That bond had been founded on my youthful seasons with the St George club in Sydney, where I'd played my junior cricket. That mighty club had once fielded Bradman and O'Reilly, and after the Second World War there was Arthur Morris and Ray Lindwall, and later on Norm O'Neill and Brian Booth. Today I still experience a tremor of pride whenever I catch sight of my red-and-white Saints cap.

There was a time when The Greatest Bowler Ever was reckoned by most cricket-lovers to have been either England's S.F.Barnes or Australia's Bill O'Reilly. One thing was certain: like Barnes (whom I had met), O'Reilly was a formidable presence. If anything, Tiger had a greater sense of humour and human warmth, though considering Barnes's chilly and uncompromising nature that isn't saying much.

In his foreword to my book on the 1978-79 Ashes series Bill wrote: "with the early confession of his 'bitter sweet schizophrenia of allegiance', my comrade in typewriter tapes [DF] sets his inflexible standard for a magnificent tale well told in The Ashes '79." How generous. He then reflects on St George's youth teams, recalling two lads under his captaincy decades earlier: Ray Lindwall and Arthur Morris.

Although he undoubtedly would have been a wise father figure for those youngsters and many more, Bill O'Reilly had firm ideas about coaches: "If you see a coach coming, run for your life." He would have growled in frustration at the sight of the army of coaches and back-up people who crowd the dressing-room today.

O'Reilly's tough bush upbringing left him with a rare independence of soul. He captured 102 wickets in his 19 Ashes Tests during the 1930s. But Maurice Leyland, the tough and rotund Yorkshire left-hander, defied him, didn't he? "How many times did I get him out?" Answer: nine times in 16 Tests. The scowl gives way to a bit of a smirk. Bill O'Reilly bagged lots of quality wickets: Hammond, Hendren, Sutcliffe, and so on.

He was not a great personal admirer of Don Bradman, and it was mutual. They were both unrelentingly competitive, both self-taught bush products. But their natures clashed. When Jock Livingston (NSW and Northamptonshire) and I mounted the Noble Stand steps one Test match morning, Bill, already seated at his front-row seat, called across: "Been to Bowral lately?"

Most endings are sad, and so it was with Bill. I knew he'd had a leg amputated, so as I drove Jock down the Princes Highway and Blakehurst came into view we agreed that it would be nice to pop in and see "Tiger". The coins clicked into the public telephone and we spoke – but only briefly. Bill sounded utterly miserable, stating that he sat in the kitchen most of the day, keeping an eye on the wall in case somebody came and took it away.

Soon afterwards he himself was taken away. The acquaintance was memorable and greatly cherished. I sometimes look at my right hand and marvel at the reality that it once shook the hand of the greatest bowler ever – maybe S.F.Barnes or Shane Warne or William Joseph O'Reilly. Rest in peace Bill – though that's hardly likely if he happens to spot Wally Hammond or Len Hutton, or even Don Bradman, in the Great Gallery in the Sky.

Above: The great Allan Border (right) was celebrated in Brisbane at the start of the International summer, when a Statue of him was unveiled at the Gabba. Pictured with him in David Cook, who was part of the Statue organising committee which included Sir Ian Botham, Fox Cricket's Steve Crawley, Brisbane businessman Steve Conry, musician Bernard Fanning.

Grimmett Injures His Foot

C. V. Grimmett, Australia's bowling mainstay for the coming Tests, injured a foot at Peterborough on Saturday. He is not badly hurt.

C. V. Grimmett

While getting out of a motor car he caught his coat in the door, and in trying to wrench it free, moved the car. The back wheel ran over his foot, tearing off his shoe.

Grimmett had to cancel his engagement to play cricket at Peterborough, although he gave hints and lectured to a large attendance at night.

Grimmett did not go to work today. He is resting his foot. He will resume work tomorrow.

Enthusiasm At Unley And Hindmarsh

Sportsmen representing almost every game attended the Unley Oval last night to say farewell to V. Y. Richardson, vice-captain of the Australian XI.

As Grimmett wished to leave early to attend a farewell to C. Walker, Mr. S. Chigwidden, secretary of Sturt Cricket Club, proposed the toast to T. W Wall, Walker and Grimmett.

Grimmett, responding, said functions of that nature were not held frequently enough. They gave players an opportunity to cement life friendships. He also suggested that in future club games, an adjournment should be made for afternoon tea to enable players to get to know one another.

Grimmett's remarks were heartily supported.

Mr. W. H. Langham, proposing the health of Richardson, said Unley was delighted to have a test player, who had been born and lived ever since in the district.

GRIMMETT THE WRECKER

9-49 v. Glenelg

TAKING nine Glenelg wickets for 49, Clarrie Grimmett on Saturday registered the best bowling feat of the season in Adelaide district cricket. The other Glenelg batsman was run out before he faced Grimmett.

KENSINGTON, declaring at six wickets for 339, had an easy first innings win.

The feature of the semi-final matches was the hard hitting of P. K. Lee, 81, whose partnership with R. G. Williams took the score from four to five for 202. That stand placed East Torrens in a winning position, as Adelaide had been dismissed for 233. Before stumps were drawn the score had been taken to 292 for eight wickets. Adelaide cannot

Kensington V. Glenelg, At Glenelg

KENSINGTON
First innings—Six wickets (dec.) for 339.

GLENELG

W. E. Catchlove, st. McArthur, b. Grimmett	38
W. S. Richardson, c. and b. Grimmett	14
F. Ward, c. Moyle, b. Grimmett	45
R. Hack, hit wicket, b. Grimmett	5
R. L. Haddrick, l.b.w., b. Grimmett	0
R. Colyer, b. Grimmett	2
W. C. Bailey, l.b.w., b. Grimmett	0
J. Reece, st. McArthur, b. Grimmett	2
M. J. Curtis, not out	2
E. Borchers, c. Johnson, b. Grimmett	12
E. J. Whitington, run out	0
Byes	8
Total	128

1	2	3	4	5	6	7	8	9
26	75	87	87	95	101	107	112	126

Bowling

	O.	M.	R.	W.
E. H. Lines	6	—	24	—
E. L. Bowley	11	3	18	—
W. S. Stirling	17	5	29	—
C. V. Grimmett	21.5	5	49	9

LONERGAN AND GRIMMETT TOP 1943/44 SEASON AVERAGES

By Deepfield

LONERGAN (Sturt) and Grimmett (Kensington) topped the batting and bowling aggregates for the district cricket season which ended on Saturday.

Larner (East-Torrens-Glenelg) finished with the best batting average. Roberts (Port Adelaide), who played in only three games had the best bowling average.

Bennett (University) was responsible for a good performance in finishing second on both batting aggregate and average lists.

Leading batting and bowling figures were —

BATTING

	I.	N.O.	H.S.	R.	Av.
Larner (E.T.-G.)	11	4	*992	495	70.7
Bennett (U.)	15	4	*122	624	56.7
Lonergan (S.)	14	2	125	655	54.5
Kierse (P.)	15	4	116	529	48.09
Teisseire (E.T.-G.)	12	1	*122	451	41.0
G. Harrison (W.T.)	12	2	85	364	36.4
Craig (P.)	16	1	71	473	31.5
Goode (U.)	14	—	102	397	28.3
McLean (P.A.)	13	1	*102	329	27.2
Pengilly (K.)	18	1	104	451	26.5
Hay (P.)	14	2	60	304	25.3

*Not out.

BOWLING

	W.	R.	Av.
Roberts (P.A.)	27	222	8.2
A. J. Smith (P.)	12	112	9.3
Grimmett (K.)	75	712	9.5
Cotton (P.)	34	352	10.3
Deguet (E.T.-G.)	43	495	11.5
Dodson (W.T.)	19	219	11.5
Churchett (E.T.-G.)	11	143	13.0
Sharpe (A.)	59	827	14.01
T. Brown (E.T.-G.)	43	627	14.5

Other good performances not in ranking order, were:—McLean (P.A.), 67 wickets, 16.7 average; Hodge (P.), 34, 18.8; Beck (P.A.), 31, 17.7; Scott (A.), 30, 18.8; Bennett (U.), 29, 16.1.

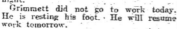

THE BROWN FOX AND AFTERNOON TEA by Andrew Faulkner

In 19 glorious seasons, he amassed 579 wickets, played every game like it was an Ashes Test, and instructed countless youngsters in his noble leg-spin art, yet perhaps Clarrie Grimmett's greatest gift to Adelaide club cricket is … afternoon tea.

Meh, you say. Afternoon tea? Afternoon tea! Is this some sort of joke?

On the contrary. Afternoon tea is serious business. I could name certain teammates whose sole motivation for playing cricket is afternoon tea. That and washouts.

Afternoon tea is a matter of pride at my club. Although judging by the recent reappearance of Tim-Tams, lamingtons and suchlike (but mercifully not the dreaded Barbecue Shapes, yet), the 'no plastic packaging' rule of the 1990s is not being enforced as rigidly as it might.

My club is Grimmett's club, Kensington, although the phrase 'Grimmett's club' comes with accompanying notes that read like the Cricinfo profile of a T20 gun for hire. Grimmett played for (deep breath) Wellington YMCA, Wellington East, Sydney, South Melbourne, Prahran, Adelaide, Colts and Kensington. So he knew a bit about club life when in 1930 he called for afternoon tea breaks during Adelaide district matches.

"(Grimmett) suggested that in future club games, an adjournment should be made for afternoon tea to enable players to get to know one another," The Register News-Pictorial reported from an Unley Oval farewell for Grimmett's fellow Ashes tourist Vic Richardson.

The assorted guests thought it a great idea, but Adelaide's club cricketers were made to wait five years for their Earl Grey and cucumber sandwiches. Grade cricket historian Geoff Sando has unearthed a clipping indicating the SACA introduced a 10-minute tea break in 1935/36.

Still, calling for something that would benefit C grade scrubbers as much as his fellow Test stars shows the mark of the man; as did Grimmett rushing from the Richardson soiree to a concurrent function at the Hindmarsh Town Hall for Ashes back-up keeper Charlie Walker.

The world's best bowler was for the game and for his mates. This shone through in his 14 seasons at Kensington from 1928/29. Grimmett always made a point of welcoming new players to the Browns. "You couldn't have got a better bloke than old Clarrie," said 1930s Kensington allrounder Kurt Koehne. "A good heart. He'd help anybody."

Grimmett collected young Koehne in his car and deposited him home after play. A diminutive leg-spinner like Grimmett, Koehne lapped up the master's voice in the car and closely studied his method on the field.

As we know, Grimmett conspired to deceive, trapping his victims with changes of pace, straight balls and his patented flipper. But Koehne said it was wrong to presume Grimmett's leg-spinner didn't rip. "He turned them a lot. There's no doubt about turning it, wrong 'uns and everything. (Although) he didn't turn them as much as Warnie."

Don Looker says Grimmett would have taken as many wickets as Shane Warne if he had played as many Tests: "I used to say to (Grimmett's son) Vic: 'They keep raving on about Warney, but they don't talk about your father – he was as good as him.'

"He was a good bloke Clarrie Grimmett," Looker says. "He was just a nice, friendly fellow. He always came up to talk to me."

Yes, 32 years was no age gap at all to Grimmett (Looker was 17 and Grimmett 49 in the young batsman's first season). The sly old fox was still bamboozling Adelaide batsmen well into his fifties: he took 75 wickets at 9.49 for Kensington in 1943/44 – aged 52. Grimmett tallied 432 wickets at 12.53 for the Browns. His 9-49 against Glenelg at Kensington Oval in 1933/34 is still a club record. The other Glenelg batsman was run out.

For 82 years Grimmett was the fastest man to 200 Test wickets; that record fell to Yasir Shah in 2018. His first-class tally of 1424 remains the best by an 'Australian' (born in New Zealand, Grimmett moved to Australia in 1914). Yet, unlike many Test stars, Grimmett respected club cricket. When free of Test and state commitments, he was at Kensington Oval with his clubmates, or coaching kids on his tennis court, or trooping off on the Browns' Easter trip to Clare.

Always fond of a lark, the celebrity spinner surprised Clare's Bentleys Hotel patrons one evening when he rode a bike into the dining room, wending through the seated diners. "When Grimmett used to come down to dinner at the Bentleys Hotel everyone greeted him as The Wizard of Oz," teammate Tom Burgess said. No prizes for guessing the most popular movie of the time.

Not every country trip was as agreeable. Grimmett missed the Browns' first three matches of the 1932/33 season after somehow running over his left foot with his own car on a trip to Peterborough. The pain lingered and the injury might have contributed to him being dropped from the Test side during that Bodyline summer.

Grimmett's 25 wickets at 26.72 helped retrieve the Ashes in 1934 but that was small beer compared with his contribution to Australia's 4-0 win in South Africa in 1935/36: 44 wickets at 14.59 is the fourth best haul in a series, ever.

That he never played another Test after South Africa is at the heart of his frosty relationship with Australian and Kensington captain Bradman. The palpable tension was obvious to the young Browns at Kensington.

Still, Kensington was blessed to have the world's best batsman and bowler in its ranks at the same time. When Grimmett rolled out to his first training after a Test tour, keeper Don McArthur sheepishly shuffled up, asking if Grimmett might bowl a few extra balls after training, as McArthur had to keep to him for the first time on the weekend. Grimmett obliged, placing a single stump in the Kensington Oval pitch and bowling six balls while McArthur crouched behind the lonely middle stump. Five of the six balls hit the middle stump. So, what made Grimmett so good, I asked McArthur 65 years after the event? "Weren't you listening sonny? Accuracy! Accuracy!"

Andrew Faulkner's Kensington District Cricket Club history will be published in early 2023.

BOOK REVIEWS by Barry Nicholls

Perhaps publisher Geoff Armstrong's observation about the paucity of sports books sales was right. People just don't buy as many books about sport anymore. Even for this reviewer there weren't as many Australian cricket books published this year. Several featured here were ordered from overseas. Perhaps younger readers no longer turn to books involving sport with the same zest of those of yesteryear. As cricket journalist Peter Lalor lamented 'sports media is in crisis at the moment.' Books about sport certainly appear to be. That said I'll proceed.

Dan Christian's The All-rounder: The Inside story of big-time cricket is revealing about a side of cricket that Australian fans rarely get to see, that is the IPL close up and personal (and in this book amid Covid chaos). The stories of limited overs cricketers tend to be relegated to newspaper articles or footnotes. So, it's refreshing to be taken inside the life of a modern globetrotting cricketer. I would have like to have read more of Christian's reflections on his Aboriginal heritage. Sadly, mainstream media's interest in Aboriginal cricket remains limited. The annual national indigenous cricket carnival held in Alice Springs each year attracts tokenistic print coverage at best.

Bernard Whimpress's Passport to Nowhere: Aborigines in Australian Cricket is still the exemplar regarding Indigenous cricketers and that was published in 1999. This year Whimpress teamed up with former SA Shield player Robert O'Shannassy to provide an illuminating and brilliantly researched and written history; *Adelaide University Cricket Club: A History.* The authors cleverly mapped out the origins of the club in 1881 through to the current day with the volume describing the role of community it played in the ever-changing student life. The book is handsomely produced with almost 400 illustrations and many historic team photos.

Queensland's 'adopted' Englishman Jonathan Northall has again provided an erudite and intriguing book, *The Life and Death of Andy Ducat.* Ducat is largely known as a dual international and for his untimely death, suffering a heart attack while batting at Lord's in 1942. Northall's latest has added substantially to the understanding of Ducat's life, career and times revealing a historian's eye for detail and research and a story teller's ability to weave together a captivating biography.

Who Only Cricket Know Hutton's men in the West Indies 1953/54 by David Woodhouse is compelling at every level. An exhaustive account (maybe the book is even a little too long) of the MCC side Len Hutton led on a trouble plagued tour better known for the controversies than the cricket (although the cricket itself was absorbing). The book's cricketing descriptions are covered from every angle while the coverage of the social and political backdrop to the lead into, the tour itself and the aftermath is unrivalled.

Elephant in the Stadium: The myth and magic of India's Epochal Win by Arunabha Sengupta covers India's 1971 win against England and so much more. The book's cover features a baby elephant perambulating The Oval's outfield on the last day of the final Test representing a symbol of Britain's one dimensional and patronising view of India. Sengupta's prose is so commanding there were times when this reviewer felt he was among the crowd on overcast dimly lit English days watching India's triumph. The book is also first-class history of post-War India while the growing military tensions in the sub-continent provide a window into the ability of Sir Garry Sobers to meld a side together for Rest of the World side that later toured Australian in 1971/72 (given it contained members of the Indian and Pakistan sides).

Cricket fans would remember where they were when they heard the news of Shane Warne's death in a Thailand hotel room. It was just hours after the announcement of Rod Marsh's passing after a major heart attack. Some months later Ken Piesse's '*On Ya Warnie: The Ultimate Celebration,*' arrived on my doorstep providing a reflective and worthwhile examination of the life and times of Shane Warne. Piesse has also written *Fifteen Minutes of Fame: Australia's One-Test Wonders* providing a salute to those who had once worn the baggy green. These are multi-dimensional portraits as the author applies his usual perceptive and layered understanding of players' lives and careers. For example, thespian and cricketer Harry Musgrove

'His entrepreneurial work in theatrical production, in combination with the American JC Williamson fuelled Melbourne's early standing as the Federation's culture capital. It was also pivotal in his remarkable rise from a bush XXII into Australia's Test team.'

Adam Zwar's Twelve Summers is a delightful yet at times poignant memoir told through a connection with childhood, adolescent and adult memories associated with cricket. Zwar's humour stands out but so too does his love of the game and sensitive handling of the topic of grief. The cover featuring a zinc creamed Shane Warne now seems even more fitting.

Ashley Mallett's passing in October 2021 reminds me of his versatility as a writer. His 2018 *The Boys from St Francis* features many Aboriginal activists' artists and athletes who came under the care of Anglican priest Father Percy Smith. Mallett writes with great perception and care about the subjects (who included Charles Perkins, John Moriarty and Vince Copley) some of whom were members of the Stolen Generation (Mallett has also written evocatively about the 1868 Aboriginal cricket tour of England).

Australia's first female Aboriginal Test cricketer Faith Thomas' (who attended Colebrook Home) is also featured. Her description of early 'cricket' experiences where they played a game 'a bit like a cross between cricket and rounders. We had a stick for a bat, and we threw stones at the girl holding the stick.' Another reminder of the challenges she faced throughout her sporting life.

Importantly it should be noted what a champion of fellow writers, Ashley Mallett was. He was always willing to offer advice and encouragement. Like the aforementioned Bernard Whimpress, Ashley Mallett was indeed someone who 'paid it forward.' A book that somehow missed my attention when it was published in 2018 is **Denis Brien's *All the King's Men: A History of the Hindmarsh Cricket Club 1857 to 1897*** (even winning the Jack Pollard Trophy for the Australian cricket book of

COUCHMATE™

SAVE SPACE, CREATE COMFORT

COUCH ARM TABLES · BATH CADDIES · LAP & PICNIC TABLES

the year!) So somewhat belatedly I mention the book is a wonderful and entertaining study of the minutiae surrounding the life of a local cricket club. Not only does it amply examine the challenges of operating a cricket club in a working-class suburb of Adelaide during pioneering times, it also brings to life some of the heart and soul of the club, its players and administrators.

Barry Nicholls' latest book The Establishment Boys was published by Wakefield Press in November 2021.

As Editor I have been doing plenty of reading over the past twelve months and really enjoyed the much awaited ***Being Geoffrey Boycott*** co-written with Jon Hotten. It is a warts and all account of his 108 Test matches from 1964 to 1981. It gives a great insight into the off and on-field pressures of Test Cricket. At various times Boycott is torn between England and Yorkshire, between himself and his captain, and doesn't hold back. His writing on batting against the West Indies in the 1980s alone is worth a read. He discusses at length personal matters, who he liked batting with and who he found hard to play with.

Mike Sexton has put out another gem of a book, entitled ***Three Summers of Sobers, South Australia 1961/62 to 1963/64.*** It's 80 pages of pictures, stories and first-hand accounts of what it was like to play with Garry Sobers, when the world's best cricketer called South Australia home in the early 1960's. Sobers enjoyed himself on and off the field and drew crowds, even to club games at Prospect.

Journalist Ron Reed passed away in 2022 but thankfully he managed to complete ***Captain Pat – cometh the hour, Cummins the man.*** It's the first book on Cummins and not only covers the new Australian Test skipper, but also looks closely at the 2021-22 Ashes series. It's an easy read which was a hallmark of Reed's style on any sporting topic. It also reflects on the departure of Tim Paine and that of coach Justin Langer. A worthy final effort from one of Australia finest sportswriters.

I also managed to obtain a copy of ***With Stoddart's team in Australia (1897-98),*** written by KS Ranjitsinhji. The Indian born batsman was a key batsman on the trip and provides an entertaining account of playing and travelling across Australia. He makes a remarkable reflection on Victor Trumper, the first time he played against him. He had only made 5 and 0 in the match and these were his impressions…how accurate they turned out to be!

"The New South Wales batting was opened by Trumper and Donnan. Trumper was the first to leave for 5, having played a loose ball rather carelessly into my hands. He created a very favourable impression on me from the way in which he was shaping at the wickets. He seemed to be all there, and the confidence with which he played the bowling, although it was for a very short time, makes me firmly believe that he will be a very great batsman in this country, and at no very distant date. Indeed, I have seen very few beginners play the ball so well, and show the same excellent style".

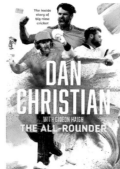
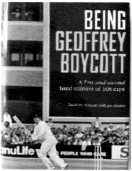
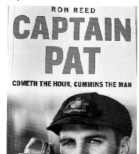
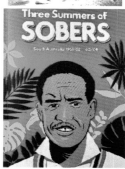
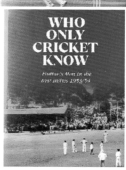
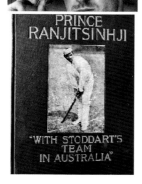

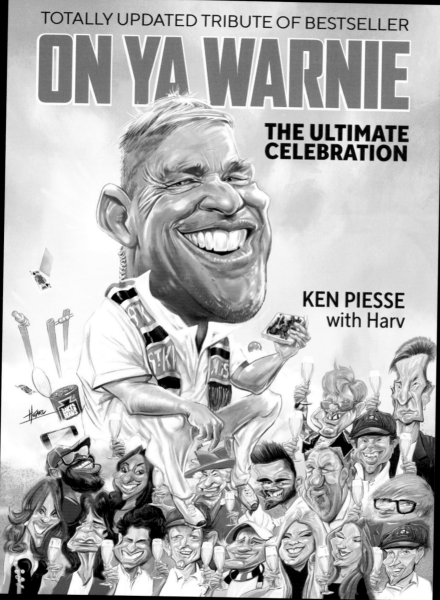

THE ASHES 2021/22
COMFORTABLY RETAINED BY AUSTRALIA 4-0

Australia easily retained the Ashes over England four matches to nil, which was a clear indication of the gulf between the two teams. The Australians had a clear advantage over England in batting, passing 400 on three occasions, where England was unable to pass 300 once in its ten innings. The numbers would suggest it was the worst England batting line-up since the 1950/51 series, where only Len Hutton (88.87) managed an average over 32 for England.

Australia had plenty of fire power in the pace bowling department, despite Josh Hazlewood going down after the first Test, while England could only respond with Mark Wood who was used in small spells until the final Test.

When the series was there to be won Australia played brilliant first days in the first three Tests, as England got too far behind to get back into the match. On the opening day at the Gabba, England were shot out for 147, when they elected to bat first under heavy skies. In Adelaide, Australia ended day one on 2-221 and at the MCG, England were all out 185, with Australia 1-61 by stumps and well on top.

Australia were also helped by England's faulty decisions at the selection table. It was odd to see that both James Anderson and Stuart Broad were both left out for the first Test and that spinner Jack Leach was picked to play at a venue with short boundaries straight down the ground. It was as obvious as the nose on your face that the Australian batsmen were going to go after Leach and so it proved as he was constantly hit over the boundary and out of the attack. Then in Adelaide where the ball does turn and the boundaries are long straight, Leach got the flick for an all-pace attack who only managed two wickets on the opening day.

For Australia, Travis Head made aggressive centuries in the first and last Tests to clinch the Man of the Series award. He backed himself to play his shots and in those two knocks it came off brilliantly. In his first Test series as skipper, Pat Cummins did a great job in charge and was always a handful for the England batsmen. Mitchell Starc had a superb first three Tests with the ball and made important runs in the lower order, while David Warner started the series well with two scores of 90 plus, setting his team well on the road to victory. Marnus Labuschagne made important runs in the first two Tests and when Nathan Lyon took his 400th Test wicket in Brisbane it freed him up to bowl well for the rest of the series.

One of the real stories of the Ashes was that of 32 year-old pace bowler Scott Boland emerging from Shield Cricket to have such a significant role for Australia. With Boland having taken 268 wickets for Victoria at 25.72 across 10 seasons, he was given the opportunity to debut at his home ground the MCG. Boland started quietly to take 1-48 in the first innings before spectacularly picking up 6-7 to destroy England in their second innings for just 68. He went on to take seven wickets in Sydney and four more in Hobart to have the series figures of 18 wickets at under 10, the second-best average of anyone in the history of the Ashes.

BEST BOWLING AVERAGE IN AN ASHES SERIES (MIN 18 WICKETS)

	Team	Series	M	Wkts	Average	Best	5w/10w
R Peel	Eng	1888	3	24	7.54	7-31	1/1
SM Boland	Aus	2021-22	3	18	9.56	6-7	1/-
JC Laker	Eng	1956	5	46	9.61	10-53	4/2
CTB Turner	Aus	1888	3	21	12.43	6-112	4/1
RM Hogg	Aus	1978-79	6	41	12.85	6-74	5/2

Usman Khawaja made his way back into the team and played splendidly in the SCG Test making a hundred in each innings. Steve Smith was well down on his output from previous Ashes series but still made useful contributions, whilst Marcus Harris played some gritty knocks, but failed to make that one big score when well set. Cameron Green finally got amongst the wickets and batted well in the last two Tests, having made some technical adjustments after struggling for runs early on. In his first Test series, Alex Carey started very well with the gloves in Brisbane, but then started to put down a few catches and looked to lose a little bit of confidence. Jhye Richardson bowled Australia to victory in Adelaide, with Michael Neser finally got his long-awaited chance at Test cricket in the same match.

For England sadly, there were too few players who could say they played to their ability. But one must be grateful that they agreed to come out at all, given the need to firstly isolate and then put up with some tough protocols throughout. Fast bowler Mark Wood was one of the real triers in the side, continually beating the bat and worrying the Aussie top order. Wood had no luck in the early Tests and got his reward in Hobart with nine wickets in the match. Jonny Bairstow came into the team mid-series and rejuvenated his Test career with a cracking hundred in the SCG Test. Skipper Joe Root battled away for three half-centuries but kept getting out caught playing away from his body, while Zak Crawley played a sparkling innings of 77 in the SCG Test and looks like one player who will feature in the 2023 series. Veteran bowlers James Anderson and Stuart Broad performed with credit and Ben Stokes gave his all and had a good SCG Test with that bat but found it hard work bowling on the Australian pitches.

TRAVIS HEAD – WINNER OF THE COMPTON/MILLER MEDAL AS MAN OF THE SERIES IN THE 2021/22 ASHES

FIRST TEST - BRISBANE

Australia had named its team well in advance of the game, with Alex Carey set to debut with the keeping gloves, while Travis Head got the nod ahead of Usman Khawaja for the number five spot. Neither James Anderson nor Stuart Broad were to turn out for England, and with the pitch having a touch of green under overcast skies, England opted to play spinner Jack Leach, a move they were to regret. England had seven of their eleven playing their first Test in Australia, Rory Burns, Haseeb Hameed, Ollie Pope, Jos Buttler, Ollie Robinson, Mark Wood and Jack Leach. England won the toss and Joe Root boldly decided to bat first.

Day One - Attendance: 30,790

In one of the most dramatic starts to an Ashes series, Mitchell Starc bowled Rory Burns behind his pads with the first ball of the match. It was a full ball on the pads and Burns went too far across and had his leg stump cleaned up, much to the delight of the Australians and the Gabba crowd. Malan eased his first ball down to the third man for four but didn't last much longer as he poked at one outside off, edging behind to give Carey's his first catch as Australia's Test keeper. Skipper Root came out and didn't last long, edging to first slip, which made it four ducks in his last eight Ashes innings. At the other end Hameed was looking composed in his first innings against Australia, as England reached drinks on 3-24 from 12 overs, Hameed 12, Stokes 5.

Straight after Stokes drove Cummins superbly through the covers for four, but a few balls later played back to one, edging it low to third slip. Hameed continued to impress, and Ollie Pope played some nice square drives as England made their way to 4-59 at Lunch with the opener on 25, Pope 17. In the first over after lunch, Hameed's good knock ended when he edged low to second slip, with all of the keeper around to third slip having now held onto catches in a sharp display in the field by the home

LAWYERS
Agency ▪ Credit Management ▪ Litigation

Making the right decisions on …..
…. and off the field

GERARD ABOOD
National Panel Umpire
Principal Solicitor at ACL Lawyers

We'll help you make the right decisions for the protection and recovery of your debts.

At ACL Lawyers, our focus is on Debt Recovery & Credit Management
Let us help you;

- Manage your debtors and debt recovery work;

- Improve your cash flow;

- Protect your future debts by reviewing & refining your

  Terms and Conditions of Trade;

We provide a professional and reliable service to ensure your debt recovery process is as smooth and efficient as possible…. every time.

(02 8677 9934   ✉ gabood@acllaw.com.au
▯ 0414 952 680   🌐 www.acllaw.com.au

side. Jos Buttler started with strong cover drive for four off Hazlewood to get off the mark and in the bowler's next over went aerial over the same area to score another. The pair looked to take the challenge up to the Australian bowlers in different ways, Pope keen on quick singles, while Buttler went for his strokes hitting regular boundaries. Buttler square drove Starc away for four to bring up the 50 stand and give England some hope, but then nicked the next ball behind to leave England 6-112.

After playing well, Pope went for a pull-shot off Green, top edging to long-leg where Hazlewood ran in and dived forward to take a fine catch, giving the young Australian all-rounder his first Test wicket. Shortly after Robinson drove meekly at a wide one and edged behind. The ninth wicket pairing smacked 22, mainly in boundaries before Wood popped a catch to short-leg and then Woakes hooked to long-leg, where Hazlewood took another fine catch diving forward, to give his skipper a five-wicket haul in his first appearance as Test skipper. England all out for 147 at 2.37pm – then the rain came and eventually play was called for the day.

Day Two - Attendance: 20,812

The sun was shining brightly at the earlier start time of 9.30am as the Australian openers headed out to the middle. How England must have regretted even more their decision to field first on the opening day. Woakes took the new ball for England with Warner getting off the mark immediately with a single to mid-off. The opening bowlers gave little away in the first half hour and got their reward when Harris came forward and edged one low to third slip. Labuschagne was off the mark easing one to the third man rope but then England thought they had Warner on 17 as Stokes sent one through his defences, but to the dismay of the visitors, the all-rounder had overstepped the front line. Had Warner been out, the score would have been 2-30 and one wonders where the day would have headed. A little later when Warner was on 26, he suffered a nasty blow to ribs from a lifter from Stokes, which was to cause him problems later in the match.

England's pace bowlers had done a good job with the 50 taking 22 overs before Labuschagne led a burst of scoring in Stokes' fifth over which went for 11. Then Leach came on in the 25th over and after conceding just a single, Warner unloaded on him in his next as he punched him to the sightboard for six, before lofting him over long-on for another, in an over that cost 17. Labuschagne continued the attack during the left-arm slow bowler's next over, advancing and lofting him over long-on for six more, with 13 coming off the over and Leach retired from the attack with figures of 0-31 off three against his name. Labuschagne cut Woakes for four past point to bring up his 50 (71 balls, 5 fours, 1 six) as Australia went to lunch on 1-113 (31 overs) with Warner 48, Labuschagne 53.

In the first over after lunch England's mood got worse as Warner (48) edged Robinson to second slip where Burns put down a straight-forward chance. Warner celebrated his luck in the next over by punching Wood away through the off-side to bring up his 50 (102 balls, 4 fours, 2 sixes) but then had more luck shortly after on 60, when he played one to Hameed at short-leg, who missed the stumps with the throw as he slipped trying to make his ground.

The partnership passed 150 and then Labuschagne advanced and lofted Leach for six, having changed from the Vulture to the Stanley Street end. But Leach had his revenge next ball and the Aussie number three made room to cut and couldn't keep it to ground, giving a catch to backward point. Smith advanced to his second ball, lofting Leach somewhat luckily through mid-wicket to the rope before playing back to Wood and edging behind just before tea, Australia going in at 3-193 (54 overs) with Warner 94 and Head yet to score.

The England fightback continued in the second over after tea as Warner lofted a slower ball to wide mid-off and next ball Green was bowled padding up to leave Australia five down with a lead of 48. After a few nervous moments for Head things changed quickly as he counter-attacked, smacking Stokes for three fours in an over before depositing Root back over his head to long-on for six. Carey had been looking good but then played a reckless pull-shot straight to mid-wicket, but this did not deter Head who despite copping a knock from Wood on his left elbow, continued to play naturally slashing a magnificent square-drive off the same bowler for four shortly after. He brought up his 50 (51 balls, 7 fours, 1 six) when he punched a Wood full-toss to the long-off rope as Australia's lead rolled past 100.

Things got worse for England as Robinson could only manage a one-over spell before heading off the field, while Head kept smacking the ball to all parts, hitting Leach straight for six and then next ball gaining a five thanks to four overthrows from Stokes at mid-off. Cummins had played a fine role in a stand worth 70 before he glanced one straight to leg-slip. With the field set deep Head had reached 97 when the new ball was taken after 80 overs with Australia 7-320. Head drove Woakes' second ball with it to the mid-on boundary to bring up his century from just 85 balls, the third equal fastest ever, behind Adam Gilchrist who called the moment in commentary for Fox Cricket.

FASTEST EVER ASHES HUNDREDS (BALLS FACED)

Adam Gilchrist (Australia)	57	WACA, Perth	2006/07
Gilbert Jessop (England)	76	The Oval, London	1902
Travis Head (Australia)	**85**	**Gabba, Brisbane**	**2021/22**
Joe Darling (Australia)	85	SCG	1897/98
Ian Botham (England)	86	Headingley, Leeds	1981
Ian Botham (England)	86	Old Trafford, Manchester	1981

In the next over Head copped a beamer from Wood and was very lucky not to be badly hurt as the ball hit his right glove which was off the bat, before it cannoned into the grille off his helmet. In the last over of the day, Starc was dropped on 10 off the inside by 'keeper Buttler, the end of the day not coming quickly enough for England, who now trailed by 196 with three days left.

Day Three - Attendance: 28,016

It was another bright day at the Gabba, when play got underway at 9.30am, Head looking fully recovered as he pulled Woakes for four in the third over of the day. In the same over Starc played a marvellous on-drive for four and continued to offer great support to his partner as the pair continued to take the shine off the second new ball. Starc magnificently straight drove the recovered Robinson for four and then Stokes came on for his first spell for the day and was bashed over long-off by Head for six. The partnership came to an end on 85 when Starc lofted Woakes straight down the throat of deep square-leg. Lyon was dropped by Woakes off his own bowling on one and in the next over pulled Stokes for four to bring up Australia's 400.

Head continued to enjoy himself, clipping Wood off his pads behind square-leg into the crowd, but then lost Lyon who mistimed a hook to short square-leg. Head reached his 150 with a powerful slog-sweep off Leach to mid-wicket for four and finally went in the next over, bowled making room to leg. Australia led by 278, as the last four wickets had added 189. This left England 37 minutes batting before lunch, with Warner unable to take the field for Australia due his rib injury.

After a three to Hameed from Starc's third ball, Burns was trapped in front of the last ball of the over, only to win a reprieve after a review which showed the ball to be just going over the stumps. Starc was pulled for four by Burns then cut for a boundary by Hameed as England went into lunch on 0-23.

In the first over after the break, Starc got one to lift at Burns who gloved it to the keeper. With Malan in, Lyon was immediately on chasing his 400th Test wicket, but the left-hander started strongly cutting Lyon for a boundary. But moments later was nearly bowled not offering a shot as he failed to pick his arm-ball. Hameed was getting the hang of the conditions as he glanced and cut Starc for boundaries, before unluckily getting a glove to one down the leg-side off the left-arm quick.

From this point England had their best period of the Test as Malan and Root settled in for a long partnership. Malan was using his feet to Lyon, while Root was picking off the Australian bowlers hitting some crisp shots as England went into tea on 2-107 (36 overs) with Malan 35, Root 26.

In the fourth over after tea, Malan on 37 advanced to Lyon which took the pad and rebounded to the bowler. It had also taken the glove, but the Australians were completely unaware and failed to review what would have been an easy decision for the third umpire. The third wicket pair continued on in style, Root hitting some sweet drives before pulling Lyon to the mid-wicket rope to bring up his 50 from 80 balls with 8 fours. With Hazlewood on the field but later revealed to be unable to bowl, Green came on for his first spell of the day and watched Malan guide him away past gully for three to reach his 50 in style.

On 64 Root had a moment of concern when Cummins got one to lift and almost hit his right glove and then Malan on 66 went close to hooking a bouncer to backward square-leg, which just fell short of Harris. Root and the England fans confidence continued to grow as he reverse swept Lyon for four to bring up England's 200. Lyon changed to the Vulture Street end late in the day, but Malan drove him for four as England finished proceedings 58 behind with some hope of making a game of it.

Day Four - Attendance: 19,228

After a great finish to the third day, England effectively lost the match in the opening half an hour of the fourth losing three wickets. In the fourth over of the day, Malan advanced to Lyon and got a touch onto his pad to silly point, giving the off-spinner his much awaited 400th Test wicket. Soon after Root flirted at a Green out-swinger to give the keeper a catch, the England skipper once again missing out on a century on Aussie soil. In the next over Pope played back to one from Lyon, gloving it to slip, England having lost 3-11 from 24 deliveries. Stokes and Buttler then played confidently, meanwhile the power went out in the TV broadcast compound at the Gabba, which meant for a period time there were no pictures going out to broadcasters worldwide.

With the TV coverage restored, the hopeful stand reached 32 but then Cummins got one to lift at Stokes who could only fend it to gully. Sadly, for England it was the beginning of the end as Buttler edged Hazlewood behind, Robinson was caught reverse sweeping and Wood bowled on the drive. When Woakes tried to uppercut Green and got a touch to the keeper, England had lost their last 5-31 to set Australia just 20 to win. Carey had also taken his eighth catch in the match, which broke the record for catches by a wicket-keeper on debut.

MOST DISMISSALS BY A KEEPER IN DEBUT TEST

Alex Carey	8	(all ct)	Australia v England, Gabba	2021-22
Brian Taber	8	(7ct/1st)	Australia v South Africa, Johannesburg	1957-58
Chris Read	8	(7ct/1st)	England v New Zealand, Edgbaston	1999

Warner was allowed to rest his injured ribs as Carey was sent out to open, his edge to the keeper the only moment of joy as Australia went one-nil up with well over a day to spare.

First Test at Gabba, Brisbane on December 8-11, 2021 – Australia won by 9 wickets

England	First innings		B	M	4	6		Second innings		B	M	4	6
RJ Burns	b Starc	0	1	1			2	c Carey b Cummins	13	27	40	2	
H Hameed	c Smith b Cummins	25	75	124	3		1	c Carey b Starc	27	58	89	2	
DJ Malan	c Carey b Hazlewood	6	9	16	1			c Labuschagne b Lyon	82	195	282	10	
JE Root *	c Warner b Hazlewood	0	9	11				c Carey b Green	89	165	245	10	
BA Stokes	c Labuschagne b Cummins	5	21	36	1			c Green b Cummins	14	49	73	3	
OJD Pope	c Hazlewood b Green	35	79	133	2			c Smith b Lyon	4	6	7	1	
JC Buttler +	c Carey b Starc	39	58	64	5			c Carey b Hazlewood	23	39	67	4	
CR Woakes	c Hazlewood b Cummins	21	24	47	4			c Carey b Green	16	47	66	2	
OE Robinson	c Carey b Cummins	0	3	7				c Head b Lyon	8	17	29		
MA Wood	c Harris b Cummins	8	15	19	1			b Lyon	6	13	14	1	
MJ Leach	not out	2	7	7				not out	0	2	7		
	5 lb, 1 w	6						4 b, 5 lb, 6 w	15				
	50.1 overs, 237 mins	147						103 overs, 464 mins	297				

1-0 (Burns), 2-11 (Malan), 3-11 (Root), 4-29 (Stokes), 5-60 (Hameed), 6-112 (Buttler), 7-118 (Pope), 8-122 (Robinson), 9-144 (Wood), 10-147 (Woakes)

1-23 (Burns), 2-61 (Hameed), 3-223 (Malan), 4-229 (Root), 5-234 (Pope), 6-266 (Stokes), 7-268 (Buttler), 8-286 (Robinson), 9-296 (Wood), 10-297 (Woakes)

Bowling	O	M	R	W	wd	nb		O	M	R	W	wd	nb
MA Starc	12	2	35	2				20	3	77	1		
JR Hazlewood	13	4	42	2				14	6	32	1		
PJ Cummins	13.1	3	38	5		1		20	6	51	2	1	
NM Lyon	9	2	21	0				34	5	91	4		
CD Green	3	1	6	1				12	3	23	2	1	
M Labuschagne								3	0	14	0		

Australia	First innings		B	M	4	6		Second innings		B	M	4	6
DA Warner	c Stokes b Robinson	94	176	275	11	2							
MS Harris	c Malan b Robinson	3	17	22				not out	9	10	24	1	
M Labuschagne	c Wood b Leach	74	117	211	6	2		not out	0	0	2		
SPD Smith	c Buttler b Wood	12	19	29	2								
TM Head	b Wood	152	148	257	14	4							
CD Green	b Robinson	0	1	2									
AT Carey +	c Pope b Woakes	12	32	43	1		1	c Buttler b Robinson	9	23	21		
PJ Cummins *	c Hameed b Root	12	27	55									
MA Starc	c Burns b Woakes	35	64	94	5								
NM Lyon	c Robinson b Wood	15	24	36	2								
JR Hazlewood	not out	0	6	11									
	4 b, 6 lb, 4 nb, 2 w	16											
	104.3 overs, 522 mins	425						5.1 overs, 24 mins	1-20				

1-10 (Harris), 2-166 (Labuschagne), 3-189 (Smith), 4-195 (Warner), 5-195 (Green), 6-236 (Carey), 7-306 (Cummins), 8-391 (Starc), 9-420 (Lyon), 10-425 (Head)

1-16 (Carey)

Bowling	O	M	R	W	wd	nb		O	M	R	W	wd	nb
CR Woakes	25	8	76	2				2	0	3	0		
OE Robinson	23	8	58	3				3	0	13	1		2
MA Wood	25.3	4	85	3	1	1		0.1	0	4	0		
BA Stokes	12	0	65	0	1	3							
MJ Leach	13	0	102	1									
JE Root	6	0	29	1									

Stumps scores:
Day 1   England (1st inns)   147
Day 2   Australia (2nd inns)   7-343   TM Head 112*, MA Starc 10*
Day 3   England (2nd inns)   2-220   DJ Malan 80, JE Root 86*

Toss: England. Umpires: PR Reiffel, RJ Tucker.
TV: P Wilson. Ref: DC Boon.
Award: TM Head (Aus). Attendance: 98,946

SECOND TEST - ADELAIDE

With Josh Hazlewood already out of the test with a side strain, Australia had more bad news in the lead up to the match as skipper Pat Cummins was deemed to have been a close contact to a positive COVID case in an Adelaide restaurant, which meant under South Australia's draconian rules he was ruled out. Steve Smith was picked as captain for the first time since 2018, while Michael Neser would make his debut and Jhye Richardson was called in. David Warner was also judged fit to play having recovered sufficiently from sore ribs suffered in Brisbane. England's veteran pairing of James Anderson and Stuart Broad came in for Mark Wood and Jack Leach.

Day One – Attendance: 32,328

England's opening bowlers gave little away, with Broad getting an early LBW decision in his favour when Harris was on just three. But the opener reviewed with technology showing the ball would have missed leg stump. It mattered little as in the quicks next over Harris gloved a leg-side pull and Buttler swooped full length to his right to bring off a great catch. Australia struggled to 1-15 off 12 overs at drinks, then Warner punched one through the off-side from Woakes just after for the day's first boundary. Broad returned for a second spell and Warner hit him to leg twice for four before Labuschagne made room to uppercut Stokes just past slip for four. Stokes gave Labuschagne a hard time cracking him on the glove and ribs in the same over as Australia went to dinner on 1-45 (25 overs) with Warner 20, Labuschagne 16.

Warner was typically strong through the off-side after lunch and then Labuschagne had some luck hooking one on 21, when Buttler was unable to hang onto to a chance high to his left off Stokes. Warner continued on, smacking Stokes through mid-off for four before pulling him to the rope to bring up his 50 (108 balls, 8 fours) as for the second test straight Australia passed 100 for just one wicket down. Labuschagne reached 50 runs and then just prior to tea brought up his 50 from 156 balls, the slowest of his career. Australia went to tea on 1-129 (53 overs) with Warner 63, Labuschagne 53.

As the floodlights slowly took over the second wicket stand rolled on, with Warner and Labuschagne both pulling Anderson for fours in the one over. The England quicks resorted to placing three deep on the leg-side fence and just as Warner looked set to secure his first ton of the series, he smacked one to cover point where Broad held the catch. Labuschagne continued to take full advantage of any short stuff, pulling boundaries away, while Smith was content take his time as the new ball loomed with Australia 2-212 after 80 overs.

Smith struck Broad square to the off-side rope for four but in the next over, Buttler grassed a regulation caught behind to his right off the bowling Anderson when Labuschagne was 95. Play ended just after 10pm, with England having created many chances but only having two wickets for their day's work.

Day Two – Attendance: 27,208

Play started with the temperature in the mid-30's as Smith cut Anderson's fourth ball of the day to the boundary. After copping a knock on the arm from Anderson, Labuschagne eased the same bowler away to the third man rope to bring up his century from 287 balls. After three overs from Anderson, Robinson came on and had Labuschagne caught behind first ball, only for cameras to reveal it was a no-ball! Thankfully for England it cost very little as in his next over, Robinson had Labuschagne leg before not offering a shot. England's bowlers were sticking to their task in the heat with both Woakes and Robinson finding edges that fell short of slip fieldsman.

Head had cracked two fine off-side shots for four before and then Smith reached his 50 (135 balls, 8 fours) as he slashed Stokes over the keeper's head to the rope. With no Leach to call upon in the spin department, Root gave himself a bowl and after being lofted straight for four by Head, bowled him with a low full-toss which he played across. In the next over Green played down the wrong line to one from Stokes to be bowled, Australia going into the dinner break on 5-302 (116 overs) with Smith 55 and Carey 6.

Australia kept the scoreboard ticking nicely after dinner and then Carey and Smith each struck Root for boundaries in an over that cost 10. Carey hit Woakes away behind point for four and then the same over Smith pulled him into the eastern stand for six to bring up the 350. Again, the pink ball was struggling to carry to the catchers behind the wicket as Carey edged Stokes just short of second slip. Smith had the benefit of a five thanks to an errant throw from Burns and then moved into the nineties, when Anderson was brought back and trapped him dead in front as he was caught on the crease. Carey reached his maiden Test 50 (104 balls, 5 fours) but then in the over before tea miscued one to cover – Australia heading in at the break on 7-390.

Straight after the break, Starc hit one through the hands of Anderson at mid-wicket as Australia looked to push the game forward. In his first test innings Neser was keen to play his shots and he took to Woakes, hitting him for two fours before lifting a shortish ball over the point rope for six. The Queensland dominated as the 50 stand was raised from 44 balls before Neser hit hard but not far enough to clear deep mid-on. Starc proceeded to hit Stokes for three fours in an over, and after lofting Woakes for six, Richardson was out caught behind which saw Australia declare leaving England around 90 minutes of batting.

Things started badly for England as Burns edged the first ball of Starc's second over to second slip and then Neser had success with his second ball in Test cricket, as Hameed punched a drive to mid-on. Fortunately for England they were to lose no further wickets that night, as lightening was spotted in the sky to the south of the Oval, which caused an early abandoned of the day's play.

Day Three – Attendance: 27,613

With the weather a much more pleasant 25 degrees, play started at 2.11pm with Neser completing his over from the night before. Things were looking good early for England as Root punched Richardson delightfully away for an early off-side boundary and then shortly after Malan hit a firm straight drive to the rope off the same bowler. Starc came on and copped some immediate stick from Malan who cracked consecutive fours off short balls behind point. Lyon was introduced and after two tight overs was lofted by Root for four over mid-on before later reverse sweeping him away for another. Malan was first to 50 (86 balls, 6 fours), celebrating with a glorious square drive for four off Lyon.

The 100 stand was raised and then Root reached his 50 (91 balls, 6 fours) with a neat glance off Richardson to the long-leg rope. Dinner then came with England 2-140 (41 overs) with Malan 68 and Root 57, with 123 having come in the session. Root scored an early boundary off Green in the over after the dinner break, but shortly after the England skipper edged the same bowler straight to Smith at first slip, playing at one he could have left alone. The stand had been worth 138, after which Green and Lyon reigned the scoring in to bowl six maidens in a row between them. Starc was recalled and was cut by Malan for four, the batsman out caught at slip from the next delivery as he looked to repeat the shot.

Stokes was taking the overly defensive approach, needing 24 balls to get off the mark before he watched Pope work one to the on-side, where he was caught at short-leg. When Buttler edged a drive to first slip, England had lost 4-19 having wasted all the good work from the first session. England dug in until tea, going to the break on 6-197 (71 overs) with Stokes 12 (71 balls) and Woakes 23 (25 balls, 5 fours) the latter having hit some fine drives and pulls.

Lyon chimed in for the first two wickets after tea as he bowled Woakes through the gate playing back and then trapped Robinson dead in front stuck on the crease. Stokes finally came out of his shell sweeping Lyon for six, before making room to launch him over cover for a four. Green then got Stokes to chop on and then the new ball was taken with Richardson banging a few in short at Broad, clunking him on the grille of his helmet before later fending one off the glove to long-leg. Broad had some revenge in the next over hooking Richardson for six, Starc actually catching the ball at long-leg whilst stepping on the rope. Starc ended the innings when Broad popped a catch to cover, England trailing by 237 – leaving 17 overs of batting for Australia under the lights.

Australia's openers started well, with both players hitting off-side boundaries before Warner was nearly run out at the bowler's end by Woakes on 11. Then within 15 minutes of stumps Harris pushed one straight to the square-leg fielder, calling for an impossible single, with Broad completing an easy run out with Warner miles short of his ground. Neser completed his night-watchman duties without trouble as the day ended with Australia leading by 282 with two days to play.

Day Four – Attendance: 17,873

England's day started badly with skipper Root unable to take the field having been struck in the abdomen in the nets before play. England's bowlers responded to the challenge ahead as Anderson breached Neser's defence before Harris edged Broad behind for Buttler to bring off a fine diving catch to his left. Smith edged the next ball, this time to Buttler's right, where the chance went down. Then off the next ball the drama continued as Smith was very close to LBW but was given not out by Umpire Tucker. England reviewed the decision with technology showing the impact was "Umpires call" but hitting the stumps – thus being not out but if the Umpire had given it out, it would have stayed that way. England were out of the luck for the second time in as many balls.

In Broad's next over, Smith drove him for four, but there was little on offer for the batsman in a period where just seven runs came in eight overs. Robinson took over from Anderson's end (his spell 4-3-1-1) and England finally had some luck as Smith got a touch to one down the leg-side, Buttler this time diving well to his left to bring off a fine catch. Australia had lost 3-10, but could still feel comfortable with a lead of 292.

The game changed after drinks as the fifth wicket pairing laid into the bowling. Head cut and pulled fours before Labuschagne hit consecutive boundaries to leg off Robinson to relieve the pressure. Root returned to the field for England, but the runs continued to flow as the England bowlers couldn't regain control. Robinson turned to some off-spin and then Stokes had a crack at the crease but went for 24 from his two overs before dinner, as Australia went in on 4-134, with Labuschagne 31 and Head 45, leading by 371.

Head reached his 50 (49 balls, 7 fours) straight after tea but went in the following over hooking a short ball to deep square-leg, where Stokes ran in and took a fine catch low to the ground. The runs continued to flow as Labuschagne reached his 50 (94 balls, 6 fours) before he slog-swept a catch to deep mid-wicket to give part-time leggie Malan his first Test wicket. Carey disappointed in chopping on and with Starc and Richardson both crunching leg-side sixes before being dismissed, Australia declared 467 ahead with 44 overs left in the day - Green having found some much needed form in an unbeaten knock.

England had just under 40 minutes batting before tea, with Hameed gloving Richardson's last ball of his first over to the keeper. At tea England was 1-20 (Burns 16, Malan 4) off 8 overs and both batsmen looked in good nick with some nice off-side shots. On 19 Malan edged Lyon to Smith at slip, who put down an absolute sitter but it mattered little as in the next over Neser trapped Malan LBW from around the wicket. Burns battled hard under the lights until he edged one low to second slip where this time Smith made no mistake. Root and Stokes had an hour to bat before stumps and were hanging tough until 15 minutes were left in the day when Starc went around the wicket and struck the England captain in the protector, which floored him having been struck in that region earlier in the day in the nets. Root recovered to bat on and when Stokes played out a maiden to Lyon there was just enough time for the final over of the day. Sadly for the England skipper he edged Starc's second ball to

Carey and was on his way, in a cruel blow to England's chances of saving the game.

Day Five – Attendance: 7,446

When Pope on-drove the second ball of day for four, England hoped for the best but in the next over he edged Starc to second slip and with England five down, it seemed only a matter of time before Australia would wrap up the test. Buttler came in on a pair and in Starc's next over edged him between keeper Carey and first slip Warner for four, with neither going for the catch. Warner was quite wide on the right in his positioning, but it was definitely Carey's catch given he had the gloves on. Defence was the order of the day until Stokes swept Lyon for four, but in the off-spinners next over he trapped Stokes, after the Aussies won a review taken with two seconds remaining.

Woakes played some nice off side strokes and he and Buttler settled into to the almost impossible task of saving the match. Woakes was almost run out by Harris in close on the off-side when on 15, but battled on to dinner where England went in without further loss on 6-142, Buttler 16 and Woakes 28.

The players returned for the second session with the new ball available in six overs, Labuschagne was tried with Woakes belting him away for two fours in his opening over. The new ball was taken straight away at 6-155 and caused no major dramas until Richardson put one through the defences of Woakes, ending his gritty innings. Buttler was gamely blocking away at the other end and almost lost Robinson straight away when he offered a low chance to Neser off his own bowling. Robinson's resistance lasted for nearly an hour until he edged one from around the wicket to Smith who took the chance.

Broad was nearly bowled second ball as he was beaten by Lyon, that just went over the top of the stumps. Shortly after Broad was adjudged LBW to Lyon, but an inside edge saw the decision reversed as England went into tea on 8-180 with 26 overs left – Buttler was 25 not out from 196 balls, having made 10 off 109 in the session.

It didn't take long after tea for the end to come as the resolute Buttler played back to one and stepped on his off-stump and then Anderson fended one low to gully – Australia winning with 20.5 overs to spare to go two up in the series. Richardson must have been close to Man of the match for his fine second innings bowling, but the award went to Labuschagne for his hundred in the first dig and fifty in the second.

Second Test at Adelaide Oval on December 16-20, 2021 (day/night) – Australia won by 275 runs

Australia	First innings		B	M	4	6		Second innings		B	M	4	6
MS Harris	c Buttler b Broad	3	28	32			2	c Buttler b Broad	23	66	78	3	
DA Warner	c Broad b Stokes	95	167	290	11		1	run out (Broad-Buttler)	13	38	55	1	
M Labuschagne	lbw b Robinson	103	305	400	8		4	c Stokes b Malan	51	96	149	6	
SPD Smith*	lbw b Anderson	93	201	329	12	1	5	c Buttler b Robinson	6	31	42	1	
TM Head	b Root	18	36	58	3		6	c Stokes b Robinson	51	54	76	7	
CD Green	b Stokes	2	5	4			7	not out	33	43	60		
AT Carey+	c Hameed b Anderson	51	107	132	5		8	b Root	6	6	5	1	
MA Starc	not out	39	39	58	5		9	c Pope b Root	19	20	21		1
MG Neser	c Broad b Stokes	35	24	41	5	1	3	b Anderson	3	13	20		
JA Richardson	c Buttler b Woakes	9	3	7		1		c Buttler b Malan	8	4	4	1	
NM Lyon													
	9 lb, 11 nb, 5 w	25						3 b, 8 lb, 5 nb, 1 w	17				
	150.4 overs, 679 mins	9-473 dec						61 overs, 259 mins	9-230 dec				

1-4 (Harris), 2-176 (Warner), 3-241 (Labuschagne), 4-291 (Head), 5-294 (Green), 6-385 (Smith), 7-390 (Carey), 8-448 (Neser), 9-473 (Richardson)

1-41 (Warner), 2-48 (Neser), 3-48 (Harris), 4-55 (Smith), 5-144 (Head), 6-173 (Labuschagne), 7-180 (Carey), 8-216 (Starc), 9-230 (Richardson)

Bowling	O	M	R	W	wd	nb		O	M	R	W	wd	nb
JM Anderson	29	10	58	2				10	6	8	1		
SCJ Broad	26	6	73	1		2		10	3	27	1		
CR Woakes	23.4	6	103	1	2	2		12	3	46	0		
OE Robinson	27	13	45	1		4		15	2	54	2		2
BA Stokes	25	2	113	3	3	3		2	0	24	0	1	3
JE Root	20	2	72	1				6	1	27	2		
DJ Malan								6	0	33	2		

England	First innings	B	M	4	6	Second innings	B	M	4	6
H Hameed	c Starc b Neser	6	21	31		2	c Carey b Richardson	0	6	8	
RJ Burns	c Smith b Starc	4	3	10	1	c Smith b Richardson	34	95	130	5
DJ Malan	c Smith b Starc	80	157	210	10	lbw b Neser	20	52	77	4
JE Root *	c Smith b Green	62	116	165	7	c Carey b Starc	24	67	100	1
BA Stokes	b Green	34	98	144	3	1	lbw b Lyon	12	77	110	1
OJD Pope	c Labuschagne b Lyon	5	19	21	1	c Smith b Starc	4	7	8	1
JC Buttler +	c Warner b Starc	0	15	22		hit wkt b Richardson	26	207	257	2
CR Woakes	b Lyon	24	40	50	5	b Richardson	44	97	118	7
OE Robinson	lbw b Lyon	0	7	9		c Smith b Lyon	8	39	61	1
SCJ Broad	c Head b Starc	9	17	42		1	not out	9	31	46	1
JM Anderson	not out	5	13	27	1	c Green b Richardson	2	5	15	
	6 lb, 1 nb	7				2 b, 3 lb, 4 nb	9			
	84.1 overs, 370 mins	236				113.1 overs, 469 mins	192			

1-7 (Burns), 2-12 (Hameed), 3-150 (Root), 4-157 (Malan), 5-164 (Pope), 6-169 (Buttler), 7-202 (Woakes), 8-204 (Robinson), 9-220 (Stokes), 10-236 (Broad)

1-4 (Hameed), 2-48 (Malan), 3-70 (Burns), 4-82 (Root), 5-86 (Pope), 6-105 (Stokes), 7-166 (Woakes), 8-178 (Robinson), 9-182 (Buttler), 10-192 (Anderson)

Bowling	O	M	R	W	wd	nb	O	M	R	W	wd	nb
MA Starc	16.1	6	37	4			27	10	43	2		1
JA Richardson	19	4	78	0		1	19.1	9	42	5		2
MG Neser	11	0	33	1			13	5	28	1		
NM Lyon	28	11	58	3			39	16	55	2		
CD Green	10	3	24	2			9	5	9	0		1
M Labuschagne							4	2	10	0		
SPD Smith							1	1	0	0		
TM Head							1	1	0	0		

Stumps scores
Day 1:   Australia (1st inns)   2-221   M Labuschagne 95*, SPD Smith 18*
Day 2:   England (1st inns)   2-17   DJ Malan 1*, JE Root 5*
Day 3:   Australia (2nd inns)   1-45   MS Harris 21*, MG Neser 2*
Day 4:   England (2nd inns)   4-82   BA Stokes 3*

Toss: Australia. Attendance: 112,468
Umpires: RJ Tucker, P Wilson,
TV: PR Reiffel, Ref: DC Boon
Award: M Labuschagne (Aus)

THIRD TEST - MELBOURNE

Australia was glad to welcome back Pat Cummins to its side, while Jhye Richardson was left out after discussions between the bowler and the selectors, the quick later confirming he had some issues with shin soreness post the Adelaide Test. At 32 years of age, Victorian pace veteran Scott Boland also gained a call up replacing Michael Neser. England punted out batsmen Burns and Pope for Crawley and Bairstow, while Broad and Woakes made way for Wood and Leach. The pitch had an extremely green tinge to it, having transformed completely from the one in the last Ashes four years ago which was white and gave little hope to the bowlers. England's players were wearing black armbands following the death on Christmas Day of former England skipper Ray Illingworth, who had led them to victory in the 1970/71 Ashes.

Day One – Attendance: 57,100

Play started 30 minutes late due to rain under overcast skies with the floodlights on. Hameed didn't last long, as he edged Cummins behind in his first over. Crawley was ticking the score over but having played well for just over half an hour, he edged Cummins low to gully. Boland came on for his first bowl and Root worked him away off his pads for the first four of the innings. Malan was battling at the other end, eventually edging a four off Boland to get off the mark after 18 balls and 44 minutes.

The pair started to play well without getting on top, Root scoring more freely than Malan as lunch approached. Lyon was tried and kept things tight (1-6 off 5 overs) and at 12.59pm there was time for one more over before lunch. Root pinched a single off the second ball from Cummins and off the next ball Malan came forward and edged a simple catch to first slip. A session which could have ended even, went Australia's way as England went into the break on 3-61, with Root not out 33.

With the sun now out, Root cut Boland for four and shortly after worked him to long-leg to reach his 50, his third for the series. Sadly, for Root he was out in the next over, caught behind looking to play one wide of his body from Starc. Stokes started to get going, pulling Starc fine for four before he advanced and mad a clean strike over long-on for six off Lyon. Green and Lyon then built the pressure with a tight spell together, giving up just five runs in six overs before Stokes poorly executed a cut shot into the hands of backward-point. Then just on tea Buttler played a poor shot when he looked to loft Lyon over long-on but miscued to deep-square leg, England going in at the break on 6-128, with Bairstow 21.

Local debutant Boland had a joyous moment grabbing his first test wicket when he hit Wood on the front pad and then Bairstow's good innings ended when he couldn't avoid a short ball from Starc, which took the glove low to gully. Leach robustly lofted Lyon back over his head for six before edging him to slip and after playing some extravagant shots Robinson lofted one out to deep mid-wicket which brought the innings to an end.

This left Australia 75 minutes batting and Harris got things off to a fine start, working Anderson away through the on-side for a boundary in the first over. Warner hit two strong off-side boundaries before getting a nasty ball from Wood which reared off a length over gully for another four. The 50 came up and then Anderson came back for one last spell and first ball had Warner well caught low down in the gully. In the last over Harris copped a nasty blow on the glove, his left finger index finger left bloodied. The opener then safely edged the last ball of the day along the ground through slip for four, Australia trailing by 124 at stumps.

Day Two – Attendance: 42,626

On a cool sunny morning, four COVID cases in the England camp (two support staff and two family) caused concerns to the match resuming, but with no players reporting positive tests play started just 30 minutes late. Early on Lyon was in aggressive mood pulling and edging Robinson for boundaries, but in the bowler's next over he edged a drive to the keeper. Wood came on for his bowl of the day and had the vital wicket of Labuschagne straight away, when he edged one to first slip. Stokes replaced the Durham quick after just a two over spell and immediately got Smith to edge one away through gully to the rope. Stokes then won an lbw decision against Harris from Umpire Reiffel on 36, but replays after the review found an inside edge.

Anderson had been giving nothing away from the Member's end and got his reward, when Smith played forward and dragged it back onto the stumps. Head came in and played and missed at his first ball from the veteran paceman before cutting Robinson for four to reach lunch on 11, Harris 48 with Australia 4-131, just 54 in arrears.

Harris punched Wood down the ground for three to reach his 50 (130 balls, 198 minutes, 5 fours) and then eased one past gully for four as 16 came from the first two overs after lunch. Leach was on from the Southern end and in what seemed odd tactics was bowling around the wicket to the two left-handers. The partnership had ticked over nicely to 61 when Head played at one that was a fraction wide, edging to first slip. Then after a quiet period of scoring Anderson found the edge of Harris' bat to end his resolute four and a half hour innings. In his two spells either side of lunch Anderson had bowled 10 overs for just three runs in an immaculate spell of swing bowling.

At tea Australia was 6-200 (Green 12, Carey 9) but lost Green straight after the break when he played back and across the line to one from Leach. England were in an even better mood when Carey edged a cover drive behind, leaving Australia only 34 ahead with two wickets in hand. The Aussie tailed wagged at the end as the last two wickets added 48 with Cummins and Starc scored the majority adding 35 off 52 balls before the Aussie skipper top edged a pull to point. Starc played responsibly for an hour and when Boland edged to second slip – Australia had a handy lead of 82 with an hour left to play for the day.

When the players went onto the field, the MCG had a gladiatorial feel to it. It wasn't long before they were shouting when Crawley got an edge to the keeper. Next ball Malan was trapped in front to one that was just clipping the top of the stumps. Starc was on a hat-trick and nearly had it when he got one to seam away from Root's bat, only just failing to take the edge. The crowd was in fever pitch but then Root off-drove Cummins for four to relieve the tension for the England fans. Their hearts were in their mouths when Root edged a drive past gully, but when Hameed hit a composed off-drive off Starc for four, England reached 2-22 with 10 minutes left to play.

Captain Cummins called up Boland for a bowl and with his third ball he struck, Hameed feathering one to the keeper. Leach came out as night-watchman and went two balls later when he let one go which hit his off-stump, which sent the crowd absolutely nuts. Cummins bowled the last over and Root calmly drove the final ball of the day for three, England 51 behind.

Day Three – Attendance: 40,945

The sun was shining as the England's best two players headed onto the MCG in an attempt to build a partnership that could get their team back into the match. Root off-drove Starc for four and then Stokes hit the same bowler straight for two more boundaries it seemed the visitors might be able to dig their way out of trouble. Sadly, it was not to be as Stokes had his stumps cleaned up as he was bowled through the gate. Root hit another sweet straight drive for four and nearly lost Bairstow on four when Green dropped a tough chance to his left in the gully off Boland. It mattered very little as in the same over Bairstow was trapped in front, which marked the beginning of the end.

Root aimed a drive at Boland and edged it to first slip, while in the next over the Victorian had a five wicket haul as he held onto a caught and bowled chance from Wood. Two balls later Robinson edged one to third slip to give Boland the remarkable figures of 6-5. Anderson calmly worked the next ball away for two and then Green finished the match off in the next over when he bowled the veteran, Australia claiming an innings victory inside seven sessions. It was a fine effort by Australia to retain the Ashes inside 12 days, England completely demoralised as their batsmen let them down once again.

ENGLAND'S LOWEST TEST TOTALS IN AUSTRALIA

45	SCG	1886/87	65	SCG	1894/95
61	MCG	1901/02	**68**	**MCG**	**2021/22**
61	MCG	1903/04			

Third Test at the MCG on December 28-30, 2021 – Australia won by an innings and 14 runs

England — First innings

Batsman	Dismissal	R	B	M	4	6
H Hameed	c Carey b Cummins	0	10	9		
Z Crawley	c Green b Cummins	12	25	36		
DJ Malan	c Warner b Cummins	14	66	110	1	
JE Root*	c Carey b Starc	50	82	113	4	
BA Stokes	c Lyon b Green	25	60	89	2	1
JM Bairstow	c Green b Starc	35	75	124	3	
JC Buttler+	c Boland b Lyon	3	11	27		
MA Wood	lbw b Boland	6	15	22		
OE Robinson	c Boland b Lyon	22	26	44	3	
MJ Leach	c Smith b Lyon	13	18	19	1	
JM Anderson	not out	0	4	8		
Extras	4 lb, 1 nb	5				
Total	65.1 overs, 304 mins	185				

1-4 (Hameed), 2-13 (Crawley), 3-61 (Malan), 4-82 (Root), 5-115 (Stokes), 6-128 (Buttler), 7-141 (Wood), 8-159 (Bairstow), 9-176 (Leach), 10-185 (Robinson)

England — Second innings

Batsman	Dismissal	R	B	M	4	6
H Hameed	c Carey b Boland	7	31	52	1	
Z Crawley	c Carey b Starc	5	16	21	1	
DJ Malan	lbw b Starc	0	1	3		
JE Root*	c Warner b Boland	28	59	101	4	
BA Stokes	(6) b Starc	11	16	30	2	
JM Bairstow	(7) lbw b Boland	5	18	31		
JC Buttler+	(8) not out	5	14	26	1	
MA Wood	(9) c & b Boland	0	3	7		
OE Robinson	(10) c Labuschagne b Boland	0	2	3		
MJ Leach	(5) b Boland	0	2	3		
JM Anderson	b Green	2	4	7		
Extras	5 lb	5				
Total	27.4 overs, 141 mins	68				

1-7 (Crawley), 2-7 (Malan), 3-22 (Hameed), 4-22 (Leach), 5-46 (Stokes), 6-60 (Bairstow), 7-61 (Root), 8-65 (Wood), 9-65 (Robinson), 10-68 (Anderson)

Bowling

Bowler	O	M	R	W	wd	nb
MA Starc	15	3	54	2		1
PJ Cummins	15	2	36	3		
SM Boland	13	2	48	1		
CD Green	8	4	7	1		
NM Lyon	14.1	3	36	3		

O	M	R	W	wd	nb
10	3	29	3		
10	4	19	0		
4	1	7	6		
3.4	0	8	1		

Australia — First innings

Batsman	Dismissal	R	B	M	4	6
MS Harris	c Root b Anderson	76	189	269	7	
DA Warner	c Crawley b Anderson	38	42	62	5	
NM Lyon	c Buttler b Robinson	10	22	28	2	
M Labuschagne	c Root b Wood	1	14	24		
SPD Smith	b Anderson	16	31	52	1	
TM Head	c Root b Robinson	27	48	82	2	
CD Green	lbw b Leach	17	63	77	2	
AT Carey+	c Buttler b Stokes	19	43	66		
PJ Cummins*	c Hameed b Anderson	21	32	53	2	
MA Starc	not out	24	37	61	1	
SM Boland	c Crawley b Wood	6	11	20		
Extras	2 b, 4 lb, 5 nb, 1 w	12				
Total	87.5 overs, 396 mins	267				

Bowling

Bowler	O	M	R	W	wd	nb
JM Anderson	23	10	33	4		
OE Robinson	19.2	4	64	2		4
MA Wood	19.5	2	71	2		
BA Stokes	10.4	1	47	1	1	1
MJ Leach	15	0	46	1		

1-57 (Warner), 2-76 (Lyon), 3-84 (Labuschagne), 4-110 (Smith), 5-171 (Head), 6-180 (Harris), 7-207 (Green), 8-219 (Carey), 9-253 (Cummins), 10-267 (Boland)

Stumps scores:
Day 1: Australia 1st inns 1-61 MS Harris 20*, NM Lyon 0*
Day 2: England 2nd inns 4-31 JE Root 12*, BA Stokes 2*

Toss: Australia. Umpires: PR Reiffel, P Wilson.
TV: RJ Tucker. Award: SM Boland (Aus).
Attendance: 140,671

FOURTH TEST - SYDNEY

Australia lost Travis Head for the Test with COVID and he was replaced by Usman Khawaja. Head wasn't the only one missing as Match Referee David Boon was also a COVID victim, Steve Bernard his replacement. England brought back Stuart Broad for Ollie Robinson as the visitors needed to turn around their form to avoid going 4-nil down.

Day One – Attendance: 25,078

With rain causing a half hour delay, the match started with a bit of a bang as Anderson's first ball took Warner on the gloves. With Australia 0-8 after just 20 minutes of play, a shower swept across the ground which caused a 40 minute delay. Warner cracked Anderson square on the off-side for a couple of boundaries, as he and Harris took Australia to 0-30 (Warner 15, Harris 11) when the rain returned once more. Lunch was taken, play resuming at 1.30 with Warner smacking Wood's second ball through cover-point for four. Stokes came on and found the edge of Warner's bat which headed near second slip on way to the rope. The 50 was raised and with the rain clouds gathering once more, Warner edged a drive off Broad to second slip. When the rain came at 2.13pm, Australia was 1-56 (21.4 overs) with Harris 14, Labuschagne 0 with tea taken at 3.40pm.

At 4.19pm play got back underway and Labuschagne impressed immediately with an off-drive off Broad for four. In Broad's next over there was plenty of action as Labuschagne edged a four, leg glanced another to the rope, before surviving an LBW shout. Harris had been driving the ball nicely through the off-side and with 100 up in the 33rd over he looked on his way to a long innings. Australia was well placed at 1-111, but things changed when Harris played back and edged to first slip and Labuschagne got a touch behind, 2-6 being lost in the space of eight balls. In the closing stages, Smith and Khawaja both hooked fours and when the rain came back at 6.23pm, most were glad when stumps were called.

Day Two – Attendance: 24,855

Play started on time at 10am on a sunny and humid morning, Broad and Wood started with the ball and gave little away to Smith and Khawaja. Rain caused a 15 minute delay at 10.44 (Australia 3-148, Smith 19, Khawaja 12) and on the restart Smith drove Anderson straight back past him for four. Khawaja reverse swept Leach for four, but the rain arrived again at 11.15am (Australia 3-163, Smith 29, Khawaja 17) causing another annoying 15 minute break.

England's bowlers were again hard to force away with singles the order of the day and then came a chance for England when Labuschagne was put down at slip by Root on 28. Things got worse for England when Stokes left the field in the 72nd over with a side strain. Lunch came with Australia in the advantage at 3-209 (78 overs) with Smith 51, Khawaja 39.

Khawaja hit Root to leg for four, with the new ball taken immediately after at 3-221. With the sun now shining, Smith cracked a couple of fours off Broad before he fiddled at one outside off and was caught behind. Khawaja reached his 50 but it turned out to be a double breakthrough for Broad as Green edged him to second slip, leaving Australia 5-242.

Khawaja continued to look completely at ease and despite an edged four by Carey, he was going well until he looked to hit Root down the ground and was well caught by mid-on running back. As Khawaja pushed on towards his ton, Cummins took stock facing 22 dot balls before getting off the mark. Khawaja moved to 99 when he eased Root away behind point for four and in the last over before tea, worked Leach off his pads for three to reach his hundred. Tea was taken with Australia 6-321, Khawaja 102, Cummins 15.

In the third over after tea, Cummins gloved a bouncer to the keeper, England needing a review to get the decision to go in their favour. Starc came in and knuckled down, while Khawaja was scoring freely against the England attack. The stand passed 50 and then Khawaja finally went, dragging an inswinger back onto his stumps to give Broad a five wicket haul. After some hitting from Lyon, which included a six off Broad, Australia declared at 6pm to have 20 minutes at England. In the fourth over Hameed was caught by Smith in the slips off Starc, but no-ball was called as England finished 403 behind.

Day Three – Attendance: 28,415

The Sydney rain returned on Jane McGrath day, preventing the start of play until 12.10pm, which left 73 overs for play. Without adding to his overnight score of two, Hameed edged Starc to the right of Carey, who dived in front of first slip and put down the chance. The opportunities came thick and fast in the shortened session as Starc blasted through Hameed's attempted drive to bowl him in the fifth over of the day. Crawley who had given a tough chance to Harris' right at short-leg off Starc when seven, hit two crisp drives to the rope before being bowled on the forward stroke. Boland and Green were giving little away as the consecutive maidens started to mount up and with ten minutes to lunch, Root flirted at a wide one and was held head high at second slip by Smith. In the last over before the break Malan copped two nasty blows on the gloves facing Green, before being caught low down at leg slip to leave England in dire straits at 4-36.

After some careful defence after lunch, England ended a streak of 70 dot balls and then Stokes decided to get on with it to hit two fours in an over from Cummins. He then had two good bits of luck, the first was surviving a caught and bowled chance on nine facing Cummins and then on 16 when he let one pass off Green which clipped the off-stump, but it didn't remove a bail. Given the bail didn't drop it seemed quite odd that Umpire Reiffel put his finger up, but after a review by Stokes the decision was reversed. Bairstow continued to build his innings and then the tide started to turn England's way when Stokes hit Starc for three fours in a row, including a fine pull-shot which aggravated his side-strain. Lyon came on and Bairstow came out of his shell to sweep him for four, before hitting a cut and lap-sweep for further fours in the spinners next over. The Yorkshireman became the senior scorer in the partnership, hitting the ball sweetly to move to tea on 45, with Stokes 52 and England 4-135.

Lyon had gone for 27 in his five over spell before tea and it got worse for the veteran off-spinner as in one over Stokes swept him behind square-leg for four, before advancing and lofting over cover for six. Bairstow joined in the fun to slog-sweep Lyon for six but in the same over the spinner broke through when he trapped Stokes LBW as he played back looking to work one to leg. On 60 Bairstow copped a nasty blow on the right thumb from a ball from Cummins, the ball rebounding way over gully. For the time being it didn't stop him as in the next over he cracked Lyon for six to the leg-side, the off-spinner's three over spell costing 32. Green came on and Bairstow was still on the attack, pulling him for six but then Buttler was out in a disappointing way, hitting a catch to short cover.

Despite the two quick wickets, England's aggressive approach continued as Wood got off the mark in spectacular fashion, hooking Cummins for six. The England fans continued to roar as the 200 came up and then Wood off-drove Lyon for four, having changed to the Paddington end. Wood continued to be up for the fight as he hooked Cummins for consecutive sixes in a row, but the shot brought his undoing as he went after another short one, getting a fine edge via his helmet to gully. With just under 20 minutes left for play Leach joined Bairstow on 94 and with Labuschagne now in the attack, Bairstow moved to within one of his hundred with the last over of the day to be bowled by Cummins. After two play and misses in the first three balls, Bairstow cracked the Aussie skipper away behind point for four to reach his hundred, the emotions flowed for him as England ended the day 158 behind.

Day Four – Attendance: 20,277

In lovely sunlight, Leach struck Starc firmly through mid-off for a boundary in the second over, but perished in the third when he had a big swing at Lyon and was caught at wide mid-on. Nursing a sore right thumb, Bairstow was a more circumspect than the previous day before his innings ended when he got a regulation edge behind. When Broad top edged a hook to the keeper, who had to run well to his right to take the catch, England had lost 3-36 in the morning, to trail overall by 122.

With both Buttler and Bairstow unable to take their place on the field, Ollie Pope was allowed to sub wicket-keep for England. He was soon into action when Warner edged him a regulation chance off Wood. Harris looked to be settling in well but after several well-timed shots, aimed a big drive at Leach and was caught behind. In the over before lunch, Smith advanced and lofted Leach back over his head for four as Australia dined on 2-66, with a lead of 188, Labuschagne 28, Smith 8.

To the fourth ball after the break, Labuschagne aimed a cut at Wood and got a thin edge behind. Smith hooked Wood for six which pleased the crowd and then superbly cover drove Broad for four before playing back to one from Leach that sneaked through and bowled him. With Australia 208 ahead and six wickets in hand, England sensed a chance, but this was soon put to rest by Khawaja and Green who put together a long partnership. Khawaja hit his first four with a fine pull-shot off Anderson and continued his faith in the reverse-sweep getting Leach away to third-man. At 4-112 Wood returned for a quick spell, troubled Green and hit him on the glove as he tried to get out of the way, the ball going away for four. After two overs from Wood, Anderson was back and Green relieved his own personal pressure when straight-drove and pulled for consecutive fours. Tea came with Australia 4-149, a lead of 271 with Khawaja 35, Green 26.

With Australia in a now safe position, Khawaja exerted greater freedom in his stroke play after tea. He lofted Leach over wide mid-on for four, then hit back-to-back square drives for four, as he passed 50 from 86 balls. Green was content to push singles, while Khawaja upped it a gear as he slog-swept Leach over mid-wicket for six. Khawaja had some luck on 70, when he got a thick edge to Leach, with Pope putting down a tough chance. The runs continued to flow with Khawaja dominant, playing fine reverses sweeps while Green increased his tempo, pulling Wood for four to bring up his 50 (96 balls) as questions about a declaration loomed.

The matter of Khawaja chasing a hundred in each innings was there as well as he moved to 94 when he slog swept Leach into the Ladies' Stand for six. Then the historic moment came when Khawaja pulled part-timer Malan through mid-wicket for two, to reach his second ton of the game, being just the third batsman to do so in an SCG Test after Doug Walters (242 & 103) v West Indies in 1969 and Ricky Ponting (120 & 143*) v South Africa in 2006. Green whacked Leach for six straight, but when his solid knock ended as he and Carey went in consecutive balls, Australia declared to set England 388 in a day and 15 overs.

As the sun still shone, Crawley hit some sparkling shots before stumps, off-driving Cummins for four before clipping Starc to leg for a boundary, before getting one that lifted off a length from Boland that took the shoulder of the bat over slips to the rope. Hameed did well to hang in there as England ended the day needing 358 to win, or a day's batting to draw.

Day Five – Attendance: 11,660

In the sixth over of the day, Hameed on 9* edged Cummins behind, only for Carey to dive to his right and drop the chance. Crawley hit two lovely leg-side fours in a Cummins over before Hameed edged Boland and this time Carey held onto the catch, moving to his right. Crawley pulled two fine fours and passed 50, but lost Malan who he tried to force away through the off-side. Green came on and was also pulled for four by Crawley, but the West Aussie won the battle of the two tall young guns when he had the opener LBW with an in-swinging yorker. In a positive start Stokes straight drove Green for four to get off the mark and then swept Lyon for a boundary. Root hooked Cummins for four and then on 11 Stokes was dropped by Harris at short-leg by Harris off Cummins. England lunched on 3-122 with Root 13, Stokes 16, 266 needed from a minimum 63 overs.

The rain came in the lunch break, which caused a delay of an hour and a loss of seven overs. Despite the chance of a win for England all but out the window, Stokes went for his shots, pulling Starc for six before hitting Green through cover to the fence. Stokes advanced and lofted Lyon to long-on for four, but next ball Boland had Root for the third time in a row when he pushed forward and got an edge to the keeper. Bairstow caused immediate concern when he took a risky second to Lyon at long-leg, the throw just missing as the Yorkshireman dived full length to make his ground. Tea came with England 4-174, Stokes 46, Bairstow, and interestingly Australia's captain not having bowled himself in the session.

With 35 overs left, a respectable draw was England's goal, as Stokes on-drove Cummins for four to reach his second 50 of the Test. Stokes continued to look to score and after lofting Lyon to long-off for four, played back to the next ball and edged a catch to slip. The new ball was taken at 5-207 with 22 overs left and after lost a review for LBW against Buttler, Cummins trapped him with a sharp inswinger. Two balls later Wood was yorked on the toe, leaving England seven down with 17 overs left. On 28 Bairstow offered Smith a low chance at second slip off Starc which was put down, but he kept battling along until he got an inside edge into his pad and was caught at silly-point. With 64 balls to go Broad came out and stuck to largely defence, while Leach played some shots. The light got worse and with three overs left, the Umpires said only spin could be used, but this worked for Australia as Leach edged Smith to slip. So two overs remained for Broad and Anderson to survive, apart from one play and miss from Broad facing Lyon, the veterans survived the day to gain some pride in the England camp.

34

Fourth Test at the SCG on January 5-9, 2022 – Match Drawn

Australia

First innings

Batsman		R	B	M	4	6
DA Warner	c Crawley b Broad	30	72	90	6	
MS Harris	c Root b Anderson	38	109	180	4	
M Labuschagne	c Buttler b Wood	28	59	97	4	
SPD Smith	c Buttler b Broad	67	141	184	5	
UT Khawaja	b Broad	137	260	403	13	
CD Green	c Crawley b Broad	5	14	17	1	
AT Carey+	c Bairstow b Root	13	39	70	2	
PJ Cummins*	c Buttler b Broad	24	47	49	4	
MA Starc	not out	34	60	100	3	
NM Lyon	not out	16	7	12	2	1
SM Boland						

8 lb, 4 nb, 12 w 24
134 overs, 605 mins   8-416 dec

1-51 (Warner), 2-111 (Harris), 3-117 (Labuschagne), 4-232 (Smith), 5-242 (Green), 6-285 (Carey), 7-331 (Cummins), 8-398 (Khawaja)

Second innings

Batsman		R	B	M	4	6
DA Warner	2 c +sub (OJD Pope) b Wood	3	18	28		
MS Harris	1 c +sub (OJD Pope) b Leach	27	61	87	3	
M Labuschagne	c +sub (OJD Pope) b Wood	29	42	72	1	
SPD Smith	b Leach	23	31	48	2	1
UT Khawaja	not out	101	138	203	10	2
CD Green	c Root b Leach	74	122	165	7	1
AT Carey+	c +sub (OJD Pope) b Leach	0	1	2		

3 lb, 5 w 8
68.5 overs, 305 mins   6-265 dec

1-12 (Warner), 2-52 (Harris), 3-68 (Labuschagne), 4-86 (Smith), 5-265 (Green), 6-265 (Carey)

Bowling – First innings

Bowling	O	M	R	W	wd	nb
JM Anderson	30	9	54	1		
SCJ Broad	29	5	101	5		1
BA Stokes	13.5	3	37	0	2	3
MA Wood	26.1	6	76	1		2
MJ Leach	24	2	89	0		
DJ Malan	3	0	15	0		
JE Root	8	0	36	1		

Bowling – Second innings

Bowling	O	M	R	W	wd	nb
JM Anderson	12	1	34	0		
SCJ Broad	11	3	31	0		
MA Wood	15	0	65	2	1	
MJ Leach	21.5	1	84	4		
DJ Malan	2	0	13	0		
JE Root	7	0	35	0		

England

First innings

Batsman		R	B	M	4	6
H Hameed	b Starc	6	26	42	1	
Z Crawley	b Boland	18	55	81	2	
DJ Malan	c Khawaja b Green	3	39	62		
JE Root*	c Smith b Boland	0	7	14		
BA Stokes	lbw b Lyon	66	91	147	9	1
JM Bairstow	c Carey b Boland	113	158	275	8	3
JC Buttler+	c Khawaja b Cummins	0	8	16		
MA Wood	c Lyon b Cummins	39	41	63	2	3
MJ Leach	c Cummins b Lyon	10	29	29	2	
SCJ Broad	c Carey b Boland	15	19	31	1	
JM Anderson	not out	4	4	6	1	

9 b, 6 lb, 2 nb, 3 w 20
79.1 overs, 387 mins   294

1-22 (Hameed), 2-36 (Crawley), 3-36 (Root), 4-36 (Malan), 5-164 (Stokes), 6-173 (Buttler), 7-245 (Wood), 8-266 (Leach), 9-289 (Bairstow), 10-294 (Broad)

Second innings

Batsman		R	B	M	4	6
H Hameed	2 c Carey b Boland	9	58	85		
Z Crawley	1 lbw b Green	77	100	152	13	
DJ Malan	b Lyon	4	29	38		
JE Root*	c Carey b Boland	24	85	130	3	
BA Stokes	c Smith b Lyon	60	123	173	10	1
JM Bairstow	c Labuschagne b Boland	41	105	154	3	
JC Buttler+	lbw b Cummins	11	38	45		
MA Wood	lbw b Cummins	0	2	3		
MJ Leach	c Warner b Smith	26	34	77	2	
SCJ Broad	not out	8	35	47		
JM Anderson	not out	0	6	6		

7 lb, 3 nb 10
102 overs, 461 mins   9-270

1-46 (Hameed), 2-74 (Malan), 3-96 (Crawley), 4-156 (Root), 5-193 (Stokes), 6-218 (Buttler), 7-218 (Wood), 8-237 (Bairstow), 9-270 (Leach)

Bowling – First innings

Bowling	O	M	R	W	wd	nb
PJ Cummins	20	6	68	2	2	1
MA Starc	16	2	56	1		
SM Boland	14.1	6	36	4		
CD Green	9	4	24	1		1
NM Lyon	17	0	88	2		
M Labuschagne	3	0	7	0		

Bowling – Second innings

Bowling	O	M	R	W	wd	nb
PJ Cummins	22	5	80	2		3
MA Starc	18	2	68	0		
SM Boland	24	11	30	3		
CD Green	10	1	38	1		
NM Lyon	22	10	28	2		
M Labuschagne	2	0	9	0		
SPD Smith	4	1	10	1		

Stumps scores:
Day 1: Australia 1st inns   3-126   SPD Smith 6*, UT Khawaja 4*
Day 2: England 1st inns   0-13   H Hameed 2*, Z Crawley 2*
Day 3: England 1st inns   7-258   JM Bairstow 103*, MJ Leach 4*
Day 4: England 2nd inns   0-30   Z Crawley 22*, H Hameed 8*

Toss: Australia
Umpires: PR Reiffel, RJ Tucker, TV: P Wilson
Ref: SR Bernard, Award: UT Khawaja (Aus)
Attendance: 110,285

FIFTH TEST - HOBART

Australia's Travis Head was back for the final Test and with Usman Khawaja moving to the top of the order, Marcus Harris was the unlucky man to make way. England made five changes as Bairstow out due to his fractured thumb, replaced by Pope, Billings debuted with the keeping gloves at the expense of Buttler, Burns replaced the out of form Hameed, while Woakes and Robinson came back for Leach and Anderson. The pitch had a very green look to it as Hobart hosted it's first Test since 2016, with a few showers of rain delaying the start by 30 minutes.

Day One – Attendance: 9,002

Broad charged in for the first ball from the Northern end, it hit Warner high on the leg, and in his follow-through he took a tumble. Both he and Robinson were beating the bat and after three runs in the opening five overs, things began to really happen from the sixth as Warner lurched forward to edge one to second slip. Then Labuschagne should have been out for a fourth ball duck, when Crawley at second slip jumped in front Root at first, to put down the chance. Khawaja then leaned forward and edged to first slip and when Smith played back and edged low to second slip, Australia was 3-12 in the 10th over.

The counterattack began immediately as Labuschagne went for anything pitched up as the boundaries started to flow. Head was also keen to be aggressive as he cover-drove Wood for four, before hitting a magnificent square-drive to the rope off Woakes first ball. Wood was trying to be a bit too aggressive with the ball as Labuschagne forced him away twice for fours through the off-side, his three over spell costing 31. Then England had the ball changed and Labuschagne got himself into all sorts of a tangle as he got too far across his stumps trying to work leg and was bowled, falling face first into the pitch in the process. In an action-packed opening session, Australia was 4-85 at dinner from 24 overs with Head 31, Green 2.

Head copped a blow on the body from Wood in the first over after the dinner break but responded well in the next by clipping Robinson off his pads to the boundary. Sadly, for Robinson he was soon off the field looking a bit worse for wear. Batting was starting to look easier as Head punched Woakes through point for four, before glancing him to the rope to bring up his 50 from 53 balls. Green was playing steadily while Head hit some magnificent drives for four through the off-side. The 100 stand was raised and then Head lifted Woakes off his pads for four to move to 96. On 99 the South Australian chopped a cut safely to the right of gully to move to his second hundred of the series, much to the delight of the Tasmanian crowd who were thoroughly enjoying themselves. Unfortunately for Head, he went to the very next ball, popping up a simple catch to mid-on. Green reached his 50 and then hit a fine off-drive off Root to the rope as Australia went into tea on 5-215 from just 52 overs, Green 57 and Carey 1.

Wood's expensive day continued straight after tea when Green hit him for two fours in an over, the first a clip to leg, before punching him through cover-point to the boundary. The quick reverted to around the wicket and Green cut him for four, but then Wood struck him on the glove with a short one. Finally, Wood's day improved when he dug another ball in short, Green went for the hook and hit it straight to deep square-leg. With more fascinating cricket looming, the rain started at 9.06pm and after a number of attempts at a restart, Stumps was called at 10.12pm.

Day Two – Attendance: 8,711

Wood's day started well when he had two early wickets with short balls, as both Starc and Cummins were caught on pull/hook at backward square-leg. At 8-252 Australia wanted a bit more wag from its tail and it came from Lyon who pulled Wood for six in one over, before repeating the shot twice in consecutive balls in the bowler's next over. Carey then dragged one onto his stumps but then the last pair advanced Australia past 300 with some fine strokes before Lyon missed a pull-shot at Broad.

Starc appeared to have Burns caught behind in the first over, but with no strong appeal play went on and it mattered little as in the next over Crawley's attempted single to the off-side saw Burns picked off by Labuschagne. The tall opener brought his SCG form with him to Hobart with some fine drives through the off-side until he got an inside edge via the pad to short-leg. Root was getting a going over from Cummins, with a couple of blows near the groin as Dinner came soon after with England 2-34, Malan 9 and Root 3.

Malan confidently drove Green for four and then next ball there was an appeal for caught behind, replays showing a fine inside edge. Malan was working to the point region in typical fashion with some nicely timed shots and was unlucky when he aimed a glance and got a touch to the keeper. Root suffered another blow in a tricky area facing Cummins and was out two balls later when a slightly fuller ball trapped him right in front. Stokes punched one hard to point where Lyon swooped low to his left to bring off a sharp catch. Pope and Billings were both keen to drive the ball and were looking good until Pope pushed at one he could have left and nicked it to the keeper.

From his first ball, Woakes edged Boland to slip where Warner dropped a simple waist high chance at first slip. Then in the last over before tea, Woakes drove at one from Boland, where Khawaja moved to his left at 3rd slip and put down the catch. Australia's slips were looking a bit closer together than normal as England went in at tea on 6-124 with Billings 19, Woakes 5.

There was plenty of confident stroke play straight after tea as Green was on-driven for four by Woakes, before Billings hit a lovely off drive to the rope. Woakes continued to make the most of his luck as he square drove Boland for a rare boundary before hooking Green over square-leg for six. The pair had added 42 before the short ball proved Billings undoing, as he found long-leg with his pull-stroke. After a couple more edged fours, Woakes luck ran out when he got a touch to one down the leg-side. When both Broad and Robinson had their stumps rattled, England were all out and trailed by 115, having lost 4-64 after tea.

Coming out to bat at 9.06pm, Australia faced the toughest time to bat and almost immediately Warner was on his way for a pair, when he poked a ball to backward-point, Pope diving to his right to hold a top catch. As in the first innings it was tough going for the Aussie batsmen while the ball was new, with Labuschagne caught down the leg-side to make it 2-5. Khawaja and Smith hit some crisp boundaries until Wood came on and bounced Khawaja, the Aussie opener unable to get his glove out of the way through to the keeper. Boland came in as nightwatchman and after some playing and missing, he and Smith survived as Australia ended a fast moving day 152 ahead with seven wickets in hand.

Day Three – Attendance: 8,088

With the players wandering out under lovely Hobart sunshine, many wondered whether this could well be the last day of the series. It started well for Wood who had Boland caught behind fending at one in the fourth over of the morning. An early on-drive from Head for four off Broad indicated he was going to approach things as he did in the first innings, but then tried to whip Wood off his hip and got a touch to the keeper. When Smith hooked Wood straight down the throat of long-leg, Australia were only 178 ahead, as Wood's figures at that moment for day three read 4.2-0-9-3.

Green and Carey weathered the end of the Wood spell, which ended at 3-12 off six overs, his longest of the series. With Woakes back into the attack, Carey hit two cracking square-drives for four off consecutive balls. But in the bowler's next over, Carey on 19 dragged a pull-shot back onto his stumps which made Australia 7-91, the lead 206. However, the TV umpire found it to be a no-ball and the Australian keeper stayed and went on to bat deep into the innings. Green continued to battle away with some edged fours until Broad trapped him in front, ending a stand worth 49.

Australia felt happier with a lead of 227, but how were England now feeling given they should have had the hosts eight down? They were to feel a bit better when Carey was adjudged leg before to Broad on 30 by Umpire Wilson, but a review showed the ball to be 51/49 pitching outside leg-stump. Carey saved once again by a matter of a few millimetres.

Wood returned to try and finish the innings off and dismissed Starc straight away, when he poked a catch to the short-leg who was crouching three metres deeper than usual. Wood had his first five for against Australia and had Cummins next ball when he yorked him LBW from the around the wicket, but again the review Gods were not helping England, as technology showed the ball to be missing off-stump. With a Cummins cut for four off Wood and a hooked boundary by Carey off Broad, Australia went into dinner on 8-141, 256 to the good, the Aussie keeper on 40 and the skipper 12.

It took half an hour for the last two wickets to fall, with Carey chasing a wide one and getting an inside edge, then Cummins was bowled having a heave to give Wood a well deserved sixth wicket. He led his teammates off the field, pleased with his best Test figures of 6-37, but those behind him knew that it would be an enormous task to make the 271 required to win the match.

With the sun starting to set, the England openers headed out with Burns edging the second ball through gully for four. On 7 the left-handed opener had some luck, as the Aussie went up for LBW but weren't convinced enough to review, technology showing shortly after the ball would have hit the top of leg-stump and been out. Crawley edged one past third slip for four off Cummins, but on-drove him for four as the confidence of the England openers grew. They had nothing to lose as the luck started to turn the visitor's way when Burns played one down off Starc which bounced over the top of the stumps.

Cummins changed ends and when Crawley hit too glorious on-drives in the same over for four, England had reached 47 without loss after nine overs. When Crawley leg-glanced Boland for four and England reached 0-60, even the CricViz people started to fly the England flag, the software deciding the match was basically 50/50. Australia thought they had Burns caught behind off Green on 26, but the review was rejected. When Crawley sweetly worked Boland off his hip for four, England was 0-68 as Green grabbed the ball for the last over before tea. The tall West Aussie ambled in, Burns left his bat hanging as he was in two minds whether to leave as the ball clipped the edge and cannoned into the stumps.

After played resumed, Malan edged a drive for four and then hit one very sweetly to the rope, before getting clunked on the helmet by a Green bumper. In the bowler's next over Malan played back and chopped onto his stumps and then Crawley's classy knock came to an end when he edged a drive to the keeper, Green now had taken three wickets in the space of 20 balls. Things were now moving fast as Stokes hooked to deep square-leg, Lyon running in and diving forward to take a fine catch. Root off-drove Starc for four but then Boland returned and hit the England skipper's off-stump with one that kept low.

The middle-order collapse continued as Billings chipped a catch to mid-on and then Pope got too far across his crease to be bowled behind his pad. Woakes had a swing and edged to Carey who dived high to his right to take a beauty and after a couple of hard-hit fours, Wood dragged a pull back onto his stumps. The end came when Robinson was bowled making room to leg, England having lost nine wickets in the session and 10-56 overall in a terrible capitulation to end the series. It was the last of many shattering England collapses throughout the series.

So, the series came to an end at 9.55pm on a chilly night, with Australia winning with two days to spare. As entertaining as the three days were for the Hobart public who turned out in good numbers and clearly enjoyed it, the pitch was too sporting for a Test match, let alone one played under lights. With Match figures of 40 wickets for 770 (average 19.25 per wicket) it was the fifth lowest batting average for a home Test in Australia since World War II.

The post-match the awards were handed out, with Travis Head's century securing him not only the Man of the match award but also the Compton-Miller Medal for Man of the series. The teams meet again for battle in mid-June 2023, one wonders who out of long-term combatants David Warner, Stuart Broad and James Anderson will be there to face one another.

Fifth Test at the Bellerive Oval, Hobart on January 15-19, 2021 (day/night) – Australia won by 146 runs

Australia — First innings

Batter	Dismissal		B	M	4	6
DA Warner	c Crawley b Robinson	0	22	27		
UT Khawaja	c Root b Broad	6	26	40		
M Labuschagne	b Broad	44	53	85	9	
SPD Smith	c Crawley b Robinson	0	2	5		
TM Head	c Robinson b Woakes	101	113	183	12	6
CD Green	c Crawley b Wood	74	109	154	8	
AT Carey+	b Woakes	24	60	100	2	
MA Starc	c Burns b Wood	3	17	25		
PJ Cummins*	c Crawley b Wood	2	12	19		
NM Lyon	b Broad	31	27	43	1	3
SM Boland	not out	10	13	27	2	
	3 b, 3 lb, 2 w	8				
	75.4 overs, 354 mins	303				

1-3 (Warner), 2-7 (Khawaja), 3-12 (Smith), 4-83 (Labuschagne),
5-204 (Head), 6-236 (Green), 7-246 (Starc), 8-252 (Cummins),
9-280 (Carey), 10-303 (Lyon)

Australia — Second innings

Batter	Dismissal		B	M	4	6
DA Warner	c Pope b Broad	0	3	3		
UT Khawaja	c Billings b Wood	11	38	63	2	
M Labuschagne	c Billings b Woakes	5	11	12		
SPD Smith	c Malan b Wood	27	62	113	4	
TM Head	c Billings b Wood	8	16	18	1	
CD Green	lbw b Broad	23	47	82	3	
AT Carey+	c Billings b Broad	49	88	125	4	
MA Starc	c Pope b Wood	1	4	13		
PJ Cummins*	b Wood	13	33	48	1	
NM Lyon	not out	4	5	5		
SM Boland	c Billings b Wood	8	33	36		
	1 b, 1 lb, 1 nb, 1 w	6				
	56.3 overs, 258 mins	155				

1-0 (Warner), 2-5 (Labuschagne), 3-33 (Khawaja),
4-47 (Boland), 5-59 (Head), 6-63 (Smith),
7-112 (Green), 8-121 (Starc), 9-151 (Carey),
10-155 (Cummins)

Bowling (England)

Bowler	O	M	R	W	wd	nb
SCJ Broad	24.4	4	59	3	1	
OE Robinson	8	3	24	2		
MA Wood	18	1	115	3		
CR Woakes	15	2	64	2		1
SCJ Broad	18	2	51	3		
OE Robinson	11	4	23	0		
MA Wood	16.3	2	37	6	1	
CR Woakes	11	3	40	1		1

England — First innings

Batter	Dismissal		B	M	4	6
RJ Burns	run out (Labuschagne)	0	6	8		
Z Crawley	c Head b Cummins	18	21	39	3	
DJ Malan	c Carey b Cummins	25	64	91	5	
JE Root*	lbw b Cummins	34	46	72	3	
BA Stokes	c Lyon b Starc	4	11	19	1	
OJD Pope	c Carey b Boland	14	23	38	3	
SW Billings+	c Boland b Green	29	48	75	6	
CR Woakes	c Carey b Starc	36	48	72	5	1
MA Wood	b Cummins	16	15	31	2	
SCJ Broad	b Starc	0	4	3		
OE Robinson	not out	0	0	2		
	4 b, 8 lb	12				
	47.4 overs, 226 mins	188				

1-2 (Burns), 2-29 (Crawley), 3-78 (Malan), 4-81 (Root), 5-85 (Stokes),
6-110 (Pope), 7-152 (Billings), 8-182 (Woakes), 9-182 (Broad),
10-188 (Wood)

England — Second innings

Batter	Dismissal		B	M	4	6
RJ Burns	b Green	26	46	78	4	
Z Crawley	c Carey b Green	36	66	109	7	
DJ Malan	b Green	10	20	23	2	
JE Root*	b Boland	11	31	56	1	
BA Stokes	c Lyon b Starc	5	15	25		
OJD Pope	b Cummins	5	26	44		
SW Billings+	c Cummins b Boland	1	9	17		
CR Woakes	c Carey b Boland	5	11	13	1	
MA Wood	b Cummins	11	7	10	2	
SCJ Broad	not out	1	1	1		
OE Robinson	b Cummins	0	1	4		
	13 lb	13				
	38.5 overs, 189 mins	124				

1-68 (Burns), 2-82 (Malan), 3-83 (Crawley),
4-92 (Stokes), 5-101 (Root), 6-107 (Billings),
7-107 (Pope), 8-115 (Woakes), 9-123 (Wood),
10-124 (Robinson)

Bowling (Australia)

Bowler	O	M	R	W	wd	nb
MA Starc	10	1	53	3		
PJ Cummins	13.4	2	45	4		
SM Boland	14	6	33	1		
CD Green	10	0	45	1		
	8	0	30	1		
	12.5	3	42	3		
	12	5	18	3		
	6	1	21	3		

Stumps scores:
Day 1: Australia 1st inns 6-241 AT Carey 10*, MA Starc 0*
Day 2: Australia 2nd inns 3-37 SPD Smith 17*, SM Boland 3*

Toss: England, Umpires: RJ Tucker, P Wilson,
TV: PR Reiffel, Ref: DC Boon,
Award: TM Head (Aus). Attendance: 25,801

TEST AVERAGES
AUSTRALIA

Batting & Fielding	M	Inn	NO	Runs	HS	Avge	100	50	S/Rate	Ct	St
UT Khawaja	2	4	1	255	137	85.00	2	0	55.19	2	-
TM Head	4	6	0	357	152	59.50	2	1	86.02	3	-
M Labuschagne	5	9	1	335	103	41.87	1	2	48.06	5	-
MA Starc	5	7	3	155	39*	38.75	0	0	64.31	1	-
DA Warner	5	8	0	273	95	34.12	0	2	50.74	5	-
CD Green	5	8	1	228	74	32.57	0	2	56.43	4	-
SPD Smith	5	8	0	244	93	30.50	0	2	47.10	11	-
MS Harris	4	7	1	179	76	29.83	0	1	37.29	1	-
NM Lyon	5	5	2	76	31	25.33	0	0	89.41	4	-
AT Carey	5	9	0	183	51	20.33	0	1	45.86	23	0
MG Neser	1	2	0	38	35	19.00	0	0	102.70	0	-
PJ Cummins	4	5	0	72	24	14.40	0	0	47.68	2	-
SM Boland	3	3	1	24	10*	12.00	0	0	42.10	4	-
JA Richardson	1	2	0	17	9	8.50	0	0	242.85	0	-
JR Hazlewood	1	1	1	0	0*	-	0	0	0.00	2	-

Bowling	M	Overs	Mdns	Runs	Wkts	Avge	Best	5i	10m	Econ	SR
SM Boland	3	81.1	31	172	18	9.55	6-7	1	0	2.11	27.0
CD Green	5	80.4	22	205	13	15.76	3-21	0	0	2.54	37.2
PJ Cummins	4	126.4	31	379	21	18.04	5-38	1	0	2.99	36.1
NM Lyon	5	163.1	47	377	16	23.56	4-91	0	0	2.31	61.1
JA Richardson	1	38.1	13	120	5	24.00	5-42	1	0	3.14	45.8
JR Hazlewood	1	27	10	74	3	24.66	2-42	0	0	2.74	54.0
MA Starc	5	152.1	32	482	19	25.36	4-37	0	0	3.16	48.0
MG Neser	1	24	5	61	2	30.50	1-28	0	0	2.54	72.0

Also bowled: TM Head 1-1-0-0, M Labuschagne 12-2-40-0, SPD Smith 5-2-10-1.

ENGLAND

Batting & Fielding	M	Inn	NO	Runs	HS	Avge	100	50	S/Rate	Ct	St
JM Bairstow	2	4	0	194	113	48.50	1	0	54.49	1	-
JE Root	5	10	0	322	89	32.20	0	3	48.27	6	
Z Crawley	3	6	0	166	77	27.66	0	1	58.65	8	-
DJ Malan	5	10	0	244	82	24.40	0	2	38.60	2	-
CR Woakes	3	6	0	146	44	24.33	0	0	54.68	0	-
BA Stokes	5	10	0	236	66	23.60	0	2	42.06	3	-
JC Buttler	4	8	1	107	39	15.28	0	0	27.43	12	0
SW Billings	1	2	0	30	29	15.00	0	0	52.63	5	0
SCJ Broad	3	6	3	42	15	14.00	0	0	39.25	2	-
RJ Burns	3	6	0	77	34	12.83	0	0	43.25	2	-
MJ Leach	3	6	2	51	26	12.75	0	0	55.43	0	-
OJ Pope	3	6	0	67	35	11.16	0	0	41.87	4	-
MA Wood	4	8	0	86	39	10.75	0	0	77.47	1	-
H Hameed	4	8	0	80	27	10.00	0	0	28.07	3	-
JM Anderson	3	6	4	13	5*	6.50	0	0	36.11	0	
OE Robinson	4	8	1	38	22	5.42	0	0	40.00	2	-

Bowling	M	Overs	Mdns	Runs	Wkts	Avge	Best	5i	10m	Econ	SR
JM Anderson	3	104	36	187	8	23.37	4-33	0	0	1.79	78.0
OE Robinson	4	106.2	34	281	11	25.54	3-58	0	0	2.64	58.0
SCJ Broad	3	118.4	23	342	13	26.30	5-101	1	0	2.88	54.7
MA Wood	4	121.1	15	453	17	26.64	6-37	1	0	3.73	42.7
DJ Malan	5	11	0	61	2	30.50	2-33	0	0	5.54	33.0
JE Root	5	57	4	234	5	46.80	2-27	0	0	4.10	68.4
MJ Leach	3	73.5	3	321	6	53.50	4-84	0	0	4.34	73.8
CR Woakes	3	88.4	22	332	6	55.33	2-64	0	0	3.74	88.6
BA Stokes	5	63.3	6	286	4	71.50	3-113	0	0	4.50	95.2

Australia A v England Lions at Ian Healy Oval, Brisbane on December 9-12, 2021 – Australia A won by 112 runs

Australia A	First innings		B	M	4	6	Second innings		B	M	4	6
BE Street	c Lees b Bess	26	91	161	4		not out	119	254	382	6	1
HJ Hunt	c Yates b Norwell	33	83	114	4		c Foakes b Fisher	40	82	128	4	
MT Renshaw	c Mahmood b Norwell	38	98	120	3	1	c Lees b Bess	43	101	147	3	1
NJ Maddinson*	c Abell b Bess	0	4	8			c Yates b Bess	71	46	65	5	4
UT Khawaja	c Foakes b Fisher	11	20	33	1	1	c Foakes b Yates	5	15	11		
MR Marsh	c Bohannon b Bess	33	45	165	6		not out	60	27	34	1	7
JP Inglis+	c & b Norwell	6	10	22	1							
MG Neser	c Foakes b Norwell	17	25	44	3							
MT Steketee	c Bohannon b Bess	39	33	46	5	2						
MJ Swepson	c Foakes b Norwell	4	16	19								
SM Boland	not out	0	2	5								
	1 b, 2 lb, 2 nb, 1 w	6					5 b, 2 lb, 3 nb, 1 w	11				
	70.5 overs, 323 mins	213					87 overs, 388 mins	4-349 dec				

1-48 (Hunt), 2-76 (Street), 3-76 (Maddinson), 4-99 (Khawaja),
5-126 (Renshaw), 6-148 (Inglis), 7-157 (Marsh), 8-195 (Neser),
9-213 (Steketee), 10-213 (Swepson)

1-87 (Hunt,), 2-175 (Renshaw),
3-269 (Maddinson), 4-278 (Khawaja)

Bowling	O	M	R	W	wd	nb	O	M	R	W	wd	nb
S Mahmood	15	4	37	0	1	2	15	5	35	0	1	2
MD Fisher	16	4	35	1			13	3	49	1		
LC Norwell	16.5	2	58	5			13	3	35	0		
DM Bess	23	5	80	4			37	3	157	2		
RM Yates							7	0	62	1		1
HC Brook							2	0	4	0		

England Lions	First innings		B	M	4	6	Second innings		B	M	4	6
RM Yates	c Inglis b Boland	2	16	24			c Renshaw b Neser	41	71	97	6	
AZ Lees*	c Renshaw b Neser	1	15	19			b Boland	1	7	8		
JR Bracey	c Khawaja b Neser	5	26	41			c Inglis b Steketee	113	295	410	9	1
TB Abell	c Inglis b Steketee	5	14	17			c Khawaja b Steketee	0	9	27		
MD Fisher	c Khawaja b Swepson	9	55	95		9	lbw b Renshaw	0	4	5		
JJ Bohannon	c Khawaja b Marsh	22	43	57	3	5	c Renshaw b Neser	51	111	132	7	
HC Brook	c Steketee b Neser	17	37	44	1	6	c Hunt b Swepson	1	8	15		
BT Foakes+	c Renshaw b Neser	12	23	30	1	7	b Renshaw	73	156	205	11	
DM Bess	b Neser	15	21	26	1	1 8	b Maddinson	25	82	92	3	
LC Norwell	b Swepson	8	13	19	1		c Hunt b Swepson	25	33	31	4	1
S Mahmood	not out	0	0	2			not out	0	5	5		
	5 lb, 2 nb	7					6 lb, 10 nb, 1 w	17				
	43.3 overs, 191 mins	103					128.2 overs, 518 mins	347				

1-3 (Lees), 2-3 (Yates), 3-13 (Abell), 4-19 (Bracey),
5-50 (Bohannon), 6-60 (Fisher), 7-80 (Brook), 8-80 (Foakes),
9-103 (Norwell), 10-103 (Bess)

1-2 (Lees), 2-68 (Yates), 3-77 (Abell), 4-172 (Bohannon),
5-174 (Brook), 6-285 (Bracey), 7-319 (Foakes),
8-319 (Fisher), 9-347 (Bess), 10-347 (Norwell)

Bowling	O	M	R	W	wd	nb	O	M	R	W	wd	nb
MG Neser	15.3	5	29	5			14	5	36	2		1
SM Boland	8	2	16	1			21	4	64	1		
MT Steketee	7	1	12	1		1	17	2	52	2	1	6
MJ Swepson	9	2	26	2			46.2	10	124	2		1
MR Marsh	4	0	15	1		1	9	2	29	0		2
MT Renshaw							14	7	26	2		
NJ Maddinson							3	1	4	1		
BE Street							4	3	6	0		

Stumps scores:
Day 1: England Lions (1st inns) 3-13   JR Bracey 5*, MD Fisher 0*
Day 2: Australia A (1st inns)   1-158   BE Street 76*, MT Renshaw 34*
Day 3: England Lions (2nd inns) 3-136   JR Bracey 57*, JJ Bohannon 29*

Toss: Australia A
Umpires: SAJ Craig, DM Koch
Ref: KC Wessels, Award: MG Neser

40

AUSTRALIA WINS FIRST ICC WORLD T20 TITLE

Australia clinched the one missing piece of silverware for their trophy cabinet when they defeated New Zealand by eight wickets with seven balls to spare to claim the 2021 ICC World T20 played in the UAE. England and Pakistan were more favoured to win the title, but Australia performed better when it counted. After winning their first two games, the Australians were soundly beaten by England, in a major dent to their chances. But they avoided meeting them again, as New Zealand took care of them with a remarkable winning chase in the Semi-final.

Player of Series David Warner was the mainstay of the batting, but it was Australia's strong bowling attack that had as much as anything to do with winning the title. Paceman Josh Hazlewood secured early wickets, Adam Zampa was economical and a key wicket taker in the middle overs, with Mitchell Starc dangerous when swinging the new ball.

Mitch Marsh played some powerful innings and Matthew Wade with his incredible 41 not out from 17 balls, ensured Australia chased down 177 in the Semi. Interestingly Aaron Finch and Glenn Maxwell were relatively quiet, the Aussie skipper didn't pass 50 and Maxwell only made 36 runs in six hits before doing well in the final and making the winning hit. Likewise, Steve Smith battled with a strike rate under 100, but took some fine catches, as once again Australia were the best fielding side.

AVERAGES - AUSTRALIA

Batting	M	I	NO	Runs	HS	Avg	SR	50	6s
MP Stoinis	7	4	3	80	40*	80.0	137	0	0
MS Wade	7	3	2	74	41*	74.0	164	0	4
MR Marsh	6	5	2	185	77*	61.6	146	2	8
DA Warner	7	7	1	289	89	48.1	146	3	10
SPD Smith	7	4	1	69	35	23.0	97	0	0
AC Agar	1	1	0	20	20	20.0	100	0	2
AJ Finch	7	7	0	135	44	19.2	116	0	6
GJ Maxwell	7	7	3	64	28*	16.0	100	0	1
MA Starc	7	1	0	13	13	13.0	216	0	1
PJ Cummins	7	1	0	12	12	12.0	400	0	2
A Zampa	7	1	0	1	1	1.0	25	0	0
JR Hazlewood	7	1	1	0	0*	-	0	0	0

Bowling	O	W	Avg	Best	Econ
A Zampa	27	13	12.0	5-19	5.81
JR Hazlewood	24	11	15.9	4-39	7.29
MA Starc	27	9	27.5	2-21	9.18
PJ Cummins	24	5	35.4	2-34	7.37
GJ Maxwell	14	2	50.0	1-6	7.14
AC Agar	2.4	1	15.0	1-15	5.62
MR Marsh	5	0	-	-	7.60
MP Stoinis	3	0	-	-	11.66

Fielding: Wade 9, Smith 8, Warner 3, Finch 3, Maxwell 3, Cummins 1, Marsh 1, Stoinis 1.

GROUP MATCHES

AUSTRALIA v SOUTH AFRICA – ABU DHABI

Bavuma started superbly for South Africa with two square-driven fours off Starc in the opening over, but in the next over he was bowled playing back to Maxwell. Van der Dussen edged to the keeper and then de Kock tried to lift one to leg, it took his gloves and landed on the stumps. When Klaasen edged a drive to gully, South Africa were 4-46 an in trouble.

Markram and Miller added 34 but then the middle order collapsed, losing 3-3 from seven balls. Miller was first when he missed a sweep, Pretorius was caught behind and then Maharaj was run out in a horrid mix-up. Markram and Rabada struck blows over the fence in the last four overs, but 9-118 was well short of what South Africa would have wanted.

Australia started poorly with Finch slashing to third-man and Warner slashing a catch to backward-point. When Marsh was miscued to deep mid-wicket, Australia was 3-38 and had plenty of work to do. Smith and Maxwell steadied things with a stand of 42 in seven overs before Smith pulled to deep mid-wicket when Markram took a great diving catch to his right. When Maxwell was bowled playing a reverse sweep, Australia had the jitters and still wanted 38 to win off 28 balls. Fortunately Wade and Stoinis kept calm and steered Australia home with two balls to spare.

Australia v South Africa at Sheikh Zayed Stadium, Abu Dhabi on October 23, 2021 - Australia won by 5 wickets

South Africa			B	4	6	Australia			B	4	6
T Bavuma*	b Maxwell		12	7	2	DA Warner	c Klaasen b Rabada		14	15	3
Q de Kock+	b Hazlewood		7	12	1	AJ Finch*	c Rabada b Nortje		0	5	
HE van der Dussen	c Wade b Hazlewood		2	3		MR Marsh	c van der Dussen				
AK Markram	c Maxwell b Starc		40	36	3	1		b Maharaj		11	17	1
H Klaasen	c Smith b Cummins		13	13	2	SPD Smith	c Markram b Nortje		35	34	3
DA Miller	lbw b Zampa		16	18		GJ Maxwell	b Shamsi		18	21	1
D Pretorius	c Wade b Zampa		1	2		MP Stoinis	not out		24	16	3
KA Maharaj	run out					MS Wade+	not out		15	10	2
	(Maxwell-Wade)		0	2		PJ Cummins					
K Rabada	not out		20	23	1	1	MA Starc					
AA Nortje	c Finch b Starc		2	3		A Zampa					
T Shamsi	not out		0	1		JR Hazlewood					
	2 b, 2 lb, 1 w	5					1 lb, 3 w		4		
6 overs: 3-29	20 overs		9-118			6 overs: 2-28	19.4 overs		5-121		

41

1-13 (Bavuma, 1.3), 2-16 (van der Dussen, 2.1), 3-23 (de Kock, 4.1), | 1-4 (Finch, 1.5), 2-20 (Warner, 4.3), 3-38 (Marsh, 7.5),
4-46 (Klaasen, 7.6), 5-80 (Miller, 13.3), 6-82 (Pretorius, 13.6), | 4-80 (Smith, 14.5), 5-81 (Maxwell, 15.2)
7-83 (Maharaj, 14.3), 8-98 (Markram, 17.1), 9-115 (Nortje, 19.4)

Bowling	O	M	R	W	wd	nb	Dots	Bowling	O	M	R	W	wd	nb	Dots
MA Starc	4	0	33	2			10	K Rabada	4	0	28	1	1		14
GJ Maxwell	4	0	24	1			7	AA Nortje	4	0	21	2	1		14
JR Hazlewood	4	1	19	2	1		15	KA Maharaj	4	0	23	1			6
PJ Cummins	4	0	17	1			14	T Shamsi	4	0	22	1			9
A Zampa	4	0	21	2			10	D Pretorius	3.4	0	26	0	1		4

Toss: Australia. Umpires: MA Gough, NN Menon, L Rusere (TV), Ref: J Srinath. Award: JR Hazlewood (Aus). Crowd: 1,950.
Points: Aus 2, SA 0

AUSTRALIA v SRI LANKA – DUBAI

Australia started well with the ball gaining the early wicket of Nissanka, but this saw Asalanka come in early and pull Cummins for four, before hitting the first ball from Maxwell well over the mid-wicket rope for six. The chunky left-hander had 25 from his first 10 balls before being subdued somewhat until he swept Zampa in the air to deep square-leg. His dismissal saw Sri Lanka lose three more wickets quickly Perera was yorked the ball after smoking Starc for six, Fernando miscued a sweep to cover and Hasaranga got a fine tickle behind.

At 5-94 in the 13th over, Rajapaksa stood up for his team adding 42 with Shanka who struggled to score quickly as Sri Lanka managed 49 off their last five overs to set Australia 155 to win. The Aussie openers flew to 43 after four overs, as Finch uppercut and drove sixes straight. Australia had a small hiccup when Finch dragged on and Maxwell was caught at deep mid-wicket, but any further trouble was averted when Smith joined Warner to add 50 for the third wicket. Warner eventually was caught at long-off but Stoinis came out and helped Smith get the team home with three overs to spare.

Australia v Sri Lanka at Dubai Sports City Stadium on October 28, 2021 (floodlit) - Australia won by 7 wickets

Sri Lanka			B	4	6	Australia			B	4	6
P Nissanka	c Warner b Cummins	7	9	1		DA Warner	c Rajapaksa b Shanaka	65	42	10	
MDKJ Perera+	b Starc	35	25	4	1	AJ Finch*	b Hasaranga	37	23	5	2
KIC Asalanka	c Smith b Zampa	35	27	4	1	GJ Maxwell	c Fernando b Hasaranga	5	6	1	
WIA Fernando	c Smith b Zampa	4	7			SPD Smith	not out	28	26	1	
PBB Rajapaksa	not out	33	26	4	1	MP Stoinis	not out	16	7	2	1
W Hasaranga	c Wade b Starc	4	2	1		MR Marsh					
MD Shanaka*	c Wade b Cummins	12	19	1		MS Wade+					
C Karunaratne	not out	9	6	1		A Zampa					
MM Theekshana						PJ Cummins					
PVD Chameera						MA Starc					
CBRLS Kumara						JR Hazlewood					
	4 lb, 1 nb, 10 w	15					2 nb, 2 w	4			
6 overs : 1-53	20 overs	6-154				6 overs : 0-63	17 overs	3-155			

1-15 (Nissanka, 2.3), 2-78 (Asalanka, 9.4), 3-86 (Perera, 10.3), | 1-70 (Finch, 6.5), 2-80 (Maxwell, 8.3), 3-130 (Warner, 14.6)
4-90 (Fernando, 11.5), 5-94 (Hasaranga, 12.2), 6-134 (Shanaka, 17.4)

Bowling	O	M	R	W	wd	nb	Dots	Bowling	O	M	R	W	wd	nb	Dots
MA Starc	4	0	27	2	1		11	C Karunaratne	2	0	19	0	1		4
JR Hazlewood	4	0	26	0	1		12	MM Theekshana	4	0	27	0			10
PJ Cummins	4	0	34	2	2	1	10	PVD Chameera	3	0	33	0		1	4
GJ Maxwell	1	0	16	0	1		3	L Kumara	3	0	48	0		1	1
MP Stoinis	3	0	35	0	1		3	W Hasaranga	4	0	22	2		1	10
A Zampa	4	0	12	2			12	MD Shanaka	1	0	6	1	1		2

Toss: Australia. Umpires: A Dar, RK Illingworth, M Erasmus (TV), Ref: JJ Crowe. Award: A Zampa (Aus). Crowd: 3,450.
Warner 50: 31 balls, 8x4   Points: Aus 2, SL 0.

AUSTRALIA v ENGLAND – DUBAI

On a slightly grassier track than one expects to find in the UAE, it was a little surprising that Marsh was left out for Australia for the extra spin option of Agar. England's bowlers ran through the Aussie top order to effectively win the game inside the first six and a bit overs. Warner was caught behind having a flirt at Woakes, Smith toed a pull-shot to mid-on to be superbly caught one-handed and then Maxwell tried to whip one to leg and was LBW. When Stoinis played back to a wrong-un from Rashid and was LBW, Australia was 4-21 and the match was effectively over. Finch and the middle order scrounged to bat the innings out, with Cummins striking two fine blows, but a target of 126 was not even close to what they were hoping for.

Roy hit Cummins for six over mid-wicket in the third over before being lbw missing a reverse-sweep, while the bowlers had no answer to Buttler who dominated proceedings, hitting sixes to all parts as England stormed home to win in 8.2 overs to spare.

Australia v England at Dubai Sports City Stadium on October 30, 2021 (floodlit) - England won by 8 wickets

Australia			B	4	6	England			B	4	6
DA Warner	c Buttler b Woakes	1	2			JJ Roy	lbw b Zampa	22	20	1	1
AJ Finch*	c Bairstow b Jordan	44	49	4		JC Buttler+	not out	71	32	5	5
SPD Smith	c Woakes b Jordan	1	5			DJ Malan	c Wade b Agar	8	8	1	
GJ Maxwell	lbw b Woakes	6	9			JM Bairstow	not out	16	11		2
MP Stoinis	lbw b Rashid	0	4			EJG Morgan*					
MS Wade+	c Roy b Livingstone	18	18	2		LS Livingstone					
AC Agar	c Livingstone b Mills	20	20		2	MM Ali					
PJ Cummins	b Jordan	12	3		2	CR Woakes					
MA Starc	c Buttler b Mills	13	6	1	1	CJ Jordan					
A Zampa	run out (Buttler-Mills)	1	4			AU Rashid					
JR Hazlewood	not out	0	0			TS Mills					
	6 lb, 3 w	9					5 b, 1 nb, 3 w	9			
6 overs: 3-21	20 overs	125				6 overs: 0-66	11.4 overs	2-126			

1-7 (Warner, 1.2), 2-8 (Smith, 2.1), 3-15 (Maxwell, 3.5),
4-21 (Stoinis, 6.1), 5-51 (Wade, 11.4), 6-98 (Agar, 17.4),
7-110 (Finch, 18.1), 8-110 (Cummins, 18.2),
9-119 (Zampa, 19.4), 10-125 (Starc, 19.6)

1-66 (Roy, 6.2), 2-97 (Malan, 9.1)

Bowling	O	M	R	W	wd	nb	Dots	Bowling	O	M	R	W	wd	nb	Dots
AU Rashid	4	0	19	1			12	MA Starc	3	0	37	0	1		6
CR Woakes	4	0	23	2	2		15	JR Hazlewood	2	0	18	0			3
CJ Jordan	4	0	17	3			12	PJ Cummins	1	0	14	0	1	1	3
LS Livingstone	4	0	15	1			10	AC Agar	2.4	0	15	1	1		7
TS Mills	4	0	45	2	1		8	A Zampa	3	0	37	1			5

Toss: England. Umpires: M Erasmus, NN Menon, K Dharmasena (TV), Ref: RS Madugalle. Award: CJ Jordan (Eng). Crowd: 8,800.

Buttler 50: 25 balls, 4x4 4x6.   Points: Eng 2, Aus 0.

AUSTRALIA v BANGLADESH – DUBAI

With Marsh back in the side for Agar, Australia trounced Bangladesh in a clash that was very one sided. Das was yorked in the first over while Hazlewood also had success in his first when Sarkar played on. When Rahim was trapped in front on the crease by Maxwell, Bangladesh was 3-10 inside the first three overs. Naim struck some nice shots before hooking a catch to square-leg and when Afif edged Zampa's first ball to slip, half the Bangladesh team were out for just 33. Shamim swept Zampa sweetly for six as he and Mahmudullah added 29, but the last five wickets fell for just 11, Zampa securing his first ever five wicket haul in T20s for Australia.

Finch hit Mustafizur hard for six over long-on and then next ball was put down when the bowler couldn't hold a return catch. The Aussie skipper cleared the ropes three more times before he had his off-stump bent back, Marsh coming in to get Australia home in just 6.2 overs, when he pulled Taskin over long-on for six to end the match.

Australia v Bangladesh at Dubai Sports City Stadium on November 4, 2021 - Australia won by 8 wickets

Bangladesh			B	4	6	Australia			B	4	6
Moh'd Naim	c Cummins b Hazlewood	17	16	3		DA Warner	b Shoriful	18	14	3	
Liton Das+	b Starc	0	1			AJ Finch*	b Taskin	40	20	2	4
Soumya Sarkar	b Hazlewood	5	8	1		MR Marsh	not out	16	5	2	1
Mushfiqur Rahim	lbw b Maxwell	1	2			GJ Maxwell	not out	0	0		
Mahmudullah*	c Wade b Starc	16	18	2		SPD Smith					
Afif Hossain	c Finch b Zampa	0	4			MP Stoinis					
Shamim Hossain	c Wade b Zampa	19	18	1	1	MS Wade+					
Mehedi Hasan	lbw b Zampa	0	1			A Zampa					
Taskin Ahmed	not out	6	11			PJ Cummins					
M Rahman	c Smith b Zampa	4	9			MA Starc					
Shoriful Islam	c Finch b Zampa	0	2			JR Hazlewood					
	1 lb, 4 w	5					1 lb, 1 nb, 2 w	4			
6 overs: 4-33	15 overs	73				6 overs: 2-67	6.2 overs	2-78			

1-1 (Das, 0.3), 2-6 (Sarkar, 1.6), 3-10 (Mushfiqur 2.5),
4-32 (Naim, 5.3), 5-33 (Afif, 6.1), 6-62 (Shamim, 10.5),
7-62 (Mehedi, 10.6), 8-65 (Mahmudullah, 12.2),
9-73 (Mustafizur, 14.4), 10-73 (Shoriful, 14.6)

1-58 (Finch, 4.6), 2-67 (Warner, 5.6)

43

Bowling	O	M	R	W	wd	nb	Dots
MA Starc	4	0	21	2	2		15
JR Hazlewood	2	0	8	2			10
GJ Maxwell	2	0	6	1	1		7
PJ Cummins	3	0	18	0			9
A Zampa	4	0	19	5	1		14

Bowling	O	M	R	W	wd	nb	Dots
Taskin Ahmed	3.2	0	36	1	1		8
Mustafizur Rahman	2	0	32	0	1		3
Shoriful Islam	1	0	9	1		1	1

Toss: Australia. Umpires: NN Menon, K Dharmasena, JS Wilson (TV), Ref: JJ Crowe.   Award: A Zampa (Eng). Crowd: 1,600.
Points: Aus 2, Ban 0.

AUSTRALIA v WEST INDIES – ABU DHABI

Australia were unchanged from their win over Bangladesh and faced an experienced West Indies side that had been performing well below its capabilities. Lewis set the ball rolling when he hit Hazlewood's first three balls for four, then Gayle pulled his fifth delivery for six, as 20 came from the over. Cummins came on and his first ball was pulled for six by Gayle, but he got his revenge next ball when Gayle chopped on. Hazlewood's day turned around completely in his second over, when Pooran mishit to cover and two balls later Chase was bowled through the "gate" on the drive.

West Indies managed a small rebuild adding 35 for the fourth wicket, before Lewis lofted a catch high to long-on which Smith did well to hold onto. Pollard was dropped by Zampa off his own bowling when three, while Hetmeyer couldn't accelerate and was out when he gloved a catch to the keeper. Bravo struck Starc over cover in fine style for six and then Pollard hooked Cummins over the rope as the final push came. Bravo was out when he was caught at straight hit and after Pollard was caught at long-on, Pollard laced Starc for two sixes from his last two balls to take West Indies to 7-157, with 48 coming from the last four overs.

Australia started well to be 18 after two overs and then in the third Warner pulled and edged fours off Holder before pulling him for six. Finch then went when he chopped on an arm ball, but Warner continued to dominate sweeping Hosein for six, before cutting him for four to reach 40 of the Aussie powerplay of 1-53.

Marsh reverse swept Walsh for four and then lofted Hosein straight for six. At 1-71 after eight overs the game went distinctly Australia's way in the next couple as Warner slog swept Walsh for six, before Marsh whipped Russell over the rope, Australia 1-98 well in control at the halfway mark. With 60 needed off the last ten overs, Australia progressed calmly, Marsh had some luck in edging two drives on the way to his 50 and then Warner cut loose facing Bravo in the 15th over, with a swap hands pull for four, before hitting him over square-leg for six. The stand of 124 off 74 balls ended with Marsh caught at mid-off, Warner finishing the job with a glance for four in the 17th over.

Australia v West Indies at Sheikh Zayed Stadium, Abu Dhabi on November 6, 2021 - Australia won by 8 wickets

West Indies			B	4	6	Australia			B	4	6
CH Gayle	b Cummins	15	9		2	DA Warner	not out	89	56	9	4
E Lewis	c Smith b Zampa	29	26	5		AJ Finch*	b Hosein	9	11	1	
N Pooran+	c Marsh b Hazlewood	4	4	1		MR Marsh	c Holder b Gayle	53	32	5	2
RL Chase	b Hazlewood	0	2			GJ Maxwell	not out	0	0		
SO Hetmyer	c Wade b Hazlewood	27	28	2		SPD Smith					
KA Pollard*	c Maxwell b Starc	44	31	4	1	MP Stoinis					
DJ Bravo	c Warner b Hazlewood	10	12		1	MS Wade+					
AD Russell	not out	18	7	1	2	A Zampa					
JO Holder	not out	1	1			PJ Cummins					
AJ Hosein						MA Starc					
HR Walsh						JR Hazlewood					
	6 lb, 3 w	9					3 lb, 1 nb, 6 w	10			
6 overs: 3-50	20 overs	7-157				6 overs: 1-53	16.2 overs	2-161			

1-30 (Gayle, 2.2), 2-35 (Pooran, 3.1), 3-35 (Chase, 3.3), 4-70 (Lewis, 9.3), 5-91 (Hetmyer, 12.5), 6-126 (Bravo, 17.3), 7-143 (Pollard, 19.2)

1-33 (Finch, 3.3), 2-157 (Marsh, 15.6)

Bowling	O	M	R	W	wd	nb	Dots
MA Starc	4	0	33	1	1		10
JR Hazlewood	4	0	39	4	1		8
PJ Cummins	4	0	37	1			10
GJ Maxwell	1	0	6	0			3
MR Marsh	3	0	16	0			7
A Zampa	4	0	20	1	1		11

Bowling	O	M	R	W	wd	nb	Dots
AJ Hosein	4	0	29	1			9
RL Chase	1.2	0	17	0	1		3
JO Holder	2	0	26	0	1		4
DJ Bravo	4	0	36	0	3		8
HR Walsh	2	0	18	0			3
AD Russell	2	0	25	0			1
CH Gayle	1	0	7	1	2		3

Toss: Australia. Umpires: RK Illingworth, L Rusere, A Dar (TV), Ref: J Srinath.   Award: DA Warner (Aus). Crowd: 1,700.
Warner 50: 29 balls, 5x4 3x6, Marsh 50: 28 balls, 5x4 2x6.   Points: Aus 2, WI 0.

This Semi-final will go down as one of the all-time Twenty20 matches. After just 11 from the first two overs Rizwan, who had failed to score from his first five balls, lofted a drive straight down the ground and Warner ran back from mid-off but couldn't hold on. Babar was playing some deft strokes to find the rope and then in the fifth over, Rizwan really lifted the tempo when he whipped Hazlewood behind square-leg for six. Rizwan was dropped low down at long-leg by Zampa on 20 off Cummins as the pair steadily reached 71 in the 10th over when Babar hit one to long-on to be caught.

Zampa gave up just seven from his first two overs, when in the 12th over Rizwan slog-swept him for six, before he lifted Hazlewood over the leg-side for another, on the way to 50 from 41 balls. Fakhar after being only three off his first six balls, started to get going, he and Rizwan both hitting sixes in the 17th over off Hazlewood which cost the paceman 21. Starc returned to have Rizwan caught at mid-off, but in the same over Fakhar lofted him straight for six in an over that went for 15. Cummins had Asif caught at long-on in an over that cost just three, but then Fakhar finished off the innings brilliantly with two sixes to wide long-on in the last over, setting Australia 177 to win.

In the opening over Shaheen looked like a man possessed, beating Warner first ball and after a single beating Finch with a sharp in ducker that hit him hard on the pad dead in front. Marsh came out and had luck on his side as he was close to LBW by a yorker first ball and was then beaten by the next in what was one of the overs of the tournament by a bowler. Australia was 1-13 after three overs and then Warner sprung to life, lofting Imad over mid-wicket for six, before taking boundaries off the next two balls as the over cost 17. Marsh greeted Rauf with a pull for six but soon after Shadab came on and Marsh was out top edging a slog-sweep high to deep backward square-leg. Warner advanced and lofted Hafeez for six before also hitting Shadab for one, but then Smith tried a similar shot which landed in the hands of deep mid-wicket. Australia reached 3-89 after 10 overs, but then Warner was given out caught behind, replays showing he had missed the ball.

Australia was feeling the pressure as the boundaries dried up and things looked terminal when Maxwell reverse swept a catch to deep backward-point to make Australia 5-92, needing 81 off the last 46 balls. Stoinis knew it was now or never and responded by lofting Shadab just over wide long-on for six, but with Rauf and Shaheen bowling tightly in the 14th and 15th overs, Australia found themselves needing 62 off the last five.

Hasan bowled the 16th, Stoinis lofting the first ball for four, in an over that cost 12, which left 50 wanted off 24 balls. A pull by Stoinis for six off Rauf in the 17th helped Australia add 13 from the over, which left 36 off 18 balls. After a single to Stonis, Wade was on strike with eight off nine balls to his name. After a two, he then lofted a Hasan slower ball for six before getting him away behind square-leg for four, leaving 22 from two overs for the win. Shaheen, who had been so good before took the ball and after a dot and leg-bye to Stoinis, bowled to Wade. After a wide and a two, Wade dramatically scooped a near yorker over long-leg for six, before winning the match with a scoop shot of a low full-toss for another six to win the match with an over to spare and put Australia in the Final.

Australia v Pakistan at Dubai Sports City Stadium on November 11, 2021 - Australia won by 5 wickets

Pakistan		B	4	6	Australia		B	4	6
Moh Rizwan+	c Smith b Starc	67	52	3	4	DA Warner	c Rizwan b Shadab	49	30	3	3
Babar Azam*	c Warner b Zampa	39	34	5		AJ Finch *	lbw b Shaheen	0	1		
Fakhar Zaman	not out	55	32	3	4	MR Marsh	c Asif b Shadab	28	22	3	1
Asif Ali	c Smith b Cummins	0	1			SPD Smith	c Fakhar b Shadab	5	6	1	
Shoaib Malik	b Starc	1	2			GJ Maxwell	c Rauf b Shadab	7	10		
Moh Hafeez	not out	1	1			MP Stoinis	not out	40	31	2	2
Imad Wasim						MS Wade +	not out	41	17	2	4
Shadab Khan						A Zampa					
Hasan Ali						PJ Cummins					
Shaheen Shah Afridi						MA Starc					
Haris Rauf						JR Hazlewood					
	5 b, 1 lb, 2 nb, 5 w	13					2 lb, 3 nb, 2 w	7			
6 overs: 0-47	20 overs	4-176				6 overs: 1-52	19 overs	5-177			

1-71 (Babar, 9.6), 2-143 (Rizwan, 17.2), 3-158 (Asif, 18.1), 4-162 (Malik, 19.2)

1-1 (Finch, 0.3), 2-52 (Marsh, 6.2), 3-77 (Smith, 8.3), 4-89 (Warner, 10.1), 5-96 (Maxwell, 12.2)

Bowling	O	M	R	W	wd	nb	Dots	Bowling	O	M	R	W	wd	nb	Dots
MA Starc	4	0	38	2	1		10	Shaheen Shah Afridi	4	0	35	1	1	1	12
JR Hazlewood	4	0	49	0	1	1	8	Imad Wasim	3	0	25	0			6
GJ Maxwell	3	0	20	0			5	Haris Rauf	3	0	32	0			6
PJ Cummins	4	0	30	1	1	1	9	Hasan Ali	4	0	44	0		1	3
A Zampa	4	0	22	1	1		9	Shadab Khan	4	0	26	4			11
MR Marsh	1	0	11	0	1		1	Mohammad Hafeez	1	0	13	0	1	1	2

Toss: Australia. Umpires: CB Gaffeney, RA Kettleborough, JS Wilson (TV), Ref: JJ Crowe.   Award: MS Wade (Aus). Crowd: 15,050.
Rizwan 50: 41 balls, 2x4 3x6, Fakhar 50: 31 balls, 3x4 4x6.

THE FINAL – DUBAI

With Australia pulling off a miracle chase in the Semi-final, they had much in common with their fellow finalists New Zealand, who chased down 57 off the last 24 balls and got there with an over to spare. Australia started as slight favourites and started well with the ball giving up only 13 off the first two overs. Mitchell lofted Maxwell for six off his first ball in the third, but in the next over he edged a drive to the keeper off Hazlewood. Australia's bowlers then gave up no boundaries in a four over patch, as a cautious New Zealand were 1-40 after eight overs. Marsh came on and was struck twice to the rope but with the Kiwis at 1-57 at the halfway point, Australia was well on top.

In the 11th over, Williamson on 21 pulled Starc to long-leg, where Hazlewood dropped the chance, with two further fours coming from the over that cost 19. Then the struggling Guptill was on his way when he slog-swept a catch to deep mid-wicket. Williamson raised New Zealand's hope with back-to-back sixes off Maxwell, as the skipper reached his fifty from 32 balls. Phillips was another to take time to get going, but in the 15th over he hit Zampa straight for six as the Kiwis were 2-114 with five overs to go.

Starc whose first two overs had gone for 28, was taken down by Williamson who hit him for 4 fours and a six in an over that cost 22. Phillips and Williamson were both caught in the deep in the same over by Hazlewood and with 23 coming from Neesham and Seifert in the last two overs, Australia were 173 set to win.

Boult bowled a good first over, finding Warner's edge while Finch was beaten and then survived a leg before shout. Warner square drove and cut fours in the second but lost his partner Finch in the third over when he advanced and pulled a catch to deep square-leg. Marsh lifted his and Milne's first ball of his hip for six, then edged and pulled fours in what was an ominous beginning for the Kiwis. When Warner pulled Southee for six, Australia was on track early being 1-40 after five overs.

Milne and Sodhi between them went for just 10 runs in the next two overs, but then the dam wall broke as Marsh swept Santner for six and then in the next over Warner pulled Sodhi for four, before lofting him back over his head for six. At 1-82 after 10 overs Neesham came on and was greeted first ball by a pull for six by Marsh, then later in the over Warner lofted him over for another six to reach his 50 from 34 balls.

With Australia 1-106 after 12 overs, New Zealand recalled Boult and second ball he had Warner bowled swinging hard across the line. This brought Maxwell in, but Marsh took the pressure off him as he hit Sodhi into the upper deck on the stand at long-on, the leg-spinner going to water a bit in an over that cost 16, including three wides. With 48 wanted off 36 balls, Milne returned and found the edge of Maxwell's bat but it rolled away to the rope. In the next over when Southee dropped one short, Maxwell swayed inside it and pulled it away for six. Needing 24 at a run a ball, Australia cruised home with Marsh pulling Boult for six and then Maxwell finished the game off with a reverse sweep off Southee for four, Australia winning with seven balls to spare to claim their first ICC World T20 title.

Australia v New Zealand at Dubai Sports City Stadium on November 14, 2021 (floodlit) - Australia won by 8 wickets

New Zealand			B	4	6
MJ Guptill	c Stoinis b Zampa	28	35	3	
DJ Mitchell	c Wade b Hazlewood	11	8		1
KS Williamson*	c Smith b Hazlewood	85	48	10	3
GD Phillips	c Maxwell b Hazlewood	18	17	1	1
JDS Neesham	not out	13	7		1
TL Seifert+	not out	8	6	1	
MJ Santner					
IS Sodhi					
AF Milne					
TG Southee					
TA Boult					
	1 b, 3 lb, 1 nb, 4 w	9			
	20 overs	4-172			

6 overs: 1-32

1-28 (Mitchell, 3.5), 2-76 (Guptill, 11.1), 3-144 (Phillips, 17.2), 4-148 (Williamson, 17.5)

Australia			B	4	6
DA Warner	b Boult	53	38	4	3
AJ Finch*	c Mitchell b Boult	5	7	1	
MR Marsh	not out	77	50	6	4
GJ Maxwell	not out	28	18	4	1
SPD Smith					
MP Stoinis					
MS Wade+					
A Zampa					
PJ Cummins					
MA Starc					
JR Hazlewood					
	4 lb, 6 w	10			
	18.5 overs	2-173			

6 overs: 1-43

1-15 (Finch, 2.3), 2-107 (Warner, 12.2)

Bowling	O	M	R	W	wd	nb	Dots
MA Starc	4	0	60	0	1	1	5
JR Hazlewood	4	0	16	3			18
GJ Maxwell	3	0	28	0			5
PJ Cummins	4	0	27	0	2		7
A Zampa	4	0	26	1			7
MR Marsh	1	0	11	0			1

Bowling	O	M	R	W	wd	nb	Dots
TA Boult	4	0	18	2	1		14
TG Southee	3.5	0	43	0	1		6
AF Milne	4	0	30	0	1		12
IS Sodhi	3	0	40	0	3		3
MJ Santner	3	0	23	0			4
JDS Neesham	1	0	15	0			1

Toss: Australia.   Umpires: M Erasmus, RA Kettleborough, NN Menon (TV), Ref: RS Madugalle   Award: MR Marsh (Aus).
Williamson 50: 32 balls, 5x4 2x6. Warner 50: 34 balls, 4x4 3x6, Marsh 31 balls, 3x4 4x6.   Crowd: 13,450

AUSTRALIA v SRI LANKA, 2021/22, HOME SIDE WINS 4-1

The start of a new era without coach Justin Langer got away to a good start, as Australia accounted for Sri Lanka. They won the first match easily, nearly got rolled in the second which went to a Superover, then convincingly won the third to wrap up the series. The fourth saw them win comfortably, while in the fifth Sri Lanka managed to win well to get something out of their time here. The crowds were low with just 55,666 attending the five games, the majority Sri Lanka supporters. Maybe the Australian fans were weary over cricket after an Ashes series and long BBL tournament.

Man of the series Glenn Maxwell and Josh Inglis showed the way with the bat for Australia, Inglis could easily have received the award. Australia's skipper Aaron Finch struggled while Ben McDermott had a good start to the series but finished poorly. With the ball Australia were strong, Josh Hazlewood excellent in his three games before being rested for the final two matches. Adam Zampa was his usual consistent self while Ashton Agar was hard to score off and didn't concede a boundary in the series. He was tried as an opening batsman in game three and four but the experiment didn't work.

For Sri Lanka they struggled with the bat, Pathum Nissanka their leading light, Dasun Shanaka had his moments and Kusal Mendis was brilliant in the last match when he steered them home to their only win of the series. With the ball spinner Maheesh Thekasanna was excellent, while paceman Dushmantha Chameera performed admirably. Lahiru Kumara bowled with pace and fire in the last two games, while Wanindu Hasaranga only played two games before contracting COVID which ruled him out of the series.

AVERAGES
AUSTRALIA

Batting	M	I	NO	Runs	HS	Avg	SR	50	6s
MS Wade	5	3	2	60	43*	60.0	166	0	3
JP Inglis	5	5	1	155	48	38.7	143	0	2
GJ Maxwell	5	5	1	138	48*	34.5	133	0	3
MP Stoinis	5	5	2	86	30	28.6	150	0	3
AC Agar	3	3	1	43	26	21.5	93	0	1
DR Sams	3	1	0	18	18	18.0	120	0	0
BR McDermott	5	5	0	83	53	16.6	93	1	3
AJ Finch	5	5	0	78	35	15.6	91	0	0
SPD Smith	2	2	0	23	14	11.5	100	0	0
PJ Cummins	2	2	1	8	6*	8.0	100	0	0
MA Starc	2	1	0	1	1	1.0	33	0	0
JR Hazlewood	3	1	1	2	2*	-	100	0	0
A Zampa	4	1	1	2	2*	-	33	0	0

Bowling	O	W	Avg	Best	Econ
JR Hazlewood	12	8	8.1	4-12	5.41
KW Richardson	15.4	8	17.1	3-21	8.74
A Zampa	16	5	20.6	3-18	6.43
AC Agar	12	3	15.6	1-14	3.91
JA Richardson	8	2	29.0	2-20	7.25
PJ Cummins	8	2	31.0	1-30	7.75
GL Maxwell	4	1	28.0	1-3	7.00
MP Stoinis	8	1	55.0	1-30	6.87
DR Sams	7.1	0	-	-	7.53
MA Starc	8	0	-	-	8.87

JA Richardson (2 matches) and KW Richardson (4 matches) did not bat.

SRI LANKA

Batting	M	I	NO	Runs	HS	Avg	SR	50	6s
K Mendis	3	3	1	100	69*	50.0	111	1	3
P Nissanka	5	5	0	184	73	36.8	115	1	3
MD Shanaka	5	5	1	116	39*	29.0	110	0	5
D Chandimal	4	4	1	71	25	23.6	101	0	2
W Hasaranga	2	2	0	26	13	13.0	130	0	0
C Asalanka	5	5	0	64	22	12.8	114	0	2
J Liyange	1	1	0	9	9	9.0	180	0	1
C Karunaratne	5	2	2	23	14*	7.6	100	0	1
PVD Chameera	5	2	2	15	5*	7.5	125	0	0
M Gunathilleke	4	4	0	27	17	6.7	96	0	1
A Fernando	2	2	0	11	6*	5.5	122	0	1
K Mishara	1	1	0	1	1	1.0	33	0	0
J Vandersay	2	1	1	5	5*	-	166	0	0
B Fernando	1	1	1	2	2*	-	100	0	0

Bowling	O	W	Avg	Best	Econ
PVD Chameera	20	7	21.8	2-30	7.65
M Theekshana	19	5	25.8	3-24	6.78
W Hasaranga	8	5	14.2	3-38	8.87
L Kumara	8	4	14.0	2-22	7.00
C Karunaratne	17	3	42.0	2-22	7.41
B Fernando	4	2	6.0	2-12	3.00
P Jayawickrama	4	1	29.0	1-29	7.25
N Thusara	5.1	1	50.0	1-40	9.67
J Vandersay	8	1	75.0	1-32	9.37
M Shanaka	1.5	0	-	-	10.36

P Jayawickrama (1 match), L Kumara (2 matches) and N Thusara (4 matches) did not bat.

MATCH ONE - SYDNEY

Australia got off to a decent start with McDermott playing with purpose in the opening overs as he swept Theekshana for four and then struck Hasaranga over mid-wicket for six. Finch wasn't at his best, surviving a review for LBW and was almost run out on seven, before being bowled on the drive. Inglis cut his third ball away for four and then McDermott smashed Hasaranga for six, but the rain came in the ninth over, which delayed the match for 25 minutes.

On resumption McDermott belted Chameera over mid-wicket for six but lost Inglis when he was yorked aiming a reverse sweep. Maxwell lifted a full-toss to deep square-leg, then Smith was beaten in flight and when McDermott played across a full ball, Australia was battling at 5-107 in the 14th over. Stoinis played a good hand, launching sixes off Theekshana and Chameera (measured at 100 metres) as Australia reached 5-140 with three overs left.

Sri Lanka's bowlers finished the innings well, in the 18th over Fernando had Wade caught at deep-point and Stoinis dragged on. In the 19th Starc was bowled making room to leg and then Cummins holed out at straight hit. The last pair could manage just three off the final over and with just nine runs coming from the final three, Sri Lanka needed just 150 to win.

Starc gave up just a wide from the opening over and the pressure was building when Hazlewood had Gunathilleke caught pulling one to mid-wicket. Nissanka was seeing the ball well as he hit a magnificent pull-shot in the Ladies stand. Avishka Fernando pulled Cummins' second ball for six to get him off the mark, but then repeated the shot next ball, top edging a catch to the keeper. Nissanka spanked Stonis straight for four but next ball should have been on his way when Cummins shelled a low chance at mid-on. Just 11 runs came in overs six to eight, but in the ninth Nissanka and Asalanka broke free to hit three boundaries between them in an over that cost 15.

Zampa returned to the attack and put the game firmly Australia's way as Nissanka top edged a slog-sweep to mid-wicket and Asalanka played a similar shot to be well held just inside the square-leg rope. Hasaranga and Shanaka were doing their best to keep up with the rate before Hasaranga was caught at cover. Then the rain returned, an over being lost which meant Sri Lanka needed 61 off the last 31 balls.

Hazlewood returned to bowl the 16th and that essentially ended Sri Lankas hopes as Shanaka was caught at deep mid-off and then two balls later Karunaratne popped a catch back to the bowler. Chandimal hit some sweet boundaries late, but it wasn't enough, Australia winning comfortably to make it six wins in a row against Sri Lanka.

First Twenty20 at the SCG on February 11, 2022 (Floodlit) – Australia won by 20 runs (DLS)

Australia			B	4	6	Sri Lanka	(DLS Target 143 off 19)		B	4	6
AJ Finch*	b Hasaranga	8	12			P Nissanka	c Starc b Zampa	36	37	5	1
BR McDermott	lbw b Karunaratne	53	41	2	3	MD Gunathilleke	c Stoinis b Hazlewood	1	5		
JP Inglis	b Karunaratne	23	18	3		WIA Fernando	c Wade b Cummins	6	3		1
GJ Maxwell	c Karunaratne					KIC Asalanka	c Smith b Zampa	16	19	2	
	b Hasaranga	7	5	1		W Hasaranga	c Smith b Zampa	13	11	1	
SPD Smith	b Hasaranga	9	8	1		MD Shanaka*	c Finch b Hazlewood	7	13		
MP Stoinis	b B Fernando	30	17	2	2	LD Chandimal+	not out	25	16	3	1
+MS Wade	c Shanaka b B Fernando	4	5			C Karunaratne	c & b Hazlewood	0	2		
PJ Cummins	c Karunaratne b Chameera	2	3			P VD Chameera	c McDermott				
MA Starc	b Chameera	1	3				b Hazlewood	5	6		
A Zampa	not out	2	6			KBU Fernando	not out	2	2		
JR Hazlewood	not out	2	2			MM Theekshana					
	4 lb, 4 w	8					4 b, 3 lb, 4 w	11			
6 overs: 1-37	20 overs	9-149				6 overs: 2-30	19 overs	8-122			

1-30 (Finch, 4.5), 2-80 (Inglis, 10.3), 3-90 (Maxwell, 11.4), 4-105 (Smith, 13.5), 5-107 (McDermott, 14.2), 6-141 (Wade, 17.3), 7-141 (Stoinis, 17.4), 8-144 (Starc, 18.3), 9-145 (Cummins, 18.5)

1-3 (Gunathilleke, 1.6), 2-21 (A Fernando, 3.3), 3-64 (Nissanka, 10.2), 4-64 (Asalanka, 10.4), 5-89 (Hasaranga, 14.3), 6-89 (Shanaka, 15.1), 7-90 (Karunaratne, 15.4), 8-104 (Chameera, 17.1)

Bowling	O	M	R	W	wd	nb	Dots	Bowling	O	M	R	W	wd	nb	Dots
P VD Chameera	4	0	38	2	1		8	MA Starc	4	0	41	0	2		11
KBU Fernando	4	0	12	2			14	JR Hazlewood	4	0	12	4			14
MM Theekshana	3	0	27	0			7	PJ Cummins	4	0	32	1	1		10
W Hasaranga	4	0	38	3			8	MP Stoinis	3	0	12	0			10
C Karunaratne	4	0	22	2	3		9	A Zampa	4	0	18	3	1		12
MD Shanaka	1	0	36	0			0								

Toss: Australia.   Umpires: SAJ Craig, SJ Nogajski, RJ Tucker (TV), Ref: DC Boon   Award: A Zampa (Aus).   Crowd: 12,098

McDermott 50: 38 balls, 2x4 3x6. Rain delay: Aus 1-58 (8.3) McDermott 30, Inglis 17 then again when SL 5-89 (14.5) Shanaka 7, Chandmal 0 which reduced the target to 143 off 19 overs.

MATCH TWO - SYDNEY

Kane Richardson came into the home side for Mitchell Starc, while Sri Lanka were unlucky to lose left-arm quick Binura Fernando to COVID, which saw Nuwan Thusara in to make his debut. Australia batted first once again and were well served by McDermott in the opening over, as he struck Chameera for consecutive fours in an over that cost 10. The opener was looking good once more until he absolutely crunched one to long-on, where the head high chance was well held. Finch showed some old form and with Inglis finding the rope early, Australia reached 1-52 at end of the first six overs.

Sadly, for the Australian captain, he walked past a wrong-un from Hasaranga and was stumped. Maxwell came in and reached the boundary twice in the tenth over, Australia 2-80 at the midway point. Inglis continued to score freely but had a shocking mix-up with Maxwell in the 12th over where both batsmen were at the same end yet survived. Three balls later

Maxwell gloved a reverse sweep to the keeper and then two overs later Inglis hit one low to cover. Stoinis cut Karunaratne to the rope twice in the 15th over, but Smith took his time getting going, being just four off his first seven balls. After adding 33 the pair went in consecutive balls, Smith hitting out to deep cover, with Stoinis slashing to short third-man. Wade only had the strike in the final over to smash 4,2,6, and 1 – Australia adding 16 in the last over to set 165 to win.

Hazlewood continued from where he left off in the first T20 having Gunathilleke was well caught at cover-point before getting Avishka Fernando caught on the drive at cover. When Asalanka chopped on to Cummins to make it 3-25, one felt we were in for an early night. But the fourth wicket pair gave Sri Lanka hope as Chandimal lifted Stoinis for six into the Ladies Stand while Nissanka hit Richardson for back to back fours, the visitors 3-64 at halfway, needing 101 to win off the last 10.

In the next over Zampa returned to have Chandimal bowled sweeping at a full ball, but then Shanaka took it upon himself to get Sri Lanka back up with the rate with some powerful strokeplay. He lifted Zampa into the Members for six in the 13th and was then dropped from the very next ball on nine by Maxwell at long-on, just inside the rope. He went hard at Richardson in the 15th, smacking him over his head for six, before whipping him off his pads for another, which left 58 to get off 30 balls.

Shanaka's knock came to an end in the 16th over when coming back for a second for Nissanka, Smith running in and hitting the stumps at the bowler's end. When Karunaratne top edged a hook to the keeper and just four came from the 17th, Sri Lanka needed 46 off the last three. But they didn't give up hope, as in the 18th over from Cummins, Hasaranga found the third man boundary twice and then Nissanka hooked him for six, leaving 29 wanted off the last two.

Hazlewood returned for the 19th and despite being lifted for six over mid-wicket by Nissanka, went for only 10, getting Hasaranga caught at deep point off the last ball, which meant Sri Lanka needed 19 off the last over. A nervous Stoinis started with a wide, then gave up a four to long-off before a full-toss to Nissanka was hit to deep square-leg, where the catch was taken. With 12 to win off three balls, Theekshana hit over mid-wicket for six with Smith diving over the rope and landing on and injuring his shoulder, which was to rule him out of the series. Stoinis then looked to bowl a wide outside off, which was not called by the umpire, the batsmen running a bye. Off the last ball Chameera lofted one straight for four, the ball landing 10 metres short of the rope, which brought about a Super Over.

After two dots from Hazlewood a bye was tried off the third, Wade's throw missed and an overthrow was attempted, but Maxwell brilliantly picked off Chandimal with a direct hit. Sri Lanka managed just five from the over, Australia winning comfortably as Stoinis hit Hasaranga for back-to-back fours, the game ending at 11.13pm local time.

Second Twenty20 at the SCG on February 13, 2022 (Floodlit) – Australia won in Super Over

Australia			B	4	6	Sri Lanka			B	4	6
BR McDermott	c Hasaranga b Thushara	18	15	3		P Nissanka	c Cummins b Stoinis	73	53	7	2
AJ Finch*	st Chandimal b Hasaranga	25	20	3		MD Gunathilleke	c McDermott b Hazlewood	0	1		
JP Inglis	b Shanaka b Hasaranga	48	32	5		WIA Fernando	c Inglis b Hazlewood	5	6	1	
GJ Maxwell	c Chandimal b Theekshana	15	12	2		KIC Asalanka	b Cummins	0	5		
SPD Smith	c Gunathilleke b Chameera	14	15	1		LD Chandimal+	b Zampa	19	22	1	1
MP Stoinis	c Theekshana b Chameera	19	18	3		MD Shanaka*	run out (Smith)	34	19	2	3
MS Wade+	not out	13	4	1	1	C Karunaratne	c Wade b Richardson	0	2		
PJ Cummins	not out	6	4			W Hasaranga	c Cummins b Hazlewood	13	9	2	
A Zampa						PVD Chameera	not out	4	1	1	
KW Richardson						MM Theekshana	not out	6	2		1
JR Hazlewood						IDN Thushara					
	2 lb, 4 w		6				1 b, 7 lb, 2 w		10		
6 overs: 1-52	20 overs		6-164			6 overs: 3-36	20 overs		8-164		

1-33 (McDermott, 3.6), 2-60 (Finch, 7.5), 3-99 (Maxwell, 11.5), 4-112 (Inglis, 13.5), 5-145 (Smith, 18.3), 6-145 (Stoinis, 18.4)

1-3 (Gunathilleke, 0.5), 2-19 (Fernando, 2.6), 3-25 (Asalanka, 4.4), 4-67 (Chandimal, 10.5), 5-115 (Shanaka, 15.6), 6-115 (Karunaratne, 16.2), 7-146 (Hasaranga, 18.6), 8-153 (Nissanka, 19.3)

Bowling	O	M	R	W	wd	nb	Dots	Bowling	O	M	R	W	wd	nb	Dots
PVD Chameera	4	0	30	2			9	JR Hazlewood	4	0	22	3			12
IDN Thushara	4	0	40	1	1		7	PJ Cummins	4	0	30	1	1		13
MM Theekshana	4	0	31	1			6	MP Stoinis	3	0	30	1	1		9
W Hasaranga	4	0	33	2			7	KW Richardson	4	0	44	1			6
C Karunaratne	4	0	28	0	3		9	A Zampa	4	0	26	1			6
								GJ Maxwell	1	0	4	0			3

Toss: Sri Lanka. Umpires: DM Koch, RJ Tucker, SAJ Craig (TV), Ref: DC Boon Award: JR Hazlewood (Aus). Crowd: 6,305
Nissanka 50: 44 balls, 6x4. Super Over - Sri Lanka 1-5 (Chandimal run out Maxwell 0 off 0, Shanaka 1 off 4, Nissanka 3 off 2, Hazlewood 0-4 with 3 dots) then Australia 0-9 off 0.3 (Maxwell 1 off 1, Stoinis 8 off 2, Hasaranga 0-9 off 0.3).

MATCH THREE - CANBERRA

Australia made three changes for this game, one forced with Smith out injured, while Cummins was being rested for the remainder of the series and Zampa was having a game off. Sams and Starc were in, plus Agar who was listed to open the batting. Batsman Kusal Mendis was a key in for Sri Lanka, having missed the first two games with COVID. Sri Lanka were off to flyer being 17 from the first two overs, before Gunathilleke was caught at short fine-leg while attempting a ramp off Richardson's first ball. In the same over Asalanka powered one over mid-wicket for six but edged the next ball behind to the keeper. Mendis couldn't get going and popped a catch back to Agar, while Nissanka swept one to deep square-leg where Sams dived to his right and took a fine catch just inside the rope.

There was a recovery of sorts with 47 added off 48 balls for the fifth wicket, before Chandimal was yorked by Richardson. Shanaka managed to find the rope a couple of times in the final three overs which added 32, but on a good pitch a target of 122 was unlikely to bother the Aussies.

Sri Lankan hopes were raised when Theekshana had McDermott edge the first ball of the innings to slip. With only run a ball wanted the home side were in no rush, Agar settled and then crunched Thushara through the covers for four before lifting Theekshana over mid-wicket for six. But the tall spinner had his revenge when he trapped Agar in front, after winning a review. Theekshana could have been on a hat-trick as next ball Maxwell slashed at one to see a sharp chance to Asalanka at slip go down.

Maxwell continued to have some luck being dropped on nine by Gunathilleke who put down a tough chance diving to his right at mid-off. Finch continued to feed him the strike with singles and then Maxwell reverse swept a full toss from Vandersay into the stand at deep cover-point. Maxwell had more luck next ball when on 22, a hard-hit drive being put down at cover by Shanaka. After a pulled six off Karunaratne, his luck finally ran out when he hit one straight down the throat of deep mid-wicket.

With Australia 3-76, Sri Lanka needed more quick wickets, and they almost came as Inglis was nearly caught and bowled twice in the same over from Chameera, once on the forward stroke as the bowler dived to his left and the second a miscued hook that landed safely. Finch and Inglis proceeded to add 26, before the Aussie skipper's sound innings ended when he was caught at slip via the keeper's gloves. Australia cruised home with 19 balls left to go to an unassailable three-nil lead.

Third Twenty20 at Manuka Oval, Canberra on February 15, 2022 (Floodlit) – Australia won by 6 wickets

Sri Lanka			B	4	6	Australia			B	4	6
P Nissanka	c Sams b Maxwell	16	21	2		BR McDermott	c Asalanka				
MD Gunathilleke	c Hazlewood						b Theekshana	0	1		
	b Richardson	9	5	1		AC Agar	lbw b Theekshana	13	13	1	1
KIC Asalanka	c Wade b Richardson	6	4		1	AJ Finch*	c Asalanka b Vandersay	35	36	3	
BKG Mendis	c & b Agar	4	11			GJ Maxwell	c Mendis b Theekshana	39	26	3	2
LD Chandimal+	b Richardson	25	29	1		JP Inglis	not out	21	18	2	
MD Shanaka*	not out	39	38	5		MP Stoinis	not out	12	8	2	
C Karunaratne	c Inglis b Hazlewood	8	11	1		MS Wade+					
P VD Chameera	not out	5	2	1		DR Sams					
JDF Vandersay						KW Richardson					
MM Theekshana						MA Starc					
						JR Hazlewood					
	4 b, 1 nb, 4 w	9					3 lb, 1 nb	4			
6 overs: 2-37	20 overs	6-121				6 overs: 2-40	16.5 overs	4-124			

1-17 (Gunathilleke, 2.1), 2-23 (Asalanka, 2.5), 3-38 (Mendis, 6.3), 4-40 (Nissanka, 7.2), 5-87 (Chandimal, 16.1), 6-115 (Karunaratne, 19.3)

1-0 (McDermott, 0.1), 2-26 (Agar, 4.4), 3-76 (Maxwell, 10.4), 4-102 (Finch, 14.1)

Bowling	O	M	R	W	wd	nb	Dots	Bowling	O	M	R	W	wd	nb	Dots
MA Starc	4	0	30	0	2	1	12	MM Theekshana	4	0	24	3			13
JR Hazlewood	4	0	31	1	1		10	IDN Thushara	1.1	0	10	0	1		4
KW Richardson	4	0	21	3			13	C Karunaratne	2.5	0	22	0			3
DR Sams	3	0	18	0			7	P VD Chameera	4	0	22	0			12
AC Agar	4	0	14	1	1		11	JDF Vandersay	4	0	32	1			5
GJ Maxwell	1	0	3	1			3	MD Shanaka	0.5	0	11	0			1

Toss: Australia. Umpires: RJ Tucker, SAJ Craig, SJ Nogajski (TV), Ref: DC Boon. Award: KW Richardson (Aus). Crowd: 6,522

MATCH FOUR - MELBOURNE

The teams headed south to Melbourne for the final two games, Australia bringing in Zampa and Jhye Richardson for game four while resting Hazlewood and Starc for the rest of the series. Sri Lanka brought in paceman Lahiru Kumara for his first game of the series at the expense of spinner Vandersay.

After being sent into bat Sri Lanka were off to a flyer, with Nissanka regularly finding the rope while Gunathilleke advanced and smashed Richardson back over his head for six, as the first four overs went for 35. Then Agar was brought on and Gunathilleke aimed to leg but miscued to point. Mendis faced four balls before getting off the mark with a great square drive for four off Jhye Richardson and then thumped Maxwell and Kane Richardson for sixes over long-on.

At 2-73 at the halfway point the visitors were well placed, but then Maxwell exerted his influence in the field as he brought off a brilliant run out to dismiss Mendis as he ran back for a second for his partner to deep mid-on. Asalanka joined Nissanka and these took Sri Lanka to 2-110 in the 16th, but from there things went awry as they lost 6-12 in the next 37 balls. Asalanka went for a big hit and skied it to backward point, Nissanka was stumped chasing a wide ball outside off, Chandimal hit a catch to cover, Shanaka clipped one down the throat of deep square-leg, Chameera was yorked, and Theekshana was run out. Sri Lanka managed 17 off the last over with Karunaratne smacking a four and six off Kane Richardson, which set Australia 140 to win.

Sri Lanka's quicks started well with the ball with Kumara bowling quickly and Chameera beating Agar several times. Theekshana was given a third over in his spell and it worked for Sri Lanka as McDermott punched one off the back foot in the air straight to him for a caught and bowled. Finch survived an appeal and review for LBW before top edging a pull shot down the throat of deep square-leg. Kumara almost had Maxwell first ball and he inside edged one just short of the keeper. When Agar mistimed a slower ball to mid-off, Australia was in some bother at 3-49 in the ninth over.

Inglis came in and immediately looked good as he pulled and reverse swept Vandersay for consecutive boundaries. Then on 19 he lofted Vandersay to long-off where Chameera took the catch but jumped over the rope to concede a six. The pair added 71 with Inglis upper-cutting Chameera for six, but he went next ball snicking one to the keeper. By now the run chase was well under control, Maxwell pulled Karunaratne for four to win the game with 11 balls to spare and put Australia 4-0 up.

Fourth Twenty20 at the MCG on February 18, 2022 (Floodlit) – Australia won by 6 wickets

Fourth T20

Sri Lanka			B	4	6	Australia			B	4	6
P Nissanka	st Wade b Zampa	46	40	4		AC Agar	c Mendis b Kumara	26	31	2	
MD Gunathilleke	c Finch b Agar	17	17	1		BR McDermott	c & b Theekshana	9	10	1	
BKG Mendis	run out (Maxwell)	27	21	1	2	AJ Finch*	c Gunathilleke b Kumara	2	5		
KIC Asalanka	c Inglis b J Richardson	22	19	3		GJ Maxwell	not out	48	39	3	
LD Chandimal+	c Finch b K Richardson	2	3			JP Inglis	c Chandimal b Chameera	40	20	3	2
MD Shanaka*	c Agar b K Richardson	1	4			MP Stoinis	not out	8	4	1	
C Karunaratne	not out	14	7	1	1	MS Wade+					
P VD Chameera	b J Richardson	1	3			DR Sams					
MM Theekshana	run out (Wade)	3	3			A Zampa					
JDF Vandersay	not out	5	3	1		JA Richardson					
L Kumara						KW Richardson					
	1 w	1					3 lb, 7 w	10			
6 overs: 1-41	20 overs	8-139				6 overs: 1-30	18.1 overs	4-143			

1-35 (Gunathilleke, 4.3), 2-76 (Mendis, 10.3),
3-110 (Asalanka, 15.4), 4-113 (Nissanka, 16.2),
5-116 (Chandimal, 17.1), 6-117 (Shanaka, 17.3),
7-119 (Chameera, 18.1), 8-122 (Theekshana, 18.5)

1-19 (McDermott, 4.1), 2-32 (Finch, 6.2),
3-49 (Agar, 8.3), 4-120 (Inglis, 16.2)

Bowling	O	M	R	W	wd	nb	Dots	Bowling	O	M	R	W	wd	nb	Dots
DR Sams	2	0	14	0			4	MM Theekshana	4	0	20	1			9
JA Richardson	4	0	20	2			13	L Kumara	4	0	22	2	4		11
KW Richardson	4	0	44	2			5	P VD Chameera	4	0	33	1	1		9
GJ Maxwell	2	0	21	0			2	C Karunaratne	2.1	0	22	0			3
AC Agar	4	0	14	1			10	JDF Vandersay	4	0	43	0	1		2
A Zampa	4	0	26	1	1		5								

Toss: Australia. Umpires: RJ Tucker, SJ Nogajski, DM Koch (TV), Ref: DC Boon. Award: GJ Maxwell (Aus). Crowd: 13,175

Australia's skipper Finch was back at the top of the order with Agar back down to number eight, as his team kept the same eleven for the final game. Sri Lanka made three changes including debuts for Mishara and Liyange as they aimed to win their first game in the series.

In the opening over McDermott was dropped off the first ball he faced when he pulled one to mid-wicket where the debutant Liyange put it down. Finch again battled before advancing and mistiming to deep mid-on, while McDermott miscued to point to leave Australia 2-12. Australia went on the counter-attack as Maxwell struck Kumara for two fours off his first three balls and then Inglis powered Jayawickrama over cover twice in the one over to the rope. In the ninth over Maxwell smacked Theekshana straight for six but lost his partner in the next over as Inglis gloved a bouncer into his helmet and was caught and bowled. Stoinis looked in great touch hitting Karunaratne straight for six before chipping one low to mid-off where a fine catch was taken and when Maxwell uppercut one to third man, Australia were under the pump at 5-82 in the 13th over

Wade and Sams came to the rescue in a stand of 62 off 36 balls, the Aussie keeping reverse sweeping Theekshana for consecutive fours before smashing Kumara and Chameera for sixes to leg. Sams was caught and deep backward square-leg and Australia could only manage seven off the last over, which set Sri Lanka 155 to win.

Sri Lanka started their chase well adding 21 in the first three overs, before Nissanka hit a catch to mid-on and then Mishara attempted a second run to Sams running in from deep square-leg. Asalanka looked dangerous, smashing boundaries through the off-side before crunching one over the rope at mid-wicket. Agar came on and the left-hander tried to lap his first ball, only to play it onto the stumps. When Liyange had a mix-up with his partner and was run out, the match was developing a familiar pattern with Sri Lanka 4-71, needing 84 off the last 11 overs.

Thankfully for the visitors that didn't happen as skipper Shanaka, who struck Zampa over long-on for six and Mendis reached his 50 as Sri Lanka needed 41 off the last five overs. The bowlers and fielders protected the boundaries well in the next three overs, but the visitors didn't panic adding 21, which meant they needed 20 for the last two to win. Jhye Richardson bowled well early in the 19th over but Mendis eased the pressure with a lapped four and then two off the last ball to reduce the target to nine off the final over.

Kane Richardson bowled the last over and went for a dot and a two before Shanaka hit one of the shots of the night, pulling him to the longest boundary for six to all but decide the issue. Richardson bowled Shanaka next ball and went off injured, leaving Sams to bowl the last two balls. Sri Lanka only needed one as Karunaratne swung hard and high to leg to complete the win and gain some pride for the Sri Lankans who were passionately cheered on by their large contingent of supporters in Australia. Maxwell was named Man of the Series for his batting and brilliant fielding, but Inglis put a very good case forward having batted very well in his first full Twenty20 series for Australia.

Fifth Twenty20 at the MCG on February 20, 2022 (Floodlit) – Sri Lanka won by 5 wickets

Australia			B	4	6
AJ Finch*	c Kumara b Chameera	8	12		
BR McDermott	c Nissanka b Jayawickrama	3	13		
JP Inglis	c & b Chameera	23	20	3	
GJ Maxwell	c Chameera b Kumara	29	21	2	1
MP Stoinis	c Karunaratne b Kumara	17	10	1	1
MS Wade+	not out	43	27	2	2
DR Sams	c sub (M Gunathilleke)				
	b Karunaratne	18	15	2	
AC Agar	not out	4	2	1	
JA Richardson					
KW Richardson					
A Zampa					
	2 lb, 7 w	9			
6 overs : 2-22	20 overs	6-154			

1-11 (Finch, 3.5), 2-12 (McDermott, 4.5), 3-55 (Inglis, 9.2), 4-79 (Stoinis, 12.2), 5-82 (Maxwell, 12.5), 6-146 (Sams, 18.5)

Bowling	O	M	R	W	wd	nb	Dots
MM Theekshana	4	0	27	0	1		9
L Kumara	4	0	34	2	1		10
P VD Chameera	4	0	30	2	2		9
P AKP Jayawickrama	4	0	29	1			7
C Karunaratne	4	0	32	1	2		6

Sri Lanka			B	4	6
P Nissanka	c Maxwell b K Richardson	13	8	1	
BKG Mendis+	not out	69	58	5	1
RVP K Mishara	run out (Sams -Wade)	1	3		
KIC Asalanka	b Agar	20	9	2	1
K Liyange	run out				
	(K Richardson-Wade)	8	9		
MD Shanaka*	b KW Richardson	35	31		2
C Karunaratne	not out	1	1		
P VD Chameera					
P AKP Jayawickrama					
MM Theekshana					
L Kumara					
	1b, 1lb, 6 w	8			
6 overs : 2-54	19.5 overs	5-155			

1-23 (Nissanka, 3.2), 2-24 (Mishara, 3.5), 3-54 (Asalanka, 6.1), 4-71 (Liyange, 8.6 ov), 5-154 (Shanaka, 19.4 ov)

Bowling	O	M	R	W	wd	nb	Dots
MP Stoinis	2	0	13	0	1		3
DR Sams	2.1	0	22	0	1		3
JA Richardson	4	0	38	0	2		6
KW Richardson	3.4	0	28	2	1		9
AC Agar	4	0	19	1			8
A Zampa	4	0	33	0			4

Toss: Australia. Umpires: DM Koch, SJ Nogajski, SAJ Craig (TV), Ref: DC Boon. Award: BKG Mendis (SL). Crowd: 17,566
K Mendis 50: 43 balls, 3x4 1x6

AUSTRALIA IN PAKISTAN, 2021/22

Australia's first full tour since 1998 was a memorable one in many, many ways. It went off without a hitch security wise which was of major importance, paving the way for future tours by other countries from now on. The Test series win was a fine triumph for Australia and its pace bowling skipper Pat Cummins given the extremely flat nature of the pitches, that made it very difficult to take 20 wickets in each match. It was also a testimony to the efforts of the Australian quick bowlers to succeed using reverse swing as well as Nathan Lyon who managed to take five wickets in the final innings of the third Test, which went a long way to securing the victory.

The performance of opener Usman Khawaja was also a major highlight, as he carried on his fine form from the SCG Ashes Test in January, where he scored a hundred in each innings. All the other batsmen played important innings at various times, but his effort at the top of the order was critical to Australia as they made first innings totals of 459, 9-556 declared and 391 in the three Tests. At times other batsman played their part, but it was Khawaja with ability to play well off the back foot to shine above everyone else in the series.

Of the other batsman, Steve Smith was patient in making three fifties, while the lesser experienced Cameron Green and Alex Carey made important contributions, with Carey doing a great job behind the stumps with the pitches playing low. Marnus Labuschagne and David Warner were slightly below par, while Travis Head was well down on his Ashes form, sometimes in too big a rush to get on with the things.

From a bowling point of view, skipper Cummins led the way and was outstanding, while Mitchell Starc proved he is still very effective in the art of reverse swing, particularly in the final Test where Pakistan lost 7-20 on the third afternoon. Nathan Lyon had to work very hard for his wickets and got his reward in the last innings of the series where he took 5-83. But throughout the series he was reluctant to bowl with a silly-point for much of the time and when he did it was noticeable the change in the attitude of the batsmen. Mitchell Swepson was called upon in the last two Tests and bowled fairly, without ever looking like he was going to run through the opposition.

From a Pakistan point of view their batting was very solid for much of the series, with the highlight being Babar Azam's magnificent 196 in 10 hours which ensured his team saved the second Test. Openers Abdullah Shafique and Imam-ul-Haq both enjoyed the flat surfaces while at 37 years of age, Azhar Ali showed his still a fine player in home conditions. Mohammad Rizwan made a magnificent hundred which helped save the second Test, but Fawad Alam struggled against the extra air speed of the Aussie quicks, being bowled or LBW in three of his four innings.

Pakistan's bowlers didn't trouble the Australians as much as expected, although quicks Shaheen Shah and youngster Nassem Shah did impress at times. Slow left-armer Nauman Ali took six wickets with negative leg side stuff in the first Test but did little after that and off-spinner Sajid Khan struggled, his four wickets coming at a strike-rate in excess of 200.

In the white ball part of the tour, Australia was without Warner, Smith and Maxwell and their first choice pace bowlers and managed to win the first ODI, before going down in the next two to lose the series. After being light on for runs in the Tests, Travis Head played two blistering innings in the first two ODIs, while Ben McDermott took his opportunity with both hands and made his maiden ODI ton in the second game. With the ball Australia lacked penetration, with only Adam Zampa making any real impression against Imam-ul-Haq and Babar Azam who starred with the bat each making two centuries in the series.

Australia finished the tour on a high with a win in the sole Twenty20 game, Nathan Ellis taking four wickets and Aaron Finch scoring some much-needed white ball runs, while Josh Inglis impressed in his one outing on the tour. Finally, a "well done" should be said to the local crowds who turned out in strong numbers to support their team. They appreciated the return of the Australians immensely and with not filling the stadiums to capacity for the Tests, turned out for the white ball segment of the tour, especially when the heat of the day ended, and the floodlights took over. This tour by Australia has undoubtedly helped foster interest in Test cricket in that part of the world, with hopefully the results to be seen in the years to come.

FIRST TEST - RAWALPINDI

Scott Boland made way for Josh Hazlewood who was back for the first time since the Ashes Test at the Gabba. Usman Khawaja kept his spot as opener ahead of Marcus Harris. Unfortunately for Pakistan, both Hasan Ali and Faheem Ashraf were unavailable due to injury.

Day One

Pakistan batted first and Shafique started well, hitting a boundary behind point off the third delivery. In his third over Starc thought he had Imam LBW and Australia reviewed the not-out decision, which was deemed too high. Lyon was on in the eighth over, as a lack of pace and bounce was apparent early on. Shafique clobbered Lyon for six over long-on and next ball was given a life on 21* when Head put down a tough chance at leg-slip. Imam took 41 balls for his first seven runs and then started to unwind, hitting regular boundaries. Australia used a fifth bowler by the 17th over as Head was introduced. Imam on drove him for two fours and then lofted Lyon straight for six and the tempo continued to increase.

Cummins returned for a second spell and when Imam hooked his first ball, he reached his 50 from 81 balls. Shafique continued to play well but then on the verge of lunch, lost concentration as he tried to loft Lyon straight, Cummins taking a well judged catch. Pakistan went in at 1-105 off 35 overs (Imam 57) in a two-and-a-half-hour session, with an hour taken for lunch to allow for Friday prayers.

Lyon and Cummins gave away little in the first half an hour after the break, the shackles broken when Imam lofted the off-spinner back over his head for six. Green finally came on in the 45th over but could find little help in the pitch in a three over spell. Azhar had started slowly but then slog-swept Lyon for six, before pulling Cummins for four. Starc returned just before tea and Imam struck him for two fours in an hour. Labuschagne bowled the last over before tea, with Imam hitting a full toss for four as Pakistan went in on 1-171 from 56 overs, Imam 92, Ahzar 30.

The Australian bowlers kept Imam quiet in the first half hour of the last session, until a cover drive for four off Starc saw him reach his first Test century. The pitch had really flattened out now as Azhar grinded out his 50 in just eight minutes short of three hours. Starc took the new ball at the start of the 83rd over, with Hazlewood bowling the 84th, before giving way to Lyon who bowled three late overs in the day. It was a tedious last period of play as the hosts went for a safety first approach, adding just 10 runs in the eight overs – the second wicket stand worth 140 when stumps were called for the day.

Day Two

Pakistan took their time in the opening session, not showing any inclination to push the score along. Australia were bowling tightly to deep fielding, as they kept the scoring rate down. When Imam was on 143, there was an appeal for caught behind off Lyon, which Carey was quick to say he felt it missed the bat, but had the Aussie's reviewed, he would have been his way. Imam reached his 150 just before lunch, as Pakistan went in on 1-302 (115 overs), Imam 154, Azhar 95.

The 200 stand was raised shortly after the break and then Azhar reached his ton, when he lofted Lyon over mid-on to the rope. Then in the next over, Cummins trapped Imam in front to end an innings that lasted just under nine hours. The crowd were electrified by the appearance of skipper Babar, a straight drive for four off Green saw them in raptures. Lyon returned to bowl his 41st over and Azhar went on the offensive, lofting him straight back over his head for six. Bad balls were few and far between and with a deep field set, the Pakistanis were content to push the singles along, as they reached tea on 2-394 (142 overs) with Azhar 151 and Babar 33.

Labuschagne started up after tea with Azhar sweeping a four and then late cutting for two more in the one over. Both went back into their shells and just after the 100 stand was raised, Babar pushed one to the leg-side and saw Labuschagne run him out at the bowlers end with a direct hit. Shortly after Azhar long innings came to an end when he didn't quite get a reverse sweep out of the middle and was well held at short third man. As conditions got gloomier, Rizwan and Iftikhar added a quick 34, with Babar declaring at 4.30pm, giving his bowlers a 50-minute crack at the visitors.

With the light fading, the roller went over time giving the required seven minutes to the pitch, and as Shaheen was shaping to bowl, the light got worse with the umpires advising that only a spinner could be used. With the break taking seven minutes longer than it should have, Sajid bowled an over which cost five, when the umpires called play for the day, 40 minutes early.

Day Three

Nassem started the bowling for Pakistan, but it was Shaheen who gave the openers some early trouble on the third morning. He beat Warner twice in his first over of the day and then in his next over had a very good shout for LBW against Khawaja, which was deemed a little high. Naseem was bowling with pace and dropped short to Khawaja who played a "no-look" hook for four, as he was done slightly for pace. Warner started to settle, but then with Khawaja on 24, Fawad put down a chance in the gully off Shaheen. From that moment in the series Khawaja rarely looked troubled, while Warner scored strongly through the off-side off Nassem. But the young quick kept running in hard on the flat surface striking Warner on the shoulder with a sharpish bouncer.

Khawaja reached his fifty and then he reverse swept Nauman for four to bring up the 100 stand. Off-spinner Iftikhar came on and Warner smacked him for three fours, as Australia were 0-138 at lunch from 33 overs, Warner 60, Khawaja 70. Pakistan's bowlers kept things tight after the break with Sajid ending the opening stand on 156, when Warner made room to cut and dragged one back on, perhaps having misjudged the length. Labuschagne opened his scoring with a fine off-drive off Naseem to the rope, while Khawaja had been content with picking up singles. The Aussie then opened up lofting and slog sweeping Sajid for fours to move within five of a hundred. After two more singles, Khawaja went for a reverse sweep and gloved the ball to short-leg, finishing up three short of what would have been a ton in his country of birth. There was no further bother for the Aussies in the rest of the session, as they went in at tea on 2-222 (61 overs) with Labuschagne 33, Smith 12.

Labuschagne started to unwind after the break as he dominated the scoring in the final session, adding 36 of the 49 scored in 12 overs, as the bad light returned – play ending at 3.53pm.

Day Four

Heavy overnight rain caused the abandonment of the first session, with play unable to start until 1pm local time. In the third over of the day Smith put Nauman away wide of mid-on for four to see Australia past the follow-on figure of 277. After a string of boundaries Labuschagne moved to 90 and looked set to reach a hundred when he edged one, being well held by slip who moved to his right. Head hit two quick fours of Shaheen, but was in too big a hurry against Sajid, toeing an edge to the keeper as he looked to force one away through the off-side. Smith continued to play patiently, reaching 50 and with Green growing in confidence, the pair was still there at tea, with Australia 4-364, Smith 61 and Green 18.

Green continued to bat positively hitting Nauman for two fours in an over which saw him removed from the attack. But the left-arm spinner returned to the attack a little later, bowling over the wicket pitching most deliveries in a negative fashion pitching well outside leg-stump. The tactic worked as he had both batsmen out sweeping, Green top-edging to short fine-leg, with Smith gloving one to the keeper.

Carey looked confident as he reverse-swept Nauman for two fours in a row, but then Naseem returned and bowled him as the played back to one. Shortly after they were off for bad light, Australia still trailing by 17.

Day Five

With a draw all but certain, Australia's lower order was quickly knocked over on the third morning. Cummins drove one to cover, which gave Nauman his fifth wicket of the innings. Shortly after Starc was beaten by a yorker and when Lyon missed a sweep – Australia all out having lost 3-10 in the morning off just 19 balls.

With 92 overs left in the day, Australia's only hope to win was to bowl Pakistan out inside 50 overs and hope they could chase down the target. Imam and Shafique were largely untroubled, much like the first innings, adding 76 before lunch in 23 overs. The pitch had not deteriorated in any shape or form as the Australians gave little away but could see their efforts were largely a waste of time. Lyon continued to wheel away at one end, while Starc and Hazlewood put their cues in the rack after both having three-over spells after lunch. Imam was first to his fifty with the 100 stand raised shortly after. Shafique reached his 50 as the pair ground on, facing purely spin for the rest of the session.

Smith was given a turn at the crease, with Shafique moving to 95 when he lofted him over wide long-on for six. He went in at tea on 99 but reaching his ton from the first ball he faced after lunch, when he worked Green to long-leg. Imam duly reached his second century of the match – eventually batted for just over 14 hours in the match.

Just before 4.30pm, Khawaja came on to bowl an over, which once completed saw the match come to an end, ending five days of cricket which saw just 14 wickets fall for 1,187 runs on one of most lifeless surfaces a Test match has ever been played on in over 140 years.

First Test at Pindi Ground, Rawalpindi on March 4-8, 2021 – Match Drawn

Pakistan

	First innings		B	M	4	6	Second innings		B	M	4	6
Abdullah Shafique	c Cummins b Lyon	44	105	146	3	1	not out	136	242	313	15	1
Imam-ul-Haq	lbw b Cummins	157	358	531	16	2	not out	111	223	313	7	2
Azhar Ali	c Green b Labuschagne	185	361	536	15	3					
Babar Azam*	run out (Labuschagne)	36	82	116	3						
Moh'd Rizwan+	not out	29	46	65	3						
Iftikhar Ahmed	not out	13	21	30	1						
Fawad Alam											
Nauman Ali											
Sajid Khan											
Shaheen Shah Afridi											
Naseem Shah											

4 b, 7 lb, 1 nb			12		2 lb, 3 nb		5
162 overs, 714 mins			4-476 dec		77 overs, 313 mins		0-252

1-105 (Shafique), 2-313 (Imam), 3-414 (Babar), 4-442 (Azhar Ali)

Bowling	O	M	R	W	wd	nb	O	M	R	W	wd	nb
MA Starc	24	5	71	0			7	1	29	0		
JR Hazlewood	26	6	53	0			5	0	8	0		
NM Lyon	52	5	161	1			26	5	75	0		
PJ Cummins	28	5	62	1			4	0	15	0		1
TM Head	3	0	13	0			13	1	35	0		
CD Green	15	3	47	0		1	4	0	14	0		2
M Labuschagne	12	0	53	1			15	0	56	0		
SPD Smith	2	0	5	0			2	0	15	0		
UT Khawaja							1	0	3	0		

Australia	First innings		B	M	4	6	Bowling	O	M	R	W	wd	nb
UT Khawaja	c Imam b Nauman	97	159	219	15		Sajid Khan	45	9	122	1		
DA Warner	b Sajid	68	114	162	12		Naseem Shah	21	2	89	1		4
M Labuschagne	c Shafique b Shaheen	90	158	190	12		Shaheen Shah Afridi	30	5	88	2		3
SPD Smith	c Rizwan b Nauman	78	196	298	8		Nauman Ali	38.1	9	107	6		1
TM Head	c Rizwan b Nauman	8	7	14	2		Iftikhar Ahmed	3	0	20	0		
CD Green	c Iftikhar b Nauman	48	109	129	4		Imam-ul-Haq	2	0	9	0		
AT Carey +	b Naseem	19	43	69	3		Babar Azam	1	0	5	0		
MA Starc	lbw b Shaheen	13	45	75	1								
PJ Cummins *	c Imam b Nauman	8	11	14	2								
NM Lyon	lbw b Nauman	3	7	13									
JR Hazlewood	not out	0	0	2									
	6 b, 13 lb, 8 nb	27											
	140.1 overs, 597 mins	459											

Fall: 1-156 (Warner), 2-203 (Khawaja), 3-311 (Labuschagne), 4-326 (Head), 5-407 (Green), 6-422 (Smith), 7-444 (Carey), 8-455 (Cummins), 9-459 (Starc), 10-459 (Lyon)

Stumps scores

Day 1	Pakistan (1st inn) 1-245	Imam-ul-Haq 132*, Azhar Ali 64*	Toss: Pakistan
Day 2	Australia (1st inn) 0-5	UT Khawaja 5*, DA Warner 0*	Umpires: Ahsan Raza, Aleem Dar,
Day 3	Australia (1st inn) 2-271	M Labuschagne 69*, SPD Smith 24*	TV: Asif Yaqoob
Day 4	Australia (1st inn) 7-449	MA Starc 12*, PJ Cummins 4*	Award: Imam-ul-Haq (Pak)

SECOND TEST - KARACHI

Australia brought in leg-spinner Mitch Swepson to make his debut, leaving out Josh Hazlewood, while Pakistan replaced Iftikhar Ahmed and Naseem Shah with Faheem Ashraf and Hasan Ali.

Day One

On another flat looking pitch, Australia won an important toss and batted. Shaheen started with a yorker to Warner, before beating him outside off-stump. Hasan bowled a good opening spell, getting both Khawaja and Warner to edge balls, but sadly for the bowler they both fell short of second slip. Both openers then hit their stride with Warner bringing up the 50 stand off Sajid, when he lofted him over long-off for six. Warner couldn't get much strike against the off-spinner but when he had the chance, he lofted him again for six over long-off.

Then came a change in the game as Faheem had Warner caught behind from a ball bowled from around the wicket and then Labuschagne drove Nauman to mid-off and charged off for a single, only to be found short when the throw from Sajid hit the stumps. Lunch came with Australia 2-100 from 27 overs, Khawaja 50, Smith 7.

In the second session, the Aussie pair progressed calmly and were completely at ease, adding 72 runs in 27 overs. Khawaja hit some nice sweeps to move to 86, while Smith took the brunt of a tidy Shaheen spell, at one stage playing out three maidens from him in a row. Half an hour after tea, Khawaja reached his hundred with a single to leg of Sajid, much to his delight as the score pressed on past 200. Both Sajid and Nauman decided to bowl over the wicket and pitch the ball outside leg, with a number of wides being called for negative bowling.

The new ball was taken after 80 overs at 2-235, with little problems for the batsmen until the second last over of the day when Smith edged a back foot drive, low to the left of second slip where Faheem brought off a splendid catch. Lyon came out to do the night-watchman duties, Australia having the better of the day's play.

Day Two

Lyon was at his aggressive best on the second morning, hooking Shaheen for a couple of boundaries as Australia scored quickly in the first 40 minutes of play. The 50 stand was raised before drinks and then shortly after, Lyon was bowled behind his pads getting too far across the crease. As he walked off one could see him ruing another chance to reach a maiden test fifty.

Head cut his third ball for four and after some nervous periods facing Sajid started to find some flow in his inning as he pulled and cut Hasan for boundaries in the one over. Khawaja duly reached his 150 (322 balls) as Australia went to lunch on 4-332 (117 overs) with Khawaja 155, Head 14.

Head looked well set, taking two fours of Sajid, before being adjudged LBW when well forward, looking to work to the on-side. Head reviewed the decision which showed the ball to be just clipping the leg-stump and looked miffed by the outcome. Pakistan were working their way back into the game as Khawaja had his defences breached by Sajid who beat the left-hander with one that turned and hit off-stump.

Green started very carefully, taking 40 balls over his first 10 runs, while Carey was careful early on, until he lofted Sajid back over his head for four. Sajid bowled unchanged since lunch and when Nauman returned, Green smacked him hard and flat for a straight six. Then on the verge of tea, Nauman hit the top of Green's off stump with one from over the wicket, the tall Aussie beaten as he came well forward in defence. Tea saw Australia 7-407, with Carey 26 and Starc 1, with 75 coming in a 29 over session.

The scoring rate limped along after tea, with Carey doing all the scoring as Starc at one stage faced 23 dot balls on the trot. Carey decided to lift the tempo as he lofted Sajid over long-on for six, before reverse-sweeping Nauman in the next over for a single to bring up his 50. A third new ball came about after 163 overs and then we saw Australia really push things forward. Carey drove Shaheen twice for fours and then Starc hooked Hasan to the rope. The spinners then returned for the final hour but Carey took too Sajid and lofted him for four and six over long-on to move closer towards his maiden hundred.

With no sign of a declaration, Australia batted on to bring up their 500 and then with three overs left in the day, Babar decided to give his tired spinners a rest and had a bowl himself. Off the last ball of the over and with Carey on 93, the Aussie keeper went to slog-sweep the Pakistani skipper and was bowled by one that kept a fraction low, the home crowd cheering wildly in delight. The ninth wicket pair carefully played out the last two overs of the day, Australia well on top after two days play.

Day Three

Australia batted on and despite losing Starc to the second ball of the day, Cummins and Swepson added 51 quick runs to take the visitors past 550. Cummins cracked Nauman Ali for sixes over long-on in consecutive overs, before doing the same to Sajid, bringing about a declaration after 35 minutes of play. Pakistan started carefully, with Imam clipping Starc to leg for four, before edging Cummins away safely for another. Cummins changed ends and Shafique drove him straight for four as the partnership started to grow. Conditions were hot once again as Lyon was on in the eighth over and debutant Swepson the 13th. In the next over, Imam played Lyon behind point for a single with Swepson gathering and hitting the stumps with a brilliant throw as Shafique was well short. Runs were hard to come by as Pakistan played carefully to be 1-38 (19 overs) at lunch, with Imam 20, Azhar 4.

Off the second ball after lunch, Azhar lifted the tempo as he lofted Lyon for six back over his head. Later in the same over Imam tried the same approach but mistimed his shot to mid-on. Babar came out and had a scary moment from his fourth ball, when Cummins pitched full and straight, the LBW shout reviewed by the Aussies when it had just hit the bat first. Starc then returned and in consecutive balls in his third over had Azhar sharply held at second slip before trapping Fawad with a big inducking yorker. Rizwan played and missed at the hat-trick ball and then had some luck when on four when he edged Cummins to Smith's left at slip, where he grassed the chance. It cost little as Rizwan was caught behind in the next over and then Green got in on the act, trapping Faheem in front. Just before tea Sajid played at one from Starc, it was taken by Carey who was the only one to appeal, he convinced his captain to review and technology showed there was an edge, much to the delight of his teammates. Pakistan had lost six wickets in the session to be 7-100 at tea, with Babar 29 and Hasan 0.

Apart from the drop by Smith, Australia's fielding had been brilliant with three direct hits in the field and in the second over after tea it was to become four as Babar pushed Starc to cover, took off for a single only to watch Labuschagne hit the stumps at the strikers end to run out Hasan. Babar's good knock came to an end when he went to loft Swepson down the ground, only to miscue to mid-off, giving the leg spinner his first Test wicket. Last pair Nauman and Shaheen found the boundary regularly to add a useful 30 for the last wicket, before Shaheen went for a sweep and was leg before. Despite leading by 408, Australia opted to bat again rather than enforce the follow-on, understandable given the heat of the day and wanting the bowl at the hosts when the pitch had deteriorated further.

Australia had 70 minutes to bat, Warner gave a catch to gully but Khawaja and Labuschagne added 61 to give Australia a lead of 489 at Stumps.

Day Four

Australia batted on for a short time, adding 16 before Labuschagne chopped a pull on, setting Pakistan 506 to win in 172 overs. Caution was the name of the game for their openers as they played out four maidens to start. Swepson came on in the fifth over and then in the sixth, Lyon had Imam leg before when well forward, with one that came on with the arm. Careful defence was the order of the day, with not a boundary to be seen as Pakistan went to lunch on 1-18 (21 overs), Shafique 14, Azhar 4.

In the second over after lunch, Azhar took evasive action at a short ball that didn't get up from Green and was adjudged LBW, replays showing he got a bit of glove on the ball. Babar looked good once again as he attempted to rebuild the innings, but should have lost Shafique on 20* when he edged a drive to Smith who dropped a straight-forward chance at slip. Had the catch been taken Pakistan would have been 3-38 and looking at a four-day defeat. The Pakistan opener put this behind him and carried on as he and his skipper slowly got on top of the bowling, the stand reaching 50 when Babar forced Lyon though the covers for four. Shafique took up the challenge to Lyon, lofting him over long-on for six as the runs started to flow. Starc and Cummins both returned for brief spells before tea, but the reverse swing wasn't forthcoming, as the hosts went in at the break on 2-104 (48 overs), Shafique 44, Babar 47.

Pakistan made careful progress after tea, with Babar reaching his 50 (83 balls, 7 fours) in the second over after the break, before Shafique eased Lyon away behind point for three to bring up his 50 (153 balls, 228 minutes) as the partnership went past 100. Australia then bowled Lyon and Swepson in tandem for a period, but despite bowling well couldn't penetrate either of the batsmen's defences. The excitement levels in the crowd continued to grow as Babar moved towards his hundred, while Shafique maintained his ultra-careful approach, only scoring the odd single. Babar reached 99* then top edged a sweep from Swepson to reach his hundred, the sixth of his Test career. The new ball was taken by Cummins with two overs to go in the day before Lyon bowled the last – the Aussies going wicket-less in the final session while Pakistan added 88 in 34 overs – the hosts needing 314 on the final day, Australia wanting eight wickets.

Day Five

With the new ball just two overs old, the Aussie quicks started at the bowling crease with Starc twice beating the edge of Babar in his third over. Swepson was then on and started with two full-tosses, Babar smashing them both to the on-side rope. Saving rather than winning was on the mind of the Pakistanis as the 200 stand was raised, as just 32 came in the opening hour of 14 overs, the hosts 2-224 at drinks, with Shafique 81, Babar 121. Lyon had been toiling away superbly from the University end and in the 100th over, finally brought in a silly-point to bring some extra pressure on the batsmen. Shafique advanced and off-drove Swepson for four to reach 91 and then just before lunch, Cummins returned for a two-over burst. Shafique cut him away for four to reach 96 but in the quick's next over, aimed a drive and edged to first slip, where this time Smith held the chance. In the over before lunch Fawad poked Starc away for a single to avoid getting a king pair, Pakistan adding 62 runs in the session to be 3-254 at lunch, Babar 133, Fawad 3, still needing 252 to win.

Cummins and Starc threw everything at the two batsmen after lunch. Babar reached his 150 with a single to leg off Lyon but then the Aussie skipper got Fawad to edge behind in the fifth over of his spell, to make Pakistan 4-277. Babar was defending hard against Lyon and in a rare attacking moment, on-drove him to the rope. Next ball came a moment of drama as he was hit on the pad coming well forward, the LBW appeal denied by Umpire Dar. A review was called for with technology showing it would have hit just under half of the leg-stump, much to the annoyance of the Aussies. Shortly after Swepson could have had Babar out twice in two balls on 161*, Head unable to hold onto a sharp one-handed chance at silly-point, which was followed by Labuschagne putting him down in a similar fashion at short-leg. In Swepson's next over Rizwan charged at him and padded one away, again the Aussies reviewed, the ball was judged to be striking leg-stump, but the batsman was past the 3m mark, which annulled that fact. Again, luck was not favouring the visitors. Swepson was bowling one of his best spells of the match as he beat both batsmen with leg-breaks in the same over, Pakistan were glad to reach tea on 4-310, Babar 168 and Rizwan 14 – with 36 overs left and having just lost two wickets in the day.

With 196 needed at 5.44 an over in the final session of the match, Rizwan hit two fours to leg off Swepson in the first over after tea and in the next Babar advanced and lofted Lyon's second ball for six – with 20 coming from the two overs. The Aussie spinners tightened things up with just eight runs coming from the next four overs, which meant 168 were needed off the last 30. Babar was starting to look tired and was defending hard only scoring the odd single, while Rizwan was looking to tick things over still and brought up a fine fifty in an over off Cummins that cost nine. The 100 stand was raised but only singles were being scored as Lyon and Swepson were giving little away. At the start of the last hour, Pakistan were 4-382 (Babar 191, Rizwan 61) with 15 overs left, the hosts needing an unlikely 124.

After a maiden from Green, Swepson rolled out his 50th over which went for nine, but then Lyon turned the game on its head, as an exhausted Babar prodded a catch to short-leg and then next ball, Faheem edged one to slip. With 12 overs left, Australia took the third new ball and could sense victory as they tried to hunt down four more wickets. A weary Starc bowled just the one over and was replaced by an equally tired Cummins who was struck for two fours in an over. With nine overs to survive, it was going to be up to the spinners to win the game for Australia.

Rizwan continued to play his shots and Sajid followed suit as he struck two in an over from Lyon before edging him to slip, Pakistan now seven down with still eight overs left. The next two were carefully played out and then Rizwan swung a Swepson full-toss for six as a hundred beckoned. Nauman blocked a Lyon maiden, which left Australia needing three wickets in four overs. Swepson bowled the next and after Rizwan hit a couple of twos, he drove one to short cover where Khawaja, for some reason still wearing his helmet, put down the low chance.

Labuschagne was finally given a long overdue bowl in the 170th over and managed to get the ball to leap out the footmarks and race away for four byes. The second last over was given to Lyon (his 55th of the innings) and after Rizwan hit two fours, he completed a magnificent hundred with a single into the off-side the game all but safe. Rizwan hit Swepson to leg for a boundary and with two balls left and three wickets in hand the match was called, Pakistan hanging on for a historic draw.

Second Test at the National Stadium, Karachi on March 12-16, 2021 – Match Drawn

Australia	First innings		B	M	4	6	Second innings		B	M	4	6
DA Warner	c Rizwan b Faheem	36	48	80	3	2	2 c Fawad b Hasan	7	16	22		
UT Khawaja	b Sajid	160	369	548	15	1	1 not out	44	70	96	4	
M Labuschagne	run out (Sajid)	0	9	14			b Shaheen	44	49	73	5	1
SPD Smith	c Faheem b Hasan	72	214	278	7							
NM Lyon	b Faheem	38	62	81	5							
TM Head	lbw b Sajid	23	48	57	5							
CD Green	b Nauman	28	73	100	2	1						
AT Carey +	b Babar	93	159	186	7	2						
MA Starc	c Azhar b Shaheen	28	97	133	2							
PJ Cummins *	not out	34	36	40	2	3						
MJ Swepson	not out	15	26	32	1							
	10 b, 7 lb, 7 nb, 5 w	29					2 lb	2				
	189 overs, 676 mins	9-556	dec				22.3 overs, 96 mins	2-97	dec			

1-82 (Warner), 2-91 (Labuschagne), 3-250 (Smith), 4-304 (Lyon),
5-347 (Head), 6-360 (Khawaja), 7-405 (Green), 8-503 (Carey),
9-505 (Starc)

1-20 (Warner), 2-97 (Labuschagne)

Bowling	O	M	R	W	wd	nb		O	M	R	W	wd	nb
Shaheen Shah Afridi	32	8	95	1		4		6.3	0	21	1		
Hasan Ali	25	7	71	1		2		7	0	23	1		
Faheem Ashraf	21	4	55	2				3	0	13	0		
Sajid Khan	57	10	167	2	3			5	0	31	0		
Nauman Ali	48	6	134	1	2			1	0	7	0		
Babar Azam	4	0	7	1									
Azhar Ali	2	0	10	0	1								

Pakistan	First innings	B	M	4	6	Second innings		B	M	4	6
Abdullah Shafique	run out (Swepson)	13	36	58	1	c Smith b Cummins	96	304	463	6	1
Imam-ul-Haq	c Cummins b Lyon	20	64	80	3	lbw b Lyon	1	18	24		
Azhar Ali	c Green b Starc	14	37	53	1	lbw b Green	6	54	62		
Babar Azam *	c Khawaja b Swepson	36	79	152	3	c Labuschagne b Lyon	196	426	602	21	1
Fawad Alam	lbw b Starc	0	1	2		c Carey b Cummins	9	27	51		
Moh Rizwan +	c Carey b Cummins	6	13	34		not out	104	177	235	11	1
Fahim Ashraf	lbw b Green	4	7	6	1	c Smith b Lyon	0	1	2		
Sajid Khan	c Carey b Starc	5	16	28	1	c Smith b Lyon	9	10	20	2	
Hasan Ali	run out (Labuschagne)	0	8	20		not out	0	18	36		
Nauman Ali	not out	20	35	52	4						
Shaheen Shah Afridi	lbw b Swepson	19	25	27	3	1					
	5 b, 3 lb, 3 nb	11				8 b, 2 lb, 5 nb, 7 w	22				
	53 overs, 251 mins	148				171.4 overs, 771 mins	7-443				

1-26 (Shafique), 2-45 (Imam-ul-Haq), 3-60 (Azhar), 4-60 (Fawad),
5-76 (Rizwan), 6-81 (Faheem), 7-97 (Sajid), 8-102 (Hasan),
9-118 (Babar), 10-148 (Shaheen)

1-2 (Imam-ul-Haq), 2-21 (Azhar), 3-249 (Shafique),
4-277 (Fawad), 5-392 (Babar), 6-392 (Faheem),
7-414 (Sajid)

Bowling	O	M	R	W	wd	nb		O	M	R	W	wd	nb
MA Starc	13	5	29	3		2		21	6	58	0	1	1
PJ Cummins	13	2	39	1				26	6	75	2		1
NM Lyon	9	5	13	1				55	20	112	4		
MJ Swepson	9	1	32	2				53.4	8	156	0	4	
CD Green	8	1	23	1		1		15	4	32	1	2	3
M Labuschagne	1	0	4	0				1	1	0	0		

Stumps scores

Day 1:	Australia 1st inns	3-251	UT Khawaja 127*, NM Lyon 0*
Day 2:	Australia 1st inns	8-505	MA Starc 28*, PJ Cummins 0*
Day 3:	Australia 2nd inns	1-81	UT Khawaja 35*, M Labuschagne 37*
Day 4	Pakistan 2nd inns	2-192	Abdullah Shafique 71*, Babar Azam 102*

Toss: Australia
Umpires: Ahsan Raza, Aleem Dar,
TV: Rashid Riaz, Ref: RS Madugalle.
Award: Babar Azam (Pak)

THIRD TEST - LAHORE

Australia elected to keep the same eleven that drew the second Test, while Pakistan recalled young quick Naseem Shah for Faheem Ashraf. The pitch had slightly more grass on it that the Karachi deck, but still appeared as though it would a very good batting surface. Australia won the toss and without hesitating, decided to bat first.

Day One

As in Karachi, the match began in hot conditions, Warner hitting the first four of the match off an inside edge just past the stumps off Hasan. Next over he met his demise when he played back and was trapped in front, beaten by some movement back into him. Then two balls later Labuschagne aimed a cover drive at a wide one, edging to the 'keeper to leave Australia 2-8 in the third over.

Smith started well with some nice drives to the boundary while Khawaja was very content on defence, having little strike in the first hour as Australia reached 2-34 from 12 overs, Khawaja 6, Smith 19. Naseem had started impressively from the College end and in his first over after drinks, almost yorked Khawaja. Nauman Ali came on in the 16th over and should have had success, as second ball Khawaja edged one through the legs of Babar at slip, the Pakistan skipper not staying lower enough in that position to take the catch. Then next ball, Smith advanced and smashed it back at Nauman, only for him to drop the chance, the ball hitting him on the fat part of his right thumb. In the left-arm spinner's next over he went for 12 as Smith hit a lofted straight drive for four and later in the over Khawaja slog swept him to leg for six. Nassem returned for a spell before lunch from the Pavilion end and did well, Australia lunching on 2-70 (24 overs) with Khawaja 31, Smith 28.

The third wicket stand continued on after lunch, until Khawaja got things moving with off-side fours off Shaheen and Sajid. He brought up a patient 50 with a cut off Sajid off 105 balls in just shy of three hours. Naseem and Sajid were bowling tightly in tandem, a restrained and careful Smith brought up his 50, twenty minutes before tea off 154 balls. Pakistan were unable to take a wicket in the session, Australia heading in at tea on 2-145 (54 overs), Khawaja 69, Smith 58.

The game got a move on after tea as Naseem struck in his first over after the break, getting one to reverse swing in to Smith, trapping him plumb in front – the partnership ending on 138. Head had some iffy moments to start, lucky not to edge on behind from the first ball he faced from Sajid. When Head was on seven, he had two bits of great luck in the one over as he nearly played on and then two balls later drove one hard back to the off-spinner, who put down his second caught and bowled for the day. Then suddenly Head looked much better as he forced Sajid for two confident looking boundaries through the off-side in the one over. At the other end Khawaja was quietly accumulating but when he was nine short of his ton, he looked to work one to leg of Sajid and was superbly held by the Pakistan skipper diving to his left at slip.

Australia moved past 200 and then Naseem came back on, Head flashing hard at his first ball, edging it away through a gap in the slips for four. In the next over the quick went around the wicket and found the edged of Head's bat, Rizwan taking a good low catch. Carey joined Green both looked assured as Pakistan took the new ball (5-211 after 83 overs) but both played out time, in what an entertaining opening day.

Day Two

The runs flowed early for Green and Carey as they looked to put Australia in a strong position. After 10 runs from the first four overs, Carey hit a cover drive off Naseem for four and then Green punched Shaheen through point to the rope. The 50 stand was raised with another sweet Carey cover driven four and then the Aussie keeper survived a bizarre incident. With Hasan bowling from around the wicket, Carey played at a yorker and missed the ball going through to the keeper. The Pakistanis appealed and Umpire Dar decided Carey was out LBW. Carey reviewed immediately and replays showed no contact with pad or boot, but that the ball had just clipped the stumps on the way through to the keeper.

The spinners returned with runs hard to come by, until Carey gained a five off Sajid, thanks to four overthrows by Hasan. In the off-spinners next over, Carey reverse swept him for four, before lofting one over mid-on for another before bringing up his 50 with a quick single to wide mid-off. The 100 stand was raised and with Green content to take singles he too reached his 50 as the score at lunch was 5-320 (116 overs), Green 56 and Carey 60, the partnership now worth 114.

Australia lifted the tempo after lunch as both batsmen found the boundary, then Carey went to hit Nauman to leg, missed and was LBW. Nassem returned and in his second over found some reverse inswing and had Green bowled through the gate. The lower order all played their shots, with Australia all out within 25 minutes of tea for 391.

With the temperature still 35 degrees, Pakistan needed a good start and the openers got to 20 before Imam was plumb in front to Cummins from the first ball of his second spell. Shafique was proving hard to move and with Azhar lofted Lyon for six over long-on, Pakistan were on the move. Swepson came on and after his first three overs went for just three runs, Shafique picked him off with some neatly struck boundaries. Late in the day Cummins thought he had Azhar LBW on 25, with the review lost. Pakistan worked their way to stumps without losing another wicket, trailing by 301.

Day Three

Azhar hit two fours in Green's first over of the day, one a leg-glance, the other from an edge along the ground between the keeper and slip. Shafique then steered Cummins behind point for four and later reached his 50 with an off-drive for two off Starc. Next ball the Aussies thought they had Shafique out LBW but lost the review which showed the ball to going well down leg-side. The 100 partnership was raised and then Azhar reached his 50 in just short of three hours. It was tight hard cricket, with little being given away in the field. Lyon then changed tack and employed a silly-point, but the Pakistani pair stayed in to reach 1-159 at lunch, Shafique 75, Azhar 63.

Australia finally achieved their first wicket for the day when in the fifth over after lunch, Shafique was given out caught behind off Lyon after the not out decision was successfully over-ruled, keeper Carey the driving force behind the review. Much to the delight of the crowd Babar entered the scene and looked well at home on the benign batting pitch. Lyon continued his long spell from the College end and was cracked over long-on for six by the Pakistani skipper. An edged four by Babar off Lyon brought up the 200 and when the home skipper struck consecutive fours off the first over of a new Cummins spell with the new ball, Pakistan were back on top in the game. But the Aussie skipper stuck to the task and when Azhar drove one back at him he snared the chance. Just before tea Australia ran out reviews when they challenged an LBW not out decision versus Fawad and lost, Pakistan heading in on 3-227 with Babar 42, Fawad 5.

Green, Lyon and then Swepson kept the run rate down in the first hour after the break. Babar reached his 50 but then Starc came back and with his third ball, hit Fawad's off-stump with a length ball that swung back in. Shortly after Rizwan bowled from around the wicket by Starc and then Cummins bowled Sajid from an inside edge. The end of the innings came quickly as Nauman was trapped in front, Hasan edged low to first slip and Naseem was yorked, Pakistan losing 7-20 off 62 balls to be bowled out 123 in arrears. Australia added 11 in the three overs before stumps, to be well on top with two days to play.

Day Four

Warner was on the move early as he struck Shaheen for three fours in his opening over of the morning. He was then fortunate in the next over on 16 when he played at one from Hasan, got a touch but neither the bowlers nor fielders appealed. Khawaja had edged a couple of fours and then on 31 was comprehensively bowled by Nassem, but it was found that he had overstepped the front line. Warner greeted the introduction of Nauman by lofting him to leg for six, before reaching his 50 the ball after. The stand reached 96 when Shaheen knocked Warner's off-stump out of the ground, the batsman shaking hands with the bowler as he walked off – as the good relations between both teams continued. Being on a pair, Labuschagne had some nervous moments, including nearly being bowled by Nauman, Australia going into lunch on 1-97, a lead of 220.

Labuschagne got off the mark with a reverse sweep for four off Sajid, while Khawaja reached his 50 hitting Shaheen away behind point for a couple. Labuschagne should have been caught at short third man on 12 by Nauman, who leapt high but failed to hang onto a reverse sweep off Sajid. The runs continued to flow until Labuschagne top edged a hard-hit sweep to deep square-leg. Hasan returned and Khawaja took him on, hitting three fours in his first over of a new spell. The lead passed 300 and then on 98 Khawaja pushed one behind point to bring up his hundred courtesy of a misfield. Tea was taken with Australia 2-202, leading by 325.

In the third over after tea, Smith edged behind as Australia batted for just one more over, as Head slog swept a six and crunched an off-side four to take Australia to a lead of 350. With 31 overs left in the day the Pakistani openers started with great care, scoring just 12 runs in the opening seven overs. Lyon was on in the sixth and offered a full toss in his second over, which was on-driven for four. On 13, Shafique was given out caught behind off Lyon, but he reviewed and the decision was overturned. Shortly after he lofted Swepson over his head for six as he and Imam ticked the score over nicely in the closing period of play. Labuschagne came on to bowl the last over of the day, Shafique (23*) edged the second last ball low to Smith's right at slip, where the chance was put down. So, the day ended with openers still at the crease, needing 278 more to win.

Day Five

In the fourth over of the morning, Australia had an early breakthrough as Green found the edge of Shafique's defensive stroke. Imam reached his 50 off Starc and in the same over Azhar hit two fours as Pakistan reached 100 being still one down. Azhar then met his end controversially as he aimed a sweep at Lyon which rebounded to slip. Technology showed the smallest murmur on "snicko" much to the disgust of the veteran who felt he had missed the ball. Babar opened his scoring with an imperious straight drive for four, much to the delight of the crowd who were riding every moment. Runs were quietly accumulated, while Lyon was starting to get some bounce and turn out of the footmarks, troubling both batsman with three close catchers around the bat. When lunch was taken, Pakistan was 2-136 (Imam 66, Babar 19) needing 215 more off 57 overs.

Imam's fine resistance came to an end in Lyon's first over after lunch, when he edged one via the pad to silly point. Fawad swept his second ball for four and after surviving a spell from Starc, Cummins returned to have him LBW from around the wicket. In the Aussie skipper's next over, he yorked Rizwan on his left toe, but despite appearing well outside off-stump and playing a shot, Umpire Dar gave him LBW. Pakistan had one review left and it to the amazement of all and sundry that he didn't use it as replays confirmed he would have been allowed to stay at the crease.

Sajid came in and showed plenty of resistance as he and Babar proceeded to bat towards tea. In the last over, the Pakistani skipper went for a big hit to deep square-leg with Head diving forward in the deep, unable to bring off the catch. With a session left, Pakistan was 5-190 (Babar 46, Sajid 8) with the new ball available and Australia needing five wickets to win.

Starc took the new ball after two deliveries and Sajid hit him powerfully away for two fours. Babar edged the last ball for four with 14 coming off the over. Then came the critical breakthrough as in Lyon's second over with the new ball, he found the edge of Babar's bat, the catch taken by Smith in front of his left foot at slip. In the next over, Sajid clipped one to mid-wicket and after a lofted straight six and reverse swept four, Hasan was bowled aiming a sweep, after the ball hit the back off his bat on the downswing. Shaheen then smashed a sweep to deep square-leg with Swepson diving to his left to bring off a fine catch. Cummins returned and fittingly spreadeagled Naseem's stumps to end the match and the series in Australia's favour. The Australian skipper was Man of the match for his match figures of 8-79, which Usman Khawaja was Man of the series for his outstanding batting at the top of the order.

Third Test at Lahore Stadium on March 21-25, 2021 – Australia won by 115 runs

Australia	First innings		B	M	4	6		Second innings		B	M	4	6
DA Warner	lbw b Shaheen	7	13	12	1		2	b Shaheen	51	91	122	6	1
UT Khawaja	c Babar b Sajid	91	219	325	9	1	1	not out	104	178	272	8	
M Labuschagne	c Rizwan b Shaheen	0	2	3				c Sajid b Nauman	36	58	87	6	
SPD Smith	lbw b Naseem	59	169	229	6			c Rizwan b Naseem	17	27	52	1	
TM Head	c Rizwan b Naseem	26	70	106	4			not out	11	7	7	1	1
CD Green	b Naseem	79	163	222	9								
AT Carey+	lbw b Nauman	67	105	172	7								
MA Starc	c Nauman b Shaheen	13	33	52	2								
PJ Cummins*	not out	11	25	51	1								
NM Lyon	b Naseem	4	3	5	1								
MJ Swepson	b Shaheen	9	7	14	2								
	13 b, 4 lb, 8 nb	25						5 b, 2 lb, 1 nb	8				
	133.3 overs, 601 mins	391						60 overs, 272 mins	3-227 dec				

1-8 (Warner), 2-8 (Labuschagne), 3-146 (Smith), 4-187 (Khawaja), 5-206 (Head), 6-341 (Carey), 7-353 (Green), 8-369 (Starc), 9-374 (Lyon), 10-391 (Swepson)

1-96 (Warner), 2-161 (Labuschagne), 3-216 (Smith)

Bowling	O	M	R	W	wd	nb		O	M	R	W	wd	nb
Shaheen Shah Afridi	24.3	3	79	4				11	2	45	1		
Hasan Ali	20	5	61	0		3		11	3	37	0		
Naseem Shah	31	13	58	4		2		12	3	23	1	1	
Nauman Ali	24	4	77	1		3		10	0	55	1		
Sajid Khan	33	4	97	1				16	1	60	0		
Babar Azam	1	0	2	0									

Pakistan	First innings		B	M	4	6		Second innings		B	M	4	6
Abdullah Shafique	c Carey b Lyon	81	228	317	11			c Carey b Green	27	80	133	3	1
Imam-ul-Haq	lbw b Cummins	11	41	53	2			c Labuschagne b Lyon	70	199	272	5	
Azhar Ali	c & b Cummins	78	208	329	7	1		c Smith b Lyon	17	47	75	2	
Babar Azam *	lbw b Starc	67	131	217	6	1		c Smith b Lyon	55	104	164	6	
Fawad Alam	b Starc	13	56	86	1			lbw b Cummins	11	20	35	1	
Moh Rizwan +	b Starc	1	14	23				lbw b Cummins	0	6	10		
Sajid Khan	b Cummins	6	17	18	1			c Khawaja b Starc	21	47	54	4	
Nauman Ali	lbw b Cummins	0	3	10				not out	1	20	44		
Hasan Ali	c Smith b Cummins	0	4	3				b Lyon	13	17	19	1	1
Shaheen Shah Afridi	not out	0	1	8				c Swepson b Lyon	5	7	8	1	
Naseem Shah	b Starc	0	3	4				b Cummins	1	7	11		
	5 b, 6 nb	11						8 b, 4 lb, 1 nb, 1 w	14				
	116.4 overs, 545 mins	268						92.1 overs, 419 mins	235				

1-20 (Imam), 2-170 (Shafique), 3-214 (Azhar), 4-248 (Fawad), 5-256 (Rizwan), 6-264 (Sajid), 7-268 (Nauman), 8-268 (Hasan), 9-268 (Babar), 10-268 (Naseem)

1-77 (Shafique), 2-105 (Azhar), 3-142 (Imam), 4-165 (Fawad), 5-167 (Rizwan), 6-213 (Babar), 7-213 (Sajid), 8-226 (Hasan), 9-232 (Shaheen),\ 10-235 (Naseem)

Bowling	O	M	R	W	wd	nb		O	M	R	W	wd	nb
MA Starc	20.4	6	33	4				17	6	53	1		
PJ Cummins	24	8	56	5		3		15.1	6	23	3		
CD Green	14	4	37	0		2		11	4	18	1	1	1
NM Lyon	40	10	95	1				37	8	83	5		
MJ Swepson	18	2	42	0		1		10	1	36	0		
M Labuschagne								2	0	10	0		

Stumps scores:
Day 1: Australia 1st inns 5-232 CD Green 20*, AT Carey 8*
Day 2: Pakistan 1st inns 1-90 Abdullah Shafique 45*, Azhar Ali 30*
Day 3: Australia 2nd inns 0-11 UT Khawaja 7*, DA Warner 4*
Day 4: Pakistan 2nd inns 0-73 Abdullah Shafique 27*, Imam-ul-Haq 42*

Toss: Australia
Umpires: Ahsan Raza, Aleem Dar, TV: Asif Yaqoob
Award: PJ Cummins.
Series: UT Khawaja

TEST AVERAGES
AUSTRALIA

Batting & Fielding	M	Inn	NO	Runs	HS	Avge	100	50	S/Rate	Ct	St
UT Khawaja	3	5	2	496	160	165.33	2	2	49.84	2	-
AT Carey	3	3	0	179	93	59.66	0	2	58.30	5	0
SPD Smith	3	4	0	226	78	56.50	0	3	37.29	6	-
PJ Cummins	3	3	2	53	34*	53.00	0	0	73.61	3	-
CD Green	3	3	0	155	79	51.66	0	1	44.92	2	-
M Labuschagne	3	5	0	170	90	34.00	0	1	61.59	2	-
DA Warner	3	5	0	169	68	33.80	0	2	59.92	0	-
MJ Swepson	2	2	1	24	15*	24.00	0	0	72.72	1	-
TM Head	3	4	1	68	26	22.66	0	0	51.51	0	-
MA Starc	3	3	0	54	28	18.00	0	0	30.85	0	-
NM Lyon	3	3	0	45	38	15.00	0	0	62.50	0	-
JR Hazlewood	1	1	1	0	0*	-	0	0	-	0	-

Bowling	M	Overs	Mdns	Runs	Wkts	Avge	Best	5i	10m	Econ	SR
PJ Cummins	3	110.1	27	270	12	22.50	5-56	1	0	2.45	55.0
MA Starc	3	102.4	29	273	8	34.12	4-33	0	0	2.65	77.0
NM Lyon	3	219	53	539	12	44.91	5-83	1	0	2.46	109.5
CD Green	3	67	16	171	3	57.00	1-18	0	0	2.55	134.0
M Labuschagne	3	31	1	123	1	123.00	1-53	0	0	3.96	186.0
MJ Swepson	2	90.4	12	266	2	133.00	2-32	0	0	2.93	272.0

Also bowled: JR Hazlewood 31-6-61-0, TM Head 16-1-48-0, UT Khawaja 1-0-3-0, SPD Smith 4-0-20-0.

PAKISTAN

Batting & Fielding	M	Inn	NO	Runs	HS	Avge	100	50	S/Rate	Ct	St
Abdullah Shafique	3	6	1	397	136*	79.40	1	2	39.85	1	-
Babar Azam	3	5	0	390	196	78.00	1	2	47.50	1	-
Imam-ul-Haq	3	6	1	370	157	74.00	2	1	40.97	2	-
Azhar Ali	3	5	0	300	185	60.00	1	1	42.43	1	-
Mohammad Rizwan	3	5	2	140	104*	46.66	1	0	54.68	6	0
Nauman Ali	3	4	3	21	20*	21.00	0	0	27.63	1	-
Shaheen Shah Afridi	3	3	1	24	19	12.00	0	0	72.72	0	-
Sajid Khan	3	4	0	41	21	10.25	0	0	45.55	1	-
Fawad Alam	3	4	0	33	13	8.25	0	0	31.73	1	-
Hasan Ali	2	3	0	13	13	4.33	0	0	44.82	0	-
Faheem Ashraf	1	2	0	4	4	2.00	0	0	50.00	1	-
Naseem Shah	2	2	0	1	1	0.50	0	0	10.00	0	-
Iftikhar Ahmed	1	1	1	13	13*	-	0	0	61.90	1	-

Bowling	M	Overs	Mdns	Runs	Wkts	Avge	Best	5i	10m	Econ	SR
Babar Azam	3	6	0	14	1	14.00	1-7	0	0	2.33	36.0
Naseem Shah	2	64	18	170	6	28.33	4-58	0	0	2.65	64.0
Faheem Ashraf	1	24	4	68	2	34.00	2-55	0	0	2.83	72.0
Shaheen Shah Afridi	3	104	18	328	9	36.44	4-79	0	0	3.15	69.3
Nauman Ali	3	121.1	19	380	9	42.22	6-107	1	0	3.13	80.7
Hasan Ali	2	63	15	192	2	96.00	1-23	0	0	3.04	189.0
Sajid Khan	3	156	24	477	4	119.25	2-167	0	0	3.05	234.0

Also bowled: Iftikhar Ahmed 3-0-20-0, Azhar Ali 2-0-10-0, Imam-ul-Haq 2-0-9-0.

ONE-DAY INTERNATIONALS
FIRST MATCH – LAHORE

With David Warner out of the ODI series, Travis Head came in at the top of the order and made the most of the opportunity as he slammed the Pakistani bowlers to all part in the opening overs. In the extreme heat Australia was 60 after seven over with Head scoring 48 of them, hitting eight fours and a hooked six off Wasim. This allowed Finch to take his time, his first 11 runs taking 26 balls without a boundary. Zahid came in for a battering as Finch lofted him over long-on for six and Head did the same twice in two overs as Australia reached 100 in the 14th over, before Finch was caught behind. McDermott came in and provided further good support for Head, who reached his second ODI in just the 25th over. Two balls later Head advanced and lofted a catch to long-off, which left Australia 2-171 at the midway point.

McDermott reached fifty in good style but was then run out after thinking a third run was possible. Pakistan's bowlers kept Australia to just 36 in overs 31-40 and with Labuschagne caught at long-on and Carey bowled leg-stump reverse sweeping, the visitors were 5-232 with ten overs to go. Stoinis was slow early with just three singles from his first 17 balls but added 47 with Green until he was bowled missing a pull-shot. Green and Abbott hit hard as 38 came off the last four overs, Australia reaching 313 which at one stage they seemed set for more.

Fakhar started well hitting two of his first three balls for four, but in the fifth over he mistimed a drive to mid-off. Babar joined Imam and the pair started to take the game away from Australia. Zampa was on in the sixth over and was keeping things tight, being well supported by some very good ground fielding. Stoinis bowled a tidy three over spell but didn't grab a wicket as Babar reached his fifty in the 23rd over. Swepson returned and had Babar leg trying to sweep and then Head had Shakeel caught at cover, as things started to turn Australia's way. When Rizwan aimed a sweep and was brilliantly caught down leg-side by Carey, Australia looked in charge and set for victory.

However, Imam was still in the way and when he launched Head and Swepson for leg-side sixes, Pakistan still had a chance. The left-handed opener reached his ton but in the next over Ellis returned and settled the issue when he bowled Imam as he tried to ease one away to third-man. Pakistan lost their last 5-21 off 39 balls as the tail crumbled to the spin of Zampa, Australia running out easy winners.

First ODI at Lahore (day/night) on March 29, 2022 – Australia won by 88 runs

Australia			B	M	4	6	Pakistan			B	M	4	6
TM Head*	c Khushdil b Iftikhar	101	72	106	12	3	Fakhar Zaman	c Head b Abbott	18	18	19	3	
AJ Finch*	c Rizwan b Zahid	23	36	64	1		Imam-ul-Haq	b Ellis	103	96	178	6	3
BR McDermott	run out (Wasim-Rizwan)	55	70	76	4		Babar Azam*	lbw b Swepson	57	72	89	6	
M Labuschagne	c Shakil b Khushdil	25	35	51	1		Saud Shakil	c Labuschagne b Head	3	8	10		
MP Stoinis	b Rauf	26	42	52		1	M Rizwan+	c Carey b Zampa	10	18	18		
AT Carey+	b Zahid	4	4	7			Iftikhar Ahmed	c Abbott b Head	2	9	11		
CD Green	not out	40	30	46	3	1	Khushdil Shah	c Carey b Zampa	19	22	47	1	
SA Abbott	b Rauf	14	9	11	2		Hasan Ali	b Zampa	2	9	11		
NT Ellis	not out	3	2	6			M Wasim	b Zampa	0	1	1		
A Zampa							Haris Rauf	c Green b Swepson	7	17	23	1	
MJ Swepson							Zahid Mahmood	not out	0	3	14		
	9 lb, 13 w	22						1 nb, 3 w	4				
	10 overs: 0-72	50 overs, 215 mins	7-313					10 overs: 1-52	45.2 overs, 216 mins	225			

1-110 (Finch, 14.4), 2-171 (Head, 24.6),
3-209 (McDermott, 32.6), 4-224 (Labuschagne, 38.1),
5-230 (Carey, 39.2), 6-277 (Stoinis, 46.4), 7-296 (Abbott, 48.5)

1-24 (Fakhar, 4.3), 2-120 (Babar, 24.1), 3-132 (Shakil, 26.4),
4-151 (Rizwan, 30.6), 5-166 (Iftikhar, 33.3),
6-204 (Imam, 38.6), 7-213 (Hasan, 41.2),
8-213 (Wasim, 41.3), 9-217 (Khushdil, 43.2), 1
10-225 (Rauf, 45.2)

Bowling	O	M	R	W	wd	nb	Bowling	O	M	R	W	wd	nb
Hasan Ali	8	0	56	0	5		SA Abbott	7	0	36	1		
Mohammad Wasim	8	0	59	0	2		CD Green	3	0	18	0		
Haris Rauf	8	0	44	2	6		A Zampa	10	0	38	4	2	
Zahid Mahmood	10	0	59	2			NT Ellis	8	0	36	1	1	1
Iftikhar Ahmed	6	0	36	1			MJ Swepson	8.2	0	53	2		
Khushdil Shah	10	0	50	1			MP Stoinis	3	0	9	0		
							TM Head	6	0	35	2		

Toss: Pakistan. Umpires: Aleem Dar, Asif Yaqoob, Ahsan Raza (TV), Ref: Mohammad Javed. Award: TM Head (Aus)
Head 50: 32 balls, 9x4 1x6; 100: 70 balls, 12x4 3x6, McDermott 50: 63 balls, 4x4. Imam 50: 57 balls, 3x4 1x6; 100: 92 balls, 6x4 3x6, Babar 50: 66 balls, 5x4

SECOND ODI – LAHORE
Australia kept an unchanged side, while Shaheen Shah Afridi returned for Pakistan. The tall left-arm quick had an immediate

impact as he trapped Finch with his third ball, a full-toss which the Australian skipper missed. With the early wicket falling Head wasn't as aggressive as in the previous game, while McDermott started slowly, taking until his 12th ball to get off the mark. It didn't take long after that for the Aussie number three to get going as he hit some fine pull-shots, including one off Shaheen that cleared the rope. Head too enjoyed the pull-stroke as lifted Rauf and then Zahid for sixes reaching his 50 in the 16th, with McDermott following suit in the next.

McDermott celebrated with a straight six off Iftikhar and when Head slog-swept the same bowler for another, Australia were 1-137 after 20 overs. Head continued to clear the rope at will as he pulled Wasim for six, before hitting Shaheeh straight for another. Just as he looked set for back-to-back hundreds, he top edged a sweep to be caught, the stand being worth 162 from 142 balls. Labuschagne came in and kept things ticking over, while McDermott continued to find the gaps, eventually launching Khushdil straight for six to bring up his maiden ODI century. His innings ended when he chipped a full-toss to mid-wicket and with Labuschagne reaching his fifty with a pull for four, Australia were 3-271 with ten overs to go.

Australia lost three wickets in the next six overs which delayed their final charge, with Labuschagne well held at long-on, Carey caught low-down by the keeper and Green caught at mid-on. Stoinis and Abbott added 42 off 23 balls and despite Shaheen taking two wickets for just five in the last over, Australia's 7-348 looked a defendable total.

After just four runs off the first two overs, Imam advanced at Abbott and lofted him for a straight six. Fakhar had some luck on 4 when he struck Abbott to deep square-leg, where Stoinis caught him but gave up a six as he had stepped on the rope. Green came on and Fakhar hit three of his first four balls for four and then Imam had some luck on 25 when McDermott dropped a catch in Zampa's first over. In the next over Imam pulled the leg-spinner for six and then Fakhar lofted Head straight for six as Pakistan reached 100 in the 16th over.

Finally the breakthrough came for Australia when Stoinis deceived Fakhar with a slower ball that moved away to hit the top of off-stump. This brought in Babar who was content to push the singles and twos and he and Imam continued to maintain the run rate required. Zampa didn't have the same influence as game one and when Babar lofted him for six, Pakistan was 1-205 after 30 overs, needing 144 off the last 20.

Imam reached his second hundred on the trot but was out to Zampa when he lofted one straight and was well held on the boundary. With 111 wanted off 14 overs, Babar then upped the ante, striking six fours as the next three overs went for 35. Pakistan needed 70 off the final 10 as Babar cruised to his century, eventually out chipping one to mid-wicket. When Rizwan was caught at long-off and just four came off the 47th over, Pakistan needed 27 off the last 18 balls. Khushdil averted any late disasters when he hit Abbott and Ellis for sixes, Pakistan home with an over to spare to level the series.

Second ODI at Lahore (day/night) on March 31, 2022 – Pakistan won by 6 wickets

Australia		B	M	4	6
TM Head	c Shaheen b Zahid	89	70	107	6	5
AJ Finch*	lbw b Shaheen	0	1	2
BR McDermott	c Rauf b Wasim	104	108	149	10	4
M Labuschagne	c Shakil b Khushdil	59	49	67	5
MP Stoinis	c Babar b Shaheen	49	33	67	5	1
AT Carey+	c Rizwan b Wasim	5	10	13
CD Green	c Iftikhar b Shaheen	5	11	9
SA Abbott	c Rauf b Shaheen	28	16	22	4
NT Ellis	not out	1	1	5
A Zampa	not out	0	1	2
MJ Swepson					
	6 lb, 2 w	8			
10 overs : 1-65	50 overs, 226 mins	8-348			

Pakistan		B	M	4	6
Fakhar Zaman	b Stoinis	67	64	82	7	2
Imam-ul-Haq	c Labuschagne b Zampa	106	97	156	6	2
Babar Azam*	c Labuschagne b Ellis	114	83	120	11	1
M Rizwan+	c Abbott b Zampa	23	26	54
Khushdil Shah	not out	27	17	25	2	2
Iftikhar Ahmed	not out	8	7	17
Saud Shakil					
M Wasim					
Shaheen Shah Afridi					
Haris Rauf					
Zahid Mahmood					
	1 b, 1 lb, 2 w	4			
10 overs _ 0-63	49 overs, 229 mins	4-349			

1-1 (Finch, 0.3), 2-163 (Head, 24.3), 3-237 (McDermott, 34.6), 4-272 (Labuschagne, 40.2), 5-295 (Carey, 43.2), 6-301 (Green, 45.2), 7-343 (Stoinis, 49.1), 8-347 (Abbott, 49.4)

1-118 (Fakhar, 18.5), 2-229 (Imam, 34.1), 3-309 (Babar, 44.2), 4-317 (Rizwan, 45.5)

Bowling	O	M	R	W	wd	nb
Shaheen Shah Afridi	10	0	63	4		
Haris Rauf	10	1	57	0		
Mohammad Wasim	10	0	56	2		
Zahid Mahmood	10	0	71	1	1	
Iftikhar Ahmed	4	0	38	0		
Khushdil Shah	6	0	57	1	1	

Bowling	O	M	R	W	wd	nb
SA Abbott	9	0	74	0	1	
CD Green	6	0	35	0		
NT Ellis	9	0	66	1		
TM Head	4	0	28	0		
A Zampa	10	0	71	2		
MJ Swepson	8	0	50	0	1	
MP Stoinis	3	0	23	1		

Toss: Pakistan. Umpires: Aleem Dar, Ahsan Raza, Asif Yaqoob (TV), Ref: Mohammad Javed. Award: Babar Azam (Pak)
Head 50: 45 balls, 4x4 2x6, McDermott 50: 52 balls, 6x4 2x6, 100: 102 balls, 10x4 4x6, Labuschagne 50: 41 balls, 5x4. Fakhar 50: 48 balls, 5x4 2x6, Imam 50: 50 balls, 2x4 2x6, 100: 90 balls, 6x4 2x6, Babar 50: 42 balls, 3x4 1x6, 100: 73 balls, 10x4 1x6

THIRD ODI - LAHORE

With Jason Behrendorff in for Swepson, Australia was hoping some extra pace might do the trick in the deciding one-dayer. In fact, the match turned out to be an anti-climax as Australia got off to one of their worst ever starts, losing 3-6 inside the first six overs. Head missed a low full-toss, Finch was trapped plumb in front and then Labuschagne edged to slip.

WORST EVER STARTS TO AN INNINGS BY AUSTRALIA IN AN ODI – THREE WICKETS DOWN

3-5	v South Africa	Cape Town	2005-06
3-6	v Pakistan	Lahore	2021-22
3-8	four times, v South Africa, Perth Stadium 2018-19, v Pakistan Sharjah 1986-87, v West Indies Mohali 1995-96 (WC), v West Indies Castries 1983-84		

A small recovery then occurred as 53 came for the fourth wicket, before Stoinis and then McDermott both got a leading edges to cover. At 5-67 in the 16th over it left plenty of time for Green and Carey to mount a recovery which they did in good style adding 89. At 5-148 after 31 overs, Australia then lost 4-18 off 29 balls as the innings fell apart for a second time. Green who was well set went for a wild swing at Wasim and Carey then lofted to wide long-on. With Behrendorff caught at square-leg and Ellis bowled it needed some hard hitting from Abbott to get Australia past 200. He struck the ball well, at one point taking 21 off a Shaheen over, before being out uppercutting to short third-man, one short of his maiden fifty.

Australia struck early with Fakhar caught at mid-off and the chance for a second came when Babar was on one, when he flicked Behrendorff to square-leg, only for Head to put down the head high chance. It was all one-way traffic from there as Imam and Babar dominated proceedings in a match winning stand. There was no pressure on the scoring rate as the Australian bowlers toiled away on a near perfect batting strip. Babar was a class above and with Imam at his side, Pakistan won comfortably with 12.1 overs to spare, to clinch the series in front of their delighted fans.

Third ODI at Lahore (day/night) on April 2, 2022 – Pakistan won by 9 wickets

Australia		B	M	4	6	Pakistan		B	M	4	6
TM Head	b Shaheen	0	1			Fakhar Zaman	c Labuschagne b Ellis	17	12	15	3
AJ Finch*	lbw b Rauf	0	3	7		Imam-ul-Haq	not out	89	100	162	6	1
BR McDermott	c Iftikhar b Wasim	36	50	78	3	1	Babar Azam*	not out	105	115	146	12
M Labuschagne	c Iftikhar b Rauf	4	10	19	1		M Rizwan+					
MP Stoinis	c Imam-ul-Haq b Zahid	19	19	38	2	1	Asif Ali					
AT Carey+	c Fakhar b Iftikhar	56	61	83	6	1	Iftikhar Ahmed					
CD Green	b Wasim	34	47	60	1	1	Khushdil Shah					
SA Abbott	c Wasim b Rauf	49	40	54	6	1	M Wasim					
JP Behrendorff	c Fakhar b Shaheen	2	8	9			Haris Rauf					
NT Ellis	b Wasim	2	4	5			Zahid Mahmood					
A Zampa	not out	0	8	28			Shaheen Shah Afridi					
	2 lb, 6 w	8					(1 lb, 2 w)	3			
10 overs: 3-31	41.5 overs, 195 mins	210				10 overs: 1-57	37.5 overs, 162 mins	1-214			

1-0 (Head, 0.1), 2-0 (Finch, 1.3), 3-6 (Labuschagne, 5.1),
4-59 (Stoinis, 12.5), 5-67 (McDermott, 15.2),
6-148 (Green, 31.1), 7-155 (Carey, 32.6),
8-162 (Behrendorff, 34.6), 9-166 (Ellis, 35.5),
10-210 (Abbott, 41.5)

1-24 (Fakhar, 3.4)

Bowling	O	M	R	W	wd	nb	Bowling	O	M	R	W	wd	nb
Shaheen Shah Afridi	8	2	40	2	1		JP Behrendorff	9	0	51	0		
Haris Rauf	8.5	1	39	3			NT Ellis	6	0	38	1	1	
Zahid Mahmood	8	0	51	1	1		A Zampa	9	0	50	0		
Mohammad Wasim	10	1	40	3	4		CD Green	3	0	19	0	1	
Iftikhar Ahmed	7	0	38	1			TM Head	2	0	9	0		
							SA Abbott	3	0	15	0		
							M Labuschagne	5.5	0	31	0		

Toss: Pakistan. Umpires: Aleem Dar, Rashid Riaz Ahsan Raza (TV), Ref: Mohammad Javed. Award: Babar Azam (Pak)
Carey 50: 55 balls, 5x4 1x6, Imam 50: 55 balls, 5x4, Babar 50: 57 balls, 7x4; 100: 110 balls, 12x4

ONLY TWENTY20 - LAHORE

Australia gave debuts to Marnus Labuschagne, Cameron Green and Ben Dwarshuis and the visitors won the toss and elected to field. Head started well in his opening over giving up just four singles from five balls, before Rizwan hammered the sixth over the rope at long-on. Babar started in imperious fashion, being very destruction in Ellis' first over, the fourth of the innings as he struck three consecutive fours. Dwarshuis came back to bowl the sixth, with the Pakistan skipper hitting him over long-off for six, as the hosts were 56 without loss in the first six overs – Babar 38 off 25 balls.

Green came on in the eighth over and bowled Rizwan with his third ball and then from the next was on a hat-trick as Fakhar chipped a full toss to mid-on. Babar started to slow somewhat being content to score singles but then with a glance to long-leg to the boundary reached his 50 off 33 balls. Iftikhar edged Ellis low to the 'keeper in the 12th over and then Babar threatened to really launch as he smashed Zampa to leg for six, but next ball he lofted a catch to deep cover.

Asif was caught at deep mid-wicket and then after belting Abbott for a six and four, Hasan was comprehensively bowled. Ellis dismissed Khushdil and Shaheen in consecutive balls, but in the last over Usman Qadir (son of the legendary Abdul) got stuck into Dwarshuis lofted him to leg for six as well as scoring two fours in an over that cost 18, which left Australia 163 to win.

Head started in a blaze cracking early boundaries off Shaheen and Hasan, before he lofted Rauf over wide mid-on for six. Next ball saw his innings come to an end as he hit one very high to deep square-leg where Qadir completed a tough catch. Finch had some early luck as he inside edged his first ball for four but looked more in control as his innings progressed. Inglis played some fine shots over the off-side and then lofted Qadir over long-on for six. The leg-spinner kept his nerve and tossed the next ball up, Inglis being caught behind aiming a drive. Shortly after Labuschagne walked past one from Qadir to be stumped, Australia 3-95 in the 11th over.

Stoinis smashed the bowlers from ball one, hitting three fours in an over from Qadir before hitting consecutive boundaries in the next over from Wasim. But both and Green were bowled in consecutive Wasim overs, Australia still 34 from 38 balls. McDermott played calmly as he and Finch added 29, before the Australian skipper was caught in the deep on the leg-side with just five wanted. Abbott was bowled first ball but with just four needed off the last over, McDermott ended the game with a leg-glance to the rope to give Australia victory with five balls to spare.

Only Twenty20 at Lahore Stadium on April 5, 2022 (floodlit) – Australia won by 3 wickets.

Pakistan		B	4	6	Australia		B	4	6
M Rizwan+	b Green	23	19	1	1	TM Head	c Qadir b Rauf	26	14	3	1
Babar Azam*	c Ellis b Zampa	66	46	6	2	AJ Finch*	c Asif b Shaheen	55	45	6
Fakhar Zaman	c Finch b Green	0	1			JP Inglis+	c Rizwan b Qadir	24	15	2	1
Iftikhar Ahmed	c Inglis b Ellis	13	13	1		M Labuschagne	st Rizwan b Qadir	2	4
Khushdil Shah	c McDermott b Ellis	24	21	3		MP Stoinis	b Wasim	23	9	5
Asif Ali	c Labuschagne b Ellis	3	5			CD Green	b Wasim	2	7
Hasan Ali	b Abbott	10	4	1	1	BR McDermott	not out	22	19	3
Shaheen Shah Afridi	c Stoinis b Ellis	0	2			SA Abbott	b Shaheen	0	1
Mohammad Wasim	not out	2	4			BJ Dwarshuis	not out	0	2
Usman Qadir	not out	18	6	2	1	NT Ellis				
Haris Rauf					A Zampa				
	2 lb, 1 nb	3					5 lb, 1 nb, 3 w	9
6 overs: 0-56	20 overs	8-162				6 overs: 1-63	19.1 overs	7-163

1-67 (Rizwan, 7.4), 2-67 (Fakhar, 7.5), 3-93 (Iftikhar, 11.5), 4-118 (Babar, 15.2), 5-127 (Asif, 16.4), 6-142 (Hasan, 17.5), 7-142 (Khushdil, 18.1), 8-142 (Shaheen, 18.2)

1-40 (Head, 3.3), 2-84 (Inglis, 8.3), 3-95 (Labuschagne, 10.1), 4-119 (Stoinis, 11.3), 5-129 (Green, 13.4), 6-158 (Finch, 18.1), 7-159 (Abbott, 18.4)

Bowling	O	M	R	W	wd	nb	Dots	Bowling	O	M	R	W	wd	nb	Dots
TM Head	2	0	17	0			3	Shaheen Shah Afridi	4	0	21	2	1		12
BJ Dwarshuis	3	0	42	0			2	Hasan Ali	3	0	30	0			3
SA Abbott	4	0	28	1		1	11	Haris Rauf	3.1	0	35	1			8
NT Ellis	4	0	28	4			8	Usman Qadir	4	0	33	2	1	1	10
A Zampa	4	0	29	1			6	Khushdil Shah	1	0	9	0			1
CD Green	3	0	16	2			7	Mohammad Wasim	4	0	30	2	1		9

Toss: Australia. Umpires: Aleem Dar, Ahsan Raza, Asif Yaqoob (TV), Ref: Mohammad Javed. Award: AJ Finch (Aus)
Babar 50: 33 balls, 6x4 1x6. Finch 50: 37 balls, 6x4

AUSTRALIA v SRI LANKA, 2021/22

Australia's first tour to Sri Lanka since 2016 saw five weeks of tremendous cricket, with the hosts more than a match for their opponents in all three formats. It also brought much joy to the people of Sri Lanka who had been suffering under an incompetent government who had ruined the economy, which was causing major fuel shortages as well as a host of other huge problems.

Given the issues in Sri Lanka, it was remarkable that the attendances for all white-ball matches were at capacity or close to it, while the two Tests in Galle has solid numbers which were boosted by several Australian tour groups who had made the trip over. The local fans were very keen to see their own team do well, but were very supportive of the Australians as well, so much so that many wore yellow T-shirts in the final one-dayer to show their thanks and gratitude to the Aussies for touring.

After Australia won the first Twenty20 comfortably there were concerns it could be a series of one-sided matches, but the hosts fought hard to make a game of it in the second just losing, before coming from nowhere to win the third match, on the back of a sensational knock by their skipper Dasun Shanaka. Sri Lanka needed 59 off the final three overs, but Shanaka blazed 54 not out off 25 balls, which won the game for his team with a ball to spare and made them more than believe they could match it with Australia. For the Aussies, David Warner had a good series with the bat making 130 runs, while Aaron Finch got 114 in his three hits and looked good. Throughout the T20 series Australia started to suffer a run of injuries as Mitchell Starc (lacerated finger) and Mitch Marsh (calf) missed games, with Kane Richardson (left hamstring) forced to head home, missing the ODI series.

The five match one-day series was a beauty, seesawing from one side to the other throughout. Australia won the first game on the back of a brilliant unbeaten 80 by Glenn Maxwell, which included six sixes. Sri Lanka fought back in the second to win after Australia lost 5-19 late in the run chase and then the hosts went 2-1 up when Pathum Nissanka made a magnificent century in their successful run chase of 292. Sri Lanka clinched the series in the fourth game with an exciting four run win in Colombo with Charith Asalanka making a brilliant 110. Australia grabbed a consolation win in the final ODI as mentioned and got a wonderful ovation of thanks from the capacity crowd as they did a lap of the ground at the end of the game. As in the T20 series, Australia suffered injuries in the ODIs with Ashton Agar and Marcus Stoinis having side strains, Steve Smith had a quad strain which saw him miss the last three 50-over games while Travis Head injured a hamstring and missed the last ODI, which put him in doubt for the First Test.

The two Tests in Galle were completely different types of matches but both were engrossing in their own way. The First Test saw the ball spin from the opening hour, Australia spinners Nathan Lyon and Mitch Swepson bowling better than the hosts, the visitors winning by ten wickets before lunch on the third day. Part-time spinner Travis Head also took his first Test wickets with a remarkable spell of 4-10 to wrap up of the Sri Lankan second innings. Cameron Green enhanced his reputation with a fine knock of 77, which earned him Man of the Match honours, while Usman Khawaja's 71 was worth its weight in gold.

In the second Test on a much more batsmen friendly surface, Australia was well placed at the end of day one on 5-298, with Steve Smith and Marnus Labuschagne both making centuries. But the lower order didn't fire on the second day, the final total of 364 a lot less than Australia would have hoped for as debutant Prabath Jayasuriya took 6-118. Then came one of the all-time great batting performances by a Sri Lankan outfit against Australia. A record total of 554 was compiled in 181 overs, with Dinesh Chandimal making 206, the first double-ton for Sri Lanka in a Test against Australia. Excellent knocks by Dimuth Karunaratne and Kusal Mendis built the base of the long innings, with Angelo Mathews and debutant Kamindu Mendis also making important half-centuries. Mitchell Starc showed a lot of character to take 4-89, but Nathan Lyon and Mitch Swepson found the going tougher, Lyon bowled 64 overs in the innings which was the most he has ever bowled in a Test innings.

With just under two sessions to bat on the fourth day, Australia crumbled after tea to lose nine wickets in the session as they slipped to their first ever innings defeat against Sri Lanka. Again Jayasuriya was the destroyer with six wickets, with good support from Ramesh Mendis and Theekshana who took two each.

Looking at some of the other Australian players not previously mentioned above, Alex Carey had a solid tour, making good runs particularly with the reverse sweep. He generally kept wicket well, apart from the last Test where he missed a number of stumpings. Travis Head played well in the ODIs following on from his excellent efforts in Pakistan but found things tough in the Tests. Josh Inglis didn't take his chances when given the opportunity, while Matt Kuhnemann made his debut in the ODI series and did pretty well. In the end, it was a terrific five weeks of cricket across three formats with both countries getting a lot out of the tour.

Meantime, the Australia A series against Sri Lanka A went on at the same time, with plenty of good cricket being played as both teams gained much needed experience at that level. The two match 50-over series was split one match each, with Australia winning both four-day matches. In the first game, Cameron Green's 119 not out ensured a comfortable seven wicket win. In the second, Travis Head made a blistering 110 from 86 balls, but 312 wasn't enough as a Sri Lanka levelled things up with a four wicket win with seven balls left.

In the first four-dayer Australia recovered from 5-98 to make 379, with Josh Philippe (94) and Nathan McAndrew (92) just falling short of hundreds. Off-spinner Todd Murphy (4-67) impressed with that ball in the first innings, while leg-spinner Tanveer Sangha (4-56) and quicks Aaron Hardie (3-35) and Nathan McAndrew (3-31) bowled Australia A to victory in the second. In the last four-day game, Scott Boland (4-38) and Mark Steketee (4-69) did well with the ball in the first innings, but

Australia trailed on first innings by 76, with only Jimmy Peirson (67*) doing enough with the bat. Tanveer Sangha (3-53) was handy with the ball once again, but Australia was set the difficult task of getting 367 to win. In serious strife at 4-67, Henry Hunt (107) and Jimmy Peirson (128*) stepped up to the plate to add 151, before Aaron Hardie (78*) and Peirson put on an unbeaten 150 to pull off a fine five-wicket win on the fourth afternoon to cap off the trip on a winning note.

FIRST TWENTY20 - COLOMBO

In front of a packed Premadasa Stadium, Starc caused himself a finger issue in the first over when he sprigged himself in his follow-through. It caused a nasty cut to his left hand and after treatment was able to continue. Sri Lanka started well with Gunathilleke lofting Marsh to long-off for four, before flipping him over the keeper's head for six. He continued to take the bowlers on until he lashed at one from Hazlewood to be caught at third man. Asalanka lifted Kane Richardson for six, hitting the grounds scoreboard as the hosts reached the end of the Powerplay on 1-50.

Asalanka continued to play the aggressive role while the slightly more sedate Nissanka was dropped on 22 by Smith at deep square-leg off Kane Richardson. Shortly after Nissanka slog swept Agar for six and when he mowed Starc to leg for four, Sri Lanka had 100 up in 11.5 overs.

After that it was all Australia with the ball, Nissanka was yorked and then Hazlewood returned to take three wickets in the 14th over. Mendis top-edged a pull, Rajapaksa edged behind and then Shanaka moved across his stumps to be plumb in front, Sri Lanka in all losing 4-3 off seven deliveries. Asalanka was then run out trying to pinch a bye and then the rain came with Sri Lanka 6-118 after 16 overs. After a short delay things did not improve as Karunaratne was picked off by Smith and then Starc returned to mop up the tail, taking three wickets in an over, Sri Lanka in all losing 9-28 from 46 balls.

Australia's chase started dramatically as Finch was adjudged leg-before from the third ball of the innings. But the Aussie slipper reviewed, with technology allowing him to stay as it showed the merest of snicks. After Warner was nearly run out in the third over the pair took control with Finch the more aggressive, lofting Hasaranga for six over long-on, the Lankan leggie going for 19 in his opening over. Theekshana was pulled for back-to-back fours by Warner, Australia 59 for no loss after six overs.

Finch lofted Hasaranga for another six over long-on, while Warner pulled and then uppercut Chameera for consecutive fours. Warner reached his 50 with a pulled four off Karunaratne and should have been caught in the same over on 55, when he was dropped by Nissanka. The 100 came up and then the rain came, with Australia 0-101 off 11.4 overs.

After a delay of 50 minutes, play resumed with Australia winning with six overs to spare when Finch uppercut Chameera for six. It was the third time Australia had won a T20 International by 10 wickets – the second time they have done it against Sri Lanka.

First Twenty20 at R Premadasa Stadium, Colombo on June 7, 2022 (Floodlit) – Australia won by 10 wickets

Sri Lanka			B	4	6	Australia			B	4	6
P Nissanka	b Starc	36	31	2	1	AJ Finch*	not out	61	40	4	4
MD Gunathilleke	c Marsh b Hazlewood	26	15	3	1	DA Warner	not out	70	44	9	
KIC Asalanka	run out (Wade-Marsh)	38	34	3	1	MR Marsh					
BKG Mendis+	c Agar b Hazlewood	1	5			GJ Maxwell					
PBB Rajapaksa	c Wade b Hazlewood	0	1			SPD Smith					
MD Shanaka*	lbw b Hazlewood	0	2			MP Stoinis					
W Hasaranga	c Finch b Starc	17	15	2		MS Wade+					
C Karunaratne	run out (Smith)	1	2			AC Agar					
P VD Chameera	c Warner b Starc	1	5			MA Starc					
MM Theekshana	c Warner b Richardson	1	4			KW Richardson					
IDN Thushara	not out	0	3			JR Hazlewood					
	7 w	7					3 w	3			
6 overs: 1-50	19.3 overs	128				6 overs: 0-59	14 overs	0-134			

1-39 (Gunathilleke, 4.2), 2-100 (Nissanka, 11.6), 3-102 (Mendis, 13.1),
4-103 (Rajapaksa, 13.4), 5-103 (Shanaka, 13.6), 6-116 (Asalanka, 15.4),
7-118 (Karunaratne, 16.1), 8-127 (Chameera, 18.1),
9-128 (Hasaranga, 18.3), 10-128 (Theekshana, 19.3)

Bowling	O	M	R	W	wd	nb	Dots	Bowling	O	M	R	W	wd	nb	Dots
MA Starc	4	0	26	3	3		13	MM Theekshana	4	0	25	0	1		11
JR Hazlewood	4	0	16	4			15	IDN Thushara	2	0	21	0	2		2
MR Marsh	2	0	21	0			3	P VD Chameera	4	0	48	0			4
GJ Maxwell	2	0	18	0			2	W Hasaranga	2	0	27	0			4
KW Richardson	3.3	0	22	1			13	C Karunaratne	2	0	13	0			2
AC Agar	4	0	25	0			7								

Toss: Australia.   Umpires: HDPK Dharmasena, LE Hannibal, RSA Palliyaguruge (TV), Ref: RS Madugalle
Finch 50: 37 balls, 3x4 3x6, Warner 50: 32 balls, 7x4   Award: JR Hazlewood (Aus).   Crowd: 26,000 (estimated)

SECOND TWENTY20 - COLOMBO

Australia brought in Jhye Richardson to replace Mitchell Starc, who required six stitches in his injured bowling hand. The visitors started with spin and it paid off as Maxwell induced Gunathilleke to slog-sweep one straight down the throat of deep mid-wicket. Hazlewood applied the pressure with a maiden to Asalanka and when Jhye Richardson had Nissanka slice one to third man, Sri Lanka were 2-7. Sri Lanka went on the counter-attack, with Asalanka lofting Jhye Richardson straight for six, then Mendis lofted Kane Richardson over cover for six more. Sri Lanka continued to clear the rope as Agar came on and Asalanka cracked him over the long-on rope. The partnership reached 66 when Asalanka tried to loft Maxwell, but the ball went straight up for Finch to take the catch.

Sri Lanka were well placed at 3-90 after 14 overs but then the extra pace of Jhye Richardson accounted for Nissanka, who tried to hook a short ball, only to hit the stumps with his bat. Rajapaksa pulled one to short fine leg and after Hasaranga hit Jhye Richardson for consecutive fours, he hit a catch to mid-off. Richardson took three wickets in his final over as the hosts lost their last 4-3 off seven balls, Australia needing 125 to clinch the series.

It was all smooth sailing in the early part of the chase, as Chameera went for 18 in his opening over as Finch pulled and cut him for fours, before Warner lifted one over square-leg for six. Hasaranga was called upon and Finch took him for 2, 4, 2 before hitting a catch to cover point, replays being needed to confirm the bowler hadn't touched the return crease and bowled a no-ball. Sri Lanka came back into the game as Marsh missed a sweep and then Smith was trapped in front and then Warner was run out, when Maxwell didn't want a second run from a cover drive to the deep.

Stoinis lofted Hasaranga to long-on for six, but in the next over mistimed a pull-shot to mid-wicket. Maxwell seemed to have the game under control before he lofted Hasaranga to long-off and then next ball Agar was bowled through the gate driving. The Sri Lankan leggie almost had a hat-trick when next ball Jhye Richardson was beaten between bat and pad to be nearly bowled. Australia had eight overs to get the remaining 26 to win, Wade and Jhye Richardson playing calmly and carefully until the Aussie keeper edged one through the vacant slip for four to clinch the victory with 14 balls to spare.

Second Twenty20 at R Premadasa Stadium, Colombo on June 8, 2022 (Floodlit) – Australia won by 3 wickets

Sri Lanka			B	4	6		Australia			B	4	6
P Nissanka	c Marsh b J Richardson	3	6				AJ Finch*	c Gunathilleke b Hasaranga	24	13	4	
MD Gunathilleke	c Marsh b Maxwell	4	4	1			DA Warner	run out (Nissanka-Mendis)	21	10	3	1
KIC Asalanka	c Finch b Maxwell	39	33	2	2		MR Marsh	lbw b Hasaranga	11	7	2	
BKG Mendis+	hit wkt b J Richardson	36	36	2	1		SPD Smith	lbw b Thushara	5	4	1	
PBB Rajapaksa	c Hazlewood b K Richardson	13	11	1			GJ Maxwell	c Gunathilleke b Hasaranga	19	19		
MD Shanaka*	c Finch b K Richardson	14	17	2			MP Stoinis	c Asalanka b Chameera	9	7		1
W Hasaranga	c Warner b J Richardson	12	8	2			MS Wade+	not out	26	26	2	
C Karunaratne	c Agar b K Richardson	0	2				AC Agar	b Hasaranga	0	1		
P VD Chameera	c Agar b K Richardson	0	1				JA Richardson	not out	9	20		
MM Theekshana	not out	1	1				KW Richardson					
IDN Thushara	not out	2	1				JR Hazlewood					
		0						(2 w)		2		
6 overs: 2-28	20 overs		9-124				6 overs: 3-63	17.5 overs		7-126		

1-5 (Gunathilleke, 0.5), 2-7 (Nissanka, 2.4), 3-73 (Asalanka, 11.5), 4-90 (Mendis, 14.1), 5-101 (Rajapaksa, 16.2), 6-121 (Hasaranga, 18.6), 7-121 (Shanaka, 19.1), 8-121 (Chameera, 19.2), 9-121 (Karunaratne, 19.4)

1-33 (Finch, 2.4), 2-53 (Marsh, 4.4), 3-58 (Smith, 5.2), 4-64 (Warner, 6.2), 5-80 (Stoinis, 8.4), 6-99 (Maxwell, 11.4), 7-99 (Agar, 11.5)

Bowling	O	M	R	W	wd	nb	Dots
GJ Maxwell	3	0	18	2			7
JR Hazlewood	4	1	16	0			13
JA Richardson	4	0	26	3			13
KW Richardson	4	0	30	4			11
AC Agar	4	0	27	0			8
MR Marsh	1	0	7	0			1

Bowling	O	M	R	W	wd	nb	Dots
MM Theekshana	4	0	29	0	1		9
P VD Chameera	4	0	31	1	1		9
W Hasaranga	4	0	33	4			9
IDN Thushara	2	0	18	1			4
KIC Asalanka	3	0	7	0			11
MD Gunathilleke	0.5	0	8	0			1

Toss: Australia.   Umpires: HDPK Dharmasena, RMPJ Rambukwella, LE Hannibal (TV), Ref: RS Madugalle
Award: MS Wade (Aus).   Crowd: 26,000 (estimated)

THIRD TWENTY20 - PALLEKELE

Australia's injury woes continued as Marsh was ruled out with a calf injury, with Inglis brought in to play his first match of the series. Sri Lanka brought in left-arm spinner Jayawickrama for Thushara on what looked a very good pitch for batting. Just four came from the opening over, but then Finch laid into Chameera and Theekshana in the next two overs, hitting four fours as Australia got going. Warner straight drove Karunaratne for four and then both players hit their boundaries as 13 from Chameera's second over, Australia 0-40 after five overs.

Theekshana bowled Finch as he went for a slog sweep, which saw the arrival of Maxwell who launched the second ball he faced from the spinner for six over square-leg. Hasaranga came on at the start of the eighth over, with Maxwell giving him the full treatment first ball, hitting him over deep square-leg for six. Just when it looked like Maxwell was going to completely take over, he hit one hard and flat to long-on. Then Australia lost two wickets from the next two balls as Warner was leg before after a Sri Lankan review, then Inglis wanted a leg bye that wasn't there and was run out trying to scramble back.

Stoinis reverse swept Hasaranga for four to bring up the 100 as Australia took few risks in reaching 4-117 with five overs to go. In the 16th over Stoinis started the final charge, sweeping Jayawickrama for six and then cutting back-to-back fours before being stumped off the last ball of the over, being well down the track. Theekshana gave up just five singles in the 17th and then Smith, who was 15 off his first 17 balls, slog swept Hasaranga for six in the 18th. Eleven came from the 19th and 16 from the last when Smith hit a full-toss behind point for a remarkable six.

Sri Lanka started the chase well, with both openers striking boundaries off the first over from Jhye Richardson, which cost 11. After an over from Hazlewood that cost just two, Kane Richardson had his first ball pulled for six by Gunathilleke. Hazlewood dismissed the opener in the fourth over, when he had the left-hander caught top-edging a pull-shot to short fine-leg. Asalanka was just two off his first seven balls, before pulling Kane Richardson for four and six as Sri Lanka reached 1-49 after the first six overs.

Asalanka powered Agar twice to the rope in his opening over before top-edging a pull-shot off Stoinis to short fine-leg. The Sri Lanka batting dropped away as Nissanka was caught at short third-man, with Rajapaksa leg before on the sweep. When Mendis was bowled off his pads and Hasaranga caught at cover, Sri Lanka had lost 5-41, which meant they needed 69 off the last 26 balls. Karunaratne hit Jhye Richardson for four to leg from the first ball he faced, but after Agar's last over went for just six, Sri Lanka needed 59 to win from the last 18 balls.

With figures of 2-3 off three overs, Hazlewood came on to bowl his final over to try and shut the game down. After a single to Karunaratne, Shanaka exploded into action as he pulled the next ball for six, before lofting another over mid-wicket. Cover and straight drive fours came from the next two balls, Hazlewood going for 22 in the over, which left the hosts needing 37 off the last two. Off the first ball of the 19th the Sri Lanka skipper pulled Jhye Richardson for six, with the full house now sensing their team could pull off a remarkable win. With two further fours coming from the over, Sri Lanka needed 19 off the last. Kane Richardson gave up two off-side wides from the first two balls and after a single and a bye, the hosts still needed 15 off the last four balls. Shanaka square drove a four, before smashing one to the long-off rope, leaving seven to win off the last two. The Sri Lanka captain the belted a low full-toss straight for six to tie the scores. Another wide saw the match come to an end, Sri Lanka winning with a ball to spare, something quite unimaginable 20 minutes earlier.

Third Twenty20 at Pallekele Cricket Stadium on June 11, 2022 (Floodlit) – Sri Lanka won by 4 wickets

Australia			B	4	6	Sri Lanka			B	4	6
DA Warner	lbw b Theekshana	39	33	6		MD Gunathilleke	c J Richardson				
AJ Finch*	b Theekshana	29	20	5			b Hazlewood	15	12	1	1
GJ Maxwell	c Gunathilleke b Hasaranga	16	9		2	P Nissanka	c Hazlewood b Stoinis	27	25	2	
SPD Smith	not out	37	27	2	2	KIC Asalanka	c Finch b Stoinis	26	19	3	1
JP Inglis	run out (Asalanka)	0	1			PBB Rajapaksa	lbw b Agar	17	13	1	1
MP Stoinis	st Mendis b Jayawickrama	38	23	3	1	BKG Mendis+	b Hazlewood	6	8	1	
MS Wade+	not out	13	8	2		MD Shanaka*	not out	54	25	5	4
AC Agar						W Hasaranga	c Finch b J Richardson	8	7	1	
JA Richardson						C Karunaratne	not out	14	10	2	
KW Richardson						P VD Chameera					
JR Hazlewood						MM Theekshana					
						P AKP Jayawickrama					
	1nb, 3 w	4					1 b, 4 lb, 5 w	10			
6 overs: 1-49	20 overs	5-176				6 overs: 1-49	19.5 overs	6-177			

1-43 (Finch, 5.4), 2-85 (Maxwell, 9.6), 3-85 (Warner, 10.1)
4-85 (Inglis, 10.2), 5-133 (Stoinis, 15.6)

1-25 (Gunathilleke), 2-67 (Asalanka, 8.2), 3-81 (Nissanka, 10.5)
4-96 (Rajapaksa, 12.2), 5-98 (Mendis, 13.5),
6-108 (Hasaranga, 15.4)

Bowling	O	M	R	W	wd	nb	Dots	Bowling	O	M	R	W	wd	nb	Dots
C Karunaratne	3	0	19	0	1		9	JA Richardson	4	0	46	1	1		6
P VD Chameera	4	0	46	0	2	1	7	JR Hazlewood	4	1	25	2			15
MM Theekshana	4	0	25	2			11	KW Richardson	2.5	0	44	0	4		3
MD Shanaka	1	0	10	0			2	AC Agar	4	0	23	1			9
W Hasaranga	4	0	33	1			8	GJ Maxwell	3	0	26	0			4
P AKP Jayawickrama	4	0	43	1			4	MP Stoinis	2	0	8	2			4

Toss: Australia. Umpires: HDPK Dharmasena, RR Wimalasiri, RSA Palliyaguruge (TV), Ref: RS Madugalle. Award: MD Shanaka (SL). Shanaka 50: 25 balls, 5x4 4x6. Crowd: 28,000 (est)

FIRST ONE-DAY INTERNATIONAL - PALLEKELE

Australia's injury list continued to grow as Kane Richardson had gone down with a left hamstring injury, which ruled him out of the remainder of the tour. This meant Australia had four players unfit on the sidelines, with Starc (lacerated finger), Marsh (calf), Agar (side) all unavailable. Sri Lanka's team had a similar look to its T20 outfit with top order batsman and spinner Dhananjaya de Silva coming in along with 19 year-old left-arm spinner Dulith Wellalage, who was set to debut.

With a bit of cloud about, Sri Lanka started well with Gunathilleke the more aggressive of the opening pair, pulling and cutting boundaries. Nissanka took his time to get going, before taking 14 from a Cummins over, including a top-edged hook for six. With the sun now out the 100 stand was raised in the 18th over, with both players reached their half centuries in the 19th. The partnership ended when Gunathilleke attempted a second run to deep square-leg, where Stoinis' rocket return to the keeper saw him just short. Soon after Nissanka reverse swept a catch to short third man and then Warner leapt high to his left at mid-on to bring off a brilliant catch to dismiss de Silva.

Sri Lanka had lost 3-19 and it could have been worse as Mendis (17) was put down by Labuschagne at deep mid-wicket off Maxwell. Things settled for the hosts as the fourth wicket added 77 before Asalanka hit one hard but straight to mid-on. Mendis reached his 50 and then smashed Maxwell over long-on for six. Labuschagne then grabbed two wickets, Shanaka superbly caught by Warner diving forward at long-on and Karunaratne who edged behind. Mendis continued to bat well but it was Hasaranga who ensured Sri Lanka reached 300, as he hit Jhye Richardson for five consecutive fours in the 49th over, before being out to the last ball of the innings.

Australia's reply started badly with Warner trapped in front from the first ball he faced from Theekshana. Smith was troubled by Theekshana's late drift in but settled quickly as he and Finch added 67, with the Aussie skipper in good touch until he edged a leg-break into the keeper's gloves. The rain came a ball later, causing a delay of nearly 90 minutes. When the players returned, Australia's DLS target was 282 off 44 overs.

Labuschagne was picking up singles while Smith was able to consistently find the rope as Australia reached 100 in the 18th over. Smith reached his 50, but then Labuschagne pulled one down the throat of deep square-leg and soon after Smith missed a pull-shot to one that kept a little low to give Wellalage his first ODI wicket. Stoinis was in tremendous touch, lofting Theekshana for six over long-off before pulling Hasaranga over the rope. Two balls later though the Sri Lankan leggie had his revenge, as Stoinis was bowled as he missed an attempted sweep.

Maxwell joined Carey and immediately made his presence felt as he twice hit Hasaranga to six for leg, the spinner now noticeably limping. Maxwell then hooked Chameera for six, which left Australia needing 54 off the last nine overs with five wickets in hand. Hasaranga returned to bowl his last over and in the space of three balls turned the game as he had Carey LBW reverse sweeping before bowling Cummins who had a dirty slog. The Sri Lankan fans were in a frenzy but Maxwell had the job in hand, pulling a Theekshana full toss for six in an over that cost 15. Maxwell reached his 50 with a reverse sweep for four but then lost Agar who was trapped in front playing back. From there it was all Maxwell as he struck Wellalage for consecutive fours in the 42nd over, before finishing the game in the next when he hit sixes off Chameera over long-off and square-leg

First ODI at Pallekele Cricket Stadium on June 14, 2022 (day/night) – Australia won by 2 wickets (DLS)

Sri Lanka			B	M	4	6	Australia			B	M	4	6
MD Gunathilleke	run out (Stoinis-Carey)	55	53	89	7		DA Warner	lbw b Theekshana	0	3	6		
P Nissanka	c Finch b Agar	56	68	99	6	1	AJ Finch*	c Mendis					
BKG Mendis+	not out	86	87	139	8	1		b Hasaranga	44	41	53	5	1
DM de Silva	c Warner b Agar	7	17	18			SPD Smith	b Wellalage	53	60	94	5	
KIC Asalanka	c Finch b Richardson	37	42	62	4		M Labuschagne	c Wellalage					
MD Shanaka*	c Warner							b Shanaka	24	31	34	1	
	b Labuschagne	6	7	14	1		MP Stoinis	b Hasaranga	44	31	43	4	2
C Karunaratne	c Carey b Labuschagne	7	7	9	1		AT Carey+	lbw b Hasaranga	21	22	56	1	
W Hasaranga	c Richardson						GJ Maxwell	not out	80	51	65	6	6
	b Hazlewood	37	19	22	6		PJ Cummins	b Hasaranga	0	2	1		
DN Wellalage							AC Agar	lbw b Wellalage	3	11	16		
P VD Chameera							JA Richardson	not out	1	3	17		
MM Theekshana							JR Hazlewood						
	1 b, 2 lb, 6 w	9						6 b, 1 lb, 5 w	12				
10 overs: 0-56	50 overs, 229 mins	7-300					9 overs: 1-49	42.3 overs, 198 mins	8-282				

1-115 (Gunathilleke, 19.4), 2-118 (Nissanka, 21.4),
3-134 (de Silva, 25.5), 4-211 (Asalanka, 39.3), 5-240 (Shanaka, 43.3),
6-258 (Karunaratne, 45.5), 7-300 (Hasaranga, 49.6)

1-5 (Warner, 1.1), 2-72 (Finch, 12.3), 3-126 (Labuschagne, 21.4),
4-141 (Smith, 24.3), 5-189 (Stoinis, 29.6), 6-228 (Carey, 35.1),
7-228 (Cummins, 35.3), 8-254 (Agar, 39.3)

Bowling	O	M	R	W	wd	nb	Bowling	O	M	R	W	wd	nb
JR Hazlewood	10	0	54	1	1		PVD Chameera	7.3	0	60	0	4	
GJ Maxwell	10	0	60	0	3		MM Theekshana	8	0	51	1	1	
PJ Cummins	8	1	48	0	1		C Karunaratne	4	0	16	0		
JA Richardson	8	0	64	1	1		W Hasaranga	9	0	58	4		
AC Agar	10	0	49	2			DN Wellalage	7	0	49	2		
MP Stoinis	1	0	3	0			DM de Silva	3	0	14	0		
M Labuschagne	3	0	19	2	-		MD Shanaka	4	0	27	1		

Toss: Sri Lanka. Umpires: HDPK Dharmasena, RSA Palliyaguruge, LE Hannibal (TV), Ref: RS Madugalle. Crowd: 25,000 (est)

Award: GJ Maxwell (Aus). Gunathilleke 50: 50 balls, 7x4, Nissanka 50: 61 balls, 4x4 2x6, Mendis 50: 59 balls, 4x4. Smith 50: 55 balls, 5x4; Maxwell 50: 35 balls, 4x4 4x6.

SECOND ONE-DAY INTERNATIONAL - PALLEKELE

Australia's injury list lengthened ahead of the second ODI, with side strains claiming Agar (slight) and Stoinis being the more severe of the two. This meant that reinforcements were called up from the Australia A four-day match in Hambantota, with batsman Travis Head into the line-up along with left-arm spinner Matt Kuhnemann who was to debut. Sri Lanka had lost Hasaranga to a groin strain with leggie Jeffrey Vandersay in as a like for like replacement.

The pitch looked dry and was expected to turn and interestingly Finch elected to field first when he won the toss of the coin. Nissanka looked in good nick once again, cutting Kuhnemann twice to the rope. In his third over the debutant took his first wicket when Nissanka pushed forward and got a faint edge to the keeper. Cummins came on in the eighth over and in his second had Gunathilleke when he pulled one hard to deep square-leg. De Silva started well against the Aussie skipper upper-cutting him for four as Sri Lanka reached 2-43 at the end of the first ten overs.

The ball was turning for Swepson who came on in the 11th over and he was dealt with by de Silva who lofted him straight for six, in a three-over spell that cost 23. Mendis was playing well sweeping Labuschagne for six but lost his partner de Silva (who was dropped by Head off Cummins on 30) when he uppercut a slower ball high to the keeper's right hand. Mendis toed a sweep back to Kuhnemann and when the unusually subdued Asalanka swept one to deep square-leg, Sri Lanka were 5-130 with still 21 overs left. Karunaratne smacked Maxwell for six to long-on as the score started to tick over but he then tried a similar short of Kuhnemann and holed out to long off. Shanaka had been batting well, but when he miscued a slog-sweep to short third-man, one wondered if Sri Lanka would get far past 200.

Wellalage was struggling, having made just a single off his first 17 balls, but in the 40th over he went after Kuhnemann, lofting him over long-off for six, before square driving him to the rope, Sri Lanka reaching 7-192 with ten overs left. Cummins then came back to have Vandersay caught behind and Wellalage bowled, before the last wicket added 21, when the rain came ending the Sri Lanka innings.

After a two hour and ten minute delay, Australia's DLS target was deemed to be 216 off 43 overs at 4.95 an over. Warner wanted to get them quickly smacking three fours in Theekshana's first over. Finch joined in as the stand reached 39 but then the Aussie skipper was trapped in front as he missed a shot to leg being bowled from around the wicket. When Warner was on 29 he aimed a sweep at Theekshana, the appeal was answered in the negative, had a review been called for he would have been on his way. De Silva had been bowling well and was finding the odd edge as he had Warner bowled as he made room to leg to play a cut shot.

Head came out and looked a little out of sorts on the spinning surface, while Smith started to limp, in what was later revealed to be a quad injury. Karunaratne came on and went for eight in his first over, but in his second Smith went for a pull and hit it straight to short fine-leg. Head started to look more in more control, but then went for a lofted sweep which went high but not far enough to be held at deep square-leg. When Labuschagne hit a catch to cover, Australia had slipped to 5-132, needing 94 off the last 88 balls.

Maxwell joined Carey and went after Wellalage, hitting him for three fours in an over. Australia needed 46 off the last 53 balls when Maxwell essayed a hook at the pacey Karunaratne but miscued it to point to signal the start of the final collapse. Carey was run out attempting a second run, Cummins top edged a pull to deep square-leg and when Swepson and then Kuhnemann were both bowled, Sri Lanka had pulled off a victory, much to the delight of their excited fans. Australia had lost their last 5-19 off 18 balls as Sri Lanka had levelled the series in a match where no fifty had been scored.

Second ODI at Pallekele Cricket Stadium on June 16, 2022 (day/night) – Sri Lanka won by 26 runs (DLS)

Sri Lanka		B	M	4	6	Australia	DLS Target 216 in 43 ov		B	M	4	6
MD Gunathilleke	c Kuhnemann b Cummins	18	30	40	1	DA Warner	b de Silva		37	51	57	5
P Nissanka	c Carey b Kuhnemann	14	17	22	3	AJ Finch *	lbw b de Silva		14	15	32	2
BKG Mendis +	c & b Maxwell	36	41	75	2	1	SPD Smith	c Theekshana b Karunaratne	28	35	53	3
DM de Silva	c Carey b Cummins	34	41	43	2	1	TM Head	c Asalanka b Wellalage	23	34	58	2
KIC Asalanka	c Kuhnemann b Maxwell	13	27	36	1		M Labuschagne	c Shanaka b Wellalage	18	30	38	
MD Shanaka *	c Maxwell b Swepson	34	36	58	5		AT Carey +	run out (Karunaratne)	15	20	44	1
C Karunaratne	c Cummins b Kuhnemann	18	17	19		1	GJ Maxwell	c Shanaka b Karunaratne	30	25	28	5
DN Wellalage	b Cummins	20	55	39	1	1	PJ Cummins	c Wellalage b Chameera	4	6	10	1
JDF Vandersay	c Carey b Cummins	7	10	15			MJ Swepson	b Karunaratne	2	2	9	
P VD Chameera	not out	7	18	25	1		MP Kuhnemann	b Chameera	1	2	8	
MM Theekshana	not out	11	14	17	1		JR Hazlewood	not out	4	3	4	1
	5 lb, 3 w	8					5 lb, 8 w	13				
10 overs : 2-43	47.4 overs, 199 mins	9-220				9 overs : 1-42	37.1 overs, 176 mins	189				

1-26 (Nissanka, 5.5), 2-35 (Gunathilleke, 9.2), 3-96 (de Silva, 20.4), 4-108 (Mendis, 23.3), 5-130 (Asalanka, 28.5), 6-159 (Karunaratne, 33.3), 7-172 (Shanaka, 37.1), 8-198 (Vandersay, 41.3), 9-199 (Wellalage, 43.3)

1-39 (Finch, 7.2), 2-62 (Warner, 13.3), 3-93 (Smith, 19.6), 4-123 (Head, 26.2), 5-132 (Labuschagne, 28.2), 6-170 (Maxwell, 34.2), 7-177 (Carey, 34.7), 8-181 (Cummins, 35.6), 9-185 (Swepson, 36.3), 10-189 (Kuhnemann, 37.1)

Bowling	O	M	R	W	wd	nb	Bowling	O	M	R	W	wd	nb
J R Hazlewood	7	1	26	0			P VD Chameera	6.1	0	19	2	1	
MP Kuhnemann	10	0	48	2	1		MM Theekshana	8	0	44	0	4	
GJ Maxwell	10	2	35	2	1		DM de Silva	6	0	26	2		
P J Cummins	8.4	0	35	4			J DF Vandersay	5	1	23	0		
MJ Swepson	10	0	58	1	1		C Karunaratne	7	0	47	3	3	
M Labuschagne	2	0	13	0			DN Wellalage	5	0	25	2		

Toss: Sri Lanka. Umpires: HDPK Dharmasena, RR Wimalasiri, RSA Palliyaguruge, LE Hannibal (TV), Ref: RS Madugalle.
Award: C Karunaratne (SL). Crowd: 25,000 (est)

THIRD ONE-DAY INTERNATIONAL - COLOMBO

With the series all tied up with three games to play, Marsh was back into the Australian line-up but it was at the expense of Smith who had sustained a quad injury. Green came in for his first game for the series while Jhye Richardson was also in, with Cummins rested and Swepson omitted. Dickwella was in for Sri Lanka for the injured Gunathilleke and took the keeping gloves off Mendis. It was a hot humid day as Australia won the toss and decided to bat.

Warner got Chameera away for some early boundaries but didn't last long as he top-edged a short ball to long-leg. Marsh struggled to get the ball away on the slow surface and eventually lost patience when he hit a catch to cover. The young spinner Wellalage was doing a good job and conceded just 16 runs in his initial six over spell. Finch was picking up the pace as he lofted Vandersay over long-on for six, with Labuschagne feeding him the strike as his first 19 runs were all singles. The stand had reached 69 when Vandersay returned for his second spell and had Labuschagne stumped, then Finch caught at slip to prevent any acceleration.

The two South Aussies Carey and Head needed to rebuild the innings, both playing carefully against the spinners. Carey advanced and lofted de Silva straight for six and then had some luck on 27 when Shanaka failed to hold a tough chance in his right hand at cover off Theekshana. Head had battled to 18 off 33 balls, before pulling Karunaratne for four to bring up the 50 stand. Then Carey went after de Silva sweeping and pulling him for four before he was given out LBW attempting a lap sweep. Maxwell was another to have luck, being dropped on two by de Silva off Wellalage as he top edged a sweep. He soon put that moment behind him as he consistently found the rope, at one stage hitting a 112kph slower ball from Karunaratne straight for six.

Just as Maxwell was about to really explode he tried to hit a wide one from Vandersay for six, but could only find the hands of long-on. Australia reached 6-258 with two overs left and then Head hit Wellalage for three sixes in his last over, with some sweetly struck shots all between the sightboard and deep mid-wicket as Australia ended up with 6-291.

Needing 5.84 per over to go one up in the series, Sri Lanka's replacement opener Dickwella was brilliant early on, at one point hitting four fours in the space of six balls off Hazlewood and Jhye Richardson in the opening overs. This took the pressure off his opening partner Nissanka, who fed his partner the strike in an opening stand of 42. Dickwella was lucky on 24 when Marsh dropped him off Maxwell, but it cost very little to the Australia as in the same over he was bowled on the drive. Mendis came out and late cut Maxwell to the rope first ball as he and Nissanka had little trouble against pace and the slow bowlers.

Mendis later drove Green for consecutive fours as Sri Lanka breezed past 100 in the 19th over, the Sri Lanka number three first to 50 (39 balls) when he pulled the returning Hazlewood for four. In the next over Nissanka reached his 50 (65 balls) and when the 100 stand was raised Sri Lanka were well on their way to victory at 1-142 after 25 overs. Nissanka lifted a cog when he smashed Hazlewood over the leg side for six, but on 68 had some luck when he was almost bowled by a Jhye Richardson ball that cut back into him.

The humidity started to give Mendis trouble as he was treated regularly for cramp at the end of each over. The Aussie bowlers had little answer to the run scoring and when Nissanka hit Head to fine-leg for four, the pair had set a new second wicket record partnership against Australia, surpassing the 163 added by Sanath Jayasuriya and Kumar Sangakkara at the SCG in 2005-06. Finally, the cramp got the better of Mendis and he was forced to retire at the end of the 38th over with Sri Lanka 1-212. De Silva swung straight into gear pulling Labuschagne for four and shortly after much to the acclaim of the home crowd, Nissanka reached his maiden ODI ton. He celebrated by lifting Kuhnemann over cover and then finally Australia had some success as de Silva hit a return catch to Hazlewood.

With 34 wanted off the last six overs, Nissanka found the rope against the returning quicks and then cleared them when he slog-swept Maxwell for six. He and Shanaka were dismissed in the space of four balls, but then Asalanka lifted Hazlewood over square-leg to tie the scores, his single to leg winning the game with nine balls to spare.

Third ODI at R Premadasa Stadium, Colombo on June 19, 2022 (day/night) – Sri Lanka won by 6 wickets

Australia			B	M	4	6
DA Warner	c Theekshana b Chameera	9	12	13	2	
AJ Finch*	c de Silva b Vandersay	62	85	112	4	1
MR Marsh	c Mendis b Wellalage	10	23	33	1	
M Labuschagne	st Dickwella b Vandersay	29	36	55	1	
AT Carey+	lbw b de Silva	49	52	66	3	1
TM Head	not out	70	65	109	3	3
GJ Maxwell	c Wellalage b Vandersay	33	18	22	3	1
CD Green	not out	15	12	26		1
JA Richardson						
MP Kuhnemann						
JR Hazlewood						
5 b, 4 lb, 3 nb, 2 w		14				
10 overs: 1-47	50 overs, 222 mins	6-291				

1-14 (Warner, 2.3), 2-47 (Marsh, 10.3), 3-116 (Labuschagne, 24.2), 4-121 (Finch, 26.4), 5-193 (Carey, 39.6), 6-233 (Maxwell, 44.3).

Sri Lanka			B	M	4	6
N Dickwella+	b Maxwell	25	26	34	5	
P Nissanka	c Warner b Richardson	137	147	210	11	2
BKG Mendis	retired hurt	87	85	132	8	
DM de Silva	c & b Hazlewood	25	17	23	4	
KJC Asalanka	not out	13	12	27		1
*MD Shanaka	b Richardson	0	2	2		
C Karunaratne	not out	0	2	5		
DN Wellalage						
P VD Chameera						
JDF Vandersay						
MM Theekshana						
2 b, 1 lb, 2 w		5				
10 overs: 1-54	48.3 overs, 219 mins	4-292				

1-42 (Dickwella, 7.5), 2-255 (de Silva, 43.2), 3-284 (Nissanka, 47.1), 4-285 (Shanaka, 47.4). Mendis retired hurt at 1-212 after 38 overs.

Bowling	O	M	R	W	wd	nb
P VD Chameera	8	0	49	1		1
MM Theekshana	10	0	37	0		2
C Karunaratne	5	0	46	0	1	
DN Wellalage	10	0	56	1		
JDF Vandersay	10	0	49	3		
DM de Silva	6	0	35	1		
MD Shanaka	1	0	10	0	1	

Bowling	O	M	R	W	wd	nb
JR Hazlewood	9.3	0	57	1		
JA Richardson	9	0	39	2	1	
GJ Maxwell	7	0	44	1		
MP Kuhnemann	10	0	61	0		
CJ Green	5	0	30	0	1	
M Labuschagne	7	0	49	0		
TM Head	1	0	9	0		

Toss: Sri Lanka. Umpires: HDPK Dharmasena, LE Hannibal, RR Wimalasiri, (TV), Ref: RS Madugalle. Award: P Nissanka (SL)
Finch 50: 68 balls, 3x4 1x6. Head 50: 59 balls, 2x4 1x6. Nissanka 50: 65 balls, 3x4; 100: 123 balls, 7x4 1x6, Mendis 50: 39 balls, 6x4

FOURTH ONE-DAY INTERNATIONAL - COLOMBO

Trailing 2-1, Australia made just the one change for the must win game when Cummins returned for Jhye Richardson. Sri Lanka lost Chameera with an ankle problem as Hasaranga returned from a groin strain. The pitch was the same one that was used for the third ODI two days before and was expected to be helpful to the spinners.

Things started well for the visitors as Dickwella missed one that went between his legs, with Carey fumbling slightly before bringing off a stumping. Mendis smashed Maxwell for six to long-on but soon after chopped Cummins on in his first over, and when Nissanka was caught behind in Marsh's first over, Sri Lanka were three down inside the first ten overs. The hosts needed a rescue mission and it came as de Silva played confidently while Asalanka was more circumspect. A cut for four by de Silva saw the 100 up in the 22nd over and in the next he magnificently drove Labuschagne to the cover rope. De Silva brought up his 50 (52 balls) and after an edge for four by Asalanka, the 100 stand was raised.

Marsh returned to the attack and had de Silva pulling one to Maxwell at mid-wicket, who brought off a brilliant right-handed catch. Asalanka reached his 50 (49 balls) but next ball was involved in a bad mix-up for a potential second run which saw Shanaka run out. Wellalage went up the order and provided fine support for Asalanka as the pair added 57 to see Sri Lanka to 5-205 with 10 overs left.

Wellalage's knock ended when he lofted one to long-off and then Karunaratne was eventually given out, on referral LBW after missing a sweep. Asalanka, who had been troubled by his groin reached his maiden ODI ton and after brilliantly lofting Cummins over mid-wicket for six, hit a catch to long-on to end a superb innings. Unnecessary runouts caused the last two wickets, with sub fielder Swepson throwing down the stumps to dismiss Theekshana with still an over left to bat.

At the start of the Aussie run chase, Karunaratne trapped Finch in front with his fourth delivery, in a fine spell of 1-6 from three overs. At the other end Theekshana was getting plenty of turn away from Warner, but he was in menacing form and he and Marsh reached the boundary with regularity. Wellalage came on and was struck over long-on for six by Marsh, but the young spinner had him with his next ball when Marsh played forward and edged to slip. Warner reached his 50 (49 balls) and when Australia reached 2-100 in the first of 19 overs, the chase seemed well under control.

But Sri Lanka fought back as Vandersay trapped Labuschagne in front when he was stuck on the crease trying to work one to leg. Hasaranga returned to the bowling crease after a first spell of 0-28 off three overs but his day changed as he dismissed Carey who tried to clear to rope with a slog-sweep but was caught at deep square-leg. Warner and Head settled in together and at 5-189 in the 36th Australia once again looked well placed to win.

As often happens in Asia the game can change quickly as Head was bowled through the gate coming forward, Maxwell like Labuschagne was trapped leg before caught on the crease and then Warner, one short of his ton was stumped missing a drive.

In nine balls Australia had lost 3-2 which made Sri Lanka clear favourites. A stand of 31 for the eighth wicket kept Australia in the game until the 46th over when Green played back to one and got a touch back onto his stumps. Just two singles came from that over and three from the next, which meant Australia needed 33 off the last three overs.

Vandersay kept calm with Cummins managing to get a full toss away in an over that conceded only eight. So, 25 were needed off the last two. After a two and a couple of dots, Cummins uppercut a four, but was then leg before leaving Australia wanting 19 off the last over. Despite various spin options, Skipper Shanaka entrusted himself with the ball as Kuhnemann swished and missed at the first, then hit a full toss behind point for four off the second. After a two off the third, Kuhnemann somehow got one away to long-leg for four, leaving nine wanted off the last two balls. After a powerful stroke over mid-off for four, Australia needed six off the last ball to win. After several minutes of deliberation with several teammates, Shanaka delivered a slightly slower ball which Kuhnemann who lofted in vain to point, where the hero from earlier in the day Asalanka held onto the catch. The fans were delirious, the Sri Lanka players delighted as they had beaten Australia for the first time in a series since November 2010 in Australia.

Fourth ODI at R Premadasa Stadium, Colombo on June 21, 2022 (day/night) – Sri Lanka won by 4 runs

Sri Lanka

Batsman	Dismissal	R	B	M	4	6
N Dickwella+	st Carey b Maxwell	1	3	7		
P Nissanka	c Carey b Marsh	13	25	44	2	
BKG Mendis	b Cummins	14	21	22	1	
DM de Silva	c Maxwell b Marsh	60	61	89	7	
KIC Asalanka	c Finch b Cummins	110	106	181	10	1
MD Shanaka	run out (Marsh-Carey)	4	8	19		
DN Wellalage	c Warner b Kuhnemann	19	35	43		
C Karunaratne	lbw b Kuhnemann	7	9	15		
W Hasaranga	not out	21	20	33	3	
JDF Vandersay	run out (Cummins-Carey)	0	2	3		
MM Theekshana	run out	0	5	3		
	(sub [MJ Swepson])					
	2 lb, 1 nb, 6 w	9				
10 overs: 3-35		258		49 overs, 235 mins		

Australia

Batsman	Dismissal	R	B	M	4	6
DA Warner	st Dickwella b de Silva	99	112	167	12	
AJ Finch*	lbw b Karunaratne	0	4	11		
MR Marsh	c de Silva b Wellalage	26	27	38	3	1
M Labuschagne	lbw b Vandersay	14	21	35		
AT Carey+	c Vandersay b Hasaranga	19	20	24	2	
TM Head	b de Silva	27	33	44	3	
GJ Maxwell	lbw b Theekshana	1	3	4		
CD Green	b Vandersay	13	25	38		
PJ Cummins	lbw b Karunaratne	35	43	50	2	
MP Kuhnemann	c Asalanka b Shanaka	15	12	29	3	
JR Hazlewood	not out	0	1	9		
	1 lb, 1 nb, 3 w	5				
10 overs: 1-45		254		50 overs, 231 mins		

1-5 (Dickwella, 1.2), 2-26 (Mendis, 6.3), 3-34 (Nissanka, 9.5), 4-135 (de Silva, 26.2), 5-150 (Shanaka, 29.4), 6-207 (Wellalage, 40.2), 7-222 (Karunaratne, 42.5), 8-256 (Asalanka, 47.4), 9-257 (Vandersay, 48.1), 10-258 (Theekshana, 48.6)

1-3 (Finch, 2.4), 2-66 (Marsh, 11.4), 3-101 (Labuschagne, 19.3), 4-131 (Carey, 25.4), 5-189 (Head, 35.5), 6-190 (Maxwell, 36.2), 7-192 (Warner, 37.1), 8-223 (Green, 45.3), 9-240 (Cummins, 48.5), 10-254 (Kuhnemann, 49.6)

Bowling	O	M	R	W	wd	nb
JR Hazlewood	10	0	45	0	1	
GJ Maxwell	8	0	49	1	1	
MP Kuhnemann	8	0	56	2	1	
PJ Cummins	9	1	37	2	2	
MR Marsh	7	0	29	2		1
CD Green	5	0	27	0		
M Labuschagne	2	0	13	0		

Bowling	O	M	R	W	wd	nb
C Karunaratne	5	1	19	2	1	
MM Theekshana	10	1	40	1		
W Hasaranga	10	0	52	1		
DN Wellalage	5	0	29	1	1	
DM de Silva	10	0	39	2		
JDF Vandersay	7	0	40	2	1	
KIC Asalanka	1	0	7	0		
MD Shanaka	2	0	27	1		1

Toss: Sri Lanka. Umpires: RSA Palliyaguruge, RMPJ Rambukwella, HDPK Dharmasena (TV), Ref: RS Madugalle.
Award KIC Asalanka (SL). De Silva 50: 52 balls, 6x4, Asalanka 50: 60 balls, 4x4; 100: 99 balls, 10x4. Warner 50: 49 balls, 8x4

FIFTH ONE-DAY INTERNATIONAL - COLOMBO

Despite the series being decided there was still plenty riding on the final game, with both sides having an eye to the first Test in five days time. Head was out for Australia with a hamstring strain, which meant that Josh Inglis would make his ODI debut. Sri Lanka made three changes, with Dinesh Chandimal in for his first game in the series, while paceman Pramod Madushan was in to make his debut.

Australia struck early with the new ball as Nissanka edged a catch to the keeper and then Gunathilleke drove one very hard to mid-off. Mendis got some early boundaries away but when Chandimal drove a catch to mid-on, Sri Lanka were three down inside the Powerplay. The fourth wicket added 22, but then Sri Lanka lost 4-6 in eight balls to make a complete hash of things. Firstly, Asalanka was run out after a mix-up with Mendis over a second run, then next ball Mendis stepped onto his stumps playing a pull shot. Wellalage hit a nice off-drive for four, but next ball was well caught at wide mid-on. When Shanaka missed an on-drive which hit leg stump, Sri Lanka were 7-62 after just 17 overs.

Karunaratne was up for the task hitting some early fours and then his partner Vandersay was run out, after being too slow to respond for a single to point. Madushan showed plenty of fight on debut as he and Karunaratne tried to rebuild the innings, as Sri Lanka reached 100 in the 29th over. Karunaratne reached his maiden ODI 50 (62 balls) when he pulled Cummins for four and had some luck on 60 when Finch dropped a low chance at long-on off Green. Madushan's innings ended when drove one back to Green and then Karunaratne went on the attack, lofting Labuschagne for consecutive sixes. The innings ended shortly after when Karunaratne top-edged a pull straight up in the air, Sri Lanka reaching 160 a fair effort after being 8-85.

Warner was wlooking for a quick chase when he took 10 off the first over, but lost Finch in the second when he gloved a sweep to slip. In the third Warner smashed one hard to mid-off and was gone as Gunathilleke dived to his left to bring off the catch, heading off injured immediately after. When Inglis glanced one to leg-slip, Australia were 3-19 and 161 looked way off.

After just two singles from his first 16 balls, Marsh started to find the rope and had steadied the innings until went after Madushan and miscued a catch to deep point. At 4-50 Australia could have buckled but Labuschagne and Carey eased things, adding 50 to reach the 100 mark in the 28th over. Wellalage then spun one that pitched on leg and would have hit middle, with Labuschagne's pad in the way, ending the stand of 51. The young left-arm spinner then bowled a similar ball which hit the stumps of Maxwell, which meant Australia had to make another 41 with four wickets left. Green was less than convincing early, but with Carey calmly finding the gaps, the pressure quickly eased. Green soon punched Asalanka straight to the boundary rope and hit Vandersay straight for six to win the game with 10.3 overs to spare. Post match the fans of Colombo stood and cheered to thank the Australians for touring, many wearing yellow T-shirts as a mark of support.

Fifth ODI at R Premadasa Stadium, Colombo on June 24, 2022 (day/night) - Australia won by 4 wickets

Sri Lanka		B	M	4	6	Australia		B	M	4	6
MD Gunathilleke	c Finch b Hazlewood	8	14	18	1	DA Warner	c Gunathilleke b Wellalage	10	8	16	2
P Nissanka	c Carey b Hazlewood	2	4	7		AJ Finch*	c Asalanka b Theekshana	0	3	9	
BKG Mendis +	hit wkt b Maxwell	26	40	59	3	MR Marsh	c Silva b Madushan	24	50	58	3
LD Chandimal	c Finch b Cummins	6	11	16	1	JP Inglis	c Silva b Theekshana	5	10	11	1
KIC Asalanka	run out (Kuhnemann-Maxwell)	14	27	29	1	M Labuschagne	lbw b Wellalage	31	58	102	2
MD Shanaka*	b Kuhnemann	1	3	10		AT Carey+	not out	45	65	106	1
DN Wellalage	c Cummins b Kuhnemann	4	2	5	1	GJ Maxwell	b Wellalage	16	17	18	2
C Karunaratne	c Carey b Cummins	75	75	117	8	2	CD Green	not out	25	26	31	2	1
JDF Vandersay	run out (Labuschagne)	4	23	29		PJ Cummins					
P Madushan	c & b Green	15	52	74	2	MP Kuhnemann					
MM Theekshana	not out	2	8	9		JR Hazlewood					
	(3 w)	3					(8 w)	8			
10 overs: 3-35	43.1 overs, 191 mins	160				10 overs: 3-34	39.3 overs, 183 mins	6-164			

1-9 (Nissanka, 2.1), 2-12 (Gunathilleke, 4.3), 3-34 (Chandimal, 8.4), 4-56 (Asalanka, 15.5), 5-56 (Mendis, 15.6), 6-61 (Wellalage, 16.4), 7-62 (Shanaka, 16.6), 8-85 (Vandersay, 24.2), 9-143 (Madushan, 41.1), 10-160 (Karunaratne, 43.1)

1-11 (Finch, 1.3), 2-14 (Warner, 2.3), 3-19 (Inglis, 5.2), 4-50 (Marsh, 14.5), 5-101 (Labuschagne, 27.6), 6-121 (Maxwell, 31.6)

Bowling	O	M	R	W	wd	nb
Hazlewood	7	3	22	2		
Maxwell	10	0	38	1		
Kuhnemann	10	3	26	2		
Cummins	6.1	1	22	2		1
Marsh	1	0	3	0		
Labuschagne	7	1	36	0	1	
Green	2	0	13	1	1	

Bowling	O	M	R	W	wd	nb
C Karunaratne	3	0	19	0	1	
MM Theekshana	10	1	26	2	4	
DN Wellalage	10	0	42	3	2	
JDF Vandersay	9.3	0	46	0		
P Madushan	3	0	13	1		
KIC Asalanka	4	0	18	0	1	

Toss: Sri Lanka. Umpires: HDPK Dharmasena, RSA Palliyaguruge, RMPJ Rambukwella (TV), Ref: RS Madugalle.
Karunaratne 50: 62 balls, 7x4

FIRST TEST - GALLE

On a dry looking pitch in hot conditions Australia's Travis Head was declared fit having recovered from a hamstring strain, while Mitch Swepson retained his spot as the second spinner, with Josh Hazlewood not making the final eleven. Sri Lanka gave a debut to leggie Jeffrey Vandersay who was one of four spinners in the team, Asitha Fernando the only pace bowler.

Day One

Sri Lanka had the luck with the toss and after scoring 14 off five overs of pace, which included an on-drive for four by Nissanka off Starc, off-spinner Lyon was introduced. The veterans first ball spun and bounced off the main section of the pitch, past the outside edge of Karunaratne's bat and into the grille off keeper Carey's helmet. Both openers made decent progress adding 38 until Nissanka edged a back of a length ball to the keeper. Soon after Starc returned to bowl and with his first delivery had Kusal Mendis caught behind aiming a big drive. Matthews off-drove Starc for four, then with Swepson on before lunch, Karunaratne struck him and Lyon to the rope for fours. Sri Lanka went to lunch on 2-68 (Karunaratne 25, Mathews 15) from 27 overs with Lyon bowling 11 overs of them (0-21) in the morning session.

Lyon struck in the third over after lunch when Karunaratne nicked one onto his pad, the ball going to gully for a simple catch. Many a ball was starting to explode off the surface and Swepson cashed in as de Silva leaned forward and edged a leg break to the keeper, then next ball Mathews was taken in gully as Warner juggled and held onto one that came via Carey's gloves.

Dickwella rode his luck, as he played handy reverse and regular sweeps alike, at one stage taking Lyon down for an over that cost 14 including three fours. Mathews was playing well at the other end until he was caught at slip and then Ramesh Mendis offered excellent support to Dickwella as the stand grew. In the over before tea Dickwella reached his 50 (42 balls, 5 fours) as Sri Lanka hit the break on 6-191 off 52 overs, with Dickwella 51, Ramesh Mendis 22.

It took Australia only seven overs after tea to mop up the tail as Ramesh Mendis played back and missed a sharp turning off-break. Dickwella's plucky knock ended when he got a fine edge to a sweep and after belting Lyon to leg for six to get off the mark, Embuldeniya was well held at mid-on. Vandersay reverse swept a four and then was caught at deep square-leg when he went for the conventional version, Sri Lanka all out 40 minutes, having lost 4-21 after tea.

Australia had a maximum 29 overs to bat and when Warner hit Fernando for back to back square driven boundaries, it seemed he was after the first innings lead by nightfall. Embuldeniya copped similar treatment from Warner in his first over with back-to-back fours, while Khawaja survived being given out on 13 when he had a LBW decision overturned facing Ramesh Mendis. At 47 after nine overs Australia was well placed but then Ramesh Mendis had Warner LBW on the forward stroke with one that didn't spin. Labuschagne had his broom out early with several boundaries via the sweep, but then he attempted a reverse against Ramesh Mendis and picked out backward point perfectly. In the same over Australia could have been three down as Khawaja on 36 advanced at one and missed, Dickwella fumbling the chance.

Sri Lanka had their third wicket when Smith wanted a run in the off-side that wasn't on, Khawaja ultimately deciding not to run much to the displeasure of Smith who was very upset when he walked off. Head's scoring began with an edged three and then on six he survived a stumping chance off Ramesh Mendis. So, when 5.30pm ticked over Australia trailed by 114 but could easily have lost another 2-3 wickets.

Day two

A considerable amount of rain and wind prevented the start of play until 1.45pm. Fortunately the outfield was fully covered, but a majority of the temporary stands had been blown away, which caused local authorities some difficulties. When play did start Head was soon back in the rooms, as he looked to work de Silva and gave a return catch. Australia's innings needed steadying and fortunately Khawaja and Green were able to do so on a pitch that was turning a little less than the previous day. Dickwella was having trouble with the gloves for Sri Lanka conceding two lots of four byes, as the partnership pushed past 50. Vandersay came on for his first bowl of the day and immediately had Khawaja caught after an inside edge to short-leg.

Carey came out and showed his love for the reverse sweep, with nine of his first 13 runs coming from the shot, including a boundary off Vandersay. Sri Lanka then went back to pace and Carey found that no problem as he square and cover drove Fernando for boundaries. At the other end Green was quietly adding to his score, as a third lot of four byes saw the fifty stand raised. Green cracked Vandersay away through mid-on for four and after Carey reverse swept Embuldeniya for four, Australia went to tea looking good on 5-233 (Green 48, Carey 43) holding a lead of 21.

Straight after tea Green brought up his 50 and then Carey's fine knock ended when he was well held by Chandimal running back at mid-on. Starc was hit on the helmet by Fernando but proceeded to stay with Green as the Australian lead grew. Green looked well set for a ton until he missed a sweep at a full ball and then Starc went in the next over when he hit a return catch to Vandersay. With the light fading Cummins took the long handle to Vandersay, hitting him for two sixes in an over, the second landing out of the ground at wide long-on. Incredibly seconds later the umpire deemed the light to bad to continue, Australia 101 ahead at day's end.

Day 3

At the start of play Mathews was ruled out with COVID, Sri Lanka allowed to replace him with Oshada Fernando. Paceman Asitha Fernando ended the Aussie innings quickly when he yorked Cummins and Swepson in the space of four balls to keep the Australian lead to 109. Sri Lanka got off to a flyer first ball when Nissanka drove Starc through mid-off for four and then Karunaratne joined in to hit three fours on the trot, 17 coming from the opening over. Lyon bowled the second over and after another from Starc which cost six, Swepson was on to bowl the fourth. It didn't take long for Lyon to strike, as he had Karunaratne caught behind when he got a fine edge to a sweep. Swepson had Nissanka LBW on the sweep but when Oshada Fernando hit him for six straight, Sri Lanka were looking ok at 2-59 off 11 overs.

Either side of drinks two wickets fell as Kusal Mendis top-edged a sweep to deep square-leg and Oshada Fernando who edged a drive to slip. Carey was having his frustrations behind the stumps giving up two lots of four byes in the one Lyon over, including a missed stumping of de Silva on five. With the score on 4-95, Pat Cummins turned to Travis Head offering him a bowl from the Fort end. Head had success with his second ball as Chandimal was bowled when he aimed a drive at an off-break that turned significantly. Three balls later de Silva let one hit him on the pads well back in the crease when he offered no shot, the Australian were all up for LBW, but Umpire Dharmasena wasn't interested. The visitors called for the review and were delighted when technology showed it was hitting, Sri Lanka 6-96 and T Head 2-1 from one!

Lyon joined in on the fun when Ramesh Mendis top-edged a sweep to deep backward square-leg and then Dickwella was caught reverse sweeping to cover point. Head bowled Vandersay "through the gate" and then won another review which saw Embuldeniya leg before to a full ball, the innings ending in just 22.5 overs – the least amount they've faced to be all out in a Test. With just five to win, Warner had a wild swing at the second ball and was hit on the pad, before reverse-sweeping a four and then clunking one over long-on to wrap up the game just after the scheduled lunch break on day three.

As entertaining as the Test was, the pitch spun far too much far too early in the match, but on the bright side for Australia it gave them a six-day break before the next Test at the same venue and more than likely on a similar surface.

First Test at Galle International Stadium on June 29 – July 1, 2022 - Australia won by 10 wickets

Sri Lanka	First innings		B	M	4	6	Second innings		B	M	4	6
P Nissanka	c Carey b Cummins	23	44	55	3		lbw b Swepson	14	19	32	1	
D Karunaratne	c Warner b Lyon	28	84	130	3		c Carey b Lyon	23	20	25	5	
BKG Mendis	c Carey b Starc	3	15	20			c Swepson b Lyon	8	15	26	1	
AD Mathews	c Warner b Lyon	39	71	120	3							
BOP Fernando						4	c Smith b Swepson	12	18	27	1	1
DM de Silva	c Carey b Swepson	14	22	29	2	5	lbw b Head	11	20	37		
LD Chandimal	c Warner b Swepson	0	1	1		6	b Head	13	21	23	1	
N Dickwella+	c Carey b Lyon	58	59	97	6	7	c Labuschagne b Lyon	3	7	18		
RT Mendis	lbw b Lyon	22	36	53	3	8	c Khawaja b Lyon	0	2	4		
JDF Vandersay	c Starc b Swepson	6	15	26	1	9	b Head	8	8	11	1	
L Embuldeniya	c Khawaja b Lyon	6	6	20		1 10	lbw b Head	0	6	8		
AM Fernando	not out	2	1	5		11	not out	5	2	4	1	
	5 b, 6 lb	11					14 b, 1 lb, 1 nb	16				
	59 overs, 278 mins	212					22.5 overs, 112 mins	113				

1-38 (Nissanka), 2-42 (K Mendis), 3-74 (Karunaratne), 4-97 (de Silva), 5-97 (Chandimal), 6-139 (Mathews), 7-193 (R Mendis), 8-198 (Dickwella), 9-206 (Embuldeniya), 10-212 (Vandersay)

1-37 (Karunaratne), 2-39 (Nissanka), 3-59 (K Mendis), 4-63 (B Fernando), 5-95 (Chandimal), 6-96 (de Silva), 7-97 (R Mendis), 8-108 (Dickwella), 9-108 (Vandersay), 10-113 (Embuldeniya)

BOM Fernando was a COVID sub for AD Matthews for the second innings

Bowling	O	M	R	W	wd	nb		O	M	R	W	wd	nb
MA Starc	9	0	31	1				2	0	23	0		
PJ Cummins	12	4	25	1									
NM Lyon	25	2	90	5				11	1	31	4		
MJ Swepson	13	0	55	3				7	0	34	2	1	
TM Head								2.5	0	10	4		

Australia	First innings		B	M	4	6	Second innings		B	M	4	6
UT Khawaja	c Silva b Vandersay	71	130	152	7		2 not out	0	0	3		
DA Warner	lbw b R Mendis	25	24	37	5		1 not out	10	4	3	1	1
M Labuschagne	c Fernando b R Mendis	13	19	25	2							
SPD Smith	run out (Dickwella-Mendis)	6	11	15								
TM Head	c & b de Silva	6	16	24								
CD Green	lbw b R Mendis	77	109	184	6							
AT Carey+	c Chandimal b R Mendis	45	47	83	6							
MA Starc	c & b Vandersay	10	30	56	1							
PJ Cummins*	b A Fernando	26	18	29	1	3						
NM Lyon	not out	15	20	29	2							
MJ Swepson	b A Fernando	1	2	3								
	20 b, 3 lb, 1 nb, 2 w	26					0.4 overs, 3 mins	0-10				
	70.5 overs, 323 mins	321										

1-47 (Warner, 9.1), 2-75 (Labuschagne, 15.2), 3-83 (Smith), 4-100 (Head), 5-157 (Khawaja), 6-241 (Carey), 7-278 (Green), 8-278 (Starc), 9-319 (Cummins), 10-321 (Swepson)

Bowling	O	M	R	W	wd	nb		O	M	R	W	wd	nb
AM Fernando	8.5	1	37	2	2								
DM de Silva	5	0	8	1									
L Ambuldeniya	15	0	73	0		1							
RT Mendis	32	0	112	4				0.4	0	10	0		
JDF Vandersay	10	0	68	2									

Stumps scores

| Day 1 | Australia (1st inn) 3-97 | UT Khawaja 46*, TM Head 6* |
| Day 2 | Australia (1st inn) 8-313 | PJ Cummins 26*, NM Lyon 8* |

Toss: Sri Lanka.
Umpires: HDPK Dharmasena, NN Menon, MA Gough (TV), Ref: J Srinath Award: CD Green (Aus)

79

SECOND TEST - GALLE

Having looked at the pitch, Australia's selectors decided against replacing Travis Head with Glenn Maxwell and kept the same side that won the First Test. Sri Lanka on the other hand had a number of forced changes and included Kamindu Mendis, Theekshana and Jayasuriya to all make their debuts.

Day One

The toss went the visitor's way, but after a Warner square drive for four in the third over, he went in the fifth when he played forward and down the wrong line to be bowled. Khawaja looked sound in employing the sweep and with Labuschagne pushing singles, Australia ended the opening hour on 0-45 after 14 overs. The pitch wasn't turning as much as in the opening Test, but care still had to be taken facing spinners Ramesh and Theekshana who joined forces at the bowling crease. Jayasuriya came on for his first bowl in a Test and in his second over Labuschagne struck him for two sweeps to the leg-side boundary. Khawaja continued to bat very soundly but within 30 minutes of lunch played back to one from Ramesh which spun past his bat and cannoned into the stumps. Then when Labuschagne was on 28, Dickwella missed a stumping off Ramesh, the ball bouncing a bit more than the keeper expected.

Rajitha returned for a brief spell before lunch, Labuschagne easing past backward point for two fours in an over as Australia went into the break on 2-99 (30 overs), Labuschagne 42, Smith 13. After just 10 runs in first six overs after lunch, Labuschagne pulled Rajitha away for four to bring up his 50. In the next over he took advantage of some short balls from Ramesh to pull and cut boundaries and when Smith swept the same bowler for another four, 13 had come from the over. On 63 Labuschagne was very nearly bowled by Jayasuriya when his edged sweep missed the off-stump by the smallest of margins.

The 100 stand was raised between the pair for the seventh time (22 innings) in Tests and then Smith reached his 50 as Australia was in sight of still being two down at tea. Ten minutes before tea Labuschagne pushed a ball from Jayasuriya to leg to reach his seventh Test ton and first away from Australia. Then in the last over before tea, Labuschagne advanced at Jayasuriya and was beaten by the turn and bounce, with Dickwella on this occasion able to adjust to the bounce and bring off a stumping. Australia was 3-204 as the players walked off, Smith 52 not out.

With Head under some notice for his spot given the speculation that Maxwell might play, the South Aussie was very careful in the early stages of his innings and looked content to push the ball into the gaps for singles. Smith was doing much the same as the pair added 34 before Head pushed forward and was beaten by a ball from Jayasuriya, the ball not turning as much as he thought, which just clipped the outside off the off-stump. Then Green who had been so impressive in the first Test, soon went when he was LBW after missing a sweep shot. Smith continued undaunted and with Carey in support reached his first ton since January 2021, when he drove Rajitha to the cover rope. The pair had added 46 by stumps, Australia well pleased to have two centurions on the opening day.

Day Two

On another bright day in Galle, Australia would have been confident of batting past lunch to see up a score in excess of 400. After a run a minute in the first half an hour this looked achievable with both Smith and Carey going on with the job from the night before. In the day's fifth over, Carey reverse swept Jayasuriya for four while Smith advanced and on-drove a boundary. But then Carey's strength with the shot caused his undoing as he aimed another reverse at Jayasuriya and top-edged it straight down the throat of the point fielder, who was slightly deeper than usual.

At 6-329 Australia still had hopes for a total near 400, but this was soon extinguished when Starc edged to slip and Cummins was leg before after a successful review by the hosts. When Lyon played back and was trapped in front, Australia had lost 4-16. Smith hadn't been getting much of the strike and when joined by last man Swepson it may have been a thought to be a bit more aggressive. The pair added 19 in seven overs when Swepson was LBW, Australia having lost 5-66 in the morning off 20 overs.

Sri Lanka had three overs to bat to lunch and made it to 0-8 (Nissanka 3, Karunaratne 5) but in Starc's third over after the break Nissanka edged high to gully where Green reached high to take a fine catch. The Aussie bowlers were giving little away with just 18 being scored from the first 14 overs. Karunaratne broke the quiet run of scoring when he on-drove Lyon for two fours in an over and then Nissanka pulled Cummins away for four. Karunaratne cut Lyon for four to bring up the 50, but then was lucky on 34, when in the last over before tea, he hit a full toss back at Swepson, who could only get his right hand to the ball but couldn't hold on. The hosts went into tea on 1-65 (30 overs), with Karunaratne 35 and Kusal Mendis 23.

With 38 overs left in ideal batting conditions, the Sri Lankans realised it was time to cash in. Both batsmen applied themselves to the task and were rewarded for their earlier patience. The Aussie attack tried hard but struggled to beat the bat or produce any chances as the pitch became more perfect for batting. Karunaratne reached his 50 (109 balls) when he advanced and lofted Swepson to leg for four, with the 100 stand raised shortly after. Cummins returned for a crack and with his first ball he thought he had Karunaratne caught down the leg side on 65, but a review came up with a negative result. As the wind picked up in the late afternoon, Kusal reached a well made 50 (118 balls, 171 minutes) when he pulled Head behind square leg for a couple.

The Aussies managed to get the ball changed but this did very little for them as Kusal played some confident strokes, including a hook for four off Cummins. Finally, the breakthrough came when Swepson, who had only bowled six of the first 54 overs returned to bowl the 55th and trapped Karunaratne playing back and across a skiddy leg-break. Mathews played with care and application supporting Kusal until the close of play, Sri Lanka well placed with eight wickets in hand and a deficit of 180.

Day Three

The first ten minutes of the day were action packed as Lyon thought he Kusal LBW on the back foot to the fifth ball of the day. Umpire Gough denied the shout, a review by Australia showing the ball to be clipping the stumps but as "Umpire call". In the off-spinner's next over though he had his man in similar circumstances, this time Umpire Gough giving him the decision, with Sri Lanka losing a review. Despite falling 15 short of another ton against Australia, Kusal should have been well proud of his efforts in setting the innings up.

Enter Chandimal who was intent to attack Lyon early, hitting him in the air through cover for four before whacking the next ball over long-off for six. In Lyon's next over Chandimal on 11 advanced and missed, the ball turning a mile and eluding Carey by some margin and missing a potential stumping. Lyon had brought in a silly point and then thought he had Mathews leg before on 36, the subsequent review showing a small under edge to the reverse sweep. In the next over Lyon thought he had Chandimal caught at silly point, but the ball had struck pad only and now Australia was out of reviews.

Australia took the new ball after 84 overs at 3-256 but Cummins and Starc could make no breakthrough in the five overs to lunch, Sri Lanka going in on 3-262 just 102 behind with Mathews 49, Chandimal 29. After having survived two LBW shouts facing Lyon in the first over after lunch, Mathews worked one behind square leg to reach a well made 50 from 114 balls. But the veteran was on his way in the next over, when he got an inside edge via his thigh to short-leg. Starc continued to cause some problems as in his next over he thought he had Chandimal caught behind uppercutting on 30. With no reviews left Australia were unable to challenge, with a replay shortly after showing the batsman had got a fine edge. Sri Lanka passed 300 and then soon after Chandimal swept Lyon for four to reach his fifty from 103 balls.

Kamindu Mendis was looking composed in his first test knock and then half an hour before tea the rain caused an early tea, with Sri Lanka 4-327, Chandimal 63, Kamindu 24. Australia's spinners were giving little away in the early overs after the resumption until Kamindu reverse swept Swepson for four and then on 33 he edged Lyon to Smith at slip, who dived a long way to his left but couldn't hang on. Soon after on 43 Kamindu had some more luck when he advanced at Lyon, Carey missing the stumping as the ball just went over the top of the off-stump. Sri Lanka took the lead, the 100 stand came and then Kamindu raised his 50 (110 balls) as the day continued to be a long one for the visitors.

Skipper Cummins was trying different things, bringing Labuschagne on, swapping Lyon from the Pavilion end to the Fort end but none of it worked as the 400 was brought up. Then came the moment for Chandimal as he pushed Lyon slowly into the off-side for a single to bring up his 13th Test ton – having faced 195 balls, hitting 8 fours and a six in five hours, ten minutes. Kamindu's first Test innings came to an end in the next over when he was bowled missing a slog-sweep, and then Dickwella went shortly after as holed out to mid-on.

Australia thought they had another wicket when Ramesh was on four, when he was adjudged caught down the leg side off Head, but the review showed no contact with the bat. Then the next over Carey missed a leg-side stumping off a full ball from Swepson when Ramesh was five, to continue a tough day for the Aussie keeper. Late in the day in between overs we saw an unusual incident when Labuschagne tried to throw his fielding helmet to a Carey, with it landing short of its target and hitting the main part of the pitch. Sri Lanka finished proceedings without further loss, having lost four wickets for the day for 247, to have an overall lead of 67.

Day Four

At the start of play Oshada Fernando was brought in as a COVID sub for the second Test in a row, with Nissanka this time the unfortunate man to have to drop out of the game. Australia's bowlers continued their hard toil, with Lyon passing the 60 over mark in an innings for the first time in his career. Ramesh offered Chandimal great support as they added 44 in the first hour to reach drinks on 6-477, with the third new ball available after 164 overs. Starc took it immediately and had Ramesh straight away, plumb LBW with an in-swinging yorker. Chandimal reached his 150 but lost Theekshana just before lunch when he had his off-stump removed by Cummins, Sri Lanka 8-499 at the break with Chandimal 153 not out.

After lunch Jayasuriya was yorked off-stump and in the next over Chandimal went after Cummins, uppercutting him for six as he went past his previous Test best of 164. He then hit Starc straight down the ground for three sixes in the bowlers next two overs to complete a memorable maiden double-ton, being the first to reach the mark in Tests for Sri Lanka against Australia. Swepson returned to trap Rajitha LBW, with Sri Lanka's leading by 190 with 56 overs left on day four. With 554 on the board it was also Sri Lanka's best ever total against Australia, surpassing the 8-547 declared made at Colombo (SSC) in 1992.

Australia had a massive task ahead of them, but if they could somehow get a lead of 150, they may have a chance to still win the match. Warner played out a maiden from Rajitha and then in the next over Theekshana beat the driving bat of Khawaja on two, only for Dickwella to miss the stumping. The runs began to flow for Australia, with Warner at one stage hitting four fours in two overs, as Australia reached 49 without loss ten minutes before tea. Warner then went for one shot too many as he went for a sweep off Ramesh and was out leg before, losing a review in the process with replays showing it was hitting middle stump, three quarters the way up. Tea came with Australia 1-52, still 138 behind with Khawaja 25 and Labuschagne 2.

Things moved rapidly after tea in the hosts favour as Australia collapsed to lose three wickets in the first 30 minutes. Khawaja got an inside edge via his pad to backward short-leg and then Smith played back four balls later to be plumb in front, but wasted another review which showed the ball to be crashing into middle and leg well below the bails. Head looked confident in sweeping an early four but then got stuck on the crease and poked at one that hit his off-stump.

Labuschagne and Green resisted well for a time but after the pair added 38, Australia suffered another mini-collapse to lose three wickets in 11 balls. Labuschagne missed a sweep at a full ball, but to his credit accepted his fate without question and didn't make it a hat-trick of wasted reviews. Replays showed he made the correct decision. Green then walked past a well flighted ball and then Starc edged one low to slip. Cummins swung Jayasuriya to long-on for six before being trapped in front by Theekshana, who in the same over also dismissed Lyon LBW on the sweep.

When Swepson was bowled it gave Sri Lanka their first innings victory over Australia and just their fifth win against them overall in 33 Tests. For Pat Cummins it was his first loss as Test skipper and he said at the post-match presentations that it wasn't good enough to lose nine wickets in a session and to be beaten with a day to spare. But he paid full credit to the Sri Lankans for the way they played a congratulated them on their fine win as well as thanking the country for being great hosts. With 12 wickets, Jayasuriya was named Man of the match, having recorded the best match figures for a Sri Lankan on debut. So came the end a five-week tour that gave plenty of joy to the fans that had turned out in great numbers. This despite having to deal with major shortages of fuel and other essential items, throughout a country on the verge of financial collapse.

Second Test at Galle International Stadium on July 8-11, 2022 – Sri Lanka won by an innings and 39 runs

Australia	First innings		B	M	4	6	Second innings		B	M	4	6
UT Khawaja	b Ramesh Mendis	37	77	90	4		2 c Fernando b Jayasuriya	29	47	74	4	
DA Warner	b Rajitha	5	13	20	1		1 lbw b Ramesh Mendis	24	44	56	4	
M Labuschagne	st Dickwella b Jayasuriya	104	156	217	12		lbw b Jayasuriya	32	59	72	3	
SPD Smith	not out	145	272	368	16		lbw b Jayasuriya	0	4	4		
TM Head	b Jayasuriya	12	36	46			b Ramesh Mendis	5	4	11	1	
CD Green	lbw b Jayasuriya	4	14	18			st Dickwella b Jayasuriya	23	32	45	2	
AT Carey+	c Ram. Mendis											
	b Jayasuriya	28	61	94	4		not out	16	28	48		
MA Starc	c K Mendis b Jayasuriya	1	8	11			c BKG Mendis b Jayasuriya	0	2	4		
PJ Cummins*	lbw b Rajitha	5	6	9	1		lbw b Theekshana	16	18	25	1	1
NM Lyon	lbw b Jayasuriya	5	6	10	1		lbw b Theekshana	5	3	4	1	
MJ Swepson	lbw b Theekshana	3	14	27			b Jayasuriya	0	5	4		
	5 b, 6 lb, 3 nb, 1 w	15					1 b	1				
	110 overs, 429 mins	364					41 overs, 178 mins	151				

1-15 (Warner), 2-70 (Khawaja), 3-204 (Labuschagne), 4-238 (Head), 5-252 (Green), 6-329 (Carey), 7-333 (Starc), 8-338 (Cummins), 9-345 (Lyon), 10-364 (Swepson)

1-49 (Warner), 2-59 (Khawaja), 3-59 (Smith), 4-74 (Head), 5-112 (Labuschagne), 6-117 (Green), 7-117 (Starc), 8-144 (Cummins), 9-150 (Lyon), 10-151 (Swepson)

Bowling	O	M	R	W	wd	nb	O	M	R	W	wd	nb
CAK Rajitha	25	4	70	2	1	3	5	1	16	0		
Ramesh Mendis	33	1	117	1			15	2	47	2		
MM Theekshana	16	2	48	1			5	0	28	2		
NGRP Jayasuriya	36	3	118	6			16	2	59	6		

Sri Lanka	First innings		B	M	4	6	Bowling	O	M	R	W	wd	nb
P Nissanka	c Green b Starc	6	25	41			MA Starc	29	3	89	4		
D Karunaratne*	lbw b Swepson	86	165	248	10		PJ Cummins	30	5	95	1	1	1
BKG Mendis	lbw b Lyon	85	161	252	9		NM Lyon	64	5	194	2		
AD Mathews	c Labuschagne b Starc	52	117	163	4		CD Green	6	0	20	0	1	
LD Chandimal	not out	206	326	482	16	5	MJ Swepson	38	2	103	3		
PHKD Mendis	b Swepson	61	137	198	7		TM Head	8	0	27	0		
N Dickwella+	c Cummins b Lyon	5	13	17			M Labuschagne	6	0	16	0		
Ramesh Mendis	lbw b Starc	29	98	119	1								
MM Theekshana	b Cummins	10	27	40	2		Fall: 1-12 (Nissanka), 2-164 (Karunaratne),						
NGRP Jayasuriya	b Starc	0	9	16			3-186 (BKG Mendis), 4-269 (Mathews),						
CAK Rajitha	lbw b Swepson	0	9	33			5-402 (PHKD Mendis), 6-409 (Dickwella)						
O Fernando							7-477 (Ramesh Mendis), 8-498 (Theekshana),						
	4 b, 6 lb, 1 nb, 3 w	14					9-505 (Jayasuriya), 10-554 (Rajitha)						
	181 overs, 843 mins	554											

Stumps scores

Day 1	Australia (1st inn) 5-298	SPD Smith 109*, AT Carey 16*
Day 2	Sri Lanka (1st inn) 2-184	Kusal Mendis 84* A Mathews 6*
Day 3	Sri Lanka (1st inn) 6-431	LD Chandimal 118*, Ramesh Mendis 7*

Toss: Australia. Umpires: HDPK Dharmasena, MA Gough, N Menon (TV), Ref: J Srinath. Award: NGRP Jayasuriya (SL). Series: LD Chandimal (SL)

82

AUSTRALIA A in SRI LANKA

First 50 over match at Sinhalese Sports Club Ground, Colombo on June 8, 2022 – Australia A won by 5 wickets

Sri Lanka A		R	B	M	4	6
L Croospulle	c Carey b Steketee	2	2	1		
O Fernando	c Hardie b Murphy	65	82	100	7	
K Mendis	c & b Kuhnemann	42	47	63	4	2
DM de Silva*	c Maddinson b Hardie	68	70	96	10	
N Dickwella+	lbw b Murphy	10	16	24		
A Bandara	run out (Carey)	48	46	72	3	1
DN Wellalage	c Murphy b Steketee	33	30	37	2	
PAD Lakshan	not out	4	5	7		
D Tharanga	not out	11	4	4	1	
D Madushanka						
P Tharanga						
	1 b, 3 lb, 2 nb, 8 w	14				
10 overs: 1-62	50 overs, 206 mins	7-297				

Australia A		R	B	M	4	6
JR Philippe	b Wellalage	5	12	28		
HJ Hunt	c Madushanka b Wellalage	36	45	51	4	
MT Renshaw	b Tharanga	68	69	92	8	
CD Green	not out	119	111	151	9	3
AT Carey*+	not out	52	51	81	5	
NJ Maddinson						
MT Steketee						
TR Murphy						
MP Kuhnemann						
TS Sangha						
AM Hardie						
	2 b, 4 lb, 2 nb, 10 w	18				
10 overs: 1-46	47.4 overs, 203 mins	3-298				

1-2 (Croospulle, 0.2), 2-89 (Mendis, 16.3), 3-133 (Fernando, 25.5), 4-171 (Dickwella, 31.5), 5-221 (de Silva, 39.5), 6-282 (Bandara, 48.2), 7-283 (Wellalage, 48.5)

1-35 (Philippe, 6.4), 2-61 (Hunt, 12.4), 3-182 (Renshaw, 30.1)

Bowling	O	M	R	W	wd	nb
MT Steketee	10	0	72	2	2	2
AM Hardie	10	1	52	1		
MP Kuhnemann	10	1	50	1	1	
TR Murphy	10	0	53	2	1	
JJ Sangha	10	0	66	0	1	

Bowling	O	M	R	W	wd	nb
D Madushanka	8	0	58	0	2	
P Madushan	8.4	1	43	0	2	
DN Wellalage	8	0	55	2	2	
DM de Silva	7	0	36	0		
P Tharanga	10	0	69	1	1	
D Lakshan	5	0	23	0	2	2
K Mendis	1	0	8	0		

Toss: Australia A. Umpires: H Boteju, R Martinesz. Ref: M Mendis. Fernando 50: 59 balls, 6x4, de Silva 50: 54 balls, 7x4.
Renshaw 50: 52 balls, 6x4, Green 50: 47 balls, 3x4 2x6, 100: 92 balls 7x4 3x6, Carey 50 balls, 5x4

Second 50 over match at Sinhalese Sports Club Ground, Colombo on June 10, 2022 – Sri Lanka A won by 4 wickets

Australia		R	B	M	4	6
JR Philippe+	c Fernando b Madushan	34	25	42	5	1
TM Head	c Fernando b Arachchige	110	86	125	15	2
MT Renshaw	b de Silva	2	9	11		
MS Harris	c & b Arachchige	31	32	41	3	
NJ Maddinson	lbw b Vandersay	8	9	8	1	
HJ Hunt*	c Bandara b Tharaka	40	53	68	1	1
AM Hardie	c Dickwella b Madushan	58	50	86	2	2
MT Steketee	b Tharaka	11	15	18	1	
TR Murphy	b Madushan	3	7	6		
MP Kuhnemann	b Madushan	0	2	2		
TS Sangha	not out	4	4	8	1	
	3 lb, 8 w	11				
10 overs: 1-85	48.4 overs, 212 mins	312				

Australia		R	B	M	4	6
N Dickwella+	c Head b Kuhnemann	83	73	97	10	1
O Fernando	c Hunt b Kuhnemann	24	24	27	3	1
K Mendis	c & b Sangha	40	53	76	2	
DM de Silva*	c Philippe b Kuhnemann	30	26	30	5	
J Liyange	c Hunt b Sangha	0	1	1		
A Bandara	not out	73	65	90	3	2
S Arachchige	c Hardie b Maddinson	31	43	58	1	
DN Wellalage	not out	17	8	9	1	1
JDF Vandersay						
N Tharaka						
P Madushan						
	3 lb, 14 w	17				
10 overs: 1-66	48.5 overs, 197 mins	6-315				

1-83 (Philippe, 9.1), 2-93 (Renshaw, 11.6), 3-155 (Harris, 21.3), 4-172 (Maddinson, 24.1), 5-200 (Head, 29.5), 6-260 (Hunt, 41.1), 7-287 (Steketee, 45.3), 8-290 (Murphy, 46.4), 9-290 (Kuhnemann, 46.6), 10-312 (Hardie, 48.4)

1-43 (Fernando, 7.2), 2-159 (Dickwella, 24.3), 3-167 (Mendis, 25.5), 4-167 (Liyange, 25.6), 5-205 (de Silva, 32.3), 6-290 (Arachchige, 46.4)

Bowling	O	M	R	W	wd	nb
N Tharaka	7	0	48	2	3	
P Madushan	8.4	0	50	4		
S Arachchige	8	0	58	2		
DM de Silva	5	0	28	1		
J Liyange	6	0	41	0	1	
JDF Vandersay	9	0	59	1		
DN Wellalage	5	0	25	0		

Bowling	O	M	R	W	wd	nb
MT Steketee	7	0	52	0	2	
MP Kuhnemann	10	1	43	3		
TR Murphy	9	0	68	0	2	
MT Renshaw	4	0	25	0		
AM Hardie	5	0	32	0		
T Sangha	9.5	0	72	2	5	
NJ Maddinson	4	0	20	1		

Toss: Australia A. Umpires: R Martinesz, R Kottahachchi, Ref: M Mendis. Head 50: 31 balls, 10x4 1x6, 100: 76 balls, 14x4 2x6.
Hardie 50: 48 balls, 2x4 1x6. Dickwella 50: 38 balls, 6x4 1x6, Bandara 47 balls, 2x4 2x6

First four-day match at Hambantota on June 14-17, 2022 – Australia A won by 68 runs

Australia A — First innings

Batsman		R	B	M	4	6
MT Renshaw	b Madushanka	2	11	10		
MS Harris *	b Madushanka	0	3	15		
HJ Hunt	b Madushanka	0	8	15		
TM Head	b Manasinghe	39	29	44	5	
NJ Maddinson	st Udara b Manasinghe	14	37	75	3	
JR Philippe+	st Udara b Lakshan	94	102	176	7	3
AM Hardie	b Lakshan	62	83	100	5	
NJ McAndrew	b Madushanka	92	132	164	5	
MT Steketee	b Lakshan	47	83	16	4	
TR Murphy	b Manasinghe	1	12	9		
MP Kuhnemann	not out	11	33	30	1	
T Sangha						
JJ Peirson						

11 b, 2 lb, 4 nb 17
88.1 overs, 361 mins 379

1-2 (Renshaw), 2-3 (Harris), 3-15 (Hunt), 4-49 (Head), 5-98 (Maddinson), 6-223 (Philippe), 7-226 (Hardie), 8-344 (Steketee), 9-349 (Murphy), 10-379 (McAndrew)

Australia A — Second innings

Batsman		R	B	M	4	6
MT Renshaw	lbw b Manasinghe	32	39	69	5	
MS Harris	lbw b Jayasuriya	32	36	49	1	
HJ Hunt	c Fernando b Manasinghe	0	5	5		
TM Head	4 c Udara b Lakshan	59	95	94	8	
NJ Maddinson	5 b Madushanka	69	70	108	10	
JR Philippe+	not out	4	9	14	1	
JJ Peirson	6 not out	13	23	42	1	

2 b, 1 nb 3
46 overs, 193 mins 5-212 dec

1-61 (Renshaw), 2-62 (Hunt), 3-67 (Harris), 4-178 (Maddinson), 5-208 (Philippe)

Bowling (vs Australia A)

	O	M	R	W	wd	nb		O	M	R	W	wd	nb
D Madushanka	14.1	2	62	4		1		8	1	43	1		
N Thiraka	12	1	61	0		1		2	0	17	0		
L Manasinghe	28	2	115	3		2		17	0	83	2		1
P Jayasuriya	18	1	69	0				13	4	45	1		
S Lakshan	16	1	59	3				5	1	16	1		
M Fernando								1	0	6	0		

Sri Lanka A — First innings

Batsman		R	B	M	4	6
P Waduge	c Head b McAndrew	30	57	71	3	
M Bhanuka	lbw b Murphy	11	27	56	1	
K Mendis *	b Murphy	0	8	11		
N Fernando	c Renshaw b Kuhnemann	86	140	164	11	1
S Samarawickrama	lbw b Steketee	29	53	65	2	
L Udara +	c Renshaw b Kuhnemann	50	62	81	5	
S Lakshan	c Philippe b Murphy	12	31	48	1	
L Manasinghe	c Philippe b Steketee	35	61	83	6	
N Tharaka	c Peirson b Murphy	0	3	2		
P Jayasuriya	c Hunt b Steketee	10	26	40	1	
D Madushanka	not out	1	7	4		

7 b, 3 lb 10
79.1 overs, 317 mins 274

1-41 (Bhanuka), 2-47 (Mendis), 3-47 (Waduge), 4-108 (Samarawickrama), 5-201 (Udara), 6-220 (Fernando), 7-242 (Lakshan), 8-242 (Tharaka), 9-273 (Jayasuriya), 10-274 (Manasinghe)

Sri Lanka A — Second innings

Batsman		R	B	M	4	6
P Waduge	2 lbw b Hardie	2	13	21		
M Bhanuka	1 c Philippe b Hardie	87	142	197	11	1
K Mendis	c Peirson b McAndrew	5	11	15		
N Fernando	c Hardie b McAndrew	3	18	30		
S Samarawickrama	c Maddinson b Sangha	105	146	229	9	
L Udara +	c Philippe b Hardie	2	15	20		
S Lakshan	c Philippe b Sangha	23	39	47	3	
L Manasinghe	b Sangha	5	9	12		
N Tharaka	c Murphy b McAndrew	0	4	6		
P Jayasuriya	c Hardie b Sangha	9	18	31	1	
D Madushanka	not out	4	17	18		

4 b 4
72 overs, 317 mins 249

1-14 (Waduge), 2-3 (Mendis), 3-41 (Fernando), 4-158 (Bhanuka), 5-168 (Udara)m, 6-213 (Lakshan), 7-229 (Manasinghe), 8-230 (Tharaka), 9-238 (Samarawickrama), 10-249 (Jayasuriya)

Bowling (vs Sri Lanka A)

	O	M	R	W	wd	nb		O	M	R	W	wd	nb
MT Steketee	15.1	5	51	3				12	1	50	0		
AM Hardie	8	2	29	0				12	3	35	3		
NJ McAndrew	13	4	38	1				15	4	31	3		
TR Murphy	23	7	67	4				18	0	62	0		
MP Kuhnemann	14	2	41	2									
TM Head	6	0	38	0									
T Sangha								13	0	56	4		
NJ Maddinson								2	0	11	0		

Stumps scores: Day 1: Australia A (1st) 379 all out, Day 2 SL A (1st) 8-250 (Manasinghe 21, Jayasuriya 1), Day 3: Aust A (2nd) 5-212 dec
Umpires: S Dissanayake, D Gunawardene, Ref: W Labrooy. Toss: Australia A. Subs for Australia A (needed for ODI series): JJ Peirson for TM Head and T Sangha for MP Kuhnemann

Second four-day match at Hambantota on June 21-24, 2022 - Australia won by 5 wickets

Sri Lanka A — First innings

Batsman	Dismissal	R	B	M	4	6
M Bhanuka +	c Harris b Steketee	7	18	15	1	
L Udara	c Peirson b Steketee	63	133	213	3	
K Mendis *	c Peirson b Steketee	14	12	21	1	
N Fernando	c Peirson b Hardie	32	77	86	3	
S Samarawickrama	c Renshaw b Boland	29	32	52	4	
N Danajaya	c Peirson b Boland	92	130	151	4	
S Arachchige	c Peirson b Boland	61	124	150	3	
S Lakshan	c Harris b Boland	4	2	3	1	
L Manasinghe	c Renshaw b Steketee	8	7	12	2	
M Shiraz	not out	1	3	25		
D Madushanka	not out	5	8	6	1	
	4 b, 4 lb, 6 nb	14				
	90 overs, 370 mins	9-330 dec				

Sri Lanka A — Second innings

Batsman	Dismissal	R	B	M	4	6
M Bhanuka	c Renshaw b Holland	8	35	45	1	
L Udara	c Peirson b Steketee	4	3	6		
K Mendis	b Holland	48	80	153	6	
N Fernando	5 c Peirson b Boland	0	7	11		
S Samarawickrama	6 c Peirson b Steketee	20	23	31	2	
N Danajaya	7 c Philippe b Sangha	77	130	180	2	
S Arachchige	8 b Sangha	58	120	144	5	
S Lakshan	10 not out	30	37	48	4	
L Manasinghe	lbw b Sangha	25	26	40	2	
M Shiraz	4 c Peirson b Boland	7	38	47		
D Madushanka	b Boland	9	24	39	1	
	2 lb, 1 nb, 1 w	4				
	87 overs, 366 mins	290				

1-12 (Bhanuka), 2-32 (Mendis), 3-91 (Fernando), 4-145 (Samarawickrama), 5-176 (Udara), 6-300 (Danajaya), 7-304 (Lakshan), 8-313 (Manasinghe), 9-325 (Arachchige)

In 2nd innings Arachige retired hunrt on 15* at 6-128 and returned at 7-172

1-6 (Udara), 2-26 (Bhanuka), 3-50 (Shiraz), 4-52 (Fernando), 5-82 (Samarawickrama), 6-99 (Mendis), 7-172 (Manasinghe), 8-247 (Dananjaya), 9-253 (Arachchige), 10-290 (Madushanka)

Bowling

Bowler	O	M	R	W	wd	nb		O	M	R	W	wd	nb
SM Boland	16	5	38	4		3		19	5	51	3		1
MT Steketee	17	2	69	4				16	4	55	2	1	
JM Holland	19	1	91	0		1		22	2	85	2		
AM Hardie	13	3	27	1		1		7	0	24	0		
T Sangha	15	1	68	0		1		16	0	53	3		
MT Renshaw	10	1	29	0				4	2	8	0		
NJ Maddinson								3	0	12	0		

Australia A — First innings

Batsman	Dismissal	R	B	M	4	6
MT Renshaw	c Bhanuka b Madushanka	35	51	71	2	
MS Harris *	b Manasinghe	39	60	92	3	
HJ Hunt	c Perera b Manasinghe	28	56	69	2	
NJ Maddinson	b Lakshan	0	12	14		
JR Philippe	lbw b Manasinghe	16	12	12	2	
JJ Peirson +	not out	67	112	187	3	
AM Hardie	c Mendis b Manasinghe	24	41	36	3	
MT Steketee	b Madushanka	19	38	53	2	
SM Boland	lbw b Madushanka	5	46	46		
TS Sangha	c Ranasinghe b Manasinghe	7	16	16	1	
JM Holland	c Fernando b Lakshan	4	9	10		
	2 b, 2 lb, 6 nb	10				
	74.3 overs, 307 mins	254				

Australia A — Second innings

Batsman	Dismissal	R	B	M	4	6
MT Renshaw	2 lbw b Manasinghe	0	1	9		
MS Harris	1 lbw b Manasinghe	11	38	53		
HJ Hunt	b Manasinghe	107	212	286	3	
	c Ranasinghe b Madushanka	18	39	44	2	
	c Ranasinghe b Madushanka	2	5	7		
	not out	128	189	307	4	
	not out	78	94	117	6	
	13 b, 1 lb, 8 nb, 4 w	26				
	95 overs,	5-370				

1-68 (Renshaw), 2-82 (Harris), 3-86 (Maddinson), 4-105 (Philippe), 5-131 (Hunt), 6-171 (Hardie), 7-207 (Steketee), 8-236 (Boland), 9-247 (Sangha), 10-254 (Holland)

1-7 (Renshaw), 2-37 (Harris), 3-65 (Maddinson), 4-69 (Philippe), 5-220 (Hunt)

Bowling

Bowler	O	M	R	W	wd	nb		O	M	R	W	wd	nb
D Madushanka	15	1	43	3				15	3	52	2	3	
M Shiraz	10	1	33	0				11	0	37	0	1	
S Arachchige	6	0	25	0				4	0	14	0		
L Manasinghe	25	1	82	5				32	4	116	3		2
S Lakshan	18.3	0	67	2		6		22	0	97	0	4	
K Mendis								7	0	15	0		1
N Fernando								2	0	11	0		
N Dananjaya								2	0	14	0		1

Stumps scores: Day 1: Sri Lanka A (1st) 9-330, Day 2 SL A (2nd) 2-27 (K Mendis 14, Shiraz 1), Day 3: Aust A (2nd) 1-37 (Harris 11, Hunt 20*) Umpires: K Bandara, P Udawatta, Ref: P Jeyapragash. Toss: Sri Lanka A.

WESTERN AUSTRALIA WIN FIRST
SHEFFIELD SHIELD SINCE 1998/99

Western Australia won their first Sheffield Shield in 23 years after a strong season which culminated in them drawing the final versus Victoria to clinch the long overdue title at the WACA. Victoria fell 24 runs short of gaining a bonus point advantage in the Final, which would have altered the home side's approach in the season decider, had they needed to win the match to win the Shield. It never came to that as Sam Whiteman and Aaron Hardie made centuries to bat the Vics out of the game.

WA had plenty of depth in their squad, with Whiteman and Hilton Cartwright doing best with the bat. Cameron Bancroft had a modest season with the bat until the last three games, where he made a century versus New South Wales at Bankstown, before making a fine 141 in the first innings of the final. With the ball, Jhye Richardson was a significant factor in the first half of the season, taking 23 wickets at just 13.43 to earn a recall to the Test side. Joel Paris and Lance Morris were the mainstays of the attack while all-rounder Aaron Hardie took wickets late in the season with the new-ball and his unbeaten innings of 174 ensured a draw in the Final when play was called at lunchtime on the final day.

Western Australia were also prepared to blood some young batting talent during the season, with Jayden Goodwin (son of ex WA and Zimbabwe batsman Murray) and Teague Wyllie both making their debuts. Skipper Shaun Marsh had a few injuries throughout the season, but he was there at the end lifting the Shield as one wondered why it had been so long since they had won the title.

Victoria was runner-up, having had an excellent season as they were unbeaten until the final round of the season. Their batting was strong with Nic Maddinson, Peter Handscomb and co-Shield player of the season Travis Dean all doing well. Marcus Harris was handy when there, it was unfortunate that he couldn't play in the Shield Final at the WACA, having contracted COVID after the tour to Pakistan.

The Vics had plenty of bowling options, Scott Boland was excellent when available, bowling his heart out in the Final having just come back from Pakistan. Will Sutherland and Mitch Perry both did well, while Jon Holland had a steady season, giving little away. The behind the wicket catching of the Victorians was excellent with Handscomb breaking the record for the most catches by a fielder in a season, despite only eight matches being played.

Tasmania went close to making the final, being one of three teams to win three matches, two of them against eventual winners Western Australia. Jordan Silk led the batting while Beau Webster filled in as skipper late in the season and made 166* versus Queensland in the last game, to lift his average above 50 for the season. Tim Ward and Caleb Jewell had steady seasons with the willow, while Jake Doran did well with the gloves, but only averaged 21 with the bat. Bowler Peter Siddle was the rock of the bowling attack, while Sam Rainbird finished the season in style, taking the remarkable match figures of 13-42, the best ever for Tasmania in a Shield game. Gabe Bell and Lawrence Neil-Smith made handy contributions.

Spin is an area where Tasmania are lacking, with Jarrod Freeman and Tom Andrews taking a combined 17 wickets at 54.70. Ben Manenti and ambidextrous spinner Nivethan Radhakrishnan were others to be given opportunities throughout the season. Veteran quick Jackson Bird (three games) and Riley Meredith (two games) were unavailable due to injury.

New South Wales slipped to fourth, having made the final last season. Chris Tremain made a major impact taking 24 wickets at a low cost in his five matches, having not played a game in 2020/21. Jason Sangha emerged as a key batsman and with injuries late in the season to senior players, was given the captaincy. Dan Hughes had a good season averaging just short of 50, he played a key role in their win at the Gabba, batting through the first innings for an unbeaten 86 in difficult conditions.

The 2021/22 season was one which New South Wales gave opportunities to younger players in Blake Nikitaras, Lachy Hearne and Ryan Hackney. Trent Copeland was tidy with the ball as was Jack Edwards, but he failed to reach 50 in his 13 innings.

Queensland had the worst drop in ladder position, going from title winners to fifth in 2021/22. At the midway point of the season, they were well placed to repeat their title of last season, but failed to win any of their last four games post BBL. They also failed to win any of their three games at the Gabba. Looking at their numbers it is hard to work out why, as Usman Khawaja and Marnus Labuschagne dominated with the bat, while Mark Steketee, Matt Kuhnemann and Gurinder Sandhu were excellent with the ball. Jack Clayton also impressed making his maiden ton in his second game. Jimmy Peirson again was reliable with bat and keeping gloves throughout.

Those who struggled included Joe Burns, Bryce Street and Matt Renshaw, who all averaged under 30. Jack Wildermuth took 15 wickets at 36 but averaged just nine with that bat, in a below average season.

South Australia once again brought up the rear end of the ladder but made significant progress in the season. Their recruits made an impression, with Nathan McAndrew doing a lot of the hackwork with the ball, as well as making handy runs. Brendan Doggett had a side strain but recovered to make an impact post BBL. Jake Carder started with a 118 v WA in September, but didn't quite kick on as he would have hoped, while Nathan McSweeney finished the season well with 99 not out to steer SA to its only win.

Henry Hunt had a solid season and was rewarded with the captaincy for the last two games, one of which SA won over New South Wales, ending a 15-game winless streak. Others to make an impact were Jake Lehmann who post-Christmas scored a fine hundred at the Gabba, followed by a brilliant 94 in SA's run chase victory versus New South Wales. Jake Weatherald averaged just 21 up to the mid-season break but made a good hundred v Victoria to finish the season with an acceptable average of 40. Skipper Travis Head made two tons when available, while paceman David Grant did well bowling largely on pretty flat pitches. Daniel Drew made a century in his return to the side, but missed the last game, when he was concussed fielding in the SACA Grade Final.

Lloyd Pope was given plenty of chances, but couldn't make a major impression, while Daniel Worrall didn't play post-Christmas and appears to have played his last game for the Redbacks, as he takes up a three-year deal with Surrey in County Cricket.

2021-22 SHEFFIELD SHIELD STATS

LADDER	Mts	Won	Lost	Drawn	Match Points	Bat Pts	Bowl Pts	Total	Pts/game
Western Australia	7	3	2	2	20	6.62	6.20	32.82	4.68
Victoria	7	3	1	3	21	3.77	5.40	30.17	4.31
Tasmania	8	3	3	2	20	5.19	5.90	31.09	3.88
New South Wales	7	2	3	2	14	1.70	5.80	21.50	3.07
Queensland	9	2	3	4	16	3.83	7.40	27.23	3.02
South Australia	8	1	2	5	11	4.96	5.70	21.66	2.70

Most Runs	Team	M	Inn	NO	Runs	HS	Average	100s	50s
PSP Handscomb	Vic	8	15	1	697	148*	49.78	2	3
SM Whiteman	WA	7	13	2	641	176*	58.27	2	2
HWR Cartwright	WA	8	15	1	601	121*	42.92	2	3
HJ Hunt	SA	8	15	1	601	134	46.23	3	1
TP Ward	Tas	8	14	0	552	144	39.42	1	3
NJ Maddinson	Vic	7	13	3	545	128	54.50	2	2
UT Khawaja	Qld	6	10	1	529	174	58.77	2	3
JC Silk	Tas	7	11	2	514	100*	57.11	1	3
CP Jewell	Tas	8	14	0	508	102	36.28	1	3
M Labuschagne	Qld	6	11	2	507	136	56.33	2	1

Highest Scores		Balls	Mins	4s	6s		Venue
SM Whiteman	176*	309	449	20	1	Western Australia v Tasmania	Bellerive Oval, Hobart
AM Hardie	174*	317	405	25	1	Western Australia v Victoria	WACA, Perth
UT Khawaja	174	294	440	14	1	Queensland v South Australia	Adelaide Oval
BJ Webster	166*	172	250	21	6	Tasmania v Queensland	Bellerive Oval, Hobart
TM Head	163	215	304	18	3	South Australia v Western Australia	Rolton Oval, Adelaide

Most Wickets	Team	M	Overs	Mdns	Runs	Wkts	Avge	Best	5wI	10wM
MT Steketee	Qld	6	209.2	59	574	32	17.93	7-44	2	1
NJ McAndrew	SA	8	302.4	69	815	27	30.18	5-84	1	-
SM Boland	Vic	5	218.3	72	444	26	17.07	5-56	3	-
GS Sandhu	Qld	6	175.1	48	479	25	19.16	6-57	2	-
MP Kuhnemann	Qld	7	289.3	80	797	25	31.88	5-25	3	1
CP Tremain	NSW	5	170.3	46	383	24	15.95	5-48	1	-
JS Paris	WA	7	185.5	59	497	24	20.70	5-63	1	-
WJ Sutherland	Vic	7	250.1	58	651	24	27.12	5-78	1	-
MJ Perry	Vic	8	273.2	71	713	24	29.70	4-31	-	-
JA Richardson	WA	4	129.2	46	309	23	13.43	5-23	1	-

Best Bowling in an Innings			Venue
SL Rainbird	8-21	Tasmania v Queensland	Bellerive Oval, Hobart
MT Steketee	7-44	Queensland v South Australia	Adelaide Oval
SA Abbott	6-38	New South Wales v Victoria	Drummoyne Oval, Sydney
GS Sandhu	6-57	Queensland v South Australia	Rolton Oval, Adelaide
SL Rainbird	5-21	Tasmania v Queensland	Bellerive Oval, Hobart
JA Richardson	5-23	Western Australia v Queensland	Gabba

Best Bowling in a Match			Venue
SL Rainbird	13-42	Tasmania v Queensland	Bellerive Oval, Hobart
MT Steketee	10-92	Queensland v South Australia	Adelaide Oval
MP Kuhnemann	10-167	Queensland v Tasmania	Riverway Stadium, Townsville

Keepers	Most Dismissals	M	Total	Ct	St
JR Philippe	Western Australia	8	37	37	-
SB Harper	Victoria	8	29	24	5
JR Doran	Tasmania	7	27	27	-
JJ Peirson	Queensland	9	27	26	1

Match 1 – South Australia v Western Australia at Rolton Oval, Adelaide on September 24-27, 2021
Match Drawn. Points: SA 3.32, WA 2.75

Western Australia

Batsman	First innings	R	B	M	4	6	Second innings	R	B	M	4	6
CT Bancroft	lbw b McAndrew	11	47	52			c Carey b Pope	27	50	55	4	
SM Whiteman	c McAndrew b Grant	44	100	132	5		c Carey b Grant	40	72	98	5	
SE Marsh *	c Kerber b McAndrew	118	190	274	14	2	c Lehmann b Pope	36	83	122	6	
CD Green	c Carey b McAndrew	106	161	180	11	4	lbw b Grant	2	2	2		
HWR Cartwright	c Weatherald b Pope	69	122	167	8	3	not out	121	186	203	12	4
JR Philippe	c Lehmann b Pope	77	107	130	10	2	st Carey b Pope	25	51	53	3	
JP Inglis +	c Worrall b Pope	28	30	57	2	1	c Weatherald b Head	13	17	31	1	
JS Paris	c Carey b Worrall	5	19	21			not out	17	49	40	2	1
ML Kelly	c Kerber b Pope	0	4	3								
CJ Rocchiccioli	not out	1	8	8								
LRT Morris												
Extras	3 lb, 3 w	6					8 b, 3 lb	11				

100 overs:4-335 131.2 overs, 516 min 9-465 dec | 85 overs, 305 mins 6-292 dec

1-23 (Bancroft), 2-82 (Whiteman), 3-281 (Green), 4-292 (Marsh),
5-401 (Philippe), 6-436 (Cartwright), 7-457 (Paris), 8-458 (Kelly),
9-465 (Inglis)

1-47 (Bancroft), 2-87 (Whiteman), 3-89 (Green),
4-142 (Marsh), 5-204 (Philippe), 6-247 (Inglis)

Bowling	O	M	R	W	wd	nb	O	M	R	W	wd	nb
Worrall	27	8	60	1			10	3	36	0		
Grant	29	5	101	1	1		17	5	34	2		
McAndrew	31	6	71	3	1		10	5	16	0		
Head	18	1	62	0			19	5	42	1		
Pope	15.2	0	92	4	1		22	2	123	3		
Kerber	11	1	76	0			7	0	30	0		

South Australia

Batsman	First innings	R	B	M	4	6
HJ Hunt	c Inglis b Kelly	36	101	115	6	
JB Weatherald	lbw b Paris	3	9	26		
JM Carder	c Bancroft b Green	118	237	315	15	
TM Head *	c Marsh b Paris	163	215	304	18	3
AT Carey +	c Rocchiccioli b Morris	37	45	48	5	
JS Lehmann	c Bancroft b Morris	12	16	20	2	
SL Kerber	run out (Inglis)	11	16	23	2	
NJ McAndrew	not out	65	80	100	7	2
DJ Worrall	b Paris	2	2	2		
DMK Grant	c Green b Morris	4	13	14	1	
LAJ Pope	c Bancroft b Rocchiccioli	12	49	66	2	
Extras	1 b, 2 lb, 15 nb, 11 w	29				

100 overs:4-392 128 overs, 521 mins 492

Bowling	O	M	R	W	wd	nb
JS Paris	26	6	73	3		3
ML Kelly	22	3	85	1		
CD Green	14	1	68	1		4
CJ Rocchiccioli	39	4	145	1		
LRT Morris	21	3	91	3	3	8
HWR Cartwright	6	1	27	0		

Fall: 1-10 (Weatherald), 2-68 (Hunt), 3-299 (Carder),
4-372 (Carey), 5-392 (Lehmann), 6-397 (Head)
7-404 (Kerber), 8-406 (Worrall),
9-418 (Grant), 10-492 (Pope)

Stumps scores:

Day 1	Western Australia (1st inns)	4-324	HWR Cartwright 13*, JR Philippe 28*
Day 2	South Australia (1st inns)	2-164	JM Carder 58*, TM Head 45*
Day 3	Western Australia (2nd inns)	1-76	SM Whiteman 35*, SE Marsh 13*

Toss: Western Australia
Umpires: MW Graham-Smith, SJ Nogajski
Ref: SD Fry. Award: TM Head (SA)

Match 2 – Queensland v Tasmania at Rolton Oval, Adelaide on October 7-10, 2021
Match Drawn. Points: Qld 2.43, Tas 2.32

Tasmania

	First innings		B	M	4	6	Second innings		B	M	4	6
CP Jewell	c Khawaja b Neser		10	14	18	2	lbw b Kuhnemann		24	50	50	3
TP Ward	lbw b Kuhnemann		144	343	461	19	b Kuhnemann		81	130	202	10
CA Wakim	c Labuschagne b Steketee		62	133	171	9 4	c Renshaw b Kuhnemann		3	61	67	
BR McDermott+	c Renshaw b Steketee		71	158	170	8 2 5	not out		1	15	16	
LH Neil-Smith	c sub (JJ Bazley) b Neser		28	64	97	2 1 3	not out		71	201	236	10 1
JC Silk	not out		100	131	157	12						
BJ Webster*	c Burns b Street		39	89	128	3						
MB Wright	not out		25	22	41	1 1						
PM Siddle												
JA Freeman												
SL Rainbird												

4 lb, 16 nb, 1 w 21 | 7 b, 2 lb, 7 nb 16

100 overs: 3-292 156.2 overs, 620 mins 6-500 dec | 75 overs, 287 mins 3-196 dec

1-14 (Jewell), 2-134 (Wakim), 3-279 (McDermott), 4-333 (Neil-Smith),
5-333 (Ward), 6-422 (Webster) | 1-52 (Jewell), 2-143 (Ward), 3-179 (Wakim)

Bowling	O	M	R	W	wd	nb		O	M	R	W	wd	nb
MG Neser	24.4	6	60	2		4		12	5	27	0		
JD Wildermuth	15	3	50	0		4		6	0	8	0		3
MP Kuhnemann	51.2	10	151	1				26	11	61	3		
MT Steketee	27	6	87	2	1	6		8	4	9	0		2
BL Edwards	16.3	2	54	0		2		6	0	33	0		2
M Labuschagne	17.5	1	71	0				9	2	27	0		
MT Renshaw	1	0	4	0				6	0	17	0		
BE Street	3	1	19	1									
JA Burns								1	1	0	0		
UT Khawaja								1	0	5	0		

Queensland

	First innings		B	M	4	6
BE Street	c Ward b Rainbird		143	334	389	14 3
JA Burns	c Neil-Smith b Freeman		26	30	43	5
M Labuschagne	b Neil-Smith		32	29	39	5
UT Khawaja*	c McDermott b Rainbird		20	60	88	3
MT Renshaw	lbw b Freeman		11	23	45	1
JJ Peirson+	not out		106	168	195	13
JD Wildermuth	not out		6	16	24	
MG Neser						
MT Steketee						
MP Kuhnemann						
BL Edwards						

5 lb, 6 nb 11

100 overs: 4-313 109 overs, 414 mins 5-355 dec

Bowling	O	M	R	W	wd	nb
PM Siddle	20	4	61	0		2
SL Rainbird	21	1	80	2		2
JA Freeman	33	6	92	2		
LH Neil-Smith	15	3	44	1		
BJ Webster	17	1	56	0		2
CA Wakim	2	0	12	0		
JC Silk	1	0	5	0		

Fall: 1-45 (Burns), 2-90 (Labuschagne),
3-144 (Khawaja), 4-172 (Renshaw), 5-334 (Street)

Stumps scores:

Day 1	Tasmania (1st inns)	3-285	TP Ward 126*, LH Neil-Smith 0*
Day 2	Queensland (1st inns)	2-122	BE Street 49*, UT Khawaja 12*
Day 3	Tasmania (2nd inns)	1-59	TP Ward 30*, LH Neil-Smith 1*

Toss: Tasmania
Umpires: DR Close, DM Koch
Referee: SD Fry
Award: TP Ward (Tas)

Match 3 – South Australia v Queensland at Adelaide Oval on October 15-18, 2021, Drawn. Points: SA 2.80, Qld 2.00

Queensland	First innings		B	M	4	6	Second innings		B	M	4	6
BE Street	c Carey b McAndrew	22	63	78	1		c Pope b Worrall	23	77	104	1	
JA Burns	c Carey b Doggett	48	99	144	7		lbw b Doggett	2	16	34		
M Labuschagne	lbw b Doggett	8	16	33			lbw b McAndrew	45	179	247	1	
UT Khawaja*	c McSweeney b McAndrew	13	52	58			c McSweeney b Worrall	174	294	440	14	1
MT Renshaw	lbw b Worrall	3	20	40			c Carey b McAndrew	41	95	102	4	
JJ Peirson+	c Carey b Worrall	16	45	57			c Nielsen b Pope	132	155	183	18	2
JD Wildermuth	lbw b Worrall	7	10	17			c Nielsen b Pope	14	16	20		1
JJ Bazley	c McSweeney b Worrall	6	11	16			not out	6	2	3		
MT Steketee	c Worrall b Doggett	17	17	35	2		not out	0	0	1		
MP Kuhnemann	c Hunt b Grant	8	12	13	1							
BL Edwards	not out	1	10	12								
	3 lb	3					6 b, 7 lb, 1 w	14				
	59.1 overs, 256 mins	152					139 overs, 570 mins	7-451 dec				

1-42 (Street), 2-78 (Labuschagne), 3-89 (Burns), 4-94 (Khawaja), 5-100 (Renshaw), 6-114 (Wildermuth), 7-124 (Bazley), 8-132 (Peirson), 9-147 (Kuhnemann), 10-152 (Steketee)

1-9 (Burns), 2-43 (Street), 3-137 (Labuschagne), 4-205 (Renshaw), 5-400 (Khawaja), 6-443 (Wildermuth), 7-445 (Peirson)

Bowling	O	M	R	W	wd	nb		O	M	R	W	wd	nb
BJ Doggett	14.1	7	25	3				28	12	67	1		
DJ Worrall	17	5	49	4				32	12	83	2	1	
DMK Grant	13	2	31	1				25	3	83	0		
NJ McAndrew	13	2	31	2				32	6	110	2		
LAJ Pope	2	0	13	0				16	1	58	2		
NA McSweeney								1	0	1	0		
TM Head								5	0	36	0		

South Australia	First innings		B	M	4	6	Second innings		B	M	4	6
JM Carder	b Steketee	1	7	7			c & b Kuhnemann	79	149	190	11	
HJ Hunt	b Steketee	37	85	135	4		c Street b Steketee	0	19	27		
NA McSweeney	c Burns b Steketee	22	49	61	2		lbw b Steketee	32	93	132	3	
TM Head*	c & b Steketee	55	62	92	8		c Renshaw b Steketee	23	41	56	1	1
AT Carey+	c Khawaja b Bazley	32	40	63	5		not out	66	115	150	3	1
HJ Nielsen	c Edwards b Wildermuth	71	126	173	8		c Bazley b Wildermuth	13	34	30	1	
NJ McAndrew	c Burns b Wildermuth	39	120	127	3		b Wildermuth	9	66	66	1	
DJ Worrall	c Peirson b Steketee	3	12	14			not out	9	19	24	2	
DMK Grant	b Steketee	5	21	32								
BJ Doggett	b Steketee	6	10	7								
LAJ Pope	not out	1	9	18								
	3 b, 2 lb, 3 nb	8					7 lb, 5 nb, 1 w	13				
	89.4 overs, 369 mins	280					88.3 overs, 341 mins	6-244				

1-5 (Carder), 2-44 (McSweeney), 3-100 (Hunt), 4-132 (Head), 5-161 (Carey), 6-262 (McAndrew), 7-265 (Nielsen), 8-265 (Worrall), 9-271 (Doggett), 10-280 (Grant)

1-8 (Hunt), 2-96 (McSweeney), 3-132 (Carder), 4-161 (Head), 5-189 (Nielsen), 6-232 (McAndrew)

Bowling	O	M	R	W	wd	nb		O	M	R	W	wd	nb
JD Wildermuth	22	5	82	2		1		18.3	7	32	2	1	1
MT Steketee	26.4	4	44	7		2		24	7	48	3		2
BL Edwards	8	1	39	0				5	0	18	0		
JJ Bazley	15	5	61	1				6	2	15	0		
M Labuschagne	5	0	14	0				12	0	46	0		2
MP Kuhnemann	13	4	35	0				23	4	78	1		

Stumps scores:

Day 1	South Australia (1st inns)	2-89	HJ Hunt 37*, TM Head 28*
Day 2	Queensland (2nd inns)	2-63	M Labuschagne 22*, UT Khawaja 15*
Day 3	Queensland (2nd inns)	4-370	UT Khawaja 158*, JJ Peirson 89*

Toss: South Australia
Umpires: SAJ Craig, DM Koch,
Referee: SJ Davis. Award: MT Steketee (Qld)

Western Australia

Batsman	First innings	R	B	M	4	6
CT Bancroft	b Bell	11	37	39	2	
SM Whiteman	c Ward b Bell	5	16	29	1	
SE Marsh *	c Doran b Neil-Smith	16	28	45	2	
CD Green	lbw b Webster	7	23	28	1	
HWR Cartwright	c Doran b Neil-Smith	30	70	73	5	
JR Philippe+	c Silk b Neil-Smith	60	143	188	7	
DJM Short	c Webster b Neil-Smith	24	89	128	3	
JS Paris	c McDermott b Siddle	19	38	54	3	
JA Richardson	c Webster b Siddle	34	49	54	6	
ML Kelly	c Doran b Neil-Smith	12	24	28	1	
LRT Morris	not out	14	12	20	3	
	4 b, 1 lb, 1 w	6				
	88.1 overs, 352 mins	238				

Batsman	Second innings	R	B	M	4	6
	c Doran b Siddle	12	25	24	1	
	lbw b Freeman	49	107	144	6	
	c Doran b Meredith	58	150	176	9	
	lbw b Siddle	13	31	45	2	
	c Doran b Meredith	0	5	5		
	c Doran b Meredith	2	7	6		
	b Siddle	4	28	35	1	
	b Webster	27	69	91	1	
	c Ward b Siddle	50	59	88	8	
	not out	1	19	22		
	c Jewell b Siddle	0	5	7		
	13 lb, 1 w	14				
	84.1 overs, 344 mins	230				

1-10 (Whiteman), 2-19 (Bancroft), 3-36 (Green), 4-40 (Marsh), 5-80 (Cartwright), 6-153 (Philippe), 7-156 (Short), 8-208 (Paris), 9-213 (Richardson), 10-238 (Kelly)

1-20 (Bancroft), 2-104 (Whiteman), 3-129 (Green), 4-130 (Cartwright), 5-142 (Philippe), 6-147 (Marsh), 7-155 (Short), 8-227 (Paris), 9-230 (Richardson), 10-230 (Morris)

Bowling	O	M	R	W	wd	nb		O	M	R	W	wd	nb
PM Siddle	20	4	53	2				22.1	9	40	5		
GT Bell	18	7	44	2				15	1	58	0		
BJ Webster	15	6	34	1	1			15	2	46	1		
LH Neil-Smith	16.1	5	43	5				2	1	2	0		
JA Freeman	19	4	59	0				11	4	26	1		
RP Meredith								19	7	45	3	1	

Tasmania

Batsman	First innings	R	B	M	4	6
CP Jewell	c Philippe b Morris	28	71	100	4	
TP Ward	c Bancroft b Richardso	0	5	7		
LH Neil-Smith	b Paris	60	126	196	8	
CA Wakim	c Short b Green	6	5	4	1	
BR McDermott	c Philippe b Cartwright	49	108	150	7	
JR Doran+	lbw b Short	1	2	4		
JC Silk	c Philippe b Cartwright	47	78	105	8	
BJ Webster*	not out	53	60	80	7	
JA Freeman	c Philippe b Cartwright	1	10	7		
PM Siddle	c Philippe b Cartwright	0	10	6		
GT Bell	b Short	0	3	3		
RP Meredith						
	5 lb, 1 nb, 1 w	7				
	79.3 overs, 339 mins	252				

	Batsman	Second innings	R	B	M	4	6
	CP Jewell	c Kelly b Richardson	52	51	69	5	
	TP Ward	c Philippe b Morris	20	49	66	2	1
3		b Richardson	50	81	113	7	
4		c Marsh b Kelly	18	58	64	2	
7		c Bancroft b Morris	19	22	35	2	
5		run out (Paris)	12	22	23	1	
6		lbw b Paris	19	20	34	3	
8		not out	21	19	23	3	
9		not out	2	1	1		
		1 nb, 3 w	4				
		53.4 overs, 221 mins	7-217				

1-0 (Ward), 2-59 (Jewell), 3-70 (Wakim), 4-127 (Neil-Smith), 5-130 (Doran), 6-173 (McDermott), 7-247 (Silk), 8-249 (Freeman), 9-251 (Siddle), 10-252 (Bell). (Meredith concussion sub for Neil-Smith)

1-74 (Ward), 2-74 (Jewell), 3-111 (McDermott), 4-142 (Silk), 5-166 (Wakim), 6-186 (Webster), 7-215 (Doran)

Bowling	O	M	R	W	wd	nb		O	M	R	W	wd	nb
JS Paris	19	3	50	1				17	4	65	1	1	
JA Richardson	2	1	5	1				14	2	37	2	1	
CD Green	12	1	51	1	1			8	2	31	1		
ML Kelly	15	6	35	0				5	0	22	0		
LRT Morris	14	2	43	1	1			4.4	1	33	2	1	
DJM Short	10.3	0	40	2				3	0	18	0		
HWR Cartwright	7	1	23	4				2	0	11	0		

Stumps scores:

Day 1:	Tasmania (1st inns)	1-8	CP Jewell 6*, LH Neil Smith 2*
Day 2:	Western Australia (2nd inns)	1-42	SM Whiteman 21*, SE Marsh 9*
Day 3:	Western Australia (2nd inns)	3-130	SE Marsh 45*, HWR Cartwright 0*

Toss: Tasmania
Umpires: MW Graham-Smith, SJ Nogajski
Ref: DA Johnston
Award: LH Neil-Smith (Tas)

Match 5 – New South Wales v Victoria at Drummoyne Oval, Sydney on October 27 – 30, 2021
Victoria won by 204 runs. Points: NSW 1.00, Vic 7.00

Victoria	First innings		B	M	4	6	Second innings		B	M	4	6
JL Seymour	lbw b Abbott	34	90	118	4	1	c Nevill b Copeland	8	33	41	1	
MS Harris	c Nevill b Abbott	9	20	22	1		c Lyon b Abbott	137	361	452	9	1
PSP Handscomb*	b Abbott	15	60	86			b Abbott	115	292	413	9	
NJ Maddinson	c T Sangha b Abbott	87	136	170	5	4	not out	2	8	14		
MW Short	c Copeland b Abbott	2	10	8			not out	4	6	11		
JA Merlo	c Nevill b T Sangha	33	53	67	3							
SB Harper+	c Nevill b T Sangha	1	8	6								
WJ Sutherland	c Gilkes b Lyon	5	19	14								
MJ Perry	c Gilkes b T Sangha	1	24	21								
SM Boland	lbw b Abbott	5	30	32	1							
JM Holland	not out	0	4	9								
	5 b, 1 lb, 1 w	7					11 b, 8 lb, 4 nb, 1 w	24				
	75.4 overs, 280 mins	199					116 overs, 467 mins	3-290 dec				

1-12 (Harris), 2-59 (Handscomb), 3-60 (Seymour), 4-64 (Short),
5-126 (Merlo), 6-128 (Harper), 7-137 (Sutherland), 8-146 (Perry),
9-187 (Boland), 10-199 (Maddinson)

1-22 (Seymour), 2-283 (Harris), 3-284 (Handscomb)

Bowling	O	M	R	W	wd	nb	O	M	R	W	wd	nb
TA Copeland	11	4	23	0			17	5	36	1		
SA Abbott	15.4	3	38	6	1		25	4	74	2	1	2
HNA Conway	12	2	29	0			18	7	36	0		
NM Lyon	22	4	59	1			29	9	64	0		
T Sangha	15	3	44	3			17	4	29	0		
JR Edwards							10	1	32	0		2

New South Wales	First innings		B	M	4	6	Second innings		B	M	4	6
DP Hughes	lbw b Boland	8	26	32			lbw b Short	18	41	43	3	
MR Gilkes	c Handscomb b Short	25	55	65	3		c Harris b Boland	20	66	97	2	
KR Patterson*	c Harper b Boland	48	143	180	4	4	b Boland	4	37	46		
HNA Conway	b Perry	20	87	100	3	3	lbw b Sutherland	5	34	32		
JJ Sangha	c Merlo b Sutherland	0	15	23			c Handscomb b Holland	4	33	42		
JR Edwards	not out	29	59	99	3		b Boland	11	66	79		
SA Abbott	c &b Holland	10	38	39			c Harris b Sutherland	16	43	49		
PM Nevill+	b Perry	4	11	10	1		not out	29	129	154	2	
TA Copeland	lbw b Holland	0	15	10			b Sutherland	17	67	76	2	
NM Lyon	lbw b Boland	2	4	6			lbw b Holland	5	33	48		
T Sangha	lbw b Boland	1	9	7			lbw b Holland	0	16	15		
	3 lb, 1 w	4					4 lb, 1 nb	5				
	77 overs, 290 mins	151					94 overs, 345 mins	134				

1-17 (Hughes), 2-43 (Gilkes), 3-89 (Conway), 4-100 (J Sangha),
5-108 (Patterson), 6-132 (Abbott), 7-141 (Nevill), 8-144 (Copeland),
9-147 (Lyon), 10-151 (T Sangha)

1-29 (Hughes), 2-38 (Conway), 3-47 (Gilkes),
4-54 (Patterson), 5-54 (J Sangha), 6-79 (Abbott),
7-85 (Edwards), 8-120 (Copeland), 9-134 (Lyon),
10-134 (T Sangha)

Bowling	O	M	R	W	wd	nb	O	M	R	W	wd	nb
SM Boland	19	6	34	4			24	9	39	3		
MJ Perry	14	4	35	2	1		18	10	32	0		
JM Holland	20	5	46	2			23	14	16	3		
WJ Sutherland	15	3	25	1			19	6	31	3	1	
MW Short	8	4	7	1			10	4	12	1		
JA Merlo	1	0	1	0								

Stumps Scores
Day 1: New South Wales (1st inns) 2-43   KR Patterson 8*, HNA Conway 0*
Day 2: Victoria (2nd inns) 1-75   MS Harris 41*, PSP Handscomb 26*
Day 3: New South Wales (2nd inns) 1-33   MR Gilkes 11*, HNA Conway 4*

Toss: Victoria
Umpires: GA Abood, GJ Davidson
Referee: DR Gilbert
Award: NJ Maddinson (Vic)

Match 6 – Queensland v Tasmania at Riverway Stadium, Townsville on October 27-30, 2021
Queensland won by 96 runs. Points: Qld 8.12, Tas 0.30

Queensland

First innings

Batsman	Dismissal	R	B	M	4	6
BE Street	c Webster b Neil-Smith	14	35	35	1	
JA Burns	b Freeman	79	188	254	10	
M Labuschagne	c Doran b Bell	136	208	287	15	1
UT Khawaja*	c Doran b Webster	119	184	234	11	4
MT Renshaw	not out	120	167	208	12	4
JJ Peirson+	c Webster b Meredith	7	25	21	1	
JD Wildermuth	b Meredith	1	6	7		
JJ Bazley	not out	1	7	12		
C Sully						
MP Kuhnemann						
GS Sandhu						

3 b, 2 lb, 4 nb, 1 w — 10

100 overs: 3-312
136 overs, 532 mins — 6-487 dec

1-20 (Street), 2-203 (Burns), 3-277 (Labuschagne), 4-432 (Khawaja),
5-450 (Peirson), 6-458 (Wildermuth)

Second innings

Batsman	Dismissal	R	B	M	4	6
BE Street	c Jewell b Bell	23	56	49	3	
JA Burns	not out	46	78	99	3	1
M Labuschagne	not out	60	46	49	4	3

3 lb — 3
30 overs, 99 mins — 1-132 dec

1-48 (Street)

Bowling

	O	M	R	W	wd	nb
RP Meredith	23	7	59	2		
GT Bell	20	4	67	1	1	
LH Neil-Smith	20	5	48	1		2
TD Andrews	28	4	98	0		
BJ Webster	18	2	86	1		2
JA Freeman	27	4	124	1		

	O	M	R	W	wd	nb
	4	2	11	0		
	4	1	11	1		
	11	1	52	0		
	4	0	20	0		
	7	0	35	0		

Tasmania

First innings

Batsman	Dismissal	R	B	M	4	6
CP Jewell	c Peirson b Sully	27	47	62	3	
T Ward	c Wildermuth b Sandhu	11	37	47	2	
CA Wakim	c Wildermuth b Kuhnemann	34	57	78	6	
JC Silk	c Peirson b Wildermuth	47	136	159	4	
JR Doran+	c Street b Kuhnemann	10	14	20	1	
BJ Webster*	c Street b Sandhu	28	78	100	3	
LH Neil-Smith	c Khawaja b Kuhnemann	0	5	6		
TD Andrews	c Labuschagne b Kuhnemann	7	25	29	1	
JA Freeman	not out	6	13	35		
GT Bell	c Peirson b Sandhu	2	17	14		
RP Meredith	c Burns b Kuhnemann	3	10	9		

1 b, 1 lb, 5 w — 7
73.1 overs, 284 mins — 182

1-39 (Ward), 2-42 (Jewell), 3-102 (Wakim), 4-112 (Doran), 5-155 (Silk),
6-156 (Neil-Smith), 7-169 (Webster), 8-171 (Andrews), 9-175 (Bell),
10-182 (Meredith)

Second innings

Batsman	Dismissal	R	B	M	4	6
CP Jewell	lbw b Labuschagne	90	157	242	11	1
T Ward	c Peirson b Bazley	54	134	145	7	
CA Wakim	b Kuhnemann	5	32	32	1	
JC Silk	lbw b Sandhu	0	3	5		
JR Doran+	c Wildermuth b Kuhnemann	47	105	118	7	
BJ Webster*	lbw b Kuhnemann	36	46	67	3	1
LH Neil-Smith	lbw b Kuhnemann	13	36	42	1	
TD Andrews	c Bazley b Kuhnemann	10	16	16	1	
JA Freeman	not out	41	60	98	4	1
GT Bell	c Peirson b Wildermuth	0	13	11		
RP Meredith	c Street b Sully	20	58	53	3	

1 b, 3 lb, 3 nb, 13 w, 5 pen — 25
109.3 overs, 336 mins — 341

1-118 (Ward), 2-135 (Wakim), 3-136 (Silk),
4-173 (Jewell), 5-238 (Doran), 6-245 (Webster),
7-254 (Andrews), 8-276 (Neil-Smith), 9-277 (Bell),
10-341 (Meredith)

Bowling

	O	M	R	W	wd	nb
JD Wildermuth	11	3	22	1	1	
GS Sandhu	18	3	44	3	4	
MT Renshaw	4	0	8	0		
MP Kuhnemann	30.1	9	60	5		
C Sully	7	0	34	1		
M Labuschagne	3	0	12	0		
JJ Bazley						

	O	M	R	W	wd	nb
	13	2	43	1	4	2
	12	3	40	1	2	1
	4	0	17	0		
	43	11	107	5		
	9.3	2	32	1	1	
	19	3	68	1		
	9	2	25	1		2

Stumps scores:

Day 1	Queensland (1st inns)	3-311	UT Khawaja 63*, MT Renshaw 13*
Day 2	Tasmania (1st inns)	4-150	JC Silk 45*, BJ Webster 20*
Day 3	Tasmania (2nd inns)	1-127	CP Jewell 65*, CA Wakim 4*

Toss: Queensland
Umpires: DM Koch, BNJ Oxenford
Ref: KC Wessels. Award: MP Kuhnemann (Qld)

Match 7 – Western Australia v South Australia at the WACA, Perth on October 27-30, 2021
Western Australia won by 6 wickets. Points: WA 7.79, SA 0.60

South Australia	First innings		B	M	4	6	Second innings		B	M	4	6
HJ Hunt	c Philippe b Richardson	10	28	39	2		b Paris	44	92	125	5	
JB Weatherald	c Philippe b Paris	4	7	9	1		c Bancroft b Paris	108	245	371	13	1
JM Carder	lbw b Morris	37	96	148	6		c Short b Cartwright	68	143	172	9	
TM Head*	c Philippe b Gannon	9	12	12	1		c Short b Cartwright	21	25	25	2	
AT Carey+	run out (Short)	0	3	2			c Bancroft b Richardson	7	10	8	1	
JS Lehmann	c Philippe b Morris	0	1	2			c Philippe b Paris	17	15	19	4	
HJ Nielsen	c Philippe b Green	18	73	74	2		c Short b Gannon	1	14	10		
NJ McAndrew	c Marsh b Richardson	17	39	50	3		c Morris b Richardson	8	21	32	2	
DJ Worrall	c Philippe b Morris	6	8	13	1		c Philippe b Paris	1	7	8		
DMK Grant	b Richardson	14	16	25	2		b Paris	10	16	15	1	
BJ Doggett	not out	2	8	8			not out	0	1	2		
	4 b, 7 lb	11					1 lb, 4 nb, 1 w	6				
	48.3 overs, 201 mins	128					97.3 overs, 403 mins	291				

1-9 (Weatherald), 2-23 (Hunt), 3-41 (Head), 4-41 (Carey),
5-41 (Lehmann), 6-78 (Nielsen), 7-90 (Carder), 8-100 (Worrall),
9-119 (McAndrew), 10-128 (Grant)

1-80 (Weatherald), 2-212 (Carder), 3-242 (Head), 4-249
(Carey), 5-270 (Lehmann), 6-271 (Nielsen), 7-271 (Hunt)
8-273 (Worrall), 9-287 (Grant), 10-291 (McAndrew)

Bowling	O	M	R	W	wd	nb	O	M	R	W	wd	nb
JS Paris	11	2	32	1			28	9	63	5		3
JA Richardson	11.3	3	22	3			21.3	4	75	2		1
LRT Morris	8	2	25	3			11	4	32	0	1	
CJ Gannon	12	5	26	1			18	5	51	1		
CD Green	6	2	12	1			10	2	33	0		
DJM Short							5	0	20	0		
HWR Cartwright							4	0	16	2		

Western Australia	First innings		B	M	4	6	Second innings		B	M	4	6
CT Bancroft	c Carey b Grant	46	134	188	5		b Worrall	8	21	20	1	
SM Whiteman	c Carey b Worrall	0	5	7			c Carey b McAndrew	6	8	16	1	
SE Marsh*	c Lehmann b McAndrew	11	32	44	2		run out (Hunt)	16	41	49	2	
CD Green	c Nielsen b Grant	61	94	142	7	1	not out	38	90	157	5	
HWR Cartwright	lbw b Grant	73	154	184	8	2	run out (Hunt)	15	44	61	3	
JR Philippe+	c Grant b McAndrew	32	66	89	4		not out	31	38	47	6	
DJM Short	b Grant	28	88	122	4							
JS Paris	c Carey b McAndrew	30	38	52	4	1						
JA Richardson	c Carey b McAndrew	9	18	20	2							
CJ Gannon	not out	1	4	9								
LRT Morris	b McAndrew	0	3	3								
	4 b, 2 lb, 2 w	8					7 lb	7				
	106 overs, 449 mins	299					40.2 overs, 179 mins	4-121				

100 overs: 6-279

1-0 (Whiteman), 2-17 (Marsh), 3-118 (Bancroft), 4-119 (Green),
5-192 (Philippe), 6-250 (Cartwright), 7-279 (Short), 8-293 (Paris),
9-298 (Richardson), 10-299 (Morris)

1-10 (Whiteman), 2-14 (Bancroft), 3-39 (Marsh),
4-77 (Cartwright)

Bowling	O	M	R	W	wd	nb	O	M	R	W	wd	nb
BJ Doggett	10.2	5	21	0								
DJ Worrall	27	8	75	1	1		16	4	40	1		
DMK Grant	25	4	76	4			10	3	40	0		
NJ McAndrew	32.4	7	84	5	1		14	3	29	1		
TM Head	9	3	28	0								
JM Carder	2	0	9	0								
JS Lehmann							0.2	0	5	0		

Stumps Scores

Day 1	Western Australia (1st inns) 2-42	CT Bancroft 13*, CD Green 17*	
Day 2	South Australia (2nd inns) 0-68	JB Weatherald 38*, HJ Hunt 28*	
Day 3	Western Australia (2nd inns) 3-55	CD Green 9*, HWR Cartwright 9*	

Toss: Western Australia
Umpires: DR Close, MW Graham-Smith
Referee: SD Fry
Award: JS Paris (WA)

Match 8 – Victoria v New South Wales at the MCG on November 5-8, 2021
Victoria won by 174 runs. Points: Vic 8.01, NSW 0.80

Victoria — First innings

Batsman	Dismissal	R	B	M	4	6
JL Seymour	c Nevill b Lyon	105	220	324	19	
MS Harris	c Edwards b Hatcher	1	14	29		
PSP Handscomb*	lbw b Abbott	27	59	80	2	
NJ Maddinson	c & b Lyon	128	206	270	14	1
MW Short	b Hatcher	9	14	19		
SB Harper+	c Lyon b Hatcher	0	6	9		
JL Pattinson	b Lyon	6	35	49	1	
WJ Sutherland	c Patterson b Hatcher	23	46	57	2	1
MJ Perry	b Abbott	0	11	10		
SM Boland	not out	2	10	28		
JM Holland	not out	0	2	4		
WJ Parker						

9 lb, 1 nb, 2 w = 12

100 overs: 8-301   103.4 overs, 444 mins   9-313 dec

1-3 (Harris), 2-59 (Handscomb), 3-250 (Seymour), 4-274 (Short), 5-278 (Harper), 6-283 (Maddinson), 7-292 (Pattinson), 8-293 (Perry), 9-313 (Sutherland)

Victoria — Second innings

Batsman	Dismissal	R	B	M	4	6
JL Seymour	c Abbott b Hatcher	8	21	26	1	
MS Harris	lbw b Abbott	0	7	11		
PSP Handscomb*	c Nevill b Edwards	90	177	250	9	
NJ Maddinson	b Edwards	33	98	145		
MW Short	c sub (H Conway) b Edwards	90	122	150	8	2
SB Harper+	not out	17	34	60	1	

8 lb, 1 nb, 1 w = 10

76.2 overs, 323 mins   5-248 dec

1-1 (Harris), 2-13 (Seymour), 3-94 (Maddinson), 4-168 (Handscomb), 5-248 (Short)

Bowling

Bowler	O	M	R	W	wd	nb		O	M	R	W	wd	nb
TA Copeland	2.3	2	0	0									
SA Abbott	29	6	83	2				16	3	33	1	1	
LC Hatcher	23.1	3	86	4	1	1		17	3	75	1		
NM Lyon	32	11	63	3				23	4	65	0		
JR Edwards	11	2	37	0		1		16.2	6	47	3	1	
JJ Sangha	6	0	35	0				4	0	20	0		

New South Wales — First innings

Batsman	Dismissal	R	B	M	4	6
DP Hughes	run out (Sutherland)	59	132	183	7	
MR Gilkes	c Short b Boland	16	55	73	1	
JJ Sangha	c Handscomb b Sutherland	10	36	39	1	
*KR Patterson	b Perry	2	13	30		
JR Edwards	c Harper b Pattinson	7	34	46	1	
LD Hearne	c Short b Sutherland	4	8	13	1	
SA Abbott	c Harper b Pattinson	0	2	2		
+PM Nevill	c Maddinson b Parker	16	45	71	1	
NM Lyon	c Short b Boland	15	39	51	2	
LC Hatcher	b Boland	0	4	3		
TA Copeland	not out	7	7	12	1	

1 b, 3 nb = 4

62 overs, 266 mins = 140

1-34 (Gilkes), 2-61 (Sangha), 3-85 (Patterson), 4-98 (Hughes), 5-102 (Edwards), 6-102 (Abbott), 7-102 (Hearne), 8-132 (Lyon), 9-132 (Hatcher), 10-140 (Nevill)

New South Wales — Second innings

Batsman	Dismissal	R	B	M	4	6
DP Hughes	not out	89	319	473	11	
MR Gilkes	c & b Boland	0	3	4		
JJ Sangha	c Harper b Pattinson	5	20	27		
*KR Patterson	lbw b Sutherland	24	64	71	4	
JR Edwards	b Boland	42	106	155	4	
LD Hearne	c Harper b Boland	2	7	9		
SA Abbott	lbw b Short	16	50	55	1	
+PM Nevill	lbw b Perry	16	50	59	1	
NM Lyon	c Seymour b Perry	0	5	7		
LC Hatcher	lbw b Boland	24	44	67	4	
TA Copeland	lbw b Boland	4	6	10	1	

4 b, 14 lb, 5 nb, 2 w = 25

111.3 overs, 473 mins = 247

1-1 (Gilkes), 2-15 (Sangha), 3-61 (Patterson), 4-146 (Edwards), 5-148 (Hearne), 6-172 (Abbott), 7-198 (Nevill), 8-198 (Lyon), 9-239 (Hatcher), 10-247 (Copeland)

Bowling

Bowler	O	M	R	W	wd	nb		O	M	R	W	wd	nb
SM Boland	18	6	33	3				29.3	10	56	5		
JL Pattinson	15	7	27	2		2		27	3	67	1	1	3
WJ Sutherland	14	1	41	2		1		23	8	40	1		2
MW Short	3	1	3	0				7	1	22	1		
MJ Perry	9	4	24	1				19	5	35	2	1	
WB Parker	3	0	11	1				6	1	9	0		

Stumps Scores

Day 1	Victoria (1st inns)	6-283	JL Pattinson 1*, WJ Sutherland 0*
Day 2	New South Wales (1st inns)	9-139	PM Nevill 16*, TA Copeland 6*
Day 3	New South Wales (2nd inns)	3-61	DP Hughes 19*, JR Edwards 0*

Toss: New South Wales
Umpires: PJ Gillespie, AK Wilds
Referee: RL Parry
Award: SM Boland (Vic)

Match 9 – Queensland v Western Australia at the Gabba, Brisbane on November 10-13, 2021
Western Australia won by 7 wickets. Points: Qld 1.00, WA 7.81

Queensland — First innings

Batsman	Dismissal	Runs	B	M	4	6
BE Street	b Paris	0	15	19		
JA Burns	c Morris b Richardson	8	22	33		
M Labuschagne	c Philippe b Paris	0	1	1		
UT Khawaja*	c Green b Morris	70	138	207	11	
MT Renshaw	c Philippe b Morris	9	50	65		
JJ Peirson+	c Philippe b Morris	4	9	11		
JD Wildermuth	c Bancroft b Richardson	8	10	16	2	
MG Neser	c Philippe b Richardson	0	7	8		
GS Sandhu	c Gannon b Green	13	37	45	2	
MT Steketee	b Morris	10	9	11	2	
MP Kuhnemann	not out	5	22	33		
	1 nb, 1 w	2				
	53.1 overs, 229 mins	129				

Queensland — Second innings

Dismissal	Runs	B	M	4	6
c Philippe b Richardson	6	31	34	1	
c Short b Richardson	49	99	158	7	
c Philippe b Richardson	36	89	112	4	
c Green b Gannon	8	13	21	2	
c Philippe b Green	43	118	173	2	1
c Bancroft b Gannon	0	5	7		
c Cartwright b Richardson	34	45	67	6	
11 c Philippe b Richardson	5	14	18	1	
8 b Short	39	69	88	4	1
9 c Cartwright b Short	0	2	4		
10 not out	4	15	21		
13 b, 1 lb, 6 nb, 2 w	22				
82.2 overs, 356 mins	246				

1-8 (Street), 2-8 (Labuschagne), 3-8 (Burns), 4-34 (Renshaw),
5-38 (Peirson), 6-52 (Wildermuth), 7-56 (Neser), 8-84 (Sandhu),
9-95 (Steketee), 10-129 (Khawaja)

1-15 (Street), 2-91 (Labuschagne), 3-98 (Burns), 4-106
(Khawaja), 5-106 (Peirson), 6-159 (Wildermuth), 7-237
(Renshaw), 8-237 (Sandhu), 9-238 (Steketee),
10-246 (Neser)

Bowling

Bowler	O	M	R	W	wd	nb		O	M	R	W	wd	nb
JS Paris	9	5	19	2				22.2	13	23	5		2
JA Richardson	14	6	38	3		1		21	6	60	2		2
CJ Gannon	12	3	26	0				15	4	41	1		
CD Green	8	4	25	1				14	2	61	0	2	2
LRT Morris	10.1	4	21	4		1		3	0	10	0		
HWR Cartwright								7	0	37	2		
DJM Short													

Western Australia — First innings

Batsman	Dismissal	Runs	B	M	4	6
CT Bancroft	c Peirson b Neser	0	1	1		
J Goodwin	c Peirson b Sandhu	10	26	34	2	
SE Marsh*	not out	10	16	24	2	
CD Green	c Burns b Steketee	53	117	172	7	
JR Philippe+	c sub (X Bartlett) b Steketee	129	222	310	14	3
HWR Cartwright	b Steketee	0	7	9		
DJM Short	b Kuhnemann	15	41	69		
JA Richardson	st Peirson b Kuhnemann	35	48	55	8	
JS Paris	b Wildermuth	5	17	25		
CJ Gannon	c Peirson b Steketee	0	1	2		
LRT Morris	c Peirson b Wildermuth	5	10	13	1	
	6 lb, 7 nb, 6 w	19				
	83.2 overs, 362 mins	281				

Western Australia — Second innings

Dismissal	Runs	B	M	4	6
not out	47	108	137	3	
b Steketee	6	12	18	1	
3 b Labuschagne	15	29	45	1	
not out	17	27	33	3	
4 c Renshaw b Steketee	7	28	38	1	
3 nb	3				
33.3 overs, 137 mins	3-95				

1-0 (Bancroft), 2-18 (Goodwin), 3-119 (Green), 4-119 (Cartwright),
5-182 (Short), 6-258 (Richardson), 7-272 (Philippe), 8-272 (Gannon),
9-272 (Paris), 10-281 (Morris)

1-13 (Goodwin), 2-47 (Green), 3-71 (Cartwright)

Bowling

Bowler	O	M	R	W	wd	nb		O	M	R	W	wd	nb
MG Neser	8.4	1	25	1				8	0	27	0		1
JD Wildermuth	12.2	0	33	2	1	2		5	0	15	0		
GS Sandhu	16	5	49	1				9	1	21	2		2
MT Steketee	22	8	74	4	1	5		10	2	21	1		
M Labuschagne	10.2	1	27	0				1	0	3	0		
MP Kuhnemann	10	0	47	2				0.3	0	8	0		
BE Street	4	0	20	0									

Stumps Scores

Day 1	Western Australia (1st inns)	2-108	CD Green 48*, JR Philippe 36*	
Day 2	Queensland (2nd inns)	0-1	BE Street 0*, JA Burns 1*	
Day 3	Queensland (2nd inns)	9-244	MP Kuhnemann 2*, MG Neser 5*	

Toss: Western Australia
Umpires: SAJ Craig, BNJ Oxenford
Referee: KC Wessels
Award: JA Richardson (WA)

Match 10 – Tasmania v South Australia at Bellerive Oval, Hobart on November 10-13, 2021
Match Drawn. Points: Tas 2.68, SA 2.00

South Australia	First innings		B	M	4	6	Second innings		B	M	4	6
HJ Hunt	c Doran b Freeman	134	236	316	16	3	2 not out		15	37	56	3
JB Weatherald	c Jewell b Bell	3	13	24			1 not out		16	45	56	2
JM Carder	c Neil-Smith b Siddle	3	18	20								
TM Head*	b Neil-Smith	14	32	63	2							
AT Carey+	c Wakim b Siddle	6	19	32								
HJ Nielsen	c McDermott b Siddle	0	5	9								
LAH Scott	c Doran b Freeman	42	75	87	3							
NJ McAndrew	c Webster b Siddle	1	16	16								
NP Winter	lbw b Freeman	4	13	14	1							
DJ Worrall	c Ward b Neil-Smith	9	24	33		1						
DMK Grant	not out	0	1	13								
	3 lb, 1 nb	4										
	75.1 overs, 316 mins	220					13.4 overs, 56 mins	0-32				

1-10 (Weatherald), 2-13 (Carder), 3-57 (Head), 4-76 (Carey),
5-78 (Nielsen), 6-148 (Scott), 7-159 (McAndrew), 8-164 (Winter),
9-192 (Worrall), 10-220 (Hunt)

Bowling	O	M	R	W	wd	nb		O	M	R	W	wd	nb
P M Siddle	24	10	42	4		1		4	3	3	0		
GT Bell	19	2	62	1				6.4	2	11	0		
LH Neil-Smith	15	1	60	2				3	0	17	0		
BJ Webster	1	0	5	0									
J A Freeman	16.1	4	48	3									

Tasmania	First innings		B	M	4	6	Bowling	O	M	R	W	wd	nb
TP Ward	c Hunt b McAndrew	29	102	162	1		DJ Worrall	26	8	55	2		
CP Jewell	c McAndrew b Worrall	2	7	10			NP Winter	19	6	50	1		
CA Wakim	b McAndrew	68	121	136	8		NJ McAndrew	23	4	50	2		
BR McDermott	lbw b Scott	45	128	170	4		DMK Grant	19.4	4	57	1		
LH Neil-Smith	c Head b Scott	10	65	99	1		LAH Scott	11	3	31	2		1
JR Doran+	lbw b Head	14	45	58	2		TM Head	6	0	22	2		
JC Silk	c Worrall b Grant	58	85	111	5								
BJ Webster*	c Carey b Winter	1	6	8			1-5 (Jewell), 2-101 (Wakim), 3-102 (Ward),						
J A Freeman	c Weatherald b Worrall	7	7	6	1		4-143 (Neil-Smith), 5-181 (McDermott), 6-181 (Doran),						
P M Siddle	st Carey b Head	30	57	83	3		7-183 (Webster), 8-190 (Freeman),						
GT Bell	not out	0	6	9			9-276 (Siddle), 10-282 (Silk)						
	4 b, 13 lb, 1nb	18											
100 overs: 8-268	104.4 overs, 429 mins	282											

Stumps Scores

Day 1	South Australia (1st inns)	2-27	HJ Hunt 14*, TM Head 5*
Day 2	Tasmania (1st inns)	3-102	BR McDermott 1*, LH Neil-Smith 0*
Day 3	Tasmania (1st inns)	8-220	JC Silk 15*, PM Siddle 13*

Toss: Tasmania
Umpires: DR Close, SJ Nogajski
Referee: DA Johnston
Award: HJ Hunt (SA)

Match 11 – New South Wales v Victoria at the SCG on November 20-23, 2021
Match Drawn. Points: NSW 2.13, Vic 2.65

New South Wales

First innings:

Batsman	Dismissal	R	B	M	4	6
DP Hughes	c Handscomb b Couch	70	154	218	11	
MR Gilkes	c Handscomb b Perry	13	13	20	2	
KR Patterson*	st Harper b Short	37	46	64	7	
MC Henriques	st Harper b Short	7	9	15	1	
JJ Sangha	c Seymour b Crone	12	48	64	1	
JR Edwards	b Crone	0	1	1		
PM Nevill+	b Pattinson	1	3	5		
HL Kerr	not out	62	75	94	9	1
CP Tremain	c Handscomb b Merlo	1	3	3		
T Sangha	c Harper b Merlo	2	13	17		
HNA Conway	c Handscomb b Pattinson	3	18	28		
Extras	9 b, 12 lb, 4 nb	25				
	63.1 overs, 269 mins	233				

1-27 (Gilkes), 2-96 (Patterson), 3-114 (Henriques), 4-145 (J Sangha),
5-145 (Edwards), 6-148 (Nevill), 7-185 (Hughes), 8-186 (Tremain),
9-210 (T Sangha), 10-233 (Conway)

Second innings:

Batsman	Dismissal	R	B	M	4	6
DP Hughes	c Short b Pattinson	0	4	2		
MR Gilkes	c Handscomb b Pattinson	18	40	55	1	
KR Patterson*	c Seymour b Crone	112	144	199	18	1
MC Henriques	c Harper b Pattinson	6	26	38		
JJ Sangha	c Harper b Pattinson	78	102	9	9	3
JR Edwards	b Crone	6	9	23	1	
PM Nevill+	b Pattinson	20	20	23	2	
HL Kerr	not out	11	8	19		1
CP Tremain	not out	11	5	8	1	1
Extras	4 b, 8 lb, 10 nb, 1 w	23				
	58 overs, 245 mins	7-285 dec				

1-1 (Hughes), 2-47 (Gilkes), 3-76 (Henriques),
4-227 (Patterson), 5-233 (Edwards), 6-253 (J Sangha),
7-265 (Nevill)

Bowling (first innings):

	O	M	R	W	wd	nb
MJ Perry	14	4	50	1		
JL Pattinson	17.1	5	32	2		
BL Couch	6	0	38	1		4
MW Short	8	0	25	2		
XA Crone	10	2	32	2		
JA Merlo	6	1	14	2		
WB Parker	2	0	21	0		

Bowling (second innings):

O	M	R	W	wd	nb
12	1	38	0		2
18	2	71	5		5
6	1	35	0		2
6	0	21	0		
11	0	71	2	1	1
2	0	15	0		
3	0	22	0		

Victoria

First innings:

Batsman	Dismissal	R	B	M	4	6
JL Seymour	b Tremain	0	1	1		
TJ Dean	not out	144	300	420	15	
PSP Handscomb*	lbw b Tremain	0	2	2		
MW Short	c Patterson b Tremain	2	8	10		
JA Merlo	lbw b Henriques	64	184	246	6	
SB Harper+	c Nevill b T Sangha	0	7	9		
JL Pattinson	lbw b T Sangha	45	83	114	8	
XA Crone	c Nevill b Kerr	0	8	9		
WB Parker	c Nevill b Kerr	0	10	7		
MJ Perry	c Nevill b T Sangha	7	10	10	1	
BL Couch	c Patterson b Tremain	1	4	4		
Extras	5 lb, 2 nb, 1 w	8				
100 overs: 8-265	102.3 overs, 420 mins	271				

1-0 (Seymour), 2-0 (Handscomb), 3-2 (Short), 4-145 (Merlo)
5-145 (Harper), 6-256 (Pattinson), 7-259 (Crone), 8-261 (Parker)
9-269 (Perry), 10-271 (Couch)

Second innings:

Batsman	Dismissal	R	B	M	4	6
JL Seymour	lbw b Conway	4	23	32		
TJ Dean	b Kerr	21	32	55	4	
PSP Handscomb*	c J Sangha b Edwards	39	73	95	6	
MW Short	b T Sangha	1	5	3		
JA Merlo	not out	7	82	110		
SB Harper+	not out	8	43	41	1	
Extras	2 b, 6 lb, 3 w	11				
	43 overs, 170 mins	4-91				

1-25 (Seymour), 2-53 (Dean), 3-54 (Short),
4-83 (Handscomb)

Bowling (first innings):

	O	M	R	W	wd	nb
CP Tremain	25.3	7	52	4		1
HNA Conway	22	5	71	0		
HL Kerr	18	3	54	2		
T Sangha	25	6	60	3		
JR Edwards	7	1	15	0		
MC Henriques	5	1	14	1		2

Bowling (second innings):

O	M	R	W	wd	nb
8	3	15	0		
5	0	29	1		
7	2	18	1	1	
14	9	15	1		
3	2	1	1		
3	1	5	0		2
3	3	0	0		

Stumps Scores

Day 1	Victoria (1st inns)	3-68	TJ Dean 32*, JA Merlo 32*
Day 2	No play due to rain		
Day 3	New South Wales (2nd inns)	2-76	KR Patterson 43*, MC Henriques 6*

Toss: Victoria
Umpires: PJ Gillespie, BC Treloar
Referee: RW Stratford, Award: TJ Dean (Vic)

Match 12 – Tasmania v Western Australia at Bellerive Oval, Hobart on November 21-24, 2021
Tasmania won by 4 wickets. Points – Tas 7.26, WA 2.51

Western Australia

First innings			B	M	4	6	Second innings		B	M	4	6
CT Bancroft	c Ward b Bell		1	3	5		lbw b Freeman	41	74	97	5	1
J Goodwin	c Hope b Bell		4	18	24	1	b Freeman	22	85	89	3	
SM Whiteman*	not out		176	309	449	20	1	c Doran b Siddle	13	29	41	1	
CD Green	c McDermott b Neil-Smith		15	35	46	2	b Hope	54	96	122	6	
HWR Cartwright	c Doran b Neil-Smith		0	5	9		c Doran b Bell	33	53	68	1	1
JR Philippe+	c Doran b Neil-Smith		53	111	149	6	1	c Hope b Bell	8	17	15	1	
DJM Short	c & b Silk		67	74	101	11	1	c Doran b Neil-Smith	30	22	31	4	
JA Richardson	c McDermott b Bell		43	44	62	6		not out	14	14	28	1	
ML Kelly	b Siddle		10	24	27	2		not out	4	1	2	1	
CJ Gannon	lbw b Siddle		8	10	7	1							
LRT Morris	not out		10	19	24								
	1 b, 11 lb, 4 nb, 2 w		18					6 lb, 1 nb	7				
	108 overs, 454 mins	9-405 dec						65 overs, 249 mins	7-226 dec				

100 overs: 7-371

1-5 (Bancroft), 2-16 (Goodwin), 3-41 (Green), 4-47 (Cartwright), 5-152 (Philippe), 6-270 (Short), 7-350 (Richardson), 8-371 (Kelly), 9-379 (Gannon)

1-69 (Goodwin), 2-72 (Bancroft), 3-96 (Whiteman), 4-166 (Cartwright), 5-178 (Philippe), 6-184 (Green), 7-222 (Short)

Bowling	O	M	R	W	wd	nb		O	M	R	W	wd	nb
PM Siddle	26	4	62	2	1	2		10	1	30	1		
GT Bell	27	7	80	3				12	4	29	2		
LH Neil-Smith	21	5	72	3	1			10	0	43	1		
BM Hope	20	3	83	0		2		11	0	41	1	1	
JA Freeman	13	1	88	0				22	1	77	2		
JC Silk	1	0	8	1									

Tasmania

First innings		B	M	4	6	Second innings		B	M	4	6
TP Ward	c Philippe b Richardson	86	217	269	11		b Short	42	95	135	6	
CP Jewell	c Short b Richardson	102	206	285	11	1	c Kelly b Gannon	60	73	94	11	
CA Wakim	c Goodwin b Gannon	16	43	59	2		lbw b Richardson	37	46	53	6	
BR McDermott	c Philippe b Richardson	4	29	35			c Philippe b Richardson	40	69	102	5	
JR Doran+	c Green b Richardson	0	7	29			c Philippe b Richardson	1	14	15		
JC Silk*	c Whiteman b Gannon	73	104	145	13	1	not out	83	100	151	9	
BM Hope	c Philippe b Kelly	6	12	20	1		lbw b Green	10	33	28	1	
LH Neil-Smith	c Philippe b Kelly	5	24	32	1		not out	25	41	48	4	
JA Freeman	b Gannon	6	10	19	1							
PM Siddle	c Gannon b Cartwright	1	14	14								
GT Bell	not out	8	32	55	1							
	6 b, 4 nb	10					8 b, 7 lb, 3 nb, 2 w	20				
	115.4 overs, 474 mins	317					78 overs, 315 mins	6-318				

100 overs: 8-256

1-197 (Ward), 2-200 (Jewell), 3-214 (McDermott), 4-218 (Wakim), 5-218 (Doran), 6-229 (Hope), 7-243 (Neil-Smith), 8-256 (Freeman), 9-259 (Siddle), 10-315 (Silk)

1-100 (Jewell), 2-133 (Ward), 3-149 (Wakim), 4-155 (Doran), 5-248 (McDermott), 6-268 (Hope)

Bowling	O	M	R	W	wd	nb		O	M	R	W	wd	nb
JA Richardson	28	13	53	4		3		16	4	56	3		3
ML Kelly	25	7	72	2				17	0	68	0		
CJ Gannon	25.4	7	87	3				18	3	78	1	1	
LRT Morris	5	0	31	0		1							
CD Green	10	5	12	0				9	0	28	1	1	
DJM Short	14	2	36	0				15	1	63	1		
HWR Cartwright	8	4	20	1				3	0	10	0		

Stumps Scores

Day 1	Western Australia (1st inns)	6-350	SM Whiteman 151*, JA Richardson 43*
Day 2	Tasmania (1st inns)	2-210	CA Wakim 8*, BR McDermott 4*
Day 3	Western Australia (2nd inns)	4-170	CD Green 52*, JR Philippe 2*

Toss: Tasmania
Umpires: NR Johnstone, BNJ Oxenford
Referee: DA Johnston
Award: CP Jewell (Tas)

Match 13 – South Australia v Queensland at Karen Rolton Oval, Adelaide on November 23-26, 2021
Queensland won by 8 wickets. Points – SA 0.40, Qld 7.22

Queensland	First innings		B	M	4	6	Second innings		B	M	4	6
BE Street	c Carey b Scott		87	226	303	11	c Carey b McAndrew		6	14	28	
JA Burns	c Weatherald b Grant		17	105	133		c Head b McAndrew		1	48	55	
M Labuschagne	b Head		110	223	304	10	not out		28	46	75	4
UT Khawaja *	c Carey b Worrall		4	17	20	1	not out		52	36	48	10
MT Renshaw	lbw b Grant		10	42	57	1						
JJ Peirson +	c Weatherald b Scott		21	32	42	1	1					
JD Wildermuth	c Weatherald b Scott		0	15	20							
JJ Bazley	c Hunt b Head		0	3	1							
GS Sandhu	c Carder b Pope		9	16	20	2						
MT Steketee	c Carey b McAndrew		11	22	36		1					
MP Kuhnemann	not out		20	24	21	3						
	3 b, 4 lb, 3 w		10				1 w		1			
100 overs : 4-222	120.5 overs, 483 mins		299				24 overs, 104 mins		2-88			

1-55 (Burns), 2-179 (Street), 3-188 (Khawaja), 4-207 (Renshaw),
5-255 (Peirson), 6-259 (Labuschagne), 7-259 (Bazley), 8-259 (Wildermuth),
9-271 (Sandhu), 10-299 (Steketee)

1-7 (Street), 2-16 (Burns)

Bowling	O	M	R	W	wd	nb		O	M	R	W	wd	nb
DJ Worrall	22	8	31	1				6	1	21	0	1	
DMK Grant	23	7	51	2	2			5	1	14	0		
NJ McAndrew	23.5	7	42	1	1			6	1	27	2		
LAH Scott	17	8	16	3				3	2	1	0		
LAJ Pope	25	1	114	1				3	0	24	0		
TM Head	10	1	38	2				1	0	1	0		

South Australia	First innings	B	M	4	6	Second innings	B	M	4	6
HJ Hunt	c Renshaw b Bazley	12	39	64	1	c Renshaw b Sandhu	26	57	72	2
JB Weatherald	c Street b Steketee	33	69	104	5	lbw b Sandhu	39	77	105	8
JM Carder	c & b Sandhu	4	9	12	1	c Burns b Sandhu	1	12	14	
TM Head *	c Renshaw b Kuhnemann	8	14	13	1	c Peirson b Kuhnemann	101	149	226	11
AT Carey +	c Steketee b Kuhnemann	2	7	9		c Street b Sandhu	3	3	3	
HJ Nielsen	b Bazley	7	21	27		c Bazley b Steketee	42	85	111	4
LAH Scott	lbw b Steketee	15	41	56	2	b Sandhu	6	16	21	1
NJ McAndrew	c Peirson b Kuhnemann	2	18	18		not out	37	118	135	4	1
DJ Worrall	c Sandhu b Kuhnemann	6	8	7	1	c Peirson b Kuhnemann	24	24	33	5
DMK Grant	not out	3	26	28		c Labuschagne b Kuhnemann	0	8	9	
LAJ Pope	c & b Kuhnemann	2	20	23		c Peirson b Sandhu	0	11	21	
	5 lb, 2 nb, 1 w	8				3 lb, 2 nb	5			
	45 overs, 185 mins	102				93 overs, 379 mins	284			

1-36 (Hunt), 2-43 (Carder), 3-58 (Head), 4-61 (Carey),
5-61 (Weatherald), 6-78 (Nielsen), 7-87 (McAndrew), 8-93 (Worrall),
9-93 (Scott), 10-102 (Pope)

1-58 (Weatherald), 2-62 (Carder), 3-73 (Hunt),
4-79 (Carey), 5-172 (Nielsen), 6-189 (Scott),
7-233 (Head), 8-263 (Worrall), 9-271 (Grant),
10-284 (Pope)

Bowling	O	M	R	W	wd	nb		O	M	R	W	wd	nb
MT Steketee	11	2	41	2	1	2		13	1	49	1		
JD Wildermuth	4	0	10	0				8	2	26	0	2	
GS Sandhu	7	2	11	1				21	5	57	6		
JJ Bazley	8	5	9	2				10	1	28	0		
MP Kuhnemann	14	8	25	5				35	10	97	3		
M Labuschagne	1	0	1	0				4	0	18	0		
								2	0	6	0		

Stumps Scores

Day 1	Queensland (1st inns)	1-87	BE Street 45*, M Labuschagne 21*
Day 2	South Australia (1st inns)	8-93	LAH Scott 15*, DMK Grant 0*
Day 3	Queensland (2nd inns)	0-5	BE Street 4*, JA Burns 0*

Toss: South Australia
Umpires: MW Graham-Smith, DM Koch
Ref: SJ Davis
Award: MP Kuhnemann (Qld)

Queensland	First innings		B	M	4	6
BE Street	c Copeland b Tremain	5	30	29	1	
UT Khawaja*	c Copeland b Edwards	63	155	226	6	
M Labuschagne	lbw b Copeland	8	26	21	2	
MT Renshaw	c Conway b Tremain	12	61	91	2	
SJ Truloff	lbw b Edwards	37	73	69	4	
JJ Peirson +	c Hughes b Kerr	7	35	57	1	
JD Wildermuth	b Tremain	7	19	21		
MG Neser	not out	24	44	63	3	
JJ Bazley	c Conway b Kerr	4	20	33		
MT Steketee	c Holt b T Sangha	0	1	3		
MJ Swepson	c Holt b T Sangha	2	7	6		
	13 lb, 8 nb, 3 w	24				
	77.1 overs, 329 mins	193				

1-9 (Street), 2-24 (Labuschagne), 3-79 (Renshaw), 4-140 (Khawaja),
5-147 (Truloff), 6-156 (Wildermuth), 7-169 (Peirson), 8-189 (Bazley),
9-189 (Steketee), 10-193 (Swepson)

Bowling	O	M	R	W	wd	nb
TA Copeland	20	5	47	1	1	8
CP Tremain	17	7	26	3		
HNA Conway	10	1	32	0		
HL Kerr	13	1	41	2	1	
JR Edwards	10	4	17	2	2	
T Sangha	7.1	0	17	2		

	Second innings		B	M	4	6
	c Hughes b Conway	14	62	74	2	
	c Holt b Tremain	6	12	16	1	
	c T Sangha b Conway	44	80	143	5	
	c Holt b Kerr	12	37	51		
	c J Sangha b T Sangha	18	32	40	4	
	b Copeland	3	22	23		
	c Hearne b Tremain	3	24	36		
	c Holt b Copeland	13	30	42	1	
	run out (J Sangha)	2	7	10		
	c Edwards b Copeland	0	6	5		
	not out	4	4	5	1	
	4 b, 3 lb, 3 w	10				
	52.4 overs, 227 mins	129				

1-12 (Khawaja), 2-39 (Street), 3-68 (Renshaw),
4-101 (Labuschagne), 5-102 (Truloff), 6-105 (Peirson),
7-115 (Wildermuth), 8-117 (Bazley), 9-118 (Steketee),
10-129 (Neser)

O	M	R	W	wd	nb
13.4	4	28	3		
13	4	31	2	2	
9	3	11	2	1	
5	1	18	1		
5	2	13	0		
7	2	21	1		

New South Wales	First innings		B	M	4	6
DP Hughes*	not out	86	155	249	14	
RP Hackney	c Truloff b Steketee	0	12	16		
JJ Sangha	lbw b Steketee	14	19	22	3	
JR Edwards	c Truloff b Neser	12	19	28	2	
LD Hearne	c Peirson b Bazley	8	16	21	1	
HL Kerr	c Street b Wildermuth	5	11	12		
BJH Holt+	c Truloff b Neser	10	21	23	2	
TA Copeland	c Labuschagne b Neser	0	2	6		
CP Tremain	c Renshaw b Steketee	37	61	74	4	
HNA Conway	c Truloff b Steketee	5	12	19	1	
T Sangha	c Swepson b Steketee	1	4	19		
	4 b, 1 nb, 3 w	8				
	55.1 overs, 249 mins	186				

1-4 (Hackney), 2-28 (J Sangha), 3-45 (Edwards), 4-58 (Hearne),
5-69 (Kerr), 6-83 (Holt), 7-86 (Copeland), 8-152 (Tremain),
9-168 (Conway), 10-186 (T Sangha)

Bowling	O	M	R	W	wd	nb
MG Neser	17	4	68	3	1	
MT Steketee	19.1	7	46	5		1
JD Wildermuth	6	0	17	1		
JJ Bazley	11	3	40	1		
MJ Swepson	2	0	11	0		

	Second innings		B	M	4	6
	c Peirson b Neser	1	5	11		
	b Steketee	1	7	6		
	lbw b Wildermuth	11	29	54	1	
	c Bazley b Steketee	24	53	62	4	
	c Labuschagne b Wildermuth	28	43	73	4	
	lbw b Neser	11	26	34	1	
	b Neser	20	75	108	4	
	lbw b Steketee	12	17	30	1	
	not out	16	46	69	2	
	not out	1	9	17		
	1 lb, 1 nb, 10 w	12				
	51.3 overs, 236 mins	8-137				

1-2 (Hackney), 2-2 (Hughes), 3-36 (J Sangha)
4-49 (Edwards), 5-79 (Kerr), 6-91 (Hearne),
7-110 (Copeland), 8-129 (Holt)

O	M	R	W	wd	nb
17	7	38	3		
19.3	6	54	3	2	1
11	2	29	2		
4	1	15	0		

Stumps Scores

Day 1	New South Wales (1st inns)	2-33	DP Hughes 15*, JR Edwards 0*
Day 2	Queensland (2nd inns)	5-105	JJ Peirson 3*, JD Wildermuth 0*

Toss: New South Wales
Umpires: BC Treloar, AK Wilds
Referee: KC Wessels, Award: CP Tremain (NSW)

Match 15 – South Australia v Victoria at Adelaide Oval on February 9-12, 2022
Match Drawn. Points – SA 2.83, Vic 2.14

South Australia	First innings		B	M	4	6	Second innings		B	M	4	6
HJ Hunt	c Harper b Perry		9	24	23	1	b Sutherland	57	95	157	2	1
JB Weatherald	c Harris b Boland		122	208	317	10	2	c Short b Holland	32	74	94	4	
JM Carder	lbw b Boland		31	62	82	1		c Harper b Perry	29	48	77	3	
TM Head*	lbw b Boland		0	2	2			c Short b Holland	46	52	79	2	3
DR Drew	c Harper b Perry		130	317	379	15	1	b Holland	7	16	19	1	
AT Carey+	b Boland		11	18	30	1		lbw b Sutherland	15	27	29		
LAH Scott	st Harper b Holland		22	78	105	1		lbw b Sutherland	10	18	33	1	
NJ McAndrew	c Harper b Perry		17	21	26	1		c Sutherland b Perry	0	4	4		
DMK Grant	c Sutherland b Short		12	17	23		1	b Boland	0	4	5		
BJ Doggett	c Sutherland b Perry		0	1	1			not out	6	7	13		
LAJ Pope	not out		6	13	13			c Harper b Boland	1	3	6		
	1 b, 4 lb, 1 nb		6					3 b, 6 lb, 1 w	10				
100 overs: 5-283	126.4 overs, 504 mins		366					58 overs, 262 mins	213				

1-13 (Hunt), 2-77 (Carder), 3-77 (Head), 4-230 (Weatherald),
5-252 (Carey), 6-320 (Scott), 7-347 (McAndrew), 8-352 (Drew),
9-352 (Doggett), 10-366 (Grant)

1-68 (Weatherald), 2-123 (Hunt), 3-129 (Carder)
4-144 (Drew), 5-173 (Carey), 6-203 (Head), 7-203
(McAndrew), 8-204 (Grant), 9-208 (Scott), 10-213 (Pope)

Bowling	O	M	R	W	wd	nb		O	M	R	W	wd	nb
SM Boland	28	8	61	4				12	2	39	2	1	
MJ Perry	30	9	57	4				13	3	45	2		
WJ Sutherland	23	7	71	0		1		14	3	42	3		
MW Short	11.4	0	59	1				5	0	23	0		
JM Holland	28	0	97	1				14	1	55	3		
JA Merlo	6	1	16	0									

Victoria	First innings		B	M	4	6	Second innings		B	M	4	6
WJ Pucovski	c Carey b Grant		54	123	197	5							
MS Harris	c Scott b McAndrew		58	140	167	5	1	c sub (RJ Gibson) b Grant	5	13	17		
PSP Handscomb*	lbw b Doggett		12	25	37	1		not out	148	280	357	21	
NJ Maddinson	b Pope		82	134	211	8	2	c Carey b Doggett	2	10	12		
JA Merlo	c Carey b Grant		0	8	13			c Carey b Doggett	5	56	95	1	
MW Short	lbw b McAndrew		6	20	24	1		c sub (RJ Gibson) b Grant	25	85	127	2	
SB Harper+	c Drew b McAndrew		18	61	69	3		lbw b Doggett	22	68	83	4	
WJ Sutherland	c Carey b Grant		0	4	5			not out	14	27	38	2	
MJ Perry	c Hunt b Doggett		11	31	44	2							
SM Boland	b Doggett		0	9	11								
JM Holland	not out		0	13	31								
TJ Dean							lbw b Doggett	0	2	5		
	1 b, 16 lb, 1 nb, 5 w		23					12 b, 1 nb, 2 w	15				
	94.3 overs, 409 mins		264					90 overs, 370 mins	6-236				

1-110 (Harris), 2-130 (Pucovski), 3-136 (Handscomb), 4-139 (Merlo),
5-145 (Short), 6-199 (Harper), 7-201 (Sutherland), 8-234 (Perry),
9-241 (Boland), 10-264 (Maddinson)

1-7 (Maddinson), 2-7 (Harris), 3-49 (Merlo),
4-128 (Short), 5-135 (Dean), 6-210 (Harper)

Bowling	O	M	R	W	wd	nb		O	M	R	W	wd	nb
BJ Doggett	26	8	72	3	1			21	6	51	4		
DMK Grant	25	6	66	3	2			22	5	43	2	2	1
NJ McAndrew	23	5	60	3	1			19	6	48	0		
LAJ Pope	11.3	2	33	1				24	4	76	0		
LAH Scott	8	3	14	0	1	1		4	1	16	0		
TM Head	1	0	2	0									

Stumps Scores

Day 1	South Australia (1st inns)	5-280	DR Drew 96*, LAH Scott 5*
Day 2	Victoria (1st inns)	5-151	NJ Maddinson 10*, SB Harper 5*
Day 3	South Australia (2nd inns)	7-203	LAH Scott 7*, DMK Grant 0*

Toss: South Australia
Umpires: GJ Davidson, D Taylor
Ref: SD Fry
Award: PSP Handscomb (Vic)

New South Wales	First innings		B	M	4	6	Second innings		B	M	4	6
MR Gilkes	c Jewell b Rainbird	20	42	49	1	1	b Andrews	64	115	149	7	
RP Hackney	c Doran b Siddle	38	129	178	4		c Doran b Bird	9	27	35	1	
KR Patterson*	c Doran b Rainbird	0	2	2			c Doran b Rainbird	5	7	11	1	
JJ Sangha	b Rainbird	5	7	9	1		c Ward b Andrews	75	178	246	7	
JR Edwards	b Andrews	24	30	43	4		c Bird b Andrews	18	33	31	2	
PM Nevill+	c Vines b Radhakrishna	34	97	106	5		c Bird b Webster	18	53	63	2	
HL Kerr	b Bird	88	129	194	12		c & b Bird	15	23	23		
TA Copeland	c Doran b Bird	9	28	33	1		c Doran b Webster	6	21	20	1	
CP Tremain	c Webster b Siddle	38	68	71	4	1	b Webster	2	6	22		
HNA Conway	not out	15	50	62	1		not out	7	30	25	1	
T Sangha	c Rainbird b Bird	2	12	8			not out	2	6	6		
	2 lb, 1 nb	3					4 lb, 1 nb	5				
	98.5 overs, 384 mins	276					83 overs, 320 mins 9-226 dec					

1-29 (Gilkes), 2-29 (Patterson), 3-41 (J Sangha), 4-78 (Edwards),
5-106 (Hackney), 6-136 (Nevill), 7-154 (Copeland), 8-224 (Tremain),
9-274 (Kerr), 10-276 (T Sangha)

1-25 (Hackney), 2-36 (Patterson), 3-106 (Gilkes),
4-129 (Edwards), 5-180 (Nevill), 6-198 (Kerr)
7-215 (Copeland), 8-215 (J Sangha), 9-219 (Tremain)

Bowling	O	M	R	W	wd	nb	O	M	R	W	wd	nb
JM Bird	19.5	7	38	3			16	9	43	2	1	
PM Siddle	21	8	31	2			13	5	22	0		
SL Rainbird	15	3	77	3			11	3	24	1		
BJ Webster	15	4	40	0		1	12	0	40	3		
TD Andrews	21	1	59	1			28	5	69	3		
N Radhakrishnan	7	2	29	1			3	0	24	0		

Tasmania	First innings		B	M	4	6	Second innings		B	M	4	6
TP Ward	c Nevill b Tremain	4	15	13	1		b T Sangha	32	76	91	1	1
CP Jewell	b T Sangha	36	101	131	5		lbw b Tremain	0	2	12		
EM Vines	c Nevill b Tremain	0	1	1			c Nevill b Conway	38	112	148	2	
MB Wright	lbw b Tremain	57	164	210	4		not out	78	186	216	8	
JR Doran+	run out (Patterson)	54	149	207	5		c Tremain b Edwards	14	46	61	1	
BJ Webster*	c Nevill b Tremain	10	13	17	2		b Copeland	9	21	32	2	
N Radhakrishnan	c Gilkes b T Sangha	4	37	49			b Edwards	13	45	53	2	
TD Andrews	lbw b T Sangha	4	3	2	1		c Patterson b Copeland	20	20	29	3	1
JM Bird	c Edwards b Kerr	4	8	13			b Tremain	4	4	4	1	
SL Rainbird	b Tremain	0	4	8			b Copeland	0	1	2		
PM Siddle	not out	31	21	20	5		c Patterson b Copeland	2	6	9		
	5 b, 3 lb, 1 w	9					3 b, 1 nb	4				
	86 overs, 341 mins	213					86.2 overs, 358 mins	214				

1-5 (Ward), 2-5 (Vines), 3-65 (Jewell), 4-120 (Wright), 5-140 (Webster),
6-159 (Radhakrishnan), 7-163 (Andrews), 8-170 (Bird), 9-174 (Rainbird),
10-213 (Doran)

1-4 (Jewell), 2-58 (Ward), 3-74 (Vines), 4-112 (Doran),
5-133 (Webster), 6-163 (Radhakrishnan), 7-200 (Andrews),
8-205 (Bird), 9-206 (Rainbird), 10-214 (Siddle)

Bowling	O	M	R	W	wd	nb	O	M	R	W	wd	nb
TA Copeland	14	4	38	0			18.2	3	46	4		
CP Tremain	17	5	48	5			18	2	49	2	1	
HL Kerr	9	1	25	1			8	3	12	0		
HNA Conway	8	2	20	0	1		10	4	14	1		
T Sangha	26	6	55	3			25	4	75	1		
JR Edwards	10	4	13	0			7	1	15	2		
JJ Sangha	2	0	6	0								

Stumps Scores

Day 1	New South Wales (1st inns)	8-272	H Kerr 88*, HNA Conway 14*
Day 2	New South Wales (2nd inns)	0-8	MR Gilkes 8*, RP Hackney 0*
Day 3	Tasmania (2nd inns)	1-19	TP Ward 12* EM Vines 5*

Toss: New South Wales
Umpires: GA Abood, AK Wilds
Referee: DR Gilbert
Award: H Kerr (NSW)

Queensland	First innings		B	M	4	6		Second innings		B	M	4	6
BE Street	lbw b Pattinson	23	98	122	2			c Harper b Perry	24	72	85	4	
JA Burns	b Perry	22	59	88	1	1		c Harper b Perry	13	21	32	2	
MT Renshaw	c Handscomb b Short	43	78	120	5	1		c Dean b Holland	6	17	24	1	
J Clayton	c Dean b Sutherland	109	235	312	12	1	6	c Handscomb b Holland	23	57	71	2	
SJ Truloff	c Harper b Short	20	77	77	2		4	c Harper b Perry	25	77	94	2	
JJ Peirson*+	run out (Sutherland)	0	3	2			5	c Maddinson b Holland	76	141	204	9	1
GS Sandhu	c Handscomb b Sutherland	19	52	62	2			c Harper b Sutherland	1	14	11		
JJ Bazley	c Sutherland b Short	64	98	152	9			not out	42	56	81	5	1
MT Steketee	c Handscomb b Short	5	5	4	1			not out	19	19	27	2	
MJ Swepson	c Harper b Sutherland	8	17	19									
MP Kuhnemann	not out	24	41	45	2	1							
	8 lb, 4 w	12						11 b, 5 lb, 1 w	17				
100 overs : 6-231	127.1 overs, 506 mins	349						79 overs, 318 mins	7-246 dec				

1-40 (Burns), 2-59 (Street), 3-115 (Renshaw), 4-157 (Truloff),
5-157 (Peirson), 6-191 (Sandhu), 7-272 (Clayton), 8-277 (Steketee),
9-296 (Swepson), 10-349 (Bazley)

1-20 (Burns), 2-34 (Renshaw), 3-53 (Street),
4-102 (Truloff), 5-149 (Clayton), 6-152 (Sandhu),
7-218 (Peirson)

Bowling	O	M	R	W	wd	nb		O	M	R	W	wd	nb
SM Boland	19	10	24	0				13	2	43	0		
JL Pattinson	24	4	64	1	2			9	4	21	0	1	
MJ Perry	20	6	41	1				17	4	61	3		
WJ Sutherland	22	2	78	3	2			5	0	14	1		
JM Holland	23	8	60	0				29	11	67	3		
MW Short	19.1	0	74	4				6	0	24	0		

Victoria	First innings		B	M	4	6		Second innings		B	M	4	6
TJ Dean	c Burns b Sandhu	4	26	32	1			c Truloff b Sandhu	1	11	12		
MS Harris	c Street b Bazley	91	222	293	9	1		lbw b Renshaw	21	53	79	4	
PSP Handscomb	b Swepson	92	213	274	11			c Peirson b Bazley	3	15	24		
NJ Maddinson	not out	110	147	225	12	1		not out	48	116	122	10	
MW Short	c sub (JD Wildermuth) b Steketee	48	128	161	7	1		not out	31	93	80	7	
SB Harper+	c Street b Sandhu	0	4	4									
JL Pattinson	c Street b Steketee	0	3	3									
WJ Sutherland	c Renshaw b Steketee	0	4	4									
MJ Perry	b Sandhu	5	8	13	1								
SM Boland	c Peirson b Sandhu	0	11	18									
JM Holland	c Peirson b Sandhu	0	4	2					0				
	4 b, 1 lb, 2 nb, 3 w	10											
100 overs : 3-250	128 overs, 519 mins	360						48 overs, 160 mins	3-104				

1-7 (Dean), 2-187 (Harris), 3-193 (Handscomb), 4-336 (Short),
5-337 (Harper), 6-338 (Pattinson), 7-338 (Sutherland), 8-351 (Perry),
9-360 (Boland), 10-360 (Holland)

1-9 (Dean), 2-18 (Handscomb), 3-33 (Harris)

Bowling	O	M	R	W	wd	nb		O	M	R	W	wd	nb
MT Steketee	28	8	92	3	1			2	0	9	0		
GS Sandhu	27	9	65	5	2	2		9	4	23	1		
JJ Bazley	16	9	38	1				6	1	10	1		
MJ Swepson	34	8	94	1				18	7	51	0		
MP Kuhnemann	23	4	66	0				9	8	1	0		
MT Renshaw								4	2	10	1		

Stumps Scores
Day 1	Queensland (1st inns)	6-221	J Clayton 71*, JJ Bazley 16*
Day 2	Victoria (1st inns)	4-177	MS Harris 88*, PSP Handscomb 74*
Day 3	Queensland (2nd inns)	3-69	SJ Truloff 15*, JJ Peirson 9*

Toss: Queensland
Umpires: GJ Davidson, SA Lightbody
Referee: RL Parry
Award: NJ Maddinson (Vic)

Match 18 – Queensland v South Australia at the Gabba on March 3-6, 2022
Match Drawn. Points – Qld 2.95, SA 2.24

Queensland First innings

Batsman		R	B	M	4	6
BE Street	c Nielsen b Scott	43	146	195	4	
JA Burns	lbw b Scott	13	26	53	1	
MT Renshaw	lbw b Doggett	63	166	220	4	
J Clayton	c & b McSweeney	85	164	220	7	
SJ Truloff	lbw b Doggett	0	10	14		
MA Bryant	c Doggett b Grant	21	31	49	4	
JJ Peirson*+	c Drew b McAndrew	65	45	72	9	
JD Wildermuth	c Nielsen b McAndrew	0	6	9		
JJ Bazley	not out	2	6	9		
XC Bartlett	not out	1	3	3		
GS Sandhu						

2 b, 7 lb, 3 nb 12
100 overs, 426 mins 8-305 dec

1-33 (Burns), 2-100 (Street), 3-150 (Renshaw), 4-154 (Truloff), 5-197 (Bryant), 6-299 (Peirson), 7-302 (Clayton), 8-302 (Wildermuth)

Queensland Second innings

Batsman		R	B	M	4	6
BE Street	c Carder b Scott	18	36	40	3	
JA Burns	b Scott	27	22	42	2	1
MT Renshaw	c & b Doggett	12	11	21	1	
J Clayton	c Weatherald b Scott	16	37	49	2	
SJ Truloff	b Grant	64	86	116	8	1
MA Bryant	lbw b Scott	6	19	32	1	
JJ Peirson*+	c McAndrew b Scott	6	13	21	1	
JD Wildermuth	b Grant	23	29	39	3	
JJ Bazley	not out	10	6	14	1	
XC Bartlett	c & b Grant	0	1	1		
GS Sandhu	c Grant b McSweeney	2	3	4		

4 b, 1 lb, 2 nb 7
43.3 overs, 194 mins 191

1-45 (Street), 2-45 (Burns), 3-64 (Renshaw), 4-95 (Clayton), 5-108 (Bryant), 6-122 (Peirson), 7-163 (Truloff), 8-186 (Wildermuth), 9-186 (Bartlett), 10-191 (Sandhu)

Bowling

	O	M	R	W	wd	nb		O	M	R	W	wd	nb
BJ Doggett	25	6	59	2		1		5	1	25	1		
DMK Grant	20	3	65	1				8	0	48	3		
LAJ Scott	17	3	67	2	2			16	5	46	5	2	
NJ McAndrew	22	5	62	2				11	1	41	0		
NA McSweeney	16	3	43	1				3.3	0	26	1		

South Australia First innings

Batsman		R	B	M	4	6
JB Weatherald	b Bartlett	24	46	63	3	2
HJ Hunt*	c Truloff b Sandhu	0	1	5		1
JM Carder	c Street b Wildermuth	25	37	44	3	
NA McSweeney	c Renshaw b Wildermuth	1	9	15		
DR Drew	c Peirson b Sandhu	37	99	155	4	
JS Lehmann	c Peirson b Bazley	102	177	254	11	
HJ Nielsen+	c Burns b Sandhu	16	49	45	2	
LAH Scott	c Peirson b Bartlett	0	2	2		
NJ McAndrew	c Renshaw b Bazley	29	39	50	2	
DMK Grant	not out	0	0	1		
BJ Doggett						

1 lb, 5 nb, 4 w 10
75.4 overs, 321 mins 9-244 dec

1-4 (Hunt), 2-46 (Carder), 3-52 (Weatherald), 4-52 (McSweeney), 5-155 (Drew), 6-188 (Nielsen), 7-189 (Scott), 8-244 (McAndrew), 9-244 (Lehmann)

South Australia Second innings

Batsman		R	B	M	4	6
JB Weatherald	not out	60	112	158	5	
HJ Hunt*	c Truloff b Bartlett	10	15	19		
JM Carder	c Street b Bartlett	11	18	26	1	
NA McSweeney	c Wildermuth b Sandhu	10	32	48	1	
DR Drew	not out	15	48	62	1	

4 b, 2 lb, 2 nb, 1 w 9
37 overs, 158 mins 3-115

1-17 (Hunt), 2-38 (Carder), 3-66 (McSweeney)

Bowling

	O	M	R	W	wd	nb		O	M	R	W	wd	nb
XC Bartlett	17	4	49	2				11	2	30	2		1
GS Sandhu	23	6	64	3	1	4		10	1	29	1		1
JD Wildermuth	14	1	61	2		3		7	0	18	0	1	
JJ Bazley	12.4	3	48	2	1			5	0	17	0		
BE Street	1	0	8	0				4	0	15	0		
MT Renshaw	8	2	13	0									

Stumps Scores

Day 1	No play		
Day 2	Queensland (1st inns)	4-158	J Clayton 31*, MA Bryant 1*
Day 3	South Australia (1st inns)	5-185	JS Lehmann 76*, HJ Neilsen 15*

Toss: South Australia
Umpires: DR Close, BNJ Oxenford
Referee: KC Wessels
Award: LAH Scott (SA)

Western Australia First innings

		B	M	4	6	Second innings		B	M	4	6
CT Bancroft	lbw b Tremain	117	262	342	9	c Holt b Tremain	2	10	13		
SM Whiteman*	c Copeland b Edwards	10	43	63	1	not out	27	111	170	2	
SE Marsh	c Holt b Edwards	58	152	204	4	b Tremain	17	40	47	3	
HWR Cartwright	c Kerr b Tremain	81	209	275	9	b J Sangha	10	19	30	1	
JR Philippe+	c & b Edwards	32	96	125	1	c Tremain b Ayre	8	31	41		
AM Hardie	not out	37	72	97	6	not out	10	29	35	1	
DJM Short	c & b Kerr	1	4	5							
JS Paris	not out	7	9	15	1						
ML Kelly											
CJ Rocchiccioli											
LRT Morris											
	11 lb, 1 nb, 1 w	13				1 lb	1				
	100 overs : 3-236 141 overs , 566 mins 6-356 dec					40 overs , 170 mins 4-75 dec					

1-28 (Whiteman), 2-169 (Marsh), 3-211 (Bancroft),
4-291 (Philippe), 5-344 (Cartwright), 6-345 (Short)

1-7 (Bancroft), 2-29 (Marsh),
3-44 (Cartwright), 4-62 (Philippe)

Bowling	O	M	R	W	wd	nb		O	M	R	W	wd	nb
TA Copeland	23	9	39	0				5	1	11	0		
CP Tremain	24	6	42	2	1			8	3	12	2		
AJ Nair	10	1	34	0				2	1	2	0		
JR Edwards	21	2	58	3		1		9	2	20	0		
HL Kerr	23	8	57	1				6	2	8	0		
T Sangha	18	2	50	0									
JJ Sangha	14	5	36	0				6	2	12	1		
RR Ayre	8	0	29	0				4	0	9	1		

New South Wales First innings

		B	M	4	6
DP Hughes	c Bancroft b Paris	6	11	11	1
KR Patterson*	lbw b Kelly	21	42	59	4
JJ Sangha	c Philippe b Paris	86	213	304	9
JR Edwards	c Bancroft b Kelly	1	8	9	
HL Kerr	b Kelly	0	3	6	
BJH Holt+	b Paris	2	11	10	
AJ Nair	c Bancroft b Hardie	0	10	17	
MC Henriques	c Philippe b Rocchiccio	23	43	50	4
CP Tremain	c Bancroft b Rocchiccio	58	102	175	2	3
TA Copeland	c Philippe b Short	5	26	27	
RR Ayre	not out	1	9	11	
TT Sangha	subbed out (concussion)				
	1 b, 1 lb, 3 nb	5			
	79.1 overs, 344 mins	208			

Bowling	O	M	R	W	wd	nb
JS Paris	20	10	42	3		
AM Hardie	9	1	17	1		
ML Kelly	16	6	27	3		
CJ Rocchiccioli	17	2	54	2		
LRT Morris	14	1	51	0		3
DJM Short	3.1	0	15	1		

1-8 (Hughes), 2-32 (Patterson), 3-34 (Edwards),
4-42 (Kerr), 5-46 (Holt), 6-56 (Nair),
7-98 (Henriques), 8-202 (J Sangha)
9-206 (Tremain), 10-208 (Copeland)

Stumps Scores
Day 1   Western Australia (1st inns) 3-231   HWR Cartwright 29*, JR Philippe 3*
Day 2   No play
Day 3   New South Wales (1st inns) 7-165   JJ Sangha 66*, CP Tremain 41*

Toss: Western Australia
Umpires: GA Abood, GJ Davidson
Referee: K Hannam
Award: CT Bancroft (WA)

Match 20 – Victoria v Tasmania at Junction Oval, Melbourne on March 15-18, 2022
Victoria won by 2 wickets - Match Drawn. Points – Vic 7.57, Tas 1.13

Tasmania

First innings

			B	M	4	6
TP Ward	b Murphy	29	89	110	4	
CP Jewell	st Harper b Murphy	27	74	99	4	
MS Wade*	c Harper b Murphy	61	129	177	8	1
BR McDermott	c Handscomb b Sutherland	94	209	257	9	2
JC Silk	c Handscomb b Holland	31	65	79	6	
JR Doran+	b Pattinson	23	50	71	4	
TS Rogers	c Handscomb b Murphy	0	7	5		
TD Andrews	c Maddinson b Holland	39	44	60	6	1
BAD Manenti	not out	19	22	31	2	1
JM Bird	b Holland	26	18	23	1	2
PM Siddle	c Handscomb b Holland	0	2	1		
	1 lb, 3 nb, 2 w	6				
100 overs : 6-263	117.4 overs, 461 mins	355				

1-53 (Jewell), 2-58 (Ward), 3-187 (Wade), 4-246 (Silk),
5-250 (McDermott), 6-251 (Rogers), 7-310 (Doran),
8-310 (Andrews), 9-355 (Bird), 10-355 (Siddle)

Bowling

	O	M	R	W	wd	nb
JL Pattinson	24	8	65	1	1	
WJ Sutherland	24	4	69	1		1
MJ Perry	17	5	40	0	1	2
TR Murphy	29	8	98	4		
JM Holland	23.4	2	82	4		
JL Seymour						

Second innings

			B	M	4	6
	lbw b Perry	5	8	7	1	
	c Handscomb b Perry	6	17	23	1	
	c Handscomb b Murphy	50	87	97	6	
	c Seymour b Murphy	21	44	72	2	
	c Handscomb b Holland	42	119	144	4	
	c Handscomb b Murphy	2	12	16		
	b Holland	3	15	11		
	run out (Fraser-McGurk)	40	49	59	8	
	c Handscomb b Perry	23	53	51	4	
	b Perry	1	7	11		
	not out	4	6	7		
	4 b, 7 lb, 1 nb	12				
	69.2 overs, 253 mins	209				

1-9 (Ward), 2-24 (Jewell), 3-86 (McDermott),
4-90 (Wade), 5-100 (Doran), 6-105 (Rogers), 7-160
(Andrews), 8-204 (Silk), 9-204 (Manenti), 10-209 (Bird)

O	M	R	W	wd	nb
10	1	26	0		
2	0	9	0		1
11.2	1	31	4		
21	6	48	3		
22	3	68	2		
3	0	16	0		

Victoria

First innings

			B	M	4	6
JL Seymour	lbw b Bird	10	26	26	1	
TJ Dean	b Andrews	146	302	413	19	
PSP Handscomb*	c Bird b Siddle	22	34	47	3	
NJ Maddinson	c & b Manenti	1	7	16		
J Fraser-McGurk	lbw b Rogers	25	54	59	4	
SB Harper+	lbw b Andrews	93	193	247	9	2
JL Pattinson	b Manenti	21	22	23	3	
WJ Sutherland	not out	5	12	14		
MJ Perry	not out	3	1	4		
TR Murphy						
JM Holland						
	2 b, 2 lb, 3 nb, 1 w	8				
100 overs : 5-297	108 overs, 428 mins	7-334 dec				

1-14 (Seymour), 2-61 (Handscomb), 3-72 (Maddinson),
4-110 (Fraser-McGurk), 5-297 (Harper), 6-310 (Dean),
7-328 (Pattinson)

Bowling

	O	M	R	W	wd	nb
JM Bird	22	6	54	1	1	3
PM Siddle	18	6	53	1		
BAD Manenti	31	7	101	2		
TS Rogers	18	2	69	1		
TD Andrews	19	2	53	2		

Second innings

			B	M	4	6
	lbw b Manenti	25	52	75	3	
	b Bird	47	46	51	8	
	lbw b Siddle	33	55	56	5	
	lbw b Andrews	23	63	82	2	
	b Manenti	9	25	30	1	
	c McDermott b Andrews	8	23	25		
	c Silk b Manenti	6	26	28		
	c Bird b Siddle	14	40	40	1	
	not out	32	59	74	3	
	not out	24	53	54	3	
	8 b, 5 lb	13				
	73.4 overs, 261 mins	8-234				

1-74 (Dean), 2-86 (Seymour), 3-121 (Handscomb),
4-134 (Fraser-McGurk), 5-148 (Maddinson),
6-151 (Harper), 7-161 (Pattinson), 8-187 (Sutherland)

O	M	R	W	wd	nb
9	3	36	1		
16	4	46	2		
31.4	4	89	3		
17	3	50	2		

Stumps Scores

Day 1   Tasmania (1st inns) 5-250   JR Doran 2*, TS Rogers 0*
Day 2   Victoria (1st inns)   4-210   TJ Dean 103*, SB Harper 42*
Day 3   Tasmania (2nd inns) 7-170   JC Silk 22*, BAD Manenti 9*

Toss: Tasmania
Umpires: SAJ Craig, NR Johnstone
Referee: RW Stratford
Award: TJ Dean (Vic)

Match 21 – Tasmania v Queensland at Bellerive Oval, Hobart on March 23-24, 2022
Tasmania won by an innings and 231 runs. Points – Tas 8.75, Qld 0.9

Queensland	First innings	B	M	4	6	Second innings	B	M	4	6
BE Street	c Bird b Rainbird	23	49	58	2	b Rainbird	1	3	6	
JA Burns	c Ward b Rainbird	28	81	132	4	c Webster b Bell	30	48	64	5
MT Renshaw	c Ward b Rainbird	1	9	11		c Doran b Rainbird	24	62	78	5
JJ Clayton	lbw b Rainbird	0	3	2		c Webster b Hope	1	10	25	
SJ Truloff	c Doran b Bell	3	7	10		c Doran b Hope	11	39	61	2
JJ Peirson*+	lbw b Rainbird	23	41	59	4	c Jewell b Hope	9	24	33	2
JD Wildermuth	b Bell	5	9	12	1	lbw b Rainbird	3	15	16	
JJ Bazley	b Rainbird	0	2	7		c Bell b Rainbird	0	2	2	
GS Sandhu	c Doran b Rainbird	5	21	22	1	c Doran b Rainbird	0	9	25	
MP Kuhnemann	b Rainbird	9	17	27	2	lbw b Bell	4	16	17	
BL Edwards	not out	0	6	9		not out	0	2	3	
	1 b, 6 lb	7				4 lb	4			
	40.5 overs, 177 mins	104				38.2 overs, 167 mins	87			

1-40 (Street), 2-42 (Renshaw), 3-42 (Clayton), 4-47 (Truloff),
5-83 (Burns), 6-86 (Peirson), 7-90 (Wildermuth),
8-90 (Bazley), 9-99 (Sandhu), 10-104 (Kuhnemann)

1-1 (Street), 2-46 (Burns), 3-56 (Renshaw),
4-58 (Clayton), 5-76 (Peirson), 6-83 (Wildermuth),
7-83 (Bazley), 8-83 (Truloff), 9-87 (Kuhnemann),
10-87 (Sandhu)

Bowling	O	M	R	W	wd	nb	O	M	R	W	wd	nb
JM Bird	10	2	29	0			10	1	29	0		
SL Rainbird	14.5	8	21	8			12.2	4	21	5		
GT Bell	12	2	29	2			7	4	18	2		
BM Hope	4	1	18	0			9	3	15	3		

Tasmania	First innings	B	M	4	6
TP Ward	c Peirson b Edwards	15	15	24	2
CP Jewell	c Renshaw b Wildermuth	44	101	161	5
MB Wright	c Peirson b Bazley	22	51	54	4
JR Doran+	run out (Truloff)	72	155	214	13	1
JC Silk	b Edwards	21	36	45	3
BJ Webster*	not out	166	172	250	21	6
BM Hope	c Peirson b Wildermuth	2	11	10	
TD Andrews	c Burns b Sandhu	21	28	32	1	2
JM Bird	c Wildermuth b Sandhu	11	5	9	2
SL Rainbird	c Peirson b Edwards	12	41	63	1
GT Bell	c Bazley b Sandhu	19	24	48	2	1
	8 lb, 8 nb, 1 w	17			
	100 overs:9-37? 105.1 overs, 457 mins	422			

Bowling	O	M	R	W	wd	nb
GS Sandhu	27.1	10	82	3		1
JD Wildermuth	24	3	87	2		5
BL Edwards	23	4	95	3	1	1
JJ Bazley	20	3	84	1		
MP Kuhnemann	11	1	66	0		

1-20 (Ward), 2-64 (Wright), 3-122 (Jewell),
4-157 (Silk), 5-228 (Doran), 6-235 (Hope)
7-279 (Andrews), 8-304 (Bird), 9-335 (Rainbird),
10-422 (Bell)

Stumps Scores
Day 1 Tasmania (1st inns) 4-157   JR Doran 48*, BJ Webster 0*

Toss: Tasmania. Umpires: MW Graham-Smith, SJ Nogajski, Ref: DA Johnston. Award: SL Rainbird (Tas)

INNINGS WINS BY TASMANIA OVER QUEENSLAND IN SHEFFIELD SHIELD MATCHES

Season		Venue	Margin
1992/93	Queensland 104 & 87 lost to Tasmania 422	Gabba	Innings and 5 runs
2001/02	Tasmania 281 def Queensland 130 & 101	Bellerive	Innings and 50 runs
2005/06	Queensland 176 & 140 lost to Tasmania 356	Bellerive	Innings and 40 runs
2021/22	**Queensland 104 & 87 lost to Tasmania 422**	**Bellerive**	**Innings and 231 runs***

Match 22 – South Australia v New South Wales at Rolton Oval, Adelaide on March 23-26, 2022
South Australia won by 5 wickets. Points – SA 7.47, NSW 1.43

New South Wales — First innings

Batsman	Dismissal		B	M	4	6
RP Hackney	c Nielsen b Doggett	0	21	24		
B Nikitaras	c Carder b Scott	44	92	123	7	1
MR Gilkes	c Lehmann b Buckingham	41	104	140	4	
JJ Sangha *	c Nielsen b McAndrew	142	235	338	17	1
LD Hearne	c Carder b McSweeney	36	115	139	2	
JR Edwards	b Buckingham	5	31	35		
BJH Holt +	c Lehmann b Buckingham	2	7	10		
CP Tremain	c Nielsen b Doggett	6	27	35	1	
TA Copeland	c Nielsen b Buckingham	7	11	12		
HNA Conway	b Doggett	4	20	22	1	
TS Sangha	not out	0	14	28		
	1 b, 1 lb, 4 nb, 1 w	7				
100 overs : 7-253	112.1 overs, 462 mins	294				

1-10 (Hackney), 2-83 (Nikitaras), 3-104 (Gilkes), 4-205 (Hearne),
5-219 (Edwards), 6-229 (Holt), 7-249 (Tremain), 8-260 (Copeland),
9-271 (Conway), 10-294 (J Sangha)

Bowling	O	M	R	W	wd	nb
BJ Doggett	28	8	58	3		
JSD Buckingham	27	7	79	4		
NJ McAndrew	22.1	5	77	1	1	
LAH Scott	19	6	43	1		4
NA McSweeney	16	5	35	1		

Second innings

Dismissal		B	M	4	6
c Capel b McAndrew	12	60	88	2	
run out (Doggett)	56	100	125	7	2
lbw b McSweeney	54	76	82	10	
c Nielsen b McSweeney	62	103	138	6	1
b McSweeney	65	107	144	9	
b McAndrew	38	44	47	5	
c McSweeney b McAndrew	10	10	18	1	
c McAndrew b McSweeney	0	1	1		
not out	1	1	6		
not out	1	3	3		
1 b, 2 lb, 1 nb, 5 w	9				
84 overs, 335 mins	8-308 dec				

1-54 (Hackney), 2-84 (Nikitaras), 3-147 (Gilkes),
4-218 (J Sangha), 5-278 (Edwards), 6-302 (Hearne),
7-302 (Tremain), 8-306 (Holt)

O	M	R	W	wd	nb
15	3	70	0	2	
13	3	41	0	3	1
20	6	67	3		
10	1	38	0		
26	1	89	4		

South Australia — First innings

Batsman	Dismissal		B	M	4	6
HJ Hunt*	c Copeland b TS Sangha	109	238	311	11	10
BT Capel	c J Sangha b Tremain	1	10	22		
JM Carder	c & b Conway	15	35	47	2	
NA McSweeney	lbw b Copeland	7	25	30	1	
JS Lehmann	c J Sangha b Copeland	0	1	1		
TJ Kelly	lbw b TS Sangha	29	34	41	3	2
HJ Nielsen +	c Edwards b Tremain	63	154	198	7	
LAH Scott	not out	30	60	86	2	1
NJ McAndrew	c Edwards b Copeland	3	14	18		
BJ Doggett	b Tremain	10	10	14	2	
JSD Buckingham	not out	0	10	19		
	1 b, 4 lb, 3 nb, 2 w	10				
	98 overs, 398 mins	9-277 dec				

1-8 (Capel), 2-35 (Carder), 3-52 (McSweeney), 4-52 (Lehmann),
5-98 (Kelly), 6-222 (Hunt), 7-241 (Nielsen), 8-248 (McAndrew),
9-261 (Doggett)

Bowling	O	M	R	W	wd	nb
TA Copeland	25	8	58	3	1	
CP Tremain	23	4	51	3	1	
HNA Conway	13	2	43	1		
TS Sangha	23	3	75	2		
JR Edwards	8	2	21	0		3
JJ Sangha	6	0	24	0		

Second innings

Dismissal		B	M	4	6
c Copeland b Edwards	25	61	78	5	
c Edwards b Copeland	8	15	18	2	
c Edwards b Conway	46	52	90	8	
not out	99	183	244	13	
c Gilkes b T Sangha	94	89	146	14	
c Hearne b Tremain	13	19	14	2	
not out	34	37	51	4	
2 b, 2 lb, 5 w	9				
76 overs, 323 mins	5-328				

1-13 (Capel), 2-61 (Hunt), 3-89 (Carder),
4-240 (Lehmann), 5-253 (Kelly)

O	M	R	W	wd	nb
15	2	57	1	1	
17	5	57	1		
10	0	38	1	1	
21	1	106	1		
13	1	66	1		2

Close of Play Scores

Day 1	New South Wales (1st inns)	6-243	JJ Sangha 104*, CP Tremain 4*
Day 2:	South Australia (1st inns)	5-219	HJ Hunt 107*, HJ Nielsen 52*
Day 3:	New South Wales (2nd inns)	4-235	LD Hearne 31*, JR Edwards 11*

Toss: South Australia
Umpires: SAJ Craig, DM Koch
Referee: SD Fry
Award: JJ Sangha (NSW)

109

Victoria	First innings		B	M	4	6		Second innings		B	M	4	6
TJ Dean	b Hardie		3	6	8		2	b Hardie		29	52	71	5
WJ Pucovski	c Philippe b Kelly		22	45	61	3	1	c Philippe b Paris		11	21	26	1
PSP Handscomb*	c Bancroft b Hardie		1	26	38			b Morris		20	53	78	3
NJ Maddinson	lbw b Hardie		4	12	19	1		lbw b Kelly		5	6	3	1
JM Fraser-McGurk	c Whiteman b Hardie		4	12	23	1		lbw b Paris		9	14	23	1
MW Short	b Paris		43	81	125	6	7	c Rocchiccioli b Hardie		35	53	105	5
SB Harper+	c Whiteman b Kelly		18	54	79	3	8	c Philippe b Morris		17	109	123	2
JL Pattinson	b Morris		1	17	24		9	b Morris		21	43	58	4
WJ Sutherland	not out		9	10	13	2	10	c Marsh b Morris		6	9	11	1
MJ Perry	c Marsh b Paris		0	2	1		6	c Whiteman b Paris		3	6	12	
CL McClure	run out (Hardie)		0	2	8			not out		0	2	7	
	5 b, 4 nb		9					5 b, 5 lb, 5 nb, 1 w		16			
	43.5 overs, 208 mins		114					60.3 overs, 265 mins		172			

1-6 (Dean), 2-23 (Handscomb), 3-27 (Pucovski), 4-31 (Maddinson),
5-44 (Fraser-McGurk), 6-91 (Harper), 7-105 (Pattinson), 8-105 (Short),
9-105 (Perry), 10-114 (McClure)

1-26 (Pucovski), 2-54 (Dean), 3-59 (Maddinson),
4-79 (Fraser-McGurk), 5-79 (Handscomb), 6-86 (Perry),
7-137 (Short), 8-151 (Harper), 9-166 (Sutherland),
10-172 (Pattinson)

Bowling	O	M	R	W	wd	nb		O	M	R	W	wd	nb
JS Paris	11.5	7	27	2		1		16	8	31	3		
AM Hardie	12	2	24	4				15	2	46	2	1	
ML Kelly	13	5	27	2				10	4	19	1		
LRT Morris	7	0	31	1		3		13.3	3	55	4		5
CJ Rocchiccioli								6	1	11	0		

Western Australia	First innings		B	M	4	6
CT Bancroft	c Harper b Perry		38	123	156	2
SM Whiteman	c Short b Sutherland		63	85	119	10
SE Marsh*	c Handscomb b Sutherland		18	47	64	2
ML Kelly	c Fraser-McGurk b Pattinson		41	51	90	7	1
HWR Cartwright	lbw b McClure		109	178	254	17	1
TA Wyllie	c Harper b Sutherland		42	95	101	5
JR Philippe+	c Short b Pattinson		4	11	12	
AM Hardie	lbw b Pattinson		4	8	9	
JS Paris	c Handscomb b Perry		10	33	46	2
CJ Rocchiccioli	not out		0	0	4	
LRT Morris	lbw b McClure		0	1	1	
	3 b, 5 lb		8			
100 overs: 7-322	105.2 overs, 441 mins		337			

Bowling	O	M	R	W	wd	nb
JL Pattinson	24	5	96	3		
MJ Perry	27	6	73	2		
CL McClure	22.2	8	67	2		
WJ Sutherland	25	4	67	3		
MW Short	7	0	26	0		

1-94 (Whiteman), 2-114 (Bancroft), 3-126 (Marsh),
4-189 (Kelly), 5-292 (Wyllie), 6-299 (Philippe),
7-307 (Hardie), 8-337 (Paris),
9-337 (Cartwright), 10-337 (Morris)

Stumps Scores

| Day 1 | Western Australia (1st inns) | 2-119 | CT Bancroft 135*, ML Kelly 3* |
| Day 2 | Victoria (2nd inns) | 5-82 | MJ Perry 0*, MW Short 3* |

Toss: Western Australia
Umpires: GA Abood, PJ Gillespie
Ref: SR Bernard

MOST CATCHES BY A FIELDER IN A SHEFFIELD SHIELD SEASON

	Team	Season	Matches	Catches
Peter Handscomb	**Victoria**	**2021/22**	**8**	**27**
Adam Voges	Western Australia	2008/09	10	23
Craig Serjeant	Western Australia	1981/82	9	23
Beau Webster	Tasmania	2017/18	10	23
Jamie Siddons	South Australia	1990/91	11	23

THE FINAL - PERTH

With Western Australia winning over Victoria in the last round at the WACA, the teams met again in the Final, set down for five days at the same venue. With the Test part of the Pakistan tour over, Victoria regained Ashes hero Scott Boland, for the injured James Pattinson. Marcus Harris could not take his place as he had contracted COVID. WA went in with the same team that had won the previous week and were solid favourites to win the Shield.

Day One: March 31, 2022 – Attendance: 1,113

On a very white looking pitch, Victoria decided to send the hosts in to bat. After just six runs from the first four overs, the WA openers started to push things along, adding 21 off the next three, Bancroft hitting some lovely drives through the off-side. There was little movement in the air for the bowlers as WA went into drinks on 0-41 (16 overs) with Bancroft 28 and Whiteman nine. After drinks it was more of the same, with the Victoria bowlers unable to penetrate. Whiteman took 53 balls over his first 11 and then proceeded to unwind, with some nice pull shots in the lead up to lunch. Bancroft continued to drive the ball well and WA went to the break on 99 without loss, Bancroft 55, Whiteman 36.

Boland found the edge of Whiteman's bat in his first over after lunch, but the ball fell short of the keeper. The 100 stand was raised and when Whiteman reached his fifty (122 balls, 167 minutes) it looked as thought it was going to be a very long day for the bowlers. Sutherland and Merlo toiled hard and each managed to find the edge of Bancroft's bat, while Whiteman continued to bat efficiently as tea loomed. Boland returned for a spell just before the break and managed to induce Whiteman to hit a catch to gully. Tea was taken immediately, with WA 1-188 (56.5 overs) with Bancroft 94 not out.

Shortly after tea Bancroft reached his ton (170 balls, 14 fours) with a clip to leg off Boland and when Marsh hit Perry for four, square on the off-side, the 200 was raised with just one wicket down. Bancroft edged Boland through a vacant second slip for four and then Marsh lost concentration and advanced at Short, to be easily stumped. Cartwright looked very assured as the runs ticked over, WA reaching 2-250 when the new ball was taken after 80 overs. Boland returned and was off his game as Cartwright hit a pull and cut to the fence, in an over that cost 15. Cartwright survived a tight LBW shout on 33 when facing Boland and then in the last over of the day, hit one hard to gully where it was well snapped up by Merlo. Kelly came out as night-watchman for one ball, which he clipped to leg for three, WA ending the opening day well on top at 3-290.

Day Two: April 1, 2022 – Attendance: 1,585

The first session was going to be critical for Victoria if they were to get themselves back into the game. Their quicks got the ball to move in the air and picked up three wickets in the first 20 minutes. Kelly edged to second slip, Wyllie to first and then Bancroft was caught down the leg side. Philippe resisted for a while before he edged on the first slip, WA having lost 4-16 from 56 balls. When Hardie edged behind to leave WA 8-322, one felt the hosts would be lucky to reach 350. Paris played well, hooking Perry for six until Boland returned and had him caught at second slip. Then Rocchiccioli proceeded to lay into the Victorian bowlers, hitting Holland for six over long-on before hooking Perry for six more. A quiet single to the on-side brought up a rapid fire 50 (28 balls) and he was bowled by the next ball he faced, having a wild swing. WA had lost 7-96 in the morning session, to still be in a strong position when lunch was called.

The Victorian openers started carefully before Pucovski started to find the rope with some well timed strokes. Dean had some luck on 13 when he was dropped by Bancroft at second slip off Kelly. The pair went in at tea with 53 from 26 overs on the board albeit a little slowly – Pucosvki 34, Dean 19. After tea the Vics picked up the rate, but lost Dean who popped a catch to short-leg. Pucovski reached his 50 (107 balls) and looked set for a long knock when he was out getting an inside edge to the keeper. WA's bowlers were giving little away, as the Vics reached the 50 over mark at 2-114. Not long after that, Short was caught at second slip with Perry coming in as night-watchman with just under 30 minutes left in the day. Handscomb hit Paris for three fours in an over and Perry completed his job, the Vics ended the day 239 behind.

Day Three: April 2, 2022 – Attendance: 2,964

Inside the first half hour Handscomb reached his 50 with a hook off Morris for four but then Perry got stuck on 20 for 29 balls. After drinks Perry started to get a move on finding the rope, barely scoring any runs on the leg-side. The new ball came with Victoria 3-213 after 80 overs, Paris being struck for boundaries by Handscomb and Perry as nine came from the over. Within minutes of lunch Handscomb drove at one from Hardie and was caught behind, ending a fine knock.

Maddinson came out after the break and edged his first ball for four, before cutting his third for another. Victoria's hopes of gaining a bonus points advantage lay with him as with 14 overs to go before the 100 over cut off, Victoria needed to score 47 more runs without losing a wicket. He continued to play aggressively, hitting five fours in 20 before edging one low to first slip where Shaun Marsh took a good catch. This left Victoria needing 36 runs in 9.3 overs without losing a wicket to gain the lead on bonus points. Merlo joined Perry and the pair played out the next 21 balls without scoring a run. The tactics seemed odd given the target was well within reach. Merlo cracked two fours in an over from Paris, as Victoria reached 5-270, needing 28 from the next 30 balls to gain the lead – as long as they didn't lose a wicket.

Perry played a maiden from Kelly and then just three came from the next, it was obvious Victoria had decided the only way to clinch the Shield was to win outright. When Merlo got a fine touch to one off Paris, the Victorian innings subsided quickly, losing their last 5-28 to be 80 behind on the first innings. Perry was eighth out, being superbly held at leg-slip.

Bancroft was caught at first slip third ball and when Shaun Marsh was out to Short for the second time in the match, it was game on. The Victorian bowlers had their tails up as Whiteman and Cartwright dug in. The stand of 41 came to an end when Cartwright edged to first slip, but Wyllie came out and batted well as he and the gritty Whiteman got to stumps, WA 171 ahead.

Day Four: April 3, 2022 – Attendance: 1,732

WA were in no hurry with just three singles coming from the first nine overs of the day. Whiteman reached his 50 and then lost Wyllie to a catch at first slip. When Philippe was well held at short cover, WA were just 190 ahead with five wickets left. The sixth wicket pair dug in until lunch, WA 5-134 (Whiteman 67, Hardie 11) having scored just 45 in the session. In the second over after lunch, Hardie (15*) appeared lucky to survive an LBW shout facing Sutherland – height the only possible reason to deny the dismissal. Had he been given out, WA would have been 220 ahead with four wickets in hand.

This appeared to be a mortal blow for the Vics as they took just one more wicket for the rest of the day. Whiteman got his ton (383 mins, 260 balls) and in another blow for the visitors, Hardie was dropped by Harper off Holland on 49 just before tea. The stand continued on against a tired looking attack, with neither batsman taking any risks. Hardie reached his 100 with a straight drive for four off Sutherland, the lead now past 350 for WA. Whiteman eventually fell, shouldering arms to Sutherland half an hour before stumps. Paris and Hardie added a further 29 before stumps, WA 393 ahead with a day to play

Day Five: April 4, 2022 – Attendance: 382

WA showed no signs of declaring adding 21 runs in the morning before Paris was adjudged LBW. Kelly put his head down, guiding Hardie to his maiden 150. Then on the verge of lunch, there was movement in the WA rooms as their players all put their whites on. Word came through that the match would end in a draw at lunch – giving the WA their first Shield in 23 years.

The Final – Western Australia v Victoria at the WACA, Perth on March 31 - April 4, 2022
Match Drawn. Bonus Points – WA 1.67, Vic 1.44

Western Australia	First innings		B	M	4	6	Second innings		B	M	4	6
CT Bancroft	c Harper b Boland		141	269	385	17	c Short b Boland		0	3	2	
SM Whiteman	c Sutherland b Boland		85	179	239	11	b Sutherland		123	338	502	11
SE Marsh	st Harper b Short		12	31	43	1	c Handscomb b Short		13	31	56	2
HWR Cartwright	c Merlo b Sutherland		41	70	77	4	c Short b Boland		12	50	80	1
ML Kelly	c Handscomb b Sutherland		4	12	9		9 not out		21	85	96	1
TA Wyllie	c Short b Sutherland		4	6	8	1	5 c Handscomb b Perry		23	86	103	3
JRP Philippe+	c Short b Sutherland		2	16	30		6 c Sutherland b Holland		1	7	4	
AM Hardie	c Harper b Perry		13	47	65	1	7 not out		174	317	405	25	1
JS Paris	c Handscomb b Boland		16	40	54	1	1	8 lbw b Holland		21	61	56	3
CJ Rocchiccioli	b Sutherland		50	29	51	4	2						
LRT Morris	not out		4	28	33								
	13 lb, 1 w		14				4 b, 8 lb		12			
100 overs : 6-307	121.1 overs, 504 mins		386				163 overs, 658 mins	7-400 dec				

1-188 (Whiteman), 2-219 (Marsh), 3-287 (Cartwright), 4-291 (Kelly), 5-301 (Wyllie), 6-301 (Bancroft), 7-307 (Philippe), 8-322 (Hardie), 9-344 (Paris), 10-386 (Rocchiccioli)

1-0 (Bancroft), 2-27 (Marsh), 3-68 (Cartwright), 4-109 (Wyllie), 5-110 (Philippe), 6-284 (Whiteman), 7-334 (Paris)

Bowling	O	M	R	W	wd	nb		O	M	R	W	wd	nb
SM Boland	31	8	80	3				25	11	35	2		
MJ Perry	24	4	90	1				28	5	61	1		
WJ Sutherland	30.1	10	78	5				34	10	86	1		
JM Holland	15	2	53	0				40	7	98	2		
JA Merlo	12	1	51	0	1			4	0	21	0		
MW Short	9	1	21	1				27	4	74	1		
NJ Maddinson								5	1	13	0		

Victoria	First innings		B	M	4	6
TJ Dean	c Wyllie b Hardie		28	87	122	4
WJ Pucovski	c Philippe b Paris		59	133	161	6
PSP Handscomb*	c Philippe b Hardie		80	141	235	9
MW Short	c Bancroft b Hardie		10	45	57	1
MJ Perry	c Paris b Morris		74	168	221	13
NJ Maddinson	c Marsh b Paris		20	12	21	5
JA Merlo	c Philippe b Paris		10	22	35	2
SB Harper+	lbw b Morris		6	10	19	1
WJ Sutherland	c Hardie b Rocchiccioli		9	5	8	1
SM Boland	not out		1	6	11	
JM Holland	c Paris b Rocchiccioli		1	5	6	
	1 b, 5 lb, 2 nb		8			
100 overs : 6-284	105.2 overs, 457 mins		306			

Bowling	O	M	R	W	wd	nb
JS Paris	28	5	95	3		
AM Hardie	24	9	54	3	1	
ML Kelly	25	10	60	0		
LRT Morris	17	1	67	2		1
CJ Rocchiccioli	11.2	0	24	2		

1-75 (Dean), 2-97 (Pucovski), 3-122 (Short), 4-233 (Handscomb), 5-262 (Maddinson), 6-278 (Merlo), 7-290 (Harper), 8-297 (Perry), 9-305 (Sutherland), 10-306 (Holland)

Stumps Scores

Day 1	Western Australia (1st inns) 3-290	CT Bancroft 135*, ML Kelly 3*	Toss: Victoria
Day 2	Victoria (1st inns) 3-147	PSP Handscomb 39*, MJ Perry 10*	Umpires: DM Koch, SJ Nogajski
Day 3	Western Australia (2nd inns) 3-91	SM Whiteman 45*, TA Wyllie 15*	TV: PJ Gillespie, Referee: RL Parry
Day 4	Western Australia (2nd inns) 6-313	AM Hardie 119*, JS Paris 11*	Award: SM Whiteman (WA)
			Attendance: 7,776

NEW SOUTH WALES AVERAGES

Batting & Fielding	M	Inn	NO	Runs	HS	Avge	100	50	S/Rate	Ct	St
B Nikitaras	1	2	0	100	56	50.00	0	1	52.08	0	-
DP Hughes	5	9	2	337	89*	48.14	0	4	39.78	2	-
JJ Sangha	7	13	0	504	142	38.76	1	4	48.55	4	-
HL Kerr	4	7	2	192	88	38.40	0	2	69.81	2	-
KR Patterson	5	9	0	253	112	28.11	1	0	50.80	5	-
MR Gilkes	5	10	0	271	64	27.10	0	2	47.62	4	-
CP Tremain	5	9	2	169	58	24.14	0	1	52.97	2	-
LD Hearne	3	6	0	143	65	23.83	0	1	48.31	2	-
PM Nevill	4	8	1	138	34	19.71	0	0	33.82	14	0
JR Edwards	7	13	1	217	42	18.08	0	0	44.01	8	-
HNA Conway	5	9	4	61	20	12.20	0	0	23.19	3	-
MC Henriques	2	3	0	36	23	12.00	0	0	46.15	0	-
LC Hatcher	1	2	0	24	24	12.00	0	0	50.00	0	-
SA Abbott	2	4	0	42	16	10.50	0	0	31.57	1	-
RP Hackney	3	6	0	60	38	10.00	0	0	23.43	0	-
BJ Holt	3	5	0	44	20	8.80	0	0	35.48	7	0
TA Copeland	6	11	2	68	17	7.55	0	0	33.83	6	-
NM Lyon	2	4	0	22	15	5.50	0	0	27.16	3	-
T Sangha	6	7	2	8	2*	1.60	0	0	10.81	2	-
AJ Nair	1	1	0	0	0	0.00	0	0	0.00	0	-
RR Ayre	1	1	1	1	1*	-	0	0	11.00	0	-

Bowling	M	Overs	Mdns	Runs	Wkts	Avge	Best	5i	10m	SR	Econ
CP Tremain	5	170.3	46	383	24	15.95	5-48	1	0	42.6	2.24
MC Henriques	2	8	2	19	1	19.00	1-14	0	0	48.0	2.37
SA Abbott	2	85.4	16	228	11	20.72	6-38	1	0	46.7	2.66
HL Kerr	4	89	21	233	8	29.12	2-41	0	0	66.7	2.61
TA Copeland	6	164.3	47	383	13	29.46	4-46	0	0	75.9	2.32
JR Edwards	7	130.2	30	355	12	29.58	3-47	0	0	65.1	2.72
T Sangha	6	198.1	40	547	17	32.17	3-44	0	0	69.9	2.76
LC Hatcher	1	40.1	6	161	5	32.20	4-86	0	0	48.2	4.00
RR Ayre	1	12	0	38	1	38.00	1-9	0	0	72.0	3.16
HNA Conway	5	117	26	323	6	53.83	2-11	0	0	117.0	2.76
NM Lyon	2	106	28	251	4	62.75	3-63	0	0	159.0	2.36
JJ Sangha	7	41	10	133	1	133.00	1-12	0	0	246.0	3-24
AJ Nair	1	12	2	36	0	-	-	0	0	-	3.00

NEW SOUTH WALES SHEFFIELD SHIELD RECORDS
Results

versus	M	W	L	D	T	%W	Toss	%toss
Queensland	186	77	48	61	0	41.40	87	46.77
South Australia	233	129	60	44	0	55.36	112	48.07
Tasmania	87	33	25	29	0	37.93	34	39.08
Victoria	244	80	80	83	1	32.79	117	47.95
Western Australia	140	59	39	42	0	42.14	71	50.71
	890	378	252	259	1	42.47	421	47.30

Highest Team Totals

Total	v	Venue	Season
918	SA	SCG	1900-01
815	Vic	SCG	1908-09
807	SA	Adelaide	1899-00
805	Vic	MCG	1905-06
802	SA	SCG	1920-21

Lowest Completed Team Totals

Total	v	Venue	Season
32*	Tas	Bellerive	2020-21
53	Tas	Bellerive	2006-07
56	WA	WACA	1998-99
64	NSW	Park 25	2020-21
66	Vic	MCG	1894-95

Includes batting one short

Leading Run Scorers

	M	Inn	NO	Runs	HS	Ave	100s	50s
MG Bevan	93	163	31	8174	216	61.92	32	33
ME Waugh	93	158	18	7232	229*	51.66	23	30
SR Waugh	85	147	14	6609	216*	49.69	22	24
AF Kippax	61	95	9	6096	315*	70.88	23	14
MA Taylor	85	147	3	6090	199	42.29	15	34
BJ Haddin	94	157	21	5712	154	42.00	11	34
J Dyson	82	150	16	5648	241	42.15	11	29
KD Walters	91	159	16	5602	253	39.17	17	24
PA Jaques	76	140	4	5581	240*	41.04	14	25
GRJ Matthews	116	177	27	5567	184	37.11	8	28

Highest Individual scores

		v	Venue	Season
452*	DG Bradman	Qld	Sydney	1929-30
359	RB Simpson	Qld	Brisbane	1963-64
340*	DG Bradman	Vic	Sydney	1928-29
315*	AF Kippax	Qld	Sydney	1927-28
306	SM Katich	Qld	Sydney	2007-08

Most Catches (Fielders)

	M	Ct
MA Taylor	85	120
ME Waugh	92	112
GRJ Matthews	116	102
TA Copeland	93	94
R Benaud	73	92

Most Appearances

	M	Start	Start
GRJ Matthews	116	12 Nov 1982	25 Oct 1997
PA Emery	109	22 Jan 1988	14 Mar 1999
GF Lawson	103	18 Feb 1978	1 April 1992
PM Nevill	**101**	**15 Feb 2009**	**21 Feb 2022**
SJ Rixon	94	25 Oct 1974	4 Jan 1988
BJ Haddin	94	19 Oct 1999	28 Nov 2014
MG Bevan	93	16 Nov 1990	7 Mar 2004
ME Waugh	93	25 Oct 1985	7 Mar 2004

Most Dismissals (Keepers)

	M	Ct	St	Total
PA Emery	109	298	41	339
PM Nevill	**89**	**296**	**23**	**319**
BJ Haddin	93	282	24	306
SJ Rixon	93	218	43	261
HB Taber	64	179	32	211
WAS Oldfield	51	109	70	179
DA Ford	56	107	51	158

Record Partnerships

Wkt	Runs			v..	Venue	Season
1	319	RB McCosker	J Dyson	WA	SCG	1980-81
2	378	LA Marks	KD Walters	SA	Adelaide	1964-65
3	363	DG Bradman	AF Kippax	Qld	SCG	1933-34
4	325	NC O'Neill	BC Booth	Vic	SCG	1957-58
5	464*	ME Waugh	SR Waugh	WA	WACA	1990-91
6	332	NG Marks	G Thomas	SA	SCG	1958-59
7	255	G Thomas	R Benaud	Vic	MCG	1961-62
8	270	VT Trumper	EP Barbour	Vic	SCG	1912-13
9	226	C Kelleway	WAS Oldfield	Vic	MCG	1925-26
10	307	AF Kippax	JEH Hooker	Vic	MCG	1928-29

Leading Wicket takers

	M	Balls	Mdns	Runs	Wkts	Ave	Best	5wI	10M	SR	Econ
GF Lawson	103	20933	870	8673	367	23.63	6-31	12	0	57.04	2.49
GRJ Matthews	116	26764	1375	10518	363	28.98	8-52	19	4	73.73	2.36
TA Copeland	93	21414	1055	8984	341	26.35	8-92	16	2	62.80	2.52
SCG MacGill	86	19189	549	11239	328	34.27	6-64	17	0	58.50	3.51
DE Bollinger	89	15668	589	8166	290	28.16	6-47	10	2	54.03	3.13
R Benaud	73	18106	474	7172	266	26.96	7-32	12	3	68.07	2.38
JW Martin	70	15890	239	7949	263	30.22	8-97	12	0	60.42	3.00
MR Whitney	77	14983	562	7314	251	29.14	7-75	10	0	59.69	2.93
AK Davidson	62	13425	275	5195	246	21.12	7-31	10	0	54.57	2.32
SR Clark	69	13854	563	6646	228	29.15	8-58	9	1	60.76	2.88

Best Bowling in an innings

		v	Venue	Season
WJ O'Reilly	9-41	SA	Adelaide	1937-38
WJ O'Reilly	9-50	Vic	MCG	1933-34
WP Howell	9-52	Vic	MCG	1902-03
DW Hourn	9-77	Vic	SCG	1978-79
RG Holland	9-83	SA	SCG	1984-85

Best Bowling in a Match

		v	Venue	Season
TR McKibbin	15-125	SA	Adelaide	1896-97
WJ O'Reilly	14-45	Qld	SCG	1939-40
WJ O'Reilly	14-98	SA	Adelaide	1937-38
TR McKibbin	14-189	SA	SCG	1894-95
HV Hordern	13-87	Vic	SCG	1910-11

QUEENSLAND AVERAGES

Batting & Fielding	M	Inn	NO	Runs	HS	Avge	100	50	S/Rate	Ct	St
UT Khawaja	6	10	1	529	174	58.77	2	3	55.04	3	-
M Labuschagne	6	11	2	507	136	56.33	2	1	53.76	5	-
J Clayton	3	6	0	234	109	39.00	1	1	46.24	0	-
JJ Peirson	9	15	1	475	132	33.92	2	2	62.25	26	1
MT Renshaw	9	15	1	410	120*	29.28	1	1	42.88	12	-
JA Burns	8	15	1	409	79	29.21	0	1	43.41	9	-
BE Street	9	17	0	475	143	27.94	1	1	35.26	12	-
MP Kuhnemann	7	7	4	74	24*	24.66	0	0	50.34	2	-
SJ Truloff	4	8	0	178	64	22.25	0	1	44.38	7	-
JJ Bazley	7	12	5	137	64	19.57	0	1	62.27	5	-
MG Neser	3	4	1	42	24*	14.00	0	0	44.21	0	-
MA Bryant	1	2	0	27	21	13.50	0	0	54.00	0	-
GS Sandhu	6	8	0	88	39	11.00	0	0	39.81	2	-
JD Wildermuth	8	13	1	111	34	9.25	0	0	50.45	5	-
MT Steketee	6	9	2	62	19*	8.85	0	0	76.54	2	-
MJ Swepson	2	3	1	14	8	7.00	0	0	50.00	1	-
XC Bartlett	1	2	1	1	1*	1.00	0	0	25.00	0	-
BL Edwards	3	3	3	1	1*	-	0	0	5.55	1	-

Also played: C Sully 1 match, did not bat.

Bowling	M	Overs	Mdns	Runs	Wkts	Avge	Best	5i	10m	SR	Econ
MT Steketee	6	209.2	59	574	32	17.93	7-44	2	1	39.2	2.74
GS Sandhu	6	175.1	48	479	25	19.16	6-57	2	0	42.0	2.73
XC Bartlett	1	28	6	79	4	19.75	2-30	0	0	42.0	2.82
MG Neser	3	79.2	23	218	9	24.22	3-38	0	0	52.8	2.74
MP Kuhnemann	7	289.3	80	797	25	31.88	5-25	3	1	69.4	2.75
C Sully	1	16.3	2	66	2	33.00	1-32	0	0	49.5	4.00
JD Wildermuth	8	179.5	28	545	15	36.33	2-29	0	0	71.9	3.03
JJ Bazley	7	122.4	35	390	10	39.00	2-9	0	0	73.6	3.17
BE Street	9	8.3	1	55	1	55.00	1-19	0	0	51.0	6.47
BL Edwards	3	58.3	7	239	3	79.66	3-95	0	0	117.0	4.08
MT Renshaw	9	33	4	90	1	90.00	1-10	0	0	198.0	2.72
M Labuschagne	6	91.1	9	305	2	152.50	1-21	0	0	273.5	3.34
MJ Swepson	2	54	15	156	1	156.00	1-94	0	0	324.0	2.88

Also bowled: JA Burns 1-1-0-0, UT Khawaja 1-0-5-0.

QUEENSLAND SHEFFIELD SHIELD RECORDS
Results

versus	M	W	L	D	T	%W	Toss	%toss
New South Wales	186	48	77	61	0	25.81	99	53.23
South Australia	178	67	56	54	1	37.64	73	41.01
Tasmania	90	40	18	32	0	44.44	44	48.89
Victoria	180	57	65	58	0	31.67	92	51.11
Western Australia	142	34	51	57	0	23.94	67	47.18
	776	**246**	**267**	**262**	**1**	**31.70**	**375**	**48.32**

Highest Team Totals

	v	Venue	Season
6-900	Vic	Gabba	2005-06
687	NSW	Exhibition	1930-31
664	SA	Gabba	1994-95
5-650	NSW	Gabba	1997-98
613	NSW	Gabba	1963-64
7-605	Vic	Junc Oval	2003-04

Lowest Completed Team Totals

	v	venue	Season
49	Vic	MCG	1936-37
52	WA	WACA	1982-83
54	Vic	Gabba	1932-33
61	Vic	AB Field	2016-17
62	Tas	Gabba	2008-09
65	Vic	MCG	1957-58
65	Vic	MCG	1970-71

Leading Run Scorers

	M	Inn	NO	Runs	HS	Ave	100s	50s
ML Love	139	244	20	10132	300*	45.23	27	43
JP Maher	141	253	22	9086	223	39.33	17	44
SG Law	142	234	28	9034	216	43.85	24	47
SC Trimble	123	230	13	8647	252*	39.85	22	40
ML Hayden	89	161	17	7913	234	54.95	25	33
PJP Burge	83	138	12	7084	283	56.22	22	31
AR Border	87	143	19	6779	196	54.67	15	37
JA Burns	**95**	**171**	**12**	**6493**	**202***	**40.84**	**14**	**34**
KD Mackay	100	162	22	6341	223	45.29	14	32
GM Ritchie	94	154	14	6096	213*	43.54	14	34
TJ Barsby	100	181	7	6052	165	34.78	13	28

Highest Individual Scores

		v..	Venue	Season
ML Love	300*	Vic	Junc Oval	2003-04
PJP Burge	283	NSW	Gabba	1963-64
FC Thompson	275*	NSW	Exhibition	1930-31
WC Andrews	253	NSW	SCG	1934-35
SC Trimble	252*	NSW	SCG	1963-64

Most Catches (Fielders)

	M	Ct
ML Love	139	158
JP Maher	141	153
SG Law	142	126
JA Burns	**95**	**110**
AR Border	87	99

Most Appearances

	M	Start	End
SG Law	142	28 Oct 1988	16 Mar 2004
JP Maher	141	25 Nov 1993	3 Mar 2008
ML Love	139	26 Mar 1993	17 Mar 2009
CD Hartley	128	19 Dec 2003	18 Mar 2017
SC Trimble	123	11 Dec 1959	19 Jan 1976
TV Hohns	105	02 Feb 1973	17 Mar 1991

Most Dismissals (Keepers)

	M	Ct	St	Total
CD Hartley	128	535	15	550
WA Seccombe	101	474	14	488
JA MacLean	86	289	24	313
ATW Grout	84	213	63	276
R Phillips	68	214	12	226
D Tallon	67	145	61	206

Record Wicket Partnerships

Wkt				v..	Venue	Season
1	388	KC Wessels	RB Kerr	Vic	Junc Oval	1982-83
2	369	CT Perren	SG Law	WA	Gabba	2003-04
3	326	ML Love	SG Law	Tas	Gabba	1994-95
4	329*	SR Watson	CT Perren	Vic	Gabba	2005-06
5	273	CA Lynn	CD Hartley	Vic	Gabba	2014-15
6	233	ML Love	CD Hartley	NSW	Gabba	2008-09
7	335	WC Andrews	EC Bensted	NSW	SCG	1934-35
8	146	TV Hohns	G Dymock	Vic	MCG	1978-79
9	152*	ATW Grout	WT Walmsley	NSW	Sydney	1956-57
10	105*	WT Walmsley	JE Freeman	NSW	Gabba	1957-58

Leading Wicket takers

	M	Balls	Mdns	Runs	Wkts	Ave	Best	5w	10m	SR	Econ
MS Kasprowicz	101	22216	927	10833	441	24.56	8-44	26	2	50.38	2.93
AJ Bichel	89	19654	785	9994	430	23.24	7-54	22	4	45.71	3.05
CG Rackemann	102	22400	921	10079	383	26.32	7-43	12	1	58.49	2.70
JR Thomson	77	15172	403	7927	328	24.17	7-27	17	3	46.26	3.13
CJ McDermott	67	14974	541	7605	303	25.10	8-44	22	2	49.42	3.05
JR Hopes	104	19172	950	19172	296	26.76	6-40	11	0	64.77	2.48
G Dymock	75	17118	446	7032	266	26.44	6-79	6	0	64.35	2.46
D Tazelaar	73	15371	623	7050	257	27.43	6-48	9	1	59.81	2.75
AA Noffke	68	13628	528	6652	242	27.49	6-24	12	0	56.31	2.93
JH Dawes	64	12442	545	5936	238	24.94	7-67	9	2	52.28	2.86

Best Bowling in an Innings

		v	Venue	Season
PJ Allan	10-61	Vic	MCG	1965-66
CJ McDermott	8-44	Tas	Gabba	1989-90
MS Kasprowicz	8-44	Vic	Gabba	2005-06
MA Polzin	8-51	Vic	MCG	1989-90
JRF Duncan	8-55	Vic	MCG	1970-71

Best Bowling in a Match

		v	Venue	Season
PJ Allan	13-110	NSW	Sydney	1968-69
JRF Duncan	13-125	Vic	MCG	1970-71
CR Swan	13-144	SA	AB Field	2010-11
PJ Allan	12-56	Vic	Gabba	1968-69
JR Thomson	12-112	NSW	Gabba	1976-77

SOUTH AUSTRALIA AVERAGES

Batting & Fielding	M	Inn	NO	Runs	HS	Avge	100	50	S/Rate	Ct	St
DR Drew	2	4	1	189	130	63.00	1	0	39.37	2	-
TM Head	6	10	0	440	163	44.00	2	1	72.84	2	-
HJ Hunt	8	15	1	601	134	42.92	3	1	46.23	4	-
JB Weatherald	6	11	2	367	122	40.77	1	1	50.13	7	-
JS Lehmann	4	6	0	225	102	37.50	1	1	75.25	5	-
NA McSweeney	3	6	1	171	99*	34.20	0	1	43.73	5	-
JM Carder	8	14	0	468	118	33.42	1	2	50.70	4	-
HJ Nielsen	6	10	1	265	71	29.44	0	2	44.31	10	0
NJ McAndrew	8	12	2	227	65*	22.70	0	1	40.82	4	-
TJ Kelly	1	2	0	42	29	21.00	0	0	79.24	0	-
LAJ Scott	5	7	1	125	42	20.83	0	0	43.10	1	-
AT Carey	6	10	1	179	66*	19.88	0	1	62.36	23	2
SL Kerber	1	1	0	11	11	11.00	0	0	68.75	2	-
DJ Worrall	5	8	1	60	24	8.57	0	0	57.69	3	-
BJ Doggett	5	6	3	24	10	8.00	0	0	64.86	2	-
DMK Grant	7	10	3	48	14	6.85	0	0	39.34	3	-
LAJ Pope	4	6	2	22	12	5.50	0	0	20.95	1	-
BT Capel	1	2	0	9	8	4.50	0	0	36.00	1	-
NP Winter	1	1	0	4	4	4.00	0	0	30.76	0	-
JS Buckingham	1	1	1	0	0*	-	0	0	0.00	0	-

Bowling	M	Overs	Mdns	Runs	Wkts	Avge	Best	5i	10m	S/Rate	Econ
LAJ Scott	5	105	32	262	13	20.15	5-46	1	0	48.4	2.49
BJ Doggett	5	172.3	56	448	17	26.35	4-51	0	0	60.8	2.59
NA McSweeney	3	62.3	9	194	7	27.71	4-89	0	0	53.5	3.10
JS Buckingham	1	40	10	120	4	30.00	4-79	0	0	60.0	3.00
NJ McAndrew	8	302.4	69	815	27	30.18	5-84	1	0	67.2	2.69
DMK Grant	7	241.4	48	709	20	35.45	4-76	0	0	72.5	2.93
DJ Worrall	5	183	57	450	12	37.50	4-49	0	0	91.5	2.45
TM Head	6	69	10	231	5	46.20	2-22	0	0	82.8	3.34
LAJ Pope	4	118.5	10	533	11	48.45	4-92	0	0	64.8	4.48
NP Winter	1	19	6	50	1	50.00	1-50	0	0	114.0	2.63
SL Kerber	1	18	1	106	0	-	-	0	0	-	5.88

Also bowled: JS Lehmann 0.2-0-5-0, JM Carder 2-0-9-0.

SOUTH AUSTRALIA SHEFFIELD SHIELD RECORDS

Results

versus	M	W	L	D	T	%W	toss	%toss
New South Wales	233	60	129	44	0	25.75	121	51.93
Queensland	178	56	67	54	1	31.46	105	58.99
Tasmania	83	29	23	31	0	34.94	47	56.63
Victoria	237	53	121	63	0	22.36	122	51.48
Western Australia	144	41	62	41	0	28.47	87	60.42
	875	239	402	233	1	27.31	482	55.09

Highest Team Totals

	v	venue	Season
7-821	Qld	Adelaide	1939-40
673	Tas	Adelaide	1987-88
7-644	Qld	Adelaide	1934-35
3-643	Tas	Adelaide	1986-87
8-642	Qld	Adelaide	1935-36
638	Tas	Bellerive	2005-06

Lowest Completed Team Totals

	v	venue	Season
27	NSW	SCG	1955-56
29	NSW	SCG	2004-05
45	Tas	Bellerive	2014-15
55	Tas	Bellerive	2010-11
56	WA	WACA	1959-60
61	NSW	Adelaide	1906-07

Leading Run Scorers

	M	Inn	NO	Runs	HS	Ave	100s	50s
DS Lehmann	119	218	14	11622	301*	56.97	39	41
GS Blewett	117	223	13	9682	268	46.10	23	48
DW Hookes	120	205	9	9364	306*	47.78	26	44
CJ Ferguson	124	235	17	8318	213	38.16	19	42
LE Favell	121	220	4	8269	164	38.28	20	43
IM Chappell	89	157	13	7665	205*	53.23	22	45
HN Dansie	107	196	6	6692	185	35.22	17	32
AMJ Hilditch	91	161	11	6504	230	43.36	17	32

Highest Individual Scores

		v	venue	Season
C Hill	365*	NSW	Adelaide	1900-01
DG Bradman	357	Vic	MCG	1935-36
BA Richards	356	WA	WACA	1970-71
CL Badcock	325	Vic	Adelaide	1935-36
DW Hookes	306*	Tas	Adelaide	1986-87

Most Catches (Fielders)

	M	Ct
DW Hookes	120	128
JD Siddons	82	113
IM Chappell	89	113
TLW Cooper	86	104
VY Richardson	77	99

Most Appearances

	M	Start	End
PR Sleep	127	4 Feb 1977	21 Mar 1993
CJ Ferguson	124	16 Oct 2004	6 Apr 2021
LE Favell	121	30 Nov 1951	16 Feb 1970
DW Hookes	120	7 Nov 1975	2 Mar 1992
DS Lehmann	119	11 Dec 1987	25 Nov 2007
GS Blewett	117	1 Nov 1991	21 Feb 2006
HN Dansie	107	27 Jan 1950	31 Jan 1967

Most Dismissals (Keepers)

	M	Ct	St	Total
GA Manou	96	307	21	328
TJ Nielsen	92	255	29	284
BN Jarman	77	193	57	250
CW Walker	57	103	87	190
TP Ludeman	47	158	7	165
AT Carey	**38**	**151**	**4**	**155**
GRA Langley	46	111	24	135

Record Wicket Partnerships

Wkt				v	venue	Season
1	293	HJ Hunt	JB Weatherald	Tas	Adelaide	2019-20
2	386	GS Blewett	DS Lehmann	Tas	Bellerive	2001-02
3	286	GS Blewett	DS Lehmann	Tas	Adelaide	1993-94
4	462*	DW Hookes	WB Phillips	Tas	Adelaide	1986-87
5	281	CL Badcock	MG Waite	Qld	Adelaide	1939-40
6	260	DS Lehmann	TJ Nielsen	Qld	Adelaide	1996-97
7	198	TLW Cooper	AT Carey	WA	WACA	2016-17
7	198	GA Bishop	TBA May	Tas	Adelaide	1990-91
8	250	GA Manou	JN Gillespie	Tas	Bellerive	2007-08
9	232	C Hill	E Walkley	NSW	Adelaide	1900-01
10	104	L Michael	EI Pynor	Vic	Adelaide	1949-50

Leading Wicket takers

	M	Balls	Mdns	Runs	Wkts	Ave	Best	5i	10m	SR	Econ
CV Grimmett	78	28144	442	12878	504	25.55	9-180	47	13	55.84	2.75
AA Mallett	77	20988	674	8171	344	23.75	7-57	19	2	61.01	2.34
CJ Sayers	71	16337	783	7216	279	25.86	8-64	14	3	58.56	2.65
TBA May	80	22575	930	9943	270	36.83	7-93	15	2	83.61	2.64
JM Mennie	69	14605	549	6941	256	27.11	7-96	6	0	57.05	2.85
PE Sleep	127	19482	671	9883	254	38.91	8-133	7	0	76.70	3.04
PE McIntyre	61	17431	576	8974	215	41.74	6-64	8	2	81.07	3.09
E Jones	39	12145	500	5516	208	26.52	8-157	19	3	58.39	2.73

Best Bowling in an Innings

		v	venue	Season
TW Wall	10-36	NSW	SCG	1932-33
JPF Travers	9-30	Vic	MCG	1900-01
G Giffen	9-147	Vic	Adelaide	1892-93
CV Grimmett	9-180	Qld	Adelaide	1934-35
JN Gillespie	8-50	NSW	SCG	2001-02

Best Bowling in a Match

	Runs	v	venue	Season
G Giffen	16-186	NSW	Adelaide	1894-95
CV Grimmett	16-289	Qld	Adelaide	1934-35
G Giffen	15-185	Vic	Adelaide	1902-03
EW Freeman	13-105	NSW	Adelaide	1970-71
PC Rofe	13-112	NSW	Adelaide	2001-02

TASMANIA AVERAGES

Batting & Fielding	M	Inn	NO	Runs	HS	Avge	100	50	S/Rate	Ct	St
MB Wright	3	4	2	182	78*	91.00	0	2	43.02	0	-
JC Silk	7	11	2	514	100*	57.11	1	3	58.47	3	-
MS Wade	1	2	0	111	61	55.50	0	2	51.38	0	-
BJ Webster	6	9	2	361	166*	51.57	1	1	71.48	8	-
BR McDermott	5	9	1	343	94	42.87	0	2	41.93	6	-
BAD Manenti	1	2	1	42	23	42.00	0	0	56.00	1	-
TP Ward	8	14	0	552	144	39.42	1	3	41.97	8	-
CP Jewell	8	14	0	508	102	36.28	1	3	52.31	5	-
LH Neil-Smith	5	8	2	212	71*	35.33	0	2	37.72	2	-
CA Wakim	5	9	0	281	68	31.22	0	3	48.53	1	-
JA Freeman	5	6	3	82	41*	27.33	0	0	68.90	0	-
JR Doran	7	12	0	257	72	21.41	0	2	41.31	27	0
TD Andrews	4	7	0	141	40	20.14	0	0	76.21	0	-
EM Vines	1	2	0	38	38	19.00	0	0	33.62	1	-
PM Siddle	6	8	3	70	31*	14.00	0	0	59.82	0	-
RP Meredith	2	2	0	23	20	11.50	0	0	33.82	0	-
JM Bird	3	5	0	46	26	9.20	0	0	109.52	6	-
N Radhakrishnan	1	2	0	17	13	8.50	0	0	20.73	0	-
GT Bell	5	6	2	29	19	7.25	0	0	30.52	1	-
BM Hope	2	3	0	18	10	6.00	0	0	32.14	2	-
SL Rainbird	3	3	0	12	12	4.00	0	0	26.08	1	-
TS Rogers	1	2	0	3	3	1.50	0	0	13.63	0	-

Bowling	M	Overs	Mdns	Runs	Wkts	Avge	Best	5i	10m	SR	Econ
SL Rainbird	3	74.1	19	223	19	11.73	8-21	2	1	23.4	3.00
JC Silk	7	2	0	13	1	13.00	1-8	0	0	12.0	6.50
RP Meredith	2	46	16	115	5	23.00	3-45	0	0	55.2	2.50
PM Siddle	6	194.1	58	443	19	23.31	5-40	1	0	61.3	2.28
LH Neil-Smith	5	102.1	20	329	13	25.30	5-43	1	0	47.1	3.22
GT Bell	5	140.4	34	409	14	29.21	3-80	0	0	60.2	2.90
JM Bird	3	86.5	28	229	7	32.71	3-38	0	0	74.4	2.63
BAD Manenti	1	62.4	11	190	5	38.00	3-89	0	0	75.2	3.03
BM Hope	2	44	7	157	4	39.25	3-15	0	0	66.0	3.56
TD Andrews	4	124	16	381	8	47.62	3-69	0	0	93.0	3.07
N Radhakrishnan	1	10	2	53	1	53.00	1-29	0	0	60.0	5.30
BJ Webster	6	97	15	327	6	54.50	3-40	0	0	97.0	3.37
JA Freeman	5	148.1	24	549	9	61.00	3-48	0	0	98.7	3.71
TS Rogers	1	18	2	69	1	69.00	1-69	0	0	108.0	3.83

Also bowled: CA Wakim 2-0-12-0.

TASMANIA SHEFFIELD SHIELD RECORDS

Results

versus	M	W	L	D	%W	toss	%toss
New South Wales	87	25	33	29	28.74	53	60.92
Queensland	90	18	40	32	20.00	46	51.11
South Australia	83	23	29	31	27.71	36	43.37
Victoria	82	20	28	34	24.39	41	50.00
Western Australia	86	21	38	27	24.42	52	60.47
	428	107	168	153	25.00	228	53.27

Highest Team Totals

	v	venue	Season
651	SA	Bellerive	2013-14
592	SA	Adelaide	1987-88
6-569	SA	Bellerive	1997-98
8-566	Vic	Bellerive	2015-16
7-553	WA	WACA	2006-07
550	NSW	Bellerive	1990-91

Lowest Team Totals

	v	Venue	Season
76	NSW	Bellerive	1991-92
82*	Qld	Gabba	2001-02
86	WA	Bellerive	2005-06
91	SA	Glenelg	2015-16
94	WA	Bellerive	2006-07

includes one batsman retired hurt

Leading Run Scorers

	M	Inn	NO	Runs	HS	Ave	100s	50s
J Cox	161	295	17	10821	245	38.92	30	47
MJ Di Venuto	140	250	11	9974	189	41.73	19	67
GJ Bailey	128	233	18	8153	200*	37.92	20	41
DC Boon	119	204	8	8029	227	40.96	20	43
DJ Marsh	133	230	33	7134	134	36.21	13	38
DF Hills	100	187	8	6887	265	38.47	18	36
RT Ponting	65	118	17	6377	233	63.14	26	21
AJ Doolan	104	190	8	5978	247*	32.85	11	30
S Young	104	176	29	5565	175*	37.86	10	35
RJ Tucker	90	153	24	4611	165	35.74	7	24

Highest Individual Scores

		v	Venue	Season
DF Hills	265	SA	Bellerive	1997-98
AJ Doolan	247*	Vic	MCG	2017-18
J Cox	245	NSW	Bellerive	1999-00
RT Ponting	233	Qld	A B Field	2000-01
EP Gulbis	229	SA	Bellerive	2013-14
DC Boon	227	Vic	MCG	1983-84

Most Catches (Fielders)

	M	Ct
DJ Marsh	133	171
MJ Di Venuto	140	151
GJ Bailey	128	105
DC Boon	119	93
BJ Webster	**59**	**84**
J Cox	161	78

Most Appearances

	M	Start	End
J Cox	161	20 Nov 1987	20 Nov 2005
MJ Di Venuto	140	13 Mar 1992	10 Mar 2008
DJ Marsh	133	07 Nov 1996	12 Mar 2010
GJ Bailey	128	16 Dec 2004	10 Dec 2019
DC Boon	119	15 Dec 1978	14 Mar 1999
S Young	104	29 Nov 1991	14 Dec 2001
AJ Doolan	104	30 Jan 2009	8 Mar 2021

Most Catches (Keepers)

	M	Ct	St	Total
TD Paine	74	263	8	271
MN Atkinson	84	237	25	262
SG Clingeleffer	74	219	12	231
RD Woolley	43	97	13	110
RE Soule	51	103	4	107
TIF Triffitt	16	70	2	70

Record Wicket Partnerships

Wkt					v	Venue	Season
1	297	DF Hills	J Cox		Vic	Bellerive	1997-98
2	294	J Cox	MJ Di Venuto		NSW	Bellerive	1999-00
3	294	BR Dunk	AJ Doolan		Vic	Bellerive	2015-16
4	319	MG Bevan	DJ Marsh		WA	Bellerive	2004-05
5	319	RT Ponting	RJ Tucker		WA	Bellerive	1994-95
6	213	BF Davison	RD Woolley		SA	Adelaide	1980-81
7	293*	RT Ponting	JJ Krejza		NSW	Bellerive	2012-13
8	148	BF Davison	PI Faulkner		SA	Adelaide	1983-84
9	125	BJ Webster	JM Bird		Tas	WACA	2020-21
10	120	SL Saunders	PM Clough		WA	WACA	1981-82

Leading Wicket takers

	M	Balls	Mdns	Runs	Wkts	Avg	Best	5i	10m	SR	Econ
JM Bird	**69**	**14543**	**628**	**6892**	**319**	**21.61**	**7-18**	**17**	**5**	**45.59**	**2.84**
BW Hilfenhaus	68	15341	604	7742	262	29.55	7-58	9	1	58.55	3.03
LR Butterworth	69	11919	573	5440	221	24.62	6-49	8	1	53.93	2.74
CR Miller	54	13846	546	6657	210	31.70	7-49	8	2	65.93	2.88
S Young	104	16399	744	7884	201	39.22	5-26	5	1	81.59	2.88
DG Wright	64	13541	655	6330	197	32.13	6-25	6	0	68.74	2.80
SL Rainbird	**54**	**9830**	**355**	**5329**	**167**	**31.91**	**8-21**	**4**	**1**	**58.86**	**3.25**
AR Griffith	45	9534	359	5179	158	32.78	7-54	8	1	60.34	3.26

Best Bowling in an Innings

		v	Venue	Season
SL Rainbird	**8-21**	**Qld**	**Bellerive**	**2021-22**
PM Clough	8-95	WA	Launceston	1983-84
JM Bird	7-18	NSW	Bellerive	2020-21
JM Bird	7-45	NSW	Bellerive	2015-16
CR Miller	7-49	Vic	MCG	1997-98
AR Griffith	7-54	Vic	Bellerive	2004-05

Best Bowling in a Match

		v	Venue	Season
SL Rainbird	**13-42**	**Qld**	**Bellerive**	**2021-22**
CR Miller	12-119	SA	Bellerive	1997-98
SR Watson	11-78	Qld	Bellerive	2001-02
JM Bird	11-95	WA	Bellerive	2011-12
SJ Jurgensen	11-103	NSW	Bellerive	2001-02
JM Bird	11-112	SA	Adelaide	2018-19

VICTORIA AVERAGES

Batting & Fielding	M	Inn	NO	Runs	HS	Avge	100	50	S/Rate	Ct	St
NJ Maddinson	7	13	3	545	128	54.50	2	2	57.06	3	-
PSP Handscomb	8	15	1	697	148*	49.78	2	3	46.31	27	-
TJ Dean	6	10	1	423	146	47.00	2	0	48.95	2	-
MS Harris	4	8	0	322	137	40.25	1	2	38.79	3	-
WJ Pucovski	3	4	0	146	59	36.50	0	2	45.34	0	-
MW Short	7	13	2	306	90	27.81	0	1	45.67	12	-
J Seymour	4	8	0	194	105	24.25	1	0	41.63	4	-
J Merlo	4	6	1	119	64	23.80	0	1	29.38	2	-
SB Harper	8	13	2	208	93	18.90	0	1	33.54	24	5
MJ Perry	8	10	2	136	74	17.00	0	1	42.50	0	-
JL Pattinson	5	7	0	100	45	14.28	0	0	43.66	0	-
W Sutherland	7	10	3	85	23	12.14	0	0	48.29	6	-
J Fraser-McGurk	2	4	0	47	25	11.75	0	0	44.76	1	-
SM Boland	5	5	2	8	5	2.66	0	0	12.12	1	-
BL Couch	1	1	0	1	1	1.00	0	0	25.00	0	-
JM Holland	6	5	3	1	1	0.50	0	0	3.57	1	-
XA Crone	1	1	0	0	0	0.00	0	0	0.00	0	-
CL McClure	1	2	1	0	0*	0.00	0	0	0.00	0	-
W Parker	2	1	0	0	0	0.00	0	0	0.00	0	-
TR Murphy	1	1	1	24	24*	-	0	0	45.28	0	

Bowling	M	Overs	Mdns	Runs	Wkts	Avge	Best	5i	10m	SR	Econ
SM Boland	5	218.3	72	444	26	17.07	5-56	1	0	50.4	2.03
T Murphy	1	50	14	146	7	20.85	4-98	0	0	42.8	2.92
XA Crone	1	21	2	103	4	25.75	2-32	0	0	31.5	4.90
W Sutherland	7	250.1	58	651	24	27.12	5-78	1	0	62.5	2.60
M Perry	8	273.2	71	713	24	29.70	4-31	0	0	68.3	2.60
JL Pattinson	5	168.1	39	469	15	31.26	5-71	1	0	67.2	2.78
JM Holland	6	237.4	53	642	20	32.10	4-82	0	0	71.3	2.70
MW Short	7	126.5	15	391	12	32.58	4-74	0	0	63.4	3.08
CL McClure	1	22.2	8	67	2	33.50	2-67	0	0	67.0	3.00
J Merlo	4	31	3	118	2	59.00	2-14	0	0	93.0	3.80
W Parker	2	14	1	63	1	63.00	1-11	0	0	84.0	4.50
BL Couch	1	12	1	73	1	73.00	1-38	0	0	72.0	6.08

Also bowled: NJ Maddinson 5-1-13-0, J Seymour 3-0-16-0.

VICTORIA SHEFFIELD SHIELD RECORDS
Results

versus	M	W	L	D	T	%W	toss	%toss
New South Wales	244	80	80	83	1	32.79	127	52.05
Queensland	180	65	57	58	0	36.11	88	48.89
South Australia	237	121	53	63	0	51.05	115	48.52
Tasmania	82	28	20	34	0	34.15	41	50.00
Western Australia	142	48	40	54	0	33.80	77	54.23
	885	342	250	292	1	38.64	448	50.62

Highest Team Totals

Total	v	venue	Season
1107	NSW	MCG	1926-27
8-806	Qld	MCG	2008-09
793	Qld	MCG	1927-28
724	SA	MCG	1920-21
710	Qld	MCG	2003-04

Lowest Completed Team Totals

Total	v	venue	Season
31	NSW	SCG	1906-07
35	NSW	SCG	1926-27
43	SA	MCG	1895-96
73	WA	MCG	1971-72
76	Qld	Gabba	1974-75

Leading Run Scorers

	M	Inn	NO	Runs	HS	Ave	100s	50s
BJ Hodge	140	254	23	10474	286*	45.34	29	49
DM Jones	110	194	16	9622	324*	54.06	31	40
MTG Elliott,	103	197	16	9470	203	52.32	32	43
DJ Hussey	105	179	15	7476	212*	45.59	19	43
CL White	135	231	25	7453	150*	36.18	11	45
WM Lawry	85	139	14	6615	266	52.92	17	41
GN Yallop	76	137	11	5881	246	46.67	18	31
AL Hassett	58	97	10	5535	229	63.62	18	27
JL Arnberger	76	144	13	5504	239*	42.02	13	28
WH Ponsford	43	70	5	5413	437	83.28	21	14

Highest Individual scores

		v	Season	Venue
WH Ponsford	437	Qld	1927-28	MCG
WH Ponsford	352	NSW	1926-27	MCG
WH Ponsford	336	SA	1927-28	MCG
DM Jones	324*	SA	1994-95	MCG
J Ryder	295	NSW	1926-27	MCG

Most Catches (Fielders)

	M	Ct
CL White	135	185
DJ Hussey	105	138
MTG Elliott	103	125
PSP Handscomb	**84**	**113**
DF Whatmore	85	109

Most Appearances

	M	Start	end
BJ Hodge	140	27 Oct 1993	13 Dec 2009
CL White	135	9 Mar 2001	1 Apr 2019
DS Berry	129	9 Nov 1990	16 Mar 2004
DM Jones	110	29 Jan 1982	15 Mar 1998
DJ Hussey	105	5 Feb 2003	25 Mar 2015
MTG Elliott	103	3 Feb 1993	13 Mar 2005
RJ Bright	101	29 Dec 1972	1 Feb 1988

Most Dismissals (Keepers)

	M	Ct	St	Dis
DS Berry	129	468	44	512
MS Wade	74	271	7	278
RD Robinson	68	212	26	238
RC Jordon	70	199	31	230
MGD Dimattina	60	149	19	168
JL Ellis	49	111	45	156
LV Maddocks	57	115	33	148

Record Partnerships

Wkt				v..	venue	Season
1	486	WJ Pucovski	MS Harris	SA	Glenelg Oval	2020-21
2	314	WH Ponsford	HSTL Hendry	Qld	MCG	1927-28
3	390*	JM Wiener	JK Moss	WA	Junction Oval	1981-82
4	309*	J Moss	DJ Hussey	WA	WACA	2003-04
5	316*	LD Harper	GB Gardiner	SA	Princess Park	1997-98
6	290	MTG Elliott	DS Berry	NSW	SCG	1996-97
7	205	CL White	IJ Harvey	Qld	Gabba	2004-05
8	215	RL Park	WW Armstrong	SA	MCG	1919-20
9	143	GR Hazlitt	A Kenny	SA	MCG	1910-11
10	211	M Ellis	TJ Hastings	SA	MCG	1902-03

Leading Wicket takers

	M	Balls	Mdns	Runs	Wkts	Ave	Best	5i	10m	SR	Econ
PR Reiffel	86	19137	843	8242	318	25.92	6-57	7	2	60.18	2.58
AN Connolly	71	17973	367	7745	297	26.08	9-67	12	4	60.52	2.59
AIC Dodemaide	94	19880	824	8884	281	31.62	6-67	12	0	70.75	2.68
SM Boland	**80**	**15649**	**632**	**7175**	**279**	**25.72**	**7-31**	**7**	**0**	**56.09**	**2.75**
MG Hughes	76	16762	582	8169	267	30.60	7-81	10	2	62.78	2.92
RJ Bright	101	22899	1013	8821	252	35.00	6-61	10	0	90.87	2.31
L O'B Fleetwood-Smith	41	11576	119	6034	246	24.53	9-135	25	8	47.06	3.13
JD Higgs	75	14962	376	7202	240	30.01	8-66	12	8	62.34	2.89
PM Siddle	61	12066	490	5623	233	24.13	8-54	11	0	57.16	2.80
JM Holland	**72**	**15593**	**537**	**7416**	**230**	**32.24**	**7-92**	**9**	**0**	**67.80**	**2.85**
DW Fleming	67	14648	654	6675	221	30.20	7-90	7	1	66.28	2.73
MHN Walker	62	15011	429	6476	220	29.44	6-49	11	0	68.23	2.59

Best Bowling in an innings

		v..	Venue	Season
EL McCormick	9-40	SA	Adelaide	1936-37
AN Connolly	9-67	Qld	Gabba	1964-65
L Fleetwood-Smith	9-135	SA	MCG	1937-38
DJ Pattinson	8-35	WA	WACA	2010-11
H Trumble	8-39	SA	MCG	1898-99

Best Bowling in a Match

		v..	Venue	Season
LOB Fleetwood-Smith	15-96	Qld	MCG	1936-37
LOB Fleetwood-Smith	15-226	NSW	Sydney	1934-35
AL Thomson	13-141	NSW	MCG	1969-70
GE Tribe	13-153	SA	Adelaide	1946-47
J Ryder	13-155	SA	MCG	1912-13

WESTERN AUSTRALIA AVERAGES

Batting & Fielding	M	Inn	NO	Runs	HS	Avge	100	50	SR	Ct	St
AM Hardie	3	5	3	238	174*	119.00	1	0	50.31	1	-
SM Whiteman	7	13	2	641	176*	58.27	2	2	45.72	4	-
CJ Rocchiccioli	4	3	2	51	50	51.00	0	1	137.83	2	2
HWR Cartwright	8	15	1	601	121*	42.92	1	3	50.08	2	-
C Green	5	10	1	364	106	40.44	1	3	53.68	4	-
JR Philippe	8	15	2	481	129	37.00	1	3	50.63	37	0
JA Richardson	4	6	1	185	50	37.00	0	1	79.74	0	-
CT Bancroft	8	15	1	502	141	35.85	2	0	43.01	15	-
SE Marsh	7	12	1	383	118	34.81	1	2	45.54	6	-
DJM Short	5	7	0	169	67	24.14	0	1	48.84	6	-
T Wyllie	2	3	0	69	42	23.00	0	0	36.89	1	-
JP Inglis	1	2	0	41	28	20.50	0	0	87.23	1	-
JS Paris	7	10	2	157	30	19.62	0	0	42.09	2	-
M Kelly	6	8	3	93	41	18.60	0	0	42.27	2	-
J Goodwin	2	4	0	42	22	10.50	0	0	29.78	1	-
LRT Morris	8	7	3	33	14*	8.25	0	0	42.30	2	-
CJ Gannon	3	3	1	9	8	4.50	0	0	60.00	2	-

Bowling	M	Overs	Mdns	Runs	Wkts	Avge	Best	5i	10m	SR	Econ
JA Richardson	4	129.2	46	309	23	13.43	5-23	1	0	33.7	2.38
AM Hardie	3	60	14	141	10	14.10	4-24	0	0	36.0	2.35
HWR Cartwright	8	33	6	117	7	16.71	4-23	0	0	28.2	3.54
JS Paris	7	185.5	59	497	24	20.70	5-63	1	0	46.4	2.67
LRT Morris	8	139.2	23	541	20	27.05	4-21	0	0	41.8	3.88
DJM Short	5	57.4	3	229	6	38.16	2-37	0	0	57.6	3.97
CJ Gannon	3	106.4	29	328	8	41.00	3-87	0	0	80.0	3.07
M Kelly	6	151	43	424	10	42.40	3-27	0	0	90.6	2.80
CJ Rocchiccioli	4	73.2	7	234	5	46.80	2-24	0	0	88.0	3.19
C Green	5	89	19	292	6	48.66	1-12	0	0	89.0	3.28

WESTERN AUSTRALIA SHEFFIELD SHIELD RECORDS

Results

versus	M	W	L	D	%W	toss	%toss
New South Wales	140	39	59	42	27.86	69	49.29
Queensland	142	51	34	57	35.92	75	52.82
South Australia	144	62	41	41	43.06	57	39.58
Tasmania	86	38	21	27	44.19	34	39.53
Victoria	142	40	48	54	28.17	65	45.77
	654	230	203	221	35.17	300	45.87

Highest Team Totals

	v	venue	Season
654	Vic	WACA	1986-87
633	SA	Glenelg	2014-15
5-615	Qld	Brisbane	1968-69
3-608	Vic	WACA	2006-07
8-607	Qld	WACA	1989-90
8-607	NSW	WACA	2004-05

Lowest Team Totals

	v	venue	Season
41	SA	Adelaide	1989-90
50	NSW	SCG	1951-52
51	NSW	WACA	1950-51
54	Qld	Gabba	1972-73
58	NSW	SCG	1998-99
67	Tas	Bellerive	2012-13

Leading Run Scorers

	M	Inn	NO	Runs	HS	Ave	100s	50s
JL Langer	108	195	15	9406	274*	52.26	29	35
TM Moody	132	228	22	8853	272	42.98	20	46
SE Marsh	**121**	**219**	**24**	**8330**	**214**	**42.73**	**20**	**43**
MEK Hussey	112	207	12	8007	223*	41.06	16	41
AC Voges	112	200	32	7522	249	44.77	19	35
MRJ Veletta	114	198	20	7306	262	41.04	18	40
MJ North	111	200	17	7277	239*	39.77	21	32
GR Marsh	100	175	12	7009	355*	43.00	21	28
DR Martyn	97	171	16	6910	203*	44.58	20	34
GM Wood	109	174	25	6904	186*	46.34	20	32

Highest Individual Scores

		v..	Season	venue
GR Marsh	355*	SA	1989-90	WACA
LM Davis	303*	NSW	2011-12	WACA
CJL Rogers	279	Vic	2006-07	WACA
JL Langer	274*	SA	1996-97	WACA
TM Moody	272	Tas	1994-95	Hobart

Most Catches (Fielders)

	M	Ct
AC Voges	112	170
RJ Inverarity	108	138
SE Marsh	**121**	**130**
TM Moody	132	114
JL Langer	108	105

Most Appearances

	M	Start	End
TM Moody	132	10 Jan 1986	5 Mar 2001
SE Marsh	**121**	**2 Mar 2001**	**4 Apr 2022**
MRJ Veletta	114	21 Oct 1983	19 Mar 1995
AC Voges	112	8 Dec 2002	19 Mar 2017
MEK Hussey	112	4 Nov 1994	17 Mar 2013
MJ North	111	15 Oct 1999	24 Mar 2014

Most Dismissals (Keepers)

	M	Ct	St	Total
TJ Zoehrer	105	320	28	348
RW Marsh	81	311	33	344
AC Gilchrist	53	257	8	265
L Ronchi	55	208	10	218
RJ Campbell	52	187	11	198
BL Buggins	57	131	18	149

Record Wicket Partnerships

Wkt	Runs			v..	Venue	Season
1	431	MRJ Veletta	GR Marsh	SA	WACA	1989-90
2	324	CT Bancroft	M Klinger	NSW	WACA	2014-15
3	459	CJL Rogers	MJ North	Vic	WACA	2006-07
4	369	CJL Rogers	MJ North	NSW	WACA	2002-03
5	301*	RB Simpson	KD Meuleman	NSW	WACA	1959-60
6	266*	AC Agar	JP Inglis	SA	Rolton Oval	2020-21
7	214	M Klinger	AC Agar	Tas	Bellerive	2015-16
8	242*	TJ Zoehrer	KH MacLeay	NSW	WACA	1990-91
9	168*	KH MacLeay	VJ Marks	NSW	WACA	1986-87
10	94	AC Agar	MG Hogan	Qld	Gabba	2012-13

Leading Wicket Takers

	M	Balls	Mdns	Runs	Wkts	Ave	Best	5i	10m	SR	Econ
J Angel	105	22351	1030	10418	419	24.86	6-35	13	0	53.34	2.80
TM Alderman	97	20482	778	9299	384	24.22	7-28	17	3	53.34	2.72
DK Lillee	70	16617	440	7544	323	23.36	7-36	18	4	51.45	2.72
GAR Lock	66	20107	555	7210	302	23.87	7-53	16	2	66.58	2.15
BP Julian	87	16149	614	8573	292	29.36	7-39	15	2	55.30	3.19
GD McKenzie	73	16565	287	7322	232	31.56	6-100	7	0	71.40	2.65
KH MacLeay	90	17761	835	7033	229	30.71	6-93	5	0	77.56	2.38
MG Hogan	60	13300	656	5989	221	27.10	6-70	6	0	60.18	2.70
TM Moody	132	14431	674	6297	220	28.62	7-38	5	1	65.60	2.62
SJ Magoffin	56	11526	566	5145	190	27.08	8-47	7	1	60.66	2.68

Best Bowling in an Innings

		v..	venue	Season
IJ Brayshaw	10-44	Vic	WACA	1967-68
JP Behrendorff	9-37	WA	WACA	2016-17
JA Richardson	8-47	NSW	Perth St	2017-18
SJ Magoffin	8-47	SA	WACA	2005-06
HR Gorringe	8-56	Qld	WACA	1952-53
DE Hoare	8-98	NSW	WACA	1964-65
CD Matthews	8-101	Qld	WACA	1987-88

Best Bowling in a Match

		v..	venue	Season
TM Alderman	14-87	NSW	WACA	1981-82
JP Behrendorff	14-89	Vic	WACA	2016-17
IJ Brayshaw	12-90	Vic	WACA	1967-68
DK Lillee	12-113	SA	Adelaide	1975-76
SP Mackin	12-163	SA	Glenelg	2016-17

SHEFFIELD SHIELD RECORDS - RECENT WINNERS

1991-92	Western Australia	2002-03	New South Wales	2013-14	New South Wales
1992-93	New South Wales	2003-04	Victoria	2014-15	Victoria
1993-94	New South Wales	2004-05	New South Wales	2015-16	Victoria
1994-95	Queensland	2005-06	Queensland	2016-17	Victoria
1995-96	South Australia	2006-07	Tasmania	2017-18	Queensland
1996-97	Queensland	2007-08	New South Wales	2018-19	Victoria
1997-98	Western Australia	2008-09	Victoria	2019-20	New South Wales
1998-99	Western Australia	2009-10	Victoria	2020-21	Queensland
1999-2000	Queensland	2010-11	Tasmania	2021-22	Western Australia
2000-01	Queensland	2011-12	Queensland		
2001-02	Queensland	2012-13	Tasmania		

Overall results

Team	M	W	L	D	T	%W	toss	%toss
New South Wales	890	378	252	259	1	42.47	421	42.47
Queensland	776	246	267	262	1	31.70	375	48.32
South Australia	875	239	402	233	1	27.31	482	55.09
Tasmania	428	107	168	153	0	25.00	228	53.27
Victoria	885	342	250	292	1	38.64	448	50.62
Western Australia	654	230	203	221	0	35.17	300	45.87

Highest Team Totals

Total	for	v..	Venue	Season
1107	Vic	NSW	MCG	1926-27
918	NSW	SA	SCG	1900-01
6-900	Qld	Vic	Gabba	2005-06
7-821	SA	Qld	Adelaide	1939-40
815	NSW	Vic	SCG	1908-09
807	NSW	SA	Adelaide	1899-00
8-806	Vic	Qld	MCG	2008-09
805	NSW	Vic	MCG	1905-06
802	NSW	SA	SCG	1920-21

Lowest Team Totals

Total	for	v..	Venue	Season
27	SA	NSW	SCG	1955-56
29	SA	NSW	SCG	2004-05
31	Vic	NSW	SCG	1906-07
32*	NSW	Tas	Bellerive	2020-21
35	Vic	NSW	SCG	1926-27
41	WA	SA	Adelaide	1989-90
43	Vic	SA	MCG	1895-96
45	SA	Tas	Adelaide	2014-15
49	Qld	Vic	MCG	1936-37
50	WA	NSW	SCG	1951-52
51*	WA	NSW	WACA	1950-51

* Includes one batsman absent hurt

Leading Run scorers

	for	M	Inn	NO	HS	Runs	Avge	100s	50s	0s
DS Lehmann	SA/Vic	147	266	18	301*	13635	54.98	45	51	15
J Cox	Tas	161	295	17	245	10821	38.92	30	47	26
JD Siddons	Vic/SA	146	259	21	245	10643	44.72	30	50	17
MG Bevan	SA/NSW/Tas	118	211	36	216	10621	60.69	42	41	9
BJ Hodge	Vic	140	254	23	286*	10474	45.34	29	49	19
MTG Elliott	SA/Vic	122	235	18	203	10263	47.29	32	48	12
ML Love	Qld	139	244	20	300*	10132	45.23	27	43	22
MJ Di Venuto	Tas	140	250	11	189	9974	41.73	19	67	23
CJL Rogers	WA/Vic	120	214	13	279	9917	49.34	33	42	10
GS Blewett	SA	117	223	13	268	9682	46.10	23	48	15

Highest Individual Scores

		for	v..	Venue	Season
DG Bradman	452*	NSW	Qld	SCG	1929-30
WH Ponsford	437	Vic	Qld	MCG	1927-28
C Hill	365*	SA	NSW	Adelaide	1900-01
RB Simpson	359	NSW	Qld	Gabba	1963-64
DG Bradman	357	SA	Vic	MCG	1935-36
BA Richards	356	SA	WA	WACA	1970-71
GR Marsh	355*	WA	SA	WACA	1989-90
WH Ponsford	352	Vic	NSW	MCG	1926-27
DG Bradman	340*	NSW	Vic	SCG	1928-29
WH Ponsford	336	Vic	SA	MCG	1927-28

Most Appearances

	M	Period
J Cox	161	1987/88-2004/05
RJ Inverarity	159	1962/63-1984/85
DS Lehmann	147	1987/88-2007/08
JD Siddons	146	1984/85-1999/00
SG Law	142	1988/89-2003/04
JP Maher	141	1993/94-2007/08
MJ Di Venuto	140	1991/92-2007/08
BJ Hodge	140	1993/94-2009/10
DS Berry	139	1989/90-2003/04
ML Love	139	1992/93-2008/09

Record Partnerships

Wkt				for	v	venue	Season
1	486	WJ Pucovski	MS Harris	Vic	SA	Glenelg Oval	2020-21
2	386	GS Blewett	DS Lehmann	SA	Tas	Bellerive	2001-02
3	459	CJL Rogers	MJ North	WA	Vic	WACA	2006-07
4	462*	DW Hookes	WB Phillips	SA	Tas	Adelaide	1986-87
5	464*	ME Waugh	SR Waugh	NSW	WA	WACA	1990-91
6	332	NG Marks	G Thomas	NSW	SA	SCG	1958-59
7	335	WC Andrews	EC Bensted	Qld	NSW	SCG	1934-35
8	270	VT Trumper	EP Barbour	NSW	Vic	SCG	1912-13
9	232	C Hill	E Walkley	SA	NSW	Adelaide	1900-01
10	307	AF Kippax	JEH Hooker	NSW	Vic	MCG	1928-29

Highest Partnerships

	Wkt			for	v	Venue	Season
486	1st	WJ Pucovski	MS Harris	Vic	SA	Glenelg Oval	2020-21
464*	5th	ME Waugh	SR Waugh	NSW	WA	WACA	1990-91
462*	4th	DW Hookes	WB Phillips	SA	Tas	Adelaide	1986-87
459	3rd	CJL Rogers	MJ North	WA	Vic	WACA	2006-07
431	1st	MRJ Veletta	GR Marsh	WA	SA	WACA	1989-90
397	5th	W Bardsley	C Kelleway	NSW	SA	SCG	1920-21
391	5th	MC Henriques	PM Nevill	NSW	Qld	SCG	2016-17
390*	3rd	JM Wiener	JK Moss	Vic	WA	Junction Oval	1981-82
388	1st	KC Wessels	RB Kerr	Qld	Vic	Junction Oval	1982-83
386	2nd	GS Blewett	DS Lehmann	SA	Tas	Bellerive	2001-02
379	3rd	N Jewell	BJ Hodge	Vic	Qld	Gabba	2007-08
379	3rd	LM Davis	AC Voges	WA	NSW	WACA	2011-12
378	2nd	LA Marks	KD Walters	NSW	SA	Adelaide	1964-65
378	4th	CJ Ferguson	JS Lehmann	SA	Tas	Bellerive	2015-16
375	1st	WM Woodfull	WH Ponsford	Vic	NSW	MCG	1926-27

Leading Wicket Takers

	for	M	Balls	Mdns	Runs	Wkts	Ave	Best	5i	10	SR	Econ
CV Grimmett	Vic/SA	79	28321	443	12976	513	25.29	9-180	48	13	55.2	2.75
MS Kasprowicz	Qld	101	22216	927	10833	441	24.56	8-44	26	2	50.3	2.93
AJ Bichel	Qld	89	19654	785	9994	430	23.24	7-54	22	4	45.7	3.05
J Angel	WA	105	22351	1030	10418	419	24.86	6-35	13	0	53.3	2.80
TM Alderman	WA	97	20482	778	9299	384	24.22	7-28	17	3	53.3	2.72
CG Rackemann	Qld	102	22400	921	10079	383	26.32	7-43	12	1	58.4	2.70
GF Lawson	NSW	103	20933	870	8673	367	23.63	6-31	12	0	57.0	2.49
GRJ Matthews	NSW	116	26764	1375	10518	363	28.98	8-52	19	4	73.7	2.36
JR Thomson	NSW/Q	84	16545	428	8591	355	24.20	7-27	18	3	46.6	3.12
AA Mallett	SA	77	20988	674	8171	344	23.75	7-57	19	2	61.0	2.34
TA Copeland	**NSW**	**93**	**21414**	**1055**	**8984**	**341**	**26.35**	**8-92**	**16**	**2**	**62.8**	**2.52**
DK Lillee	WA/Tas	75	17813	476	8086	338	23.92	7-36	18	4	52.7	2.72
SCG MacGill	WA/NSW	87	19363	551	11330	328	34.54	6-64	17	0	59.0	3.51
JM Bird	**Tas**	**69**	**14543**	**628**	**6892**	**319**	**21.61**	**7-18**	**17**	**5**	**45.5**	**2.84**
PR Reiffel	Vic	86	19137	843	19137	318	25.92	6-57	7	2	60.1	2.58
CD Matthews	WA/Tas	79	17663	610	8912	307	29.03	8-101	18	0	57.5	3.03
CR Miller	V/SA/T	84	20285	810	9738	304	32.03	7-49	11	2	66.7	2.88
CJ McDermott	Qld	67	14974	541	7605	303	25.10	8-44	22	2	49.4	3.05
GAR Lock	WA	66	20107	555	7210	302	23.87	7-53	16	2	66.5	2.15

Best Bowling in an Innings

		Venue	Season
TW Wall	10-36	SCG	SA v NSW	1932-33
IJ Brayshaw	10-44	WACA	WA v Vic	1967-68
PJ Allan	10-61	MCG	Qld v Vic	1965-66
JPF Travers	9-30	SA v Vic	MCG	1900-01
JP Behrendorff	9-37	WA v Vic	WACA	2016-17
EL McCormick	9-40	Vic v SA	Adel	1936-37
WJ O'Reilly	9-41	NSW v SA	Adel	1937-38
WJ O'Reilly	9-50	NSW v Vic	MCG	1933-34
WP Howell	9-52	NSW v Vic	MCG	1902-03
AN Connolly	9-67	Vic v Qld	Gabba	1964-65
DW Hourn	9-77	NSW v Vic	SCG	1979-80
RG Holland	9-83	NSW v SA	SCG	1984-85

Best Bowling in a Match

		for	Venue	Season
G Giffen	16-186	SA v NSW	Adel	1894-95
CV Grimmett	16-289	SA v Qld	Adel	1934-35
LO'B Fleetwood-Smith	15-96	Vic v Qld	MCG	1936-37
TR McKibbin	15-125	NSW v SA	Adel	1896-97
G Giffen	15-185	SA v Vic	Adel	1902-03
LO'B Fleetwood-Smith	15-226	Vic v NSW	SCG	1934-35
WJ O'Reilly	14-45	NSW v Qld	SCG	1939-40
TM Alderman	14-87	WA v NSW	WACA	1981-82
WJ O'Reilly	14-98	NSW v SA	Adel	1937-38
JP Behrendorff	14-89	WA v Vic	WACA	2016-17
TR McKibbin	14-189	NSW v SA	SCG	1894-95

Leading Wicket-Keepers

	for	M	Ct	St	Total	Byes/Inn	Runs	Avge	100
CD Hartley	Qld	128	535	15	550	1.33	6038	34.70	10
DS Berry	SA/Vic	139	499	47	546	2.73	3963	21.77	4
WA Seccombe	Qld	101	474	14	488	1.91	3207	25.05	4
TJ Zoehrer	WA	105	320	28	348	1.89	4177	30.71	6
RW Marsh	WA	81	311	33	344	1.72	4306	35.01	6
PA Emery	NSW	109	298	41	339	3.02	3081	25.67	1
PM Nevill	**NSW**	**93**	**310**	**23**	**333**	**3.74**	**4834**	**39.95**	**10**
MS Wade	**Vic/Tas**	**89**	**321**	**7**	**328**	**2.96**	**4988**	**43.00**	**9**
GA Manou	SA	96	307	21	328	3.49	3827	25.68	6
JA MacLean	Qld	86	289	24	313	2.42	3277	25.21	2
BJ Haddin	NSW	93	282	24	306	3.93	5629	42.01	11
TJ Nielsen	SA	92	255	29	284	2.49	3531	26.16	4
ATW Grout	Qld	84	213	63	276	3.21	3016	24.13	2

Leading Fielders

	For	M	Ct
JD Siddons	Vic/SA	146	189
RJ Inverarity	WA/SA	159	188
CL White	Vic	185	135
DJ Marsh	SA/Tas	137	172
AC Voges	WA	112	170
ML Love	Qld	139	158
JP Maher	Qld	141	153
MJ Di Venuto	Tas	140	151
MTG Elliott	Vic/SA	122	143
DJ Hussey	Vic	105	138
SE Marsh	**WA**	**121**	**130**
DW Hookes	SA	120	128
SG Law	Qld	142	126
M Klinger	V/SA/WA	122	122
MA Taylor	NSW	85	120

Captains Records – most games as skipper

	For	M	W	L	D	%W
LE Favell	SA	80	30	29	21	37.50
DM Wellham	NSW/Tas/Q	78	19	16	43	24.36
DW Hookes	SA	78	20	22	36	25.64
CL White	Vic	77	38	22	17	49.35
GJ Bailey	Tas	77	28	33	16	36.36
JD Siddons	SA	74	20	27	27	27.03
PL Ridings	SA	70	11	28	31	15.71
SG Law	Qld	69	35	10	24	50.72
VY Richardson	SA	64	23	37	4	35.94
TM Head	**SA**	**59**	**12**	**33**	**14**	**20.34**
DC Boon	Tas	58	13	25	20	22.41
WM Lawry	Vic	56	18	13	25	32.14
AC Voges	WA	55	24	20	11	43.64
RJ Inverarity	WA/SA	55	23	13	19	41.82
DS Lehmann	SA	55	17	23	15	30.91

SHEFFIELD SHIELD CRICKETERS OF THE SEASON

Season	
1975-76	Ian Chappell (SA) & Greg Chappell (Qld)
1976-77	Richie Robinson (Vic)
1977-78	David Ogilvie (Qld)
1978-79	Peter Sleep (SA)
1979-80	Ian Chappell (SA)
1980-81	Greg Chappell (Qld)
1981-82	Kepler Wessels (Qld)
1982-83	Kim Hughes (WA)
1983-84	Brian Davison (Tas) & John Dyson (NSW)
1984-85	David Boon (Tas)
1985-86	Allan Border (Qld)
1986-87	Craig McDermott (Qld)
1987-88	Dirk Tazelaar (Qld) & Mark Waugh (NSW)
1988-89	Tim May (SA)
1989-90	Mark Waugh (NSW)
1990-91	Stuart Law (Qld)
1991-92	Tony Dodemaide (Vic)
1992-93	Jamie Siddons (SA)
1993-94	Matthew Hayden (Qld)
1994-95	Dean Jones (Vic)
1995-96	Matthew Elliott (Vic)
1996-97	Andy Bichel (Qld)
1997-98	Dene Hills (Tas)
1998-99	Matthew Elliott (Vic)

Season	
1999-2000	Darren Lehmann (SA)
2000-01	Jamie Cox (Tas)
2001-02	Brad Hodge (Vic) & Jimmy Maher (Qld)
2002-03	Clinton Perren (Qld)
2003-04	Matthew Elliott (Vic)
2004-05	Michael Bevan (Tas)
2005-06	Andy Bichel (Qld)
2006-07	Chris Rogers (WA)
2007-08	Simon Katich (NSW)
2008-09	Phillip Hughes (NSW)
2009-10	Chris Hartley (Qld)
2010-11	James Hopes (Qld)
2011-12	Jackson Bird (Tas)
2012-13	Ricky Ponting (Tas)
2013-14	Marcus North (WA)
2014-15	Adam Voges (WA)
2015-16	Travis Head (SA)
2016-17	Chadd Sayers (SA)
2017-18	Chris Tremain (Vic)
2018-19	Scott Boland (Vic)
2019-20	Moises Henriques (NSW) and Nic Maddinson (Vic)
2020-21	Nathan Lyon (NSW)
2021-22	Henry Hunt (SA) and Travis Dean (Vic)

CAREER RECORDS to the end of 2021-22

	M	I	NO	Runs	HS	Avge	100	50	Ct	St	Balls	Runs	Wkt	Avge	BB	5	10
SA Abbott	62	91	9	1886	102*	23.00	1	10	34	0	10648	5550	174	31.89	7-45	5	0
AC Agar	49	73	7	1824	114*	27.63	3	9	19	0	10412	5330	126	42.30	6-110	6	2
WA Agar	13	20	9	137	41	12.45	0	0	3	0	2747	1380	37	37.29	5-53	1	0
TD Andrews	15	25	4	572	101	27.23	1	3	5	0	3100	1664	32	52.00	6-40	1	0
RR Ayre	1	1	1	1	1*		0	0	0	0	72	38	1	38.00	1-9	0	0

	M	I	NO	Runs	HS	Avge	100	50	Ct	St	Balls	Runs	Wkt	Avge	BB	5	10
CT Bancroft	73	133	6	4837	228*	38.08	15	15	95	1	24	10	1	10.00	1-10	0	0
XC Bartlett	10	14	6	87	25	10.87	0	0	2	0	1931	986	35	28.17	5-85	1	0
JJ Bazley	8	13	5	163	64	20.37	0	1	5	0	784	423	10	42.30	2-9	0	0
JP Behrendorff	30	45	13	389	39*	12.15	0	0	11	0	5587	2934	126	23.28	9-37	6	2
GT Bell	29	44	15	172	22	5.93	0	0	8	0	5484	2722	103	26.42	4-17	0	0
JM Bird	69	104	26	1044	64	13.38	0	3	46	0	14543	6892	319	21.60	7-18	17	5
SM Boland	80	97	32	811	51	12.47	0	2	24	0	15655	7175	279	25.71	7-31	7	0
MA Bryant	2	4	0	32	21	8.00	0	0	0	0							
JSD Buckingham	1	1	1	0	0*		0	0	0	0	240	120	4	30.00	4-79	0	0
JA Burns	95	171	12	6493	202*	40.83	14	34	110	0	90	34	1	34.00	1-0	0	0
BT Capel	1	2	0	9	8	4.50	0	0	1	0							
JM Carder	15	27	3	730	118	30.41	1	3	8	0	335	259	5	51.80	3-134	0	0
AT Carey	41	74	7	2263	143	33.77	5	10	153	4							
HWR Cartwright	53	95	10	3237	170*	38.08	6	16	23	0	1895	1248	32	39.00	4-23	0	0
J Clayton	3	6	0	234	109	39.00	1	1	0	0							
HNA Conway	36	50	27	221	31	9.60	0	0	13	0	5862	2576	95	27.11	6-39	6	1
TA Copeland	93	137	23	1822	106	15.98	1	6	95	0	21408	8984	341	26.34	8-92	16	2
BL Couch	1	1	0	1	1	1.00	0	0	0	0	72	73	1	73.00	1-38	0	0
XA Crone																0	0
TJ Dean	56	100	6	3134	154*	33.34	8	13	41	0	102	53	0		-	0	0
BJ Doggett	22	24	9	156	43*	10.40	0	0	9	0	4164	2173	73	29.76	5-77	2	0
JR Doran	54	95	2	2679	123	28.80	3	15	97	1	162	124	2	62.00	1-5	0	0
BL Edwards	4	4	2	10	8	5.00	0	0	1	0	519	331	7	47.28	3-95	0	0
JR Edwards	22	38	4	779	101	22.91	1	0	22	0	1172	571	18	31.72	3-47	0	0
NT Ellis	7	10	0	164	41	16.40	0	0	2	0	1570	879	35	25.11	6-43	2	0
ZK Evans	1	0	0	0	0		0	0	0	0	186	105	1	105.00	1-31	0	0
J Fraser-McGurk	8	14	1	237	51	18.23	0	1	4	0	18	13	0		-	0	0
JA Freeman	11	16	5	208	41*	18.90	0	0	4	0	1816	1129	24	47.04	4-72	0	0
CJ Gannon	41	52	11	571	58	13.92	0	1	28	0	8489	3865	135	28.62	6-53	3	0
MR Gilkes	12	21	0	636	83	30.28	0	5	12	0							
J Goodwin	2	4	0	42	22	10.50	0	0	1	0							
DMK Grant	14	20	10	83	14	8.30	0	0	5	0	2705	1371	34	40.32	4-38	0	0
CD Green	28	48	8	2119	251	52.97	7	6	12	0	2203	1190	37	32.16	6-30	2	0
RP Hackney	3	6	0	60	38	10.00	0	0	0	0							
PSP Handscomb	84	138	7	5288	215	40.36	13	30	152	4	54	58	0		-	0	0
AM Hardie	10	16	5	486	174*	44.18	2	0	5	0	1354	696	28	24.85	4-24	0	0
SB Harper	27	43	7	864	106*	24.00	1	4	92	7						0	0
MS Harris	91	163	10	6208	250*	40.57	15	26	42	0	78	64	0		-	0	0
LC Hatcher	5	7	1	52	27	8.66	0	0	1	0	895	622	18	34.55	4-86	0	0
JR Hazlewood	33	37	9	265	43*	9.46	0	0	13	0	6047	2809	118	23.80	6-35	2	0
TM Head	86	159	4	6175	223	39.83	13	36	41	0	4523	2849	47	60.61	3-42	0	0
LD Hearne	4	8	0	197	65	24.62	0	2	2	0							
SD Heazlett	39	70	4	2015	135	30.53	4	9	36	0	12	5	0		-	0	0
MC Henriques	86	142	15	4956	265	39.02	13	17	40	0	4902	2600	79	32.91	5-17	1	0
JM Holland	72	83	35	703	55	14.64	0	1	25	0	15593	7421	230	32.26	7-82	9	0
BJH Holt	6	10	1	133	29	14.77	0	0	21	0							
BM Hope	3	5	0	31	10	6.20	0	0	3	0	300	178	4	44.50	3-15	0	0
DP Hughes	60	113	12	3786	136	37.48	7	22	45	0							
HJ Hunt	24	46	1	1716	134	38.13	6	6	16	0							
JP Inglis	40	67	9	1980	153*	34.13	3	11	134	3							
CP Jewell	19	35	1	937	140	27.55	2	4	10	0							
ML Kelly	38	50	12	644	89	16.94	0	1	16	0	6961	3270	112	29.19	6-67	5	0
TJ Kelly	1	2	0	42	29	21.00	0	0	0	0							
SL Kerber	2	3	0	99	55	33.00	0	1	3	0	285	198	3	66.00	3-92	0	0
HL Kerr	4	7	2	192	88	38.40	0	2	2	0	534	233	8	29.12	2-41	0	0
UT Khawaja	74	123	13	5311	214	48.28	16	25	48	0	108	73	1	73.00	1-21	0	0
MP Kuhnemann	10	9	5	87	24*	21.75	0	0	3	0	2217	1024	29	35.31	5-25	3	1
M Labuschagne	61	109	9	4080	192	40.00	10	21	57	0	2490	1608	27	59.55	3-85	0	0
JS Lehmann	52	96	8	3118	205	35.43	7	15	36	0	308	194	4	48.50	2-17	0	0
NM Lyon	54	79	17	764	75	12.32	0	2	22	0	12886	5879	172	34.18	6-21	4	1
CL McClure	1	2	1	0	0*	0.00	0	0	0	0	134	67	2	33.50	2-67	0	0
NA McSweeney	8	16	2	297	99*	21.21	0	1	7	0	477	236	9	26.22	4-89	0	0
NJ Maddinson	89	155	11	5753	224	39.95	13	27	57	0	376	261	4	65.25	2-10	0	0
BAD Manenti	1	2	1	42	23	42.00	0	0	1	0	376	190	5	38.00	3-89	0	0
MR Marsh	51	94	7	2501	151	28.74	4	12	31	0	4269	2418	82	29.48	6-84	1	0
SE Marsh	121	219	24	8330	214	42.71	20	43	131	0	210	148	2	74.00	2-20	0	0
NJ McAndrew	8	12	2	227	65*	22.70	0	1	4	0	1817	815	27	30.18	5-84	1	0
BR McDermott	42	74	8	2247	104	34.04	1	17	32	0	102	75	0		-	0	0
RP Meredith	20	26	17	105	20	11.66	0	0	3	0	3170	1867	56	33.33	5-98	1	0
JA Merlo	5	8	1	123	64	17.57	0	1	3	0	204	132	2	66.00	2-14	0	0

128

	M	I	NO	Runs	HS	Avge	100	50	Ct	St	Balls	Runs	Wkt	Avge	BB	5	10
LRT Morris	13	11	6	39	14*	7.80	0	0	5	0	1539	983	32	30.71	5-94	1	0
TR Murphy	2	2	1	58	34	58.00	0	0	1	0	582	273	8	34.12	4-98	0	0
AJ Nair	4	5	0	64	37	12.80	0	0	2	0	566	245	3	81.66	2-71	0	0
LH Neil-Smith	11	16	5	327	71*	29.72	0	2	2	0	1523	920	28	32.85	5-43	1	0
MG Neser	54	80	12	1778	121	26.14	1	11	23	0	9859	4650	183	25.40	6-57	5	0
PM Nevill	101	161	30	5137	235*	39.21	10	27	314	23	6	8	0		-	0	0
HJ Nielsen	30	56	4	1520	114	29.23	2	9	68	4							
B Nikitaras	1	2	0	100	56	50.00	0	1	0	0							
TD Paine	88	154	17	3958	215	28.89	3	21	276	8	36	23	0		-	0	0
JS Paris	27	36	8	732	102*	26.14	1	1	11	0	4896	2287	103	22.20	6-23	5	0
WB Parker	4	2	0	4	4	2.00	0	0	1	0	360	192	6	32.00	3-54	0	0
KR Patterson	73	132	10	4484	157	36.75	9	25	51	0							
JL Pattinson	45	64	9	979	80	17.80	0	2	14	0	7774	3864	161	24.00	6-32	5	0
JJ Peirson	50	79	9	2262	132	32.31	3	14	174	2							
MJ Perry	16	16	2	210	74	15.00	0	1	1	0	2637	1249	39	32.02	4-31	0	0
JR Philippe	27	51	3	1469	129	30.60	2	10	54	0							
LAJ Pope	13	20	9	42	12	3.81	0	0	3	0	2496	1838	29	63.37	7-87	2	0
WJ Pucovski	21	32	3	1822	255*	62.82	6	7	4	0							
N Radhakrishnan	1	2	0	17	13	8.50	0	0	0	0	60	53	1	53.00	1-29	0	0
SL Rainbird	54	82	20	882	59	14.22	0	2	16	0	9824	5325	167	31.88	8-21	4	1
MT Renshaw	54	97	7	3232	170	35.91	9	8	51	0	372	184	3	61.33	1-10	0	0
JA Richardson	18	26	2	561	71	23.37	0	4	11	0	3748	1671	81	20.62	8-47	3	1
KW Richardson	33	51	4	645	49	13.72	0	0	10	0	6879	3454	98	35.24	5-69	1	0
CJ Rocchiccioli	4	3	2	51	50	51.00	0	1	2	0	440	234	5	46.80	2-24	0	0
JW Rogers	11	21	0	447	95	21.28	0	2	13	0	12	4	0		-	0	0
TS Rogers	15	21	0	365	80	17.38	0	1	3	0	1948	1048	47	22.29	4-9	0	0
GS Sandhu	31	41	5	575	97*	15.97	0	2	14	0	5009	2552	75	34.03	6-57	3	0
JJ Sangha	23	41	2	1097	142	28.12	3	4	13	0	890	480	13	36.92	3-19	0	0
TS Sangha	6	7	2	8	2*	1.60	0	0	2	0	1189	547	17	32.17	3-44	0	0
LAH Scott	13	23	3	414	61	20.70	0	1	2	0	1464	683	16	42.68	5-46	1	0
JL Seymour	5	9	0	254	105	28.22	1	1	5	0	24	16	0		-	0	0
DJM Short	21	36	2	945	67	27.79	0	6	18	0	1675	1103	27	40.85	3-78	0	0
MW Short	35	55	6	1489	98	30.38	0	9	34	0	1985	986	23	42.86	4-74	0	0
PM Siddle	73	102	20	1301	87	15.86	0	2	19	0	14503	6574	270	24.34	8-54	12	0
JC Silk	69	131	6	4039	127	32.31	8	22	46	0	257	144	2	72.00	1-4	0	0
SPD Smith	42	74	6	3411	177	50.16	12	14	64	0	3010	2066	41	50.39	7-64	1	0
DL Solway	13	22	4	714	133*	39.66	1	5	6	0							
MA Starc	35	41	14	625	86*	23.14	0	3	22	0	5931	3255	119	27.35	8-73	6	2
MT Steketee	47	64	13	753	53	14.76	0	2	17	0	8890	4364	165	26.44	7-44	3	1
MP Stoinis	54	95	6	2969	170	33.35	3	23	20	0	4250	2363	57	41.45	4-73	0	0
BE Street	25	42	2	1355	143	33.87	4	5	29	0	69	72	1	72.00	1-19	0	0
C Sully	1	0	0	0			0	0	0	0	99	66	2	33.00	1-32	0	0
WJ Sutherland	20	26	6	301	34*	15.05	0	0	14	0	3496	1567	60	26.11	6-67	3	0
MJ Swepson	43	58	11	635	37	13.51	0	0	30	0	7914	4520	130	34.76	5-55	4	1
CP Tremain	64	85	18	991	111	14.79	1	1	14	0	11689	5779	249	23.20	7-82	8	1
SJ Truloff	14	26	2	456	64	19.00	0	1	15	0							
EM Vines	6	10	0	163	38	16.30	0	0	5	0							
MS Wade	105	167	25	6447	152	45.40	12	45	327	7	484	319	8	39.87	3-13	0	0
CA Wakim	20	38	1	1092	160	29.51	1	6	8	0	90	79	1	79.00	1-27	0	0
TP Ward	9	16	0	591	144	36.93	1	3	9	0							
DA Warner	22	39	3	1565	144	43.47	5	6	10	0	199	125	1	125.00	1-0	0	0
JB Weatherald	54	103	3	3495	198	34.95	8	17	47	0	42	44	1	44.00	1-14	0	0
BJ Webster	59	104	9	2941	187	30.95	7	11	84	0	4832	2945	67	43.95	4-50	0	0
SM Whiteman	68	113	8	3912	176*	37.25	8	22	153	5							
JD Wildermuth	57	93	6	2221	110	25.52	2	11	17	0	7599	3835	132	29.05	5-40	1	0
NP Winter	22	36	8	431	53*	15.39	0	1	3	0	5094	2407	78	30.85	5-48	4	1
DJ Worrall	49	78	32	593	39	12.89	0	0	15	0	10548	5342	184	29.03	7-64	7	1
A Zampa	38	61	7	1177	74	21.79	0	6	9	0	7697	5068	105	48.26	6-62	2	1

FIRST CLASS AVERAGES 2021-22

	M	I	NO	Runs	HS	Avge	100	50	Ct	St	Balls	Runs	Wkt	Avge	BB	5	10
SA Abbott	2	4	0	42	16	10.50	0	0	1	0	514	228	11	20.72	6-38	1	1
TB Abell	1	2	0	5	5	2.50	0	0	1	0							
JM Anderson	3	6	4	13	5*	6.50	0	0	0	0	624	187	8	23.37	4-33	0	0
TD Andrews	4	7	0	141	40	20.14	0	1	0	0	744	381	8	47.62	3-69	0	0
RR Ayre	1	1	1	1	1*		0	0	0	0	72	38	1	38.00	1-9	0	0
JM Bairstow	2	4	0	194	113	48.50	1	0	1	0	0	0	0		-	0	0
CT Bancroft	8	15	1	502	141	35.85	2	0	15	0	0	0	0		-	0	0
XC Bartlett	1	2	1	1	1*	1.00	0	0	0	0	168	79	4	19.75	2-30	0	0
JJ Bazley	7	12	5	137	64	19.57	0	1	5	0	736	390	10	39.00	2-9	0	0
GT Bell	5	6	2	29	19	7.25	0	0	1	0	844	409	14	29.21	3-80	0	0

129

	M	I	NO	Runs	HS	Avge	100	50	Ct	St	Balls	Runs	Wkt	Avge	BB	5	10
DM Bess	1	2	0	40	25	20.00	0	0	0	0	360	237	6	39.50	4-80	0	0
SW Billings	1	2	0	30	29	15.00	0	0	5	0	0	0	0		-	0	0
JM Bird	3	5	0	46	26	9.20	0	0	6	0	521	229	7	32.71	3-38	0	0
JJ Bohannon	1	2	0	73	51	36.50	0	1	2	0	0	0	0		-	0	0
SM Boland	9	9	4	32	10*	6.40	0	0	5	0	1972	696	46	15.13	6-7	2	0
JR Bracey	1	2	0	118	113	59.00	1	0	0	0	0	0	0		-	0	0
SCJ Broad	3	6	3	42	15	14.00	0	0	2	0	712	342	13	26.30	5-101	1	0
HC Brook	1	2	0	18	17	9.00	0	0	0	0	12	4	0		-	0	0
MA Bryant	1	2	0	27	21	13.50	0	0	0	0	0	0	0		-	0	0
JSD Buckingham	1	1	1	0	0*		0	0	0	0	240	120	4	30.00	4-79	0	0
JA Burns	8	15	1	409	79	29.21	0	1	9	0	6	0	0		-	0	0
RJ Burns	3	6	0	77	34	12.83	0	0	2	0	0	0	0		-	0	0
JC Buttler	4	8	1	107	39	15.28	0	0	12	0	0	0	0		-	0	0
BT Capel	1	2	0	9	8	4.50	0	0	1	0	0	0	0		-	0	0
JM Carder	8	14	0	468	118	33.42	1	2	4	0	12	9	0		-	0	0
AT Carey	11	19	1	362	66*	20.11	0	2	46	2	0	0	0		-	0	0
HWR Cartwright	8	15	1	601	121*	42.92	2	3	2	0	198	117	7	16.71	4-23	0	0
J Clayton	3	6	0	234	109	39.00	1	1	0	0	0	0	0		-	0	0
HNA Conway	5	9	4	61	20	12.20	0	0	3	0	702	323	6	53.83	2-11	0	0
TA Copeland	6	11	2	68	17	7.55	0	0	6	0	987	383	13	29.46	4-46	0	0
BL Couch	1	1	0	1	1	1.00	0	0	0	0	72	73	1	73.00	1-38	0	0
Z Crawley	3	6	0	166	77	27.66	0	1	8	0	0	0	0		-	0	0
XA Crone	1	1	0	0	0	0.00	0	0	0	0	126	103	4	25.75	2-32	0	0
PJ Cummins	4	5	0	72	24	14.40	0	0	2	0	760	379	21	18.04	5-38	1	0
TJ Dean	6	10	1	423	146	47.00	2	0	2	0	0	0	0		-	0	0
BJ Doggett	5	6	3	24	10	8.00	0	0	2	0	1035	448	17	26.35	4-51	0	0
JR Doran	7	12	0	257	72	21.41	0	2	27	0	0	0	0		-	0	0
DR Drew	2	4	1	189	130	63.00	1	0	2	0	0	0	0		-	0	0
BL Edwards	3	2	2	1	1*		0	0	1	0	351	239	3	79.66	3-95	0	0
JR Edwards	7	13	1	217	42	18.08	0	0	8	0	782	355	12	29.58	3-47	0	0
MD Fisher	1	2	0	9	9	4.50	0	0	0	0	174	84	2	42.00	1-35	0	0
BT Foakes	1	2	0	85	73	42.50	0	1	5	0	0	0	0		-	0	0
J Fraser-McGurk	2	4	0	47	25	11.75	0	0	1	0	0	0	0		-	0	0
JA Freeman	5	6	3	82	41*	27.33	0	0	0	0	889	549	9	61.00	3-48	0	0
CJ Gannon	3	3	1	9	8	4.50	0	0	2	0	640	328	8	41.00	3-87	0	0
MR Gilkes	5	10	0	271	64	27.10	0	2	4	0	0	0	0		-	0	0
J Goodwin	2	4	0	42	22	10.50	0	0	1	0	0	0	0		-	0	0
DMK Grant	7	10	3	48	14	6.85	0	0	3	0	1450	709	20	35.45	4-76	0	0
CD Green	10	18	2	592	106	37.00	1	5	8	0	1018	497	19	26.15	3-21	0	0
RP Hackney	3	6	0	60	38	10.00	0	0	0	0	0	0	0		-	0	0
H Hameed	4	8	0	80	27	10.00	0	0	3	0	0	0	0		-	0	0
PSP Handscomb	8	15	1	697	148*	49.78	2	3	27	0	0	0	0		-	0	0
AM Hardie	3	5	3	238	174*	119.00	1	0	1	0	360	141	10	14.10	4-24	0	0
SB Harper	8	13	2	208	93	18.90	0	1	24	5	0	0	0		-	0	0
MS Harris	8	15	1	501	137	35.78	1	3	4	0	0	0	0		-	0	0
LC Hatcher	1	2	0	24	24	12.00	0	0	0	0	241	161	5	32.20	4-86	0	0
JR Hazlewood	1	1	1	0	0*		0	0	2	0	162	74	3	24.66	2-42	0	0
TM Head	10	16	0	797	163	49.81	4	2	5	0	420	231	5	46.20	2-22	0	0
LD Hearne	3	6	0	143	65	23.83	0	1	2	0	0	0	0		-	0	0
MC Henriques	2	3	0	36	23	12.00	0	0	0	0	48	19	1	19.00	1-14	0	0
JM Holland	6	5	3	1	1	0.50	0	0	1	0	1426	642	20	32.10	4-82	0	0
BJH Holt	3	5	0	44	20	8.80	0	0	7	0	0	0	0		-	0	0
BM Hope	2	3	0	18	10	6.00	0	0	2	0	264	157	4	39.25	3-15	0	0
DP Hughes	5	9	2	337	89*	48.14	0	4	2	0	0	0	0		-	0	0
HJ Hunt	9	17	1	674	134	42.12	3	1	6	0	0	0	0		-	0	0
JP Inglis	2	3	0	47	28	15.66	0	0	4	0	0	0	0			0	0
CP Jewell	8	14	0	508	102	36.28	1	3	5	0	0	0	0		-	0	0
ML Kelly	6	8	3	93	41	18.60	0	0	2	0	906	424	10	42.40	3-27	0	0
TJ Kelly	1	2	0	42	29	21.00	0	0	0	0	0	0	0		-	0	0
UT Khawaja	9	16	2	800	174	57.14	4	3	9	0	6	5	0		-	0	0
MP Kuhnemann	7	7	4	74	24*	24.66	0	0	2	0	1737	797	25	31.88	5-25	3	1
M Labuschagne	11	20	3	842	136	49.52	3	3	10	0	619	345	2	172.50	1-21	0	0
MJ Leach	3	6	2	51	26	12.75	0	0	0	0	443	321	6	53.50	4-84	0	0
AZ Lees	1	2	0	2	1	1.00	0	0	2	0	0	0	0		-	0	0
JS Lehmann	4	6	0	225	102	37.50	1	1	5	0	2	5	0		-	0	0
NM Lyon	7	9	2	98	31	14.00	0	0	7	0	1615	628	20	31.40	4-91	0	0
CL McClure	1	2	1	0	0*	0.00	0	0	0	0	134	67	2	33.50	2-67	0	0
NA McSweeney	3	6	1	171	99*	34.20	0	1	5	0	375	194	7	27.71	4-89	0	0
NJ Maddinson	8	15	3	616	128	51.33	2	3	3	0	48	17	1	17.00	1-4	0	0
S Mahmood	1	2	2	0	0*		0	0	1	0	180	72	0		-	0	0

	M	I	NO	Runs	HS	Avge	100	50	Ct	St	Balls	Runs	Wkt	Avge	BB	5	10
DJ Malan	5	10	0	244	82	24.40	0	2	2	0	66	61	2	30.50	2-33	0	0
BAD Manenti	1	2	1	42	23	42.00	0	0	1	0	376	190	5	38.00	3-89	0	0
MR Marsh	1	2	1	93	60*	93.00	0	1	0	0	78	44	1	44.00	1-15	0	0
SE Marsh	7	12	1	383	118	34.81	1	2	6	0	0	0	0		-	0	0
NJ McAndrew	8	12	2	227	65*	22.70	0	1	4	0	1817	815	27	30.18	5-84	1	0
BR McDermott	5	9	1	343	94	42.87	0	2	6	0	0	0	0		-	0	0
RP Meredith	2	2	0	23	20	11.50	0	0	0	0	276	115	5	23.00	3-45	0	0
JA Merlo	4	6	1	119	64	23.80	0	1	2	0	186	118	2	59.00	2-14	0	0
LRT Morris	8	7	3	33	14*	8.25	0	0	2	0	836	541	20	27.05	4-21	0	0
TR Murphy	1	1	1	24	24*		0	0	0	0	300	146	7	20.85	4-98	0	0
AJ Nair	1	1	0	0	0	0.00	0	0	0	0	72	36	0		-	0	0
LH Neil-Smith	5	8	2	212	71*	35.33	0	2	2	0	613	329	13	25.30	5-43	1	0
MG Neser	5	7	1	97	35	16.16	0	0	0	0	797	344	18	19.11	5-29	1	0
PM Nevill	4	8	1	138	34	19.71	0	0	14	0	0	0	0		-	0	0
HJ Nielsen	6	10	1	265	71	29.44	0	2	10	0	0	0	0		-	0	0
B Nikitaras	1	2	0	100	56	50.00	0	1	0	0	0	0	0		-	0	0
LC Norwell	1	2	0	33	25	16.50	0	0	1	0	179	93	5	18.60	5-58	1	0
JS Paris	7	10	2	157	30	19.62	0	0	2	0	1115	497	24	20.70	5-63	1	0
WB Parker	2	1	0	0	0	0.00	0	0	0	0	84	63	1	63.00	1-11	0	0
KR Patterson	5	9	0	253	112	28.11	1	0	5	0	0	0	0		-	0	0
JL Pattinson	5	7	0	100	45	14.28	0	0	0	0	1009	469	15	31.26	5-71	1	0
JJ Peirson	9	15	1	475	132	33.92	2	2	26	1	0	0	0		-	0	0
MJ Perry	8	10	2	136	74	17.00	0	1	0	0	1640	713	24	29.70	4-31	0	0
JR Philippe	8	15	2	481	129	37.00	1	3	37	0	0	0	0		-	0	0
LAJ Pope	4	6	2	22	12	5.50	0	0	1	0	713	533	11	48.45	4-92	0	0
OJD Pope	3	6	0	67	35	11.16	0	0	4	0	0	0	0		-	0	0
WJ Pucovski	3	4	0	146	59	36.50	0	2	0	0	0	0	0		-	0	0
N Radhakrishnan	1	2	0	17	13	8.50	0	0	0	0	60	53	1	53.00	1-29	0	0
SL Rainbird	3	3	0	12	12	4.00	0	0	1	0	445	223	19	11.73	8-21	2	1
MT Renshaw	10	17	1	491	120*	30.68	1	1	16	0	282	116	3	38.66	2-26	0	0
JA Richardson	5	8	1	202	50	28.85	0	1	0	0	1005	429	28	15.32	5-23	2	0
OE Robinson	4	8	1	38	22	5.42	0	0	2	0	638	281	11	25.54	3-58	0	0
CJ Rocchiccioli	4	3	2	51	50	51.00	0	1	2	0	440	234	5	46.80	2-24	0	0
TS Rogers	1	2	0	3	3	1.50	0	0	0	0	108	69	1	69.00	1-69	0	0
JE Root	5	10	0	322	89	32.20	0	3	6	0	342	234	5	46.80	2-27	0	0
GS Sandhu	6	8	0	88	39	11.00	0	0	2	0	1051	479	25	19.16	6-57	2	0
JJ Sangha	7	13	0	504	142	38.76	1	4	4	0	246	133	1	133.00	1-12	0	0
TS Sangha	6	7	2	8	2*	1.60	0	0	2	0	1189	547	17	32.17	3-44	0	0
LAH Scott	5	7	1	125	42	20.83	0	0	1	0	630	262	13	20.15	5-46	1	0
JL Seymour	4	8	0	194	105	24.25	1	0	4	0	18	16	0		-	0	0
DJM Short	5	7	0	169	67	24.14	0	1	6	0	346	229	6	38.16	2-37	0	0
MW Short	7	13	2	306	90	27.81	0	1	12	0	761	391	12	32.58	4-74	0	0
PM Siddle	6	8	3	70	31*	14.00	0	0	0	0	1165	443	19	23.31	5-40	1	0
JC Silk	7	11	2	514	100*	57.11	1	3	3	0	12	13	1	13.00	1-8	0	0
SPD Smith	5	8	0	244	93	30.50	0	2	11	0	30	10	1	10.00	1-10	0	0
MA Starc	5	7	3	155	39*	38.75	0	0	1	0	913	482	19	25.36	4-37	0	0
MT Steketee	7	10	2	101	39	12.62	0	0	3	0	1400	638	35	18.22	7-44	2	1
BA Stokes	5	10	0	236	66	23.60	0	2	3	0	381	286	4	71.50	3-113	0	0
BE Street	10	19	1	620	143	34.44	2	1	12	0	75	61	1	61.00	1-19	0	0
C Sully	1	0	0	0	0		0	0	0	0	99	66	2	33.00	1-32	0	0
WJ Sutherland	7	10	3	85	23	12.14	0	0	6	0	1501	651	24	27.12	5-78	1	0
MJ Swepson	3	4	1	18	8	6.00	0	0	1	0	656	306	5	61.20	2-26	0	0
CP Tremain	5	9	2	169	58	24.14	0	1	2	0	1023	383	24	15.95	5-48	1	0
SJ Truloff	4	8	0	178	64	22.25	0	1	7	0	0	0	0		-	0	0
EM Vines	1	2	0	38	38	19.00	0	0	1	0	0	0	0		-	0	0
MS Wade	1	2	0	111	61	55.50	0	2	0	0	0	0	0		-	0	0
CA Wakim	5	9	0	281	68	31.22	0	3	1	0	12	12	0		-	0	0
TP Ward	8	14	0	552	144	39.42	1	3	8	0	0	0	0		-	0	0
DA Warner	5	8	0	273	95	34.12	0	2	5	0	0	0	0		-	0	0
JB Weatherald	6	11	2	367	122	40.77	1	1	7	0	0	0	0		-	0	0
BJ Webster	6	9	2	361	166*	51.57	1	1	8	0	582	327	6	54.5	3-40	0	0
SM Whiteman	7	13	2	641	176*	58.27	2	2	4	0	0	0	0		-	0	0
JD Wildermuth	8	13	1	111	34	9.25	0	0	5	0	1079	545	15	36.33	2-29	0	0
NP Winter	1	1	0	4	4	4.00	0	0	0	0	114	50	1	50	1-50	0	0
CR Woakes	3	6	0	146	44	24.33	0	0	2	0	532	332	6	55.33	2-64	0	0
MA Wood	4	8	0	86	39	10.75	0	0	1	0	727	453	17	26.64	6-37	1	0
DJ Worrall	5	8	1	60	24	8.57	0	0	3	0	1098	450	12	37.5	4-49	0	0
MB Wright	3	4	2	182	78*	91.00	0	2	0	0	0	0	0		-	0	0
TA Wyllie	2	3	0	69	42	23.00	0	0	1	0	0	0	0		-	0	0
RM Yates	1	2	0	43	41	21.50	0	0	2	0	42	62	1	62	1-62	0	0

WESTERN AUSTRALIA WIN THEIR 15ᵗʰ DOMESTIC TITLE

Western Australia won the Marsh Cup in a classic low scoring final against New South Wales at the Junction Oval, grabbing their fourth title in the past six seasons. They had plenty of bowling depth with AJ Tye leading the way with 15 wickets, while Jason Behrendorff and Matt Kelly were also very good. The batsman made four tons, but it was Behrendorff and Kelly who were called upon to do their bit with the bat in the final, their last wicket stand of 52 crucial to the outcome.

New South Wales made the final despite having four matches washed out, but grabbed two wins, one a massive victory over Victoria before beating Queensland at the Gabba. They looked set to win the final but lost their last three to get rolled.

Tasmania was a bit stiff to miss the final, as they were the only team to beat eventual champions Western Australia. Veteran Peter Siddle was a constant with the ball with 12 wickets at an economy under four per over. Queensland won three games, but also lost three, with Matt Renshaw dominating with the bat to claim the player of the series award.

South Australia and Victoria brought up the bottom of the ladder, Travis Head's double ton for SA was the innings of the tournament. Alex Carey made two splendid centuries which helped him into the Australian Test side. The Vics managed to beat SA but did little else, with the exception of Marcus Harris who made their only hundred in his one hit.

LADDER	M	W	L	NR	BP	Points	Net Run Rate
Western Australia	6	4	2	-	2	18	+0.940
New South Wales	6	2	-	4	1	17	+2.619
Tasmania	6	3	1	2	1	17	+0.800
Queensland	6	3	3	-	2	14	+0.119
South Australia	6	1	4	1	-	6	-0.503
Victoria	6	1	4	1	-	6	-2.085

Most Runs	Team	M	Inn	NO	Runs	HS	Average	S/Rate	100s	50s	Sixes
MT Renshaw	Qld	6	6	1	377	156*	75.40	111.53	1	3	6
TM Head	SA	4	4	-	306	230	76.50	153.76	1	-	8
JR Philippe	WA	7	7	-	265	137	37.85	98.88	1	-	9
AT Carey	SA	5	5	1	258	128*	64.50	109.32	2	-	3
AJ Turner	WA	7	7	1	242	100	40.33	100.41	1	1	4
CT Bancroft	WA	4	4	2	219	124*	109.50	95.63	1	-	1
BR McDermott	Tas	3	3	-	207	133	69.00	89.22	1	1	5
JC Silk	Tas	4	4	1	207	90*	69.00	84.14	-	2	1
JJ Peirson	Qld	6	6	2	200	62	50.00	109.28	-	2	6

Highest Scores		Balls	4s	6s		Venue	Date
TM Head	230	127	28	8	South Australia v Queensland	Rolton Oval	Oct 13, 2021
MT Renshaw	156*	109	15	5	Queensland v South Australia	Adelaide Oval	Nov 28, 2021
JR Philippe	137	116	10	7	Western Australia v South Australia	Rolton Oval	Sep 22, 2021
BR McDermott	133	140	8	5	Tasmania v Western Australia	Bellerive Oval	Nov 26, 2021
AT Carey	128*	106	15	1	South Australia v Western Australia	Rolton Oval	Sep 22, 2021

Most Wickets	Team	M	Overs	Mdns	Runs	Wkts	Avge	Econ	Best
AJ Tye	WA	7	58.3	3	285	15	19.00	4.87	4-30
PM Siddle	Tas	4	34.1	4	134	12	11.16	3.92	4-22
GS Sandhu	Qld	4	32.1	1	211	9	15.25	5.68	4-42
LAJ Pope	SA	4	32.5	1	211	9	23.44	6.42	4-78
JJ Bazley	Qld	5	34.4	1	175	8	21.87	5.04	3-12
JP Behrendorff	WA	5	44.3	2	218	8	27.25	4.89	4-39
ML Kelly	WA	7	47.2	2	256	8	32.00	5.40	2-37

Best Bowling				Venue	Date
T Sangha	4-21	New South Wales v Victoria		SCG	Nov 24, 2021
PM Siddle	4-22	Tasmania v Victoria		Bellerive	Mar 6, 2022
AJ Tye	4-30	Western Australia v New South Wales		Junction Oval	Mar 11, 2022
JP Behrendorff	4-39	Western Australia v South Australia		Rolton Oval	Sep 22, 2021
AJ Tye	4-39	Western Australia v Tasmania		WACA	Oct 15, 2021
C Sully	4-39	Queensland v Tasmania		Townsville	Nov 1, 2021
GS Sandhu	4-42	Queensland v Victoria		Junction Oval	Feb 23, 2022

Match 1 – South Australia v Western Australia at Rolton Oval, Adelaide on September 22, 2021
WA won by 78 runs (DLS)

Western Australia		B	M	4	6
JR Philippe +	c Worrall b Richardson	137	116	184	10	7
SE Marsh	c Head b Richardson	1	4	10		
MR Marsh*	b Worrall	111	124	143	14	3
JP Inglis	b McAndrew	3	6	5		
AJ Turner	c McSweeney b Agar	46	28	47	4	1
DJM Short	c Kerber b Agar	15	10	16	2	
AC Agar	not out	11	8	11		1
CD Green	not out	13	5	4	1	1
AJ Tye					
ML Kelly					
JP Behrendorff					
	9 lb, 1 nb, 5 w	15			
10 overs: 1-42	50 overs, 213 mins	6-352			

1-15 (S Marsh, 2.4), 2-232 (M Marsh, 38.1), 3-237 (Inglis, 39.3), 4-293 (Philippe, 44.5), 5-328 (Short, 47.4), 6-328 (Turner, 47.5)

South Australia		B	M	4	6
AT Carey+	not out	128	106	154	15	1
JB Weatherald	c Agar b Behrendorff	14	9	11	1	1
TM Head*	c Short b Behrendorff	19	16	24	4	
NA McSweeney	c Kelly b Behrendorff	1	4	8		
HJ Nielsen	c Inglis b Tye	5	9	8	1	
RJ Gibson	lbw b Green	0	3	3		
SL Kerber	c Inglis b M Marsh	12	19	24	1	
NJ McAndrew	b Agar	18	17	18	1	1
DJ Worrall	c Turner b Agar	1	7	6		
KW Richardson	c M Marsh b Tye	18	26	26	3	
WA Agar	c Kelly b Behrendorff	18	15	20	1	1
	3 w	3			
9 overs: 2-71	38.3 overs, 157 mins	237			

1-27 (Weatherald, 2.5), 2-71 (Head, 8.5), 3-77 (McSweeney, 10.4), 4-85 (Nielsen, 12.6), 5-90 (Gibson, 13.5), 6-118 (Kerber, 19.2), 7-150 (McAndrew, 24.1), 8-159 (Worrall, 26.1), 9-203 (Richardson, 33.2), 10-237 (Agar, 38.3)

Bowling	O	M	R	W	wd	nb
KW Richardson	10	0	61	2		
DJ Worrall	10	0	61	1		
WA Agar	10	1	68	2	5	
SL Kerber	9	0	74	0		
NJ McAndrew	10	0	70	1		
NA McSweeney	1	0	9	0		

Bowling	O	M	R	W	wd	nb
JP Behrendorff	7.3	0	39	4		
ML Kelly	3	0	32	0		
MR Marsh	6	0	41	1	1	
CD Green	5	0	21	1		
AJ Tye	8	0	57	2	1	
AC Agar	9	1	47	2	1	

Toss: South Australia. Umpires: MW Graham-Smith, SJ Nogajski, Ref: SD Fry. Award: JR Philippe (WA)

Philippe 50: 61 balls, 5x4 1x6, 100: 96 balls, 8x4 5x6. Marsh 50: 71 balls, 6x4 1x6, 100: 111 balls, 12x4 2x6.
Carey 50: 41 balls, 8x4, 100: 86 balls, 11x4 1x6.   Pts: WA 5, WA 0.

Match 2 – South Australia v Queensland at Rolton Oval, Adelaide on October 13, 2021
SA won by 67 runs (DLS)

South Australia		B	M	4	6
AT Carey+	c Peirson b Wildermuth	12	17	14	2	
JB Weatherald	c Khawaja b Sandhu	97	103	139	8	3
TM Head*	c Labuschagne b Neser	230	127	184	28	8
NA McSweeney	b Wildermuth	37	27	41	3	1
RJ Gibson	c Labuschagne b Sandhu	1	6	11		
NJ McAndrew	c Sandhu b Neser	0	1	7		
HJ Nielsen	c &b Sandhu	2	2	4		
NP Winter	not out	1	2	7		
DJ Worrall	c Burns b Sandhu	0	1	1		
BJ Doggett	not out	4	2	2		
LAJ Pope					
	1 b, 6 w	7			
10 overs: 1-52	48 overs, 209 mins	8-391			

1-22 (Carey, 3.4), 2-266 (Weatherald, 35.2), 3-350 (McSweeney, 43.2), 4-364 (Gibson, 45.3), 5-383 (Head, 46.4), 6-383 (McAndrew, 46.5), 7-386 (Nielsen, 47.2), 8-387 (Worrall, 47.4)

Queensland		B	M	4	6
SD Heazlett	st Carey b Pope	93	59	71	11	4
UT Khawaja	lbw b Winter	12	8	14	2	
M Labuschagne	c Weatherald b Doggett	6	11	20		
MT Renshaw	c McSweeney b Doggett	52	53	74	4	
JA Burns	c Carey b Doggett	27	34	45	1	1
JJ Peirson+	c Worrall b Pope	8	9	14		
JD Wildermuth	c Carey b Pope	37	18	30	2	3
MG Neser	c Gibson b Doggett	55	30	37	1	5
GS Sandhu	c Gibson b Pope	10	9	9	1	
C Sully	c Carey b McAndrew	3	7	12		
MP Kuhnemann	not out	4	5	7	1	
	4 lb, 1 w	5			
10 overs: 2-76	40.3 overs, 171 mins	312			

1-33 (Khawaja, 3.4), 2-66 (Labuschagne, 8.2), 3-132 (Heazlett, 16.5), 4-193 (Renshaw, 26.5), 5-199 (Burns, 28.2), 6-206 (Peirson, 30.1), 7-270 (Wildermuth, 35.3), 8-300 (Sandhu, 37.5), 9-306 (Neser, 38.5), 10-312 (Sully, 40.3)

Bowling	O	M	R	W	wd	nb
MG Neser	10	0	85	2	1	
JD Wildermuth	9	0	62	2	2	
MT Renshaw	6	0	44	0	2	
GS Sandhu	10	0	73	4		
C Sully	5	0	51	0		
MP Kuhnemann	6	0	52	0		
M Labuschagne	2	0	23	0	1	

Bowling	O	M	R	W	wd	nb
DJ Worrall	7	0	41	0	1	
NP Winter	8	0	63	1		
BJ Doggett	9	0	75	4		
NJ McAndrew	7.3	0	51	1		
LAJ Pope	9	0	78	4		

Toss: South Australia. Umpires: SAJ Craig, DM Koch, TV: NR Johnstone (TV), Ref: SJ Davis. Award: TM Head (SA)

Weatherald 50: 71 balls, 4x4. Head 50: 35 balls, 8x4 1x6; 100: 65 balls, 15x4, 3x6; 150: 91 balls, 19x4, 6x6; 200: 114 balls, 25x4, 7x4
Heazlett 50: 52 balls, 4x4, Renshaw 50: 52 balls, 7x4, Neser 50: 25 balls, 1x4 5x6.   Pts: SA 4, Qld 0

Match 3 – Western Australia v Tasmania at the WACA, Perth on October 15, 2021 - Tasmania won by 4 wickets

Western Australia			B	M	4	6
JR Philippe+	lbw b Rainbird	0	7	9		
SM Whiteman	lbw b Meredith	3	10	16		
SE Marsh	c Jewell b Webster	15	27	39	2	
CD Green	lbw b Meredith	5	10	8	1	
AJ Turner*	c Meredith b Siddle	100	121	163	14	1
DJM Short	c Jewell b Meredith	5	7	8	1	
HWR Cartwright	c McDermott b Andrews	10	18	25	1	
ML Kelly	c McDermott b Siddle	3	9	5		
AJ Tye	c Jewell b Webster	44	31	33	5	2
JP Behrendorff	c Silk b Siddle	23	38	51		1
LCJ Guthrie	not out	2	5	10		
	4 lb, 4 w	8				
10 overs: 3-26	47.1 overs, 202 mins	218				

1-2 (Philippe, 2.1), 2-10 (Whiteman, 3.3), 3-16 (Green, 5.3),
4-53 (Marsh, 16.2), 5-58 (Short, 17.6), 6-78 (Cartwright, 24.2),
7-81 (Kelly, 25.5), 8-140 (Tye, 34.1), 9-211 (Turner, 44.3),
10-218 (Behrendorff, 47.1)

Bowling	O	M	R	W	wd	nb
SL Rainbird	10	1	43	1	1	
RP Meredith	10	1	41	3	1	
PM Siddle	8.1	1	31	3		2
BJ Webster	9	1	48	2		
TD Andrews	10	1	51	1		

Tasmania			B	M	4	6
BR McDermott+	c Short b Tye	57	63	74	10	
CP Jewell	b Behrendorff	9	12	20	1	
MB Wright	c Marsh b Kelly	0	4	2		
JC Silk*	not out	90	99	153	9	1
JR Doran	c Philippe b Tye	1	6	7		
BJ Webster	c Kelly b Tye	39	59	67	4	
MJ Owen	b Tye	2	5	5		
TD Andrews	not out	14	16	18	1	1
SL Rainbird						
PM Siddle						
RP Meredith						
	5 lb, 1nb, 3 w	9				
10 overs: 2-48	43.5 overs, 179 mins	6-221				

1-21 (Jewell, 4.6), 2-22 (Wright, 5.5), 3-100 (McDermott, 17.5),
4-106 (Doran, 19.4), 5-186 (Webster, 36.5), 6-192 (Owen, 38.2)

Bowling	O	M	R	W	wd	nb
JP Behrendorff	9	0	48	1	1	
ML Kelly	8	0	34	1	2	
CD Green	5	0	23	0		
LCJ Guthrie	3	0	19	0		
AJ Tye	10	2	39	4		1
DJM Short	8.5	0	53	0		

Toss: Western Australia.   Umpires: MW Graham-Smith, SJ Nogajski, NR Johnstone (TV), Ref: DA Johnston.   Award: JC Silk (Tas).
Turner 50: 92 balls, 7x4, 100: 120 balls, 14x4 1x6. McDermott 50: 58 balls, 9x4, Silk 50: 50 balls, 5x4 1x6. Points: Tas 4, WA 0. Crowd: 1,558

Match 4 – Western Australia v South Australia at the WACA, Perth on October 25, 2021
Western Australia won by 6 wickets (DLS)

South Australia			B	M	4	6
AT Carey+	c Philippe b Guthrie	5	7	7	1	
JB Weatherald	c Green b Kelly	60	81	119	3	2
TM Head*	c Philippe b Morris	28	19	23	5	
NA McSweeney	c Philippe b Green	0	4	4		
HJ Nielsen	b Guthrie	21	39	54		1
RJ Gibson	c Philippe b Kelly	14	20	26	1	
NJ McAndrew	not out	21	15	32	4	
DJ Worrall	not out	31	25	30	5	
WA Agar						
BJ Doggett						
LAJ Pope						
	5 lb, 8 w	13				
35 overs, 154 mins	6-193					

1-7 (Carey, 1.5), 2-47 (Head, 7.3), 3-48 (McSweeney, 8.3),
4-114 (Nielsen, 22.3), 5-138 (Weatherald, 28.1), 6-138 (Gibson, 28.2)

Bowling	O	M	R	W	wd	nb
ML Kelly	7	0	37	2	1	
LCJ Guthrie	7	0	48	2		
LRT Morris	8	0	36	1	4	
CD Green	7	0	38	1	1	
AJ Tye	6	0	29	0	2	

Western Australia			B	M	4	6
JR Philippe+	c Weatherald b Agar	26	28	39	5	
SM Whiteman	c Agar b Doggett	7	23	28		
SE Marsh	not out	80	63	82	11	1
CD Green	c McAndrew b Pope	9	15	24	1	
AJ Turner*	c Agar b Pope	0	1	1		
DJM Short	not out	35	27	43	3	1
HWR Cartwright						
ML Kelly						
AJ Tye						
LCJ Guthrie						
LRT Morris						
	1 b, 4 lb, 3 nb, 2 w	10				
25.4 overs, 112 mins	4-167					

1-30 (Whiteman, 7.1), 2-41 (Philippe, 9.4),
3-73 (Green, 15.4), 4-74 (Turner, 15.6)

Bowling	O	M	R	W	wd	nb
DJ Worrall	5	0	39	0	1	
BJ Doggett	6	1	29	1	1	
NJ McAndrew	4	1	15	0		
WA Agar	5.4	0	44	1	1	2
LAJ Pope	5	0	35	2		

Toss: South Australia.   Umpires: MW Graham-Smith, SJ Nogajski, NR Johnstone (TV), Ref: SD Fry.   Award: SE Marsh (WA).
Weatherald 50: 65 balls, 3x4 2x6. S Marsh 50: 43 balls, 8x4.   Pts: WA 4, SA 0.   Crowd: 288

Match 5 – Queensland v Tasmania at the Riverway Stadium, Townsville on November 1, 2021
Queensland won by 45 runs (DLS)

Queensland			B	M	4	6
SD Heazlett	c Jewell b Meredith	0	3	3		
UT Khawaja*	c Manenti b Siddle	3	14	18		
M Labuschagne	lbw b Manenti	27	33	58	3	
MT Renshaw	c Webster b Siddle	76	62	95	13	
J A Burns	b Manenti	10	13	18		
JJ Peirson+	c Webster b Siddle	42	27	34	3	3
JD Wildermuth	c Rogers b Meredith	7	6	41	1	
JJ Bazley	not out	9	11	15		
GS Sandhu	c & b Rogers	2	5	8		
C Sully						
MP Kuhnemann						
	1 b, 3 lb, 6 w	10				
	29 overs, 132 mins	8-186				

1-1 (Heazlett, 0.3), 2-8 (Khawaja, 3.3v), 3-62 (Labuschagne, 13.4), 4-90 (Burns, 17.4), 5-164 (Renshaw, 25.1), 6-165 (Peirson, 25.2), 7-175 (Wildermuth, 26.5), 8-186 (Sandhu, 28.6)

Tasmania			B	M	4	6
CP Jewell+	c Labuschagne b Sully	27	21	27	4	1
BR McDermott	c Renshaw b Kuhnemann	17	29	49	2	
MB Wright	lbw b Sully	5	7	8	1	
JC Silk*	c Peirson b Sully	35	43	65	2	
CA Wakim	c Peirson b Bazley	9	16	22		
BJ Webster	c Renshaw b Bazley	2	4	7		
TS Rogers	run out (Labuschagne)	2	4	7		
TD Andrews	run out (Labuschagne)	10	9	10	1	
BAD Manenti	not out	15	13	21	1	1
P M Siddle	c Renshaw b Sully	0	2	2		
RP Meredith	b Bazley	5	12	15		
	1 lb, 3 w	4				
	26.4 overs, 121 mins	131				

1-38 (Jewell, 6.2 ov), 2-44 (Wright, 8.1), 3-68 (McDermott, 11.1), 4-86 (Wakim, 16.3), 5-92 (Webster, 18.2), 6-96 (Rogers, 19.3), 7-110 (Andrews, 21.5), 8-111 (Silk, 22.1), 9-111 (Siddle, 22.3), 10-131 (Meredith, 26.4)

Bowling	O	M	R	W	wd	nb
RP Meredith	6	0	18	2	2	
P M Siddle	6	0	30	3	4	
BJ Webster	3	0	32	0		
TS Rogers	6	0	39	1		
BAD Manenti	6	0	43	2		
TD Andrews	2	0	20	0		

Bowling	O	M	R	W	wd	nb
GS Sandhu	4	0	24	0		
JD Wildermuth	6	0	34	0	2	
C Sully	6	0	39	4	1	
MP Kuhnemann	6	0	21	1		
JJ Bazley	4.4	0	12	3		

Toss: Tasmania.   Umpires: DM Koch, BNJ Oxenford, Ref: DR Gilbert.   Award: MT Renshaw (Qld).
Renshaw 50: 45 balls, 9x4   Pts: Qld 5, Tas 0   Crowd: 403

Match 6 – Victoria v New South Wales at the MCG on November 12, 2021 – Match Abandoned due to rain

Match 7 – Western Australia v Queensland at the Gabba, Brisbane on November 15, 2021
Western Australia won by 70 runs

Western Australia			B	M	4	6
JR Philippe+	c & b Kuhnemann	45	49	81	7	
NR Hobson	c Bryant b Bazley	33	50	58	4	
CT Bancroft	not out	124	105	151	12	
CD Green	c Wildermuth b Bazley	70	55	66	3	5
AJ Turner*	not out	71	41	61	6	2
DJM Short						
HWR Cartwright						
ML Kelly						
AJ Tye						
JP Behrendorff						
LCJ Guthrie						
	10 lb, 8 w	18				
10 overs: 0-52	50 overs, 210 mins	3-361				

1-74 (Hobson, 14.1), 2-102 (Philippe, 19.1), 3-217 (Green, 34.6)

Queensland			B	M	4	6
MA Bryant	c Kelly b Green	32	45	66	6	
UT Khawaja*	c Hobson b Kelly	7	10	15	1	
M Labuschagne	b Behrendorff	20	19	20	3	
MT Renshaw	st Philippe b Short	36	34	51	5	
J A Burns	c Hobson b Tye	73	74	103	7	2
JJ Peirson+	c Cartwright b Tye	62	50	74	9	
JD Wildermuth	c Green b Short	12	17	20		1
JJ Bazley	c Green b Short	8	9	11	1	
MT Steketee	c Green b Tye	0	2	5		
C Sully	c Turner b Kelly	15	19	25	1	
MP Kuhnemann	not out	15	15	21	1	
	6 lb, 1 nb, 4 w	11				
10 overs: 2-49	48.5 overs, 210 mins	291				

1-13 (Khawaja, 3.3), 2-38 (Labuschagne, 8.3), 3-87 (Bryant, 15.3), 4-113 (Renshaw, 20.1), 5-237 (Peirson, 37.3), 6-243 (Burns, 39.3), 7-254 (Bazley, 42.3), 8-260 (Wildermuth, 42.6), 9-262 (Steketee, 43.5), 10-291 (Sully, 48.5)

Bowling	O	M	R	W	wd	nb
JD Wildermuth	10	0	66	0	4	
MT Steketee	10	1	57	0	2	
JJ Bazley	10	0	73	2	1	
C Sully	7	0	57	0	1	
MP Kuhnemann	9	0	65	1		
M Labuschagne	4	0	33	0		

Bowling	O	M	R	W	wd	nb
JP Behrendorff	10	1	52	1	1	
ML Kelly	6.5	0	40	2	1	
CD Green	6	0	43	1		
LCJ Guthrie	6	0	48	0	1	
DJM Short	10	0	56	3		
AJ Tye	10	0	46	3	1	1

Toss: Western Australia. Umpires: SAJ Craig, DM Koch, BNJ Oxenford (TV), Ref: KC Wessels. Award: CT Bancroft (WA). Pts: WA 4, Qld 0.
Bancroft 50: 52 balls, 5x4, 100: 90 balls, 9x4, Green 50: 34 balls, 2x4 4x6. Burns 50: 51 balls, 6x4 1x6, Peirson 50: 43 balls, 7x4. Crowd: 391

Match 8 – New South Wales v Victoria at the SCG on November 24, 2021 - New South Wales won by 174 runs (BP)

New South Wales		B	M	4	6	Victoria		B	M	4	6
DP Hughes	c Harper b Couch	40	47	52	7	SB Harper+	lbw b Tremain	6	7	7	1
MR Gilkes	c Harper b Couch	51	49	66	6	2	MWG Harvey	c Hughes b Zampa	55	72	122	5	1
MC Henriques	c Harper b Merlo	39	41	56	5	J Fraser-McGurk	c Kerr b Sams	45	33	33	8
KR Patterson*	c Harper b Pattinson	22	30	34	3	PSP Handscomb*	c Holt b Kerr	3	8	12	
JR Edwards	c Seymour b Short	33	38	50	3	JA Merlo	c Patterson b Kerr	5	7	9	
H Kerr	lbw b Short	43	41	16	1	2	JL Seymour	b Sangha	13	20	20	1
DR Sams	b Murphy	21	13	70		2	MW Short	lbw b Sangha	0	2	1	
BJH Holt+	not out	41	21	34	3	3	JL Pattinson	b Zampa	8	12	11	1
CP Tremain	not out	27	20	24	1	1	SM Elliott	lbw b Sangha	2	6	7	
T Sangha						TR Murphy	b Sangha	12	20	17	1
A Zampa						BL Couch	not out	3	7	8	
	2 b, 16 lb, 9 w	27					2 b, 11 lb, 5 w	18			
10 overs: 0-67	50 overs, 205 mins	7-344				10 overs: 2-77	32.2 overs, 131 mins	170			

1-89 (Gilkes, 13.5), 2-104 (Hughes, 17.2), 3-166 (Patterson, 27.3), 4-168 (Henriques, 28.5), 5-237 (Edwards, 38.5), 6-267 (Sams, 42.3), 7-280 (Kerr, 44.2)

1-8 (Harper, 1.4), 2-75 (Fraser-McGurk, 9.3), 3-86 (Handscomb, 12.1), 4-100 (Merlo, 14.2), 5-128 (Seymour, 20.3), 6-128 (Short, 20.5), 7-141 (Pattinson, 23.6), 8-148 (Elliott, 26.3), 9-158 (Harvey, 29.1), 10-170 (Murphy, 32.2)

Bowling	O	M	R	W	wd	nb	Bowling	O	M	R	W	wd	nb
MW Short	8	0	38	2	1		DR Sams	4	0	32	1	1	
JL Pattinson	10	0	54	1	4		CP Tremain	3	0	22	1		
SM Elliott	7	0	55	0	2		A Zampa	8	1	44	2	1	
BL Couch	7	0	65	2			H Kerr	5	1	16	2		
TR Murphy	10	1	60	1			JR Edwards	5	0	22	0		
JA Merlo	8	0	54	1	2		T Sangha	7.2	1	21	4		

Toss: New South Wales. Umpires: GJ Davidson, BC Treloar, AK Wilds (TV), Ref: DR Gilbert. Points: NSW 5, Vic 0
Gilkes 50: 48 balls, 6x4 2x6, Harvey 50: 69 balls, 4x4 1x6

Match 9 – Tasmania v Western Australia at Bellerive Oval, Hobart on November 26, 2021 (Day/night)
Tasmania won by 5 wickets

Western Australia		B	M	4	6	Tasmania		B	M	4	6
JR Philippe+	c Wright b David	45	53	62	3	BR McDermott+	c Cartwright b Kelly	133	140	195	8	5
SM Whiteman	c McDermott b Rogers	79	65	100	7	2	CP Jewell	b Guthrie	10	9	14	2
CT Bancroft	lbw b Hope	46	48	68	3	1	CA Wakim	b Tye	42	41	54	6
CD Green	lbw b Rogers	6	10	14	1	JC Silk*	c sub (CJ Gannon) b Tye	0	4	4	
AJ Turner*	c McDermott b Siddle	16	24	46	1	MB Wright	b Guthrie	55	70	87	2	1
DJM Short	c Silk b Andrews	6	6	6	1	TH David	not out	36	23	35	5
HWR Cartwright	lbw b Siddle	50	45	66	4	1	BM Hope	not out	5	4	5	1
ML Kelly	c Silk b David	0	7	6		TD Andrews					
AJ Tye	c McDermott b Rainbird	34	36	43	3	TS Rogers					
LCJ Guthrie	not out	3	6	8		PM Siddle					
DJM Moody	not out	0	1	1		SL Rainbird					
	1 lb, 1 nb, 7 w	9					6 lb, 11 w	17			
10 overs: 0-50	50 overs, 205 mins	9-294				10 overs: 1-50	48.3 overs, 196 mins	5-298			

1-93 (Philippe, 15.1), 2-164 (Whiteman, 24.6), 3-179 (Green, 28.1), 4-189 (Bancroft, 31.2), 5-196 (Short, 32.3), 6-225 (Turner, 38.1), 7-226 (Kelly, 39.3), 8-290 (Cartwright, 48.1), 9-293 (Tye, 49.4)

1-13 (Jewell, 2.6), 2-88 (Wakim, 16.2), 3-88 (Silk, 16.3), 4-224 (Wright, 40.3), 5-283 (McDermott, 47.2)

Bowling	O	M	R	W	wd	nb	Bowling	O	M	R	W	wd	nb
SL Rainbird	10	0	64	1	1		LCJ Guthrie	10	0	46	2	1	
PM Siddle	10	1	51	2	1	1	ML Kelly	9	0	60	1	3	
TS Rogers	10	0	49	2			DJM Moody	10	0	49	0	5	
BM Hope	6	0	42	1	1		AJ Tye	9.3	1	52	2	2	
TH David	4	0	25	2			DJM Short	7	0	56	0		
TD Andrews	10	0	62	1			AJ Turner	3	0	29	0		

Toss: Tasmania. Umpires: DR Close, SJ Nogajski, BNJ Oxenford (TV), Ref: KC Wessels. Award: BR McDermott (Tas).
Whiteman 50: 42 balls, 5x4 1x6, Cartwright 50: 44 balls, 4x4 1x6, McDermott 50: 69 balls, 3x4 1x6, 100: 112 balls, 6x4 3x6,
Wright 50: 66 balls, 2x4 1x6 Pts: Tas 4, WA 0.

Match 10 – South Australia v Queensland at Adelaide Oval on November 28, 2021
Queensland won by 6 wickets

South Australia

			B	M	4	6
AT Carey+	b Labuschagne	101	93	121	14	1
HJ Hunt	c Bryant b Sandhu	61	74	107	7	
TM Head*	c Steketee b Kuhnemann	29	37	58	1	
JS Lehmann	c Peirson b Bazley	21	20	27	4	
NA McSweeney	c Labuschagne b Sandhu	26	32	36	3	
TJ Kelly	c Steketee b Sandhu	12	14	17		
NJ McAndrew	b Sandhu	1	2	8		
CJ Kelly	c Khawaja b Kuhnemann	7	3	3	1	
DJ Worrall	b Kuhnemann	0	2	1		
WA Agar	not out	0	0	6		
LAJ Pope	c Heazlett b Steketee	1	6	5		
	1 b, 5 lb, 9 w	15				
	47.1 overs, 199 mins	274				

1-159 (Hunt, 26.2), 2-180 (Carey, 29.4), 3-217 (Lehmann, 35.6), 4-232 (Head, 40.1), 5-265 (T Kelly, 44.5), 6-265 (McSweeney, 44.6), 7-273 (C Kelly, 45.4), 8-273 (Worrall, 45.6), 9-273 (McAndrew, 46.1), 10-274 (Pope, 47.1)

Queensland

			B	M	4	6
SD Heazlett	c Carey b Worrall	7	10	13		
UT Khawaja*	c C Kelly b McAndrew	16	25	45	3	
M Labuschagne	run out (Hunt)	11	29	34		
MT Renshaw	not out	156	109	126	15	5
MA Bryant	c McSweeney b McAndrew	68	67	99	3	2
JJ Peirson+	not out	6	13	23		
JD Wildermuth						
JJ Bazley						
GS Sandhu						
MT Steketee						
MP Kuhnemann						
	7 lb, 4 w	11				
	42.1 overs, 172 mins	4-275				

1-14 (Heazlett, 3.1), 2-38 (Khawaja, 10.2), 3-38 (Labuschagne, 10.4), 4-215 (Bryant, 36.6)

Bowling	O	M	R	W	wd	nb
MT Steketee	8.1	1	40	1	2	
JD Wildermuth	4	0	38	0		
GS Sandhu	9	0	44	4	1	
JJ Bazley	10	1	39	1	3	
MP Kuhnemann	9	0	54	3	1	
M Labuschagne	7	0	53	1		

10 overs: 0-46

Bowling	O	M	R	W	wd	nb
WA Agar	10	1	76	0		
DJ Worrall	7	0	37	1	3	
NJ McAndrew	7	0	54	2		
CJ Kelly	5	0	24	0		
LAJ Pope	9.1	0	47	0	1	
TM Head	4	0	30	0		

10 overs: 1-34

Toss: South Australia.   Umpires: MW Graham-Smith, DN Koch, E Sheridan (TV) Ref: SJ Davis.   Pts: Qld 4, SA 0.   Crowd: 381
Carey 50: 59 balls, 6x4, 100: 90 balls, 14x4, 1x6, Hunt 50: 63 balls, 6x4. Renshaw 50: 44 balls, 7x4, 100: 91 balls, 10x4, 150: 108 balls, 15x4 4x6
Bryant 50: 49 balls, 2x4 2x6. Sandhu took a hat-trick in the South Australia innings (Kelly, McSweeney, McAndrew)

Match 11 – Queensland v New South Wales at the Gabba, Brisbane on February 14, 2022 (Day/night)
New South Wales won by 5 wickets (DLS)

Queensland

			B	M	4	6
SD Heazlett	c Holt b Dwarshuis	10	15	17	2	
UT Khawaja*	c Edwards b Tremain	7	13	22	1	
M Labuschagne	c Larkin b Kerr	13	22	36	1	
MT Renshaw	c & b Tremain	0	4	4		
JA Burns	lbw b Edwards	18	28	45	2	
JJ Peirson+	not out	26	37	58	2	
MG Neser	c Holt b Hatcher	7	6	6		
JJ Bazley	c Davies b Tremain	8	15	18		
XC Bartlett	not out	2	7	13		
MT Steketee						
MJ Swepson						
	3 lb, 1 nb, 10 w	14				
	24.2 overs, 113 mins	7-105				

1-22 (Heazlett, 4.3), 2-22 (Khawaja, 5.1), 3-23 (Renshaw, 5.5), 4-46 (Labuschagne, 11.1), 5-70 (Burns, 15.2), 6-78 (Neser, 16.3), 7-92 (Bazley, 20.4)

New South Wales (DLS Target 101 in 24 overs)

			B	M	4	6
H Kerr	b Steketee	31	51	75	3	
LD Hearne	c Burns b Bartlett	2	11	21		
JJ Sangha*	c Burns b Bartlett	0	5	3		
JR Edwards	c Peirson b Bazley	13	15	21	1	
NCR Larkin	lbw b Swepson	0	1	4		
O Davies	not out	26	29	44	4	
BJH Holt+	not out	21	14	21	2	1
BJ Dwarshuis						
CP Tremain						
T Sangha						
LC Hatcher						
	4 lb, 4 w	8				
	21 overs, 97 mins	5-101				

1-13 (Hearne, 5.1), 2-17 (JJ Sangha, 5.6), 3-38 (Edwards, 10.2), 4-42 (Larkin, 11.1), 5-66 (Kerr, 16.3)

Bowling	O	M	R	W	wd	nb
BJ Dwarshuis	5	1	18	1	1	
CP Tremain	6	0	25	3	3	
LC Hatcher	5	0	18	1		1
H Kerr	3.2	0	18	1	1	
JR Edwards	1	0	8	1	1	
T Sangha	4	0	15	0		

Bowling	O	M	R	W	wd	nb
MT Steketee	5	1	15	1		
MG Neser	0.1	0	2	0	1	
M Labuschagne	2.5	0	12	0		
XC Bartlett	4	1	17	2	1	
MJ Swepson	5	0	31	1	1	
JJ Bazley	4	0	20	1	1	

Toss: New South Wales.   Umpires: BC Treloar, AK Wilds, Ref: KC Wessels.   Award: OHL Davies (NSW). Pts: NSW 4, Qld 0.

Match 12 –South Australia v Victoria at Rolton Oval, Adelaide on February 15, 2022 – Victoria won by 5 wickets

South Australia		R	B	M	4	6
HJ Hunt	c Merlo b Murphy	30	34	45	5	
JB Weatherald	b Couch	13	24	32	2	
AT Carey*+	c Merlo b Murphy	12	13	19		1
JS Lehmann	c Handscomb b Merlo	49	74	112	3	
NA McSweeney	c Maddinson b Sutherland	53	84	93	7	
T Kelly	c Maddinson b Merlo	12	17	19		
LAH Scott	not out	42	33	42	3	1
NJ McAndrew	b Sutherland	25	19	20	3	
DMK Grant	not out	2	2	13		
LAJ Pope						
BJ Doggett						
	5 lb, 16 w	21				
10 overs : 1-62	50 overs, 201 mins	7-259				

1-52 (Weatherald, 7.6), 2-64 (Hunt, 10.5), 3-69 (Carey, 12.2),
4-169 (McSweeney, 36.6), 5-180 (Lehmann, 39.5), 6-189 (Kelly, 41.6),
7-228 (McAndrew, 46.6)

Victoria		R	B	M	4	6
J Fraser-McGurk	c Carey b Grant	36	29	45	5	1
MWG Harvey	b McSweeney	61	71	96	7	
MS Harris	not out	102	105	132	6	3
PSP Handscomb*+	c Carey b Pope	45	29	38	7	
NJ Maddinson	lbw b Pope	0	1	2		
JA Merlo	st Carey b Pope	9	30	30		
MW Short	not out	1	9	8		
WJ Sutherland						
BL Couch						
HTRJ Y Thornton						
TR Murphy						
	3 lb, 5 w	8				
10 overs : 0-65	45.4 overs, 178 mins	5-262				

1-69 (Fraser-McGurk, 10.4), 2-132 (Harvey, 24.6),
3-207 (Handscomb, 33.5), 4-207 (Maddinson, 33.6), 5-249 (Merlo, 43.1)

Bowling	O	M	R	W	wd	nb
WJ Sutherland	10	0	62	2	6	
H Thornton	10	1	54	0		
BL Couch	10	0	46	1		4
TR Murphy	10	0	42	2		
MW Short	4	0	27	0		
JA Merlo	6	0	23	2	2	

Bowling	O	M	R	W	wd	nb
LAH Scott	4	0	17	0		1
BJ Doggett	8	0	64	0		
DMK Grant	6	0	33	1		
NJ McAndrew	8	2	62	0	2	
NA McSweeney	10	0	32	1		
LAJ Pope	9.4	1	51	3		

Toss: South Australia. Umpires: GJ Davidson, D Taylor, Ref: SD Fry.
Award: MS Harris (Vic). Pts: Vic 4, SA 0
McSweeney 50: 78 balls, 7x4. Harvey 50: 58 balls, 2x4 2x6, Harris 50: 66 balls, 100: 105 balls, 6x4 3x6

Match 13 – Victoria v Queensland at Junction Oval, Melbourne on February 23, 2022
Queensland won by 92 runs (BP)

Queensland		R	B	M	4	6
MA Bryant	c Harper b Sutherland	0	4	4		
SD Heazlett	run out (Couch-Maxwell)	15	28	39	1	
MT Renshaw	c Harper b Thornton	57	76	104	3	1
JA Burns	c Sutherland b Maxwell	22	38	47	2	
SJ Truloff	b Thornton	80	85	106	7	1
JJ Peirson*+	b Thornton	56	47	67	3	3
JJ Bazley	not out	28	15	28	1	2
XC Bartlett	not out	10	7	9	1	
GS Sandhu						
MP Kuhnemann						
W Prestwidge						
	4 lb, 13 w	17				
10 overs : 2-45	50 overs, 206 mins	6-285				

1-4 (Bryant, 0.6), 2-38 (Heazlett, 9.4), 3-95 (Burns, 22.2),
4-126 (Renshaw, 27.6), 5-228 (Peirson, 43.6), 6-262 (Truloff, 47.2)

Victoria		R	B	M	4	6
MWG Harvey	b Renshaw	32	38	49	5	
J Fraser-McGurk	c Bryant b Bazley	35	26	36	4	2
NJ Maddinson	run out (Truloff)	52	64	86	5	1
PSP Handscomb*	lbw b Kuhnemann	6	16	19		
GJ Maxwell	b Sandhu	2	10	13		
JA Merlo	c Peirson b Sandhu	0	2	2		
SB Harper+	c Bryant b Bartlett	25	27	38	3	
WJ Sutherland	c Renshaw b Sandhu	16	16	35	2	
TR Murphy	b Bartlett	0	2	3		
HTRJ Y Thornton	c Bazley b Sandhu	18	23	23	1	1
BL Couch	not out	0	6	6		
	2 lb, 4 w	7				
10 overs : 1-64	38.1 overs, 159 mins	193				

1-58 (Fraser-McGurk, 8.4), 2-71 (Harvey, 11.4),
3-91 (Handscomb, 17.1), 4-102 (Maxwell, 20.4), 5-102 (Merlo, 20.6),
6-157 (Maddinson, 30.2), 7-157 (Harper, 30.3), 8-157 (Murphy, 30.5),
9-189 (Thornton, 36.4), 10-193 (Sutherland, 38.1)

Bowling	O	M	R	W	wd	nb
WJ Sutherland	10	0	63	1	5	
H Thornton	10	1	45	3	2	
GJ Maxwell	2	0	18	1	1	
TR Murphy	10	0	41	0	2	
BL Couch	8	0	55	0		
JA Merlo	10	0	59	0	1	

Bowling	O	M	R	W	wd	nb
GS Sandhu	9.1	0	42	4		
XC Bartlett	6	0	44	2	2	1
W Prestwidge	5	0	29	0		
JJ Bazley	6	0	31	1	1	
MT Renshaw	3	0	7	1		
MP Kuhnemann	9	1	38	1		

Toss: Victoria. Umpires: PJ Gillespie, SA Lightbody, Ref: RW Stratford.
Award: SJ Truloff (Qld).
Renshaw 50: 69 balls, 2x4 1x6, Truloff 50: 63 balls, 5x4, Peirson 50: 45 balls, 3x4 2x6. Maddinson 50: 61 balls, 5x4 1x6. Pts: Qld 5, Vic 0

Match 14 – New South Wales v Tasmania at North Sydney Oval on February 23, 2022 – Match Abandoned due to rain

Match 15 – New South Wales v Tasmania at North Sydney Oval on February 25, 2022 – Match Abandoned due to rain

Match 16 – Tasmania v Victoria at the Bellerive Oval, Hobart on March 6, 2022 – Tasmania won by 139 runs (BP)

Tasmania		B	M	4	6
J R Doran+	c Harvey b Thornton	12	21	18	
CP Jewell	c Handscomb b McClure	4	12	21	1
MB Wright	c Handscomb b Couch	49	76	84	5
JC Silk*	c Harvey b Couch	82	100	164	8
MS Wade	c Couch b Merlo	86	55	65	11	1
BJ Webster	b Thornton	26	22	28	2
TS Rogers	not out	15	10	16	1	1
NT Ellis	not out	9	4	4		1
TD Andrews					
PM Siddle					
JM Bird					
	3 lb, 9 w	12			
10 overs: 2-31	50 overs, 199 mins	6-295			

1-17 (Doran, 4.6), 2-17 (Jewell, 5.3), 3-119 (Wright, 28.4), 4-230 (Wade, 42.4), 5-263 (Silk, 46.3), 6-284 (Webster, 49.1)

Victoria		B	M	4	6
J Fraser-McGurk	c Silk b Siddle	19	22	31	3
MWG Harvey	c Doran b Siddle	3	9	18	
AJ Finch	c Doran b Siddle	0	1	1	
PSP Handscomb*+	c Jewell b Ellis	27	33	48	3
GJ Maxwell	c Rogers b Siddle	44	66	97	3	1
NJ Maddinson	c & b Andrews	9	20	31	1
JA Merlo	c Doran b Ellis	7	18	21	
TR Murphy	c Doran b Andrews	5	12	18	
HTRJY Thornton	not out	25	36	43	2	1
BL Couch	lbw b Webster	6	18	21	1
CL McClure	st Doran b Andrews	2	9	7	
	2 lb, 7 w	9			
10 overs: 3-48	40.4 overs, 168 mins	156			

1-17 (Harvey, 4.1), 2-17 (Finch, 4.2), 3-30 (Fraser-McGurk, 6.3), 4-65 (Handscomb, 15.4), 5-93 (Maddinson, 22.4), 6-113 (Merlo, 27.5), 7-115 (Maxwell, 28.3), 8-119 (Murphy, 31.3), 9-141 (Couch, 37.5), 10-156 (McClure, 40.4)

Bowling	O	M	R	W	wd	nb
H Thornton	10	2	55	2	1	
CL McClure	10	1	55	1	2	
BL Couch	10	0	63	2		3
NJ Maddinson	9	0	42	0	1	
TR Murphy	6	0	40	0		
JA Merlo	5	0	37	1	2	

Bowling	O	M	R	W	wd	nb
TS Rogers	6	0	26	0		
JM Bird	8	0	34	0		1
PM Siddle	10	2	22	4	1	
NT Ellis	7	1	19	2	2	
TD Andrews	7.4	1	34	3		1
BJ Webster	2	0	19	1		2

Toss: Victoria. Umpires: DM Koch, SJ Nogajski, Ref: DA Johnston. Award: MS Wade (Tas). Pts: Tas 5, Vic 0.
Silk 50: 65 balls, 4x4, Wade 50: 37 balls, 7x4 1x6

Match 17 – New South Wales v South Australia at North Sydney Oval on March 8, 2022
Match Abandoned due to rain

Match 18 – Victoria v Western Australia at Junction Oval, Melbourne on March 8, 2022
Western Australia won by 6 wickets (BP)

Victoria		B	M	4	6
MWG Harvey	c Turner b Behrendorff	4	16	30	
J Fraser-McGurk	c Richardson b Behrendorff	10	11	16	2
AJ Finch	c Bancroft b Hardie	67	100	153	7
PSP Handscomb*+	c Marsh b Kelly	12	26	32	
GJ Maxwell	c Bancroft b Hardie	2	5	5	
NJ Maddinson	run out (Kelly)	4	14	19	
F O'Neill	c Philippe b Richardson	7	17	18	
JL Pattinson	b Richardson	1	11	11	
HTRJY Thornton	c Philippe b Short	16	34	39	3
TR Murphy	not out	0	3	11	
CL McClure	c Philippe b Hardie	0	2	1	
	8 lb, 1 nb, 11 w	20			
10 overs: 2-31	39.4 overs, 172 mins	143			

1-13 (Fraser-McGurk, 3.4), 2-27 (Harvey, 7.1), 3-51 (Handscomb, 14.4), 4-55 (Maxwell, 15.5), 5-66 (Maddinson, 19.5), 6-82 (O'Neill, 24.2), 7-86 (Pattinson, 26.6), 8-126 (Thornton, 36.6), 9-143 (Finch, 39.2), 10-143 (McClure, 39.4)

Western Australia		B	M	4	6
JR Philippe+	c Maxwell b Pattinson	8	9	11	2
DJM Short	b McClure	54	49	67	9
SE Marsh	c Harvey b McClure	31	51	63	5
CT Bancroft	not out	10	19	49	1
AJ Turner*	b McClure	9	25	28	2
HWR Cartwright	not out	22	11	12	5
AM Hardie					
JA Richardson					
AJ Tye					
ML Kelly					
JP Behrendorff					
	3 lb, 1 nb, 7 w	11			
10 overs: 1-57	27.1 overs, 117 mins	4-145			

1-22 (Philippe, 2.3), 2-96 (Short, 16.6), 3-97 (Marsh, 18.2), 4-117 (Turner, 24.3)

Bowling	O	M	R	W	wd	nb
JA Richardson	8	1	12	2	1	
JP Behrendorff	8	1	27	2	1	
ML Kelly	6	2	20	1	1	
AM Hardie	7.4	1	28	3	2	
AJ Tye	7	0	32	0	1	1
DJM Short	3	1	16	1	1	

Bowling	O	M	R	W	wd	nb
JL Pattinson	8	1	37	1	2	1
H Thornton	6	0	40	0		
CL McClure	8	0	38	3	3	
F O'Neill	5	0	23	0	1	
NJ Maddinson	0.1	0	4	0		

Toss: Western Australia. Umpires: SAJ Craig, PJ Gillespie, DR Close (TV) Ref: RL Parry. Award: DJM Short (WA). Pts: WA 5, Vic 0.
Finch 50: 85 balls, 5x4. Short 50: 40 balls, 9x4

THE FINAL - MELBOURNE

On a cool day at the Junction Oval, Western Australia stole victory from the jaws of defeat to clinch their 15th domestic one-day title. With 22 wanted off the last six overs with three wickets in hand, Henriques hit Short hard to deep long-on, where Cartwright ran ten metres and dived full-length to his left to bring off a sensational catch. New South Wales lost their last three wickets for three from 15 balls to miss out on going back-to-back, having beaten WA in last season's final.

With a 10.30am start, WA won the toss and batted and were in early trouble as both Philippe and Short edged behind in Sam's opening two overs. Shaun Marsh and Bancroft rescued things with a stand of 61 from 90 balls, before Zampa bowled both Marsh and Turner in consecutive balls. Shortly after Zampa caught and bowled Cartwright and when Bancroft was adjudged leg before to Sandhu, WA found themselves 6-89 in the 23rd over.

Hardie and Jhye Richardson played intelligently to add 59 from 90 balls, before Hardie was caught behind, but when Tye and Richardson (who made his career best) went in quick succession, WA were 9-173 with still more than seven overs to bat. WA's long batting line-up proved to be needed and thanks to Kelly (dropped on 2 by Gilkes off Kerr) and Behrendorff the pair added 52 for the last wicket from 44 balls, with 19 coming from the final over with Behrendorff crunching two sixes from Kerr.

New South Wales' target was a modest 4.52 per over but they were well under pressure early from Richardson, who beat Hughes three times outside off in his opening over. The quick bowled an impressive spell of 0-8 off five overs, keeping NSW to 22 from the first nine overs. But NSW broke away in the next two overs and at 42 without loss after 11 overs, they looked well on their way to the title.

Hardie then came on with immediate effect, having Gilkes caught behind from his first ball, while in his next over Hughes hit him a return catch. The third wicket added 38 but then Tye came on and had an impact in his first over as Patterson was caught driving to point and next ball Edwards chipped a catch to mid-wicket. Tye grabbed a third when Kerr was bowled driving at a big inswinger and in the next over Richardson returned to bowl Holt who failed to offer a shot. This left NSW 6-108 needing 118 from 23 overs.

Richardson returned to the crease, but in the second over his spell pulled up lame with a leg injury and had to leave the field. Watching this all unfold was the experienced Henriques, who was playing calmly. He found a great ally in Sams, who played aggressively to take the pressure off the veteran as their partnership got going. Sams started to find the rope and one of the shots of the day was when he whacked Behrendorff over long-on for six.

When the partnership reached 60 and the chase was seemingly under control, Sams flicked Hardie off his pads straight down the throat off long-leg. Dwarshuis entered the fray and found the rope with some fine off-drives and once again NSW looked set to win, until Cartwright's brilliant catch to dismiss Henriques. Tye finished the game off having Zampa caught behind and Sangha caught at point mistiming a pull to give WA a narrow win in a classic low-scoring final.

The Final – Western Australia v New South Wales at Junction Oval, Melbourne on March 11, 2022
Western Australia won by 18 runs

Western Australia			B	M	4	6	New South Wales			B	M	4	6
J R Philippe+	c Holt b Sams	4	6	4	1		DP Hughes	c & b Hardie	20	44	55	3	
DJ M Short	c Holt b Sams	3	4	10			MR Gilkes	c Philippe b Hardie	20	26	46	3	
SE Marsh	b Zampa	29	47	68	5		MC Henriques	c Cartwright b Short	43	75	152	4	
CT Bancroft	lbw b Sangha	39	57	81	4		KR Patterson*	c Short b Tye	23	30	36	4	
AJ Turner*	b Zampa	0	1	1			J R Edwards	c Turner b Tye	0	1	1	
HWR Cartwright	c & b Zampa	6	9	9	1		H Kerr	b Tye	16	19	18	2	
AM Hardie	c Holt b Kerr	27	47	60			BJH Holt+	b Richardson	0	2	4	
J A Richardson	c Gilkes b Sams	44	64	77	2		DR Sams	c Kelly b Hardie	42	41	52	5	1
AJ Tye	b Kerr	8	13	11	1		BJ Dwarshuis	not out	31	33	40	4	
M L Kelly	not out	27	30	43	3		A Zampa	c Philippe b Tye	0	6	7	
J P Behrendorff	not out	24	22	31	1	2	T Sangha	c sub (SM Whiteman) b Kelly	0	3	4	
	4 b, 5 lb, 5 w	14						7 lb, 1 nb, 4 w	12				
10 overs: 2-49	50 overs, 202 mins 9-225						10 overs: 0-36	46.3 overs, 212 mins	207				

1-4 (Philippe, 0.6), 2-15 (Short, 2.2), 3-76 (Marsh, 17.2), 4-76 (Turner, 17.3), 5-87 (Cartwright, 19.6), 6-89 (Bancroft, 22.1), 7-148 (Hardie, 37.1), 8-161 (Tye, 39.6), 9-173 (Richardson, 42.4)

1-42 (Gilkes, 11.1), 2-47 (Hughes, 13.1), 3-85 (Patterson, 21.2), 4-85 (Edwards, 21.3), 5-107 (Kerr, 25.6), 6-108 (Holt, 26.4), 7-168 (Sams, 37.3), 8-204 (Henriques, 44.1), 9-206 (Zampa, 45.5), 10-207 (Sangha, 46.3)

Bowling	O	M	R	W	wd	nb
DR Sams	10	0	45	3	1	
BJ Dwarshuis	7	0	30	0		
H Kerr	10	0	52	2		
J R Edwards	3	0	12	0	1	
A Zampa	10	1	40	3		
T Sangha	10	0	37	1	3	

Bowling	O	M	R	W	wd	nb
J A Richardson	6.4	1	13	1	1	1
J P Behrendorff	10	0	52	0	1	
M L Kelly	7.3	0	33	1		
AM Hardie	8	0	41	3		
AJ Tye	8	0	30	4	2	
DJ M Short	6.2	0	31	1		

Toss: WA. Umpires: PJ Gillespie, MW Graham-Smith, SAJ Craig (TV), Ref: RW Stratford. Award: AJ Tye (WA). Series: MT Renshaw (Qld)

2021-22 AVERAGES
New South Wales

Batting & Fielding	M	Inn	NO	Runs	HS	Avge	S/Rate	100s	50s	6s	Ct	St
BJ Holt	3	3	2	62	41*	62.00	167.56	0	0	4	6	0
MC Henriques	2	2	0	82	43	41.00	70.68	0	0	0	0	-
MR Gilkes	2	2	0	71	51	35.50	94.66	0	1	2	1	-
DR Sams	2	2	0	63	42	31.50	116.66	0	0	3	0	-
H Kerr	3	3	0	90	43	30.00	81.08	0	0	2	1	-
DP Hughes	2	2	0	60	40	30.00	65.93	0	0	0	1	-
KR Patterson	2	2	0	45	23	22.50	75.00	0	0	0	1	-
JR Edwards	3	3	0	46	33	15.33	85.18	0	0	0	1	-
LD Hearne	1	1	0	2	2	2.00	18.18	0	0	0	0	-
NCR Larkin	1	1	0	0	0	0.00	0.00	0	0	0	1	-
JJ Sangha	1	1	0	0	0	0.00	0.00	0	0	0	0	-
T Sangha	3	1	0	0	0	0.00	0.00	0	0	0	0	-
A Zampa	2	1	0	0	0	0.00	0.00	0	0	0	1	-
BJ Dwarshuis	2	1	1	31	31*	-	93.93	0	0	0	0	-
CP Tremain	2	1	1	27	27*	-	135.00	0	0	1	1	-
OHL Davies	1	1	1	26	26*	-	89.65	0	0	0	1	-

Played but did not bat: LC Hatcher (1 match).

Bowling	M	Overs	Mdns	Runs	Wkts	Avge	Econ	Best	4w	SR
T Sangha	3	21.2	1	73	5	14.60	3.42	4-21	1	25.6
A Zampa	2	18	2	84	5	16.80	4.66	3-40	-	21.6
H Kerr	3	18.2	1	86	5	17.20	4.69	2-16	-	22.0
CP Tremain	2	9	0	47	4	11.75	5.22	3-25	-	13.5
DR Sams	2	14	0	77	4	19.25	5.50	3-45	-	21.0
LC Hatcher	1	5	0	18	1	18.00	3.60	1-18	-	30.0
BJ Dwarshuis	2	12	1	48	1	48.00	4.00	1-18	-	72.0
JR Edwards	3	9	0	42	1	42.00	4.66	1-8	-	54.0

Queensland

Batting & Fielding	M	Inn	NO	Runs	HS	Avge	S/Rate	100s	50s	6s	Ct	St
SJ Truloff	1	1	0	80	80	80.00	94.11	0	1	1	0	-
MT Renshaw	6	6	1	377	156*	75.40	111.53	1	3	6	4	-
JJ Peirson	6	6	2	200	62	50.00	109.28	0	2	6	6	0
M Bryant	3	3	0	100	68	33.33	86.20	0	1	2	0	-
MG Neser	2	2	0	62	55	31.00	172.22	0	1	5	0	-
JA Burns	5	5	0	150	73	30.00	80.21	0	1	3	3	-
JJ Bazley	5	4	2	53	28*	26.50	106.00	0	0	2	1	-
SD Heazlett	5	5	0	125	93	25.00	108.69	0	1	5	1	-
JD Wildermuth	4	3	0	56	37	18.66	136.58	0	0	4	1	-
M Labuschagne	5	5	0	77	27	15.40	67.54	0	0	0	4	-
UT Khawaja	5	5	0	45	16	9.00	64.28	0	0	0	2	-
C Sully	3	2	0	18	15	9.00	69.23	0	0	0	0	-
GS Sandhu	4	2	0	12	10	6.00	85.71	0	0	1	2	-
MT Steketee	3	1	0	0	0	0.00	0.00	0	0	0	2	-
MP Kuhnemann	5	2	2	19	15*	-	95.00	0	0	0	1	-
XC Bartlett	2	2	2	12	10*	-	85.71	0	0	0	0	-

Played but did not bat: W Prestwidge (1 match), MJ Swepson (1 match).

Bowling	M	Overs	Mdns	Runs	Wkts	Avge	Econ	Best	4w	SR
GS Sandhu	4	32.1	0	183	12	15.25	5.68	4-42	3	16.0
JJ Bazley	5	34.4	1	175	8	21.87	5.04	3-12	-	26.0
MP Kuhnemann	5	39	1	230	6	38.33	5.89	3-54	-	39.0
XC Bartlett	2	10	1	61	4	15.25	6.10	2-17	-	15.0
C Sully	3	18	0	147	4	36.75	8.16	4-39	1	27.0
MT Steketee	3	23.1	3	112	2	56.00	4.83	1-15	-	69.5
JD Wildermuth	4	29	0	200	2	100.00	6.89	2-62	-	87.0
MG Neser	2	10.1	0	87	2	43.50	8.55	2-85	-	30.5
MT Renshaw	6	9	0	51	1	51.00	5.66	1-7	-	54.0
M Labuschagne	5	15.5	0	121	1	121.00	7.64	1-53	-	95.0

Also bowled: W Prestwidge (1 match) 5-0-29-0, MJ Swepson (1 match) 5-0-31-1

South Australia

Batting & Fielding	M	Inn	NO	Runs	HS	Avge	S/Rate	100s	50s	6s	Ct	St
TM Head	4	4	0	306	230	76.50	153.76	1	0	8	1	-
AT Carey	5	5	1	258	128*	64.50	109.32	2	0	3	6	2
JB Weatherald	4	4	0	184	97	46.00	84.79	0	2	6	2	-
HJ Hunt	2	2	0	91	61	45.50	84.25	0	1	0	0	-
JS Lehmann	2	2	0	70	49	35.00	74.46	0	0	0	0	-
NA McSweeney	5	5	0	117	53	23.40	77.48	0	1	1	3	-
WA Agar	3	2	1	18	18	18.00	120.00	0	0	1	2	-
KW Richardson	1	1	0	18	18	18.00	69.23	0	0	0	0	-
NJ McAndrew	5	5	1	65	25	16.25	120.37	0	0	1	1	-
TJ Kelly	2	2	0	24	12	12.00	77.41	0	0	0	0	-
SL Kerber	1	1	0	12	12	12.00	63.15	0	0	0	1	-
DJ Worrall	4	4	1	32	31*	10.66	91.42	0	0	0	2	-
HJ Nielsen	3	3	0	28	21	9.33	56.00	0	0	1	0	-
CJ Kelly	1	1	0	7	7	7.00	233.33	0	0	1	1	-
RJ Gibson	3	3	0	15	14	5.00	51.72	0	0	0	2	-
LAJ Pope	4	1	0	1	1	1.00	16.66	0	0	0	0	-
LAH Scott	1	1	1	42	42*	-	127.27	0	0	1	0	-
BJ Doggett	3	1	1	4	4*	-	200.00	0	0	0	0	-
DMK Grant	1	1	1	2	2*	-	100.00	0	0	0	0	-
NP Winter	1	1	1	1	1*	-	50.00	0	0	0	0	-

Bowling	M	Overs	Mdns	Runs	Wkts	Avge	Econ	Best	4w	SR
LAJ Pope	4	32.5	1	211	9	23.44	6.42	4-78	1	21.8
BJ Doggett	3	23	1	168	5	33.60	7.30	4-75	1	27.6
NJ McAndrew	5	36.3	3	252	4	63.00	6.90	2-54	-	54.7
WA Agar	3	25.4	2	188	3	62.66	7.32	2-68	-	51.3
DJ Worrall	4	29	0	178	2	89.00	6.13	1-37	-	87.0
NA McSweeney	5	11	0	41	1	41.00	3.72	1-32	-	66.0

Also bowled in one match: DMK Grant 6-1-33-1, TM Head 4-0-30-0, CJ Kelly 5-0-24-0, SL Kerber 9-0-74-0, KW Richardson 10-0-61-2, LAH Scott 4-0-17-0, NP Winter 8-0-63-1

Tasmania

Batting & Fielding	M	Inn	NO	Runs	HS	Avge	S/Rate	100s	50s	6s	Ct	St
MS Wade	1	1	0	86	86	86.00	156.36	0	1	3	0	-
BR McDermott	3	3	0	207	133	69.00	89.22	1	1	5	5	0
JC Silk	4	4	1	207	90*	69.00	84.14	0	2	1	4	-
MB Wright	4	4	0	109	55	27.25	69.42	0	1	1	1	-
CA Wakim	2	2	0	51	42	25.50	89.47	0	0	0	0	-
TD Andrews	4	2	1	24	14*	24.00	96.00	0	0	1	1	-
BJ Webster	3	3	0	67	39	22.33	78.82	0	0	0	2	-
TS Rogers	3	2	1	17	15*	17.00	121.42	0	0	1	3	-
CP Jewell	4	4	0	50	27	12.50	92.59	0	0	1	5	-
JR Doran	2	2	0	13	12	6.50	48.14	0	0	0	4	1
RP Meredith	2	1	0	5	5	5.00	41.66	0	0	0	1	-
MJ Owen	1	1	0	2	2	2.00	40.00	0	0	0	0	-
PM Siddle	4	1	0	0	0	0.00	0.00	0	0	0	0	-
TH David	1	1	1	36	36*	-	156.52	0	0	0	0	-
BAD Manenti	1	1	1	15	15*	-	115.38	0	0	1	1	-
NT Ellis	1	1	1	9	9*	-	225.00	0	0	1	0	-
BM Hope	1	1	1	5	5*	-	125.00	0	0	0	0	-

Played but did not bat: JM Bird (1 match), SL Rainbird (2 matches)

Bowling	M	Overs	Mdns	Runs	Wkts	Ave	Econ	Best	4w	SR
PM Siddle	4	34.1	4	134	12	11.16	3.92	4-22	17.0	1
RP Meredith	2	16	0	59	5	11.80	3.68	3-41	19.2	-
TD Andrews	4	29.4	2	167	5	33.40	5.62	3-34	35.6	-
TS Rogers	3	22	0	114	3	38.00	5.18	2-49	44.0	-
BJ Webster	3	14	1	99	3	33.00	7.07	2-48	28.0	-
SL Rainbird	2	20	1	107	2	53.50	5.35	1-43	60.0	-

Also bowled in one match: JM Bird 8-0-34-0, TH David 4-0-25-2, NT Ellis 7-1-19-2, BM Hope 6-0-42-1, BAD Manenti 6-0-43-2.

Victoria

Batting & Fielding	M	Inn	NO	Runs	HS	Avge	S/Rate	100s	50s	6s	Ct	St
MS Harris	1	1	1	102	102*	-	97.14	1	0	3	0	-
AJ Finch	2	2	0	67	67	33.50	66.33	0	1	0	0	-
MWG Harvey	5	5	0	155	61	31.00	75.24	0	2	1	3	1
HTRJY Thornton	4	3	1	59	25*	29.50	63.44	0	0	2	0	-
J Fraser-McGurk	5	5	0	145	45	29.00	119.83	0	0	3	0	-
PSP Handscomb	5	5	0	93	45	18.60	83.03	0	0	0	3	0
NJ Maddinson	4	4	0	65	52	16.25	65.65	0	1	1	2	-
GJ Maxwell	3	3	0	48	44	16.00	59.25	0	0	1	1	-
WJ Sutherland	2	1	0	16	16	16.00	100.00	0	0	0	1	-
SB Harper	2	2	0	31	25	15.50	91.17	0	0	0	6	0
JL Seymour	1	1	0	13	13	13.00	65.00	0	0	0	1	-
BL Couch	4	3	2	9	6	9.00	29.03	0	0	1	1	-
F O'Neill	1	1	0	7	7	7.00	41.17	0	0	0	0	-
TR Murphy	5	4	1	17	12	5.66	45.94	0	0	0	0	-
JA Merlo	4	4	0	21	9	5.25	36.84	0	0	0	2	-
JL Pattinson	2	2	0	9	8	4.50	39.13	0	0	1	0	-
SM Elliott	1	1	0	2	2	2.00	33.33	0	0	0	0	-
CL McClure	2	2	0	2	2	1.00	18.18	0	0	0	0	-
MW Short	2	2	1	1	1*	1.00	9.09	0	0	0	0	-

Bowling	M	Overs	Mdns	Runs	Wkts	Avge	Econ	Best	4w	SR
HTRJY Thornton	4	36	4	194	5	38.80	5.38	3-45	43.2	-
BL Couch	4	35	0	229	5	45.80	6.54	2-63	42.0	-
CL McClure	2	18	1	93	4	23.25	5.16	3-38	27.0	-
JA Merlo	4	29	0	173	4	43.25	5.96	2-23	43.5	-
TR Murphy	5	36	1	183	3	61.00	5.08	2-42	72.0	-
WJ Sutherland	2	20	0	125	3	41.66	6.25	2-62	40.0	-
JL Pattinson	2	18	1	91	2	45.50	5.05	1-37	54.0	-
MW Short	2	12	0	65	2	32.50	5.41	2-38	36.0	-

Also bowled: SM Elliott (1 match) 7-0-55-0, NJ Maddinson (4 matches) 9.1-0-46-0, GL Maxwell (2 matches) 2-0-18-1, F O'Neill (1 match) 5-0-23-0,

Western Australia

Batting & Fielding	M	Inn	NO	Runs	HS	Avge	S/Rate	100s	50s	6s	Ct	St
MR Marsh	1	1	0	111	111	111.00	89.51	1	0	3	1	-
CT Bancroft	4	4	2	219	124*	109.50	95.63	1	0	1	2	-
JP Behrendorff	5	2	1	47	24*	47.00	78.33	0	0	3	0	-
JA Richardson	2	1	0	44	44	44.00	68.75	0	0	0	1	-
AJ Turner	7	7	1	242	100	40.33	100.41	1	1	4	4	-
SE Marsh	5	5	1	156	80*	39.00	81.25	0	1	1	2	-
JR Philippe	7	7	0	265	137	37.85	98.88	1	0	9	10	1
NR Hobson	1	1	0	33	33	33.00	66.00	0	0	0	2	-
SM Whiteman	3	3	0	89	79	29.66	90.81	0	1	2	0	-
HWR Cartwright	6	4	1	88	50	29.33	106.02	0	1	1	3	-
AJ Tye	7	3	0	86	44	28.66	107.50	0	0	2	0	-
AM Hardie	2	1	0	27	27	27.00	57.44	0	0	0	1	-
CD Green	5	5	1	103	70	25.75	108.42	0	1	6	4	-
DJM Short	7	6	1	118	54	23.60	114.56	0	1	1	3	-
ML Kelly	7	3	1	30	27*	15.00	65.21	0	0	0	5	-
JP Inglis	1	1	0	3	3	3.00	50.00	0	0	0	2	-
AC Agar	1	1	1	11	11*	-	137.50	0	0	1	1	-
LCJ Guthrie	4	2	2	5	3*	-	45.45	0	0	0	0	-
DJM Moody	1	1	1	0	0*	-	0.00	0	0	0	0	-

Played in one match: LRT Morris (did not bat).

Bowling	M	Overs	Mdns	Runs	Wkts	Avge	Econ	Best	4w	SR
AJ Tye	7	58.3	3	285	15	19.00	4.87	4-30	2	23.40
JP Behrendorff	5	44.3	2	218	8	27.25	4.89	4-39	1	33.30
ML Kelly	7	47.2	2	256	8	32.00	5.40	2-37	-	35.50
AM Hardie	2	15.4	1	69	6	11.50	4.40	3-28	-	15.60
DJM Short	7	35.1	1	212	5	42.40	6.02	3-56	-	42.20
LCJ Guthrie	4	26	0	161	4	40.25	6.19	2-46	-	39.00
JA Richardson	2	14.4	2	25	3	8.33	1.70	2-12	-	29.30
CD Green	5	23	0	125	3	41.66	5.43	1-21	-	46.00

Also bowled: AC Agar (1 match) 9-1-47-2, MR Marsh (1 match) 6-0-41-1, DJM Moody (1 match) 10-0-49-0, LRT Morris 8-0-36-1, AJ Turner (7 matches) 3-0-29-0.

DOMESTIC ONE DAY FINALISTS

Season	Winner	Runner-up	Man of Series
			Not awarded until 1998-99
1969-70	New Zealand	Victoria	
1970-71	Western Australia	Queensland	
1971-72	Victoria	South Australia	
1972-73	New Zealand	Queensland	
1973-74	Western Australia	New Zealand	
1974-75	New Zealand	Western Australia	
1975-76	Queensland	Western Australia	
1976-77	Western Australia	Victoria	
1977-78	Western Australia	Tasmania	
1978-79	Tasmania	Western Australia	
1979-80	Victoria	New South Wales	
1980-81	Queensland	Western Australia	
1981-82	Queensland	New South Wales	
1982-83	Western Australia	New South Wales	
1983-84	South Australia	Western Australia	
1984-85	New South Wales	South Australia	
1985-86	Western Australia	Victoria	
1986-87	South Australia	Tasmania	
1987-88	New South Wales	South Australia	
1988-89	Queensland	Victoria	
1989-90	Western Australia	South Australia	
1990-91	Western Australia	New South Wales	
1991-92	New South Wales	Western Australia	
1992-93	New South Wales	Victoria	
1993-94	New South Wales	Western Australia	
1994-95	Victoria	South Australia	
1995-96	Queensland	Western Australia	
1996-97	Western Australia	Queensland	
1997-98	Queensland	New South Wales	
1998-99	Victoria	New South Wales	Matthew Hayden (Qld)
1999-00	Western Australia	Queensland	Matthew Hayden (Qld)
2000-01	New South Wales	Western Australia	Shaun Young (Tas) & Darren Lehmann (SA)
2001-02	New South Wales	Queensland	Darren Lehmann (SA)
2002-03	New South Wales	Western Australia	Justin Langer (WA)
2003-04	Western Australia	Queensland	Not awarded
2004-05	Tasmania	Queensland	Not awarded
2005-06	New South Wales	South Australia	Not awarded
2006-07	Queensland	Victoria	Matthew Elliott (SA)
2007-08	Tasmania	Victoria	Matthew Elliott (SA)
2008-09	Queensland	Victoria	Shane Harwood (Vic)
2009-10	Tasmania	Victoria	Brad Hodge (Vic)
2010-11	Victoria	Tasmania	Brad Hodge (Vic)
2011-12	South Australia	Tasmania	Tom Cooper (SA)
2012-13	Queensland	Victoria	Aaron Finch (Vic)
2013-14	Queensland	New South Wales	Cameron White (Vic)
2014-15	Western Australia	New South Wales	Cameron White (Vic)
2015-16	New South Wales	South Australia	Mitchell Starc (NSW)
2016-17	New South Wales	Queensland	Marnus Labuschagne (Qld)
2017-18	Western Australia	South Australia	Shaun Marsh (WA)
2018-19	Victoria	Tasmania	Ben McDermott (Tas)
2019-20	Western Australia	Queensland	Usman Khawaja (Qld)/Marnus Labuschagne (Qld)
2020-21	New South Wales	Western Australia	David Warner (NSW)/Tom Andrews (Tas)
2021-22	Western Australia	New South Wales	Matt Renshaw (Qld)

Titles won: WA 15, New South Wales 12, Queensland 10, Victoria 6, Tasmania 4, South Australia 3, New Zealand 3, CA XI 0

How teams have finished in the recent seasons

State	21/22	20/21	19/20	18/19	17/18	16/17	15/16	14/15	13/14	12/13
New South Wales	2	1	6	6	4	1	1	2	2	4
Queensland	4	3	2	4	5	2	6	3	1	1
South Australia	5	6	3	5	2	6	2	6	6	3
Tasmania	3	4	4	2	6	5	4	4	4	5
Victoria	6	5	5	1	3	3	3	5	3	2
W Australia	1	2	1	3	1	4	5	1	5	6
Cricket Aust XI			-	-	7	7	7			

OVERALL RECORDS – AUSTRALIAN DOMESTIC ONE-DAY CRICKET

Results	M	W	L	T	NR	Titles	R-up
ACT	18	3	15	0	0	0	0
Cricket Aust XI	18	2	16	0	0	0	0
New South Wales	293	160	126	4	3	12	9
New Zealand	10	7	3	0	0	3	1
Queensland	297	164	128	0	5	10	9
South Australia	288	119	164	4	1	3	8
Tasmania	272	106	157	4	5	4	5
Victoria	298	141	148	2	7	6	10
Western Australia	312	180	125	2	5	15	11

Highest Team Totals

Total	for	v..	Venue	Season
7-420	SA	CA XI	Hurstville	2016-17
4-405	Qld	WA	Gabba	2003-04
3-402	Qld	Tas	Nth Sydney	2014-15
1-398	Tas	Qld	Nth Sydney	2014-15
4-397	NSW	Tas	Bankstown	2001-02
8-391	SA	Qld	Rolton Oval	2021-22
387	WA	Qld	Hurstville	2018-19
8-386	WA	Vic	WACA	2019-20
2-379	Vic	Qld	Gabba	2012-13
5-372	Qld	Vic	Nth Sydney	2014-15
5-369	WA	SA	WACA	2020-21

Lowest Team Totals

Total	for	v..	Venue	Season
51	SA	Tas	Bellerive	2002-03
59	CA	NSW	Bankstown	2015-16
59	WA	Vic	MCG	1969-70
62	Qld	WA	WACA	1976-77
62	Tas	WA	Gabba	2014-15
65	Vic	Qld	Ballarat	2002-03
76	WA	NZ	MCG	1974-75
77	WA	Qld	WACA	1976-77
78	Vic	Qld	Gabba	1989-90
79	CA XI	Vic	Hurstville	2015-16
79	Qld	WA	MCG	1970-71

Most Runs

Most Runs	for	M	Inn	NO	Runs	HS	Ave	SR	100	50s	0s	Sixes
BJ Hodge	Vic	139	137	18	5597	144	47.03	81.0	20	25	8	64
M Klinger	Vic/SA/WA	129	128	11	5124	140*	43.79	73.8	12	30	7	57
JP Maher	Qld	112	112	10	4589	187	44.99	75.0	10	25	0	34
DS Lehmann	SA/Vic	98	96	15	4155	142*	51.30	87.5	7	31	6	30
CJ Ferguson	SA	114	111	10	4085	169	40.45	86.2	11	20	6	33
GJ Bailey	Tas	130	123	12	3892	126	35.06	83.7	5	25	3	84
MTG Elliott	Vic/SA	103	101	10	3804	146	41.80	74.2	10	22	8	34
SE Marsh	WA	91	88	6	3672	186	44.78	80.1	10	19	4	57
CL White	Vic	120	110	13	3643	165	37.56	80.5	7	22	10	103
DJ Hussey	Vic	101	96	15	3546	140*	43.78	93.9	6	25	3	87

Highest Scores

Highest Scores		Balls	4s	6s	for	v	Venue	Season
DJM Short	257	148	15	23	WA	Qld	Hurstville	2018-19
TM Head	230	127	28	8	SA	Qld	Rolton Oval	2021-22
BR Dunk	229*	157	15	13	Tas	Qld	North Sydney	2014-15
TM Head	202	120	20	12	SA	WA	Hurstville	2015-16
DA Warner	197	141	20	10	NSW	Vic	North Sydney	2013-14
AJ Finch	188*	151	11	14	Vic	Qld	Junction Oval	2019-20
JP Maher	187	129	26	3	Qld	WA	Gabba	2003-04
SE Marsh	186	148	23	6	WA	CA	North Sydney	2015-16
DLR Smith	179*	122	13	11	NSW	Vic	North Sydney	2011-12
CT Bancroft	176	155	14	8	WA	SA	Hurstville	2015-16
PA Jaques	171*	143	20	2	NSW	Qld	SCG	2009-10

Partnerships

Wkt	Record		Partnerships	for	v	Venue	Season
1	280	UT Khawaja	CD Hartley	Qld	Tas	North Sydney	2014-15
2	263*	MG Dighton	RT Ponting	Tas	NSW	North Sydney	2007-08
3	278	TM Head	CJ Ferguson	SA	WA	Hurstville	2015-16
4	205	DJ Hussey	CL White	Vic	Qld	Gabba	2005-06
4	205	PSP Handscomb	JA Merlo	Vic	SA	Junction Oval	2020-21
5	180	JP Maher	CT Perren	Qld	SA	Gabba	2003-04
6	173*	MEK Hussey	GB Hogg	WA	Vic	MCG	1999-00
7	124	GT Cunningham	CM Smart	ACT	Vic	Punt Rd, Richmond	1999-00
8	110*	L Ronchi	NJ Rimmington	WA	SA	Adelaide	2011-12
9	96	TIF Triffitt	XJ Doherty	Tas	Vic	MCG	2011-12
9	96*	SM Thompson	SD Bradstreet	NSW	Qld	North Sydney	1998-99
10	61	CD Hartley	NJ Rimmington	Qld	Tas	Gabba	2010-11

Highest Partnerships

	Wkt			for	v..	Season	Venue
280	1st	UT Khawaja	CH Hartley	Qld	Tas	2014-15	North Sydney
278	3rd	TM Head	CJ Ferguson	SA	WA	2015-16	Hurstville
277	1st	BR Dunk	TD Paine	Tas	Qld	2014-15	North Sydney
263*	2nd	MG Dighton	RT Ponting	Tas	NSW	2007-08	North Sydney
260	2nd	ML Hayden	SG Law	Qld	Tas	1993-94	Brisbane
257	3rd	MW Goodwin	MEK Hussey	WA	NSW	2000-01	Perth
253	1st	RB McCosker	J Dyson	NSW	SA	1981-82	Sydney
250	1st	ML Hayden	JP Maher	Qld	ACT	1999-00	Canberra
241	3rd	M Klinger	MR Marsh	WA	SA	2017-18	Drummoyne
240	3rd	SR Waugh	ME Waugh	NSW	Vic	1991-92	North Sydney

Quickest Innings

Fastest Fifties

	BF	Venue	Season
GJ Maxwell	19	Vic v Tas	Bellerive	2011-12
DW Hookes	21	SA v WA	Perth	1990-91
JS Lehmann	22	SA v Vic	Nth Sydney	2017-18
TLW Cooper	22	SA v Vic	Bellerive	2017-18
MA Bryant	23	Qld v SA	Hurstville	2018-19
DT Christian	23	SA v NSW	Nth Sydney	2010-11
DA Nash	24	NSW v WA	Nth Sydney	2000-11
MR Marsh	24	WA v NSW	Perth	2009-10
TLW Cooper	24	SA v Tas	Bellerive	2009-10
L Ronchi	24	WA v Tas	Bunbury	2010-11
JP Inglis	24	CA XI v SA	Hurstville	2016-17
CJ Boyce	24	Tas v Qld	Bellerive	2017-18
MS Wade	24	Vic v Qld	Townsville	2018-19

Fastest Hundreds

	BF	Venue	Season
L Ronchi	56	WA v NSW	Perth	2006-07
MP Stoinis	58	WA v Vic	WACA	2019-20
DJ Hussey	60	Vic v NSW	SCG	2007-08
AC Voges	62	WA v NSW	Nth Sydney	2004-05
AC Gilchrist	63	WA v Qld	Perth	2006-07
DJ Hussey	63	Vic v NSW	Nth Sydney	2012-13
RJ Quiney	64	Vic v SA	Adelaide	2010-11
CA Lynn	64	Qld v SA	Hurstville	2018-19
MS Wade	65	Tas v Vic	Town'ville	2018-19
TM Head	**65**	**SA v Qld**	**Rolton Oval**	**2021-22**
JB Weatherald	66	SA v CA XI	Hurstville	2016-17
TM Head	68	SA v WA	WACA	2020-21
SG Law	69	Qld v Tas	Bellerive	2003-04

Leading Wicket Takers

	for	M	Balls	Mdns	Runs	Wkts	Ave	Best	4i	SR	Econ
JR Hopes	Qld	114	5594	51	4236	155	27.33	5-29	9	36.09	4.54
SCG MacGill	NSW	62	3173	24	2773	124	22.36	5-40	11	25.59	5.24
NM Hauritz	Qld/NSW	100	4938	24	3759	120	31.33	4-39	4	41.15	4.57
XJ Doherty	Tas	106	5059	40	3865	120	32.21	4-18	5	42.16	4.58
SR Clark	NSW	84	4500	57	3153	104	30.32	4-24	5	43.27	4.20
SW Tait	SA	53	2733	21	2361	103	22.92	8-43	7	26.53	5.18
KM Harvey	WA	80	3488	33	2794	103	27.13	4-8	6	33.86	4.81
MS Kasprowicz	Qld	83	4207	51	2941	101	29.12	4-19	3	41.65	4.19
DE Bollinger	NSW	72	3816	37	3034	100	30.34	4-24	5	38.16	4.77
GS Sandhu	**NSW/Tas/Qld**	**45**	**2342**	**17**	**2040**	**94**	**21.70**	**7-56**	**8**	**24.91**	**5.23**

Best Bowling

		for	v	Season	Venue
SW Tait	8-43	SA	Tas	2003-04	Adelaide
CG Rackemann	7-34	Qld	SA	1988-89	Adelaide
JR Hazlewood	7-36	NSW	SA	2014-15	AB Field
GS Sandhu	7-56	Tas	Vic	2018-19	Junction Oval
JR Thomson	6-18	Qld	SA	1978-79	Gabba
B Laughlin	6-23	Qld	NSW	2008-09	Cairns
MA Starc	6-25	NSW	CA XI	2015-16	Bankstown
BE McNamara	6-25	NSW	Tas	1996-97	SCG
JM Holland	6-29	Vic	SA	2011-12	Adelaide
SW Tait	6-41	SA	NSW	2005-06	Adelaide

Hat- Tricks

	for	Venue	Season
AG Hurst	Vic v WA	WACA	1978-79
RM Baker	WA v ACT	WACA	1999-00
NW Bracken	NSW v Vic	MCG	2001-02
DE Bollinger	NSW v SA	Manuka	2004-05

	for	Venue	Season
KM Harvey	WA v Tas	Devenport	2004-05
NJ Rimmington	WA v Tas	Gabba	2009-10
MA Beer	Vic v SA	WACA	2016-17
GS Sandhu	Tas v Vic	Junc Oval	2018-19

Leading Wicket-keepers

	for	M	Ct	St	Total	b/Inn	Runs	Ave	100s
BJ Haddin	ACT/NSW	94	128	36	164	0.78	3010	34.60	6
GA Manou	SA	109	144	15	159	0.58	1554	22.20	0
DS Berry	SA/Vic	87	105	29	134	0.72	812	18.04	0
WA Seccombe	Qld	77	104	22	126	0.35	794	19.85	0
L Ronchi	WA	71	107	15	122	0.61	1803	29.56	4
TD Paine	Tas	74	107	14	121	0.51	2395	37.42	6
CD Hartley	Qld	90	107	14	121	0.76	2033	33.33	1
PM Nevill	NSW	66	92	10	102	0.41	1069	23.24	0

Captaincy Records – most games as Skipper

	Team	M	W	L	T	NR	%W
CL White	Vic	73	39	33	1	0	53.42
GJ Bailey	Tas	61	31	28	1	1	50.82
JP Maher	Qld	54	30	23	0	1	55.56
DS Lehmann	SA	51	25	25	1	0	49.02
DJ Marsh	Tas	49	23	24	1	1	46.94
SG Law	Qld	42	23	17	0	2	54.76
AC Voges	WA	42	19	22	1	0	45.24

Leading Fielders

	for	M	Ct
CL White	Vic	120	56
DJ Hussey	Vic	101	54
DJ Marsh	SA/Tas	115	54
GJ Bailey	Tas	130	51
JP Maher	Qld	112	50
MJ Di Venuto	Tas	103	50

Most Successful Run Chases

Team		Overs	Defeated		Venue	Season
Queensland	3-402	47.2	Tasmania	1-398	North Sydney	2014-15
South Australia	4-354	46.3	Western Australia	4-350	Hurstville Oval	2015-16
Victoria	4-352	46.4	New South Wales	350	North Sydney	2012-13
New South Wales	6-324	49.3	Victoria	9-321	North Sydney	2013-14
Queensland	5-319	49.1	New South Wales	6-317	North Sydney	2013-14
New South Wales	3-318	40.3	Victoria	7-317	North Sydney	2011-12

Most Successful Run Chases – Other Venues

Venue	Team		Overs	Versus		Season
Adelaide Oval	South Australia	4-313	48.4	Tasmania	5-310	2008-09
Allan Border Field	Queensland	6-307	48	New South Wales	5-305	2019-20
Bellerive Oval	**Tasmania**	**5-298**	**48.3**	**Western Australia**	**9-294**	**2021-22**
Gabba	Victoria	6-302	48.3	South Australia	8-299	2014-15
Junction Oval	Victoria	1-305	44.2	Queensland	6-304	2019-20
MCG	Victoria	6-301	49.2	Tasmania	7-300	2009-10
North Sydney	Victoria	4-352	46.4	New South Wales	350	2012-13
SCG	Queensland	7-277	47.2	New South Wales	6-275	2005-06
WACA	Western Australia	3-298	46.2	Queensland	5-297	2003-04

Most Successful Run Chases – By Team

Team		Overs	Versus		Venue	Season
New South Wales	6-324	49.3	Victoria	9-321	North Sydney	2013-14
Queensland	3-402	47.2	Tasmania	1-398	North Sydney	2014-15
South Australia	4-354	46.3	Western Australia	4-350	Hurstville Oval	2015-16
Tasmania	6-317	49	Queensland	6-316	Townsville	2018-19
Victoria	4-352	46.4	New South Wales	350	North Sydney	2012-13
Western Australia	3-298	46.2	Queensland	5-297	Perth	2003-04

Tied matches (8)

		Versus		Venue	Season	Notes
New South Wales	6-243	Western Australia	9-243	WACA	1986-87	
South Australia	7-222	Victoria	6-222	Adelaide Oval	1986-87	SA into Final beat Tas
Tasmania	8-228	New South Wales	228	Devonport	2002-03	
Victoria	7-235	New South Wales	8-235	MCG	2003-04	
South Australia	5-160	Tasmania	8-171	Adelaide Oval	2005-06	Tied on D/L
Tasmania	8-291	New South Wales	7-291	Bellerive	2008-09	
South Australia	285	Tasmania	4-285	Adelaide Oval	2011-12	SA won Final
Western Australia	9-242	South Australia	242	WACA	2016-17	

NEW SOUTH WALES RECORDS

Results

v..	M	W	L	NR	T
A.C.T	3	3	0	0	0
Cricket Aust XI	2	2	0	0	0
New Zealand	1	0	1	0	0
Queensland	63	34	28	1	0
South Australia	50	27	23	0	0
Tasmania	49	31	16	0	2
Victoria	61	28	30	2	1
Western Australia	63	34	28	0	1
	293	160	126	3	4

Highest team scores

Total	v	Venue	Season
4-397	Tas	Bankstown	2001-02
350	Vic	Nth Sydney	2012-13
6-348	WA	Drummoyne	2019-20

Lowest team scores

Total	v	Venue	Season
92	Qld	Gabba	1972-73
112	SA	SCG	2008-09
116	WA	SCG	1994-95

Leading Run Scorers

	M	Inn	NO	Runs	HS	Ave	SR	100	50s	Sixes
BJ Haddin	87	86	6	2724	138*	34.05	93.8	5	16	56
MC Henriques	87	79	11	2648	164*	38.94	88.2	3	12	61
MG Bevan	58	58	19	2400	135*	61.54	73.1	1	21	6
PA Jaques	65	64	5	2341	171*	39.68	88.0	5	9	32
SR Waugh	55	54	10	2269	131	51.57	84.2	5	13	25
ME Waugh	64	60	6	1984	123	36.74	80.6	3	10	20

Highest Scores

		BF	4s	6s	v	venue	Season
DA Warner	197*	141	20	10	Vic	North Sydney	2013-14
DLR Smith	179*	122	13	11	Vic	North Sydney	2011-12
PA Jaques	171*	143	20	2	Qld	SCG	2009-10
DA Warner	165*	112	19	9	Tas	Hurstville	2008-09
MC Henriques	164	135	17	4	CA XI	Hurstville	2016-17
RB McCosker	164	144	15	5	SA	SCG	1981-82

Record Partnerships

Wkt				v	Venue	Season
1	253	RB McCosker	J Dyson	SA	SCG	1981-82
2	190	R Chee Quee	MG Bevan	WA	SCG	1993-94
3	240	SR Waugh	ME Waugh	Vic	North Sydney	1991-92
4	181	SPD Smith	MC Henriques	Qld	Drummoyne	2015-16
5	171*	PA Jaques	DJ Thornely	SA	Adelaide	2005-06
6	105*	SR Waugh	MA Higgs	Qld	SCG	2001-02
6	105*	PJ Forrest	SNJ O'Keefe	WA	Hurstville	2010-11
6	105	MG Bevan	GRJ Matthews	WA	Perth	1990-91
7	116	CJ Richards	BJ Haddin	SA	North Sydney	2000-01
8	93	SNJ O'Keefe	NM Hauritz	Vic	SCG	2010-11
9	96*	SM Thompson	SD Bradstreet	Qld	North Sydney	1998-99
10	54	BE McNamara	GR Robertson	SA	Adelaide	1996-97

Leading Wicket takers

	M	Balls	Mdns	Runs	Wkts	Ave	Best	4w	SR	Econ
SCG MacGill	62	3173	24	2773	124	22.36	5-40	11	25.59	5.24
SR Clark	84	4500	57	3153	104	30.32	4-24	5	43.27	4.20
DE Bollinger	72	3816	37	3034	100	30.34	4-24	5	38.16	4.77
NW Bracken	68	3622	57	2588	87	29.75	5-38	3	41.63	4.29
SA Abbott	51	2201	13	2005	82	26.84	5-43	2	26.84	5.47
MA Starc	22	1252	14	1252	63	15.43	6-25	7	19.87	4.66
JR Hazlewood	41	2262	27	1776	61	29.11	7-36	2	37.08	4.71

Best Bowling

		v	Venue	Season
JR Hazlewood	7-36	SA	AB Field	2014-15
MA Starc	6-25	CA XI	Bankstown	2015-16
BE McNamara	6-25	Tas	Sydney	1996-97
SJ Coyte	6-60	Tas	Hobart	2011-12
AC Bird	5-26	Qld	Sydney	2008-09

Wicket keeping

	M	Total	Ct	St
BJ Haddin	85	155	119	36
PM Nevill	66	102	92	10
PA Emery	58	81	69	12
SJ Rixon	25	31	25	6
DLR Smith	21	21	19	2

Fielders

	M	Ct
ME Waugh	64	37
MC Henriques	87	33
S Lee	59	31
NJ Maddinson	56	28
SPD Smith	46	27
DJ Thornley	78	27

QUEENSLAND RECORDS

Results

v..	M	W	L	NR
A.C.T	3	3	0	0
Cricket Australia	2	2	0	0
New South Wales	63	28	34	1
New Zealand	1	0	1	0
South Australia	54	36	18	0
Tasmania	56	34	21	1
Victoria	57	32	24	1
Western Australia	60	28	30	2
	297	**164**	**128**	**5**

Highest team scores

Total	v	Venue	Season
4-405	WA	Gabba	2003-04
3-402	Tas	Nth Sydney	2014-15
5-372	Vic	Nth Sydney	2014-05

Lowest team scores

Total	v	Venue	Season
62	WA	WACA	1976-77
79	WA	MCG	1970-71
99	NSW	Gabba	2005-06

Leading Run Scorers

	M	Inn	NO	Runs	HS	Ave	SR	100	50s	Sixes
JP Maher	112	112	10	4589	187	44.99	75.0	10	25	34
CT Perren	98	90	14	2844	117	37.42	68.0	2	21	28
ML Hayden	61	61	9	2616	152*	50.31	73.7	8	15	25
SG Law	85	78	7	2534	159	35.69	93.1	6	10	17
NJ Reardon	87	85	8	2466	116	32.03	81.4	2	20	65
ML Love	82	79	11	2412	127*	35.47	76.8	4	9	13
UT Khawaja	**45**	**45**	**2**	**2366**	**166**	**55.02**	**88.4**	**6**	**14**	**32**

Highest Scores

		BF	4s	6s	v	Venue	Season
JP Maher	187	129	26	3	WA	Gabba	2003-04
UT Khawaja	166	110	18	7	Tas	North Sydney	2014-15
SG Law	159	136	18	0	Tas	Gabba	1993-94
MT Renshaw	**156***	**109**	**15**	**5**	**SA**	**Adelaide Oval**	**2021-22**
ML Hayden	152*	167	15	1	Vic	MCG	1998-99

Record Partnerships

Wkt				v	Venue	Season
1	280	UT Khawaja	CD Hartley	Tas	North Sydney	2014-15
2	260	ML Hayden	SG Law	Tas	Gabba	1993-94
3	217	UT Khawaja	M Labuschagne	NSW	Drummoyne	2017-18
4	**177**	**MT Renshaw**	**MA Bryant**	**SA**	**Adelaide Oval**	**2021-22**
5	180	JP Maher	CT Perren	SA	Gabba	2003-04
6	123*	CA Philipson	CP Simpson	Vic	MCG	2009-10
7	112	JR Hopes	BCJ Cutting	NSW	Blacktown	2014-15
8	58	MG Neser	CJ Gannon	WA	Drummoyne	2017-18
9	84*	BCJ Cutting	MG Gale	Vic	North Sydney	2013-14
10	61	CD Hartley	NJ Rimmington	Tas	Gabba	2010-11

Leading Wicket Takers

	M	Balls	Mdns	Runs	Wkts	Ave	Best	4w	SR	Econ
JR Hopes	114	5594	51	4236	155	27.33	5-29	9	36.09	4.54
MS Kasprowicz	83	4207	51	2941	101	29.12	4-19	3	41.65	4.19
AJ Bichel	78	4001	45	2941	87	33.80	4-45	1	45.99	4.41
BCJ Cutting	61	3060	28	2749	82	33.52	4-50	4	37.32	5.39
NM Hauritz	66	3140	11	2432	80	30.40	4-39	4	39.25	4.65
AA Noffke	68	3395	42	2635	73	36.10	4-32	2	46.51	4.66

Best Bowling

		v	Venue	Season
CG Rackemann	7-34	SA	Adelaide	1988-89
JR Thomson	6-18	SA	Brisbane	1978-79
B Laughlin	6-23	NSW	Cairns	2008-09
G Dymock	5-27	NSW	Sydney	1981-82
JR Hopes	5-29	SA	Adelaide	2000-01
IH King	5-33	NSW	SCG	1969-70

Wicket keeping

	M	Total	Ct	St
WA Seccombe	77	126	104	22
CD Hartley	90	121	107	14
IA Healy	29	54	47	7
JJ Peirson	**40**	**50**	**47**	**3**
JA MacLean	19	33	32	1

Fielders

	M	Ct
JP Maher	112	50
A Symonds	77	40
SG Law	85	35
CT Perren	98	34
ML Love	82	31

SOUTH AUSTRALIA RECORDS

Results

v..	M	W	L	NR	T
A.C.T	3	3	0	0	0
Cricket Aust XI	2	2	0	0	0
New South Wales	50	23	27	0	0
New Zealand	2	0	2	0	0
Queensland	53	18	36	0	0
Tasmania	53	25	25	1	2
Victoria	59	23	35	0	1
Western Australia	64	25	38	0	1
	288	119	164	1	4

Highest team scores

Total	v	Venue	Season
7-420	CA XI	Hurstville	2016-17
8-391	**Qld**	**Rolton Oval**	**2021-22**
6-356	Vic	Nth Syd	2017-18
356	WA	WACA	2020-21

Lowest team scores

Total	v	Venue	Season
51	Tas	Bellerive	2002-03
83	Qld	Gabba	2002-03
87	WA	WACA	1989-90

Leading Run Scorers

	M	Inn	NO	Runs	HS	Ave	SR	100	50s	Sixes
CJ Ferguson	114	111	10	4085	169	40.45	86.2	11	20	33
DS Lehmann	87	86	14	3963	142*	55.04	88.6	7	30	29
GS Blewett	100	98	9	3544	125	39.82	68.5	6	19	26
TLW Cooper	88	85	9	3023	139	39.78	85.6	6	21	64
M Klinger	51	51	3	2524	140*	52.58	76.5	7	16	26
MJ Cosgrove	64	64	3	1978	121	32.43	83.5	3	12	30

Highest Scores

		BF	4s	6s	v	venue	Season
TM Head	**230**	**127**	**28**	**8**	**Qld**	**Rolton Oval**	**2021-22**
TM Head	202	120	20	12	WA	Hurstville	2015-16
CJ Ferguson	169	138	23	2	WA	Drummoyne	2017-18
CJ Ferguson	154	113	17	3	CA XI	Hurstville	2016-17
MTG Elliott	146	141	14	3	WA	Perth	2007-08
DS Lehmann	142*	119	14	2	Tas	Adelaide	1994-95
TM Head	142	86	15	6	WA	WACA	2020-21

Record Partnerships

Wkt				v	Venue	Season
1	217	DS Lehmann	PC Nobes	Tas	Adelaide	1994-95
2	226	HJ Nielsen	TM Head	WA	WACA	2020-21
3	278	TM Head	CJ Ferguson	WA	Hurstville	2015-16
4	138	JB Weatherald	AI Ross	NSW	Hurstville	2017-18
5	150	M Klinger	DT Christian	NSW	Wollongong	2009-10
6	130	DS Lehmann	MC Miller	NSW	Adelaide	2003-04
7	111	GA Manou	MF Cleary	NSW	Adelaide	2003-04
8	70	CJ Borgas	AW O'Brien	WA	Perth	2010-11
9	65*	CJ Ferguson	NM Lyon	WA	Adelaide	2011-12
10	57	A Zampa	PR George	Qld	North Sydney	2013-14

Leading Wicket Takers

	M	Balls	Mdns	Runs	Wkts	Ave	Best	4wI	SR	Econ
SW Tait	53	2733	21	2361	103	22.92	8-43	7	26.53	5.18
KW Richardson	52	2856	26	2513	82	30.65	6-48	5	34.83	5.28
P Wilson	46	2540	42	1676	70	23.94	4-23	2	36.29	3.96
MF Cleary	49	2440	23	2072	67	30.93	4-55	1	36.42	5.10
JN Gillespie	52	2906	35	2001	65	30.78	4-46	2	44.71	4.13
GS Blewett	100	2394	15	2051	62	33.08	4-16	2	38.61	5.14

Best Bowling

		v	Venue	Season
SW Tait	8-43	Tas	Adelaide	2003-04
SW Tait	6-41	NSW	Adelaide	2005-06
DT Christian	6-48	Vic	Geelong	2010-11
KW Richardson	6-48	Qld	Adelaide	2012-13
KW Richardson	6-51	NSW	SCG	2012-13

Wicket keeping

	M	Ct	St	Total
GA Manou	109	144	15	159
TJ Nielsen	45	55	3	58
AT Carey	**36**	**37**	**3**	**40**
TP Ludeman	33	28	3	31
WB Phillips	13	18	0	18

Fielders

	M	Ct
TLW Cooper	88	50
GS Blewett	100	32
CJ Ferguson	114	31
DS Lehmann	87	27
BE Young	42	27
M Klinger	51	23

TASMANIA RECORDS

Results

v..	M	W	L	NR	T
A.C.T	3	2	1	0	0
Cricket Aust XI	2	1	1	0	0
New South Wales	49	16	31	0	2
New Zealand	1	0	1	0	0
Queensland	56	21	34	1	0
South Australia	53	25	25	1	2
Victoria	52	21	29	2	0
Western Australia	55	19	35	1	0
	272	106	157	5	4

Highest team scores

Total	v	Venue	Season
1-398	Qld	North Sydney	2014-15
5-340	SA	Bellerive	2004-05
7-334	CA XI	Hurstville	2017-18

Lowest team scores

Total	v	Venue	Season
62	WA	Gabba	2014-15
80	NSW	Devonport	1984-85
89	Qld	Gabba	1976-77

Leading Run Scorers

	M	Inn	NO	Runs	HS	Ave	SR	100	50s	Sixes
GJ Bailey	130	123	12	3892	126	35.06	83.7	5	25	84
MJ Di Venuto	103	101	7	2891	129*	30.76	79.3	5	12	10
DJ Marsh	104	96	18	2575	106*	33.01	76.6	4	13	32
TD Paine	80	78	9	2564	125	37.16	70.4	6	11	21
MG Dighton	73	72	1	2476	146*	34.87	78.1	3	17	32
TR Birt	72	70	8	2097	145	33.82	90.6	1	14	67

Highest Scores

		BF	4s	6s	v	Venue	Season
BR Dunk	229*	157	15	13	NSW	North Sydney	2007-08
MG Dighton	146*	138	13	7	NSW	North Sydney	2007-08
TR Birt	145	143	13	6	SA	Hobart	2004-05
BR McDermott	**133**	**140**	**8**	**5**	**WA**	**Bellerive**	**2021-22**
EJM Cowan	131*	120	9	2	NSW	SCG	2010-11
MJ Di Venuto	129*	150	10	0	SA	Hobart	1996-97

Record Partnerships

Wkt				v	Venue	Season
1	277	BR Dunk	TD Paine	Qld	North Sydney	2014-15
2	263*	MG Dighton	RT Ponting	NSW	North Sydney	2007-08
3	221	MJ Cosgrove	GJ Bailey	Vic	Bellerive	2010-11
4	174	GJ Bailey	RT Ponting	SA	Adelaide	2011-12
5	172	EJM Cowan	TR Birt	NSW	SCG	2010-11
6	129	JW Wells	EP Gulbis	Vic	AB Field	2014-15
7	114	JP Faulkner	EP Gulbis	WA	Burnie	2012-13
8	82*	XJ Doherty	AJ Doolan	Vic	North Sydney	2016-17
9	96	TIF Triffitt	XJ Doherty	Vic	MCG	2011-12
10	42	CJ Duval	BW Hilfenhaus	Qld	Bellerive	2008-09

Leading Wicket Takers

	M	Balls	Mdns	Runs	Wkts	Ave	Best	4w	SR	Econ
XJ Doherty	106	5059	40	3865	120	32.21	4-18	5	42.16	4.58
B Geeves	64	3144	34	2671	89	30.01	5-45	1	35.33	5.10
JP Faulkner	52	2526	17	2164	71	30.48	4-20	4	35.58	5.14
BG Drew	46	2139	13	1983	70	28.33	4-38	2	30.56	5.56
DG Wright	55	2939	44	1895	65	29.15	4-23	2	45.22	3.87
BW Hilfenhaus	51	2875	36	2070	58	35.69	4-24	1	49.57	4.32

Best Bowling

		v..	Venue	Season
GS Sandhu	7-56	Vic	Junction Oval	2018-19
JM Bird	6-25	NSW	Bellerive	2019-20
B Laughlin	6-53	NSW	Canberra	2011-12
JJ Krejza	6-55	NSW	Bellerive	2011-12
JP Marquet	5-23	Qld	Bellerive	1995-96
PJ Hutchison	5-27	SA	Bellerive	1996-97
SL Rainbird	5-29	Vic	AB Field	2014-15

Wicket keeping

	M	Ct	St	Total
TD Paine	74	98	12	110
MN Atkinson	35	43	7	50
SG Clingeleffer	40	39	3	42
BR McDermott	**9**	**19**	**0**	**19**
RD Woolley	17	16	1	17

Fielders

	M	Ct
GJ Bailey	130	51
MJ Di Venuto	103	50
DJ Marsh	104	50
XJ Doherty	106	33
RT Ponting	42	25

VICTORIA RECORDS

Results

v..	M	W	L	NR	T
A.C.T	3	1	2	0	0
Cricket Aust XI	2	2	0	0	0
New South Wales	61	30	28	2	1
New Zealand	2	1	1	0	0
Queensland	57	24	32	1	0
South Australia	59	35	23	0	1
Tasmania	52	29	21	2	0
Western Australia	61	18	41	2	0
	298	141	148	7	2

Highest team scores

Total	v	Venue	Season
2-379	Qld	Gabba	2012-13
4-352	NSW	Nth Sydney	2012-13
8-352	NSW	SCG	2007-08

Lowest team scores

Total	v	Venue	Season
65	Qld	Ballarat	2002-03
78	Qld	Gabba	1989-90
90	Qld	MCG	1988-89

Leading Run Scorers

	M	Inn	NO	Runs	HS	Ave	SR	100	50s	Sixes
BJ Hodge	139	137	18	5597	144	47.03	81.0	20	25	64
CL White	120	110	13	3643	165	37.56	80.5	7	22	103
DJ Hussey	101	96	15	3546	140*	43.78	93.9	6	25	87
MTG Elliott	78	76	6	2640	118*	37.71	71.5	6	17	17
AJ Finch	64	64	6	2420	188*	41.72	88.0	4	15	66
RJ Quiney	74	69	5	2361	119	36.89	90.7	2	20	48

Highest Scores

		BF	4s	6s	v	Venue	Season
AJ Finch	188*	151	11	14	Qld	Junction Oval	2019-20
CL White	165	154	16	6	Tas	Perth	2017-18
AJ Finch	154	141	14	5	Qld	Brisbane	2012-13
CL White	145	130	12	4	SA	Perth	2016-17
BJ Hodge	144	123	14	6	NSW	North Sydney	2011-12
BJ Hodge	140*	121	11	8	Qld	Brisbane	2010-11
DJ Hussey	140*	84	15	4	NSW	North Sydney	2012-13
CJL Rogers	140	116	14	3	SA	Melbourne	2009-10
AJ Finch	140	121	8	10	NSW	North Sydney	2012-13

Record Partnerships

Wkt				v	Venue	Season
1	226	RJ Quiney	AJ Finch	Qld	Gabba	2012-13
2	222	MTG Elliott	BJ Hodge	Qld	Gabba	2003-04
3	227	BJ Hodge	DJ Hussey	SA	Adelaide	2003-04
4	205	PSP Handscomb	JA Merlo	SA	Junction Oval	2020-21
4	205	DJ Hussey	CL White	Qld	Brisbane	2005-06
5	171	CL White	RJ Quiney	SA	Adelaide	2010-11
6	149	BJ Hodge	RJ Quiney	NSW	North Sydney	2011-12
7	106	CJL Rogers	JW Hastings	SA	MCG	2009-10
8	73*	AM Smith	AIC Dodemaide	Qld	MCG	1996-97
9	77	DJ Hussey	CJ McKay	Tas	AB Field	2014-15
10	40	Fawad Ahmed	AL Fekete	WA	Junction Oval	2018-19

Leading Wicket Takers

	M	Balls	Mdns	Runs	Wkts	Ave	Best	4w	SR	Econ
SM Harwood	54	2786	28	2088	88	23.73	6-46	5	31.66	4.50
ML Lewis	62	3063	42	2365	83	28.49	4-41	1	36.90	4.63
IJ Harvey	69	3007	30	2220	81	27.41	5-34	3	37.12	4.43
JW Hastings	48	2644	22	2271	78	29.12	4-30	4	33.90	5.15
AB McDonald	84	3292	20	2753	72	38.24	5-38	2	45.72	5.02
JM Holland	54	2784	13	2274	68	33.44	6-29	2	40.94	4.90

Best Bowling

		v	Venue	Season
JM Holland	6-29	SA	Adelaide	2011-12
SM Harwood	6-46	WA	Perth	2010-11
JL Pattinson	6-48	NSW	Sydney	2009-10
GD Watson	5-20	WA	MCG	1969-70
DJ Hickey	5-26	WA	MCG	1985-86
IJ Harvey	5-34	ACT	Punt Road	1999-2000

Wicket keeping

	M	Total	Ct	St
DS Berry	83	127	100	27
AJ Crosthwaite	54	78	69	9
MS Wade	49	65	56	9
PSP Handscomb	26	51	47	4

Fielders

	M	Ct
CL White	120	56
DJ Hussey	101	54
BJ Hodge	139	45
RJ Quiney	74	36

WESTERN AUSTRALIA RECORDS

Results

v..	M	W	L	NR	T
A.C.T	3	3	0	0	0
Cricket Aust XI	2	2	0	0	0
New South Wales	63	28	34	0	1
New Zealand	3	2	1	0	0
Queensland	60	30	28	2	0
South Australia	64	38	25	0	1
Tasmania	55	35	19	1	0
Victoria	61	61	18	2	0
	312	180	125	5	2

Highest team scores

Total	v	Venue	Season
387	Qld	Hurstville	2018-19
8-386	Vic	WACA	2019-20
5-369	SA	WACA	2020-21

Lowest team scores

Total	v	Venue	Season
59	Vic	MCG	1969-70
76	NZ	MCG	1974-75
77	Qld	WACA	1976-77

Leading Run Scorers

	M	Inn	NO	Runs	HS	Ave	SR	100	50s	Sixes
SE Marsh	91	88	6	3672	186	44.78	80.1	10	19	57
JL Langer	100	96	9	3374	146	38.78	70.5	7	23	32
AC Voges	91	90	17	3133	112	42.92	75.7	3	26	27
MJ North	86	82	12	2935	134*	41.93	78.9	5	20	37
MEK Hussey	84	80	10	2720	106	38.86	75.2	3	21	18
DR Martyn	58	54	7	2217	140	47.17	76.6	4	16	14

Highest Scores

		BF	4s	6s	v	Venue	Season
DJM Short	257	148	15	23	Qld	Hurstville	2018-19
SE Marsh	186	148	23	6	SA	Hurstville	2015-16
CT Bancroft	176	155	14	8	SA	Hurstville	2015-16
MW Goodwin	167	138	21	0	NSW	Perth	2000-01
SEMarsh	155*	147	12	6	Qld	Brisbane	2012-13
JL Langer	146	148	13	2	SA	Perth	1999-00

Record Partnerships

Wkt					v	Venue	Season
1	216	CT Bancroft	SE Marsh		SA	Hurstville	2015-16
2	188*	JL Langer	DR Martyn		Vic	MCG	1997-98
3	257	MW Goodwin	MEK Hussey		NSW	Perth	2000-01
4	167	SM Katich	MEK Hussey		Vic	Perth	2001-02
5	141	AC Voges	TM Beaton		Qld	Perth	2010-11
6	173*	MEK Hussey	GB Hogg		Vic	MCG	1999-00
7	111*	RW Marsh	B Yardley		NSW	SCG	1973-74
8	110*	L Ronchi	NJ Rimmington		SA	Adelaide	2011-12
9	87	MJ North	BR Dorey		NSW	Perth	2008-09
10	52*	ML Kelly	JP Behrendorff		NSW	Junction Oval	2021-22

Leading Wicket Takers

	M	Balls	Mdns	Runs	Wkts	Ave	Best	4w	SR	Econ
KM Harvey	80	3488	33	2794	103	27.13	4-8	6	33.86	4.81
J Angel	74	3686	52	2524	94	26.85	5-16	2	39.21	4.11
NM Coulter-Nile	39	2174	18	1800	82	21.95	5-26	4	26.51	4.97
AJ Tye	35	1733	8	1604	78	20.56	6-46	4	22.22	5.55
TM Moody	75	3205	42	2131	70	30.44	4-30	1	45.79	3.99
GB Hogg	77	2338	7	1953	60	32.55	4-37	2	38.97	5.01

Best Bowling

		v	Venue	Season
AJ Tye	6-46	Qld	Hurstville	2018-19
DL Boyd	5-15	Vic	Perth	1982-83
J Angel	5-16	Vic	Perth	2001-02
NM Coulter-Nile	5-26	Vic	Blacktown	2014-15
JP Behrendorff	5-27	NSW	SCG	2014-15
KH MacLeay	5-30	Tas	Perth	1984-85

Wicket keeping

	M	Total	Ct	St
L Ronchi	71	122	107	15
RJ Campbell	47	88	82	6
AC Gilchrist	42	81	74	7
RW Marsh	33	51	50	1
TJ Zoehrer	35	45	41	4

Fielders

	M	Ct
JL Langer	100	49
MEK Hussey	84	45
AC Voges	86	39
SE Marsh	91	36
MJ North	86	33

	M	Runs	HS	Avge	SR	100	50	Ct/St	Wkt	Avge	Econ	Best	4w
SA Abbott	51	477	50	14.90	94.5	0	1	25	82	24.45	5.46	5-43	3
AC Agar	31	464	64	24.42	96.3	0	1	14	32	38.00	5.19	3-8	2
WA Agar	20	72	18	10.28	77.4	0	0	6	29	36.93	6.40	5-40	2
TD Andrews	26	88	14*	5.86	62.9	0	0	11	29	40.82	5.34	4-41	1
CT Bancroft	44	1438	176	38.86	86.9	2	10	29/1	0			-	0
XC Bartlett	17	45	28	11.25	45.5	0	0	7	21	33.23	5.38	3-43	0
JJ Bazley	17	177	45	13.61	83.5	0	0	4	11	42.27	6.06	3-12	0
JP Behrendorff	42	195	35*	15.00	60.7	0	0	8	57	27.92	4.80	5-27	2
NL Bertus	5	87	69*	21.75	93.5	0	1	1	0			-	0
JM Bird	38	169	28*	14.08	102.4	0	0	16	49	33.89	4.77	6-25	1
SM Boland	42	120	19	6.66	59.1	0	0	7	46	44.82	5.64	5-63	2
MA Bryant	23	666	89	28.95	116.2	0	5	19	0			-	0
JA Burns	64	1904	115	34.61	78.8	1	12	26	1	33.00	11.00	1-20	0
JM Carder	11	367	102	33.36	89.3	1	2	0				-	0
AT Carey	38	1299	128*	36.08	86.2	2	8	40/3	0			-	0
HWR Cartwright	46	855	99	25.14	83.7	0	4	20	9	47.33	6.04	2-14	0
HNA Conway	10	30	10*	30.00	48.4	0	0	4	14	33.35	5.48	3-30	0
BL Couch	6	10	6	10.00	27.8	0	0	2	6	49.33	6.16	2-63	0
XA Crone	5	25	16*	8.33	54.3	0	0	3	7	42.85	7.50	2-60	0
PJ Cummins	20	180	49	25.71	98.4	0	0	8	34	25.52	4.99	4-26	2
TH David	1	36	36*		156.5	0	0	0	2	12.50	6.25	2-25	0
OHL Davies	5	170	57	56.66	116.4	0	1	3	0			-	0
BJ Doggett	11	26	11	8.66	49.1	0	0	3	16	38.87	6.67	4-75	1
JR Doran	19	238	34*	18.30	64.3	0	0	18/1	0			-	0
BJ Dwarshuis	9	48	31*	16.00	85.7	0	0	1	13	26.92	5.22	4-50	1
JR Edwards	17	557	116	37.13	89.1	2	2	11	1	165.00	6.11	1-8	0
SM Elliott	2	2	2	2.00	33.3	0	0	0	2	57.50	7.18	2-60	0
NT Ellis	12	103	31	20.60	82.4	0	0	0	18	22.16	4.69	5-38	1
ZK Evans	2	7	6	3.50	50.0	0	0	0	2	50.50	5.94	2-68	0
AJ Finch	64	2420	188*	41.72	88.1	4	15	21	1	37.00	5.69	1-2	0
J Fraser-McGurk	9	243	54	30.37	114.6	0	1	1	0			-	0
JA Freeman	2	4	4	4.00	200.0	0	0	0	2	30.50	4.69	2-17	0
RJ Gibson	17	453	106	26.64	83.4	1	3	4	0			-	0
MR Gilkes	12	280	82	25.45	102.2	0	2	11/1	0			-	0
SE Gotch	17	347	61	24.78	73.1	0	2	13/1	0			-	0
DMK Grant	4	2	2*		100.0	0	0	0	4	46.25	5.44	2-44	0
CD Green	18	472	144	33.71	97.3	1	2	10	7	68.28	5.71	3-44	0
LCJ Guthrie	9	27	19	13.50	77.1	0	0	3	9	36.11	5.41	2-46	0
PSP Handscomb	68	1989	131	36.83	88.0	2	10	65/4	0			-	0
AM Hardie	7	77	27	19.25	72.6	0	0	1	10	23.40	5.70	3-28	0
SB Harper	19	347	60	19.27	97.7	0	2	20/2	0			-	0
MS Harris	48	1358	102*	30.86	87.1	1	7	12	0			-	0
MWG Harvey	9	186	61	20.66	71.3	0	2	4	0			-	0
LC Hatcher	11	55	31	13.75	82.1	0	0	4	16	35.56	6.54	3-46	0
JR Hazlewood	41	50	17	4.54	52.6	0	0	8	61	29.11	4.71	7-36	2
TM Head	32	1270	230	42.33	120.0	3	3	13	6	74.00	6.25	2-9	0
LD Hearne	1	2	2	2.00	18.2	0	0	0	0			-	0
SD Heazlett	22	971	107	44.13	106.9	1	9	7	0			-	0
MC Henriques	87	2648	164*	38.94	88.2	3	12	33	59	38.72	5.20	4-17	1
NR Hobson	3	71	36	35.50	77.2	0	0	3	0			-	0
BJH Holt	3	62	41*	62.00	167.6	0	0	6	0			-	0
BM Hope	1	5	5*		125.0	0	0	0	1	42.00	7.00	1-42	0
JP Inglis	18	579	91	32.16	112.9	0	6	30/3	0			-	0
CP Jewell	16	468	104	31.20	92.5	1	2	8	0			-	0
CJ Kelly	6	81	27	13.50	75.0	0	0	1	2	107.00	6.29	1-63	0
ML Kelly	19	77	27*	12.83	77.8	0	0	11	26	27.19	5.08	4-25	1
TJ Kelly	2	24	12	12.00	77.4	0	0	0	0			-	0
SL Kerber	3	37	22	12.33	67.3	0	0	2	1	210.00	7.77	1-70	0
H Kerr	4	104	43	26.00	84.6	0	0	2	6	17.16	3.91	2-16	0
UT Khawaja	57	2863	166	52.05	86.8	9	15	23	0			-	0
MP Kuhnemann	22	87	18*	17.40	71.9	0	0	10	33	29.45	5.85	4-37	1
M Labuschagne	31	1177	135	39.23	90.3	1	10	14	2	128.50	7.17	1-53	0
NCR Larkin	10	135	36	16.87	66.5	0	0	3	0		6.50	-	0
JS Lehmann	37	933	87	30.09	77.9	0	6	12	0			-	0
NM Lyon	42	137	37*	10.53	107.9	0	0	20	49	37.77	4.80	4-10	2
NJ McAndrew	7	67	25	13.40	106.3	0	0	2	6	53.83	6.77	2-54	0
CL McClure	2	2	2	1.00	18.2	0	0	0	4	23.25	5.16	3-38	0
BR McDermott	26	1211	133	50.45	80.9	4	7	26	0			-	0

	M	Runs	HS	Avg	SR	100	50	Ct/St	Wkt	Avg	Eco	Best	4I
NA McSweeney	5	117	53	23.40	77.5	0	1	3	1	41.00	3.72	1-32	0
NJ Maddinson	77	2415	137	34.01	89.2	5	13	37	7	57.71	5.17	4-29	1
BAD Manenti	1	15	15*		115.4	0	0	1	2	21.50	7.16	2-43	0
MR Marsh	43	1425	124	43.18	94.9	3	8	23	23	33.00	5.16	4-40	1
SE Marsh	91	3672	186	44.78	80.2	10	19	35	1	31.00	5.16	1-14	0
GJ Maxwell	48	1000	80	25.64	100.4	0	7	30	28	35.75	5.17	3-30	0
RP Meredith	22	16	5	5.33	29.1	0	0	9	33	29.78	5.14	4-42	1
JA Merlo	11	179	101	19.88	77.2	1	0	4	17	29.70	5.97	5-71	1
DJM Moody	9	2	1*		40.0	0	0	3	8	47.37	6.03	3-47	0
LRT Morris	3	12	12	6.00	75.0	0	0	0	2	50.00	5.88	1-27	0
TR Murphy	7	32	12	8.00	60.4	0	0	1	5	53.00	4.73	2-42	0
MG Neser	45	660	122	27.50	88.4	1	2	14	54	33.40	5.17	4-41	2
HJ Nielsen	17	417	110	29.78	87.4	1	2	9/1	0			-	-
F O'Neil	1	7	7	7.00	41.2	0	0	0	0		4.60	-	0
MJ Owen	3	16	13	5.33	72.7	0	0	0	0		8.50	-	0
JS Paris	18	61	16*	20.33	62.2	0	0	7	36	17.11	4.41	4-13	3
WB Parker	1	7	7	7.00	50.0	0	0	1	1	44.00	6.00	1-44	0
KR Patterson	44	1134	84	30.64	79.2	0	5	16	0			-	0
JL Pattinson	28	245	54	13.61	79.8	0	1	4	52	25.26	5.08	6-48	3
JJ Peirson	46	1153	85	29.56	88.1	0	8	48/4	0			-	0
JR Philippe	22	729	137	33.13	103.8	1	5	26/3	0			-	0
LAJ Pope	7	1	1	1.00	16.7	0	0	1	11	31.63	6.34	4-78	1
W Prestwidge	1	0	0			0	0	0	0		5.80	-	0
WJ Pucovski	7	66	34	9.42	58.9	0	0	3	0			-	0
SL Rainbird	20	38	9*	4.75	52.8	0	0	5	23	37.26	5.35	5-29	1
MT Renshaw	25	888	156*	40.36	89.2	1	9	10	4	43.75	5.30	1-7	0
JA Richardson	22	164	44	23.42	79.6	0	0	16	33	30.00	5.16	3-23	0
KW Richardson	53	329	36	11.75	86.1	0	0	12	84	30.64	5.29	6-48	5
TS Rogers	13	116	38	14.50	67.1	0	0	9	15	38.13	5.52	4-53	1
DR Sams	14	302	62	27.45	106.7	0	2	4	21	24.71	5.17	5-46	1
GS Sandhu	43	203	51	12.68	68.8	0	1	15	91	21.20	5.21	7-56	8
JJ Sangha	5	43	23	8.60	57.3	0	0	3	0		6.56	-	0
T Sangha	3	0	0	0.00	0.0	0	0	0	5	14.60	3.42	4-21	1
LAH Scott	1	42	42*		127.3	0	0	0	0		4.25	-	0
JL Seymour	2	22	13	22.00	78.6	0	0	1	0			-	0
DJM Short	34	1025	257	37.96	109.7	3	3	11	24	34.79	5.65	3-53	0
MW Short	36	808	88	27.86	88.2	0	4	14	20	46.10	5.58	3-44	0
PM Siddle	41	209	62	11.61	105.0	0	1	5	59	27.96	4.52	4-22	2
JC Silk	41	1314	90*	38.64	83.4	0	13	22	0		6.25	-	0
SPD Smith	46	1948	143*	59.03	89.5	3	14	27	19	43.26	5.44	3-43	0
B Stanlake	21	11	4*	3.66	20.8	0	0	5	27	35.07	5.08	4-24	2
MA Starc	22	129	34*	21.50	91.5	0	0	6	63	15.42	4.65	6-25	7
MT Steketee	34	267	30	19.07	96.0	0	0	9	53	27.67	5.30	4-25	5
MP Stoinis	39	1113	109	32.73	84.0	2	7	14	29	32.62	5.36	4-43	2
C Sully	3	18	15	9.00	69.2	0	0	0	4	36.75	8.16	4-39	1
WJ Sutherland	17	189	66	14.53	85.5	0	2	9	30	29.60	5.90	5-45	2
MJ Swepson	26	139	77	15.44	87.4	0	1	11	23	52.78	5.99	3-52	0
HTRJY Thornton	7	74	25*	14.80	56.1	0	0	0	7	50.28	5.50	3-45	0
SJ Truloff	1	80	80	80.00	94.1	0	1	0	0			-	0
AJ Turner	37	875	100	31.25	93.8	1	4	14	4	71.50	5.95	2-26	0
AJ Tye	42	255	44	15.93	109.4	0	0	11	93	20.31	5.43	6-46	6
MS Wade	69	2170	120	35.57	89.3	5	10	68/10	0			-	0
CA Wakim	5	63	42	12.60	74.1	0	0	2	0			-	0
DA Warner	39	1619	197	43.75	105.3	5	5	12	3	39.33	5.90	1-11	0
JB Weatherald	34	1315	141	39.84	94.1	4	7	9	0			-	0
BJ Webster	29	595	121	24.79	68.2	1	2	19	10	57.60	5.81	2-28	0
SM Whiteman	42	827	79	24.32	74.2	0	6	29/3	0			-	0
JD Wildermuth	22	325	66	16.25	86.7	0	2	4	23	41.34	5.47	4-39	1
NP Winter	8	12	7*	12.00	44.4	0	0	0	6	78.50	7.59	2-94	0
DJ Worrall	26	105	31*	11.66	77.8	0	0	10	28	42.67	5.39	5-62	1
MB Wright	12	377	104	37.70	73.2	1	2	3	0		9.42	-	0
A Zampa	40	440	66	18.33	112.2	0	2	10	62	30.79	5.14	4-18	2

SOME AUSTRALIAN LIST A RECORDS

Most runs

	Years	M	Inn	NO	Runs	HS	Ave	100	50s
RT Ponting	1992-2013	456	455	53	16363	164	41.74	34	99
MG Bevan	1989-2006	427	385	124	15103	157*	57.86	13	116
ME Waugh	1985-2004	434	417	42	14663	173	39.10	27	85
DS Lehmann	1998-2007	367	341	61	13122	191	46.86	19	94
MEK Hussey	1996-2013	381	346	71	12123	123	44.08	12	90
ML Hayden	1991-2008	308	299	29	12051	181*	44.63	27	67
SG Law	1998-2009	392	371	28	11812	163	34.43	20	64
SR Waugh	1984-2004	436	393	81	11764	140*	37.70	13	67
MW Goodwin	1994-2014	383	364	42	11477	167	35.64	14	71
AC Gilchrist	1992-2010	356	343	19	11326	172	34.95	18	63

Highest Scores

		Balls	4s	6s		Venue	Season
DJM Short	257	148	15	23	Western Australia v Queensland	Hurstville	2018-19
TM Head	**230**	**127**	**28**	**8**	**South Australia v Queensland**	**Rolton Oval**	**2021-22**
BR Dunk	229	157	15	13	Tasmania v Queensland	North Sydney	2014-15
PJ Hughes	202*	151	18	6	Australia A v South Africa A	Darwin	2014
TM Head	202	120	20	12	South Australia v Western Australia	Hurstville	2015-16
DA Warner	197	141	20	10	New South Wales v Victoria	North Sydney	2013-14
CJ Ferguson	192	143	21	5	Worcestershire v Leicestershire	Worcester	2018
DS Lehmann	191	103	20	11	Yorkshire v Nottinghamshire	Scarborough	2001
AJ Finch	188*	151	11	14	Victoria v Queensland	Junction Oval	2019-20
JP Maher	187	129	26	3	Queensland v Western Australia	Gabba	2003-04
SE Marsh	186	148	23	6	Western Australia v Cricket Aust XI	North Sydney	2015-16
SR Watson	185*	96	15	15	Australia v Bangladesh	Dhaka	2010-11
ML Hayden	181*	166	11	10	Australia v New Zealand	Hamilton	2006-07

Highest Totals

		versus	Venue	Season
Australia	4-434	South Africa	Johannesburg	2005-06
South Australia	7-420	Cricket Aust XI	Hurstville Oval	2015-16
Australia	6-417	Afghanistan	WACA	2014-15
Queensland	4-405	Western Australia	Gabba	2003-04
Queensland	3-402	Tasmania	North Sydney	2014-15
Tasmania	1-398	Queensland	North Sydney	2014-15
New South Wales	4-397	Tasmania	Bankstown	2001-02

Most Wickets

		M	Balls	Runs	Wkts	Ave	Best	Econ
SK Warne	1991-2007	311	16419	11642	473	24.61	6-42	4.25
GD McGrath	1992-2007	305	15808	10004	463	21.60	7-15	3.79
IJ Harvey	1993-2010	305	13607	9952	445	22.36	5-19	4.38
B Lee	1997-2012	262	13475	10524	438	24.05	5-22	4.69
AJ Bichel	1992-2007	235	11433	8362	320	26.13	7-20	4.38
MS Kasprowicz	1990-2008	226	11037	7977	298	26.76	5-45	4.33
NW Bracken	1998-2010	205	10339	7520	286	26.29	5-38	4.36
MG Johnson	2003-2015	184	9228	7386	284	26.00	6-31	4.80
A Symonds	1994-2009	424	11713	9379	282	33.25	6-14	4.80
GB Hogg	1994-2008	233	9297	7213	257	28.06	5-23	4.65
SR Waugh	1984-2004	436	11233	8610	257	33.50	4-32	4.59

Best Bowling

			Venue	Season
SW Tait	8-43	South Australia v Tasmania	Adelaide	2003-04
GD McGrath	7-15	Australia v Namibia	Potchefstroom	2002-03
AJ Bichel	7-20	Australia v England	Port Elizabeth	2002-03
JR Thomson	7-22	Middlesex v Hampshire	Lord's	1981
CG Rackemann	7-34	Queensland v South Australia	Adelaide	1998-99
JR Hazlewood	7-36	New South Wales v South Australia	Allan Border Field	2014-15

BBL11 – SCORCHERS WIN FOURTH TITLE

The Perth Scorchers won BBL11, becoming the first team to win the title four times. It was a marvellous triumph for the team, who were restricted to just one home match out of a possible seven, due to the harsh COVID border restrictions. While the title winners had plenty of stars and experienced players, they got the best out of Kurtis Patterson who had a breakout season as an opener making four half-centuries, striking at 142. Mitchell Marsh dominated in the eight games he played while Colin Munro was excellent mainly batting at four, having scored a club record 114 not out as an opener versus the Strikers on December 11. Laurie Evans was solid and saved his best until it was most needed when he came in at 4-25 in the final and peeled off a magnificent 76 off 41 balls. The Scorchers had the best bowling attack as AJ Tye was as effective as ever to take 25 wickets, while Jason Behrendorff in the powerplay and Ashton Agar in the middle overs were as reliable as can be. Unorthodox leg-spinner Peter Hatzoglou did well having come across from the Renegades and Matt Kelly was excellent in the early part of the tournament. Only available for the finals, Jhye Richardson was a dominant figure and with the team superbly and calmly led by Ashton Turner, it's no wonder they won the title.

The Sixers came a gallant second ably led by Moises Henriques who made his reliable contribution with the bat. Josh Philippe was again a fine contributor before missing the final with COVID while Dan Hughes made three fifties in a handy season. With the ball Hayden Kerr took 25 wickets and will be remembered for his remarkable innings of 98 not out which secured the Sixers a spot in the final. Sean Abbott did well with the ball and made some handy runs, with Ben Dwarshuis and Steve O'Keefe as fixtures of the bowling attack. James Vince was down on his batting form of BBL10, while Tom Curran injured his back and was only able to play four games.

The Strikers finished third having won just two of their first ten games, before winning four straight to qualify fourth. They were smart enough to gain 10 boost points for having a better score at the 10-over mark which was worth an extra win on the competition ladder. The recruitment of Gloucestershire batsmen Ian Cockbain had much to do with the turnaround in form for the Strikers, while Jon Wells had a fine tournament, and it surprised many when he was released by the club at the end of the season. Matt Short was excellent with the bat and handy with the ball, particularly in the powerplay where he scored at a strike rate of 160 and conceded just 7.23 an over. The ageless warrior Peter Siddle was brilliant once again and took the responsibility of bowling in the Power Surge, while Rashid Khan was always a constant threat before having to return to play for his native Afghanistan. Pace bowler Henry Thornton also came in at the back end of the tournament and did very well.

The Thunder lost its one and only final to finish fourth for the second season in a row. Jason Sangha great with the bat while Sam Billings was dangerous before England commitments took him away. Daniel Sams efforts with bat, ball and in the field were strong while Alex Hales was always a constant threat in what was a decent season for him. Alex Ross did well and scored three fifties in nine hits, while Gurinder Sandhu performed capably with the ball. Usman Khawaja returned after the Ashes to play and Thunder fans could argue that his dismissal in the Knockout final against the Strikers may have cost them a chance of high glory.

The Hurricanes came fifth and were glad for the wonderful form of Ben McDermott who took out the competition's MVP. Tom Rogers was a fine performer with the ball, while Matthew Wade was one of the biggest hitters in the competition, whilst Tim David was always a dangerous proposition. D'Arcy Short lacked the firepower of previous seasons with the bat, but still passed 400 runs while Riley Meredith did well when fit and firing. The Hurricanes were also unlucky to lose Nathan Ellis to a side strain for the second half of the tournament. Their Yorkshire recruits in Harry Brook and Jordan Thompson made little impression.

The Stars were one of the hardest hit teams by COVID, using 26 players across the summer. Captain Glenn Maxwell had a good season in tough circumstances making two tons, as his team missed out on the finals by one point. Nottinghamshire's Joe Clarke had a shocking start with just 58 runs from his first seven digs (including three ducks) but he then struck form with four consecutives fifties in what turned out to be for him a good summer. Hilton Cartwright hit hard when needed and fielded like a demon, while Marcus Stoinis wasn't as strong as in previous years. With the ball rookie paceman Brody Couch did well in his first full season, Qais Ahmad was hard to get away with his spinners while Adam Zampa was reliable in his appearances.

The Heat were another team savaged by COVID, using 29 players across the BBL. Ben Duckett did best with the bat while Max Bryant had a reasonable season. Chris Lynn became the first Heat player to play 100 games but was down on previous seasons and has parted way with the club after great service. Sadly, Jimmy Peirson couldn't repeat his efforts with that bat from BBL10, while with the ball Mujeeb was hard to get away when available. Quicks James Bazley, Mark Steketee and Xavier Bartlett all plugged away as best they could in what was a tough season for the club.

The Renegades continue to be a concern for the competition, having finished last for the third season in a row, having won just 10 out of 41 completed games across that period. Aaron Finch did his best with four half-centuries while Mackenzie Harvey had a decent season with two fifties. Kane Richardson took 19 wickets before electing to miss the last few games, while leg-spinner Cameron Boyce provided one of the highlights of the season, taking a double hat-trick against the Thunder in their final game. Since their title success in 2018-19 the Renegades have released a number of players and on August first it was announced that Boyce had signed a deal with the Strikers.

Apart from the struggles for some teams having to deal with COVID cases, the decision to prevent Steve Smith playing for the Sixers late in the tournament seemed to be a bad one. With the New Zealand white-ball series for late-January early February postponed on January 19, Smith was available and it seemed a great opportunity to give him a game, particularly as he had always been a Sixers player. The Sixers had a spot open on their list when James Vince was called up by England to leave early for international duties in the West Indies. With many saying the competition needed the best players available it seemed a logical move in the circumstances to let him play. Behind the scenes there were other issues at play involving the states, concerning matters that had happened in previous seasons and in the end Smith to play was rejected by the BBL's technical committee. Days later when the Sixers were struck down by COVID in the finals there was another chance for Smith to be included, but this too was rejected in what ended up being a bad PR exercise for the competition and Cricket Australia.

BBL11 - STATISTICS AND SCORES

LADDER	M	W	L	NR	Boost	Pts	Net Run Rate
Perth Scorchers (1)	14	11	3	-	8	40	+0.926
Sydney Sixers (2)	14	9	4	1	6	35	+1.027
Sydney Thunder (4)	14	9	5	-	8	32	+0.725
Adelaide Strikers (3)	14	6	8	-	10	28	+0.237
Hobart Hurricanes (5)	14	7	7	-	5	27	-0.332
Melbourne Stars (6)	14	7	7	-	5	26	-0.222
Brisbane Heat (7)	14	3	11	-	7	16	-0.910
Melbourne Renegades (8)	14	3	10	1	5	16	-1.477

Most Runs

	Team	M	Inn	NO	Runs	HS	Average	S/Rate	100s	50s	6s
BR McDermott	Hurricanes	13	13	1	577	127	48.08	153.86	2	3	29
JW Wells	Strikers	17	17	4	501	73	38.53	128.79	0	4	10
MW Short	Strikers	16	16	1	493	89	32.86	155.52	0	3	26
GJ Maxwell	Stars	13	13	2	468	154*	42.54	159.72	2	1	12
JJ Sangha	Thunder	12	12	3	445	91*	49.44	132.04	0	3	13
DJM Short	Hurricanes	15	15	3	444	73*	37.00	113.26	0	2	11
MC Henriques	Sixers	16	15	3	440	76*	36.66	133.33	0	2	12
JR Philippe	Sixers	15	14	1	429	99*	33.00	143.47	0	4	16
JM Clarke	Stars	13	13	0	419	85	32.23	151.26	0	5	17
KR Patterson	Scorchers	14	13	0	391	78	30.07	142.18	0	4	18

Highest Scores

	Balls	4s	6s		Venue	
GJ Maxwell	154*	64	22	4	Stars v Hurricanes	MCG	Jan 19, 2022
BR McDermott	127	65	9	9	Hurricanes v Renegades	Docklands	Dec 29, 2021
C Munro	114*	73	8	6	Scorchers v Strikers	Sydney Showgrounds	Dec 11, 2021
BR McDermott	110*	60	12	5	Hurricanes v Strikers	Bellerive	Dec 27, 2021
GJ Maxwell	103	57	12	3	Stars v Sixers	MCG	Dec 15, 2021
MR Marsh	100*	60	6	5	Scorchers v Hurricanes	Bellerive	Dec 14, 2021

Most Wickets

	Team	M	Overs	Mdns	Runs	Wkts	Avge	Econ	Best
PM Siddle	Strikers	17	63.5	0	532	30	17.73	8.33	5-23
HL Kerr	Sixers	17	50	0	375	25	15.00	7.50	4-32
AJ Tye	Scorchers	16	52.3	0	424	25	16.96	8.07	3-15
Rashid Khan	Strikers	11	44	0	279	20	13.95	6.34	6-17
TS Rogers	Hurricanes	13	49	0	386	20	19.30	7.87	3-24
KW Richardson	Renegades	11	38	1	312	19	16.42	8.21	4-32
SA Abbott	Sixers	14	46.1	0	378	19	19.89	8.18	4-31
DR Sams	Thunder	15	55	0	467	19	24.57	8.49	4-33
GS Sandhu	Thunder	11	39.1	0	298	18	16.55	7.60	4-22
AC Agar	Scorchers	15	58	0	394	18	21.88	6.79	2-16

Five wickets in an innings

	Figures		Venue	Date
Rashid Khan	6-17	Strikers v Heat	Gabba	Jan 12, 2022
CJ Boyce	5-21	Renegades v Thunder	MCG	Jan 19, 2022
PM Siddle	5-23	Strikers v Hurricanes	Adelaide Oval	Jan 5, 2022
BJ Dwarshuis	5-26	Sixers v Renegades	Geelong	Jan 11, 2022

Hat-tricks

GS Sandhu	Thunder v Scorchers	Cararra	Jan 6, 2022
CJ Boyce*	Renegades v Thunder	MCG	Jan 19, 2022

* Boyce took a double hat-trick – 4 wickets in 4 balls.

Match 1 – Sixers v Stars at the SCG on December 5, 2021 – Sixers won by 152 runs

Sixers			B	4	6
J R Philippe+	c Cartwright b Rainbird	83	47	8	3
J M Vince	c Zampa b Maxwell	44	29	6	
M C Henriques*	not out	76	38	8	3
D T Christian	c Cartwright b Couch	5	5	1	
T K Curran	c Larkin b Couch	0	1		
J C Silk	not out	0	0		
D P Hughes					
S N J O'Keefe					
C J Jordan					
S A Abbott					
H Kerr					
	1 lb, 4 w	5			
4 overs: 0-40	20 overs	4-213			

1-90 (Vince, 9.4), 2-192 (Philippe, 18.1), 3-206 (Christian, 19.2), 4-207 (Curran, 19.4)

Bowling	O	M	R	W	wd	nb	Dots
S M Elliott	3	0	29	0			6
S L Rainbird	4	0	59	1	2		4
Syed Faridoun	4	0	37	0		1	8
A Zampa	4	0	34	0			6
B L Couch	3	0	36	2	1		3
G J Maxwell	2	0	17	1			1

Stars			B	4	6
J M Clarke+	c Kerr b O'Keefe	1	2		
P M Nevill	c O'Keefe b Kerr	18	14	2	
N C R Larkin	lbw b O'Keefe	0	2		
G J Maxwell*	b Abbott	5	9		
H W R Cartwright	c Vince b Kerr	10	9		1
B J Webster	c Philippe b Abbott	2	4		
S M Elliott	c Abbott b O'Keefe	2	7		
S L Rainbird	c Philippe b Abbott	0	2		
A Zampa	st Philippe b O'Keefe	1	3		
B L Couch	c Christian b Curran	8	10	1	
Syed Fariuddin	not out	6	5	1	
	2 b, 6 w	8			
4 overs: 3-26	11.1 overs	61			

1-2 (Clarke, 0.3), 2-4 (Larkin, 0.5), 3-18 (Maxwell, 3.1), 4-41 (Nevill, 5.5), 5-41 (Cartwright, 5.6), 6-45 (Webster, 7.1), 7-45 (Rainbird, 7.3), 8-47 (Elliott, 8.3), 9-47 (Zampa, 8.4), 10-61 (Couch, 11.1)

Bowling	O	M	R	W	wd	nb	Dots
S N J O'Keefe	4	0	14	4	1		14
S A Abbott	3	0	14	3			11
C J Jordan	2	0	16	0		1	7
T K Curran	1.1	0	9	1			2
H Kerr	1	0	6	2			3

Toss: Stars. Umpires: PJ Gillespie, MW Graham-Smith, GA Abood (TV). Ref: DR Gilbert. Award: JR Philippe (SS). Crowd: 10,013
Philippe 50: 33 balls, 5x4 1x6: Henriques 50: 29 balls, 6x4 2x6. No Subs. Points: SS 4, MS 0.
10 overs: SS 1-92, MS 9-55

Match 2 – Thunder v Heat at Manuka Oval, Canberra on December 6, 2021 – Thunder won by 7 wickets

Heat			B	4	6
C A Lynn	c Whiteman b Sams	9	7	1	
M A Bryant	c Ross b McAndrew	5	11	1	
B M Duckett	c Billings b Sandhu	46	35	4	
S D Heazlett	c&b Sams	42	37	3	
J D Wildermuth	c Billings b Sandhu	1	2		
J J Peirson*+	c Ross b Sangha	3	5		
J J Bazley	c Cutting b Sams	1	3		
X C Bartlett	not out	26	18	3	1
Mujeeb-ur-Rahman	c Green b McAndrew	0	1		
M P Kuhnemann	not out	1	1		
L C J Guthrie					
	4 lb, 2 w	6			
4 overs: 2-20	20 overs	8-140			

1-13 (Bryant, 2.4), 2-16 (Lynn, 3.1), 3-99 (Heazlett, 14.1), 4-107 (Wildermuth, 15.1), 5-110 (Duckett, 15.4), 6-111 (Peirson, 16.2), 7-124 (Bazley, 18.2), 8-130 (Mujeeb, 19.1)

Bowling	O	M	R	W	wd	nb	Dots
G S Sandhu	4	0	17	2			16
D R Sams	4	0	22	3			12
N J McAndrew	4	0	33	2			8
C J Green	4	0	32	0			3
T Sangha	3	0	22	1	2		4
B C J Cutting	1	0	10	0			0

Thunder			B	4	6
A D Hales	c Duckett b Bartlett	0	2		
S M Whiteman	c Kuhnemann b Guthrie	11	9	2	
M R Gilkes	lbw b Guthrie	20	10	2	1
S W Billings+	not out	45	36	5	1
A I Ross	not out	61	46	7	2
B C J Cutting					
D R Sams					
C J Green*					
T Sangha					
G S Sandhu					
N J McAndrew					
	1 lb, 3 w	4			
4 overs: 3-37	17.1 overs	3-141			

1-0 (Hales, 0.2), 2-28 (Whiteman, 3.1), 3-32 (Gilkes, 3.3)

Bowling	O	M	R	W	wd	nb	Dots
X C Bartlett	3.1	0	21	1	1		11
L C J Guthrie	3	0	32	2			7
J D Wildermuth	2	0	23	0			3
Mujeeb	4	0	25	0			11
M P Kuhnemann	2	0	21	0		1	3
J J Bazley	3	0	18	0		1	7

Toss: Thunder. Umpires: GJ Davidson, AK Wilds, D Taylor (TV). Ref: SR Bernard. Award: AI Ross (ST). Crowd: 6,824
Ross 50: 38 balls, 6x4 2x6 Points: ST 4, BH 0. 10 overs: BH 2-58, ST 3-71 No Subs.

Match 3 – Renegades v Strikers at Marvel Stadium, Melbourne on December 7, 2021 – Renegades won by 2 runs

Renegades		B	4	6	Strikers		B	4	6
SB Harper+	c & b Short	33	28	2	1	MW Short	c Harvey b Zahir	29	18	1	2
MWG Harvey	b Rashid Khan	56	46	2	2	JB Weatherald	c Fraser-McGurk b Zahir	18	16	2
J Fraser-McGurk	c Weatherald b Siddle	8	11		HJ Nielsen+	c Harvey b Sutherland	30	30	1
JL Seymour	c Gibson b Worrall	24	14	1	2	JW Wells	lbw b Zahir Khan	8	9
Mohammad Nabi	c Worrall b Siddle	12	9	1	RJ Gibson	retired hurt	8	7
WJ Sutherland	c Short b Worrall	0	1		DR Drew	not out	17	16	2
JA Merlo	c Short b Siddle	2	3		GHS Garton	b Sutherland	5	3	1
JL Pattinson	c Wells b Garton	3	3		Rashid Khan	c Richardson b Topley	11	7	2
KW Richardson*	c Agar b Garton	2	2		DJ Worrall	b Richardson	9	6	2
RJW Topley	not out	2	2		WA Agar	c Nabi b Pattinson	1	3
Zahir Khan	not out	0	0		PM Siddle*	not out	6	4
	5 lb, 6 w	11				1 lb, 8 w	9
4 overs: 0-22	20 overs	9-153			4 overs: 0-38	20 overs	8-151

1-65 (Harper, 8.5), 2-92 (Fraser-McGurk, 13.2),
3-114 (Harvey, 14.5), 4-142 (Seymour, 17.4),
5-142 (Sutherland, 17.5), 6-144 (Merlo, 18.3),
7-146 (Nabi, 18.5), 8-149 (Richardson, 19.2), 9-151 (Pattinson, 19.4)

1-45 (Short, 4.6), 2-50 (Weatherald, 6.1), 3-84 (Wells, 10.4),
4-96 (Nielsen, 13.1), 5-111 (Garton, 15.2), 6-131 (Rashid, 17,4)
7-140 (Worrall, 18.4), 8-145 (Agar, 19.2)

Bowling	O	M	R	W	wd	nb	Dots
GHS Garton	4	0	23	2	1		10
DJ Worrall	4	0	26	2			11
Rashid Khan	4	0	30	1	1		8
PM Siddle	4	0	43	3			6
WA Agar	3	0	21	0			6
MW Short	1	0	5	1			3

Bowling	O	M	R	W	wd	nb	Dots
RJW Topley	4	0	43	1	1		10
JL Pattinson	4	0	27	1	1		9
KW Richardson	4	0	24	1			9
Zahir Khan	4	0	24	3	2		8
Mohammad Nabi	2	0	19	0			1
WJ Sutherland	2	0	13	2	1		4

Toss: Renegades. Umpires: MW Graham-Smith, PJ Gillespie, T Penman (TV), Ref: RW Stratford. Award: Z Khan (MR). Crowd: 8,932
Harvey 50: 42 balls, 1x4 2x6. No Subs. Points: MR 3, AS 1. 10 overs: MR 1-70, AS 2-82

Match 4 – Hurricanes v Sixers at York Park, Launceston on December 8, 2021 – Sixers won by 14 runs

Sixers		B	4	6	Hurricanes		B	4	6
JR Philippe+	b Ellis	5	11		MS Wade*+	c Silk b Kerr	20	18	1
JM Vince	st Wade b David	13	12	1	DJM Short	b Manenti	21	36	1
DP Hughes	c Wade b Rogers	3	6		PSP Handscomb	c Silk b Curran	47	31	3	2
MC Henriques*	c Cox b Ellis	73	48	6	2	CP Jewell	c Manenti b Jordan	20	11	1	1
JC Silk	lbw b Rogers	0	2		TA Lammonby	c & b O'Keefe	0	2
DT Christian	c Cox b Lamichhane	5	10		TH David	c Christian b Kerr	4	5	1
TK Curran	c Handscomb b Paris	27	21	4		JM Cox	b Curran	10	12
H Kerr	b Rogers	2	3		NT Ellis	c Philippe b Curran	3	4
CJ Jordan	run out (Cox)	9	6	1	TS Rogers	not out	0	0
BAD Manenti	not out	1	1		JS Paris	not out	0	1
SNJ O'Keefe					S Lamichhane			
	1 b, 2 lb, 3 w	6				1 lb, 4 w	5
4 overs: 1-22	20 overs	9-144			4 overs: 0-17	20 overs	8-130

1-20 (Philippe, 3.3), 2-22 (Vince, 4.1), 3-26 (Hughes, 5.2),
4-26 (Silk, 5.4), 5-39 (Christian, 8.1), 6-101 (Curran, 15.6),
7-123 (Kerr, 17.5), 8-142 (Henriques, 19.4), 9-144 (Jordan, 19.6)

1-38 (Wade, 8.2), 2-41 (Short, 9.1), 3-70 (Jewell, 11.5),
4-73 (Lammonby, 12.3), 5-78 (David, 13.3), 6-118 (Cox, 17.2),
7-126 (Ellis, 19.2), 8-130 (Handscomb, 19.5)

Bowling	O	M	R	W	wd	nb	Dots
JS Paris	4	0	20	1	2		9
TS Rogers	4	0	28	3	1		7
NT Ellis	4	0	34	2			7
TH David	1	0	4	1			2
S Lamichhane	4	0	24	1			9
DJM Short	2	0	15	0			3
TA Lammonby	1	0	10	0			1

Bowling	O	M	R	W	wd	nb	Dots
CJ Jordan	4	0	20	1			9
TK Curran	4	0	27	3	3		9
H Kerr	3	0	15	2			11
BA Manenti	3	0	18	1			6
DT Christian	2	0	21	0	1		5
SNJ O'Keefe	4	0	28	1			6

Toss: Hurricanes. Umpires: DR Close, BNJ Oxenford, AK Wilds (TV), Ref: DR Gilbert. Award: MC Henriques (SS). Crowd: 3,316
Points: HH 1, SS 3. 10 overs: SS 5-49, HH 2-50 No Subs.

Match 5 – Heat v Scorchers at Perth Stadium on December 8, 2021 – Scorchers won by 6 runs

Scorchers		R	B	4	6
C Munro	b Guthrie	3	5		
CT Bancroft+	b Bazley	25	21	4	
KR Patterson	c Duckett b Gannon	55	30	6	2
LJ Evans	not out	33	33	2	
AJ Turner*	c Cooper b Mujeeb	28	19	1	2
AM Hardie	c Peirson b Gannon	5	6		
AC Agar	c Peirson b Bartlett	2	4		
AJ Tye	not out	1	2		
ML Kelly					
JP Behrendorff					
P Hatzoglou					
	1 lb, 4 w	5			
4 overs: 1-40	20 overs	6-157			

1-7 (Munro, 1.3), 2-75 (Bancroft, 8.1), 3-92 (Patterson, 10.4),
4-137 (Turner, 16.1), 5-150 (Hardie, 18.1), 6-153 (Agar, 19.1)

Heat		R	B	4	6
CA Lynn	c Hardie b Agar	27	33	2	
MA Bryant	c Evans b Kelly	2	5		
BM Duckett	b Kelly	1	5		
SD Heazlett	c Kelly b Tye	34	17	2	3
JJ Peirson*+	c Patterson b Tye	6	11		
TLW Cooper	c Behrendorff b Hatzoglou	13	7	3	
JJ Bazley	b Behrendorff	14	7		2
XC Bartlett	not out	34	25	5	
CJ Gannon	c Bancroft b Kelly	1	3		
Mujeeb-ur-Rahman	b Kelly	0	1		
LCJ Guthrie	run out	6	6	1	
	(Hardie-Behrendorff)				
	2 b, 2 lb, 1 nb, 8 w	13			
4 overs: 2-20	19.5 overs	151			

1-12 (Bryant, 1.6), 2-16 (Duckett, 3.2), 3-59 (Heazlett, 7.4),
4-72 (Peirson, 11.1), 5-90 (Cooper, 12.3), 6-105 (Bazley, 13.5),
7-107 (Lynn, 14.3), 8-110 (Gannon, 15.2), 9-110 (Mujeeb, 15.3),
10-151 (Guthrie, 19.5)

Bowling	O	M	R	W	wd	nb	Dots
XC Bartlett	4	0	34	1	1		11
LCJ Guthrie	4	0	40	1			8
Mujeeb-ur-Rahman	4	0	23	1			9
JJ Bazley	4	0	27	1	2		9
CJ Gannon	4	0	32	2	1		8

Bowling	O	M	R	W	wd	nb	Dots
JP Behrendorff	3.5	0	31	1	1		11
ML Kelly	4	0	28	4	2		13
P Hatzoglou	4	0	40	1	5		6
AC Agar	4	0	16	1			10
AJ Tye	4	0	32	2	1		13

Toss: Scorchers. Umpires: GA Abood, GJ Davidson, SA Lightbody (TV), Ref: SR Bernard. Award: ML Kelly (PS). Crowd: 16,108
Patterson 50: 27 balls, 6x4 2x6.   No Subs.   Points: PS 4, BH 0.   10 overs: PS 2-89, BH 3-65

Match 6 – Strikers v Renegades at Adelaide Oval on December 9, 2021 – Strikers won by 49 runs

Strikers		R	B	4	6
MW Short	c Merlo b Zahir	32	17	1	3
JB Weatherald	b Zahir	11	8	2	
HJ Nielsen+	b Pattinson	14	15	1	
JW Wells	c Harper b Richardson	37	30		2
DR Drew	lbw b Richardson	12	12	1	
LAH Scott	c Nabi b Topley	1	6		
Rashid Khan	c Nabi b Topley	13	7	3	
GHS Garton	c Nabi b Richardson	19	11	3	
DJ Worrall	c Harper b Topley	3	6		
WA Agar	b Richardson	1	3		
PM Siddle*	not out	0	0		
	1 lb, 1 nb, 4 w	6			
4 overs: 1-48	19 overs	149			

1-34 (Weatherald, 2.6), 2-50 (Short, 4.3), 3-81 (Nielsen, 8.6),
4-104 (Drew, 12.4), 5-111 (Wells, 14.2), 6-125 (Rashid, 15.3),
7-125 (Scott, 15.4), 8-139 (Worrall, 17.2), 9-149 (Garton, 18.5),
10-149 (Agar, 18.6)

Renegades		R	B	4	6
SB Harper+	c Short b Agar	33	31	1	1
MWG Harvey	run out (Agar-Nielsen)	19	12	3	
JL Seymour	c Nielsen b Rashid	10	13	1	
Mohammad Nabi	c Weatherald b Worrall	12	14		
JA Merlo	lbw b Rashid	4	9		
J Fraser-McGurk	c Nielsen b Agar	3	6		
WJ Sutherland	c Weatherald b Garton	0	1		
JL Pattinson	c Nielsen b Agar	0	3		
KW Richardson*	c Garton b Siddle	4	8		
RJW Topley	not out	9	12	1	
Zahir Khan	b Worrall	0	3		
	1 lb, 5 w	6			
4 overs: 0-36	18.4 overs	100			

1-39 (Harvey, 4.5), 2-59 (Seymour, 8.2), 3-72 (Harper, 10.4),
4-80 (Merlo, 12.4), 5-84 (Nabi, 13.5), 6-85 (Fraser-McGurk, 14.1),
7-85 (Pattinson, 14.4), 8-89 (Sutherland, 15.3),
9-99 (Richardson, 17.4), 10-100 (Zahir, 18.4)

Bowling	O	M	R	W	wd	nb	Dots
RJW Topley	4	0	32	3			10
JL Pattinson	3	0	27	1	1		5
Zahir Khan	4	0	33	2	2		10
KW Richardson	4	0	32	4	1	1	10
Mohammad Nabi	3	0	16	0			3
WJ Sutherland	1	0	8	0			3

Bowling	O	M	R	W	wd	nb	Dots
MW Short	2	0	17	0	1		4
DJ Worrall	3.4	0	18	2	1		9
GHS Garton	3	0	19	1			5
PM Siddle	3	0	11	1			10
Rashid Khan	4	0	17	2			11
WA Agar	3	0	17	3	3		10

Toss: Strikers. Umpires: MW Graham-Smith, BC Treloar, PJ Gillespie (TV), Ref: SJ Davis. Award: WA Agar (AS). Crowd: 8,408
Points: AS 4, MR 0   No Subs.   10 overs: AS 3-86, MR 2-69

Match 7 – Stars v Thunder at the MCG on December 10, 2021 – Stars won by 4 runs

Stars		B	4	6	Thunder		B	4	6
MP Stoinis	run out				AD Hales	lbw b Zampa	10	10	2
	(Ross-Green-McAndrew)	13	13	2	SM Whiteman	b Coulter-Nile	10	8	2
JM Clarke+	c Ross b McAndrew	13	12	2	MR Gilkes	c Clarke b Coulter-Nile	56	49	4	1
GJ Maxwell*	b Sangha	16	16		SW Billings+	c Maxwell b Qais	43	31	2	2
NCR Larkin	not out	52	43	5	DR Sams	c Clarke b Couch	1	3	
HWR Cartwrigh	c Cutting b Sangha	42	30	3	2	AI Ross	not out	17	11	1
AD Russell	not out	17	9	2	BCJ Cutting	not out	12	8	2
BJ Webster					NJ McAndrew				
NM Coulter-Nile					CJ Green*				
A Zampa					GS Sandhu				
Qais Ahmed					T Sangha				
BL Couch									
	1 lb, 3 nb, 8 w	12				2 lb, 10 w	12		
4 overs: 1-30	20 overs	4-165			4 overs: 2-30	20 overs	5-161		

1-18 (Clarke, 2.6), 2-31 (Stoinis, 4.3),
3-61 (Maxwell, 9.3), 4-141 (Cartwright, 17.4)

1-20 (Hales, 1.6), 2-29 (Whiteman, 3.1), 3-118 (Billings, 14.1),
4-123 (Sams, 15.5), 5-135 (Gilkes, 17.2)

Bowling	O	M	R	W	wd	nb	Dots	Bowling	O	M	R	W	wd	nb	Dots
GS Sandhu	4	0	32	0	2	1	8	NM Coulter-Nile	4	1	27	2	1		10
DR Sams	4	0	50	0	4	1	5	A Zampa	4	0	31	1			6
NJ McAndrew	4	0	27	1	1	1	12	GJ Maxwell	1	0	9	0			3
T Sangha	4	0	29	2			9	Qais Ahmed	3	0	23	1	1		6
CJ Green	2	0	16	0	1		4	AD Russell	4	0	40	0	4		6
BCJ Cutting	2	0	10	0			6	BL Couch	3	0	23	1			8
								HWR Cartwright	1	0	6	0			1

Toss: Thunder. Umpires: DR Close, GJ Davidson, TM Penman (TV), Ref: RW Stratford.   Award: NCR Larkin (MS) Crowd: 10,888
Larkin 50: 41 balls, 5x4. Gilkes 50: 44 balls, 4x4 1x6.   No Subs.   Points: MS 3, ST 1.   10 over scores: MS 3-62, ST 2-79

Match 8 – Sixers v Hurricanes at the SCG on December 11, 2021 – Hurricanes won by 44 runs (DLS)

Hurricanes		B	4	6	Sixers	DLS 196 off 18	B	4	6
MS Wade*+	c Silk b Curran	93	46	9	5	JR Philippe+	c Thompson b Paris	72	46	6	3
DJM Short	not out	73	51	7	3	JM Vince	c Ellis b Paris	26	22	2	
CP Jewell	c Silk b Jordan	42	23	6	1	MC Henriques*	not out	26	25	2	
TH David	not out	0	0			DT Christian	b Paris	12	9	2	
PSP Handscomb					DP Hughes	c Rogers b Ellis	2	3		
JA Thompson					TK Curran	not out	6	3	1	
NT Ellis					JC Silk					
TS Rogers					CJ Jordan					
JS Paris					H Kerr					
S Lamichhane					SNJ O'Keefe					
JJ Kann					SA Abbott					
	5 w	5				3 lb, 4 w	7		
4 overs: 0-54	20 overs	2-213			4 overs: 0-36	18 overs	4-151		

1-111 (Wade, 11.2), 2-203 (Jewell, 19.1)

1-61 (Vince, 7.1), 2-118 (Philippe, 13.5), 3-136 (Christian, 16.1),
4-145 (Hughes, 17.3)

Bowling	O	M	R	W	wd	nb	Dots	Bowling	O	M	R	W	wd	nb	Dots
SA Abbott	4	0	42	0	1		9	TH David	2	0	8	0			4
TK Curran	3	0	46	1	2		4	JS Paris	4	0	35	3	1		10
H Kerr	1	0	8	0			1	TS Rogers	3	0	36	0			2
CJ Jordan	4	0	51	1			7	NT Ellis	4	0	37	1	3		6
SNJ O'Keefe	4	0	30	0			8	JJ Kann	1	0	8	0			1
DT Christian	4	0	36	0	2		7	S Lamichhane	4	0	24	0			8

Toss: Hurricanes. Umpires: MW Graham-Smith, BNJ Oxenford, SA Lightbody (TV), Ref: SR Bernard.   Award: MS Wade (HH).
Wade 50: 19 balls, 7x4 2x6; Short 50: 42 balls, 5x4 2x6; Philippe 50: 36 balls, 5x4 2x6.   Points: SS 0, HH 4.   Crowd: 11,070
HH Sub: JJ Kann for TA Lammonby.

Match 9 – Scorchers v Strikers at Sydney Showgrounds on December 11, 2021 – Scorchers won by 49 runs

Scorchers			B	4	6	Strikers			B	4	6
C Munro	not out		114	73	8	M W Short	c Bancroft b Kelly		63	47	4	2
CT Bancroft+	run out (Wells-Nielsen)		45	37	5	J B Weatherald	c Turner b Behrendorff		17	9	2	1
AJ Turner*	not out		14	10	1	HJ Nielsen+	run out (Hardie)		9	12	
KR Patterson						J W Wells	b Hatzoglou		6	7	
LJ Evans						DR Drew	c Bancroft b Agar		10	6	1
AM Hardie						T Kelly	c Patterson b Tye		26	15	2	2
AC Agar						LAH Scott	b Tye		2	3	
AJ Tye						Rashid Khan	c Hardie b Tye		0	1	
M L Kelly						DJ Worrall	c Patterson b Behrendorff		2	3	
J P Behrendorff						P M Siddle*	b Behrendorff		0	3	
P Hatzoglou						Fawad Ahmed	not out		1	1	
	11 lb, 11 w		22				4 b, 6 w		10		
4 overs: 0-35	20 overs		1-195			4 overs: 1-34	17.5 overs		146		

1-132 (Bancroft, 15.3)

1-28 (Weatherald, 2.5), 2-58 (Nielsen, 7.1), 3-86 (Wells, 10.5), 4-97 (Drew, 11.6), 5-134 (Short, 15.3), 6-143 (Kelly, 16.2), 7-143 (Scott, 16.3), 8-144 (Rashid, 16.5), 9-145 (Siddle, 17.3), 10-146 (Worrall, 17.5)

Bowling	O	M	R	W	wd	nb	Dots	Bowling	O	M	R	W	wd	nb	Dots
DJ Worrall	4	0	28	0	1		13	J P Behrendorff	2.5	0	22	3	1		7
P M Siddle	4	0	46	2			5	M L Kelly	3	0	30	1			5
WA Agar	1	0	14	0	2		2	P Hatzoglou	4	0	26	1	4		8
Rashid Khan	4	0	40	0	1		7	AJ Turner	1	0	9	0			2
Fawad Ahmed	4	0	33	0			3	AC Agar	4	0	34	1			4
M W Short	3	0	23	0	1		4	AJ Tye	3	0	21	3			10

Toss: Scorchers. Umpires: NR Johnstone, AK Wilds, GA Abood (TV), Ref: RL Perry.   Award: C Munro (PS).   Crowd: None
Munro 50: 48 balls, 1x4 2x6; 100: 69 balls, 6x4 5x6. Short 50: 40 balls 2x4 2x6. AS Sub: LAH Scott for WA Agar. Points: PS 3, AS 1.

Match 10 – Thunder v Stars at Sydney Showgrounds on December 12, 2021 – Stars won by 6 wickets

Thunder			B	4	6	Stars			B	4	6
AD Hales	c Clarke b Couch		28	21	4	1	MP Stoinis	c Sams b Sangha		31	30	3	
SM Whiteman	c Clarke b Maxwell		4	7			JM Clarke+	c Billings b McAndrew		0	4	
MR Gilkes	b Qais		7	6	1		NCR Larkin	c McAndrew b Cutting		6	11	1	
S W Billings+	c Coulter-Nile b Qais		9	19			GJ Maxwell*	c Cutting b Sangha		40	25	3	2
AI Ross	not out		77	49	4	4	AD Russell	not out		42	21	1	5
DR Sams	c Qais b Couch		22	18	1	2	HWR Cartwright	not out		23	13	1	2
BCJ Cutting	not out		0	0			BJ Webster					
NJ McAndrew							BL Couch					
CJ Green*							Qais Ahmad					
GS Sandhu							A Zampa					
T Sangha							NM Coulter-Nile					
	1 b, 2 lb, 1 w		4					4 b, 4 lb, 1 nb, 4 w		13		
4 overs: 1-31	20 overs		5-151				4 overs: 1-24	17.1 overs		4-155		

1-24 (Whiteman, 3.2), 2-33 (Gilkes, 4.5), 3-40 (Hales, 6.1), 4-65 (Billings, 11.5), 5-149 (Sams, 19.5)

1-15 (Clarke, 2.1), 2-24 (Larkin, 4.2), 3-83 (Stoinis, 11.2), 4-83 (Maxwell, 11.3)

Bowling	O	M	R	W	wd	nb	Dots	Bowling	O	M	R	W	wd	nb	Dots
NM Coulter-Nile	4	0	31	0			8	DR Sams	3	0	36	0	1	1	6
A Zampa	3	0	29	0			5	GS Sandhu	3.1	0	27	0	3		9
Qais Ahmad	4	0	17	2	1		13	NJ McAndrew	4	0	37	1			10
Gj Maxwell	1	0	7	1			2	BCJ Cutting	2	0	17	1			4
AD Russell	4	0	38	0			10	T Sangha	4	1	20	2			14
BL Couch	4	0	26	2			9	CJ Green	1	0	10	0			

Toss: Stars. Umpires: GA Abood, BC Treloar, PJ Gillespie (TV), Ref: DR Gilbert. Award: AD Russell (MS).   Crowd: 4.314
Ross 50: 41 balls, 3x4 2x6.   No subs   Points: ST 0, MS 4.   10 overs: ST 3-58, MS 2-77

Match 11 – Heat v Renegades at Metricon Stadium, Gold Coast on December 13, 2021 – Heat won by 5 wickets

Renegades			B	4	6	Heat			B	4	6
MWG Harvey	not out	71	56	8		MA Bryant	c Richardson b Nabi	18	17	2	
SB Harper+	c Mujeeb b Bazley	12	13	2		CA Lynn	b Zahir	32	15	5	1
NJ Maddinson*	c Bartlett b Swepson	19	21	2		BM Duckett	lbw b Zahir	11	10	2	
M Nabi	c Heazlett b Bazley	3	6			SD Heazlett	not out	44	29	1	3
JL Seymour	c Bryant b Bazley	8	11			TB Abell	c Zahir b Prestwidge	9	13		
J Fraser-McGurk	lbw b Guthrie	6	5			JJ Peirson*+	c Harvey b Richardson	4	5		
WJ Sutherland	c Heazlett b Bartlett	10	7		1	JJ Bazley	not out	16	12	1	1
JA Prestwidge	not out	1	1			XC Bartlett					
KW Richardson						MJ Swepson					
RJW Topley						Mujeeb-ur-Rahman					
Zahir Khan						LCJ Guthrie					
	2 b, 2 lb, 6 w	10					1 b, 2 lb, 4 w	7			
4 overs: 0-28	20 overs	6-140				4 overs: 0-46	16.5 overs	5-141			

1-38 (Harper, 6.1), 2-84 (Maddinson, 12.2), 3-90 (Nabi, 13.4), 4-117 (Seymour, 16.4), 5-126 (Fraser-McGurk, 18.2), 6-137 (Sutherland, 19.4)

1-46 (Lynn, 4.1), 2-65 (Bryant, 6.5), 3-67 (Duckett, 7.2), 4-92 (Abell, 11.4), 5-107 (Peirson, 13.2)

Bowling	O	M	R	W	wd	nb	Dots	Bowling	O	M	R	W	wd	nb	Dots
XC Bartlett	4	0	48	1	3		7	NJ Maddinson	1	0	4	0			2
LCJ Guthrie	4	0	10	1	1		15	WJ Sutherland	1	0	21	0			0
JJ Bazley	4	0	28	3	1		9	Zahir Khan	4	0	27	2	2		8
Mujeeb-ur-Rahman	4	0	19	0	1		10	RJW Topley	2.5	0	26	0			5
MJ Swepson	4	0	31	1			7	KW Richardson	3	0	26	1			7
								Mohammad Nabi	3	0	19	1			4
								JA Prestwidge	2	0	15	1			4

Toss: Heat. Umpires: BNJ Oxenford, D Taylor, AK Wilds (TV), Ref: SR Bernard. Award: JJ Bazley (BH). Crowd: 6,459
Harvey 50: 43 balls, 5x4. No subs. 10 overs MR 1-58, BH 3-84. Points: BH 4, MR 0.

Match 12 – Hurricanes v Scorchers at Bellerive Oval, Hobart on December 14, 2021 – Scorchers won by 53 runs

Scorchers			B	4	6	Hurricanes			B	4	6
KR Patterson	c McDermott b Ellis	13	10	2		MS Wade*+	c Patterson b Behrendorff	4	5	1	
C Munro	c Brook b Paris	0	2			DJM Short	c Marsh b Agar	31	29	1	2
MR Marsh	not out	100	60	6	5	CP Jewell	lbw b Mills	2	2		
JP Inglis+	c Jewell b Lamichhane	2	3			BR McDermott	c Inglis b Mills	41	29	3	3
AJ Turner*	c Ellis b Boland	17	14		1	HC Brook	st Inglis b Hatzoglou	1	4		
LJ Evans	c McDermott b Ellis	40	24	5	1	PSP Handscomb	c Munro b Tye	3	5		
AC Agar	not out	7	8			TH David	c Behrendorff b Tye	17	10	1	1
AJ Tye						NT Ellis	b Mills	1	2		
JP Behrendorff						SM Boland	st Inglis b Agar	10	13	2	
P Hatzoglou						S Lamichhane	not out	13	9		1
TS Mills						JS Paris	c Marsh b Turner	2	7		
	1 lb, 1 nb, 1 w	3					1 nb, 3 w	4			
4 overs: 2-34	20 overs	5-182				4 overs: 2-15	19 overs	129			

1-3 (Munro, 0.4), 2-33 (Patterson, 3.4), 3-40 (Inglis, 5.1), 4-74 (Turner, 9.4), 5-141 (Evans, 17.1)

1-5 (Wade, 0.5), 2-7 (Jewell, 1.2), 3-76 (McDermott, 9.5), 4-79 (Brook, 10.5), 5-82 (Handscomb, 11.4), 6-86 (Short, 12.4), 7-88 (Ellis, 13.1), 8-106 (David, 14.6), 9-114 (Boland, 16.4), 10-129 (Paris, 18.6)

Bowling	O	M	R	W	wd	nb	Dots	Bowling	O	M	R	W	wd	nb	Dots
JS Paris	1.4	0	13	1	1		5	JP Behrendorff	3	0	14	1	1		14
SM Boland	4	0	45	1			3	TS Mills	4	0	23	3	1		17
TH David	2.2	0	17	0			1	AC Agar	4	0	21	2			9
NT Ellis	4	0	33	2			8	P Hatzoglou	4	0	28	1			6
DJM Short	4	0	41	0	1		4	AJ Tye	3	0	31	2		1	7
S Lamichhane	4	0	32	1			6	AJ Turner	1	0	12	1	1		2

Toss: Scorchers. Umpires: GA Abood, DM Koch, DR Close (TV), Ref: DA Johnston. Award: MR Marsh (PS). Crowd: 5,673
Marsh 50: 37 balls, 4x4 1x6; 100: 60 balls, 6x4 5x6. Points: PS 3, HH 1. No Subs. 10 overs: PS 4-75, HH 3-76

Stars		B	4	6
MP Stoinis	c Philippe b Dwarshuis	3	5	
JM Clarke+	st Philippe b O'Keefe	0	3	
NCR Larkin	b Christian	23	25	2
GJ Maxwell*	c Hughes b Jordan	103	57	12	3
HWR Cartwright	b Kerr	23	20	3
AD Russell	not out	12	8	1
BJ Webster	not out	4	2	1
NM Coulter-Nile				
Qais Ahmad				
A Zampa				
BL Couch				
	1 b, 5 lb, 3 w	9		
4 overs: 2-12	20 overs	5-177		

1-3 (Stoinis, 1.1), 2-6 (Clarke, 2.1), 3-59 (Larkin, 8.4), 4-144 (Cartwright, 17.1), 5-162 (Maxwell, 18.5)

Bowling	O	M	R	W	wd	nb	Dots
SNJ O'Keefe	4	0	24	1			10
BJ Dwarshuis	4	0	51	1	1		8
CJ Jordan	4	0	24	1	1		10
LAJ Pope	1	0	12	0			1
TK Curran	1	0	11	0			2
DT Christian	2	0	17	1	1		1
MC Henriques	1	0	5	0			1
H Kerr	3	0	27	1			6

Sixers		B	4	6
JR Philippe+	not out	99	61	11	2
JM Vince	c Webster b Coulter-Nile	9	9	1
MC Henriques*	lbw b Zampa	29	20	1	2
DP Hughes	c & b Couch	11	10		1
JC Silk	not out	25	19	1
DT Christian				
TK Curran				
CJ Jordan				
BJ Dwarshuis				
SNJ O'Keefe				
H Kerr				
	5 lb, 1 nb, 3 w	9		
4 overs: 1-31	19.4 overs	3-182		

1-30 (Vince, 3.5), 2-84 (Henriques, 9.6), 3-116 (Hughes, 13.1)

Bowling	O	M	R	W	wd	nb	Dots
GJ Maxwell	2	0	20	0			2
BL Couch	3	0	22	1			5
A Zampa	4	0	28	1			7
NM Coulter-Nile	4	0	43	1	1	1	5
Qais Ahmad	3.4	0	40	0			2
AD Russell	3	0	24	0	1		4

Toss: Sixers. Umpires: SAJ Craig, BNJ Oxenford, SA Lightbody (TV), Ref: RL Parry. Award: JR Philippe (SS). Crowd: 11,037
Maxwell 50: 35 balls, 5x4 1x6; 100: 54 balls, 12x4 2x6. Sub: H Kerr in for LAJ Pope (SS). Points: MS 0, BH 4.
10 overs MS 3-66, SS 2-84

Thunder		B	4	6
MR Gilkes	c sub (TLW Cooper) b Swepson	28	22	2	1
AD Hales	c Duckett b Bartlett	35	26	3	2
JJ Sangha	b Swepson	39	28	3	1
SW Billings+	lbw b Bazley	64	27	5	5
DR Sams	c Steketee b Bartlett	1	3	
BCJ Cutting	c Peirson b Steketee	8	11	1
AI Ross	c Peirson b Steketee	4	2	1
NJ McAndrew	not out	1	1	
CJ Green*				
S Mahmood				
T Sangha				
	6 lb, 10 w	16		
4 overs: 0-39	20 overs	7-196		

1-55 (Gilkes, 5.5), 2-81 (Hales, 10.2), 3-146 (J Sangha, 15.3), 4-156 (Sams, 16.3), 5-186 (Billings, 18.5), 6-195 (Ross, 19.3), 7-196 (Cutting, 19.6)

Heat		B	4	6
CA Lynn	c Hales b Mahmood	4	3	1
MA Bryant	run out (Gilkes-Billings)	2	3	
BM Duckett	c Gilkes b Mahmood	2	2	
SD Heazlett	c Sams b Mahmood	5	6	1
TLW Cooper	c Sams b Green	32	18	3	2
JJ Peirson*+	c Cutting b Mahmood	0	3	
JJ Bazley	c McAndrew b T Sangha	9	14	1
XC Bartlett	not out	42	29	3	1
MT Steketee	c J Sangha b Sams	33	24	2	1
MJ Swepson	b T Sangha	4	2	1
Mujeeb-ur-Rahman	lbw b T Sangha	0	1	
	1 b, 1 lb, 8 w	10		
4 overs: 5-28	17.3 overs	143		

1-4 (Lynn, 0.3), 2-8 (Duckett, 0.5), 3-14 (Heazlett, 2.1), 4-15 (Bryant, 2.2), 5-15 (Peirson, 2.5), 6-59 (Cooper, 7.5), 7-60 (Bazley, 8.1), 8-139 (Steketee, 16.6), 9-143 (Swepson, 17.2), 10-143 (Mujeeb, 17.3)

Bowling	O	M	R	W	wd	nb	Dots
XC Bartlett	4	0	45	2	5		9
MT Steketee	4	0	32	2			10
Mujeeb-ur-Rahman	4	0	34	0	1		10
JJ Bazley	4	0	52	1	3		8
MJ Swepson	4	0	27	2	1		7

Bowling	O	M	R	W	wd	nb	Dots
S Mahmood	3	0	22	4	2		12
DR Sams	3	0	30	1	1		5
NJ McAndrew	3	0	25	0	2		8
CJ Green	4	0	29	1	2		8
T Sangha	3.3	0	26	3	1		7
BCJ Cutting							0

Toss: Heat. Umpires: DM Koch, DR Close, BC Treloar, Ref: KC Wessels. Award: S Mahmood (ST). Crowd: 16,189
Billings 50: 24 balls, 4x4 4x6. Points: BH 0, ST 4. BH sub: TLW Cooper for TB Abell. 10 overs: ST 6-81 BH 7-77

Match 15 – Hurricanes v Scorchers at Bellerive Oval, Hobart on December 20, 2021 – Scorchers won by 42 runs

Scorchers			B	4	6
KR Patterson	c & b Thompson	78	48	6	5
JP Inglis+	c Brook b Meredith	0	4		
MR Marsh	b Rogers	21	21	1	1
C Munro	run out (Thompson)	10	16		
AJ Turner*	b Rogers	12	10	1	
LJ Evans	c Ellis b Thompson	9	10		
AC Agar	not out	30	11	3	2
AJ Tye	c Brook b Thompson	0	1		
JP Behrendorff					
P Hatzoglou					
TS Mills					
	3 lb, 1 nb, 3 w	7			
4 overs: 1-18	20 overs	7-167			

1-1 (Inglis, 0.6), 2-73 (Marsh, 8.3), 3-98 (Munro, 12.6),
4-119 (Turner, 15.5), 5-126 (Patterson, 16.3),
6-149 (Evans, 19.1), 7-167 (Tye, 19.6)

Hurricanes			B	4	6
MS Wade*+	c Marsh b Tye	13	14	2	
DJM Short	lbw b Agar	13	18		
CP Jewell	c Marsh b Tye	13	17	1	
BR McDermott	c sub (NR Hobson) b Tye	8	10		
HC Brook	b Hatzoglou	2	3		
TH David	run out				
	(sub NR Hobson-Inglis)	6	8		
JA Thompson	c Munro b Mills	2	3		
NT Ellis	st Inglis b Agar	20	15	2	
TS Rogers	c sub (NR Hobson)				
	b Hatzoglou	9	9	1	
WB Parker	not out	25	17	1	1
S Lamichhane	not out	8	7		
	1 nb, 5 w	6			
4 overs: 1-20	20 overs	9-125			

1-18 (Wade, 3.2), 2-42 (Jewell, 7.6), 3-45 (Short, 8.3),
4-48 (Brook, 9.1), 5-58 (McDermott, 10.5), 6-60 (Thompson, 11.3),
7-64 (David, 12.3), 8-83 (Rogers, 14.5), 9-108 (Ellis, 17.4)

Bowling	O	M	R	W	wd	nb	Dots
RP Meredith	1	0	1	1			5
TH David	2	0	16	0	1		11
TS Rogers	4	0	21	2		1	11
MT Ellis	4	0	35	0			4
S Lamichhane	4	0	40	0			4
WB Parker	1	0	18	0			4
JA Thompson	4	0	33	3	2		12

Bowling	O	M	R	W	wd	nb	Dots
JP Behrendorff	2	0	10	0			6
TS Mills	3	0	15	1	1		9
AJ Tye	4	0	19	3	2	1	12
P Hatzoglou	4	0	29	2	1		6
MR Marsh	2	0	13	0			4
AC Agar	4	0	31	2	1		4
AJ Turner	1	0	8	0			0

Toss: Scorchers. Umpires: GJ Abood, AK Wilds, NR Johnstone (TV), Ref: DR Gilbert. Award: KR Patterson (PS). Crowd: 1,917
Patterson 50: 26 balls, 4x4, 3x6.   Points: HH 0, PS 4. 10 overs: PS 2-79, HH 4-53   HH Sub: JA Thompson for RP Meredith

Match 16 – Sixers v Strikers at the SCG on December 21, 2021 – Sixers won by 4 wickets

Strikers			B	4	6
MW Short	c Christian b Abbott	16	8	2	1
JB Weatherald	c Henriques b Abbott	6	11	1	
MT Renshaw	c Kerr b Christian	24	23	2	
JW Wells	c Philippe b Christian	32	19	2	2
TJ Kelly	c Vince b Abbott	41	34	4	
HJ Nielsen+	b Christian	1	3		
GHS Garton	c Abbott b Pope	11	11	1	
Rashid Khan	c Vince b Kerr	2	3		
DJ Worrall	not out	5	8		
PM Siddle*					
Fawad Ahmed					
	3 lb, 6 w	9			
4 overs: 2-31	20 overs	8-147			

1-20 (Short, 1.6), 2-25 (Weatherald, 3.1), 3-84 (Wells, 9.4),
4-89 (Renshaw, 11.1), 5-92 (Nielsen, 11.6), 6-107 (Garton, 14.5),
7-115 (Rashid, 15.6), 8-147 (Kelly, 19.6)

Sixers			B	4	6
JR Philippe+	c Wells b Garton	23	20	1	1
JM Vince	b Fawad Ahmed	21	24	3	
MC Henriques*	lbw b Rashid	28	26	2	1
DP Hughes	c Nielsen b Rashid	7	9	1	
JC Silk	c sub (HJ Hunt) b Garton	36	24	5	
DT Christian	lbw b Rashid	0	1		
SA Abbott	not out	19	10	2	
H Kerr	not out	8	2		1
CJ Jordan					
BJ Dwarshuis					
LAJ Pope					
	2 lb, 6 w	8			
4 overs: 0-35	19.2 overs	6-150			

1-44 (Vince, 6.5), 2-52 (Philippe, 7.5), 3-63 (Hughes, 9.5),
4-115 (Henriques, 16.2), 5-115 (Christian, 16.3), 6-134 (Silk, 18.3)

Bowling	O	M	R	W	wd	nb	Dots
BJ Dwarshuis	2	0	30	0	2		3
SA Abbott	4	0	24	3	1		12
H Kerr	2	0	11	1			5
LAJ Pope	4	0	33	1	1		4
CJ Jordan	4	0	38	0	1		7
MC Henriques	1	0	8	0			1
DT Christian	3	0	8	3			10

Bowling	O	M	R	W	wd	nb	Dots
DJ Worrall	3	0	27	0	1		6
GHS Garton	4	0	41	2	1		12
PM Siddle	3.2	0	40	0			4
Fawad Ahmed	4	0	16	1			9
Rashid Khan	4	0	20	3			11
MW Short	1	0	4	0			2

Toss: Strikers. Umpires: BNJ Oxenford, D Taylor, GJ Davidson (TV), Ref: SR Bernard. Award: SA Abbott (SS). Crowd: 8,359
Points: SS 3, AS 1.   No subs. 10 overs: AS 3-85, SS 3-63

Match 17 – Renegades v Scorchers at Marvel Stadium, Melbourne on December 22, 2021 - Scorchers won by 21 runs

Scorchers		B	4	6
CT Bancroft	c Harper b Sutherland	24	21	3
JP Inglis +	c Maddins on b Pattinson	2	4	
MR Marsh	c Maddinson			
	b Richardson	86	53	5 5
C Munro	b Richardson	20	17	1 1
AJ Turner*	c Harper b Richardson	20	11	1 1
LJ Evans	not out	42	16	4 2
AC Agar	not out	0	0	
AJ Tye				
JP Behrendorff				
P Hatzoglou				
TS Mills				
	2 b, 3 lb, 2 nb, 5 w	12		
4 overs: 1-31	20 overs	5-206		

1-6 (Inglis, 1.4), 2-68 (Bancroft, 8.3), 3-138 (Munro, 15.4),
4-139 (Marsh, 15.6), 5-192 (Turner, 19.2)

Bowling	O	M	R	W	wd	nb	Dots
RJW Topley	4	0	44	0		2	10
JL Pattinson	4	0	39	1	2		9
Zahir Khan	4	0	45	0	2		4
KW Richardson	4	0	33	3			8
NJ Maddinson	1	0	8	0			2
WJ Sutherland	2	0	24	1	1		3
Mohammad Nabi	1	0	8	0			3

Renegades		B	4	6
MWG Harvey	b Behrendorff	0	2	
AJ Finch	c Behrendorff b Agar	68	43	4 5
NJ Maddinson*	c Inglis b Marsh	67	41	8 3
J Fraser-McGurk	c Behrendorff			
	b Hatzoglou	30	24	2 1
M Nabi	lbw b Agar	0	1	
WJ Sutherland	not out	15	8	2
SB Harper+	not out	0	1	
JL Pattinson				
RJW Topley				
KW Richardson				
Zahir Khan				
	3 lb, 2 w	5		
4 overs: 1-47	20 overs	5-185		

1-0 (Harvey, 0.2), 2-130 (Maddinson, 13.1), 3-141 (Finch, 15.2),
4-142 (Nabi, 15.4), 5-172 (Fraser-McGurk, 19.2)

Bowling	O	M	R	W	wd	nb	Dots
JP Behrendorff	2	0	25	1			3
TS Mills	4	0	38	0	2		9
AJ Tye	4	0	36	0			11
MR Marsh	3	0	20	1			7
AC Agar	3	0	23	2			7
P Hatzoglou	4	0	40	1			9

Toss: Scorchers. Umpires: DM Koch, BC Treloar, SAJ Craig (TV), Ref: RL Parry. Award: MR Marsh (PS).   No subs.   Crowd: 9,487
Marsh 50: 30 balls, 1x4 4x6; Finch 50: 32 balls, 1x4, 5x6, Maddinson 50: 30 balls, 5x4 3x6. Points: MR 1, PS 3.
10 overs: PS 2-87, MR 1-94

Match 18 – Strikers v Heat at Adelaide Oval on December 23, 2021 – Heat won by 39 runs

Heat		B	4	6
CA Lynn	c Nielsen b Agar	10	5	2
MA Bryant	c Agar b Rashid	32	20	5 1
TLW Cooper	lbw b Siddle	16	5	2 1
BM Duckett	c Wells b Rashid	78	47	10 2
SD Heazlett	c Short b Rashid	49	30	3 3
JJ Peirson*+	b Siddle	11	5	1 1
JJ Bazley	c Garton b Agar	2	3	
MT Steketee	not out	6	3	
MP Kuhnemann	not out	1	2	
Mujeeb-ur-Rahman				
LCJ Guthrie				
	3 w	3		
4 overs: 2-50	20 overs	7-208		

1-10 (Lynn, 0.5), 2-34 (Cooper, 2.4), 3-74 (Bryant, 6.6),
4-188 (Duckett, 17.4), 5-188 (Heazlett, 17.5),
6-197 (Bazley, 18.4), 7-202 (Peirson, 19.2)

Bowling	O	M	R	W	wd	nb	Dots
WA Agar	4	0	39	2	1		7
GHS Garton	3	0	48	0	1		6
PM Siddle	4	0	42	2			7
Rashid Khan	4	0	34	3	1		9
Fawad Ahmed	4	0	25	0			7
MW Short	1	0	20	0			0

Strikers		B	4	6
JB Weatherald	b Steketee	1	3	
MW Short	c Peirson b Kuhnemann	14	4	2
MT Renshaw	c Duckett b Bazley	22	23	
JW Wells	c Guthrie b Kuhnemann	55	41	6 1
TJ Kelly	c Duckett b Steketee	27	22	1
HJ Nielsen+	c Guthrie b Steketee	10	8	
GHS Garton	lbw b Kuhnemann	19	6	3
Rashid Khan	b Bazley	4	4	
WA Agar	not out	9	9	
PM Siddle *	not out	0	0	
Fawad Ahmed				
	1 b, 1 lb, 6 w	8		
4 overs: 1-34	20 overs	8-169		

1-15 (Short, 0.5), 2-17 (Weatherald, 1.3), 3-88 (Renshaw, 11.1),
4-97 (Wells, 12.4), 5-127 (Nielsen, 15.3), 6-147 (Garton, 16.5),
7-152 (Rashid, 17.4), 8-166 (Kelly, 19.5)

Bowling	O	M	R	W	wd	nb	Dots
MP Kuhnemann	4	0	47	3			6
MT Steketee	4	0	27	3	1		8
LCJ Guthrie	4	0	28	0	1		7
JJ Bazley	4	0	27	2			7
Mujeeb-ur-Rahma	4	0	38	0	1		7

Toss: Heat. Umpires: NR Johnstone, BNJ Oxenford, PJ Gillespie (TV), Ref: SD Fry. Award: BM Duckett (BH). Crowd: 7,581
Duckett 50: 32 balls, 6x4 1x6, Wells 50: 37 balls, 5x4 1x6. Points: AS 0, BH 4. No subs. 10 overs: BH 3-94, AS 2-82

Match 19 – Hurricanes v Stars at Bellerive Oval, Hobart on December 24, 2021 – Hurricanes won by 24 runs

Hurricanes		B	4	6
BR McDermott	c Cartwright b Russell	67	43	4	4
MS Wade*+	c Cartwright b Coulter-Nile	39	27	2	2
DJM Short	c Burns b Russell	26	24	2	1
PSP Handscomb	c Webster b Coulter-Nile	12	12		
TH David	not out	22	12	1	1
HC Brook	b Russell	0	2		
JA Thompson	c Hinchliffe b Couch	3	3		
NT Ellis	not out	0	0		
TS Rogers					
RP Meredith					
S Lamichhane					
	1 lb, 3 nb, 7 w	11			
4 overs: 0-35	20 overs	6-180			

Stars		B	4	6
MP Stoinis	c David b Rogers	18	16	1	1
JM Clarke+	st Wade b Short	52	40	2	3
GJ Maxwell*	c Brook b Meredith	12	9		
JA Burns	b Ellis	22	17	2	
AD Russell	c McDermott b Ellis	12	13	2	
HWR Cartwright	c Brook b Rogers	26	18	2	1
BJ Webster	c Ellis b Meredith	1	2		
NM Coulter-Nile	c Short b Meredith	0	1		
CD Hinchliffe	c & b Rogers	1	2		
Qais Ahmad	not out	2	2		
BL Couch	not out	0	1		
	1 lb, 1 nb, 3 w, 5 pen	10			
4 overs: 0-34	20 overs	9-156			

1-93 (Wade, 9.3), 2-115 (McDermott, 13.1), 3-150 (Short, 16.4), 4-157 (Handscomb, 17.5), 5-170 (Brook, 18.5), 6-173 (Thompson, 19.2)

1-32 (Stoinis, 5.2), 2-50 (Maxwell, 7.4), 3-105 (Clarke, 12.6), 4-107 (Burns, 13.3), 5-134 (Russell, 17.4), 6-143 (Webster, 18.3), 7-143 (Coulter-Nile, 18.4), 8-148 (Cartwright, 19.1), 9-150 (Hinchliffe, 19.4)

Bowling	O	M	R	W	wd	nb	Dots
GJ Maxwell	2	0	20	0	1		2
BL Couch	4	0	33	1	2	2	9
NM Coulter-Nile	4	0	22	2		1	10
Qais Ahmad	4	0	35	0	1		3
CD Hinchliffe	2	0	21	0			2
AD Russell	4	0	48	3	1		6

Bowling	O	M	R	W	wd	nb	Dots
RP Meredith	4	0	32	3	1		9
TS Rogers	4	0	29	3			10
TH David	1	0	8	0			4
NT Ellis	4	0	27	2	2		9
S Lamichhane	4	0	32	0			7
JA Thompson	1	0	8	0		1	3
DJM Short	2	0	14	1			1

Toss: Hurricanes. Umpires: DR Close, MW Graham-Smith, GA Abood (TV), Ref: SJ Davis. Award: NT Ellis (HH). Crowd: 4,967
McDermott 50: 28 balls, 4x4, 3x6. Clarke 50: 37 balls, 2x4 3x6. Points: HH 4, MS 0. No subs: 10 overs: HH 1-95, MS 2-84

Match 20 – Thunder v Sixers at Sydney Showgrounds on December 26, 2021 – Sixers won by 30 runs (DLS)

Sixers		B	4	6
JR Philippe+	c Green b Sams	13	10	1	
JM Vince	c Billings b Sams	31	29	5	
DP Hughes	b Mahmood	50	26	1	5
MC Henriques*	c Cutting b Green	10	4	1	
JC Silk	not out	18	12	3	
DT Christian	not out	41	17	4	2
SA Abbott					
H Kerr					
BJ Dwarshuis					
LAJ Pope					
MW Edwards					
	2 lb, 2 nb, 1 w	5			
4 overs: 1-29	16 overs	4-168			

Thunder	(DLS 173 in 16)	B	4	6
MR Gilkes	c Edwards b Dwarshuis	6	6	1	
AD Hales	c Edwards b Abbott	14	6		2
JJ Sangha	c Henriques b Kerr	47	30	6	1
SW Billings+	c Henriques b Pope	9	6	1	
AI Ross	st Philippe b Pope	16	14	1	
DR Sams	c Abbott b Edwards	28	11	4	
BCJ Cutting	c Hughes b Dwarshuis	10	9	1	
NJ McAndrew	c Edwards b Kerr	1	2		
CJ Green*	c Dwarshuis b Kerr	6	3	1	
S Mahmood	not out	2	3		
T Sangha	c Silk b Abbott	0	1		
	1 lb, 2 w	3			
4 overs: 2-40	15.1 overs	142			

1-24 (Philippe, 3.2), 2-62 (Vince, 8.3), 3-75 (Henriques, 9.2), 4-117 (Hughes, 12.4)

1-6 (Gilkes, 0.6), 2-39 (Hales, 3.4), 3-59 (Billings, 5.6), 4-93 (J Sangha, 9.5), 5-108 (Ross, 10.5), 6-125 (Sams, 12.4), 7-127 (McAndrew, 13.1), 8-136 (Green, 13.6), 9-140 (Cutting, 14.3), 10-142 (T Sangha, 15.1)

Bowling	O	M	R	W	wd	nb	Dots
S Mahmood	4	0	38	1			11
NJ McAndrew	3	0	39	0	1	1	5
DR Sams	3	0	29	2		1	8
CJ Green	3	0	19	1			6
T Sangha	2	0	26	0			4
BCJ Cutting	1	0	15	0			2

Bowling	O	M	R	W	wd	nb	Dots
BJ Dwarshuis	3	0	21	2			8
SA Abbott	3.1	0	29	2			8
H Kerr	3	0	29	3			5
MW Edwards	2	0	19	1	1		4
LAJ Pope	3	0	33	2			4
DT Christian	1	0	10	0	1		1

Toss: Thunder. Umpires: GJ Davidson, BNJ Oxenford, D Taylor (TV), Ref: SR Bernard. Award: DT Christian (SS). Crowd: 10,061
Hughes 50: 25 balls, 1x4 5x6. Points: SS 0, ST 4. SS Sub: MW Edwards for TR Murphy

Match 21 – Renegades v Scorchers at Marvel Stadium, Melbourne on December 26, 2021
Scorchers won by 8 wickets

Renegades			B	4	6
AJ Finch	c Marsh b Mills	8	7	1	
MWG Harvey	run out (Evans)	45	40	1	1
SB Harper+	c Bancroft b Agar	32	25	4	
NJ Maddinson*	b Mills	3	6		
J Fraser-McGurk	c Tye b Behrendorff	6	4		1
M Nabi	c Inglis b Marsh	7	13		
WJ Sutherland	c Tye b Behrendorff	2	3		
JA Prestwidge	not out	22	11	2	
JL Pattinson	b Agar	16	8	2	1
RJW Topley	not out	8	3		1
Zahir Khan					
	1 lb, 1 w	2			
4 overs: 1-28	20 overs	8-151			

1-12 (Finch, 1.5), 2-68 (Harper, 8.5), 3-76 (Maddinson, 10.4), 4-83 (Fraser-McGurk, 11.3), 5-99 (Nabi, 15.1), 6-105 (Harvey, 16.1), 7-105 (Sutherland, 16.2), 8-129 (Pattinson, 18.3)

Scorchers			B	4	6
CT Bancroft	lbw b Maddinson	23	19	2	1
JP Inglis+	st Harper b Zahir	23	18	2	
MR Marsh	not out	42	33	2	1
C Munro	not out	58	32	6	2
AJ Turner*					
LJ Evans					
AC Agar					
AJ Tye					
JP Behrendorff					
P Hatzoglou					
TS Mills					
	2 lb, 1 nb, 3 w	6			
4 overs: 0-30	16.5 overs	2-152			

1-49 (Inglis, 5.5), 2-53 (Bancroft, 6.4)

Bowling	O	M	R	W	wd	nb	Dots
JP Behrendorff	4	0	19	2			11
TS Mills	4	0	36	2	1		9
MR Marsh	3	0	18	1			7
AC Agar	4	0	38	2			7
AJ Tye	3	0	22	0			3
P Hatzoglou	2	0	17	0			4

Bowling	O	M	R	W	wd	nb	Dots
RJW Topley	4	0	36	0			8
JL Pattinson	3	0	35	0	2	1	4
Zahir Khan	4	0	30	1			6
Nj Maddinson	1	0	5	1			2
JA Prestwidge	2.5	0	25	0	1		4
WJ Sutherland	2	0	19	0			3

Toss: Renegades. Umpires: PJ Gillespie, NR Johnstone, DM Koch (TV), Ref: K Hannam. Award: MR Marsh (PS). Crowd: 1,771
Munro 50: 30 balls, 5x4 2x6.   Points: MR 0, PS 4.   No subs.   10 overs: MR 2-73, PS 2-80

Match 22 – Hurricanes v Strikers at Bellerive Oval, Hobart on December 27, 2021 – Hurricanes won by 7 wickets

Strikers			B	4	6
JB Weatherald	c David b Meredith	51	43	6	
MW Short	lbw b Rogers	2	3		
MT Renshaw	c McDermott b Meredith	63	41	9	
JW Wells	c McDermott b Meredith	17	13	2	
TJ Kelly	c & b Ellis	28	18	1	1
GHS Garton	not out	1	2		
HJ Nielsen+	not out	0	0		
Rashid Khan					
WA Agar					
PM Siddle*					
Fawad Ahmed					
	1 b, 6 lb, 6 w	13			
4 overs: 1-29	20 overs	5-175			

1-7 (Short, 1.1), 2-125 (Weatherald, 14.2), 3-130 (Renshaw, 14.5), 4-162 (Wells, 18.4), 5-174 (Kelly, 19.5)

Hurricanes			B	4	6
BR McDermott	not out	110	60	12	5
MS Wade*+	c Weatherald b Garton	6	7	1	
DJM Short	lbw b Siddle	37	32	3	1
HC Brook	lbw b Rashid	6	8		
TH David	not out	6	4	1	
PSP Handscomb					
JA Thompson					
NT Ellis					
TS Rogers					
RP Meredith					
S Lamichhane					
	5 lb, 6 w	11			
4 overs: 1-28	18.3 overs	3-176			

1-19 (Wade, 1.5), 2-100 (Short, 12.3), 3-135 (Brook, 15.3)

Bowling	O	M	R	W	wd	nb	Dots
RP Meredith	4	0	37	3	1		10
TS Rogers	4	0	30	1	1		6
NT Ellis	4	0	31	1	3		7
TH David	2	0	15	0	1		2
S Lamichhane	3	0	31	0			3
DJM Short	2	0	13	0			2
JA Thompson	1	0	11	0			

Bowling	O	M	R	W	wd	nb	Dots
MW Short	1	0	6	0			3
GHS Garton	3	0	30	1	1		5
WA Agar	3.3	0	44	0			3
PM Siddle	3	0	25	1	1		8
Fawad Ahmed	4	0	36	0	1		6
Rashid Khan	4	0	30	1			7

Toss: Strikers. Umpires: SA Lightbody, SJ Nogajski, SA Lightbody (TV), Ref: SJ Davis. Award: BR McDermott (HH).   Crowd: 4,896
Weatherald 50: 40 balls, 6x4; Renshaw 50: 31 balls, 7x4. McDermott 50: 36 balls, 6x4 1x6, 100: 58 balls, 11x4 5x6.
Points: HH 4, AS 0. No Subs. 10 overs: AS 1-79, HH 1-82.

Match 23 – Heat v Stars at the Gabba, Brisbane on December 27, 2021 – Stars won by 20 runs

Stars		B	4	6
MP Stoinis	c Peirson b Steketee	0	2	
JM Clarke+	b Mujeeb Zadran	85	44	7	5
JA Burns	b Guthrie	2	6	
GJ Maxwell*	c Guthrie b Steketee	2	4	
HWR Cartwright	c Duckett b Guthrie	79	44	1	8
AD Russell	lbw b Kuhnemann	0	2	
BJ Webster	c Steketee b Bazley	6	7	
NM Coulter-Nile	c Bryant b Steketee	1	4	
Qais Ahmad	c Duckett b Bazley	16	6	2	1
A Zampa	not out	4	2	1	
BL Couch				
	1 b, 1 lb, 1 nb, 9 w	12		
4 overs: 3-27	20 overs	9-207		

Heat		B	4	6
MA Bryant	c Russell b Couch	2	2	
CA Lynn	c Russell b Qais	57	34	3	5
TLW Cooper	c Maxwell b Couch	8	3	2	
BM Duckett	c Cartwright b Coulter-Nile	54	35	6	2
SD Heazlett	c Webster b Couch	26	15	2	1
JJ Peirson*+	run out (Cartwright)	2	2	
JJ Bazley	b Qais	2	5	
MT Steketee	b Zampa	3	11	
MP Kuhnemann	c Maxwell b Qais	9	4	2	
Mujeeb-ur-Rahman	not out	3	5	
LCJ Guthrie	not out	11	4	1	1
	5 b, 1 lb, 4 w	10		
4 overs: 2-38	20 overs	9-187		

1-0 (Stoinis, 0.2), 2-9 (Burns, 1.5), 3-16 (Maxwell, 2.5), 4-167 (Cartwright, 14.6), 5-167 (Russell, 15.2), 6-179 (Clarke, 16.6), 6-179 (Clarke, 16.6), 7-181 (Coulter-Nile, 18.1), 8-195 (Webster, 19.1), 9-207 (Qais, 19.6)

1-2 (Bryant, 0.2), 2-12 (Cooper, 0.6), 3-99 (Duckett, 10.3), 4-129 (Lynn, 12.4), 5-131 (Peirson, 13.1), 6-134 (Bazley, 14.1), 7-154 (Steketee, 16.6), 8-162 (Heazlett, 17.5), 9-172 (Kuhnemann, 18.6)

Bowling	O	M	R	W	wd	nb	Dots
MT Steketee	4	0	40	3	1		10
LCJ Guthrie	4	0	70	2	6	1	5
MP Kuhnemann	4	0	24	1			9
JJ Bazley	4	0	40	2	2		7
Mujeeb-ur-Rahman	4	0	31	1			10

Bowling	O	M	R	W	wd	nb	Dots
BL Couch	3	0	34	3	1		5
GJ Maxwell	4	0	30	0			8
NM Coulter-Nile	3	0	32	1			7
A Zampa	4	0	37	1			11
Qais Ahmad	4	1	26	3			12
AD Russell	2	0	22	0	3	2	

Toss: Heat. Umpires: GA Abood, AK Wilds, TM Penman (TV), Ref: KC Wessels. Award: JM Clarke (MS). Crowd: 14,803
Clarke 50: 26 balls, 4x4, 3x6, Cartwright 50: 31 balls, 1x4 5x6. Lynn 50: 28 balls, 2x4 5x6, Duckett 50: 33 balls, 6x4 2x6. No subs.
Points: BH 1, MS 3. 10 overs: MS 3-85, BH 2-91

Match 24 – Thunder v Scorchers at Manuka Oval, Canberra on December 28, 2021 – Thunder won by 34 runs

Thunder		B	4	6
MR Gilkes	c sub (NR Hobson) b Kelly	2	3	
AD Hales	b Kelly	13	11	1	1
JJ Sangha	not out	56	46	5	
SW Billings+	c Inglis b Tye	67	35	10	2
AI Ross	b Marsh	6	6	1	
DR Sams	lbw b Marsh	10	4	1	1
BCJ Cutting	c Agar b Behrendorff	10	6	2	
NJ McAndrew	b Kelly	6	5	1	
CJ Green*	not out	14	6	2	
S Mahmood				
T Sangha				
	6 lb, 2 nb, 8 w	16		
4 overs: 2-27	20 overs	7-200		

Scorchers		B	4	6
KR Patterson	c Green b McAndrew	10	12	1	
JP Inglis+	b Mahmood	0	1	
MR Marsh	c Gilkes b McAndrew	6	10	1	
C Munro	not out	64	43	6	
AJ Turner*	b McAndrew	13	10	1	
LJ Evans	c McAndrew b Mahmood	12	10	1	
AC Agar	b Sams	5	5	1	
AJ Tye	c Hales b Green	44	25	3	3
ML Kelly	c J Sangha b Green	1	2	
JP Behrendorff	not out	2	2	
LRT Morris				
	3 lb, 6 w	9		
4 overs: 3-17	20 overs	8-166		

1-5 (Gilkes, 1.3), 2-23 (Hales, 3.5), 3-136 (Billings, 14.3), 4-147 (Ross, 15.1), 5-158 (Sams, 15.5), 6-177 (Cutting, 17.5), 7-185 (McAndrew, 18.5)

1-1 (Inglis, 0.2), 2-16 (Marsh, 3.3), 3-17 (Patterson, 3.6), 4-44 (Turner, 6.5), 5-87 (Evans, 11.1), 6-97 (Agar, 12.4), 7-152 (Tye, 18.1), 8-155 (Kelly, 18.5)

Bowling	O	M	R	W	wd	nb	Dots
JP Behrendorff	4	0	34	1	2		9
ML Kelly	4	0	30	3			10
AC Agar	4	0	35	0	1		5
AJ Tye	1.3	0	26	1	1	2	3
P Hatzoglou	1	0	3	0		1	4
MR Marsh	4	0	50	2	1		7
LRT Morris	1.3	0	16	0	1		2

Bowling	O	M	R	W	wd	nb	Dots
S Mahmood	4	0	29	2			12
DR Sams	4	0	30	1	2		11
NJ McAndrew	4	0	40	3	2		7
CJ Green	4	0	29	2	1		6
T Sangha	3	0	25	0	1		7
BCJ Cutting	1	0	10	0			0

Toss: Scorchers. Umpires: DM Koch, D Taylor, GJ Davidson (TV), Ref: SR Bernard. Award: SW Billings (ST). Crowd: 9,740
J Sangha 50: 42 balls, 5x4, Munro 50: 33 balls, 5x4. Points ST 4, PS 0. 10 overs: ST 2-83, PS 4-77. PS Sub: LRT Morris for P Hatzoglou.

Match 25 – Sixers v Heat at the SCG on December 29, 2021 – Sixers won by 2 wickets

Heat			B	4	6
JJ Peirson*+	c Vince b Dwarshuis	0	4		
CA Lynn	c Abbott b Dwarshuis	2	6		
TLW Cooper	b Abbott	7	4		
BM Duckett	c Kerr b Abbott	21	19	2	
SD Heazlett	b Christian	4	10		
MA Bryant	c Silk b Abbott	22	23	1	1
XC Bartlett	c Philippe b Kerr	1	5		
JD Wildermuth	b Abbott	27	26	1	
JJ Bazley	c Abbott b Kerr	8	9		
MT Steketee	not out	10	9	1	
Mujeeb-ur-Rahman	run out				
	(Abbott-Christian)	0	0		
	2 lb, 1 w	3			
4 overs : 3-13	19.1 overs	105			

Sixers			B	4	6
JRP Philippe+	c Bazley b Steketee	0	2		
JM Vince	c Cooper b Bartlett	0	1		
DP Hughes	c Cooper b Bazley	6	13		
MC Henriques *	c Peirson b Mujeeb	15	15	1	
JC Silk	c Cooper b Wildermuth	3	4		
DT Christian	c Heazlett b Bartlett	2	7		
SA Abbott	not out	37	43	2	2
H Kerr	c Bryant b Bazley	2	6		
Shadab Khan	c Duckett				
	b Wildermuth	8	9	1	
BJ Dwarshuis	not out	23	20	3	
LAJ Pope					
	10 lb	10			
4 overs : 3-21	20 overs	8-106			

1-0 (Peirson, 0.4), 2-8 (Cooper, 1.6), 3-13 (Lynn, 3.2),
4-21 (Heazlett, 5.3), 5-41 (Duckett, 9.1), 6-46 (Bartlett, 10.3),
7-63 (Bryant, 12.5), 8-86 (Bazley, 16.2), 9-104 (Wildermuth, 18.6),
10-105 (Mujeeb, 19.1)

1-0 (Philippe, 0.2), 2-0 (Vince, 1.1), 3-21 (Hughes, 3.6),
4-26 (Silk, 5.1), 5-29 (Christian, 6.4), 6-30 (Henriques, 7.1),
7-35 (Kerr, 8.6), 8-47 (Shadab, 12.5)

Bowling	O	M	R	W	wd	nb	Dots
BJ Dwarshuis	4	1	13	2			15
SA Abbott	4	0	31	4			9
H Kerr	4	0	18	2			9
Shadab Khan	4	0	27	0			6
DT Christian	2.1	0	8	1	1		8
LAJ Pope	1	0	6	0			3

Bowling	O	M	R	W	wd	nb	Dots
MT Steketee	4	1	25	1			14
XC Bartlett	4	0	22	2			13
JJ Bazley	4	0	19	2			10
Mujeeb-ur-Rahma	4	0	12	1			12
JD Wildermuth	4	0	18	2			13

Toss: Heat. Umpires: DR Close, SJ Nogajski , BNJ Oxenford (TV), Ref: DR Gilbert. Award: SA Abbott (SS). Crowd: 11,354
BH Sub: JD Wildermuth for MP Kuhnemann. Points: SS 3, BH 1. 10 overs BH 5-45, SS 7-36.

Match 26 – Renegades v Hurricanes at Marvel Stadium, Melbourne on December 29, 2021 – Hurricanes won by 85 runs

Hurricanes			B	4	6
MS Wade*+	c Fraser-McGurk b Topley	0	3		
BR McDermott	run out (Harper)	127	65	9	9
DJM Short	c Harper b Topley	5	7		
HC Brook	c Harvey b Maddinson	11	16		
PSP Handscomb	c Richardson b Prestwidge	24	20	2	
TH David	not out	30	9	1	4
JA Thompson					
NT Ellis					
TS Rogers					
RP Meredith					
S Lamichhane					
	2 b, 1 lb, 6 w	9			
4 overs : 2-19	20 overs	5-206			

Renegades			B	4	6
SB Harper+	run out (Ellis-Wade)	57	35	4	3
AJ Finch	c Thompson b Rogers	1	2		
NJ Maddinson*	c Short b Rogers	3	7		
MWG Harvey	c Meredith b Rogers	0	1		
J Fraser-McGurk	c Short b Lamichhane	21	13	1	1
M Nabi	c Short b Lamichhane	2	3		
JA Prestwidge	c Brook b Meredith	10	13		
JLP attinson	run out				
	(Lamichhane-Short)	0	1		
KW Richardson	c Handscomb b Short	0	1		
RJW Topley	not out	14	11	1	1
Zahir Khan	st Wade b Lamichhane	3	8		
	2 lb, 8 w	10			
4 overs : 3-39	15.5 overs	121			

1-0 (Wade, 0.3), 2-17 (Short, 3.2), 3-52 (Brook, 8.5),
4-167 (Handscomb, 17.4), 5-206 (McDermott, 19.6),

1-19 (Finch, 1.1), 2-30 (Maddinson, 3.2), 3-31 (Harvey, 3.4),
4-69 (Fraser-McGurk, 7.2), 5-73 (Nabi, 7.6), 6-102 (Harper, 11.6),
7-102 (Pattinson, 12.1), 8-103 (Richardson, 12.3)
9-109 (Prestwidge, 13.1), 10-121 (Zahir, 15.5)

Bowling	O	M	R	W	wd	nb	Dots
RJW Topley	4	0	17	2			13
Mohammad Nabi	1	0	6	0			2
KW Richardson	4	0	63	0			6
Zahir Khan	3	0	37	0	3		4
JLP attinson	3	0	31	0	3		4
NJ Maddinson	2	0	13	1			4
JA Prestwidge	3	0	31	1			5

Bowling	O	M	R	W	wd	nb	Dots
RP Meredith	3	0	31	1	2		5
TS Rogers	3	0	24	3			6
NT Ellis	3	0	14	0	1		10
S Lamichhane	3.5	0	32	3	1		7
JA Thompson	1	0	7	0			3
DJM Short	2	0	11	1			6

Toss: Renegades. Umpires: MW Graham-Smith, AK Wilds, NR Johnstone (TV), Ref: RL Parry. Award: BR McDermott (HH).
McDermott 50: 37 balls, 4x4, 2x6; 100: 53 balls, 7x4 7x6. Harper 50: 34 balls, 4x4 3x6. Points: MR 1, HH 3. Crowd: 8,314
No subs: 10 over scores: HH 3-66, MR 5-85

Match 27 – Strikers v Thunder at Adelaide Oval on December 31, 2021 – Thunder won by 22 runs

Thunder		B	4	6
MR Gilkes	c Short b Fawad	13	10	1	1
BCJ Cutting	c Nielsen b Siddle	37	32	3	2
JJ Sangha	not out	91	55	6	6
SW Billings+	c Short b Worrall	18	11	1	1
O Davies	not out	26	12	1	2
DR Sams				
AJ Nair				
NJ McAndrew				
CJ Green*				
BJ Doggett				
S Mahmood				
	2 w	2		
4 overs: 0-37	20 overs	3-187		

Strikers		B	4	6
JB Weatherald	c Green b Sams	31	29	2	
MW Short	lbw b Mahmood	16	12	2	1
MT Renshaw	c Green b Mahmood	38	26	5	
JW Wells	c McAndrew b Sams	46	26	5	1
TJ Kelly	c sub (LD Hearne) b Sangha	1	3		
GHS Garton	c Mahmood b Sams	8	11		
HJ Nielsen+	not out	13	11	1	
Rashid Khan	c Billings b Sams	0	1		
DJ Worrall	not out	1	1		
PM Siddle*				
Fawad Ahmed				
	1 lb, 10 w	11		
4 overs: 1-29	20 overs	7-165		

1-37 (Gilkes, 4.3), 2-62 (Cutting, 9.3), 3-98 (Billings, 13.2)

1-23 (Short, 2.6), 2-91 (Renshaw, 10.6), 3-96 (Weatherald, 11.3), 4-102 (Kelly, 12.3), 5-119 (Garton, 15.3), 6-161 (Wells, 19.2), 7-162 (Rashid, 19.4)

Bowling	O	M	R	W	wd	nb	Dots
DJ Worrall	4	0	34	1			11
GHS Garton	3	0	47	0			6
PM Siddle	4	0	47	1	2		5
Fawad Ahmed	4	0	22	1			7
Rashid Khan	4	0	23	0			10
MW Short	1	0	14	0			

Bowling	O	M	R	W	wd	nb	Dots
S Mahmood	4	0	35	2	1		10
DR Sams	4	0	33	4	2		6
CJ Green	4	0	20	0			9
NJ McAndrew	3	0	32	0	2		5
AJ Nair	1	0	8	0			1
BJ Doggett	3	0	33	0	1		2
JJ Sangha	1	0	3	1			3

Toss: Thunder. Umpires: DR Close, GJ Davidson, E Sheridan (TV), Ref: SD Fry. Award: JJ Sangha (ST). Crowd: 9,555
J Sangha 50: 39 balls, 1x4 4x6. Points: AS 1, ST 3. No subs. 10 overs: ST 2-65, AS 1-81

Match 28 – Hurricanes v Heat at Bellerive Oval, Hobart on January 1, 2022 – Heat won by 14 runs

Heat		B	4	6
CA Lynn	c Meredith b Ellis	13	15	2	
JJ Peirson*+	c Wade b Meredith	5	3	1	
BM Duckett	c Handscomb b Rogers	5	4	1	
SD Heazlett	c David b Rogers	26	28	2	1
MA Bryant	c Ellis b Thompson	9	10	1	
XC Bartlett	lbw b Ellis	7	7	1	
JD Wildermuth	c Short b Lamichhane	28	21	2	1
JJ Bazley	not out	44	27	3	2
MT Steketee	c Brook b Ellis	10	5	1	
MP Kuhnemann	not out	0	0		
Mujeeb-ur-Rahman				
	3 w	3		
4 overs: 2-16	20 overs	8-150		

Hurricanes		B	4	6
MS Wade*+	c Peirson b Bartlett	1	5		
BR McDermott	lbw b Bartlett	0	3		
DJM Short	c Steketee b Bartlett	27	38	3	
HC Brook	lbw b Mujeeb	22	20	3	
PSP Handscomb	c Bryant b Mujeeb	14	10	1	1
TH David	c Peirson b Bartlett	7	8	1	
JA Thompson	b Mujeeb	7	4	1	
NT Ellis	c Bartlett b Steketee	18	10	2	1
TS Rogers	not out	33	20	4	2
RP Meredith	not out	3	2		
S Lamichhane				
	2 lb, 2 w	4		
4 overs: 2-18	20 overs	8-136		

1-7 (Peirson, 1.2), 2-14 (Duckett, 2.3), 3-26 (Lynn, 5.1), 4-47 (Bryant, 8.1), 5-64 (Bartlett, 10.3), 6-77 (Heazlett, 12.1), 7-119 (Wildermuth, 17.4), 8-142 (Steketee, 19.4)

1-1 (Wade, 1.1), 2-6 (McDermott, 1.5), 3-38 (Brook, 7.6), 4-58 (Handscomb, 11.1), 5-68 (David, 13.4), 6-72 (Short, 13.6), 7-93 (Thompson, 15.2), 8-120 (Ellis, 18.1)

Bowling	O	M	R	W	wd	nb	Dots
TS Rogers	4	0	15	2			12
RP Meredith	4	0	23	1	1		11
TH David	1	0	10	0			2
NT Ellis	4	0	41	3	2		8
S Lamichhane	4	0	37	1			6
JA Thompson	3	0	24	1			5

Bowling	O	M	R	W	wd	nb	Dots
MT Steketee	4	0	30	1			13
XC Bartlett	4	0	30	4	1		10
JD Wildermuth	4	0	34	0	1		9
JJ Bazley	4	0	20	0			10
Mujeeb-ur-Rahma	4	0	20	3			16

Toss: Hurricanes. Umpires: MW Graham-Smith, NR Johnstone, BC Treloar (TV), Ref: DA Johnston. Award: Mujeeb-ur-Rahman (BH).
Points: HH 0, BH 4. 10 overs: BH 4-61, HH 3-44. BH Sub: JD Wildermuth for LCJ Guthrie. Crowd: 5,137

Match 30 – Stars v Scorchers at Junction Oval, Melbourne on January 2, 2022 – Scorchers won by 50 runs

Scorchers			B	4	6
CT Bancroft+	run out (O'Connell)	5	7		
KR Patterson	c Wakim b Haris	54	39	4	2
C Munro	c Cartwright b O'Connell	40	20	1	4
LJ Evans	lbw b Couch	2	3		
AJ Turner*	run out (Couch)	27	19	2	
AM Hardie	b Qais	5	7		
AC Agar	c O'Connell b Qais	19	16	2	1
AJ Tye	not out	7	6	1	
JP Behrendorff	b Haris Rauf	3	4		
P Hatzoglou					
TS Mills					
	4 b, 2 lb, 1 nb, 11 w	18			
4 overs: 1-41	20 overs	8-180			

1-27 (Bancroft, 2.4), 2-95 (Munro, 8.6), 3-103 (Evans, 9.6),
4-116 (Patterson, 11.6), 5-129 (Hardie, 14.1 ov),
6-164 (Turner, 17.6 ov), 7-165 (Agar, 18.3 ov),
8-180 (Behrendorff, 19.6 ov)

Bowling	O	M	R	W	wd	nb	Dots
GJ Maxwell	4	0	38	0	1	1	6
BL Couch	4	0	36	1	2		9
Haris Rauf	4	0	40	2			8
XA Crone	2	0	16	0			3
Qais Ahmad	4	0	26	2	1		5
TL O'Connell	2	0	18	1			2

Stars			B	4	6
JM Clarke+	c Evans b Tye	52	32	9	1
TF Rogers	c Munro b Hatzoglou	32	25	4	1
GJ Maxwell*	b Hatzoglou	4	7		
CA Wakim	c Mills b Behrendorff	20	24	1	1
HWR Cartwright	c Evans b Mills	12	10	1	1
TL O'Connell	c Hardie b Tye	0	2		
JJ Avendano	c Evans b Agar	6	5	1	
XA Crone	run out (Bancroft-Mills)	1	4		
Qais Ahmad	c Hardie b Mills	1	2		
BL Couch	lbw b Mills	0	2		
Haris Rauf	not out	0	0		
	2 w	2			
4 overs: 0-39	18.5 overs	130			

1-78 (Clarke, 8.3), 2-86 (Rogers, 9.5), 3-95 (Maxwell, 11.5),
4-111 (Cartwright, 14.5), 5-115 (O'Connell, 15.2),
6-122 (Wakim, 16.5), 7-129 (Avendano, 17.4), 8-130 (Crone, 18.2),
9-130 (Qais, 18.3), 10-130 (Couch, 18.5)

Bowling	O	M	R	W	wd	nb	Dots
TS Mills	3.5	0	28	3			14
JP Behrendorff	4	0	33	1			13
AJ Tye	3	0	11	2			11
AC Agar	4	0	31	1	1		11
P Hatzoglou	4	0	27	2	1		11

Toss: Scorchers. Umpires: GJ Davidson, BNJ Oxenford, CA Polosak (TV), Ref: RL Parry. Award: P Hatzoglou (PS). Crowd: 3,272
Patterson 50: 34 balls, 4x4, 2x6. Clarke 50: 29 balls, 9x4 1x6. Points: MS 0, PS 4. No subs. 10 overs: PS 3-103, MS 2-87

Match 31 – Thunder v Strikers at Sydney Showgrounds on January 2, 2022 – Thunder won by 28 runs

Thunder			B	4	6
MR Gilkes	c Renshaw b Agar	93	57	9	3
BCJ Cutting	c Wells b Agar	34	25	3	2
JJ Sangha	c Fawad b Rashid	6	9		
SW Billings+	c Kelly b Siddle	11	9	1	
O Davies	lbw b Siddle	14	12	2	
DR Sams	b Siddle	1	2		
CJ Green*	c Wells b Agar	5	6		
AJ Nair	not out	0	0		
GS Sandhu					
Mohammad Hasnain					
S Mahmood					
	5 lb, 3 w	8			
4 overs: 0-38	20 overs	7-172			

1-64 (Cutting, 7.3), 2-73 (Sangha, 9.3), 3-97 (Billings, 12.3),
4-140 (Davies, 16.6), 5-154 (Sams, 18.1), 6-172 (Gilkes, 19.5),
7-172 (Green, 19.6)

Bowling	O	M	R	W	wd	nb	Dots
MW Short	4	0	28	0	1		8
WA Agar	4	0	26	3	2		12
PM Siddle	4	0	36	3			9
Fawad Ahmed	4	0	51	0			2
Rashid Khan	4	0	26	1			9

Strikers			B	4	6
JB Weatherald	lbw b Hasnain	10	9	2	
MW Short	c Sams b Hasnain	13	6	2	
MT Renshaw	c Green b Sangha	30	21	2	
JW Wells	c Cutting b Hasnain	0	2		
HJ Hunt	st Billings b Sangha	5	11		
T Kelly	run out (Gilkes)	19	15	2	
HJ Nielsen+	c Cutting b Green	39	31	4	1
Rashid Khan	c sub (JD Cook) b Mahmood	1	2		
WA Agar	c Green b Sams	9	13		
PM Siddle*	b Mahmood	4	3	1	
Fawad Ahmed	not out	4	2	1	
	2 lb, 8 w	10			
4 overs: 3-30	19.1 overs	144			

1-25 (Short, 2.2), 2-25 (Weatherald, 2.3), 3-25 (Wells, 2.5),
4-50 (Hunt, 6.6), 5-65 (Renshaw, 8.6), 6-110 (Kelly, 13.5),
7-111 (Rashid, 14.1), 8-135 (Agar, 17.6), 9-140 (Siddle, 18.4),
10-144 (Nielsen, 19.1)

Bowling	O	M	R	W	wd	nb	Dots
S Mahmood	4	0	44	2	2		8
GS Sandhu	2	0	14	0			5
Mohammad Hasnain	4	1	20	3	1		14
DR Sams	4	0	26	1	5		8
CJ Green	3.1	0	22	1			6
JJ Sangha	2	0	16	2			2

Toss: Thunder. Umpires: GA Abood, SA Lightbody, TM Penman (TV), Ref: K Hannam. Award: MR Gilkes (ST). Crowd: 5,784
Gilkes 50: 39 balls, 4x4, 2x6. Points: ST 3, AS 1. No subs. 10 overs: ST 2-73, AS 5-74

Match 32 – Stars v Renegades at the MCG on January 3, 2022 – Renegades won by 5 wickets

Stars			B	4	6
TJ Dean	b Maddinson	32	26	3	
JJ Avendano	c &b Maddinson	6	9	1	
CA Wakim	c Harper b Maddinson	12	11	1	
GJ Maxwell*	c Harvey b Topley	7	9		
HWR Cartwright	c Harvey b Topley	41	29	4	1
PJ Rowe+	c Harvey b Prestwidge	3	6		
TL O'Connell	c Marsh b Richardson	3	8		
Qais Ahmad	c Marsh b Richardson	10	14	1	
BL Couch	c Harper b Richardson	0	1		
Haris Rauf	b Topley	8	5	1	
Ahmed Daniyal	not out	1	2		
	1 lb, 2 w	3			
4 overs: 1-28	20 overs	126			

1-13 (Avendano, 2.1), 2-43 (Wakim, 6.2), 3-54 (Dean, 8.3),
4-61 (Maxwell, 9.5), 5-68 (Rowe, 11.5), 6-72 (O'Connell, 13.3),
7-99 (Qais, 16.6), 8-109 (Couch, 18.2), 9-117 (Cartwright, 19.1),
10-126 (Haris, 19.6)

Bowling	O	M	R	W	wd	nb	Dots
RJW Topley	4	0	27	3	1		12
Mohammad Nabi	2	0	20	0			2
NJ Maddinson	4	0	20	3			8
Zahir Khan	4	0	25	0	1		10
KW Richardson	4	1	24	3			11
JA Prestwidge	2	0	9	1			4

Renegades			B	4	6
SB Harper+	st Rowe b Qais	7	7	1	
AJ Finch	c Rauf b O'Connell	50	40	3	2
SE Marsh	c Couch b Daniyal	21	17	2	
NJ Maddinson*	lbw b O'Connell	4	5		
MWG Harvey	not out	23	25	3	
M Nabi	b Rauf	0	1		
JL Seymour	not out	17	14	2	
WJ Sutherland					
JA Prestwidge					
KW Richardson					
RJW Topley					
Zahir Khan					
	2 lb, 1 nb, 4 w	7			
4 overs: 1-23	18 overs	5-129			

1-10 (Harper, 1.5), 2-71 (Marsh, 9.1), 3-87 (Maddinson, 11.1),
4-90 (Finch, 11.6), 5-91 (Nabi, 12.2)

Bowling	O	M	R	W	wd	nb	Dots
Ahmed Daniyal	3	0	24	1	1	1	7
Qais Ahmad	4	0	33	1	1		11
Haris Rauf	4	0	26	1			11
GJ Maxwell	3	0	19	0			3
BL Couch	2	0	14	0			4
TL O'Connell	2	0	11	2			5

Toss: Stars. Umpires: BNJ Oxenford, GJ Davidson, PJ Gillespie (TV), Ref: RW Stratford. Award: KW Richardson (MR) Crowd: 21,562
Finch 50: 39 balls, 3x4 2x6. MR Sub: JL Seymour for WJ Sutherland. Points: MS 0, MR 4. 10 over scores: MS 4-61, MR 2-78

Match 33 – Scorchers v Sixers at Metricon Stadium, Gold Coast on January 4, 2022 – Scorchers won by 10 runs

Scorchers			B	4	6
KR Patterson	c Abbott b Christian	27	25	1	1
CT Bancroft+	c Philippe b Bird	6	7	1	
C Munro	c Abbott b Kerr	27	36	1	
LJ Evans	c Philippe b Christian	0	3		
AJ Turner*	c Christian b Kerr	2	4		
AM Hardie	c Christian b Kerr	45	24	3	2
AC Agar	c Silk b Kerr	29	20	3	
AJ Tye	c Silk b Abbott	0	1		
P Hatzoglou	not out	0	0		
TS Mills					
LRT Morris					
	5 lb, 2 w	7			
4 overs: 1-23	20 overs	8-143			

Sixers			B	4	6
JR Philippe+	c Bancroft b Morris	0	3		
JM Vince	b Mills	5	9		
JR Edwards	c Munro b Mills	1	3		
MC Henriques*	c Munro b Morris	5	7	1	
JC Silk	c Munro b Tye	16	19	1	
DT Christian	c sub (CJM Sabburg) b Tye	73	61	5	4
SA Abbott	c Bancroft b Tye	4	2	1	
H Kerr	not out	13	11	1	
BJ Dwarshuis	b Mills	6	5		
JM Bird	not out	1	1		
SNJ O'Keefe					
	3 lb, 1 nb, 5 w	9			
4 overs: 4-20	20 overs	8-133			

1-15 (Bancroft, 2.1), 2-62 (Patterson, 10.1), 3-62 (Evans, 10.4),
4-68 (Turner, 12.2), 5-69 (Munro, 12.5), 6-118 (Agar, 17.6),
7-118 (Tye, 18.1), 8-143 (Hardie, 19.6)

1-0 (Philippe, 0.3), 2-5 (J Edwards, 1.2), 3-16 (Henriques, 2.6),
4-16 (Vince, 3.3), 5-61 (Silk, 12.1), 6-67 (Abbott, 12.5),
7-124 (Christian, 18.5), 8-132 (Dwarshuis, 19.5)

Bowling	O	M	R	W	wd	nb	Dots
JM Bird	3	0	22	1	1		7
SA Abbott	4	0	28	1			9
BJ Dwarshuis	3	0	27	0			8
H Kerr	4	0	32	4	1		10
SNj O'Keefe	2	0	15	0			2
DT Christian	4	0	14	2			11

Bowling	O	M	R	W	wd	nb	Dots
LRT Morris	4	0	25	2	1	1	13
TS Mills	4	0	29	3	3		14
AJ Tye	4	0	17	3	1		15
P Hatzoglou	4	0	30	0			8
AC Agar	4	0	29	0			8

Toss: Scorchers. Umpires: GA Abood, TM Penman, D Taylor (TV), Ref: KC Wessels. Award: AM Hardie (PS). Crowd: 5,970
Christian 50: 51 balls, 4x4 2x6. Points: PS 4, SS 0. No subs. 10 overs: PS 1-62, SS 4-41

Match 34 – Strikers v Hurricanes at Adelaide Oval on January 5, 2022 – Strikers won by 7 wickets

Hurricanes			B	4	6
BR McDermott	c Kelly b Siddle	11	12	1	
MS Wade *+	b Conway	1	4		
DJM Short	b Short	32	32	3	
PSP Handscomb	run out				
	(Agar-Nielsen-Short)	14	13	1	
CP Jewell	c & b Rashid	2	4		
TH David	b Siddle	28	18	2	1
MB Wright	c Wells b Rashid	6	14		
MJ Owen	b Siddle	16	10	3	
TS Rogers	b Siddle	8	9		
RP Meredith	not out	1	1		
S Lamichhane	b Siddle	2	2		
	2 lb, 3 w	5			
4 overs: 2-18	19.5 overs	126			

1-6 (Wade, 1.3), 2-13 (McDermott, 3.2), 3-49 (Handscomb, 8.1), 4-53 (Jewell, 9.1), 5-88 (Short, 12.5), 6-96 (David, 15.4), 7-106 (Wright, 16.5), 8-123 (Owen, 19.1), 9-124 (Rogers, 19.3), 10-126 (Lamichhane, 19.5)

Strikers			B	4	6
MW Short	not out	72	44	4	5
HJ Hunt	c Short b Lamichhane	18	14	3	
MT Renshaw	c David b Lamichhane	19	21	1	
JW Wells	c Owen b Short	11	11	1	
JB Weatherald	not out	0	1		
TJ Kelly					
Rashid Khan					
HJ Nielsen+					
HNA Conway					
WA Agar					
PM Siddle*					
	7 lb, 2 w	9			
4 overs: 0-38	15.1 overs	3-129			

1-38 (Hunt, 4.3), 2-106 (Renshaw, 12.1), 3-125 (Wells, 14.5)

Bowling	O	M	R	W	wd	nb	Dots
MW Short	4	0	25	1	1		6
HNA Conway	4	0	24	1	1		12
WA Agar	4	0	26	0	1		10
PM Siddle	3.5	0	23	5			10
Rashid Khan	4	0	26	2			8

Bowling	O	M	R	W	wd	nb	Dots
TH David	3	0	23	0			9
TS Rogers	4	0	29	0			9
RP Meredith	1	0	12	0	1		3
S Lamichhane	4	0	22	2	1		8
DJM Short	2	0	23	1			4
MJ Owen	1.1	0	13	0			3

Toss: Strikers. Umpires: PJ Gillespie, AK Wilds, SJ Nogajski (TV), Ref: SJ Davis. Award: MW Short (AS). Crowd: 5,575
Short 50: 36 balls, 2x4 4x6. HH Sub: MB Wright for WB Parker. Points: AS 4, HH 0. 10 overs: HH 4-65, AS 1-80

Match 35 – Renegades v Heat at Kardinia Park, Geelong on January 6, 2022 – Renegades won by 5 wickets

Heat			B	4	6
JS Lehmann	c Nabi b Richardson	65	52	8	
JJ Clayton	lbw b Zahir	15	15	3	
Fakhar Zaman	c Evans b Zahir	3	8		
SD Heazlett	c Harper b Nabi	12	16		1
TLW Cooper*	c Harvey b Nabi	4	7		
LDP feffer+	c Sutherland				
	b Richardson	6	6		
S McGiffin	not out	14	11	1	
W Prestwidge	not out	2	6		
RH McDonald					
DMK Grant					
Mujeeb-ur-Rahman					
	1 b, 1 nb, 5 w	7			
4 overs: 0-33	20 overs	6-128			

1-36 (Clayton, 4.4), 2-42 (Fakhar, 6.3), 3-63 (Heazlett, 10.5), 4-80 (Cooper, 13.4), 5-98 (Pfeffer, 15.5), 6-124 (Lehmann, 18.5)

Renegades			B	4	6
SB Harper+	b Grant	0	3		
AJ Finch	c McDonald b Grant	37	28	2	2
SE Marsh	c Fakhar b Mujeeb	57	35	6	3
NJ Maddinson*	not out	22	14		2
WJ Sutherland	c Mujeeb b Grant	5	7		
MWG Harvey	c Lehmann				
	b McDonald	0	2		
JL Seymour	not out	3	1		
KW Richardson					
ZK Evans					
Zahir Khan					
M Nabi					
	3 lb, 2 w	5			
4 overs: 1-26	15 overs	5-129			

1-0 (Harper, 0.3), 2-96 (Marsh, 10.1), 3-106 (Finch, 11.4), 4-114 (Sutherland, 13.3), 5-118 (Harvey, 14.3)

Bowling	O	M	R	W	wd	nb	Dots
ZK Evans	3	0	26	0	1		6
JL Pattinson	1	0	10	0	1		4
WJ Sutherland	3	0	25	0	1	1	6
KW Richardson	4	0	22	2			10
Zahir Khan	4	0	21	2	1		10
JL Seymour	1	0	4	0			2
Mohammad Nabi	4	0	19	2			6

Bowling	O	M	R	W	wd	nb	Dots
DMK Grant	4	0	20	3			11
RH McDonald	2	0	21	1	1		3
W Prestwidge	2	0	22	0			5
Mujeeb-ur-Rahman	4	0	16	1	1		13
S McGiffin	1	0	16	0			1
SD Heazlett	1	0	15	0			1
TLW Cooper	1	0	16	0			1

Toss: Renegades. Umpires: BNJ Oxenford, BC Treloar, GJ Davidson (TV), Ref: K Hannam. Award: SE Marsh (MR). Crowd: 4,611
Lehmann 50: 42 balls, 6x4. Marsh 50: 31 balls, 5x4 3x6. MR Sub: M Nabi for JL Pattinson. Points: MR 4, BH 0.
10 overs: BH 2-58, MR 1-96

Match 36 – Scorchers v Thunder at Carrara Stadium, Gold Coast on January 6, 2022 – Thunder won by 6 wickets (DLS)

Scorchers			B	4	6
KR Patterson	c Cutting b Sandhu	19	14	2	
CT Bancroft+	c Sangha b Green	30	31	2	1
C Munro	c Cutting b Sandhu	18	20		1
LJ Evans	c Billings b Sandhu	20	18		
AJ Turner*	c Billings b Mahmood	8	4	2	
AM Hardie	c Gilkes b Sandhu	4	5		
AC Agar	run out (Billings-Mahmood)	22	10	1	2
AJ Tye	c Sangha b Sams	1	3		
ML Kelly	b Mahmood	1	2		
TS Mills	not out	1	1		
LRT Morris					
	2 lb, 7 w	9			
4 overs: 0-31	18 overs	9-133			

Thunder			B	4	6
MR Gilkes	c & b Tye	32	23	4	1
AD Hales	c Munro b Tye	26	32	1	1
JJ Sangha	b Kelly	34	26	2	2
SW Billings+	not out	19	11	4	
O Davies	run out (Tye)	19	10	1	2
DR Sams	not out	1	1		
BCJ Cutting					
NJ McAndrew					
CJ Green*					
GS Sandhu					
S Mahmood					
	2 lb, 1 nb, 3 w	6			
4 overs: 0-31	17 overs	4-137			

1-33 (Patterson, 4.2), 2-61 (Bancroft, 9.4), 3-80 (Munro, 11.6), 4-97 (Turner, 13.4), 5-107 (Hardie, 15.1), 6-107 (Evans, 15.2), 7-111 (Tye, 16.2), 8-126 (Kelly, 17.3), 9-133 (Agar, 17.6)

1-51 (Gilkes, 6.3), 2-90 (Hales, 12.6), 3-95 (Sangha, 13.4), 4-131 (Davies, 16.5)

Bowling	O	M	R	W	wd	nb	Dots
S Mahmood	4	0	42	2	1		8
GS Sandhu	4	0	22	4	1		10
NJ McAndrew	3	0	23	0			10
DR Sams	4	0	28	1	2		3
CJ Green	2	0	9	1	1		4
BCJ Cutting	1	0	7	0			1

Bowling	O	M	R	W	wd	nb	Dots
LRT Morris	3	0	26	0			6
ML Kelly	4	0	29	1			11
TS Mills	3	0	21	0	2		10
AJ Tye	4	0	38	2	1	1	12
AC Agar	3	0	21	0			6

Toss: Scorchers. Umpires: GA Abood, TM Penman, MW Graham-Smith (TV), Ref: KC Wessels. Award: GS Sandhu (ST). Crowd: 556. Rain delay with PS 0-24 (3.2) reduced match to 18 overs per side. No subs. Points: PS 0, ST 4. 9 overs: PS 1-59, ST 1-62

Match 37 – Renegades v Thunder at Marvel Stadium, Melbourne on January 8, 2022 – Thunder won by 129 runs

Thunder			B	4	6
MR Gilkes	c & b Evans	10	8	1	1
AD Hales	c Evans b Zahir Khan	63	28	3	5
JJ Sangha*	b Sutherland	21	23	2	
DR Sams	not out	98	44	7	8
O Davies	c Harper b Richardson	2	3		
BCJ Cutting	c & b Maddinson	6	5	1	
BJH Holt+	c Harvey b Richardson	2	7		
NJ McAndrew	run out (Harper-Richardson)	2	3		
GS Sandhu	not out	0	0		
T Sangha					
M Hasnain					
	2 lb, 1 nb, 2 w	5			
4 overs: 1-33	20 overs	7-209			

Renegades			B	4	6
SB Harper+	c J Sangha b Sandhu	4	7		
AJ Finch	b T Sangha	17	12	2	
SE Marsh	run out (Hasnain-Holt)	8	5	1	
NJ Maddinson*	c Holt b Hasnain	1	2		
MWG Harvey	c Holt b Sams	2	3		
JL Seymour	b Hasnain	25	23	3	
WJ Sutherland	lbw b McAndrew	4	5		
KW Richardson	b Sandhu	17	21	3	
JK Lalor	c Holt b T Sangha	1	5		
ZK Evans	not out	0	2		
Zahir Khan	b Hasnain	0	1		
	1 w	1			
4 overs: 3-29	14.2 overs	80			

1-12 (Gilkes, 1.4), 2-78 (J Sangha, 8.2), 3-118 (Hales, 11.4), 4-132 (Davies, 13.1), 5-162 (Cutting, 15.3), 6-182 (Holt, 17.5), 7-205 (McAndrew, 19.5)

1-5 (Harper, 1.3), 2-27 (Marsh, 3.2), 3-29 (Maddinson, 3.6), 4-32 (Harvey, 4.4), 5-38 (Finch, 5.4), 6-46 (Sutherland, 6.5), 7-78 (Richardson, 12.4), 8-79 (Lalor, 13.3), 9-80 (Seymour, 14.1), 10-80 (Zahir, 14.2)

Bowling	O	M	R	W	wd	nb	Dots
JK Lalor	4	0	38	0	1	1	10
ZK Evans	2	0	22	1			5
KW Richardson	4	0	39	2	1		9
Zahir Khan	3	0	49	1			2
NJ Maddinson	4	0	36	1			8
WJ Sutherland	3	0	23	1			9

Bowling	O	M	R	W	wd	nb	Dots
M Hasnain	3.2	0	22	3			11
GS Sandhu	3	0	8	2			11
NJ McAndrew	2	0	23	1	1		3
DR Sams	2	0	10	1			6
T Sangha	3	0	12	2			10
JJ Sangha	1	0	5	0			4

Toss: Renegades. Umpires: BNJ Oxenford, BC Treloar, NR Johnstone (TV), Ref: RL Parry. Award: DR Sams (ST). Crowd: 4,351. Hales 50: 24 balls, 3x4 4x6, Sams 50: 25 balls, 1x4 5x6. Points: MR 0, ST 4. No subs. 10 overs: ST 2-96, MR 6-59

Match 38 – Heat v Hurricanes at the Gabba, Brisbane on January 8, 2022 - Hurricanes won by 8 wickets

Heat		B	4	6	Hurricanes		B	4	6
JS Lehmann	lbw b Lamichhane	9	14	1	CP Jewell	c Pfeffer b Prestwidge	9	5	1	
J Clayton	b Rogers	6	8	1	BR McDermott+	c Dooley b Prestwidge	93	61	10	2
LDP feffer+	c Lammonby b Owen	69	51	6	3	PSP Handscomb	not out	27	33	1
SD Heazlett	c Lammonby b David	4	6		DJM Short	not out	12	5	1	1
TLW Cooper*	c Short b Owen	1	5		TH David				
JP Wood	c McDermott				TA Lammonby				
	b Lamichhane	12	13	1	MJ Owen				
S McGiffin	c Jewell b Meredith	6	12		TS Rogers				
WP restwidge	run out (McDermott)	21	7	1	2	W Sanders				
PG Dooley	not out	4	3	1	RP Meredith				
DMK Grant	not out	1	1		S Lamichhane				
Mujeeb-ur-Rahman									
	3 lb, 8 w	11				1 lb, 3 w	4		
4 overs: 1-28	20 overs	8-144			4 overs: 1-25	17.2 overs	2-145		

1-9 (Clayton, 1.4), 2-44 (Lehmann, 5.4), 3-64 (Heazlett, 7.6), 4-69 (Cooper, 9.2), 5-86 (Wood, 12.6), 6-106 (McGiffin, 16.5), 7-138 (Pfeffer, 19.1), 8-139 (Prestwidge, 19.4)

1-14 (Jewell, 2.4), 2-131 (McDermott, 15.4)

Bowling	O	M	R	W	wd	nb	Dots	Bowling	O	M	R	W	wd	nb	Dots
RP Meredith	4	0	28	1	5		11	PG Dooley	4	0	25	0			9
TS Rogers	4	0	28	1			15	DMK Grant	4	0	28	0			8
W Sanders	1	0	9	0	1		3	WP restwidge	3.2	0	37	2	2		7
TH David	2	0	17	1	1		2	Mujeeb-ur-Rahman	4	0	34	0			4
S Lamichhane	4	0	23	2			12	S McGiffin	1	0	7	0	1		1
DJM Short	1	0	11	0			2	JP Wood	1	0	13	0			1
MJ Owen	4	0	25	2	1		10								

Toss: Hurricanes. Umpires: GA Abood, D Taylor, TM Penman (TV), Ref: KC Wessels. Award: BR McDermott (HH). Crowd: 9,704
Pfeffer 50: 33 balls, 5x4 3x6. McDermott 50: 42 balls, 4x4 1x6. HH Sub: M Wright in for W Sanders. Points: BH 1, HH 3.
10 overs: BH 4-72, HH 1-68

Match 39 – Sixers v Scorchers at Coffs Harbour International Stadium on January 9, 2022 – Scorchers won by 5 wickets

Sixers		B	4	6	Scorchers		B	4	6
JR Philippe+	c & b Agar	32	22	1	3	KR Patterson	c Christian b Dwarshuis	11	8	1	
JJ Avendano	b Agar	23	22	2	1	CT Bancroft+	b Dwarshuis	5	10	
JR Edwards	lbw b Hatzoglou	8	10		LJ Evans	c Edwards b Shadab	19	15	3	
DP Hughes*	c Agar b Kelly	24	25	1	AJ Turner*	c Hughes b Bird	69	41	7	2
JC Silk	not out	26	22	2		AM Hardie	c Shadab b Kerr	35	31	1	1
DT Christian	not out	35	20	4	1	AC Agar	not out	4	6	
H Kerr					CJM Sabburg	not out	7	3	1
Shadab Khan					AJ Tye				
BJ Dwarshuis					ML Kelly				
JM Bird					P Hatzoglou				
TR Murphy					LRT Morris				
	1 lb, 1 nb, 1 w	3				2 w	2		
4 overs: 0-33	20 overs	4-151			4 overs: 2-22	19 overs	5-152		

1-56 (Philippe, 7.1), 2-57 (Avendano, 7.4), 3-72 (Edwards, 11.1), 4-101 (Hughes, 15.3)

1-17 (Patterson, 2.5), 2-17 (Bancroft, 2.6), 3-44 (Evans, 6.2), 4-135 (Turner, 15.6), 5-144 (Hardie, 18.2)

Bowling	O	M	R	W	wd	nb	Dots	Bowling	O	M	R	W	wd	nb	Dots
LRT Morris	2	0	16	0			7	JM Bird	3	0	24	1	1		7
ML Kelly	4	0	37	1			8	H Kerr	4	0	30	1			7
P Hatzoglou	3	0	21	1			6	BJ Dwarshuis	4	0	34	2	1		10
AC Agar	4	0	23	2			10	Shadab Khan	4	0	36	1			7
AJ Tye	4	0	39	0	1	1	6	DT Christian	2	0	17	0			2
AJ Turner	2	0	10	0			3	TR Murphy	2	0	11	0			4
AM Hardie	1	0	4	0			3								

Toss: Sixers. Umpires: SJ Nogajski, AK Wilds, PJ Gillespie (TV), Ref: SJ Davis. Award: AJ Turner (PS). Crowd: 7,022
Turner 50: 29 balls, 6x4 1x6. Points: SS 0, PS 4. No subs. 10 overs: SS 2-68, PS 3-72

Match 40 – Hurricanes v Thunder at the MCG on January 10, 2022 – Thunder won by 9 wickets

Hurricanes		R	B	4	6
CP Jewell	c Sandhu b McAndrew	4	8		
BR McDermott+	c Cutting b McAndrew	38	34	3	1
PSP Handscomb*	st Holt b T Sangha	21	25	1	
HC Brook	c Davies b Sandhu	2	5		
DJM Short	c J Sangha b Sandhu	29	24	3	
TH David	c J Sangha b Sams	15	14	1	
JA Thompson	not out	15	9		2
MJ Owen	not out	3	1		
TS Rogers					
RP Meredith					
S Lamichhane					
	5 b, 2 lb, 5 w	12			
4 overs: 1-23	20 overs	6-139			

Thunder		R	B	4	6
MR Gilkes	st McDermott b Short	19	17	4	
AD Hales	not out	80	56	11	1
JJ Sangha*	not out	35	31	1	1
DR Sams					
O Davies					
BCJ Cutting					
BJH Holt+					
NJ McAndrew					
GS Sandhu					
T Sangha					
M Hasnain					
	1 b, 4 lb, 1 w	6			
4 overs: 0-32	17.2 overs	1-140			

1-9 (Jewell, 2.2), 2-62 (McDermott, 9.4), 3-67 (Brook, 11.1), 4-78 (Handscomb, 12.6), 5-102 (David, 16.5), 6-128 (Short, 19.2)

1-34 (Gilkes, 4.6)

Bowling	O	M	R	W	wd	nb	Dots
M Hasnain	3	0	15	0	3		10
GS Sandhu	4	0	32	2	1		8
NJ McAndrew	4	0	31	2			8
DR Sams	4	0	29	1	1		10
T Sangha	4	0	22	1			9
JJ Sangha	1	0	3	0			3

Bowling	O	M	R	W	wd	nb	Dots
RP Meredith	3	0	29	0	1		11
TS Rogers	3	0	33	0			6
DJM Short	3	0	9	1			10
S Lamichhane	3.2	0	21	0			8
MJ Owen	2	0	25	0			2
TH David	2	0	18	0			1

Toss: Hurricanes. Umpires: GA Abood, D Taylor, BC Treloar (TV), Ref: DA Johnston. Award: AD Hales (ST). Crowd: 809
Hales 50: 44 balls, 5x4. Points: HH 1, ST 3. No subs: HH 2-63, ST 1-62

Match 41 – Stars v Strikers at the MCG on January 10, 2022 – Stars won by 5 wickets

Strikers		R	B	4	6
MW Short	c Webster b Zampa	8	8	1	
HJ Hunt	lbw b Couch	12	9	1	1
JB Weatherald	c Larkin b Qais	8	9	1	
JW Wells	c Webster b Zampa	68	56	5	1
TJ Kelly	c Cartwright b Hinchliffe	13	15		
RJ Gibson	st Clarke b Qais	0	2		
HJ Nielsen+	b Rauf	14	15	1	
Rashid Khan	not out	7	4	1	
PM Siddle*	b Rauf	0	1		
HNA Conway	run out (Crone-Clarke)	1	1		
Fawad Ahmed	did not bat				
	1 b, 3 lb, 4 w	8			
4 overs: 2-30	20 overs	9-139			

Stars		R	B	4	6
JM Clarke+	c Kelly b Siddle	83	58	3	4
CD Hinchliffe	lbw b Conway	2	6		
NCR Larkin	st Nielsen b Fawad	3	6		
JA Burns	c Hunt b Rashid	9	14	1	
HWR Cartwright	c Hunt b Siddle	17	11	1	1
BJ Webster	not out	14	20	1	
Qais Ahmad	not out	6	1		1
XA Crone					
A Zampa*					
Haris Rauf					
BL Couch					
	1 nb, 5 w	6			
4 overs: 1-24	19.1 overs	5-140			

1-21 (Hunt, 2.3), 2-29 (Short, 3.3), 3-34 (Weatherald, 5.3), 4-81 (Kelly, 12.1), 5-91 (Gibson, 13.6), 6-128 (Wells, 18.3), 7-138 (Nielsen, 19.4), 8-138 (Siddle, 19.5), 9-139 (Conway, 19.6)

1-7 (Hinchliffe, 1.4), 2-25 (Larkin, 4), 3-43 (Burns, 7.5), 4-83 (Cartwright, 11.6), 5-133 (Clarke, 18.5)

Bowling	O	M	R	W	wd	nb	Dots
Haris Rauf	4	0	25	2	2		10
Qais Ahmad	4	0	21	2			12
BL Couch	3	0	31	1	2		4
A Zampa	4	0	24	2			8
CD Hinchliffe	4	0	21	1			9
XA Crone	1	0	13	0			1

Bowling	O	M	R	W	wd	nb	Dots
MW Short	3.1	0	27	0	2		5
HNA Conway	4	0	37	1			7
Rashid Khan	4	0	16	1			14
Fawad Ahmed	4	0	34	1	3		6
PM Siddle	4	0	26	2		1	11

Toss: Stars. Umpires: NR Johnstone, TM Penman, SA Lightbody (TV), Ref: K Hannam. Award: JM Clarke (MS). Crowd: 5,802
Wells 50: 44 balls, 4x4 1x6. Clarke 50: 36 balls, 2x4 2x6. Points: MS 4, AS 0.
No subs. 10 overs: AS 3-66, MS 3-69

Match 42 – Stars v Scorchers at Kardinia Park, Geelong on January 11, 2022 – Scorchers won by 47 runs

Scorchers

Batter		R	B	4	6
KR Patterson	c Clarke b Rauf	8	5	1	
NR Hobson	c Rauf b Zampa	46	36	6	
LJ Evans+	lbw b Rauf	69	46	2	5
AJ Turner*	not out	47	26	3	3
AM Hardie	not out	15	7	2	
CJM Sabburg					
AC Agar					
AJ Tye					
ML Kelly					
P Hatzoglou					
JP Behrendorff					
	2 b, 2 lb, 7 w	11			
4 overs: 1-33	20 overs	3-196			

1-22 (Patterson, 2.2), 2-105 (Hobson, 11.3), 3-176 (Evans, 18.1)

Stars

Batter		R	B	4	6
NCR Larkin	b Kelly	1	3		
BJ Webster	c Patterson b Tye	63	47	7	2
JA Burns	c & b Kelly	20	17	2	
GJ Maxwell	c Hobson b Hatzoglou	5	8		
HWR Cartwright	b Kelly	10	8	1	
JM Clarke+	c Turner b Behrendorff	17	11	1	1
CD Hinchliffe	st Evans b Agar	1	3		
Qais Ahmad	c Agar b Kelly	9	8	1	
SL Rainbird	not out	10	11		
A Zampa*	run out (Sabburg-Hardie)	3	3		
Haris Rauf	not out	1	1		
	3 lb, 6 w	9			
4 overs: 1-21	20 overs	9-149			

1-1 (Larkin, 1.1), 2-59 (Burns, 8.1), 3-68 (Maxwell, 9.5), 4-103 (Cartwright, 13.1), 5-121 (Webster, 14.6), 6-124 (Hinchliffe, 15.5), 7-128 (Clarke, 16.4), 8-139 (Qais, 17.6), 9-146 (Zampa, 19.2)

Bowling	O	M	R	W	wd	nb	Dots
SL Rainbird	4	0	33	0			5
BJ Webster	1	0	13	0			2
Haris Rauf	4	0	38	2			6
BL Couch	1	0	7	0	1		3
Qais Ahmad	4	0	40	0	2		7
A Zampa	4	0	34	1	2		9
CD Hinchliffe	2	0	27	0			1

Bowling	O	M	R	W	wd	nb	Dots
JP Behrendorff	4	0	26	1			11
ML Kelly	4	0	25	4			11
P Hatzoglou	4	0	35	1	1		7
AJ Tye	3	0	30	1	2		7
AC Agar	4	0	25	1			8
AM Hardie	1	0	5	0			1

Toss: Scorchers. Umpires: PJ Gillespie, SA Lightbody, DM Koch (TV), Ref: SJ Davis. Award: LJ Evans (PS). Crowd: 5,821

Evans: 33 balls, 1x4 4x6. Webster 50: 38 balls, 6x4 2x6. MS Sub: CD Hinchliffe for BL Couch. Points: MS 0, PS 4. 10 overs: PS 1-79, MS 3-69

Match 43 – Renegades v Sixers at Kardinia Park, Geelong on January 11, 2022 – Sixers won by 45 runs

Sixers

Batter		R	B	4	6
JR Philippe+	c Fraser-McGurk b Lalor	0	3		
JR Edwards	c Fraser-McGurk b Boyce	40	34	3	1
DP Hughes	c Maddinson b Boyce	17	16	1	1
MC Henriques*	c Harvey b Richardson	49	35	4	1
DT Christian	c Harper b Sutherland	22	21	3	
Shadab Khan	c Harper b Richardson	12	7	2	
SA Abbott	not out	1	1		
H Kerr	not out	5	3		
BJ Dwarshuis					
JM Bird					
TR Murphy					
	4 w	4			
4 overs: 1-33	20 overs	6-150			

1-0 (Philippe, 0.3), 2-44 (Hughes, 6.4), 3-71 (Edwards, 10.1), 4-124 (Christian, 16.6), 5-144 (Henriques, 19.1), 6-144 (Shadab, 19.2)

Renegades

Batter		R	B	4	6
AJ Finch	lbw b Abbott	3	4		
J Fraser-McGurk	lbw b Bird	6	4	1	
SE Marsh	b Kerr	39	36	4	1
NJ Maddinson*	c Philippe b Murphy	9	16		
MWG Harvey	c Philippe b Dwarshuis	7	11		
SB Harper+	c Abbott b Dwarshuis	15	7	2	
WJ Sutherland	c Edwards b Dwarshuis	3	4		
CJ Boyce	b Abbott	0	1		
KW Richardson	not out	15	10	1	
JK Lalor	b Dwarshuis	5	6		
Zahir Khan	b Dwarshuis	0	3		
	3 lb	3			
4 overs: 2-22	17 overs	105			

1-7 (Fraser-McGurk, 0.5), 2-11 (Finch, 1.4), 3-41 (Maddinson, 7.5), 4-65 (Harvey, 11.2), 5-68 (Marsh, 12.1), 6-73 (Sutherland, 13.1), 7-85 (Harper, 13.4), 8-85 (Boyce, 14.1), 9-105 (Lalor, 16.3), 10-105 (Zahir, 16.6)

Bowling	O	M	R	W	wd	nb	Dots
JK Lalor	4	0	30	1	1		14
KW Richardson	4	0	37	2			6
WJ Sutherland	3	0	30	1	2		4
CJ Boyce	4	0	15	2			9
Zahir Khan	4	0	27	1			7
NJ Maddinson	1	0	11	0			

Bowling	O	M	R	W	wd	nb	Dots
JM Bird	3	0	19	1			9
SA Abbott	3	0	18	2			11
TR Murphy	3	0	13	1			5
H Kerr	3	0	18	1			5
BJ Dwarshuis	4	0	26	5			12
Shadab Khan	1	0	8	0			1

Toss: Sixers. Umpires: MW Graham-Smith, D Taylor, BNJ Oxenford (TV), Ref: RW Stratford. Award: BJ Dwarshuis (SS).

Points: MR 0, SS 4. No subs. 10 overs: SS 2-71, MR 3-55

Match 44 – Heat v Strikers at the Gabba, Brisbane on January 13, 2022 – Strikers won by 71 runs

Strikers			B	4	6
MW Short	c Pfeffer b Prestwidge	27	19	3	
HJ Hunt	b Kuhnemann	25	26	1	
JB Weatherald	c Lehmann b Prestwidge	35	31	1	1
JW Wells	not out	23	24		
Rashid Khan	b Mujeeb Zadran	13	4		2
TJ Kelly	not out	24	16	1	1
LAH Scott					
HJ Nielsen+					
HTRJY Thornton					
PM Siddle*					
HNA Conway					
	1 b, 2 lb, 11 w	14			
4 overs: 1-33	20 overs	4-161			

1-32 (Short, 3.5), 2-85 (Hunt, 11.2),
3-108 (Weatherald, 14.3), 4-125 (Rashid, 16.1)

Bowling	O	M	R	W	wd	nb	Dots
XC Bartlett	4	0	40	0	1		8
LCJ Guthrie	3	0	24	0	2		7
WP Prestwidge	4	0	34	2			7
NA McSweeney	1	0	5	0			2
MP Kuhnemann	4	0	27	1			4
Mujeeb-ur-Rahman	4	0	28	1	3		11

Heat			B	4	6
NA McSweeney	c Conway b Short	5	5	1	
CA Lynn*	b Thornton	7	7		1
LD Pfeffer+	run out (Siddle-Nielsen)	23	24	2	
BM Duckett	b Short	24	18	3	
SD Heazlett	c Nielsen b Rashid	0	1		
JS Lehmann	b Rashid	0	1		
XC Bartlett	not out	19	20	3	
WP Prestwidge	c Weatherald b Rashid	0	6		
MP Kuhnemann	b Rashid Khan	1	5		
Mujeeb-ur-Rahma	c Short b Rashid	0	1		
LCJ Guthrie	c Short b Rashid	0	2		
	6 lb, 5 w	11			
4 overs: 2-37	15 overs	90			

1-6 (McSweeney, 0.6), 2-17 (Lynn, 2.2), 3-62 (Pfeffer, 8.1),
4-62 (Heazlett, 8.2), 5-62 (Lehmann, 8.3), 6-67 (Duckett, 10.2),
7-73 (Prestwidge, 12.3), 8-89 (Kuhnemann, 14.2),
9-89 (Mujeeb, 14.3), 10-90 (Guthrie, 14.6)

Bowling	O	M	R	W	wd	nb	Dots
MW Short	3	0	13	2	1		10
HNA Conway	2	0	23	0	2		5
HTRJY Thornton	3	0	12	1	1		8
PM Siddle	3	0	19	0	1		11
Rashid Khan	4	0	17	6			14

Toss: Strikers. Umpires: PJ Gillespie, SA Lightbody , NR Johnstone (TV), Ref: K Hannam   Award: Rashid Khan (AS). Crowd: 8,386
No subs.   Points: BH 0, AS 4.   10 overs: AS 1-79, BH 5-67.

Match 45 – Thunder v Hurricanes at Marvel Stadium, Melbourne on January 13, 2022 – Hurricanes won by 9 runs

Hurricanes			B	4	6
CP Jewell	c Davies b Sandhu	51	32	5	3
BR McDermott+	c T Sangha b Sams	18	15	1	1
MS Wade*	not out	83	54	8	2
DJM Short	c Holt b Sandhu	4	4	1	
TH David	c Holt b T Sangha	3	4		
PSP Handscomb	run out (Gilkes-Holt)	1	1		
JA Thompson	b Hasnain	2	3		
MJ Owen	not out	7	7	1	
TS Rogers					
RP Meredith					
S Lamichhane					
	1 b, 7 w	8			
4 overs: 0-27	20 overs	6-177			

1-29 (McDermott, 4.3), 2-118 (Jewell, 12.2), 3-122 (Short, 12.6),
4-136 (David, 15.1), 5-137 (Handscomb, 15.2),
6-140 (Thompson, 16.1)

Bowling	O	M	R	W	wd	nb	Dots
M Hasnain	4	0	31	1			11
GS Sandhu	3	0	27	2	1		7
NJ McAndrew	4	0	36	0			8
DR Sams	4	0	32	1	3		7
T Sangha	4	0	30	1	1		6
BCJ Cutting	1	0	20	0	2		0

Thunder			B	4	6
MR Gilkes	c David b Meredith	1	4		
AD Hales	c Rogers b Thompson	38	17	7	1
JJ Sangha*	lbw b Thompson	31	19	3	1
DR Sams	c McDermott b Short	18	17	1	1
O Davies	b Meredith	6	9		
BCJ Cutting	b Meredith	0	1		
BJH Holt+	c Jewell b Lamichhane	17	20	1	
NJ McAndrew	c Jewell b Lamichhane	30	20	3	1
GS Sandhu	not out	11	9	1	
T Sangha	c Short b Thompson	2	3		
M Hasnain	not out	4	2	1	
	1 b, 1 lb, 1 nb, 7 w	10			
4 overs: 1-56	20 overs	9-168			

1-5 (Gilkes, 0.5), 2-67 (Hales, 4.4), 3-92 (J Sangha, 8.1),
4-102 (Davies, 10.4), 5-102 (Cutting, 10.5), 6-102 (Sams, 11.1),
7-147 (Holt, 17.1), 8-151 (McAndrew, 17.4),
9-161 (T Sangha, 18.6)

Bowling	O	M	R	W	wd	nb	Dots
RP Meredith	4	0	29	3	4		12
TH David	1	0	20	0			1
TS Rogers	4	0	41	0	2		7
JA Thompson	3	0	24	3	1	1	7
S Lamichhane	4	0	26	2			8
MJ Owen	1	0	6	0			7
DJM Short	3	0	20	1			7

Toss: Hurricanes. Umpires: SAJ Craig, TM Penman, AK Wilds (TV), Ref: SJ Davis. Award: RP Meredith (HH). Points: HH 3, ST 1.
Jewell 50: 31 balls, 5x4 3x6, Wade 50: 33 balls, 4x4 1x6. HH Sub: MJ Owen for WB Parker.   10 overs: HH 1-87, ST 3-100

Match 46 – Renegades v Stars at Marvel Stadium, Melbourne on January 13, 2022 – Stars won by 6 wickets

Renegades			B	4	6
SE Marsh	c Rainbird b Rauf	7	6	1	
J Fraser-McGurk	b Qais	32	39	2	
NJ Maddinson*	b Rauf	0	2		
MWG Harvey	c Rauf b Zampa	8	7	1	
AJ Finch	b Couch	45	44	3	1
SB Harper+	st Clarke b Qais	1	2		
J A Prestwidge	b Zampa	6	7		
CJ Boyce	not out	8	9		
KW Richardson	not out	5	4	1	
JK Lalor					
Zahir Khan					
	5 lb, 5 w	10			
4 overs: 2-23	20 overs	7-122			

1-9 (Marsh, 1.2), 2-9 (Maddinson, 1.4), 3-25 (Harvey, 5.2), 4-76 (Fraser-McGurk, 13.2), 5-79 (Harper, 13.6), 6-100 (Prestwidge, 16.4), 7-111 (Finch, 18.2)

Stars			B	4	6
JM Clarke+	c Harper b Lalor	10	6	1	1
GJ Maxwell*	not out	68	45	8	1
BJ Webster	b Zahir	0	2		
JA Burns	c Maddinson b Boyce	17	19	1	
HWR Cartwright	c Maddinson b Richardson	12	15	1	
NCR Larkin	not out	0	0		
Qais Ahmad					
SL Rainbird					
BL Couch					
A Zampa					
Haris Rauf					
	4 b, 3 lb, 9 w	16			
4 overs: 2-39	14.3 overs	4-123			

1-15 (Clarke, 0.6), 2-15 (Webster, 1.2), 3-67 (Burns, 8.2), 4-95 (Cartwright, 12.5)

Bowling	O	M	R	W	wd	nb	Dots
SL Rainbird	4	0	32	0			8
Haris Rauf	4	0	28	2	1		7
BL Couch	4	0	24	1	1		9
Qais Ahmad	4	0	15	2	1		12
A Zampa	4	0	18	2			9

Bowling	O	M	R	W	wd	nb	Dots
JK Lalor	2	0	25	1	1		6
Zahir Khan	3.3	0	33	1	1		8
KW Richardson	3	0	12	1			7
CJ Boyce	4	0	30	1			7
JA Prestwidge	2	0	16	0	3		2

Toss: Renegadess. Umpires: GA Abood, BC Treloar, DR Close (TV), Ref: DA Johnston. Award: GJ Maxwell (MS). Crowd: 10,014
Maxwell 50: 38 balls, 5x4, 1x6.   Points: MS 4, MR 0.   No subs.   10 overs: MR 3-53, MS 3-73

Match 47 – Strikers v Scorchers at Adelaide Oval on January 14, 2022 (Day) – Strikers won by 6 wickets

Scorchers			B	4	6
KR Patterson	c Siddle b Fawad	25	19	2	1
NR Hobson	c &b Siddle	4	9		
LJ Evans+	c Nielsen b Fawad	39	31	4	1
AJ Turner*	c Short b Thornton	28	15	2	2
AM Hardie	c Thornton b Siddle	0	3		
CJM Sabburg	run out (Kelly-Siddle)	3	7		
AJ Tye	b Thornton	2	4		
JP Behrendorff	b Fawad	0	2		
P Hatzoglou	not out	12	13		
DJM Moody	b Short	8	15		
LRT Morris	not out	0	2		
	3 lb, 3 w	6			
4 overs: 1-19	20 overs	9-127			

1-10 (Hobson, 3.1), 2-32 (Patterson, 5.5), 3-80 (Turner, 9.6), 4-80 (Hardie, 10.3), 5-90 (Sabburg, 12.4), 6-105 (Evans, 14.2), 7-105 (Behrendorff, 14.4), 8-107 (Tye, 15.4), 9-127 (Moody, 19.4)

Strikers			B	4	6
MW Short	c Patterson b Hatzoglou	34	28	4	1
HJ Hunt	c Tye b Hardie	27	23	2	1
IA Cockbain	not out	35	24	5	
JW Wells	b Hardie	6	12	1	
JB Weatherald	c Turner b Hardie	8	6	1	
T Kelly	not out	14	9	1	1
HJ Nielsen+					
HTRJ Y Thornton					
PM Siddle*					
Fawad Ahmed					
HNA Conway					
	1 lb, 5 w	6			
4 overs: 0-38	17 overs	4-130			

1-52 (Short, 7.1), 2-78 (Hunt, 10.1), 3-91 (Wells, 12.5), 4-107 (Weatherald, 14.5)

Bowling	O	M	R	W	wd	nb	Dots
MW Short	4	0	15	1			9
HNA Conway	4	0	29	0	3		7
HTRJ Y Thornton	4	0	30	2			9
PM Siddle	4	0	20	2			13
Fawad Ahmed	4	0	30	3			11

Bowling	O	M	R	W	wd	nb	Dots
JP Behrendorff	2	0	23	0	2		6
DJM Moody	1	0	9	0			3
P Hatzoglou	4	0	24	1	2		10
AJ Tye	2	0	12	0			4
LRT Morris	3	0	21	0			8
AM Hardie	4	0	31	3			10
AJ Turner	1	0	9	0			1

Toss: Strikers. Umpires: MW Graham-Smith, BNJ Oxenford, D Taylor (TV), Ref: RW Stratford. Award: Fawad Ahmed (AS).
Points: AS 3, PS 1.   No subs. 10 overs: PS 3-80, AS 1-78.   Crowd: 2,869

Match 48 – Strikers v Stars at Adelaide Oval on January 15, 2022 (day) – Strikers won by 23 runs

Strikers			B	4	6
M W Short	c & b Hinchliffe	33	22	5	1
M T Renshaw	b Rainbird	2	4		
IA Cockbain	st Clarke b Hinchliffe	17	17	1	
J W Wells	run out (Webster-Clarke)	73	49	6	1
J B Weatherald	c Cartwright b Rainbird	17	23		
T Kelly	b Daniyal	5	4	1	
HJ Nielsen+	not out	1	1		
HTRJY Thornton					
HNA Conway					
P M Siddle*					
Fawad Ahmed					
	3 b, 3 lb, 1 w	7			
4 overs: 1-36	20 overs	6-155			

1-22 (Renshaw, 2.2), 2-42 (Short, 5.4), 3-69 (Cockbain, 8.6), 4-130 (Weatherald, 17.4), 5-145 (Kelly, 19.2), 6-155 (Wells, 19.6)

Bowling	O	M	R	W	wd	nb	Dots
S L Rainbird	4	0	25	2	1		9
Ahmed Daniyal	4	0	37	1			5
A Zampa	4	0	35	0			6
BL Couch	4	0	25	0			7
CD Hinchliffe	3	0	21	2			5
GJ Maxwell	1	0	6	0			1

Stars			B	4	6
JM Clarke+	b Short	9	11		
GJ Maxwell*	b Thornton	16	10	2	
BJ Webster	c Nielsen b Thornton	8	11		
MP Stoinis	c Short b Fawad	1	4		
HWR Cartwright	c Short b Thornton	49	35	2	3
JA Burns	b Siddle	25	26	1	
CD Hinchliffe	c Kelly b Conway	15	12		1
SL Rainbird	b Thornton	1	4		
BL Couch	not out	4	6		
A Zampa	not out	1	1		
Ahmed Daniyal					
	1 b, 1 lb, 1 w	3			
4 overs: 1-31	20 overs	8-132			

1-21 (Maxwell, 2.2), 2-32 (Clarke, 4.5), 3-33 (Stoinis, 5.3), 4-37 (Webster, 6.3), 5-79 (Burns, 13.6), 6-121 (Hinchliffe, 17.5), 7-125 (Cartwright, 18.2), 8-127 (Rainbird, 18.6)

Bowling	O	M	R	W	wd	nb	Dots
M W Short	4	0	23	1			9
HNA Conway	4	0	26	1	1		10
HTRJY Thornton	4	0	26	4			9
P M Siddle	4	0	22	1			7
Fawad Ahmed	4	0	33	1			8

Toss: Stars. Umpires: MW Graham-Smith, BNJ Oxenford, D Taylor (TV), Ref: RW Stratford. Award: H Thornton (AS). Crowd: 3,511
Wells 50: 36 balls, 3x4 1x6   Points: AS 4, MS 0.   No subs.   10 overs: AS 3-74, MS 4-49

Match 49 – Sixers v Thunder at the SCG on January 15, 2022 – Sixers won by 60 runs

Sixers			B	4	6
JR Edwards	c McAndrew b Sandhu	2	5		
JR Philippe+	c Ross b McAndrew	57	35	5	2
DP Hughes	c Green b McAndrew	66	48	7	2
MC Henriques*	not out	47	27	4	1
DT Christian	c T Sangha b Sams	4	2	1	
JC Silk	c Sandhu b Sams	8	3	2	
SA Abbott	not out	6	1		1
H Kerr					
SNJ O'Keefe					
JM Bird					
BJ Dwarshuis					
	1 lb, 1 nb, 5 w	7			
4 overs: 1-8	20 overs	5-197			

1-5 (Edwards, 1.2), 2-87 (Philippe, 10.6), 3-164 (Hughes, 17.6), 4-168 (Christian, 18.2), 5-176 (Silk, 18.5)

Bowling	O	M	R	W	wd	nb	Dots
M Hasnain	4	0	22	0	2		11
GS Sandhu	4	0	46	1	3		5
DR Sams	4	0	43	2		1	7
CJ Green	3	0	36	0			0
Nj McAndrew	3	0	30	2			4
T Sangha	2	0	19	0			3

Thunder			B	4	6
MR Gilkes+	c Henriques b Kerr	6	7	1	
AD Hales	b O'Keefe	23	18	4	
JJ Sangha	c Christian b Dwarshuis	22	22	2	
AI Ross	c Philippe b O'Keefe	0	3		
DR Sams	c Abbott b O'Keefe	10	12	1	
O Davies	st Philippe b O'Keefe	1	2		
NJ McAndrew	b Dwarshuis	1	3		
CJ Green*	c Abbott b Henriques	50	31	4	1
GS Sandhu	run out (Abbott-Philippe)	0	0		
T Sangha	not out	17	21	2	
M Hasnain	not out	0	1		
	7 w	7			
4 overs: 1-36	20 overs	9-137			

1-25 (Gilkes, 3.1), 2-42 (Hales, 5.1), 3-42 (Ross, 5.4), 4-58 (Sams, 9.1), 5-61 (Davies, 9.5), 6-62 (McAndrew, 10.2), 7-79 (J Sangha, 12.4), 8-80 (Sandhu, 12.5), 9-136 (Green, 19.4)

Bowling	O	M	R	W	wd	nb	Dots
JM Bird	3	0	19	0			9
SA Abbott	2	0	16	0			5
H Kerr	4	0	32	1			9
BJ Dwarshuis	4	0	23	2	2		11
SNJ O'Keefe	4	0	18	4			10
DT Christian	2	0	23	0	1		4
MC Henriques	1	0	6	1			2

Toss: Thunder. Umpires: GA Abood, PJ Gillespie, BC Treloar (TV), Ref: K Hannam. Award: SNJ O'Keefe (SS). Crowd: 20,306
Philippe 50: 32 balls, 4x4 2x6, Hughes 50: 37 balls, 6x4 1x6. Green 50: 30 balls, 4x6 1x6. Points: SS 4, ST 0.   No subs.
10 overs: Sixers 1-73, Thunder 5-62

Heat		B	4	6
NA McSweeney	lbw b Daniyal	20	20	2
CA Lynn*	c Coulter-Nile b Maxwell	28	22	2	1
BM Duckett	b Zampa	51	42	3	2
LD Pfeffer+	c Larkin b Maxwell	11	14	1
SD Heazlett	c Maxwell b Coulter-Nile	9	8	1
JJ Peirson	not out	15	10	2
JJ Bazley	c Rainbird b Zampa	5	5
MG Neser	not out	0	0
MJ Swepson				
MT Steketee				
MP Kuhnemann				
	5 lb, 1 nb, 4 w	10		
4 overs: 0-33	20 overs	6-149		

1-50 (Lynn, 6.3), 2-53 (McSweeney, 7.2), 3-82 (Pfeffer, 12.3), 4-103 (Heazlett, 15.5), 5-130 (Duckett, 17.6), 6-145 (Bazley, 19.5)

Bowling	O	M	R	W	wd	nb	Dots
SL Rainbird	2	0	19	0			5
A Zampa	4	0	20	2	1		10
Ahmed Daniyal	3	0	30	1	2		7
BL Couch	1	0	12	0			1
NM Coulter-Nile	4	0	32	1	2		6
GJ Maxwell	4	0	19	2			9
BJ Webster	2	0	12	0			3

Stars		B	4	6
JM Clarke+	c Steketee b Bazley	62	36	9	1
GJ Maxwell*	c Lynn b Steketee	37	30	4
HWR Cartwright	not out	16	7		2
MP Stoinis	not out	29	10	1	3
BJ Webster				
JA Burns				
NM Coulter-Nile				
A Zampa				
SL Rainbird				
NCR Larkin				
Ahmed Daniyal				
	1 lb, 5 w	6		
4 overs: 0-48	13.5 overs	2-150		

1-104 (Maxwell, 10.4), 2-110 (Clarke, 11.2)

Bowling	O	M	R	W	wd	nb	Dots
MG Neser	3	0	27	0	2		4
MT Steketee	3	0	43	1	1		5
JJ Bazley	3.5	0	34	1	2		8
MJ Swepson	3	0	38	0			3
MP Kuhnemann	1	0	7	0			2

Toss: Heat. Umpires: SAJ Craig, AK Wilds, SA Lightbody (TV), Ref: SJ Davis. Award: GJ Maxwell (MS). Crowd: 7,009
Duckett 50: 37 balls, 3x4, 2x6, Clarke 50: 28 balls, 7x4 1x6. MS Sub: RP Larkin in for BL Couch. Points: MS 4, BH 0.
10 overs: BH 2-67, MS 0-94

Sixers		B	4	6
JR Edwards	b Fawad	34	34	1
JR Philippe+	b Fawad	22	19	2
MC Henriques*	b Renshaw	17	14	2
DT Christian	c Cockbain b Thornton	22	17		1
DP Hughes	c Nielsen b Fawad	0	1	
JJ Avendano	c Cockbain b Siddle	52	29	1	5
SA Abbott	b Siddle	5	6	
H Kerr	not out	0	0	
BJ Dwarshuis	not out	1	1	
JM Bird				
TR Murphy				
	4 b, 2 lb, 1 nb, 1 w	8		
4 overs: 0-29	20 overs	7-161		

1-44 (Philippe, 6.3), 2-72 (Henriques, 10.3), 3-83 (Edwards, 12.3), 4-83 (Hughes, 12.4), 5-146 (Christian, 17.6), 6-160 (Avendano, 19.4), 7-160 (Abbott, 19.5)

Bowling	O	M	R	W	wd	nb	Dots
MT Renshaw	4	0	38	1			5
HNA Conway	4	0	30	0			5
HTRJY Thornton	4	0	39	1		1	8
PM Siddle	4	0	32	2	1		7
Fawad Ahmed	4	0	16	3			10

Strikers		B	4	6
MT Renshaw	b Kerr	50	31	7
HJ Hunt	c Murphy b Dwarshuis	15	9	1	1
IA Cockbain	not out	71	42	5	4
JW Wells	not out	27	23	3
JB Weatherald				
T Kelly				
HJ Nielsen+				
HTRJY Thornton				
PM Siddle*				
HNA Conway				
Fawad Ahmed				
	2 w	2		
4 overs: 1-49	17.3 overs	2-165		

1-45 (Hunt, 3.5), 2-98 (Renshaw, 9.4)

Bowling	O	M	R	W	wd	nb	Dots
JM Bird	2	0	11	0			4
SA Abbott	3	0	44	0	1		2
H Kerr	4	0	37	1	1		5
BJ Dwarshuis	3	0	37	1			5
DT Christian	1.3	0	14	0			2
TR Murphy	4	0	22	0			6

Toss: Strikers. Umpires: DR Close, PJ Gillespie, NR Johnstone (TV), Ref: K Hannam. Award: IA Cockbain (AS). Crowd: 4,255
Avendano: 50 27 balls, 1x4 5x6, Renshaw 50: 30 balls, 7x4, Cockbain 50: 30 balls, 4x4 2x6   Points: AS 4, SS 0. No subs.
10 overs: SS 1-70, AS 2-98

Match 52 – Scorchers v Heat at Marvel Stadium, Melbourne on January 17, 2022 – Scorchers won by 6 wickets

Heat			B	4	6
MA Bryant	c Patterson b Behrendorff	81	56	7	4
CA Lynn	c Patterson b Marsh	7	11		
BM Duckett	c Morris b Hatzoglou	6	12		
SD Heazlett	c Inglis b Agar	10	9	1	
NA McSweeney	c Morris b Hatzoglou	6	6	1	
JJ Peirson*+	not out	31	19	1	2
JJ Bazley	c Turner b Tye	9	5	2	
MG Neser	c Patterson b Behrendorff	0	1		
MT Steketee	not out	0	1		
MP Kuhnemann					
MJ Swepson					
	1 b, 2 lb, 2 w	5			
4 overs: 0-39	20 overs	7-155			

Scorchers			B	4	6
KR Patterson	lbw b Swepson	26	20	1	3
JP Inglis +	c Heazlett b Neser	18	15	3	
MR Marsh	c Peirson b Swepson	59	34	6	3
C Munro	c Neser b Kuhnemann	24	28	1	1
AJ Turner*	not out	18	14	2	
AM Hardie	not out	6	1	1	
AC Agar					
AJ Tye					
JP Behrendorff					
P Hatzoglou					
LRT Morris					
	1 b, 1 lb, 3 w	5			
4 overs: 0-34	18.4 overs	4-156			

1-44 (Lynn, 5.3), 2-71 (Duckett, 9.1), 3-85 (Heazlett, 12.1), 4-94 (McSweeney, 13.4), 5-132 (Bryant, 17.3), 6-144 (Bazley, 18.5), 7-144 (Neser, 19.1)

1-45 (Inglis, 5.2), 2-48 (Patterson, 6.2), 3-132 (Marsh, 15.5), 4-147 (Munro, 17.6)

Bowling	O	M	R	W	wd	nb	Dots
JP Behrendorff	4	0	25	2	1		9
LRT Morris	2	0	21	0			5
AC Agar	4	0	26	1			8
P Hatzoglou	4	0	17	2			10
MR Marsh	3	0	26	1	1		7
AJ Tye	3	0	37	1			5

Bowling	O	M	R	W	wd	nb	Dots
MG Neser	3	0	22	1	1		10
MT Steketee	3.4	0	39	0	1		9
JJ Bazley	3	0	39	0	1		4
MJ Swepson	4	0	19	2			11
MP Kuhnemann	4	0	28	1			10
NA McSweeney	1	0	7	0			4

Toss: Heat. Umpires: SAJ Craig, BC Treloar, AK Wilds (TV), Ref: RW Stratford.
Bryant 50: 29 balls, 5x4 3x6. Marsh 50: 29 balls, 5x4 3x6. Points: PS 3, BH 1. No subs.
Award: MR Marsh (PS). Crowd: 480
10 overs: BH 2-77, PS 2-67

Match 53 – Renegades v Hurricanes at Marvel Stadium, Melbourne on January 18, 2022 – Hurricanes won by 6 runs

Hurricanes			B	4	6
CP Jewell	c Lalor b Boyce	35	28	3	1
BR McDermott+	c Evans b Lalor	3	7		
MS Wade*	c Zahir b Evans	48	39	4	1
DJM Short	c Marsh b Lalor	37	22	4	1
JA Thompson	c Harper b Boyce	9	4	1	
TH David	not out	46	20	2	4
PSP Handscomb	not out	0	0		
JJ Kann					
TS Rogers					
RP Meredith					
S Lamichhane					
	1 lb, 3 w	4			
4 overs: 1-26	20 overs	5-182			

Renegades			B	4	6
JL Seymour	c Kann b Rogers	24	13	4	1
AJ Finch*	c David b Rogers	75	52	6	4
SE Marsh	c David b Lamichhane	51	38	7	1
U Chand	c Jewell b Lamichhane	6	8		
JA Merlo	c Short b Rogers	1	3		
SB Harper+	not out	3	3		
WJ Sutherland	c Wade b Meredith	6	4	1	
CJ Boyce					
ZK Evans					
JK Lalor					
Zahir Khan					
	2 b, 6 lb, 1 nb, 1 w	10			
4 overs: 1-43	20 overs	6-176			

1-12 (McDermott, 2.2), 2-79 (Jewell, 10.5), 3-96 (Wade, 13.2), 4-119 (Thompson, 15.3), 5-170 (Short, 19.1)

1-37 (Seymour, 3.2), 2-138 (Marsh, 14.5), 3-161 (Chand, 17.4), 4-166 (Finch, 18.4), 5-166 (Merlo, 18.5), 6-176 (Sutherland, 19.6)

Bowling	O	M	R	W	wd	nb	Dots
JK Lalor	4	0	37	2	1		8
ZK Evans	3	0	39	1			4
JL Seymour	3	0	18	0			7
Zahir Khan	4	0	33	0	2		7
JA Merlo	1	0	4	0			2
CJ Boyce	4	0	37	2			6
WJ Sutherland	1	0	13	0			0

Bowling	O	M	R	W	wd	nb	Dots
RP Meredith	4	0	27	1			9
JJ Kann	2	0	28	0			4
S Lamichhane	4	0	27	2			13
TS Rogers	4	0	35	3			9
DJM Short	4	0	29	0	1		10
JA Thompson	2	0	22	0		1	2

Toss: Hurricanes. Umpires: SAJ Craig, AK Wilds, SA Lightbody (TV), Ref: SJ Davis.
Finch 50: 37 balls, 4x4 3x6. S Marsh 50: 36 balls, 7x4 1x6. Points: MR 1, HH 3. No subs.
Award: AJ Finch (MR). Crowd: 1,324
10 overs: HH 1-76, MR 1-89

Match 54 – Heat v Sixers at the Gabba, Brisbane on January 19, 2022 (day) – Sixers won by 27 runs

Sixers

Batter			B	4	6
JR Edwards	run out (Labuschagne-Peirson)	25	13	5	
JR Philippe+	c Duckett b Neser	18	12		1
DP Hughes	c Lynn b Steketee	59	45	7	
MC Henriques*	c Peirson b Labuschagne	28	18	3	
DT Christian	c Swepson b Neser	32	24	2	1
JJ Avendano	c Labuschagne b Neser	12	8	1	
SA Abbott	not out	0	0		
H Kerr					
BJ Dwarshuis					
NM Lyon					
SNJ O'Keefe					
	1 nb, 3 w	4			
4 overs: 1-43	20 overs	6-178			

1-31 (Edwards, 2.6), 2-63 (Philippe, 6.6), 3-120 (Henriques, 13.3), 4-142 (Hughes, 16.1), 5-176 (Avendano, 19.4), 6-178 (Christian, 19.6)

Heat

Batter			B	4	6
MA Bryant	b Dwarshuis	57	55	4	
CA Lynn	c Lyon b Kerr	19	14	2	
M Labuschagne	c Philippe b Dwarshuis	3	6		
BM Duckett	c & b Kerr	3	6		
SD Heazlett	c Henriques b Lyon	1	3		
JJ Peirson*+	c Abbott b O'Keefe	42	23	5	1
JJ Bazley	not out	12	8	1	
MG Neser	c Dwarshuis b Abbott	4	5		
MT Steketee	lbw b Kerr	0	1		
MJ Swepson	not out	1	1		
MP Kuhnemann					
	1 lb, 2 nb, 6 w	9			
4 overs: 1-23	20 overs	8-151			

1-22 (Lynn, 3.4), 2-28 (Labuschagne, 5.2), 3-40 (Duckett, 7.3), 4-43 (Heazlett, 8.2), 5-127 (Peirson, 16.5), 6-132 (Bryant, 17.4), 7-142 (Neser, 18.6), 8-147 (Steketee, 19.3)

Bowling	O	M	R	W	wd	nb	Dots
MT Steketee	4	0	38	1		1	8
MG Neser	4	0	39	3	1		5
JJ Bazley	2	0	20	0	1		4
MJ Swepson	4	0	31	0			5
MP Kuhnemann	3	0	27	0			3
M Labuschagne	3	0	23	1			3

Bowling	O	M	R	W	wd	nb	Dots
SNJ O'Keefe	4	0	21	1	1		7
BJ Dwarshuis	4	0	36	2	3	2	11
SA Abbott	4	0	39	1	1		6
H Kerr	4	0	23	3			9
NM Lyon	4	0	31	1			4

Toss: Heat. Umpires: PJ Gillespie, D Taylor, DR Close (TV), Ref: K Hannam.
Hughes 50: 39 balls, 6x4. Bryant 50: 43 balls, 4x4.. Points: BH 0, SS 4.
Award: DP Hughes (SS). Crowd: 5,239
No subs. 10 overs: SS 2-92, BH 4-52

Match 55 – Renegades v Thunder at the MCG on January 19, 2022 (day) – Thunder won by 1 run

Thunder

Batter			B	4	6
AD Hales	c Chand b Boyce	44	32	7	1
UT Khawaja*	b Evans	77	86	8	1
JJ Sangha	st Harper b Boyce	2	8		
AI Ross	lbw b Boyce	0	2		
DR Sams	lbw b Boyce	0	2		
MR Gilkes+	c Lalor b Boyce	2	10		
BCJ Cutting	run out (Boyce)	20	26	1	
NJ McAndrew	c Chand b Lalor	13	18	1	
CJ Green	c Chand b Lalor	7	8		
GS Sandhu	not out	0	2		
T Sangha					
	5 w	5			
4 overs: 0-54	20 overs	8-170			

1-80 (Hales, 6.6), 2-85 (J Sangha, 8.1), 3-85 (Ross, 8.2), 4-85 (Sams, 8.3), 5-93 (Gilkes, 10.1), 6-136 (Cutting, 16.2), 7-152 (Khawaja, 18.2), 8-164 (Green, 19.4)

Heat

Batter			B	4	6
JL Seymour	c Sams b Sandhu	2	2		
AJ Finch*	c Sams b Sandhu	82	64	4	2
SE Marsh	c Hales b T Sangha	19	16	2	
U Chand	c Green b T Sangha	29	22	1	2
JA Merlo	b Sams	15	9	2	
SB Harper+	run out	1	4		
	(JJ Sangha-Sandhu)				
WJ Sutherland	not out	7	2	1	
CJ Boyce	c JJ Sangha b Sandhu	0	1		
ZK Evans					
JK Lalor					
Zahir Khan					
	1 b, 1 lb, 12 w	14			
4 overs: 1-34	20 overs	7-169			

1-2 (Seymour, 0.2), 2-61 (Marsh, 7.4), 3-129 (Chand, 15.3), 4-161 (Merlo, 18.4), 5-162 (Harper, 19.2), 6-162 (Finch, 19.3), 7-169 (Boyce, 19.5)

Bowling	O	M	R	W	wd	nb	Dots
JK Lalor	4	0	48	1	1		6
ZK Evans	3	0	31	1	1		5
WJ Sutherland	2	0	31	0	1		0
Zahir Khan	4	0	18	0	2		12
CJ Boyce	4	0	21	5			10
JA Merlo	1	0	5	0			2
JL Seymour	1	0	6	0			1
AJ Finch	1	0	10	0			0

Bowling	O	M	R	W	wd	nb	Dots
GS Sandhu	4	0	33	3	1		9
NJ McAndrew	4	0	48	0	3		6
DR Sams	4	0	22	1	1		11
CJ Green	3	0	21	0			2
T Sangha	4	0	32	2	3		5
JJ Sangha	1	0	11	0			1

Toss: Renegades. Umpires: SA Lightbody, AK Wilds, SAJ Craig (TV), Ref: SJ Davis. Award: CJ Boyce (MR).
Khawaja 50: 34 balls, 4x4, 1x6. Finch 50: 40 balls, 2x4 2x6. Points: MR 0, ST 4. No subs. 10 overs: ST 4-93, MR 2-77

Match 56 – Stars v Sixers at the MCG on January 26, 2021 – Stars won by 106 runs

Stars			B	4	6
GJ Maxwell*	not out	154	64	22	4
JM Clarke+	c Parker b Kann	35	18	3	1
NCR Larkin	b Thompson	3	7		
MP Stoinis	not out	75	31	4	6
BJ Webster					
HWR Cartwright					
CD Hinchliffe					
TL O'Connell					
NM Coulter-Nile					
SM Elliott					
BL Couch					
1 lb, 5 w		6			
4 overs : 0-63	20 overs	2-273			

1-97 (Clarke, 6.6), 2-141 (Larkin, 10.6)

Heat			B	4	6
CP Jewell	b Couch	3	6		
BR McDermott	c Cartwright b Couch	55	33	2	4
JA Thompson	c & b O'Connell	11	5	1	1
MS Wade*	c O'Connell b Hinchliffe	10	12		
DJM Short	not out	41	36	3	
PSP Handscomb	c Maxwell b Webster	28	18	2	1
TH David	c Maxwell b Couch	13	10		1
MJ Owen	not out	0	0		
JJ Kann					
WB Parker					
S Lamichhane					
6 w		6			
4 overs : 1-39	20 overs	6-167			

1-20 (Jewell, 2.5), 2-46 (Thompson, 4.4), 3-67 (Wade, 7.5), 4-94 (McDermott, 11.1), 5-138 (Handscomb, 16.5), 6-164 (David, 19.4)

Bowling	O	M	R	W	wd	nb	Dots
TH David	2	0	33	0	1		0
DJM Short	2	0	34	0	2		1
S Lamichhane	4	0	52	0			4
W Sanders	1	0	17	0			1
MJ Owen	3	0	32	0			4
JJ Kann	2	0	40	1			1
WB Parker	3	0	32	0			4
JA Thompson	3	0	32	1			4

Bowling	O	M	R	W	wd	nb	Dots
SM Elliott	4	0	32	0	1		5
NM Coulter-Nile	2	0	15	0	1		4
BL Couch	4	0	30	3	1		10
BJ Webster	2	0	23	1			2
TL O'Connell	4	0	32	1	1		6
CD Hinchliffe	4	0	35	1			5

Toss: Hurricanes. Umpires: GA Abood, DM Koch, BC Treloar (TV), Ref: RW Stratford. Award: GJ Maxwell (MS). Crowd: 8,886
Maxwell 50: 20 balls, 8x4, 1x6; 100: 41 balls, 14x4 3x6; 150: 62 balls, 22x4 4x6, Stoinis 50: 23 balls, 3x4 4x6.
McDermott 50: 29 balls 4x4 2x6. Points: MS 4, HH 0. HH Sub: JA Thompson for W Sanders. 10 overs: MS 1-130, HH 3-86

Maxwell's 154 not out – Ball by ball

186

ELIMINATOR FINAL - MELBOURNE

Carey and Short got the Strikers off to a brilliant start as the boundaries flowed off their bats. Carey hit some fine drives and Short a crunching pull as 35 arrived from the first three overs. In the fourth over, Short on 15 lofted Boland towards mid-off where Rogers dropped a catch he should have taken. Short made the most of his luck as he later top edged a pull shot off Meredith over the keeper's head for six. After reaching his fifty from 29 balls, Carey on 51 smashed one hard back at leg-spinner Parker who put the tough chance down. The 100 came up in the 11th over and this was the signal for Short to up the tempo as he pulled Meredith for six in the 12th to bring up a 32-ball fifty. In the next over on 57 Short pulled his namesake to the deep mid-wicket rope where Parker dived high to his right to nearly bring off a remarkable catch, sadly for the fielder he had touched the rope before disposing of the ball which meant a six.

Short pulled Parker for six and then finally the Hurricanes had some joy as Carey pulled one down the throat of deep square-leg. Short then went into overdrive straight-driving and sweeping sixes before the young leggie got him to miscue a sweep in the air to the keeper. This sparked a late order collapse as a rusty looking Head was caught at wide long-on, with Cockbain and Renshaw out to catches at deep mid-wicket. Wells managed a boundary off the last ball of the innings, but the Hurricanes had fought back taking 5-39 off the last five overs.

Spinner Short took the new ball and McDermott glanced his second ball away for four. To the next delivery, McDermott made room to leg and lifted a drive straight down the throat of deep mid-off. Jewell hit two early fours with reverse and regular sweeps and then the Strikers dismissed Wade when he lofted a square drive straight down the throat of deep point. Jewell continued to play some neat sweeps but then was out when he made room to pull and got a touch to the keeper.

The Hurricanes reached 3-85 after 12 overs when they took the Power Surge, Short whacked Siddle for two fours in an over that cost 14. Their revitalised chase continued when Short lofted Conway straight for six, 17 coming from the over, which meant the Hurricanes needed 74 off the last eight overs.

However things went sour for the Hurricanes in the 15th over when Thornton had Short caught by long-off diving and then Handscomb miscued a pull-shot to mid-on. Thompson and Rogers went in quick succession, but David smacked Fawad for consecutive sixes to leg, which left 46 wanted off the last 18 balls. Siddle bowled the 18th over and after being glanced for four first ball by David, the burly Hurricane holed out to long-off which ensured the Strikers victory and passage to the last four.

Strikers v Hurricanes at the MCG on January 21, 2022 – Strikers won by 22 runs

Strikers		B	4	6	Hurricanes			B	4	6
AT Carey+	c Thompson b Boland	67	45	8	BR McDermott+	c Siddle b Short		6	3	1
M W Short	c McDermott b Parker	89	48	4	6	CP Jewell	c Carey b Conway	35	31	4
TM Head	c Handscomb b Meredith	5	7		MS Wade*	c Renshaw b Siddle		7	7	1
IA Cockbain	c Short b Meredith	3	6		DJM Short	c Cockbain b Thornton		56	34	4	2
MT Renshaw	c Jewell b Rogers	7	5	1	PSP Handscomb	c Cockbain b Thornton	15	13	2
J W Wells	not out	12	8	1	TH David	c sub (JB Weatherald)				
T Kelly	c McDermott b Rogers	0	1			b Siddle	21	11	1	2
HTRJY Thornton	not out	0	0		J A Thompson	c Kelly b Conway		3	3	
P M Siddle*					TS Rogers	c Carey b Fawad		1	2	
HNA Conway					WB Parker	b Siddle		4	2	1
Fawad Ahmed					SM Boland	not out		5	5	
					RP Meredith	b Siddle		10	7	1
	2 lb, 3 w	5				2 lb, 1 w		3		
4 overs: 0-44	20 overs	6-188			4 overs: 2-28	19.4 overs	166			

1-145 (Carey, 14.2), 2-164 (Short, 15.6), 3-169 (Head, 17.2), 4-169 (Cockbain, 17.4), 5-179 (Renshaw, 19.1), 6-184 (Kelly, 19.5)

1-6 (McDermott, 0.3), 2-28 (Wade, 3.6), 3-67 (Jewell, 9.1), 4-122 (Short, 14.3), 5-122 (Handscomb, 14.5), 6-128 (Thompson, 15.4), 7-130 (Rogers, 16.1), 8-147 (David, 17.2), 9-152 (Parker, 17.5), 10-166 (Meredith, 19.4)

Bowling	O	M	R	W	wd	nb	Dots	Bowling	O	M	R	W	wd	nb	Dots
SM Boland	4	0	32	1			6	M W Short	4	0	33	1			7
RP Meredith	4	0	37	2			7	HNA Conway	4	0	32	2			6
TS Rogers	4	0	37	2	1		6	P M Siddle	3.4	0	32	4			8
DJM Short	3	0	28	0	1		2	Fawad Ahmed	4	0	33	1			8
J A Thompson	1	0	10	0			0	HTRJY Thornton	3	0	25	2			3
WB Parker	4	0	42	1	1		9	TM Head	1	0	9	0	1		1

Toss: Strikers. Umpires: PJ Gillespie, DM Koch, DR Close (TV), Ref: SJ Davis. Award: MW Short (AS). Crowd: 2,942

Carey 50: 29 balls, 6x4; MW Short 50: 32 balls, 4x4 2x6. DJM Short 50: 31 balls 3x4 2x6. No Subs

In the lead up to this final, the Sixers were trying to get Steve Smith a permit to play, but Cricket Australia refused to give in, even though there was a spot on the list available given James Vince had left for England's tour to the West Indies. The Sixers bad luck continued as after the toss Daniel Hughes injured his ankle during warmups, being replaced by Nick Bertus.

Lyon took the new ball and conceded just six but then the boundaries started to flow as Inglis and Patterson skipped into action. With 38 coming from the opening four overs the Scorchers were up and away, which was further improved in the next over when Patterson whipped Dwarshuis over the fence behind square-leg. O'Keefe came on for the seventh and Patterson immediately swept him for six to raise the 50 in just 5.1 overs. At the other end Inglis wasn't hitting the ball as hard or far but was scoring off virtually every ball as the Scorchers reached 94 without loss at the halfway mark, with Patterson bringing up his 50 off 33 balls (4x4 2x6) from the last ball of the 10th over.

In the next over Patterson celebrated his 50 with a hard hit drive for four off Abbott and then Inglis reached his half-ton (32 balls) when he slog-swept O'Keefe over mid-wicket for six. Patterson pulled Kerr into the second tier for six, but then next ball hit a catch to long-on, ending an opening stand of 120 from 74 balls. From his third ball Marsh hit O'Keefe over cover for four and then Inglis cleverly reverse swept Kerr to third man for four. With the surge taken in the 16th over, Inglis struck Dwarshuis for three fours as the Scorchers reached 1-150 with four overs left.

Abbott did well to concede only seven off the 17th over and then in the 18th O'Keefe tossed one up wide and Inglis was well stumped to end an excellent knock. Marsh took Abbott for three fours in the 19th before being out from the second last ball of the innings, the Scorchers setting the Sixers 190 to win.

Richardson set the standard early when he thought he had Philippe caught behind second ball in what was a brilliant opening over. This was soon forgotten as Behrendorff had Avendano caught behind top edging a pull and then Philippe dragged Richardson on as he attempted a similar shot. Silk poked a catch to short third-man and then Bertus missed a sweep, which left the Sixers 4-21. Christian made an aggressive start from his first ball when he smacked Agar over long-on for six but shortly after top edged a sweep to deep square-leg which ended the match as a contest.

Kerr hit some sweet shots but then was smartly thrown out by Turner, the Sixers had slipped to 7-55. This saw the arrival of Dwarshuis to the crease and his rapid fire knock at least put some interest in the closing overs. He started his knock by hitting 18 off Hatzoglou's third over, including a six over long-off. In the 18th he whacked Behrendorff for six over deep square-leg and then in the 19th smashed Tye for 24 in the over, including two sixes and three fours. He reached his maiden fifty from 24 balls and in doing so became the first number nine to reach a half-century in BBL history. He was stumped in the final over, which put the Scorchers into their seventh BBL Grand Final.

Scorchers v Sixers at Marvel Stadium, Melbourne on January 22, 2022 – Scorchers won by 49 runs

Scorchers		B	4	6
J P Inglis +	st Philippe b O'Keefe	79	49 9	1
K R Patterson	c Christian b Kerr	64	41 5	3
M R Marsh	c Henriques b Kerr	28	21 4	
C Munro	not out	12	9	1
A J Turner*	not out	0	0	
L J Evans				
A C Agar				
J A Richardson				
A J Tye				
J P Behrendorff				
P Hatzoglou				
	3 lb, 3 w	6		
	4 overs : 0-38 20 overs	3-189		

1-120 (Patterson, 12.2), 2-159 (Inglis, 17.1), 3-187 (Marsh, 19.5)

Sixers		B	4	6
J R Philippe+	b Richardson	5	8	1
J J Avendano	c Inglis b Behrendorff	0	3	
M C Henriques *	c Inglis b Richardson	17	30	1
J C Silk	c Hatzoglou b Behrendorff	1	5	
N L Bertus	b Agar	4	7	
D T Christian	c Munro b Agar	7	4	1
S A Abbott	run out (Turner)	3	7	
H Kerr	c Inglis b Tye	22	18 2	1
B J Dwarshuis	st Inglis b Hatzoglou	66	29 7	4
N M Lyon	c Behrendorff b Tye	2	2	
S N J O'Keefe	not out	2	3	
	1 b, 5 lb, 5 w	11		
	4 overs : 3-12 19.2 overs	140		

1-5 (Avendano, 1.3), 2-8 (Philippe, 2.3), 3-11 (Silk, 3.5), 4-21 (Bertus, 6.5), 5-33 (Christian, 8.1), 6-41 (Henriques, 10.2), 7-55 (Abbott, 11.6), 8-96 (Kerr, 16.2), 9-98 (Lyon, 16.4), 10-140 (Dwarshuis, 19.2)

Bowling	O	M	R	W	wd	nb	Dots
N M Lyon	3	0	31	0	1		2
S A Abbott	4	0	39	0			6
H Kerr	4	0	37	2	1		5
B J Dwarshuis	3	0	29	0			8
S N J O'Keefe	4	0	14	1	1		5
D T Christian	2	0	14	0			4

Bowling	O	M	R	W	wd	nb	Dots
J A Richardson	4	0	21	2			15
J P Behrendorff	4	0	31	2	4		8
A C Agar	4	0	16	2	1		14
P Hatzoglou	3.2	0	28	1			8
A J Tye	4	0	38	2			9

Toss: Scorchers. Umpires: GA Abood, SAJ Craig, AK Wilds (TV), Ref: RW Stratford.   Award: JP Inglis (PS).   Crowd: 2,071

Inglis 50: 32 balls, 4x4 1x6, Patterson 50: 33 balls, 4x4 2x6. Dwarshuis 50: 24 balls, 5x4 3x6. No Subs.

With the Strikers happy to bat first again, Carey looked in top touch as he pumped Sandhu past mid-off in the first over for four, before lifting Sams over mid-wicket for six in the third. In the same over Short also joined in the fun as he clipped Sams twice to leg for four as the Strikers reached 34 from the first three. Sams' tough start to the game continued when he put down a high ball at deep mid-wicket from the bat of Short off Green on 13. But as can often happen in the Twenty20 game fortunes can change quickly and when Carey hit his first ball from Tanveer Sangha right out of the screws to deep mid-wicket, Sams leapt high to his left to bring off a brilliant catch just inside the rope.

Short smashed Jason Sangha to the sightboard for six and then Cockbain stepped up to pull McAndrew over the fence at long-leg, the Strikers hitting the halfway mark well placed at 1-85. Short pulled Jason Sangha for six at the start of the 11th over, but in the same over missed a sweep to be LBW. Head looked rusty once again before hitting a catch to deep square-leg, the Thunder back in the game having claimed 2-3 from seven balls.

Cockbain continued to time the ball sweetly and went into overdrive when he lofted Jason Sangha for six over long-off and then swept him for four to reach his 50 (30 balls) in the 14th over which cost 18. At 3-124 with six overs left the Strikers called for the Power Surge, Wells lofting Sams over long-on for six in an over that added 12. Cockbain lifted McAndrew for six but later in the same over was caught at point. Shortly after Wells was caught at short third-man, but Kelly cleverly found the third man rope a couple of times as he and Renshaw added 31 from 20 balls to set the Thunder 185 to win.

The Thunder took 15 off the first two overs of the chase but then Thornton struck with his first ball when Hales drive failed to clear deep mid-off. Jason Sangha joined Khawaja and the pair regularly found the rope, taking the Thunder 1-40 after four overs. At 1-56 in the seventh over, came the most controversial moment of the game when Khawaja advanced to Short and got an edge to short third-man, with Fawad diving forward to claim the low catch. Replays indicated that some part of the ball may have hit the ground, but the umpires felt the evidence wasn't there to change the "out" decision, so Khawaja was on his way. Ross smoked Thornton over the leg-side for six in the ninth over and at the halfway point the Thunder needed 103 to win. Jason Sangha and Ross continued to find the rope with some wristy and powerful shots, Sangha lofting Fawad for six in the 16th over which left the Thunder wanting 43 off the last four overs with eight wickets in hand and the Surge to come.

As he had for much of the season, Siddle rose to the occasion when needed and had Sangha caught at deep mid-on and in the same over trapped Sams in front with a yorker. With 35 to win off 18, Conway bowled the second over of the surge and with Cutting hitting two fours, the target was down to 23 off 12. In the 19th over where Ross reached a fine 50, Siddle gave up nine, so with 14 to win, Conway took the ball. After a leg bye first ball, Ross edged a four to third man and then had a swing and a miss at a slower ball. Nine wanted off three balls. Ross swung hard at the fourth ball, it went high towards long-leg, Carey ran back towards it, but Thornton ran in from the rope and calmly caught it, the pair narrowly avoiding a nasty collision. Off the second last ball Cutting hit hard but not far enough, being caught at long-on, which meant the Strikers were winners and through to Challenger Final in three days time.

Thunder v Strikers at the MCG on January 23, 2022 – Strikers won by 6 runs

Strikers			B	4	6	Thunder			B	4	6
AT Carey+	c Sams b T Sangha	23	14	2	1	AD Hales	c Siddle b Thornton	9	9	1	
MW Short	lbw b J Sangha	39	28	2	2	UT Khawaja*	c Fawad b Short	23	17	4	
IA Cockbain	c J Sangha b McAndrew	65	38	6	3	JJ Sangha	c Wells b Siddle	61	43	6	1
TM Head	c Ross b Sandhu	3	6			AI Ross	c Thornton b Conway	56	39	4	1
JW Wells	c Cutting b T Sangha	18	12		1	DR Sams	lbw b Siddle	1	2		
MT Renshaw	not out	15	9			BCJ Cutting	c Cockbain b Conway	16	10	3	
T Kelly	c Green b Sandhu	16	13	2		NJ McAndrew	not out	2	1		
HTRJY Thornton	not out	0	0			MR Gilkes+	not out	0	0		
Fawad Ahmed						CJ Green					
PM Siddle*						T Sangha					
HNA Conway						GS Sandhu					
	1 b, 1 lb, 3 w	5					2 lb, 1 nb, 7 w	10			
4 overs : 0-40	20 overs	6-184				4 overs : 1-40	20 overs	6-178			

1-41 (Carey, 4.3), 2-91 (Short, 10.4), 3-94 (Head, 11.4), 4-146 (Cockbain, 15.5), 5-151 (Wells, 16.3), 6-182 (Kelly, 19.5)

1-15 (Hales, 2.1), 2-56 (Khawaja, 6.3), 3-146 (J Sangha, 16.2), 4-150 (Sams, 16.6), 5-176 (Ross, 19.4), 6-176 (Cutting, 19.5)

Bowling	O	M	R	W	wd	nb	Dots
GS Sandhu	4	0	40	2	1		5
NJ McAndrew	3	0	28	1	1		9
DR Sams	4	0	47	0	1		5
CJ Green	2	0	16	0			2
T Sangha	4	0	15	2			11
JJ Sangha	3	0	36	1			5

Bowling	O	M	R	W	wd	nb	Dots
MW Short	4	0	28	1	1		10
HNA Conway	4	0	33	2	1		8
HTRJY Thornton	3	0	35	1	2	1	6
PM Siddle	4	0	41	2	1		3
Fawad Ahmed	4	0	34	0			7
TM Head	1	0	5	0			2

Toss: Strikers. Umpires: PJ Gillespie, DM Koch, BC Treloar (TV), Ref: K Hannam.   Award: IA Cockbain (AS).   Crowd: 2,760

Cockbain 50: 30 balls, 5x4 2x6. J Sangha 50: 37 balls, 5x4; Ross 50: 35 balls, 3x4 1x6   No Subs.

CHALLENGER FINAL – SYDNEY

On Australia Day, the Sixers had a major blow when Josh Philippe was ruled out with COVID. Hayden Kerr was named to open with Jake Carder coming in to make his BBL debut. The Strikers kept the same side and on a glorious night the Sixers got off to a brilliant start with the ball as Carey lofted a simple catch to mid-off in the opening over. Short was then well held at slip and Head's poor BBL form continued when he was bowled having a heave at a length ball. A rebuild came as gradually Cockbain and Wells developed a stand, but just 4 fours came in the first ten overs as the Strikers reached 3-62 after 10 overs.

The Strikers got a crack on in the 11th over when Cockbain slammed Kerr over cover point for six in an over that cost 14. O'Keefe completed his four-over spell in the 12th over without conceding a boundary and headed off the field with what looked a calf complaint. Cockbain pulled Christian for six but then met his fate in the first over of the Surge when he dragged a slower ball from Abbott onto the stumps, ending a stand of 83 off 63 balls. A dozen came from the second over of the Surge and in that time Silk headed from the field with what was a hamstring injury. In the last three overs the Strikers scored 38 as Renshaw hit Lyon and Dwarshuis for sixes, Wells smacked Abbott over the long-on rope, their stand worth 63 off 37 deliveries.

With 168 needed, the Strikers should have got off to the dream start when Kerr advanced at Short and Carey missed the stumping. It was to prove to be one of most costly misses of the competition as the opener was to play a magnificent innings. Just seven came off the first two overs and then in the third Thornton struck with his second ball, as Avendano top edged a pull-shot to the keeper. Kerr's luck continued, as on 16 he skied a catch to deep square-leg off Siddle where Renshaw shelled the straight-forward chance.

Kerr continued to go for broke slog sweeping Short for six and four in the 6th over before losing Carder who mistimed a pull to mid-on. Kerr reached his fifty (33 balls) and after hitting some further boundaries, the Sixers reached 2-95 after 13 overs, when they took the Surge. Siddle yorked Henriques in the first surge over and in the next Christian was caught at cover-point. Abbott took the pressure off Kerr immediately by finding the gaps for three twos, then hit a six over mid-wicket off Thornton, which left 47 wanted off the final 24 balls.

With 12 coming from the 17th over from Short and then just four off the first five balls from 18th by Siddle, Abbott powered a slower ball away for four off the last which left 27 to win from the last two overs. The target got down to 19 off eight and then Abbott effortlessly lifted Thornton over backward square-leg for six. With 12 to get, Conway took the ball and first ball Abbott was caught at wide long-off. Kerr flicked the second to leg, Dwarshuis wanted a second run but was run out after being sent back. Silk limped out and scored a single to deep mid-wicket as he was barely able to complete the run. Then Kerr stepped up and lofted a slower ball for six, just clearing the leaping deep mid-wicket fielder on the rope. With four to get off two, Kerr smashed one past the bowler straight, with Silk just able to make it back for two and then after some yelling and flapping of arms from Sixers coach Greg Shipperd, Silk was retired hurt which brought out a fully fit Lenton at the non-striker's end. With two to win off the last, Kerr clipped to deep square-leg, two was always on but Wells missed the ball and it crossed the rope, putting the Sixers into their sixth BBL Grand Final.

Sixers v Strikers at the SCG on January 26, 2022 – Sixers won by 4 wickets

Strikers			B	4	6
AT Carey+	c Christian b O'Keefe	1	2		
MW Short	c Christian b Abbott	6	5	1	
IA Cockbain	b Abbott	48	42	2	2
TM Head	b Abbott	3	5		
JW Wells	not out	62	47	5	1
MT Renshaw	not out	36	20	3	2
T Kelly					
HNA Conway					
PM Siddle*					
HTRJY Thornton					
Fawad Ahmed					
	1 b, 3 lb, 1 nb, 6 w	11			
4 overs: 3-21	20 overs	4-167			

1-5 (Carey, 0.3), 2-13 (Short, 1.6), 3-21 (Head, 3.4), 4-104 (Cockbain, 14.2)

Sixers			B	4	6
H Kerr	not out	98	58	10	2
JJ Avendano	c Carey b Thornton	1	8		
JM Carder	c Cockbain b Thornton	10	13		
MC Henriques*	b Siddle	13	16		
DT Christian	c Renshaw b Conway	1	4		
SA Abbott	c Head b Conway	41	20	2	2
BJ Dwarshuis	run out (Renshaw-Carey)	0	0		
JC Silk	retired hurt	1	1		
JS Lenton+	not out	0	0		
NM Lyon					
SNJ O'Keefe					
	2 lb, 3 w	5			
4 overs: 1-23	20 overs	6-170			

1-7 (Avendano, 2.2), 2-51 (Carder, 7.1), 3-96 (Henriques, 13.2), 4-101 (Christian, 14.1), 5-156 (Abbott, 19.1), 6-157 (Dwarshuis, 19.2)

Bowling	O	M	R	W	wd	nb	Dots
SNJ O'Keefe	4	0	21	1	1		7
SA Abbott	4	0	27	3		1	11
H Kerr	3	0	32	0			4
NM Lyon	3	0	25	0			4
BJ Dwarshuis	4	0	38	2			6
DT Christian	2	0	20	0	1		2

Bowling	O	M	R	W	wd	nb	Dots
MW Short	4	0	35	0	1		7
HNA Conway	4	0	37	2			6
HTRJY Thornton	4	0	40	2	1		4
PM Siddle	4	0	28	1	1		8
Fawad Ahmed	4	0	28	0			6

Toss: Sixers. Umpires: DM Koch, SJ Nogajski, GA Abood (TV), Ref: RW Stratford. Award: H Kerr (SS). Crowd: 10,896
Wells 50: 41 balls, 4x4. Kerr 50: 33 balls, 5x4 1x6. No Subs.

The Sixers welcomed back Dan Hughes for the final, also bringing in Nick Bertus and Jackson Bird, the trio replacing Justin Avendano, Jake Carder and the injured Jordan Silk. The Scorchers kept the same XI that won the Qualifier final, as both teams were chasing their fourth BBL title. The Scorchers were under pressure early as Patterson was out when he top-edged a pull high to the keeper, while Inglis was dropped on 12 off Kerr's first ball, when Henriques failed to hold a simple chance running in from mid-off. The drop cost the Sixers very little as O'Keefe had Inglis stumped in the next over with his first ball and then Marsh who had taken until his ninth ball to get off the mark, hit Lyon's first ball straight down the throat of long-on. The misery for the Scorchers continued as from the last ball of the Lyon over, Munro was caught reverse sweeping to short third-man, leaving the men from the west in total despair at 4-25 after six overs.

But like all great teams they found a way out of trouble as Turner and Evans combined to retrieve the situation. At 4-40 after eight overs, Evans decided that O'Keefe had to be dealt with, hitting him for two fours and a swept six over deep square-leg as the bowler went for 19 off the over. After some more free scoring overs the Scorchers reached 4-85 after 12 and then took the Surge. Turner hit Kerr for two fours in the first surge over that went for 14, and when 10 came from the 14th, the Scorchers were 4-109 with six to go. On 43 Turner top edged a pull off Christian, with Hughes running back towards square-leg but unable to hang on and then Evans reached his fifty (25 balls) with a low, hard and flat strike over mid-wicket for six off Christian. In the 16th over, Turner swept O'Keefe for six for reach is fifty (32 balls) and in doing so brought up the 100 stand.

The remarkable stand came to an end on 104 when the Scorchers skipper edged a drive to short third-man. Evans played an imperious lofted drive over cover off Christian for six, while Agar made room to leg to smash Lyon for two fours to the off-side in the one over. Agar was out when he missed a full-toss from Kerr but then Evans struck one last major blow, another magnificent cover driven six off Dwarshuis in the last over, the Scorchers setting the Sixers 172 to win.

Things went bad early in the chase for the Sixers when the hero of the previous game Kerr, was caught at short third-man in the second over. Hughes was hitting the ball well, but lost Bertus when he got a leading edge to point. Henriques missed a sweep and then Christian smashed a pull-shot flat like a rocket to deep square-leg but was brilliantly caught by Patterson diving forward. Hughes defiantly slog-swept Agar for six, but then lost Avendano who dragged one on. Abbott couldn't repeat his good batting in the previous game and when he called for a quick single to third-man, Marsh picked off Hughes who struggled in vain to make his ground.

The tail failed to wag and when O'Keefe was trapped in front by Richardson, the Scorchers were champions for a record fourth time, much to the delight of the squad, their families and supporters, who had been restricted to just one home game through Western Australia's overly harsh COVID border restrictions.

BBL11 FINAL, Sixers v Scorchers at Marvel Stadium, Melbourne on January 28, 2022 – Scorchers won by 79 runs

Scorchers		B	4	6
KR Patterson	c Lenton b Bird	1	4	
JP Inglis +	st Lenton b O'Keefe	13	13	2
MR Marsh	c Christian b Lyon	5	11	1
C Munro	c Bird b Lyon	1	5	
AJ Turner*	c Hughes b O'Keefe	54	35	4	1
LJ Evans	not out	76	41	4	4
AC Agar	lbw b Kerr	15	9	3	
JA Richardson	not out	1	2	
AJ Tye				
JP Behrendorff				
P Hatzoglou				
	1 lb, 4 w	5		
4 overs: 1- 14	20 overs	6-171		

1-7 (Patterson, 1.4), 2-14 (Inglis, 4.1), 3-20 (Marsh, 5.1), 4-25 (Munro, 5.6), 5-129 (Turner, 15.5), 6-158 (Agar, 18.5)

Sixers		B	4	6
HL Kerr	c Hatzoglou b Behrendorff	2	4	
NL Bertus	c Behrendorff b Turner	15	15	
DP Hughes	run out (Marsh-Inglis)	42	33	2	1
MC Henriques *	lbw b Agar	7	7	1
DT Christian	c Patterson b Tye	3	7	
JJ Avendano	b Hatzoglou	1	4	
SA Abbott	c Patterson b Tye	1	9	
BJ Dwarshuis	c Inglis b Tye	0	2	
JS Lenton+	not out	10	9	1
NM Lyon	b Richardson	3	3	
SNJ O'Keefe	lbw b Richardson	2	5	
	1 lb, 5 w	6		
4 overs: 1-26	16.2 overs	92		

1-5 (Kerr, 1.3), 2-32 (Bertus, 4.6), 3-46 (Henriques, 6.6), 4-62 (Christian, 9.4), 5-71 (Avendano, 11.2), 6-77 (Hughes, 12.5), 7-77 (Abbott, 13.2), 8-77 (Dwarshuis, 13.3), 9-82 (Lyon, 14.3), 10-92 (O'Keefe, 16.2)

Bowling	O	M	R	W	wd	nb	Dots
SA Abbott	4	0	27	0			8
JM Bird	1	0	6	1			3
H Kerr	3	0	20	1			7
SNJ O'Keefe	4	0	43	2	2		7
NM Lyon	3	0	24	2			7
BJ Dwarshuis	2	0	22	0	1		2
DT Christian	3	0	28	0	1		4

Bowling	O	M	R	W	wd	nb	Dots
JA Richardson	3.2	0	20	2			6
JP Behrendorff	2	0	12	1	1		6
AJ Turner	1	0	6	1			1
P Hatzoglou	3	0	13	1	4		11
AC Agar	4	0	25	1			8
AJ Tye	3	0	15	3			9

Toss: Scorchers. Umpires: PJ Gillespie, SJ Nogajski, DM Koch (TV), Ref: SJ Davis. Award: LJ Evans (PS). Crowd: 10,392
Turner 50: 32 balls, 4x4, 1x6, Evans 50: 25 balls, 4x4 2x6.
SS Sub: JM Avendano for JM Bird.

TEAM BY TEAM STATISTICS
ADELAIDE STRIKERS – THIRD

Batting & Fielding	M	Inn	NO	Runs	HS	Avge	100s	50s	6s	S/Rate	Ct	St
JW Wells	17	17	4	501	73	38.53	0	4	10	128.79	7	0
MW Short	16	16	1	493	89	32.86	0	3	26	155.52	12	-
MT Renshaw	11	11	2	306	63	34.00	0	2	2	136.60	3	-
IA Cockbain	6	6	2	239	71*	59.75	0	2	9	141.42	6	-
TJ Kelly	15	12	2	214	41	21.40	0	0	6	129.69	5	-
JB Weatherald	14	13	1	213	51	17.75	0	1	2	107.03	5	-
HJ Nielsen	14	10	3	131	39	18.71	0	0	1	103.96	10	1
HJ Hunt	6	6	0	102	27	17.00	0	0	3	110.86	2	-
AT Carey	3	3	0	91	67	30.33	0	1	1	149.18	3	0
GHS Garton	6	6	1	63	19	12.60	0	0	3	143.18	2	-
Rashid Khan	11	9	1	51	13	6.37	0	0	2	154.54	1	-
DR Drew	3	3	1	45	23*	22.50	0	0	0	118.42	0	-
WA Agar	7	4	1	20	9*	6.66	0	0	0	71.42	2	-
DJ Worrall	5	5	2	20	9	6.66	0	0	0	83.33	1	-
TM Head	3	3	0	11	5	3.66	0	0	0	61.11	1	-
RJ Gibson	2	2	1	8	8*	8.00	0	0	0	88.88	1	-
Fawad Ahmed	13	2	2	5	4*	-	0	0	0	166.66	2	-
PM Siddle	17	6	3	4	4	1.33	0	0	0	57.14	4	-
LAJ Scott	3	2	0	3	2	1.50	0	0	0	33.33	0	-
HNA Conway	9	1	0	1	1	1.00	0	0	0	100.00	1	-
HTRJY Thornton	7	2	2	0	0*	-	0	0	0	-	2	-

Bowling	M	Overs	Mdns	Runs	Wkts	Avge	Best	Econ	4w	SR	Dot %
PM Siddle	17	63.5	0	532	30	17.73	5-23	8.33	2	12.7	35
Rashid Khan	11	44	0	279	20	13.95	6-17	6.34	1	13.2	41
HTRJY Thornton	7	25	0	207	13	15.92	4-26	8.28	1	11.5	31
Fawad Ahmed	13	52	0	391	11	35.54	3-16	7.51	0	28.3	27
HNA Conway	9	34	0	271	9	30.11	2-32	7.97	0	22.6	33
MW Short	16	44.1	0	316	8	39.50	2-13	7.15	0	33.1	33
WA Agar	7	22.3	0	187	8	23.37	3-17	8.31	0	16.8	40
GHS Garton	6	20	0	208	6	34.66	2-23	10.40	0	20.0	37
DJ Worrall	5	18.4	0	133	5	26.60	2-18	7.12	0	22.4	45
MT Renshaw	11	4	0	38	1	38.00	1-38	9.50	0	24.0	21
TM Head	3	2	0	14	0	-	-	7.00	0	-	25

BBL11 Powerplays

Batting	Out	Runs	Balls	SR	Bowling	Ov	Figs	Econ	Dot %
AT Carey	0	53	30	177	DJ Worrall	8	0-51	6.38	67
MW Short	7	276	173	160	HNA Conway	11	2-72	6.55	48
HJ Hunt	2	60	43	140	HTRJY Thornton	6	4-41	6.83	39
MT Renshaw	1	60	45	133	MW Short	13	2-94	7.23	37
JB Weatherald	5	79	77	103	GHS Garton	8	1-69	8.63	46

Power Surge	Ov	Figs	Econ	Dot %
Rashid Khan	9	5-81	8.80	37
PM Siddle	17	10-161	9.47	35
HNA Conway	6	2-68	11.33	17
GHS Garton	2	0-40	20.00	20

ADELAIDE STRIKERS - HONOUR ROLL

Season	Finished	Captain	Coach	MVP	Minor Rd W/L/NR
2011-12	6th	M Klinger	DS Berry	M Klinger	2/5
2012-13	5th	J Botha	DS Berry	J Botha	4/4
2013-14	7th	J Botha/PJ Hughes	DS Berry	MG Neser	2/5
2014-15	Lost Semi	J Botha	DS Berry	A Zampa	6/1 NR 1
2015-16	Lost Semi	BJ Hodge	JN Gillespie	AU Rashid	7/1
2016-17	6th	BJ Hodge	JN Gillespie	BR Dunk	3/5
2017-18	Won title	TM Head/CA Ingram	JN Gillespie	Rashid Khan	7/3
2018-19	7th	TM Head/CA Ingram	JN Gillespie	JW Wells	6/8
2019-20	4th	TM Head/AT Carey	JN Gillespie	JW Wells	8/5/1
2020-21	5th	TM Head/PM Siddle/AT Carey	JN Gillespie	WA Agar	7/7
2021-22	3rd	PM Siddle	JN Gillespie	MW Short	6/8

Most Runs	M	Runs	HS	Avge	SR	Most Wickets	M	W	Avge	Best	Econ
JB Weatherald	77	1881	115	26.4	129	Rashid Khan	61	92	16.7	6-17	6.44
JW Wells	71	1740	73	37.8	123	PM Siddle	61	85	18.4	5-16	7.42
AT Carey	51	1679	101	34.9	128	MG Neser	62	62	26.9	3-24	8.34
TM Head	53	1360	101*	29.5	132	B Laughlin	50	60	22.6	4-26	8.07

Highest Individual scores

	Runs	Bls	4s	6s	Versus	Venue	Season
JB Weatherald	115	70	9	8	Hurricanes	Adelaide	2017-18
TM Head	101*	53	4	9	Sixers	Adelaide	2015-16
AT Carey	101	62	10	3	Heat	Adelaide	2020-21
AT Carey	100	56	12	4	Hurricanes	Adelaide	2017-18

Fastest Fifties / Fastest Hundreds

	Bls	Versus	Venue	Season		Bls	Versus	Venue	Season
TP Ludeman	18	Stars	Adelaide	2014-15	TM Head	53	Sixers	Adelaide	2015-16
AT Carey	21	Scorch	Perth St	2019-20	AT Carey	54	Hurricanes	Adelaide	2017-18
PD Salt	23	Reneg	Dockland	2019-20	JB Weatherald	58	Hurricanes	Adelaide	2017-18

Highest Team totals / Lowest Team totals

	Versus	Venue	Season			Versus	Venue	Season
8-207	Hurricanes	Adelaide	2019-20	68	Stars	MCG	2020-21
2-202	Hurricanes	Adelaide	2017-18	87	Sixers	Adelaide	2011-12
6-198	Scorchers	WACA	2013-14	88	Scorchers	Perth St	2018-19
6-196	Heat	Adelaide	2016-17	9-90	Stars	MCG	2013-14

Best Bowling

		Overs	Dots	Versus	Venue	Season
HS Sodhi	6-11	3.3	12	Thunder	Syd Showground	2016-17
Rashid Khan	**6-17**	**4**	**14**	**Heat**	**Gabba**	**2021-22**
PM Siddle	5-16	3.3	12	Hurricanes	Launceston	2020-21
PM Siddle	**5-23**	**3.5**	**10**	**Hurricanes**	**Adelaide**	**2021-22**

Most Economical Bowling (Min 4 overs)

		Dots	Versus	Venue	Season
Rashid Khan	0-9	17	Scorchers	Perth Stadium	2018-19
B Laughlin	2-10	13	Sixers	Adelaide	2016-17
J Botha	2-11	14	Heat	Adelaide	2013-14
AW O'Brien	0-12	14	Stars	MCG	2011-12
DJ Worrall	2-12	18	Sixers	Bellerive	2020-21

Most Expensive Bowling (Min 4 overs)

		Versus	Venue	Season
KW Richardson	2-54	Sixers	SCG	2014-15
B Laughlin	1-51	Sixers	Adelaide	2014-15
Fawad Ahmed	**0-51**	**Thunder**	**Syd Showground**	**2021-22**
B Stanlake	2-50	Heat	Gabba	2018-19
BS Oakley	0-50	Scorchers	Adelaide	2013-14

BRISBANE HEAT – SEVENTH

Batting & Fielding	M	Inn	NO	Runs	HS	Avge	100s	50s	6s	S/Rate	Ct	St
BM Duckett	12	12	0	302	78	25.16	0	3	6	128.51	9	-
SD Heazlett	14	14	1	266	49	20.46	0	0	12	123.72	4	-
MA Bryant	10	10	0	230	81	23.00	0	2	6	113.86	4	-
CA Lynn	12	12	0	215	57	17.91	0	1	8	125.00	2	-
XC Bartlett	7	6	4	129	42*	64.50	0	0	2	124.03	2	-
JJ Bazley	11	11	3	122	44*	15.25	0	0	5	124.48	1	-
JJ Peirson	11	11	2	119	42	13.22	0	0	4	132.22	11	0
LD Pfeffer	4	4	0	109	69	27.25	0	1	3	114.73	2	0
TLW Cooper	7	7	0	81	32	11.57	0	0	4	165.30	5	-
JS Lehmann	3	3	0	74	65	24.66	0	1	0	110.44	2	-
S McGiffin	2	2	1	20	14*	20.00	0	0	0	86.95	1	-
MT Steketee	8	7	3	62	33	15.50	0	0	2	114.81	4	-
JD Wildermuth	3	3	0	56	28	18.66	0	0	1	114.28	0	-
NA McSweeney	3	3	0	31	20	10.33	0	0	0	100.00	0	-
W Prestwidge	3	3	1	23	21	11.50	0	0	2	121.05	0	-
J Clayton	2	2	0	21	15	10.50	0	0	0	91.30	0	-
LCJ Guthrie	6	3	1	17	11*	8.50	0	0	1	141.66	3	-
JP Wood	1	1	0	12	12	12.00	0	0	1	92.30	0	-
MP Kuhnemann	9	5	3	12	9	6.00	0	0	0	100.00	1	-
TB Abell	2	1	0	9	9	9.00	0	0	0	69.23	1	-
MJ Swepson	5	2	1	5	4	5.00	0	0	0	166.66	1	-
MG Neser	3	3	1	4	4	2.00	0	0	0	66.66	1	-
PG Dooley	1	1	1	4	4*	-	0	0	0	133.33	1	-
Fakhar Zaman	1	1	0	3	3	3.00	0	0	0	37.50	1	-
M Labuschagne	1	1	0	3	3	3.00	0	0	0	50.00	1	-
Mujeeb Ur Rahman	11	6	1	3	3*	0.60	0	0	0	33.33	2	-
CJ Gannon	1	1	0	1	1	1.00	0	0	0	33.33	0	-
DMK Grant	2	1	1	1	1*	-	0	0	0	100.00	0	-

Also played: RH McDonald (1 match) did not bat and took a catch.

Bowling	M	Overs	Mdns	Runs	Wkts	Avge	Best	Econ	4w	SR	Dot %
JJ Bazley	11	39.5	0	324	12	27.00	3-28	8.13	0	19.9	35
MT Steketee	8	30.4	1	274	12	22.83	3-27	8.93	0	15.3	43
XC Bartlett	7	27.1	0	239	11	21.72	4-30	8.79	1	14.8	42
Mujeeb Ur Rahman	11	44	0	280	8	35.00	3-20	6.36	0	33.0	43
MP Kuhnemann	9	22	0	181	6	30.16	3-47	8.22	0	22.0	28
LCJ Guthrie	6	22	0	204	6	34.00	2-32	9.27	0	22.0	37
MJ Swepson	5	19	0	146	5	29.20	2-19	7.68	0	22.8	29
MG Neser	3	10	0	88	4	22.00	3-39	8.80	0	15.0	32
W Prestwidge	3	9.2	0	93	4	23.25	2-34	9.96	0	14.0	34
DMK Grant	2	8	0	48	3	16.00	3-20	6.00	0	16.0	40
JD Wildermuth	3	10	0	75	2	37.50	2-18	7.50	0	30.0	42

Also bowled: TLW Cooper (7 matches) 1-0-16-0 (17%), PG Dooley (1 match) 4-0-25-0 (38% dot), CJ Gannon (1 match) 4-0-32-2 (33%), SD Heazlett (14 matches) 1-0-15-0 (17%), M Labuschagne (1 match) 3-0-23-1 (17%), RH McDonald (1 match) 2-0-21-1 (25%), S McGiffin (2 matches) 2-0-23-0 (17%), NA McSweeney (3 matches) 2-0-12-0 (50%), JP Wood (1 match) 1-0-13-0 (17%).

BBL11 Powerplays

Batting	Out	Runs	Balls	SR	Bowling	Ov	Figs	Econ	Dot %
CA Lynn	6	133	102	133	MT Steketee	13	4-85	6.54	56
MA Bryant	4	80	66	121	JJ Bazley	6	2-43	7.17	42
BM Duckett	3	42	35	120	XA Bartlett	11	4-88	8.00	47

Power Surge	Ov	Figs	Econ	Dot %
Mujeeb-Ur-Rahman	4	1-29	7.25	54
MT Steketee	7	2-84	12.00	26
XC Bartlett	5.1	2-72	13.93	42

BRISBANE HEAT - HONOUR ROLL

Season	Finished	Captain	Coach	MVP	Minor Rd W/L
2011-12	5th	JR Hopes/PJ Forrest	DS Lehmann	A McDermott	3/4
2012-13	Won Title	JR Hopes/CD Hartley	DS Lehmann	LA Pomersbach	4/4
2013-14	5th	JR Hopes/DL Vettori	SG Law	DL Vettori	3/5
2014-15	Last	JR Hopes	SG Law	PJ Forrest	2/6
2015-16	6th	CA Lynn	DL Vettori	CA Lynn	3/5
2016-17	3rd	BB McCullum/JA Burns	DL Vettori	BB McCullum	5/3
2017-18	7th	BB McCullum	DL Vettori	Yasir Shah	4/6
2018-19	5th	CA Lynn	DL Vettori	Mujeeb ur Rahman	6/7/NR 1
2019-20	7th	CA Lynn	DS Lehmann	MT Renshaw	6/8
2020-21	3rd	CA Lynn/JJ Peirson	DS Lehmann	CA Lynn	7/7
2021-22	7th	JJ Peirson/TLW Cooper/CA Lynn	WA Seccombe	BM Duckett	3/11

Most Runs	M	Runs	HS	Avge	SR		Most Wickets	M	W	Avge	Best	Econ
CA Lynn	102	3005	101	34.5	148		MT Steketee	61	78	24.4	4-33	8.91
JJ Peirson	88	1279	69*	21.3	124		BCJ Cutting	79	63	30.1	3-25	8.83
BCJ Cutting	79	1199	81*	21.8	145		MJ Swepson	54	53	26.6	3-14	7.54
JA Burns	59	1192	69	26.4	123		JK Lalor	36	42	23.5	5-26	7.77

Highest Individual scores

	Runs	Bls	4s	6s	Versus	Venue	Season
LA Pomersbach	112*	70	15	2	Renegades	Docklands	2012-13
CA Lynn	101	51	5	7	Hurricanes	Brisbane	2015-16
CA Lynn	98*	49	3	11	Scorchers	Perth	2016-17
CA Lynn	94	35	4	11	Sixers	SCG	2019-20

Fastest Fifties

	Bls	Versus	Venue	Season
T Banton	16	Thunder	Showg	2019-20
BCJ Cutting	17	Stars	Gabba	2018-19
BB McCullum	18	Renegades	Gabba	2016-17
CA Lynn	18	Hurricanes	Gabba	2014-15

Fastest Hundreds

	Bls	Versus	Venue	Season
CA Lynn	49	Hurricanes	Gabba	2015-16
L Pomersbach	65	Renegades	Dock	2012-13

Highest Team totals

	Versus	Venue	Season
3-212	Hurricanes	Bellerive	2019-20
3-209	Hurricanes	Gabba	2013-14
4-209	Sixers	SCG	2019-20
6-208	Hurricanes	Hobart	2014-15

Lowest Team totals

	Versus	Venue	Season
73	Sixers	SCG	2017-18
80	Renegades	Docklands	2014-15
90	Strikers	Gabba	2021-22
91	Strikers	Adelaide	2017-18

Best Bowling

		Overs	Dots	Versus	Venue	Season
Mujeeb-ur-Rahmann	5-15	4	14	Hurricanes	Gabba	2020-21
S Badree	5-22	4	12	Stars	MCG	2015-16
DT Christian	5-26	4	10	Thunder	Stadium Australia	2012-13
JK Lalor	5-26	4	12	Sixers	SCG	2018-19
JL Pattinson	5-33	4	11	Strikers	Gabba	2019-20
BJ Doggett	5-35	4	9	Scorchers	Gabba	2017-18

Most Economical Bowling (Min 4 overs)

		Dots	Versus	Venue	Season
JR Hopes	1-8	17	Renegades	Docklands	2014-15
LCJ Guthrie	1-10	15	Renegades	Gold Coast	2021-22
Mujeeb Ur Rahman	2-10	16	Scorchers	Perth Stadium	2018-19
DL Vettori	2-10	15	Strikers	Adelaide	2013-14

Most Expensive Bowling (Min 4 overs)

		Versus	Venue	Season
LCJ Guthrie	2-70	Stars	Gabba	2021-22
B Laughlin	0-60	Scorchers	Perth Stadium	2019-20
MT Steketee	0-54	Scorchers	Adelaide Oval	2020-21
LW Feldman	1-53	Hurricanes	Gabba	2015-16

HOBART HURRICANES – FIFTH

Batting & Fielding	M	Inn	NO	Runs	HS	Avge	100s	50s	6s	S/Rate	Ct	St
BR McDermott	13	13	1	577	127	48.08	2	3	29	153.86	9	1
DJM Short	15	15	3	444	73*	37.00	0	2	11	113.26	10	-
MS Wade	13	13	1	325	93	27.08	0	2	10	134.85	3	3
TH David	15	14	5	218	46*	24.22	0	0	14	163.90	7	-
CP Jewell	11	11	0	216	51	19.63	0	1	6	129.34	6	-
PSP Handscomb	14	12	2	206	47	20.60	0	0	4	113.81	4	-
JA Thompson	11	8	1	52	15*	7.42	0	0	3	152.94	3	-
TS Rogers	13	5	2	51	33*	17.00	0	0	3	127.50	3	-
HC Brook	7	7	0	44	22	6.28	0	0	0	75.86	7	-
NT Ellis	8	5	1	42	20	10.50	0	0	1	135.48	7	-
WB Parker	5	2	1	29	25*	29.00	0	0	1	152.63	1	-
MJ Owen	5	4	3	26	16	26.00	0	0	0	144.44	1	-
S Lamichhane	14	3	2	23	13*	23.00	0	0	1	127.77	0	-
SM Boland	2	2	1	15	10	15.00	0	0	0	83.33	0	-
RP Meredith	11	3	2	14	10	14.00	0	0	0	140.00	2	-
JM Cox	1	1	0	10	10	10.00	0	0	0	83.33	2	-
MB Wright	1	1	0	6	6	6.00	0	0	0	42.85	0	-
JS Paris	3	2	1	2	2	2.00	0	0	0	25.00	0	-
TA Lammonby	3	1	0	0	0	0.00	0	0	0	0.00	2	-
J Kann	3	-	-	-	-	-	-	-	-	-	1	-
W Sanders	2	-	-	-	-	-	-	-	-	-	0	-

Bowling	M	Overs	Mdns	Runs	Wkts	Avge	Best	Econ	4w	SR	Dot %
TS Rogers	13	49	0	386	20	19.30	3-24	7.87	0	14.7	36
RP Meredith	11	36	0	286	16	17.87	3-29	7.94	0	13.5	43
S Lamichhane	14	54.1	0	422	14	30.14	3-32	7.79	0	23.2	32
NT Ellis	8	31	0	252	11	22.90	3-41	8.12	0	16.9	32
JA Thompson	11	19	0	171	8	21.37	3-24	9.00	0	14.2	32
JS Paris	3	9.4	0	74	5	14.80	3-35	7.65	0	11.6	42
DJM Short	15	30	0	248	5	49.60	1-9	8.26	0	36.0	29
MJ Owen	5	12.1	0	101	2	50.50	2-25	8.30	0	36.5	29
TH David	15	21.2	0	189	2	94.50	1-4	8.85	0	64.0	25
SM Boland	2	8	0	77	2	38.50	1-32	9.62	0	24.0	19
W Parker	5	8	0	92	1	92.00	1-42	11.50	0	48.0	29
J Kann	3	5	0	76	1	76.00	1-40	15.20	0	30.0	21
TA Lammonby	3	1	0	10	0	-	-	10.00	0	-	17

BBL11 Powerplays

Batting	Out	Runs	Balls	SR	Bowling	Ov	Figs	Econ	Dot %
MS Wade	7	116	93	125	NT Ellis	7	2-43	6.14	36
BR McDermott	4	144	126	114	TH David	7	0-53	7.23	53
CP Jewell	4	55	58	95	RP Meredith	15	3-124	8.27	51
DJM Short	1	40	67	60	TS Rogers	17	7-148	8.71	41

Power Surge	Ov	Figs	Econ	Dot %
TS Rogers	10	1-89	8.90	28
NT Ellis	8	0-95	11.88	21
RP Meredith	4	1-41	10.25	38

HOBART HURRICANES - HONOUR ROLL

Season	Finished	Captain	Coach	MVP	Minor Rd W/L
2011-12	Lost Semi	XJ Doherty	AS de Winter	TR Birt	5/2
2012-13	6th	GJ Bailey/TD Paine	TC Coyle	B Laughlin	4/4
2013-14	Lost Final	GJ Bailey/TD Paine	DG Wright	BR Dunk	3/4 NR1
2014-15	5th	GJ Bailey/TD Paine	DG Wright	BW Hilfenhaus	3/5
2015-16	7th	GJ Bailey/TD Paine	DG Wright	DT Christian	3/5
2016-17	7th	TD Paine	DG Wright	SCJ Broad	3/5
2017-18	R-up	GJ Bailey	G Kirsten	DJM Short	5/5
2018-19	Lost Semi	MS Wade	AR Griffith	DJM Short	10/4
2019-20	5th	MS Wade/BR McDermott	AR Griffith	DJM Short	6/7/1
2020-21	6th	PSP Handscomb/MS Wade	AR Griffith	SM Boland	7/7
2021-22	5th	MS Wade/PSP Handscomb	AR Griffith	BR McDermott	7/7

Most Runs	M	Runs	HS	Avge	SR		Most Wickets	M	W	Avge	Best	Econ
DJM Short	72	2553	122*	39.8	133		**RP Meredith**	45	59	22.0	4-21	8.04
BR McDermott	70	2100	127	38.1	139		CJ Boyce	40	43	25.7	3-11	8.23
MS Wade	52	1624	130*	36.0	149		**NT Ellis**	37	43	25.6	4-34	8.13
GJ Bailey	72	1559	74*	36.4	137		JP Faulkner	25	36	19.0	3-21	8.02

Highest Individual scores

	Runs	Bls	4s	6s	Versus	Venue	Season
MS Wade	130*	61	11	7	Strikers	Adelaide	2019-20
BR McDermott	**127**	65	9	9	**Renegades**	**Docklands**	**2021-22**
DJM Short	122*	69	8	8	Heat	Gabba	2017-18
BR McDermott	114	52	8	9	Renegades	Docklands	2016-17
BR McDermott	**110***	60	12	5	**Strikers**	**Bellerive**	**2021-22**
DJM Short	103*	70	3	7	Scorchers	Perth Stadium	2019-20

Fastest Fifties

	Bls	Versus	Venue	Season
MS Wade	19	Sixers	SCG	2021-22
BR Dunk	20	Heat	Gabba	2013-14
DJM Short	21	Sixers	SCG	2016-17
DT Christian	21	Heat	Gabba	2015-16

Fastest Hundreds

	Bls	Versus	Venue	Season
BR McDermott	47	Renegades	Docklands	2016-17
MS Wade	48	Strikers	Adelaide	2019-20
BR McDermott	53	**Renegades**	**Docklands**	**2021-22**
BR McDermott	58	**Strikers**	**Bellerive**	**2021-22**

Highest Team totals

	Versus	Venue	Season
8-223	Renegades	Docklands	2016-17
2-213	**Sixers**	**SCG**	**2021-22**
1-217	Strikers	Adelaide	2019-20
7-210	Heat	Gabba	2013-14
4-210	Scorchers	Perth Stadium	2017-18

Lowest Team totals

	Versus	Venue	Season
91	Sixers	SCG	2015-16
98	Scorchers	Bellerive	2019-20
9-102	Renegades	Docklands	2012-13
109	Thunder	Launceston	2017-18

Best Bowling

	Overs	Dots	Versus	Venue	Season
DT Christian	5-14	4	15	Strikers	Hobart	2016-17
DJM Short	5-21	4	10	Thunder	Hobart	2019-20
JK Reed	4-11	4	18	Thunder	Syd Showgrounds	2014-15
Qais Ahmed	4-12	4	16	Sixers	Alice Springs	2019-20

Most Economical Bowling (Min 4 overs)

		Dots	Versus	Venue	Season
BW Hilfenhaus	2-10	18	Scorchers	WACA	2011-12
RP Meredith	1-10	15	Sixers	Alice Springs	2019-20
JK Reed	4-11	18	Thunder	Syd Showgrounds	2014-15
NT Ellis	2-11	17	Stars	Bellerive	2020-21

Most Expensive Bowling (Min 4 overs)

		Versus	Venue	Season
SW Tait	0-56	Stars	Bellerive	2016-17
TS Mills	2-56	Stars	MCG	2017-18
RP Meredith	1-55	Sixers	MCG	2020-21
SW Tait	1-54	Hurricanes	Gabba	2015-16
JK Reed	2-54	Renegades	Docklands	2016-17

MELBOURNE RENEGADES – LAST

Batting & Fielding	M	Inn	NO	Runs	HS	Avge	100s	50s	6s	S/Rate	Ct	St
AJ Finch	11	10	0	386	82	38.60	0	4	18	130.40	0	-
MWG Harvey	12	11	2	231	71*	25.66	0	2	3	112.68	9	-
SE Marsh	7	7	0	202	57	28.85	0	2	5	132.02	3	-
SB Harper	14	13	2	198	57	18.00	0	1	7	119.27	14	2
NJ Maddinson	9	9	1	128	67	16.00	0	1	5	112.28	7	-
J Seymour	9	8	2	112	25	18.66	0	0	4	123.07	0	-
J Fraser-McGurk	9	8	0	112	32	14.00	0	0	3	105.66	4	-
WJ Sutherland	12	10	2	52	15*	6.50	0	0	4	120.93	1	-
KW Richardson	11	6	2	43	17	10.75	0	0	1	93.47	3	-
JA Prestwidge	6	4	2	39	22*	19.50	0	0	1	121.87	0	-
Mohammad Nabi	9	7	0	36	12	5.14	0	0	0	76.59	5	-
UBT Chand	2	2	0	35	29	17.50	0	0	2	116.66	2	-
RJW Topley	8	4	4	33	14*	-	0	0	2	117.85	0	-
JA Merlo	4	4	0	22	15	5.50	0	0	0	91.66	1	-
JL Pattinson	6	4	0	19	16	4.75	0	0	1	126.66	0	-
CJ Boyce	4	3	1	8	8*	4.00	0	0	0	72.72	0	-
JK Lalor	5	2	0	6	5	3.00	0	0	0	54.54	2	-
Zahir Khan	14	5	1	3	3	0.75	0	0	0	20.00	2	-
ZK Evans	4	1	1	0	0*	-	0	0	0	0.00	4	-

Bowling	M	Overs	Mdns	Runs	Wkts	Avge	Best	Econ	4w	SR	Dot %
KW Richardson	11	38	1	312	19	16.42	4-32	8.21	1	12.0	36
Zahir Khan	14	49.3	0	402	12	33.50	3-24	8.12	0	24.7	32
CJ Boyce	4	16	0	103	10	10.30	5-21	6.43	1	9.6	33
RJW Topley	8	26.5	0	225	9	25.00	3-27	8.38	0	17.8	42
NJ Maddinson	9	14	0	97	6	16.16	3-20	6.92	0	14.0	32
JK Lalor	5	18	0	178	5	35.60	2-37	9.88	0	21.6	41
WJ Sutherland	12	20	0	207	5	41.40	2-13	10.35	0	24.0	27
Mohammad Nabi	9	16	0	107	3	35.66	2-19	6.68	0	32.0	27
JA Prestwidge	6	11.5	0	101	3	33.66	1-9	8.53	0	23.6	27
JL Pattinson	6	18	0	169	3	56.33	1-27	9.38	0	36.0	32
ZK Evans	4	11	0	118	3	39.33	1-22	10.72	0	22.0	30
JA Merlo	4	2	0	9	0	-	-	4.50	0	-	33
J Seymour	9	5	0	28	0	-	-	5.60	0	-	38
AJ Finch	11	1	0	10	0	-	-	10.00	0	-	0

BBL11 Powerplays

Batting	Out	Runs	Balls	SR	Bowling	Ov	Figs	Econ	Dot %
MWG Harvey	2	64	49	131	RJW Topley	11	2-68	6.18	55
AJ Finch	3	92	74	124	KW Richardson	7	1-53	7.57	36
SE Marsh	2	66	55	120	JK Lalor	10	3-91	9.10	53
SB Harper	3	76	77	98	JL Pattinson	6	1-61	10.17	47

Power Surge	Ov	Figs	Econ	Dot %
KW Richardson	9	6-85	9.44	43
ZK Evans	3	1-36	12.00	17
RJW Topley	6	3-76	12.67	28

MELBOURNE RENEGADES - HONOUR ROLL

Season	Finished	Captain	Coach	MVP	Minor Rd W/L
2011-12	7th	AB McDonald	S Helmot	AJ Finch	2/5
2012-13	Lost Semi	AJ Finch/BJ Rohrer	S Helmot	AJ Finch	7/1
2013-14	6th	AJ Finch/BJ Rohrer	S Helmot	AJ Finch	3/5
2014-15	6th	AJ Finch/BJ Rohrer	S Helmot	JL Pattinson	3/5
2015-16	5th	AJ Finch/CL White	DJ Saker	DJ Bravo	3/5
2016-17	5th	AJ Finch	AB McDonald	AJ Finch	4/4
2017-18	Lost Semi	AJ Finch/DJ Bravo/CL White	AB McDonald	TLW Cooper	6/4
2018-19	Champions	AJ Finch/TLW Cooper	AB McDonald	DT Christian	8/6
2019-20	Last	AJ Finch/DT Christian	M Klinger	BJ Webster	3/11
2020-21	Last	AJ Finch/SE Marsh	M Klinger	SB Harper	4/10
2021-22	Last	KW Richardson/NJ Maddinson/AJ Finch	DJ Saker	KW Richardson	3/10/1

Most Runs	M	Runs	HS	Avge	SR		Most Wickets	M	W	Avge	Best	Econ
AJ Finch	87	2817	111*	34.7	134		KW Richardson	54	80	19.9	4-22	7.83
TLW Cooper	70	1202	65*	23.1	125		CJ Boyce	34	40	22.1	5-21	6.86
SB Harper	56	1169	73	23.3	131		NJ Rimmington	35	34	25.8	4-26	8.14
SE Marsh	31	963	87	31.0	126		DJ Bravo	27	33	24.6	5-28	8.08

Highest Individual scores

	Runs	Bls	4s	6s	Versus	Venue	Season
AJ Finch	111*	65	12	4	Stars	Docklands	2012-13
AJ Finch	109	68	6	7	Sixers	SCG	2019-20
AD Hales	89	52	5	8	Sixers	SCG	2012-13
SE Marsh	87	48	5	5	Thunder	Gold Coast	2020-21

Fastest Fifties

	Bls	Versus	Venue	Season
CH Gayle	12	Strikers	Docklands	2015-16
AJ Finch	20	Heat	Gabba	2016-17
TLW Cooper	22	Hurricanes	Docklands	2016-17
CJ Boyce	22	Thunder	Docklands	2018-19

Fastest Hundreds

	Bls	Versus	Venue	Season
AJ Finch	60	Stars	Docklands	2012-13
AJ Finch	63	Sixers	SCG	2019-20

Highest Team totals

	Versus	Venue	Season
4-222	Hurricanes	Docklands	2016-17
3-210	Heat	Docklands	2013-14
5-199	Heat	Gabba	2016-17
6-189	Thunder	Canberra	2017-18

Lowest Team totals

	Versus	Venue	Season
57	Stars	Docklands	2014-15
60	Sixers	Bellerive	2020-21
80	Thunder	Manuka	2020-21
80	**Thunder**	**Manuka**	**2021-22**

Best Bowling

		Overs	Dots	Versus	Venue	Season
CJ Boyce	**5-21**	**4**	**10**	**Thunder**	**MCG**	**2021-22**
DJ Bravo	5-28	4	10	Hurricanes	Hobart	2017-18
ZK Evans	5-33	4	8	Hurricanes	MCG	2020-21
Shakib-al-Hasan	4-13	4	15	Heat	Docklands	2014-15
CJ Boyce	4-15	4	12	Heat	Gabba	2019-20

Most Economical Bowling (Min 4 overs)

		Dots	Versus	Venue	Season
Fawad Ahmed	1-7	18	Heat	Docklands	2014-15
DT Christian	1-9	15	Thunder	Docklands	2018-19
CP Tremain	3-9	17	Scorchers	Perth Stadium	2018-19
DP Nannes	0-10	14	Thunder	Stadium Australia	2011-12

Most Expensive Bowling (Min 4 overs)

		Versus	Venue	Season
KW Richardson	**0-63**	**Hurricanes**	**Docklands**	**2021-22**
NLTC Perera	0-59	Hurricanes	Docklands	2016-17
KW Richardson	2-55	Hurricanes	Bellerive	2018-19
HF Gurney	1-55	Scorchers	Perth Stadium	2019-20

MELBOURNE STARS – SIXTH

Batting & Fielding	M	Inn	NO	Runs	HS	Avge	100	50s	6s	S/Rate	Ct	St
GJ Maxwell	13	13	2	468	154*	42.54	2	1	12	159.72	6	-
JM Clarke	13	13	0	419	85	32.23	0	5	17	151.26	5	-
HWR Cartwright	14	13	2	360	79	32.72	0	1	22	144.57	9	-
MP Stoinis	8	8	2	170	75*	28.33	0	1	10	153.15	0	-
BJ Webster	12	8	2	98	63	16.33	0	1	2	103.15	5	-
JA Burns	7	6	0	95	25	15.83	0	0	2	95.95	1	-
NCR Larkin	9	8	2	88	52*	14.66	0	1	0	90.72	3	-
AD Russell	5	5	3	83	42*	41.50	0	0	5	156.60	2	-
Qais Ahmad	10	6	2	44	16	11.00	0	0	4	133.33	1	-
TJ Dean	1	1	0	32	32	32.00	0	0	0	123.07	0	-
TF Rogers	1	1	0	32	32	32.00	0	0	1	128.00	0	-
CA Wakim	2	2	0	32	20	16.00	0	0	1	91.42	1	-
CD Hinchliffe	5	4	0	19	15	4.75	0	0	1	82.60	2	-
PM Nevill	1	1	0	18	18	18.00	0	0	0	128.57	0	-
Haris Rauf	5	3	2	9	8	9.00	0	0	1	150.00	3	-
J Avendano	2	2	0	12	6	6.00	0	0	0	85.71	0	-
BL Couch	14	5	2	12	8	4.00	0	0	0	60.00	2	-
SL Rainbird	5	3	1	11	10*	5.50	0	0	0	68.75	2	-
A Zampa	10	4	2	9	4*	4.50	0	0	0	90.00	1	-
Syed Faridoun	1	1	1	6	6*	-	0	0	0	120.00	0	-
P Rowe	1	1	0	3	3	3.00	0	0	0	50.00	0	1
TL O'Connell	3	2	0	3	3	1.50	0	0	0	30.00	3	-
SM Elliott	2	1	0	2	2	2.00	0	0	0	28.57	0	-
XA Crone	2	1	0	1	1	1.00	0	0	0	25.00	0	-
NM Coulter-Nile	7	2	0	1	1	0.50	0	0	0	20.00	2	-
Ahmed Daniyal	3	1	1	1	1*	-	0	0	0	50.00	0	-

Bowling	M	Overs	Mdns	Runs	Wkts	Avge	Best	Econ	4w	SR	Dot %
BL Couch	14	43	0	353	16	22.06	3-30	8.20	0	16.1	33
Qais Ahmad	10	38.4	1	276	13	21.23	3-26	7.13	0	17.8	36
A Zampa	10	39	0	290	10	29.00	2-18	7.43	0	23.4	33
Haris Rauf	5	20	0	157	9	17.44	2-25	7.85	0	13.3	35
NM Coulter-Nile	7	25	1	202	7	28.85	2-22	8.08	0	21.4	33
TL O'Connell	3	8	0	61	4	15.25	2-11	7.62	0	12.0	27
GJ Maxwell	13	24	0	185	4	46.25	2-19	7.70	0	36.0	26
CD Hinchliffe	5	15	0	125	4	31.25	2-21	8.33	0	22.5	24
Ahmed Daniyal	3	10	0	91	3	30.33	1-24	9.10	0	20.0	32
SL Rainbird	5	18	0	168	3	56.00	2-25	9.33	0	36.0	29
AD Russell	5	17	0	172	3	57.33	3-48	10.11	0	34.0	27
BJ Webster	12	5	0	48	1	48.00	1-23	9.60	0	30.0	23
SM Elliott	2	7	0	61	0	-	-	8.71	0	-	26
Syed Faridoun	1	4	0	37	0	-	-	9.25	0	-	33
XA Crone	2	3	0	29	0	-	-	9.66	0	-	22
HWR Cartwright	14	1	0	6	0	-	-	6.00	0	-	17

BBL11 Powerplays

Batting	Out	Runs	Balls	SR	Bowling	Ov	Figs	Econ	Dot %
GJ Maxwell	2	97	57	170	Qais Ahmad	4	1-22	5.50	58
JM Clarke	5	166	110	151	A Zampa	7	2-41	5.86	50
MP Stoinis	2	40	40	120	NM Coulter-Nile	7	2-54	7.71	48
					GJ Maxwell	8	1-67	8.38	31

Power Surge	Ov	Figs	Econ	Dot %
NM Coulter-Nile	6	3-62	10.33	33
Haris Rauf	4	0-44	11.00	33
A Russell	4	1-46	11.50	25
A Zampa	6	1-70	11.67	39

MELBOURNE STARS - HONOUR ROLL

Season	Finished	Captain	Coach	MVP	Minor Rd W/L
2011-12	Lost Semi	CL White	G Shipperd	DJ Hussey	4/3
2012-13	Lost Semi	SK Warne/CL White	G Shipperd	LS Malinga	5/3
2013-14	Lost Semi	CL White/BJ Hodge	G Shipperd	LJ Wright	8/-
2014-15	Lost Semi	CL White	G Shipperd	JW Hastings	5/3
2015-16	Lost Final	DJ Hussey	SP Fleming	KP Pietersen	5/3
2016-17	Lost Semi	DJ Hussey	SP Fleming	LJ Wright	4/4
2017-18	Last	JW Hastings	SP Fleming	GJ Maxwell	2/8
2018-19	Runner-up	GJ Maxwell/NJ Maddinson	SP Fleming	GJ Maxwell	7/7
2019-20	Runner-up	GJ Maxwell/PSP Handscomb	DJ Hussey	MP Stoinis	10/4
2020-21	7th	GJ Maxwell	DJ Hussey	A Zampa	7/7
2021-22	6th	GJ Maxwell/A Zampa	DJ Hussey	JM Clarke	7/7

Most Runs	M	Runs	HS	Avge	SR	Most Wickets	M	W	Avge	Best	Econ
GJ Maxwell	94	2549	154*	34.9	151	A Zampa	67	82	21.7	5-17	7.18
MP Stoinis	79	2297	147*	37.0	133	JW Hastings	38	50	21.2	4-29	7.88
LJ Wright	57	1479	117	29.0	131	JP Faulkner	45	44	23.8	4-46	7.61
KP Pietersen	33	1110	76	37.0	137	MP Stoinis	79	36	20.9	4-21	8.48

Highest Individual scores

	Runs	Bls	4s	6s	Versus	Venue	Season
GJ Maxwell	154	64	22	4	Hurricanes	MCG	2021-22
MP Stoinis	147*	79	13	8	Sixers	MCG	2019-20
LJ Wright	117	60	8	9	Hurricanes	Hobart	2011-12
LJ Wright	109*	63	11	4	Renegades	MCG	2015-16
PSP Handscomb	103*	64	6	5	Scorchers	MCG	2014-15
GJ Maxwell	103	57	12	3	Sixers	MCG	2021-22

Fastest Fifties

	Bls	Versus	Venue	Season
N Pooran	17	Sixers	G/Coast	2020-21
GJ Maxwell	20	Hurric	MCG	2021-22
P Handscomb	22	Sixers	SCG	2018-19

Fastest Hundreds

	Bls	Versus	Venue	Season
GJ Maxwell	41	Hurric	MCG	2021-22
LJ Wright	44	Hurric	Bellerive	2011-12
GJ Maxwell	54	Sixers	MCG	2021-22

Highest Team totals

	Versus	Venue	Season
2-273	Hurricanes	MCG	2021-22
1-219	Sixers	SCG	2019-20
7-208	Renegades	MCG	2013-14
9-207	Heat	Gabba	2021-22

Lowest Team totals

	Versus	Venue	Season
61	Sixers	SCG	2021-22
99	Sixers	MCG	2019-20
115	Heat	MCG	2019-20
126	Scorchers	WACA	2014-15

Best Bowling

	Overs	Dots	Versus	Venue	Season
SL Malinga	6-7	4	19	Scorchers	WACA	2012-13
A Zampa	5-17	3.2	9	Strikers	MCG	2020-21
Haris Rauf	5-27	4	14	Hurricanes	Moe	2019-20
NM Coulter-Nile	4-10	3.5	15	Heat	Manuka Oval	2020-21
MP Stoinis	4-21	4	10	Heat	MCG	2018-19

Most Economical Bowling (Min 4 overs)

		Dots	Versus	Venue	Season
SL Malinga	6-7	19	Scorchers	WACA	2012-13
SL Malinga	2-8	16	Strikers	MCG	2013-14
JP Faulkner	3-9	17	Strikers	MCG	2013-14
A Zampa	2-10	15	Thunder	Manuka	2020-21

Most Expensive Bowling (Min 4 overs)

		Versus	Venue	Season
DJ Worrall	0-60	Hurricanes	MCG	2014-15
SL Rainbird	1-59	Sixers	SCG	2021-22
Dilbar Hussain	1-56	Heat	MCG	2019-20
SM Boland	2-55	Strikers	Adelaide Oval	2015-16

PERTH SCORCHERS – CHAMPIONS

Batting & Fielding	M	Inn	NO	Runs	HS	Avge	100s	50s	6s	S/Rate	Ct	St
KR Patterson	14	13	0	391	78	30.07	0	4	18	142.18	11	-
C Munro	13	13	4	390	114*	43.33	1	2	16	127.45	8	-
LJ Evans	15	12	3	361	76*	40.11	0	2	14	144.40	4	1
AJ Turner	16	15	4	357	69	32.45	0	2	16	153.87	4	-
MR Marsh	8	8	2	347	100*	57.83	1	2	15	142.79	5	-
CT Bancroft	8	8	0	163	45	20.37	0	0	2	106.53	6	-
JP Inglis	8	8	0	137	79	17.12	0	1	3	128.03	9	4
AC Agar	15	10	4	133	30*	22.16	0	0	8	149.43	4	-
AM Hardie	9	8	2	115	45	19.16	0	0	6	136.90	4	-
AJ Tye	16	7	2	55	44	11.00	0	0	3	130.95	4	-
NR Hobson	2	2	0	50	46	25.00	0	0	0	111.11	1	-
P Hatzoglou	15	2	2	12	12*	-	0	0	0	92.30	2	-
CJM Sabburg	3	2	1	10	7*	10.00	0	0	0	100.00	0	-
DJM Moody	1	1	0	8	8	8.00	0	0	0	53.33	0	-
JP Behrendorff	13	3	1	5	3	2.50	0	0	0	62.50	6	-
ML Kelly	6	2	0	2	1	1.00	0	0	0	50.00	2	-
TS Mills	7	1	1	1	1*	-	0	0	0	100.00	1	-
JA Richardson	2	1	1	1	1*	-	0	0	0	50.00	0	-
LRT Morris	6	1	1	0	0*	-	0	0	0	0.00	2	-

Bowling	M	Overs	Mdns	Runs	Wkts	Avge	Best	Econ	4w	SR	Dot %
AJ Tye	16	52.3	0	424	25	16.96	3-15	8.07	0	12.6	44
AC Agar	15	58	0	394	18	21.88	2-16	6.79	0	19.3	35
JP Behrendorff	13	41.4	0	305	16	19.06	3-22	7.32	0	15.6	45
P Hatzoglou	15	52.1	0	379	15	25.26	2-17	7.26	0	20.8	36
ML Kelly	6	23	0	179	14	12.78	4-25	7.78	2	9.8	42
TS Mills	7	25.5	0	190	12	15.83	3-23	7.35	0	12.9	53
MR Marsh	8	15	0	127	5	25.40	2-50	8.46	0	18.0	36
JA Richardson	2	7.2	0	41	4	10.25	2-20	5.59	0	11.0	49
AM Hardie	9	6	0	40	3	13.33	3-31	6.66	0	12.0	39
AJ Turner	16	7	0	54	2	27.00	1-6	7.71	0	21.0	21
LRT Morris	6	15.3	0	125	2	62.50	2-25	8.06	0	46.5	45
DJM Moody	1	1	0	9	0	-	-	9.00	0	-	50

BBL11 Powerplays

Batting	Out	Runs	Balls	SR		Bowling	Ov	Figs	Econ	Dot %
KR Patterson	5	188	136	138		ML Kelly	10	5-58	5.80	55
JP Inglis	3	65	54	120		TS Mills	10	4-69	6.90	57
MR Marsh	1	53	46	115		JP Behrendorff	23	6-163	7.09	47
CT Bancroft	3	67	75	89						

Power Surge	Ov	Figs	Econ	Dot %
TS Mills	6	2-52	8.67	50
AJ Tye	12.3	10-120	9.60	47
ML Kelly	3	3-29	9.67	22

PERTH SCORCHERS - HONOUR ROLL

Season	Finished	Captain	Coach	MVP (Katich Medal)	Minor Rd W/L
2011-12	R-up	MJ North	LM Stevens	HH Gibbs	5/2
2012-13	R-up	SM Katich	JL Langer	SE Marsh	5/3
2013-14	Champions	SM Katich	JL Langer	CJ Simmons	5/3
2014-15	Champions	AC Voges	JL Langer	JP Behrendorff	5/3
2015-16	Lost Semi	M Klinger/ AC Voges	JL Langer	DJ Willey	5/3
2016-17	Champions	AC Voges/M Klinger	JL Langer	AJ Tye	5/3
2017-18	Lost Semi	AC Voges/AJ Turner	JL Langer	AC Agar	8/2
2018-19	Last	MR Marsh/AJ Turner/M Klinger	AC Voges	AJ Turner	4/10
2019-20	6th	MR Marsh	AC Voges	JA Richardson	6/8
2020-21	R-up	AJ Turner	AC Voges	JA Richardson	8/5/1
2021-22	Champions	AJ Turner	AC Voges	AC Agar	11/3

Most Runs	M	Runs	HS	Avge	SR		Most Wickets	M	W	Avge	Best	Econ
MR Marsh	70	1904	100*	38.8	135		AJ Tye	82	116	19.0	5-23	7.73
AJ Turner	100	1637	70	24.4	142		JP Behrendorff	72	86	20.7	4-22	6.92
SE Marsh	37	1435	99*	49.4	129		JA Richardson	55	73	16.4	4-19	7.70
M Klinger	49	1284	105*	28.5	117		AC Agar	66	51	28.4	3-19	7.23

Highest Individual scores

	Runs	Bls	4s	6s	Versus	Venue	Season
C Munro	114	73	8	6	Strikers	Syd Showg	2021-22
CJ Simmons	112	58	4	11	Sixers	SCG	2013-14
M Klinger	105*	60	7	4	Renegades	WACA	2014-15
CJ Simmons	102	41	8	8	Strikers	WACA	2013-14
MR Marsh	100*	60	6	5	Hurricanes	Bellerive	2021-22

Fastest Fifties

	Bls	Versus	Venue	Season
MR Marsh	21	Renegades	Perth St	2019-20
LS Livingstone	21	Strikers	Adel	2019-20
AJ Turner	22	Sixers	Perth St	2018-19

Fastest Hundreds

	Bls	Versus	Venue	Season
CJ Simmons	39	Strikers	WACA	2013-14
CJ Simmons	53	Sixers	SCG	2013-14
M Klinger	60	Renegades	WACA	2014-15
MR Marsh	60	Hurricanes	Bellerive	2021-22

Highest Team totals

	Versus	Venue	Season
3-213	Heat	Perth Stadium	2019-20
5-206	Renegades	Docklands	2021-22
7-203	Strikers	WACA	2013-14

Lowest Team totals

	Versus	Venue	Season
69	Stars	WACA	2012-13
79	Renegades	Perth Stadium	2018-19
86	Stars	Perth Stadium	2019-20

Best Bowling

		Overs	Dots	Versus	Venue	Season
AJ Tye	5-23	4	14	Stars	WACA	2017-18
AC Thomas	4-8	3.1	12	Renegades	WACA	2012-13
AJ Tye	4-18	4	13	Stars	WACA	2014-15
AJ Tye	4-18	4	13	Stars	MCG	2018-19

Most Economical Bowling (Min 4 overs)

		Dots	Versus	Venue	Season
MG Johnson	3-3	21	Stars	WACA	2016-17
GB Hogg	2-8	16	Thunder	Stadium Australia	2011-12
NM Coulter-Nile	1-9	16	Sixers	SCG	2012-13
GB Hogg	2-11	16	Strikers	Adelaide	2014-15
JP Behrendorff	0-11	19	Heat	Gabba	2018-19

Most Expensive Bowling (Min 4 overs)

		Versus	Venue	Season
JA Richardson	0-55	Renegades	WACA	2017-18
DJ Willey	0-54	Strikers	Adelaide Oval	2015-16
MR Marsh	0-53	Hurricanes	Perth Stadium	2017-18
Fawad Ahmed	0-52	Heat	Adelaide Oval	2020-21

SYDNEY SIXERS – RUNNER UP

Batting & Fielding	M	Inn	NO	Runs	HS	Avge	100s	50s	6s	S/Rate	Ct	St
MC Henriques	16	15	3	440	76*	36.66	0	2	12	133.33	6	-
JR Philippe	15	14	1	429	99*	33.00	0	4	16	143.47	12	5
DP Hughes	14	12	0	287	66	23.91	0	3	11	122.12	4	-
DT Christian	17	15	2	264	73	20.30	0	1	10	126.31	11	-
H Kerr	17	9	5	152	98*	38.00	0	1	4	144.76	4	-
JM Vince	9	8	0	149	44	18.62	0	0	0	110.37	4	-
JC Silk	13	11	5	134	36	22.33	0	0	0	120.72	5	-
SA Abbott	14	10	5	117	41	23.40	0	0	5	118.18	11	-
J Edwards	6	6	0	110	40	18.33	0	0	1	110.00	2	-
BJ Dwarshuis	14	6	2	96	66	24.00	0	1	4	171.42	2	-
J Avendano	6	6	0	89	52	14.83	0	1	7	120.27	0	-
TK Curran	4	3	1	33	27	16.50	0	0	0	132.00	0	-
Shadab Khan	4	2	0	20	12	10.00	0	0	0	125.00	1	-
NL Bertus	2	2	0	19	15	9.50	0	0	0	86.36	0	-
JM Carder	1	1	0	10	10	10.00	0	0	0	76.92	0	-
JS Lenton	2	2	2	10	10*	-	0	0	0	111.11	1	1
CJ Jordan	5	1	0	9	9	9.00	0	0	0	150.00	0	-
NM Lyon	4	2	0	5	3	2.50	0	0	0	100.00	1	-
SNJ O'Keefe	11	2	1	4	2*	4.00	0	0	0	50.00	2	-
JM Bird	6	1	1	1	1*	-	0	0	0	100.00	1	-
BAD Manenti	1	1	1	1	1*	-	0	0	0	100.00	1	-

Also played but did not bat: MW Edwards (1 match) 3 catches, TR Murphy (4 matches) 1 catch, LAJ Pope (4 matches).

Bowling	M	Overs	Mdns	Runs	Wkts	Avge	Best	Econ	4w	SR	Dot%
H Kerr	17	50	0	375	25	15.00	4-32	7.50	1	12.00	34
SA Abbott	14	46.1	0	378	19	19.89	4-31	8.18	1	14.50	39
BJ Dwarshuis	14	44	1	387	17	22.76	5-26	8.79	1	15.50	41
SNJ O'Keefe	11	38	0	250	15	16.66	4-14	6.57	2	15.20	33
DT Christian	17	30.4	0	230	7	32.85	3-8	7.50	0	26.20	33
TK Curran	4	9.1	0	93	5	18.60	3-27	10.14	0	11.00	31
JM Bird	6	15	0	101	4	25.25	1-6	6.73	0	22.50	43
CJ Jordan	5	18	0	140	3	46.66	1-20	7.77	0	36.00	37
NM Lyon	4	13	0	111	3	37.00	2-24	8.53	0	26.00	22
LAJ Pope	4	9	0	84	3	28.00	2-33	9.33	0	18.00	22
Shadab Khan	4	9	0	71	1	71.00	1-36	7.88	0	54.00	26
TR Murphy	4	9	0	46	1	46.00	1-13	5.11	0	54.00	28
MC Henriques	16	3	0	19	1	19.00	1-6	6.33	0	18.00	22
MW Edwards	1	2	0	19	1	19.00	1-19	9.50	0	12.00	33

BBL11 Powerplays

Batting	Out	Runs	Balls	SR	Bowling	Ov	Figs	Econ	Dot %
JR Edwards	3	60	47	128	SNJ O'Keefe	6	5-27	4.50	58
JR Philippe	6	143	122	117	BJ Dwarshuis	8	7-46	5.75	67
JM Vince	3	95	81	117	JM Bird	10	3-62	6.20	50
DP Hughes	1	28	42	67	SA Abbott	20	8-136	6.80	53

Power Surge	Ov	Figs	Econ	Dot %
SA Abbott	9	3-79	8.78	26
CJ Jordan	4	1-34	8.50	29
H Kerr	3	0-36	12.00	11
BJ Dwarshuis	8	3-118	14.75	27

SYDNEY SIXERS - HONOUR ROLL

Season	Finished	Captain	Coach	MVP	Minor Rd W/L/NR
2011-12	Champions	BJ Haddin/SPD Smith	TH Bayliss	MC Henriques	5/2
2012-13	7th	BJ Haddin/MC Henriques	TH Bayliss	JR Hazlewood	3/5
2013-14	Lost Semi	SPD Smith/MC Henriques/ MJ North	TH Bayliss	NJ Maddinson	6/2
2014-15	R-up	MC Henriques/NJ Maddison	TH Bayliss	MC Henriques	5/3
2015-16	Last	MC Henriques/NJ Maddison/ BJ Haddin	G Shipperd	MJ Lumb	2/6
2016-17	R-up	MC Henriques	G Shipperd	SA Abbott/DP Hughes	5/3
2017-18	5th	MC Henriques/J Botha	G Shipperd	SW Billings	4/6
2018-19	3rd	MC Henriques	G Shipperd	TK Curran	8/6
2019-20	Champions	MC Henriques/DP Hughes	G Shipperd	JR Philippe	9/4/1
2020-21	Champions	DP Hughes/MC Henriques	G Shipperd	JM Vince	9/5
2021-22	R-up	MC Henriques/DP Hughes	G Shipperd	H Kerr	9/4/1

Most Wickets	M	Runs	HS	Avge	SR		Most Wickets	M	W	Avge	Best	Econ
MC Henriques	103	2340	77	29.2	131		SA Abbott	81	115	19.7	5-16	8.42
DP Hughes	81	1897	96	28.3	122		BJ Dwarshuis	83	102	16.8	5-26	8.17
JR Philippe	62	1728	99*	33.2	143		SNJ O'Keefe	85	78	23.9	4-14	6.75
JC Silk	97	1654	78	29.5	124		TK Curran	32	47	19.5	4-22	8.48

Highest Individual scores

	Runs	Bls	4s	6s	Versus	Venue	Season
JR Philippe	99*	61	11	2	Stars	MCG	2021-22
JM Vince	98*	53	14	1	Scorchers	Manuka Oval	2020-21
H Kerr	98*	58	10	2	Strikers	SCG	2021-22
DP Hughes	96	51	6	7	Stars	Gold Coast	2020-21

Fastest Fifties

	Balls	Versus	Venue	Season
DT Christian	15	Strikers	Bellerive	2020-21
NJ Maddinson	22	Thunder	SCG	2015-16
NJ Maddinson	22	Stars	SCG	2017-18
NJ Maddinson	23	Stars	MCG	2017-18

Highest Team totals

	Versus	Venue	Season
4-213	Stars	SCG	2021-22
4-205	Renegades	Bellerive	2020-21
5-197	Thunder	SCG	2021-22

Lowest Team totals

	Versus	Venue	Season
74	Stars	MCG	2018-19
76	Thunder	Syd Showg	2019-20
92	Scorchers	Docklands	2021-22

Best Bowling

		Overs	Dots	Versus	Venue	Season
SA Abbott	5-16	4	12	Strikers	Adelaide	2016-17
NM Lyon	5-23	3.5	12	Hurricanes	SCG	2015-16
BJ Dwarshuis	5-26	4	12	Renegades	Geelong	2021-22
SA Abbott	4-11	4	15	Heat	SCG	2017-18

Most Economical Bowling (Min 4 overs)

		Dots	Versus	Venue	Season
BJ Dwarshuis	3-7	18	Strikers	SCG	2018-19
SA Abbott	4-11	15	Heat	SCG	2017-18
SCG MacGill	2-12	15	Strikers	Adelaide	2011-12

Most Expensive Bowling (Min 4 overs)

		Versus	Venue	Season
BJ Dwarshuis	0-61	Stars	MCG	2019-20
TK Curran	1-58	Stars	MCG	2019-20
TK Curran	1-58	Renegades	Docklands	2019-20
TK Curran	0-52	Heat	SCG	2019-20

SYDNEY THUNDER – FOURTH

Batting & Fielding	M	Inn	NO	Runs	HS	Avge	100s	50s	6s	S/Rate	Ct	St
JJ Sangha	12	12	3	445	91*	49.44	0	3	13	132.04	9	-
AD Hales	13	13	1	383	80*	31.91	0	2	15	148.44	3	-
MR Gilkes	15	15	1	295	93	21.07	0	2	9	129.95	3	-
SW Billings	9	9	2	284	67	40.57	0	2	12	153.51	7	1
AI Ross	9	9	3	237	77*	39.50	0	3	7	138.59	5	-
DR Sams	15	12	2	191	98*	19.10	0	1	16	161.86	8	-
BCJ Cutting	14	11	2	153	37	17.00	0	0	5	118.60	11	-
UT Khawaja	2	2	0	100	77	50.00	0	1	1	147.05	0	-
CJ Green	12	5	1	82	50	20.50	0	1	2	157.69	10	-
OHL Davies	7	6	1	68	26*	13.60	0	0	4	141.66	2	-
NJ McAndrew	14	8	3	56	30	11.20	0	0	1	133.33	5	-
SM Whiteman	3	3	0	25	11	8.33	0	0	0	104.16	1	-
BJ Holt	3	2	0	19	17	9.50	0	0	0	70.37	5	1
T Sangha	12	3	1	19	17*	9.50	0	0	0	76.00	2	-
GS Sandhu	11	4	3	11	11*	11.00	0	0	0	122.22	2	-
Mohammad Hasnain	5	2	2	4	4*	-	0	0	0	133.33	0	-
S Mahmood	6	1	1	2	2*	-	0	0	0	66.66	1	-
AJ Nair	2	1	1	0	0*	-	0	0	0	-	0	-
BJ Doggett	1	-	-	-	-	-	-	-	-	-	0	-

Bowling	M	Overs	Mdns	Runs	Wkts	Avge	Best	Econ	4w	SR	Dot%
DR Sams	15	55	0	467	19	24.57	4-33	8.49	1	17.3	33
GS Sandhu	11	39.1	0	298	18	16.55	4-22	7.60	1	13.0	40
T Sangha	12	40.3	1	278	16	17.37	3-26	6.86	0	15.1	37
S Mahmood	6	23	0	210	13	16.15	4-22	9.13	1	10.6	44
NJ McAndrew	14	48	0	452	13	34.76	3-40	9.41	0	22.1	36
Mohammad Hasnain	5	18.2	1	110	7	15.71	3-20	6.00	0	15.7	52
CJ Green	12	35.1	0	259	6	43.16	2-29	7.36	0	35.1	24
JJ Sangha	12	9	0	74	4	18.50	2-16	8.22	0	13.5	33
BCJ Cutting	14	10	0	98	1	98.00	1-17	9.80	0	60.0	22
AJ Nair	2	1	0	8	0	-	-	8.00	0	-	17
BJ Doggett	1	3	0	33	0	-	-	11.00	0	-	11

Best BBL11 Powerplays

Batting	Out	Runs	Balls	SR	Bowling	Ov	Figs	Econ	Dot %
JJ Sangha	0	69	42	164	M Hasnain	9	4-32	3.56	65
AD Hales	5	202	124	163	GS Sandhu	13	3-82	6.31	45
BCJ Cutting	0	46	34	135	DR Sams	14	2-100	7.14	45
MR Gilkes	6	116	98	118	S Mahmood	10	6-72	7.20	58
					NJ McAndrew	12	6-94	7.83	53

Power Surge	Ov	Figs	Econ	Dot %
S Mahmood	4	4-32	8.00	38
DR Sams	14	4-154	11.00	26
NJ McAndrew	7	1-80	11.43	33

SYDNEY THUNDER - HONOUR ROLL

Season	Finished	Captain	Coach	MVP	Minor Rd W/L/NR
2011-12	Last	DA Warner/DLR Smith	S Duff	CH Gayle	2/5
2012-13	Last	CJR Rogers/CH Gayle	S Duff	DP Nannes	0/8
2013-14	Last	MEK Hussey	C Hathurusinghe	GS Sandhu	1/7
2014-15	7th	MEK Hussey/CD Hartley	P Upton	JH Kallis	2/5/1
2015-16	Champions	MEK Hussey/SR Watson	P Upton	SR Watson/UT Khawaja	4/4
2016-17	Last	BJ Rohrer/SR Watson	P Upton	PJ Cummins	3/5
2017-18	6th	SR Watson	P Upton	SR Watson	4/6
2018-19	6th	SR Watson/JC Buttler	SE Bond	CJ Ferguson	6/7/1
2019-20	3rd	CJ Ferguson	SE Bond	DR Sams	6/7/1
2020-21	4th	CJ Ferguson	SE Bond	AD Hales	8/6
2021-22	4th	CJ Green/JJ Sangha/UT Khawaja	TH Bayliss	SW Billings	

Most Runs	M	Runs	HS	Avge	SR
UT Khawaja	97	1818	109*	34.3	129
AD Hales	45	1502	110	36.6	152
CJ Ferguson	53	1325	113*	30.1	126
SR Watson	40	1040	100	26.6	133

Most Wickets	M	W	Avge	Best	Econ
DR Sams	56	75	20.0	4-33	8.34
GS Sandhu	58	59	26.1	4-22	7.98
CJ Green	74	52	30.8	4-34	7.40
Fawad Ahmed	42	40	25.4	4-14	6.97

Highest Individual scores

	Runs	Bls	4s	6s	Versus	Venue	Season
CJ Ferguson	113*	53	8	8	Scorchers	Perth Stadium	2018-19
AD Hales	110	56	9	8	Sixers	Adelaide Oval	2020-21
UT Khawaja	109*	70	12	3	Stars	MCG	2015-16
UT Khawaja	104*	59	13	3	Strikers	Adelaide	2015-16
DA Warner	102*	51	6	6	Stars	MCG	2011-12

Fastest Fifties

	Bls	Versus	Venue	Season
AD Hales	21	Stars	Manuka	2020-21
DR Sams	23	Heat	Manuka	2020-21
CJ Ferguson	24	Scorchers	Perth St	2018-19
UT Khawaja	24	Strikers	Adel Ov	2015-16
SW Billings	24	Heat	Gabba	2021-22
AD Hales	24	Reneg	Dock	2021-22

Fastest Hundreds

	Bls	Versus	Venue	Season
CJ Ferguson	48	Scorchers	Perth St	2018-19
DA Warner	50	Stars	MCG	2011-12
AD Hales	51	Sixers	Adel Ov	2020-21
CH Gayle	53	Strikers	Syd Oly	2012-13

Highest Team totals

	Versus	Venue	Season
5-232	Sixers	Adel Oval	2020-21
7-219	Stars	Manuka	2020-21
7-209	Renegades	Docklands	2021-22
8-209	Renegades	Manuka	2020-21

Lowest Team totals

	Versus	Venue	Season
94	Hurricanes	Hobart	2013-14
99	Scorchers	Stad Aus	2011-12
101	Strikers	Syd Show	2016-17

Best Bowling

	Overs	Dots	Versus	Venue	Season
Fawad Ahmed	4-14	4	13	Sixers	SCG	2016-17
T Sangha	4-14	3.2	12	Renegades	Manuka Oval	2020-21
DP Nannes	4-17	4	12	Strikers	Stadium Australia	2012-13
JD Cook	4-21	4	7	Hurricanes	Bellerive	2019-20

Most Economical Bowling (Min 4 overs)

		Dots	Versus	Venue	Season
AF Milne	1-6	20	Strikers	Adelaide Oval	2020-21
Fawad Ahmed	2-11	13	Sixers	Syd Showground	2017-18
JD Cook	1-13	12	Scorchers	Syd Showground	2018-19
AD Russell	3-13	18	Sixers	Syd Showground	2015-16

Most Expensive Bowling (Min 4 overs)

		Versus	Venue	Season
NJ McAndrew	0-57	Sixers	Adelaide Oval	2020-21
GS Sandhu	0-55	Heat	Gabba	2015-16
DR Sams	0-54	Hurricanes	Bellerive	2018-19

OVERALL RECORDS

Season	PREVIOUS FINALS	Margin	Venue	Crowd	Man of Match
2011-12	Sixers 3-158 d Scorchers 5-156	Sixers 7 wkts	WACA	16,255	MC Henriques (SS)
2012-13	Heat 5-167 d Scorchers 9-133	Heat 34 runs	WACA	18,517	NM Hauritz (BH)
2013-14	Scorchers 4-191 d Hurricanes 7-152	Scorchers 39 runs	Perth	18,517	GB Hogg (PS)
2014-15	Sixers 5-147 lost to Scorchers 6-148	Scorchers 4 wkts	Manuka	11,741	SE Marsh (PS)
2015-16	Stars 9-176 lost to Thunder 7-181	Thunder 3 wkts	MCG	47,672	UT Khawaja (ST)
2016-17	Sixers 9-141 lost to Scorchers 1-144	Scorchers 9 wkts	WACA	21,832	JA Richardson (PS)
2017-18	Strikers 2-202 d Hurricanes 5-177	Strikers 25 runs	Adel Oval	40,732	JB Weatherald (AS)
2018-19	Renegades 5-145 d Stars 7-132	Renegades 13 runs	Docklands	40,816	DT Christian (MR)
2019-20	Sixers 5-116 d Stars 6-97	Sixers 17 runs	SCG	10,121	JP Philippe (SS)
2020-21	Sixers 6-188 d Scorchers	Sixers 27 runs	SCG	25,295	JM Vince (SS)
2021-22	**Scorchers 6-171 d Sixers 92**	**Scorchers 79 runs**	**Docklands**	**10,392**	**LJ Evans (PS)**

WIN/LOSS RECORD OF EACH TEAM

	Matches	Wins	Losses	No Result	Titles	Runners-up
Adelaide Strikers	122	62	57	3	1	0
Brisbane Heat	119	50	68	1	1	0
Hobart Hurricanes	121	58	61	2	0	2
Melbourne Renegades	117	48	68	0	1	0
Melbourne Stars	125	65	59	1	0	3
Perth Scorchers	130	78	51	1	4	3
Sydney Sixers	128	74	52	1	3	3
Sydney Thunder	120	49	68	3	1	0

MOST RUNS – THE TOP TEN

	M	Inn	NO	Runs	HS	Avge	SR	100s	50s	Sixes
Chris Lynn	102	100	13	3005	101	34.54	148.6	1	24	180
Aaron Finch	87	86	5	2817	111*	34.78	134.0	2	22	104
Glenn Maxwell	100	95	16	2673	154*	33.84	150.8	2	18	109
Jonathan Wells	112	103	30	2554	73	34.99	122.7	0	14	40
D'Arcy Short	72	72	8	2554	122*	39.89	133.6	2	20	90
Shaun Marsh	68	68	8	2398	99*	39.97	128.5	0	22	77
Moises Henriques	103	98	18	2340	77	29.25	131.7	0	12	72
Marcus Stoinis	82	79	15	2307	147*	36.05	132.9	1	15	80
Matthew Wade	81	77	10	2156	130*	32.18	142.5	1	15	74
Ben McDermott	74	71	13	2139	127	36.88	138.9	3	10	102

HUNDREDS (32)

		Balls		Venue	Season
Glenn Maxwell	**154***	**64**	**Stars v Hurricanes**	**MCG**	**2021-22**
Marcus Stoinis	147*	79	Stars v Sixers	MCG	2019-20
Matthew Wade	130*	61	Hurricanes v Strikers	Adelaide Oval	2019-20
Ben McDermott	**127**	**65**	**Hurricanes v Renegades**	**Docklands**	**2021-22**
Darcy Short	122*	69	Hurricanes v Heat	Gabba	2017-18
Luke Wright	117	60	Stars v Hurricanes	Hobart	2011-12
Jake Weatherald	115	70	Strikers v Hurricanes	Adelaide	2017-18
Colin Munro	**114***	**73**	**Scorchers v Strikers**	**Sydney Showgrounds**	**2021-22**
Ben McDermott	114	52	Hurricanes v Renegades	Docklands	2016-17
Callum Ferguson	113*	53	Thunder v Scorchers	Perth Stadium	2018-19
Luke Pomersbach	112*	70	Heat v Renegades	Docklands	2012-13
Craig Simmons	112	58	Scorchers v Sixers	SCG	2013-14
Aaron Finch	111*	65	Renegades v Stars	Docklands	2012-13
Ben McDermott	**110***	**60**	**Hurricanes v Strikers**	**Bellerive**	**2021-22**
Alex Hales	110	56	Thunder v Sixers	Adelaide Oval	2020-21
Usman Khawaja	109*	70	Thunder v Stars	MCG	2015-16
Luke Wright	109*	63	Stars v Renegades	MCG	2015-16
Aaron Finch	109	68	Renegades v Sixers	SCG	2019-20
Michael Klinger	105*	60	Scorchers v Renegades	WACA	2014-15
Usman Khawaja	104*	59	Thunder v Strikers	Adelaide	2015-16
Glenn Maxwell	**103**	**57**	**Stars v Sixers**	**MCG**	**2021-22**
Peter Handscomb	103*	64	Stars v Scorchers	MCG	2014-15
D'Arcy Short	103*	70	Hurricanes v Scorchers	Perth Stadium	2019-20
David Warner	102*	51	Thunder v Stars	MCG	2011-12
Craig Simmons	102	41	Scorchers v Strikers	WACA	2013-14
Travis Head	101*	53	Strikers v Sixers	Adelaide	2015-16
Alex Carey	101	62	Strikers v Heat	Adelaide Oval	2020-21

Chris Lynn	101	51	Heat v Hurricanes	Gabba		2015-16
Mitchell Marsh	**100***	**60**	**Scorchers v Hurricanes**	**Bellerive**		**2021-22**
Chris Gayle	100*	54	Thunder v Strikers	Stadium Australia		2011-12
Alex Carey	100	56	Strikers v Hurricanes	Adelaide		2017-18
Shane Watson	100	62	Heat v Thunder	Gabba		2018-19

SCORES OF 99 (2)

Shaun Marsh	99*	(52)	Scorchers v Renegades	Docklands	2011-12
Marcus Stoinis	99	(51)	Stars v Heat	Gabba	2017-18

FASTEST FIFTIES (Balls faced)

Chris Gayle	12	Renegades v Strikers	Docklands	2015-16
Daniel Christian	15	Sixers v Strikers	Bellerive Oval	2020-21
Tom Banton	16	Heat v Thunder	Sydney Showgrounds	2019-20
Ben Cutting	17	Heat v Stars	Gabba	2018-19
Nicolas Pooran	17	Stars v Sixers	Carrara	2020-21
Brendon McCullum	18	Heat v Renegades	Gabba	2016-17
Tim Ludeman	18	Strikers v Stars	Adelaide	2014-15
Chris Lynn	18	Heat v Hurricanes	Gabba	2014-15

FASTEST HUNDREDS (Balls Faced)

Craig Simmons	39	Scorchers v Strikers	WACA	2013-14
Glenn Maxwell	**41**	**Stars v Hurricanes**	**MCG**	**2021-22**
Luke Wright	44	Stars v Hurricanes	Hobart	2011-12
Ben McDermott	47	Hurricanes v Renegades	Docklands	2016-17
Matthew Wade	48	Hurricanes v Strikers	Adelaide Oval	2019-20
Callum Ferguson	48	Thunder v Scorchers	Perth Stadium	2018-19
Chris Lynn	49	Heat v Hurricanes	Gabba	2015-16

RUN CHASES WON OFF THE LAST BALL OF THE MATCH (Full 20-over games only)

Winner				Venue	Season	Notes on end of Match
Heat	7-186	Strikers	8-185	Adelaide Oval	2012-13	Chris Hartley hits Gary Putland for four
Stars	7-154	Renegades	6-153	MCG	2014-15	Tom Triffit gets single off Nathan Rimmington
Sixers	6-155	Thunder	4-154	SCG	2014-15	23 needed off last over, Steve O'Keefe hits Josh Lalor for 4 off last ball
Scorchers	6-148	Sixers	5-147	Manuka Oval	2014-15	BBL04 Final – Arafat single to mid-wicket off Brett Lee, poss Run out miss
Strikers	4-146	Hurricanes	143	Adelaide Oval	2015-16	4 to win, new bat in Jake Lehmann hits Simon Milenko over long-off for 6
Scorchers	6-152	Renegades	8-148	Docklands	2016-17	3 to win, A Agar hits Aaron Finch for 6
Thunder	4-168	Stars	8-166	Sydney Showground	2016-17	5 needed Eoin Morgan hits Ben Hilfenhaus back over his head for six
Hurricanes	8-223	Renegades	4-222	Docklands	2016-17	Stuart Broad hits Thisara Perera for a single to win in a record chase
Thunder	5-150	Sixers	9-149	Sydney Showground	2017-18	16 to win off last over off Sean Abbott, Arjun Nair/Aiden Blizzard hit 44141 before Nair single wins it off last ball
Sixers	2-157	Thunder	6-156	SCG	2017-18	Two needed, Moises Henriques hits Chris Green for a couple to clinch win
Sixers	7-152	Heat	148	Carrara	2020-21	One needed off last ball, Dan Christian hits Xavier Bartlett for four
Sixers	**8-106**	**Heat**	**105**	**SCG**	**2021-22**	**Abbott scored single off Bartlett**
Sixers	**6-170**	**Strikers**	**4-167**	**SCG**	**2021-22**	**Kerr hits last ball off Conway for 4**

RECORD PARTNERSHIPS

Wkt					for	v..	Venue	Season
1	207	MP Stoinis	HWR Cartwright		Stars	Sixers	MCG	2019-20
2	167*	JR Philippe	JM Vince		Sixers	Hurricanes	SCG	2018-19
3	151	BR McDermott	GJ Bailey		Hurricanes	Renegades	Docklands	2016-17
4	**151**	**JM Clarke**	**HWR Cartwright**		**Stars**	**Heat**	**Gabba**	**2021-22**
5	137*	CT Bancroft	HWR Cartwright		Scorchers	Thunder	Syd Showg	2017-18
5	137	MP Stoinis	JP Faulkner		Stars	Heat	Gabba	2017-18
6	94*	M Nabi	DT Christian		Renegades	Strikers	Adelaide	2018-19
7	88	TK Curran	SA Abbott		Sixers	Thunder	Syd Showg	2018-19
8	**60**	**XC Bartlett**	**MT Steketee**		**Heat**	**Thunder**	**Gabba**	**2021-22**
9	60	JJ Peirson	Mujeeb-ur-Rahman		Heat	Strikers	Gabba	2020-21
10	61*	DJ Worrall	DJ Briggs		Strikers	Hurricanes	Bellerive	2020-21

HIGHEST SCORES BY TEAM

Score	Match	Venue	Season
2-273	Stars v Hurricanes	MCG	2021-22
5-232	Thunder v Sixers	Adelaide Oval	2020-21
8-223	Hurricanes v Renegades	Docklands	2016-17
4-222	Renegades v Hurricanes	Docklands	2016-17
1-219	Stars v Sixers	MCG	2019-20
7-219	Thunder v Stars	Manuka Oval	2020-21

LOWEST COMPLETED SCORES BY TEAM

Score	Match	Venue	Season
57	Renegades v Stars	Docklands	2014-15
60	Renegades v Sixers	Bellerive Oval	2020-21
61	Stars v Sixers	SCG	2021-22
68	Strikers v Stars	MCG	2020-21
69	Scorchers v Stars	Perth	2012-13

MOST RUNS OFF AN OVER

Runs	Details	Bowler		Venue	Season
30	T Banton (066666)	AJ Nair	BH v ST	Syd Showg	2019-20
30	CA Lynn (066666)	BW Hilfenhaus	BH v MS	MCG	2015-16
29	EP Gulbis (1) DJG Sammy (wide, 6646, wide 4)	DJ Worrall	HH v MS	MCG	2014-15
28	TR Birt (0446 6nb 6nb wkt) OA Shah (0)	CJ McKay	HH v MS	Bellerive	2014-15
28	JC Buttler (661, 6nb 6 1) SR Watson (1)	TS Rogers	ST v HH	Launceston	2018-19
28	BJ Rohrer (644644)	JD Wildermuth	ST v MR	Manuka	2017-18

SUPEROVER MATCHES (Full 20-over games only)

				Won by	Season	Venue
Scorchers	9-153	Sixers	5-153	Scorchers	2013-14	SCG
Sixers	6-150	Stars	4-150	Stars	2014-15	MCG
Heat	9-167	Sixers	8-167	Sixers	2016-17	Gabba
Thunder	8-149	Sixers	7-149	Sixers	2019-20	SCG

MOST WICKETS

	M	Balls	Mdns	Runs	Wkts	Ave	Best	4i	Econ
Sean Abbott	95	1847	1	2609	125	20.87	5-16	4	8.47
Andrew Tye	85	1777	1	2283	118	19.34	5-23	6	7.70
Kane Richardson	90	1949	5	2557	117	21.85	4-22	5	7.87
Ben Laughlin	96	1999	1	2693	111	24.26	4-26	2	8.08
Ben Dwarshuis	83	1720	3	2341	102	22.95	5-26	2	8.16
Adam Zampa	85	1849	1	2228	98	22.73	5-17	1	7.22
Rashid Khan	61	1430	1	1536	92	16.69	6-17	2	6.44
Peter Siddle	68	1413	2	1747	90	19.41	5-16	4	7.41
Cameron Boyce	80	1672	0	2114	89	23.75	5-21	2	7.58
Daniel Christian	121	1790	0	2468	89	27.73	5-14	4	8.27

BEST BOWLING

		Dots		Venue	Season
Lasith Malinga	6-7	19	Stars v Scorchers	WACA	2012-13
Ish Sodhi	6-11	12	Strikers v Thunder	Syd Showground	2016-17
Rashid Khan	6-17	14	Strikers v Heat	Gabba	2021-22
Daniel Christian	5-14	15	Hurricanes v Strikers	Hobart	2016-17
Mujeeb-ur-Rahman	5-15	14	Heat v Hurricanes	Gabba	2020-21
Sean Abbott	5-16	12	Sixers v Strikers	Adelaide	2016-17
Peter Siddle	5-16	12	Strikers v Hurricanes	York Park	2020-21

BEST ECONOMY IN A FOUR OVER SPELL

		Dots		Venue	Season
Mitchell Johnson	3-3	21	Scorchers v Sixers	WACA	2016-17
Adam Milne	1-6	20	Thunder v Strikers	Adelaide Oval	2020-21
Lasith Malinga	6-7	19	Stars v Scorchers	WACA	2012-13
Fawad Ahmed	1-7	18	Renegades v Heat	Docklands	2014-15
Ben Dwarshuis	3-7	18	Sixers v Strikers	SCG	2018-19

WORST ECONOMY IN A FOUR OVER SPELL

			Venue	Season
Liam Guthrie	2-70	Heat v Stars	Gabba	2021-22
Kane Richardson	0-63	Renegades v Hurricanes	Docklands	2021-22
Ben Dwarshuis	0-61	Sixers v Stars	MCG	2019-20

HAT TRICKS (8)

Bowler		Venue	Season
Xavier Doherty	Hurricanes v Thunder	Hobart	2012-13
Andrew Tye	Scorchers v Heat	Gabba	2016-17
Andrew Tye	Scorchers v Sixers	SCG	2017-18
Josh Lalor	Heat v Scorchers	Gabba	2018-19
Rashid Khan	Strikers v Sixers	Adelaide Oval	2019-20
Haris Rauf	Stars v Thunder	MCG	2019-20
Gurinder Sandhu	**Thunder v Scorchers**	**Gold Coast**	**2021-22**
Cameron Boyce	**Renegades v Thunder**	**MCG**	**2021-22**

PLAYERS OF THE TOURNAMENT

Season	Winner	Votes	Runner-up	Votes
2011-12	David Hussey (Stars)	19	Herschelle Gibbs (Scorchers)	18
2012-13	Aaron Finch (Renegades)	21	Shaun Marsh (Scorchers)	17
2013-14	Ben Dunk (Hurricanes)	18	Luke Wright (Stars)	17
2014-15	Jacques Kallis (Thunder)	n/a	Not known	n/a
2015-16	Chris Lynn (Heat)	22	Adil Rashid (Strikers)	17
2016-17	Chris Lynn (Heat)	18	Ben Dunk (Strikers), Sean Abbott (Sixers)	16
2017-18	D'Arcy Short (Hurricanes)	26	Shane Watson (Thunder)	18
2018-19	D'Arcy Short (Hurricanes)	41	Marcus Stoinis (Stars)	32
2019-20	Marcus Stoinis (Stars)	26	Tom Curran (Sixers)	24
2020-21	Josh Philippe (Sixers)	22	Alex Hales (Thunder)	20
2021-22	**Ben McDermott (Hurricanes)**	25	Glenn Maxwell/Joe Clarke (Stars)	22

SEASON BY SEASON TABLES and VOTES

2011-12 Table (7 matches) - **Scorchers 10 (NRR +0.626), Hurricanes 10 (+0.569), Sixers 10 (+0.262), Stars 8,** Heat 6, Strikers 4 (-0.338), Renegades 4 (-0.582), Thunder 4 (-1.25). **MVP: David Hu ssey (Stars) 19,** Herschelle Gibbs (Scorchers) 18, Chris Gayle (Thunder) 16

2012-13 Table (8 matches) – **Renegades 14, Scorchers 10 (+1.322), Stars 10, Heat 8 (+0.464),** Strikers 8 (-0.162), Hurricanes 8 (-0.569), Sixers 6, Thunder 0. **MVP: Aaron Finch (Renegades) 21,** Shaun Marsh (Scorchers) 17, Lasith Malinga (Stars) 16,

2013-14 Table (8 matches) - **Stars 16, Sixers 12, Scorchers 10, Hurricanes 7,** Heat 6 (-0.197), Renegades 6 (-0.475), Strikers 4, Thunder 2. **MVP: Ben Dunk (Hurricanes) 18,** Luke Wright (Stars) 17, Moises Henriques (Sixers) 12, Jackson Bird (Stars) 11, John Hastings (Stars) 11, Brad Hodge (Stars) 11, Michael Hussey (Thunder) 11, Chris Lynn (Heat) 11

2014-15 Table (8 matches) - **Strikers 13, Scorchers 10 (+0.705), Stars 10 (+0.336), Sixers 10 (-0.014),** Hurricanes 6 (-0.280), Renegades 6 (-0.331), Thunder 5, Heat 4. **MVP: Jacques Kallis (Thunder),** *No other Votes*

2015-16 Table (8 matches) **Strikers 14, Stars 10 (+0.366), Scorchers 10 (+0.181), Thunder 8 (+0.375),** Renegades 6 (-0.141), Heat 6 (-0.204), Hurricanes 6 (-0.955), Sixers 4. **MVP: Chris Lynn (Heat) 22,** Adil Rashid (Strikers) 17. Mahela Jayawardena (Strikers) 15, Travis Head (Strikers) 14,

2016-17 Table (8 matches) - **Scorchers 10 (+0.61), Heat 10 (+0.51), Sixers 10 (-0.84), Stars 8,** Renegades 6 (-0.04), Strikers 6 (-0.33), Hurricanes 6 (-0.53), Thunder 6 (-0.60). **MVP: Chris Lynn (Heat) 18,** Ben Dunk (Strikers) 16, Sean Abbott (Sixers) 16, Aaron Finch (Renegades) 14, Michael Klinger (Scorchers) 12.

2017-18 Table (10 matches) - **Scorchers 16, Strikers 14, Renegades 12, Hurricanes 10,** Sixers 8 (+0.331), Thunder 8 (-0.039), Heat 8 (-0.437), Stars 4 (-0.926). **MVP: D'Arcy Short (Hurricanes) 26,** Shane Watson (Thunder) 18, Alex Carey (Strikers) 16, Ashton Agar (Scorchers) 15.

2018-19 Table (14 matches) - **Hurricanes 20, Renegades 16 (+0.173), Sixers 16 (+0.047), Stars 14, Heat 13, (+0.249),** Thunder 13 (NRR Even), Strikers 12, Scorchers 8. **MVP: D'Arcy Short (Hurricanes) 41,** Marcus Stoinis (Stars) 32, Matthew Wade (Hurricanes) 28, Chris Lynn (Heat) 21, Ashton Turner (Scorchers) 17

2019-20 Table (14 matches) - **Stars 20, Sixers 19, Strikers 17, Hurricanes 13 (-0.355), Thunder 13 (-0.446),** Scorchers 12 (-0.023), Heat 12 (-0.237), Renegades 6 (-0.348). **MVP: Marcus Stoinis (Stars) 26,** Tom Curran (Sixers) 24, Alex Hales (Thunder) 23, Jono Wells (Strikers) 22, Glenn Maxwell (Stars) 21, D'Arcy Short (Hurricanes) 21, Rashid Khan (Strikers) 18

2020-21 Table (14 matches) - **Sixers 36, Scorchers 32, Thunder 31, Heat 29, Strikers 28 (NRR +0.105),** Hurricanes 28 (-0.187), Stars 24, Renegades 16 **MVP: Josh Philippe (Sixers) 22,** Alex Hales (Thunder) 20, Jhye Richardson 19, Glenn Maxwell 18, Ben McDermott (Hurricanes) 17, Chris Lynn (Heat) 17, Colin Munro (Scorchers) 17,

2021-22 Table (14 matches) – **Scorchers 40, Sixers 35 (NRR +1.027), Thunder 35 (+0.735), Strikers 28, Hurricanes 27,** Stars 26, Heat 16 (-0.91), Renegades 16 (-1.477). **MVP: Ben McDermott (Hurricanes) 25,** Glenn Maxwell (Stars) 22, Joe Clarke (Stars) 22, Mitchell Marsh (Scorchers) 21, Matt Short (Strikers) 21, Daniel Sams (Thunder) 17, Josh Philippe (Sixers) 16.

AUSSIES IN OVERSEAS TWENTY 20 TOURNAMENTS
THE IPL 2022 FINAL ON MAY 29, 2022 AT AHMEDABAD ON MAY 29, 2022

The Final – Rajasthan Royals 9-130 cc (JS Buttler 39; HH Pandya 3-17 (4), **Rashid Khan 1-18 (4 overs, 9 dots) lost Gujarat Titans 3-133** (18.1 overs) (S Gill 45*, **MS Wade 8) by seven wickets.**

STATS OF THOSE INVOLVED WITH BBL CLUBS AND OTHERS OF INTEREST

	Club	M	I	NO	Runs	HS	Avge	SR	100	50	Sixes	Overs	Wkt	Avge	Best	Econ
SA Abbott	Sun Hyder	1	1	0	7	7	7.00	140.0	0	0	0	4	1	11.75	1-47	11.75
NM Coulter-Nile	Rajasthan	1	1	1	1	1*		50.0	0	0	0	3				16.00
PJ Cummins	KKR	5	5	1	63	56*	15.75	262.5	0	1	6	19.5	7	30.28	3-22	10.68
TH David	Mumbai	8	8	3	186	46	37.20	216.2	0	0	16					
NT Ellis	Punjab	2	1	0	0	0	0.00	0.0	0	0	0	6	3	18.33	3-40	9.16
AJ Finch	KKR	5	5	0	86	58	17.20	140.9	0	1	3					
JR Hazlewood	RCB	12	5	5	18	7*		69.2	0	0	0	46.3	20	18.85	4-25	8.10
MR Marsh	Delhi	8	8	0	251	89	31.37	132.8	0	2	14	12	4	25.50	2-25	8.50
GJ Maxwell	RCB	13	13	2	301	55	27.36	169.1	0	1	15	24	6	27.50	2-22	6.87
RP Meredith	Mumbai	8	1	1	0	0*	0.00	0.0	0	0	0	28	8	29.50	2-24	8.42
Rashid Khan	Gujarat	16	8	4	91	40	22.75	206.8	0	0	9	63.5	19	22.15	4-24	6.59
DR Sams	Mumbai	11	10	3	38	15	5.42	105.5	0	0	3	42	13	28.46	4-30	8.80
MP Stoinis	Lucknow	11	10	2	156	38*	19.50	147.1	0	0	13	7	4	19.75	3-23	11.28
AJ Tye	Lucknow	3	0									11	2	53.50	2-40	9.72
MS Wade	Gujarat	10	10	0	157	35	15.70	113.7	0	0	2	7 ct	1 st			
DA Warner	Delhi	12	12	3	432	92*	48.00	150.5	0	5	15					

VITALITY T20 BLAST FINALS DAY SCORES AT EDGBASTON on July 16, 2022

Semi Finals - Yorkshire 7-204 cc (T Kohler-Cadmore 66, JA Thompson 50) **lost to Lancashire 4-208** (18.4 overs) (KK Jennings 75, DJ Vilas 63*) **by six wickets.** *Jordan Thompson faced 18 balls reached his fifty off just 17 balls, with 6 sixes and 1 four.* **Hampshire 6-190 cc** (BR McDermott 31, T Prest 64) **defeated Somerset 153** (19.3 overs) (NT Ellis 3-30)

The Final – Hampshire 8-152 cc (BR McDermott 62, MW Parkinson 4-26) **defeated Lancashire 8-151 cc** (SJ Croft 36; NT **Ellis 0-23 (4 overs, 10 dots) by one run.** *With 11 needed to win, Nathan Ellis bowled the last over of the match and after several dramas, in particular a late call for no-ball when Hampshire had thought they had won and begun to celebrate, Ellis kept calm and conceded just nine to ensure Hampshire the title. Earlier opener Ben McDermott faced just 36 balls, hitting 4 fours and 4 sixes.*

STATS OF THOSE INVOLVED WITH BBL CLUBS AND OTHERS OF INTEREST

	Club	M	I	NO	Runs	HS	Avge	SR	100	50	Sixes	Overs	Wkts	Avge	Best	Econ
Qais Ahmad	Kent	14	9	2	59	24	8.42	137.2	0	0	3	55	14	29.28	3-28	7.45
TM Banton	Som	16	16	0	359	73	22.43	129.1	0	2	14					
JP Behrendorff	Midd	11	4	3	38	22*	38.00	131.0	0	0	4	39.1	11	29.63	3-30	8.32
SW Billings	Kent	12	12	2	253	48*	25.30	117.1	0	0	5	6 ct	1 st			
HWR Cartwright	Derby	2	2	0	48	38	24.00	150.0	0	0	2					
DT Christian	Notts	13	11	3	196	56	24.50	130.6	0	1	9	15.0	4	41.75	2-22	11.13
JM Clarke	Notts	14	14	0	305	86	21.78	151.7	0	3	14					
IA Cockbain	Glouc	12	11	0	162	64	14.72	111.7	0	1	3					
TH David	Lancs	17	17	3	405	66	28.92	174.5	0	2	27	16	4	37.50	1-15	9.37
BM Duckett	Notts	14	14	3	396	63	36.00	160.3	0	3	9					
NT Ellis	Hamp	13	11	8	29	7	9.66	85.2	0	0	0	45.3	15	20.86	3-4	6.87
CJ Green	Midd	14	12	5	177	46*	25.28	147.5	0	0	3	46.4	14	27.14	3-16	8.14
AD Hales	Notts	14	14	0	374	91	26.71	193.7	0	3	25					
AM Hardie	Surrey	3	3	0	29	15	9.66	138.0	0	0	1	5	1	62.00	1-33	12.40
MG Hogan	Glam	11	2	1	1	1*	1.00	50.0	0	0	0	41	20	16.65	5-18	8.12
CA Ingram	Glam	8	7	2	152	57	30.40	134.5	0	1	6					
CJ Jordan	Surrey	14	10	3	173	73	24.71	160.1	0	1	8	47	17	22.11	4-31	8.00
HL Kerr	Derby	13	8	1	129	29	18.42	132.9	0	0	3	39.3	15	24.06	2-6	9.13
M Labuschagne	Glam	6	5	0	118	41	23.60	132.5	0	0	3	12	3	34.33	2-27	8.58
LS Livingstone	Lancs	7	6	0	164	75	27.33	137.8	0	1	10	24.4	7	26.57	3-33	7.54
CA Lynn	North	11	10	2	516	113*	64.50	159.2	2	4	29					
BR McDermott	Hamp	17	17	0	494	83	29.05	146.1	0	5	34	16 ct	2 st			
TS Mills	Sussex	9	4	3	13	5*	13.00	81.2	0	0	0	33.4	15	21.26	4-32	9.47
MG Neser	Glam	10	2	1	17	11	17.00	121.4	0	0	0	31	13	18.53	3-13	7.77
JL Pattinson	Notts	2										4.0	2	28.50	2-38	14.25
JR Philippe	Sussex	6	6	0	142	70	23.66	129.0	0	1	6	2 ct	1st			
Rashid Khan	Sussex	6	5	1	47	25*	11.75	123.6	0	0	2	24	8	21.87	3-30	7.29
DR Sams	Essex	12	10	3	165	71	23.57	171.8	0	1	13	43.5	14	28.35	3-20	9.05
PM Siddle	Som	11	4	2	17	11*	8.50	106.2	0	0	0	36.1	17	17.88	3-10	8.40
AJ Turner	Durham	8	7	1	124	33	20.66	158.9	0	0	7	4.2	3	12.33	2-24	8.53
AJ Tye	Durham	10	4	3	29	13*	29.00	161.1	0	0	3	34.4	21	14.76	5-38	8.94
DJ Worrall	Surrey	10	2	2	4	2*	-	44.4	0	0	0	28	8	30.00	1-9	8.57

Batting	M	Runs	Avge	HS	100s	50s		Bowling	M	Overs	Wkts	Avge	Best
Ashley Chandrasinghe (Vic)	3	423	84.60	112	1	4		**Tom O'Connell (Vic)**	4	144.2	19	24.95	5-56
Teague Wyllie (WA)	2	382	191.00	153*	2	1		Iain Carlisle (Tas)	4	127.3	15	25.80	4-64
Jake Fraser-McGurk (Vic)	2	378	94.50	146	3	-		Fergus O'Neil (Vic)	4	110.5	14	19.00	4-83
Blake Niktaras (ACT/NSW)	4	355	50.71	112	1	3		Sam Kerber (SA)	4	90.4	13	19.00	6-53
Aryan Jain (Qld)	3	336	84.00	111*	2	2		Spencer Johnson (SA)	4	121.5	13	28.62	3-82
Nathan McSweeney (SA)	4	329	47.00	96*	-	3		Hunar Verma (NSW Metro)	3	66	12	20.25	4-33
Daniel Drew (SA)	4	312	44.57	161*	1	1		Sam Skelly (ACT/NSW)	4	108.5	12	28.92	4-46
Nivethan Radhakrishnan (Tas)	3	284	47.33	133	1	1		Toby Gray (ACT/NSW)	4	106.1	11	26.64	6-64
Jack Clayton (Qld)	2	275	91.67	102*	1	3		Riley Ayre (ACT/NSW)	4	86	10	26.30	5-37
Jake Lehmann (SA)	4	268	44.67	101	1	1		Jordan Buckingham (SA)	4	127	10	35.80	3-34

Wicket keeping: Patrick Rowe (Vic) 15 (13 ct/2st), Tyran Liddiard (NSW Metro) 13 (11/2), Jaron Morgan (WA) 10 (8/2), Tim Paine (Tas) 9 (all caught).

MATCHES PLAYED: At Adelaide Oval No 2 on October 11-14, 2021 – South Australia won by 86 runs. South Australia 6-**428 dec** (DG Drew 161*, TJ Kelly 50, CJ Kelly 86) and 7-240 dec (TJ Kelly 63, CJ Kelly 51) **def Western Australia 286** (TA Wyllie 79, C Connolly 65; CJ Kelly 5-57) **and 296** (TA Wyllie 112, AM Hardie 60; J Medew-Ewen 5-79)

At Campbelltown Memorial Oval, Adelaide on November 8-11, 2021 – Match Drawn. Queensland 7-404 dec (SD Heazlett 102, A Jain 108, J Clayton 102) and 3-232 dec (A Jain 111*, J Clayton 62) **drew with South Australia 223** (JS Lehmann 101; BL Edwards 4-53) **and 4-209** (JS Lehmann 68*)

At Blacktown International Sports Park No 1 on November 15-18, 2021 – Victoria won by 137 runs. Victoria 8-381 dec (JM Fraser-McGurk 146) **and 178** (H Verma 4-33) **def New South Metro 184** (RP Hackney 50, LD Hearne 54; JF Garner 3-24, TR Murphy 3-41) **and 238** (AJ Nair 68)

At Lindisfarne Oval, Hobart on November 22-25, 2021 – Tasmania won by 6 wickets. South Australia 165 (NA McSweeney 96; AJ Pyecroft 3-31, IJ Carlisle 3-27) **and 304** (NA McSweeney 55, SL Kerber 59; IJ Carlisle 4-64) **lost to Tasmania 317** (MB Wright 95, N Radhakrishnan 72, AJ Pycroft 51; SL Kerber 6-53) **and 4-153** (EM Vines 61*). *Tim Paine made 1 & 7, took 9 catches but elected to take a break from cricket following this game.*

At the MCG on November 29-December 2, 2021 – Match Drawn. Victoria 8-352 dec (J Rudd 50, A Chandrasinghe 56, XA Crone 51*; S Skelly 3-71) **and 162** (A Chandrasinghe 68; RR Ayre 5-37) **drew with ACT/NSW Country 309** (RP Hackney 83, B Nikitaras 74; FP O'Neill 3-43) **and 5-152** (BD Macdonald 63; TR Murphy 4-38)

At the WACA, Perth on December 6-9, 2021 – Western Australia won by 7 wickets. Tasmania 292 (BM Hope 121, JA Freeman 84; CH Stobo 3-51, SJ Greer 3-68) **and 288** (N Radhakrishnan 133; CH Stobo 3-54, CJ Rocchiccioli 3-64, B Jackson 3-24) **lost to Western Australia 445** (ST Fanning 115, TA Wyllie 153*; JA Freeman 5-118) **and 3-139**

At the Campbelltown Memorial Oval, Adelaide on January 24-27, 2022 – South Australia won by 5 wickets. Queensland 6-**325 dec** (BE Street 105, A Jain 55, J Clayton 60) **and 7-169 dec** (A Jain 58, J Clayton 51; JSD Buckingham 3-34) **lost to South Australia 191** (SL Kerber 57; JJ Bazley 3-39) **and 5-304** (K Brazell 72, BT Capel 125, DG Drew 66; JP Wood 3-61)

At Bellerive Oval, Hobart on February 7-10, 2022 – New South Wales Metro won by 7 wickets. Tasmania 367 (TP Ward 139; H Verma 4-90) **and 5-275 dec** (TP Ward 64, JR Doran 91) **lost to New South Wales Metro 182** (IJ Carlisle 3-25) **and 3-461** (DL Solway 80, JR Attenborough 80, L Ohrynowsky 112*, T Liddiard 114*)

At Alexandra Park (Ian Barker Fields), Albury on February 7-10, 2022 – Victoria won by 46 runs. Victoria 359 (JM Fraser-McGurk 100; TW Gray 6-64) **and 5-231 dec** (J Seymour 72, JM Fraser-McGurk 100; S Skelly 4-46) **def ACT/NSW Country 244** (NCR Larkin 77, NJ Cutler 68; FP O'Neil 3-31, TL O'Connell 5-56) **and 300** (B Nikitaras 63, NCR Larkin 66, RR Pawson 61; TL O'Connell 4-70)

At Jubilee Oval, Ringwood, Melbourne on February 21-24, 2022 – South Australia won by 8 wickets. Victoria 368 (A Chandrasinghe 112, CJ Kellaway 67, FP O'Neil 68; SH Johnson 3-82, SL Kerber 3-52) **and 9-248 dec** (J Seymour 67, A Chandraisnghe 91; JSD Buckingham 3-69, LAJ Pope 4-89) **lost to South Australia 390** (JJ Doyle 112, RJ Gibson 128; FP O'Neil 3-36) **and 2-229** (JJ Doyle 110, NA McSweeney 79)

At Ian Healy Oval, Brisbane on February 21-24, 2022 – Match Drawn. ACT/NSW Country 287 (B Nikitaras 93, JM Avendano 55; PG Dooley 3-53) **drew with Queensland 3-207** (LD Pfeffer 87, C Taylor 55)

At Rosedale Oval, Sydney on March 14-17, 2022 – New South Wales Metro won by 9 wickets. ACT/NSW Country 131 (BJ Dwarshuis 4-25) **and 211** (B Nikitaras 112; BJ Dwarshuis 3-48, CJ Green 3-48) **lost to New South Wales Metro 323** (JR Attenborough 50, DL Solway 65, LD Hearne 87; TW Gray 3-57, RR Ayre 4-45) **and 1-20**

At Merv Hughes Oval, Melbourne on March 14-17, 2022 – Victoria won 79 runs. Victoria 233 and 8-408 dec (A Chandrasinghe 74, TF Rogers 81, JA Merlo 65; BM Hope 3-65) **defeated Tasmania 371** (EM Vines 97, MJ Owen 61, CT Valente 56; FP O'Neil 4-83, TL O'Connell 3-55) **and 191** (MJ Owen 64; JA Merlo 5-45)

UNDER 19'S – QUEENSLAND METRO WINS TITLE IN MACKAY

Matches Played (50 overs each unless otherwise stated). Round one - April 7, 2022
Vic Metro 8-213 cc (J Lemire 66, W Townsend 55) **lost to NSW Metro 4-215** (46.5 overs) (J Davies 86*, JN Watson 72*) **at George Gorrie Oval.** *NSW Metro were 4-44 in the run chase before Joel Davies and Jordan Watson added 171 for the fifth wicket* **ACT/NSW Country 158** (37.4 overs) (A McTaggart 65; S Voss 3-15, J Willmott 3-31, N Radhakrishnan 3-31) **lost to Tasmania 4-160** (28.1 overs) (A Wynwood 58*, S Wright 44) **at Jack Lancaster Oval. Qld Metro 6-260 cc** (N McFadyen 102, LW Crump 65; JJ Ryan 4-51) **def Qld Country 88** (21 overs) (A Stockdale 4-9) **at Roy Trevaskis Oval.** *Qld Metro skipper Noah McFadyen faced 79 balls, hit 8 fours and 3 sixes.* **NT 5-223 cc** (A Naqvi 78, B Waring 59) **lost to Vic Country 9-228** (47 overs) (AD Buxton 69, RT Mark 45*; C Smith 3-43) **at Harrup Park No 1. NSW Under 17s 153** (46.5 overs) (S Konstas 78; S Young 3-16, JM Reuther 3-50) **lost to SA 2-154** (34 overs) (C Arnold 66*, Z McCabe 46*) **at Magpie Sportsground.**
Round two - April 8, 2022. NSW Metro 9-221 cc (LD Shaw 47; TH Balkin 3-35) **def Qld Metro 207** (48.2 overs) (W Salzman 3-35) **at Harrup Park No 1. Vic Metro 218** (49.1 overs) (SJ Wood 59, JR Koduru 50; NE Hurley 3-33, JF Garner 3-38) **def Vic Country 177** (42.5 overs) (J Doherty 58; W Townsend 3-48) **at Magpie Sportsground. ACT/NSW Country 9-259 cc** (AP Cahill 89, Z Keogh 60) **def SA 186** (41.2 overs) (HP Townsend 5-35, E Fitzpatrick 3-36) **at George Gorrie Oval. Qld Country 157** (45.5 overs) (MB Wilkins 40; A Parsons 3-33) **lost to NSW Under 17s 3-159** (19.5 overs) (H Singh 104) **at Jack Lancaster Oval.** *Harjas Singh (52 balls, 15x4, 4x6).* **Tasmania 8-273 cc** (NR Davis 52, S Hayes 51*; C Kemp 3-38) **def NT 188** (41.2 overs) **at Roy Trevaskis Oval.**
Round three - April 10, 2022 (20 overs) all matches at Harrup Park No 1. SA 9-94 cc (T Menzies 3-13) **lost to NT 6-97** (19.2 overs) (A Naqvi 37*). **Qld Metro 8-143 cc** (T Snell 36, N McFadyen 30; RT Mark 4-18) **def Vic Country 4-137** (LS Blackford 61). **April 11, 2022, all matches at Harrup Park No 1. ACT/NSW Country 9-63 cc lost to NSW Under 17s 2-68** (12 overs) (H Singh 34*). **NSW Metro 5-92** (13.3 overs) (J Davies 39*) **lost to Qld Country 4-103** (13 overs) (FS Thomasson 47, EG Ramsbotham 38). *Qld Country DLS target of 100 from 13, Jem Ryan came in on a hat-trick with seven to win and whacked Joel Davies for six and four to clinch the win.* **Vic Metro 7-120 cc** (J Koduru 34, W Townsend 30) **lost to Tasmania 7-124** (19.5 overs) (N Radhakrishnan 62*).

STANDINGS (3 matches per team)

POOL A	W	L	Pts	NRR	POOL B	W	L	Pts	NRR
Qld Metro	2	1	9	+1.366	Tasmania	3	0	14	+1.800
NSW Metro	2	1	7	+0.242	NSW Under 17s	2	1	9	+1.047
Vic Metro	1	2	4	+0.168	SA	1	2	5	-0.092
Vic Country	1	2	4	-0.234	ACT/NSW Country	1	2	5	-0.591
Qld Country	1	2	4	-3.173	NT	1	2	4	-0.828

April 12, 2022 – Fifth place playoff from Pool A and B. Qld Country 183 (48.3 overs) (FS Thomasson 68; T Menzies 3-28) **lost to NT 4-184** (42.5 overs) (T Kelaart 52*, H Brimbal 43) **at Harrup Park No 1.**
Semi Finals on April 13, 2022. Qld Metro 9-222 cc (N McFadyen 63; L Callanan 3-35) **def NSW Under 17s 182** (47.1 overs) (H Singh 67 S Konstas 51; J Sinfield 3-45) **at George Gorrie Oval. NSW Metro 9-240 cc** (L Shaw 74; L Smith 3-50) **def Tasmania 175** (41.4 overs) (O Cole 5-41) **at Harrup Park No 1**
Playoff games - Vic Country 145 (H McGregor 3-23) **lost to ACT/NSW Country 2-148** (29.1 overs) (Z Keogh 70*) **at Roy Trevaskis Oval. Vic Metro 4-281 cc** (J Lemire 102* H Kannan 71* J Koduru 69) **def SA 8-264** (Z McCabe 91, S Rahaley 61 I Higgins 52) **at Jack Lancaster Oval.**
The Final on April 14, 2022. Queensland Metro 9-198 cc (S Muller 74 T Whitney 36) **def NSW Metro 171** (42.4 overs) (L Shaw 38; A Stockdale 3-21). *Player of the match was Stephan Muller (111 balls, 3 fours).*
3rd v 4th Playoff - Tasmania 212 (44.4 overs) (N Radhakrishnan 42; L Callanan 4-54) **lost to NSW Under 17s 5-214** (39.1 overs) (R MacMillan 59* R Hicks 45*) **at George Gorrie Oval. Other playoff matches – 50 overs per side. Vic Metro 9-199 cc lost to ACT/NSW Country 9-203** (47.2 overs) (T Martin 57; T Nelson 4-35) **at Jack Lancaster Oval. Other playoff matches – 20 overs per side, both at Roy Trevaskis Oval. Qld Country 7-119 cc lost to Vic Country 5-123** (18.2 overs) (L Blackford 60; D McAteer 3-23). **NT 5-127 cc** (J Naganayagam 51; P Weckert 3-5) **lost to SA 3-130** (18.2 overs) (Z McCabe 44, S Rahaley 40). **Final Positions:** 1. Qld Metro, 2. NSW Metro, 3. NSW U17s, 4. Tas, 5. ACT/NSW Country, 6. SA, 7. Vic Metro, 8. NT, 9. Vic Country, 10. Qld Country.

Leading Batting	M	Runs	Avge	HS	100/50	Leading Bowling	M	Wkts	Avge	Best	5wI
Noah McFadyen (Qld M)	5	221	44.20	102	1/1	Jesse Willmott (Tas)	5	10	17.20	3-31	-
Harjas Singh (NSW U17)	5	211	52.75	104	1/1	Aubrey Stockdale (Qld M)	5	9	10.22	4-9	-
Jai Lemire (Vic M)	5	205	51.25	102*	1/1	Harrison Townsend (ACT/NSW C)	5	9	15.44	5-35	1
Zac McCabe (SA)	5	201	67.00	91	-/1	Jem Ryan (Qld Country)	5	9	17.00	4-51	-
Liam Blackford (Vic M)	5	189	37.80	61	-/2	Thomas Nelson (Vic M)	5	9	19.89	4-35	-

Wicket-Keeping: Tobias Snell (Qld M) 17 (14ct/3st), Harry Matthias (SA) 12 (10ct/2st), Daniel Gauci (NSW M) 10 (all ct)
Team of the Championships (batting order) - Zac McCabe (SA), Nivethan Radhakrishnan (Qld Metro), Harjas Singh (NSW U17), Jagadeswara Koduru (Vic Metro), Noah McFadyen (Qld Metro), Joel Davies (NSW Metro), Jai Lemire (WK) (Vic Metro), Tom Menzies (NT), Aubrey Stockdale (Qld Metro), Max Birthistle (Vic Metro), Jessie Wilmot (Tas), Jem Ryan (Qld Country).
Player of the tournament - Noah McFadyen (Queensland Metro). Spirit of Cricket – NSW Under 17s

PREMIER LEAGUE CRICKET 2021/22

ACT PREMIER CRICKET LADDER
(8 sides, 7 matches, top four, 50 overs per side)
Was meant to be two-day competition but changed to one-day

	Won First inns	Drawn	Lost First inns	Points	Quotient
Queanbeyan	3	4	-	23	1.35
Tuggeranong	3	4	-	22	0.92
Western District	3	2	2	17	-0.46
Eastlake	2	3	2	16	-0.20
Ginninderra	2	1	4	14	0.61
North Canberra-Gungahlin	3	1	3	14	-0.75
Western Creek Molonglo	2	2	3	13	-0.16
ANU	1	1	5	6	-0.98

Leading Batting	M	Inns	NO	HS	Runs	Avge	100/50
Dean Solway (Queanbeyan)	6	6	2	124*	305	76.25	2/-
John Rogers (West Creek-Molonglo)	6	5	2	65	218	72.67	-/3
Daniel Leerdam (ANU)	6	6	1	75	206	41.20	-/2
Scott Murn (Western District)	7	7	2	63*	193	38.60	-/1
William Todd (Queanbeyan)	5	5	-	71	191	38.20	-/2

Leading Bowling	M	Overs	Wkts	Avge	Best	5/10
Kai Brunker (Queanbeyan)	6	54.1	15	14.73	4-13	-/-
Shane Devoy (Tuggeranong Valley)	7	44.3	12	10.33	4-24	-/-
Blake Faunce (West Creek-Molonglo)	6	41	12	16.25	4-24	-/-
Matthew Shean (Tuggeranong Valley)	7	38	11	11.09	5-36	1/-
Siddartha Sharma (Western District)	7	51	10	14.10	4-27	-/-

Keeping: Josh Staines (Tuggeranong) 13 (12ct/1st), **Mikey McNamara** (Queanbeyan) 13 (6ct/7st).

AWARDS

DB Robin Medal: Tied between Mark Solway (Queanbeyan) and Scott Murn (Western District)
Grade team of the year: John Rogers (WCM), Dean Solway (Queanbeyan), Mark Solway (Queanbeyan), John Staines (Tuggeranong), Scott Murn (Western District), Brad Thomas (Ginninderra), Shane Devoy (Tuggeranong Valley), Hanno Jacobs (ANU), Luke Powell (Western District), Blake Faunce (WCM), Kai Brunker (Queanbeyan), Coach: Peter Solway (Queanbeyan). Club Championship: Queanbeyan. Greg Lord Administrator of the Year: Damien Eaton (Eastlake). Paul Egan Volunteer award: Luke Hickey (WCM*)*. Lord's Taverners Spirit of Cricket Award: ANU

KONICA MINOLTA REGIONAL TWENTY 20 FINAL at Phillip Oval on Sunday February 20, 2022 – Queanbeyan won by 7 wickets. Tuggeranong 7-106 cc (WH Todd 2-19) **lost to Queanbeyan 3-110** (12.4 overs) (MA Higgs 43; C Devoy 2-19).

50 OVER FINAL (John Gallup Cup Final) at Freebody Oval on Sunday January 23, 2022 – Western Creek Molonglo won by 54 runs. Western Creek Molonglo 6-270 cc (RW Trickett 42, J Myburgh 52, J Low-McMahon 71) **def Queanbeyan 216** (45.3 overs) (M Solway 40, M Curtale 56, GD Gillespie 47; JD McNally 4-44, BA Faunce 3-28).

GRADE FINAL (Douglas Cup) at Phillip Oval on March 19, 2022 – Tuggeranong won by 32 runs. Tuggeranong 7-202 cc (M Barrington-Smith 43, A Floros 40; K Brunker 4-46) **def Queanbeyan 170** (46.5 overs) (WH Todd 39; M Shean 5-36, C Devoy 3-27). *Matt Shean won the Greg Irvine Medal.*

Recent Titles and Awards

Season	First Grade	50 over (Gallup Cup)	Twenty 20	DB Robin Medal winners
2012/13	Western District UC	Eastlake	Albury Wodonga	Ben Oakley (WDUC)
2013/14	Western District UC	Queanbeyan	Western District UC	Shane Devoy (TV)
2014/15	Western Creek Molonglo	Western District UC	Nth Canb/Gungahlin	Blake Dean (WCM)
2015/16	Western District UC	Queanbeyan	Queanbeyan	Mark Bennett (WCM)
2016/17	Tuggeranong Valley	Tuggeranong Valley	West Creek Molonglo	Shane Devoy (TV)
2017/18	Weston Creek Molonglo	Weston Creek Molonglo	Western District UC	Tied – Tom Engelbrecht (WDUC) & Tim Floros (TV)
2018/19	Ginninderra	Weston Creek Molonglo	Tuggeranong Valley	Ethan Bartlett (WDUC)
2019/20	Western District	Weston Creek Molonglo	Western District	Shane Devoy (TV)
2020/21	Weston Creek Molonglo	Tuggeranong Valley	Queanbeyan	Shane Devoy (TV)
2021/22	Tuggeranong	Weston Creek Molonglo	Queanbeyan	M Solway (Q)/S Murn (WD)

DARWIN CRICKET 2021 (7 sides, 12 matches, top four)

	Won First inns	Drawn	Lost First inns	Points	Quotient
Waratah	8	1	3	44	1.3085
Darwin	7	1	4	40	1.2452
Southern Districts	7	-	5	38	1.3414
Tracy Village	6	1	5	35	1.2427
PINT T CASS First XI	5	1	6	25	0.7014
Palmerston	4	1	7	21	0.7485
Nightcliff	2	1	9	13	0.6844

Leading Batting	M	Inns	NO	HS	Runs	Avge	100/50
Ashley Chandrasinghe (Waratah)	13	12	2	172	741	74.10	2/4
Jackson Isakka (Southern Districts)	12	11	2	171*	739	82.11	4/2
Anthony Adlam (Darwin)	12	12	2	100*	644	64.40	1/7
Josh Kann (Tracy Village)	12	12	2	162*	629	62.90	2/4
Lochie Hardy (Southern Districts)	12	12	1	178*	585	53.18	2/2

Leading Bowling	M	Overs	Wkts	Avge	Best	5/10
Udara Weerasinghe (Waratah)	14	154.4	31	19.32	5-28	1/-
Hamish Martin (Palmerston)	11	179	29	21.00	6-66	1/-
Blade Baxter (PINT)	12	174	25	22.80	5-57	1/-
Matthew Hammond (Southern Districts)	13	132.1	24	16.58	5-38	1/-
Ryan McElduff (Nightcliff)	11	153.4	23	25.57	5-51	1/-

Keeping: Daniel Mylius (Southern Districts) 22 (17ct/5st), Corey McDean (Palmerston) 13 (11ct/2st), Max Hatzoglou (Tracy Village) 13 (10 ct/3 st)

AWARDS

Ralph Wiese Medal was tied between Southern Districts' Jackson Isakka and Tracy Village's Josh Kann. Third came Ryan McElduff from Nightcliff. Carlton Mid Premier Club Cricketer of the year: Jackson Isakka (Southern Districts) Bob Vowles Curator's Award – Nightcliff. Club Championship – Darwin.

Fielding – Tied between Palmerston's Alex Bleakley and PINT's Josh Neill. Spirit of Cricket award: Southern Districts
The NT News/Sunday Territorian Team of the Year: Anthony Adlam (Darwin), Blade Baxter (PINT),
Matthew Hammond (Southern Districts), Lochie Hardy (Southern Districts), Dylan Hunter (Waratah),
Jackson Isakka (Southern Districts), Josh Kann (TV), Hamish Martin (Palmerston), Ryan McElduff (Nightcliff),
Daniel Mylius (Southern Districts), Auston Umpherston (Waratah), Udara Weerasinghe (Waratah).

CARLTON MID TWENTY20 FINAL at Gardens Oval on July 15, 2021 – Darwin won by 8 wickets
Waratah 9-136 cc (DJ Hunter 70; L Zanchetta 3-21) **lost to Darwin 2-137** (16.4 overs)

CARLTON MID PREMIER GRADE FINAL at Marrara Oval on September 11-12, 2021 – Southern Districts won by 7 wickets.
Waratah 247 (A Chandrasinghe 63, DJ Hunter 56) **defeated Southern Districts 3-251** (L Hardy 71, MR Gilkes 126*). *Matt Gilkes faced 128 balls, hit 11 fours and 3 sixes.*

Recent Titles and Awards

Season	First Grade	Ralph Wiese Medal winners
2010	Nightcliff	Craig Cachopa (Tracy Village)
2011	Palmerston	Jake Fawcett (Darwin)/Nick Berry (PINT)
2012	PINT	Nick Berry (PINT)
2013	PINT	Greg Clarence (PINT)
2014	PINT	Jason Mackay (Tracy Village)
2015	Darwin	Jake Weatherald (Tracy Village)
2016	Darwin	Luke Shelton (Darwin)
2017	Darwin	Brad Schmulian (Waratah)
2018	Palmerston	Christian Leopard (Palmerston)
2019	Southern Districts	Josh Clarkson (PINT)
2020	Waratah	Luke Shelton (Darwin)
2021	Southern Districts	Josh Kann (TV) and Jackson Isakka (Southern Districts)

NEW SOUTH WALES PREMIER CRICKET - LADDER (20 sides, 17 matches, top six)

The Belvidere Cup	Won Out	Won First inns	Drawn	Lost First inns	Lost Out	Points	Quotient
Northern District	-	14	2	1	-	91	1.7059
Mosman	1	11	3	2	-	85	1.5697
Randwick-Petersham	-	13	2	2	-	81	1.3106
Manly-Warringah	1	10	2	4	-	75	1.5551
St George	-	9	3	5	-	59	1.3906
Sydney	-	9	3	5	-	58	1.2419
Western Suburbs	-	8	2	7	-	51	1.0728
Sydney University	-	7	3	7	-	46	1.1021
Uni of NSW	-	7	3	7	-	46	1.0599
Eastern Suburbs	-	7	2	8	-	44	0.9809
Parramatta	-	6	5	6	-	42	0.9442
UTS North Sydney	-	6	4	7	-	40	1.1786
Fairfield-Liverpool	-	6	3	8	-	40	0.8124
Bankstown	-	5	3	9	-	36	0.8046
Gordon	-	4	4	8	1	28	0.7074
Sutherland	-	3	4	10	-	23	0.7022
Penrith	-	3	4	9	1	22	0.8585
Hawkesbury	-	3	4	10	-	22	0.6519
Blacktown Mounties	-	3	3	11	-	21	0.6741
Campbelltown-Camden	-	2	5	10	-	17	0.5204

Leading Batting

	M	Inns	NO	HS	Runs	Avge	100/50
Josh Clarke (Western Suburbs)	15	15	2	134*	742	57.08	2/3
Scott Rodgie (Northern District)	18	18	5	147	738	56.77	3/2
Justin Avendano (UTS North Sydney)	10	10	1	171	707	78.56	3/3
Peter Forrest (Mosman)	13	14	4	121*	696	69.60	1/5
Ryan Hackney (Paramatta)	12	12	2	113*	610	61.00	1/5

Leading Bowling

	M	Overs	Wkts	Avge	Best	5/10
Adam Semple (Randwick-Petersham)	16	153.4	30	19.37	6-37	1/-
Scott Rodgie (Northern District)	18	145.4	29	14.76	5-32	1/-
Sam Skelly (Eastern Suburbs)	14	139.1	29	22.38	6-37	1/-
Jonathon Craig Dobson (St George)	14	111.2	28	17.18	6-45	1/-
Ryan Felsch (Sydney)	14	125.1	28	19.07	4-35	-/-
Jake Turner (Mosman)	15	187.5	28	25.46	5-102	1/-

Keeping: Anthony Sams (Randwick-Petersham) 28 (25ct/3st), Andrew Deitz (Sutherland) 25 (23ct/2st)

AWARDS

The Bill O'Reilly Medal won by Scott Rodgie (Northern District) on 25 votes.

The Kingsgrove Sports First Grade team of the season: Scott Rodgie (Captain, Northern District), Justin Avendano (UTS North Sydney), Joshua Clarke (Western Suburbs), Daniel Solway (Bankstown), Angus Robson (Eastern Suburbs), Raveesh Srivastava (Fairfield-Liverpool), Tim Cummins (Sydney University), Devlin Malone (Sydney University), Ryan Felsch (Sydney), Hunar Verma (Blacktown Mounties), Luke Courtney (Hawkesbury), Sam Skelly (Eastern Suburbs).

Sydney Smith Cup Club Championship: Northern District. Spirit of cricket: Northern District. Captain of the Year: Josh Clarke (Western Suburbs). Coach (Bob Simpson award) of the Year: Peter Forrest (Mosman), Ground of the year: Pratten Park (Western Suburbs)

KINGSGROVE SPORTS TWENTY20 FINAL at University Oval on Sunday February 6, 2022 - Randwick Petersham won by 31 runs.

Randwick Petersham 114 (18.1 overs) (C Hawkins 52; D Malone 3-13, R McElduff 4-16) **def Sydney University 83** (18.1 overs) (H Kerr 37; DR Sams 2-8, A Semple 3-11, D Singh 2-29). *Camden Hawkins (41 balls, 5 fours) was Man of the match,*

Leading Twenty20 Stats 2021-22

Batting	Runs	Avge	HS	SR	100s	Bowling	Wkts	Avge	Econ	Best
Liam Robertson (Syd U)	242	48.4	73*	150	-	Devlin Malone (Syd Uni)	13	11.0	5.26	3-9
Anthony Sams (Rand/Peter)	215	53.7	115*	174	1	Dugald Holloway (Sud Uni)	12	14.0	7.30	5-24
Tyran Liddiard (Penrith)	185	61.6	104*	144	1	Tom Brooks (Western Suburbs)	11	10.0	5.55	3-25
Adam Semple (Rand/Peter)	183	61.0	100*	174	1	Jack Preddey (Eastern Suburbs)	9	9.4	5.43	3-14
Daniel Solway (Bankstown)	181	50.3	72*	108	-	Hanno Jacobs (Western Suburbs)	9	13.6	6.15	2-11

First Grade Grand Final at Bankstown Oval on April 1, 2 & 3, 2022 - Mosman won on first innings

Mosman		B	M	4	6
LM O'Farrell +	c Shaw b Furrer	12	16	14	
NJ Hinton *	c Shaw b Furrer	5	8	23	
LD Hearne	lbw b Green	144	336	424	
HJ Dalton	run out (Pawson)	0	5	4	
PJ Forrest	run out (Green)	29	107	131	
MM Moran	c Shaw b Anderson	5	8	9	
MJ Calder	c & b Green	28	34	42	
EA Eales	c Gray b Green	18	60	63	
JD Park	lbw b Green	0	1	1	
DJ Crawford	c Pawson b Gray	46	94	139	
JM Turner	not out	2	13	19	
	4 b, 6 lb, 1 nb	11			
	113.3 overs	300			

Northern District		B	M	4	6
DA Lowery	c Dalton b Turner	34	203	260	1
CD Miller	b Turner	0	1	4	
BJ Davis *	c Forrest b Park	21	55	88	
CJ Green	lbw b Crawford	80	293	424	6
SA Rodgie	b Eales	6	22	36	
LD Shaw +	c O'Farrell b Turner	4	34	41	1
DA Anderson	c Dalton b Turner	72	243	375	7
RR Pawson	b Eales	22	45	62	5
TW Gray	c Forrest b Park	8	95	91	
CF Anderson	b Turner	4	15	20	1
GW Furrer	not out	0	5	19	
	4 b, 8 lb, 15 nb, 1 w	28			
	166 overs	279			

1-17 (O'Farrell), 2-20 (Hinton). 3-20 (Dalton), 4-94 (Forrest), 5-99 (Moran), 6-140 (Calder), 7-176 (Eales), 8-176 (Park), 9-281 (Crawford), 10-300 (Hearne)

1-1 (Miller), 2-46 (Davis), 3-104 (Lowery), 4-118 (Rodgie), 5-131 (Shaw), 6-195 (Green), 7-231 (Pawson), 8-257 (Gray), 9-266 (Anderson), 10-279 (Anderson)

Bowling	O	M	R	W	wd	nb
RR Pawson	14	1	51	0		
GW Furrer	12	5	24	2		
CJ Green	39.3	10	82	4		
SA Rodgie	19	5	46	0		
TW Gray	19	4	58	1		
CF Anderson	10	3	29	1	1	

Bowling	O	M	R	W	wd	nb
JM Turner	42	12	102	5		12
EA Eales	34	14	51	2		1
JD Park	51	23	58	2		1
DJ Crawford	23	10	33	1		1
MM Moran	10	5	8	0		
HJ Dalton	2	0	5	0		
NJ Hinton	4	2	10	0		

Toss: Northern District.   Umpires: GJ Davidson, BC Treloar.   Benaud Medal: JM Turner (Mosman). Stumps Day One: Mosman 8-190 (80 overs) LD Hearne 79*, DJ Crawford 5. Day Two: Northern District 4-128 (76 overs) CJ Green 47*, LD Shaw 4*. **Mosman won their first A grade flag since 1938/39 which was captained by Stan McCabe.**

Recent Premierships

2000-01	St George	2011-12	Sydney University
2001-02	Fairfield-Liverpool	2012-13	St George
2002-03	Sydney University	2013-14	Sydney University
2003-04	Eastern Suburbs	2014-15	Manly-Warringah
2004-05	Sydney University	2015-16	Bankstown
2005-06	Fairfield-Liverpool	2016-17	Sydney University
2006-07	Bankstown	2017-18	Paramatta
2007-08	St George	2018-19	Penrith
2008-09	St George	2019-20	Randwick-Petersham
2009-10	St George	2020-21	Sydney
2010-11	Sydney University	2021-22	Mosman

Most Premierships won by (Current teams): St George 17, Western Suburbs (inc Burwood) 11, Sydney University 9, Eastern Suburbs (inc Waverley) 8, Bankstown 7, Gordon 6, Northern District 6, Manly-Warringah 5, UTS North Sydney 5, Sydney (inc Balmain) 5, Mosman 5, Paramatta (inc Central Cumberland) 4, Penrith 3, Fairfield-Liverpool 2, Sutherland 2, University of NSW 2, Randwick-Petersham 1.

Recent One-day Titles

2006-07	Bankstown	2013-14	Northern District
2007-08	Northern District and Eastern Suburbs (joint)	2014-15	Bankstown
		2015-16	Bankstown
2008-09	Mosman	2016-17	Penrith
2009-10	Sutherland	2017-18	Sydney University
2010-11	Sydney University	2018-19	Sydney
2011-12	Randwick Petersham	2019-20	Sydney University
2012-13	North Sydney	2020-21	Randwick Petersham

Twenty20 Cup Winners

2008-09	Northern District		2015-16	Randwick Petersham
2009-10	Manly-Warringah		2016-17	Northern District
2010-11	Sydney		2017-18	Sydney
2011-12	Randwick Petersham		2018-19	Sutherland
2012-13	Fairfield-Liverpool		2019-20	Sydney
2013-14	Randwick Petersham		2020-21	Bankstown
2014-15	St George		2021-22	Randwick-Petersham

Recent Bill O'Reilly Medal winners

2000-01	Robert Aitken (Parramatta)		2013-14	Patrick Jackson (Penrith)
2001-02	Richard Chee Quee (Rand-Peter)		2014-15	Ahillen Beadle (Manly-Warringah)
2002-03	Grant Lambert (Fairf-Liverpool)		2015-16	Charlie Stobo (Gordon)
2003-04	Trent Johnston (Mosman)		2016-17	Mason Crane & Elliot Richtor (both Gordon)
2004-05	Jarrad Burke (Campb-Camden)		2017-18	Jonathan Cook (Western Suburbs)
2005-06	Ian Moran (Sydney Univ)		2018-19	Nick Bertus (Paramatta)
2006-07	Grant Lambert (Fairf-Liverpool)		2019-20	Will Affleck (Randwick Petersham),
2007-08	Anthony Clark (Fairf-Liverpool)		4-way	Hayden Kerr (Sydney University)
2008-09	Jonathan Moss (Sydney)		tie	Nivethan Radhakrishnan (Hawkesbury)
2009-10	Greg Mail (Syd Uni)			Scott Rodgie (Northern District)
	Trent Copeland (St George)			
2010-11	Dominic Thornely (Sydney)		2020-21	Nic Stapleton (St George)
2011-12	Greg Mail (Sydney Uni)		tied	Tom Jagot (UTS North Sydney)
2012013	Harry Evans (Gordon)		2021-22	Scott Rodgie (Northern District)

Most runs ever in Competition

	Clubs	Career	Inns	NO	HS	Runs	Avge	100s
GJ Mail	Parramatta, Hawkesbury, Balmain, Sydney Uni	1995-2017	382	54	214*	15230	46.43	44
GJ Hayne	UTS-Balmain, Gordon	1987-2007	365	30	161	12354	36.87	26
W Bardsley*	Glebe, Western Suburbs	1898-1933	291	49	217*	12118	50.07	36
R Chee Quee	Randwick, Randwick-Petersham	1987-2006	346	24	182	11886	36.91	20
RJ Bower	Bankstown-Canterbury, Penrith, Balmain	1977-1998	322	40	200	11841	41.98	24

Run tally of Warren Bardsley amended after publishing of recent book on him by Peter Lloyd

Most wickets

	Clubs	Career Span	Wickets	Avge	Best	5 w I
HC Chilvers	Northern District	1925-52	1153	15.99	9/46	105
KC Gulliver	Mosman	1930-63	1029	18.26	8/92	70
WJ O'Reilly	North Sydney, St George	1926-1949	962	9.44	9/27	104
OP Asher	Sydney, Paddington	1910-1933	861	17.30	9/46	65
AA Mailey	Redfern, Balmain, Middle Harbour, Manly, Waverley	1906-1935	828	18.84	9/53	79

QUEENSLAND PREMIER LEAGUE CRICKET - LADDER (12 sides, 11 matches, two-day games. top four)

Cam Battersby Cup/ Bob Spence Shield	Won Out	Won 1st inn	Drawn	Lost 1st inn	Lost Out	Points	Quotient
Ipswich	-	7	4	-	-	160.50	1.4051
Western Suburbs	-	6	4	1	-	145.25	1.6258
Gold Coast	-	5	5	1	-	137.75	1.6501
Redlands	-	4	4	3	-	120.50	0.9332
Toombul	-	4	4	3	-	116.75	0.9413
University of Queensland	-	3	4	4	-	110.25	0.9156
Sunshine Coast	-	2	7	2	-	106.25	1.1546
South Brisbane	-	2	6	3	-	105.75	0.8914
Northern Suburbs	-	3	2	6	-	103.75	0.8865
Valley	-	2	5	4	-	97.50	0.8566
Sandgate-Redcliffe	-	1	4	6	-	81.50	0.6988
Wynnum/Manly	-	2	1	8	-	72.25	0.6892

Leading Batting	M	Inns	NO	HS	Runs	Avge	100/50
Sam Truloff (Western Suburbs)	**13**	**12**	**2**	**219**	**1116**	**111.60**	**5/4**
Isaiah Snell (Western Suburbs)	13	12	-	119	680	56.67	2/4
Jack Clayton (Uni of Qld)	11	11	-	123	614	55.82	1/5
Emmanuel Peterson (South Brisbane)	10	10	2	182*	599	74.88	2/3
Max Bryant (Gold Coast)	10	10	1	157	587	65.22	2/4

Leading Bowling	M	Overs	Wkts	Avge	Best	5/10
Simon Milenko (Redlands)	**12**	**387.1**	**47**	**21.36**	**6-32**	**5/-**
Noah McFadyen (Northern Suburbs)	11	231.2	30	26.40	5-84	1/-
Adam Smith (Ipswich)	13	244	26	22.19	4-39	-/-
Chathura Kaluthanthri (Sandgate-Redcliffe)	10	138.1	25	18.16	7-41	1/-
Liam Hope-Shackley (Wynnum-Manly)	11	162.4	25	29.32	4-48	-/-

Keeping: Isaiah Snell (Western Suburbs) 24 (all ct), Tom Healy (Northern Suburbs) 22 (19ct/3st).

AWARDS - Peter Burge Medal: Won by Harry Wood (Ipswich)
Bob Spence Trophy for most improved Under 21: Hugo Burdon (Gold Coast). Groundsman's Award: Chris Hepburn (Redlands).
Umpire of Season (Bruce Oxenford Medal): Dave Taylor.
Team of the season: Max Bryant (Gold Coast), Angus Lovell (Uni Q), Sam Truloff (Wests, Captain), Jack Clayton (Uni Q), Hugo Burdon (Gold Coast), Harrison Wood (Ipswich), Isaiah Snell (Wests), Liam Hope-Shackley (Wynnum-Manly), Noah McFadyen (Norths), Simon Milenko (Redlands), Chathrura Kaluthanthri (Sandgate-Redcliffe), Emmanuel Peterson (South Brisbane). Coach: Aaron Moore (Ipswich)

KOOKABURRA/JOHN McKNOULTY 50 OVER FINAL at Bill Pippen Field on Sunday October 24, 2021 – Gold Coast won by 108 runs. Gold Coast 6-280 cc (H Burdon 105, S Palombo 68; W Prestwidge 2-44) **defeated Northern Suburbs 172** (38.5 overs) (JA Burns 66; J Kann 5-20, N Buchanan 3-36, MP Kuhnemann 2-56).
Jimmy Maher Medal - Hugo Burdon (Gold Coast) faced 118 balls, hit 9 fours and 1 six.

Leading 50-over Stats 2021/22

Batting	Runs	Avge	HS	SR	100s	Bowling	Wkts	Avge	Econ	Best
Hugo Burdon (Gold Coast)	324	64.8	105	79	1	Josh Kann (Gold Coast)	12	13.4	4.13	5-20
Hayden Kerr (Gold Coast)	265	88.3	150*	110	2	Connor Sully (Norths)	12	17.6	4.75	5-29
Ryan Hackney (Ipswich)	250	83.3	116*	84	1	Will Prestwidge (Norths)	11	16.3	4.00	4-38
Harrison Wood (Ipswich)	244	81.3	121*	98	2	Will Sanders (Uni Qld)	11	20.9	5.23	4-49
Andy Grewal (Northern Suburbs)	237	39.5	100	91	1	Matt Willans (Uni Qld)	10	19.3	4.35	4-53

KOOKABURRA/TOM VEIVERS CUP TWENTY20 FINAL at the Gabba on Sunday December 19, 2021 – Gold Coast won by 6 wickets. Sunshine Coast 91 (19.4 overs) (B Munro 3-14, C Taylor 3-23) **lost to Gold Coast 4-93** (16.4 overs) (J Markham 42).

Leading Twenty20 Stats 2021/22

Batting	Runs	Avge	HS	SR	100s	Bowling	Wkts	Avge	Econ	Best
Callum Taylor (Gold Coast)	**185**	**92.5**	**85***	**125**	**-**	**Thomas Olsen (Sun Coast)**	**10**	**9.2**	**6.27**	**3-14**
Simon Milenko (Redlands)	175	35.0	83	165	-	Jackson Smith (Gold Coast)	9	7.3	5.08	4-17
Logan Duval (South Brisbane)	159	31.8	66	116	-	Conor McInerney (Redlands)	9	13.4	6.05	3-27
Jack Beath (Valley)	151	30.2	89	235	-	Stephen Shaw (Sand-Redcl)	8	9.3	5.00	3-16
Conor McInerney (Redlands)	139	27.8	56	128	-	Donal Whyte (Valley)	8	11.5	6.65	3-14

Sci-Fi Fleet Motors First Grade Final at Ivor Marsden Memorial Park (Baxter Oval) on March 26, 27, April 2 & 3, 2022 - Western Suburbs won on first innings

Ipswich			B	M	4	6	Western Suburbs			B	M	4	6
B Llewellyn	b Edwards		58	150	187	3	1	I Snell +	b Lutter		75	253	283	4
LJ Thomson								P Collins *	c Wilson b Smith		54	182	255	4
-Matthews	lbw b Dooley		23	65	119			SJ Truloff	c H Wood b J Wood		92	262	400	5
HL Austin	b Edwards		6	27	38	1		S McGiffin	lbw b Smith		125	289	449	10	2
H Wood	c Snell b Edwards		0	2	3			J Del Simone	c Cross b Wood		6	22	23	1
J P Wood	lbw b Whitney		19	26	45	2	1	J Sippel	not out		55	107	148	5	2
DP Wilson	c McGiffin b Whitney		29	119	198	2		SR Dennien	b Lutter		11	55	83	1	
AG Wilson*	run out (McGiffin)		46	98	124	4		P G Dooley	not out		4	11	10		
J W Cross +	b Watterson		5	24	28			A Watterson							
A Smith	b Edwards		5	17	21			BL Edwards							
J Creevey	c Collins b Whitney		4	14	21			TN Whitney							
S Lutter	not out		3	13	18										
	4 b, 3 lb, 7 nb, 1 w		15						6 b, 4 lb, 11 nb		21				
	91.3 overs		213						195 overs		6-443				

1-65 (Thomson-Matthews), 2-92 (Austin), 3-92 (H Wood), 4-101 (Llewellyn), 5-113 (J Wood), 6-187 (Wilson), 7-195 (Cross), 8-202 (Smith), 9-202 (Wilson), 10-213 (Creevey)

1-134 (Collins), 2-140 (Snell), 3-322 (Truloff), 4-338 (Del Simone), 5-383 (McGiffin), 6-437 (Dennien)

Bowling	O	M	R	W	wd	nb
BL Edwards	21	8	38	4		
TN Whitney	19.3	2	52	3		5
A Watterson	18	3	41	1		2
S McGiffin	16	3	49	0		
PG Dooley	17	6	26	1	1	

Bowling	O	M	R	W	wd	nb
A Smith	40	6	88	2		6
H Wood	27	7	67	0		1
S Lutter	35	8	56	2		
J Creevey	17	5	30	0		2
JP Wood	51	11	130	2		2
DP Wilson	22	8	36	0		
B Llewellyn	3	0	6	0		

Toss: Ipswich   Umpires: D Taylor, SE Dionysius.   Man of Match: (Andy Bichel Award): Blake Edwards

Stumps Scores - Day One: Ipswich 7-195 (83 overs) Wilson 27, Smith 0. Day Two: Western Suburbs 2-161 (84 overs) Truloff 16, McGiffin 6, Day Three: Western Suburbs 5-395 (180 overs) Sippel 22, Dennien 3.

WESTS WIN IN 2021/22
(Photo Courtesy - Queensland Cricket)

QUEENSLAND GRADE RECORDS

Most Premierships (Since 1897-98): South Brisbane 21, Toombul 19, Western Suburbs 15, University/Uni of Queensland 14, Northern Suburbs 9, Eastern Suburbs 7, Fortitude Valley 6, Sandgate-Redcliffe 5, Valley 5, Wynnum/Manly 5, Colts 4, Gold Coast 2, Toombul/Windsor 2, Redlands 1, Sunshine Coast 1, Toowong 1.

Recent First Grade Premiers

2001-02	Sandgate-Redcliffe	2012-13	Toombul
2002-03	Gold Coast	2013-14	Valley
2003-04	Sandgate-Redcliffe	2014-15	University of Queensland
2004-05	Western Suburbs	2015-16	Redlands
2005-06	Sunshine Coast	2016-17	Western Suburbs
2006-07	University of Queensland	2017-18	Northern Suburbs
2007-08	Western Suburbs	2018-19	University of Queensland
2008-09	Gold Coast	2019-20	University of Queensland
2009-10	Toombul	2020-21	University of Queensland
2010-11	Wynnum-Manly	2021-22	Western Suburbs
2011-12	University of Queensland		

Recent One-Day Premiers - John McKnoulty Cup

2005-06	Western Suburbs	2014-15	Wynnum-Manly
2006-07	University of Queensland	2015-16	University of Queensland
2007-08	University of Queensland	2016-17	University of Queensland
2008-09	University of Queensland	2017-18	Sandgate-Redcliffe
2009-10	Gold Coast	2018-19	Valley
2010-11	University of Queensland	2019-20	Western Suburbs
2011-12	University of Queensland	2020-21	Redlands
2012-13	Toombul	2021-22	Gold Coast
2013-14	University of Queensland		

Recent Twenty20 Premiers - Tom Veivers Cup

2005-06	University of Queensland	2014-15	University of Queensland
2006-07	Norths	2015-16	Sandgate-Redcliffe
2007-08	University of Queensland	2016-17	Sandgate-Redcliffe
2008-09	Wynnum-Manly	2017-18	Sandgate-Redcliffe
2009-10	Toombul	2018-19	University of Queensland
2010-11	University of Queensland	2019-20	Valley
2011-12	University of Queensland	2020-21	Gold Coast
2012-13	Valley	2021-22	Gold Coast
2013-14	Valley		

Recent Peter Burge Medals winners

1995-96	Adam Dale (Wynnum-Manly)	2009-10	Chris Lynn (Toombul)
1996-97	Jeff Pfaff (Gold Coast)	2010-11	Nick Fitzpatrick (Sunshine Coast)
1997-98	Paul Argent (South Brisbane)	2011-12	Brian May (South Bris)
1998-99	Mick Miller (Norths)	2012-13	Brad Ipson (Gold Coast)
1999-2000	Brendan Creevey (Sand-Red)	2013-14	Simon Milenko (Redlands)
2000-01	Dale Turner (Souths)	2014-15	Scott Walter (Uni of Qld)
2001-02	Greg Rowell (Wests)	2015-16	Sam Truloff (Wests)
2002-03	Aaron Nye (Wests)	2016-17	Michael Philipson (Uni of Qld)
2003-04	Nathan Rimmington (Sand-Red)	2017-18	Alecz Day (Sunshine Coast)
2004-05	Derek Tate (Toombul)	2018-19	Andrew Gode (Valley)
2005-06	Ben Laughlin (Wynnum-Manly)	2019-20	Jason Floros (Wynnum-Manly)
2006-07	Aaron Nye (Wests)	2020-21	Nathan McSweeney (Norths)
2007-08	Glen Batticciotto (Sand-Red)	2021-22	Harry Wood (Ipswich)
2008-09	Craig Philipson (Uni of Qld)		

SACA PREMIER CRICKET LADDER (13 sides, 12 matches, top four)

	Won Out	Won First inns	Drawn	Lost First inns	Lost Out	Points	Quotient
Sturt	1	7	2	2	-	185	1.2081
Tea Tree Gully	1	7	1	3	-	180	0.9854
Kensington	-	7	1	3	1	170	1.6241
West Torrens	-	7	3	2	-	165	1.4494
Glenelg	-	7	2	3	-	155	1.6068
Adelaide University	1	5	3	3	-	150	1.6495
Woodville	-	6	1	5	-	130	1.1235
Port Adelaide	1	5	1	5	-	120	0.9358
Northern Districts	-	4	2	6	-	100	0.8366
East Torrens	-	3	1	7	1	90	0.8402
Prospect	1	3	1	6	1	80	0.8070
Adelaide	-	2	1	7	2	50	0.5313
Southern District	-	-	1	11	-	5	0.5044

Leading Batting	M	Inns	NO	HS	Runs	Avge	100s	50s
Will Bosisto (Adelaide Uni)	11	12	4	166*	854	106.75	3	6
Thomas Kelly (Sturt)	10	8	2	211*	836	139.33	3	3
Josh Doyle (Kensington)	13	15	2	97	699	53.77	-	7
Daniel Drew (West Torrens)	10	8	2	180*	663	110.50	3	1
Kelvin Smith (West Torrens)	12	13	1	206*	654	54.50	2	1
Kyle Brazell (Adelaide Uni)	12	12	2	179*	633	63.30	2	1

Leading Bowling

	M	Overs	Wkts	Avge	Best	5/10
Adam Somerfield (TTG)	**14**	**189.5**	**33**	**17.48**	**5-14**	**1/-**
Daniel Fallins (West Torrens)	12	208.1	31	22.84	4-43	-/-
Tim Oakley (TTG)	14	202.1	31	23.58	7-30	1/-
Spencer Johnson (West Torrens)	11	175.4	29	16.90	5-55	1/-
Jordan Buckingham (West Torrens)	11	199.4	27	23.07	3-35	-/-

Keeping– Warren Peters (West Torrens) 23 (20 ct/3 st), Damon Kerr (Southern Districts) 21 (20ct/1st)

AWARDS

Bradman Medal: Won by Will Bosisto (Adelaide University) with 34 votes then came Thomas Kelly (Sturt) 29, Antum Naqvi, Northern Districts on 25.

Grade Cricket Team of the Year - voted by captains and coaches in batting order:
Kyle Brazell (Adelaide University), Isaac Higgins (Glenelg), Will Bosisto (c) (Adelaide University), Thomas Kelly (Sturt), Daniel Drew (West Torrens), Josh Doyle (Kensington), Isaac Conway (wk, Port Adelaide), Daniel Fallins (West Torrens), Spencer Johnson (West Torrens), Adam Somerfield (Tea Tree Gully), Tim Oakley (Tea Tree Gully), Elliot Opie (Kensington)
Coach of the Year – Peter Muggleton (Sturt). Grade Cricket Umpire of the Year – Craig Thomas. Spirit of Cricket – Glenelg. Talbot Smith (Fielding) Trophy - Michael McDonald (Port Adelaide), Thomas Kelly (Sturt). Grade Cricket Volunteer of the Year – David Boschma (Glenelg). C W Walker Memorial (First Grade keeper) – Josh Barrett (Southern Districts).
Fred Godson Medal (West End One Day Cup) – Lewis Evans (East Torrens)
The Darren Lehmann Medal (West End Twenty20 Cup Player of the series) – Will Bosisto (Adelaide University)
Jason Gillespie Medal for Premier Cricket's rising star – Harry Matthias (Sturt)

WEST END TWENTY20 FINAL at Rolton Oval on Sunday January 16, 2022 (Floodlit) – Port Adelaide won by 6 runs.
Port Adelaide 7-158 cc (S Chatto 45*) **defeated East Torrens 152** (19.5 overs) (R King 46; JS Lehmann 44; M McDonald 3-35, NJ Benton 3-18))

Leading Twenty20 Stats 2020-21

Batting	Runs	Avge	HS	SR	100s	Bowling	Wkts	Avge	Econ	Best
Thomas Kelly (Sturt)	**289**	**72.2**	**105***	**180**	**1**	**David Grant (Kensington)**	**17**	**8.3**	**5.92**	**5-16**
Will Bosisto (Adel Uni)	280	40.0	108	142	1	Joe Medew-Ewen (Port Adel)	14	12.2	5.83	5-21
Josh Barrett (Southern Dists)	264	52.8	91*	148	-	Matt Spoors (Sturt)	13	9.3	5.95	5-26
Matt Spoors (Sturt)	256	64.0	71*	128	-	Nick Benton (Port Adel)	11	14.0	5.60	3-18
Henry Hunt (Kensington)	242	121.0	110	150	1					

WEST END ONE DAY CUP FINAL at Karen Rolton Oval on Sunday February 13, 2022 – West Torrens won by 17 runs. West Torrens 9-232 (RJ Gibson 75; LAH Scott 3-55, LE Thompson 3-46) **defeated Glenelg 215** (49.4 overs) (JL Winter 105; JS Buckingham 4-27).

First Grade Final at Glenelg Oval on March 19 & 20, 2022 - West Torrens won on First innings

West Torrens			B	M	4	6
KR Smith	c Gatting b Atkinson	17	37	43	1	
BT Capel	run out (Somerfield)	9	23	50		
RJ Gibson	c Barrett b Oakley	103	163	254	7	1
DG Drew *	c Weaver b Barrett	43	88	119	5	
HJ Nielsen	lbw b Barrett	0	1	1		
D Fallins	b Oakley	16	32	54	2	
WA Peters +	not out	65	103	153	6	
MJ Short	c Holliday b Somerfield	6	20	30	1	
SH Johnson	c Holliday b Atkinson	10	23	42	1	
JM Reuther	not out	4	6			
JS Buckingham						
	1 lb, 4 nb, 3 w	8				
	82 overs	8-281 dec				

1-29 (Smith), 2-32 (Capel), 3-120 (Drew), 4-120 (Nielsen), 5-159 (Fallins), 6-195 (Short), 7-219 (Johnson) 8-271 (Gibson)

Tea Tree Gully			B	M	4	6
JS Holliday +	c Peters b Fallins	23	92	134	3	
D Ironside	c Short b Johnson	2	4	4		
Z Worden	lbw b Johnson	0	1	1		
P Page	lbw b Johnson	0	4	3		
FW Pannell	c Smith b Short	14	50	67	1	
JS Gatting *	c Smith b Fallins	20	48	60	4	
MK Weaver	c Peters b Buckingham	24	43	51	4	
AJ Somerfield	lbw b Short	61	104	144	9	
TN Barrett	c Nielsen b Fallins	2	13	32		
TL Oakley	c sub (Pointon) b Fallins	26	62	84	3	
B Atkinson	not out	3	13	13		
	2 b, 9 lb, 2 nb	13				
	71.5 overs	188				

1-3 (Ironside), 2-3 (Worden), 3-3 (Page), 4-34 (Pannell), 5-60 (Holliday), 6-65 (Gatting), 7-113 (Weaver), 8-132 (Barrett), 9-182 (Somerfield), 10-188 (Atkinson)

Bowling	O	M	R	W	wd	nb
TL Oakley	19	2	70	2	2	3
B Atkinson	19	2	73	2		
AJ Somerfield	21	7	60	1		1
JS Gatting	3	0	11	0		
TN Barrett	20	2	66	2	1	

Bowling	O	M	R	W	wd	nb
SH Johnson	23	7	55	3		
JS Buckingham	15	4	30	1		
MJ Short	10	2	31	2		1
D Fallins	23.5	5	61	4		1

Toss: Tea Tree Gully.   Umpires: C Thomas, H Singh.   David Hookes Medal: RJ Gibson (West Torrens)
Stumps Day One: Tea Tree Gully 3-20 (12 overs) Holliday 7, Pannell 7.

Photo thanks to West Torrens Cricket Club

Most A Grade Premierships since 1897/98: East Torrens 17, Kensington 17, Sturt 14, West Torrens 14, Prospect 10, Salisbury 9, Adelaide 7, Glenelg 6, Port Adelaide 6, Adelaide University 5, Woodville 5, North Adelaide 4, East Adelaide 3, Tea Tree Gully 3, Northern Districts 1, Southern District 1.

SACA GRADE STATISTICS
Recent First Grade Premierships

2001-02	Kensington	2012-13	Glenelg
2002-03	Kensington	2013-14	Port Adelaide
2003-04	Adelaide	2014-15	Tea Tree Gully
2004-05	Northern Districts	2015-16	Southern Districts
2005-06	Sturt	2016-17	West Torrens
2006-07	West Torrens	2017-18	Tea Tree Gully
2007-08	Woodville	2018-19	Kensington
2008-09	Woodville	2019-20	Kensington
2009-10	Sturt	2020-21	Adelaide University
2010-11	Kensington	2021-22	West Torrens
2011-12	Woodville		

Recent Limited-overs Titles

2007-08	Sturt	2015-16	Glenelg
2008-09	Glenelg	2016-17	West Torrens
2009-10	Kensington	2017-18	Port Adelaide
2010-11	Glenelg	2018-19	Kensington
2011-12	Tea Tree Gully	2019-20	East Torrens
2012-13	Tea Tree Gully	2020-21	Kensington
2013-14	Tea Tree Gully	2021-22	West Torrens
2014-15	East Torrens		

Twenty20 Titles

2005-06	Sturt	2014-15	Glenelg
2006-07	Kensington	2015-16	Tea Tree Gully
2007-08	Tea Tree Gully	2016-17	West Torrens
2008-09	Port Adelaide	2017-18	Tea Tree Gully
2009-10	Northern Districts	2018-19	East Torrens
2010-11	Sturt	2019-20	Adelaide University
2011-12	Tea Tree Gully	2020-21	Adelaide University
2012-13	Tea Tree Gully	2021-22	Port Adelaide
2013-14	Tea Tree Gully		

Recent Bradman Medal winners

2000-01	Mike Smith (University)	2012-13	Sam Miller (Prospect)
2001-02	Tim Haysman (Sturt)	2013-14	Jake Brown (Kensington)
2002-03	Ryan Harris (Northern Dists)	2014-15	Jake Brown (Kensington)
2003-04	Shane Deitz (Southern Dists)	2015-16	Simon Roberts (Sturt)
2004-05	Ben Johnson (Adelaide)	2016-17	Daniel Drew (West Torrens)
2005-06	Luke Williams (Adelaide)	2017-18	Kelvin Smith (West Torrens)
2006-07	Ben Hook (Glenelg)	2018-19	Jake Brown (Kensington)
2007-08	Luke Williams (Adelaide)	2019-20	Cam Valente (Adelaide)
2008-09	Matthew Weeks (Port Adel)	2020-21	Brad Davis (Sturt) tied w
2009-10	Luke Williams (Adelaide)	tied	Sam Kerber (Adelaide Uni)
2010-11	Chadd Sayers (Woodville)	2021-22	Will Bosisto (Adelaide Uni)
2011-12	Sam Raphael (Adelaide)		

Batting - 8000 or more Runs

	Career	Inns	NO	HS	Runs	Avge	100s
CW Bradbrook	1971/72-1996/97	325	24	169	9509	31.59	17
RJ Zadow	1971/72-1995/96	326	47	166	9505	34.06	16
JM Brown	**2004/05-2021/22**	**255**	**31**	**181**	**9325**	**41.62**	**15**
MP Faull	1983/84-2002/03	278	24	208*	9094	35.80	20
DE Pritchard	1910/11-1935/36	249	27	327*	8817	39.71	25
GW Harris	1915/16-1939/40	234	24	205*	8744	41.63	27
BJ Hook	1990/91-2006/07	256	35	156	8605	38.93	22
CR Bradbrook	1987/88-2009/10	314	31	257	8309	29.36	10
CLB Starr	1925/26-1952/53	259	32	183*	8285	36.49	20

Bowling - 600 or more Wickets

	Career Span	Wickets	Avge	Best	5 w I
NL Williams	1918/19-1941/42	894	18.85	9-22	84
JPF Travers	1890/91-1921/22	819	17.11	9-86	74
AT Sincock	1966/67-1994/95	762	20.66	9-50	30
G Giffen	1874/75-1910/11	744	12.69	10-67	74
GC Clarke	1955/56-1978/79	724	16.57	10-21	43
DJ Lambert	1963/64-1984/85	636	20.40	9-80	39
RJ Stratfold	1956/57-1974/75	624	18.08	9-39	39
PH Coombe	1898/99-1921/22	623	19.57	8-12	34

TASMANIA PREMIER LEAGUE CRICKET - LADDER (9 sides, 20 matches, top four)

	Won Out	Won First	Drawn	Lost First	Lost Out	Points	Quotient
South Hobart/Sandy Bay	-	12	4	4	-	64	1.52
Greater Northern	-	11	2	7	-	56	1.05
New Town	1	8	4	7	-	54	1.24
Lindisfarne	-	10	4	6	-	54	1.06
Glenorchy	1	8	1	10		51	0.88
Kingborough	-	7	6	7	-	40	0.95
North Hobart	-	5	5	10	-	33	0.84
Clarence	-	5	5	8	2	33	0.83
University of Tasmania	-	5	5	12	-	29	0.82

Leading Batting

	M	Inns	NO	HS	Runs	Avge	100/50
Anthony Mosca (New Town)	**18**	**18**	**2**	**139**	**841**	**52.56**	**3/5**
Dylan Hay (Kingborough)	19	21	4	181*	830	48.82	1/5
Harry Manenti (New Town)	19	19	2	107	737	43.35	1/6
Sean Willis (South Hobart)	22	21	2	85*	733	38.58	-/6
Navrojdeep Virk (Sth Hob/Sandy Bay)	21	22	3	205*	724	38.11	2/2

Leading Bowling

	M	Overs	Wkts	Avge	Best	5/10
Cameron Valente (Sth Hob/S Bay)	**24**	**256.2**	**47**	**17.79**	**7-55**	**1/-**
Harry Manenti (New Town)	19	215.2	43	18.23	7-40	1/1
Jonathon Chapman (Greater Northern)	20	189.5	39	16.74	4-25	-/-
Tushaar Garg (Glenorchy)	21	244.1	37	26.68	5-16	1/-
Alex Vincent (Kingborough)	19	175.2	33	24.94	4-100	-/-

Keeping: Josh Pride (Kingborough) 24 (22ct/2st), Thomas McGann (Lindisfarne) 24 (23ct/1st), Michael Jones (Clarence) 20 (19ct/1st).

PREMIER LEAGUE TWENTY 20 FINAL at Bellerive Oval on Wednesday January 26, 2022 – Greater Northern won by 3 wickets. South Hobart/Sandy Bay 7-143 cc (J Chapman 4-25) **lost to Greater Northern 7-144** (19 overs) (C Eastoe 43; CT Valente 2-25, TD Andrews 3-25). *Jono Chapman (Award) who took four wickets including Tom Andrews (13) and Cam Valente (6).*

KOOKABURRA CUP - 50 OVER FINAL at Bellerive Oval on Sunday February 13, 2022 – South Hobart/Sandy Bay won by 147 runs. South Hobart/Sandy Bay 6-292 cc (EM Vines 56, TD Andrews 65, CT Valente 57, AJ Doolan 48*; D Singh 4-57) **def Glenorchy 145** (35.4 overs) (RW Graham-Daft 65*; CT Valente 3-17). *Man of the match (Danny Buckingham Medal): Cam Valente faced 63 balls and hit 5 fours and took two early wickets at Glenorchy slipped to 4-23 in the run chase. It was the merged clubs seventh one-day title.*

AWARDS: Emerson Rodwell Medal won by Harry Manenti (New Town) with 22 votes. Cam Valente (SHSB) was runner up on 20. Then came Tushaar Garg (Glenorchy) 16 and Jarrod Freeman (Lindisfarne) and Jono Chapman (Greater Northern) on 14. Club Championship: Kingborough. Spirit of Cricket: Clarence. Ground of the Year: Kingstown Twin Ovals (James Di Saia). Under 17 Player of the Year (Michael Di Venuto Medal): Luke Quinlan (Lindisfarne).
Under 15 Player of the Year (Tim Paine Medal): Cooper Stubbs (South Hobart/Sandy Bay).
Inductees to Cricket Tasmania Hall of Fame: Michael GH Allen, Maxwell Coombes and Belinda Page.
First Grade Team of the Year: Eammon Vines (SHSB), Mac Wright (Captain, Lindisfarne), Dylan Hay (Kingborough), Jake Doran (University of Tasmania), Navrojdeep Virk (Glenorchy), Jarrod Freeman (Lindisfarne), Cam Valente (SHSB), Harry Manenti (New Town), Tom Andrews (SHSB), Tushaar Garg (Glenorchy), Jono Chapman (Greater Northern). Coach: Tim Coyle (Greater Northern), Umpires of the Year: Wade Stewart and Sam Burns.

Premier League Grand Final at TCA Ground, Hobart on March 25, 26 & 27, 2022 – New Town won on first innings.

South Hobart/Sandy Bay		B	M	4	6	New Town		B	M	4	6
TW Willoughby	c Wright b Mupariwa	22	48	61	3	J Randall	c Hine b Bell	11	57	71	
EM Vines	c Mosca b B Manenti	33	79	96	3	AJ Mosca	c Nicholls b Kuepper	139	297	400	15
S Willis *	c Mupariwa b B Manenti	72	160	207	9	1	MJ Owen *	c Vines b Valente	10	22	26	2
CT Valente	c Wright b Owen	9	20	23	1	HJ Manenti	b Andrews	83	169	194	9
TD Andrews	c Di Venuto b Montgomery	130	140	140	22	BA Manenti	b Kuepper	86	102	136	10	1
H Nicholls	c Di Venuto b H Manenti	35	75	75	7	T Mupariwa	not out	4	22	30	
S Voss	c Di Venuto b Montgomery	5	19	19		S Wright	not out	6	5	6	1
K Hine +	c Di Venuto b H Manenti	7	31	31	1	JW Di Venuto +					
U Butt	c Mosca b B Manenti	2	31	31		J Vince					
GT Bell	b H Manenti	10	28	28		T Pybus					
C Kuepper	not out	9	23	23		J Montgomery					
	8 b, 3 lb, 1w	12					4 b, 4 lb, 2 nb, 1w	11			
	109 overs	346					112.2 overs	5-350			

1-48 (Willoughby), 2-72 (Vines), 3-95 (Valente), 4-270 (Willis), 5-274 (Andrews), 6-288 (Voss), 7-310 (Hine), 8-323 (Butt), 9-327 (Nichols), 10-346 (Bell).

1-37 (Randall), 2-54 (Owen), 3-202 (H Manenti), 4-324 (Mosca), 5-343 (B Manenti)

Bowling	O	M	R	W	wd	nb	Bowling	O	M	R	W	wd	nb
HJ Manenti	24	8	64	3	1		GT Bell	28	5	87	1		1
T Pybus	4	1	9	0			CT Valente	32	3	105	1		1
T Mupariwa	18	7	42	1			U Butt	11.2	0	47	0	1	
BA Manenti	39	8	116	3			TD Andrews	24	3	50	1		
J Montgomery	15	2	55	2			C Kuepper	17	2	53	2		
MJ Owen	9	1	49	1									

Toss: New Town. Umpires: DR Close, M Qureshi. Roger Woolley Medal: AJ Mosca (New Town). Stumps Day One: South Hobart/Sandy Bay 8-323 (100 overs) H Nicholls 35, Day Two: New Town 3-241 (85 overs) Mosca 107, B Manenti 19

Recent Premierships

2008-09	University	2015-16	South Hobart/Sandy Bay
2009-10	North Hobart	2016-17	South Hobart/Sandy Bay
2010-11	Lindisfarne	2017-18	Clarence
2011-12	Clarence	2018-19	Lindisfarne
2012-13	Glenorchy	2019-20	Lindisfarne
2013-14	Glenorchy	2020-21	University of Tasmania
2014-15	Kingborough	2021-22	New Town

Recent One-day Titles

2008-09	South Hobart/Sandy Bay	2015-16	South Hobart/Sandy Bay
2009-10	North Hobart	2016-17	Clarence
2010-11	Kingborough	2017-18	University of Tasmania
2011-12	Clarence	2018-19	South Hobart/Sandy Bay
2012-13	University of Tasmania	2019-20	Lindisfarne
2013-14	Lindisfarne	2020-21	University of Tasmania
2014-15	Glenorchy	2021-22	South Hobart/Sandy Bay

Twenty20 Winners

2008-09	Clarence		2015-16	Lindisfarne
2009-10	North Hobart		2016-17	New Town
2010-11	University		2017-18	South Hobart/Sandy Bay
2011-12	Kingborough		2018-19	North Hobart
2012-13	Lindisfarne		2019-20	Lindisfarne
2013-14	Glenorchy		2020-21	North Hobart
2014-15	South Hobart/Sandy Bay		2021-22	Greater Northern

Recent Emerson Rodwell Medal winners

2007-08	Alex Doolan (SH/SB)		2015-16	Daniel Salpietro (Clarence)
2008-09	Adam Polkinghorne (SH/SB)		2016-17	Harry Evans (Kingborough)
2009-10	Andrew Kealy (Uni)		2017-18	Harry Allanby (Clarence)
2010-11	Mark Divin (Kingborough)		tied with	Caleb Jewell (North Hobart)
2011-12	Mark Divin (Kingborough)		2018-19	Harry Allanby (Clarence)
2012-13	Brett Geeves (Glenorchy)		2019-20	Trent Keep (Kingborough)
2013-14	Jonathon Wells (Clarence)		2020-21	Alex Doolan (SH/SB)
2014-15	Luke Butterworth (Glenorchy)		2021-22	Harry Manenti (New Town)

Overall Records
Batting - 9000 or more Runs

	Career	Mts	Inns	NO	HS	Runs	Avge	100s
Ron Morrisey	1930/31 − 1962/63	360	456	76	197	19170	50.45	48
Emerson Rodwell	1938/39 − 1963/64	293	344	35	215	11703	37.87	29
Kenneth Burn	1883/84 − 1909/10	164	222	39	365*	11450	62.57	31
James Dykes	1988/89 − 2008/09	272	273	51	189	9793	44.11	25
Brian Richardson	1951/52 − 1977/78	269	314	41	181*	9612	35.21	15
Brian Patterson	1954/55 − 1980/81	265	314	40	179*	9609	35.07	14
Gerald James	1924/25 − 1952/53	322	398	36	166*	9455	26.12	12
Charles Eady	1884/85 − 1912/13	157	216	33	566	9446	51.62	20
Roger Woolley	1971/72 − 1997/98	275	275	63	162*	9117	43.00	15

Bowling - 700 or more Wickets

	Career Span	Mts	Wickets	Avge	Best	5 w I
Gerald James	1924/25 − 1952/53	322	949	15.90	9-11	61
Alan Newton	1906/07 − 1935/36	218	853	15.58	8-43	69
Colin Richardson	1943/44 − 1960/61	224	845	11.46	9-35	64
Don Broughton	1947/48 − 1972/73	260	766	16.77	7-37	45
Noel Diprose	1938/39 − 1962/63	279	762	13.49	8-30	38
Charles Eady	1884/85 − 1912/13	157	752	12.85	10-44	79
Mark Colegrave	1986/87 − 2008/09	296	744	17.13	9-42	45
Brian Patterson	1954/55 − 1980/81	265	731	15.06	8-33	44
James Tringrove	1931/32 − 1948/49	219	722	14.99	10-53	41

VICTORIAN PREMIER LEAGUE CRICKET LADDER - (18 sides, 16 matches, top eight)

	Won First inns	Lost First inns	Drawn	Points	NRR
St Kilda	14	1	1	78	0.960
Carlton	11	2	3	66	0.852
Melbourne	11	3	2	63	0.624
Casey-South Melbourne	10	5	1	58	0.632
Footscray	9	4	3	55	0.183
Richmond	9	6	1	52	0.438
Geelong	9	6	1	49	0.190
Essendon	9	7	1	46	-0.163
Northcote	7	8	1	40	0.243
Prahran	7	8	1	40	0.015
Melbourne Uni	6	8	2	38	-0.014
Ringwood	6	9	1	35	-0.297
Fitzroy Doncaster	6	9	1	32	-0.308
Dandenong	5	10	1	30	-0.330
Frankston Peninsula	5	10	1	29	-0.186
Greenvale Kangaroos	3	11	2	20	-1.198
Camberwell Magpies	3	12	1	18	-0.994
Kingston Hawthorn	2	12	2	15	-0.668

Leading Batting

	M	Inns	NO	HS	Runs	Avge	100/50
Tom Rogers (Ringwood)	11	11	1	**200***	**898**	**89.80**	**4/2**
Hayden Butterworth (Geelong)	16	16	-	117	781	48.81	4/2
Harrison Smythe (Carlton)	16	16	5	100*	684	62.18	1/6
Adam Crosthwaite (St Kilda)	17	16	4	105*	681	56.75	1/2
Luke Manders (Casey/Sth Melb)	16	16	1	116	671	44.73	2/3

Leading Bowling

	M	Overs	Wkts	Avge	Best	5/10
Ruwantha Kellepotha (Casey/SM)	**18**	**170.5**	**37**	**15.59**	**5-25**	**1/-**
Dominic Matarazzo (Richmond)	17	104.1	32	11.41	8-16	3/-
Liam Bowe (Essendon)	16	145.1	32	20.44	4-24	-/-
Evan Gulbis (Carlton)	14	100.4	29	11.55	5-29	1/-

Keeping: Devin Pollock 33 **(28ct/5st)**, Jai Lemire (Carlton) 26 (23ct/3st), Patrick Rowe (St Kilda) 26 (23ct/3st)

AWARDS: Jack Ryder Medal: Won by Dean Russ of Footscray polling 30 votes, with Geelong all-rounder Hayden Butterworth and Carlton batter Harrison Smyth equal second on 28.

Club Championship: St Kilda.

Team of the year: Adam Crosthwaite (St Kilda, Captain), Tom Rogers (Ringwood), Hayden Butterworth (Geelong), Harrison Smyth (Carlton), Jack Harper (Melbourne, wk), Jack Lalor (Northcote), Dean Russ (Footscray), Fergus O'Neill (Melbourne), Ruwantha Kellepotha (Casey South Melbourne), Dominic Matarazzo (Richmond), Michael Topp (Northcote), Liam Bowe (Essendon).

Aaron Finch Medal (Vic Super Slam) James Nanopoulos (Frankston Peninsula).

Premier League Grand Final at the Albert Ground on April 2, 2022 – Carlton won by 4 wickets

Casey-South Melbourne

			B	M	4	6
A Chandrasinghe	c & b Smyth	25	58	64	2	
L Manders	c Lemire b O'Sullivan	63	103	146	6	
MT Wallace *	c Harvey b Crone	14	25	35	2	
HA Kannan	run out (Stevenson-Lemire)	16	18	24	1	1
DJ Pollock +	b O'Sullivan	17	27	44	1	
LJ Shelton	not out	32	35	58	2	1
RP Kellepotha	lbw b Gulbis	22	18	22	2	1
LJ Sperling	c sub (McKenna) b O'Sullivan	3	7	9		
DB Webb	b Gulbis	2	2	4		
N Lambden	c Stevenson b Gulbis	0	1	2		
JN Fry	not out	0	0	2		
	1 b, 2 lb, 3 w	6				
	49 overs	9-200				

1-56 (Chandrasinghe), 2-85 (Wallace), 3-106 (Kannan), 4-133 (Manders), 5-146 (Pollock), 6-181 (Kellepotha), 7-193 (Sperling), 8-198 (Webb), 9-198 (N Lambden)

Bowling	O	M	R	W	wd	nb
CA Stevenson	5	0	25	0		
EP Gulbis	10	2	35	3	1	
C Rutland	5	1	19	0		
TJ Smyth	9	0	44	1		
XA Crone	10	1	42	1		
EC O'Sullivan	10	1	32	3	2	

Carlton

			B	M	4	6
EP Gulbis *	c Pollock b Fry	28	25	48	6	
MW Harvey	b Fry	5	12	18	1	
B Stepien	c Sheldon b Sperling	51	72	93	8	
HJ Smyth	c Pollock b Fry	0	2	8		
NJ Ross	c Kellepotha b Fry	0	4	4		
TJ Smyth	not out	52	101	140	2	
C Rutland	c Sperling b Kellepotha	45	56	77	2	2
XA Crone	not out	18	9	12	2	1
CA Stevenson						
J Lemire +						
EC O'Sullivan						
	1 b, 2 lb, 3 w	6				
	46.5 overs	6-205				

1-18 (Harvey), 2-60 (Gulbis), 3-66 (H Smyth), 4-66 (Ross), 5-110 (Stepien), 6-185 (Rutland)

Bowling	O	M	R	W	wd	nb
N Lambden	8	0	51	0	1	
JN Fry	10	3	28	4	2	
DB Webb	1.5	0	25	0		
RP Kellepotha	10	0	34	1		
LJ Shelton	10	0	30	0		
LJ Sperling	7	0	34	1		

Toss: Carlton.   Umpires: C Grant, M van Eck.   John Scholes Medal: TJ Smyth (Carlton)

Recent Premierships

2003-04	St Kilda	2013-14	Footscray-Edgewater
2004-05	St Kilda	2014-15	Ringwood
2005-06	St Kilda	2015-16	Fitzroy-Doncaster
2006-07	Dandenong	2016-17	Fitzroy-Doncaster
2007-08	Ringwood	2017-18	Dandenong
2008-09	Ringwood	2018-19	Carlton
2009-10	Melbourne	2019-20	Melbourne
2010-11	Dandenong	2020-21	Prahran
2011-12	Richmond	2021-22	Carlton
2012-13	Melbourne		

Recent One-day/White-ball Titles

2006-07	St Kilda	2012-13	Melbourne
2007-08	Carlton	2013-14	Melbourne
2008-09	Melbourne	2014-15	Monash Tigers
2009-10	St Kilda	2015-16	Fitzroy Doncaster
2010-11	Carlton	2016-17	Melbourne
2011-12	Prahran	2017-18	Dandenong

Recent Twenty20 Titles

2007-08	Melbourne	2013-14	Footscray Edgewater
2008-09	St Kilda	2014-15	to 2017-18 No Final contested
2009-10	Geelong		***Became Super Slam in 2018-19***
2010-11	No Final Played	2018-19	Carlton
2011-12	Prahran	2019-20	Carlton
2012-13	Melbourne	2020-21	Not held

Recent Jack Ryder Medal winners

2007-08	S Spoljaric (Hawth/Mon Uni)	2015-16	Steven Taylor (Northcote)
2008-09	GD Cross (St Kilda)	2016-17	Brendan Drew (Camberwell Magpies)
2009-10	GC Rummans (St Kilda)	2017-18	Trent Lawford (Fitzroy-Doncaster)
2010-11	Theo Doropoulos (Northcote)	2018-19	Brett Forsyth (Dandenong)
2011-12	Clive Rose (Casey/Sth Melb)	2019-20	David King (Ringwood)
2012-13	Brenton McDonald (Melbourne)	tied with	James Seymour (Essendon)
2013-14	James Miller (Prahran)	2020-21	Scott Edwards (Richmond)
2014-15	Ian Holland (Ringwood)	2021-22	Dean Russ (Footscray)

Most runs ever in Competition

	Clubs	Career	Inns	NO	HS	Runs	Avge	100s
WG Ayres	Melbourne, Dandenong	1983-2008	396	36	218	15277	42.43	41
GM Watts	Fitzroy-Doncaster	1975-2001	344	38	260*	12933	42.26	25
WJ Scholes	Carlton, Fitzroy-Doncaster	1965-1996	400	47	156	12693	35.96	26
J Ryder	Collingwood, Northcote,	1906-1943	364	61	267	12677	41.83	37
PA McAlister	E Melb, Hawthorne E Melb	1889-1922	331	45	265*	11893	41.58	31

Most wickets

	Clubs	Career Span	Wickets	Avge	Best	5 wI	10wM
H Ironmonger	Melbourne, St Kilda	1913-1935	862	13.03	9-30	80	11
DD Blackie	St Kilda, Prahran	1905-1935	803	15.09	10-64	70	8
JL Keating	Collingwood, Richmond	1910-1942	636	18.49	9-13	35	-
TA Carlton	North Melbourne, Essendon	1908-1941	632	16.14	9-58	46	3
KW Kirby	Essendon	1959-1982	623	19.67	9-34	39	2

WACA FIRST GRADE CRICKET - LADDER (16 sides, 15 matches, top six)

	Won Out	Won First inn	Drawn	Lost First inn	Lost Out	Points	Quotient
South Perth	1	10	-	3	1	87	1.1747
Subiaco Floreat	-	11	1	3	-	85	1.7623
Willeton	-	11	-	4	-	78	1.4747
Perth	-	11	-	4	-	78	1.3886
Midland-Guildford	1	7	-	6	-	76	1.1611
Melville	-	10	1	4	-	75	1.2893
Fremantle	-	9	-	6	-	70	1.3441
Mount Lawley	-	9	-	6	-	58	1.1466
Bayswater-Morley	1	7	1	7	-	57	1.1023
Claremont-Nedlands	-	7	-	8	-	50	1.0500
Rockingham-Mandurah	1	6	1	8	-	47	0.9013
Wanneroo	-	4	1	10	-	35	0.6229
Scarborough	-	5	-	10	-	34	0.7056
University	-	4	-	11	-	32	0.8115
Joondalup	-	4	-	11	-	28	0.7469
Gosnells	-	-	-	14	1	0	0.3568

Leading Batting	M	Inns	NO	HS	Runs	Avge	100/50
Sam Fanning (Perth)	16	19	2	166*	867	**51.00**	4/1
Geremy Fatouros (Subiaco-Floreat)	19	20	2	140	745	41.39	1/4
Shayne Wornes (Willeton)	17	17	1	125	715	44.69	1/4
Fraser Hay (Melville)	16	16	1	101	714	47.60	3/4
Jayden Goodwin (Subiaco-Floreat)	17	17	-	131	684	40.24	2/4

Leading Bowling	M	Overs	Wkts	Avge	Best	5/10
Hamish McKenzie (Subiaco-Floreat)	**19**	**260.3**	**58**	**12.86**	**7-45**	**5/-**
Daniel Turkich (Clarmont-Nedlands)	15	242.1	39	16.05	6-46	3/-
Alex Bevilaqua (South Perth)	18	212.4	37	15.70	6-45	3/-
Michael Hart (Subiaco-Floreat)	18	209.4	36	14.89	7-47	1/-
Jay Chislett (University)	15	182.5	35	17.06	7-85	2/-

Keeping: Ben Tredget (Subiaco-Floreat) 42 (29ct/13st), Andrew Bottege (Mt Lawley) 41 (35ct/6 st), Joel Curtis (Perth) 40 (30ct/10st).

2021/22 AWARDS – Olly Cooley Medal: Hamish McKenzie (Subiaco-Floreat) with 16 votes, then came Clint Hinchliffe (Mt Lawley) 14, Alex Bevilaqua (South Perth) 13 and Kaiden Cookson (Fremantle) 13.

Team of the Year: Sam Fanning (Perth), Jayden Goodwin (Subiaco-Floreat), Fraser Hay (Melville, Captain), Nick Maiolo (Scarborough), Shayne Wornes (Willetton), Darius D'Silva (Mount Lawley), Abdrew Bottega (Mount Lawley, WK), Hamish McKenzie (Subiaco-Floreat), Daniel Turkich (Claremont-Nedlands), Alex Bevilaqua (South Perth), Justin Kandiah (Midland-Guildford), Kyle Wiggers (Bayswater-Morley)

Club Championship: Subiaco-Floreat. Male Spirit of Cricket Award: Gosnells.

Coach of Year: Wayne Clark (Subiaco-Floreat). Best First Grade Umpire: Todd Rann. Peter McConnell Medal: Dennis Smallwood. Best Pitch (Roy Abbott) Award: Stevens Reserve West. Most Improved Pitch Award: UWA Sports Park.

PREMIER TWENTY 20 FINAL at the WACA on Sunday February 6, 2022 (Floodlit) – Melville won by 6 wickets.
Subiaco-Floreat 119 (20 overs) (J Goodwin 47; B Jackson 2-16, B Reed 2-24, T Kerr-Shephard 2-21) **lost to Melville 4-120** (19.4 overs) (F Hay 58; M Hart 2-33, C Hansberry 2-15)
Man of the Match: Fraser Hay faced 42 balls, hit 5 fours and 2 sixes

Leading Twenty20 Stats 2021-22

Batting	Runs	Avge	HS	SR	100s	Bowling	Wkts	Avge	Econ	Best
Daniel Kennedy (Frem)	276	69.0	70*	160	-	**Kaiden Cookson (Frem)**	11	8.4	4.65	5-9
Fraser Hay (Melville)	234	46.8	73	151	-	Liam Stevens (Scarborough)	11	9.3	5.15	4-13
Nick Maiolo (Scraborough)	206	34.3	75	132	-	Mark Turner (Melville)	11	10.2	5.38	3-9
Aaron Hardie (Willeton)	184	92.0	99*	154	-	Brad Turner (Melville)	11	12.4	5.71	4-30
Tim Monteleone (Sub-Floreat)	175	35.0	65	125	-	Chris Hansberry (Sub-Flor)	9	8.5	4.28	3-13

50 OVER FINAL at the WACA on Sunday February 20, 2022 – Subiaco Floreat won by 51 runs
Subiaco Floreat 9-209 cc (B Tredget 57) **def Mount Lawley 158** (43.2 overs) (SJ Walters 54; H McKenzie 5-30)
Man of the match was Mt Lawley's Hamish McKenzie for his five wicket haul.

Grand Final at the WACA on March 12 & 13, 2022 – Subiaco Floreat won on first innings

Subiaco-Floreat First innings		B	M	4	6	Second innings		B	M	4	6
B Tredget+	c Hale b Bevilaqua	14	55	77	1	c Dallimore b Ringrose	2	19	27		
J Goodwin	lbw b Gannon	1	17	25		c Leaver b Bevilaqua	21	65	78	2	
TJ Monteleone	lbw b Dallimore	0	6	13		c Moore b Botha	51	98	136	8	
G Fatouros *	c Gannon b Botha	46	100	127	7	not out	50	121	142	10	
H McKenzie	c Moore b Dallimore	38	61	103	7	c Stuart b Botha	0	3	5		
AC Lilly	b Botha	6	13	17	1	not out	15	26	52	3	
C Hansberry	c Moore b Botha	1	12	19							
M Hart	b Botha	0	2	1							
C Moldrich	c Gannon b Botha	0	1	1							
M Sculthorpe	lbw b Botha	1	14	17							
T Massey	not out	0	0	6							
	8 lb, 2 nb, 1 w	11				4 b, 4 lb, 2 nb, 1 w	11				
	46.3 overs	118				55 overs	4-150				

1-5 (Goodwin), 2-6 (Monteleone), 3-28 (Tredget), 4-98 (Fatouros), 5-116 (McKenzie), 6-116 (Lilly), 7-116 (Hart), 8-116 (Moldrich), 9-117 (Hansberry), 10-118 (Sculthorpe)

1-12 (Tredget), 2-41 (Goodwin), 3-97 (Monteleone), 4-97 (McKenzie)

Bowling	O	M	R	W	wd	nb		O	M	R	W	wd	nb
CJ Gannon	10	4	19	1									
LC Dallimore	16	6	36	2		2		9	3	26	0		
S Ringrose	3	0	13	0				7	3	15	1		
AA Bevilaqua	11	4	29	1				12	5	23	1	1	1
EG Botha	6.3	2	13	6	1			15	2	45	2		1
S Stuart								6	1	16	0		
J Mulder								6	1	17	0		

South Perth		B	M	4	6	Bowling	O	M	R	W	wd	nb
D Cleary	c Fatouros b Moldrich	5	23	23	1	M Hart	22.3	7	47	7	2	
B Guest	c Fatouros b Sculthorpe	12	36	73	1	C Moldrich	10	1	29	1		
T Hale	c Lilly b Hart	3	8	7		M Sculthorpe	5	0	14	1		
D Moore+	lbw b Hart	1	10	10		T Massey	2	1	5	0		
CJ Gannon	b Hart	15	35	50	3	H McKenzie	9	1	22	1		5
S Stuart *	lbw b McKenzie	23	40	55	4							
EG Botha	lbw b Hart	3	10	17								
AA Bevilaqua	lbw b Hart	9	21	38	2							
J Mulder	c Monteleone b Hart	13	26	41	1							
LC Dallimore	c Monteleone b Hart	14	58	72								
S Ringrose	not out	12	29	44	1							
	5 nb, 2 w	7										
	48.3 overs	117										

1-7 (Cleary), 2-10 (Hale), 3-12 (Moore), 4-33 (Guest), 5-43 (Gannon), 6-53 (Botha), 7-74 (Stuart), 8-81 (Bevilaqua), 9-90 (Mulder), 10-117 (Dallimore)

Toss: South Perth.   Umpires: T Steenholdt, T Rann.   Man of match: M Hart (Subiaco-Floreat)

Stumps Day One: South Perth 8-81 (33 overs), Mulder 5, Dallimore 0

Recent Premierships

2002-03	Subiaco-Floreat		2012-13	Joondalup
2003-04	Melville		2013-14	Wanneroo
2004-05	Melville		2014-15	Joondalup
2005-06	Claremont-Nedlands		2015-16	Rockingham-Mandurah
2006-07	Scarborough		2016-17	Subiaco-Floreat
2007-08	Scarborough		2017-18	Claremont-Nedlands
2008-09	Scarborough		2018-19	Claremont-Nedlands
2009-10	Scarborough		2019-20	Claremont-Nedlands
2010-11	Subiaco-Floreat		2020-21	Wanneroo
2011-12	Wanneroo		2021-22	Subiaco-Floreat

Most Premierships won by: North Perth 12, Fremantle 10, Scarborough 9, University 8, Subiaco 7, South Perth 7, Claremont 7, Subiaco-Floreat 7, Mt Lawley 6, East Perth 6, Claremont-Nedlands 5, Midland Guildford 4, West Perth 4, Bayswater-Morley 3, Melville 3, Wanneroo 3, Joondalup 2, Nedlands 2, Claremont-Cottesloe 2, Rockingham-Mandurah 1.

Recent One-day League Premierships

2011-12	Melville		2017-18	Claremont-Nedlands
2012-13	Melville		2018-19	Claremont-Nedlands
2013-14	Subiaco-Floreat		2019-20	Claremont-Nedlands
2014-15	Joondalup		2020-21	Claremont-Nedlands
2015-16	Claremont-Nedlands		2021-22	Subiaco-Floreat
2016-17	Claremont-Nedlands			

Recent Statewide Twenty20 Titles

2009-10	Rockingham-Mandurah		2016-17	Fremantle
2010-11	Melville		2017-18	Wanneroo Districts
2011-12	Scarborough		2018-19	Melville
2012-13	Melville		2019-20	Fremantle
2013-14	Melville		2020-21	South Perth
2014-15	Claremont-Nedlands		2021-22	Melville
2015-16	Joondalup			

Recent Cooley Medal winners

2002-03	CG Mason (Bays-Morley)		2011-12	T Hopes (Scarborough)
2003-04	Jim Allenby (Claremont-Nedlands)		2012-13	Craig Simmons (Rockingham-Mandurah)
tied w	David Bandy (Scarborough)		2013-14	Tim Armstrong (Fremantle)
2004-05	PM Kennan (Perth)		2014-15	Justin Coetzee (Scarborough)
2005-06	S Howman (Subiaco-Floreat)		2015-16	Stewart Walters (Midland-Guildford)
2006-07	Stewart Walters (Mid-Guildford)			Brendon Diamanti (Rockingham-Mandurah)
2007-08	Wes Robinson (Claremont-Nedlands)		2016-17	Tim David (Claremont-Nedlands)
2008-09	G Dixon (Wanneroo)		2017-18	Dane Ugle (Rockingham-Mandurah)
2009-10	P Davis (Mt Lawley)		2018-19	Craig Simmons (Rockingham-Mandurah)
tied w	M Johnston (Willeton)		2019-20	Brooke Guest (South Perth)
2010-11	David Bandy (Subiaco-Floreat)		2020-21	Brad Hope (Claremont-Nedlands)
tied w	Matt Johnston (Willeton)		2021-22	Hamish McKenzie (Subiaco-Floreat)

WOMENS CRICKET
ANOTHER BRILLIANT TWELVE MONTHS FOR AUSTRALIA
RECORD FROM SEPTEMBER 1, 2021 TO SEPTEMBER 1, 2022

Format	Matches	Won	Lost	Drawn/NR
Tests	2	0	0	2
ODIs	15	14	1	0
T20s	14	10	0	4
Total	31	24	1	6

The Australian Women's Team had one of their most successful periods in the past twelve months, winning multi-format series over India and England, before going unbeaten to win the 50-over World Cup in New Zealand and then win Gold at the Birmingham Commonwealth games. They lost just once in 31 games over the period, the defeat in an ODI to India on September 26, 2021 ending a winning streak of 26 matches.

There were some star individual performances over the time, none better than the Alyssa Healy's 170 off 138 balls in the 50-over World Cup Final at Christchurch. Tahlia McGrath was one the big improvers in the period to hold her own as an all-rounder. Here are the combined numbers of the leading run scorers and wicket takers across the period since September 2021.

Batting	Inn	NO	Runs	Avg	HS	100	50		Bowling	Wkts	Avg	Best
Beth Mooney	26	10	1000	62.5	125*	1	8		Jess Jonassen	32	17.3	4-17
Meg Lanning	29	8	995	47.3	135*	1	7		Alana King	31	20.8	4-8
Alyssa Healy	30	2	833	29.7	170	2	3		Tahlia McGrath	29	23.0	3-4
Rachael Haynes	20	4	795	49.6	130	1	5		Ash Gardner	26	22.9	3-16
Tahlia McGrath	20	6	758	54.1	74	-	6		Megan Schutt	25	24.8	3-20

On January 29, 2022 it was announced that Ash Gardner had won the Belinda Clark Medal. Across 10 innings Gardner struck 281 runs at an average of 35.1 that included four half centuries and a top score of 73 not out in a memorable T20 win against New Zealand in Hamilton. A valuable asset in the field, Gardner's off-spin broke through for nine wickets, two shy of Sophie Molineux's year-leading 11.

The quintessential allrounder, Gardner finished the voting period inside Australia's top three run scorers and top five wicket takers across all formats. Gardner won her first Belinda Clark Award with 54 votes from Beth Mooney (47) and Alyssa Healy (39) who finished second and third respectively in the voting.

The One-Day International Player of the Year went to Alyssa Healy for the third consecutive year. Healy claimed top honours with 13 votes ahead of Rachael Haynes (10) and Megan Schutt (10). Mooney took out the Female Twenty20 Player of the Year with 13 votes, ahead of Tahlia McGrath (10) and Gardner (6).

Ash Gardner with the Belinda Clark Medal	Alyssa Healy – ODI Player of the year

Domestically, the Scorchers won their first WBBL title, having been runner-up in 2016/17 and 2017/18. The Renegades Harmanpreet Kaur was the MVP with 31 votes, finishing ahead of Perth Scorchers pair Beth Mooney and Sophie Devine on 28. The Heat's Grace Harris (25) was fourth with teammate Georgia Redmayne tied for fifth with Hurricanes batter Mignon du Preez, both on 24.

Tasmania won their first ever WNCL title, with a strong win in the final by nine wickets over South Australia.

ACT Meteor Zoe Cooke was named Community Champion for her work to support, promote and advocate for the women's game in the ACT through coaching and mentoring roles, particularly in the pathway system.

In addition to the volunteer roles she plays within community cricket, Zoe also puts her hand up for several other charitable causes such as the Grizzly Bear Adoption Program for the World Wildlife Foundation, One Foot Forward challenge for Black Dog Institute and Breast Cancer Awareness Month.

AUSTRALIA v INDIA – HOSTS WIN 11 POINTS TO FIVE
FIRST TWENTY20 INTERNATIONAL – MACKAY

On a bright sunny morning, Brown gave Australia an excellent start with the ball when she had Verma caught down the leg-side on the pull and Mandhana driving a catch to backward point. Raj took her time to get going and when on 11 copped a nasty blow on the helmet from a Perry short ball. She and Bhatia added 77 in 21 overs to pass the 100 mark, but then Brown returned and took two wickets to reduce India to 4-129. Raj was slow in taking 90 balls to get to her fifty and eventually went to a fine stumping by Healy, which bounced and turned considerably. India at one stage looked like they were going to battle to get to 200, but Ghosh and Goswami made some good hits in adding 45 to set Australia 226 to win.

On a good pitch India looked about 50 short and so it proved as the openers dominated the Indian pace bowlers, with Healy hitting some magnificent pull-shots early in her knock. She also dominated the spinners, lofting Yadav straight for six on the way to passing 2,000 ODI runs for Australia. After being caught at mid-off, Haynes hit a nice sweep for four to reach her 50 as she and Lanning continued the comfortable progress to victory. The Aussie skipper found the gaps with ease as the second added 101 to complete a comfortable win, their 25th in a row.

First ODI at Harrup Park, Mackay on September 21, 2021 - Australia won by 9 wickets

India			B	M	4	6	Australia			B	M	4	6
S Verma	c Healy b Brown	8	10	17	2		RL Haynes	not out	93	100	171	7	
SS Mandhana	c Haynes b Brown	16	18	26	1		AJ Healy+	c Vastrakar b Yadav	77	77	87	8	2
YH Bhatia	c Haynes b Brown	35	51	90	2		MM Lanning*	not out	53	69	83	7	
MD Raj*	st Healy b Molineux	63	107	127	3		EA Perry						
DB Sharma	c Wareham b Brown	9	19	20	1		BL Mooney						
P Vastrakar	c Molineux b Darlington	17	29	34	1		AK Gardner						
RM Ghosh+	not out	32	29	47	3	1	TM McGrath						
S Rana	b Darlington	2	11	8			SG Molineux						
JN Goswami	st Healy b Molineux	20	24	25	1	1	GL Wareham						
Meghna Singh	not out	1	2	2			HJ Darlington						
P Yadav							DR Brown						
	3 lb, 19 w	22						1 lb, 3 w	4				
10 overs : 2-51	50 overs, 202 mins	8-225					10 overs : 0-52	41 overs, 171 mins	1-227				

1-31 (Verma, 3.3), 2-38 (Mandhana, 5.1), 3-115 (Bhatia, 26.1),
4-129 (Sharma, 30.3), 5-166 (Raj, 37.4), 6-172 (Vastrakar, 40.1),
7-178 (Rana, 42.5), 8-223 (Goswami, 49.3)

1-126 (Healy, 21.2)

Bowling	O	M	R	W	wd	nb	Bowling	O	M	R	W	wd	nb
EA Perry	4	0	37	0	6		JN Goswami	10	0	38	0		
DR Brown	9	1	33	4	3		Meghna Singh	6	0	27	0	2	
TM McGrath	6	0	34	0	4		P Vastrakar	2	0	26	0		
AK Gardner	4	0	14	0			DB Sharma	4	0	31	0		
SG Molineux	9	0	39	2	1		P Yadav	10	0	58	1	1	
GL Wareham	10	0	36	0			S Rana	9	1	46	0		
HJ Darlington	8	1	29	2	1								

Toss: Australia. Umpires: PJ Gillespie, CA Polosak, BNJ Oxenford (TV), Ref: RW Stratford. Award: DR Brown (Aus).
Raj 50: 90 balls, 3x4. Haynes 50: 55 balls, 3x4, Healy 50: 56 balls, 5x4 1x6, 67 balls, 7x4   Crowd: 720. Points: Aus 2, India 0

SECOND ONE-DAY INTERNATIONAL – MACKAY

On another gorgeous Mackay day, India realised they needed to go harder in the early overs and did so with Mandhana putting away several short deliveries away to the fence, as the visitors raced to 50 inside the first eight overs. At 0-74 after 11 overs, things then came undone as India lost 3-21, with Verma dragging one on, Raj run out by Lanning after a mix-up with Mandhana and then Bhatia pulled a catch to mid-wicket. Mandhana and Ghosh retrieved the situation adding 76 in 13 overs, before the Indian opener's excellent knock ended when she drove a catch to point. Ghosh and the middle order all punished the Aussie bowlers and with 274 on the board, India had a formidable total.

India's defence of their total started perfectly when Healy was bowled between bat and pad from the third ball of the run chase. Lanning top-edged a pull to deep square-leg and then Haynes pushed one to cover, with Vastrakar's throw finding Perry short to leave Australia 3-34. When Gardner edged a catch to slip, Australia was 4-52 and facing their first ODI defeat since England beat them at Coff's Harbour on October 29, 2017.

McGrath came in to join Mooney and hit the gaps early to score some valuable boundaries as Australia looked to rebuild. She dominated the partnership and was first to reach 50, which was her first in ODIs. She had some luck being put down on 51 at deep mid-off off Sharma but continued to be the lead figure in an excellent stand of 126 from 23 overs, before being caught at backward square-leg.

With 97 still wanted off 69 balls, India were still favourites but couldn't contain the runs with Mooney reaching her second

ODI ton in the 46th over. Carey was playing a feisty innings and with heavy due making the ball tough to grip, Australia were still maintaining the charge, getting the target down to 13 required from the final over.

The experienced Goswami took the dewy ball and started with a full-toss that Mooney hit for three which included an overthrow. Carey scored two from the next delivery, which left eight wanted off the last four balls. Goswami then bowled a beamer which hit Mooney on the helmet and after a concussion check was allowed to continue. From the next ball Carey backed up well to pinch a bye and then Haynes scored a leg-bye which left five to win over two balls. Carey managed two off the fifth ball which left Australia wanting three to win off the last ball. Goswami bowled a high full-toss, Carey pulled a catch to square-leg and India think they have won the match. But it is referred upstairs and is deemed to be a no-ball, which means the last ball has to be re-bowled with Australia wanting two to win. Carey strikes it to wide long-on, Haynes races back for a second and Australia win, keeping their long winning streak alive.

Second ODI at Harrup Park, Mackay on September 24, 2021 (day/night) - Australia won by 5 wickets

India		B	M	4	6	Australia			B	M	4	6
SS Mandhana	c Mooney b McGrath	86	94	135	11	AJ Healy+	b Goswami		0	3	2	
S Verma	b Molineux	22	23	47	4	BL Mooney	not out		125	133	242	12
MD Raj*	run out (Lanning-Carey)	8	23	22	1	MM Lanning*	c Gayakwad b Meghna		6	21	24	1
YH Bhatia	c Gardner b Brown	3	14	12		EA Perry	run out (Vastrakar)		2	7	18	
RM Ghosh+	b McGrath	44	50	21	3	1	AK Gardner	c Bhatia b Vastrakar		12	24	27	2
DB Sharma	c Perry b McGrath	23	34	42	2	TM McGrath	c Bhatia b Sharma		74	77	100	9
P Vastrakar	b Molineux	29	37	57	1	NJ Carey	not out		39	38	66	2
JN Goswami	not out	28	25	32	3	SG Molineux						
Meghna Singh						GL Wareham						
RS Gayakwad						HJ Darlington						
P Yadav						DR Brown						
	5 b, 9 lb, 17 w	31					3 b, 4 lb, 3 nb, 7 w	17				
10 overs: 0-68	50 overs, 2 13 mins	7-274				10 overs: 3-34	50 overs, 242 mins	5-275				

1-74 (Verma, 11.1), 2-88 (Raj, 16.3), 3-95 (Bhatia, 19.4),
4-171 (Mandhana, 32.1), 5-199 (Ghosh, 36.6),
6-221 (Sharma, 42.1), 7-274 (Vastrakar, 50)

1-0 (Healy, 0.3), 2-11 (Lanning, 5.5), 3-34 (Perry, 9.4),
4-52 (Gardner, 15.5), 5-178 (McGrath, 38.3)

Bowling	O	M	R	W	wd	nb		Bowling	O	M	R	W	wd	nb
EA Perry	5	0	32	0	1			JN Goswami	8	0	40	1	3	3
DR Brown	10	0	63	1	4			Meghna Singh	9	2	38	1	2	
AK Gardner	6	0	30	0	1			RS Gayakwad	10	0	49	0		
SG Molineux	8	0	28	2	1			P Vastrakar	8	0	43	1		
NJ Carey	8	1	26	0	1			P Yadav	6	0	38	0		
HJ Darlington	4	0	36	0	2			DB Sharma	9	0	60	1	2	
TM McGrath	9	0	45	3	3									

Toss: New Zealand. Umpires: BNJ Oxenford, E Sheridan, PJ Gillespie (TV), Ref: RW Stratford. Award: BL Mooney (Aus). Crowd: 1,414.
Mandhana 50: 56 balls, 7x4. Mooney 50: 78 balls, 5x4 100: 117 balls, 10x4, McGrath 50: 57 balls, 7x4. Points: Aus 2, India 0

THIRD ONE-DAY INTERNATIONAL – MACKAY

After a solid opening stand of 41, Haynes hit one down the ground to be caught at mid-on. Lanning edged a drive to the keeper four balls later for a rare duck and when Perry smacked a full-toss straight to Gayakwad, it hit the stumps at the bowlers with Healy out of her ground. When Perry hit a cut shot to point, Australia was under pressure at 4-87 in the 25th over. A rebuild started for the fifth wicket, but on 29 Mooney was dropped at cover of Gayakwad which would have made Australia 5-128 in the 33rd over. Mooney had more luck on 38 when Rana dropped a caught and bowled, the partnership of 98 in 15 overs with Gardner ending when Mooney was bowled when she missed a sweep.

Gardner had batted well and brought up her run a ball 50 when she lofted a six over wide long-off. The Indians put down another chance with Gardner on 61, but she was soon out hitting a sweep to backward square-leg. McGrath hit the ball hard in the late part of the innings as Australia added 79 from the last ten overs to set India 265 to win, helped all up by four catches that went down.

India started the chase well to be 59 in the 11th over, when Mandhana was out to a fine catch at cover by Sutherland running back with the flight of the ball. Then came some of the best batting in the series at Verma and Bhatia dominated the attack to add 101 in 19 overs. Verma brought up her maiden ODI fifty as did Bhatia and at 2-160 in the 30th over, India were well on their way to a win. But the game changed as Verma was bowled missing a sweep and then Ghosh hit a catch to square-leg. Bhatia's good knock ended she went for a pull and was out when the long-leg fielder ran in and dived forward to bring off an excellent catch. When the experienced Raj was out, India needed 57 off 56 balls, but Sharma and Rana kept up with the rate, Rana having some luck on 11 when she was dropped by Carey at square-leg. With 26 wanted off 25, Rana was caught and bowled by Carey, but replays showed it to be a no-ball. Rana kept her cool and saw India within six of victory, with Goswami hitting the winning four to gain an important win and a vital two points in the series.

234

Third ODI at Harrup Park, Mackay on September 26, 2021 (day/night) - India won by 2 wickets

Australia			B	M	4	6
RL Haynes	c Verma b Goswami	13	28	34	3	
AJ Healy+	run out (Gayakwad)	35	47	69	5	
MM Lanning*	c Ghosh b Goswami	0	4	3		
EA Perry	c Sharma b Vastrakar	26	47	60	2	
BL Mooney	b Rana	52	64	96	6	
AK Gardner	c Raj b Vastrakar	67	62	89	8	2
TM McGrath	c Ghosh b Vastrakar	47	32	42	7	
NJ Carey	not out	12	15	29		
AJ Sutherland	c Sharma b Goswami	0	1	2		
SG Molineux	run out					
	(Gayakwad-Goswami)	1	1	3		
S Campbell	not out	0	0	1		
	1b, 3 lb, 1nb, 6 w	11				
10 overs: 2-41	50 overs, 2 18 mins	9-264				

India			B	M	4	6
S Verma	b Molineux	56	91	120	7	
SS Mandhana	c Sutherland b Gardner	22	25	44	3	
YH Bhatia	c sub (MR Strano)					
	b Campbell	64	69	97	9	
RM Ghosh+	c Gardner b Sutherland	0	4	5		
MD Raj*	b Sutherland	16	28	26	1	1
P Vastrakar	b Sutherland	3	14	16		
DB Sharma	c Carey b McGrath	31	30	40	3	
S Rana	c sub (HJ Darlington) b Carey	30	27	39	5	
JN Goswami	not out	8	7	17	1	
Meghna Singh	not out	2	3	4		
RS Gayakwad						
	2 lb, 1 nb, 31 w	34				
10 overs: 0-55	49.3 overs, 2 18 mins	8-266				

1-41 (Haynes, 8.1), 2-41 (Lanning, 8.5), 3-62 (Healy, 17.1), 4-87 (Perry, 24.3), 5-185 (Mooney, 39.6), 6-224 (Gardner, 44.2), 7-260 (McGrath, 48.6), 8-261 (Sutherland, 49.2 ov), 9-263 (Molineux, 49.5 ov)

1-59 (Mandhana, 10.3), 2-160 (Verma, 29.3), 3-161 (Ghosh, 30.3), 4-180 (Bhatia, 33.5), 5-192 (Vastrakar, 38.1), 6-208 (Raj, 40.4), 7-241 (Sharma, 46.2), 8-259 (Rana, 48.4)

Bowling	O	M	R	W	wd	nb
JN Goswami	10	2	37	3	1	
Meghna Singh	6	0	37	0	1	
RS Gayakwad	9	1	38	0	1	
S Rana	9	1	56	1		1
DB Sharma	7	0	46	0		
P Vastrakar	9	1	46	3	3	

Bowling	O	M	R	W	wd	nb
EA Perry	5	0	34	0	8	
TM McGrath	6	0	46	1	4	
SG Molineux	9.3	1	41	1	1	
AK Gardner	6	0	30	1		
S Campbell	9	1	41	1	3	
NJ Carey	7	0	42	1	1	1
AJ Sutherland	7	0	30	3	2	

Toss: Australia. Umpires: PJ Gillespie, BNJ Oxenford, CA Polosak (TV), Ref: RW Stratford. Award: JN Goswami (Ind). Crowd: 1,012
Mooney 50: 63 balls, 6x4, Gardner 50: 50 balls, 7x4 1x6. Verma 50: 86 balls, 6x4, Y Bhatia 50: 56 balls, 7x4. Points: Aus 0, India 2

TEST MATCH – GOLD COAST

There was a new look to the Australian side who were playing in their first Test since July 2019, with Darcie Brown, Stella Campbell, Anabel Sutherland and Georgia Wareham all making their debuts. With the sun shining but rain forecast for later, India were sent in and got off to a fine start against some loose bowling. Mandhana played nicely square through the off-side and hit some fine pull-shots on her way to 50 off just 51 balls with 11 fours. Verma joined in to enjoy the good batting conditions but had some luck on 19 when she edged Molineux to Lanning at slip, who couldn't hold onto the chance to her left. Verma had some more luck on 25 when Sutherland dropped her at mid-on off Molineux, but then at 93 the breakthrough came when Verma was safely held at mid-off. Dinner saw India reach 1-101 from 33 overs, Mandhana 64, Raut 1. At the break Mandhana continued to play nicely, but rain caused one delay and then ended play for the day as only 11.1 overs were able to be played post the dinner-break.

On day two, Mandhana again played some fine shots with a pull-shot behind square-leg off Perry for four seeing her reach her 100 off 170 balls. At the other end Raut was scoring too slowly and just after the 100 stand came up, Mandhana's excellent knock ended when she drove a catch to short mid-off. Raut got the slightest of edges to the keeper and walked despite the Umpire saying not out. Yastika Bhatia struck the ball well before getting a leading edge to gully and then Raj was out when she played a ball to square-leg, was sent back and found short of her ground. First the lightning arrived and then the rain, with no more playing possible, with India having added 4-134 in the 57.4 overs possible.

India added 43 runs at the start of the day before Taniya Bhatia edged a catch behind to give Campbell her first test wicket. Vastrakar fell to a fine diving catch in the gully while Deepti Sharma was slow but effective in reaching fifty from 148 balls, being last out as India declared after batting on after the dinner break. Needing 228 to avoid the follow-on, Mooney was first to go when she was bowled playing across the line. The second wicket partnership added 49 in fine style until just before tea when Healy got a touch behind. Lanning was trapped in front by Vastrakar on the forward stroke, but there were suggestions maybe some bat was involved. McGrath hit some crisp shots before smashing a cut straight to point and then Perry and Gardner saw their team to stumps, Australia was 85 away from avoiding the follow-on.

Australia's fifth wicket pairing went about their business as they headed towards the follow-on target, Perry playing patiently to bring up her 50 (155) with a leg-glance for four. Australia passed 200 and Gardner too reached 50 (80 balls) until the partnership of 89 came to an end when she was held low down at mid-off. India took the new ball and shortly after Sutherland got the finest of touches to the keeper. With Molineux LBW and Wareham edging behind, Australia still needed five to avoid the follow-on with two wickets in hand. Brown hit a four to avoid the follow-on which virtually made the game safe for Australia, the hosts declaring 136 behind.

Madhana played well again before being superbly caught at long-on, India batting for 37 overs before setting Australia 272 to win in just under a session. Australia lost two wickets but were under no threat as the match was called off without the need to play the mandatory final hour. The draw meant two points for each team, with Australia ahead 6-4 with the three T20s to play.

Only Test at Metricon Stadium, Gold Coast on September 30 – October 3, 2021 – Match Drawn

India

First innings		B	M	4	6		Second innings		B	M	4	6
SS Mandhana	c McGrath b Gardner	127	216	243	22	1	2 c Gardner b Molineux	31	48	70	6	
S Verma	c McGrath b Molineux	31	64	99	4		1 lbw b Wareham	52	91	131	6	
P G Raut	c Healy b Molineux	36	165	189	2		4 not out	41	62	60	6	
MD Raj*	run out (Sutherland)	30	86	120	5							
YH Bhatia	c Mooney b Perry	19	40	52	3		3 b Gardner	3	12	12		
DB Sharma	lbw b Campbell	66	167	192	8		5 not out	3	9	12		
T Bhatia+	c Healy b Campbell	22	75	104	3							
P Vastrakar	c Mooney b Perry	13	48	60	2							
JN Goswami	not out	7	5	22	1							
Meghna Singh	not out	2	6	7								
RS Gayakwad												

3 b, 6 lb, 2 nb, 13 w 24   5 b 5
145 overs, 542 mins   8-377 dec   37 overs, 144 mins   3-135 dec

1-93 (Verma), 2-195 (Mandhana), 3-217 (Raut), 4-261 (Y Bhatia), 5-274 (Raj), 6-319 (T Bhatia), 7-359 (Vastrakar), 8-369 (Sharma)

1-70 (Mandhana), 2-74 (Y Bhatia), 3-122 (Verma)

Bowling	O	M	R	W	wd	nb	O	M	R	W	wd	nb
Perry	27	4	76	2	2		5	1	14	0		
Brown	10	0	49	0	1		4	0	15	0		
Campbell	14	2	47	2	1		4	1	19	0		
McGrath	16	3	40	0	1		2	0	6	0		
Molineux	23	8	45	2			7	0	23	1		
Gardner	30	11	52	1			10	1	31	1		
Sutherland	17	6	31	0	2		2	0	10	0		
Wareham	8	2	28	0			3	0	12	1		

Australia

First innings		B	M	4	6	Second innings		B	M	4	6
AJ Healy+	c T Bhatia b Goswami	29	66	91	3	b Goswami	6	5	10	1	
BL Mooney	b Goswami	4	16	28		c Gayakwad b Vastrakar	11	28	40	1	
MM Lanning*	lbw b Vastrakar	38	78	99	7	not out	17	43	49	2	
EA Perry	not out	68	203	311	9	not out	1	14	19		
TM McGrath	c Mandhana b Vastrakar	28	68	70	4						
AK Gardner	c Raj b Sharma	51	86	117	6						
AJ Sutherland	c T Bhatia b Singh	3	20	25							
SG Molineux	lbw b Singh	2	14	18							
GL Wareham	c T Bhatia b Vastrakar	2	11	13							
DR Brown	lbw b Sharma	8	18	21	2						
S Campbell	not out	0	1	4							

6 lb, 1 nb, 1 w 8   1 lb 1
96.4 overs, 403 mins   9-241 dec   15 overs, 60 mins   2-36

1-14 (Mooney), 2-63 (Healy), 3-80 (Lanning), 4-119 (McGrath), 5-208 (Gardner), 6-216 (Sutherland), 7-220 (Molineux), 8-223 (Wareham), 9-240 (Brown)

1-8 (Healy), 2-28 (Mooney)

Bowling	O	M	R	W	wd	nb	O	M	R	W	wd	nb
Goswami	22	7	33	2			6	2	8	1		
Meghna Singh	19	2	54	2	1	1	2	0	12	0		
Vastrakar	21.4	6	49	3			5	1	13	1		
Gayakwad	18	1	63	0			2	1	2	0		
Sharma	16	6	36	2								

Stumps Scores
Day 1   India 1st inns   1-132   Mandhana 80*, Raut 16*; 44.1 overs
Day 2   India 1st inns   5-276   Sharma 12*, T Bhatia 0*; 101.5 overs
Day 3   Australia 1st inns   4-143   Perry 27*, Gardner 13*; 60 overs

Toss: Australia. Umpires: PJ Gillespie, CA Polosak, BNJ Oxenford (TV), Ref: RW Stratford
Award: SS Mandhana (Ind)
Attendance: 1,641. Points: Aus 2, India 2

FIRST TWENTY20 – GOLD COAST

India was sent in to bat as Verma started the ball rolling in the opening over, hitting her first ball off Vlaeminck over point for six. She cleared the rope on two more occasions before she and Mandhana fell in the same over to Gardner. Kaur hit a cracking hook for four to get off the mark, but it was a clever innings from Rodrigues that put India in a good position until the rain came to end what was promising to be a brilliant contest.

First Twenty20 at Metricon Stadium, Gold Coast on October 7, 2021 (floodlit) – No result

India				B	4	6	Australia
SS Mandhana	c Darlington b Gardner	17	10	2	1		AJ Healy+
S Verma	c Wareham b Gardner	18	14		3		BL Mooney
JI Rodrigues	not out	49	36	7			MM Lanning*
H Kaur*	lbw b Molineux	12	5	3			AK Gardner
YH Bhatia	c Vlaeminck b Wareham	15	15	2			EA Perry
RM Ghosh+	not out	17	13	3			TM McGrath
P Vastrakar							NJ Carey
DB Sharma							SG Molineux
SS Pandey							GL Wareham
RS Gayakwad							HJ Darlington
Renuka Singh							TJ Vlaeminck
	1nb, 2w	3					
6 overs: 3-55	15.2 overs	4-131					

1-31 (Mandhana, 3.2), 2-37 (Verma, 3.5), 3-55 (Kaur, 5.5),
4-106 (Bhatia, 12.1)

Bowling	O	M	R	W	wd	nb	Dots
TJ Vlaeminck	4	0	32	0	2	1	13
SG Molineux	2	0	23	1			6
AK Gardner	3	0	28	2			5
EA Perry	1	0	3	0			3
NJ Carey	2	0	17	0			4
HJ Darlington	1	0	11	0			1
GL Wareham	1.2	0	3	1			5
TM McGrath	1	0	14	0			1

Toss: Australia. Umpires: BNJ Oxenford, E Sheridan, CA Polosak (TV), Ref: RW Stratford. Award: none. Crowd: 702.
Points: Aus 1, India 1

SECOND TWENTY20 – GOLD COAST

After electing to field first, Australia was well on top early as Mandhana was caught at forward square-leg and Verma's ugly heave lobbed to mid-on. India could have been 3-15 had Gardner held onto a tough left-handed chance at mid-wicket when Rodrigues was six but it mattered little as the Indian number three was out soon after when she hit a catch to wide mid-on. Kaur hit some crisp strokes but she was out when she had a wild swing at Wareham and was well stumped. India lost their way in the middle overs with two bad mix-ups which resulted in run outs, as they slipped to 9-81. But Vastrakar hit the ball hard as 37 came from the last three overs to set Australia 119 to win.

In the chase Healy hooked the first ball for four but was castled by the next which cut back a mile from well outside off, to hit the top of middle stump. With the ball moving in the air significantly Australia did well to reach 1-33 at the end of the powerplay before losing their next three wickets quickly. Lanning advanced and got a touch behind and was stumped for good measure, while Gardner was caught at point and Perry at cover, leaving Australia a precarious 4-46 in the 10th over. McGrath came in and on three edged Vastrakar to Ghosh, who failed to hold the chance in her right glove, which if held would have seen Australia 5-55. McGrath rode her luck and with 48 wanted off 42 balls, Mooney advanced and was well stumped. After a valuable 23 were added, Carey was stumped after a Ghosh fumble saw the ball knock a bail off. Wareham helped take the pressure off with two boundaries as McGrath ensured Australia got home with five balls to spare, to go nine points to five up in the series.

Second Twenty20 at Metricon Stadium, Gold Coast on October 9, 2021 (floodlit) – Australia won by 4 wickets

India			B	4	6	Australia			B	4	6
SS Mandhana	c Carey b Vlaeminck	1	5			AJ Healy+	b Pandey	4	2	1	
S Verma	c Darlington b Vlaeminck	3	7			BL Mooney	st Ghosh b Gayakwad	34	36	4	
JI Rodrigues	c Darlington b Molineux	7	13			MM Lanning*	c Ghosh b Gayakwad	15	20	2	
H Kaur*	st Healy b Wareham	28	20	5		AK Gardner	c Gayakwad b Kaur	1	5		
YH Bhatia	run out (Wareham-Healy)	8	11	1		EA Perry	c Kaur b Sharma	2	4		
RM Ghosh+	c Carey	2	10			TM McGrath	not out	42	33	6	
DB Sharma	run out (McGrath-Healy)	16	19	1		NJ Carey	st Ghosh b Gayakwad	7	8		
P Vastrakar	not out	37	26	3	2	GL Wareham	not out	10	7	2	
SS Pandey	b Gardner	1	3			SG Molineux					
Renuka Singh	b Molineux	1	3			HJ Darlington					
RS Gayakwad	not out	0	4			TJ Vlaeminck					
	2 lb, 1 nb, 11 w	14					3 lb, 1 w	4			
6 overs: 3-25	20 overs	9-118				6 overs: 1-33	19.1 overs	6-119			

1-5 (Mandhana, 0.6), 2-12 (Verma, 2.5), 3-24 (Rodrigues, 5.3),
4-50 (Kaur, 8.5), 5-52 (Bhatia, 9.4), 6-61 (Ghosh, 11.6),
7-76 (Sharma, 15.2), 8-78 (Pandey, 15.6), 9-81 (Renuka Singh, 16.6)

1-4 (Healy, 0.2), 2-35 (Lanning, 6.3), 3-38 (Gardner, 7.5),
4-46 (Perry, 9.1), 5-71 (Mooney, 13.1), 6-94 (Carey, 16.4)

Bowling	O	M	R	W	wd	nb	Dots	Bowling	O	M	R	W	wd	nb	Dots
TJ Vlaeminck	3	0	18	2	2	1	11	SS Pandey	4	0	27	1	1		11
SG Molineux	4	0	11	2			14	Renuka Singh	4	1	27	0			9
EA Perry	2	0	17	0	1		5	P Vastrakar	3.1	0	21	0			8
AK Gardner	4	0	12	1	1		13	RS Gayakwad	4	0	21	3			12
GL Wareham	2	0	14	1			5	H Kaur	2	0	9	1			6
NJ Carey	3	0	25	1	3		9	DB Sharma	2	0	11	1			4
HJ Darlington	2	0	19	0			5								

Toss: Australia. Umpires: PJ Gillespie, BNJ Oxenford, E Sheridan (TV), Ref: RW Stratford. Award: TM McGrath (Aus). Crowd: 2,033
Points: Aus 2, India 0

THIRD TWENTY20 – GOLD COAST

India started well with the ball, bowling a maiden with Pandey's appeal for LBW appeal off the fifth ball going unrewarded against Healy, with replays showing it was out. It mattered little as Healy was caught behind in the next over and then Mooney hit some nice drives to get the innings moving. Lanning was out in odd fashion after she clipped her stumps when going for a cut and then Gardner got a snick behind to a drive to leave Australia 3-58 off which Mooney had 39 off 24 balls. India pressed home their advantage when Perry was caught at long-on, but then McGrath came out and teamed up with Mooney for a stand of 44 in six overs. Mooney reached her 50 with a nice cover-drive for four and finally went to a brilliant diving catch at cover. McGrath cleared the rope straight in the 18th over and with Wareham added 32 from 16 balls to set India 150 to win.

Verma was out in the second over of the chase when she pulled a catch to short backward square-leg, but then Mandhana got a bit stuck, scoring just five off her first 15 balls. India reached 1-54 after the midway point, needing 96 off the last 10 and lost Rodrigues when she lofted a catch to wide long-off. Mandhana passed 50, but it took 46 balls as the run rate needed by India kept increasing. Her dismissal to a catch at deep cover saw a collapse of 4-10 which effectively decided the match. Kaur drove a catch to cover, Vastrakar was bowled by a yorker and Deol was run out going for a second. With a three ball needed, India fought hard but were well beaten in the end, as Australia won the series 11 points to five.

Third Twenty20 at Metricon Stadium, Gold Coast on October 10, 2021 (floodlit) – Australia won by 14 runs

Australia			B	4	6	India			B	4	6
AJ Healy+	c Ghosh b Renuka Singh	4	8	1		SS Mandhana	c Lanning b Carey	52	49	8	
BL Mooney	c Kaur b Gayakwad	61	43	10		S Verma	c Vlaeminck b Gardner	1	3		
MM Lanning*	hit wkt b Gayakwad	14	14	2		JI Rodrigues	c Vlaeminck b Wareham	23	26	1	
AK Gardner	c Ghosh b Vastrakar	1	5			H Kaur*	c Lanning b Sutherland	13	16	1	
EA Perry	c Vastrakar b Sharma	8	11			P Vastrakar	b Carey	5	3	1	
TM McGrath	not out	44	31	6	1	RM Ghosh+	not out	23	11	2	2
GL Wareham	not out	13	8	1		H Deol	run out (Wareham-Healy)	2	4		
NJ Carey						DB Sharma	not out	9	8	1	
AJ Sutherland						SS Pandey					
SG Molineux						Renuka Singh					
TJ Vlaeminck						RS Gayakwad					
	4 lb	4						7			
6 overs: 1-38	20 overs	5-149				6 overs: 1-28	20 overs	6-135			

1-5 (Healy, 1.5), 2-44 (Lanning, 6.6), 3-58 (Gardner, 8.3),
4-73 (Perry, 11.1), 5-117 (Mooney, 17.2)

1-3 (Verma, 1.2), 2-60 (Rodrigues, 10.4), 3-92 (Mandhana, 14.5),
4-95 (Kaur, 15.5), 5-99 (Vastrakar, 16.2), 6-102 (Deol, 17.1)

238

Bowling	O	M	R	W	wd	nb	Dots
SS Pandey	3	1	23	0			8
Renuka Singh	4	0	23	1			10
RS Gayakwad	4	0	37	2			7
P Vastrakar	4	0	24	1			12
H Kaur	1	0	14	0			1
DB Sharma	4	0	24	1			7

Bowling	O	M	R	W	wd	nb	Dots
TJ Vlaeminck	3	0	18	0	2		11
AK Gardner	4	0	22	1	1		9
SG Molineux	4	0	22	0			8
GL Wareham	2	0	15	1			2
NJ Carey	4	0	42	2	1		8
AJ Sutherland	3	0	13	1			8

Toss: India. Umpires: CA Polosak, E Sheridan, PJ Gillespie (TV), Ref: RW Stratford. Award: TM McGrath (Aus). Crowd: 1,008
Mooney 50: 36 balls, 8x4. Mandhana 50: 46 balls, 8x4. Points: Aus 2, India 0

AUSTRALIA v ENGLAND, 2021-22
THE HOSTS TOO STRONG 12 POINTS TO FOUR
FIRST TWENTY20 – ADELAIDE

Beth Mooney was ruled out of the T20 leg of the series, having suffered a fractured jaw at training. Grace Harris made it into the final XI, with Meg Lanning up the order from number three to open. England only made one change from their last T20 played in September against New Zealand, with Fran Davies in for Tash Farrant.

Beaumont suffered a nasty blow in the second over of the game when she was hit on the helmet by a Vlaeminck bouncer, but recovered quickly to ramp McGrath in the next over for four. In the same over Wyatt on three smashed one back at the bowler who failed to hold on. The Aussies pace bowlers were bowling too short as Beaumont played some nice pulls, while Wyatt lofted Jonassen straight for consecutive sixes as 51 came up in the first powerplay. At 82 without loss at the half-way England were well placed, but then King landed a nice leg-break and had Wyatt caught and bowled to take her first T20 wicket for Australia.

Wyatt reached her 50 and continued to strike the ball well as she lofted King over mid-wicket for six. In the 14th over Sciver was adjudged leg before off Schutt on five, but after a review the decision was overturned as bat was involved. The pair added 59 in six overs before both were yorked by McGrath in the same over and with 27 off the last three overs, Australia needed 170 to win.

Healy glanced her first ball for four but England started well to have her caught at short mid-wicket in the fourth over. In front of her home crowd McGrath started to unleash some powerful shots, including a hard-hit pull off Davies for six. Lanning was forced to play second fiddle in the stand as McGrath continued to find the gaps, reaching her maiden T20 fifty from just 28 balls. England had no answer as the pair ended up adding a record second wicket stand for Australia worth 144 in 13 overs to win comfortably with three overs to spare.

First Twenty20 at Adelaide Oval on January 20, 2022 (floodlit) - Australia won by 9 wickets

England			B	4	6	Australia			B	4	6
TT Beaumont	c & b King		30	24	4	MM Lanning*	not out		64	44	8
DN Wyatt	b McGrath		70	54	6 3	AJ Healy+	c Sciver b Ecclestone		7	9	1
NR Sciver	b McGrath		32	23	4	TM McGrath	not out		91	49	13 1
HC Knight *	not out		10	9		RL Haynes					
AE Jones+	c Harris b McGrath		4	6		AK Gardner					
SIR Dunkley	not out		10	5	1	GM Harris					
ME Bouchier						NJ Carey					
KH Brunt						JL Jonassen					
S Ecclestone						AM King					
S Glenn						TJ Vlaeminck					
FR Davies						M Schutt					
	4 b, 1 lb, 1 nb, 4 w		13				1 lb, 7 w		8		
6 overs : 0-51	20 overs		4-169			6 overs : 1- 42	17 overs		1-170		

1-82 (Beaumont, 10.1), 2-141 (Sciver, 16.3),
3-142 (Wyatt, 16.5), 4-154 (Jones, 18.4)

1-26 (Healy, 3.5)

Bowling	O	M	R	W	wd	nb	Dots
M Schutt	4	0	28	0			11
TJ Vlaeminck	4	0	29	0	3		11
TM McGrath	4	0	26	3		1	9
JL Jonassen	2	0	23	0			2
NJ Carey	2	0	27	0			2
AM King	4	0	28	1			7

Bowling	O	M	R	W	wd	nb	Dots
KH Brunt	3	0	24	0	1		8
S Ecclestone	4	0	29	1	1		11
NR Sciver	3	0	31	0		2	2
FR Davies	3	0	29	0	2		2
S Glenn	3	0	39	0			4
HC Knight	1	0	17	0			1

Toss: Australia. Umpires: BNJ Oxenford, CA Polosak, MW Graham-Smith (TV), Ref: SR Bernard. Award: TM McGrath (Aus).
Wyatt 50: 39 balls, 5x4 2x6. Lanning 50: 38 balls, 5x4, McGrath 50: 28 balls, 6x4 1x6. Points: Aus 2, Eng 0. Crowd: 1,930

SECOND TWENTY20 – ADELAIDE

After a delayed start, a 14 overs per side match was attempted, but the rain returned to give no chance of getting a result.

Second Twenty20 at Adelaide Oval on January 22, 2022 (day/night) - No result

England			B	4	6	Australia
DN Wyatt	not out		14	12	2	MM Lanning*
TT Beaumont	not out		6	14	1	AJ Healy+
NR Sciver						TM McGrath
HC Knight*						RL Haynes
AE Jones+						AK Gardner
SIR Dunkley						GM Harris
CE Dean						NJ Carey
KH Brunt						JL Jonassen
S Ecclestone						AM King
S Glenn						DR Brown
FR Davies						M Schutt
	1 b, 1 lb, 1 nb, 2 w	5				
	4.1 overs	0-25				

Bowling	O	M	R	W	wd	nb	Dots
AK Gardner	1	0	6	0			3
DR Brown	1	0	3	0		1	5
TM McGrath	1	0	6	0	2		5
M Schutt	1	0	8	0			3
AM King	0.1	0	0	0			1

Toss: Australia.   Umpires: MW Graham-Smith, BNJ Oxenford, CA Polosak (TV), Ref: SR Bernard.   Points: Aus 1, Eng 1.

THIRD TWENTY20 – ADELAIDE

Rain washed out this match, with not even a toss able to be made, Australia leading four points to two heading into the Test

Third Twenty20 at Adelaide Oval on January 23, 2022 – Abandoned without a ball being bowled

Toss: Not made.   Umpires: CA Polsak, E Sheridan, MW Graham-Smith (TV), Ref: SR Bernard. Points: Aus 1, Eng 1.

TEST MATCH - CANBERRA

Australia selected leg-spinner Alana King to make her Test debut, while England awarded off-spinning all-rounder Charlie Dean her first cap. Beth Mooney proved she was fit to play, despite fracturing her jaw on January 18.

DAY ONE – Attendance 2,197

England started well in the field as they disposed of both Healy and Mooney when both edged drives to the keeper in the first four overs. Haynes and Perry both drove and cut the ball well to add 39, but then Perry got herself into bother when she miscued a hook-shot. Australia could well have been 4-44, as Lanning on zero edged a drive low to the left of second slip and Cross. England made a terrible waste of a review for LBW when Lanning was eight and then in the over before lunch, Lanning on 14 edged Ecclestone to Sciver at slip who put down the chance. At Lunch it was 3-79 from 28 overs, Haynes 41, Lanning 15.

Sciver put down another chance, this time at second slip when Haynes on 44 edged one to her off Brunt. Haynes soon brought her fifty (107 balls) with a pull-shot for four, as she and her skipper made England pay with a long partnership. Lanning pulled Ecclestone for four to reach her fifty (97 balls) and then England lost another review, after an LBW appeal against Lanning when she was 51. She dominated making 67 in the middle session to be 82 at tea, Australia 3-199 off 60 overs, Haynes 82

England had double joy soon after tea with the score on 212, when Lanning edged catch to slip and then Haynes gloved a catch to the keeper. The quick loss of two wickets didn't phase Gardner who hooked Sciver for six, nor McGrath who hit some nice drives as Australia pushed on. Brunt took the new ball for England, but Gardner wasn't troubled as she drove her for four to bring up her fifty from 63 balls. The veteran speedster had her revenge soon after when she trapped Gardner in front, ending a stand of 84. In the last over of the day with McGrath on 48, she cut one to point and was dropped by Dunkley off Sciver, the resultant runs seeing the South Aussie to her fifty from 83 balls. Then off the last ball of the day, McGrath aimed a big drive and got a touch behind to give Jones her fifth catch, Australia at 7-327 having the better of the opening day.

DAY TWO – Attendance: 1,989

Brunt steamed in to hit the top of Sutherland's off stump in the fourth over of the morning and when Jonassen was caught behind off her to give Jones her sixth catch, Brunt was delighted to complete her third five wicket haul in Tests. Australia declared and struck early with the ball as Winfield-Hill drove at Brown, edging to second slip. After batting nearly an hour, Beaumont was trapped in front by Perry as England went to lunch on 2-38 from 19 overs with Knight 14, Sciver 11.

Sciver went after lunch caught behind off an inside edge to give Sutherland her first Test wicket while Dunkley was keen to put the short ball away before she played back and dragged one on. Knight drove the ball well and reached her 50 from 130 balls before England slipped from 4-118 to 6-120 at tea. Jones miscued a pull that was superbly held by Brown running back to her right, while Brunt was trapped LBW playing back, giving King her first Test wicket.

Needing 68 to avoid the follow-on, Knight and Dean added 30, when Dean was dropped on nine at short-leg off Gardner. It cost Australia nothing as next ball Dean top-edged a sweep straight down the throat of deep square-leg. When Shrubsole was caught at cover-point, England was 8-169 still 19 away from the follow-on. At 8-175 Australia went for a LBW review off Gardner against Ecclestone on one, but technology showed the ball to be missing leg. Then with Knight on 99, she drove one off King past cover to reach her second Test ton, scored out of 172 runs while she was at the crease.

Australia continued to overdo it with the reviews when Ecclestone was on two, an appeal for LBW rejected upstairs on the grounds that it pitched outside leg. For the rest of the day Ecclestone proved to be a worthy partner for her skipper as the pair survived through the new ball and added 66, England ending the day 102 behind.

DAY THREE – Attendance: 2,476

Ecclestone edged the third ball of the day low to the right of Lanning at first slip where she put down the chance. Knight went on the attack to reach her 150 when she cracked Jonassen over wide mid-on for four. On 33 Ecclestone was put down by Lanning off McGrath when she dived to her right but couldn't hold on. The 100 stand was raised and then Ecclestone was plumb LBW, playing all across one. There was one last wag in the tail as Cross hung around to help add 28 with Knight, before top-edging a hook to long-leg. England had added 128 for last two wickets to trail by just 40. As the skies got gloomier, Healy edged behind to record a pair and then Haynes was caught at short-leg. The rain came which ruined everything, preventing any further play.

DAY FOUR – Attendance: 1,299

With 109 overs available on the final day, Australia started with purpose to try and engineer a win. Some firm drives were hit as the runs flowed until both batters gave chances to keeper Jones, with Cross being the unlucky bowler each time. Mooney on 40 was a regulation edge and then Perry on 33, was tougher as the keeper dived in front of slip. The stand reached 91 when Perry was LBW when well forward, and in the over before lunch Mooney missed a sweep, Australia going in 163 ahead. Lanning edged a catch to slip straight after the break, but then McGrath and Gardner added 48 to take the Aussie lead past 200. Jonassen cracked three fours as Australia declared to set England 257 to win in 48 overs at a rate of 5.35 per over.

Beaumont dominated the opening stand of 52 before driving hard to short cover's left, where a fine catch was held. Knight was at her aggressive best and just as Winfield-Hill got going, she hit a catch to short mid-wicket. Then came some of the best batting of the match as Knight and Sciver added 72 in 11 overs as England reached 2-166, needing 91 off the last 15. Brown trapped Knight in front and then next ball thought she had Dunkley LBW, but England won the review on height. Dunkley then played a whirlwind knock adding 52 in seven overs with Sciver which made the visitors favourites, needing just 39 off 46 balls. Then a bit of panic set in as Sciver hit a pull to square-leg and Jones was caught at deep mid-wicket. Dunkley's knock ended when she was superbly caught at long-on. Six down with 21 to win off 24 balls, England were still a chance but Brunt edged a hook behind and in the next over Shrubsole was run out. When Dean top-edged a sweep to the keeper, England were nine down needing 13 off 13 balls. Cross put the shutters up facing Sutherland but took a single to keep the strike and then with fielders surrounding her, she blocked out the last over from King, the match ending in a draw.

Test Match at Manuka Oval, Canberra on January 27-30, 2022 – Match Drawn

Australia	First innings		B	M	4	6	Second innings		B	M	4	6
RL Haynes	c Jones b Brunt	86	180	264	10		c Beaumont b Brunt	4	10	20		
AJ Healy+	c Jones b Brunt	0	8	10			c Jones b Brunt	0	2	1		
BL Mooney	c Jones b Shrubsole	3	3	3			lbw b Dean	63	137	172	6	
EA Perry	c Jones b Sciver	18	34	51	3		lbw b Ecclestone	41	83	121	5	
MM Lanning*	c Knight b Sciver	93	170	193	13		c Knight b Brunt	12	26	39		
TM McGrath	c Jones b Sciver	52	88	126	7		b Dean	34	67	78	4	
AK Gardner	lbw b Brunt	56	74	88	8	1	c Ecclestone b Sciver	38	38	46	5	
AJ Sutherland	b Brunt	8	35	44	1		not out	7	15	29		
JL Jonassen	c Jones b Brunt	2	12	28			not out	14	6	6	3	
AM King	not out	7	21	16	1							
DR Brown												
	8 b, 4 lb	12					3 lb	3				
	104.1 overs, 415 mins	9-337 dec					64 overs, 259 mins	7-216 dec				

1-1 (Healy), 2-4 (Mooney), 3-43 (Perry), 4-212 (Lanning), 5-212 (Haynes), 6-296 (Gardner), 7-327 (McGrath), 8-328 (Sutherland), 9-337 (Jonassen)

1-1 (Healy), 2-12 (Haynes), 3-103 (Perry), 4-123 (Mooney), 5-130 (Lanning), 6-178 (Gardner), 7-199 (McGrath)

Bowling	O	M	R	W	wd	nb		O	M	R	W	wd	nb
KH Brunt	21.1	4	60	5				9	2	24	3		
A Shrubsole	18	5	38	1				8	1	30	0		
KL Cross	17	4	67	0				9	1	38	0		
NR Sciver	16	4	41	3				7	1	29	1		
S Ecclestone	20	2	74	0				24	4	68	1		
CE Dean	12	0	45	0				7	1	24	2		

England — First innings

Batsman	How out	R	B	M	4	6
L Winfield-Hill	c Mooney b Brown	4	7	7	1	
TT Beaumont	lbw b Perry	5	33	50		
HC Knight*	not out	168	294	427	17	1
NR Sciver	c Healy b Sutherland	15	42	48	2	
SIR Dunkley	b Perry	15	34	43	3	
AE Jones+	c Brown b Sutherland	13	25	42	2	
KH Brunt	lbw b King	1	12	12		
CE Dean	c McGrath b Gardner	9	40	46		9
A Shrubsole	c McGrath b Jonassen	3	21	22		8
S Ecclestone	lbw b McGrath	34	117	137	3	
KL Cross	c Brown b Perry	11	22	28	2	
Extras	1 b, 3 lb, 12 nb, 3 w	19				
Total	105.5 overs, 435 mins	297				

England — Second innings

Batsman	How out	R	B	M	4	6
L Winfield-Hill	c Haynes b Perry	33	65	83	5	
TT Beaumont	c Haynes b McGrath	36	42	51	7	
HC Knight*	lbw b Brown	48	54	82	5	
NR Sciver	c Lanning b Sutherland	58	62	86	8	
SIR Dunkley	c Mooney b King	45	32	53	5	2
AE Jones+	c Mooney b Sutherland	4	7	10		
KH Brunt	c Healy b Sutherland	4	6	11		
CE Dean	c Healy b King	3	5	10		
A Shrubsole	run out (Healy-King)	6	6	12		
S Ecclestone	not out	0	1	15		
KL Cross	not out	1	12	12		
Extras	3 lb, 4 nb	7				
Total	48 overs, 2 17 mins	9-245				

1-6 (Winfield-Hill), 2-23 (Beaumont), 3-46 (Sciver), 4-79 (Dunkley), 5-118 (Jones), 6-120 (Brunt), 7-150 (Dean), 8-169 (Shrubsole), 9-269 (Ecclestone), 10-297 (Cross)

1-52 (Beaumont), 2-94 (Winfield-Hill), 3-166 (Knight), 4-218 (Sciver), 5-224 (Jones), 6-233 (Dunkley), 7-236 (Brunt), 8-244 (Shrubsole), 9-244 (Dean)

Bowling	O	M	R	W	wd	nb		O	M	R	W	wd	nb
DR Brown	12	3	39	1	1	3		5	0	18	1		
EA Perry	20.5	2	57	3	1	3		5	0	28	1	2	
TM McGrath	10	1	35	1		5		4	0	26	1	2	
AJ Sutherland	21	5	62	2	1	1		13	0	69	3		
AM King	26	4	58	1				7	0	37	0		
JL Jonassen	7	1	15	1				5	1	25	1		
AK Gardner	9	0	27	1				9	1	39	2		

Stumps Scores
Day 1 Australia (1st inns) 7-327   AJ Sutherland 7*; 97 overs
Day 2 England (1st inns) 8-235   HC Knight 127*, S Ecclestone 27*; 87 overs
Day 3 Australia (2nd inn) 2-12   BL Mooney 7*, EA Perry 0*; 4.5 overs

Toss: England. Player of Match: HC Knight (Eng)
Umpires: MW Graham-Smith, E Sheridan,
BNJ Oxenford (TV), Ref: SR Bernard. Crowd: 7,961

FIRST ONE-DAY INTERNATIONAL – CANBERRA

With England needing to win all three ODIs to regain the Ashes, things started well for them when Haynes top-edged a pull to the keeper in the fourth over. The second wicket stand was worth 47 but then England grabbed three quick wickets as Lanning was bowled by a breakback, Perry popped one back to the bowler and Healy was smartly stumped. The fifth wicket stand stood firm to add 58 in 14 overs, but then the run out of McGrath saw Australia lose three quick wickets to slip to 7-152 after 41 overs. Mooney continued to hit the ball nicely straight and reached her 50, getting great support from King as they added 52 in nine overs to pass the 200 mark.

Brown started brilliantly with the ball as she had Beaumont caught low at slip and Knight plumb LBW in consecutive deliveries to reduce England to 2-10. Sciver survived the hat-trick ball and started to play some good shots, but lost Winfield-Hill when she pulled a ball straight down the throat of deep square-leg. This was Schutt's 100th ODI wicket, joining Cathryn Fitzpatrick, Elyse Perry, Lisa Sthalekar and Jess Jonassen on the list for Australia.

Jones hit some strong shots straight but was out when she hit an innocuous full-toss to deep square-leg and when Dunkley was LBW, England were 5-83 in the 22nd over. Brown returned to the crease and took a brilliant caught and bowled diving forward to capture a leading edge to dismiss Sciver. Schutt bowled a ripper to just clip Wyatt's off stump and with Ecclestone and Shrubsole also soon out, England needed 52 off 69 balls when Cross joined Brunt for the last wicket. For a time they reduced the target to worry Australia until Cross hit a low drive back to Jonassen, who completed a sharp caught and bowled to retain the Ashes for Australia.

242

First One-Day International at Manuka Oval on February 3, 2022 (day/night) - Australia won by 27 runs

Australia		B	M	4	6	England		B	M	4	6
RL Haynes	c Jones b Shrubsole	4	13	12	1	L Winfield-Hill	c Gardner b Schutt	13	29	40	2
AJ Healy+	st Jones b Cross	27	42	83	4	TT Beaumont	c Lanning b Brown	3	12	12	
MM Lanning*	b Cross	28	51	54	4	HC Knight*	lbw b Brown	0	1	1	
EA Perry	c & b Ecclestone	0	1	2		NR Sciver	c & b Brown	45	66	91	3
BL Mooney	c Winfield-Hill b Brunt	73	91	133	8	1	AE Jones+	c Perry b McGrath	16	29	39	3
TM McGrath	b Brunt	29	48	57	3	SIR Dunkley	lbw b McGrath	5	6	5	1
AK Gardner	run out (Knight-Jones)	12	14	13	1	DN Wyatt	b Schutt	20	39	49	2
JL Jonassen	c Beaumont b Cross	4	10	11	1	KH Brunt	not out	32	46	75	1
AM King	b Brunt	18	29	34	2	S Ecclestone	lbw b Brown	3	9	11	
M Schutt	not out	1	1	1		A Shrubsole	b Jonassen	1	8	10	
DR Brown						KL Cross	c & b Jonassen	17	26	22	3
	1 b, 4 lb, 4 w	9					5 b, 2 lb, 1 nb, 15 w	23			
10 overs: 1-34	50 overs, 204 mins	9-205				10 overs: 2-39	45 overs, 182 mins	178			

1-13 (Haynes, 3.3), 2-60 (Lanning, 16.6), 3-61 (Perry, 17.2),
4-67 (Healy, 20.1), 5-125 (McGrath, 34.1), 6-141 (Gardner, 37.6),
7-152 (Jonassen, 40.6), 8-204 (King, 49.4), 9-205 (Mooney, 49.6)

1-10 (Beaumont, 3.3), 2-10 (Knight, 3.4),
3-39 (Winfield-Hill, 10.1), 4-74 (Jones, 19.6), 5-83 (Dunkley, 21.3),
6-103 (Sciver, 26.2), 7-134 (Wyatt, 32.5), 8-143 (Ecclestone, 35.4),
9-154 (Shrubsole, 38.3), 10-178 (Cross, 44.6)

Bowling	O	M	R	W	wd	nb	Bowling	O	M	R	W	wd	nb
KH Brunt	10	1	40	3	1		ML Schutt	9	1	39	2	4	
A Shrubsole	10	0	44	1			DR Brown	10	0	34	4	5	1
KL Cross	10	0	33	3			EA Perry	5	0	16	0		
S Ecclestone	10	0	36	1			JL Jonassen	8	0	30	2		
NR Sciver	10	0	47	0	2		TM McGrath	10	1	34	2	1	
							AM King	2	0	11	0	1	
							AK Gardner	1	0	7	0		

Toss: England. Umpires: MW Graham-Smith, CA Polosak, BNJ Oxenford (TV), Ref: SR Bernard. Award: BL Mooney (Aus).
Mooney 50: 73 balls, 5x4 1x6. Points: Aust 2, Eng 0. Crowd: 1,267

SECOND ONE-DAY INTERNATIONAL – MELBOURNE

On a sunny day the at Junction Oval, Perry found the edge of Beaumont's bat in the fourth over, with Healy diving to her right to bring off a fine catch. England appeared on their way at 1-40 after 10 overs, but things then went pear-shaped as the Aussie bowlers took control. Winfield-Hill had been hitting the ball well but missed a lap-sweep and then Sciver advanced and miscued to mid-off. Knight played back to one and was LBW after a review, Dunkley also trapped in front and then Wyatt edged Sutherland to Lanning at slip, who dived well to her right to bring off a brilliant catch. When Dean top-edged a pull to the keeper, England had lost 6-28 in 15 overs to be 7-68 in the 26th.

Ecclestone and Jones saw England past 100 with a stand of 39, but then McGrath trapped Jones in the same over. The last wicket added 22, but a target of just 130 was hardly going to trouble Australia. England had some success with the new ball as the hosts were reduced to 2-18 when Haynes edged a drive to the keeper and Lanning was bowled off her pads for a rare duck. When Healy hit hard to mid-off and was caught, England had a sniff with Australia 3-49, but Perry and McGrath added 36 to stabilise the innings. McGrath was bowled through the gate and then Perry was run out at mid-on after some sharp work from Cross at mid-on. But Gardner took control with some typically powerful shots to steer Australia home with time to spare.

Second One-Day International at Junction Oval, Melbourne on February 6, 2022 - Australia won by 5 wickets

England		B	M	4	6	Australia		B	M	4	6
L Winfield-Hill	lbw b King	24	36	44	4	AJ Healy+	c Winfield-Hill b Sciver	22	40	55	1
TT Beaumont	c Healy b Perry	6	15	15	1	RL Haynes	c Jones b Shrubsole	10	20	20	1
HC Knight*	lbw b Jonassen	18	36	61	1	MM Lanning*	b Cross	0	4	4	
NR Sciver	c Sutherland b Jonassen	8	25	23		EA Perry	run out (Cross)	40	64	77	5	1
AE Jones+	lbw b McGrath	28	54	86	2	TM McGrath	b Cross	19	30	35	2
SIR Dunkley	lbw b Perry	2	15	15		AK Gardner	not out	31	34	40	3	1
DN Wyatt	c Lanning b Sutherland	0	4	4		AJ Sutherland	not out	2	20	28	
CE Dean	c Healy b Perry	0	4	4		NJ Carey					
S Ecclestone	not out	32	65	71	2	1	JL Jonassen					
KL Cross	lbw b McGrath	0	3	2		AM King					
A Shrubsole	c Healy b McGrath	7	15	16	1	M Schutt					
	1 lb, 3 w	4					6 lb, 1 w	7			
10 overs: 1-40	45.2 overs, 175 mins	129				10 overs: 2-29	35.2 overs, 132 mins	5-131			

243

1-11 (Beaumont, 3.6), 2-40 (Winfield-Hill, 10.3),
3-57 (Sciver, 17.2), 4-59 (Knight, 19.3), 5-66 (Dunkley, 23.4),
6-67 (Wyatt, 24.4), 7-68 (Dean, 25.4), 8-107 (Jones, 39.3),
9-107 (Cross, 39.6), 10-129 (Shrubsole, 45.2)

1-17 (Haynes, 5.5), 2-18 (Lanning, 6.4), 3-49 (Healy, 14.4),
4-85 (McGrath, 24.6), 5-99 (Perry, 27.2)

Bowling	O	M	R	W	wd	nb
M Schutt	7	1	20	0		
EA Perry	7	1	12	3	2	
AJ Sutherland	9	0	44	1	1	
AM King	10	1	23	1		
JL Jonassen	9	1	25	2		
TM McGrath	3.2	1	4	3		

Bowling	O	M	R	W	wd	nb
NR Sciver	6	0	25	1		
A Shrubsole	9	1	28	1	1	
KL Cross	8	0	46	2		
S Ecclestone	10	1	20	0		
CE Dean	2.2	0	6	0		

Toss: Australia. Umpires: BNJ Oxenford, E Sheridan, CA Polosak (TV), Ref: SR Bernard. Award: EA Perry (Aus). Crowd: 2,402
Points: Aust 2, Eng 0.

THIRD ONE-DAY INTERNATIONAL – MELBOURNE

Lamb replaced Winfield-Hill to make her debut in the England side and sadly her first knock didn't last long as she was bowled second ball. Knight hit two neat boundaries before bottom edging a hook into her stomach which caused some discomfort. The skipper's day got worse when McGrath went through her defences with a fine yorker to leave England 2-19. Australia's bowlers were giving little away, England not reaching 50 until the 20th over. Beaumont battled to 29 off 86 balls, then hit Jonassen straight for six in the 31st over, the third wicket adding 88 in 26 overs, before another batting collapse.

Beaumont reached her fifty but then drove a catch to mid-off, while Wyatt smacked a six over long-off before looking to repeat the shot and was caught at deep cover-point. Sciver was leg before, Ecclestone was yorked and then Jones had a wild swing and was bowled. When Haynes swooped on a catch at point to dismiss Shrubsole, England had lost 6-32 across 11 overs. The tail wagged a little, but once again England were well short of competitive total.

Australia were rock solid at the top of their chase with Healy taking advantage of some short bowling, before she was dropped low down by keeper Jones off Davies on 24. With 74 added for the first wicket, both openers went in the space of seven balls, Healy getting a leading edge to point with Haynes mis-timing a drive to mid-off. Davies was bowling some lovely out-swingers without success and eventually Australia's experienced third wicket partnership took the game away from England to complete another easy victory, Lanning clearing the rope at long-off to make the winning hit.

Third One-Day International at Junction Oval, Melbourne on February 8, 2022 - Australia won by 8 wickets

England		B	M	4	6
TT Beaumont	c McGrath b King	50	101	130	3	1
EL Lamb	b Perry	0	2	4	
HC Knight*	b McGrath	9	24	30	2
NR Sciver	lbw b Schutt	46	95	118	2
DN Wyatt	c Schutt b Sutherland	9	12	17	1
AE Jones+	b Schutt	4	9	21	
S Ecclestone	b Sutherland	2	7	5	
CE Dean	not out	18	28	36	
A Shrubsole	c Haynes b Sutherland	2	6	4	
NE Farrant	c Healy b Sutherland	7	11	16	
FR Davies	b Jonassen	1	2	4	
	4 lb, 11 w	15			
10 overs: 2-20	49.3 overs, 197 mins	163			

Australia		B	M	4	6
AJ Healy+	c Beaumont b Davies	42	56	57	6
RL Haynes	c Lamb b Ecclestone	31	46	60	4
MM Lanning*	not out	57	70	67	7	1
EA Perry	not out	31	46	64	3	1
TM McGrath					
AK Gardner					
AJ Sutherland					
NJ Carey					
JL Jonassen					
AM King					
M Schutt					
	1 b, 2 w	3			
10 overs: 0-47	36.2 overs, 125 mins	2-164			

1-2 (Lamb, 1.2), 2-19 (Knight, 8.6), 3-107 (Beaumont, 34.2),
4-124 (Wyatt, 38.3), 5-125 (Sciver, 39.2), 6-128 (Ecclestone, 40.5),
7-136 (Jones, 43.2), 8-139 (Shrubsole, 44.3), 9-159 (Farrant, 48.4),
10-163 (Davies, 49.3)

1-74 (Healy, 15.6), 2-74 (Haynes, 16.6)

Bowling	O	M	R	W	wd	nb
M Schutt	10	1	25	2	1	
EA Perry	8	2	18	1		
TM McGrath	6	0	23	1	4	
AJ Sutherland	9	0	31	4	3	
AM King	8	0	29	1		
NJ Carey	4	0	13	0	3	
JL Jonassen	4.3	0	20	1		

Bowling	O	M	R	W	wd	nb
A Shrubsole	5	0	20	0		
NE Farrant	6.2	0	44	0	1	
FR Davies	10	1	46	1	1	
S Ecclestone	10	2	18	1		
CE Dean	5	0	35	0		

Toss: England. Umpires: CA Polosak, E Sheridan, MW Graham-Smith (TV), Ref: SR Bernard. Award: AJ Sutherland (Aus).
Beamont 50: 98 balls, 3x4 1x6. Lanning 50: 62 balls, 7x4. Points: Aust 2, Eng 0. Crowd: 1,008

WOMEN'S WORLD CUP IN NEW ZEALAND
AUSTRALIA GOES UNBEATEN TO WIN SEVENTH TITLE

Australia won the 2022 ICC Women's World Cup, going unbeaten throughout the tournament to take the trophy for the seventh time. Although unbeaten they were tested by England in their opening match, winning by 12 runs and India, who they defeated by six wickets with two balls to spare. Alyssa Healy was a key figure, with two centuries including 170 against England in the Final. Rachael Haynes, Meg Lanning and Beth Mooney all dominated with the bat, whilst with the ball it was the success of the spinners that was a highlight. Jess Jonassen, Alana King and Ash Gardner all each took 10 wickets or more, while veteran quick Megan Schutt and rookie opening bowler Darcie Brown both had their moments.

Warm-up games. Australia v West Indies at Lincoln Green, Lincoln on February 27, 2022 – Australia won by 90 runs.
Toss: West Indies. **Australia 7-259 cc** (EA Perry 62, AJ Sutherland 54, SR Taylor 3-51) **def West Indies 169** (50 overs) (SR Taylor 66).

Australia v New Zealand at Bert Sutcliffe Oval, Lincoln on March 1, 2022 – New Zealand won by 9 wickets.
Toss: New Zealand. **Australia 321** (49.3 overs) (AJ Healy 64, MM Lanning 87, BL Mooney 55, AK Gardner 60) **lost to New Zealand 1-325** (43.1 overs) (SW Bates 63, SFM Devine 161*, AC Kerr 92*).

AUSTRALIA v ENGLAND - HAMILTON

After Healy chipped a catch to mid-wicket in the ninth over, Haynes and Lanning dominated to add 196 in 34 overs, which was a record stand for any wicket for Australia versus England. Haynes scored her second ODI ton in what was her highest score as she saw Australia past 300. England's Beaumont and Knight added 92 and then Sciver played a fine knock to give her side every chance when they need 88 off the last 10 overs. Scoring her fourth ODI ton she gave England a chance and with 19 to win off nine balls, but the wicket of Brunt in the last over ensured Australia of a first up win.

Australia v England at Seddon Park, Hamilton on March 5, 2022 – Australia won by 12 runs

Australia			B	M	4	6	England			B	M	4	6
RL Haynes	c Wyatt b Sciver	130	131	203	14	1	L Winfield-Hill	c Sutherland b Schutt	0	4	6		
AJ Healy+	c Brunt b Sciver	28	35	39	4		TT Beaumont	st Healy b King	74	82	106	7	
MM Lanning*	c Beaumont b Brunt	86	110	141	7	1	HC Knight*	c Lanning b McGrath	40	51	68	3	1
BL Mooney	not out	27	19	28	3		NR Sciver	not out	109	85	117	13	
EA Perry	not out	14	5	4	3		AE Jones+	c Haynes b King	4	11	7		
TM McGrath							DN Wyatt	b McGrath	7	11	18	1	
AJ Sutherland							SIR Dunkley	b King	28	32	30	2	
JL Jonassen							KH Brunt	c & b Jonassen	25	21	27	1	1
AM King							S Ecclestone	c Mooney b Jonassen	1	3	4		
M Schutt							KL Cross						
DR Brown							A Shrubsole						
	4 1b, 2 1 w		25					4 b, 4 1b, 2 w		10			
10 overs: 1-37	50 overs		3-310				10 overs: 1-53	50 overs		8-298			

1-35 (Healy, 8.6), 2-231 (Lanning, 42.6), 3-291 (Haynes, 48.5)

1-0 (Winfield-Hill, 0.4), 2-92 (Knight, 18.5), 3-149 (Beaumont, 27.3) 4-153 (Jones, 29.2), 5-177 (Wyatt, 32.5), 6-232 (Dunkley, 41.5) 7-296 (Brunt, 49.2), 8-298 (Ecclestone 49.6)

Bowling	O	M	R	W	wd	nb	Bowling	O	M	R	W	wd	nb
KH Brunt	10	1	54	1	4		M Schutt	10	0	52	1		
A Shrubsole	10	0	45	0	2		DR Brown	6	0	40	0	1	
NR Sciver	10	0	68	2	1		JL Jonassen	3	0	18	2		
Kl Cross	10	0	62	0	2		AJ Sutherland	6	0	42	0		
S Ecclestone	10	0	77	0			EA Perry	5	0	28	0	1	
							TM McGrath	10	0	51	2		
							AM King	10	0	59	3		

Toss: England.   Umpires: Ahmed Shah Pakteen, JM Williams, KD Cotton (TV), Ref: GAV Baxter.   Award: RL Haynes (Aus).
Points: Aus 2, Eng 0. Haynes 50: 73 balls, 5x4; 100: 115 balls, 11x4, Lanning 50: 75 balls, 5x4. Beaumont 50: 54 balls, 5x4, Sciver 50: 43 balls, 6x4; 100: 79 balls, 12x4.

AUSTRALIA v PAKISTAN – MT MAUNGANUI

Australia's bowlers dominated early to reduce Pakistan to 4-44, before Maroof and Riaz combined to add 99 in 31 overs. They did well to reach 6-190, but it was never going to trouble the Australians, Healy timing the ball well in her first 50 of the tournament, as the top order all chipped in to ensure a comfortable win with 15 overs to spare.

Australia v Pakistan at Bay Oval, Mount Maunganui on March 8, 2022 – Australia won by 7 wickets

Pakistan			B	M	4	6	Australia			B	M	4	6
Sidra Ameen	c Lanning b Perry		2	9	13		AJ Healy+	c Sandhu b Sohail		72	79	102	7
Nahida Khan	c Mooney b Schutt		9	10	10	2	RL Haynes	c Maroof b Sandhu		34	34	41	7
Bismah Maroof*	not out		78	122	175	8	MM Lanning*	b Sohail		35	37	44	6
Omaima Sohail	b King		12	25	33	2	EA Perry	not out		26	33	43	2
Nida Dar	c Lanning b Wellington		5	8	5	1	BL Mooney	not out		23	26	24	2
Aliya Riaz	lbw b Carey		53	109	108	4	AJ Sutherland						
Fatima Sana	c Healy b King		14	15	22	1	NJ Carey						
Diana Baig	not out		7	4	4	1	JL Jonassen						
Sidra Nawaz+							AM King						
Nashra Sandhu							A Wellington						
Anam Amin							M Schutt						
	2 b, 2 nb, 6 w		10					1 lb, 1 nb, 1 w		3			
10 overs: 2-37	50 overs		6-190				10 overs: 0-59	34.4 overs		3-193			

1-11 (Nahida, 2.6), 2-11 (Ameen, 3.1), 3-38 (Sohail, 10.6)
4-44 (Nida, 12.5), 5-143 (Riaz, 44.2), 6-177 (Sana, 48.4)

1-60 (Haynes, 10.3), 2-123 (Lanning, 21.1), 3-153 (Healy, 27.1)

Bowling	O	M	R	W	wd	nb	Bowling	O	M	R	W	wd	nb
M Schutt	10	1	43	1	2		Diana Baig	4	0	35	0		1
EA Perry	5	1	27	1	3		Anam Amin	6	0	31	0		
AM King	9	0	24	2			Nida Dar	5.4	0	33	0		
JL Jonassen	10	0	33	0			Fatima Sana	4	0	24	0		
A Wellington	8	1	25	1			Nashra Sandhu	7	0	30	1		
NJ Carey	8	0	36	1	1	2	Omaima Sohail	8	0	39	2	1	

Toss: Australia. Umpires: KD Cotton, AG Wharf, JM Williams (TV), Ref: GAV Baxter. Award: AJ Healy (Aus).
Points: Aus 2, Pak 0. Maroof 50: 96 balls, 5x4, Riaz 50: 107 balls, 4x4. Healy 50: 55 balls, 6x4.

AUSTRALIA v NEW ZEALAND – WELLINGTON

Australia took on the hosts at home in front of a good crowd and were struggling early at 3-56 before Perry and Mooney stabilised the innings to add 57. Perry and McGrath then took over to add 101 in 15 overs, before Perry was superbly caught by Green at long-on diving to her left in front of the sightboard. Australia scored 55 of the last five as Gardner dominated the late overs, hitting four massive sixes in a whirlwind knock. New Zealand reached 0-22, but then lost 5-13 which ended their chances. Devine was bowled through the gate and then Amelia Kerr superbly held by Mooney diving to her right at second slip. Bates top edged a pull, Green got a touch behind and then Mackay was LBW as Australia won their third game on the trot.

Australia v New Zealand at Basin Reserve, Wellington on March 13, 2022 – Australia won by 141 runs

Australia			B	M	4	6	New Zealand			B	M	4	6
RL Haynes	b Tahuhu		30	44	62	4	SW Bates	c McGrath b Brown		16	28	33	1
AJ Healy+	c A Kerr b Mackay		15	31	37	2	SFM Devine*	b Perry		6	6	18	1
MM Lanning*	c Martin b Jensen		5	15	19		AC Kerr	c Mooney b Brown		1	3	3	
EA Perry	c Green b Tahuhu		68	86	114	6	1	AE Satterthwaite	c Lanning b Gardner		44	67	97	5
BL Mooney	b A Kerr		30	44	50	2	ML Green	c Healy b McGrath		3	10	12	
TM McGrath	c Bates b Rowe		57	56	66	8	FL Mackay	lbw b Brown		1	2	3	
AK Gardner	not out		48	18	23	4	4	KJ Martin+	lbw b Wellington		19	27	35	2
AM King	c Bates b Tahuhu		2	5	4		HNK Jensen	c McGrath b Wellington		0	1	1	
A Wellington	run out (Mackay)		1	3	6		HM Rowe	c Perry b Schutt		6	8	8	1
M Schutt	not out		0	0	3		LM Tahuhu	c Mooney b Gardner		23	25	32	2	1
DR Brown							JM Kerr	not out		6	5	7	1
	1 lb, 2 nb, 10 w		13					3 w		3			
10 overs: 1-37	50 overs		8-269				10 overs: 3-29	30.2 overs		128			

1-37 (Healy, 9.5), 2-54 (Lanning, 14.3), 3-56 (Haynes, 15.1),
4-113 (Mooney, 29.1), 5-214 (Perry, 44.6),
6-229 (McGrath, 46.3), 7-238 (King, 47.4),
8-253 (Wellington, 49.1)

1-22 (Devine, 4.3), 2-23 (A Kerr, 5.2), 3-24 (Bates, 7.3)
4-30 (Green, 10.4), 5-35 (Mackay, 11.1), 6-73 (Martin, 19.5)
7-73 (Jensen, 19.6), 8-86 (Rowe, 22.3), 9-121 (Satterthwaite, 28.3),
10-128 (Tahuhu, 30.2)

Bowling	O	M	R	W	wd	nb	Bowling	O	M	R	W	wd	nb
JM Kerr	8	1	34	0	2		EA Perry	5	0	18	1	1	
HM Rowe	9	0	50	1	2		DR Brown	7	1	22	3		
FL Mackay	7	0	34	1			TM McGrath	3	0	17	1		
HNK Jensen	8	0	55	1	4	2	A Wellington	6	0	34	2		
LM Tahuhu	9	0	53	3	1		M Schutt	6	0	22	1	2	
AC Kerr	9	0	42	1	1		AK Gardner	3.2	0	15	2		

Toss: New Zealand. Umpires: L Agenbag, L Rusere, S Redfern (TV), Ref: GS Lakshmi. Award: EA Perry (Aus). Points: Aus 2, NZ 0.
Perry 50: 74 balls, 4x4, McGrath 50: 47 balls, 8x4.

AUSTRALIA v WEST INDIES – WELLINGTON

Perry dented the West Indies chances with consecutive balls in her opening over, when she hit the top of Matthews off-stump and then had Knight caught behind. Dottin was smartly held at slip by Lanning moving to her left, but then West Indies steadied to reach 3-70 in the 23rd over before two wickets in an over for the second time in the innings. Campbelle was caught at short mid-wicket and then Nation was bowled playing down the wrong line. Taylor carried on to reach 50 before being eighth out, West Indies total of 131 well short of par.

Australia had some early hiccups when Matthews took two fine catches, the first off her own bowling to dismiss Healy, before she took a head high chance at slip to dismiss Lanning for a duck. Haynes was nearly run out on 34 and went on to pass 50, adding 51 with Perry and 74 with Mooney as Australia strolled to victory with just under 20 overs to spare.

Australia v West Indies at Basin Reserve, Wellington on March 15, 2022 – Australia won by 7 wickets

West Indies			B	M	4	6	Australia			B	M	4	6
DJS Dottin	c Lanning b Perry	16	36	45	2		AJ Healy+	c & b Matthews	3	8	8		
HK Matthews	b Perry	0	4	7			RL Haynes	not out	83	95	107	9	
KA Knight	c Healy b Perry	0	1	1			MM Lanning*	c Matthews b Connell	0	6	3		
SR Taylor*	lbw b Gardner	50	91	25	3		EA Perry	c Matthews b Henry	10	31	41		
SA Campbelle+	c Mooney b Gardner	20	51	43	2		BL Mooney	not out	28	42	54	3	
CN Nation	b Gardner	0	4	2			TM McGrath						
CA Henry	run out (King-Healy)	10	11	13	2		AK Gardner						
AA Alleyne	c Sutherland b Schutt	10	34	17			AJ Sutherland						
SC Selman	b Jonassen	6	19	15			JL Jonassen						
K Ramharack	c Gardner b Jonassen	4	17	12			AM King						
SS Connell	not out	2	7	5			M Schutt						
	8 lb, 5 w	13						2 lb, 6 w	8				
10 overs: 3-34	45.5 overs	131					10 overs: 2-33	30.2 overs	3-132				

1-4 (Matthews, 1.2), 2-4 (Knight, 1.3), 3-34 (Dottin, 9.5),
4-70 (Campbelle, 22.2), 5-70 (Nation, 22.6), 6-85 (Henry, 26.5),
7-111 (Alleyne, 36.5), 8-119 (Taylor, 40.3), 9-126 (Selman, 43.1),
10-131 (Ramharack, 45.5)

1-6 (Healy, 2.1), 2-7 (Lanning, 3.2), 3-58 (Perry, 15.6)

Bowling	O	M	R	W	wd	nb	Bowling	O	M	R	W	wd	nb
M Schutt	9	2	23	1			HK Matthews	8	2	31	1		
EA Perry	8	0	22	3	3		SS Connell	6	0	32	1	3	
TM McGrath	4	0	17	0	1		K Ramharack	6	0	21	0	3	
AM King	7	1	18	0			CA Henry	5	0	20	1		
AK Gardner	10	1	25	3	1		SC Selman	4	0	18	0		
JL Jonassen	7.5	1	18	2			SR Taylor	1.2	0	8	0		

Toss: West Indies.   Umpires: S Redfern, AG Wharf, L Rusere (TV), Ref: GS Lakshmi.   Award: EA Perry (Aus).   Points: Aus 2, WI 0.
Taylor 50: 89 balls, 3x4. Haynes 50: 66 balls, 5x4.

AUSTRALIA v INDIA – AUCKLAND

At New Zealand's most iconic sporting venue, young quick bowler Brown dominated early to have Mandhana caught at slip and then Verma superbly caught at backward-point. Bhatia and Raj both reached fifties in adding 130 in 26 overs but things slowed when both were caught in the deep. Ghosh and Rana were out consecutive overs but Kaur and Vastrakar added 62 off the last overs to give Australia a challenging target of 278 to win.

Australia got ahead of the rate early as Healy dominated the India bowlers and and along with Haynes added 121 for the first wicket. Both were out in consecutive overs, but then Lanning took charge as she and Perry added 103 in 20 overs. The Aussie skipper was caught at point within sight of a hundred, but Mooney saw the team home, lofting Goswami straight for four with three balls to spare.

Australia v India at Eden Park, Auckland on March 19, 2022 – Australia won by 6 wickets

India			B	M	4	6	Australia			B	M	4	6
SS Mandhana	c Lanning b Brown	10	11	12	1		RL Haynes	c Ghosh b Vastrakar	43	53	95	5	
S Verma	c Mooney b Brown	12	16	25	1	1	AJ Healy+	c Raj b Rana	72	65	87	9	
YH Bhatia	c Perry b Brown	59	83	107	6		MM Lanning*	c Vastrakar b M Singh	97	107	118	13	
MD Raj*	c Perry b King	68	96	122	4	1	EA Perry	c Raj b Vastrakar	28	51	83	1	
H Kaur	not out	57	47	78	6		BL Mooney	not out	30	20	32	4	
RM Ghosh+	st Healy b King	8	14	19			TM McGrath	not out	0	2	5		
S Rana	b Jonassen	0	5	6			AK Gardner						
P Vastrakar	run out (Jonassen)	34	28	31	1	2	JL Jonassen						
JN Goswami							AM King						
Meghna Singh							M Schutt						
RS Gayakwad							DR Brown						
	2 b, 3 lb, 24 w	29						1 lb, 9 w	10				
10 overs: 2-39	50 overs	7-277					10 overs: 0-67	49.3 overs	4-280				

1-11 (Mandhana, 3.1), 2-28 (Verma, 5.6), 3-158 (Bhatia, 31.4), 4-186 (Raj, 37.3), 5-212 (Ghosh, 41.1), 6-213 (Rana, 42.1), 7-277 (Vastrakar, 49.6)

1-121 (Healy, 19.2), 2-123 (Haynes, 20.6), 3-226 (Perry, 41.3), 4-270 (Lanning, 48.4)

Bowling	O	M	R	W	wd	nb
M Schutt	10	0	57	0		
DR Brown	8	0	30	3	3	
JL Jonassen	7	0	40	1		
EA Perry	3	0	24	0	6	
AK Gardner	6	1	34	0	4	
TM McGrath	6	0	35	0	1	
AM King	10	1	52	2	2	

Bowling	O	M	R	W	wd	nb
JN Goswami	9.3	0	64	0		1
Meghna Singh	10	0	68	1	5	
RS Gayakwad	10	0	48	0	1	
P Vastrakar	10	0	43	2	2	
S Rana	10	0	56	1		

Toss: Australia. Umpires L Agenbag, Sharfuddoula, RSA Palliyaguruge (TV), Ref: SA Fritz. Award: MM Lanning (Aus).
Points: Aus 2, India 0. Y Khatia 50: 77 balls, 5x4, Raj 50: 77 balls, 3x4 1x6, Kair 50: 42 balls, 6x4, Healy 50: 49 balls, 6x4, Lanning 50: 56 balls, 8x4.

AUSTRALIA v SOUTH AFRICA - WELLINGTON

South Africa's openers were on their way with Woolvardt being the dominant partner, finding the rope in the early stages. Lee took 16 overs to hit her first four and was starting to look dangerous until she tried to turn a straight ball to leg and was LBW. Woolvardt slowed a bit to reach her fifty from 86 balls, but later Luus hit some fine shots. Both were out in consecutive overs to good catches in the deep by McGrath, but they were bettered by Gardner's one-handed effort to catch du Preez at deep mid-wicket. South Africa's final push came from Kapp and Tryon who added 43 in the last five overs setting Australia 272 to win. Australia were under pressure early when Healy nicked off, but Lanning came out and hit the ball sweetly from the word go. Haynes was superbly caught at deep square-leg, but then Mooney came out and helped her skipper add 60 as Australia kept up with the rate needed. When Mooney was picked off by a throw from square-leg, McGrath filled the breach as she and Lanning took control of the game with a stand of 93 in just 13 overs. Lanning reached her century off 92 balls, when she disposed of a short ball behind square-leg for four and went on to be there at the end, as Australia made it to the winning post with 28 balls to spare.

Australia v South Africa at Basin Reserve, Wellington on March 22, 2022 – Australia won by 5 wickets

South Africa			B	M	4	6
L Lee	lbw b King	36	44	72	3	
L Wolvaardt	c McGrath b Gardner	90	134	152	6	
L Goodall	c King b Sutherland	15	29	26	1	
SE Luus*	c McGrath b Schutt	52	51	58	6	
M du Preez	c Gardner b Jonassen	14	13	12	2	
M Kapp	not out	30	21	22	4	
CL Tryon	not out	17	9	14		1
T Chetty+						
S Ismail						
A Khaka						
TS Sekhukhune						
4 lb, 1 nb, 12 w		17				
10 overs: 0-41	50 overs	5-271				

Australia			B	M	4	6
RL Haynes	c du Preez b Tryon	17	29	42	2	
AJ Healy+	c Chetty b Ismail	5	6	9	1	
MM Lanning*	not out	135	130	166	15	1
BL Mooney	run out (Sekhukhune)	21	23	36	3	
TM McGrath	c Kapp b Ismail	32	35	51	1	
AK Gardner	c Sekhukhune b Tryon	22	26	26	4	
AJ Sutherland	not out	22	23	17	2	1
EA Perry						
JL Jonassen						
AM King						
M Schutt						
6 lb, 12 w		18				
10 overs: 1-44	45.2 overs	5-272				

1-88 (Lee, 19.4), 2-118 (Goodall, 27.1), 3-209 (Wolvaardt, 42.3), 4-216 (Luus, 43.4), 5-228 (du Preez, 45.5)

1-14 (Healy, 2.1), 2-45 (Haynes, 10.3), 3-105 (Mooney, 19.2), 4-198 (McGrath, 32.4), 5-241 (Gardner, 39.2)

Bowling	O	M	R	W	wd	nb
M Schutt	10	0	55	1	1	
EA Perry	3	0	18	0	2	1
JL Jonassen	10	0	52	1		
AK Gardner	10	1	52	1	2	
AJ Sutherland	6	0	26	1	2	
TM McGrath	4	0	29	0	5	
AM King	7	1	35	1		

Bowling	O	M	R	W	wd	nb
S Ismail	7	1	33	2		
M Kapp	8	0	38	0	2	
A Khaka	9.2	0	48	0	4	
CL Tryon	8	0	44	2	1	
TS Sekhukhune	7	0	68	0	5	
SE Luus	6	0	35	0		

Toss: Australia. Umpires KD Cotton, AG Wharf, S Redfern (TV), Ref: GS Lakshmi. Award: MM Lanning (Aus).
Points: Aus 2, SA 0. Wolvaardt 50: 86 balls, 4x4, Luus 50: 48 balls, 6x4. Lanning 50: 56 balls, 7x4 1x6: 100: 92 balls, 13x4 1x6.

AUSTRALIA v BANGLADESH - WELLINGTON

On a typically windy day in Wellington, Australia was without Perry who had been suffering from back spasms. Bangladesh struggled to get the scoring rate up against some good Australian bowling and fielding. Australia was in trouble early in the run chase as Healy lofted a sweep to deep square-leg, Lanning was bowled and Haynes hit a catch to mid-off. An upset was in the offing when Gardner was leg before to make Australia 4-41. Gardner helped add 29 with Mooney before being bowled but then Sutherland came in and ensured the win as she and Mooney added an unbeaten 66 from 15 overs.

Australia v Bangladesh at Basin Reserve, Wellington on March 25, 2022 – Australia won by 5 wickets

Bangladesh			B	M	4	6
Murshida Khatun	c Haynes b Gardner	12	17	38	1	
Sharmin Akter	lbw b Jonassen	24	56	75	2	
Farzana Haque	c Healy b Sutherland	8	22	18		
Nigar Sultana*+	c McGrath b Jonassen	7	30	30		
Rumana Ahmed	c Jonassen b Gardner	15	45	55	2	
Lata Mondal	st Healy b Schutt	33	63	78	2	
Salma Khatun	not out	15	23	38	1	
Nahida Akter	not out	3	3	2		
Ritu Moni						
Fahima Khatun						
Jahanara Alam						
	1 b, 3 lb, 1 nb, 13 w	18				
9 overs: 1-38	43 overs	6-135				

1-33 (Murshida, 8.1), 2-48 (Farzana, 13.5), 3-58 (Sharmin, 18.1), 4-62 (Sultana, 22.2), 5-95 (Rumana, 34.2), 6-131 (Mondal, 42.1).

Bowling	O	M	R	W	wd	nb
M Schutt	8	2	25	1	2	
DR Brown	6	0	25	0	5	1
AK Gardner	8	1	23	2	2	
JL Jonassen	9	3	13	2	1	
AJ Sutherland	6	0	22	1	3	
AM King	6	1	23	0		

Australia			B	M	4	6
AJ Healy+	c Jahanara b Salma	15	22	26	3	
RL Haynes	c Farzana b Khatun	7	23	45		
MM Lanning*	b Salma	0	8	12		
BL Mooney	not out	66	75	95	5	
TM McGrath	lbw b Nahida	3	11	13		
AK Gardner	b Rumana	13	16	21	2	
AJ Sutherland	not out	26	39	54	1	
JL Jonassen						
AM King						
M Schutt						
DR Brown						
	2 lb, 1 nb, 3 w	6				
9 overs: 2-26	32.1 overs	5-136				

1-22 (Healy, 5.3), 2-23 (Lanning, 7.4), 3-26 (Haynes, 9.2), 4-41 (McGrath, 12.5), 5-70 (Gardner, 17.4).

Bowling	O	M	R	W	wd	nb
Jahanara Alam	4	1	13	0		1
Salma Khatun	9	0	23	3	1	
Lata Mondal	2	0	12	0		
Nahida Akter	5	0	33	1		
Rumana Ahmed	8.1	0	35	1		
Ritu Moni	2	0	11	0		
Fahima Khatun	2	0	7	0	2	

Toss: Australia. Umpires: L Agenbag, AG Wharf, AS Pakteen (TV), Ref: SA Fritz. Award: BL Mooney (Aus). Points: Aus 2, Ban 0.
Mooney 50: 60 balls, 4x4.

GROUP STANDINGS

	Won	Lost	NR	Points	Net RR
Australia	7	-	-	14	+1.283
South Africa	5	1	1	11	+0.078
England	4	3	-	8	+0.949
West Indies	3	3	1	7	-0.885
India	3	4	-	6	+0.642
New Zealand	3	4	-	6	+0.027
Bangladesh	1	6	-	2	-0.999
Pakistan	1	6	-	2	-1.313

SEMI FINAL - WELLINGTON

Australia had their second comfortable win over the West Indies in the space of two weeks to progress to the Final. Haynes and Healy led the way with a stand of 216, which was the third best ever ODI partnership for Australia. Healy was dropped on five when Henry dropped a tough caught and bowled chance but eased her way to her fourth ODI ton. Australia passed 300 for the second time in the tournament, thanks to a great cameo from Mooney, who smacked an unbeaten 43 off just 31 balls. West Indies reply started badly when Williams was superbly caught by Mooney diving to her right at square-leg. Despite useful innings by Dottin, Matthews and skipper Taylor, West Indies were never up with the rate. They also batted two short with Mohammed injury and Henry unwell, Australia winning easily to make it to the Final.

Semi Final, Australia v West Indies at Basin Reserve, Wellington on March 30, 2022 – Australia won by 157 runs

Australia			B	M	4	6
RL Haynes+	c Dottin b Henry	85	100	156	9	
AJ Healy	c sub (SC Selman) b Connell	129	107	144	17	1
AK Gardner	c Campbelle b Henry	12	8	13	2	
MM Lanning*	not out	26	26	38	1	
BL Mooney	not out	43	31	34	3	
TM McGrath						
AJ Sutherland						
JL Jonassen						
AM King						
M Schutt						
DR Brown						
	2 nb, 8 w	10				
9 overs: 0-37	45 overs	3-305				

West Indies			B	M	4	6
DJS Dottin	c Sutherland b McGrath	34	35	39	5	
RS Williams	c Mooney b Schutt	0	10	14		
HK Matthews	c King b Jonassen	34	49	75	2	
SR Taylor*	c Jonassen b King	48	75	105	4	
SA Campbelle+	c Jonassen b Sutherland	8	23	21		
CN Nation	run out (Healy)	7	6	5	1	
KA Knight	b Jonassen	0	2	1		
K Ramharack	lbw b Gardner	7	15	18		
SS Connell	not out	1	7	9		
CA Henry	absent					
A Mohammed	absent					
	1 lb, 8 w	9				
9 overs: 1-39	37 overs	148				

1-216 (Healy, 32.4), 2-231 (Haynes, 35.1), 3-236 (Gardner, 35.6)

1-12 (Williams, 3.5), 2-44 (Dottin, 9.3), 3-91 (Matthews, 22.4)
4-117 (Campbelle, 28.3), 5-126 (Nation, 29.4),
6-126 (Knight, 29.6), 7-146 (Ramharack, 35.2),
8-148 (Taylor, 36.6)

Bowling	O	M	R	W	wd	nb
SS Connell	8	0	45	1	3	
CA Henry	9	0	51	2	1	
HK Matthews	9	0	45	0		
A Mohammed	2	0	20	0	1	
K Ramharack	9	0	65	0		2
DJS Dottin	3	0	31	0	2	
SR Taylor	5	0	48	0	1	

Bowling	O	M	R	W	wd	nb
DR Brown	6	0	37	0	4	
M Schutt	4	0	8	1	1	
AJ Sutherland	6	0	26	1	2	
TM McGrath	4	0	17	1	1	
AM King	6	0	19	1		
AK Gardner	6	0	26	1		
JL Jonassen	5	0	14	2		

Toss: West Indies.   Umpires: L Agenbag, KD Cotton, S Redfern (TV), Ref: SA Fritz.   Award: AJ Healy (Aus).
Haynes 50: 66 balls, 6x4, Healy 50: 63 balls, 6x4, 100: 91 balls, 13x4 1x6.

THE FINAL - CHRISTCHURCH

Australia made just one change for the Final with Perry back in the side, having recovered from back spasms, Sutherland the player who made way. Australia started quietly only adding 16 in the first six overs against tidy bowling from Brunt and Shrubsole. Haynes then hooked and pull fours in the seventh over, while Healy did score her first four until the ninth over. A straight drive from Healy for four off Shrubsole saw Australia reach 37 at the end of the powerplay. The Aussie scoring picked up as 31 came from the next five overs and then in the 16th England reviewed an LBW shout by Ecclestone versus Healy, but the replays showed an inside edge.

Haynes had some luck on 47 when she cut Cross to backward-point, only for Wyatt to drop the chance. Then in the next over when Healy was on 43, she pulled Ecclestone to Sciver at mid-wicket who put down the catch. The stand reached 100 in the 22nd over, Healy in the 25th smacking Dean for two fours in the over through mid-off. The stand came to an end in 30th over, when Haynes sliced a catch into the off-side. Mooney joined Healy and the pair continued to score freely, with the Aussie keeper reaching her 100 in the 35th over with a cut off Shrubsole for a single.

From there on it was a boundary-fest for Healy, her 100 had come from as many balls, but she motored to 150 in just another 29. She was severe on Sciver in the 43rd over, smacking her for three fours in a row, the second a dropped chance on 136* to Beaumont who leapt high at short fine-leg but couldn't hold on. In the 44th over she hit Ecclestone for three fours in an over but started to tire and was eventually stumped in the 46th, her innings the highest by either male or female in a World Cup Final.

Wickets fell in the later overs, as Gardner was run out and Lanning top edged to short third man in her 100th ODI. Mooney's top innings ended when she pulled a catch to deep mid-wicket. Australia 5-331 midway through the 48th over, McGrath and Perry combined to add 25 from 15 balls, including 15 off the last over to take Australia past 350. Only Shrubsole could be happy with her effort with ball, as the rest floundered in an inning which remarkably didn't see a six all.

With England needing more than seven runs per over, Schutt as she often has over the years, chiming in with an early wicket as Wyatt was bowled by an inswinger. Beaumont looked in fine touch hitting the ropes with regularity until she too was dismissed by one from Schutt that swung in. In the same over Sciver was struck on the pad, the Aussies review of the LBW a bad one as the ball was clearly missing leg. Knight started to hit her straps, thumping Brown for three fours in an over and when Sciver lofted King for six over long-on, England were 2-71 after 11 overs. England hopes grew as Sciver hit McGrath for two fours in the 14th over but then hit rock bottom when Knight played back to King when she should have been forward and was palpably LBW.

Jones was another to get a start and again at 3-127 after 20 overs, England was building a good base for the chase. But in the next over she lofted one to mid-off and King ran back and took a good catch. Dunkley on nine gave Lanning a tough chance at cover but she settled well with Sciver as the pair added 50 from 45 balls. But then King went around the wicket and offered a gap behind square-leg, Dunkley went the sweep and was bowled behind her pads. Australia then took control as Brunt walked past one and was stumped, Ecclestone battled to turn over the strike before being trapped plumb in front. When Cross popped a catch back to Jonassen, England were 8-213 and it seemed the end would come quickly.

But England had one last bit of fight in them as Dean joined Sciver, who reached her second hundred in the tournament against Australia when she pulled McGrath fine for two. The ninth wicket pairing did well to really kick the total along, Sciver finding the gaps for boundaries with Dean doing a good job feeding her strike. With 98 to win off the last 10 overs, England were still a chance, but Jonassen brought the field up and just three singles came from the 41st over. Gardner came on for the 42nd, with Sciver brilliantly reverse sweeping her first ball through cover-point for four. Ten came from the over but then in Gardner's next over Dean struck a reverse sweep to short third-man, ending a stand of 65 from 53 balls. The end was nigh as Jonassen claimed the final wicket, Shrubsole trying to lift one over mid-off off Jonassen to be well held by Gardner running back at mid-off. Australia had won comfortably in the end, having gone through undefeated in nine matches and celebrated accordingly, while Sciver could be proud of her efforts as she walked off having played one the great innings in a World Cup Final.

The Final, Australia v England at Hagley Oval, Christchurch on April 3, 2022 – Australia won by 71 runs

Australia			B	M	4	6
AJ Healy +	st Jones b Shrubsole	170	138	188	26	
RL Haynes	c Beaumont b Ecclestone	68	93	112	7	
BL Mooney	c Sciver b Shrubsole	62	47	87	8	
AK Gardner	run out (Cross-Shrubsole)	1	2	2		
MM Lanning *	c Beaumont b Shrubsole	10	5	7	2	
TM McGrath	not out	8	5	8	1	
EA Perry	not out	17	10	8	2	
JL Jonassen						
AM King						
M Schutt						
DR Brown						
	4 b, 2 lb, 14 w	20				
10 overs: 0-37	50 overs	5-356				

1-160 (Haynes, 29.1), 2-316 (Healy, 45.3), 3-318 (Gardner, 45.6), 4-331 (Lanning, 47.2), 5-331 (Mooney, 47.3),

England			B	M	4	6
TT Beaumont	lbw b Schutt	27	26	27	5	
DN Wyatt	b Schutt	4	5	10	1	
HC Knight*	lbw b King	26	25	51	4	
NR Sciver	not out	148	121	145	15	1
AE Jones+	c King b Jonassen	20	18	19	2	
SIR Dunkley	b King	22	22	30	1	
KH Brunt	st Healy b King	1	4	7		
S Ecclestone	lbw b McGrath	3	10	13		
KL Cross	c & b Jonassen	2	3	4		
CE Dean	c Jonassen b Gardner	21	24	31	1	
A Shrubsole	c Gardner b Jonassen	1	4	5		
	4 lb, 6 w	10				
10 overs: 2-59	43.4 overs	285				

1-12 (Wyatt, 2.1), 2-38 (Beaumont, 6.3), 3-88 (Knight, 14.6), 4-129 (Jones, 20.3), 5-179 (Dunkley, 27.6), 6-191 (Brunt, 29.4), 7-206 (Ecclestone, 32.4), 8-213 (Cross, 33.4), 9-278 (Dean, 42.3), 10-285 (Shrubsole, 43.4)

Bowling	O	M	R	W	wd	nb
KH Brunt	10	0	69	0	1	
A Shrubsole	10	0	46	3	1	
NR Sciver	8	0	65	0	1	
CE Dean	4	0	34	0	1	
S Ecclestone	10	0	71	1	2	
KL Cross	8	0	65	0	8	

Bowling	O	M	R	W	wd	nb
M Schutt	8	0	42	2	2	
DR Brown	7	0	57	0	4	
AM King	10	0	64	3		
TM McGrath	8	0	46	1		
JL Jonassen	8.4	0	57	3		
AK Gardner	2	0	15	1		

Toss: England.   Umpires: L Agenbag, KD Cotton, JM Williams (TV), Ref: GS Lakshmi.   Award: AJ Healy (Aus).   Crowd: approx. 9,000
Healy 50: 62 balls, 6x4, 100: 100 balls, 13x4, 150: 129 balls, 22x4. Haynes 50: 69 balls, 6x4. Sciver 50: 53 balls, 5x4 1x6, 100: 90 balls, 10x4 1x6

AVERAGES

Batting	M	I	NO	Runs	HS	Avg	SR	100s	50s
BL Mooney	9	9	6	330	66*	110.0	101.8	0	2
RL Haynes	9	9	1	497	130	62.1	82.5	1	3
AJ Healy	9	9	0	509	170	56.5	103.6	2	2
MM Lanning	9	9	2	394	135*	56.2	88.7	1	2
EA Perry	7	6	3	163	68	54.3	75.4	0	1
TM McGrath	8	5	2	100	57	33.3	91.7	0	1
AK Gardner	7	5	1	96	48*	24.0	137.1	0	0
AJ Sutherland	6	2	2	48	26*	-	77.4	0	0
AM King	9	1	0	2	2	2.0	40.0	0	0
SK Moloney	1	1	0	1	1	1.0	0	0	0
M Schutt	9	1	1	0	0*	-	0	0	0

Bowling	O	W	Avg	Best	Econ
JL Jonassen	60.3	13	18.8	3-57	4.05
AM King	65	12	24.5	3-59	4.52
AK Gardner	45.2	10	19.0	3-25	4.19
M Schutt	75	9	36.3	2-42	4.36
DR Brown	40	6	35.1	3-22	5.27
TM McGrath	39	5	42.4	2-51	5.44
EA Perry	29	5	27.4	3-22	4.72
AJ Sutherland	24	3	38.6	1-22	4.83
SK Moloney	6	2	17.0	2-34	5.67
AJ Wellington	8	1	25.0	1-25	3.13
NJ Carey	8	1	36.0	1-36	4.50

DR Brown (6 matches), NJ Carey (1 match), JL Jonassen (8 matches) and AJ Wellington (1 match) did not bat.

Fielding – Healy 8 (4ct/4st), Mooney 7, Lanning 6, Jonassen 6, McGrath 5, Gardner 3, King 3, Perry 3, Haynes 2.

WOMEN'S WORLD CUP TITLES

1973	England	1993	England	2009	England
1978	Australia	1997	Australia	2013	Australia
1982	Australia	2000	New Zealand	2017	England
1988	Australia	2005	Australia	2022	Australia

AUSTRALIA IN IRELAND, 2022

In the lead up to the Commonwealth Games, Australia stopped off in Ireland for a brief T20 series. Australia beat Ireland on both occasions, while rain ruined both games against Pakistan, with Australia well on top.

Australia v Pakistan at Bready on July 16, 2022 – No result

Pakistan			B	4	6
Iram Javed	b Schutt	12	10	2	
Muneeba Ali+	b Gardner	4	14	1	
Bismah Maroof*	b Gardner	1	5		
Nida Dar	not out	10	14	1	
Kainat Imtiaz	lbw b King	0	1		
Ayesha Naseem	lbw b King	0	1		
Aliya Riaz	lbw b King	0	1		
Fatima Sana	not out	1	4		
Tooba Hassan					
Diana Baig					
Anam Amin					
	5 lb, 2 nb, 21 w	28			
6 overs: 3-39	8 overs	6-56			

Australia: AJ Healy+, BL Mooney, MM Lanning*, TM McGrath, RL Haynes, AK Gardner, GM Harris, NJ Carey, AM King, M Schutt, DR Brown

1-29 (Javed, 3.1), 2-33 (Bismah, 4.1), 3-35 (Muneeba, 4.6),
4-44 (Imtiaz, 6.1), 5-47 (Naseem, 6.2), 6-47 (Riaz, 6.3)

Bowling	O	M	R	W	wd	nb	Dots
M Schutt	2	0	6	1	3		9
DR Brown	2	0	22	0	9	2	8
AK Gardner	2	0	11	2	1		8
TM McGrath	1	0	4	0			5
AM King	1	0	8	3	8		6

Toss: Pakistan. Umpires: M Hawthorne, A Seaver, Ref: P Thompson. Award: None given. Points: Aus 1, Pak 1.

Australia v Ireland at Bready on July 17, 2022 – Australia won by 9 wickets

Ireland			B	4	6
RK Stokell	b King	22	33	2	
GH Lewis	c Gardner b Schutt	0	4		
O Prendergast	b Brown	12	9	2	
LK Delany*	b Brown	0	4		
R Delaney	lbw b King	1	5		
MV Waldron+	c Schutt b Carey	7	16		
AN Kelly	c Brown b McGrath	5	11		
L Paul	c Healy b King	12	17		
A Canning	not out	14	16		
J A Maguire	not out	3	7		
C Murray					
	10 lb, 2 nb, 11 w	23			
6 overs: 3-26	20 overs	8-99			

Australia			B	4	6
AJ Healy+	c Maguire b Kelly	10	11	18	1
BL Mooney	not out	45	33	53	4
MM Lanning*	not out	39	33	33	5
TM McGrath					
RL Haynes					
AK Gardner					
GM Harris					
NJ Carey					
AM King					
M Schutt					
DR Brown					
	1 lb, 8 w	9			
6 overs: 1-43	12.5 overs	1-103			

1-35 (Healy, 4.3)

1-1 (Lewis, 0.6), 2-16 (Prendergast, 3.2), 3-16 (Delany, 3.6),
4-27 (Delaney, 6.4), 5-44 (Waldron, 10.6), 6-44 (Stokell, 11.4),
7-69 (Kelly, 14.6), 8-90 (Paul, 18.1)

Bowling	O	M	R	W	wd	nb	Dots
M Schutt	3	0	21	1	1		10
DR Brown	4	1	9	2		1	16
TM McGrath	2	0	17	1	3		6
AM King	4	0	9	3			16
AK Gardner	3	0	14	0			8
NJ Carey	4	0	19	1	1	1	7

Bowling	O	M	R	W	wd	nb	Dots
J A Maguire	2.5	0	29	0	7		6
A Canning	2	0	18	0			2
LK Delaney	2	0	12	0		1	7
AN Kelly	3	0	19	1			6
L Paul	2	0	14	0			2
C Murray	1	0	10	0			2

Ireland v Pakistan at Bready on July 19, 2022 – Pakistan won by 13 runs (DLS)

Toss: Pakistan. **Pakistan 5-92** (14 overs) **def Ireland 6-83** (14 overs) (GH Lewis 47). Award: Nida Dar (Pak). Points: Pak 2, Ire 0.

Australia v Ireland at Bready on July 21, 2022 – Australia won by 63 runs

Australia

Batter	Dismissal	R	B	4	6
AJ Healy+	lbw b Dempsey	1	9		
BL Mooney	c Kelly b Delaney	9	9	1	
MM Lanning*	c Dempsey b Kelly	74	49	9	2
TM McGrath	c Murray b Dempsey	70	45	11	
RL Haynes	not out	11	5	2	
AK Gardner	not out	5	3	1	
AJ Sutherland					
JL Jonassen					
AM King					
M Schutt					
DR Brown					
	4 b, 2 lb, 6 w	12			
6 overs: 2-39	20 overs	4-182			

1-7 (Healy, 1.6), 2-31 (Mooney, 4.4),
3-166 (Lanning, 18.3), 4-176 (McGrath, 19.2)

Ireland

Batter	Dismissal	R	B	4	6
RK Stokell	c Haynes b Schutt	1	4		
GH Lewis	c Lanning b Jonassen	7	11	1	
O Prendergast	b King	25	22	4	
LK Delany*	c Haynes b Brown	21	31	1	
R Delaney	st Healy b King	3	6		
MV Waldron+	b Schutt	15	18	1	
AN Kelly	b Jonassen	12	15		
L Paul	not out	12	12		
G Dempsey	not out	3	3		
A Canning					
C Murray					
	3 lb, 2 nb, 15 w	20			
6 overs: 2-42	20 overs	7-119			

1-2 (Stokell, 0.5), 2-26 (Lewis, 3.5), 3-62 (Prendergast, 8.4),
4-66 (Delaney, 10.1), 5-89 (Waldron, 14.4), 6-91 (Delany, 15.1),
7-108 (Kelly, 18.3)

Bowling	O	M	R	W	wd	nb	Dots
A Canning	3	0	18	0			11
G Dempsey	4	0	35	2	3		9
R Delaney	2	0	23	1			3
AN Kelly	4	0	41	1	1		7
L Paul	3	0	20	0			8
C Murray	2	0	25	0	2		3
LK Delany	2	0	14	0			2

Bowling	O	M	R	W	wd	nb	Dots
M Schutt	3	0	16	2	5		10
DR Brown	4	0	18	1	2		12
JL Jonassen	4	0	27	2			10
AJ Sutherland	3	0	26	0	7	2	8
AK Gardner	3	0	18	0			3
AM King	3	0	11	2	1		9

Toss: Ireland. Umpires: M Hawthorne, J Kennedy, Ref: P Thompson. Award: TM McGrath (Aus)
Lanning 50: 31 balls, 6x4 2x6, McGrath 50: 30 balls, 9x4   Points: Aus 2, Ire 0

Australia v Pakistan at Bready on July 23, 2022 – No result

Pakistan

Batter	Dismissal	R	B	4	6
Muneeba Ali+	c Mooney b Carey	19	23	2	
Iram Javed	b Gardner	9	14	1	
Omaima Sohail	c Gardner b Jonassen	2	5		
Bismah Maroof*	not out	32	39	1	
Ayesha Naseem	c Lanning b Carey	0	6		
Aliya Riaz	run out (Schutt-Healy)	14	17	1	
Kainat Imtiaz	st Healy b Jonassen	11	13	1	
Fatima Sana	b Jonassen	0	1		
Diana Baig	b Jonassen	1	2		
Anam Amin					
Tooba Hassan					
	3 lb, 3 w	6			
6 overs: 2-30	20 overs	8-94			

1-21 (Javed, 4.3), 2-30 (Sohail, 5.6), 3-38 (Muneeba, 8.5),
4-42 (Naseem, 10.3), 5-72 (Riaz, 15.4), 6-92 (Imtiaz, 19.2),
7-92 (Sana, 19.3 ov), 8-94 (Baig)

Australia

Batter	Dismissal	R	B	4	6
BL Mooney	not out	11	13	1	
AJ Healy+	not out	12	14	1	
MM Lanning*					
TM McGrath					
RL Haynes					
AK Gardner					
NJ Carey					
JL Jonassen					
AM King					
M Schutt					
GM Harris					
	1 lb, 1 nb, 3 w	5			
	4.2 overs	0-28			

Bowling	O	M	R	W	wd	nb	Dots
AK Gardner	4	0	16	1			13
M Schutt	4	0	24	0			11
JL Jonassen	4	0	17	4	2		13
AM King	4	0	18	0	1		12
NJ Carey	4	0	16	2			10

Bowling	O	M	R	W	wd	nb	Dots
Diana Baig	2	0	15	0	3	1	5
Anam Amin	2	0	10	0			5
Fatima Sana	0.2	0	2	0			1

Toss: Pakistan. Umpires: A Seaver, M Hawthorne, Ref: P Thompson. Award: None given. Points: Aust 1, Pak 1.

Ireland v Pakistan at Bready on July 24, 2022 – Match abandoned without a ball bowled
Final Points table: Australia 6, Pakistan 5, Ireland 1.

AUSTRALIA WINS GOLD AT COMMONWEALTH GAMES

Australia added another trophy to its cabinet when it won gold at the Birmingham Commonwealth Games. They were tested in their opening match, being 5-49 chasing 155 to win, before Ash Gardner got them over the line. Barbados and Pakistan provided them with little to worry about, which saw the team cruise into the Medal playoffs. New Zealand tested them in the Semi-final, which again went to the last over, while the final was a classic encounter, Australia defending well enough in the end to take the Gold.

Australia v India at Edgbaston on July 29, 2022 – Australia won by 3 wickets

India			B	4	6
SS Mandhana	c Healy b Brown	24	17	5	
S Verma	c Healy b Jonassen	48	33	9	
YH Bhatia+	run out (Harris-Healy)	8	12	1	
H Kaur*	b Schutt	52	34	8	1
JI Rodrigues	c Mooney b Jonassen	11	12	1	
DB Sharma	c and b Jonassen	1	2		
H Deol	c McGrath b Jonassen	7	6	1	
RP Yadav	not out	2	3		
Meghna Singh	c McGrath b Schutt	0	1		
RS Gayakwad					
Renuka Singh					
	1 w	1			
6 overs: 1-35	20 overs	8-154			

Australia			B	4	6
AJ Healy+	c Sharma b Renuka Singh	0	2		
BL Mooney	b Renuka Singh	10	9	1	
MM Lanning*	c Yadav b Renuka Singh	8	5	1	
TM McGrath	b Renuka Singh	14	8	3	
RL Haynes	c Yadav b Sharma	9	14		
AK Gardner	not out	52	35	9	
GM Harris	c Kaur b Meghna Singh	37	20	5	2
JL Jonassen	c&b Sharma	3	5		
AM King	not out	18	16	3	
M Schutt					
DR Brown					
	1 lb, 5 w	6			
6 overs: 4-41	19 overs	7-157			

1-25 (Mandhana, 3.3), 2-68 (Bhatia, 9.1), 3-93 (Verma, 11.4), 4-115 (Rodrigues, 15.1), 5-117 (Sharma, 15.5), 6-140 (Deol, 18.2), 7-154 (Kaur, 19.5), 8-154 (Meghna Singh, 19.6)

1-0 (Healy, 0.2), 2-20 (Lanning, 2.1), 3-21 (Mooney, 2.5), 4-34 (McGrath, 4.1), 5-49 (Haynes, 7.2), 6-100 (Harris, 12.6), 7-110 (Jonassen, 14.2)

Bowling	O	M	R	W	wd	nb	Dots
DR Brown	3	0	30	1			9
M Schutt	4	0	26	2			12
AK Gardner	4	0	23	0			13
AM King	4	0	36	0			5
JL Jonassen	4	0	22	4			13
TM McGrath	1	0	17	0		1	

Bowling	O	M	R	W	wd	nb	Dots
Renuka Singh	4	0	18	4	3		16
Meghna Singh	4	0	38	1			10
RS Gayakwad	2	0	24	0			4
DB Sharma	4	0	24	2	1		12
RP Yadav	4	0	42	0			8
H Kaur	1	0	10	0	1		0

Toss: India.   Umpires: L Agenbag, S Redfern, KD Cotton (TV), Ref: SA Fritz.   Points: Aus 2, India 0.
Kaur 50: 31 balls, 5x4 1x6, Gardner 50: 34 balls, 9x4

Australia v Barbados at Edgbaston on July 31, 2022 – Australia won by 9 wickets

Barbados			B	4	6
DJS Dottin	lbw b King	8	22	1	
HK Matthews*	c Harris b Brown	18	13	4	
Kycia A Knight+	c Schutt b McGrath	9	11		
Kyshona A Knight	c Harris b Gardner	5	9		
AA Alleyne	b King	8	16		
T Holder	c Healy b Gardner	0	5		
A Scantlebury	b McGrath	8	19		
SC Selman	lbw b King	0	3		
SS Connell	lbw b King	0	1		
KO Elliott	lbw b McGrath	2	13		
SJ Bruce	not out	1	9		
	1 b, 1 lb, 1 nb, 2 w	5			
6 overs: 1-29	20 overs	64			

Australia			B	4	6
AJ Healy+	not out	23	24	4	
BL Mooney	st Kycia A Knight b Bruce	2	6		
MM Lanning*	not out	36	21	5	2
TM McGrath					
RL Haynes					
AK Gardner					
GM Harris					
JL Jonassen					
AM King					
M Schutt					
DR Brown					
	2 nb, 5 w	7			
	8.1 overs	1-68			

1-20 (Matthews, 3.5), 2-37 (Dottin, 7.2),
3-39 (Kycia A Knight, 8.2), 4-49 (Kys A Knight, 11.1),
5-49 (Holder, 11.6), 6-51 (Alleyne, 12.6), 7-53 (Selman, 14.3),
8-53 (Connell, 14.4), 9-60 (Scantlebury, 17.5), 10-64 (Elliott, 19.6)

1-5 (Mooney, 1.2)

Bowling	O	M	R	W	wd	nb	Dots
M Schutt	2	0	6	0			7
DR Brown	3	0	22	1	1		12
JL Jonassen	3	1	7	0	1		15
AM King	4	1	8	4			17
TM McGrath	4	0	13	3		1	14
AK Gardner	4	1	6	2			19

Bowling	O	M	R	W	wd	nb	Dots
SS Connell	2	0	10	0	1		7
SJ Bruce	2	0	7	1			8
HK Matthews	2	1	9	0			9
DJS Dottin	1	0	25	0	1	2	3
KO Elliott	1	0	11	0			1
SC Selman	0.1	0	6	0	1		

Toss: Australia.   Umpires: S Mishra, S Redfern, KD Cotton (TV), Ref: SA Fritz.   Points: Aus 2, Barb 0.

Australia v Pakistan at Edgbaston on August 3, 2022 – Australia won by 44 runs

Australia			B	4	6
AJ Healy+	b Fatima Sana	4	8	1	
BL Mooney	not out	70	49	8	1
MM Lanning*	b Sadia Iqbal	4	12	1	
TM McGrath	not out	78	51	10	1
RL Haynes					
AK Gardner					
GM Harris					
JL Jonassen					
AM King					
M Schutt					
DR Brown					
	1 lb, 3 w	4			
6 overs : 2-22	20 overs	2-160			

1-9 (Healy, 1.4), 2-19 (Lanning, 5.2)

Pakistan			B	4	6
Muneeba Ali+	c Brown b Schutt	0	3		
Bismah Maroof*	c Jonassen b McGrath	23	32	1	
Iram Javed	c Harris b Brown	6	8	1	
Omaima Sohail	b King	23	23	3	
Aliya Riaz	run out (McGrath)	1	4		
Ayesha Naseem	c King b McGrath	8	14	1	
Fatima Sana	not out	35	26	2	2
Tooba Hassan	lbw b McGrath	0	1		
Diana Baig	lbw b Jonassen	2	7		
Aimen Anwar	not out	2	2		
Sadia Iqbal					
	4 b, 12 w	16			
6 overs : 2-32	20 overs	8-116			

1-0 (Muneeba, 0.3), 2-8 (Javed, 1.6), 3-44 (Sohail, 8.1), 4-47 (Riaz, 9.1), 5-60 (Naseem, 12.4), 6-81 (Bismah, 16.2), 7-81 (Hassan, 16.3), 8-104 (Baig, 18.6)

Bowling	O	M	R	W	wd	nb	Dots
Diana Baig	4	0	16	0			17
Fatima Sana	4	0	41	1	1		10
Sadia Iqbal	4	0	28	1			3
Omaima Sohail	3	0	28	0	1		7
Tooba Hassan	1	0	9	0			3
Aimen Anwar	4	0	37	0	1		6

Bowling	O	M	R	W	wd	nb	Dots
M Schutt	4	0	29	1	3		11
DR Brown	4	0	23	1	5		14
JL Jonassen	3	0	26	1	2		6
TM McGrath	3	1	13	3			11
AK Gardner	3	0	11	0			10
AM King	3	0	10	1			8

Toss: Australia.   Umpires: L Agenbag, S Redfern, KD Cotton (TV), Ref: SA Fritz.   Points: Aus 2, Pak 0.

STANDINGS: Group A – Australia 6 points, India 4, Barbados 2, Pakistan 0. Group B – England 6, New Zealand 4, South Africa 2, Sri Lanka 0.

First Semi-Final: England v India at Edgbaston on August 6, 2022 – India won by 4 runs. India 5-164 cc (S Mandhana 61, J Rodrigues 44*) **defeated England 6-160 cc** (NR Sciver 41).

Second Semi Final – Australia v New Zealand at Edgbaston on August 6, 2022 (floodlit) – Australia won by 5 wickets

New Zealand			B	4	6
SFM Devine*	c Mooney b Jonassen	53	48	6	1
SW Bates	b Schutt	0	1		
GEP limmer	b Schutt	17	16	3	
AC Kerr	c Brown b McGrath	40	36	4	
LM Tahuhu	b McGrath	3	4		
BM Halliday	c Mooney b Schutt	16	10	2	
ML Green	run out (Mooney)	2	4		
HNK Jensen	not out	1	1		
IC Gaze+					
HM Rowe					
FC Jonas					
	2 lb, 10 w	12			
6 overs : 2-39	20 overs	7-144			

1-6 (Bates, 0.5, 2-39 (Plimmer, 5.2), 3-112 (Devine, 15.6), 4-122 (Kerr, 16.6), 5-136 (Tahuhu, 18.4), 6-142 (Halliday, 19.3), 7-144 (Green 19.6)

Australia			B	4	6
AJ Healy+	c Gaze b Tahuhu	14	10	3	
BL Mooney	c Rowe b Tahuhu	36	29	5	
MM Lanning*	b Tahuhu	7	11		1
TM McGrath	run out (Kerr-Gaze)	34	23	6	
RL Haynes	c Bates b Devine	19	18	2	
AK Gardner	not out	19	20	2	
GM Harris	not out	8	7	1	
JL Jonassen					
AM King					
M Schutt					
DR Brown					
	1 b, 3 lb, 1 nb, 3 w	8			
6 overs : 2-40	19.3 overs	5-145			

1-18 (Healy, 2.1), 2-28 (Lanning, 4.4), 3-84 (McGrath, 10.4), 4-103 (Mooney, 13.1), 5-129 (Haynes, 17.2)

Bowling	O	M	R	W	wd	nb	Dots
M Schutt	4	0	20	3	1		14
DR Brown	4	0	19	0	2		13
JL Jonassen	4	0	41	1	1		9
TM McGrath	4	0	30	2	1		8
AM King	3	0	25	0			6
AK Gardner	1	0	7	0			0

Bowling	O	M	R	W	wd	nb	Dots
FC Jonas	4	0	21	0	1		12
HNK Jensen	4	0	38	0			7
LM Tahuhu	4	1	20	3	1		15
AC Kerr	4	0	31	0			9
SFM Devine	3.3	0	31	1	1	1	8

Toss: Australia.   Umpires: L Agenbag, JM Williams, S Redfern (TV), Ref: GS Lakshmi.   Devine 50: 46 balls, 6x4 1x6

Bronze Medal Playoff: England v New Zealand at Edgbaston on August 7, 2022 – New Zealand won by 8 wickets. England 9-110 cc (HNK Jensen 3-24) **lost to New Zealand 2-111** (11.5 overs) (SFM Devine 51*)

255

GOLD MEDAL MATCH – BIRMINGHAM

The toss was delayed ahead of the Gold Medal match, when Tahlia McGrath was found to have COVID, Australia seeking and gaining approval for her to play. After just nine runs off the first two overs, Healy was leg before in the third after India needed a review to remove her. Mooney and Lanning both found the gaps with regular boundaries, Lanning's lofted off-drive for six off Renuka Singh the best shot of the powerplay that realised 1-43. Mooney hit a fine lofted drive straight for four in the eighth over and in the 10th, Kaur went for 17, as Lanning hit the last three balls for fours, Australia 1-83 at the halfway mark. India fought back when Mooney drove one back at Yadav, who cleverly flicked the ball back onto the stumps with Lanning unable to get back. Then McGrath hit a cut to be brilliantly caught at backward point, Australia having lost 2-4 from seven balls. Gardner cut and edged early boundaries and in the 15th over lofted Yadav straight for six, as Australia reached 3-125 after 15 overs. India again bounced back as Gardner was bowled going for a big hit and then Harris miscued to mid-on. Mooney's fine knock ended when she was superbly caught by Sharma who ran backwards towards long-on and held the chance one-handed. Haynes hit Rana for six but late wickets saw Australia only get 11 from the last two overs, India 162 to win.

Verma went hard from the opening over which cost 12 as she edged Schutt for four before advancing and driving her for four. Mandhana sweetly drove Brown's third ball for four, but two balls later went way across her crease, had a swing and was bowled leg stump. Off-spinner Gardner came on for the third over and should have had Verma first ball, when she hit a high ball to Schutt at cover who dropped it. Three balls later the Aussies were relieved when Verma hit a catch to mid-on. India quickly rebounded with Kaur striking Brown for fours via a hook and square-drive to end the powerplay. Their stand grew as the eighth over from McGrath went for 11 as Kaur lapped a four with Rodrigues putting away a full-toss. Kaur hit Jonassen long-on for six in the 10th over that cost 11, India 1-73 at the halfway mark. Kaur got to 50 and then hit King over long-on for six, India wanting 50 off the last six.

The stand of 96 ended when Rodrigues had a wild swing and was bowled. In the next over wickets fell off consecutive balls as Vastrakar was caught at deep mid-wicket, then Kaur top-edged a lap-sweep via the helmet to be caught by a diving Healy. India scored 13 in the 17th bowled by King which included five wides, which left 28 wanted off 18 balls. Rana hit Gardner wide of mid-off for four, the target now 23 off 16. Rana played one behind square-leg, where Brown was quick to get the throw to the bowler Gardner who ran her out. With 17 wanted off 12 Yadav hit Schutt to mid-off, Harris calmly picking her off with the throw. Sharma struck the next ball straight for four, but then Schutt changed to around the wicket and had her LBW. India wanted 11 off the last over, Yastika hit the first ball to long-on but didn't run. She hit the next to long-off and wanted an impossible second with Meghna run out by miles. The end came when Yastika missed a reverse sweep to be LBW, Australia across the line in a fine struggle to obtain the Gold Medal.

Gold Medal Match – Australia v India at Edgbaston on August 9, 2022 – Australia won by 9 runs

Australia			B	4	6	India			B	4	6
AJ Healy+	lbw b Renuka Singh	7	12	1		S Verma	c McGrath b Gardner	11	7	2	
BL Mooney	c Sharma b Rana	61	41	8		SS Mandhana	b Brown	6	7	1	
MM Lanning*	run out (Yadav)	36	26	5	1	JI Rodrigues	b Schutt	33	33	3	
TM McGrath	c Yadav b Sharma	2	4			H Kaur*	c Healy b Gardner	65	43	7	2
AK Gardner	st T Bhatia b Rana	25	15	2	1	P Vastrakar	c Mooney b Gardner	1	5		
GM Harris	c Meghna Singh					DB Sharma	lbw b Schutt	13	8	2	
	b Renuka Singh	2	4			S Rana	run out (Brown-Gardner)	8	6	1	
RL Haynes	not out	18	10	1	1	RP Yadav	run out (Harris)	1	2		
AM King	c Meghna Singh b Yadav	1	5			YH Bhatia	lbw b Jonassen	2	5		
JL Jonassen	run out (Mandhana)	1	2			Meghna Singh	run out (King-Jonassen)	1	1		
M Schutt	not out	1	1			Renuka Singh	not out	0	0		
DR Brown	did not bat										
	4 b, 3 w	7					5 b, 6 w	11			
6 overs: 1-43	20 overs	8-161				6 overs: 2-42	19.3 overs	152			

1-9 (Healy, 2.2), 2-83 (Lanning, 10.1), 3-87 (McGrath, 11.1),
4-125 (Gardner, 15.1), 5-133 (Harris, 16.2), 6-142 (Mooney, 17.2),
7-150 (King, 18.3), 8-157 (Jonassen, 19.2)

1-16 (Mandhana, 1.5), 2-22 (Verma, 2.4), 3-118 (Rodrigues, 14.3)
4-121 (Vastrakar, 15.4), 5-121 (Kaur, 15.5), 6-139 (Rana, 17.3)
7-145 (Yadav, 18.1), 8-149 (Sharma, 18.3),
9-152 (Meghna Singh, 19.2), 10-152 (Y Bhatia, 19.3)

Y Bhatia was subbed in for T Bhatia after suffering from concussion.

Bowling	O	M	R	W	wd	nb	Dots	Bowling	O	M	R	W	wd	nb	Dots
Renuka Singh	4	0	25	2	1		13	M Schutt	4	0	27	2			10
Meghna Singh	2	0	11	0			5	DR Brown	3	0	19	1			11
DB Sharma	4	0	30	1	1		7	AK Gardner	3	0	16	3			8
RP Yadav	4	0	24	1			8	JL Jonassen	3.3	0	21	1			7
S Rana	4	0	38	2	1		6	AM King	4	0	40	0	2		3
P Vastrakar	1	0	12	0			1	TM McGrath	2	0	24	0			2
H Kaur	1	0	17	0			1								

Toss: Australia. Umpires: KD Cotton, JM Williams, S Redfern (TV), Ref: SA Fritz. Mooney 50: 36 balls, 7x4. Kaur 50: 34 balls, 6x4 1x6

INDIVIDUAL CAREER RECORDS (up to September 1, 2022)

TESTS

	M	Inns	NO	Runs	HS	Avge	100	50	Ct	St	Balls	Runs	Wkt	Avge	Best	5	10
DR Brown	2	1	0	8	8	8.00	0	0	2	0	186	121	2	60.50	1-18	0	0
S Campbell	1	1	1	0	0*		0	0	0	0	108	66	2	33.00	2-47	0	0
AK Gardner	3	5	1	157	56	39.25	0	2	1	0	432	171	4	42.75	1-27	0	0
RL Haynes	6	11	0	383	98	34.82	0	3	3	0	156	54	2	27.00	1-0	0	0
AJ Healy	6	10	0	236	58	23.60	0	1	12	1							
JL Jonassen	4	7	1	238	99	39.67	0	2	1	0	679	245	6	40.83	2-16	0	0
AM King	1	1	1	7	7*	-	0	0	0	0	210	97	3	32.33	2-39	0	0
MM Lanning	6	12	1	345	93	31.36	0	2	3	0	48	10	0				
TM McGrath	3	4	0	161	52	40.25	0	1	4	0	372	164	5	32.80	2-45	0	0
SG Molineux	2	3	0	64	41	21.33	0	0	0	0	402	163	7	23.29	4-95	0	0
BL Mooney	4	7	0	184	63	26.29	0	2	5	0							
EA Perry	10	17	7	752	213*	75.20	2	3	5	0	1881	739	37	19.97	6-32	2	0
AJ Sutherland	2	3	1	18	8	9.00	0	0	0	0	318	172	5	34.40	3-69	0	0
GL Wareham	1	1	0	2	2	2.00	0	0	0	0	66	40	1	40.00	1-12	0	0

ONE-DAY INTERNATIONALS

	M	Inns	NO	Runs	HS	Avge	S/R	100	50	Ct	St	Balls	Runs	Wkt	Avge	Best	Econ
DR Brown	10	0						0	0	1	0	420	347	15	23.13	4-33	4.96
S Campbell	1	1	1	0	0*			0	0	0	0	54	41	1	41.00	1-41	4.56
NJ Carey	23	11	5	153	39*	25.50	98.0	0	0	8	0	809	551	17	32.41	3-19	4.09
HJ Darlington	2	0						0	0	0	0	72	65	2	32.50	2-29	5.42
AK Gardner	49	35	8	667	67	24.70	116.8	0	4	22	0	1953	1353	53	25.53	3-25	4.16
RL Haynes	77	71	6	2585	130	39.77	77.9	2	19	25	0	108	94	7	13.43	3-10	5.22
AJ Healy	94	83	11	2639	170	36.65	100.1	5	15	63	30						
JL Jonassen	85	44	14	554	39	18.47	81.9	0	0	26	0	3912	2576	131	19.66	5-27	3.95
AM King	12	2	0	20	18	10.00	58.8	0	0	3	0	510	357	14	25.50	3-59	4.20
MM Lanning	100	100	16	4463	152*	53.13	92.1	15	19	52	0	132	114	1	114.00	1-30	5.18
TM McGrath	19	14	4	327	74	32.70	91.6	0	2	6	0	584	494	16	30.88	3-4	5.06
SG Molineux	9	6	1	62	26	12.40	84.9	0	0	7	0	455	226	17	13.29	4-14	3.12
SK Moloney	1	1	0	1	1	1.00	33.3	0	0	0	0	36	34	2	17.00	2-34	5.67
BL Mooney	54	49	14	1751	125*	50.03	85.5	2	12	22	0						
EA Perry	128	103	36	3369	112*	50.28	76.2	2	29	43	0	5524	4010	161	24.91	7-22	4.36
M Schutt	77	23	9	98	18	7.00	64.0	0	0	19	0	3677	2574	112	22.98	4-18	4.20
AJ Sutherland	12	6	3	102	35	34.00	60.3	0	0	8	0	386	294	13	22.62	4-31	4.59
GL Wareham	23	5	4	58	19*	58.00	76.3	0	0	6	0	966	704	24	29.33	2-18	4.24
A Wellington	13	7	2	16	11	3.20	61.5	0	0	3	0	636	502	16	31.38	3-24	4.74

TWENTY20 INTERNATIONALS

	M	Inns	NO	Runs	HS	Avge	S/R	100	50	Ct	St	Balls	Runs	Wkt	Avge	Best	Econ
DR Brown	10	0						0	0	3	0	192	191	8	23.88	2-9	5.97
NJ Carey	26	11	9	54	10*	27.00	79.4	0	0	16	0	360	428	18	23.78	3-15	6.76
HJ Darlington	2	0					-	0	0	3	0	18	30	0			10.00
AK Gardner	60	46	9	916	93	24.76	130.3	0	5	15	0	724	747	35	21.34	3-16	6.19
GM Harris	21	14	3	167	39*	15.18	154.6	0	0	7	0	144	143	6	23.83	2-15	5.96
RL Haynes	84	56	24	850	69*	26.56	117.7	0	3	29	0	44	74	4	18.50	3-19	10.09
AJ Healy	132	114	19	2207	148*	23.23	127.0	1	12	51	54						
JL Jonassen	94	41	9	432	47	13.50	89.8	0	0	26	0	1804	1662	87	19.10	5-12	5.53
AM King	11	2	1	19	18*	19.00	90.4	0	0	2	0	215	193	14	13.79	4-8	5.65
MM Lanning	124	114	26	3211	133*	36.49	116.5	2	15	43	0	36	39	4	9.75	2-17	6.50
TM McGrath	14	8	4	375	91*	93.75	153.6	0	3	3	0	138	164	12	13.67	3-13	7.13
SG Molineux	27	7	1	47	18	7.83	88.6	0	0	10	0	543	538	26	20.69	4-16	5.94
BL Mooney	70	65	15	1893	117*	37.86	123.1	2	13	29	0						
EA Perry	126	76	31	1253	60*	27.84	105.4	0	4	36	0	2285	2237	115	19.45	4-12	5.87
M Schutt	84	10	4	26	8*	4.33	96.3	0	0	10	0	1671	1685	108	15.60	4-18	6.05
AJ Sutherland	8	4	2	32	22*	16.00	139.1	0	0	2	0	84	110	3	36.67	1-13	7.86
TJ Vlaeminck	15	1	0	0	0	0.00	0.0	0	0	6	0	282	284	13	21.85	3-13	6.04
GL Wareham	35	6	3	49	13*	16.33	122.5	0	0	14	0	503	487	36	13.53	3-12	5.81

WOMENS CRICKET RECORDS SECTION (up to September 1, 2022)
ASHES SERIES 1934-35 TO 2021-22

Year	Host	M	Winner	Result	Holder	Year	Host	M	Winner	Result	Holder
1934-35	Aus	3	Eng	2-0	Eng	1987	Eng	3	Aus	1-0	Aus
1937	Eng	3		1-1	Eng	1991-92	Aus	1	Aus	1-0	Aus
1948-49	Aus	3	Aus	1-0	Aus	1998	Eng	3		0-0	Aus
1951	Eng	3		1-1	Aus	2001	Eng	2	Aus	2-0	Aus
1957-58	Aus	3		0-0	Aus	2002-03	Aus	2	Aus	1-0	Aus
1963	Aus	3	Eng	1-0	Eng	2005	Eng	2	Eng	1-0	Eng
1968-69	Aus	3		0-0	Eng	2007-08	Aus	1	Eng	1-0	Eng
1976	Eng	3		0-0	Eng	2009	Eng	1		0-0	Eng
1984-85	Aus	5	Aus	2-1	Aus	2010-11	Aus	1	Aus	1-0	Aus

In 2013 a points system came in combining points for the Test, ODIs and Twenty20s to decide the winner

Year	Host	Test	Result	ODIs	T20s	Winner	Result	Holder
2013	Eng	1	Drawn	Eng 2-1	Eng 3-0	Eng	12-4	Eng
2013-14	Aus	1	Eng	Aus 2-1	Aus 2-1	Eng	10-8	Eng
2015	Eng	1	Aus	Aus 2-1	Eng 2-1	Aus	10-6	Aus
2017-18	Aus	1	Drawn	Aus 2-1	Eng 2-1	Drawn	8-8	Aus
2019	Eng	1	Drawn	Aus 3-0	Aus 2-1	Aus	12-4	Aus
2021-22	Aus	1	Drawn	Aus 1-0	Aus 3-0	Aus	12-4	Aus

AUSTRALIA IN TEST CRICKET

Versus	Tests	Won	Lost	Drawn	Tied
England	51	12	9	30	0
India	10	4	0	6	0
New Zealand	13	4	1	8	0
West Indies	2	0	0	2	0
Total	**76**	**20**	**10**	**46**	**0**

HIGHEST TEAM SCORES

	Versus	Season	Venue
6-569	England	1998	Guildford
525	India	1983-84	Ahmedabad
9-448	England	2017-18	North Sydney
4-427	England	1998	Worcester

LOWEST TEAM SCORES

	Versus	Season	Venue
38	England	1957-58	Junction Oval
47	England	1934-35	Gabba
78	England	2002-03	Gabba
83	England	1951	The Oval

MOST RUNS

	M	Inn	NO	HS	Runs	Avge	100s	50s	0s
KL Rolton	14	22	4	209*	1002	55.66	2	5	3
BJ Clark	15	25	5	136	919	45.95	2	6	2
ER Wilson	11	16	1	127	862	57.46	3	3	0
DA Annetts	10	13	3	193	819	81.90	2	6	0

HIGHEST SCORES

	Balls	versus	Season	Venue
EA Perry	213	374 England	2017-18	Nth Sydney
KL Rolton	209*	313 England	2001	Headingley
MAJ Goszko	204	345 England	2001	Shenley
J Broadbent	200	476 England	1998	Guildford

MOST WICKETS

	M	Balls	Runs	Wkts	Avge	Best	5i	10m	SR
ER Wilson	11	2885	803	68	11.80	7/7	4	2	42.4
CL Fitzpatrick	13	303	1147	60	19.11	5/29	2	0	60.0
R Thompson	16	4304	1040	57	18.24	5/33	1	0	75.5
DL Wilson	11	2812	880	48	18.33	5/27	2	0	58.5

BEST BOWLING

		versus	Season	Venue
ER Wilson	7-7	England	1957-58	St Kilda
A Palmer	7-18	England	1934-35	Brisbane
L Johnston	7-24	New Zealand	1971-72	Junction Oval
ER Wilson	6-23	England	1948-49	Adelaide Oval

WICKET KEEPING

	M	Total	Ct/St	Byes/Inns
C Matthews	20	60	46/14	3.49
MJ Jennings	8	24	14/10	4.64
JC Price	10	22	20/2	3.89

FIELDING

	M	Total
LA Fullston	12	20
DA Annetts	10	12

ONE-DAY INTERNATIONAL RECORDS

RESULTS

Team	M	Won	Lost	NR	Tied
Bangladesh	1	1	0	0	0
Denmark	2	2	0	0	0
England	83	57	22	3	1
India	50	40	10	0	0
International XI	4	3	0	1	0
Ireland	15	15	0	0	0
Jamaica	1	1	0	0	0
Netherlands	5	5	0	0	0
New Zealand	133	100	31	2	0
Pakistan	13	13	0	0	0
South Africa	15	14	0	1	0
Sri Lanka	11	11	0	0	0
Trinidad & Tobago	1	1	0	0	0
West Indies	15	14	1	0	0
Young England	1	1	0	0	0
Total	**350**	**278**	**64**	**6**	**2**

HIGHEST TEAM SCORES

	Versus	Venue	Season
3-412	Denmark	Mumbai	1997-98
4-397	Pakistan	Wesley Col, Melb	1996-97
5-356	**England**	**Hagley Oval**	**2021-22**
7-332	India	Vadodara	2017-18
5-325	New Zealand	AB Field	2020-21

LOWEST TEAM SCORES

	Versus	Venue	Season
77	New Zealand	Beckenham	1993
77	India	Chennai	2004-05
86	New Zealand	St Peters Coll, Adelaide	1995-96

MOST RUNS

	M	Inn	NO	Runs	HS	Avge	S/Rate	100s	50s	Sixes
BJ Clark	118	114	12	4844	229*	47.49	66.2	5	30	5
KL Rolton	141	132	32	4814	154*	48.14	74.1	8	33	12
MM Lanning	**100**	**100**	**16**	**4463**	**152***	**53.13**	**92.1**	**15**	**19**	**39**
AJ Blackwell	144	124	27	3492	114	36.01	66.2	3	25	8
EA Perry	**128**	**103**	**36**	**3369**	**112***	**50.28**	**76.2**	**2**	**29**	**27**
LC Sthalekar	125	111	22	2728	104*	30.65	68.7	2	16	3
AJ Healy	**94**	**83**	**11**	**2639**	**170**	**36.65**	**100.1**	**5**	**15**	**27**

HIGHEST SCORES

		Balls	4s	6s	versus	Venue	Season
BJ Clark	229*	155	22	0	Denmark	Mumbai	1997-98
AJ Healy	**170**	**138**	**26**	**0**	**England**	**Hagley Oval, Christchurch**	**2021-22**
LM Keightley	156*	147	15	0	Pakistan	Wesley Coll, Melbourne	1996-97
KL Rolton	154*	118	19	0	Sri Lanka	Hagley Oval, Christchurch	2000-01
MM Lanning	152*	135	19	1	Sri Lanka	Bristol	2017
KL Rolton	151	114	20	1	Ireland	Dublin	2005

FASTEST HALF CENTURIES

	Balls	Versus	Venue	Season
MM Lanning	23	New Zealand	North Sydney	2012-13
AK Gardner	23	West Indies	North Sound	2019-20
AJ Healy	27	West Indies	North Sound	2019-20
AJ Healy	31	Sri Lanka	AB Field	2019-20

FASTEST CENTURIES

	Balls	Versus	Venue	Season
MM Lanning	45	New Zealand	North Sydney	2012-13
KL Rolton	57	South Africa	Lincoln	2000-01
AJ Healy	71	Sri Lanka	AB Field	2019-20
BL Clark	72	Pakistan	Wesley College	1996-97

MOST WICKETS

	M	Balls	Runs	Wkts	Avge	Best	5i	4i	Econ
CL Fitzpatrick	109	6017	3023	180	16.79	5-14	4	11	3.01
EA Perry	**128**	**5524**	**4010**	**161**	**24.90**	**7-22**	**3**	**4**	**4.36**
LC Sthalekar	125	5965	3646	146	24.97	5-35	1	2	3.67
JL Jonassen	**85**	**3912**	**2577**	**131**	**19.67**	**5-27**	**2**	**8**	**3.95**
M Schutt	**77**	**3677**	**2574**	**112**	**22.98**	**4-18**	**0**	**5**	**4.20**
S Nitschke	80	3626	2159	98	22.03	7-24	1	3	3.57
KL Rolton	141	3267	1769	85	20.81	4-29	0	1	3.25
CL Mason	46	2366	1150	83	13.85	5-9	2	6	2.92
LA Fullston	41	2366	968	73	13.26	5-27	2	6	2.45

BEST BOWLING

		versus	Season	Venue
EA Perry	7-22	England	2019	Canterbury
S Nitschke	7-24	England	2005	Kidderminster
CL Mason	5-9	England	1999-2000	Newcastle
J Broadbent	5-10	New Zealand	1992-93	Lismore

WICKET KEEPING

	M	Ct/St	Total
JC Price	83	69/30	99
AJ Healy	**94**	**60/30**	**90**
JM Fields	60	55/19	74

FIELDING

	M	Total
AJ Blackwell	144	55
MM Lanning	**100**	**50**
LC Sthalekar	125	49

TWENTY20 INTERNATIONAL RECORDS

Team	M	Won	Lost	NR	Tied
Bangladesh	1	1	0	0	0
Barbados	1	1	0	0	0
England	39	19	19	1	0
India	25	18	6	1	0
Ireland	8	8	0	0	0
New Zealand	47	25	21	1	0
Pakistan	13	11	0	2	0
South Africa	5	5	0	0	0
Sri Lanka	6	6	0	0	0
West Indies	13	12	1	0	0
Total	**158**	**106**	**47**	**5**	**0**

HIGHEST TEAM SCORES

	Versus	Venue	Season
3-226	England	Chelmsford	2019
2-226	Sri Lanka	North Sydney	2019-20
4-217	Sri Lanka	North Sydney	2019-20
4-209	England	Brab Stadium	2017-18
3-195	Pakistan	Kuala Lumpur	2018-19

LOWEST TEAM SCORES

	Versus	Venue	Season
66	New Zealand	Adelaide Oval	2016-17
73	New Zealand	WTS, Wellington	2009-10
9-80	New Zealand	Lincoln	2007-08
89	India	Visag	2011-12
7-91	England	Chester-le-Street	2013

MOST RUNS

	M	Inn	NO	Runs	HS	Avge	S/Rate	100s	50s	Sixes
MM Lanning	124	114	26	3211	133*	36.48	116.5	2	15	45
AJ Healy	132	114	19	2207	148*	23.23	127.0	1	12	41
BL Mooney	70	65	15	1893	117*	37.86	123.1	2	13	10
EJ Villani	62	58	10	1369	90*	28.52	118.2	0	12	12
AJ Blackwell	95	81	19	1314	61	21.19	92.9	0	1	1
EA Perry	126	76	31	1253	60*	27.84	105.4	0	4	23
JE Duffin	64	55	10	941	68*	20.91	107.5	0	3	20

HIGHEST SCORES

		Balls	4s	6s	versus	Venue	Season
AJ Healy	148*	61	19	7	Sri Lanka	North Sydney	2019-20
MM Lanning	133*	63	17	7	England	Chelmsford	2019
MM Lanning	126	65	18	4	Ireland	Sylhet	2013-14
BL Mooney	117*	70	19	1	England	Canberra	2017-18
BL Mooney	113	61	20	0	Sri Lanka	North Sydney	2019-20
KL Rolton	96*	53	16	1	England	Taunton	2005

FASTEST HALF CENTURIES

	Balls	Versus	Venue	Season
AJ Healy	21	Ireland	Providence	2018-19
MM Lanning	24	England	Chelmsford	2019
AJ Healy	25	Sri Lanka	North Sydney	2019-20
AJ Healy	26	Bangladesh	Manuka Oval	2019-20
MM Lanning	27	England	Mumbai	2017-18

FASTEST CENTURIES

	Balls	Versus	Venue	Season
AJ Healy	46	Sri Lanka	North Sydney	2019-20
MM Lanning	51	England	Chelmsford	2019
MM Lanning	53	Ireland	Sylhet	2013-14
BL Mooney	54	Sri Lanka	North Sydney	2019-20
BL Mooney	65	England	Manuka Oval	2017-18

MOST WICKETS

	M	Balls	Mdns	Runs	Wkts	Avge	Best	5i	4i	Econ
EA Perry	126	2285	6	2237	115	19.45	4-12	0	4	5.87
M Schutt	84	1671	6	1685	108	15.60	4-18	0	3	6.05
JL Jonassen	94	1810	7	1673	87	19.22	5-12	1	4	5.54
LC Sthalekar	54	1196	1	1161	60	19.35	4-18	0	1	5.82
RM Farrell	54	1113	5	1150	55	20.91	4-15	0	1	6.20
EA Osborne	59	1124	0	1080	48	22.50	4-19	0	1	5.77
SJ Coyte	47	962	1	979	47	20.83	4-5	0	1	6.11

BEST BOWLING

		Versus	Venue	Season
MR Strano	5-10	New Zealand	Geelong	2016-17
JL Jonassen	5-12	India	Junction Oval	2019-20
JL Hunter	5-22	West Indies	Colombo (RPS)	2012-13
SJ Coyte	4-5	India	Billericay	2011
JL Jonassen	4-7	West Indies	Bridgetown	2019-20

WICKET KEEPING

	M	Ct/St	Total
AJ Healy	117	49/54	103
JM Fields	37	25/15	40

FIELDING

	M	Total
MM Lanning	124	43
EA Perry	126	36
AJ Blackwell	95	34
JE Cameron	64	33

WBBL07 – SCORCHERS WIN FIRST TITLE

After being beaten in two previous finals, the **Perth Scorchers** won their first trophy in 2021-22 when they beat the Adelaide Strikers by 14 runs at Perth Stadium. At the top of the order Sophie Devine and Beth Mooney were by far the best opening combination, adding 828 runs together at 63, with three century stands and another three past fifty. Chloe Piparo and Sri Lankan Chamari Atapattu topped off the batting, while they had five reliable bowling options with Heather Graham, Alana King, Lilly Mills, Devine and South African Marizanne Kapp all fine performers.

The **Adelaide Strikers** did brilliantly to finish runner-up, having won two finals from fourth spot in the minor round. Katie Mack was their dominant batter with five half-centuries, South African duo Laura Woolvardt and Dane van Niekerk also doing well with the bat. All-rounder Tahlia McGrath had a solid season, as the Strikers had plenty of seam bowling options with Megan Schutt and Sarah Coyte doing well, while young quick Darcie Brown was excellent. Amanda-Jade Wellington took 23 wickets was a star in the back end of the season, with brilliant figures of 5-8 versus the Renegades in the Eliminator Final.

The **Melbourne Renegades** had their best ever season to finish third, with Indian Harmanpreet Kaur dominating with the bat and ball to take out the WBBL MVP. Her compatriot Jemimah Rodrigues was good with the bat while Sophie Molineux and Ellie Falconer did well with the ball.

The ever-consistent **Brisbane Heat** came fourth after bombing out in the Eliminator Final to the Strikers. Their batting was dominated by Georgia Redmayne and Grace Harris, who made nine half-centuries between them, their average opening stands worth 597 runs at 42.64 with one hundred stand and four with fifty plus. Jess Jonassen was very good, with Nicola Hancock and Courtney Sippel were good with the ball also.

The **Melbourne Stars** slipped from second to fifth, despite Elyse Villani leading their batting. Meg Lanning managed only two scores over fifty in what was a below par season for her. Irish All-rounder Kim Garth made useful runs and led the bowling with Annabel Sutherland also having some tidy all-round performances. England's Maia Boucher didn't do as well as expected, failing to pass fifty and had a strike-rate of just 95.

The **Hurricanes** strength lay in their bowling, with Molly Strano, Tayla Vlaeminck, Ruth Johnston and Nicola Carey also having good seasons. With the bat they struggled, their average opening stand was just eight, with a best of 28 as they only passed 150 in three games. South Africa's Mignon du Preez did well to make made four half-centuries and while Rachel Priest blasted a brilliant 107 not out against the Stars, she fell well short of what she would have hoped for with the bat.

Last season's winners **Sydney Thunder** dropped to seventh, despite the fine efforts of Indian all-rounder Deepti Sharma. Smriti Mandhana did well while young tyro Phoebe Litchfield made useful runs. New skipper Hannah Darlington had a great year with the ball, while Sam Bates was a consistent performer once again. Last came the **Sydney Sixers**, who had their worst season ever. Elyse Perry led their batting but her strike-rate was just 91, while the usually dominant Alyssa Healy battled with just two scores over 50 and Ash Gardner was down on her usual output. Nicole Bolton had good numbers, but didn't pass 40 in her 12 innings.

TABLE	W	L	NR	Points	Net Run Rate
Perth Scorchers (1)	9	3	2	20	+0.64
Melbourne Renegades (3)	8	4	2	18	-0.14
Brisbane Heat (4)	8	5	1	17	+0.51
Adelaide Strikers (2)	7	6	1	15	+0.70
Melbourne Stars (5)	5	7	2	12	-0.38
Hobart Hurricanes (6)	5	8	1	11	-0.28
Sydney Thunder (7)	4	8	2	10	-0.30
Sydney Sixers (8)	4	9	1	9	-0.70

MOST RUNS

	Team	M	Inns	NO	Runs	HS	Avge	S/Rate	100s	50s	6s
BL Mooney	PS	14	14	3	547	101*	49.72	128.7	1	4	1
KM Mack	AS	17	15	7	513	89*	64.12	115.2	-	5	1
SFM Devine	PS	14	14	1	442	101	34.00	128.4	1	2	14
EJ Villani	MS	12	12	2	439	100*	43.90	122.2	1	3	5
GP Redmayne	BH	14	14	1	437	71	33.61	120.0	-	5	3
GM Harris	BH	14	14	1	420	75	32.30	123.1	-	4	9
M du Preez	HH	14	14	1	414	87*	31.84	115.0	-	4	10
H Kaur	MR	13	12	5	406	81*	58.00	130.9	-	3	18
L Woolvardt	AS	17	16	3	381	54	29.30	121.3	-	2	7
S Mandhana	ST	13	13	2	377	114*	34.27	130.4	1	2	7

HUNDREDS (5)

		Balls	4s	6s		Venue
S Mandhana	114*	64	14	3	Thunder v Renegades	Mackay
RH Priest	107*	68	10	7	Hurricanes v Stars	Bellerive Oval
BL Mooney	101*	63	13	0	Scorchers v Renegades	WACA, Perth
SFM Devine	101	60	8	6	Scorchers v Thunder	York Park, Launceston
EJ Villani	100*	65	13	2	Stars v Strikers	Adelaide Oval

MOST WICKETS

Bowling	Team	M	Overs	Mdns	Runs	Wkts	Avge	Econ	Best	4i
A Wellington	AS	17	57	2	374	23	16.26	6.56	5-8	1
JL Jonassen	BH	14	48.1	0	313	21	14.90	6.49	3-10	-
DR Brown	AS	15	55	0	334	20	16.70	6.07	3-19	-
HL Graham	PS	14	47	0	300	18	16.66	6.38	3-16	-
L Mills	PS	14	30	0	205	16	12.81	6.83	4-23	1
AM King	PS	14	50	0	292	16	18.25	5.84	4-11	1
HJ Darlington	ST	13	52	0	332	16	20.75	6.38	3-21	-
SJ Coyte	AS	17	55	0	389	16	24.31	7.07	3-12	-
KJ Garth	MS	12	45	3	281	15	18.73	6.24	3-11	-
H Kaur	MR	13	42	0	313	15	20.86	7.45	3-22	-
MR Strano	HH	14	48.3	1	356	15	23.75	7.34	3-19	-

BEST BOWLING

	Figures	Overs	Dots		Venue
A Wellington	5-8	4	18	Strikers v Heat	Adelaide Oval
R Johnston	4-8	3.2	13	Hurricanes v Stars	Bellerive Oval
M Kapp	4-10	4	19	Scorchers v Hurricanes	WACA, Perth
AM King	4-11	4	16	Scorchers v Thunder	York Park, Launceston
L Mills	4-25	3	7	Scorchers v Renegades	WACA, Perth
EM Falconer	4-29	4	7	Renegades v Heat	Rolton Oval, Adelaide

HAT TRICK (1)

DR Brown	Strikers v Heat	Invermay Park, Launceston

MATCHES PLAYED
Match 1 – Stars v Sixers at Bellerive Oval on October 14, 2021 (day/night) - Sixers won by 6 wickets

Stars			B	4	6	Sixers			B	4	6
EJ Villani	not out	54	31	5	1	AJ Healy+	b Day	57	27	11	
AJ Sutherland	run out (Verma)	14	19	1		S Verma	b Sutherland	8	10	1	
MM Lanning*	not out	23	17	4		AK Gardner	c Sutherland b Garth	7	12		
ME Bouchier						EA Perry*	c A Lanning b McKenr	7	8	1	
KJ Garth						NE Bolton	not out	7	4	1	
NM Faltum+						AR Reakes	not out	3	3		
TM Flintoff						RP Yadav					
AJ Lanning						MJ Brown					
M Darke						CF Moore					
SF Day						SR Campbell					
RM McKenna						EL Hughes					
	1 lb, 1 nb, 6 w	8					2 lb, 2 nb, 7 w	11			
3 overs : 0-28	11 overs	1-99				3 overs : 0-33	10.2 overs	4-100			

1-49 (Sutherland, 5.5)

1-40 (Verma, 3.5), 2-83 (Gardner, 7.4), 3-89 (Healy, 8.5), 4-95 (Perry, 9.4)

Bowling	O	M	R	W	wd	nb	Dots	Bowling	O	M	R	W	wd	nb	Dots
NE Bolton	2	0	17	0			3	TM Flintoff	2	0	26	0		1	4
S Campbell	3	0	25	0	3		9	KJ Garth	3	0	16	1		1	8
RP Yadav	2	0	15	0	1		4	AJ Sutherland	2	0	27	1	3		4
MJ Brown	2	0	14	0		1	4	SF Day	2	0	18	1			5
EA Perry	2	0	27	0			3	RM McKenna	1	0	9	1			1
								AJ Lanning	0.2	0	2	0			1

Toss: Sixers.   Umpires: R Howard, D Taylor, SA Lightbody (TV), Ref: K Hannam.   Award: AJ Healy (SS)
Villani 50: 29 balls, 5x4 1x6, Healy 50: 24 balls, 10x4.

Match 2 – Hurricanes v Renegades at Bellerive Oval, Hobart on October 16, 2021 – Renegades won by 6 wickets

Hurricanes			B	4	6
R H Priest*+	c Wareham b Leeson	21	24	3	
R Johnston	c sub (MA Blows) b Wareham	20	20	3	
M du Preez	lbw b Wareham	5	10		
R M Ghosh	c Ferling b Kaur	21	14	2	1
N J Carey	b Molineux	8	10		
N E Stalenberg	run out (Kaur)	28	27	3	
S K Moloney	b Falconer	0	2		
M R Strano	c & b Wareham	4	5		
B W Vakarewa	b Molineux	1	5		
T J Vlaeminck	run out (Ferling)	1	1		
A Smith	not out	1	2		
	2 b, 3 lb, 6 w	11			
6 overs: 1-36	20 overs	121			

1-28 (Johnston, 4.4), 2-38 (du Preez, 6.6), 3-59 (Priest, 10.2), 4-73 (Ghosh, 11.4), 5-92 (Carey, 14.6), 6-95 (Moloney, 15.6), 7-115 (Strano, 18.3), 8-117 (Stalenberg, 18.6), 9-119 (Vakarewa, 19.3), 10-121 (Vlaeminck, 19.6)

Renegades			B	4	6
SG Molineux*	run out (Ghosh)	16	16	2	
JI Rodrigues	c du Preez b Vakarewa	33	34	2	1
CA Webb	c Johnston b Vakarewa	31	35	4	
H Kaur	not out	24	19	1	1
E Jones	c Ghosh b Smith	4	7	1	
GL Wareham	not out	5	7		
JE Duffin					
JE Dooley+					
CM Leeson					
EM Falconer					
HL Ferling					
	1 b, 3 lb, 2 nb, 6 w	12			
6 overs: 1-32	19.2 overs	4-125			

1-22 (Molineux, 4.4), 2-90 (Rodrigues, 13.3), 3-90 (Webb, 13.5), 4-96 (Jones, 15.6)

Bowling	O	M	R	W	wd	nb	Dots
HL Ferling	3	0	22	0			10
EM Falconer	4	0	29	1	1		8
SG Molineux	4	0	12	2			15
GL Wareham	4	0	13	3	3		15
CM Leeson	2	0	20	1	1		3
H Kaur	3	0	20	1			6

Bowling	O	M	R	W	wd	nb	Dots
B W Vakarewa	4	0	21	2	1		12
TJ Vlaeminck	4	0	19	0	2	1	14
MR Strano	4	0	26	0			9
NJ Carey	4	0	31	0	2		9
A Smith	2.2	0	16	1	1		8
SK Moloney	1	0	8	0		1	4

Toss: Hurricanes. Umpires: AR Crozier, CA Polosak, SA Lightbody (TV), Ref: K Hannam. Award: GL Wareham (MR)

Match 3 – Strikers v Thunder at Bellerive Oval, Hobart (floodlit) on October 16, 2021 – Strikers won by 30 runs

Strikers			B	4	6
D van Niekerk	c Darlington b Johnson	11	13	2	
KM Mack	b Bates	6	5	1	
L Wolvaardt	c Johnson b Sharma	0	1		
TM McGrath*	c Litchfield b L Smith	42	34	4	
BE Patterson	b Darlington	11	10	1	
M Penna	st E Smith b L Smith	35	37	4	
A Wellington	not out	15	11	1	
TJ McPharlin+	st E Smith b Johnson	6	10		
SJ Coyte					
JL Barsby					
DR Brown					
Extras	3 lb, 1 nb, 10 w	14			
6 overs: 3-45	20 overs	7-140			

1-16 (Mack, 1.6), 2-20 (van Niekerk, 2.6), 3-26 (Wolvaardt, 3.4), 4-46 (Patterson, 6.2), 5-115 (McGrath, 16.2), 6-117 (Penna, 16.5), 7-140 (McPharlin, 19.6)

Thunder			B	4	6
SJ Johnson	c Penna b Brown	4	4	1	
SS Mandhana	c Wolvaardt b McGrath	4	4	1	
PES Litchfield	c McPharlin b Barsby	16	16	3	
CL Hall	c Patterson b McGrath	38	35	3	
A Learoyd	c McGrath b Coyte	23	31	2	
DB Sharma	c McGrath b Coyte	4	6		
HJ Darlington*	st McPharlin b Wellington	0	2		
LG Smith	run out (Brown)	2	6		
IECM Wong	c Patterson b Wellington	6	7	1	
EJ Smith+	not out	5	4		
SL Bates	st McPharlin b Coyte	0	1		
	2 lb, 6 w	8			
6 overs: 3-34	19.2 overs	110			

1-4 (Johnson, 0.4), 2-14 (Mandhana, 1.5), 3-34 (Litchfield, 5.3), 4-93 (Hall, 14.5), 5-93 (Learoyd, 14.6), 6-94 (Darlington, 15.4), 7-99 (Sharma, 17.1), 8-99 (LG Smith, 17.2), 9-106 (Wong, 18.4), 10-110 (Bates, 19.2)

Bowling	O	M	R	W	wd	nb	Dots
IECM Wong	2	0	17	0	3		6
SL Bates	4	0	27	1	2		8
SJ Johnson	4	0	22	2			11
DB Sharma	4	0	32	1	2	1	6
HJ Darlington	4	0	22	1	2		12
LG Smith	2	0	17	2			4

Bowling	O	M	R	W	wd	nb	Dots
DR Brown	3	0	22	1	1		10
TM McGrath	4	0	17	3	1		15
JL Barsby	2	1	9	1			6
D van Niekerk	3	0	22	0	2		4
A Wellington	4	0	20	2			11
SJ Coyte	3.2	0	18	2			8

Toss: Thunder. Umpires: SA Lightbody, M van Eck, D Taylor (TV), Ref: SR Bernard. Award: TM McGrath (AS)

Match 4 – Hurricanes v Sixers at Bellerive Oval, Hobart on October 17, 2021 – Sixers won by 5 wickets

Hurricanes		B	4	6	Sixers		B	4	6
RH Priest*+	c Gardner b Perry	2	5		S Verma	c Vlaeminck b Strano	57	50	6
R Johnston	c Verma b Perry	10	14	2	AJ Healy+	b Vlaeminck	3	6	
M du Preez	c Yadav b Brown	1	4		AK Gardner	c Priest b Strano	3	3	
RM Ghosh	c Reakes b Yadav	46	46	1 3	EA Perry*	st Priest b Strano	27	33	3
NJ Carey	b Gardner	12	17		NE Bolton	not out	17	19	1
NE Stalenberg	lbw b Bolton	1	5		AR Reakes	b Carey	4	4	1
SK Moloney	c Gardner b Yadav	22	16	4	MJ Brown	not out	4	2	1
MR Strano	not out	11	7	2	RP Yadav				
BW Vakarewa	b Brown	2	3		CF Moore				
TJ Vlaeminck	b Bolton	1	2		SR Campbell				
A Smith	not out	2	2		EL Hughes				
	1 b, 2 lb, 1 nb, 11 w	15				4 lb, 10 w	14		
6 overs: 3-26	20 overs	9-125			6 overs: 2-39	19.3 overs	5-129		

1-4 (Priest, 1.3), 2-11 (du Preez, 2.2), 3-26 (Johnston, 5.6),
4-75 (Carey, 12.2), 5-76 (Stalenberg, 13.1),
6-108 (Moloney, 17.2), 7-108 (Ghosh, 17.4),
8-116 (Vakarewa, 18.5), 9-117 (Vlaeminck, 19.1)

1-7 (Healy, 1.3), 2-14 (Gardner, 2.2), 3-77 (Perry, 12.3),
4-119 (Verma, 18.3), 5-124 (Reakes, 19.1)

Bowling	O	M	R	W	wd	nb	Dots	Bowling	O	M	R	W	wd	nb	Dots
NE Bolton	4	0	29	2			8	BW Vakarewa	4	0	30	0	3		8
EA Perry	2	0	9	2	2		9	TJ Vlaeminck	4	0	37	1	3		8
MJ Brown	4	0	23	2	4		16	MR Strano	4	0	19	3			11
RP Yadav	4	0	31	2			9	NJ Carey	3.3	0	21	1	2		8
SR Campbell	2	0	14	0	1	1	7	A Smith	2	0	10	0	1		3
AK Gardner	4	0	16	1			12	R Johnston	2	0	8	0	1		6

Toss: Sixers.   Umpires: R Howard, D Taylor, SA Lightbody, Ref: SR Bernard   Award: S Verma (SS)
Verma 50: 45 balls, 5x4

Match 5 – Heat v Scorchers at Bellerive Oval, Hobart on October 17, 2021 – Scorchers won in Superover

Scorchers		B	4	6	Heat		B	4	6
SFM Devine*	c Prestwidge b Jonassen	19	12	2 1	GM Harris	lbw b Kapp	41	27	4 2
BL Mooney+	b Yadav	40	37	3 1	GP Redmayne+	c Atapttu b Devine	18	13	4
C Atapattu	c Harris b Jonassen	14	14	1	JL Jonassen*	b Mills	18	22	2 1
M Kapp	c Harris b Prestwidge	9	14	1	G Voll	c Graham b King	12	15	1
HL Graham	c Hancock b Yadav	6	12		AE Bosch	c King b Graham	14	18	2
AM King	b Hancock	12	11	2	LM Kimmince	c & b King	8	9	1
CL Piparo	not out	20	14	2	MC Hinkley	c King b Mills	1	5	
MG Carmichael	c & b Jonassen	5	6		N de Klerk	run out (Graham)	11	9	1
LG Mills	not out	2	2		GK Prestwidge	b Mills	0	1	
TCJ Peschel					NM Hancock	not out	3	2	
SM Betts					P Yadav	not out	0	0	
	2 lb, 2 nb, 6 w	10				2 lb, 1nb, 8 w	11		
6 overs: 1-44	20 overs	7-137			6 overs: 1-51	20 overs	9-137		

1-25 (Devine, 3.1), 2-67 (Atapattu, 8.2), 3-85 (Kapp, 11.6),
4-87 (Mooney, 12.6), 5-97 (Graham, 15.4), 6-114 (King, 17.1),
7-123 (Carmichael, 18.5)

1-42 (Redmayne, 3.5), 2-87 (Jonassen, 9.5), 3-92 (Harris, 11.3),
4-103 (Voll, 13.2), 5-116 (Kimmince, 15.4),
6-117 (Hinkley, 16.3), 7-127 (Bosch, 18.6),
8-133 (Prestwidge, 19.3), 9-135 (de Klerk, 19.5)

Bowling	O	M	R	W	wd	nb	Dots	Bowling	O	M	R	W	wd	nb	Dots
N de Klerk	3	0	29	0	2		5	M Kapp	4	1	18	1	1		17
NM Hancock	4	0	16	1	2	1	16	TCJ Peschel	2	0	22	0	3	1	5
JL Jonassen	4	0	16	3			11	SFM Devine	2	0	20	1			5
GM Harris	3	0	25	0			6	AM King	4	0	24	2			12
GK Prestwidge	3	0	24	1	2	1	7	L Mills	4	0	28	3			13
P Yadav	3	0	25	2			6	HL Graham	3	0	14	1			9
								SM Betts	1	0	9	0			3

Toss: Heat.   Umpires: CA Polosak, M van Eck, SA Lightbody (TV), Ref: K Hannam   Award: AM King (PS).
Superover: BH 0-12 (Harris run out 1 off 1, Kimmince 0* (1), Bosch run out 11 (4) 2x4; Kapp 1-0-12-0. PS: 0-14 (0.4) Devine 13* (3),
Mooney 1* (1); Jonassen 0.4-0-14-0

Match 6 – Hurricanes v Stars at Bellerive Oval, Hobart on October 19, 2021 – Hurricanes won by 63 runs

Hurricanes

Batter	Dismissal	Runs	B	4	6
RH Priest*+	not out	107	68	10	7
R Johnston	c Sutherland b Smith	2	8		
M du Preez	c Bouchier b Sutherland	1	2		
RM Ghosh	c Villani b Sutherland	2	10		
NJ Carey	c Garth b Flintoff	14	19	1	
NE Stalenberg	not out	17	13	3	
SK Moloney					
MR Strano					
BW Vakarewa					
TJ Vlaeminck					
A Smith					
Extras	1 lb, 8 w	9			
6 overs: 2-29	20 overs	4-152			

1-20 (Johnston, 3.2), 2-22 (du Preez, 4.1), 3-39 (Ghosh, 6.6), 4-93 (Carey, 14.1)

Stars

Batter	Dismissal	Runs	B	4	6
EJ Villani	c Stalenberg b Strano	0	2		
AJ Sutherland	c Moloney b Strano	2	8		
MM Lanning*	b Johnston	25	28	3	
ME Bouchier	c Strano b Vlaeminck	10	16	1	
KJ Garth	lbw b Johnston	13	16		
AJ Lanning	b Smith	3	9		
NM Faltum+	c Ghosh b Carey	3	7		
TM Flintoff	b Carey	5	6		
LCN Smith	b Johnston	12	13	1	
SF Day	b Johnston	4	6		
RM McKenna	not out	2	5		
Extras	3 lb, 7 w	10			
6 overs: 2-29	19.2 overs	89			

1-0 (Villani, 0.2), 2-3 (Sutherland, 2.2), 3-30 (Bouchier, 6.3), 4-57 (Garth, 11.1), 5-62 (A Lanning, 12.6), 6-62 (M Lanning, 13.1), 7-70 (Flintoff, 15.1), 8-71 (Faltum, 15.3), 9-82 (Day, 17.3), 10-89 (Smith, 19.2)

Bowling	O	M	R	W	wd	nb	Dots
KJ Garth	4	0	35	0			12
TM Flintoff	4	0	23	1	1		14
LCN Smith	4	0	35	1	2		8
AJ Sutherland	4	1	22	2	3		13
SF Day	3	0	22	0	1		7
RM McKenna	1	0	14	0			3

Bowling	O	M	R	W	wd	nb	Dots
MR Strano	4	0	21	2			13
BW Vakarewa	3	0	18	0	2		9
TJ Vlaeminck	3	0	15	1	4		11
NJ Carey	3	0	11	2			9
A Smith	3	0	13	1	1		8
R Johnston	3.2	0	8	4			13

Toss: Stars. Umpires: SA Lightbody, M van Eck, Ref: K Hannam. Award: RH Priest (HH)
Priest 50: 37 balls, 7x4, 2x6; 100: 65 balls, 9x4 7x6.

Match 7 – Heat v Scorchers at Bellerive Oval, Hobart on October 19, 2021 (day/night) – Heat won by 59 runs

Heat

Batter	Dismissal	Runs	B	4	6
GM Harris	lbw b Devine	34	30	6	
GP Redmayne+	not out	59	52	6	
G Voll	c Peschel b Betts	24	17	4	
LM Kimmince	c Piparo b Graham	9	8	1	
AE Bosch	st Mooney b King	3	4		
MC Hinkley	c Atapattu b Graham	2	6		
JL Jonassen*	not out	19	6	4	
N de Klerk					
GK Prestwidge					
NM Hancock					
P Yadav					
Extras	1 b, 5 lb, 3 nb, 3 w	12			
6 overs: 0-50	20 overs	5-162			

1-68 (Harris, 7.5 ov), 2-112 (Voll, 13.5 ov), 3-131 (Kimmince, 16.2 ov), 4-138 (Bosch, 17.3 ov), 5-143 (Hinkley, 18.5 ov)

Scorchers

Batter	Dismissal	Runs	B	4	6
SFM Devine*	c Hinkley b Hancock	18	15	3	
BL Mooney+	c Bosch b Hancock	0	1		
C Atapattu	c Bosch b Jonassen	11	14	1	
M Kapp	c Redmayne b Prestwidge	6	11		
HL Graham	c Redmayne b Harris	17	16	2	
CL Piparo	c Redmayne b Yadav	10	11	1	
MG Carmichael	st Redmayne b Yadav	9	11	1	
AM King	c de Klerk b Harris	5	11		
LG Mills	c Redmayne b Hancock	4	6		
TCJ Peschel	not out	5	7		
SM Betts	b Harris	0	2		
Extras	6 lb, 12 w	18			
6 overs: 3-48	17.2 overs	103			

1-7 (Mooney, 0.2), 2-34 (Atapattu, 4.1), 3-42 (Devine, 5.2), 4-56 (Kapp, 7.3), 5-78 (Piparo, 10.5), 6-87 (Graham, 12.3), 7-94 (Carmichael, 14.5), 8-94 (King, 15.1), 9-103 (Mills, 16.5), 10-103 (Betts, 17.2)

Bowling	O	M	R	W	wd	nb	Dots
M Kapp	4	1	27	0	2		12
TCJ Peschel	2	0	27	0	1	3	5
SFM Devine	4	0	37	1			8
AM King	4	0	25	1			7
HL Graham	4	0	15	2			14
LG Mills	1	0	12	0			0
SM Betts	1	0	13	1			1

Bowling	O	M	R	W	wd	nb	Dots
NM Hancock	3	0	19	3	3		13
GK Prestwidge	2	0	9	1	3		9
N de Klerk	1	0	13	0			2
GM Harris	3.2	0	16	3			9
JL Jonassen	3	0	14	1	2		9
P Yadav	4	0	15	2			6
AE Bosch	1	0	11	0			1

Toss: Scorchers. Umpires: AR Crozier, TJ Matibiri, Ref: SR Bernard. Award: GP Redmayne (BH)
Redmayne 50: 43 balls, 6x4

Match 8 - Strikers v Renegades at Bellerive Oval, Hobart on October 20, 2021 – Strikers won by 8 wickets

Renegades		B	4	6
SG Molineux*	c Patterson b Coyte	9	16	
JI Rodrigues	c Mack b Wellington	13	17	1
CA Webb	b Barsby	1	4	
H Kaur	c Patterson b Brown	41	37	4 1
E Jones	not out	36	29	2
JE Duffin	c Wellington b Coyte	2	7	
GL Wareham	c Penna b Coyte	13	10	2
JE Dooley+	not out	1	1	
CM Leeson				
EM Falconer				
HL Ferling				
	5 lb, 1 nb, 4 w	10		
6 overs: 2-27	20 overs	6-126		

1-19 (Molineux, 4.1), 2-21 (Webb, 5.1), 3-53 (Rodrigues, 9.4),
4-78 (Kaur, 14.1), 5-90 (Duffin, 16.5), 6-113 (Wareham, 18.6)

Bowling	O	M	R	W	wd	nb	Dots
DR Brown	4	0	16	1	3		16
TM McGrath	4	0	31	0		1	7
JI Barsby	2	0	11	1			7
SJ Coyte	4	0	20	3	1		14
A Wellington	4	0	33	1			5
D van Niekerk	2	0	10	0			3

Strikers		B	4	6
D van Niekerk	c Molineux b Falconer	29	14	7
KM Mack	st Dooley b Kaur	13	13	2
L Wolvaardt	not out	36	39	4
TM McGrath*	not out	50	39	3 1
BE Patterson				
M Penna				
A Wellington				
TJ McPharlin+				
SJ Coyte				
JL Barsby				
DR Brown				
Extras	1 w	1		
6 overs: 2-47	17.3 overs	2-129		

1-35 (van Niekerk, 3.5), 2-47 (Mack, 5.2)

Bowling	O	M	R	W	wd	nb	Dots
SG Molineux	3.3	0	19	0			9
HL Ferling	1	0	12	0			3
GL Wareham	3	0	13	0			12
EM Falconer	1	0	14	1			2
H Kaur	4	0	31	1			6
CM Leeson	3	0	22	0	1		5
CA Webb	1	0	6	0			1
E Jones	1	0	12	0			0

Toss: Renegades.   Umpires: M Qureshi, D Taylor, Ref: K Hannam   Award: TM McGrath (AS)
McGrath 50: 39 balls, 3x4 1x6

Match 9 – Stars v Sixers at Bellerive Oval, Hobart on October 20, 2021 (Floodlit) – Stars won by 30 runs

Stars		B	4	6
EJ Villani	b Gardner	10	6	2
AJ Sutherland	b Gardner	57	50	9
MM Lanning*	c Healy b Campbell	10	19	1
ME Bouchier	not out	32	25	4
KJ Garth	not out	24	21	
NM Faltum+				
T Flintoff				
AJ Lanning				
LCN Smith				
SF Day				
RM McKenna				
	2 lb, 1 nb, 3 w	6		
6 overs: 1-34	20 overs	3-139		

1-28 (Villani, 3.1), 2-60 (M Lanning, 10.1), 3-88 (Sutherland, 13.5)

Sixers		B	4	6
S Verma	c Faltum b Garth	0	3	
AJ Healy+	c Bouchier b Sutherland	14	13	2
AK Gardner	c Smith b Day	31	33	4
EA Perry*	c Flintoff b Garth	40	43	4
NE Bolton	b Flintoff	8	11	1
MJ Brown	c Faltum b Flintoff	0	1	
AR Reakes	st Faltum b Smith	6	10	
RP Yadav	b Garth	2	6	
CF Moore	not out	0	0	
SR Campbell				
JE Allen				
	6 lb, 2 w	8		
6 overs: 2-30	20 overs	8-109		

1-0 (Verma, 0.3), 2-29 (Healy, 5.3), 3-61 (Gardner, 10.6),
4-81 (Bolton, 14.3), 5-81 (Brown, 14.4), 6-98 (Reakes, 17.6),
7-109 (Perry, 19.4), 8-109 (Yadav, 19.6)

Bowling	O	M	R	W	wd	nb	Dots
NE Bolton	4	0	31	0			9
EA Perry	1	0	13	0	2	1	3
MJ Brown	4	0	38	0			8
AK Gardner	4	0	16	2			12
RP Yadav	4	0	17	0			9
SR Campbell	3	0	22	1	1		9

Bowling	O	M	R	W	wd	nb	Dots
KJ Garth	4	0	17	3			14
T Flintoff	4	0	23	2	1		15
LCN Smith	4	0	15	1			12
AJ Sutherland	4	0	24	1	1		10
SF Day	4	0	24	1			6

Toss: Sixers.   Umpires: R Howard, M van Eck, Ref: SR Bernard   Award: AJ Sutherland (MS)
Sutherland 50: 47 balls, 8x4

Match 10 – Hurricanes v Strikers at Invermay Park, Launceston on October 23, 2021 – No result

Hurricanes		B	4	6	Strikers		B	4	6
R H Priest*+	c McGrath b Brown	13	16	1	D van Niekerk				
R Johnston	c Wellington b Brown	2	8		KM Mack				
M du Preez	c Barsby b Coyte	39	35	2	3	L Wolvaardt				
NJ Carey	c McPharlin b Wellington	19	18	1	TM McGrath*				
RM Ghosh	lbw b Wellington	4	3	1	BE Patterson				
NE Stalenberg	not out	21	17	2	M Penna				
SK Moloney	not out	0	0		A Wellington				
MR Strano					TJ McPharlin+				
BW Vakarewa					SJ Coyte				
TJ Vlaeminck					JL Barsby				
A Smith					DR Brown				
	2 b, 1 nb, 6 w	9							
6 overs : 2-29	16 overs	5-107							

1-11 (Johnston, 2.2), 2-27 (Priest, 4.5), 3-70 (Carey, 11.2),
4-74 (Ghosh, 11.5), 5-106 (du Preez, 15.5).

Bowling	O	M	R	W	wd	nb	Dots
DR Brown	4	0	21	2	2	1	15
TM McGrath	2	0	16	0	1		5
SJ Coyte	3	0	18	1			8
A Wellington	3	0	16	2			8
D van Niekerk	3	0	21	0	1		7
M Penna	1	0	13	0			2

Toss: Strikers.   Umpires: S Burns, R Howard, Ref: K Hannam.   No Award.   Crowd: 314

Match 11 – Thunder v Sixers at York Park, Launceston on October 23, 2021 – Match Abandoned due to rain
Match 12 – Heat v Stars at Invermay Park, Launceston on October 23, 2021 – Match Abandoned due to rain
Match 13 – Renegades v Scorchers at York Park, Launceston on October 23, 2021 – Match Abandoned due to rain

Match 14 – Heat v Strikers at Invermay Park, Launceston on October 24, 2021 – Heat won by 5 runs

Heat		B	4	6	Strikers		B	4	6
GM Harris	c McPharlin b Coyte	16	11	4		D van Niekerk	lbw b Jonassen	24	22	30	2
GP Redmayne+	c Mack b Brown	28	14	4	1	L Wolvaardt	c Kimmince b Prestwidge	54	30	39	5
E Johnston	c McGrath b Brown	9	10	1	TM McGrath*	c & b Jonassen	0	1	2	
LM Kimmince	c Wolvaardt b Brown	0	1		M Penna	c Redmayne b Prestwidge	2	6	9	
JL Jonassen*	c Penna b Coyte	9	10	1	A Wellington	not out	7	3	8	1
G Voll	not out	31	17	2	2	SJ Coyte	not out	5	4	6	1
AE Bosch	not out	5	3	1	KM Mack					
MC Hinkley					BE Patterson					
GK Prestwidge					TJ McPharlin+					
NM Hancock					JL Barsby					
P Yadav					DR Brown					
	3 lb, 3 w	6				2 b, 5 w	7			
3 overs : 1-35	11 overs	5-104			3 overs : 0-21	11 overs	4-99			

1-35 (Harris, 2.5), 2-57 (Redmayne, 5.4), 3-57 (Johnston, 5.5),
4-57 (Kimmince, 5.6), 5-98 (Jonassen, 10.2)

1-68 (van Niekerk, 7.5), 2-68 (McGrath, 7.6), 3-83 (Wolvaardt, 9.4),
4-85 (Penna, 9.5)

Bowling	O	M	R	W	wd	nb	Dots
DR Brown	3	0	28	3	3		10
TM McGrath	2	0	20	0			3
SJ Coyte	2	0	19	2			5
A Wellington	2	0	18	0			3
D van Niekerk	2	0	16	0			5

Bowling	O	M	R	W	wd	nb	Dots
NM Hancock	2	0	20	0	1		5
JL Jonassen	2	0	17	2			5
GK Prestwidge	3	0	24	2	4		8
GM Harris	2	0	17	0			3
P Yadav	2	0	19	0			4

Toss: Strikers.   Umpires: R Howard, M Qureshi, Ref: SR Bernard   Award: SL Bates (ST)   Crowd: 224
Woolvardt 50: 29 balls, 5x4 3x6

267

Match 15 – Renegades v Sixers at York Park, Launceston on October 24, 2021 – Renegades won by 7 wickets

Sixers		R	B	4	6
AJ Healy+	c&b Kaur	5	10		
S Verma	c Kaur b Molineux	0	1		
AK Gardner	c Dooley b Kaur	7	9	1	
EA Perry*	not out	50	51	3	1
NE Bolton	c Ferling b Webb	38	41	2	
AR Reakes	not out	11	9	1	
MJ Brown					
RP Yadav					
CF Moore					
LR Cheatle					
SR Campbell					
	1 nb, 6 w	7			
6 overs: 3-17	20 overs	4-118			

Renegades		R	B	4	6
E Jones	c Perry b Campbell	38	30	4	1
JI Rodrigues	run out (Yadav)	14	15	1	
CA Webb	c&b Yadav	23	25	1	
H Kaur	not out	35	29	1	2
JE Duffin	not out	6	4	1	
SG Molineux*					
JE Dooley+					
CM Leeson					
EL Hayward					
EM Falconer					
HL Ferling					
	1 nb, 3 w	4			
6 overs: 1-44	17 overs	3-120			

1-1 (Verma, 0.3), 2-8 (Gardner, 1.6), 3-12 (Healy, 4.1), 4-92 (Bolton, 17.2)

1-43 (Rodrigues, 5.3), 2-66 (Jones, 9.1), 3-100 (Webb, 15.4)

Bowling	O	M	R	W	wd	nb	Dots
SG Molineux	4	0	18	1			12
H Kaur	4	0	17	2			12
EL Hayward	4	0	21	0			10
CA Webb	4	0	30	1	1		5
CM Leeson	3	0	22	0	1		7
EM Falconer	1	0	10	0		1	2

Bowling	O	M	R	W	wd	nb	Dots
LR Cheatle	2	0	17	0			1
AK Gardner	4	0	41	0			8
NE Bolton	3	0	12	0	1		8
MJ Brown	3	0	25	0		1	6
RP Yadav	2	0	12	1			4
SR Campbell	3	0	13	1	2		8

Toss: Renegades.　Umpires: SAJ Craig, M van Eck, CA Polosak (TV), Ref: DA Johnston.　Award: H Kaur (MR).　Crowd: 561

Perry 50: 49 balls, 3x4 1x6

Match 16 – Scorchers v Thunder at York Park, Launceston on October 24, 2021 – Scorchers won by 81 runs

Scorchers		R	B	4	6
SFM Devine*	c Mandhana b Darlington	101	60	8	6
BL Mooney+	c Wilson b Wong	65	54	6	
C Atapattu	not out	12	6	2	
M Kapp	not out	0	0		
MG Carmichael					
HL Graham					
L Griffith					
AM King					
LG Mills					
TCJ Peschel					
CL Piparo					
	8 w	8			
6 overs: 0-35	20 overs	2-186			

Thunder		R	B	4	6
TB Wilson+	b King	15	19	1	
SS Mandhana	c Peschel b Griffith	9	8	1	
PES Litchfield	c Carmichael b Graham	24	34	3	
SJ Johnson	b King	0	3		
CL Hall	c Devine b King	5	7		
AB Learoyd	lbw b King	4	10		
DB Sharma	c Atapattu b Griffith	20	20	2	
HJ Darlington*	b Mills	2	6		
IECM Wong	b Kapp	4	4	1	
LG Smith	not out	17	10	3	
SL Bates	not out	0	0		
Extras	1 nb, 4 w	5			
6 overs: 1-30	20 overs	9-105			

1-173 (Mooney, 18.5), 2-175 (Devine, 19.2)

1-14 (Mandhana, 2.2), 2-49 (Wilson, 9.3), 3-49 (Johnson, 9.6), 4-53 (Litchfield, 10.5), 5-61 (Learoyd, 13.1), 6-62 (Hall, 13.4), 7-73 (Darlington, 15.6), 8-79 (Wong, 16.5), 9-101 (Sharma, 19.3)

Bowling	O	M	R	W	wd	nb	Dots
SL Bates	4	0	28	0	1		9
IECM Wong	3	0	24	1	1		8
DB Sharma	3	0	29	0	2		6
SJ Johnson	3	0	28	0			4
HJ Darlington	4	0	35	1	2		9
LG Smith	1	0	11	0			1
AB Learoyd	2	0	31	0	1		2

Bowling	O	M	R	W	wd	nb	Dots
LG Mills	3	0	17	1			4
M Kapp	3	0	24	1	2		7
L Griffith	3	0	17	2	1		11
SFM Devine	1	0	2	0			4
TCJ Peschel	3	0	21	0	1	1	9
AM King	4	0	11	4			16
HL Graham	3	0	13	1			9

Toss: Thunder.　Umpires: AR Crozier, SA Lightbody, D Taylor (TV) Ref: K Hannam.　Award: SFM Devine (PS).　Crowd: 234

Devine 50: 32 balls, 4x4 3x6, 100: 58 balls, 8x4 6x6, Mooney 50: 48 balls, 3x4

Match 17 – Stars v Thunder at York Park, Launceston on October 26, 2021 – Stars won by 12 runs

Stars		B	4	6
EJ Villani	c Sharma b Bates	52	63	3
AJ Sutherland	lbw b Wong	3	7	
MM Lanning*	c Mandhana b Wong	6	8	1
ME Bouchier	c Litchfield b Smith	31	28	4
KJ Garth	c Peterson b Sharma	9	8	1
EA Osborne	c Peterson b Darlington	0	2	
NM Faltum+	run out (Mandhana)	4	4	
TM Flintoff	not out	0	0	
M Darke				
LCN Smith				
SF Day				
	3 w	3		
6 overs: 2-18	20 overs	7-108		

1-10 (Sutherland, 3.4), 2-18 (Lanning, 5.5), 3-81 (Bouchier, 15.3), 4-98 (Garth, 17.5), 5-100 (Osborne, 18.3), 6-107 (Villani, 19.5), 7-108 (Faltum, 19.6)

Bowling	O	M	R	W	wd	nb	Dots
SL Bates	4	0	11	1			14
IECM Wong	4	0	19	2			14
DB Sharma	4	0	28	1	2		6
HJ Darlington	4	0	20	1			6
KE Peterson	2	0	18	0	1		5
LG Smith	2	0	12	1			4

Thunder		B	4	6
TB Wilson+	c Darke b Garth	0	3	
SS Mandhana	c Garth b Sutherland	3	10	
PES Litchfield	lbw b Garth	0	1	
CL Hall	c Lanning b Garth	3	8	
DB Sharma	not out	44	48	4
A Learoyd	b Day	21	35	1
HJ Darlington*	not out	17	15	1
LG Smith				
IECM Wong				
KE Peterson				
SL Bates				
	1 lb, 7 w	8		
6 overs: 4-13	20 overs	5-96		

1-0 (Wilson, 0.3), 2-0 (Litchfield, 0.4), 3-12 (Mandhana, 3.3), 4-12 (Hall, 4.1), 5-54 (Learoyd, 14.3)

Bowling	O	M	R	W	wd	nb	Dots
KJ Garth	4	3	11	3	1		19
TM Flintoff	2	0	15	0	1		6
AJ Sutherland	3	0	8	1	1		12
EA Osborne	4	0	20	0			10
LCN Smith	4	0	22	0			6
SF Day	3	0	19	1			5

Toss: Stars.   Umpires: AR Crozier, D Taylor, Ref: K Hannam   Award: KJ Garth (MS)
Villani 50: 60 balls, 3x4

Match 18 – Hurricanes v Heat at York Park, Launceston on October 26, 2021 – Heat won by 8 wickets

Hurricanes		B	4	6
RH Priest*+	b Sippel	0	1	
R Johnston	c Voll b Jonassen	47	42	5	1
M du Preez	c Bosch b Sippel	2	4	
NJ Carey	c Kimmince b Prestwidge	5	4	1
SK Moloney	b Jonassen	0	5	
RM Ghosh	c Johnston b Bosch	22	27	3
NE Stalenberg	c & b Jonassen	0	4	
MR Strano	c Redmayne b Sippel	33	24	4
TJ Vlaeminck	not out	11	6	1
A Smith	not out	4	3	
CL Rafferty				
	8 w	8		
6 overs: 4-33	20 overs	8-132		

1-0 (Priest, 0.1), 2-2 (du Preez, 0.5), 3-9 (Carey, 1.3), 4-15 (Moloney, 3.2), 5-60 (Ghosh, 10.6), 6-60 (Stalenberg, 11.4), 7-107 (Johnston, 17.3), 8-128 (Strano, 19.3)

Bowling	O	M	R	W	wd	nb	Dots
CG Sippel	4	0	25	3			13
GK Prestwidge	2	0	19	1	6		8
JL Jonassen	4	0	14	3	1		15
P Yadav	4	0	26	0			11
GM Harris	3	0	29	0			7
AE Bosch	3	0	19	1	1		9

Heat		B	4	6
GM Harris	not out	57	46	5	2
GP Redmayne+	c Ghosh b Carey	22	22	2
G Voll	b Carey	0	3	
MC Hinkley	not out	49	40	5	1
JL Jonassen*				
LM Kimmince				
AE Bosch				
E Johnston				
GK Prestwidge				
CG Sippel				
P Yadav				
	2 lb, 8 w	10		
6 overs: 0-44	18.3 overs	2-138		

1-52 (Redmayne, 7.1), 2-52 (Voll, 7.4)

Bowling	O	M	R	W	wd	nb	Dots
TJ Vlaeminck	4	0	26	0	2		14
CL Rafferty	1	0	14	0	1		2
MR Strano	3.3	0	34	0	1		8
R Johnston	2	0	10	0			5
A Smith	2	0	16	0	1		3
NJ Carey	3	0	16	2			8
SK Moloney	3	0	20	0	2		6

Toss: Heat.   Umpires: SAJ Craig, M Qureshi, Ref: DA Johnston.   Award: GM Harris (BH)   Crowd: 367
G Harris 50: 41 balls, 4x4 2x6

269

Match 19 – Renegades v Thunder at York Park, Launceston on October 27, 2021 – Renegades won by 9 runs

Renegades			B	4	6
JE Dooley+	c Smith b Bates	37	34	4	
JI Rodrigues	not out	75	56	9	
JE Duffin	c Bates b Sharma	11	13		
H Kaur	lbw b Peterson	3	4		
CA Webb	run out (Mandhana)	6	9		
CM Leeson	b Darlington	2	4		
MA Blows					
SG Molineux*					
EM Falconer					
EL Hayward					
HL Ferling					
	1 b, 2 lb, 5 w	8			
6 overs: 0-31	20 overs	5-142			

1-84 (Dooley, 11.1), 2-106 (Duffin, 14.6), 3-120 (Kaur, 16.1),
4-134 (Webb, 18.6), 5-142 (Leeson, 19.6)

Bowling	O	M	R	W	wd	nb	Dots
IECM Wong	4	0	36	0	1		5
SL Bates	4	0	16	1			10
DB Sharma	4	0	23	1			7
HJ Darlington	4	0	34	1	1		8
LG Smith	2	0	20	0			3
K Peterson	2	0	10	1			5

Thunder			B	4	6
TB Wilson+	c Leeson b Hayward	6	13	1	
SS Mandhana	b Kaur	64	44	4	1
PES Litchfield	c Dooley b Webb	14	19	1	
CL Hall	lbw b Molineux	10	12	1	
AB Learoyd	run out (Molineux)	3	5		
LG Smith	c Dooley b Webb	9	13		
IECM Wong	c Duffin b Leeson	1	3		
DB Sharma	not out	23	10	4	
HJ Darlington*	c & b Webb	0	1		
KE Peterson	not out	0	0		
SL Bates					
	1 lb, 2 w	3			
6 overs: 1-43	20 overs	8-133			

1-9 (Wilson, 2.3), 2-62 (Litchfield, 9.4), 3-88 (Hall, 13.3),
4-99 (Mandhana, 15.2), 5-101 (Learoyd, 15.5),
6-104 (Wong, 16.6), 7-129 (Smith, 19.4), 8-129 (Darlington, 19.5)

Bowling	O	M	R	W	wd	nb	Dots
SG Molineux	4	0	21	1			11
H Kaur	4	0	35	1	1		8
EL Hayward	4	0	15	1			10
EM Falconer	1	0	19	0	1		0
CM Leeson	4	0	21	1			7
CA Webb	3	0	21	3			6

Toss: Renegades. Umpires: AR Crozier, R Howard, Ref: DA Johnston. Award: JI Rodridges (MR)

Rodrigues 50: 37 balls, 7x4. Mandhana 50: 34 balls, 4x4 1x6

Match 20 – Hurricanes v Stars at York Park, Launceston on October 27, 2021 – Hurricanes won by 6 wickets

Stars			B	4	6
EJ Villani	b Vlaeminck	35	29	4	
AJ Sutherland	b Vlaeminck	12	27	1	
MM Lanning*	b Vlaeminck	3	4		
ME Bouchier	c Vlaeminck b Strano	42	33	3	2
KJ Garth	not out	44	29	6	
EA Osborne	not out	0	0		
NM Faltum+					
TM Flintoff					
M Darke					
LCN Smith					
SF Day					
	2 nb, 6 w	8			
6 overs: 0-43	20 overs	4-144			

1-48 (Sutherland, 7.5), 2-55 (Lanning, 9.3), 3-57 (Villani, 9.5),
4-140 (Bouchier, 19.5)

Bowling	O	M	R	W	wd	nb	Dots
R Johnston	4	0	24	0	1		9
TJ Vlaeminck	4	0	27	3	3	1	14
MR Strano	4	0	40	1	1		8
CL Rafferty	1	0	6	0		1	4
NJ Carey	4	0	27	0	1		9
A Smith	3	0	20	0			4

Hurricanes			B	4	6
RH Priest*+	c & b Day	23	27	25	5
R Johnston	b Garth	0	1	4	
M du Preez	c Osborne b Sutherland	62	45	61	5
NJ Carey	run out (Sutherland)	24	23	31	1
RM Ghosh	not out	24	16	19	4
NE Stalenberg	not out	3	4	10	
SK Moloney					
MR Strano					
TJ Vlaeminck					
A Smith					
CL Rafferty					
	4 lb, 7 w	11			
6 overs: 1-30	19.2 overs	4-147			

1-2 (Johnston, 0.4), 2-33 (Priest, 6.5), 3-107 (Carey, 14.4),
4-124 (du Preez, 16.5)

Bowling	O	M	R	W	wd	nb	Dots
KJ Garth	4	0	25	1	2		13
LCN Smith	3.2	0	20	0			12
AJ Sutherland	4	0	32	1	5		11
SF Day	2	0	17	1			3
EA Osborne	3	0	26	0			3
TM Flintoff	3	0	23	0			6

Toss: Hurricanes. Umpires: SA Lightbody, CA Polosak, Ref: SR Bernard. Award: M du Preez (HH). Crowd: 367

du Preez 50: 34 balls, 4x4 3x6

Match 21 – Renegades v Sixers at Lilac Hill, Perth on October 30, 2021 – Renegades won by 12 runs

Renegades			B	4	6
E Jones	c Gardner b Perry	4	11	1	
J I Rodrigues	c Campbell b Cheatle	25	27	2	
CA Webb	c Verma b Campbell	9	7	2	
H Kaur	c &b Yadav	43	32	4	1
J E Duffin	not out	41	32	3	2
SG Molineux*	c Campbell b Gardner	10	10		
J E Dooley+	b Gardner	0	1		
CM Leeson	run out (Reakes-Bolton)	1	1		
EM Falconer	not out	0	0		
EL Hayward					
HL Ferling					
	5 lb, 1 nb, 3 w	9			
6 overs: 2-45	20 overs	7-142			

1-5 (Jones, 1.6), 2-21 (Webb, 4.2), 3-72 (Rodrigues, 10.5), 4-108 (Kaur, 15.5), 5-125 (Molineux, 18.5), 6-125 (Dooley, 18.6), 7-136 (Leeson, 19.5)

Bowling	O	M	R	W	wd	nb	Dots
LR Cheatle	4	1	17	1			14
EA Perry	2	0	15	1			7
MJ Brown	3	0	16	0	1		9
SR Campbell	1	0	17	1	1	1	3
NE Bolton	4	0	37	0	1		5
RP Yadav	4	0	27	1			8
AK Gardner	2	0	8	2			6

Sixers			B	4	6
AJ Healy+	b Molineux	1	4		
EA Perry*	c Kaur b Hayward	28	28	3	
AK Gardner	run out (Rodrigues-Dooley)	4	4	1	
NE Bolton	run out (Dooley)	9	13		
S Verma	c Dooley b Falconer	20	15	2	
AR Reakes	c Falconer b Webb	3	10		
MJ Brown	c Rodrigues b Falconer	31	20	4	
RP Yadav	not out	11	12		
CF Moore	run out (Rodrigues-Dooley)	1	3		
LR Cheatle	run out (Kaur-Dooley)	14	9	1	
SR Campbell	not out	3	2		
	(1b, 4 w)	5			
6 overs: 2-30	20 overs	9-130			

1-2 (Healy, 0.6), 2-12 (Gardner, 3.1), 3-44 (Perry, 8.1), 4-44 (Bolton, 8.2), 5-50 (Reakes, 10.3), 6-100 (Brown, 15.3), 7-101 (Verma, 15.5), 8-107 (Moore, 16.6), 9-127 (Cheatle, 19.3)

Bowling	O	M	R	W	wd	nb	Dots
SG Molineux	4	0	17	1			11
EL Hayward	4	0	22	1			10
H Kaur	3	0	19	0			6
CM Leeson	2	0	23	0	2		2
CA Webb	3	0	20	1	1		7
EM Falconer	4	0	28	2	1		9

Toss: Sixers.   Umpires: T Steenholdt, J Thomas, Ref: K Hannam   Award: JE Duffin (MR)
Mack 50: 36 balls, 8x4. Redmayne 50: 37 balls, 6x4 1x6

Match 22 – Stars v Thunder at York Park, Launceston on October 30, 2021 – Thunder won by 19 runs

Thunder			B	4	6
TB Wilson+	run out (Smith-Faltum)	53	53	5	
SS Mandhana	c Sutherland b Garth	3	4		
PES Litchfield	c Sutherland b Osborne	49	42	7	
CL Hall	c Day b Osborne	3	4		
DB Sharma	run out (Villani)	16	14	2	
SJ Johnson	not out	0	1		
HJ Darlington*	not out	1	1		
LG Smith					
IECM Wong					
KE Peterson					
SL Bates					
	4 b, 2 lb, 2 w	8			
6 overs: 1-26	20 overs	5-133			

1-9 (Mandhana, 2.2), 2-90 (Litchfield, 13.5), 3-101 (Hall, 15.5), 4-126 (Sharma, 19.2), 5-131 (Wilson, 19.4)

Bowling	O	M	R	W	wd	nb	Dots
KJ Garth	4	0	17	1	1		12
EA Osborne	4	0	25	2			8
AJ Sutherland	4	1	22	0			12
LCN Smith	3	0	15	0			7
T Flintoff	4	0	32	0			6
SF Day	1	0	16	0	1		1

Stars			B	4	6
EJ Villani	lbw b Johnson	38	31	5	
MM Lanning*	b Bates	2	6		
AJ Sutherland	b Wong	4	6	1	
ME Bouchier	lbw b Bates	20	23	2	
KJ Garth	c &b Sharma	3	12		
EA Osborne	b Sharma	11	16	1	
NM Faltum+	c &b Sharma	4	7		
T Flintoff	b Darlington	17	12	3	
M Darke	not out	7	6		
LCN Smith	not out	1	1		
SF Day					
	2 lb, 5 w	7			
6 overs: 2-32	20 overs	8-114			

1-5 (Lanning, 1.5), 2-10 (Sutherland, 2.6), 3-69 (Bouchier, 10.5), 4-69 (Villani, 11.1), 5-84 (Garth, 15.2), 6-85 (Osborne, 15.5), 7-98 (Faltum, 17.4), 8-113 (Flintoff, 19.5)

Bowling	O	M	R	W	wd	nb	Dots
IECM Wong	3	0	17	1	2		10
SL Bates	4	0	14	2			12
SJ Johnson	3	0	22	1	1		9
HJ Darlington	4	0	16	1			13
DB Sharma	4	0	25	3			10
K Peterson	1	0	15	0	1		2
LG Smith	1	0	3	0			3

Toss: Thunder.   Umpires: R Howard, TJ Matibiri, Ref: DA Johnston   Award: SL Bates (ST).   Crowd: 284

Match 23 – Scorchers v Strikers at Lilac Hill, Perth on October 30, 2021 – Scorchers won in Superover

Scorchers			B	4	6
SFM Devine*	st McPharlin b van Niekerk	20	21	2	
BL Mooney+	c Brown b Wellington	36	33	5	
C Atapattu	c Coyte b Wellington	20	23	2	
M Kapp	b McGrath	2	8		
HL Graham	c Coyte b Schutt	22	20	3	
AM King	not out	11	12		
CLP iparo	not out	7	3	1	
MG Carmichael					
L Griffith					
LG Mills					
TCJ Peschel					
	2 lb, 1 w	3			
6 overs: 0-36	20 overs	5-121			

Strikers			B	4	6
D van Niekerk	c Mooney b Kapp	10	9	2	
KM Mack	b Mills	24	30	1	
L Wolvaardt	c Mooney b Griffith	5	9	1	
TM McGrath*	c Atapattu b Peschel	17	17	2	
BE Patterson	c Griffith b Graham	12	18		
M Penna	run out (Devine)	0	2		
A Wellington	c Peschel b Mills	11	9	2	
TJ McPharlin+	not out	21	16	3	
SJ Coyte	run out (Mills)	14	10	1	
M Schutt					
DR Brown					
	1 lb, 6 w	7			
6 overs: 2-27	20 overs	8-121			

1-59 (Devine, 8.5), 2-63 (Mooney, 9.4), 3-73 (Kapp, 12.6),
4-93 (Atapttu, 15.4), 5-111 (Graham, 19.1)

1-12 (van Niekerk, 2.1), 2-19 (Wolvaardt, 3.6),
3-48 (McGrath, 9.2), 5-64 (Penna, 12.1), 6-84
(Wellington, 15.3), 7-88 (Patterson, 16.1), 8-121 (Coyte, 19.6)

Bowling	O	M	R	W	wd	nb	Dots
M Schutt	4	0	19	1			13
DR Brown	3	0	19	0			9
TM McGrath	3	0	28	1			7
D van Niekerk	2	0	12	1			2
SJ Coyte	4	0	29	0	1		7
A Wellington	4	0	12	2			14

Bowling	O	M	R	W	wd	nb	Dots
M Kapp	4	0	26	1	1		9
C Atapattu	1	0	10	0			2
L Griffith	2	0	5	1			7
SFM Devine	1	0	4	0			3
AM King	4	0	16	0	1		11
TCJ Peschel	2	0	16	1	2		5
HL Graham	3	0	25	1	1		5
LG Mills	3	0	18	2			9

Toss: Scorchers.   Umpires: J Buscall, NR Johnstone, Ref: K Hannam.   Award: BL Mooney (PS).
Superover: AS 1-9 Woolvardt 6 (3), McGrath 3 (2) Coyte 0* (0) - Kapp 0-9. Scorchers 0-12 (0.2) Devine 12* (6) 2x6, Mooney 0* (0),
Schutt 0.2-0-12-0

Match 24 – Hurricanes v Heat at York Park, Launceston on October 30, 2021 – Heat won by 14 runs

Heat			B	4	6
GM Harris	run out (Smith)	75	51	6	2
GP Redmayne+	c Ghosh b Strano	64	50	9	
LM Kimmince	b Johnston	2	3		
G Voll	run out (Ghosh)	12	9	1	
AE Bosch	st Priest b Johnston	3	6		
MC Hinkley	run out (Johnston)	2	2		
JL Jonassen*	not out	0	0		
CR Knott					
NM Hancock					
CG Sippel					
P Yadav					
	2 lb, 1 nb, 9 w	12			
6 overs: 0-42	20 overs	6-170			

Hurricanes			B	4	6
RH Priest*+	lbw b Jonassen	9	12	2	
R Johnston	lbw b Sippel	3	5		
M du Preez	c Redmayne b Bosch	73	49	9	1
RM Ghosh	b Jonassen	16	9	3	
NJ Carey	c Redmayne b Sippel	31	26	3	
NE Stalenberg	c Sippel b Jonassen	3	5		
MR Strano	c Yadav b Hancock	12	9	1	
SK Moloney	c Kimmince b Hancock	1	2		
TJ Vlaeminck	c Harris b Hancock	0	1		
BW Vakarewa	not out	3	2		
A Smith	not out	0	0		
	5 w	5			
6 overs: 2-36	20 overs	9-156			

1-140 (Harris, 15.1), 2-142 (Kimmince, 15.4), 3-163 (Voll, 18.1),
4-166 (Redmayne, 18.6), 5-170 (Hinkley, 19.5),
6-170 (Bosch, 19.6)

1-13 (Priest, 2.2), 2-16 (Johnston, 3.5), 3-50 (Ghosh, 7.2),
4-137 (du Preez, 16.4), 5-137 (Carey, 17.1),
6-149 (Stalenberg, 18.4), 7-152 (Strano, 19.1),
8-153 (Vlaeminck, 19.3), 9-156 (Moloney, 19.4)

Bowling	O	M	R	W	wd	nb	Dots
TJ Vlaeminck	4	0	10	0			15
BW Vakarewa	3	0	26	0	1		6
MR Strano	3	0	29	1	2		5
NJ Carey	3	0	30	0	1	1	4
A Smith	3	0	27	0			1
R Johnston	4	0	30	2			7
SK Moloney	1	0	16	0	3		1

Bowling	O	M	R	W	wd	nb	Dots
NM Hancock	4	0	33	3	1		12
CG Sippel	4	0	25	2	1		10
JL Jonassen	4	0	25	3			10
GM Harris	2	0	18	0			4
P Yadav	2	0	24	0	2		2
CR Knott	2	0	19	0	1		3
AE Bosch	2	0	12	1			6

Toss: Hurricanes.   Umpires: S Burns, AR Crozier, Ref: SR Bernard.   Award: GM Harris (BH).   Crowd: 544
Harris 50: 39 balls 4x4 1x6, Redmayne 50: 39 balls, 8x4. M du Preez 50: 38 balls, 7x4

Match 25 – Strikers v Renegades at Lilac Hill, Perth on October 31, 2021 - Renegades won by 6 wickets

Strikers			B	4	6
D van Niekerk	lbw b Leeson	62	47	6	2
KM Mack	b Molineux	19	21	2	
L Wolvaardt	c Ferling b Kaur	47	35	4	1
TM McGrath*	c Kaur b Falconer	7	6		
M Penna	st Dooley b Kaur	4	5		
BE Patterson	not out	11	5	1	
A Wellington	not out	1	1		
TJ McPharlin+					
SJ Coyte					
M Schutt					
DR Brown					
	9 w	9			
6 overs: 0-43	20 overs	5-160			

1-43 (Mack, 6.2), 2-116 (van Niekerk, 15.2),
3-127 (McGrath, 16.6), 4-148 (Wolvaardt, 18.5), 5-148 (Penna, 18.6)

Bowling	O	M	R	W	wd	nb	Dots
SG Molineux	4	0	34	1	1		10
EL Hayward	3	0	23	0			6
EM Falconer	4	0	25	1			9
H Kaur	4	0	31	2	4		10
HL Ferling	1	0	13	0			1
CM Leeson	4	0	34	1			4

Renegades			B	4	6
E Jones	c McPharlin b McGratl	3	15		
J I Rodrigues	c van Niekerk b Schutt	27	16	4	1
JE Dooley+	c Coyte b Schutt	29	28	2	
H Kaur	not out	73	46	3	5
JE Duffin	c McPharlin b Coyte	14	11	1	
SG Molineux*	not out	8	3	2	
CM Leeson					
EM Falconer					
EL Hayward					
HL Ferling					
RK O'Donnell					
	2 lb, 1 nb, 5 w	8			
6 overs: 2-38	19.4 overs	4-162			

1-32 (Rodrigues, 4.5), 2-33 (Jones, 5.2), 3-103 (Dooley, 14.5),
4-151 (Duffin, 18.4)

Bowling	O	M	R	W	wd	nb	Dots
M Schutt	4	1	18	2			15
DR Brown	4	0	39	0	2	1	8
TM McGrath	3.4	0	26	1	1		7
SJ Coyte	4	0	33	1			8
D van Niekerk	3	0	28	0			3
A Wellington	1	0	16	0	2		2

Toss: Strikers.   Umpires: NR Johnstone, J Thomas, Ref: K Hannam
van Niekerk 50: 38 balls, 5x4 2x6. Kaur 50: 36 balls, 2x4 3x6

Award: H Kaur (MR).

Match 26 – Hurricanes v Thunder at York Park, Launceston on October 31, 2021 – Thunder won by 37 runs

Thunder			B	4	6
SS Mandhana	c Moloney b Carey	50	50	4	1
TB Wilson+	b Vlaeminck	3	7		
PES Litchfield	c du Preez b Smith	31	25	3	1
CL Hall	c Vakarewa b Carey	12	13	1	
DB Sharma	run out (Vakarewa)	20	15	2	
SJ Johnson	lbw b Johnston	13	9	3	
A Learoyd	not out	3	2		
HJ Darlington*	not out	0	0		
LG Smith					
IECM Wong					
SL Bates					
	1 lb, 1 nb, 12 w	14			
6 overs: 1-42	20 overs	6-146			

1-6 (Wilson, 2.1), 2-76 (Litchfield, 10.2), 3-100 (Hall, 14.3),
4-111 (Mandhana, 16.2), 5-139 (Johnson, 19.2),
6-144 (Sharma, 19.5)

Bowling	O	M	R	W	wd	nb	Dots
TJ Vlaeminck	4	0	27	1	6		12
BW Vakarewa	3	0	18	0			8
MR Strano	4	0	29	0	1		8
NJ Carey	4	0	36	2	1		9
R Johnston	3	0	25	1	1	1	4
A Smith	2	0	10	1			5

Hurricanes			B	4	6
RH Priest*+	c Sharma b Wong	0	2		
R Johnston	c Darlington b Sharma	7	14		
M du Preez	c Smith b Sharma	41	39	2	1
NJ Carey	c Learoyd b Johnson	29	28	2	1
RM Ghosh	c & b Darlington	3	6		
NE Stalenberg	c Bates b Darlington	11	12	1	
SK Moloney	c Litchfield b Sharma	10	13		
MR Strano	not out	4	6		
TJ Vlaeminck	run out (Litchfield)	0	0		
BW Vakarewa	not out	0	0		
A Smith					
	4 lb	4			
6 overs: 2-25	20 overs	8-109			

1-0 (Priest, 0.2), 2-24 (Johnston, 5.2), 3-66 (du Preez, 11.5),
4-82 (Ghosh, 14.3), 5-84 (Carey, 15.1), 6-104 (Stalenberg, 18.4),
7-106 (Moloney, 19.3), 8-107 (Vlaeminck, 19.4)

Bowling	O	M	R	W	wd	nb	Dots
IECM Wong	4	0	19	1			10
SL Bates	3	0	21	0			6
DB Sharma	4	0	13	4			14
HJ Darlington	4	0	20	2			8
SJ Johnson	3	0	17	1			8
LG Smith	2	0	15	0			5

Toss: Thunder.   Umpires: SAJ Craig, R Howard, CA Polosak (TV), Ref: SR Bernard. Award: DB Sharma (ST). Crowd: 422
Mandhana 50: 49 balls, 4x4 1x6

Match 27 – Heat v Stars at York Park, Launceston on October 31, 2021 – Stars won by 8 wickets

Heat			B	4	6
GP Redmayne+	lbw b Garth	1	2		
GM Harris	b Flintoff	28	23	4	
JL Jonassen*	c Smith b Sutherland	6	11	1	
G Voll	lbw b Flintoff	2	10		
MC Hinkley	b Sutherland	20	26	1	
LM Kimmince	c Faltum b Sutherland	5	10		
CR Knott	c Bouchier b Osborne	4	8		
N de Klerk	c Flintoff b Smith	2	10		
NM Hancock	not out	11	13		
CG Sippel	lbw b Garth	4	5		
P Yadav	not out	3	2		
	5 lb, 4 w	9			
6 overs: 2-36	20 overs	9-95			

1-8 (Redmayne, 0.6), 2-25 (Jonassen, 3.6), 3-38 (Voll, 6.4), 4-43 (Harris, 8.1), 5-55 (Kimmince, 10.5), 6-64 (Knott, 13.4), 7-77 (Hinkley, 16.2), 8-79 (de Klerk, 17.3), 9-90 (Sippel, 19.3)

Stars			B	4	6
EJ Villani	c Redmayne b Sippel	26	20	5	
MM Lanning*	not out	27	37	1	
AJ Sutherland	c de Klerk b Hancock	5	9	1	
ME Bouchier	not out	32	34	3	
KJ Garth					
EA Osborne					
NM Faltum+					
T Flintoff					
LCN Smith					
SF Day					
RM McKenna					
	1 lb, 8 w	9			
6 overs: 2-36	16.4 overs	2-99			

1-30 (Villani, 3.6), 2-36 (Sutherland, 5.5)

Bowling	O	M	R	W	wd	nb	Dots
KJ Garth	4	0	19	2	2		15
TM Flintoff	4	0	21	2			10
AJ Sutherland	4	0	21	3	1		12
LCN Smith	4	0	16	1			12
RM McKenna	1	0	3	0			3
EA Osborne	3	0	10	1	1		9

Bowling	O	M	R	W	wd	nb	Dots
JL Jonassen	3	0	24	0	1		7
NM Hancock	3	0	14	1	1		12
N de Klerk	3	0	10	0	2		10
CG Sippel	2	0	18	1	3		6
GM Harris	2.4	0	20	0	1		4
P Yadav	2	0	9	0			3
CR Knott	1	0	3	0			3

Toss: Heat.   Umpires: AR Crozier, D Taylor, CA Polosak (TV), Ref: DA Johnston.   Award: TM Flintoff (MS).   Crowd: 180

Match 28 – Scorchers v Sixers at Lilac Hill, Perth on October 31, 2021 – Sixers won by 44 runs

Sixers			B	4	6
AJ Healy+	not out	94	57	12	2
EA Perry*	b Peschel	31	39	3	
AK Gardner	c Graham b Peschel	8	16		
S Verma	run out (Kapp)	8	6	1	
MJ Brown	not out	6	5	1	
NE Bolton					
AR Reakes					
RP Yadav					
JE Allen					
LR Cheatle					
S Campbell					
	4 b, 3 nb, 7 w	14			
6 overs: 0-42	20 overs	3-161			

1-101 (Perry, 12.4), 2-119 (Gardner, 16.3), 3-139 (Verma, 18.2)

Scorchers			B	4	6
SFM Devine*	c Cheatle b Perry	6	12	1	
BL Mooney+	c Cheatle b Yadav	30	29	1	
CL Piparo	b Bolton	29	29	2	
C Atapattu	c Yadav b Bolton	0	3		
HL Graham	c Perry b Yadav	19	14	2	
M Kapp	c Cheatle b Bolton	2	3		
AM King	c Bolton b Cheatle	14	16		
MG Carmichael	not out	12	12		
LG Mills	b Cheatle	0	1		
TCJ Peschel	c Bolton b Gardner	0	1		
L Griffith					
	3 lb, 2 w	5			
6 overs: 1-31	20 overs	9-117			

1-19 (Devine, 3.4), 2-67 (Piparo, 11.2), 3-67 (Atapattu, 11.5), 4-71 (Mooney, 12.5), 5-74 (Kapp, 13.3), 6-98 (Graham, 16.5), 7-107 (King, 18.2), 8-110 (Mills, 18.6), 9-117 (Peschel, 19.6)

Bowling	O	M	R	W	wd	nb	Dots
M Kapp	4	0	18	0	1		10
LG Mills	2	0	12	0			5
TCJ Peschel	4	0	34	2	1	3	11
L Griffith	2	0	28	0	1		2
HL Graham	4	0	38	0			7
AM King	4	0	27	0			9

Bowling	O	M	R	W	wd	nb	Dots
LR Cheatle	4	0	13	2			14
MJ Brown	4	0	31	0	2		6
EA Perry	1	0	5	1			4
AK Gardner	3	0	17	1			7
SR Campbell	2	0	15	0			1
RP Yadav	4	0	22	2			10
NE Bolton	2	0	11	3			5

Toss: Sixers.   Umpires: J Buscall, T Steenholdt, Ref: K Hannam.   Award: AJ Healy (SS).
Healy 50: 31 balls, 7x4 1x6

Match 29 – Hurricanes v Sixers at the WACA, Perth on November 3, 2021 – Sixers won by 31 runs

Sixers			B	4	6
EA Perry*	lbw b Carey	47	52	4	1
AJ Healy+	c Carey b Vlaeminck	0	2		
AK Gardner	c Vakarewa b Johnston	51	49	8	
S Verma	st Priest b Strano	3	4		
MJ Brown	not out	7	6	1	
NE Bolton	not out	18	9	3	
AR Reakes					
RP Yadav					
CE Moore					
LR Cheatle					
SR Campbell					
	2 lb, 2 nb, 11 w	15			
6 overs: 1-40	20 overs	4-141			

1-1 (Healy, 0.4), 2-104 (Gardner, 15.5), 3-111 (Verma, 17.2), 4-119 (Perry, 18.3)

Hurricanes			B	4	6
RH Priest*+	c Bolton b Perry	27	29	4	
R Johnston	c Verma b Cheatle	3	7		
M du Preez	c Gardner b Brown	5	10	1	
NJ Carey	c Gardner b Yadav	15	15	2	
RM Ghosh	st Healy b Bolton	11	17	1	
NE Stalenberg	c Reakes b Bolton	14	17	1	1
MR Strano	not out	22	16	1	
SK Moloney	c Yadav b Brown	5	6		
TJ Vlaeminck	not out	2	3		
BW Vakarewa					
A Smith					
	1 lb, 5 w	6			
6 overs: 2-30	20 overs	7-110			

1-9 (Johnston, 1.5), 2-28 (du Preez, 4.6), 3-54 (Carey, 9.5), 4-54 (Priest, 10.2), 5-81 (Stalenberg, 15.4), 6-81 (Ghosh, 15.5), 7-104 (Moloney, 18.5)

Bowling	O	M	R	W	wd	nb	Dots
TJ Vlaeminck	4	1	22	1	4		18
MR Strano	4	0	34	1		2	7
BW Vakarewa	2	0	18	0			5
NJ Carey	4	0	26	1	1		10
R Johnston	4	0	23	1			13
A Smith	2	0	16	0	2		3

Bowling	O	M	R	W	wd	nb	Dots
NE Bolton	4	0	28	2	2		10
LR Cheatle	2	0	10	1	1		6
EA Perry	2	1	9	1			9
MJ Brown	4	0	15	2	1		14
AK Gardner	3	0	15	0	1		10
SR Campbell	2	0	12	0			3
RP Yadav	3	0	20	1			5

Toss: Hurricanes.
Gardner 50: 47 balls, 8 fours

Umpires: T Steenholdt, DC Trigg, Ref: K Hannam.

Award: AK Gardner (SS)

Match 30 – Scorchers v Renegades at the WACA, Perth on November 3, 2021 - Scorchers won by 40 runs

Scorchers			B	4	6
SFM Devine*	c Hayward b Webb	72	49	8	2
BL Mooney+	not out	101	63	13	
HL Graham	c Molineux b Kaur	7	5	1	
C Atapattu	not out	4	5		
MG Carmichael					
L Griffith					
M Kapp					
AM King					
LG Mills					
TCJ Peschel					
CL Piparo					
	4 lb, 2 nb, 4 w	10			
6 overs: 0-63	20 overs	2-194			

1-165 (Devine, 16.2), 2-177 (Graham, 17.4)

Renegades			B	4	6
JI Rodrigues	c Kapp b Mills	9	10	1	
JE Dooley+	c Mooney b Mills	6	6	1	
CA Webb	c King b Mills	46	34	5	1
H Kaur	lbw b King	13	17	2	
JE Duffin	b Mills	23	22	4	
SG Molineux*	not out	31	18	6	
CM Leeson	c Carmichael b Pesche	4	2	1	
E Jones	not out	8	11		
EM Falconer					
E Hayward					
HL Ferling					
	9 b, 4 lb, 1 w	14			
6 overs: 2-41	20 overs	6-154			

1-15 (Dooley, 2.2), 2-17 (Rodrigues, 2.4), 3-59 (Kaur, 9.2), 4-101 (Duffin, 14.3), 5-102 (Webb, 14.6), 6-106 (Leeson, 15.2)

Bowling	O	M	R	W	wd	nb	Dots
SG Molineux	4	0	29	0	1		9
H Kaur	3	0	32	1			5
E Hayward	2	0	17	0	1		2
EM Falconer	2	0	22	0			3
CA Webb	4	0	33	1	2		3
CM Leeson	2	0	23	0			3
HL Ferling	2	0	22	0	2		1
JI Rodrigues	1	0	12	0			1

Bowling	O	M	R	W	wd	nb	Dots
M Kapp	4	0	24	0	1		11
TCJ Peschel	3	0	16	1			11
LG Mills	3	0	25	4			7
L Griffith	2	0	14	0			7
HL Graham	4	0	28	0			9
AM King	4	0	34	1			9

Toss: Scorchers.

Umpires J Buscall, NR Johnstone, Ref: K Hannam

Award: BL Mooney (BH)

Devine 50: 35 balls, 7x4, Mooney 50: 31 balls, 7x4, 100: 62 balls, 13x4

Match 31 – Heat v Renegades at Rolton Oval, Adelaide on November 6, 2021 – Renegades won by 15 runs

Renegades		B	4	6
JI Rodrigues	lbw b Jonassen	52	31	10
E Jones	c Hancock b Sippel	62	46	9
CA Webb	st Redmayne b Harris	7	5	1
H Kaur	c Sippel b Hancock	65	32	4	6
JE Duffin	not out	4	7	
SG Molineux*				
JE Dooley+				
EM Falconer				
RK O'Donnell				
EL Hayward				
HL Ferling				
	2 b, 6 lb, 1 nb, 8 w	17		
6 overs: 0-59	20 overs	4-207		

Heat		B	4	6
GM Harris	c Dooley b O'Donnell	23	20	5
GP Redmayne+	c sub (AE Price) b Falconer	2	3	
G Voll	c Duffin b O'Donnell	40	28	5	1
MC Hinkley	c & b Hayward	7	8	
AE Bosch	c Kaur b Falconer	14	12	1
LM Kimmince	run out (Dooley)	42	21	4	3
JL Jonassen*	c Dooley b Falconer	0	1	
CR Knott	c Ferling b Falconer	15	10	2
N de Klerk	c sub (AE Price) b Kaur	15	6	1	1
NM Hancock	run out (Ferling)	21	9	3
CG Sippel	not out	6	3	1
	2 lb, 1 nb, 4 w	7		
6 overs: 1-50	20 overs	192		

1-101 (Rodrigues, 9.4), 2-115 (Webb, 11.1), 3-159 (Jones, 16.2), 4-207 (Kaur, 19.6)

1-13 (Redmayne, 1.5), 2-50 (Harris, 6.1), 3-74 (Hinkley, 9.3), 4-76 (Voll, 10.1), 5-119 (Bosch, 14.1), 6-119 (Jonassen, 14.2), 7-136 (Kimmince, 15.6), 8-154 (de Klerk, 17.2), 9-168 (Knott, 18.2), 10-192 (Hancock, 19.6)

Bowling	O	M	R	W	wd	nb	Dots
N de Klerk	3	0	32	0			6
CG Sippel	4	0	37	1	1		9
NM Hancock	4	0	44	1		1	9
JL Jonassen	4	0	33	1	2		10
GM Harris	3	0	29	1			6
CR Knott	1	0	15	0	1		2
AE Bosch	1	0	9	0			1

Bowling	O	M	R	W	wd	nb	Dots
SG Molineux	4	0	46	0			6
EM Falconer	4	0	29	4	2		11
HL Ferling	3	0	40	0	2		7
H Kaur	2	0	19	1			5
RK O'Donnell	4	0	25	2			6
EL Hayward	3	0	31	1		1	4

Toss: Heat.   Umpires: SAJ Craig, H Singh, Ref: SD Fry   Award: H Kaur (MR)

Rodrigues 50: 28 balls, 10x4; Jones 50: 36 balls, 8x4; Kaur 50: 27 balls 4x4 4x6

Match 32 – Strikers v Stars at Rolton Oval, Adelaide on November 6, 2021 – Stars won by 37 runs

Stars		B	4	6
EJ Villani	c & b Wellington	23	23	3
MM Lanning*	c McPharlin b Schutt	82	45	9	3
AJ Sutherland	c McGrath b van Niekerk	1	2	
ME Bouchier	c Brown b van Niekerk	11	7	1
KJ Garth	not out	5	5	
TM Flintoff	not out	1	2	
EA Osborne				
NM Faltum+				
LCN Smith				
SF Day				
RM McKenna				
Extras	2 lb, 1 w	3		
4 overs: 0-21	14 overs	4-126		

Strikers		B	4	6
D van Niekerk	c Smith b Flintoff	14	18	1
L Wolvaardt	c Lanning b Smith	14	9	3
TM McGrath*	c Lanning b Flintoff	8	8	1
M Penna	c Smith b McKenna	3	5	
BE Patterson	c Smith b McKenna	6	6	1
A Wellington	c Garth b Sutherland	9	11	
SJ Coyte	b Smith	11	9		1
KM Mack	not out	14	8	1
TJ McPharlin+	run out (Garth)	8	10	
M Schutt	not out	0	0	
DR Brown				
Extras	2 w	2		
4 overs: 1-24	14 overs	8-89		

1-63 (Villani, 8.2), 2-78 (Sutherland, 9.1), 3-101 (Bouchier, 11.5), 4-124 (Lanning, 13.3)

1-20 (Wolvaardt, 2.5), 2-38 (McGrath, 5.3), 3-39 (van Niekerk, 5.6), 4-46 (Patterson, 7.1), 5-48 (Penna, 7.5), 6-66 (Coyte, 10.3), 7-70 (Wellington, 11.2), 8-83 (McPharlin, 13.4)

Bowling	O	M	R	W	wd	nb	Dots
DR Brown	3	0	24	0			7
M Schutt	3	0	20	1	1		5
SJ Coyte	3	0	30	0			5
TM McGrath	1	0	13	0			0
A Wellington	2	0	22	1			3
D van Niekerk	2	0	15	2			5

Bowling	O	M	R	W	wd	nb	Dots
KJ Garth	3	0	26	0	1		4
TM Flintoff	2	0	12	2			7
LCN Smith	3	0	19	2			6
AJ Sutherland	3	0	12	1	1		9
EA Osborne	2	0	17	0			3
RM McKenna	1	0	3	2			3

Toss: Strikers.   Umpires: SA Lightbody, D Taylor. Ref: SJ Davis   Award: MM Lanning (MS).   Crowd: 877

Lanning 50: 30 balls, 6x4 2x6

Match 33 – Scorchers v Hurricanes at the WACA on November 6, 2021 – Hurricanes won by 2 runs

Hurricanes			B	4	6
RH Priest*+	c Atapattu b Peschel	54	48	5	3
NE Stalenberg	b King	15	19	1	
M du Preez	c & b Mills	23	20	2	
RM Ghosh	c King b Mills	0	2		
NJ Carey	b Kapp	3	3		
MR Strano	not out	15	10	2	
R Johnston	c Kapp b King	4	6		
SK Moloney	c Carmichael b Graham	5	4	1	
TJ Vlaeminck	c Kapp b Graham	7	9	1	
BW Vakarewa					
A Smith					
	2 b, 2 lb, 1 nb, 6 w	11			
6 overs: 0-38	20 overs	8-137			

1-40 (Stalenberg, 6.6), 2-90 (Priest, 13.3), 3-97 (Ghosh, 14.1),
4-101 (du Preez, 14.5), 5-106 (Carey, 15.3), 6-115 (Johnston, 16.5),
7-122 (Moloney, 17.5), 8-137 (Vlaeminck, 19.6)

Bowling	O	M	R	W	wd	nb	Dots
M Kapp	3	0	21	1	2		9
TCJ Peschel	3	0	19	1	1	1	11
LG Mills	4	0	27	2			7
HL Graham	4	0	31	2	1		10
AM King	4	0	20	2			11
PM Cleary	2	0	15	0	2		7

Scorchers			B	4	6
SFM Devine*	c Priest b Strano	25	15	3	2
BL Mooney+	c Stalenberg b Vakarewa	1	5		
CL Piparo	st Priest b Smith	20	24	2	
C Atapattu	c Stalenberg b Vakarewa	33	31	5	
HL Graham	lbw b Carey	24	19	2	1
M Kapp	c and b Strano	9	8	1	
MG Carmichael	lbw b Johnston	2	3		
AM King	not out	12	10	1	
TCJ Peschel	b Carey	2	2		
L Mills	not out	0	3		
PM Cleary					
	3 lb, 4 w	7			
6 overs: 2-42	20 overs	8-135			

1-7 (Mooney, 2.1), 2-28 (Devine, 3.3), 3-71 (Piparo, 10.4),
4-102 (Atapattu, 14.4), 5-115 (Graham, 16.3),
6-118 (Carmichael, 17.1), 7-126 (Kapp, 18.3), 8-132 (Peschel, 19.2)

Bowling	O	M	R	W	wd	nb	Dots
BW Vakarewa	3	1	23	2			12
TJ Vlaeminck	3	0	22	0	1		6
MR Strano	4	0	30	2	1		7
NJ Carey	4	0	17	2	1		15
R Johnston	4	0	24	1			10
A Smith	2	0	16	1	1		3

Toss: Hurricanes. Umpires: NR Johnstone, DC Trigg, Ref: K Hannam. Award: RH Priest (HH). Crowd: 1,545
Priest 50: 46 balls 5x4 3x6

Match 34 – Heat v Thunder at Adelaide Oval on November 7, 2021 – Heat won by 5 wickets

Thunder			B	4	6
SS Mandhana	c Harris b Yadav	37	24	6	1
TB Wilson+	c Yadav b Harris	4	8	1	
PES Litchfield	c Hancock b Yadav	40	32	4	
CL Hall	lbw b Yadav	0	1		
DB Sharma	c Voll b Knott	8	12	1	
SJ Johnson	c Harris b Prestwidge	12	15	1	
AB Learoyd	b Jonassen	4	7		
HJ Darlington*	not out	19	15	1	
LG Smith	not out	7	6		
IECM Wong					
SL Bates					
	5 lb, 7 w	12			
6 overs: 1-51	20 overs	7-143			

1-24 (Wilson, 2.5), 2-63 (Mandhana, 7.3), 3-63 (Hall, 7.4),
4-89 (Sharma, 11.1), 5-99 (Litchfield, 13.4), 6-109 (Learoyd, 15.6),
7-116 (Johnson, 16.3)

Bowling	O	M	R	W	wd	nb	Dots
GK Prestwidge	3	0	34	1	6		9
NM Hancock	4	0	21	0			12
GM Harris	2	0	18	1			6
JL Jonassen	4	0	35	1	1		6
P Yadav	4	0	17	3			12
AE Bosch	2	0	10	0			6
CR Knott	1	0	3	1			4

Heat			B	4	6
GP Redmayne+	c Mandhana b Sharma	57	45	7	
GM Harris	c Wong b Bates	6	11		
G Voll	b Darlington	25	21	3	1
MC Hinkley	c Litchfield b Darlington	33	25	2	1
LM Kimmince	c Sharma b Darlington	11	6	1	1
AE Bosch	not out	2	2		
JL Jonassen*	not out	0	0		
CR Knott					
NM Hancock					
GK Prestwidge					
P Yadav					
	3 lb, 7 w	10			
6 overs: 1-42	18.2 overs	5-144			

1-22 (Harris, 3.3), 2-63 (Voll, 9.2), 3-122 (Redmayne, 15.5),
4-142 (Hinkley, 17.5), 5-142 (Kimmince, 17.6v)

Bowling	O	M	R	W	wd	nb	Dots
IECM Wong	3	0	33	0	4		3
SL Bates	3.2	0	23	1	1		10
DB Sharma	3	0	24	1			7
HJ Darlington	4	0	21	3			10
SJ Johnson	3	0	24	0	1		8
LG Smith	2	0	16	0	1		2

Toss: Thunder. Umpires: CA Polosak, H Singh, SAJ Craig (TV), Ref: SJ Davis. Award: GP Redmayne (BH)
Redmayne 50: 40 balls, 6x4

Match 35 – Renegades v Stars at Adelaide Oval on November 7, 2021 – Renegades won by 7 wickets

Stars			B	4	6	Renegades			B	4	6
EJ Villani	c Rodrigues b Kaur	1	2			JI Rodrigues	c McKenna b Garth	45	38	6	
MM Lanning*	b Hayward	17	19	3		E Jones	b Flintoff	0	5		
AJ Sutherland	c Duffin b Falconer	9	9		1	CM Leeson	lbw b Garth	41	33	5	
ME Bouchier	c Molineux b O'Donnell	5	16			H Kaur	not out	12	9	1	
KJ Garth	run out (Ferling)	32	24	3		JE Duffin	not out	0	0		
EA Osborne	c Kaur b Molineux	29	36			SG Molineux*					
T Flintoff	c Hayward b Molineux	1	3			JE Dooley+					
NM Faltum+	run out (Kaur)	5	7			EM Falconer					
LCN Smith	st Dooley b Kaur	2	3			RK O'Donnell					
R McKenna	c Ferling b Kaur	0	1			EL Hayward					
S Day	not out	0	0			HL Ferling					
	2 lb	2					1 lb, 5 w	6			
6 overs: 2-31	20 overs	103				6 overs: 1-46	14.1 overs	3-104			

1-1 (Villani, 1.1), 2-17 (Sutherland, 3.4), 3-31 (Lanning, 7.1),
4-41 (Bouchier, 8.3), 5-83 (Garth, 15.3), 6-87 (Flintoff, 16.3),
7-99 (Osborne, 18.4), 8-103 (Smith, 19.4), 9-103 (McKenna, 19.5),
10-103 (Faltum, 19.6)

1-4 (Jones, 1.4), 2-85 (Rodrigues, 11.2), 3-100 (Leeson, 13.6)

Bowling	O	M	R	W	wd	nb	Dots	Bowling	O	M	R	W	wd	nb	Dots
SG Molineux	4	0	10	2			15	KJ Garth	4	0	23	2	1		14
H Kaur	4	0	22	3			7	TM Flintoff	4	0	27	1	1		9
EM Falconer	3	0	24	1			9	AJ Sutherland	1	0	15	0	2		0
HL Ferling	1	0	4	0			3	LCN Smith	1	0	10	0			2
RK O'Donnell	4	1	19	1			13	EA Osborne	1	0	12	0			0
EL Hayward	4	0	22	1			6	R McKenna	1.1	0	8	0			3
								S Day	2	0	8	0			6

Toss: Stars. Umpires: SA Lightbody, E Sheridan, D Taylor (TV). Ref: SD Fry. Award: SG Molineux (MR). Crowd: 460
Perry 50: 52 balls, 6x4. Priest 50: 41 balls, 9x4

Match 36 – Scorchers v Hurricanes at the WACA, Perth on November 7, 2021 - Scorchers won by 5 wickets

Hurricanes			B	4	6	Scorchers			B	4	6
RH Priest*+	b Kapp	1	8			SFM Devine*	b Vlaeminck	11	7	1	1
NE Stalenberg	c Graham b Kapp	0	1			BL Mooney+	b Vlaeminck	6	5	1	
M du Preez	c Graham b Devine	4	11			CL Piparo	c & b Strano	29	33	3	
NJ Carey	lbw b Kapp	5	8			C Atapattu	lbw b Vlaeminck	18	17	3	
RM Ghosh	b Devine	0	4			HL Graham	run out (Moloney)	10	16	1	
MR Strano	c Mooney b Kapp	3	2			M Kapp	not out	18	15	4	
R Johnston	c King b Mills	38	40	3	2	MG Carmichael	not out	0	1		
SK Moloney	c Graham b Mills	15	21	2		P M Cleary					
TJ Vlaeminck	b Graham	9	9	1		AM King					
BW Vakarewa	c Piparo b Mills	11	13	1		LG Mills					
A Smith	not out	3	3			TCJ Peschel					
	2 lb, 5 w	7					1 nb, 6 w	7			
6 overs: 5-17	20 overs	96				6 overs: 2-43	15.3 overs	5-99			

1-1 (Priest, 1.2), 2-2 (Stalenberg, 1.4), 3-8 (Carey, 3.3),
4-10 (Ghosh, 4.4), 5-13 (Strano, 5.1), 6-19 (du Preez, 6.5),
7-73 (Johnston, 15.4), 8-73 (Moloney, 15.5),
9-86 (Vlaeminck, 18.3), 10-96 (Vakarewa, 19.6)

Bowling	O	M	R	W	wd	nb	Dots	Bowling	O	M	R	W	wd	nb	Dots
TCJ Peschel	4	0	11	0	1		16	BW Vakarewa	1	0	13	0	2		3
M Kapp	4	0	10	4	1		19	TJ Vlaeminck	4	0	21	3	3		15
SFM Devine	3	0	15	2	1		11	NJ Carey	3	0	16	0			9
P M Cleary	1	0	8	0	2		4	MR Strano	4	1	25	1		1	14
AM King	2	0	20	0			3	R Johnston	2.3	0	18	0			6
HL Graham	3	0	12	0			9	A Smith	1	0	6	0			3
LG Mills	3	0	18	3			6								

Toss: Hurricanes.   Umpires: J Buscall, T Steenholdt, Ref: K Hannam.   Award: M Kapp (PS).   Crowd: 1,339

278

Match 37 – Heat v Sixers at Rolton Oval, Adelaide on November 9, 2021 – Heat won by 8 wickets

Sixers			B	4	6
AJ Healy+	c Voll b Hancock	16	26	1	
EA Perry*	c Kimmince b Prestwidge	14	18	2	
AK Gardner	not out	86	52	6	5
NE Bolton	not out	38	24	6	
S Verma					
AR Reakes					
MJ Brown					
RP Yadav					
CF Moore					
JE Allen					
SR Campbell					
	5 w	5			
6 overs: 1-33	20 overs	2-159			

1-28 (Perry, 5.1), 2-72 (Healy, 11.6)

Heat			B	4	6
GM Harris	c Bolton b Yadav	54	39	4	2
GP Redmayne+	run out (Gardner)	27	18	3	1
G Voll	not out	48	41	7	
LM Kimmince	not out	23	15	1	2
MC Hinkley					
AE Bosch					
JL Jonassen*					
CR Knott					
NM Hancock					
GK Prestwidge					
P Yadav					
	1 lb, 2 nb, 7 w	10			
6 overs: 0-51	18.3 overs	2-162			

1-53 (Redmayne, 6.2), 2-100 (Harris, 12.1)

Bowling	O	M	R	W	wd	nb	Dots
NM Hancock	4	0	41	1	3		9
GK Prestwidge	3	0	23	1	2		8
JL Jonassen	4	0	37	0			9
GM Harris	4	0	20	0			11
P Yadav	4	0	32	0			7
AE Bosch	1	0	6	0			3

Bowling	O	M	R	W	wd	nb	Dots
NE Bolton	3.3	0	27	0	1		4
MJ Brown	3	0	36	0	4	1	8
SR Campbell	3	0	22	0	1		6
EA Perry	3	0	18	0	1	1	10
RP Yadav	4	0	33	1			7
AK Gardner	2	0	25	0			4

Toss: Sixers. Umpires: D Bhatt, D Taylor, Ref: SJ Davis Award: AK Gardner (SS)
Gardner 50: 37 balls, 6x4 1x6. G Harris 50: 34 balls, 4x4 2x6.

Match 38 – Strikers v Thunder at Rolton Oval on November 9, 2021 (Floodlit) – Strikers won by 18 runs

Strikers			B	4	6
D van Niekerk	c Litchfield b Johnson	58	46	3	3
KM Mack	b Smith	31	28	3	
L Wolvaardt	c Litchfield b Darlington	54	32	2	3
TM McGrath*	lbw b Johnson	8	6	1	
M Penna	not out	14	9	1	1
BE Patterson	not out	0	0		
A Wellington					
TJ McPharlin+					
SJ Coyte					
JL Barsby					
M Schutt					
	4 b, 4 lb, 3 w	11			
6 overs: 0-28	20 overs	4-176			

1-65 (Mack, 9.6), 2-105 (van Niekerk, 14.3), 3-126 (McGrath, 16.3), 4-170 (Wolvaardt, 19.5)

Thunder			B	4	6
SS Mandhana	c Coyte b Barsby	7	7		1
TB Wilson+	lbw b McGrath	42	46	3	
PES Litchfield	c Patterson b Wellington	40	28	3	1
SJ Johnson	c & b Schutt	2	4		
IECM Wong	b Wellington	43	17		6
DB Sharma	not out	17	14	1	
HJ Darlington*	b McGrath	1	2		
LG Smith	not out	2	2		
CL Hall					
AB Learoyd					
SL Bates					
	2 lb, 2 w	4			
6 overs: 1-34	20 overs	6-158			

1-13 (Mandhana, 1.6), 2-86 (Litchfield, 12.4), 3-90 (Johnson, 13.4), 4-95 (Wilson, 14.4), 5-143 (Wong, 18.2), 6-153 (Darlington, 19.2)

Bowling	O	M	R	W	wd	nb	Dots
IECM Wong	3	2	8	0			13
SL Bates	4	0	37	0			9
HJ Darlington	4	0	33	1			5
DB Sharma	2	0	35	0	2		2
SJ Johnson	4	0	25	2			9
LG Smith	3	0	30	1	1		4

Bowling	O	M	R	W	wd	nb	Dots
M Schutt	4	0	23	1			12
JL Barsby	3	0	23	1			8
TM McGrath	4	0	20	2	1		10
D van Niekerk	3	0	34	0			4
A Wellington	4	0	38	2	1		4
SJ Coyte	2	0	18	0			5

Toss: Strikers. Umpires: NR Johnstone, SA Lightbody, Ref: SD Fry. Award: L Woolvardt (AS). Crowd: 549
van Niekerk 50: 38 balls, 3x4 3x6, Woolvardt 50: 30 balls, 2x4 3x6.

Match 39 – Stars v Scorchers at Rolton Oval, Adelaide on November 10, 2021 – Scorchers won by 10 wickets

Stars			B	4	6	Scorchers			B	4	6
EJ Villani	b King	16	21	2		BL Mooney+	not out	57	38	10	
MM Lanning*	b Kapp	1	6			SFM Devine*	not out	35	27	4	1
AJ Sutherland	c Griffith b Devine	0	9			C Atapattu					
ME Bouchier	b King	0	6			MG Carmichael					
KJ Garth	c Piparo b Devine	31	31	5		HL Graham					
EA Osborne	c Piparo b Graham	5	16			L Griffith					
LCN Smith	run out (Kapp)	3	6			M Kapp					
NM Faltum+	c & b Mills	0	3			AM King					
TM Flintoff	lbw b Graham	14	11	2		LG Mills					
SF Day	not out	10	9	1		TCJ Peschel					
RM McKenna	not out	8	4	1		CL Piparo					
	(9 w)	9					4 lb, 2 w	6			
6 overs: 3-20	20 overs	9-97				6 overs: 0-44	10.5 overs	0-98			

1-2 (Lanning, 1.4), 2-19 (Sutherland, 4.5), 3-20 (Bouchier, 5.6),
4-24 (Villani, 7.2), 5-48 (Osborne, 12.4), 6-58 (Smith, 14.4),
7-60 (Faltum, 15.2), 8-66 (Garth, 16.3), 9-83 (Flintoff, 18.5)

Bowling	O	M	R	W	wd	nb	Dots	Bowling	O	M	R	W	wd	nb	Dots
TCJ Peschel	2	0	15	0	2		7	KJ Garth	3	0	25	0			9
M Kapp	3	1	5	1			16	TM Flintoff	2	0	19	0	1		4
SFM Devine	3	1	22	2	2		14	AJ Sutherland	1	0	8	0			4
AM King	4	0	18	2			13	LCN Smith	2	0	11	0			6
L Griffith	2	0	11	0	1		5	SF Day	1	0	12	0	1		1
HL Graham	3	0	19	2			8	RM McKenna	1	0	9	0			1
L Mills	3	0	18	1			6	EA Osborne	0.5	0	10	0			0

Toss: Stars.   Umpires: D Bhatt, SA Lightbody, Ref: SJ Davis   Award: SFM Devine (PS).
Mooney 50: 35 balls, 9x4

Match 40 – Strikers v Sixers at Rolton Oval, Adelaide on November 10, 2021 – Strikers won by 8 wickets

Sixers			B	4	6	Strikers			B	4	6
EA Perry*	run out (van Niekerk)	24	19	3		KM Mack	not out	67	55	6	
AJ Healy+	c Penna b Brown	13	10	2		D van Niekerk	b Brown	0	1		
AK Gardner	b Brown	0	1			L Wolvaardt	run out (Moore)	33	27	5	
NE Bolton	c Patterson b Wellington	34	38	2		TM McGrath*	not out	40	30	3	1
S Verma	not out	53	43	6	1	BE Patterson					
MJ Brown	not out	15	9	2		M Penna					
AR Reakes						A Wellington					
RP Yadav						TJ McPharlin+					
CF Moore						SJ Coyte					
SR Campbell						M Schutt					
EL Hughes						DR Brown					
	2 lb, 1 w	3					1 nb, 7 w	8			
6 overs: 3-43	20 overs	4-142				6 overs: 1-47	18.4 overs	2-148			

1-29 (Perry, 3.5), 2-29 (Gardner, 3.6), 3-38 (Healy, 5.1),
4-122 (Bolton, 17.4)

1-5 (van Niekerk, 0.6), 2-79 (Wolvaardt, 9.6)

Bowling	O	M	R	W	wd	nb	Dots	Bowling	O	M	R	W	wd	nb	Dots
M Schutt	4	0	27	0			12	MJ Brown	4	0	30	1	1	1	6
DR Brown	4	0	34	2	1		13	EA Perry	3	0	17	0			8
TM McGrath	3	0	20	0			6	SR Campbell	4	0	28	0	1		8
SJ Coyte	4	0	25	0			4	AK Gardner	1	0	12	0			1
A Wellington	4	0	26	1			8	RP Yadav	4	0	30	0			5
D van Niekerk	1	0	8	0			1	EL Hughes	1.4	0	17	0	4		4
								NE Bolton	1	0	14	0			0

Toss: Strikers.   Umpires: NR Johnstone, D Taylor, Ref: SD Fry.   Award: KM Mack (AS)   Crowd: 582
Verma 50: 40 balls, 6x4 1x6, Mack 50: 40 balls, 5x4

Match 41 – Scorchers v Thunder at Rolton Oval, Adelaide on November 11, 2021 – No result

Scorchers		B	4	6
SFM Devine*	b Johnson	16	15	3
BL Mooney+	not out	83	53	13
CLP iparo	c Wilson b Darlington	10	10	2
C Attapattu	not out	70	42	8 2
SM Betts				
PM Cleary				
HL Graham				
M Kapp				
AM King				
LG Mills				
TCJ Peschel				
	2 lb, 3 w	5		
6 overs: 1-48	20 overs	2-184		

1-18 (Devine, 2.6), 2-49 (Piparo, 6.3)

Thunder		B	4	6
SS Mandhana	not out	12	8	2
HJ Darlington*	b Kapp	4	2	1
PES Litchfield	not out	3	5	
TB Wilson+				
DB Sharma				
SJ Johnson				
AB Learoyd				
IECM Wong				
LG Smith				
KE Peterson				
SL Bates				
	2 w	2		
2.3 overs		1-21		

Bowling	O	M	R	W	wd	nb	Dots
IECM Wong	2	0	20	0	1		5
SL Bates	4	0	31	0	1		4
SJ Johnson	4	0	38	1			10
DB Sharma	3	0	25	0	1		6
HJ Darlington	4	0	32	1			9
KE Peterson	2	0	27	0			2
LG Smith	1	0	9	0			1

Bowling	O	M	R	W	wd	nb	Dots
M Kapp	1.3	0	8	1			4
LG Mills	1	0	13	0	1		2

Toss: Scorchers. Umpires: D Bhatt, NR Johnstone, Ref: SD Fry
Mooney 50: 34 balls, 6x4, Atapattu 50: 33 balls, 6x4 1x6

No Award. Crowd: 88

Match 42 – Renegades v Stars at Rolton Oval, Adelaide on November 11, 2021 – Abandoned due to rain
Toss: None made. Umpires: E Sheridan, D Taylor, Ref: SJ Davis

Match 43 – Strikers v Hurricanes at Harrup Park, Mackay on November 13, 2021 – Strikers won by 48 runs

Strikers		B	4	6
KM Mack	b Vlaeminck	1	5	
D van Niekerk	c Smith b Strano	44	38	5
L Wolvaardt	c Priest b Strano	25	25	3
TM McGrath*	not out	38	37	3
BE Patterson	c Priest b Carey	25	17	2 1
M Penna				
A Wellington				
TJ McPharlin+				
SJ Coyte				
M Schutt				
DR Brown				
	1 lb, 2 nb, 6 w	9		
6 overs: 1-35	20 overs	4-142		

1-2 (Mack, 0.6), 2-49 (Wolvaardt, 8.2), 3-88 (van Niekerk, 14.1), 4-142 (Patterson, 19.6)

Hurricanes		B	4	6
NE Stalenberg	c Patterson b Brown	2	8	
RH Priest*+	c Wellington b Brown	5	7	1
M du Preez	c Penna b McGrath	21	24	4
NJ Carey	run out (Wellington)	8	14	
RM Ghosh	b Brown	4	5	1
MR Strano	lbw b Schutt	12	10	1
SK Moloney	c and b van Niekerk	8	11	1
TJ Vlaeminck	c Schutt b Wellington	17	14	1 1
A Genford	st McPharlin b Wellington	8	12	
BW Vakarewa	c Wellington b Coyte	2	4	
A Smith	not out	2	2	
	1 b, 1 lb, 1 nb, 2	5		
6 overs: 2-27	18.2 overs	94		

1-3 (Stalenberg, 1.4), 2-16 (Priest, 3.2), 3-38 (du Preez, 8.2), 4-44 (Carey, 9.3), 5-44 (Ghosh, 9.4), 6-64 (Strano, 12.6), 7-64 (Moloney, 13.1), 8-90 (Genford, 17.1), 9-91 (Vlaeminck, 17.3), 10-94 (Vakarewa, 18.2)

Bowling	O	M	R	W	wd	nb	Dots
TJ Vlaeminck	4	0	16	1	1		12
BW Vakarewa	4	0	29	0			9
NJ Carey	4	0	43	1	1	2	6
MR Strano	4	0	23	2	1		9
A Smith	2	0	16	0	2		2
SK Moloney	2	0	14	0	1		3

Bowling	O	M	R	W	wd	nb	Dots
M Schutt	4	0	17	1			15
DR Brown	4	0	19	3	2		17
SJ Coyte	2.2	0	7	1			8
A Wellington	3	0	15	2			7
TM McGrath	3	0	23	1	1		7
D van Niekerk	2	0	11	1			7

Toss: Hurricanes. Umpires: SJ Farrell, SA Lightbody, D Taylor (TV), Ref: K Hannam.

Award: DR Brown (AS).

Match 44 – Heat v Sixers at Harrup Park, Mackay on November 13, 2021 – Heat won by 3 wickets

Sixers			B	4	6
AJ Healy+	c Redmayne b Sippel	4	5		
EA Perry*	c Redmayne b Jonasser	2	12		
AK Gardner	c de Klerk b Sippel	0	5		
NE Bolton	c Hinkley b Jonassen	25	31	2	
S Verma	c Harris b Yadav	7	13		
AR Reakes	st Redmayne b de Klerk	10	19		
MJ Brown	c Harris b Jonassen	10	14	1	
RP Yadav	not out	17	15		
LR Cheatle	not out	4	6		
SR Campbell					
EL Hughes					
	5 lb, 7 w	12			
6 overs: 3-23	20 overs	7-91			

Heat			B	4	6
GP Redmayne+	c Gardner b Cheatle	19	16	3	
GM Harris	lbw b Cheatle	0	1		
G Voll	c Reakes b Cheatle	13	12	2	
MC Hinkley	c Hughes b Brown	11	19		
AE Bosch	b Brown	1	5		
JLJonassen*	c Bolton b Gardner	15	18	2	
LM Kimmince	lbw b Campbell	16	10	2	1
N de Klerk	not out	5	3		
CG Sippel	not out	2	4		
GKP restwidge					
P Yadav					
	1 lb, 3 nb, 6 w	10			
6 overs: 4-37	14.1 overs	7-92			

1-6 (Healy, 1.1), 2-6 (Gardner, 1.6), 3-21 (Perry, 5.4),
4-34 (Verma, 8.6), 5-56 (Bolton, 13.3), 6-64 (Reakes, 15.2),
7-76 (Brown, 17.4)

Bowling	O	M	R	W	wd	nb	Dots
GKP restwidge	3	0	20	0	3		8
CG Sippel	4	1	12	2			15
N de Klerk	4	0	18	1	2		11
JLJonassen	4	0	15	3	1		12
P Yadav	4	0	17	1			11
GM Harris	1	0	4	0			2

Bowling	O	M	R	W	wd	nb	Dots
LR Cheatle	4	0	16	3			15
MJ Brown	4	1	14	2	1	1	18
EA Perry	2	0	23	0	2	1	3
SR Campbell	2	0	20	1	2	1	6
AK Gardner	2	0	15	1			6
RP Yadav	0.1	0	3	0			0

Toss: Heat. Umpires: SE Dionysius, E Sheridan, CA Polosak, Ref: SD Fry. Award: CG Sippel (BH)

Match 45 – Heat v Strikers at Harrup Park, Mackay on November 14, 2021 – Strikers won by 8 wickets

Heat			B	4	6
GM Harris	b Schutt	7	9		
GP Redmayne+	c & b Wellington	14	24	2	
G Voll	c Brown b Wellington	12	19	2	
MC Hinkley	c McPharlin b Coyte	15	29	1	
CR Knott	c and b Barsby	1	4		
JLJonassen*	c McGrath b Brown	13	20		
LM Kimmince	not out	22	11	2	1
N de Klerk	run out (Mack)	3	5		
NM Hancock					
CG Sippel					
P Yadav					
	1 lb, 1 nb, 5 w	7			
6 overs: 1-26	20 overs	7-94			

Strikers			B	4	6
D van Niekerk	c Voll b Sippel	5	5	1	
KM Mack	not out	54	48	8	
L Wolvaardt	c Redmayne b Sippel	0	1		
TM McGrath*	not out	31	44	2	
BE Patterson					
A Wellington					
TJ McPharlin+					
SJ Coyte					
JL Barsby					
M Schutt					
DR Brown					
	1 lb, 7 w	8			
6 overs: 2-35	16.2 overs	2-98			

1-8 (Harris, 2.3), 2-39 (Redmayne, 8.2), 3-40 (Voll, 8.5),
4-43 (Knott, 9.6), 5-67 (Hinkley, 16.5), 6-70 (Jonassen, 17.3),
7-94 (de Klerk, 19.6)

1-10 (van Niekerk, 1.2), 2-10 (Wolvaardt, 1.3)

Bowling	O	M	R	W	wd	nb	Dots
M Schutt	4	0	17	1			16
DR Brown	4	0	16	1		1	12
TM McGrath	1	0	7	0	1		4
SJ Coyte	2	0	17	1			4
D van Niekerk	2	0	7	0			5
A Wellington	4	1	21	2			14
JL Barsby	3	0	8	1			10

Bowling	O	M	R	W	wd	nb	Dots
NM Hancock	3	0	14	0	1		11
CG Sippel	4	0	22	2	3		13
N de Klerk	1	0	11	0			2
JLJonassen	2	0	17	0			5
P Yadav	3.2	0	19	0	1		8
GM Harris	2	0	7	0			5
CR Knott	1	0	7	0			2

Toss: Heat. Umpires: SJ Farrell, CA Polosak, E Sheridan (TV), Ref: K Hannam. Award: KM Mack (AS)

Match 46 – Sixers v Thunder at Harrup Park, Mackay on November 14, 2021 – Thunder won by 6 wickets

Sixers			B	4	6	Thunder			B	4	6
AJ Healy+	c Sharma b Wong		7	16		SS Mandhana	c Gardner b Campbell		45	39	6
S Verma	run out (Sharma)		8	14	1	SJ Johnson	c Healy b Cheatle		12	9	2
EA Perry*	not out		40	40	3	P ES Litchfield	c Verma b Cheatle		3	5	
AK Gardner	b Wong		0	1		CL Hall	b Cheatle		19	28	2
NE Bolton	b Darlington		19	29	2	TB Wilson+	not out		4	10	
AR Reakes	c Litchfield b Darlington		16	16	1	1	DB Sharma	not out		4	2	1
MJ Brown	st Wilson b Johnson		0	3		A Learoyd					
RP Yadav	not out		1	1		HJ Darlington*					
LR Cheatle						IECM Wong					
SR Campbell						LG Smith					
EL Hughes						SL Bates					
	3 w		3				1 nb, 8 w		9		
6 overs : 3-22	20 overs		6-94			6 overs : 2-33	15.2 overs		4-96		

1-13 (Verma, 4.2), 2-22 (Healy, 5.5), 3-22 (Gardner, 5.6), 4-61 (Bolton, 14.2), 5-88 (Reakes, 18.6), 6-88 (Brown, 19.3)

1-21 (Johnson, 2.6), 2-24 (Litchfield, 4.4), 3-77 (Hall, 12.3), 4-90 (Mandhana, 14.2)

Bowling	O	M	R	W	wd	nb	Dots	Bowling	O	M	R	W	wd	nb	Dots
SL Bates	4	1	14	0			16	LR Cheatle	4	0	15	3			15
IECM Wong	4	0	27	2			9	MJ Brown	2	0	22	0	1		4
SJ Johnson	4	0	19	1			9	AK Gardner	3	0	17	0	1		10
HJ Darlington	4	0	15	2	2		14	SR Campbell	3	0	16	1	6		11
DB Sharma	4	0	19	0	1		10	EA Perry	1	0	8	0		1	2
								NE Bolton	2.2	0	18	0			5

Toss: Sixers. Umpires: SE Dionysius, D Taylor, SA Lightbody (TV), Ref: SD Fry Award: IECM Wong (ST)

Match 47 – Strikers v Scorchers at Rolton Oval, Adelaide on November 17, 2021 – Scorchers won by 12 runs

Scorchers			B	4	6	Strikers			B	4	6
SFM Devine*	c Brown b Schutt		61	52	7	1	KM Mack	not out		84	61	10
BL Mooney+	c Barsby b Coyte		78	53	10		D van Niekerk	c Graham b Kapp		5	11	1
HL Graham	c Patterson b McGrath		22	11		2	L Wolvaardt	c Carmichael b Devine		40	28	7
AM King	not out		8	4	1	TM McGrath*	c Piparo b Graham		14	10	2
M Kapp	not out		0	0		BE Patterson	c Devine b Graham		6	4	1
MG Carmichael						A Wellington	c Graham b Devine		4	6	
PM Cleary						SJ Coyte	not out		0	0	
L Griffith						TJ McPharlin+					
LG Mills						JL Barsby					
TCJ Peschel						M Schutt					
CL Piparo						DR Brown					
	5 lb, 3 w		8				1 lb, 11 w		12		
6 overs : 0-50	20 overs		3-177			6 overs : 1-40	20 overs		5-165		

1-137 (Devine, 16.3), 2-152 (Mooney, 18.2), 3-171 (Graham, 19.4)

1-9 (van Niekerk, 2.4), 2-99 (Wolvaardt, 12.3), 3-133 (McGrath, 16.2), 4-151 (Patterson, 18.1), 5-160 (Wellington, 19.4)

Bowling	O	M	R	W	wd	nb	Dots	Bowling	O	M	R	W	wd	nb	Dots
DR Brown	3	0	14	0	1		11	M Kapp	3	0	21	1	3		9
M Schutt	4	0	31	1			8	TCJ Peschel	3	0	23	0	3		6
TM McGrath	3	0	40	1			5	L Griffith	1	0	10	0	1		3
D van Niekerk	2	0	17	0			2	SFM Devine	4	0	30	2	2		8
A Wellington	3	0	25	0			4	HL Graham	4	0	30	2			6
JL Barsby	2	0	18	0		1	1	AM King	4	0	39	0	1		8
SJ Coyte	3	0	27	1			4	LG Mills	1	0	11	0			1

Toss: Scorchers. Umpires: H Singh, D Taylor, Ref: SJ Davis. Award: BL Mooney (BH). Crowd: 277

Devine 50: 48 balls, 6x4, Mooney 50: 36 balls, 7x4. Mack 50: 40 balls, 7x4

Match 48 – Renegades v Thunder at Harrup Park, Mackay on November 17, 2021 (Floodlit) - Renegades won by 4 runs

Renegades			B	4	6
J I Rodrigues	c Wilson b Bates	2	4		
E Jones	c Hall b Bates	42	33	6	1
CM Leeson	c Smith b Wong	7	7	1	
H Kaur	not out	81	55	11	2
J E Duffin	run out (Peterson)	33	22	2	1
J E Dooley+					
EL Hayward					
SG Molineux*					
EM Falconer					
RK O'Donnell					
HL Ferling					
	2 b, 2 lb, 1 nb, 5 w	10			
6 overs : 2-36	20 overs	4-175			

Thunder			B	4	6
SS Mandhana	not out	114	64	14	3
SJ Johnson	c Duffin b Kaur	12	14	2	
P ES Litchfield	c Hayward b O'Donnell	1	3		
TB Wilson+	not out	38	39	3	
CL Hall					
DB Sharma					
HJ Darlington*					
IECM Wong					
LG Smith					
KE Peterson					
SL Bates					
	2 b, 2 lb, 2 w	6			
6 overs : 1-46	20 overs	2-171			

1-2 (Rodrigues, 0.4), 2-9 (Leeson, 1.6), 3-100 (Jones, 13.1), 4-175 (Duffin, 19.6)

1-31 (Johnson, 4.6), 2-46 (Litchfield, 6.1)

Bowling	O	M	R	W	wd	nb	Dots
SL Bates	4	0	21	2			14
IECM Wong	4	0	34	1	1		13
SJ Johnson	4	0	45	0	1		5
HJ Darlington	4	0	31	0	2		9
DB Sharma	2	0	17	0		1	3
KE Peterson	2	0	23	1			5

Bowling	O	M	R	W	wd	nb	Dots
EL Hayward	4	0	25	0			9
SG Molineux	4	0	27	0			9
H Kaur	4	0	27	1	1		9
EM Falconer	1	0	15	0			2
RK O'Donnell	3	0	25	1			4
CM Leeson	1	0	12	0	1		1
HL Ferling	3	0	36	0			3

Toss: Thunder. Umpires: J Adie, N James, Ref: SD Fry Award: SS Mandhana (ST)

Kaur 50: 38 balls, 5x4, 2x6. Mandhana 50: 31 balls, 8x4 1x6; 100: 57 balls, 13x4 3x6

Match 49 – Hurricanes v Renegades at Harrup Park, Mackay on November 19, 2021 – Hurricanes won by 52 runs

Hurricanes			B	4	6
RH Priest*+	c Dooley b Molineux	0	2		
R Johnston	c Falconer b Kaur	63	46	8	1
M du Preez	c Kaur b Webb	50	46	4	1
RM Ghosh	c Duffin b Kaur	7	8	1	
NE Stalenberg	lbw b Webb	21	12	3	1
NJ Carey	not out	6	6		
MR Strano	not out	6	3	1	
SK Moloney					
TJ Vlaeminck					
BW Vakarewa					
A Smith					
	4 b, 3 nb, 1 w	8			
6 overs : 1-52	20 overs	5-161			

Renegades			B	4	6
J I Rodrigues	b Strano	19	21	3	
E Jones	c Smith b Vlaeminck	8	11	1	
CA Webb	b Carey	14	11	2	
H Kaur	c Priest b Johnston	9	15	1	
J E Duffin	c Vakarewa b Johnston	17	21	1	
SG Molineux*	c Priest b Vlaeminck	1	5		
J E Dooley+	c Stalenberg b Moloney	2	3		
CM Leeson	run out (Johnston)	0	0		
EM Falconer	not out	24	12		3
RK O'Donnell	c & b Moloney	1	2		
E Hayward	b Moloney	6	7		
	1 lb, 7 w	8			
6 overs : 1-42	18 overs	109			

1-0 (Priest, 0.2), 2-120 (du Preez, 14.5), 3-121 (Johnston, 15.1), 4-138 (Ghosh, 17.5), 5-151 (Stalenberg, 18.5)

1-29 (Jones, 3.6), 2-46 (Webb, 6.5), 3-48 (Rodrigues, 7.4), 4-66 (Kaur, 10.5), 5-69 (Molineux, 11.6), 6-75 (Dooley, 13.2), 7-77 (Leeson, 13.6), 8-79 (Duffin, 14.6), 9-81 (O'Donnell, 15.3), 10-109 (Hayward, 17.6)

Bowling	O	M	R	W	wd	nb	Dots
SG Molineux	4	0	12	1			13
EM Falconer	2.3	0	29	0	1	3	6
H Kaur	3	0	28	2			7
EL Hayward	1	0	13	0			2
RK O'Donnell	4	0	37	0			8
CA Webb	4	0	27	2			7
CM Leeson	1.3	0	11	0			3

Bowling	O	M	R	W	wd	nb	Dots
BW Vakarewa	2	0	17	0	2		5
TJ Vlaeminck	4	0	23	2	2		14
R Johnston	4	0	17	2			13
MR Strano	3	0	26	1			6
NJ Carey	2	0	8	1	1		7
SK Moloney	3	0	17	3			7

Toss: Hurricanes. Umpires: SE Dionysius, N James, Ref: K Hannam Award: R Johnston (HH)

Johnston 50: 35 balls, 7x4 1x6, du Preez 50: 43 balls, 4x4 1x6

284

Match 50 – Heat v Thunder at Harrup Park on November 19, 2021 – Thunder won by 9 runs

Thunder			B	4	6
SS Mandhana	c Redmayne b de Klerk	29	24	5	
SJ Johnson	run out (Sippel)	52	36	6	1
P ES Litchfield	c Harris b Jonassen	24	21	3	
IECM Wong	c Harris b Hancock	1	2		
DB Sharma	not out	24	21	1	
TB Wilson+	c Jonassen b Sippel	10	11	1	
HJ Darlington*	not out	12	6	2	
AB Learoyd					
LG Smith					
KE Peterson					
SL Bates					
	1 nb, 9 w	10			
6 overs : 0-53	20 overs	5-162			

1-58 (Mandhana, 6.3), 2-110 (Johnson, 13.1),
3-114 (Litchfield, 13.3), 4-116 (Wong, 14.1),
5-144 (Wilson, 18.2)

Bowling	O	M	R	W	wd	nb	Dots
CG Sippel	3	0	26	1	3		5
NM Hancock	3	0	23	1	2	1	10
JL Jonassen	4	0	38	1			6
N de Klerk	3	0	15	1	3		9
GM Harris	3	0	27	0			4
P Yadav	4	0	33	0			4

Heat			B	4	6
GP Redmayne+	c Sharma b Johnson	54	52	6	
GM Harris	c Mandhana b Bates	50	34	7	1
LM Kimmince	c Darlington b Bates	0	2		
E Johnston	run out (Litchfield)	1	3		
G Voll	run out (Learoyd)	2	3		
MC Hinkley	c Litchfield b Darlington	18	13		1
JL Jonassen*	c Peterson b Darlington	9	6		1
N de Klerk	b Sharma	5	4		
NM Hancock	c Litchfield b Sharma	1	2		
CG Sippel	not out	1	1		
P Yadav	not out	2	2		
	2 lb, 2 nb, 6 w	10			
6 overs : 0 -52	20 overs	9-153			

1-99 (Harris, 11.1), 2-99 (Kimmince, 11.3), 3-103 (Johnston, 12.5),
4-114 (Voll, 14.4), 5-130 (Redmayne, 16.4), 6-144 (Jonassen, 18.2),
7-144 (Hinkley, 18.3), 8-148 (Hancock, 19.1),
9-150 (de Klerk, 19.3)

Bowling	O	M	R	W	wd	nb	Dots
SL Bates	4	0	25	2			12
IECM Wong	2	0	21	0	1	1	4
SJ Johnson	3	0	32	1	2		7
DB Sharma	4	0	21	2	-		9
HJ Darlington	4	0	23	2	2	1	9
LG Smith	3	0	29	0	1		3

Toss: Thunder.   Umpires: J Adie, SJ Farrell, Ref: K Hannam   Award: SJ Johnson (BH)
Johnson 50: 34 balls, 6x4 1x6, G Harris 50: 33 balls, 7x4 1x6. Redmayne 50: 45 balls, 6x4

Match 51 – Stars v Scorchers at Adelaide Oval, on November 20, 2021 - Scorchers won by 4 wickets

Stars			B	4	6
EJ Villani	c King b Graham	84	66	9	2
MM Lanning*	b King	4	12		
AJ Sutherland	run out (Devine)	9	14	1	
ME Bouchier	c Mills b Graham	2	6		
KJ Garth	c Kapp b Devine	3	8		
TM Flintoff	run out (King)	5	12		
AJ Lanning	st Mooney b Graham	0	1		
NM Faltum+	not out	1	1		
EA Osborne	not out	0	1		
LCN Smith					
RM McKenna					
	2 b, 2 lb, 1 nb, 9 w	14			
6 overs : 0-35	20 overs	7-122			

1-35 (M Lanning, 6.1), 2-61 (Sutherland, 10.3),
3-64 (Bouchier, 11.3), 4-77 (Garth, 14.3), 5-119 (Villani, 19.2),
6-120 (A Lanning, 19.4), 7-121 (Flintoff, 19.5)

Bowling	O	M	R	W	wd	nb	Dots
M Kapp	4	0	11	0	1		17
TCJ Peschel	2	1	15	0	3		8
SFM Devine	4	0	36	1	4		8
AM King	4	0	16	1			12
SM Betts	2	0	24	0		1	3
HL Graham	4	0	16	3			12

Scorchers			B	4	6
SFM Devine*	b Flintoff	5	10	1	
BL Mooney+	st Faltum b Garth	5	5	1	
CL Piparo	c Villani b Sutherland	27	28	4	
HL Graham	b Sutherland	13	22	1	
M Kapp	not out	29	25	2	
MG Carmichael	c Garth b Smith	30	20	5	
AM King	run out (Flintoff)	9	9	1	
TCJ Peschel	not out	1	1		
SM Betts					
P M Cleary					
LG Mills					
	2 lb, 2 w	4			
6 overs : 2029	20 overs	6-123			

1-12 (Mooney, 2.2), 2-16 (Devine, 3.1), 3-39 (Graham, 8.4),
4-69 (Piparo, 13.2), 5-112 (Carmichael, 18.1), 6-122 (King, 19.5)

Bowling	O	M	R	W	wd	nb	Dots
KJ Garth	4	0	27	1			12
TM Flintoff	4	0	24	1	2		12
LCN Smith	4	0	15	1			14
AJ Sutherland	4	0	20	2			11
RM McKenna	2	0	18	0			4
EA Osborne	2	0	17	0			3

Toss: Scorchers.   Umpires: CA Polosak, E Sheridan, SAJ Craig (TV), Ref: SJ Davis.   Award: HL Graham (PS)
Villani 50: 48 balls, 6x4

Match 52 – Stars v Sixers at Adelaide Oval on November 20, 2021 - Strikers won by 8 wickets

Sixers		R	B	4	6
AJ Healy+	c Wellington b Schutt	0	2		
EA Perry*	lbw b Brown	9	12	2	
AK Gardner	c McPharlin b Brown	0	1		
NE Bolton	run out (Mack)	15	17	2	
S Verma	run out (Schutt)	0	0		
AR Reakes	c Brown b Wellington	3	7		
MJ Brown	lbw b Coyte	6	13	1	
RP Yadav	c Coyte b McGrath	12	15	1	
LR Cheatle	c Patterson b Coyte	16	16	2	
SR Campbell	st McPharlin b Coyte	12	25		
EL Hughes	not out	2	8		
	3 lb, 4 w	7			
6 overs: 5-28	19.2 overs	82			

Strikers		R	B	4	6
D van Niekerk	c Verma b Brown	33	22	5	1
KM Mack	c Gardner b Yadav	24	20	4	
L Wolvaardt	not out	10	14	1	
TM McGrath*	not out	9	8	2	
BE Patterson					
A Wellington					
TJ McPharlin+					
SJ Coyte					
JL Barsby					
M Schutt					
DR Brown					
	2 nb, 6 w	8			
6 overs: 1-55	10.2 overs	2-84			

1-1 (Healy, 0.2), 2-1 (Gardner, 1.1), 3-24 (Perry, 3.6),
4-24 (Verma, 4.1), 5-28 (Bolton, 5.5), 6-30 (Reakes, 6.6),
7-47 (Brown, 10.3), 8-52 (Yadav, 11.2), 9-76 (Cheatle, 16.5),
10-82 (Campbell, 19.2)

1-54 (van Niekerk, 5.4), 2-65 (Mack, 7.5)

Bowling	O	M	R	W	wd	nb	Dots
M Schutt	4	0	16	1	1		15
DR Brown	4	0	25	2	1		13
A Wellington	4	0	18	1			12
TM McGrath	4	1	8	1			19
SJ Coyte	3.2	0	12	3	1		11

Bowling	O	M	R	W	wd	nb	Dots
LR Cheatle	4	0	32	0	3		10
EA Perry	1	0	15	0	1		1
MJ Brown	2	0	13	1		2	7
SR Campbell	1.2	0	8	0	2		5
RP Yadav	2	0	16	1			5

Toss: Sixers. Umpires: H Singh, D Taylor, Ref: SD Fry. Award: DR Brown (AS)

Match 53 – Thunder v Hurricanes at Harrup Park, Mackay on November 20, 2021 – Hurricanes won by 4 runs

Hurricanes		R	B	4	6
RH Priest*+	b Wong	0	3		
R Johnston	c Sharma b Johnson	15	15	1	1
M du Preez	not out	87	61	11	1
NJ Carey	lbw b Sharma	2	6		
RM Ghosh	st Wilson b Bates	2	3		
NE Stalenberg	c Wong b Bates	15	18	1	
MR Strano	not out	23	14	2	
SK Moloney					
TJ Vlaeminck					
BW Vakarewa					
A Smith					
	1 lb, 2 w	3			
6 overs: 2-36	20 overs	5-147			

Thunder		R	B	4	6
SS Mandhana	c Priest b Vakarewa	0	3		
SJ Johnson	c du Preez b Carey	39	21	5	2
TB Wilson+	c Moloney b Vakarewa	3	9		
DB Sharma	c Ghosh b Johnston	31	36	2	
AB Learoyd	c Smith b Vakarewa	34	27	5	
IECM Wong	c Johnston b Strano	1	3		
PES Litchfield	c Stalenberg b Molone	18	10	2	1
HJ Darlington*	c Strano b Johnston	4	7		
LG Smith	not out	4	2		
K Peterson	lbw b Moloney	0	1		
SL Bates	not out	2	2		
	1 lb, 1 nb, 5 w	7			
6 overs: 2-41	20 overs	9-143			

1-0 (Priest, 0.3), 2-35 (Johnston, 5.3), 3-56 (Carey, 8.6),
4-61 (Ghosh, 9.6), 5-99 (Stalenberg, 15.5)

1-0 (Mandhana, 0.3), 2-10 (Wilson, 2.6), 3-48 (Johnson, 6.6),
4-107 (Learoyd, 14.6), 5-113 (Wong, 15.5), 6-116 (Sharma, 16.5),
7-137 (Darlington, 18.6), 8-140 (Litchfield, 19.2),
9-140 (Peterson, 19.3)

Bowling	O	M	R	W	wd	nb	Dots
IECM Wong	2	0	16	1	1		5
SJ Johnson	4	0	27	1			9
DB Sharma	4	0	31	1			8
SL Bates	4	0	22	2			10
LG Smith	2	0	20	0			5
HJ Darlington	4	0	30	0	1		8

Bowling	O	M	R	W	wd	nb	Dots
BW Vakarewa	4	0	8	3			16
TJ Vlaeminck	2	0	26	0	1		5
MR Strano	3	0	20	1	3		6
NJ Carey	2	0	19	1		1	4
SK Moloney	4	0	17	2			10
R Johnston	4	0	39	2			6
A Smith	1	0	13	0	1		1

Toss: Hurricanes. Umpires: J Adie, SE Dionysius, Ref: K Hannam. Award: BW Vakarewa (ST)
du Preez 50: 42 balls, 7x6

Match 54 – Heat v Renegades at Harrup Park, Mackay on November 20, 2021 (Floodlit) – Heat won by 43 runs

Heat			B	4	6
GM Harris	st Dooley b Molineux	12	12	2	
GP Redmayne+	c Rodrigues b Webb	71	51	8	1
G Voll	c Hayward b O'Donnell	41	30	5	1
LM Kimmince	c Duffin b Hayward	7	5	1	
MC Hinkley	c Molineux b O'Donnell	3	6		
JL Jonassen*	not out	11	9	1	
E Johnston	not out	7	7	1	
N de Klerk					
NM Hancock					
CG Sippel					
P Yadav					
	1 lb, 3 w	4			
6 overs: 1-47	20 overs	5-156			

1-37 (Harris, 4.6), 2-119 (Voll, 14.3), 3-130 (Kimmince, 15.6), 4-135 (Redmayne, 16.5), 5-138 (Hinkley, 17.4)

Renegades			B	4	6
JI Rodrigues	b Hancock	3	4		
E Jones	b de Klerk	17	18	1	1
CA Webb	c Hinkley b Jonassen	7	14	1	
JE Dooley+	c Kimmince b Poonam	35	27	5	
JE Duffin	c Kimmince b Hancock	7	11	1	
SG Molineux*	c Kimmince b Harris	2	4		
RK O'Donnell	c Harris b Jonassen	19	17	1	
EM Falconer	c sub b Jonassen	10	11		
E Hayward	st Redmayne b de Klerk	2	3		
HL Ferling	not out	2	1		
H Kaur					
	1 b, 1 lb, 1 nb, 6 w	9			
6 overs: 2-35	18.1 overs	113			

1-4 (Rodrigues, 0.5), 2-27 (Webb, 4.5), 3-43 (Jones, 7.2), 4-54 (Duffin, 9.4), 5-58 (Molineux, 10.2), 6-86 (O'Donnell, 14.3), 7-103 (Dooley, 16.5), 8-111 (Hayward, 17.5), 9-113 (Falconer, 18.1)

Bowling	O	M	R	W	wd	nb	Dots
SG Molineux	4	0	23	1	1		12
EL Hayward	4	0	29	1	1		5
EM Falconer	2	0	18	0	1		6
CA Webb	4	0	34	1			9
H Kaur	3	0	25	0			5
RK O'Donnell	3	0	26	2			6

Bowling	O	M	R	W	wd	nb	Dots
NM Hancock	3	0	12	2	1		7
CG Sippel	3	0	18	0	2		11
GM Harris	2	0	22	1		1	4
N de Klerk	4	0	23	2	3		12
JL Jonassen	3.1	0	10	3			12
P Yadav	3	0	26	1			4

Toss: Heat. Umpires: SJ Farrell, N James, Ref: K Hannam.
Devine 50: 34 balls, 9x4, Mooney 50: 38 balls, 6x4

Award: GP Redmayne (BH)

Match 55 – Scorchers v Sixers at Adelaide Oval on November 21, 2021 – Scorchers won by 8 wickets

Sixers			B	4	6
S Verma	lbw b King	27	22	3	1
AJ Healy+	b King	17	22	1	
EA Perry*	not out	39	37	3	1
NE Bolton	b King	19	21	1	
AR Reakes	c Kapp b Graham	22	17	3	
MJ Brown	not out	0	1		
CF Moore					
LR Cheatle					
SR Campbell					
JE Allen					
EL Hughes					
	4 w	4			
6 overs: 0-41	20 overs	4-128			

1-46 (Healy, 7.1), 2-47 (Verma, 7.3), 3-86 (Bolton, 14.4), 4-127 (Reakes, 19.4)

Scorchers			B	4	6
SFM Devine*	c Cheatle b Campbell	18	16	3	
BL Mooney+	c & b Bolton	26	24	3	
CL Piparo	not out	50	39	6	
HL Graham	not out	34	24	5	
MG Carmichael					
PM Cleary					
AL Edgar					
M Kapp					
AM King					
L Mills					
TCJ Peschel					
	1 lb, 2 w	3			
6 overs: 1-44	17.1 overs	2-131			

1-34 (Devine, 4.4), 2-57 (Mooney, 7.6v)

Bowling	O	M	R	W	wd	nb	Dots
M Kapp	3	0	18	0			7
TCJ Peschel	4	0	25	0	3		9
SFM Devine	2	0	18	0	1		4
PM Cleary	1	0	14	0			3
HL Graham	4	0	29	1			6
AM King	4	0	18	3			10
LG Mills	2	0	6	0			6

Bowling	O	M	R	W	wd	nb	Dots
NE Bolton	3	0	20	1			5
LR Cheatle	3	0	25	0			6
MJ Brown	3.1	0	24	0			8
SR Campbell	4	0	24	1	1		12
EA Perry	2	0	16	0			2
JE Allen	2	0	21	0	1		2

Toss: Sixers. Umpires: D Bhatt, SA Lightbody, E Sheridan (TV) Ref: SD Fry. Award: AM King (PS).
Piparo 50: 39 balls, 6x4

Match 56 – Strikers v Stars at Adelaide Oval on November 21, 2021 – Stars won by 9 wickets

Strikers		B	4	6
KM Mack	not out	89	67	13
D van Niekerk	b Garth	0	1	
L Wolvaardt	b Sutherland	13	14	1
BE Patterson	c Garth b Sutherland	6	4	1
M Penna	not out	56	34	7 2
TM McGrath*				
A Wellington				
TJ McPharlin+				
SJ Coyte				
JL Barsby				
M Schutt				
3 lb, 8 w		11		
6 overs: 1-45	20 overs	3-175		

Stars		B	4	6
EJ Villani	not out	100	65	13 2
MM Lanning*	c Wellington b Schutt	50	39	5 2
AJ Sutherland	not out	27	13	2 1
ME Bouchier				
KJ Garth				
EA Osborne				
NM Faltum+				
TM Flintoff				
AJ Lanning				
LCN Smith				
LP Cripps				
2 b, 2 lb		4		
6 overs: 0-44	19.3 overs	1-181		

1-2 (van Niekerk, 0.3), 2-51 (Wolvaardt, 7.2), 3-57 (Patterson, 7.6)

1-119 (M Lanning, 14.4)

Bowling	O	M	R	W	wd	nb	Dots
KJ Garth	4	0	40	1	2		10
TM Flintoff	4	0	29	0	1		10
LCN Smith	4	0	33	0			8
AJ Sutherland	4	0	33	2	1		11
EA Osborne	2	0	12	0			6
LP Cripps	2	0	25	0	3		3

Bowling	O	M	R	W	wd	nb	Dots
M Schutt	4	0	20	1			13
TM McGrath	4	0	43	0			7
SJ Coyte	4	0	34	0			3
D van Niekerk	2.3	0	27	0			4
A Wellington	3	0	37	0			3
JL Barsby	2	0	16	0			3

Toss: Strikers. Umpires: SAJ Craig, CA Polosak, Ref: SJ Davis Award: EJ Villani (MS). Crowd: 1,533

Mack 50: 45 balls, 8x4. Penna 50: 31 balls, 7x4 2x6. Villani 50: 33 balls, 9x4; 100: 65 balls, 13x4 2x6, M Lanning 50: 36 balls, 5x4 2x6

Eliminator Final – Strikers v Heat (Floodlit) at Adelaide Oval on November 24, 2021 (Floodlit)
Strikers won by 8 wickets

Heat		B	4	6
GM Harris	st McPharlin b Wellington	17	27	2
GP Redmayne+	c McPharlin b Brown	1	2	
G Voll	c Wolvaardt b Wellington	20	24	3
MC Hinkley	c van Niekerk b Wellington	0	2	
JL Jonassen*	b Wellington	1	5	
LM Kimmince	c Patterson b Wellington	3	4	
AE Bosch	c McPharlin b Brown	4	4	1
N de Klerk	not out	18	25	2
NM Hancock	c Schutt b Coyte	40	26	6 1
CG Sippel	not out	1	1	
P Yadav				
1 lb, 8 w		9		
6 overs: 1-25	20 overs	8-114		

Strikers		B	4	6
D van Niekerk	c de Klerk b Hancock	12	14	2
KM Mack	not out	50	42	5
L Wolvaardt	lbw b Yadav	16	16	3
TM McGrath*	not out	38	27	4 1
BE Patterson				
MM Penna				
A Wellington				
TJ McPharlin+				
SJ Coyte				
M Schutt				
DR Brown				
2 w		2		
6 overs: 1-39	16.3 overs	2-118		

1-15 (Redmayne, 3.1), 2-27 (Harris, 6.3), 3-27 (Hinkley, 6.5),
4-40 (Jonassen, 8.6), 5-47 (Kimmince, 10.3), 6-47 (Voll, 10.4),
7-52 (Bosch, 11.4), 8-108 (Hancock, 19.3)

1-16 (van Niekerk, 2.4), 2-47 (Wolvaardt, 7.5)

Bowling	O	M	R	W	wd	nb	Dots
M Schutt	4	0	24	0			15
DR Brown	4	0	18	2	5		14
TM McGrath	3	0	19	0	1		11
A Wellington	4	1	8	5			18
D van Niekerk	2	0	18	0			5
SJ Coyte	3	0	26	1	1		6

Bowling	O	M	R	W	wd	nb	Dots
NM Hancock	3.3	1	29	1	1		10
CG Sippel	3	0	28	0	1		6
N de Klerk	3	0	14	0			7
JL Jonassen	3	0	18	0			8
P Yadav	3	0	19	1			7
AE Bosch	1	0	10	0			2

Toss: Strikers. Umpires: CA Polosak, D Taylor, SAJ Craig (TV), Ref: K Hannam. Award: A Wellington (AS). Crowd: 1,329

Mack 50: 42 balls, 5x4

Challenger Final – Renegades v Strikers at Adelaide Oval on November 25, 2021 (Floodlit)
Strikers won by 9 wickets

Renegades			B	4	6
J E Dooley+	b Schutt	0	1		
J I Rodrigues	c Wolvaardt b Brown	16	13	3	
C M Leeson	c Wellington b Brown	2	4		
H Kaur	lbw b McGrath	7	15	1	
J E Duffin	c McGrath b Wellington	2	11		
E Jones	run out (Coyte)	14	21		1
C A Webb	run out (Wellington)	0	0		
R K O'Donnell	lbw b Schutt	10	22		
E L Hayward	not out	18	23	1	
H L Ferling	not out	11	10	1	
S G Molineux*					
	2 lb, 1 w	3			
6 overs: 3-27	20 overs	8-83			

1-0 (Dooley, 0.1), 2-5 (Leeson, 1.3), 3-20 (Rodrigues, 3.3),
4-28 (Duffin, 6.5), 5-30 (Kaur, 7.6), 6-30 (Webb, 8.2),
7-47 (Jones, 11.6), 8-66 (O'Donnell, 16.5)

Bowling	O	M	R	W	wd	nb	Dots
M Schutt	4	0	23	2	1		11
DR Brown	4	0	9	2			18
SJ Coyte	4	0	16	0			14
A Wellington	4	0	21	1			12
TM McGrath	4	0	12	1			13

Strikers			B	4	6
D van Niekerk	c Kaur b Leeson	43	30	5	1
KM Mack	not out	31	29	5	
L Wolvaardt	not out	9	6	1	
TM McGrath*					
BE Patterson					
MM Penna					
A Wellington					
TJ McPharlin+					
SJ Coyte					
M Schutt					
DR Brown					
	3 w	3			
6 overs: 0-48	10.5 overs	1-86			

1-72 (van Niekerk, 9.3)

Bowling	O	M	R	W	wd	nb	Dots
SG Molineux	2	0	22	0	1		3
HL Ferling	1	0	8	0			2
EL Hayward	2	0	16	0			7
RK O'Donnell	2.5	0	18	0	1		8
CA Webb	1	0	10	0	1		3
H Kaur	1	0	7	0			0
CM Leeson	1	0	5	1			4

Toss: Strikers. Umpires: SA Lightbody, E Sheridan, CA Polosak (TV), Ref: SD Fry. Award: DR Brown (AS). Crowd: 1,184

The Final – Scorchers v Strikers at Perth Stadium on November 27, 2021 – Scorchers won by 12 runs

Scorchers			B	4	6
SFM Devine*	run out (van Niekerk)	35	33	6	
BL Mooney+	c Wellington b McGrath	19	25	2	
CL Piparo	c McPharlin b Brown	14	10	2	
HL Graham	c McGrath b Wellington	23	20	1	1
M Kapp	not out	31	23	4	
MG Carmichael	c Coyte b Schutt	2	5		
AM King	not out	14	5	3	
L Griffith					
LG Mills					
TCJ Peschel					
PM Cleary					
	1 lb, 1 nb, 6 w	8			
6 overs: 0-37	20 overs	5-146			

1-52 (Mooney, 7.5), 2-67 (Devine, 10.4), 3-75 (Piparo, 11.3),
4-116 (Graham, 16.5), 5-128 (Carmichael, 18.4)
(Wellington, 18.2)

Bowling	O	M	R	W	wd	nb	Dots
M Schutt	4	0	19	1			12
DR Brown	4	0	30	1	2	1	13
SJ Coyte	4	0	40	2			7
A Wellington	4	0	28	1			11
TM McGrath	2	0	14	1	2		6
D van Niekerk	2	0	14	0			5

Strikers			B	4	6
KM Mack	c King b Devine	6	13	1	
D van Niekerk	c Mooney b Peschel	6	13	1	
L Wolvaardt	c Griffith b Graham	25	28	2	
TM McGrath*	c Piparo b Peschel	36	29	3	1
BE Patterson	c Mills b Kapp	17	11	2	
MM Penna	not out	30	21	2	1
A Wellington	c Devine b Graham	4	4		
TJ McPharlin+	not out	2	1		
SJ Coyte					
M Schutt					
DR Brown					
	2 lb, 6 w	8			
6 overs: 2-16	20 overs	6-134			

1-12 (Mack, 4.1), 2-12 (van Niekerk, 5.1), 3-77 (McGrath, 13.3),
4-81 (Wolvaardt, 14.2), 5-105 (Patterson, 16.4), 6-120

Bowling	O	M	R	W	wd	nb	Dots
M Kapp	4	1	25	1			13
TCJ Peschel	4	0	23	2	5		13
AM King	4	0	24	0			8
SFM Devine	3	1	23	1			9
L Griffith	1	0	7	0			2
HL Graham	4	0	30	2	1		7

Toss: Strikers. Umpires: NR Johnstone, SA Lightbody, CA Polosak (TV), Ref: K Hannam. Award: M Kapp (PS) Crowd: 15,511

WBBL07 Stats

ADELAIDE STRIKERS

Batting & Fielding	M	Inn	NO	Runs	HS	Avge	100s	50s	6s	S/Rate	Ct	St
KM Mack	17	15	7	513	89*	64.12	0	5	1	115.28	2	-
L Wolvaardt	17	16	3	381	54	29.30	0	2	7	121.33	4	-
D van Niekerk	17	16	0	356	62	22.25	0	2	7	117.10	3	-
TM McGrath	17	14	6	338	50*	42.25	0	1	4	114.18	7	-
MM Penna	14	8	3	144	56*	28.80	0	1	4	121.00	5	-
BE Patterson	17	9	2	94	25	13.42	0	0	1	125.33	11	-
A Wellington	17	7	3	51	15*	12.75	0	0	0	113.33	10	-
TJ McPharlin	17	4	2	37	21*	18.50	0	0	0	100.00	11	6
SJ Coyte	17	4	2	30	14	15.00	0	0	1	130.43	6	-
M Schutt	13	1	1	0	0*	-	0	0	0	-	3	-
JL Barsby	9	-	-	-	-	-	-	-	-	-	3	-
DR Brown	15	-	-	-	-	-	-	-	-	-	5	-

Bowling	M	Overs	M	Runs	Wkts	Avge	Best	Econ	SR	4w	Dot %
A Wellington	17	57	2	374	23	16.26	5-8	6.56	14.8	1	41
DR Brown	15	55	0	334	20	16.70	3-19	6.07	16.5	0	56
SJ Coyte	17	55	0	389	16	24.31	3-12	7.07	20.6	0	37
M Schutt	13	51	1	274	13	21.07	2-18	5.37	23.5	0	54
TM McGrath	17	50.4	1	357	12	29.75	3-17	7.04	25.3	0	44
D van Niekerk	17	33.3	0	260	4	65.00	2-15	7.76	50.2	0	30
JL Barsby	9	14	1	85	4	21.25	1-8	6.07	21.0	0	42
MM Penna	14	1	0	13	0	-	-	13.00	-	0	33

BRISBANE HEAT

Batting & Fielding	M	Inn	NO	Runs	HS	Avge	100s	50s	6s	S/Rate	Ct	St
GP Redmayne	14	14	1	437	71	33.61	0	5	3	120.05	13	4
GM Harris	14	14	1	420	75	32.30	0	4	9	123.16	10	-
G Voll	14	14	2	282	48*	23.50	0	0	7	113.25	4	-
MC Hinkley	14	12	1	161	49*	14.63	0	0	3	88.95	3	-
LM Kimmince	14	13	2	148	42	13.45	0	0	8	140.95	7	-
JL Jonassen	14	12	4	101	19*	12.62	0	0	2	93.51	4	-
NM Hancock	12	5	2	76	40	25.33	0	0	1	146.15	3	-
N de Klerk	9	7	2	59	18*	11.80	0	0	1	95.16	4	-
AE Bosch	10	8	2	46	14	7.66	0	0	0	85.18	3	-
CR Knott	6	3	0	20	15	6.66	0	0	0	90.90	0	-
ER Johnston	4	3	1	17	9	8.50	0	0	0	85.00	1	-
CG Sippel	9	5	4	14	6*	14.00	0	0	0	100.00	2	-
P Yadav	13	3	3	5	3*	-	0	0	0	125.00	2	-

Bowling	M	Overs	M	Runs	Wkts	Avge	Best	Econ	SR	4w	Dot %
JL Jonassen	14	48.1	0	313	21	14.90	3-10	6.49	13.7	0	43
NM Hancock	12	40.3	1	286	14	20.42	3-19	7.06	17.3	0	52
CG Sippel	9	31	1	211	12	17.58	3-25	6.80	15.5	0	47
P Yadav	13	42.2	0	281	10	28.10	3-17	6.63	25.4	0	35
GK Prestwidge	7	19	0	153	7	21.85	2-24	8.05	16.2	0	50
GM Harris	14	33	0	252	6	42.00	3-16	7.63	33.0	0	36
N de Klerk	9	25	0	165	4	41.25	2-23	6.60	37.5	0	43
AE Bosch	10	11	0	77	2	38.50	1-12	7.00	33.0	0	42
CR Knott	6	6	0	47	1	47.00	1-3	7.83	36.0	0	39

HOBART HURRICANES

Batting & Fielding	M	Inn	NO	Runs	HS	Avge	100s	50s	6s	S/Rate	Ct	St
M du Preez	14	14	1	414	87*	31.84	0	4	1	115.00	3	-
RH Priest	14	14	1	262	107*	20.15	1	1	1	103.96	7	4
RG Johnston	13	13	0	214	63	16.46	0	1	5	94.69	2	-
NJ Carey	14	14	1	181	31	13.92	0	0	1	91.87	1	-
RM Ghosh	14	14	1	162	46	12.46	0	0	4	95.29	5	-
NE Stalenberg	14	14	3	151	28	13.72	0	0	2	93.20	5	-
MR Strano	14	11	6	145	33	29.00	0	0	0	136.79	4	-
SK Moloney	14	10	1	66	22	7.33	0	0	0	82.50	4	-
TJ Vlaeminck	14	9	2	48	17	6.85	0	0	2	106.66	2	-
BW Vakarewa	12	6	2	19	11	4.75	0	0	0	70.37	3	-
A Smith	14	6	6	12	4*	-	0	0	0	100.00	3	-
AA Genford	1	1	0	8	8	8.00	0	0	0	66.66	0	-
CL Rafferty	2	-	-	-	-	-	-	-	-	-	0	-

Bowling	M	Overs	M	Runs	Wkts	Avge	Best	Econ	SR	4w	Dot
MR Strano	14	48.3	1	356	15	23.73	3-19	7.34	19.4	0	38
TJ Vlaeminck	14	48	1	291	13	22.38	3-21	6.06	22.1	0	51
RG Johnston	13	36.5	0	226	13	17.38	4-8	6.13	17.0	1	42
NJ Carey	14	43.3	0	301	13	23.15	2-11	6.91	20.0	0	41
BW Vakarewa	12	33	1	221	7	31.57	3-8	6.69	28.2	0	47
SK Moloney	14	14	0	92	5	18.40	3-17	6.57	16.8	0	37
A Smith	14	24.2	0	179	4	44.75	1-10	7.35	36.5	0	30
CL Rafferty	2	2	0	20	0	-	-	10.00	-	0	50

MELBOURNE RENEGADES

Batting & Fielding	M	Inn	NO	Runs	HS	Avge	100s	50s	6s	S/Rate	Ct	St
H Kaur	13	12	5	406	81*	58.00	0	3	18	130.96	8	-
JI Rodrigues	13	13	1	333	75*	27.75	0	2	2	116.43	3	-
E Jones	12	12	2	236	62	23.60	0	1	5	99.57	0	-
JE Duffin	13	12	4	160	41*	20.00	0	0	3	99.37	6	-
CA Webb	10	10	0	144	46	14.40	0	0	1	100.00	1	-
JE Dooley	13	8	1	110	37	15.71	0	0	0	108.91	7	4
SG Molineux	13	7	2	77	31*	15.40	0	0	0	106.94	4	-
CM Leeson	11	7	0	57	41	8.14	0	0	0	111.76	4	-
EM Falconer	12	3	2	34	24*	34.00	0	0	3	147.82	2	-
RK O'Donnell	7	3	0	30	19	10.00	0	0	0	73.17	0	-
EL Hayward	11	3	1	26	18*	13.00	0	0	0	78.78	5	-
GL Wareham	2	2	1	18	13	18.00	0	0	0	105.88	2	-
HL Ferling	12	2	2	13	11*	-	0	0	0	118.18	5	-
MA Blows	1	-	-	-	-	-	-	-	-	-	0	-

Bowling	M	Overs	M	Runs	Wkts	Avge	Best	Econ	SR	4w	Dot %
H Kaur	13	42	0	313	15	20.86	3-22	7.45	16.8	0	34
SG Molineux	13	49.3	0	290	10	29.00	2-10	5.85	29.7	0	46
EM Falconer	12	29.3	0	262	10	26.20	4-29	8.88	17.7	1	37
CA Webb	10	24	0	181	9	20.11	3-21	7.54	16.0	0	28
RK O'Donnell	7	20.5	1	150	6	25.00	2-25	7.20	20.8	0	37
EL Hayward	11	35	0	234	5	46.80	1-15	6.68	42.0	0	34
CM Leeson	11	23.3	0	193	4	48.25	1-5	8.21	35.2	0	28
GL Wareham	2	7	0	26	3	8.66	3-13	3.71	14.0	0	64
HL Ferling	12	15	0	157	0	-	-	10.46	-	0	33
E Jones	12	1	0	12	0	-	-	12.00	-	0	0
JI Rodrigues	13	1	0	12	0	-	-	12.00	-	0	17

MELBOURNE STARS

Batting & Fielding	M	Inn	NO	Runs	HS	Avge	100s	50s	6s	S/Rate	Ct	St
EJ Villani	12	12	2	439	100*	43.90	1	3	5	122.28	2	-
MM Lanning	12	12	2	250	82	25.00	0	2	5	104.16	3	-
ME Bouchier	12	10	2	185	42	23.12	0	0	3	95.36	3	-
KJ Garth	12	9	3	164	44*	27.33	0	0	0	106.49	5	-
AJ Sutherland	12	12	1	143	57	13.00	0	1	2	82.65	4	-
EA Osborne	9	6	2	45	29	11.25	0	0	0	63.38	1	-
TM Flintoff	12	7	2	43	17	8.60	0	0	0	93.47	2	-
LCN Smith	11	4	1	18	12	6.00	0	0	0	78.26	5	-
NM Faltum	12	6	1	17	5	3.40	0	0	0	62.96	3	2
SF Day	10	3	2	14	10*	14.00	0	0	0	93.33	2	-
RM McKenna	8	3	2	10	8*	10.00	0	0	0	100.00	1	-
MC Darke	4	1	1	7	7*	-	0	0	0	116.66	1	-
AJ Lanning	5	2	0	3	3	1.50	0	0	0	30.00	1	-
LP Cripps	1	-	-	-	-	-	-	-	-	-	0	-

Bowling	M	Overs	M	Runs	Wkts	Avge	Best	Econ	SR	4w	Dot %
KJ Garth	12	45	3	281	15	18.73	3-11	6.24	18.0	0	53
AJ Sutherland	12	38	2	244	14	17.42	3-21	6.42	16.2	0	48
TM Flintoff	12	39	0	274	9	30.44	2-12	7.02	26.0	0	43
LCN Smith	11	36.2	0	211	6	35.16	2-19	5.80	36.3	0	43
SF Day	10	18	0	136	4	34.00	1-17	7.55	27.0	0	31
EA Osborne	9	21.5	0	149	3	49.66	2-25	6.82	43.6	0	33
RM McKenna	8	8.1	0	64	3	21.33	2-3	7.83	16.3	0	37
AJ Lanning	5	0.2	0	2	0	-	-	6.00	-	0	50
LP Cripps	1	2	0	25	0	-	-	12.50	-	0	25

PERTH SCORCHERS

Batting & Fielding	M	Inn	NO	Runs	HS	Avge	100s	50s	6s	S/Rate	Ct	St
BL Mooney	14	14	3	547	101*	49.72	1	4	1	128.70	5	2
SFM Devine	14	14	1	442	101	34.00	1	2	14	128.48	3	-
CL Piparo	14	10	3	216	50*	30.85	0	1	0	107.46	6	-
HL Graham	14	11	1	197	34*	19.70	0	0	4	110.05	7	-
C Atapattu	10	9	3	182	70*	30.33	0	1	3	117.41	5	-
M Kapp	14	10	5	106	31*	21.20	0	0	0	99.06	5	-
AM King	14	8	4	85	14*	21.25	0	0	0	108.97	8	-
MG Carmichael	13	7	2	60	30	12.00	0	0	0	103.44	4	-
TCJ Peschel	14	4	2	8	5*	4.00	0	0	0	80.00	3	-
LG Mills	14	4	2	6	4	3.00	0	0	0	50.00	4	-
SM Betts	4	1	0	0	0	0.00	0	0	0	0.00	0	-
PM Cleary	7	-	-	-	-	-	-	-	-	-	0	-
AL Edgar	1	-	-	-	-	-	-	-	-	-	0	-
L Griffith	7	-	-	-	-	-	-	-	-	-	3	-

Bowling	M	Overs	M	Runs	Wkts	Avge	Best	Econ	SR	4w	Dot%
HL Graham	14	47	0	300	18	16.66	3-16	6.38	15.6	0	39
AM King	14	50	0	292	16	18.25	4-11	5.84	18.7	1	43
LG Mills	14	30	0	205	16	12.81	4-25	6.83	11.2	1	37
M Kapp	14	48.3	4	256	12	21.33	4-10	5.27	24.2	1	55
SFM Devine	14	27	2	196	10	19.60	2-11	7.25	16.2	0	46
TCJ Peschel	14	38	1	267	7	38.14	2-23	7.02	32.5	0	51
L Griffith	7	13	0	92	3	30.66	2-17	7.07	26.0	0	25
SM Betts	4	4	0	46	1	46.00	1-13	11.5	24.0	0	29
PM Cleary	7	4	0	37	0	-	-	9.25	-	0	58
C Atapattu	10	1	0	10	0	-	-	10.00	-	0	33

SYDNEY SIXERS

Batting & Fielding	M	Inn	NO	Runs	HS	Avge	100s	50s	6s	S/Rate	Ct	St
EA Perry	13	13	3	358	50*	35.80	0	1	4	91.32	2	-
NE Bolton	13	12	4	247	38*	30.87	0	0	0	96.10	6	-
AJ Healy	13	13	1	231	94*	19.25	0	2	2	115.50	2	1
AK Gardner	12	12	1	197	86*	17.90	0	2	5	105.91	8	-
S Verma	13	12	1	191	57	17.36	0	2	4	105.52	5	-
MJ Brown	13	10	5	79	31	15.80	0	0	0	106.75	0	-
AR Reakes	13	9	2	78	22	11.14	0	0	1	82.10	3	-
RP Yadav	12	5	3	43	17*	21.50	0	0	0	87.75	5	-
LR Cheatle	8	3	1	34	16	17.00	0	0	0	109.67	4	-
SR Campbell	13	2	1	15	12	15.00	0	0	0	55.55	2	-
EL Hughes	7	1	1	2	2*	-	0	0	0	25.00	1	-
CF Moore	9	2	1	1	1	1.00	0	0	0	33.33	0	-
JE Allen	4	-	-	-	-	-	-	-	-	-	0	-

Bowling	M	Overs	M	Runs	Wkts	Avge	Best	Econ	4w	Dot %
LR Cheatle	8	27	1	145	10	14.50	3-15	5.37	0	50
RP Yadav	12	33.1	0	226	9	25.11	2-22	6.81	0	33
MJ Brown	13	42.1	1	301	8	37.62	2-14	7.13	0	45
NE Bolton	13	32.5	0	244	8	30.50	3-11	7.43	0	32
AK Gardner	12	28	0	182	7	26.00	2-8	6.50	0	45
SR Campbell	13	33.2	0	236	6	39.33	1-13	7.08	0	44
EA Perry	13	22	1	175	5	35.00	2-9	7.95	0	46
EL Hughes	7	1.4	0	17	0	-	-	10.20	0	0
JE Allen	4	2	0	21	0	-	-	10.50	0	17

SYDNEY THUNDER

Batting & Fielding	M	Inn	NO	Runs	HS	Avge	100s	50s	6s	S/Rate	Ct	St
S Mandhana	13	13	2	377	114*	34.27	1	2	7	130.44	4	-
PES Litchfield	13	13	1	263	49	21.91	0	0	3	109.12	9	-
DB Sharma	13	11	5	211	44*	35.16	0	0	0	106.56	8	-
TB Wilson	12	11	2	178	53	19.77	0	1	0	81.65	3	2
SJ Johnson	11	10	1	146	52	16.22	0	1	3	125.86	1	-
AB Learoyd	11	7	1	92	34	15.33	0	0	0	78.63	1	-
CL Hall	10	8	0	90	38	11.25	0	0	0	83.33	1	-
HJ Darlington	13	11	5	60	19*	10.00	0	0	1	105.26	4	-
IECM Wong	13	6	0	56	43	9.33	0	0	6	155.55	2	-
LG Smith	13	6	4	41	17*	20.50	0	0	0	105.12	3	-
EJ Smith	1	1	1	5	5*	-	0	0	0	125.00	0	2
SL Bates	13	3	2	2	2*	2.00	0	0	0	66.66	2	-
KE Peterson	7	2	1	0	0*	0.00	0	0	0	0.00	3	-

	M	Overs	M	Runs	Wkts	Avge	Best	Econ	SR	4w	Dot %
HJ Darlington	13	52	0	332	16	20.75	3-21	6.38	19.5	0	38
DB Sharma	13	45	0	322	13	24.76	3-13	7.15	20.7	0	44
SL Bates	13	50.2	1	290	12	24.16	2-14	5.76	25.1	0	44
SJ Johnson	11	39	0	299	10	29.90	2-22	7.66	23.4	0	38
IECM Wong	13	40	2	291	9	32.33	2-19	7.27	26.6	0	44
LG Smith	13	21	0	182	4	45.50	2-17	8.66	31.5	0	28
KE Peterson	7	9	0	93	1	93.00	1-10	10.33	54.0	0	35
AB Learoyd	11	2	0	31	0	-	-	15.50	-	0	

WBBL COMPETITION RECORDS
THE FINALS

Season	Batted first	Batted Second	Venue	Player of match	Player of series
2015-16	Sixers 7-115	lost to Thunder 7-116	MCG	Erin Osborne (ST)	Meg Lanning (MS)
2016-17	Sixers 5-124	def Scorchers 7-117	WACA	Sarah Aley (SS)	Beth Mooney (BH)
2017-18	Scorchers 99	lost to Sixers 1-100	Adelaide Oval	Sarah Coyte (SS)	Amy Satterthwaite (MR)
2018-19	Sixers 7-131	lost to Heat 7-132	Drummoyne	Beth Mooney (BH)	Ellyse Perry (SS)
2019-20	Strikers 7-161	lost to Heat 4-162	Border Field	Beth Mooney (BH)	Sophie Devine (AS)
2020-21	Stars 9-86	lost to Thunder 3-87	North Syd No 1	Shabnim Ismail (ST)	Sophie Devine (PS)
2021-22	Scorchers 5-146	def Strikers 6-134	Perth Stadium	Marizanne Kapp (PS)	H Kaur (MR)

RESULTS

Team	Matches	Won	Lost	NR	Titles	R-up
Adelaide Strikers	102	48	51	3	0	2
Brisbane Heat	103	61	41	1	2	0
Hobart Hurricanes	97	31	64	2	0	0
Melbourne Renegades	98	43	53	2	0	0
Melbourne Stars	97	40	54	3	0	1
Perth Scorchers	104	57	45	2	1	2
Sydney Sixers	104	60	43	1	2	2
Sydney Thunder	101	54	43	3	2	0

LEADING RUN SCORERS

	M	Inn	NO	Runs	HS	Avge	S/Rate	100s	50s	6s
BL Mooney	103	103	25	3674	102	47.10	122.7	2	33	20
EA Perry	96	95	28	3361	103*	50.16	102.7	2	21	51
SFM Devine	92	92	15	3076	103*	39.95	128.8	3	19	120
EJ Villani	99	98	11	2849	100*	32.75	115.2	1	24	28
MM Lanning	78	77	13	2725	101	42.58	120.1	1	27	52
AJ Healy	100	99	5	2646	112*	28.15	136.2	4	14	61

HUNDREDS (21)

		Balls	4s	6s		Venue	Season
S Mandhana	114*	64	14	3	Renegades v Thunder	Mackay	2021-22
AK Gardner	114	52	9	10	Sixers v Stars	North Sydney	2017-18
AJ Healy	112*	69	17	2	Sixers v Strikers	Hurstville	2018-19
AJ Healy	111	52	15	6	Sixers v Stars	North Sydney	2020-21
RH Priest	107*	68	10	7	Hurricanes v Stars	Bellerive Oval	2021-22
AJ Healy	106*	53	13	4	Sixers v Stars	WACA	2019-20
AJ Healy	106	66	13	3	Sixers v Strikers	Hurstville Oval	2017-18
L Lee	103*	65	13	3	Stars v Scorchers	WACA	2019-20
SFM Devine	103	68	5	7	Scorchers v Sixers	Hurstville Oval	2020-21
SFM Devine	103*	48	10	8	Strikers v Hurricanes	Glenelg Oval	2016-17
EA Perry	103*	64	10	5	Sixers v Heat	SCG	2018-19
GM Harris	103	55	14	4	Heat v Sixers	Aquinas Coll, Perth	2015-16
L Lee	102*	56	16	3	Stars v Sixers	Junction Oval	2018-19
EA Perry	102*	59	14	2	Sixers v Scorchers	North Sydney No 1	2018-19
BL Mooney	102	55	14	1	Heat v Thunder	Cairns	2018-19
SW Bates	102	65	15	0	Strikers v Hurricanes	Glenelg Oval	2017-18
BL Mooney	101*	63	13	0	Scorchers v Renegades	WACA	2021-22
GM Harris	101*	42	13	6	Heat v Stars	Gabba	2018-19
MM Lanning	101	67	12	3	Scorchers v Hurricanes	Lilac Hill	2019-20
SFM Devine	101	60	8	6	Scorchers v Thunder	York Park, Launceston	2021-22
EJ Villani	100*	65	13	2	Stars v Strikers	Adelaide Oval	2021-22

HIGHEST TEAM SCORES

Total		Venue	Season
4-242	SS v MS	North Sydney No 1	2017-18
4-207	MR v BH	KRO, Adelaide	2021-22
1-206	SS v AS	Hurstville Oval	2018-19
6-200	ST v MR	North Sydney No 1	2017-19
0-199	SS v MS	WACA	2019-20
6-196	HH v MS	Burnie	2018-19
2-194	PS v MR	WACA	2021-22

LOWEST TEAM SCORES

		Venue	Season
66	BH v MR	Docklands	2017-18
66	HH v SS	Gabba	2016-17
68	MR v ST	Manuka Oval	2017-18
73	SS v BH	Nth Syd No 1	2019-20
76	PS v AS	Traeger Park	2017-18
76	MR v BH	Drumm Oval	2020-21
77	HH v AS	Hurstville Oval	2020-21

FASTEST MILESTONE INNINGS

Fifty	Bls		Venue/Season		Century	Bls		Venue/Season
AK Gardner	22	SS v MS	Nth Syd 1, 2017-18		GM Harris	42	BH v MS	Gabba, 2018-19
L Lee	22	MS v SS	Nth Syd 1, 2017-18		AK Gardner	47	SS v MS	Nth Syd 1, 2017-18
H Kaur	23	ST v BH	Nth Syd 1, 2018-19		AJ Healy	47	SS v MS	Nth Syd 1, 2020-21
GM Harris	23	BH v MS	Gabba, 2018-19		SFM Devine	48	AS v HH	Glenelg, 2016-17
MM Lanning	23	MS v BH	Nth Syd 1, 2020-21		GM Harris	53	BH v SS	Aquin Coll, 2015-16
					BL Mooney	53	BH v ST	Cairns, 2018-19

RECORD PARTNERSHIPS

						Venue	Season
1	156	BL Mooney	GM Harris	Heat v Sixers		Aquinas College, Perth	2015-16
2	156*	MM Lanning	M du Preez	Stars v Strikers		Junction Oval	2015-16
3	135	BL Mooney	C Atapattu	Scorchers v Thunder		Rolton Oval, Adelaide	2021-22
4	121	HC Knight	RL Haynes	Thunder v Strikers		Syd Showground	2020-21
5	126	EA Osborne	M du Preez	Stars v Hurricanes		Burnie	2018-19
6	76*	TT Beaumont	A Wellington	Strikers v Heat		Gabba	2016-17
7	83*	NJ Carey	RM Farrell	Thunder v Renegades		North Sydney No 1	2017-18
8	60*	LK Ebsary	PM Cleary	Scorchers v Renegades		Camberwell	2017-18
9	55	GP Redmayne	BL Hepburn	Hurricanes v Sixers		Bellerive	2018-19
10	30	DM Kimmince	HP Birkett	Heat v Thunder		North Sydney No 1	2018-19

LEADING WICKET TAKERS

	M	Balls	M	Runs	Wkts	Avge	Best	4i	5i	Econ
MR Strano	99	2082	4	2305	119	19.37	5-15	2	1	6.64
JL Jonassen	113	2181	3	2266	113	20.05	4-13	4	0	6.23
A Wellington	103	1940	3	2178	103	21.15	5-8	1	1	6.74
M Kapp	102	2112	15	1869	102	18.32	4-10	3	0	5.31
HL Graham	100	1882	2	2154	102	21.12	3-16	0	0	6.87
NJ Carey	99	1990	2	2291	99	23.14	4-12	1	0	6.91
SJ Coyte	91	1805	2	2011	93	21.62	3-9	0	0	6.68

FIVE WICKETS IN AN INNINGS (5)

			Venue	Season
A Wellington	5-8	Strikers v Heat	Adelaide Oval	2021-22
MR Strano	5-15	Renegades v Stars	MCG	2015-16
AE Satterthwaite	5-17	Hurricanes v Thunder	Bellerive	2016-17
HK Matthews	5-19	Hurricanes v Heat	Bellieve	2016-17
SFM Devine	5-41	Strikers v Stars	Junction Oval	2017-18

MOST ECONOMCAL/EXPENSIVE IN A FOUR OVER SPELL

Economical		v	Venue	Season		Expensive		v	Venue	Season
NR Sciver	1-7	MS v MR	MCG	2015-16		SG Molineux	2-54	MR v BH	Geelong	2018-19
KM Beams	1-7	MS v BH	Mackay	2015-16		NJ Carey	1-52	HH v SS	Mowbray	2019-20
LMM Tahuhu	0-7	MR v SS	Geelong	2018-19		KM Beams	2-51	MS v SS	Nth Syd No 1	2017-18
M Schutt	3-7	AS v SS	Drummoyne	2020-21		RM Farrell	0-50	ST v SS	Nth Syd No 1	2018-19
						NJ Carey	1-50	ST v HH	Launceston	2016-17
						M Penna	3-50	MS v AS	K Rolton Ov	2019-20

HAT TRICKS (6)

		Venue	Season
NE Bolton	Scorchers v Hurricanes	Blacktown	2015-16
GL Triscari	Stars v Thunder	Sydney Showground	2015-16
AE Sattherwaite	Hurricanes v Thunder	Bellerive	2016-17
D van Niekerk	Sixers v Hurricanes	Bellerive	2017-18
M Kapp	Sixers v Stars	Hurstville Oval	2019-20
DR Brown	Strikers v Heat	Invermay Park, Launceston	2021-22

SUPEROVERS (10)

	Winner	Venue	Season
Renegades 8-141 v Strikers 141	Renegades	Adelaide No 2	2015-16
Renegades 7-120 v Sixers 7-120	Renegades	Geelong	2017-18
Stars 6-118 v Renegades 6-118	Stars	MCG	2017-18
Strikers 5-114 v Thunder 4-144	Strikers	Wagga Wagga	2017-18
Strikers 5-189 v Hurricanes 8-189	Strikers	Karen Rolton Oval	2018-19
Sixers 4-131 v Renegades 6-131	Sixers	Drummoyne Oval	2018-19
Strikers 6-161 v Thunder 6-161	Strikers	Bellerive Oval	2019-20
Stars 8-165 v Renegades 7-165	Renegades	Sydney Showground	2020-21
Scorchers 7-137 v Heat 9-137	Scorchers	Bellerive Oval	2021-22
Scorchers 5-121 v Strikers 8-121	Scorchers	Lilac Hill, Perth	2021-22

ADELAIDE STRIKERS - HONOUR ROLL

Season	Finished	Captain	Coach	MVP	Minor Rd W/L/NR
2015-16	Seventh	LK Ebsary	Andrea McCauley	SJ Taylor	6/8
2016-17	Last	TJ McPharlin	Andrea McCauley	CM Edwards	3/9/2
2017-18	Fourth	SW Bates	Andrea McCauley	SFM Devine	8/6
2018-19	Sixth	SW Bates	Andrea McCauley	SFM Devine	5/8/1
2019-20	Runner-up	SW Bates	Luke Williams	SFM Devine	10/4
2020-21	Sixth	M Schutt/SW Bates	Luke Williams	SJ Coyte	6/7/1
2021-22	Runner-up	TM McGrath	Luke Williams	KM Mack	7/6/1

Leading team records

Most Runs	M	Runs	HS	Avge	100/50	SR	Most Wickets	M	W	Econ	Best
SFM Devine	66	2174	103*	39.53	1/14	129.4	A Wellington	102	103	6.74	5-8
TM McGrath	100	1579	65*	20.78	-/5	101.7	M Schutt	98	87	5.68	3-7
BE Patterson	102	1293	60	17.24	-/3	98.7	SJ Coyte	87	83	6.78	3-9
SW Bates	46	1208	102	28.76	1/6	107.7	TM McGrath	100	66	6.97	3-17

Highest Individual scores

		Balls	4s	6s		Venue	Season
SFM Devine	103*	48	10	8	Hurricanes	Glenelg Oval	2016-17
SW Bates	102	65	15	0	Hurricanes	Glenelg Oval	2017-18
SFM Devine	99*	53	10	4	Hurricanes	Karen Rolton Oval	2018-19
SFM Devine	95	60	8	5	Stars	Adelaide Oval	2018-19

Fastest Fifties

	Balls	Versus	Venue	Season
SFM Devine	26	Hurricanes	Glenelg	2016-17
BE Patterson	27	Scorchers	Karen Rolton Oval	2019-20
SFM Devine	29	Renegades	Karen Rolton Oval	2019-20
L Woolvardt	29	Heat	Mowbray	2021-22
SFM Devine	30	Heat	Junction Oval	2018-19

Highest Team totals

	Versus	Venue	Season
5-189	Hurricanes	Karen Rolton Oval	2018-19
3-183	Hurricanes	Glenelg Oval	2017-18
4-176	Thunder	Karen Rolton Oval	2021-22
6-176	Hurricanes	Glenelg	2017-18

Lowest Team totals

	Versus	Venue	Season
9-82	Scorchers	Adelaide Oval	2016-17
83	Hurricanes	Launceston	2015-16
88	Stars	Lilac Hill	2016-17
9-94	Stars	MCG	2016-17
94	Sixers	Adelaide Oval	2016-17

Best Bowling

		Overs	Versus	Venue	Season
A Wellington	5-8	4	Heat	Adelaide Oval	2021-22
SFM Devine	5-41	4	Stars	Adelaide Oval	2018-19
A Wellington	4-24	3	Heat	Drummoyne Oval	2020-21
M Schutt	3-7	4	Sixers	Drummoyne Oval	2020-21
M Schutt	3-8	4	Hurricanes	Launceston	2015-16

Most Economical/Expensive Bowling (Min 4 overs)

Economical		v	Venue	Season	Expensive		v	Venue	Season
M Schutt	3-8	HH	Launceston	2015-16	D Hazell	0-46	SS	Hurstville	2018-19
A Wellington	5-8	BH	Adel Oval	2021-22	TM McGrath	2-43	ST	Syd Showg	2020-21
TM McGrath	1-8	SS	Adel Oval	2021-22	SFM Devine	5-41	MS	Adel Oval	2018-19
M Schutt	3-8	HH	York Park	2015-16	SJ Coyte	1-41	ST	Bellerive	2019-20
A Wellington	2-8	BH	Gabba	2016-17					

BRISBANE HEAT - HONOUR ROLL

Season	Finished	Captain	Coach	MVP	Minor Rd W/L/NR
2015-16	Sixth	DM Kimmince	Andy Richards	BL Mooney	7/7
2016-17	Third	DM Kimmince/KLH Short	Andy Richards	BL Mooney	8/6
2017-18	Fifth	KLH Short	Peter McGiffin	BL Mooney	7/7
2018-19	Won Title	KLH Short	Peter McGiffin	SJ Johnson	9/5
2019-20	Won Title	KLH Short	Ashley Noffke	JL Jonassen	10/4
2020-21	Third	JL Jonassen	Ashley Noffke	AC Kerr	8/4/2
2021-22	Fourth	JL Jonassen	Ashley Noffke	GM Harris	8/5/1

Leading team records

Most Runs	M	Runs	HS	Avge	100/50	SR	Most Wickets	M	W	Econ	Best
BL Mooney	75	2576	102	45.19	1/25	122.6	JL Jonassen	103	113	6.23	4-13
JL Jonassen	103	1712	67*	24.81	-/6	111.5	DM Kimmince	86	77	7.02	4-18
GM Harris	76	1652	103	25.03	2/8	126.6	GM Harris	76	57	6.79	4-15
KLH Short	67	945	79	19.68	-/3	91.2	JL Barsby	58	53	6.68	4-2

Highest Individual scores

		Balls	4s	6s	Versus	Venue	Season
GM Harris	103	55	14	4	Sixers	Aquinas College, Perth	2015-16
BL Mooney	102	55	14	1	Thunder	Cazaly's Oval, Cairns	2018-19
GM Harris	101*	42	13	6	Stars	Gabba	2018-19
DM Kimmince	87*	54	9	3	Scorchers	North Sydney No 1	2017-18

Fastest Fifties

	Balls	Versus	Venue	Season
GM Harris	23	Stars	Gabba	2018-19
JL Jonassen	25	Renegades	Junction Oval	2019-20
GM Harris	26	Thunder	North Sydney Oval No 1	2018-19
BL Mooney	27	Thunder	Cairns	2018-19
BL Mooney	27	Stars	Junction Oval	2019-20

Highest Team totals

	Versus	Venue	Season
192	Renegades	Rolton Oval, Adelaide	2021-22
3-190	Sixers	Aquinas College, Perth	2015-16
4-183	Renegades	Allan Border Field	2019-20
8-174	Renegades	Geelong	2018-19
7-172	Thunder	Cazaly's Oval, Cairns	2018-19

Lowest Team totals

	Versus	Venue	Season
66	Renegades	Docklands	2017-18
9-83	Sixers	Drummoyne Oval	2016-17
8-93	Stars	Mackay	2017-18
94	Thunder	Kingston Twin Oval	2015-16
7-94	Stars	Allan Border Field	2016-17

Best Bowling

		Overs	Versus	Venue	Season
JL Barsby	4-2	2	Thunder	Allan Border Field	2017-18
HL Ferling	4-8	3	Scorchers	Aquinas Coll, Perth	2015-16
GK Prestwidge	4-12	3.2	Renegades	Drummoyne Oval	2020-21
JL Barsby	4-13	3	Renegades	Allan Border Field	2016-17
JL Jonassen	4-13	4	Thunder	Drummoyne Oval	2019-20

Most Economical/Expensive Bowling (Min 4 overs)

Economical		v	Venue	Season	Expensive		v	Venue	Season
SJ Johnson	2-9	PS	Nth Sydney	2018-19	JL Jonassen	0-48	MR	AB Field	2019-20
JL Jonassen	3-11	AS	Gabba	2015-16	JL Jonassen	2-46	ST	Nth Syd No 1	2018-19
SJ Johnson	1-11	SS	Nth Sydney	2019-20	JL Jonassen	0-46	HH	Bellerive	2019-20
JL Barsby	2-12	PS	WACA	2016-17	AC Kerr	0-45	MS	Junc Oval	2019-20
SJ Johnson	3-12	MS	Gabba	2018-19	NM Hancock	1-44	MR	Rolton Oval	2021-22
GM Harris	1-12	MS	Gabba	2018-19					
SJ Johnson	1-12	ST	Drummoyne	2018-19					

HOBART HURRICANES - HONOUR ROLL

Season	Finished	Captain	Coach	MVP	Minor Rd W/L/NR
2015-16	Third	HC Knight	Julia Price	HC Knight	8/6
2016-17	Fourth	HC Knight	Julia Price	AE Satterthwaite	7/6/1
2017-18	Last	CL Hall/IMHC Joyce	Julia Price	HK Matthews	2/12
2018-19	Last	SK Moloney	Salliann Briggs	HC Knight	2/12
2019-20	Seventh	CL Hall	Salliann Briggs	BW Vakarewa	4/9/1
2020-21	Last	CL Hall	Salliann Briggs	RH Priest	3/9/2
2021-22	Sixth	RH Priest	Salliann Briggs	TJ Vlaeminck	5/8/1

Leading team records

Most Runs	M	Runs	HS	Avge	100/50	SR	Most Wickets	M	W	Econ	Best
HC Knight	55	1353	82*	26.52	/-8	107.6	BL Hepburn	65	44	6.94	3-24
CL Hall	81	955	53*	17.05	-/2	103.8	HK Matthews	56	41	6.64	5-19
HK Matthews	56	865	77	18.02	-/1	98.1	V Pyke	54	41	6.63	4-17
GP Redmayne	42	797	64*	22.14	-/3	93.4	HC Knight	55	39	6.92	3-7

Highest Individual scores

		Balls	4s	6s		Venue	Season
RH Priest	107*	68	10	7	Stars	Bellerive Oval	2021-22
RH Priest	92*	63	15	1	Sixers	Sydney Showground	2020-21
M du Preez	87*	61	11	1	Thunder	Mackay	2021-22
RH Priest	83*	64	9	4	Thunder	Hurstville Oval	2020-21
HC Knight	82*	55	9	3	Stars	Burnie	2018-19

Fastest Fifties

	Balls	Versus	Venue	Season
SS Mandhana	23	Strikers	Karen Rolton Oval	2018-19
SS Mandhana	24	Stars	Burnie	2018-19
M du Preez	34	Stars	York Park	2021-22
HC Knight	34	Sixers	Bellerive Oval	2018-19
CL Hall	34	Renegades	Junction Oval	2019-20

Highest Team totals

	Versus	Venue	Season
6-196	Stars	Burnie	2018-19
8-189	Strikers	Karen Rolton Oval	2018-19
7-173	Scorchers	Bellerive Oval	2018-19
3-171	Thunder	Launceston	2016-17

Lowest Team totals

	Versus	Venue	Season
66	Sixers	Gabba	2016-17
77	Strikers	Hurstville Oval	2020-21
80	Heat	Launceston	2018-19
82	Heat	Drummoyne Oval	2020-21
84	Strikers	Hurstville Oval	2020-21

Best Bowling

		Overs	Versus	Venue	Season
AE Satterthwaite	5-17	4	Thunder	Bellerive Oval	2016-17
HK Matthews	5-19	3.4	Heat	Bellerive Oval	2016-17
R Johnston	4-8	3.2	Stars	Bellerive Oval	2021-22
V Pyke	4-17	4	Strikers	Glenelg Oval	2017-18
BW Vakarewa	4-19	4	Sixers	North Sydney No 1	2019-20
HK Matthews	4-23	4	Renegades	Bendigo	2016-17

Most Economical/Expensive Bowling (Min 4 overs)

Economical		v	Venue	Season	Expensive		v	Venue	Season
BW Vakarewa	3-8	ST	Mackay	2021-22	NJ Carey	1-52	SS	Mowbray	2019-20
HK Matthews	2-9	MR	Blacktown	2020-21	HC Knight	1-49	AS	Karen Rolton	2018-19
TJ Vlaeminck	0-10	BH	York Park	2021-22	HK Matthews	0-47	AS	Glenelg	2017-18
JL Hunter	1-11	SS	Hurstville	2016-17	NJ Carey	2-44	AS	Hurstville	2020-21
JL Hunter	1-11	PS	Blacktown	2015-16					

MELBOURNE RENEGADES - HONOUR ROLL

Season	Finished	Captain	Coach	MVP	Minor Rd W/L
2015-16	Last	SJ Elliott/MR Strano/ RH Priest/KL Britt	Lachlan Stevens	MR Strano	4/10
2016-17	Seventh	RH Priest	Lachlan Stevens	MR Strano	6/8
2017-18	Sixth	AE Satterthwaite/C Atapattu	Tim Coyle	AE Satterthwaite	6/8
2018-19	Fourth	AE Satterthwaite	Tim Coyle	SG Molineux	7/6/1
2019-20	Fourth	JE Duffin/MR Strano	Tim Coyle	JE Duffin	8/6
2020-21	Seventh	AE Satterthwaite	Lachlan Stevens	CA Webb	4/8/2
2021-22	Third	SG Molineux	Simon Helmot	H Kaur	8/4/2

Leading team records

Most Runs	M	Runs	HS	Avge	100/50	SR	Most Wickets	M	W	Econ	Best
SG Molineux	87	1376	78*	21.50	-/6	104.4	MR Strano	85	104	6.53	5-15
DN Wyatt	55	1346	87	28.04	-/7	114.0	SG Molineux	87	67	6.55	4-18
JE Duffin	50	1205	81	33.47	-/6	119.5	LMM Tahuhu	61	53	6.02	3-13
AE Satterthwaite	42	897	66	26.38	-/3	97.3	MJ Brown	59	44	6.84	3-17

Highest Individual scores

	Balls	4s	6s		Venue	Season
DN Wyatt	87	55	11	2	Heat	Allan Border Field	2019-20
H Kaur	81	55	11	2	Thunder	Mackay	2021-22
JE Duffin	81	47	12	1	Thunder	North Sydney Oval No 1	2017-18
SG Molineux	78*	54	12	-	Stars	MCG	2018-19
JE Duffin	76*	57	9	2	Stars	Junction Oval	2019-20

Fastest Fifties

	Balls	Versus	Venue	Season
H Kaur	27	Heat	Rolton Oval, Adelaide	2021-22
JE Duffin	27	Heat	Allan Border Field	2019-20
GL Wareham	27	Sixers	Sydney Showground	2020-21
JI Rodrigues	28	Heat	Rolton Oval, Adelaide	2021-22
DN Wyatt	29	Strikers	Karen Rolton Oval	2019-20

Highest Team totals

	Versus	Venue	Season
4-207	Heat	Rolton Oval, Adelaide	2021-22
6-189	Thunder	North Sydney Oval No 1	2017-18
4-185	Heat	Allan Border Field	2019-20
4-175	Thunder	Mackay	2021-22
4-169	Sixers	North Sydney Oval No 1	2020-21

Lowest Team totals

	Versus	Venue	Season
68	Thunder	Manuka Oval	2017-18
76	Heat	Drummoyne Oval	2020-21
81	Hurricanes	Blacktown	2020-21
8-83	Strikers	Adelaide Oval	2021-22
86	Hurricanes	Launceston	2015-16

Best Bowling

		Overs	Versus	Venue	Season
MR Strano	5-15	4	Stars	MCG	2015-16
DN Wyatt	4-13	4	Heat	Gabba	2015-16
E Hayward	4-16	4	Stars	Sydney Showground	2020-21
SG Molineux	4-18	4	Strikers	North Sydney Oval No 2	2016-17
D van Niekerk	4-20	4	Heat	Gabba	2015-16

Most Economical/Expensive Bowling (Min 4 overs)

Economical		v	Venue	Season	Expensive		v	Venue	Season
LMM Tahuhu	0-7	SS	Geelong	2018-19	SG Molineux	2-54	BH	Geelong	2018-19
S Ismail	3-10	MS	MCG	2015-16	SG Molineux	0-46	BH	Rolton Oval	2021-22
SG Molineux	2-10	MS	Adel Oval	2021-22	SG Molineux	0-44	AS	Rolton Oval	2019-20
MJ Brown	0-12	MS	MCG	2016-17	LMM Tahuhu	1-43	ST	Nth Syd No 1	2017-18
LMM Tahuhu	1-12	ST	Manuka Oval	2017-18					

MELBOURNE STARS - HONOUR ROLL

Season	Finished	Captain	Coach	MVP	Minor Rd W/L/NR
2015-16	Fifth	MM Lanning	David Hemp	MM Lanning	7/7
2016-17	Fifth	MM Lannig/KM Beams	David Hemp	MM Lanning	7/7
2017-18	Seventh	KM Beams/EA Osborne	David Hemp	EA Osborne	5/9
2018-19	Seventh	EA Osborne/KM Beams	David Hemp	AM King	5/8/1
2019-20	Last	EJ Villani	David Hemp	L Lee	2/12
2020-21	Runner-up	MM Lanning	Trent Woodhill	NR Sciver	8/3/3
2021-22	Fifth	MM Lanning	Jarrad Loughman	KJ Garth	5/7/2

Leading team records

Most Runs	M	Runs	HS	Avge	100/50	SR	Most Wickets	M	W	Econ	Best
MM Lanning	**54**	**1805**	**97***	**41.98**	-/18	117.5	AM King	68	54	7.11	3-13
M du Preez	64	1498	88	26.75	-/10	111.6	MR Sciver	37	45	6.63	4-29
EJ Villani	**41**	**1143**	**100***	**30.89**	1/8	115.6	**KM Beams**	**61**	**40**	**6.67**	**4-20**
L Lee	40	1100	103*	29.72	2/7	125.5	**AJ Sutherland**	**58**	**38**	**6.92**	**4-20**

Highest Individual scores

		Balls	4s	6s		Venue	Season
L Lee	103*	65	13	3	Scorchers	WACA	2019-20
L Lee	102*	56	16	3	Sixers	Junction Oval	2018-19
EL Villani	**100***	**65**	**13**	**2**	**Strikers**	**Adelaide Oval**	**2021-22**
MM Lanning	97*	72	11	3	Heat	Allan Border Field	2016-17

Fastest Fifties

	Balls	Versus	Venue	Season
L Lee	22	Sixers	North Sydney Oval No 1	2017-18
MM Lanning	23	Heat	North Sydney Oval No 1	2020-21
L Lee	28	Sixers	Junction Oval	2018-19
E Villani	**29**	**Sixers**	**Bellerive Oval**	**2021-22**

Highest Team totals

	Versus	Venue	Season
1-181	**Strikers**	**Adelaide Oval**	**2021-22**
4-178	Sixers	North Sydney No 1	2020-21
9-177	Heat	North Sydney No 1	2020-21
3-169	Renegades	Ballarat	2019-20
3-166	Sixers	Junction Oval	2018-19

Lowest Team totals

	Versus	Venue	Season
9-85	Renegades	MCG	2015-16
9-86	Thunder	North Sydney No 1	2020-21
88	Heat	Gabba	2018-19
89	**Hurricanes**	**Bellerive Oval**	**2021-22**

Best Bowling

		Overs	Versus	Venue	Season
GL Triscari	4-10	2	Thunder	Sydney Showground	2015-16
KM Beams	4-11	4	Sixers	Drummoyne Oval	2015-16
AJ Sutherland	4-20	4	Strikers	Adelaide Oval	2017-18
EA Osborne	4-20	4	Heat	Mackay	2017-18
M Penna	4-20	4	Thunder	Bankstown Oval	2019-20

Most Economical/Expensive Bowling (Min 4 overs)

Economical		v	Venue	Season	Expensive		v	Venue	Season
KM Beams	1-7	BH	Mackay	2017-18	KM Beams	0-51	SS	Nth Syd No 1	2017-18
NR Sciver	1-7	MR	MCG	2015-16	M Penna	3-50	AS	K Rolton Ov	2019-20
KM Beams	4-11	SS	Drummoyne	2015-16	NM Hancock	1-48	HH	Burnie	2018-19
KM Beams	1-11	HH	MCG	2017-18	M Penna	0-46	SS	WACA	2019-20
AJ Sutherland	2-11	MR	MCG	2017-18	KH Brunt	0-45	SS	Nth Syd No 1	2020-21
EM Kearney	1-11	PS	Lilac Hill	2016-17					
KM Beams	3-11	HH	Bellerive	2016-17					
KJ Garth	**3-11**	**ST**	**York Pk**	**2021-22**					

PERTH SCORCHERS - HONOUR ROLL

Season	Finished	Captain	Coach	MVP	Minor Rd W/L
2015-16	Fourth	NE Bolton	Lisa Keightley	KH Brunt	7/7
2016-17	Second	SW Bates	Lisa Keightley	KH Brunt	8/6
2017-18	Second	EJ Villani	Lisa Keightley	KH Brunt	8/6
2018-19	Fifth	MM Lanning/EJ Villani	Lisa Keightley	HL Graham	7/7
2019-20	Third	MM Lanning	Lisa Keightley	NC Sciver	9/5
2020-21	Fourth	MM Lanning/SFM Devine	Shelley Nitschke	BL Mooney	6/6/2
2021-22	Champions	SFM Devine	Shelley Nitschke	SFM Devine	9/3/2

Leading team records

Most Runs	M	Runs	HS	Avge	100/50	SR	Most Wickets	M	W	Econ	Best
EJ Villani	58	1706	84*	34.12	-/16	114.8	HL Graham	100	102	6.87	3-16
NE Bolton	86	1494	71	22.29	-/5	95.2	KH Brunt	44	49	5.15	4-17
MM Lanning	24	920	101	43.80	1/9	125.6	EL King	54	41	6.42	3-17
HL Graham	100	1026	44*	16.82	-/-	98.1	NE Bolton	86	41	6.80	3-20

Highest Individual scores

		Balls	4s	6s		Venue	Season
SFM Devine	103	68	5	7	Sixers	Hurstville Oval	2020-21
BL Mooney	101*	63	13	0	Renegades	WACA, Perth	2021-22
SFM Devine	101	60	8	6	Thunder	York Park, Launceston	2021-22
MM Lanning	101	67	12	3	Hurricanes	Lilac Hill	2019-20

Fastest Fifties

	Balls	Versus	Venue	Season
MM Lanning	24	Thunder	Lilac Hill	2018-19
AE Jones	26	Sixers	North Sydney	2018-19
NR Sciver	28	Heat	North Sydney	2017-18
EJ Villani	30	Hurricanes	Junction Oval	2018-19
MM Lanning	30	Strikers	Alice Springs	2018-19
EJ Villani	30	Stars	WACA, Perth	2017-18

Highest Team totals

	Versus	Venue	Season
2-194	Renegades	WACA, Perth	2021-22
6-188	Heat	North Sydney	2017-18
2-186	Thunder	York Park, Launceston	2021-22
2-184	Thunder	Rolton Oval, Adelaide	2021-22
4-183	Sixers	Hurstville Oval	2020-21

Lowest Team totals

	Versus	Venue	Season
76	Strikers	Traeger Park, Alice Springs	2017-18
7-90	Stars	Casey Fields	2018-19
9-94	Heat	WACA	2016-17
99	Sixers	Adelaide Oval	2017-18

Best Bowling

		Overs	Versus	Venue	Season
M Kapp	4-10	4	Hurricanes	WACA, Perth	2021-22
AM King	4-11	4	Thunder	York Park, Launceston	2021-22
KH Brunt	4-17	4	Heat	Aquinas College, Perth	2015-16
S Glenn	4-18	4	Strikers	North Sydney Oval	2020-21
KJ Hartshorn	4-23	4	Hurricanes	Blacktown ISP	2015-16

Most Economical/Expensive Bowling (Min 4 overs)

Economical		v	Venue	Season	Expensive		v	Venue	Season
SW Bates	2-9	SS	Aquinas Coll	2015-16	TCJ Peschel	0-42	AS	Nth Syd No 1	2020-21
KJ Hartshorn	1-9	SS	SCG	2015-16	HL Graham	1-41	SS	Lilac Hill	2018-19
M Kapp	4-10	HH	WACA	2021-22	HNK Jensen	1-40	HH	Bellerive	2018-19
EL King	2-10	BH	WACA	2016-17	AM King	0-39	AS	Rolton Oval	2021-22
KH Brunt	3-11	MR	Camberwell	2017-18	KJ Hartshorn	0-39	MS	WACA	2017-18
KH Brunt	2-11	MS	WACA	2015-16	EL King	0-39	SS	Lilac Hill	2018-19

SYDNEY SIXERS - HONOUR ROLL

Season	Finished	Captain	Coach	MVP	Minor Rd W/L
2015-16	Second	EA Perry	Ben Sawyer	M Kapp	8/6
2016-17	Won Title	EA Perry/AJ Healy	Ben Sawyer	AJ Healy	9/5
2017-18	Won Title	EA Perry	Ben Sawyer	EA Perry	10/4
2018-19	Second	EA Perry	Ben Sawyer	EA Perry	10/4
2019-20	Fifth	EA Perry/AJ Healy	Ben Sawyer	M Kapp	7/7
2020-21	Fifth	EA Perry	Ben Sawyer	AJ Healy	6/6/2
2021-22	Last	EA Perry	Ben Sawyer	NE Bolton	4/9/1

Leading team records

Most Runs	M	Runs	HS	Avge	100/50	SR	Most Wickets	M	W	Econ	Best
EA Perry	96	3661	103*	50.16	2/21	102.7	M Kapp	83	90	5.31	4-18
AJ Healy	100	2646	112*	28.15	4/14	136.2	SE Aley	81	89	6.58	4-8
AK Gardner	95	1876	114	22.07	1/10	120.1	D van Niekerk	62	65	6.45	4-13
SJ McGlashan	64	923	79*	20.51	-/3	106.7	EA Perry	96	45	6.91	3-14

Highest Individual scores

		Balls	4s	6s		Venue	Season
AK Gardner	114	52	9	10	Stars	North Sydney No 1	2017-18
AJ Healy	112*	69	17	2	Strikers	Hurstville	2018-19
AJ Healy	111	52	15	6	Stars	North Sydney No 1	2020-21
AJ Healy	106*	53	13	4	Stars	WACA	2019-20
AJ Healy	106	66	13	3	Strikers	Hurstville Oval	2017-18
EA Perry	103*	64	10	5	Heat	SCG	2018-19
EA Perry	102*	59	14	2	Scorchers	North Sydney No 1	2018-19

Fastest Innings

Fastest 50	Balls	v	Venue	Season		Fastest 100	Balls	v	Venue	Season
AK Gardner	22	MS	Nth Syd No 1	2017-18		AK Gardner	47	MS	Nth Syd No 1	2017-18
AJ Healy	24	MS	Bellerive	2021-22		AJ Healy	47	MS	Nth Syd No 1	2020-21
SJ McGlashan	25	BH	Aquin Coll	2015-16		AJ Healy	52	MS	WACA	2019-20
AJ Healy	25	BH	SCG	2017-18		EA Perry	59	PS	Nth Syd No 1	2018-19
AJ Healy	26	AS	Hurst Oval	2019-20		AJ Healy	60	AS	Hurstville	2017-18
AJ Healy	26	MS	Nth Syd No 1	2020-21						

Highest Team totals

	Versus	Venue	Season
4-242	Stars	North Sydney Oval No 1	2017-18
1-206	Strikers	Hurstville Oval	2018-19
0-199	Stars	WACA	2019-20
6-192	Thunder	North Sydney Oval No 1	2019-20

Lowest Team totals

	Versus	Venue	Season
73	Heat	North Sydney No 1	2019-20
9-80	Stars	Drummoyne Oval	2015-16
81	Scorchers	Aquinas College, Perth	2015-16
82	Strikers	Adelaide Oval	2021-22

Best Bowling

		Overs	Versus	Venue	Season
SE Aley	4-8	3	Hurricanes	Waverley Oval, Sydney	2015-16
D van Niekerk	4-13	4	Renegades	Docklands	2017-18
M Kapp	4-18	4	Thunder	SCG	2015-16
SE Aley	4-18	4	Strikers	Adelaide Oval	2017-18

Most Economical/Expensive Bowling (Min 4 overs)

Economical		v	Venue	Season	Expensive		v	Venue	Season
M Kapp	1-8	MS	Drummoyne	2015-16	AK Gardner	0-41	MR	York Park	2021-22
M Kapp	3-9	PS	SCG	2015-16	EA Perry	0-40	PS	Hurstville	2020-21
M Kapp	2-9	MS	MCG	2018-19	SE Aley	0-39	MR	Geelong	2017-18
M Kapp	0-9	AS	Adel Oval	2016-17	MJ Brown	0-38	MS	Bellerive	2021-22
M Kapp	0-10	HH	Bellerive	2017-18	NE Bolton	0-37	MR	Lilac Hill	2021-22
					D van Niekerk	0-36	MR	Nth Syd No 1	2020-21

SYDNEY THUNDER - HONOUR ROLL

Season	Finished	Captain	Coach	MVP	Minor Rd W/L/NR
2015-16	Won Title	AJ Blackwell	Joanne Broadbent	SR Taylor	9/5
2016-17	Sixth	AJ Blackwell	Joanne Broadbent	H Kaur	6/7/1
2017-18	Third	AJ Blackwell	Joanne Broadbent	RL Haynes	10/4
2018-19	Third	AJ Blackwell	Joanne Broadbent	RH Priest	9/4/1
2019-20	Sixth	RL Haynes/AJ Blackwell	Trevor Griffin	HJ Darlington	5/8/1
2020-21	Won Title	RL Haynes	Trevor Griffin	HC Knight	7/5/2
2021-22	Seventh	HJ Darlington	Trevor Griffin	S Mandhana	4/8/2

Leading team records

Most Runs	M	Runs	HS	Avge	100/50	SR	Most Wickets	M	W	Econ	Best
RL Haynes	85	1919	78*	25.58	-/10	105/6	SL Bates	88	83	6.09	3-9
AJ Blackwell	72	1752	81*	34.35	-/6	106.1	RM Farrell	66	79	6.30	4-18
SR Taylor	58	1041	68	26.69	-/6	101.2	NJ Carey	59	62	6.72	4-12
NE Stalenberg	68	929	55	17.20	-/1	105.5	HJ Darlington	40	51	6.48	3-19

Highest Individual scores

	Balls	4s	6s		Venue	Season
S Mandhana	114*	64	14	3	Renegades	Mackay	2021-22
HC Knight	83	39	11	3	Strikers	Syd Showground	2020-21
AJ Blackwell	81*	58	10	1	Scorchers	WACA	2017-18
RL Haynes	78*	49	4	3	Stars	Howell, Penrith	2017-18

Fastest Fifties

	Balls	Versus	Venue	Season
H Kaur	23	Heat	North Sydney No 1	2018-19
RH Priest	26	Strikers	Wagga Wagga	2017-18
NJ Carey	30	Sixers	SCG	2015-16
HC Knight	30	Strikers	Sydney Showground	2020-21

Highest Team totals

	Versus	Venue	Season
6-200	Renegades	North Sydney Oval No 1	2017-18
4-192	Heat	North Sydney Oval No 1	2018-19
6-190	Strikers	Sydney Showground	2020-21
5-179	Scorchers	Lilac Hill	2018-19
7-171	Heat	Cazaly's Oval, Cairns	2018-19

Lowest Team totals

	Versus	Venue	Season
96	Heat	Drummoyne Oval	2019-20
5-96	Stars	York Park, Launceston	2021-22
97	Scorchers	Sydney Showgrounds	2020-21
5-102	Strikers	Howell Oval, Penrith	2016-17
103	Renegades	Docklands	2015-16

Best Bowling

		Overs	Versus	Venue	Season
NJ Carey	4-12	3.2	Hurricanes	Kingston Twin Ovals	2015-16
SR Taylor	4-15	4	Hurricanes	Launceston	2017-18
RM Farrell	4-18	4	Stars	Sydney University Oval	2015-16
LR Cheatle	4-20	4	Sixers	SCG	2015-16
SJ Johnson	4-26	4	Renegades	Hurstville Oval	2020-21
H Kaur	4-27	4	Stars	Albury	2016-17

Most Economical/Expensive Bowling (Min 4 overs)

Economical		v	Venue	Season	Expensive		v	Venue	Season
RM Farrell	1-8	SS	SCG	2015-16	RM Farrell	0-50	SS	Nth Syd No 1	2018-19
SL Bates	3-9	PS	Blacktown	2020-21	NJ Carey	1-50	HH	Launceston	2016-17
S Ismail	3-10	HH	Drummoyne	2020-21	SL Bates	2-49	BH	Nth Syd No 1	2018-19
S Ismail	1-11	MR	Junc Oval	2019-20	SJ Johnson	0-45	MR	Mackay	2021-22
RC Trenaman	2-11	SS	Syd Showgr	2018-19	RM Farrell	2-44	MR	Nth Syd No 1	2017-18
SJ Johnson	2-11	MS	Nth Syd No 1	2020-21	Nida Dar	2-44	SS	Nth Syd No 1	2019-20
SL Bates	1-11	MS	York Park	2021-22					

INTERSTATE 50 OVER COMPETITION
TASMANIA WINS FIRST WNCL TITLE

LADDER (8 games)

	W	L	NR	Bonus	Pts	Net Run Rate
Tasmania	7	1	-	3	31	+0.511
South Australia	4	2	2	3	23	+0.455
New South Wales	4	2	2	2	22	+0.807
Australian Capital Territory	4	3	1	4	22	+0.475
Queensland	4	3	1	3	21	+0.169
Victoria	1	6	1	1	7	-1.200
Western Australia	0	7	1	0	2	-1.215

MOST RUNS

	Team	M	Inns	NO	Runs	HS	Avge	S/Rate	100s	50s
CA Webb	SA	8	8	0	367	88	45.87	87.1	0	4
EJ Villani	Tas	9	9	1	356	111*	75.58	75.5	1	2
MC Hinkley	Qld	8	7	1	319	121*	53.16	76.8	1	2
RH Priest	Tas	9	9	0	309	110	34.33	73.7	1	1
E Manix-Geeves	Tas	9	9	2	300	104*	42.85	56.7	1	1
BE Patterson	SA	8	8	0	288	118	36.00	69.7	1	0

BEST SCORES

		Balls	4s	6s		Venue
MC Hinkley	121*	141	12	3	Qld v WA	Chisholm Oval, Canberra
EA Perry	120	94	10	4	Vic v NSW	Junction Oval
RL Haynes	118	132	13	1	NSW v ACT	Philip Oval, Canberra
BE Patterson	118	138	10	1	SA v Vic	Junction Oval
EJ Villani	111*	124	14	0	Tas v SA	Bellerive Oval

MOST WICKETS

Bowling	Team	M	Overs	Mdns	Runs	Wkts	Avge	Econ	Best	4i
SL Bates	Vic	7	61.3	4	269	16	16.81	4.37	5-29	1
EM Falconer	SA	8	61.3	3	288	14	20.57	4.68	5-56	2
GK Prestwidge	Qld	8	60	4	250	13	19.23	4.16	4-42	1
ML Gibson	Tas	9	73	5	288	13	22.15	3.94	5-19	1
SJ Coyte	Tas	8	71.4	3	299	13	23.00	4.17	3-39	-
ZE Cooke	ACT	8	53.5	8	187	12	15.58	3.47	3-5	-

BEST BOWLING

	Figures	Overs		Venue
S Campbell	7-25	8	NSW v ACT	Philip Oval, Canberra
ML Gibson	5-19	10	Tas v Vic	Shepley Oval, Dandenong
JL Jonassen	5-24	9.2	Qld v Tas	Bellerive Oval, Hobart
SL Bates	5-29	9.2	Vic v Qld	Kippax Oval, Canberra
SM Betts	5-46	10	SA v WA	Rolton Oval, Adelaide
Z Britcliffe	5-53	10	WA v Qld	Chisholm Oval, Canberra
EM Falconer	5-56	10	SA v ACT	Philip Oval, Canberra

Matches Played

December 17, 2021

Queensland 8-265 cc (G Voll 40, GM Harris 64, MC Hinkley 72; HL Graham 3-42) **defeated Tasmania 199** (44.2 overs) (NJ Carey 74; JL Jonassen 5-24) **by 66 runs at Bellerive Oval, Hobart.** *Award: JL Jonassen.*

Victoria 8-270 cc (AJ Sutherland 57, NM Faltum 88*: HJ Darlington 3-54) **lost to New South Wales 5-274** (43.1 overs) (RL Haynes 96, AJ Healy 51, EA Burns 80: SL Bates 3-61) **by five wickets at Junction Oval.** *Award: RL Haynes (119 balls, 12 fours).*

December 19, 2021

Queensland 6-223 cc (GP Redmayne 63: SJ Coyte 3-40) **lost to Tasmania 5-233** (45.1 overs) (NJ Carey 100*, HL Graham 55) **by five wickets at Bellerive Oval, Hobart.** *Award: NJ Carey (109 balls, 10 fours) added 101 in 21 overs with Heather Graham (65 balls, 5 fours).*

New South Wales 7-300 (46 overs) (TB Wilson 54, AK Gardner 57, PES Litchfield 88) **defeated Victoria 9-229** (35 overs) (EA Perry 120, NM Faltum 49) **by 26 runs (DLS Method).** *Elyse Perry (Award) faced 94 balls, hit 10 fours and 4 sixes.*

January 5, 2022

New South Wales 260 (49.5 overs) (RL Haynes 118; AB Yates 4-56, CM Leeson 3-42) **def ACT 53** (16 overs) (S Campbell 7-25) **by 207 runs at Philip Oval, Canberra.** *Award: Stella Campbell.*

February 22, 2022

New South Wales 0-15 (1.5 overs) **v ACT at North Sydney Oval – Match Abandoned due to rain.**

February 24, 2022

Victoria 87 (31.2 overs) (EA Osborne 4-15, ZE Cooke 3-5) **lost to ACT 5-91** (21.3 overs) (R McKenna 3-9) **by 5 wickets at Junction Oval, Melbourne.** *Award: Zoe Cooke.*

February 27, 2022

Western Australia 8-228 cc (MG Carmichael 75; SM Betts 5-46) **lost to South Australia 8-230** (47.5 overs) (E de Broughe 58; AL Edgar 4-35) **by 2 wickets at Rolton Oval, Adelaide.** *Award: Sam Betts.*

March 1, 2022

South Australia 7-296 cc (E de Broughe 93, CA Webb 61) **defeated Western Australia 210** (46.1 overs) (SM Betts 3-29, K Peterson 3-41) **by 86 runs at Rolton Oval, Adelaide.** *Award: Emma de Broughe (SA) faced 107 balls, hit 12 fours.*

March 2, 2022

Tasmania 9-212 cc (SJ Coyte 69*; R McKenna 3-41) **defeated Victoria 165** (44.4 overs) (SJ Coyte 3-39) **by 47 runs at Junction Oval, Melbourne.** *Award: Sarah Coyte batted at nine, came in at 7-83 and faced 79 balls, hit 7 fours, 2 sixes.*

March 6, 2022

South Australia 8-140 (35.3 overs) (GE Parsons 4-33) **v Queensland at North Sydney Oval. No result.**

Western Australia 6-188 cc (CL Piparo 54, M Darke 50) **lost to Tasmania 5-189** (45 overs) (E Manix-Geeves 68; Z Britcliffe 3-33) **by 5 wickets at Kippax Oval, Canberra.** *Award: Emma Manix-Geeves faced 125 balls.*

March 9, 2022

Tasmania 7-241 cc (RH Priest 110, EJ Villani 78; CM Leeson 3-43) **defeated ACT 222** (48.1 overs) (KM Mack 53) **by 19 runs at Philip Oval, Canberra.** *Award: Rachel Priest (124 balls, 14 fours) added 152 in 32 overs with Elyse Villani (108 balls, 6 fours)*

March 10, 2022

Victoria 8-180 cc (MA Blows 64; CG Sippel 4-47) **lost to Queensland 116** (39.2 overs) (SL Bates 5-29, E Hayward 3-13) **by 64 runs at Kippax Oval, Canberra.** *Award: Sam Bates.*

March 11, 2022

Western Australia 9-195 cc (AL Edgar 85*; SJ Johnson 3-39) **lost to New South Wales 2-196** (39.4 overs) (RC Trenaman 90*) **by 8 wickets at North Sydney Oval.** *Award: Rachel Trenaman 109 balls, hit 8 fours, 1 six and added 149 in 32 overs with Tahlia Wilson (110 balls, 6 fours)*

South Australia 8-222 cc (EM Falconer 50*; A Smith 3-47) **lost to Tasmania 5-223** (39.2 overs) (EJ Villani 63) **by 5 wickets at Philip Oval, Canberra.** *Award: Molly Strano for 2-44 and making 49* off 40 balls, with 6 fours.*

March 13, 2022

ACT 9-224 cc (EA Osborne 58, CM Leeson 50; GK Prestwidge 4-42) **defeated Queensland 138** (36.2 overs) (CG Sippel 54*) **by 86 runs at Philip Oval, Canberra.** *Award: Erin Osborne (102 balls, 3 fours, 1 six) also took 1-24.*

March 15, 2022

ACT 166 (46 overs) (EA Osborne 53; JL Barsby 3-36) **lost to South Australia 3-167** (35.3 overs) (CA Webb 72, JE Dooley 65*) **by 7 wickets at Philip Oval, Canberra.** *Award: Courtney Webb faced 89 balls, hit 6 fours, she and Josie Dooley (94 balls, 2 fours) added 137 for the third wicket.*

New South Wales 198 (48.3 overs) (A Learoyd 51; A Smith 3-32, ML Gibson 3-43) **lost to Tasmania 6-199** (42.4 overs) (RH Priest 84; MJ Brown 3-31, SJ Johnson 3-43) **by 4 wickets at North Sydney Oval.** *Award: Rachel Priest faced 94 balls, hit 13 fours.*

Queensland 231 (49 overs) (MC Hinkley 64; Z Britcliffe 5-53) **defeated Western Australia 162** (39.3 overs) (ME Bouchier 79; G Voll 3-20) **by 69 runs at Chisholm Oval, Canberra.** *Award: G Voll.*

March 17, 2022

Victoria 130 (50 overs) (ML Gibson 5-19) **lost to Tasmania 3-131** (31.1 overs) **by 7 wickets.** *Award: Maisy Gibson.*

March 18, 2022

ACT 8-282 cc (KM Mack 107; EM Falconer 5-56) **defeated South Australia 172** (43 overs) (CA Webb 57, E de Broughe 54; CL Rafferty 3-16, GJ Sutcliffe 3-24) **by 110 runs at Philip Oval, Canberra.** *Award: Katie Mack faced 134 balls, hit 12 fours.*

Western Australia 7-208 cc lost to Queensland 7-213 (47.1 overs) (MC Hinkley 121*; PM Cleary 3-36) **by 3 wickets at Chisholm Oval, Canberra.** *Award: Mikayla faced 141 balls, hit 12 fours and 3 sixes.*

March 20, 2022

Western Australia 117 (37.4 overs) (ZE Cooke 3-29) **lost to ACT 4-120** (18.1 overs) (OP Porter 58) **by 6 wickets at Philip Oval, Canberra.** *Award: Erin Osborne who also made 32 not out.*

March 21, 2022

South Australia 5-264 cc (BE Patterson 118, JE Dooley 63; KJ Garth 3-42) **defeated Victoria 139** (43.3 overs) (EM Falconer 4-30, JL Barnsy 3-23) **by 125 runs at Junction Oval, Melbourne.** *Award: Bridget Patterson (138 balls, 10 fours, 1 six) added 144 in 28 overs with Josie Dooley (96 balls, 5 fours)*

March 22, 2022

Queensland 7-214 cc (G Voll 52) **defeated New South Wales 9-152 cc** (CR Knott 3-24) **by 62 runs at Hurstville Oval.** *Award: Charli Knott.*

March 27, 2022 – The Final at Bellerive Oval Hobart.

South Australia 8-242 cc (CA Webb 88, JE Dooley 66; A Smith 3-33) **lost to Tasmania 1-245** (47.4 overs) (EJ Villani 111*, E Manix-Geeves 104*) **by 9 wickets.** *Award: Elyse Villani (124 balls, 14 fours) and opener Emma Manix-Geeves (133 balls, 8 fours) added 205 in 39 overs to steer Tasmania home to its first ever WNCL title. Earlier Josie Dooley (82 balls, 6 fours) and Courtney Webb (78 balls, 11 fours) added 113 in 20 overs for the third wicket, but at 2-208 in the 45th over, lost 6-34 in the last 33 balls.*

AUSTRALIAN CAPITAL TERRITORY

Batting & Fielding	M	Inn	NO	Runs	HS	Avge	100s	50s	S/Rate	Ct	St
EA Osborne	8	7	2	180	58	36.00	0	2	64.28	6	-
ZE Cooke	8	5	2	82	30	27.33	0	0	79.61	2	-
KM Mack	8	7	0	186	107	26.57	1	1	76.54	6	-
OP Porter	8	7	0	152	58	21.71	0	1	83.51	1	-
RL Carter	5	4	0	84	33	21.00	0	0	57.93	2	-
EJ Kershaw	7	6	0	104	39	17.33	0	0	56.52	5	2
CM Leeson	8	7	1	82	50	13.66	0	1	58.57	2	-
AS Wikman	4	3	0	30	20	10.00	0	0	65.21	3	-
NM Hancock	6	5	1	36	16	9.00	0	0	62.06	2	-
CL Rafferty	7	5	2	25	20	8.33	0	0	86.20	0	-
AB Yates	8	5	0	30	24	6.00	0	0	75.00	3	-
MM Penna	1	1	0	6	6	6.00	0	0	31.57	1	-
AR Reakes	1	1	0	5	5	5.00	0	0	83.33	1	-
KR Burton	1	1	0	2	2	2.00	0	0	25.00	3	-
AJ Bates	5	3	3	19	13*	-	0	0	76.00	0	-

Also played: GJ Sutcliffe (3 matches) did not bat, 1 catch.

Bowling	M	Overs	M	Runs	Wkts	Avge	Best	Econ	SR	4w
ZE Cooke	8	53.5	8	187	12	15.58	3-5	3.47	26.9	1
CM Leeson	8	40.3	1	164	8	20.50	3-42	4.04	30.3	0
CL Rafferty	7	37	2	150	8	18.75	3-16	4.05	27.7	0
AB Yates	8	32	1	180	8	22.50	4-56	5.62	24.0	0
EA Osborne	8	51.4	4	178	7	25.42	4-15	3.44	44.2	0
GJ Sutcliffe	3	14	1	50	5	10.00	3-24	3.57	16.8	0
NM Hancock	6	34	1	140	4	35.00	2-27	4.11	51.0	0
AJ Bates	5	15	0	77	4	19.25	2-24	5.13	22.5	0

Also bowled: M Penna 2-0-19-0, O Porter 3-0-15-0, A Wikman 2.3-0-11-0,

NEW SOUTH WALES

Batting & Fielding	M	Inn	NO	Runs	HS	Avge	100s	50s	S/Rate	Ct	St
RL Haynes	3	3	0	238	118	79.33	1	1	81.50	2	-
RC Trenaman	4	4	2	112	90*	56.00	0	1	72.72	2	-
EA Burns	7	5	1	166	80*	41.50	0	1	133.87	3	-
HJ Darlington	3	1	0	32	32	32.00	0	0	84.21	1	-
TB Wilson	7	7	1	163	67	27.16	0	2	67.35	6	1
AK Gardner	3	3	0	81	57	27.00	0	1	96.42	4	-
AJ Healy	2	2	0	51	51	25.50	0	1	77.27	3	-
AB Learoyd	7	5	1	98	51	24.50	0	1	63.63	2	-
PES Litchfield	7	6	1	119	88	23.80	0	1	89.47	4	-
MJ Brown	7	4	1	64	43	21.33	0	0	56.14	3	-
LG Smith	5	3	0	47	30	15.66	0	0	48.95	2	-
SM Horley	3	1	0	13	13	13.00	0	0	81.25	0	-
JE Allen	4	2	1	11	8*	11.00	0	0	52.38	1	-
SJ Johnson	5	3	0	24	19	8.00	0	0	43.63	1	-
CF Moore	3	2	0	5	5	2.50	0	0	20.00	0	-
AA Genford	2	1	1	45	45*	-	0	0	72.58	0	-
SR Campbell	4	2	2	4	4*	-	0	0	50.00	0	-

Also played: EL Hughes (1 match) did not bat.

Bowling	M	Overs	M	Runs	Wkts	Avge	Best	Econ	SR	4w
SR Campbell	4	23	1	135	10	13.50	7-25	5.86	13.8	0
MJ Brown	7	50.4	4	221	9	24.55	3-31	4.36	33.7	0
SJ Johnson	5	25	1	132	9	14.66	3-39	5.28	16.6	0
EA Burns	7	43.5	0	186	6	31.00	2-18	4.24	43.8	0
HJ Darlington	3	17	1	91	5	18.20	3-54	5.35	20.4	0
AK Gardner	3	16	0	76	3	25.33	2-41	4.75	32.0	0
JE Allen	4	28	0	139	3	46.33	2-55	4.96	56.0	0
LG Smith	5	17	0	69	1	69.00	1-37	4.05	102.0	0

Also bowled: E Hughes 9-0-41-1, A Genford 4-0-14-0, S Horley 10.1-3-25-0.

QUEENSLAND

Batting & Fielding

Batting & Fielding	M	Inn	NO	Runs	HS	Avge	100s	50s	S/Rate	Ct	St
MC Hinkley	8	7	1	319	121*	53.16	1	2	76.86	2	-
GM Harris	2	2	0	99	64	49.50	0	1	81.81	1	-
CG Sippel	7	5	3	77	54*	38.50	0	1	53.10	2	-
GP Redmayne	2	2	0	68	63	34.00	0	1	70.10	0	-
G Voll	8	7	0	187	52	26.71	0	1	64.48	5	-
CR Knott	8	7	0	148	36	21.14	0	0	61.15	2	-
CE Mair	6	5	3	41	14*	20.50	0	0	64.06	12	4
ER Johnston	8	7	1	104	34	17.33	0	0	57.77	2	-
HL Ferling	6	5	0	83	44	16.60	0	0	85.56	3	-
JL Jonassen	2	2	0	27	15	13.50	0	0	93.10	0	-
TA Wheeler	5	4	0	53	18	13.25	0	0	34.41	1	-
GK Prestwidge	8	4	2	21	14	10.50	0	0	72.41	4	-
LM Kimmince	6	5	0	33	14	6.60	0	0	137.50	4	-
GE Parsons	6	3	0	13	8	4.33	0	0	61.90	4	-
MR Dixon	2	2	1	2	1*	2.00	0	0	66.66	1	-
LK Hamilton	2	2	0	3	3	1.50	0	0	21.42	0	-

Also played: LG Mills (2 matches) did not bat, 1 catch.

Bowling

Bowling	M	Overs	M	Runs	Wkts	Avge	Best	Econ	SR	4w
GK Prestwidge	8	60	4	250	13	19.23	4-42	4.16	27.6	1
CG Sippel	7	53	3	232	10	23.20	4-47	4.37	31.8	1
CR Knott	8	43	3	157	9	17.44	3-24	3.65	28.6	0
JL Jonassen	2	19.2	1	62	6	10.33	5-24	3.20	19.3	0
GE Parsons	6	47	1	188	6	31.33	4-33	4.00	47.0	1
G Voll	8	33.1	1	153	6	25.50	3-20	4.61	33.1	0
HL Ferling	6	55.3	10	144	5	28.80	2-18	2.59	66.6	0
MR Dixon	2	17	1	74	3	24.66	2-28	4.35	34.0	0
GM Harris	2	16	1	78	2	39.00	1-34	4.87	48.0	0
LK Hamilton	2	12.3	0	70	2	35.00	2-35	5.60	37.5	0

Also bowled: LG Mills 8-0-57-0

SOUTH AUSTRALIA

Batting & Fielding

Batting & Fielding	M	Inn	NO	Runs	HS	Avge	100s	50s	S/Rate	Ct	St
CA Webb	8	8	0	367	88	45.87	0	4	87.17	1	-
BE Patterson	8	8	0	288	118	36.00	1	0	69.73	1	-
E de Broughe	8	8	0	287	93	35.87	0	3	64.34	2	-
JE Dooley	8	8	1	243	66	34.71	0	3	61.36	5	-
EM Falconer	8	7	4	103	50*	34.33	0	1	119.76	1	-
SM Betts	8	4	3	28	17*	28.00	0	0	63.63	5	-
AV O'Neil	8	8	1	135	48	19.28	0	0	84.90	3	-
TJ McPharlin	8	7	1	78	37	13.00	0	0	85.71	3	2
JL Barsby	8	6	2	43	20	10.75	0	0	61.42	5	-
K Peterson	8	6	1	36	26*	7.20	0	0	64.28	3	-
BL Harris	8	1	1	1	1*	-	0	0	20.00	1	-

Bowling

Bowling	M	Overs	M	Runs	Wkts	Avge	Best	Econ	SR	4w
EM Falconer	8	61.3	3	288	14	20.57	5-56	4.68	26.3	2
SM Betts	8	60.1	3	249	11	22.63	5-46	4.13	32.8	1
JL Barsby	8	60.2	2	271	11	24.63	3-23	4.49	32.9	0
BL Harris	8	60.4	3	279	8	34.87	2-23	4.59	45.5	0
K Peterson	8	63	0	290	7	41.42	3-41	4.60	54.0	0
CA Webb	8	17	1	93	1	93.00	1-28	5.47	102.0	0

TASMANIA

Batting & Fielding	M	Inn	NO	Runs	HS	Avge	100s	50s	S/Rate	Ct	St
NJ Carey	2	2	1	174	100*	174.00	1	1	85.29	0	-
EJ Villani	9	9	1	356	111*	44.50	1	2	75.58	2	-
E Manix-Geeves	9	9	2	300	104*	42.85	1	1	56.71	2	-
RH Priest	9	9	0	309	110	34.33	1	1	73.74	8	5
CL Hall	7	6	2	134	48	33.50	0	0	87.01	4	-
HL Graham	2	2	0	56	55	28.00	0	1	77.77	0	-
A Smith	8	2	0	40	36	20.00	0	0	90.90	2	1
NE Stalenberg	9	8	2	119	31	19.83	0	0	82.06	4	-
MR Strano	9	7	2	98	49*	19.60	0	0	85.21	2	-
SK Moloney	9	6	3	58	24*	19.33	0	0	82.85	5	-
ML Gibson	9	4	1	41	16*	13.66	0	0	54.66	4	-
BW Vakarewa	2	1	0	0	0	0.00	0	0	0.00	1	-
SJ Coyte	8	2	2	69	69*	-	0	1	87.34	2	-
C Scott	4	1	1	1	1*	-	0	0	100.00	1	-

Also played: HI Silver-Holmes (3 matches) did not bat.

Bowling	M	Overs	M	Runs	Wkts	Avge	Best	Econ	SR	4w
ML Gibson	9	73	5	288	13	22.15	5-19	3.94	33.6	1
SJ Coyte	8	71.4	3	299	13	23.00	3-39	4.17	33.0	0
MR Strano	9	82.3	3	331	11	30.09	3-39	4.01	45.0	0
A Smith	8	50	3	207	11	18.81	3-32	4.14	27.2	0
SK Moloney	9	61.1	7	219	9	24.33	3-26	3.58	40.7	0
HL Graham	2	20	1	88	5	17.60	3-42	4.40	24.0	0
C Scott	4	25	4	109	3	36.33	2-39	4.36	50.0	0
HI Silver-Holmes	3	15	1	79	2	39.50	1-19	5.26	45.0	0
BW Vakarewa	2	20	1	79	1	79.00	1-50	3.95	120.0	0
NJ Carey	2	18	1	106	1	106.00	1-47	5.88	108.0	0

Also bowled: NE Stalenberg 3-0-19-0.

VICTORIA

Batting & Fielding	M	Inn	NO	Runs	HS	Avge	100s	50s	S/Rate	Ct	St
EA Perry	2	2	0	132	120	66.00	1	0	126.92	1	-
NM Faltum	7	7	1	189	88*	31.50	0	1	68.23	9	3
AJ Sutherland	2	2	0	57	57	28.50	0	1	76.00	1	-
MA Blows	5	5	0	106	64	21.20	0	1	43.44	1	-
SF Day	7	6	2	67	27*	16.75	0	0	55.83	1	-
KJ Garth	7	7	0	111	35	15.85	0	0	60.32	1	-
EL Hayward	5	5	1	62	24	15.50	0	0	45.58	2	-
RM McKenna	4	4	0	60	33	15.00	0	0	70.58	0	-
AJ Lanning	7	7	1	78	40	13.00	0	0	48.44	3	-
S Reid	3	3	0	37	22	12.33	0	0	60.65	2	-
TJ Vlaeminck	2	2	1	10	10	10.00	0	0	71.42	0	-
AJ Vine	4	4	0	36	25	9.00	0	0	36.00	1	-
RK O'Donnell	7	7	0	52	15	7.42	0	0	41.60	1	-
TM Flintoff	7	7	0	51	15	7.28	0	0	52.04	1	-
SL Bates	7	4	2	14	13	7.00	0	0	32.55	4	-
T Atkinson	1	1	0	6	6	6.00	0	0	75.00	0	-

Bowling	M	Overs	M	Runs	Wkts	Avge	Best	Econ	SR	4w
SL Bates	7	61.3	4	269	16	16.81	5-29	4.37	23.0	0
KJ Garth	7	54	3	221	7	31.57	3-42	4.09	46.2	0
RM McKenna	4	22.1	1	99	6	16.50	3-9	4.46	22.1	1
EL Hayward	5	25	1	92	3	30.66	3-13	3.68	50.0	0
SF Day	7	33.3	1	184	3	61.33	2-60	5.49	67.0	0
TM Flintoff	7	35	1	186	2	93.00	1-23	5.31	105.0	0
AJ Sutherland	2	16	1	100	2	50.00	1-41	6.25	48.0	0
EA Perry	2	7	0	34	1	34.00	1-10	4.85	42.0	0
RK O'Donnell	7	13	0	79	1	79.00	1-18	6.07	78.0	0
TJ Vlaeminck	2	14	0	88	1	88.00	1-49	6.28	84.0	0

WESTERN AUSTRALIA

Batting & Fielding	M	Inn	NO	Runs	HS	Avge	100s	50s	S/Rate	Ct	St
C Bekker	5	3	2	47	36*	47.00	0	0	82.45	0	-
AL Edgar	7	7	2	199	85*	39.80	0	1	62.18	1	-
PM Cleary	5	5	2	103	36	34.33	0	0	61.30	0	-
MG Carmichael	7	7	0	164	75	23.42	0	1	70.99	1	-
CL Piparo	7	7	0	157	54	22.42	0	1	50.64	4	-
ME Bouchier	6	6	0	130	79	21.66	0	1	88.43	3	-
AL Day	5	5	0	103	34	20.60	0	0	48.35	1	-
MC Darke	7	7	0	135	50	19.28	0	1	60.00	12	2
P Stockwell	2	2	0	34	25	17.00	0	0	69.38	0	-
GL Wyllie	6	4	1	30	13	10.00	0	0	54.54	1	-
SA Cooper	3	2	1	9	5	9.00	0	0	69.23	0	-
MB Healy	4	4	0	27	19	6.75	0	0	49.09	0	-
TCJ Peschel	6	6	0	31	9	5.16	0	0	40.25	1	-
ZR Britcliffe	5	3	1	9	8	4.50	0	0	39.13	1	-
J Naidoo	2	2	1	2	2*	2.00	0	0	40.00	0	-

Bowling	M	Overs	M	Runs	Wkts	Avge	Best	Econ	SR	4w
ZR Britcliffe	5	34.5	2	174	10	17.40	5-53	4.99	20.9	1
AL Edgar	7	46.1	1	209	7	29.85	4-35	4.52	39.5	1
PM Cleary	5	39	4	150	6	25.00	3-36	3.84	39.0	0
C Bekker	5	34.5	0	151	5	30.20	2-25	4.33	41.8	0
GL Wyllie	6	44	2	215	5	43.00	2-49	4.88	52.8	0
TCJ Peschel	6	51	5	270	4	67.50	2-62	5.29	76.5	0
MB Healy	4	23	1	117	2	58.50	1-28	5.08	69.0	0
J Naidoo	2	15	0	102	1	102.00	1-71	6.80	90.0	0

Also bowled: S Cooper 9-0-62-0

WNCL RECORDS, RECENT WINNERS
(The modern WNCL came into being in 1996-97)

1989-90	New South Wales	1996-97 to 2001-02	New South Wales	2017-18	New South Wales
1990-91	Victoria	2002-03	Victoria	2018-19	New South Wales
1991-92	South Australia	2003-04	New South Wales	2019-20	Western Australia
1992-93	South Australia	2004-05	Victoria	2020-21	Queensland
1993-94	New South Wales	2005-06 to 2014-15	New South Wales	2021-22	Tasmania
1994-95	South Australia	2015-16	South Australia		
1995-96	Victoria	2016-17	New South Wales		

RESULTS

Team	Matches	Won	Lost	Tied	NR
Australian Capital Territory	88	41	46	0	1
New South Wales	229	179	46	2	2
Queensland	195	80	107	2	6
South Australia	193	83	105	1	4
Tasmania	78	23	54	1	0
Victoria	214	124	86	1	3
Western Australia	195	53	139	1	2

LEADING RUN SCORERS

	M	Inn	NO	Runs	HS	Avge	S/Rate	100s	50s	Sixes
KL Rolton	114	111	14	5521	173	56.92	73.97	14	41	23
AJ Blackwell	139	129	27	4788	157	46.94	71.48	11	30	12
RL Haynes	**116**	**113**	**8**	**4528**	**156**	**43.12**	**76.31**	**9**	**27**	**28**
BJ Clark	89	89	13	4059	122*	53.41	66.55	7	35	5
EJ Villani	**100**	**99**	**7**	**3657**	**173**	**39.75**	**83.30**	**9**	**18**	**33**
MJ Bulow	122	120	1	3617	130	30.39	60.13	7	16	9
KL Britt	114	111	17	3471	145*	36.93	66.83	2	21	14
LC Sthalekar	145	128	28	3393	108*	33.93	69.80	2	17	0
M Jones	122	120	10	3338	95	30.35	58.82	0	21	8
NE Bolton	92	90	7	3162	170*	38.10	70.53	9	13	5
LM Keightly	91	91	8	3108	144*	37.45	54.16	3	21	2

HIGHEST SCORES

MM Lanning	190	(153)	Vic v Tas	Bellerive Oval	2016-17
MM Lanning	175	(143)	Vic v ACT	Manuka Oval	2012-13
KL Rolton	173	(136)	SA v WA	Adel Oval No 2	1998-99
EJ Villani	173	(129)	Vic v SA	Camberwell	2012-13
NE Bolton	170*	(156)	Vic v Tas	Bellerive Oval	2014-15
BL Mooney	163	(139)	Qld v WA	Allan Border Field	2020-21

RECORD PARTNERSHIPS

					Venue	Season
1	267	NE Bolton	EJ Villani	WA v Vic	Junction Oval	2015-16
2	288	MM Lanning	JE Duffin	Vic v Tas	Bellerive Oval	2016-17
3	232	AJ Blackwell	EA Perry	NSW v ACT	Manuka Oval	2015-16
4	194	CL Piparo	MG Carmichael	WA v ACT	Murdoch Uni, Perth	2017-18
5	163	JC Price	TE Brown	Qld v NSW	Allan Border Field	2004-05
6	**117**	**EA Perry**	**NM Faltum**	**Vic v NSW**	**Junction Oval**	**2021-22**
7	125*	M Penna	NM Hancock	ACT v WA	WACA, Perth	2020-21
8	103*	KLH Short	DM Kimmince	Qld v NSW	Allan Border Field	2012-13
9	80*	KM Beams	NM Faltum	Vic v Qld	Allan Border Field	2017-18
10	56	RS Dick	GA Elwiss	ACT v Tas	Launceston	2010-11

LEADING WICKET TAKERS

	M	Balls	Runs	Wkts	Avge	Best	4i	Econ
LC Sthalekar	145	7194	3628	167	21.72	4-7		3.03
CL Fitzpatrick	103	5487	2614	148	17.66	6-22	2	2.86
RM Farrell	82	3921	2538	134	18.94	6-17	5	3.88
CR Smith	117	6006	3065	128	23.95	5-10	5	3.06
EA Perry	**85**	**3916**	**2459**	**117**	**21.02**	**5-11**	**6**	**3.77**
JL Jonassen	**74**	**3782**	**2356**	**116**	**20.31**	**5-24**	**4**	**3.74**
J Hayes	111	5731	3026	114	26.54	4-12	3	3.17
EA Osborne	**96**	**4294**	**2601**	**112**	**23.22**	**4-15**	**4**	**3.63**
KM Beams	76	3367	2149	107	20.08	6-20	8	3.83
KL Rolton	114	3969	1946	106	18.36	5-7	6	2.94

BEST BOWLING

SR Theodore	7-14	Vic v WA	Kingsway, Perth	1998-99
S Campbell	**7-25**	**NSW v ACT**	**Philip Oval, Canberra**	**2021-22**
RM Farrell	6-17	NSW v Qld	Robina	2018-19
KM Beams	6-20	Vic v ACT	Central Res, Melb	2011-12
CL Fitzpatrick	6-22	Vic v NSW	Central Res, Melb	2006-07

BEST ECONOMY IN AN INNINGS (10 over spells)

C Dittmar	1-5	SA v Vic	Punt Road	1998-99
LC Sthalakar	2-7	NSW v SA	Bankstown Oval	2007-08
KL Rolton	5-7	SA v WA	Adel Oval No 2	2004-05
B Matheson	2-8	Qld v Vic	Allan Border Field	2003-04

WICKET KEEPING

		M	Ct/St	Total
EJ Inglis	Vic/WA	90	68/46	114
AJ Healy	**NSW**	**75**	**80/30**	**110**
JCL Wallace	NSW/WA	76	69/31	100
LA Coleman	NSW/ACT	101	61/39	100

FIELDING

		M	Total
KL Britt	SA/ACT	114	70
AJ Blackwell	NSW	139	57
BJ Clark	NSW/Vic	89	53
LC Sthalekar	NSW	145	52

MOST RUNS/WICKETS FOR EACH STATE

		M	Runs	HS	Avge	100/50		M	Wkts	Avge	Best
ACT	KM Mack	58	2076	113*	37.75	4/14	SL Bates	41	48	27.92	4-7
NSW	AJ Blackwell	139	4788	157	46.94	11/30	LC Sthalekar	145	167	21.72	4-7
Qld	MJ Bulow	122	3617	130	30.39	7/16	JL Jonassen	74	116	20.31	5-24
SA	KL Rolton	114	5521	173	56.92	14/41	KL Rolton	114	106	18.36	5-7
Tas	CL Hall	63	1626	95	29.56	0/11	V Pyke	53	56	35.82	3-19
Vic	M Jones	122	3338	95	30.35	0/21	CL Fitzpatrick	103	148	17.66	6-22
WA	NE Bolton	85	2762	129	35.41	7/13	AJ Fahey	124	92	33.96	5-8

STATE BY STATE AWARDS

Australian Capital Territory: Meteors WNCL award (Calver Medal) – Erin Osborne.

New South Wales (Belinda Clark Medal): Maitlan Brown. WNCL Award: Erin Burns. Sydney Sixers Award: Nicole Boland. Sydney Thunder (Alex Blackwell Medal): Smriti Mandhana

Queensland Fire Player of the Year: Georgia Redmayne. Brisbane Heat MVP: Mikayla Hinkley

South Australia (Andrea McCauley trophy - WNCL MVP): Courtney Webb. Adelaide Strikers MVP: Katie Mack

Tasmania Player of the Year: Emma Manix-Geeves. Hobart Hurricanes MVP: Tayla Vlaeminck

Victoria (Sharon Tredrea Medal - WNCL MVP): Nicole Faltum. Renegades MVP: Harmanpreet Kaur. Stars: Kim Garth

Western Australia WNCL MVP (Zoe Goss Medal): Amy Edgar, Scorchers: Sophie Devine

STATE BY STATE PREMIER COMPETITIONS

ACT A Grade Final (Lynne O'Meara Cup – 40 over Final) at Kingston Oval on March 12, 2022. Western District 127 (36.4 overs) (E Edwards 3-21) **lost to Eastlake 4-128** (28.4 overs) (E Edwards 37*) **by 6 wickets. T20 Grand Final (Glenda Hall Shield) at Philip Oval on March 6, 2022. Queanbeyan 6-125 cc** (A Horsfall 39, S Wilde 35) **defeated Ginninderra 86** (20 overs) (E Rebus 4-12). **SJ Moore Medal: Cherie Taylor (Western District). Most Promising player (Sarah Hodgson Shield): Alana Horsfall. Team of the season:** Katie Mack (Tuggeranong), Janet King (Eastlake), Rebecca Carter (Ginninderra), Angela Reakes (Weston Creek Molonglo), Claire Koski (Ginninderra), Carly Leeson (Eastlake), Erica Kershaw (Eastlake), Mali Vanderstoep (Queanbeyan), Stella Wilde (Queanbeyan), Amber Smith (Weston Creek Molonglo), Sophie Gould (Ginninderra). Coach of the Year – Michael Minns (Western District)

NEW SOUTH WALES First Grade (50-over) Final at Drummoyne Oval on April 3, 2022. Penrith 96 (48.2 overs) (NE Bryson-Smith 6-18) **lost to Sydney 2-98** (25.2 overs) (NJ McDonald 40) **by 8 wickets. Player of the match: Nell Bryson-Smith (Sydney).** *It was Penrith's second flag in three seasons. This was the second attempt at the final after the first effort on March 27 could not be completed due to rain. Scores from that game – Penrith 114 (41.1 overs) (SJ Johnson 4-11) v Sydney 3-41 (14 overs)* **Player of the year: Saskia Horley (Manly-Warringah).** Team of the year: Saskia Horley (Captain, Manly-Warringah), Heidi Cheadle (Gordon), Rhiannon Dick (St George-Sutherland), Grace Dignam (Northern District), Anika Learoyd (Campbelltown-Camden), Naomi McDonald (Sydney), Kate Pelle (Keeper, Parramatta), Samantha Devlin (Bankstown), Ebony Hoskin (Campbelltown-Camden), Jannatul Sumona (Bankstown), Jaclyn Vickery (St George-Sutherland), Kira Churchland (Sydney)

Leading Batting	Runs	Avg	HS	100	50	Leading Bowling	Wkt	Avge	Econ	Best
Saskia Horley (Manly-Warr)	**646**	**92.2**	**129***	**2**	**3**	**Samantha Devlin (Bankstown)**	**21**	**13.6**	**3.33**	**5-22**
Rhiannon Dick (St G-Sutherland)	413	68.8	82	-	3	Ebony Hoskin (Camp-Camden)	19	13.6	3.55	5-25
Naomi McDonald (Sydney)	398	66.3	113*	1	1	Rhiannon Dick (St G-Sutherland)	18	12.2	3.61	3-33
Heidi Cheadle (Gordon)	397	44.1	107*	1	3	Jaclyn Vickery (St G-Sutherland)	18	29.6	3.44	4-16

QUEENSLAND A Grade Final (Kathryn Raymont Shield – 50 over final) at Norman Gray Oval on Marcgh 27, 2022. University of Queensland 9-128 cc (GK Prestwidge 3-20, CR Coulson 3-29) **lost to Valley 9-129** (49.2 overs) (L Scheiwe 3-24) **by 1 wicket. Twenty20 Final at Ian Healy Oval on January 22, 2022: Western Suburbs 9-89 cc lost to Sunshine Coast 8-90** (20 overs) (HL Ferling 2-13, L Hamilton 2-7) **by 2 wickets. Kath Smith Medal: Tied between Ruby Strange (Uni of Qld) and Tara Wheeler (Gold Coast).** Loretta Moore Trophy (Most improved Under 21) - Ruby Strange (University of Qld). **Team of the year:** Tara Wheeler (Gold Coast), Annie Wikman (Captain, Wests), Georgia Voll (Sandgate-Redcliffe), Mikayla Hinkley (Valley), Chelsea Gan (Wynnum-Manly/Redlands), Charlotte Lutz (Sunshine Coast), Kira Holmes (Valley), Ruby Strange (UQ), Holly Ferling (Wests), Darcey Johnson (Sandgate-Redcliffe), Charni Bloxsom (UQ), Emmie Blamey (UQ), Coach: Mark Daldy (UQ)

Leading Batting	Runs	Avg	HS	100	50	Leading Bowling	Wkt	Avge	Econ	Best
Tara Wheeler (Gold Coast)	**813**	**33.8**	**103**	**1**	**7**	**Emmie Blamey (Uni of Qld)**	**38**	**16.7**	**3.92**	**4-34**
Carly Fuller (Gold Coast)	665	31.6	74	-	4	Ruby Strange (Uni of Qld)	35	13.4	3.92	5-17
Kira Holmes (Valley)	640	27.8	73	-	4	Charlotte Briggs (Sunshine Coast)	34	18.2	4.34	3-16
Charlotte Lutz (Sunshine Coast)	590	34.7	82	-	3	Christina Coulson (Valley)	31	16.0	3.16	5-37

SOUTH AUSTRALIA First Grade (50 overs) Final at Glenelg Oval on March 27, 2022. Kensington 8-199 cc (SJ Lowe 79; T Saville 3-24, A Mushangwe 3-25) **defeated Glenelg 166** (46.4 overs) (A Mushangwe 47, E Larosa 47*) **by 33 runs.** *Player of the final was Kensington skipper Sarah Lowe (117 balls, 6 fours, 1 six).*
T20 Grand Final at Rolton Oval on Dec 22, 2021 (floodlit): Northern Districts 6-134 cc (TJ McPharlin 66; K Peterson 3-11) **defeated Glenelg 7-114** (20 overs) (TM McGrath 35, CA Webb 35; DR Brown 2-10, EL Filsell 2-29, C Rosenzweig 2-17) **by 20 runs.**
Karen Rolton Medal: Won by Courtney Webb (Glenelg) on 20 votes, runner-up was Sanigdha Bansal (Kensington) on 13, with Jemma Barsby (Northern Districts) on 12. Spirit of Cricket: Adelaide University. Marg Jude Wicketkeeping Trophy: Rachel Church (Kensington). Joanne Broadbent Fielding Trophy: Maggie Clark (West Torrens). Shelley Nitschke Medal (Twenty20 Cup Player of the Series): Eliza Doddridge (Kensington).

SACA Team of the season: Josie Dooley (wk) (Sturt), Emma de Broughe (Sturt), Courtney Webb (Glenelg), Paris Hall (West Torrens), Eliza Doddridge (Kensington), Kate Peterson (Glenelg), Kelly Armstrong (West Torrens), Sarah Lowe (Captain, Kensington), Anesu Mushangwe (Glenelg), Lucy Bowering (Glenelg), Abbie Cawse (Sturt) Nicole Hobbs (Sturt).

Leading Batting	Runs	Avg	HS	100	50	Leading Bowling	Wkt	Avge	Econ	Best
Courtney Webb (Glenelg)	**325**	**108.3**	**159***	**1**	**2**	**Abbie Cawse (Sturt)**	**17**	**13.7**	**2.99**	**4-19**
Sarah Lowe (Kensington)	270	33.7	79	-	3	Nicole Hobbs (Sturt)	16	13.2	3.46	3-57
Josie Dooley (Sturt)	269	67.2	125	1	1	Shae Daly (Kensington)	15	19.4	3.75	4-35
Paris Hall (West Torrens)	236	39.3	89	-	2	Sanigdha Bansal (Kensington)	15	19.6	3.68	4-8

TASMANIA First Grade (50 over) Final at TCA Ground, Hobart on March 20, 2022. Greater Northern 7-218 cc (E Manix-Geeves 122, A Duggan 48) **lost to North Hobart 8-219** (50 overs) (M Armstrong 40, C Scott 56*; S Lowry 4-41) **by 2 wickets.** *Emma Manix-Geeves faced 135 balls and hit 11 fours in a losing cause.*
Twenty20 final at Bellerive Oval on December 5, 2021. Greater Northern 9-88 cc (E Manix-Geeves 42; E Marsh 3-11) **lost to North Hobart 2-89** (10 overs) (NE Stalenberg 40) **by 8 wickets.** *Naomi Stalenberg faced 22 balls, hit 3 fours and 3 sixes.*
Fazackerly Medal: Emma Manix-Geeves (Greater Northern) 16 votes from Stef Daffara (North Hobart) 13 and Maddison Brooks (Clarence) 11. **Team of the season:** Emma Manix-Geeves (WK, Greater Northern), Stef Daffara (North Hobart), Amy Smith (New Town), Naomi Stalenberg (North Hobart), Sasha Moloney (Greater Northern), Rachel Priest (New Town), Emily Misfud (New Town), Erin Fazackerley (Clarence), Maddison Brooks (Clarence), Clare Scott (North Hobart), Kristin Palfrey (North Hobart), Coach: Darren Simmonds (Greatern Northern)

Leading Batting	Runs	Avg	HS	100	50	Leading Bowling	Wkt	Avge	Econ	Best
Emma Geeves-Manix (Great N)	**682**	**68.2**	**122**	**1**	**6**	**Emily Misfud (New Town)**	**24**	**17.8**	**4.64**	**4-45**
Stef Daffara (North Hobart)	598	42.7	88	-	4	Maddison Brooks (Clarence)	21	15.7	4.11	5-14
Amy Smith (New Town)	452	75.3	110	2	1	Clare Scott (North Hobart)	21	24.7	4.54	3-29
Emily Misfud (New Town)	421	24.7	81	-	4	Kristin Palfrey (North Hobart)	20	13.9	3.77	5-7

VICTORIA Premier Firsts (50-over) Final at the Albert Ground on March 13, 2022: Carlton 135 (47.5 overs) (N Hansika 42; HM Brennan 3-17) **lost to Melbourne 4-139** (31.2 overs) (SG Townsend 41, HM Brennan 32*) **by 6 wickets.** *Player of the match; Hayleigh Brennan (Melbourne).* **No Twenty20 Final. Una Paisley Medal: Bhavi Devchand (Ringwood) 33 votes,** then came Sophie Reid (Carlton) on 27, while Zoe Griffiths (Box Hill) finished in third place on 26.
Team of the Year: Bhavi Devchand (Captain, Ringwood), Sophie Reid (WK, Carlton), Amy Vine (Melbourne), Una Raymond-Hoey (Ringwood), Kim Garth (Dandenong), Cailin Green (Carlton), Zoe Griffiths (Box Hill), Ella Hayward (Melbourne), Holly Spencer (Box Hill), Hasrat Gill (Melbourne), Samantha Bates (Essendon Maribyrnong Park), Madison Albers (Carlton)

Leading Batting	Runs	Avg	HS	100	50	Leading Bowling	Wkt	Avge	Econ	Best
Amy Vine (Melbourne)	**586**	**83.7**	**116***	**1**	**4**	**Hasrat Gill (Melbourne)**	**26**	**11.9**	**3.39**	**3-15**
Bhavi Devchand (Ringwood)	557	46.4	116	2	3	Ella Hayward (Melbourne)	25	10.1	2.31	3-7
Una Raymond-Hoey (Ringwood)	493	44.8	76*	-	5	Isabel White (Box Hill)	25	16.1	3.86	5-26
Sophie Reid (Carlton)	484	37.2	110	1	2	Madison Albers (Carlton)	25	16.4	3.67	4-22

WESTERN AUSTRALIA A Grade (50 over) Final at Floreat Park on March 13, 2022. South Perth 157 (49.4 overs) (R West 54; J Emery 4-31, T Price 3-14) **lost to Subiaco Floreat 5-161** (28.1 overs) (M Banting 43, NE Bolton 54) **by 5 wickets**
T20 Grand Final at the WACA on December 19, 2021: Melville 4-121 cc (A Edgar 45; GL Wyllie 2-11) **defeated South Perth 8-120** (20 overs) **by 1 run. Player of the year (Karen Read Medal): Rebecca West (South Perth) won with 19 votes,** ahead of Nicole Bolton (Subiaco-Floreat) and Meg Banting (Subiaco-Floreat) on 12.
Team of the year: Nicole Bolton (Subiaco-Floreat), Rebecca West (South Perth), Megan Banting (Subiaco-Floreat), Sarah Fragomeni (Midland-Guildford), Shenae Reichelt (Waneroo), Amy Edgar (Melville), Annelies Gevers (Keeper, Midland-Guildford) - Jessica Emery (Captain, Subiaco-Floreat), Sarah Sribala-Sundaram (South Perth), Kayla van Spall (Melville), Chloe Wain (Melville), Jaqueline Naidoo (Subiaco-Floreat).

Leading Batting (50 over)	Runs	Avg	HS	100	50	Leading Bowling	Wkt	Avge	Econ	Best
Nicole Bolton (Subiaco-Floreat)	**471**	**67.2**	**120**	**2**	**2**	**Jessica Emery (Subiaco-Floreat)**	**22**	**8.5**	**2.88**	**8-14**
Rebecca West (South Perth)	326	40.7	85	-	3	Sarah Sribala-Sundaram (Sth Perth)	17	11.0	3.13	6-22
Meg Banting (Subiaco-Floreat)	286	35.7	99*	-	2	Kayla Van Spall (Melville)	16	15.8	4.04	5-25
Bree Hyde (Midland-Guildford)	261	43.5	77*	-	2	Rebecca West (South Perth)	14	15.2	3.95	4-9

UNDER 19 FEMALE CHAMPIONSHIPS IN ADELAIDE

April 7, 2022 – Day One, morning Twenty20 games
Vic Metro 7-94 cc (M Perrin 32) **lost to NSW Metro 2-96** (18.4 overs) (CF Moore 38*) **at Park 25 No 3**
ACT/NSW Country 4-139 cc (PES Litchfield 70*, C McGuirk 34) **lost to South Australia 8-140 cc** (K Peterson 30; M McGuigan 4-16) **at at Rolton Oval.** *SA won off the last ball of the match*
Queensland 4-147 cc (CR Knott 90*) **def Vic Country 8-102 cc** (S Ginger 3-9) **at Park 25 No 1.** *Charli Knott (63 balls) 10x4 3x6*
Afternoon games
Queensland 6-135 cc (E Johnston 65) **def NSW Metro 7-115 cc at Rolton Oval**
ACT/NSW Country 5-103 cc (PES Litchfield 43) **def Vic Country 7-102 cc** (S Shelley 3-23) **at Park 25 No 1**
Tasmania 5-108 cc (A Smith 39) **lost to South Australia 3-109** (16.1 overs) **at Park 25 No 3**

April 8, 2022 - Day Two, morning Twenty20 games
ACT/NSW Country 8-71 cc **lost to Queensland 0-72** (8.5 overs) (CR Knott 37*) **at Park 25 No 3**
Vic Metro 2-151 cc (TM Flintoff 65) **def Tasmania 3-94 cc at Park 25 No 1**
NSW Metro 7-110 cc (CF Moore 38) **lost to South Australia 2-111** (S Beazleigh 36*) **at Parl 25 No 2**
Afternoon games
Vic Country 87 (18.4 overs) (E Carroll 3-15) **lost to Vic Metro 2-90** (15 overs) **at Park 25 No 2**
ACT/NSW Country 1-167 cc (CK McGuirk 71*, PES Litchfield 55*) **def Tasmania 4-133 cc** (A Smith 84) **at Park 25 No 3**
Queensland 7-123 cc **lost to South Australia 9-124 cc** (E Worthley 34, G Parsons 3-23) **at Park 25 No 1**

April 10, 2022 – Day Three, 50 overs per side
Tasmania 6-222 cc (H Silver-Holmes 78*) **lost to NSW Metro 4-226** (41 overs) (CF Moore 81 A Genford 47; A Smith 3-35) **at Park 25 No 1**
ACT/NSW Country 9-209 cc (C McGurk 52 G Lyons 50; L Page 3-39) **def Vic Metro 149** (39.5 overs) (EL Hayward 52; C Black 4-22, M McGuigan 3-25) **at Rolton Oval**
South Australia 255 (48 overs) (A Rault 85; A Cheeran 3-37) **def Vic Country 166** (38.4 overs) (E Wilson 4-24) **at Park 25 No 3**

April 11, 2022 – Day Four, 50 overs per side
Vic Country 113 (25 overs) **lost to NSW Metro 2-114** (20 overs) (CF Moore 57*) **at Park 25 No 3**
Queensland 227 (46 overs) (E Johnston 51) **def Tasmania 41** (20.3 overs) (no one in double figures) **at Park 25 No 2**
South Australia 205 (48.2 overs) (E Worthley 41 S Beazleigh 40; I White 4-51) **lost to Vic Metro 7-208** (48.3 overs) (EL Hayward 76*, Z Samuel 46; E Larosa 4-29) **at Park 25 No 1**

April 13 – Day Five, 50 overs per side
ACT/NSW Country 8-257 cc (PES Litchfield 161*; L Kua 3-24) **def NSW Metro 199** (46.2 overs) (S Dimeglio 42; E Hoskin 3-29 S Shelley 3-39) **at Park 25 No 1.** *Phoebe Litchfield batted at three and faced 143 balls, hitting 20 fours and a six*
Vic Metro 83 (27 overs) (G Parsons 4-13) **lost to Queensland 4-84** (20.3 overs) (CR Knott 50*) **at Park 25 No 2**
Tasmania 207 (48.3 overs (M Armstrong 75 HI Silver-Holmes 42; G Jones 3-27) **def Vic Country 140** (32 overs) (P Bowdler 40; A Smith 3-18) **at Rolton Oval**

Final ladder: Qld 20 points, SA 20, ACT/NSW Country 16, NSW Metro 12, Vic Metro 12, Tasmania 4, NT 0

April 14 – Day Six, The Final played at Rolton Oval - Queensland won by 131 runs
Queensland 7-273 cc (G Voll 121, E Johnston 50; S Bansal 3-64) **def South Australia 142** (38.3 overs) (G Parsons 3-34). *Georgia Voll faced 133 balls, hit 14 fours and 2 sixes as she and Elle Johnston (63 balls, 7 fours) added 161 for the second wicket.*
Playoff matches - Morning
Vic Country 99 (19.5 overs) **lost to NSW Metro 8-102** (19 overs) (CF Moore 39, G Jones 3-17) **at Park 25 No 2**
Vic Metro 3-124 cc (M Perrin 60*) **def Tasmania 9-101 cc** (LF Page 5-16) **at Park 25 No 1**
Playoff matches - Afternoon
Vic Country 90 (19.5 overs) (EL Hayward 3-11, Z Samuel 3-15) **lost to Vic Metro 3-91** (12,4 overs) (EL Hayward 40*) **at Park 25 No 1.**
Tasmania 8-95 cc (M Armstrong 33) **lost to ACT/NSW Country 4-97** (18 overs) (G Lyons 34*)
Final standings: 1. Qld, 2. SA, 3. ACT/NSW Country, 4. Vic Metro, 5. NSW Metro, 6. Tasmania, 7. Vic Country.
Team of the Championships – Phoebe Litchfield (ACT/NSW Country), Charli Knott (Qld), Claire Moore (NSW Metro), Amy Smith (Tas), Claire McGuirk (ACT/NSW Country), Georgia Voll (Qld), Caitlin Mair (WK, Qld), Grace Parsons (Qld), Maddison McGuigan (ACT/NSW Country), Ananaya Sharma (NSW Metro), Eleanor Larosa (South Australia).
Charlie Knott won the Betty Wilson award. Vic Country won the Spirit of Cricket award.

Leading Batting	M	Runs	Avge	HS	100/50
Phoebe Litchfield (ACT/N)	**7**	**340**	**85.00**	**161***	**1/2**
Charli Knott (Qld)	7	276	69.00	90*	-/2
Claire Moore (NSW M)	7	267	53.40	81	-/2
Ella Hayward (Vic M)	8	257	64.25	76	-/2
Georgia Voll (Qld)	7	225	37.50	121	1/-

Leading Bowling	M	Wkts	Avge	Best	5wl
Grace Parsons (Qld)	**7**	**15**	**7.13**	**4-13**	**-**
Maddison McGuigan (ACT/NSW C)	7	10	11.60	4-16	-
Ella Hayward (Vic M)	8	10	14.30	3-11	-
Zoe Samuel (Vic M)	8	8	11.63	3-15	-
Bonnie Berry (Qld)	7	8	11.88	2-13	-

Wicket-Keeping	M	Catches	Stumpings	Total
Caitlan Mair (Qld)	**7**	**9**	**6**	**15**
Lara Shannon (Vic M)	8	5	4	9
Katie Letcher (ACT/NSW C)	7	6	1	7

MENS RECORDS
AUSTRALIA IN TEST CRICKET

Leading Run Scorers

	M	Inn	NO	Runs	HS	Avge	100s	50s
RT Ponting	168	287	29	13378	257	51.85	41	62
AR Border	156	265	44	11174	205	50.56	27	63
SR Waugh	168	260	46	10927	200	51.06	32	50
MJ Clarke	115	198	22	8643	329*	49.10	28	27
ML Hayden	103	184	14	8625	380	50.73	30	29
SPD Smith	**87**	**154**	**18**	**8161**	**239**	**60.00**	**28**	**36**
ME Waugh	128	209	17	8029	153*	41.81	20	47
DA Warner	**96**	**176**	**8**	**7817**	**335***	**46.52**	**24**	**34**
JL Langer	105	182	12	7696	250	45.27	23	30
MA Taylor	104	186	13	7525	334*	43.49	19	40
DC Boon	107	190	20	7422	200	43.65	21	32

Triple Centuries

	Balls	Mins	4s	6s	Versus	Venue	Season
ML Hayden	380	437	622	38	11 Zimbabwe	WACA	2003-04
DA Warner	335*	418	554	39	1 Pakistan	Adelaide	2019-20
MA Taylor	334*	564	720	32	1 Pakistan	Peshawar	1998-99
DG Bradman	334	446	383	46	0 England	Headingley	1930
MJ Clarke	329*	468	609	39	1 India	SCG	2011-12
RB Simpson	311	743	762	23	1 England	Old Trafford	1964
RM Cowper	307	589	727	20	0 England	MCG	1965-66
DG Bradman	304	465	430	44	2 England	Headingley	1934

Record Partnerships

Wkt				Versus	Venue	Season
1st	382	WM Lawry	RB Simpson	West Indies	Bridgetown	1964-65
2nd	451	WH Ponsford	DG Bradman	England	The Oval	1934
3rd	315	RT Ponting	DS Lehmann	West Indies	Port-of-Spain	2002-03
4th	449	AC Voges	SE Marsh	West Indies	Hobart	2015-16
5th	405	SG Barnes	DG Bradman	England	SCG	1946-47
6th	346	JHW Fingleton	DG Bradman	England	MCG	1936-37
7th	217	KD Walters	GJ Gilmour	New Zealand	Christchurch	1976-77
8th	243	MJ Hartigan	C Hill	England	Adelaide	1907-08
9th	154	SE Gregory	JM Blackham	England	SCG	1894-95
10th	163	PJ Hughes	AC Agar	England	Trent Bridge	2013

Quickest Innings

Fastest Fifties

	Bls	Versus	Venue	Season
DA Warner	23	Pak	SCG	2016-17
B Yardley	29	WI	Bridgetown	1977-78
MA Starc	32	SA	WACA	2012-13
JA Burns	33	India	SCG	2014-15
DA Warner	34	SL	MCG	2012-13
GN Yallop	35	Eng	Old Trafford	1981
DA Warner	35	Eng	Edgbaston	2015

Fastest Hundreds

	Bls	Versus	Venue	Season
AC Gilchrist	57	Eng	WACA	2006-07
JM Gregory	67	SA	Johannesburg	1921-22
DA Warner	69	India	WACA	2011-12
DA Warner	78	Pak	SCG	2014-15
DA Warner	82	WI	SCG	2015-16
AC Gilchrist	84	Ind	Mumbai	2000-01
AC Gilchrist	84	Zim	WACA	2003-04
ML Hayden	84	Zim	SCG	2003-04

Fastest Double Hundreds

	Bls	Versus	Venue	Season
AC Gilchrist	212	SA	Johannesburg	2001-02
MJ Clarke	226	SA	Adelaide	2012-13
AC Voges	226	WI	Hobart	2015-16
VT Trumper	236	SA	Adelaide	1910-11
DA Warner	236	NZ	WACA	2015-16
DG Bradman	242	Eng	The Oval	1934
MJ Clarke	255	India	Adelaide	2011-12

Fastest Triple Hundreds

	Bls	Versus	Venue	Season
ML Hayden	362	Zim	WACA	2003-04
DA Warner	389	Pak	Adelaide	2019-20
DG Bradman	410	Eng	Headingley	1930
MJ Clarke	432	India	SCG	2011-12
DG Bradman	457	Eng	Headingley	1934
MA Taylor	520	Pak	Peshawar	1998-99
RW Cowper	570	Eng	MCG	1965-66

Leading Wicket takers

	M	Balls	Mdns	Runs	Wkts	Ave	Best	5WI	10WM
SK Warne	145	40704	1761	17995	708	25.41	8-71	37	10
GD McGrath	124	29248	1470	12186	563	21.64	8-24	29	3
NM Lyon	**110**	**28583**	**923**	**14047**	**438**	**32.07**	**8-50**	**20**	**3**
DK Lillee	70	18467	650	8493	355	23.92	7-83	23	7
MG Johnson	73	16001	514	8892	313	28.40	8-61	12	3
B Lee	76	16531	547	9554	310	30.81	5-30	10	0
CJ McDermott	71	16586	577	8332	291	28.63	8-97	14	2
MA Starc	**71**	**14344**	**480**	**7929**	**287**	**27.62**	**6-50**	**13**	**2**
JN Gillespie	71	14234	630	6770	259	26.13	7-37	8	0
R Benaud	63	19108	805	6704	248	27.03	7-72	16	1

Best Bowling

In Innings

		Versus	Venue	Season
AA Mailey	9-121	Eng	MCG	1920-21
GD McGrath	8-24	Pak	WACA	2004-05
FJ Laver	8-31	Eng	Old Trafford	1909
GD McGrath	8-38	Eng	Lord's	1997
AE Trott	8-43	Eng	Adelaide	1894-95
NM Lyon	8-50	India	Bangalore	2016-17

In match

		Versus	Venue	Season
RAL Massie	16-137	Eng	Lord's	1972
FR Spofforth	14-90	Eng	The Oval	1882
CV Grimmett	14-199	RSA	Adelaide	1931-32
MA Noble	13-77	Eng	MCG	1901-02
FR Spofforth	13-110	Eng	MCG	1878-79
BA Reid	13-148	Eng	MCG	1990-91
CV Grimmett	13-173	RSA	Durban	1935-36
MG Hughes	13-217	WI	WACA	1988-89
AA Mailey	13-236	Eng	MCG	1920-21

Wicket Keeping/Fielding

KEEPERS	M	Ct	St	Total
AC Gilchrist	96	379	37	416
IA Healy	119	366	29	395
RW Marsh	96	343	12	355

FIELDERS	M	Total
RT Ponting	168	196
ME Waugh	128	181
MA Taylor	104	157

Most Dismissals in a series

	M	Ct	St	Total	versus	Venue	Season
BJ Haddin	5	29	-	29	England	England	2013
RW Marsh	5	28	-	28	England	Australia	1982-83
IA Healy	6	25	2	27	England	England	1997
AC Gilchrist	5	24	2	26	England	Australia	2006-07
RW Marsh	6	26	-	26	West Indies	Australia	1975-76
AC Gilchrist	5	24	2	26	England	England	2001
IA Healy	6	21	5	26	England	England	1993
TD Paine	5	25	1	26	England	Australia	2017-18

AUSTRALIA IN ONE DAY INTERNATIONALS – UP TO AUGUST 27, 2022

Leading Run Scorers

	M	Inn	NO	Runs	HS	Avge	S/Rate	100s	50s
RT Ponting	374	364	39	13589	164	41.81	80.0	29	82
AC Gilchrist	286	278	11	9595	172	35.93	96.9	16	55
ME Waugh	244	236	20	8500	173	39.35	76.6	18	50
MJ Clarke	245	223	44	7981	130	44.58	78.9	8	58
SR Waugh	325	288	58	7569	120*	32.90	75.8	3	45
MG Bevan	232	196	67	6912	108*	53.58	74.0	6	46
AR Border	273	252	39	6524	127*	30.62	71.4	3	39
ML Hayden	160	154	15	6131	181*	44.10	78.9	10	36
DM Jones	164	161	25	6068	145	44.61	72.6	7	46

Highest Scores

		BF	4s	6s	Versus	Venue	Season
SR Watson	185*	96	15	15	Bangladesh	Mirpur	2010-11
ML Hayden	181*	166	11	10	New Zealand	Hamilton	2006-07
DA Warner	179	128	19	5	Pakistan	Adelaide	2016-17
DA Warner	178	133	19	5	Afghanistan	WACA	2014-15
ME Waugh	173	148	16	3	West Indies	MCG	2000-01
DA Warner	173	136	24	0	South Africa	Cape Town	2016-17
AC Gilchrist	172	126	13	3	Zimbabwe	Hobart	2003-04

Quickest Innings

Fastest Fifties

	Bls	Versus	Venue	Season
SP O'Donnell	18	SL	Sharjah	1989-90
GJ Maxwell	18	India	Bangalore	2013-14
AJ Finch	18	SL	Dambulla	2016
DJ Hussey	19	WI	St Kitts	2008
GL Maxwell	21	Afgh	WACA	2014-15
DR Martyn	22	Bang	Cairns	2003
L Ronchi	22	WI	St Kitts	2008

Fastest Hundreds

	Bls	Versus	Venue	Season
GJ Maxwell	51	SL	SCG	2014-15
JP Faulkner	57	India	Bangalore	2013-14
SPD Smith	62	India	SCG	2020-21
SPD Smith	62	India	SCG	2020-21
ML Hayden	66	SA	St Kitts	2006-07
AC Gilchrist	67	SL	Gabba	2005-06
SR Watson	69	Bang	Mirpur	2010-11

Record Partnerships

Wkt				Versus	Venue	Season
1st	284	DA Warner	TM Head	Pakistan	Adelaide	2016-17
2nd	260	DA Warner	SPD Smith	Afghanistan	WACA	2014-15
3rd	242	SPD Smith	GJ Bailey	India	WACA	2015-16
4th	237	RT Ponting	A Symonds	Sri Lanka	SCG	2005-06
5th	220	A Symonds	MJ Clarke	New Zealand	Wellington-W	2005-06
6th	212	AT Carey	GJ Maxwell	England	Old Trafford	2020
7th	123	MEK Hussey	B Lee	South Africa	Gabba	2005-06
8th	119	PR Reiffel	SK Warne	South Africa	Port Elizabeth	1993-94
9th	115	JP Faulkner	CJ McKay	India	Bangalore	2013-14
10th	63	SR Watson	AJ Bichel	Sri Lanka	SCG	2002-03

Leading Wicket takers

	M	Balls	Mdns	Runs	Wkts	Ave	Econ	Best	4wI
GD McGrath	249	12928	278	8354	380	21.98	3.87	7-15	16
B Lee	221	11191	141	8879	380	23.36	4.76	5-22	23
SK Warne	193	10600	110	7514	291	25.82	4.25	5-33	13
MG Johnson	153	7489	74	6038	239	25.26	4.83	6-31	12
CJ McDermott	138	7461	101	5018	203	24.71	4.03	5-44	5
MA Starc	**99**	**5099**	**42**	**4379**	**195**	**22.45**	**5.15**	**6-28**	**19**
SR Waugh	325	8883	55	6761	195	34.67	4.56	4-33	3
NW Bracken	116	5759	90	4239	174	24.36	4.41	5-47	7
SR Watson	190	6460	35	5341	168	31.79	4.96	4-36	3

Best Bowling

		Versus	Venue	Season
GD McGrath	7-15	Namibia	Potchefstroom	2002-03
AJ Bichel	7-20	England	Port Elizabeth	2002-03
GJ Gilmour	6-14	England	Headingley	1975
MA Starc	6-28	New Zealand	Auckland	2014-15
MG Johnson	6-31	Sri Lanka	Pallekele	2011
KH MacLeay	6-39	India	Trent Bridge	1983

WICKET KEEPING/FIELDING

KEEPERS	M	Ct	St	Total		FIELDERS	M	Total
AC Gilchrist	286	416	54	470		RT Ponting	374	159
IA Healy	168	194	39	233		AR Border	273	127
BJ Haddin	126	170	11	181		SR Waugh	325	111

AUSTRALIA IN TWENTY20 INTERNATIONALS

Leading Run Scorers

	M	Inn	NO	Runs	HS	Avge	S/Rate	100s	50s	Sixes
AJ Finch	92	92	11	2855	172	35.24	145.2	2	17	117
DA Warner	91	91	11	2684	100*	33.55	140.8	1	22	100
GJ Maxwell	87	79	13	2017	145*	30.56	153.3	3	9	99
SR Watson	58	56	6	1462	124	29.24	145.3	1	10	83
CL White	47	44	14	984	85	32.80	132.9	0	5	44
SPD Smith	57	45	10	928	90	26.51	125.7	0	4	23
MR Marsh	38	36	7	896	77*	30.89	125.3	0	6	35
MS Wade	63	47	11	828	80	23.00	128.5	0	3	32
DJ Hussey	39	36	3	756	88	22.90	121.3	0	3	34

Centuries

		BF	4s	6s	Versus	Venue	Season
AJ Finch	172	76	16	10	Zimbabwe	Harare	2018
AJ Finch	156	63	11	14	England	Southampton	2013
GJ Maxwell	145*	65	14	9	Sri Lanka	Pallekele	2016
SR Watson	124*	71	10	6	India	SCG	2015-16
GJ Maxwell	113*	55	7	9	India	Bangalore	2018-19
GJ Maxwell	103*	58	10	4	England	Hobart	2017-18
DA Warner	100*	56	10	4	Sri Lanka	Adelaide	2019-20

Quickest Innings

Fastest Fifties

	Bls	Versus	Venue	Season
DA Warner	18	WI	SCG	2009-10
GJ Maxwell	18	Pak	Mirpur	2013-14
GJ Maxwell	18	SL	Colombo-RPS	2016
DA Warner	19	SA	MCG	2008-09
SR Watson	20	SL	Pallekele	2011
DA Warner	20	NZ	Auckland	2017-18
CL White	21	NZ	Christchurch-LP	2009-10

Fastest Hundreds

	Bls	Versus	Venue	Season
AJ Finch	47	Eng	Southampton	2013
GL Maxwell	49	SL	Pallekele	2016
AJ Finch	50	Zim	Harare	2018
GJ Maxwell	50	India	Bangalore	2018-19
DA Warner	56	SL	Adelaide	2019-20
GJ Maxwell	58	Eng	Hobart	2017-18
SR Watson	60	India	SCG	2015-16

Record Partnerships

Wkt				Versus	Venue	Season
1st	223	AJ Finch	DJM Short	Zimbabwe	Harare	2018
2nd	**124**	**DA Warner**	**MR Marsh**	**West Indies**	**Abu Dhabi**	**2021-22**
3rd	118	AJ Finch	GJ Maxwell	Pakistan	Mirpur	2013-14
4th	161	DA Warner	GJ Maxwell	South Africa	Johannesburg	2015-16
5th	83	RT Ponting	SM Katich	New Zealand	Auckland	2004-05
6th	101*	CL White	MEK Hussey	Sri Lanka	Bridgetown	2010
7th	92	MP Stoinis	DR Sams	New Zealand	Dunedin	2020-21
8th	53*	MEK Hussey	MG Johnson	Pakistan	Gros Islet	2010
9th	23*	NM Coulter-Nile	CJ McKay	West Indies	Gabba	2012-13
10th	23	JA Richardson	A Zampa	New Zealand	Christchurch	2020-21

Leading Wicket takers

	M	Balls	Mdns	Runs	Wkts	Ave	Econ	Best	4wI
A Zampa	62	1331	1	1507	71	21.22	6.79	5-19	1
MA Starc	51	1158	1	1458	63	23.14	7.55	3-11	0
SR Watson	58	930	2	1187	48	24.72	7.65	4-15	1
AJ Tye	32	683	1	997	47	21.21	8.76	4-23	1
AC Agar	46	970	1	1048	47	22.29	6.48	6-30	2
JR Hazlewood	30	688	4	829	46	18.02	7.22	4-12	4
PJ Cummins	39	852	3	1002	44	22.77	7.05	3-15	0
KW Richardson	33	690	0	938	42	22.33	8.15	4-30	1
MG Johnson	30	656	2	797	38	20.97	7.28	3-15	0

Best Bowling

		Dots	Versus	Venue	Season
AC Agar	6-30	12	New Zealand	Wellington	2020-21
A Zampa	**5-19**	14	**Bangladesh**	**Dubai**	**2021-22**
AC Agar	5-24	12	South Africa	Johannesburg	2019-20
JP Faulkner	5-27	10	Pakistan	Mohali	2015-16
B Stanlake	4-8	18	Pakistan	Harare	2018
JR Hazlewood	**4-12**	14	**Sri Lanka**	**SCG**	**2021-22**
SR Watson	4-15	11	England	Adelaide	2010-11
JR Hazlewood	**4-16**	15	**Sri Lanka**	**Colombo – RPS**	**2022**
DP Nannes	4-18	14	Bangladesh	Bridgetown	2010

WICKET KEEPING/FIELDING

KEEPERS	M	Ct	St	Total
MS Wade	59	39	4	43
AT Carey	38	14	9	23
BJ Haddin	34	17	6	23
AC Gilchrist	13	17	0	17

FIELDERS	M	Total
DA Warner	91	50
AJ Finch	92	45
GJ Maxwell	87	39
SPD Smith	57	39

OBITUARIES

NOEL ALLANSON was 96 when he died on February 7, having played one first-class match for Victoria against Tasmania in 1956/57. He made 24 in that one match and played 18 seasons with Essendon in VCA club cricket, making 4,463 runs at 24.65 with four hundreds and a best score of 110. Allanson also played 57 VFL games with Essendon, being part of the 1950 flag. Noel served as an able seaman in the Royal Australian Navy towards the end of WWII and was present in Tokyo Bay in 1945 when the Japanese surrender was signed aboard the battleship USSS Missouri.

DALE ANDERSON the Tasmanian cricketer and Aussie rules footballer, died on September 29, 2021 at the age on 90. He played six first-class matches for his state between 1952/53 and 1963/64, making 123 runs at 15.37, taking 14 wickets at 40.35 as a pace bowler. His most notable wicket was that of England's Ken Barrington, who he dismissed in 1962/63. He also played six seasons of VCA club cricket, starting with Melbourne in 1953/54, before playing for Northcote from 1955/56 to 1959/60, all up taking 171 wickets at 17.71. Anderson also played seven VFL games for Melbourne during 1953 and 1954.

BRIAN BOOTH died on April 9 at the age of 97, having played eight first-class matches for Tasmania between the 1946/47 and 1959/60 seasons. He only averaged 18.80 with the bat but managed one century, 113 against Victoria at the NTCA Ground in Launceston in 1950/51, a match Victoria won by just nine runs. He was also an Able Seaman in the Royal Australian Navy in World War Two.

KEITH BRADHSAW, the popular administrator and Tasmanian batsman, died on November 8, 2021 aged 58. Bradshaw started with Tasmania in 1984/85 and had a solid first season in Sheffield Shield, making 419 runs at 41.90, with one century, 121 v Queensland at the Gabba. The 1985/86 season was tougher for him with 450 at 25.00 with 112 v Western Australia at the TCA Ground in Hobart. The 1986/87 season was a quiet one for him in Shield cricket, but he did make 37 off 30 balls to help Tasmania chase down 268 against Western Australia at the WACA in a one-day semi-final, South Australia beating them in the final a month later   .

His form slipped after that and making double figures in just two of his last 11 innings. He played his last game in 1987-88 having finished with 1083 runs at 25.78 in 25 first-class matches, not one of them yielding an outright victory. In his mid 20s Bradshaw completed his degree at University of Tasmania and later took up positions with big accounting firms Price Waterhouse and Deloitte, being promoted to partner at the latter. By 2006, he got tipped off by a friend in global recruitment that the MCC was after a new CEO and on October 1, 2006, he had the job.

Bradshaw was a popular boss at Lord's, and did some fine things, like regularly ringing members, being out meeting and greeting them when they queued up before big matches and getting celebrities and ex-players to ring the five-minute bell before start of play. He also stepped into to help Pakistan host Australia at Lord's for a Test in 2010, when they couldn't play in their own country for security reasons. He was first diagnosed with cancer in 2008 and left Lord's during 2011 and was snapped up almost immediately by the South Australian Cricket Association.

He had plenty to do at the SACA, overseeing the $535 million redevelopment of Adelaide Oval and then went about investigating a push for day/night Test matches. In June 2014 it was revealed that Adelaide would host the first day/night test after extensive research had been commissioned. Bradshaw at the time said "We had to invest in the pink ball. A lot of that revolves around getting the dye to infuse into the leather so when the ball deteriorates the colour is still within the leather itself." This was achieved and Australia hosted New Zealand under lights in the first pink ball test in 2015, which attracted 47,441 fans on the first day, and 123,736 across what ended up being a three-day match.

After a successful time with the SACA, the cancer returned mid-way through 2021, and on June 16 he went on indefinite sick leave to beat the cancer, which had spread to his spine and brain, making him unable to walk. Sadly for Keith it was a battle he couldn't win and he passed away in November.

PHIL CARLSON died on July 29, aged 70. The former Queensland all-rounder played two Ashes Tests in 1978/79 and represented Queensland across 12 seasons from 1969/70 to 1980/81. He was a very capable right-hand batsman and a medium pace bowler who swung the ball.

With just one game in his debut summer, he became a regular member of the team from 1970/71, doing well in 1971/72 with 571 runs at 38.07, plus 12 wickets at 18.58. He was a steady performer in subsequent seasons, making two centuries in 1977/78, before being called up to the Australian Ashes squad for the first Test at the Gabba in 1978/79. He was the twelfth man in Brisbane Test and Perth Test, eventually getting his chance in the fifth Test in Adelaide.

Australia won the toss and sent England in, Carlson taking a brilliant right-handed diving catch in the gully off Alan Hurst to dismiss Derek Randall. He was unlucky to be given out behind for a duck off Ian Botham in the first innings by Umpire Max O'Connell. Years later he told *The Age's* Peter Hanlon ""I'd had a few run-ins with Max O'Connell. I thought he was hopeless. We moved into each other's dressing rooms that night, and Botham said, 'Bad luck, Port, you didn't get near that. But cricket's cricket.' "

Carlson took two wickets in the second innings, trapping Mike Brearley LBW and bowling Graham Gooch. Australia needed 366 to win, Carlson hitting some nice drives in his 21 before being well caught by David Gower off Mike Hendrick. Carlson played in the sixth and final Test, but managed just two and a duck, while also going wicketless in ten overs. Overall, in 1978/79 first-class cricket he made 545 runs at 30.28 and took 31 wickets at 15.61.

With World Series Cricket over, Carlson kept his spot for the 1979/80 season and did well making 415 runs at 27.67, while taking 27 wickets and was also runner-up to South Australian skipper Ian Chappell as Sheffield Shield player of the season. Things changed the next season, and by December 1980 he decided to give the game away at 29 and concentrate on starting a family with wife, Sandy. After retirement he helped struggling local farmers in and around Childers sell their farms and was later was later on the board of the Queensland Cricketer's Club for over 15 years.

ALAN CROMPTON OAM the former Chairman of the Australian Cricket Board (1992-95), died on April 20 aged 80. In an administrative career that lasted 60 years, he started with Sydney University in 1961 which included his being the honorary secretary of the club, a vice president, a Trustee of the SUCC Foundation, a delegate to CNSW, President of the club for 22 years and its Patron for another 20 years until 2020.

Crompton served as the NSW Cricket Association's Chair from 1988-1997 and was described on the Cricket NSW site as someone with a "generous heart and with graciousness". He was also manager of three touring Australian Test teams, including the Tied Test tour of India in 1986. Playing wise he had an impressive grade record with Waverley and Sydney University, scoring 7266 runs and taking over 350 dismissals was a keeper between 1958 and 83.

COLIN HARBURN who died on January 12 aged 83, was a top-order batsman for Western Australia in seven first class matches between 1961/62 and 1964/65. His only first-class hundred was 139 at the WACA for WA against the 1964 Ashes touring team on its way by boat to England. After his last game for WA, he was transferred with the RAAF to Melbourne where he played club cricket for Footscray.

STEVE MILOSZ the Western Australian and Tasmania leg-spinner died aged 66 on July 20. Milosz played 21 first-class games in all, taking 44 wickets at 44.88. WA journalist John Townsend wrote of him on the Sport Fm website "He was armed with (Shane) Warne's control, had a fizzing leg-break to match MacGill's best and could deliver a flipper as deadly as any bowler before or since. Jim Higgs, Peter Sleep, Terry Jenner and Trevor Hohns all played Test cricket in the past 50 years without being significantly better bowlers than Milosz."

He started his career in 1983/84 and only took six wickets at 45 but played in the Sheffield Shield final win over Queensland at the Gabba. He was overlooked for the Shield team in the next two seasons, but work sent him to Tasmania in 1986-87, where he took 24 wickets at 46 including 6-153 against Queensland at the Gabba.

Milosz was back in the WA side for the start of 1987/88 and took 3-13 and 4-53 in the opening game v Tasmania, at the WACA. But the wickets dried up after that and after match figures of 1-141 from 55 overs in the game v Victoria, he was out of the side for good.

He was a legitimate number 11, with just 67 runs in Shield cricket at 7.44 but did score 29 batting at number 11 for Tasmania against New South Wales in 1986/87 and in doing so helped Roger Woolley to complete his century. Milosz also played club cricket with Midland-Guildford and Bayswater-Morley and had a stint with the VCA club Ringwood in 1989/90.

COLIN MINSON the veteran Western Australian broadcaster died on March 14 aged 75. Known in Perth as Mr Cricket, "Mino" was popular figure in the Media landscape there covering Cricket and Football for well over 25 years. After working for a number of stations in the West, he ended up at Sport FM and helped transform the station into a fine sporting station.

He covered Western Australian Cricket to all parts of the country, commentating Shield matches back into Perth. He was also very successful in business and died following an eight-month battle with leukemia.

PETER PHILPOTT OAM was 86 when he passed away on October 31, 2021. Born in Manly in 1934, Philpott was a leg-spinner and handy lower order batsman who played eight Tests, taking 26 wickets at 38.46 between March 1965 and January 1966. Early in life he was diagnosed with a heart condition, but thankfully medication enabled him to have a long and productive life, largely centred around cricket, but also as a school-teacher.

He started to become well known in the Sydney cricket circles in 1950/51, when he took 40 wickets at 6.33 in the Green Shield. He also made his first-grade debut in that season, taking 38 wickets, and in all cricket during that summer took an amazing 118 wickets at 9.33. He made his Sheffield Shield debut when 20 in 1954/55 against Queensland, scoring 71 and taking two wickets.

In 1955 he took up the opportunity to play Lancashire League cricket with Ramsbottom, making 861 runs at 43 and taking 77 wickets at 12.67. Philpott returned from England but only made five Shield appearances across the next two seasons but in 1957/58 with Richie Benaud absent in South Africa, he took 23 wickets at 34.96. This included his first five wicket haul, 5-81 against South Australia in Adelaide. In that season he was also part of the Manly Premiership side. After four Shield games with New South Wales in 1958/59, he was off to Ramsbottom again in the 1959, where he had made 1016 runs at 56, with three hundreds and took 37 wickets at 23. The following year he dominated again with the bat again to make 1069 runs at 53, taking 82 wickets at 12.06. Whilst at Ramsbottom he worked as a geography and physical education teacher at Peel Brow School. One of his students, Maurice Haslam was quoted in *The Bury Times* ""He was my hero, he introduced me to my favourite sport and it has stayed with me my whole life. "I was a young lad, and he had an Aussie accent, which you don't get much of around here, so he was remarkably cool and he had a certain aura about him that made other people enthusiastic about cricket. "And it wasn't just me – there were lots of other young lads he taught cricket to and passed on a real love of the sport". In 1962 he moved to East Lancashire and repeated his 1960 season with 82 wickets at just 9.81, making 956 runs at 56.23. All up in four seasons, he made 3,902 runs at 52 (5 hundreds) and took 278 wickets at 13.08.

Philpott returned to Australia and in 1963/64 had a strong season taking 29 wickets at 24 and with 20 wickets in five games in 1964/65, was selected to go on the Test tour to the West Indies. He made his debut in the First Test at Kingston and did well in what was a loss for Australia taking 2-56 and 4-109, including the wicket of skipper Garry Sobers in the second innings. On a turning pitch in the third Test at Bourda, also lost by Australia, he took 4-49 in the second innings. Australia lost the series 2-1, but Philpott had a credible series taking 18 wickets at 34.

On his return to Australia, he played in the 1965/66 Ashes, taking 5-90 in the rain affected first Test at the Gabba, the match where Doug Walters made his debut at 19 and scored 155. With 0-133 in the drawn second Test in Melbourne, he took 2-86 in the third Test, dismissing both Geoff Boycott (84) and John Edrich (103) caught and bowled. But England won by an innings, and he was left out of the Fourth Test, with Keith Stackpole coming in to make his debut as a leg-spinner who batted at eight.

After being overlooked for the 1966/67 tour to South Africa, Philpott retired at 32, with 245 first-class wickets at 30.31 and 2886 runs at 31.36 including four centuries. He continued to turn out for Manly, taking 60 wickets in 1967/68 and played his last season in 1969/70, finishing with 5,535 runs for the club at 31.63, taking 499 wickets at 18.93.

Coaching then played a significant role in his life, doing the role for Australia on the 1981 Ashes tour. He also coached Yorkshire, Surrey, Sri Lanka and South Australia and helped England in 1998, as they tried to combat Shane Warne. He wrote his autobiography, *A spinner's yarn* published in 1990, and *Two Times Thirty Five* in 2006.

JOHN RUTHERFORD, who played one Test for Australia, died on April 26, aged 92. He played for his country at a time when Western Australians were shunned from Australian selection. He started with WA in 1952/53 and cracked his first ton the following season, with 121 against South Australia in Perth. In 1954/55 he scored two centuries, 167 versus South Australia in Adelaide, before making 108 in the return match at the WACA. His 125 against Queensland at the WACA in December 1955, put him right in contention for a spot on the 1956 Ashes tour, and he was selected for Ian Johnson's XI versus Ray Lindwall's XI in January 1956 to be played at the SCG.

With little assistance from those running the match, and barely any practice before the game, Rutherford made 113 and shared a long stand of 244 with Ken "Slasher" Mackay, who made 143. Rutherford was now on the Ashes tour, but again faced hiccups. He was told to stay in Perth, where he would be picked up by the boat, while the Australian touring party played matches in Tasmania. He was having none of it, went to Skipper Ian Johnson and selector Don Bradman and joined the team from their departure point in Sydney. Only trouble was no-one had booked him a room at the team hotel in Tassie, so had to get a mattress and share a room with Neil Harvey and Len Maddocks.

He didn't get a run in the 1956 Ashes, but on the way home played in the second Test against India, scoring 30 at the Brabourne Stadium, before being caught behind off leg-spinner Fergie Gupte. He also managed a wicket, bowling Vijay Manjrekar. After his return he made runs for WA, scoring 655 at 50 in 1957/58, but wasn't selected on any further tours of Australia. He played with Rishton in the Lancashire League in 1959, scoring 831 runs at 39.57 and took 53 wickets at 18.67. His final first-class match for WA was against the touring West Indians at the WACA in 1960/61, in the end he made 3367 runs at 31.76 with six tons, and 29 wickets at 45.27 with his leg-breaks.

Playing that one Test meant a lot to him as he told Cricinfo's Brydon Coverdale in 2015, ""It's made a colossal difference to me," Rutherford says. "As soon as I say I've got a baggy green, up goes people's attention. It's helped me quite a lot in a number of ways. And I was very fortunate in getting eight months with the Australian XI; guys like Miller and Lindwall, I was with them all the time. What chance did I ever really have of being the first Western Australian to play Test cricket for Australia?"

ERICA SAINSBURY died at aged 62 on Christmas Eve, 2021. Sainsbury played 10 games for NSW between 1978 and 1980, but it was work as a scorer and statistician she was best known for, performing both roles between 1987 and 2003. She was also a life member of the Gordon CC in the Women's division and away from cricket Sainsbury was a registered pharmacist and highly regarded in the education sector where she held a PhD in Educational psychology.

LAWRIE SAWLE the Western Australian left-hand batsman and former Chairman of Australia Test Selectors, died on July 26, aged 96. Before playing representative cricket for WA, Sawle served in the 7th Australian Infantry Battalion during World War II. He enlisted in January 1944 and fought in Bougainville as a teenager.

It took him nearly a decade of grade cricket before Sawle played the first of his 35 first-class games with WA in 1954/55. He had his best season the following summer when he made 317 runs at 45.29, with 109 not out against New South Wales at the WACA. He had a good record against New South Wales, averaging 36.07, despite the fact that Alan Davidson dismissed him five times. His final season with WA was in 1960/61, when he made 35 and 40 against the touring West Indies. In all he made 1701 runs at 28.83, with nine 50s to go with the one century made back in 1955/56.

After his retirement as a player, the man known as "Colonel" became a selector for WA, being in the job from 1962-80, a period where the men in the west won six Sheffield Shields and four limited-overs titles. He talented spotted John Inverarity from an early age, picking him as an 18 year-old to make his debut. Sawle also was one of the first to notice a young tearaway in Dennis Lillee, bowling fast in the 1960's.

From 1982 to 1995 he was an Australian selector, being chairman for 11 years. Some of the Australia's triumphs of that period included the 1987 World Cup, four Ashes wins including the 4-0 drubbing of England in 1989 and Australia's 2-1 victory in the West Indies in 1995. Post retirement he was a regular attendee of Shield matches and Tests at the WACA. The Lawrie Sawle Medal is now the highest award for Men's cricket in Western Australia.

NEW SOUTH WALES
Coach: Phil Jacques

	No.	DOB	Place	Bat	Bowl
Sean Abbott	77	29/2/92	Windsor, NSW	RHB	RFM
Trent Copeland	9	14/3/86	Gosford, NSW	RHB	RM
Patrick Cummins *	30	5/8/93	Westmead, Sydney	RHB	RF
Ollie Davies	14	14/10/00	Curl Curl, NSW	RHB	ROS
Ben Dwarshuis	27	23/6/94	Woronora Heights, Sydney	RHB	LFM
Jack Edwards	18	19/4/00	Allambie Heights, NSW	RHB	RFM
Mickey Edwards	15	23/12/94	Sydney, NSW	RHB	RFM
Matt Gilkes	99	21/8/99	Ulladulla, NSW	LHB	WK
Ryan Hackney	1	15/7/99	Faulconbridge, NSW	LHB	SLA
Ryan Hadley		17/11/98	Blacktown, NSW	RHB	RFM
Liam Hatcher	7	17/9/96	Liverpool, NSW	RHB	RFM
Josh Hazlewood *	8	8/1/91	Tamworth, NSW	RHB	RFM
Lachlan Hearne	22	19/12/00	Camperdown, NSW	LHB	ROS
Moises Henriques	21	1/2/87	Funchal, Portugal	RHB	RFM
Baxter Holt	27	21/10/99	Carlingford, NSW	RHB	WK
Daniel Hughes	3	2/7/79	Bathurst, NSW	LHB	RFM
Nathan Lyon *	67	20/11/87	Young, NSW	RHB	ROB
Kurtis Patterson	17	5/5/93	Hurstville, NSW	LHB	RM
Daniel Sams	60	27/10/92	Milperra, NSW	RHB	LFM
Jason Sangha	23	8/9/99	Randwick, Sydney	RHB	LEG
Tanveer Sangha	2	26/11/01	Liverpool, NSW	RHB	LEG
Steve Smith *	49	2/6/89	Sydney, NSW	RHB	LEG
Mitchell Starc *	56	30/1/90	Baulkham Hills, Sydney	LHB	LF
Chris Tremain	4	10/8/91	Dubbo, NSW	RHB	RFM
David Warner *	31	27/10/86	Paddington, Sydney	LHB	LEG
Adam Zampa *	66	31/3/92	Shellharbour, NSW	RHB	LEG
Rookie Contracts:					
Liam Doddrell		27/9/02		RHB	RFM
Blake Nikitaras	74	29/4/00		LHB	
Jack Nisbet		27/1/03		RHB	RFM
Lachlan Shaw		26/12/02		RHB	WK
Will Salzman		19/11/03		RHB	RMF
Hunar Verma		13/9/01		RHB	RFM

*CA Contract

Ins: Liam Doddrell (rookie), Ryan Hadley (upgraded), Hayden Kerr, Blake Nikitaras (rookie), Lachlan Shaw (rookie), Will Salzmann (rookie)

Off Contract list for 2022-23

	No.	DOB	Place			Reason
Peter Nevill	20	13/10/85	Hawthorn, Melbourne	RHB	WK	Retired
Harry Conway	5	17/9/92	Darlinghurst, Sydney	RHB	RFM	SA

2021-22 Award Winners
Steve Waugh Medalist – Chris Tremain
Sheffield Shield Award – Chris Tremain
Marsh Cup Award (Michael Bevan Medal) – Hayden Kerr

Recent Steve Waugh Medal winners

2012-13	Gurinder Sandhu	2017-18	Daniel Hughes
2013-14	Sean Abbott	2018-19	Sean Abbott
2014-15	Peter Nevill	2019-20	Moises Henrqiues
2015-16	Nic Maddinson	2020-21	Sean Abbott
2016-17	Ed Cowan	2021-22	Chris Tremain

QUEENSLAND
Coach – Wade Seccombe

	No.	DOB	Place	Bat	Bowl
Xavier Bartlett	19	17/12/98	Adelaide, SA	RHB	RFM
James Bazley	28	8/4/95	Buderim, Qld	RHB	RMF
Max Bryant	17	10/3/99	Murwillumbah, NSW	RHB	RM
Joe Burns	15	6/9/89	Herston, Brisbane	RHB	ROS
Jack Clayton	21	25/2/99	Brisbane	LHB	
Blake Edwards	22	26/10/99	Brisbane	RHB	RFM
Sam Heazlett	47	12/9/95	Sunnybank, Qld	LHB	SLA
Usman Khawaja *	18	18/12/86	Islamabad, Pakistan	LHB	ROS
Matthew Kuhnemann	30	20/9/96	Brisbane	LHB	SLA
Marnus Labuschagne *	9	22/6/94	Klerksdorp, South Africa	RHB	RM
Michael Neser	20	29/3/90	Pretoria, South Africa	RHB	RFM
Jimmy Peirson	59	13/10/92	Sydney	RHB	WK
Matthew Renshaw	94	28/3/96	Middlesborough, UK	LHB	ROS
Mark Steketee	16	17/1/94	Monto, Qld	RHB	RFM
Bryce Street	25	25/1/98	Gosford, NSW	LHB	RM
Connor Sully	42	24/10/00	Brisbane	RHB	RFM
Mitch Swepson *	4	4/10/93	Brisbane	RHB	LEG
Sam Truloff	52	24/3/93		RHB	LEG
Jack Wildermuth	24	1/9/93	Toowoomba, Qld	RHB	RMF
Rookie Contracts:					
Hugo Burdon				RHB	RFM
Corey Hunter		23/6/00	Everton Park, Brisbane	RHB	LEG
Will Prestwidge	8	15/1/02	Brisbane	LHB	RFM
Jackson Sinfield		27/4/03		LHB	ROS
Matthew Willans		18/2/00	Auchenflower, Qld	RHB	LMF

*CA Contract

In – Jack Clayton (upgrade from rookie), Liam Guthrie (ex-WA), Kane Richardson (ex-SA), Gurinder Sandhu, Connor Sully (upgrade from rookie), Sam Truloff.

Off Contract list for 2022-23

					Reason
Lachlan Pfeffer	8/4/91	Beaudesert, Qld	LHB	WK	
Billy Stanlake	4/11/94	Hervey Bay, Qld	RHB	RFM	Tas
Jack Wood	1/10/96	Ipswich, Qld	RHB	SLC	

2021-22 Award Winners
Bulls player of the season (Ian Healy Medalist) – Mark Steketee
Sheffield Shield player of the season – Mark Steketee
Marsh One Day Cup player of the season – Matthew Renshaw
Bulls Players' player award – Mark Steketee

Recent Ian Healy Medal winners

2012-13	Chris Hartley	2017-18	Michael Neser
2013-14	James Hopes	2018-19	Mark Steketee
2014-15	Joe Burns	2019-20	Michael Neser
2015-16	Chris Hartley	2020-21	Marnus Labuschagne
2016-17	Michael Neser	2021-22	Mark Steketee

SOUTH AUSTRALIA
Coach – Jason Gillespie

	No.	DOB	Place		
Wes Agar	13	5/2/97	Malvern, Vic	RHB	RFM
Jordan Buckingham	21	17/3/00	Bundoora, Vic	RHB	RFM
Jake Carder	26	11/12/95	Perth, WA	LHB	RM
Alex Carey *	5	27/8/91	Loxton, SA	LHB	WK
Harry Conway		17/9/92	Darlinghurst, Sydney	RHB	RFM
Brendan Doggett	35	3/5/94	Rockhampton, Qld	RHB	RFM
Daniel Drew	47	22/5/96	Ashford, Adelaide	RHB	R
David Grant	14	24/5/97	North Adelaide	RHB	RFM
Travis Head ©	34	29/12/93	Adelaide	LHB	ROS
Henry Hunt	22	7/1/97	Cowra, NSW	RHB	RM
Spencer Johnson	10	16/11/95	Adelaide	LHB	LFM
Jake Lehmann	33	8/7/92	Adelaide	LHB	SLA
Thomas Kelly	31	14/12/00	Ashford, Adelaide	RHB	
Nathan McAndrew	0	14/7/93	Wollongong, NSW	RHB	RFM
Nathan McSweeney	38	8/3/99	Brisbane	RHB	ROS
Ben Manenti		23/3/97	Alexandria, NSW	RHB	ROS
Harry Nielsen	4	3/5/95	Adelaide	LHB	WK
Lloyd Pope	24	1/12/99	Adelaide	RHB	LEG
Liam Scott	6	12/12/00	Crows Nest, NSW	RHB	RM
Henry Thornton		16/12/96	Kogarah, NSW	RHB	RFM
Jake Weatherald	28	4/11/94	Darwin, NT	LHB	LEG
Nick Winter	44	19/6/93	Garran, ACT	LHB	LFM
Rookie Contracts:					
Kyle Brazell		20/9/01	Campbelltown, SA	LHB	SLA
Aiden Cahill		20/3/03		RHB	RFM
Bailey Capel	12	15/4/00	Henley Beach, SA	LHB	
Issac Higgins		8/9/02		RHB	SLA
Ryan King		2/11/01	Mt Barker, SA	LHB	LEG
Harry Matthias		25/6/03		RHB	WK

*CA Contract

In – Jordan Buckingham (upgraded), Harry Conway, Spencer Johnson, Thomas Kelly (upgraded), Ben Manenti (Tas), Henry Thornton, Aidan Cahill (rookie list), Isaac Higgins (rookie list), Harry Matthias (rookie list).

Off Contract list for 2022-23

	No	DOB	Place			Reason
Ryan Gibson	2	30/12/93	Penrith, NSW	RHB	RM	De-listed
Corey Kelly	24	14/12/00	Ashford, SA	RHB	RM	De-listed
Sam Kerber	20	26/7/94	Shepparton, Vic	LHB	SLA	De-listed
Joe Mennie	15	24/12/88	Coffs Harbour, NSW	RHB	RFM	UK
Tim Oakley	58	29/8/97	Golden Grove, SA	LHB	RFM	De-listed
Kane Richardson	55	12/2/91	Eudunda, SA	RHB	RFM	Qld
Daniel Worrall	1	10/7/91	Melbourne, Vic	RHB	RFM	Surrey

2021-22 Award Winners
Neil Dansie (MVP) Medalist – Henry Hunt (99 votes), Runner-up: Nathan McAndrew (93)
Marsh Cup Award – Alex Carey
Barry Jarman award (Most improved) – Thomas Kelly
Barry "Nuggett" Rees award – Jordan Buckingham

Recent Neil Dansie Medal winners

2012-13	Chadd Sayers	2017-18	Joe Mennie
2013-14	Tom Cooper	2018-19	Jake Lehmann
2014-15	Callum Ferguson	2019-20	Wes Agar
2015-16	Joe Mennie	2020-21	Travis Head
2016-17	Chadd Sayers	2021-22	Henry Hunt

TASMANIA
Coach: Jeff Vaughan

	No.	DOB	Place	Bat	Bowl
Tom Andrews	54	7/10/94	Darwin, NT	LHB	SLA
Gabe Bell	5	3/7/95	Trevallyn, Tas	RHB	RFM
Jackson Bird	22	11/12/86	Sydney	RHB	RFM
Iain Carlisle		5/1/00		LHB	RMF
Jake Doran	2	2/10/96	Blacktown, NSW	LHB	WK
Nathan Ellis	72	22/9/94	Greenacre, NSW	RHB	RFM
Brad Hope	30	13/7/99	Perth	RHB	RM
Caleb Jewell	1	21/4/97	Hobart, Tas	LHB	
Ben McDermott	28	12/12/94	Caboolture, Qld	RHB	RM
Riley Meredith	12	21/6/96	Bellerive, Tas	LHB	RFM
Lawrence Neil-Smith	27	1/6/99	NSW	RHB	RMF
Sam Rainbird	43	5/6/92	Hobart, Tas	RHB	LMF
Peter Siddle	46	25/11/84	Traralgon, Vic	RHB	RFM
Jordan Silk	21	18/1/91	Penrith, NSW	RHB	
Matthew Wade *	31	26/10/87	Hobart	LHB	WK
Charlie Wakim	9	9/7/91	Paddington, NSW	RHB	RM
Tim Ward	61	16/2/98	Sydney	LHB	
Beau Webster	20	1/12/93	Snug, Hobart	RHB	ROB
Mac Wright	33	22/1/98	Ferntree Gully, Vic	RHB	LEG
Rookie Contracts:					
Nick Davis		27/9/02		RHB	RFM
Jarrod Freeman	19	15/7/00	Launceston, Tas	RHB	ROB
Mitch Owen	16	16/9/01		RHB	RFM
Nivethan Radhakrishnan	3	25/11/02		LHB	R/L

*CA Contract.

In for 2022-23: Ian Carlisle (ex NSW underage), Nick Davis (Tas underage/Glenorchy), Billy Stanlake (Qld).

Off Contract list for 2022-23

Tim Paine *	36	8/12/84	Hobart, Tas		RHB	WK

2021-22 Award Winners

Ricky Ponting Medalist – Tied between Peter Siddle and Jordan Silk (134 votes), Caleb Jewell (90), Ben McDermott (82)

David Boon Medalist (Sheffield Shield) – Caleb Jewell (87 votes), Peter Siddle (73), Jordan Silk (66), Tim Ward (62)

Jack Simmons Medalist (Marsh Cup) – Jordan Silk. Jamie Cox Young Player of the year – Tim Ward
Scott Mason Memorial Captain's Award – Caleb Jewell

Recent Ricky Ponting Medal winners

2012-13	James Faulkner	2017-18	George Bailey
2013-14	Evan Gulbis	2018-19	Matthew Wade
2014-15	Andrew Fekete	2019-20	Jackson Bird
2015-16	Ben Dunk	2020-21	Jackson Bird
2016-17	Alex Doolan	2021-22	Peter Siddle and Jordan Silk

VICTORIA
Coach: Chris Rogers

	No.	DOB	Place	Type	
Scott Boland	25	11/4/89	Parkdale, Vic	RHB	RFM
Xavier Crone	26	19/12/97	Strathfieldsaye, Vic	RHB	RFM
Travis Dean	29	1/2/92	Williamstown, Vic	RHB	
Zak Evans	21	26/3/00	Westmead, NSW	RHB	RFM
Aaron Finch *	5	17/11/86	Colac, Victoria	RHB	SLA
Jake Fraser-McGurk	23	11/4/02	Melbourne	RHB	LEG
Peter Handscomb	54	26/4/91	Melbourne	RHB	WK
Sam Harper	7	10/12/96	Knoxfield, Vic	RHB	WK
Marcus Harris	14	21/7/92	Scarborough, WA	LHB	
Mackenzie Harvey	15	18/9/00	East St Kilda, Vic	LHB	RMF
Jon Holland	18	29/5/87	Sandringham, Vic	RHB	SLA
Cameron McLure	13	25/9/01	Maryborough, Vic	RHB	RFM
Nic Maddinson	53	21/12/91	Shoalhaven, NSW	LHB	SLA
Glenn Maxwell *	32	14/10/88	Kew. Melbourne	RHB	ROS
Jonathan Merlo	11	15/12/98	Melbourne	RHB	RMF
Todd Murphy	28	15/11/00	Echuca, Vic	LHB	ROS
Tom O'Connell	16	14/6/00	Brighton, SA	LHB	LEG
Will Parker	8	27/5/02			LEG
James Pattinson	19	3/5/90	Melbourne	LHB	RFM
Mitch Perry	35	27/4/00	Melbourne	LHB	RFM
Will Pucovski	10	2/2/98	Malvern, Vic	RHB	
Matthew Short	2	8/11/95	Ballarat, Vic	RHB	RM
Will Sutherland	12	27/10/99	East Melbourne	RHB	RFM
Rookie Contracts:					
Ashley Chandrasinghe		12/12/01		LHB	LEG
Brody Couch	24	5/12/99	Timboon, Vic	LHB	RFM
Sam Elliott	1	18/2/00	Mitcham, Melbourne	RHB	RFM
Campbell Kellaway		1/11/02		LHB	LFM
Fergus O'Neil		27/3/01		RHB	RM

*CA Contract

In for 2022-23: Ashley Chandrasinghe, Campbell Kellaway (both new rookies)

Off Contract list for 2022-23

	No	DOB	Place			Reason
Xavier Crone	26	19/12/97	Strathfieldsaye, Vic	RHB	RFM	De-listed
Seb Gotch	36	12/7/93	Hughesdale, Vic	RHB	WK	Retired
Tom Jackson		17/12/00	Warrnambool, Vic	RHB		De-listed
James Seymour	27	13/3/92		LHB		De-listed

2021-22 Award Winners
Bill Lawry Medal (Sheffield Shield): Nic Maddinson
Dean Jones Medal (Marsh Cup): Henry Thornton

Recent Bill Lawry Medal winners

2012-13	Chris Rogers	2017-18	Chris Tremain
2013-14	Cameron White	2018-19	Marcus Harris
2014-15	Fawad Ahmed	2019-20	Nic Maddinson
2015-16	Scott Boland	2020-21	Marcus Harris
2016-17	Jon Holland	2021-22	Nic Maddinson

WESTERN AUSTRALIA
Coach: Adam Voges

	No.	DOB	Place			
Ashton Agar *	18	14/10/93	Melbourne		LHB	SLA
Cameron Bancroft	4	19/11/92	Attadale, Perth		RHB	WK
Jason Behrendorff	5	23/4/81	Camden, NSW		RHB	LFM
Hilton Cartwright	35	14/2/92	Harare, Zimbabwe		RHB	RM
Cameron Gannon	24	23/1/89	Baulkham Hills, Sydney		RHB	RFM
Cameron Green *	31	3/6/99	Subiaco, WA		RHB	RMF
Sam Fanning	28	20/10/00			LHB	ROS
Aaron Hardie	21	7/1/99	Bournemouth, England		RHB	RM
Josh Inglis *	95	4/3/95	Leeds, Yorkshire		RHB	WK
Bryce Jackson		28/11/99			RHB	FM
Matt Kelly	12	7/12/94	Durban, Sth Africa		RHB	RFM
Mitchell Marsh *	10	20/10/91	Attadale, Perth		RHB	RFM
Shaun Marsh	20	9/7/83	Narrogin, WA		LHB	SLA
David Moody	15	28/4/95	Mt Lawley, WA		RHB	RFM
Lance Morris	1	28/3/98	Busselton, WA		RHB	RFM
Joel Paris	3	11/12/92	Subiaco, WA		LHB	LMF
Josh Philipee	27	1/6/97	Subiaco, WA		RHB	WK
Jhye Richardson	2	20/9/96	Murdoch, WA		LHB	RFM
Corey Rocchiccioli	77	8/10/97	Subiaco, WA		RHB	ROB
D'Arcy Short	23	9/8/90	Katherine, NT		LHB	SLC
Charlie Stobo		8/3/95	Sydney		RHB	RMF
Marcus Stoinis *	16	16/8/89	Perth, WA		RHB	RM
Ashton Turner	17	25/1/93	Perth, WA		RHB	ROS
Sam Whiteman	9	19/3/92	Doncaster, Yorkshire		LHB	WK
Teague Wyllie	48	24/4/04	Mandurah, WA		RHB	
Rookie Contracts:						
Cooper Connolly		22/8/03			LHB	SLA
Jayden Goodwin	7	13/12/01	Bunbury, WA		LHB	LEG
Sam Greer						
Hamish McKenzie		21/9/99			LHB	SLC

*CA Contract

In for 2022-23 – Sam Greer, Hamish McKenzie, Teague Wyllie

Off Contract list for 2022-23

	No	DOB	Place			Reason
Liam Guthrie	6	3/4/97	Subiaco, WA	LHB	LFM	Qld

2021-22 Award Winners
Lawrie Sawle Medal: Hilton Cartwright (82 votes), Jhye Richardson (77), Cameron Bancroft (52)
Four Day Player of the Year – Hilton Cartwright
Marsh Cup Player of the Year – Andrew Tye
Gold Cup (Best WA player across all levels): Mitchell Marsh

Recent Lawrie Sawle Medal winners

2012-13	Nathan Coulter-Nile	2017-18	Mitchell Marsh
2013-14	Marcus North	2018-19	Shaun Marsh
2014-15	Adam Voges	2019-20	Shaun Marsh
2015-16	Cameron Bancroft	2020-21	Cameron Green
2016-17	Hilton Cartwright	2021-22	Hilton Cartwright

WNCL SQUADS

AUSTRALIAN CAPITAL TERRITORY (Coach – Jono Dean)

	No.	DOB	Place	Club	Bat	Bwl/k
Alisha Bates		18/3/02			L	LM
Kayla Burton		2/9/02		Campbelltown-Camden	R	LEG
Rebecca Carter	32	16/7/96		Box Hill (Vic)	L	
Zoe Cooke	15	17/9/95	Bruce, ACT	Western Dist-Uni of Can	R	RM
Holly Ferling		22/12/95	Kingaroy, Qld		R	RMF
Angelina Genford		30/10/02			R	RM
Erica Kershaw	*12*	*23/12/91*	*Castlemaine, Vic*	*Prahran (Vic)*	*L*	*LEG*
Carly Leeson	74	9/11/98	St Leonards, NSW	Universities (NSW)	R	RM
Matilda Lugg	3	12/11/99	Moruya, NSW	Sawtell	R	WK
Katie Mack	2	14/9/93	Melbourne	Box Hill (Vic)	R	LEG
Olivia Porter	33	14/11/01		Universities (NSW)	R	RM
Chloe Rafferty	7	16/6/99	Williamstown, Vic		R	RM
Angela Reakes	8	27/12/90	Byron Bay, NSW	Melbourne (Vic)	R	LEG
Gabrielle Sutcliffe	6	11/4/02		Penrith (NSW)	R	RM
Annie Wikman		27/4/01			R	RM
Amy Yates	88	30/9/98	Frankston, Vic	Melbourne (Vic)	R	

In - Holly Ferling (Queensland), Alisha Bates, Annie Wikman, Angelina Genford (NSW).
Out: – Erin Osborne (retired), Madeline Penna (SA), Nicola Hancock (delisted), Erica Kershaw (delisted)

NEW SOUTH WALES (Coach – Gavan Twining)

	No.	DOB	Place	Club	Bat	Bwl/k
Jade Allen	9	13/11/03		Universities	R	LEG
Maitlan Brown	66	5/6/97	Taree, NSW		R	RM
Erin Burns	29	22/6/88	Wollongong, NSW	Bankstown	R	ROS
Stella Campbell	14	15/6/02	Mona Vale, NSW	Universities	R	RM
Lauren Cheatle	25	6/11/98	Bowral, NSW	Campbelltown-Camden	L	LMF
Hannah Darlington	30	25/1/01	Sydney, NSW	Campbelltown-Camden	R	RM
Ash Gardner *	6	15/4/97	Bankstown, NSW	Bankstown	R	ROS
Rachael Haynes *	15	26/12/86	Carlton, Vic	Sydney	L	LM
Alyssa Healy © *	77	24/3/90	Gold Coast, Qld	Sydney	R	WK
Saskia Horley		23/2/00		Manly Warringah	R	SLA
Emma Hughes	22	13/11/00		Penrith	R	RM
Sammy-Jo Johnson	58	5/11/92	Lismore, NSW	Sydney	R	RM
Anika Learoyd	44	14/4/02		Northern District	R	RM
Phoebe Litchfield	18	18/4/03	Orange, NSW	Parramatta	L	
Claire Moore		28/10/03		Parramatta	R	RM
Lauren Smith	2	6/10/96	Central Coast, NSW	Northern District	R	ROS
Tahlia Wilson	21	21/10/99	Figtree, NSW	St George-Sutherland	R	RM

In – Saskia Horley. **Out –** Rachel Trenaman (Tas)

QUEENSLAND (Coach – Ashley Noffke)

	No.	DOB	Place	Club	Bat	Bwl/k
Lucy Hamilton		8/5/06		Sunshine Coast	L	LM
Grace Harris	17	18/9/93	Ipswich, Qld	Wests	R	ROS
Nicola Hancock		8/11/95	Prahran, Vic		R	RM
Laura Harris	4	6/8/90	Ipswich, Qld	University of Qld	R	
Mikayla Hinkley	14	1/5/88	Penrith, NSW	Valley	R	ROS
Ellie Johnston	77	29/1/03		Ipswich/Logan	R	LEG
Ruth Johnston		28/2/03		Ipswich/Logan	R	ROS
Jess Jonassen *	21	5/11/92	Emerald, Qld	University of Qld	L	SLA
Charli Knott	88	29/11/02	Hervey Bay, Qld	Valley	R	ROS
Caitlyn Mair	7	5/5/03		Sandgate-Redcliffe	R	WK
Grace Parsons	34	18/8/03		Gold Coast	R	LEG
Georgia Prestwidge	16	17/12/97	Brisbane	Valley	R	RMF
Georgia Redmayne	8	8/12/93	Lismore, NSW	Gold Coast	L	WK
Courtney Sippel	37	27/4/01	Kingaroy, Qld	Wests	L	RM
Georgia Voll	19	5/8/03		Sandgate-Redcliffe	R	ROS

In – Lucy Hamilton, Nicola Hancock (ACT), Grace Parsons. **Out –** Meagan Dixon (delisted), Holly Ferling (ACT), Lily Mills (WA), Beth Mooney (WA)

327

SOUTH AUSTRALIA (Coach - Luke Williams)

	No.	DOB	Place	Club	Bat	Bwl/k
Jemma Barsby	15	4/10/95	Herston, Qld	Northern Districts	L	ROS
Samantha Betts	14	16/2/96	Orroroo, SA	Northern Districts	R	RM
Darcie Brown *	20	7/3/03	Kapunda, SA	Northern Districts	R	RM
Emma de Broughe	2	6/9/00	Adelaide	Sturt	R	RM
Josie Dooley	11	21/1/00	Brisbane	Sturt	L	ROS
Ellen Falconer	3	3/8/99	Selkirk, Scotland	West Torrens	R	RM
Paris Hall		10/11/03		West Torrens	L	WK
Brooke Harris	31	27/8/97	Adelaide	West Torrens	R	RM
Tahlia McGrath *	9	10/11/95	Adelaide	West Torrens	R	RM
Annie O'Neil	5	18/2/99	Murray Bridge	Sturt	R	LEG
Bridget Patterson	21	12/4/94	Kingscote, SA	Kensington	R	ROS
Madeline Penna		30/8/00			R	LEG
Kate Peterson		3/12/02	North Sydney	Glenelg	R	RM
Megan Schutt © *	27	15/1/93	Adelaide	Sturt	R	RMF
Courtney Webb	17	30/11/99	Launceston, Tas	Glenelg	R	LEG
Amanda Wellington	10	29/5/97	Adelaide	Port Adelaide	R	LEG
Ella Wilson		17/11/03		Glenelg	R	RM

In: Madeline Penna (ACT), Ella Wilson (Glenelg), Paris Hall (West Torrens).
Out: Tegan McPharlin (Retired), Alex Price (delisted), Eliza Doddridge (delisted).

TASMANIA (Coach – Salliann Beams)

	No.	DOB	Place	Club	Bat	Bwl/k
Sam Bates	34	17/8/92	Newcastle, NSW	Kingborough	R	SLA
Nicola Carey *	16	10/9/93	Camperdown, NSW	North Hobart	L	RM
Julia Cavanough		17/3/04			R	LM
Maisy Gibson	13	14/9/96	Singleton, NSW	Clarence	L	LEG
Heather Graham	11	5/10/96	Subiaco, WA	Clarence	R	RM
Brooke Hepburn	12	19/4/90	Launceston, Tas	Kingborough	R	RM
Emma Manix-Geeves	7	12/8/00		Greater Northern	R	ROS
Sasha Moloney	99	14/7/92	Longford, Tas	University of Tasmania	R	
Meg Phillips	10	2/2/96	Evandale, Tas	New Town	R	RM
Hayley Silver-Holmes	4	18/8/03	Wahroonga, NSW	Parramatta	R	RF
Amy Smith	14	16/11/04		New Town	R	LEG
Naomi Stalenberg	5	19/4/94	Blacktown, NSW	North Hobart	R	RM
Molly Strano	26	5/10/92	Sunshine, Vic	Essendon Maribyrnong	R	ROS
Emma Thompson	74	12/2/90	Baulkham Hills, NSW	Clarence	R	RM
Rachel Trenaman		18/4/01	Broken Hill, NSW		R	LEG
Elyse Villani	2	6/10/89	Greensborough, Vic	Essendon Maribyrnong	R	RM
Callie Wilson		1/11/03			R	RM

In: Julie Cavanough (Qld underage/Sandgate Redcliffe)), Emma Manix-Geeves, Clare Scott, Rachel Trenaman (NSW), Callie Wilson (SA underage/Sturt). **Out:** Corinne Hall (retired), Chloe Abel, Rachel Priest, Emily Smith, Belinda Vakarewa

VICTORIA (Coach – Jarrad Loughman)

	No.	DOB	Place	Club	Bat	Bwl/k
Tiana Atkinson	16	30/4/02		Dandenong	L	RM
Sam Bates	34	17/8/92	Newcastle, NSW	Essendon Maribyrnong	R	SLA
Makinley Blows	15	12/12/97	Broken Hill, NSW	Essendon Maribyrnong	L	RM
Lucy Cripps	24	6/12/01	Melbourne	Dandenong	R	RM
Sophie Day	6	2/9/98	Greensborough, Vic	Prahran	L	
Nicole Faltum	4	17/6/00	Traralgon, Vic	Dandenong	R	WK
Tess Flintoff	25	31/3/03	Melbourne	Ringwood	R	RM
Kim Garth	11	25/4/96	Dublin, Ireland	Dandenong	R	RM
Ella Hayward	18	8/9/03		Melbourne	R	ROS
Olivia Henry		27/1/04		Ringwood	R	ROS
Meg Lanning © *	7	25/3/92	Singapore	Box Hill	R	RM
Rhys McKenna	8	17/8/04		Prahran	R	RM
Sophie Molineux *	23	17/1/98	Bairnsdale, Vic	Dandenong	L	SLA
Rhiann O'Donnell	14	14/4/98	Mildura	Melbourne	R	RM
Ellyse Perry *	20	3/11/90	Wahroonga, NSW	Dandenong	R	RMF
Sophie Reid				Carlton	L	
Annabel Sutherland	3	12/10/01	East Melbourne	Prahran	R	RM
Tayla Vlaeminck *	17	27/10/98	Bendigo, Vic	Plenty Valley	R	RM
Georgia Wareham *	32	26/5/99	Terang, Vic	Essendon Maribyrnong	R	RM

In: Olivia Henry, Sophie Reid. **Out:** Anna Lanning, Lara Shannon, Amy Vine

	No.	DOB	Place	Club	Bat	Bwl/k
Anna Lanning	9	25/3/94	Sydney	Box Hill	R	RM
Lara Shannon				Box Hill		
Amy Vine	10	22/12/91	Carlton, Vic	Melbourne	R	LEG

WESTERN AUSTRALIA – (Coach: Becky Grundy)

	No.	DOB	Place	Club	Bat	Bwl/k
Charis Bekker	26	30/11/01		Subiaco-Floreat	R	SLA
Zoe Britcliffe	46	15/9/01		South Perth	R	RM
Mathilda Carmichael	5	4/4/94	St Leonards, NSW	Melville	R	RM
Piepa Cleary		17/7/96	Subiaco, WA		R	RM
Sheldyn Cooper	17	29/7/00	Swan Districts, WA	Midland-Guildford	R	RM
Maddy Darke	17	30/3/01	Randwick, Sydney	Subiaco-Floreat	R	WK
Ashley Day	64	17/9/99	Penrith, NSW	South Perth	R	LEG
Amy Edgar	9	27/12/97	Cowra, NSW	Penrith, NSW	R	RM
Lisa Griffith		28/8/92	Bathurst, NSW		R	RMF
Molly Healy	20	15/7/03	Subiaco, WA	South Perth	R	RM
Alana King *	23	22/11/95	Clarinda, Vic	Prahran	R	LEG
Lily Mills	56	2/1/01		Sandgate-Redcliffe	R	RM
Beth Mooney *	6	14/1/94	Shepparton, Vic		L	WK
Courtney Neale		4/7/98	Officer, Vic		R	RM
Taneale Peschel		29/8/92	Rockingham, WA	Midland-Guildford	R	RM
Chloe Piparo	28	5/9/94	Bunbury, WA	Midland-Guildford	R	RS
Poppy Stockwell		24/10/03		South Perth	R	LM
Georgia Wyllie	3	3/5/02		South Perth	R	LM

In – Charis Bekker, Piepa Cleary, Lilly Mills (Queensland), Beth Mooney (Queensland), Poppy Stockwell.
Out – Nicole Bolton (retired), Molly Healy (delisted), Courtney Neale (delisted)

Squads for BBL12 plus any known changes and those picked up in Draft
Squads correct to September 1, 2022
Players in italics yet to be confirmed

ADELAIDE STRIKERS
Coach: Jason Gillespie

	No.	DOB	Place	Ht	Bt	Bwl/k
Wes Agar	21	5/2/97	Malvern, Vic	193	R	RFM
Cameron Boyce	13	27/7/89	Charleville, Qld	178	R	LEG
Alex Carey	5	27/8/91	Loxton, SA	182	L	WK
Harry Conway	13	17/9/92	Darlinghurst, Sydney	200	R	RFM
Colin de Grandhomme		22/7/86	Harare, Zimbabwe	184	R	RM
Ryan Gibson	88	30/12/93	Penrith, NSW	183	R	RM
Travis Head	34	29/12/83	Adelaide	180	L	ROS
Adam Hose		25/10/92	Newport, Isle of Wight	188	R	RMF
Henry Hunt		7/1/97	Cowra, NSW		R	
Spencer Johnson	*42*	*16/12/95*	*Adelaide*	*193*	*L*	*LFM*
Thomas Kelly		14/12/00	Ashford, Adelaide		R	
Rashid Khan	19	20/9/98	Nangarhar, Afghanistan	168	R	LEG
Chris Lynn		10/4/90	Brisbane	180	R	SLA
Harry Nielsen	4	24/12/88	Adelaide	177	L	WK
Liam O'Connor	*9*	*20/6/93*	*Perth, WA*	*177*	*R*	*LEG*
Liam Scott	12	12/12/00	Crows Nest, NSW	192	R	RFM
Matt Short	2	8/11/95	Melbourne	187	R	ROS
Peter Siddle	64	25/11/84	Traralgon, Vic	187	R	RFM
Jake Weatherald	28	4/11/94	Darwin, NT	178	L	LEG

In: Cameron Boyce (Renegades), Colin de Grandhomme (NZ), Adam Hose (Birmingham), Chris Lynn (Heat)
Out: Fawad Ahmed, Matthew Renshaw (Heat), Jonathan Wells (Renegades), Daniel Worrell (Surrey)

	No.	DOB	Place	Ht	Bt	Bwl/k
Matthew Renshaw	77	28/3/96	Middlesborough, UK	186	L	ROS
Jonathan Wells	29	13/8/88	Hobart	170	R	RM

BRISBANE HEAT
Coach: Wade Seccombe

	No.	DOB	Place	Ht	Bt	Bwl/k
Xavier Bartlett	19	17/12/98	Adelaide		R	RFM
James Bazley	7	8/4/95	Buderim, Qld		R	RMF
Sam Billings		15/6/91	Pembury, Kent	183	R	WK
Max Bryant	1	10/3/99	Murwillumbah, NSW	178	R	RM
Tom Cooper	*26*	*26/11/86*	*Wollongong, NSW*	*187*	*R*	*ROB*
Sam Heazlett	47	12/9/95	Sunnybank, Qld		L	SLA
Usman Khawaja		18/12/86	Islamabad, Pakistan	177	L	ROS
Matthew Kuhnemann	30	20/9/96	Brisbane	183	L	SLA
Marnus Labuschagne	9	22/6/94	Klerksdrop, Sth Africa	182	R	RM
Colin Munro		11/3/87	Durban, South Africa	178	L	
Michael Neser	20	29/3/90	Pretoria, South Africa	183	R	RFM
James Peirson	59	13/10/92	Sydney	178	R	WK
Matt Renshaw		28/3/96	Middlesborough, Eng	186	L	ROS
Mark Steketee	6	17/1/94	Monto, Qld	187	R	RFM
Mitch Swepson	4	4/10/93	Brisbane	187	R	RFM
Ross Whiteley		13/2/88	Sheffield, England	189	L	LM
Jack Wildermuth	10	1/9/93	Toowoomba, Qld	191	R	RFM

In: Sam Billings (Thunder), Usman Khawaja (Thunder), Colin Munro (Scorchers), Matt Renshaw (Strikers), Ross Whiteley (Hampshire/Southern Brave)
Out: Ben Laughlin, Chris Lynn (Strikers), Mujeeb-ur-Rahman (Renegades),

HOBART HURRICANES
Coach: Jeff Vaughan

	No.	DOB	Place	Ht	Bt	Bwl/k
Asif Ali		1/10/91	Faisalabad, Pakistan	180	R	ROS
Faheem Ashraf		16/1/94	Kasur, Pakistan		L	RMF
Scott Boland	25	11/4/89	Parkdale, Vic	189	R	RFM
Tim David	8	16/3/96	Singapore	196	R	ROS
Nathan Ellis	72	22/9/94	Greenacre, NSW		R	RFM
Peter Handscomb	54	26/4/91	Melbourne	183	R	WK
Caleb Jewell	1	21/4/97	Hobart		L	
Josh Kann		15/11/99	Southport, Qld		R	RFM
Shadab Khan		4/10/98	Mianwali, Pakistan	178	R	LEG
Ben McDermott	28	12/12/94	Caboolture, Qld	183	R	
Riley Meredith	21	21/6/96	Hobart		L	RFM
Mitch Owen	16	16/9/01		187	R	RMF
Joel Paris	3	11/12/92	Subiaco, WA	191	L	LFM
Will Parker	17	27/5/02		184	R	LEG
D'Arcy Short	23	9/8/90	Katherine, NT	180	L	SLC
Billy Stanlake		4/9/03	Hervey Bay, Qld	204	L	RFM
Matthew Wade	13	26/12/84	Hobart	170	L	WK
Nick Winter	4	19/6/93	Garran, ACT	186	L	LMF
Mac Wright	33	22/1/98	Ferntree Gully, Vic	183	R	LEG

In – Asif Ali (Pakistan), Faheem Ashraf (Pakistan), Shabab Khan (Pakistan), Billy Stanlake (Stars)
Out – Harry Brook, Sandeep Lamichhane, Tom Lammondby, Tom Rogers (Renegades), Jordan Thompson,

MELBOURNE RENEGADES
Coach: David Saker (until end of 2022/23)

	No.	DOB	Place	Ht	Bt	Bwl/k
Zak Evans	2	26/3/2000	Westmead, NSW	189	R	RMF
Aaron Finch	5	17/11/86	Colac, Victoria	176	R	SLA
Jake Fraser-McGurk	23	11/4/02	Melbourne	178	R	LEG
Sam Harper	6	10/12/96	Knoxfield, Vic	168	R	WK
Marcus Harris	14	21/7/92	Scarborough, WA	173	L	
Mackenzie Harvey	3	18/9/00	St Kilda, Melbourne	182	L	RM
Jon Holland	18	29/5/87	Sandringham, Vic	183	R	SLA
Akeal Hosein		25/4/93	Port-of-Spain, Trinidad	178	L	SLA
Josh Lalor	11	2/11/87	Mount Druitt, NSW	183	R	LFM
Liam Livingstone		4/8/93	Barrow-in-Furness, Eng	186	R	LEG
Nic Maddinson	53	21/12/91	Nowra, NSW	185	L	SLA
Shaun Marsh	9	9/7/83	Narrogin, WA	186	L	
Mitchell Perry	16	27/4/00	Melbourne	185	L	RFM
Jack Prestwidge	61	28/2/96	Brisbane	187	R	RFM
Mujeeb-Ur-Rahman		28/3/01	Khost, Afghanistan	180	R	ROS
Kane Richardson	55	12/2/91	Eudunda, SA	190	R	RFM
Will Sutherland	12	27/10/99	East Melbourne	195	R	RFM
Jonathan Wells		13/8/88	Hobart	170	R	RM

In: Akeal Hosein (West Indies), Liam Livingstone (England), Mujeeb-Ur-Rahman (Heat), Jonathan Wells (Strikers)
Out: Unmukt Chand, Zahir Khan, Mohammad Nabi, James Pattinson, Reece Topley,

MELBOURNE STARS
Coach: David Hussey

	No.	DOB	Place	Ht	Bt	Bwl
Trent Boult		22/7/89	Rotorua, New Zealand	180	R	LFM
Joe Burns	15	6/9/89	Herston, Brisbane	182	R	RM
Hilton Cartwright	35	11/10/87	Osborne Park, WA	191	R	RFM
Joe Clarke	33	26/5/96	Shrewsbury, Eng	180	R	WK
Brody Couch	24	5/12/99	Timboon, Vic	19	L	RFM
Nathan Coulter-Nile	7	11/10/87	Osborne Park, WA	191	R	RFM
Sam Elliott	*1*	*18/2/00*	*Mitcham, Melbourne*		*R*	*RFM*
Liam Hatcher	19	17/9/96	Liverpool, NSW	190	R	RFM
Clint Hinchliffe	23	23/10/96	Duncraig, WA	179	L	SLA
Zahir Khan	*88*	*20/12/98*	*Paktika, Afghanistan*	*172*	*L*	*SLC*
Nick Larkin	36	1/5/90	Taree, NSW	187	R	
Glenn Maxwell ©	32	14/10/88	Kew, Melbourne	182	R	ROS
Jonathan Merlo	*12*	*15/12/98*	*East Melbourne, Vic*	*182*	*R*	*RMF*
Tom O'Connell	*6*	*14/6/00*	*Brighton, SA*	*181*	*L*	*LEG*
Sam Rainbird	*43*	*5/6/92*	*Hobart*	*188*	*R*	*SLA*
Marcus Stonis	16	16/8/89	Perth, WA	185	R	RFM
Beau Webster	20	1/12/93	Snug, Hobart	194	R	ROS
Luke Wood		2/8/95	Sheffield, England	177	L	LFM
Adam Zampa	88	31/3/92	Shellharbour, NSW	175	R	RLG

In: Trent Boult (New Zealand), Luke Wood (Lancashire)

Out: Qais Ahmad, Ahmed Daniyal, Syed Faridoun, Seb Gotch (Retired), Haris Rauf, Andre Russell, Billy Stanlake (Hurricanes)

PERTH SCORCHERS
Coach: Adam Voges (until end of 2023/24)

	No.	DOB	Place	Ht	Bat	Bwl/k
Ashton Agar	*18*	*14/10/93*	*Melbourne*	*187*	*L*	*SLA*
Cameron Bancroft	4	19/11/82	Attadale, Perth	182	R	
Jason Behrendorff	5	23/4/81	Camden, NSW	194	R	LFM
Cooper Connolly		22/8/03			L	SLA
Laurie Evans	32	12/10/87	Lambeth, England	183	R	RM
Aaron Hardie	21	7/1/99	Bournemouth, England	193	R	RMF
Peter Hatzoglou	34	27/11/98		188	R	LEG
Nick Hobson	19	22/8/94	Perth		L	RM
Josh Inglis	95	4/3/95	Leeds, Yorkshire	172	R	WK
Matt Kelly	12	7/12/94	Durban, South Africa	193	R	RFM
Mitchell Marsh	10	20/10/91	Attadale, Perth	193	R	RFM
Tymal Mills	72	12/8/92	Dewsbury, England	185	R	LF
David Moody	*15*	*28/4/95*	*Mt Lawley, WA*	*195*	*R*	*RFM*
Lance Morris	1	28/3/98	Busselton, WA	185	R	RFM
Jhye Richardson	2	20/9/96	Murdoch, WA	180	L	RFM
Phil Salt		28/8/96	Bodelwyddan, UK	178	R	ROS
Ashton Turner	17	25/1/93	Perth	191	R	ROS
Andrew Tye	68	12/12/86	Perth	192	R	RMF
Sam Whiteman	*9*	*19/3/92*	*Doncaster, Yorks*	*183*	*L*	*WK*

In: Phil Salt (Lancashire)

Out: Colin Munro (Heat), Kurtis Patterson (Sixers),

SYDNEY SIXERS
Coach: Greg Shipperd (until end of 2023/24)

	No.	DOB	Place	Ht	Bt	Bwl/k
Sean Abbott	77	29/2/92	Windsor, NSW	184	R	RFM
Justin Avendano	32	11/8/93	Terrigal, NSW	183	R	
Jackson Bird	33	11/12/86	Sydney	195	R	RFM
Daniel Christian	54	4/5/83	Camperdown, NSW	183	R	RFM
Ben Dwarshuis	23	23/6/94	Kareela, NSW	183	L	LFM
Jack Edwards	18	19/4/00	Allambie Heights, NSW	198	R	RFM
Mickey Edwards	78	23/12/94	Sydney	198	R	RFM
Moises Henriques ©	21	1/2/87	Funchal, Portugal	189	R	RFM
Daniel Hughes	16	2/7/79	Bathurst, NSW	188	L	
Chris Jordan	34	4/10/88	Christchurch, Barbados	185	R	RFM
Hayden Kerr	50	10/7/96	Bowral, NSW	184	R	LFM
Nathan Lyon	67	20/11/87	Young, NSW	181	R	ROS
Ben Manenti	46	23/3/97	Alexandria, Sydney	185	R	ROS
Izharulhaq Naveed		10/11/03			R	LEG
Stephen O'Keefe	72	9/10/84	Malaysia	175	R	SLA
Kurtis Patterson	41	5/5/93	Hurstville, NSW	192	L	
Josh Philippe	22	1/6/97	Subiaco, WA	177	R	
Lloyd Pope	7	1/2/99	Adelaide	185	R	LEG
Jordan Silk	14	18/1/91	Penrith, Sydney	187	R	
James Vince	9	14/2/91	Cuckfield, Sussex, UK	183	R	RM

In: Kurtis Patterson (Scorchers), Izharulhaq Naveed
Out: Tom Curran, Shadab Khan (Hurricanes)

SYDNEY THUNDER
Coach: Trevor Bayliss (until end of 2023/24)

	No.	DOB	Place	Ht	Bt	Bwl/k
Jono Cook	50	14/12/89	Port Macquarie, NSW	184	R	LEG
Ben Cutting	31	30/1/87	Sunnybank, Brisbane	192	R	RFM
Oliver Davies	9	14/10/00	Manly, NSW	179	R	ROB
Brendan Doggett	35	3/5/94	Rockhampton	188	R	RFM
Matt Gilkes	22	21/8/99	Ulladulla, NSW	177	L	WK
Chris Green	93	1/10/93	Durban, South Africa	190	R	ROS
Alex Hales	6	3/1/89	Hillingdon, UK	195	R	
Baxter Holt	27	21/10/99	Carlingford, NSW	181	L	WK
Nathan McAndrew	44	14/7/93	Wollongong, NSW	189	R	RFM
Arjun Nair	7	12/4/98	Canberra	176	R	ROS
Alex Ross	49	17/4/92	Melbourne	179	R	ROS
Rilee Rossouw		9/10/89	Bloemfontein, South Africa	182	L	ROS
Daniel Sams	60	27/10/92	Milperra, NSW	181	R	LFM
Gurinder Sandhu	28	14/6/93	Blacktown, Sydney	194	L	RFM
Jason Sangha	3	8/9/99	Randwick, Sydney	183	R	LEG
Tanveer Sangha	17	26/11/01	Liverpool, Sydney	176	R	LEG
Chris Tremain	20	10/8/91	Dubbo, NSW	188	R	RFM
David Warner	31	27/10/86	Paddington, Sydney	170	L	
David Willey		28/2/90	Northampton, England	185	L	LFM

In: Rilee Rossouw (South Africa), David Warner, David Willey (England)
Out: Sam Billings (Heat), Usman Khawaja (Heat)

ADELAIDE STRIKERS
Coach: Luke Williams

	No.	DOB	Place	Bat	Bwl/k
Jemma Barsby	4	4/10/95	Brisbane	L	ROS
Darcie Brown	20	7/3/03	Kapunda, SA	R	RM
Deandra Dottin		21/6/91	Barbados	R	RM
Tahlia McGrath	9	10/11/95	Adelaide	R	RM
Tegan McPharlin	7	7/8/98	Balaklava, SA	R	WK
Bridget Patterson	21	12/4/94	Kangaroo Island	R	ROS
Annie O'Neill	5	18/2/99	Murray Bridge, SA	R	LEG
Maddy Penna	8	30/8/00	Sydney	R	LEG
Megan Schutt	27	15/1/93	Adelaide	R	RMF
Amanda Wellington	10	29/5/97	Adelaide	R	LEG
Laura Woolvardt	14	26/4/99	Milnerton, Sth Africa	R	

In: Deandra Dottin (WI)

Off:

BRISBANE HEAT
Coach: Ashley Noffke

	No.	DOB	Place	Bat	Bwl/k
Zoe Cooke		17/9/95	Bruce, ACT	R	RM
Nicola Hancock	44	8/11/95	Prahran, Vic	R	RM
Grace Harris	17	18/9/93	Ipswich, Qld	R	ROS
Laura Harris	4	18/8/90	Ipswich, Qld	R	
Mikayla Hinkley	14	1/5/98	Penrith, NSW	R	ROS
Ellie Johnston	77	29/1/03		R	LEG
Jess Jonassen ©	21	5/11/92	Emerald, Qld	L	SLA
Charli Knott	88	29/11/02	Hervey Bay, Qld	R	ROS
Amelia Kerr (NZ)	48	13/10/00	Wellington, NZ	R	LEG
Charli Knott	88	5/5/03	Hervey Bay, Qld	R	RM
Grace Parsons		18/8/03		R	LEG
Georgia Redmayne	8	8/12/93	Lismore, NSW	L	WK
Courtney Sippel	37	27/4/01	Ballina, NSW	L	LM
Pooja Vastrakar		25/9/99	Bilaspur, India	R	RM
Georgia Voll	19	5/8/03		R	ROS
Danni Wyatt		22/4/91	Stoke-on-Trent, Eng	R	ROS

In: Danni Wyatt (Eng)

Off:

HOBART HURRICANES
Coach: Salliann Briggs

	No.	DOB	Place	Bat	Bwl/k
Nicola Carey	16	10/9/93	Sydney	L	RM
Maisy Gibson	13	14/9/96	Singleton, NSW	L	LEG
Heather Graham		10/5/96	Subiaco, WA	R	RM
Mignon du Preez (SA)	22	13/7/89	Pretoria, South Africa	R	
Ruth Johnston	28	28/2/03		R	ROS
Lizelle Lee (SA)	67	2/4/92	Ermelo, Sth Africa	R	
Emma Manix-Geeves		12/8/00		R	ROS
Hayley Silver-Holmes		18/8/03	Wahroonga, NSW	R	RM
Amy Smith	14	16/11/04		R	LEG
Naomi Stalenberg	10	19/4/94	Blacktown, NSW	R	RM
Molly Strano	26	5/10/92	Sunshine, Vic	R	ROS
Rachel Trenaman	46	18/4/01	Broken Hill, NSW	R	LEG
Elyse Villani	2	6/10/89	Melbourne	R	RM
Izzy Wong		15/5/02	Chelsea, London	R	RM

In: Mignon du Preez (Stars), Heather Graham (Scorchers), Ruth Johnston, Lizelle Lee (Renegades), Hayley Silver-Holmes (Sixers), Molly Strano (Hurricanes), Rachel Trenaman (Thunder), Elyse Villani (Renegades), Izzy Wong (Thunder)
Off:

MELBOURNE RENEGADES
Coach: Simon Helmot

	No.	DOB	Place	Bat	Bwl/k
Sarah Coyte		30/3/91	Camden, NSW	R	RM
Josie Dooley	3	21/1/00	Brisbane	R	WK
Ellie Falconer		3/8/99	Clare, SA	R	RM
Holly Ferling	9	22/12/95	Kingaroy, Qld	R	RMF
Kim Garth	34	25/4/96	Dublin, Ireland	R	RM
Ella Hayward	12	8/9/03		R	ROS
Shabnim Ismail (SA)		5/10/88	Cape Town, South Africa	L	RM
Harmanpreet Kaur	7	8/8/89	Punjab, India	R	ROS
Carly Leeson	74	9/11/98	Grafton, NSW	R	RM
Sophie Molineux ©	23	17/1/98	Bairnsdale, Vic	L	SLA
Rhiann O'Donnell	26	14/4/98	Mildura, Vic	R	RM
Tayla Vlaeminck		27/10/98	Bendigo, Vic	R	RM
Georgia Wareham	32	26/5/99	Terang, Vic	R	RM
Courtney Webb	11	30/11/99	Launceston, Tas	R	RM

In: Sarah Coyte (Strikers), Ellie Falconer (Strikers), Holly Ferling (Stars), Kim Garth, Shabnim Ismail (Thunder)
Out: Maitlan Brown (Sixers), Lizelle Lee (Hurricanes), Molly Strano (Hurricanes)

MELBOURNE STARS
Coach: Jarrad Loughman

	No.	DOB	Place	Bat	Bwl/k
Lucy Cripps	24	6/12/01	Melbourne	R	RM
Maddy Darke	17	30/3/01	Randwick, Sydney	R	WK
Sophie Day	6	2/9/98	Greensborough, Vic	R	RM
Nicole Faltum	4	17/1/00	Traralgon, Vic	R	WK
Tess Flintoff	25	31/3/03	Melbourne	R	RM
Georgia Gall	**16**	**30/7/04**	**Euroa, Vic**	**L**	**LM**
Meg Lanning	7	25/3/92	Singapore	R	RM
Rhys McKenna	11	17/8/04		R	RM
Sasha Moloney		14/7/92	Longford, Tas	R	
Sophie Reid				L	WK
Annabel Sutherland	3	12/10/01	East Melbourne	R	RM

In: Maddy Darke (Sixers)
Out: Katherine Brunt, Holly Ferling (Renegades), Alana King (Scorchers), Mignon du Preez (Hurricanes)

PERTH SCORCHERS
Coach: Shelley Nitschke

	No.	DOB	Place	Bat	Bwl/k
Chamari Atapattu	58	9/2/90	Gokarella, Sri Lanka	L	ROS
Meg Banting	**4**	**11/2/96**	**Subiaco, WA**	**R**	**RM**
Samantha Betts	14	6/2/96	Orroroo, SA	R	RM
Mathilda Carmichael	5	4/4/94	St Leonards, Sydney	R	RM
Piepa Cleary	8	17/7/96	Subiaco, WA	R	RM
Sophie Devine (NZ)	77	1/9/89	Wellington, NZ	R	RM
Sarah Glenn (Eng)	**33**	**27/8/99**	**Derby, England**	**R**	**LEG**
Lisa Griffith	54	28/8/92	Bathurst, NSW	R	RM
Mariazanne Kapp	7	4/1/90	Port Elizabeth, South Africa	R	RM
Alana King	23	22/11/95	Clarinda, Vic	R	LEG
Lilly Mills	56	2/1/01		R	RM
Emma King	**2**	**25/3/92**	**Subiaco, WA**	**R**	**ROS**
Beth Mooney	10	14/1/94	Shepparton, Vic	L	WK
Taneale Peschel	6	29/8/94	Rockingham, WA	R	RM
Chloe Piparo	28	5/9/94	Bunbury, WA	R	RS

In:
Off: Heather Graham (Hurricanes)

SYDNEY SIXERS
Coach: Ben Sawyer

	No.	DOB	Place	Bat	Bwl/k
Jade Allen		13/11/03		R	LEG
Nicole Bolton	12	17/1/89	Subiaco, WA	L	ROS
Maitlan Brown	77	5/6/97	Taree, NSW	R	RM
Erin Burns	29	22/6/88	Wollongong, NSW	R	RM
Stella Campbell	18	15/6/02	Mona Vale, NSW	R	RM
Lauren Cheatle	5	6/11/98	Sydney	L	LM
Ashleigh Gardner	6	15/4/97	Bankstown, NSW	R	ROS
Lisa Griffith	**28**	**28/8/92**	**Bathurst, NSW**	**R**	**RM**
Alyssa Healy	77	24/3/90	Gold Coast, Qld	R	WK
Emma Hughes	22	13/11/00		R	RM
Matilda Lugg		12/11/99	Moruya, NSW	R	WK
Claire Moore		28/10/03		R	
Ellyse Perry ©	8	3/11/90	Wahroonga, NSW	R	RMF
Angela Reakes	30	27/12/90	Byron Bay, NSW	R	LEG
Dane Van Niekerk (SA)	*23*	*14/5/93*	*Pretoria, Sth Africa*	*R*	*LEG*

In: – Maitlan Brown (Renegades)

Off – Hayley Silver Holmes (Hurricanes), Maddy Darke (Stars)

SYDNEY THUNDER
Coach: Trevor Griffin

	No.	DOB	Place	Bat	Bwl/k
Sam Bates	34	17/8/92	Newcastle, NSW	R	SLA
Tammy Beaumont	*91*	*11/3/91*	*Dover, Kent*	*R*	*WK*
Hannah Darlington	25	25/1/01	Sydney	R	RM
Jessica Davidson		3/5/03		R	RM
Corinne Hall	27	12/10/87	Gosford, NSW	R	ROS
Rachael Haynes ©	15	26/12/86	Carlton, Vic	L	LM
Saskia Horley	*23*	*23/2/00*	*St Leonards, NSW*	*R*	*SLA*
Sammy-Jo Johnson	58	5/11/92	Lismore, NSW	R	RM
Heather Knight (Eng)	**5**	**26/12/90**	**Plymouth, UK**	**R**	**ROS**
Anika Learoyd	4	14/4/02		R	RM
Phoebe Litchfield	36	18/4/03	Orange, NSW	L	
Kate Paterson	*33*	*3/12/02*		*R*	*RM*
Olivia Porter	14	14/11/01		R	RM
Lauren Smith	2	6/10/96	Central Coast, NSW	R	ROS
Tahlia Wilson	21	21/10/99	Figtree, NSW	R	RM

In: Corinne Hall (ex Hurricanes)

Off: Shabnim Ismail (Renegdaes) Rachel Trenaman (Hurricanes), Izzy Wong (Hurricanes)

Miscellaneous info ahead of 2022-23
AUSTRALIAN CRICKET HALL OF FAME

Name	Inducted	Career	Details
Jack Blackham	1996	1877-1894	35 Tests, 800 runs at 15.69, 37ct/24 st
Fred Spofforth	1996	1877-1887	18 Tests, 94 wickets at 18.41, Best 7-44
Victor Trumper	1996	1899-1912	48 Tests, 3163 runs at 39.05, HS 214*
Clarrie Grimmett	1996	1925-1936	37 Tests, 216 wickets at 24.22, Best 7-40
Bill Ponsford	1996	1924-1934	29 Tests, 2122 runs at 48.23, HS 266
Sir Donald Bradman	1996	1928-1948	52 Tests, 6996 runs at 99.94, HS 334
Bill O'Reilly	1996	1932-1946	27 Tests, 144 wickets at 22.59, Best 7-54
Keith Miller	1996	1946-1956	55 Tests, 2958 runs at 36.98, HS 147, 170 wkts at 22.98
Ray Lindwall	1996	1946-1960	61 Tests, 1502 runs at 21.15, HS 118, 228 wkts at 23.03
Dennis Lillee	1996	1971-1984	70 Tests, 355 wickets at 23.92, Best 7-83
Warwick Armstrong	2000	1902-1921	50 Tests, 2863 runs at 38.69, HS 159*, 87 wkts at 33.60
Neil Harvey	2000	1948-1963	79 Tests, 6149 runs at 48.42, Best 205
Allan Border	2000	1979-1994	156 Tests, 11174 runs at 50.56, 27 tons, 273 ODIs, 6524 runs at 30.62 ICC World Cup winning captain 1987
Bill Woodfull	2001	1926-1934	35 Tests, 2300 runs at 46.00, HS 161
Arthur Morris	2001	1946-1955	46 Tests, 3533 runs at 46.49, HS 206
Greg Chappell	2002	1971-1984	87 Tests, 7110 runs at 53.86, HS 247*
Stan McCabe	2002	1930-1938	39 Tests, 2748 runs at 48.21, HS 232
Ian Chappell	2003	1964-1980	75 Tests, 5345 runs at 42.42, HS 196
Lindsay Hassett	2003	1938-1953	43 Tests, 3073 runs at 46.56, HS 198*
Hugh Trumble	2004	1890-1904	32 Tests, 851 runs at 19.79, HS 70, 141 wkts at 21.79
Alan Davidson	2004	1953-1963	44 Tests, 1328 runs at 24.59, 186 wickets at 20.53
Clem Hill	2005	1896-1912	49 Tests, 3412 runs at 39.22, HS 191
Rod Marsh	2005	1970-1984	96 Tests, 3633 runs at 26.52, HS 132, 343 ct-12 st
Bob Simpson	2006	1957-1978	62 Tests, 4869 runs at 46.82, HS 311
Monty Noble	2006	1898-1909	42 Tests, 1997 runs at 30.26, HS 133, 121 wkts at 25.00
Charlie Macartney	2007	1907-1926	35 Tests, 2131 runs at 41.78, HS 170, 45 wickets at 27.56
Richie Benaud	2007	1952-1964	63 Tests, 2201 runs at 24.46, 248 wickets at 27.03
George Giffen	2008	1881-1896	31 Tests, 1238 runs at 23.35, 103 wickets at 27.09
Ian Healy	2008	1988-1999	119 Tests, 4356 runs at 30.22, HS 161* (366 ct/29 st)
Steve Waugh	2009	1985-2004	168 Tests, 10927 runs at 51.06, 32 tons, 325 ODIs, 7569 runs at 32.90 ICC World Cup winning captain 1999
Bill Lawry	2010	1961-1971	67 Tests, 5234 runs at 47.15, Best 210
Graham McKenzie	2010	1961-1971	60 Tests, 246 wickets at 29.78, Best 8-71
Mark Taylor	2011	1988-1999	104 Tests, 7525 runs at 43.49, HS 334*, Captained 3 Ashes series wins
Doug Walters	2011	1965-1981	74 Tests, 5357 runs at 48.26, HS 250, 49 wickets at 29
Shane Warne	2012	1992-2007	145 Tests, 708 wickets at 25.41, Best 8-71, 194 ODIs, 293 wkts at 25.73 ICC World Cup win in 1999
Glenn McGrath	2013	1993-2007	124 Tests, 563 wickets at 21.64, Best 8-24, 250 ODIs, 381 wkts at 22.02 ICC World Cup wins in 1999, 2003 & 2007
Charlie Turner	2013	1997-1895	17 Tests, 101 wickets at 16.53, Best 7-43
Belinda Clark	2014	1990-2005	15 Tests, 919 runs at 45.95, 118 ODIs, 4844 runs at 47.49, HS 229* ICC World Cup winning skipper 1997
Mark Waugh	2014	1988-2004	128 Tests, 8029 runs at 41.81, HS 153*, 244 ODIs, 8500 runs at 39.35 ICC WC win 1999
Jack Ryder	2015	1912-1932	20 Tests, 1394 runs at 51.62, HS 201*
Adam Gilchrist	2015	1999-2008	96 Tests, 5570 runs at 47.60, 379 ct/37 st, 287 ODIs, 9619 runs at 35.89 ICC World Cup wins 1999, 2003 & 2007
Wally Grout	2016	1946-1966	51 Tests, 890 runs at 12.81, 163 ct, 24 st
Jeff Thomson	2016	1974-1986	51 Tests, 200 wickets at 28.00
David Boon	2017	1984-1996	107 Tests, 7422 runs at 43.56, HS 200, 181 ODIs, 5964 runs at 37.04 ICC WC win 1987
Matthew Hayden	2017	1993-2009	103 Tests, 8625 runs at 50.73, HS 380, 161 ODIs, 6133 runs at 43.80 ICC WC wins 2003 & 2007
Betty Wilson	2017	1948-1958	11 Tests, 862 runs at 57.46, 68 wkts at 11.80, Best 7-7
Norman O'Neill	2018	1958-1965	42 Tests, 2779 runs at 45.55, HS 181
Ricky Ponting	2018	1995-2012	168 Tests, 13378 runs at 51.85, 41 tons, 375 ODIs, 13704 runs at 42.03 ICC World Cup win in 1999, Capt ICC WC wins in 2003 & 2007
Karen Rolton	2018	1995-2009	14 Tests, 1002 runs at 55.66, 2x100; 141 ODIs, 4814 runs at 48.14, 8x100 ICC WC wins in 1997 & 2005

Name	Year	Career	Stats
Cathryn Fitzpatrick	2019	1991-2006	13 Tests, 60 wkts at 19.11, 109 ODIs, 180 wkts @ 16.79, ICC WC wins in 1997, 2005
Dean Jones	2019	1984-1994	52 Tests, 3631 runs at 46.55, 164 ODIs, 6068 runs @ 44.61, ICC WC win 1987
Billy Murdoch	2019	1875-1904	19 Tests, 908 runs at 31.31, HS 211
Craig McDermott	2020	1984-1996	71 Tests, 291 wkts at 28.63, 138 ODIs, 203 wkts. ICC WC win 1987
Sharon Tredrea	2020	1975-1988	10 Tests, 30 wkts at 26.13, 31 ODIs, 32 wkts ICC WC wins 1978, 82, 88
Johnny Mullagh	2020	1868	Aboriginal tour to England
Lisa Sthalekar	2021	2003-2011	8 Tests, 125 ODIs (2728 runs, 146 wkts), 54 T20s ICC WC wins 2009, 10
Justin Langer	2022	1993-2007	105 Tests, 7696 runs at 45.27, HS 250, 23 tons
Raelee Thompson	2022	1972-1985	16 Tests, 57 wkts at 18.24, 23 ODI, 24 wkts at 18.86. 1982 WC Win

CRICKET AUSTRALIA UMPIRES/MATCH REFEREES PANEL

Name	State	DOB Date of Birth	Matches Shield	umpired DOD	BBL
Gerard Abood	NSW	28-2-1972	64	48	100
Shawn Craig	VIC	23-6-1973	34	24	61
Greg Davidson	NSW	7-11-1970	30	24	58
Phillip Gillespie	VIC	23-10-1975	31	21	58
Mike Graham-Smith	TAS	5-8-1969	38	29	73
Nathan Johnstone	WA	8-10-1980	5	11	16
Donovan Koch	Qld	11-10-1976	18	13	37
Simon Lightbody	NSW	26-9-1964	15	11	28
Sam Nogajski	TAS	1-1-1979	48	35	67
Bruce Oxenford	Qld	5-3-1960	60	38	27
Ben Treloar	NSW	12-7-1982	3	4	7
Paul Wilson	NSW	12-1-1972	47	45	73
Elite Umpires					
Paul Reiffel	Vic	19-4-1966	41	40	23
Rod Tucker	NSW	28-8-1964	30	20	13

Supplementary Umpire Panel Members for 2022-23

Name	State	Date of Birth	Matches Shield	umpired DOD	BBL
Stephen Dionysius	Qld	13-6-1980			
Sharad Patel	NSW				
Troy Penman	NSW	1-5-1987	0	1	4
Claire Polosak	NSW	7-4-1988	0	3	0
Eloise Sheridan	SA	3-9-1985	0	0	0
David Taylor	NSW	6-4-1974	1	1	11
Not offered Contracts for 2022-23					
Darren Close	Tas	31-3-1968	26	8	19
Tony Wilds	NSW	1-11-1963	23	15	52

International Panel: Phil Gillespie, Donovan Koch, Sam Nogajski, Paul Wilson. Elite Panel – Paul Reiffel, Rod Tucker.
Referees Panel – Steve Bernard, Steve Davis, Simon Fry, David Gilbert, Kent Hannam, Bob Parry, Bob Stratford, Kepler Wessels.

CRICKET AUSTRALIA AWARDS 2021-22

Sheffield Shield Player of the year: Henry Hunt (SA) and Travis Dean (Vic) on 12, in third place was Scott Boland (Vic) 11.
Marsh Cup Player of the year: Matthew Renshaw (Queensland). KFC Big Bash: Ben McDermott (Hobart Hurricanes).
WNCL Player of the year: Erin Osborne (ACT). WBBL Player of the year: Harmanpreet Kaur (Melbourne Renegades).
Benaud Spirit of Cricket Awards: Mens – Queensland, Womens – Victoria. Umpire Award: Phil Gillespie.
ACA Big Bash League All*Star Team of the Year: Ben McDermott (Hurricanes), Joe Clarke (Stars), Glenn Maxwell (Stars, Captain), Mitchel Marsh (Scorchers), Josh Philippe (Sixers, WK), Sam Billings (Thunder), Hayden Kerr (Sixers), Rashid Khan (Strikers), Kane Richardson (Renegades), Peter Siddle (Strikers), 12th – Sean Abbott (Sixers)
Lord's Taverners Indigenous Cricketer of the Year: Scott Boland
ACA WBBL All*Star Team of the Year: Sophie Devine (Captain, Scorchers), Beth Mooney (Scorchers), Katie Mack (Strikers), Harmanpreet Kaur (Renegades), Elyse Villani (Stars), Georgia Redmayne (Heat, WK), Grace Harris (Heat), Jess Jonassen (Heat), Kim Garth (Stars), Darcie Brown (Strikers), Tayla Vlaeminck (Hurricanes), Alana King (12th – Scorchers)
ACA WNCL All*Star Team of the Year: Bridget Patterson (SA), Katie Mack (ACT), Elyse Villani (Captain, Tas), Racehl Priest (Tas), Courtney Webb (SA), Mikayla Hinkley (Qld), Ellie Falconer (SA), Zoe Cooke (ACT), Sarah Coyte (Tas), Maisy Gibson (Tas), Sam Bates (Vic), Rachael Haynes (12th - NSW)

CRICKET AUSTRALIA CONTRACT LIST 2022-23

Men
Ashton Agar (WA)
Scott Boland (Vic)
Alex Carey (SA)
Pat Cummins (NSW)
Aaron Finch (Vic)
Cameron Green (WA)
Josh Hazlewood (NSW)
Travis Head (SA)
Josh Inglis (WA)
Usman Khawaja (Qld)
Marnus Labuschagne (Qld)
Nathan Lyon (NSW
Mitchell Marsh (WA)
Glenn Maxwell (Vic)
Steve Smith (NSW)
Mitchell Starc (NSW)
Marcus Stoinis (WA)
David Warner (NSW)
Adam Zampa (WA)

Women
Darcie Brown (SA)
Nicola Carey (Tas)
Ashleigh Gardner (NSW)
Rachael Haynes (NSW)
Alyssa Healy (NSW)
Jess Jonassen (Qld)
Alana King (WA)
Meg Lanning (Vic)
Tahlia McGrath (SA)
Beth Mooney (Qld)
Ellyse Perry (Vic)
Megan Schutt (SA)
Annabel Sutherland (Vic)
Tayla Vlaeminck (Vic)
Georgia Wareham (Vic)

GILLESPIE SPORTS UNDER 13 TRIP TO DUBAI

RESULTS - Played 8, Won 5, Lost 2, Drawn 1.

April 14, 2022 v Dubai College at Rugby 7's Oval - 30 overs per side. GS 128 (H Stephens 24, Aarav 4-6, Arush 4-10) lost to Dubai 4-213 (Aryan 50, Aarav 50).

Game 2 v ICC Academy at The Seven Stadium, Dubai on April 15th - 20 overs per side. ICC Academy 6-112 (Dhairya 25*, M.Tresidder 2-15, L.Allen 1-7) lost to GS 3-113 (R Bihari 37, R Tissen 28*)

Game 3 v Desert Cubs U13 at Sharjah. On April 17th — 35 overs per side. Desert Cubs 269 (M Nafees 100*, E Carneiro 55, H Stephens 1-25) drew with GS 5-105 (R Bihari 45, H Stephens 16) off 25 overs. Game abandoned.

Game 4 v Shazad XI at Ajman on April 20th - 40 overs over per side. GS 194 (J Murphy 41, J Thomas 35, Sai 2-12) lost to Shazad 9-199 (Arav 41, Aron 37, Aryan 25, B.Wilson 4-34, P.Biswas 1-20)

Game 5 v Rajasthan Royals at Sevens Stadium on April 18th - 20 overs per side. GS 4-165 (R Tissen 70*, R.Bihari 50*, Dhariah 2/3◗) Defeated Rajasthan Royals 69 (P.Biswan 5-7, M.Tresidder 2-12)

Game 6. v IJC.Academy at Sevens Stadium on April 21st -20 overs side. IJC.Academy 6-124 (Pasasramka 33, Liam 23, N.McCleary 2/22) lost to G.S. 5-156 (R Tissen 38*, P Biswas 31, R Bihari 27)

Game 7 v Zayed Academy at Sharjah Stadium on April 23rd- 40 overs per side. GS 8-190 (R Tissen 59, J Murphy 52 H Stephens 32, Bhatia 2-9) defeated Zayed Academy 9-178 (Bhaha 54* L Simon 35, P Biswas 3-24, N McCleary 1-11)

Game 8 v Rajasthan Royals U14 at Sevens Stadium on April 24th – 20 overs per side. GS 3-137 (R.Tissen 78*, R.Bihari 22, Zaidan 1-16) defeated Rajasthan Royals U14 8-95 (Aaria 47, H Stephens, J Murphy 1-6)

AVERAGES	M	I	NO	Runs	HS	Avge	Ct	St	RO	O	M	R	W	Avge	Econ
Lincoln Allen	7	5	2	19	14*	6.33	0	0	0	23	0	142	5	28.40	6.2
Euan Beavan	8	4	0	18	7	4.50	4	0	0	20	0	123	2	61.50	6.2
Rayan Bihari	8	8	1	211	50	30.14	2	0	7	2	0	14	0		7.0
Puffin Biswas	8	5	3	54	31	27.00	3	0	1	27	1	107	11	9.72	4.0
Harvey Stephens	8	6	0	97	32	16.17	2	0	0	32.2	0	123	7	17.57	3.8
Nate McCleary	7	7	3	49	17	12.25	2	0	1	12	0	64	4	16.00	5.3
James Murphy	8	5	0	96	52	19.20	0	0	1	36	1	208	6	34.67	5.8
Jett Thomas	7	4	2	35	16	17.50	0	0	0	14	0	69	0		4.9
Jude Thomas	6	5	0	82	35	16.40	7	1	1	2	0	11	1	11.00	5.5
Riley Tissen	8	8	4	285	78*	71.25	0	0	3	3	2	5	0		1.7
Max Tresidder	8	3	1	11	9*	5.50	1	0	0	19	1	117	4	29.25	6.2
Brad Wilson	7	5	1	28	15	7.00	3	0	0	33	1	215	7	30.70	6.5

First ODI, Australia v Zimbabwe at Riverway Stadium, Townsville on August 28, 2021 – Australia won by 5 wickets

Zimbabwe			B	M	4	6
I Kaia	c & b Marsh	17	40	50	2	
TR Marumani	b Zampa	45	61	95	4	
WN Madhevere	c and b Zampa	72	91	138	4	
TT Munyonga	c Smith b Zampa	7	14	15	1	
Sikandar Raza	c Zampa b Green	5	24	32		
RW Chakabva *+	c Starc b Green	31	33	52	3	
RP Burl	c Hazlewood b Green	2	7	10		
LM Jongwe	c Maxwell b Green	3	6	9		
BN Evans	c Maxwell b Green	5	5	7		
R Ngarava	not out	0	2	6		
VM Nyauchi	b Starc	2	3	3		
	6 lb, 1 nb, 4 w	11				
10 overs : 0-36	47.3 overs	200				

1-42 (Kaia, 10.5), 2-87 (Marumani, 20.5), 3-104 (Munyonga, 24.4),
4-122 (Raza, 31.2), 5-185 (Madhevere, 42.6),
6-188 (Chakabva, 44.3), 7-190 (Burl, 44.6), 8-196 (Jongwe, 46.2),
9-198 (Evans, 46.4), 10-200 (Nyauchi, 47.3).

Bowling	O	M	R	W	wd	nb
MA Starc	8.3	1	27	1		
JR Hazlewood	10	1	36	0		
MR Marsh	6	0	22	1	1	
CD Green	9	0	33	5		1
A Zampa	10	0	57	3	3	
GJ Maxwell	4	0	19	0		

Australia			B	M	4	6
AJ Finch *	b Ngarava	15	21	30	2	
DA Warner	b Sikandar Raza	57	66	96	7	1
SPD Smith	not out	48	80	116	6	
AT Carey+	c Nyauchi b Burl	10	8	11	2	
MP Stoinis	c Raza b Burl	19	14	13	2	1
MR Marsh	c Chakabva b Burl	2	3	1		
GJ Maxwell	not out	32	9	19	3	3
CD Green						
MA Starc						
A Zampa						
JR Hazlewood						
	5 lb, 13 w	18				
10 overs : 1-50	33.3 overs	5-201				

1-43 (Finch, 7.3), 2-108 (Warner, 22.1), 3-128 (Carey, 25.2),
4-153 (Stoinis, 29.2), 5-155 (Marsh, 29.5)

Bowling	O	M	R	W	wd	nb
WN Madhevere	1	0	9	0		
VM Nyauchi	5	0	20	0		
R Ngarava	5.3	0	26	1	1	
BN Evans	6	0	33	0	2	
Sikandar Raza	8	0	45	1	3	
RP Burl	7	0	60	3	1	
LM Jongwe	1	0	3	0	2	

Toss: Australia.   Umpires: SJ Nogajski, RJ Tucker, PR Reiffel (TV), Ref: DC Boon. Award: CD Green.   Crowd: 2,750

Madhevere 50: 67 balls, 2x4. Warner 50: 57 balls, 6x4, 1x6.

Second ODI, Australia v Zimbabwe at Riverway Stadium, Townsville on August 31, 2021 – Australia won by 8 wickets

Zimbabwe			B	M	4	6
I Kaia	b Starc	2	8	15		
TR Marumani	c sub (M Labuschagne) b Starc	4	18	32		
WN Madhevere	lbw b Starc	0	3	7		
SC Williams	c Green b Zampa	29	45	91	3	
Sikandar Raza	c Stoinis b Hazlewood	17	37	39	1	1
RW Chakabva *+	c Starc b Agar	10	14	11	2	
TT Munyonga	c Carey b Green	10	15	20	1	
RP Burl	c Carey b Green	10	16	17	2	
LM Jongwe	b Zampa	1	3	16		
BN Evans	lbw b Zampa	2	6	8		
R Ngarava	not out	1	2	4		
	4 lb, 6 w	10				
10 overs : 3-25	27.5 overs	96				

1-13 (Kaia, 2.6), 2-13 (Madhevere, 4.3), 3-14 (Marumani, 6.1),
4-46 (Raza, 14.5), 5-59 (Chakabva, 17.5), 6-79 (Munyonga, 22.3),
7-83 (Williams, 23.6), 8-93 (Burl, 26.2), 9-95 (Jongwe, 27.2),
10-96 (Evans, 27.5).

Bowling	O	M	R	W	wd	nb
MA Starc	8	1	24	3	6	
JR Hazlewood	6	2	16	1		
MP Stoinis	4	0	9	0		
AC Agar	3	0	15	1		
A Zampa	3.5	0	21	3		
CD Green	3	0	7	2		

Australia			B	M	4	6
DA Warner	c Evans b Ngarava	13	9	9	2	
AJ Finch *	c Raza b Ngarava	1	6	12		
SPD Smith	not out	47	41	53	8	1
AT Carey+	not out	26	33	50	2	
MP Stoinis						
CD Green						
GJ Maxwell						
AC Agar						
MA Starc						
A Zampa						
JR Hazlewood						
	4 b, 1 lb, 1 nb, 7 w	13				
10 overs : 2-57	14.4 overs	2-100				

1-15 (Warner, 2.1), 2-16 (Finch, 2.3)

Bowling	O	M	R	W	wd	nb
R Ngarava	4	0	16	2	3	
BN Evans	4	0	29	0		
Sikandar Raza	2	0	23	0		
LM Jongwe	3	0	13	0	2	
SC Williams	1.4	0	14	0	1	1

Toss: Australia.   Umpires: DM Koch, PR Reiffel, RJ Tucker (TV), Ref: DC Boon. Award: A Zampa.   Crowd: 1,158

Third ODI, Australia v Zimbabwe at Riverway Stadium, Townsville on September 3, 2021
Zimbabwe won by 3 wickets

Australia			B	M	4	6
DA Warner	c Evans b Burl	94	96	124	14	2
AJ Finch*	c Burl b Ngarava	5	11	18		
SPD Smith	lbw b Nyauchi	1	6	6		
AT Carey+	c Chakabva b Evans	4	9	13	1	
MP Stoinis	c Chakabva b Evans	3	15	22		
CD Green	c Burl b Williams	3	11	16		
GJ Maxwell	c and b Burl	19	22	32	3	
AC Agar	c Madhevere b Burl	0	2	1		
MA Starc	b Burl	2	6	13		
A Zampa	not out	1	6	10		
JR Hazlewood	c Chakabva b Burl	0	2	3		
	3 lb, 6 w	9				
10 overs: 3-37	31 overs	141				

Zimbabwe			B	M	4	6
T Kaitano	c Smith b Hazlewood	19	25	36	4	
TR Marumani	c Carey b Green	35	47	93	4	
WN Madhevere	c Agar b Hazlewood	2	7	9		
SC Williams	c Carey b Hazlewood	0	1	1		
Sikandar Raza	c Starc b Stoinis	8	19	27	1	
RW Chakabva*+	not out	37	72	98	3	
TT Munyonga	b Agar	17	40	48		
RP Burl	c Green b Starc	11	17	26	1	1
BN Evans	not out	2	7	7		
R Ngarava						
VM Nyauchi						
	8 1b, 1 nb, 2 w	11				
10 overs: 1-44	39 overs	7-142				

1-9 (Finch, 4.2), 2-10 (Smith, 5.4), 3-31 (Carey, 8.5), 4-59 (Stoinis, 14.2), 5-72 (Green, 17.6), 6-129 (Maxwell, 26.4), 7-129 (Agar, 26.6), 8-135 (Warner, 28.6), 9-136 (Starc, 30.3), 10-141 (Hazlewood, 30.6)

1-38 (Kaitano, 8.2), 2-44 (Madhevere, 10.3), 3-44 (Williams, 10.4), 4-66 (Raza, 15.4), 5-77 (Marumani, 18.3), 6-115 (Munyonga, 31.2), 7-130 (Burl, 36.6)

Bowling	O	M	R	W	wd	nb
R Ngarava	6	1	27	1		
VM Nyauchi	6	3	15	1		
BN Evans	6	1	35	2		
SC Williams	6	0	36	1		
Sikandar Raza	4	0	15	0		
RP Burl	3	0	10	5	2	

Bowling	O	M	R	W	wd	nb
MA Starc	8	0	33	1	2	
JR Hazlewood	10	2	30	3		
CD Green	6	0	17	1		
MP Stoinis	2	0	6	1		
A Zampa	8	0	32	0		1
AC Agar	5	0	16	1		

Toss: Zimbabwe. Umpires: RJ Tucker, P Wilson, PR Reiffel (TV), Ref: DC Boon. Award: RP Burl. Crowd: 2,483

Warner 50: 47 balls, 9x4 1x6. **Match reports on this series will appear in the next edition.**

FUTURE TOURS PROGRAM

MEN

2022-23

✈ Three T20 tour of India (Mohali, Nagpur and Hyderabad)
October: Two T20s v West Indies. Three T20s v England
October-November: T20 World Cup (Australia)
November: Three ODIs v England
December: Two Tests v West Indies
December-January: Three Tests v South Africa
✈ February-March: Four Test tour of India

2023-24

✈ June: World Test Championship final – Lord's (if qualified)
✈ June-July: Five Test Ashes tour of England
✈ September: Five ODIs and three T20s tour of South Africa.
✈ Three ODI tour of India
✈ October-November: ODI World Cup India
✈ November-December: Five T20 tour of India
December: Three Tests v Pakistan
January: Two Tests v West Indies
February: Three ODIs and three T20s v West Indies
✈ February-March: Two Tests and three T20s tour of NZ

2024-25

✈ June: T20 World Cup – USA/Windies
✈ August: Three T20s v Afghanistan (location TBC)
✈ August-September: Three ODIs, one T20 tour of Ireland
✈ September: Five ODIs and three T20s tour of England
November: Three ODIs and three T20s v Pakistan
December-January: Five-Test Border-Gavaskar series v India
✈ February: Two-Test tour of Sri Lanka
✈ February-March: ICC Champions Trophy (50-over) tournament in Pakistan.

WOMEN

2022-23 (Multi-format series = one Test, three ODI & T20s)

✈ December: Five T20s tour of India
January: Three ODIs and three T20s v Pakistan
✈ February: T20 World Cup – South Africa

2023-24

✈ June-July: Multi-format series in England
✈ July: Three ODIs tour of Ireland
September-October: Three ODIs and three T20s v West Indies
✈ December-January: Multi-format series in India
January-February: Multi-format series v South Africa
✈ March: three ODIs and three T20s tour of Bangladesh

2024-25

✈ September-October: T20 World Cup – Bangladesh
December: Three ODIs* v India. ✈ Three ODIs* tour of New Zealand
January-February: Multi-format Ashes series against England. One Test, three ODIs and three T20s
✈ March: Three T20 tour of New Zealand

For more info, search online for ICC Future Tours Program

FIXTURES 2022-23

* Indicates some or all match under lights

NEW ZEALAND ODI SERIES

Tue Sep 6	First ODI *	Cairns
Thu Sep 8	Second ODI *	Cairns
Sun Sep 11	Third ODI *	Cairns

WEST INDIES TWENTY20 SERIES

Wed Oct 5	First T20*	Gold Coast
Fri Oct 7	Second T20*	Gabba

ENGLAND TWENTY20 SERIES

Sun Oct 9	First T20*	Perth Stadium
Tue Oct 12	Second T20*	Manuka Oval
Thu Oct 14	Third T20*	Manuka Oval

ENGLAND ODI SERIES

Thu Nov 17	First ODI *	Adelaide Oval
Sat Nov 19	Second ODI *	SCG
Tue Nov 22	Third ODI*	MCG

WEST INDIES TEST SERIES

Nov 30-Dec 4	First Test *	Perth Stadium
Dec 8-12	Second Test *	Adelaide Oval

SOUTH AFRICA TEST SERIES

Tests FOX Cricket/Seven, Tour matches FOX Cricket

Dec 17-21	First Test	Gabba
Dec 26-30	Second Test	MCG
Jan 4-8	Third Test	SCG

MARSH CUP

* Some part floodlit, + TV via FOX CRICKET

Fri Sep 23	Vic v NSW	Junction Oval
Sun Sep 25	Vic v WA	Junction Oval
Mon Sep 26	Qld v SA	AB Field
Wed Sep 28	SA v Tas*	AB Field
Fri Sep 30	Qld v Tas *	AB Field
Sat Oct 1	WA v NSW *	WACA
Fri Oct 21	SA v Tas	Adelaide Oval
Sat Oct 22	Vic v WA	Junction Oval
Wed Oct 26	Tas v Vic	Launceston
Sat Nov 5	NSW v SA	North Sydney
	WA v Qld	WACA
Tue Nov 15	Qld v Vic	AB Field
Wed Nov 16	WA v SA	WACA
Thu Nov 17	Tas v NSW	Bellerive Oval
Sun Nov 27	NSW v Qld*	North Sydney
Tue Feb 14	Vic v Qld*	MCG
Wed Feb 15	SA v WA*	Adelaide Oval
Thu Feb 16	NSW v Tas	North Sydney
Sun Feb 26	SA v Vic	TBC
	Tas v WA	Bellerive Oval
	Qld v NSW*	Gabba
Wed Mar 8	The Final	TBC

This schedule is current at September 1, 2022. Cricket Australia reserves the right in its absolute discretion to change or amend the program at any time, without notice.

BBL12 – All LIVE on FOX CRICKET

F - indicates 16 Exclusive Fox games

All games at night unless indicated * as Day

Dec 13	Thunder v Stars	Manuka Oval
Dec 14	Strikers v Sixers	Adelaide Oval
Dec 15	Heat v Renegades	Gabba
Dec 16	Stars v Hurricanes	MCG
	Thunder v Strikers	Syd Showground
Dec 17	Scorchers v Sixers F	Perth Stadium
Dec 18	Renegades v Thunder	Marvel Stadium
Dec 19	Hurricanes v Scorchers	Uni of Tas, Launc
Dec 20	Strikers v Thunder	Adelaide Oval
Dec 21	Renegades v Heat	Kardinia Park
Dec 22	Sixers v Hurricanes	SCG
Dec 23	Stars v Scorchers F	Junction Oval *
	Heat v Strikers F	Gabba
Dec 24	Hurricanes v Renegades F	Bellerive Oval *
Dec 26	Sixers v Stars	SCG
	Scorchers v Strikers	Perth Stadium
Dec 27	Thunder v Heat	Syd Showground
Dec 28	Sixers v Renegades	SCG
Dec 29	Heat v Thunder	Metricon Stadium
	Scorchers v Stars	Perth Stadium
Dec 30	Renegades v Sixers F	Kardinia Park
Dec 31	Thunder v Hurricanes F	Albury*
	Strikers v Stars F	Adelaide Oval
Jan 1	Renegades v Scorchers	Marvel Stadium*
	Heat v Sixers	Gabba
Jan 2	Hurricanes v Strikers	Bellerive Oval
Jan 3	Stars v Renegades	MCG
Jan 4	Sixers v Heat	North Syd Oval
	Scorchers v Thunder	Perth Stadium
Jan 5	Strikers v Hurricanes	Adelaide Oval
Jan 6	Stars v Sixers F	MCG
Jan 7	Renegades v Hurricanes F	Marvel Stadium
	Scorchers v Heat F	Perth Stadium
Jan 8	Thunder v Sixers	Syd Showground
Jan 9	Hurricanes v Stars	Bellerive Oval
Jan 10	Strikers v Renegades	Adelaide Oval
Jan 11	Heat v Scorchers	Gabba
Jan 12	Stars v Strikers	MCG
Jan 13	Thunder v Scorchers F	Syd Showground
Jan 14	Strikers v Heat F	Adelaide Oval*
	Renegades v Stars F	Marvel Stadium
Jan 15	Hurricanes v Thunder	Bellerive Oval *
	Sixers v Scorchers	SCG
Jan 16	Stars v Heat	MCG
Jan 17	Sixers v Strikers	Coffs Harbour
Jan 18	Scorchers v Hurricanes	Perth Stadium
Jan 19	Thunder v Renegades	Manuka Oval
Jan 20	Strikers v Scorchers F	Adelaide Oval *
	Heat v Hurricanes F	Gabba
Jan 21	Sixers v Thunder F	SCG
Jan 22	Heat v Stars	Gabba *
	Scorchers v Renegades	Perth Stadium
Jan 23	Hurricanes v Sixers	Bellerive Oval
Jan 24	Renegades v Strikers	Marvel Stadium
Jan 25	Hurricanes v Heat	Uni of Tas, Launc
	Stars v Thunder	MCG
Jan 27	Playoff – 4th v 5th	The Eliminator
Jan 28	Playoff – 1st v 2nd	The Qualifier
Jan 29	3rd v winner Eliminator	The Knockout
Feb 2	Loser Qual v win KO	Prelim Final
Feb 4	BBL 12 Final	

SHEFFIELD SHIELD - Qld 10.00 start; all others 10.30

Oct 3-6	WA v NSW	WACA
Oct 6-9	Qld v Tas	AB Field
	SA v Vic	Rolton Oval
Oct 16-19	SA v Tas	Adelaide Oval
Oct 17-20	Vic v WA	Junction Oval
Oct 18-21	NSW v Qld	Drummoyne Oval
Oct 29-Nov 1	Tas v Vic	Bellerive Oval
Oct 31-Nov 3	NSW v SA	North Dalton Park
	WA v Qld	WACA
Nov 10-13	Qld v Vic	AB Field
Nov 11-14	WA v SA	WACA

Nov 12-15	Tas v NSW	Bellerive Oval
Nov 20-23	SA v Qld	Adelaide Oval
Nov 22-25	NSW v WA	SCG
Nov 24-27	Vic v Tas	MCG
Dec 1-4	Vic v NSW	Junction Oval
	Tas v SA	Bellerive Oval
	Qld v WA	Gabba
Feb 9-12	Vic v Qld	MCG
Feb 10-13	SA v WA	Adelaide Oval
Feb 11-14	NSW v Tas	SCG
Feb 20-23	Vic v SA	Junction Oval
Feb 21-24	Tas v WA	Bellerive Oval
	Qld v NSW	Gabba
March 2-5	NSW v Vic	SCG
	Qld v SA	Gabba
	WA v Tas	WACA
March 14-17	Tas v Qld	Bellerive Oval
	SA v NSW	Rolton Oval
	WA v Vic	WACA
March 23-27	The Final	TBA (Fox)

WOMENS CRICKET
PAKISTAN IN AUSTRALIA - (All Live on Seven/Fox)

Jan 16	First ODI	AB Field
Jan 18	Second ODI	AB Field
Jan 21	Third ODI	North Sydney Oval
Jan 24	First T20	North Sydney Oval
Jan 26	Second T20 *	North Sydney Oval
Jan 29	Third T20	Manuka Oval

WNCL – 50 over competition (CA/Kayo Live)

Sep 23	SA v WA	Rolton Oval
	NSW v Qld	North Sydney Oval
	WA v ACT	WACA
Sep 25	SA v Vic	Rolton Oval
	WA v ACT	WACA
Sep 30	NSW v WA	North Sydney Oval
Oct 1	Qld v ACT	TBC
Oct 2	NSW v WA	North Sydney Oval
Oct 3	Qld v ACT	TBC
Oct 4	Vic v Tas	Junction Oval
Oct 6	Vic v Tas	Junction Oval
Dec 18	ACT v SA	TBC
	Tas v NSW	TBC
Dec 20	Tas v NSW	TBC
	ACT v SA	TBC
Dec 21	WA v Qld	WACA
Dec 23	WA v Qld	WACA
Jan 4	WA v SA	WACA
Jan 5	Vic v NSW	Junction Oval
Jan 6	Qld v Tas	AB Field
	WA v SA	WACA
Jan 7	Vic v NSW	Junction Oval
Jan 17	Qld v Vic	Ian Healy Oval
Jan 19	ACT v Tas	TBC
	SA v NSW	Rolton Oval
	Qld v Vic	Ian Healy Oval
Jan 21	ACT v Tas	
	SA v NSW	Rolton Oval
Feb 6	Tas v SA	Bellerive Oval
Feb 8	Vic v WA	Junction Oval
	Tas v SA	Bellerive Oval
Feb 10	NSW v ACT	Wade Pk, Orange
	Vic v WA	Junction Oval
Feb 12	NSW v ACT	Wade Pk, Orange
Feb 14	Tas v WA	Bellerive Oval
Feb 16	Tas v WA	Bellerive Oval
Feb 17	ACT v Vic	Solar Pk, Canberra
	SA v Qld	Rolton Oval
Feb 19	ACT v Vic	Solar Pk, Canberra
	SA v Qld	Rolton Oval
Feb 25	The Final	TBC

WBBL08 - * Indicate Floodlit game
7 = Televised by Seven/Fox, F = Excl to Fox Cricket

All via Kayo Sports

Thu Oct 13	Heat v Sixers* 7	Mackay
Fri Oct 14	Scorchers v Heat F	Blacktown
Sat Oct 15	Strikers v Sixers 7	Mackay
	Heat v Stars * 7	Mackay
Sun Oct 16	Renegades v Strikers 7	Mackay
	Sixers v Stars 7	Mackay
	Thunder v Scorchers F	Blacktown
Mon Oct 17	Hurricanes v Scorchers * F	Blacktown
Tue Oct 18	Heat v Renegades F	Mackay
	Hurricanes v Thunder F	Mackay
Thu Oct 20	Scorchers v Stars 7	WACA
Fri Oct 21	Renegades v Heat F	Rolton Oval
	Strikers v Sixers F	Rolton Oval
Sat Oct 22	Scorchers v Thunder F	WACA
Sun Oct 23	Thunder v Stars 7	WACA
	Scorchers v Hurricanes	WACA
Mon Oct 24	Strikers v Renegades F	Rolton Oval
Tue Oct 25	Heat v Thunder F	AB Field
Thu Oct 27	Heat v Strikers *7	AB Field
Fri Oct 28	Strikers v Scorchers F	Rolton Oval
Sat Oct 29	Hurricanes v Sixers F	Ballarat
	Renegades v Stars F	Ballarat
	Heat v Scorchers *7	AB Field
Sun Oct 30	Renegades v Sixers F	Ballarat
Mon Oct 31	Stars v Thunder F	Ballarat
Wed Nov 2	Strikers v Stars F	Blacktown
	Thunder v Sixers *F	Blacktown
Thu Nov 3	Hurricanes v Renegades 7	Bellerive
Fri Nov 4	Thunder v Heat F	Bellerive
Sat Nov 5	Stars v Strikers F	Lilac Hill
	Scorchers v Sixers F	Lilac Hill
Sun Nov 6	Hurricanes v Heat 7	Bellerive
	Renegades v Thunder 7	Bellerive
	Scorchers v Strikers F	Lilac Hill
Mon Nov 7	Renegades v Hurricanes F	Bellerive
Wed Nov 9	Scorchers v Heat F	Lilac Hill
Thu Nov 10	Renegades v Sixers F	Junc Oval
Fri Nov 11	Hurricanes v Strikers* F	Rolton Oval
Sat Nov 12	Renegades v Scorchers 7	Junc Oval
	Stars v Sixers 7	Junc Oval
	Heat v Hurricanes *F	Rolton Oval
Sun Nov 13	Sixers v Scorchers 7	Junc Oval
	Stars v Renegades 7	Junc Oval
	Strikers v Thunder F	Nuriootpa
Mon Nov 14	Strikers v Heat 7	Rolton Oval
Tue Nov 15	Hurricanes v Stars F	TBC
	Thunder v Renegades F	Manuka Oval
Wed Nov 16	Stars v Hurricanes F	TBC
	Sixers v Heat * F	North Syd
Fri Nov 18	Strikers v Hurricanes 7	North Syd
	Sixers v Thunder* 7	North Syd
Sat Nov 19	Stars v Scorchers F	Moe
Sun Nov 20	Scorchers v Renegades F	Moe
	Sixers v Hurricanes 7	North Syd
	Stars v Heat F	Moe
	Thunder v Strikers* 7	North Syd
Nov 25-27	Finals	TBC